TH

TUDOR LITERATURE, 1485–1603

This is the first major collection of essays to look at the literature of the entire Tudor period, from the reign of Henry VII to death of Elizabeth I. It pays particularly attention to the years before 1580. Those decades saw, amongst other things, the establishment of print culture and growth of a reading public; the various phases of the English Reformation and process of political centralization that enabled and accompanied them; the increasing emulation of Continental and classical literatures under the influence of humanism; the self-conscious emergence of English as a literary language and determined creation of a native literary canon; the beginnings of English empire and the consolidation of a sense of nationhood. However, study of Tudor literature prior to 1580 is not only of worth as a context, or foundation, for an Elizabethan 'golden age'. As this much-needed volume shows, it is also of artistic, intellectual, and cultural merit in its own right. Written by experts from Europe, North America, and the United Kingdom, the forty-five chapters in *The Oxford Handbook of Tudor Literature* recover some of the distinctive voices of sixteenth-century writing, its energy, variety, and inventiveness. As well as essays on well-known writers, such as Philip Sidney or Thomas Wyatt, the volume contains the first extensive treatment in print of some of the Tudor era's most original voices.

Mike Pincombe is Professor of Tudor and Elizabethan Literature at the University of Newcastle upon Tyne; he convened the Tudor Symposium between 1998 and 2009. He has written books on John Lyly (1996) and Elizabethan Humanism (2001), and also essays and articles on a range of mid-Tudor topics. He is presently working on a study of early Elizabethan Poetry.

Cathy Shrank is Professor of Tudor and Renaissance Literature at the University of Sheffield. Her publications include *Writing the Nation in Reformation England*, 1530–1580 (Oxford University Press, 2004, 2006) and essays and articles on various Tudor and Shakespearean topics, including language reform, civility, travel writing, cheap print, and mid-sixteenth-century sonnets. She is currently working on an edition of Shakespeare's poems and a monograph on non-dramatic dialogue in the sixteenth and early seventeenth centuries.

THE OXFORD HANDBOOK OF

TUDOR LITERATURE, 1485–1603

Edited by

MIKE PINCOMBE

and

CATHY SHRANK

OXFORD

UNIVERSITY PRESS

To Meg and Mimo

ACKNOWLEDGEMENTS

This book would not have happened without the Arts Humanities Research Council, who funded the project—'The origins of early modern literature: recovering mid-Tudor writing for a modern readership'—out of which this volume grew. We are also indebted to Andrew McNeillie at Oxford University Press, who came to the initial colloquium, held at the University of Aberdeen in July 2005, and was convinced by the case for mid-Tudor writing laid out during those two days. This volume offers a controversial version of what matters in the literature of the long sixteenth century: we are tremendously grateful for Andrew's belief in the project, and for giving us such free rein.

Many thanks are also due to our contributors: we could not have wished for a more friendly and hard-working group. They have done exactly as we asked, and have produced essays which are provocative and informed. Astoundingly, given the numbers involved, and that many were also having babies, these were delivered on time. We are especially grateful to Dermot Cavanagh, Jennifer Richards, Jessica Winston, and Phil Withington for their helpful comments on the Prologue (and the immense tact with which they made them, at the eleventh hour).

We would also like to thank Jacqueline Baker, Lindsey Hall, our splendid copy-editor Laurien Berkeley, and the production team at OUP, as well as the libraries, museums, and archives who helped us and our contributors. In particular, thanks are due to the Bodleian Library; the British Library; Cambridge University Library; Hatfield House; the Huntington Library; Kuntsmuseum, Basel; Lambeth Palace, the Pepys Library, Magdalene College, Cambridge; Newcastle University; the University of Sheffield; the Warburg Institute; and the Wren Library, Trinity College, Cambridge. We are also very grateful to Louise Wilson (and her Swiss bank account), and to Rita and Peter Redford, who suggested the cover image.

Last, but not least, thanks are also due to Ewa Dąbrowska and Phil Withington. They have listened to us drone on and on and on.

M.P., C.S.

Contents

PART III. 1560–1579

PART IV. 1580–1603

LIST OF ILLUSTRATIONS

Abbreviations and Conventions

A list of primary material consulted appears after each essay. Secondary material for all essays is listed in one large bibliography at the back of the volume. To save space, we have used an author–date system.

Titles of works have been modernized within the text of essays, in order to ensure that the same text is presented in the same orthographic form across the volume. However, to enable readers to locate the works consulted more easily (especially if using electronic texts), we retained old spelling in the lists of primary texts (and also in the captions to the illustrations).

The spelling of proper names follows *The Oxford Dictionary of National Biography* in the first instance; for people omitted from *ODNB* (e.g. some printers), we have followed the English Short-Title Catalogue.

In quotations from primary material in old spelling, u/v and i/j have been standardized. Interpolations, including ellipses, have been given in square brackets.

AHR	*American Historical Review*
AUMLA	*AUMLA: Journal of the Australasian Universities, Language and Literature Association*
BHR	*Bibliothèque d'Humanisme et Renaissance*
BJRL	*Bulletin of the John Rylands University Library*
BL	British Library
Bodl.	Bodleian Library
CahiersE	*Cahiers Élisabéthains*
CJ	*Classical Journal*
CML	*Classical and Modern Literature*
CP	*Classical Philology*
CPR	*Calendar of Patent Rolls Preserved in the Public Record Office*
CritI	*Critical Inquiry*
CrSurv	*Critical Survey*
CSP	*Calendar of State Papers*
CUL	Cambridge University Library
EEBO	Early English Books On-line

EETS	Early English Text Society
EHR	*English Historical Review*
EiC	*Essays in Criticism*
ELH	*English Literary History*
ELN	*English Language Notes*
ELR	*English Literary Renaissance*
ELWIU	*Essays in Literature*
e.s.	extra series
ES	*English Studies*
ESTC	English Short-Title Catalogue
ETREED	*Early Theatre*
GLQ	*GLQ: A Journal of Lesbian and Gay Studies*
HJ	*Historical Journal*
HLQ	*Huntington Library Quarterly*
HMSO	His/Her Majesty's Stationery Office
IJCT	*International Journal of the Classical Tradition*
JBS	*Journal of British Studies*
JEBS	*Journal of the Early Book Society*
JEGP	*Journal of English and Germanic Philology*
JEH	*Journal of Ecclesiastical History*
JHI	*Journal of the History of Ideas*
JMEMSt	*Journal of Medieval and Early Modern Studies*
JMRS	*Journal of Medieval and Renaissance Studies*
JWCI	*Journal of the Warburg and Courtauld Institutes*
L&H	*Literature and History*
LP	*Letters and Papers, Foreign and Domestic, of the Reign of Henry VIII, 1509–47*, ed. J. S. Brewer, J. Gairdner, and R. H. Brodie, 21 vols in 33 (1862–1910)
MED	*Middle English Dictionary*, gen. ed. Robert E. Lewis (Ann Arbor: University of Michigan Press, 1954–2001); repr. in *Middle English Compendium* (Ann Arbor: University of Michigan Press, 2006), <http://quod.lib.umich.edu/m/mec>, accessed 6 Jan. 2009
METh	*Medieval English Theatre*
MLN	*Modern Language Notes*
MLQ	*Modern Language Quarterly*

MLR	*Modern Language Review*
MLS	*Modern Language Studies*
MP	*Modern Philology*
MS	manuscript
NA	The National Archives, Kew (formerly PRO)
N&Q	*Notes and Queries*
Neophil	*Neophilologus*
n.s.	new series
ODNB	*Oxford Dictionary of National Biography* (on-line version)
OED	*Oxford English Dictionary* (on-line version)
o.s.	original series
PBSA	*Papers of the Bibliographical Society of America*
PMLA	*Publications of the Modern Language Association*
PQ	*Philological Quarterly*
PRO	Public Record Office, Kew
PubHist	*Publishing History*
ReFo	*Renaissance Forum*
Ren&R	*Renaissance and Reformation*
RenQ	*Renaissance Quarterly*
RenSt	*Renaissance Studies*
RES	*Review of English Studies*
RMSt	*Reading Medieval Studies*
RORD	*Research Opportunities in Renaissance Drama*
SB	*Studies in Bibliography*
SCJ	*Sixteenth-Century Journal*
SCRev	*South Central Review*
SEL	*Studies in English Literature*
ShS	*Shakespeare Survey*
SiJ	*Sidney Journal*
SP	*Studies in Philology*
SQ	*Shakespeare Quarterly*
s.s.	supplementary series
SSt	*Spenser Studies*
STC2	Short Title Catalogue (2nd edn)

TCBS	*Transactions of the Cambridge Bibliographical Society*
TLS	*Times Literary Supplement*
Tr&Lit	*Translation and Literature*
TSLL	*Texas Studies in Literature and Language*
YES	*The Yearbook of English Studies*

LIST OF CONTRIBUTORS

Thomas Betteridge is Professor of Early Modern Literature and Drama at Oxford Brookes University. His books include *Literature and Politics in the English Reformation* (Manchester University Press, 2004) and *Tudor Histories of the English Reformations* (Ashgate, 1999). He is currently working on a study of Sir Thomas More's writing to be published by the University of Notre Dame Press in 2010. He is also co-editor, with Greg Walker, of the *Oxford Handbook of Tudor Drama*.

David Bevington is the Phyllis Fay Horton Distinguished Service Professor Emeritus in the Humanities at the University of Chicago. His numerous books include *From 'Mankind' to Marlowe* (Oxford University Press, 1962), *Tudor Drama and Politics* (Harvard University Press, 1968), *Shakespeare: The Seven Ages of Human Experience* (Blackwell, 2005), and *Shakespeare's Ideas* (Blackwell, 2008). He is the editor of *Medieval Drama* (1975), *The Bantam Shakespeare*, and *The Complete Works of Shakespeare*, 6th edition (Longman, 2008). He is a senior editor of the Revels Student Editions, the Revels Plays, *The Norton Anthology of Renaissance Drama*, and the forthcoming Cambridge edition of the works of Ben Jonson.

Joyce Boro is an Associate Professor in the English Studies Department at the University of Montreal. She has published on medieval and early modern romance, Lord Berners, feminist historiography, and sixteenth-century translators and printers. Her first book is a critical edition and a study of the reception of Lord Berners's *Castell of Love*. She is currently editing Margaret Tyler's *Mirror of Princely Deeds and Knighthood* for the MHRA Tudor and Stuart Translations series.

Alan Bryson is a Postdoctoral Research Associate in the School of English at the University of Sheffield. His articles include 'Gamaliell Pye, Citizen of London', *British Art Journal*, 6 (2005), and 'Edward VI's "speciall men"', *Historical Research*, 82 (2009). He currently works on mid-Tudor lordship, politics, and warfare, mid-Tudor literature, and the correspondence of Bess of Hardwick. His monograph *Lordship and Politics in the Reign of Edward VI* (Pickering & Chatto) is in progress for publication in 2011.

Kent Cartwright is Professor of English and Chair of the English Department at the University of Maryland. His primary areas of research are Tudor literature and Shakespeare. He is the author of *Theatre and Humanism: English Drama in the Sixteenth Century* (Cambridge University Press, 1999) and *Shakespearean Tragedy* *and its Double: The Rhythms of Audience Response* (Pennsylvania State University Press, 1991), and he is the editor of the forthcoming *Blackwell Companion to Tudor Literature and Culture* (2009). He is also currently editing *The Comedy of Errors* for Arden Shakespeare, third series.

Dermot Cavanagh teaches literature at the University of Edinburgh. He is the author of *Language and Politics in the Sixteenth-Century History Play* (Palgrave Macmillan, 2003) and co-editor of *Shakespeare's Histories and Counter-Histories* (Manchester University Press, 2006). He is currently working on a study of the early modern mourning play.

Helen Cooper is Professor of Medieval and Renaissance English at the University of Cambridge. Her books include *Pastoral: Medieval into Renaissance* (Brewer, 1978), *The Structure of the Canterbury Tales* (Duckworth, 1983), *The Canterbury Tales*, Oxford Guides to Chaucer (Oxford University Press, 1989), *The English Romance in Time: Transforming Motifs from Geoffrey of Monmouth to the Death of Shakespeare* (Oxford University Press, 2004), and *Shakespeare and the Medieval World* (Arden Shakespeare, 2010). She has particular interests in links between the medieval and the early modern.

Janette Dillon is Professor of Drama at the University of Nottingham. Her books include *Language and Stage in Medieval and Renaissance England* (Cambridge University Press, 1998), *Performance and Spectacle in Hall's Chronicle* (Society for Theatre Research, 2002), and *The Cambridge Introduction to Early English Theatre* (Cambridge University Press, 2006). She is currently working on a book provisionally entitled *The Language of Space in Court Performance 1400–1625*.

Andrew Escobedo, an Associate Professor at Ohio University, is the author of *Nationalism and Historical Loss in Renaissance England: Foxe, Dee, Spenser, Milton* (Cornell University Press, 2004). He is currently writing a book about personification as an expression of Renaissance ideas about volition.

Jonathan Gibson is an academic coordinator at the English Subject Centre. His publications include *Women and Early Modern Manuscript Culture* (Ashgate, 2004), co-edited with Victoria Burke; *A Companion to the Gawain-Poet* (Brewer, 1997), co-edited with Derek Brewer; and essays on a wide variety of early modern topics, including letters, manuscript culture, Tudor poetry, and Shakespeare. Current research interests include manuscript miscellanies.

Alexandra Gillespie is an Associate Professor at the University of Toronto. She is co-editor of *John Stow and the Making of the English Past* (British Library, 2004) and the author of *Print Culture and the Medieval Author* (Oxford University Press, 2006). She is currently co-editing *The Production of Books in England 1350–1530* for

Cambridge University Press and working on a study of book and documentary production in the century before the invention of printing.

Jane Griffiths is a Senior Lecturer in English Literature at the University of Bristol. She has published articles on late medieval and early modern poetry and poetics in a variety of journals including the *Huntington Library Quarterly*, *Mediaevalia et Humanistica*, *Renaissance Studies*, and the *Yearbook of English Studies*. Her books include *John Skelton and Poetic Authority: Defining the Liberty to Speak* (Clarendon Press, 2006) and *Another Country: New and Selected Poems* (Bloodaxe Books, 2008), which was shortlisted for the Forward Prize. She is now working on a study of the marginal gloss in the period of transition from manuscript to print.

Andrew Hadfield is Professor of English at the University of Sussex and editor of *Renaissance Studies*. He is the author of a number of works on early modern literature, culture, and politics, including *Literature, Politics and National Identity: Reformation to Renaissance* (Cambridge University Press, 1994), Spenser's *Irish Experience* (Clarendon Press, 1997), and *Shakespeare and Republicanism* (Cambridge University Press, 2005; paperback, 2008). He has co-edited, with Raymond Gillespie, *The Oxford History of the Irish Book*, iii: *The Irish Book in English, 1550–1800* (Oxford University Press, 2006), and, with Matthew Dimmock, *Religions of the Book: Co-existence and Conflict, 1400–1660* (Palgrave Macmillan, 2008).

Hannibal Hamlin is an Associate Professor in the Department of English at Ohio State University. He is the author of *Psalm Culture and Early Modern English Literature* (Cambridge University Press, 2004), and articles and reviews in *Renaissance Quarterly*, *Spenser Studies*, the *Sidney Journal*, the *Yale Review*, the *Spenser Review*, and *Early Modern Literary Studies*. Current projects include co-editing the Psalms of Philip and Mary Sidney and a book-length study of biblical allusion in Shakespeare's plays.

Peter Happé is the retired Principal of Barton Peveril Sixth Form College, and is at present Visiting Fellow in the Department of English at the University of Southampton. Recent publications include *Cyclic Form and the English Mystery Plays* (Rodopi, 2004) and *The Towneley Cycle: Unity and Diversity* (University of Wales Press, 2007), and he has co-edited *Urban Theatre in the Low Countries 1400–1625* (Brepols, 2006) and *Interludes and Early Modern Society: Studies in Gender, Power and Theatricality* (Rodopi, 2007). He is editing Jonson's *A Tale of a Tub* (Cambridge University Press) and is working on a study of his Caroline plays.

Elizabeth Heale was a Senior Lecturer in English at the University of Reading and is now an Honorary Fellow. Her books include *Wyatt, Surrey and Early Tudor Poetry* (Longman, 1998) and *Autobiography and Authorship in Renaissance Verse: Chronicles of the Self* (Palgrave Macmillan, 2003). She is currently working on sixteenth-century verse and Elizabethan travel-writing.

Andrew Hiscock is Professor of English at Bangor University, Wales. He edited the MHRA's 2008 double issue of the *Yearbook of English Studies* devoted to Tudor literature and his last monograph was *The Uses of this World: Thinking Space in Shakespeare, Marlowe, Cary and Jonson* (University of Wales Press, 2004). He is series co-editor for the *Continuum Renaissance Drama*, co-editor of the journal *English*, and from autumn 2011 editor (English) for *MLR*. His new monograph is entitled *Reading Memory in Early Modern Literature* (Cambridge University Press, 2011).

Alice Hunt is Lecturer in Early Modern English Literature at the University of Southampton. She is the author of *The Drama of Coronation: Medieval Ceremony in Early Modern England* (Cambridge University Press, 2008) and the editor, with Anna Whitelock, of *Tudor Queenship: The Reigns of Mary and Elizabeth* (Palgrave Macmillan, 2010).

Lorna Hutson is Berry Professor of English Literature at the University of St Andrews. She is the author of *Thomas Nashe in Context* (Oxford University Press, 1989), *The Usurer's Daughter* (Routledge, 1994), and *The Invention of Suspicion: Law and Mimesis in Shakespeare and Renaissance Drama* (Oxford, 2007). She is interested in the legal and rhetorical underpinnings of Renaissance literature, and is currently editing a special forum of *Representations* on Ernst Kantorowicz.

John N. King is Distinguished University Professor Emeritus and Humanities Distinguished Professor Emeritus of English and Religious Studies in the Department of English at Ohio State University. His numerous books include *English Reformation Literature: The Tudor Origins of the Protestant Tradition* (Princeton University Press, 1982), *Spenser's Poetry and the Reformation Tradition* (Princeton University Press, 1990), and Foxe's *Book of Martyrs and Early Modern Print Culture* (Cambridge University Press, 2006). He is the editor of the journal *Reformation*.

Scott Lucas is Professor of English at the Citadel, the Military College of South Carolina. He is the author of the monograph *A Mirror for Magistrates and the Politics of the English Reformation* (University of Massachusetts Press, 2009), as well as articles and book chapters on Tudor and Stuart literature, history, and culture. He is currently working on studies of the Tudor chronicler Edward Hall's *Union of the Two Noble and Illustre Famelies* and of Holinshed's *Chronicles*.

R. W. Maslen is Senior Lecturer at the University of Glasgow. His books include *Elizabethan Fictions* (Clarendon Press, 1997), *Shakespeare and Comedy* (Arden Critical Companions, 2005), and a revision of Geoffrey Shepherd's edition of Sir Philip Sidney's *Apology for Poetry* (Manchester University Press, 2002). He is currently working on a history of comic fiction in the sixteenth century.

Steven W. May is adjunct Professor of English at Emory University, Atlanta, and Honorary Research Fellow at the University of Sheffield. His books include an edition of *Queen Elizabeth I: Selected Works* (Simon & Schuster, 2004) and *Elizabethan Poetry: A Bibliography and First-Line Index of English Verse, 1559–1603* (3 vols, Thoemmes Continuum, 2004). His research interests include English Renaissance manuscript culture, the Tudor court, and editing early modern documents.

Helen Moore is Fellow and Tutor in English at Corpus Christi College, Oxford. She has edited *Amadis de Gaule* (Ashgate, 2004) and *The Tragical History of Guy, Earl of Warwick* (Malone Society, 2007). She has published essays on the English reception of Continental and classical romance, and on early modern drama, and is currently working on a book about Anglo-French cultural relations in the early modern period.

Janel Mueller is William Rainey Harper Distinguished Service Professor Emerita in the Department of English, University of Chicago. She has co-edited for University of Chicago Press *Elizabeth I: Collected Works* (2000), *Elizabeth I: Autograph Compositions and Foreign Language Originals* (2003), and *Elizabeth I: Translations* (2008). She is presently completing her edition of *Queen Katherine Parr: Complete Works and Correspondence* under the auspices of an Andrew Mellon Foundation Emeritus Fellowship.

Wolfgang G. Müller is Emeritus Professor of English Studies at the University of Jena. His books include *Die politische Rede bei Shakespeare* (Narr, 1979); *Topik des Stilbegriffs: Zur Geschichte des Stilverständnisses von der Antike bis zur Gegenwart* (Wissenschaftliche Buchgesellschaft, 1981), *Die englisch-schottische Volksballade* (Francke, 1983), *William Shakespeare. Hamlet. Einleitung und Kommentar* (Stauffenburg Verlag, 2006). He is currently working on the construction of an ethical narratology and on the tradition of Cervantes in the English novel.

Mike Pincombe is Professor of Tudor and Elizabethan Literature at Newcastle University; he convened the Tudor Symposium between 1998 and 2009. He has written books on John Lyly (1996) and Elizabethan Humanism (2001), and also essays and articles on a range of mid-Tudor topics. He is presently working on a study of early Elizabethan poetry.

Jason Powell is an Assistant Professor of English at St Joseph's University in Philadelphia. His articles have appeared in *Huntington Library Quarterly*, *Poetica*, *English Manuscript Studies 1100–1700*, and the *Sixteenth Century Journal*. His scholarly edition of Thomas Wyatt's complete works is forthcoming in two volumes from Oxford University Press.

Syrithe Pugh lectures on English literature at the University of Aberdeen. She is the author of *Spenser and Ovid* (2005), *Herrick, Fanshawe and the Politics of Intertextuality: Classical Literature and Seventeenth-Century Royalism* (in press), and articles on Spenser, Sidney, Jonson, Herrick, and Fanshawe.

Mark Rankin is Assistant Professor of English at James Madison University. He is the author of articles and chapters on Tudor literature and book history and the co-editor of *Henry VIII and His Afterlives* (Cambridge, 2009). He is currently working on a monograph on the afterlife of Henry VIII in early modern literature and polemical writing.

Jennifer Richards is Professor of English at Newcastle University. Her publications include *Rhetoric and Courtliness in Early Modern Literature* (Cambridge University Press, 2003, 2007) and *Rhetoric* (Routledge, 2008). She is the editor of *Early Modern Civil Discourses* (Palgrave Macmillan, 2003). She is currently working on 'Diet, Dialogue and the Early Modern Body Politic'.

Fred Schurink is Lecturer in Early Modern English Literature at Northumbria University. He is the author of the *Review of English Studies* Prize Essay ' "Like a hand in the margine of a booke": William Blount's Marginalia and the Politics of Sidney's *Arcadia*' (2008) and other articles and chapters on Tudor literature, reading practices, and education, and is co-author of the online database 'The Origins of Early Modern Literature' (hriOnline, 2009). He is currently writing a book on Tudor translations of the classics and editing a two-volume selection of sixteenth-century translations of Plutarch's *Essays* and *Lives*.

Philip Schwyzer is Associate Professor in English at the University of Exeter. His books include *Literature, Nationalism and Memory in Early Modern England and Wales* (Cambridge University Press, 2004) and *Archaeologies of English Renaissance Literature* (Oxford University Press, 2007). He is currently working on a study of the textual and material remains of Richard III in the Tudor era.

Laurie Shannon is Wender-Lewis Associate Professor of English at Northwestern University. She works on topics in political thought, natural history, animal studies, and affect, gender, and sexuality in early modern literature and culture. She is the author of *Sovereign Amity: Figures of Friendship in Shakespearean Contexts* (University of Chicago Press, 2002) and *The Accommodated Animal: Cosmopolity in Shakespearean Locales* (University of Chicago Press, 2012); both studies explore broadly constitutional questions to chart diverse conceptions of political membership.

Cathy Shrank is Professor of Tudor and Renaissance Literature at the University of Sheffield. Her publications include *Writing the Nation in Reformation England, 1530–1580* (Oxford University Press, 2004, 2006) and essays and articles on various Tudor and Shakespearean topics, including language reform, civility, travel writing, cheap print, and mid-sixteenth-century sonnets. She is currently working on an edition of Shakespeare's poems and a monograph on non-dramatic dialogue in the sixteenth and early seventeenth centuries.

James Simpson is Donald P. and Katherine B. Loker Professor of English at Harvard University (2004–). He is a Life Fellow of Fellow of Girton College and an Honorary Fellow of the Australian Academy of the Humanities. His books include *Reform and Cultural Revolution*, being volume 2 in the *Oxford English Literary History* (Oxford University Press, 2002) (winner of the British Academy Sir Israel Gollancz Prize, 2007); and *Burning to Read: English Fundamentalism and its Reformation Opponents* (Harvard University Press, 2007); and *Under the Hammer: Iconoclasm in the Anglo-American Tradition* (OUP, 2010).

D. J. B. Trim is a Lecturer in History at Newbold College and associate editor of the *Journal of the Society for Army Historical Research*. His publications include *The Chivalric Ethos and Military Professionalism* (Brill, 2002); *Religious Minorities and the Development of Pluralism in Modern Britain and France* (Peter Lang, 2004) with Richard Bonney; and *Cross, Crown and Community: Religion, Government and Culture in Early Modern Europe* (Peter Lang, 2004) with Peter J. Balderstone. He is currently working on a book about English and Welsh mercenaries during the European wars of religion, 1562–1610.

Margaret Tudeau-Clayton is Professor of English Literature and head of the Institute of English Studies at the University of Neuchâtel, Switzerland. She is author of *Jonson, Shakespeare and early modern Virgil* (Cambridge 1998; reprinted as pbk 2006) and numerous articles on English Renaissance literature, especially on translation and on Shakespeare. She has co-edited three collections of essays: with Martin Warner, *Addressing Frank Kermode* (Macmillan 1991); with Philippa Berry, *Textures of Renaissance Knowledge* (Manchester 2003); and with Willy Maley, *This England, That Shakespeare* (Ashgate 2010). She is currently working on two related projects: *Shakespeare's Englishes* and 'Shakespeare and Immigration'.

Daniel Wakelin is a Lecturer in English at the University of Cambridge and a Fellow of Christ's College. He has published a book entitled *Humanism, Reading, and English Literature 1430–1530* (Oxford University Press, 2007) and articles on Middle English and early Tudor literature and the history of the book. He is currently co-editing *The Production of Books in England 1350–1530* for Cambridge University Press.

Christopher Warley teaches Renaissance literature and critical theory at the University of Toronto. He is the author of *Sonnet Sequences and Social Distinction in Renaissance England* (Cambridge University Press, 2005), and is currently working on *Specters of Horatio: Reading Class in Renaissance Literature*.

Paul Whitfield White is Professor of English in the Department of English, Purdue University. His publications include *Theatre and Reformation: Protestantism, Patronage, and Playing in Tudor England* (Cambridge University Press, 1993); *Marlowe, History, and Sexuality: New Critical Essays on Christopher Marlowe* (AMS, 1998); *Shakespeare and Theatrical Patronage in Early Modern England*

(Cambridge University Press, 2002), co-edited with Suzanne R. Westfall; and *Drama and Religion in English Provincial Society, 1485–1660* (Cambridge University Press, 2008).

Katharine Wilson has taught at Newcastle University and the University of Oxford. She is the author of *Fictions of Authorship in Late Elizabethan Narratives: Euphues in Arcadia* (Oxford, 2006) and has contributed an essay to *Writing Robert Greene*, edited by Kirk Melnikoff and Edward Gieskes (Ashgate, 2008).

Jessica Winston is an Associate Professor of English at Idaho State University. Her articles include 'Seneca in Early Elizabethan England' (*Renaissance Quarterly*, 2006) and 'Expanding the Political Nation: *Gorboduc* at the Inns of Court and Succession Revisited' (*Early Theatre*, 2005). She is currently working on a book on the literary community of the Inns of Court in the 1560s.

Phil Withington is a Lecturer in Social and Economic History at the University of Cambridge. He is the author of *The Politics of Commonwealth: Citizens and Freemen in Early Modern England* (Cambridge University Press, 2005) and *Society in Early Modern* England (Polity, 2010), co-edited *Communities in Early Modern England* (Manchester University Press, 2000), and has written articles on the social history of citizenship for *Past and Present, Historical Journal, English Historical Review*, and *American Historical Review*. He is currently researching the history of intoxicants and intoxication during the sixteenth and seventeenth centuries.

Jonathan Woolfson is Academic Director of the Istituto Lorenzo de' Medici, Florence. He is the author of *Padua and the Tudors: English Students in Italy, 1485–1603* (University of Toronto Press, 1998) and the editor of *Reassessing Tudor Humanism* (Palgrave Macmillan, 2002) and *Palgrave Advances in Renaissance Historiography* (Palgrave Macmillan, 2004). He has written widely on Anglo-Italian cultural and intellectual relations during the sixteenth century.

PROLOGUE

THE TRAVAILS OF
TUDOR LITERATURE

MIKE PINCOMBE

CATHY SHRANK

'WE must learn to do without the Tudors,' wrote the distinguished historian C. S. L. Davies (2008: 15), just as the editors of the present volume embarked upon this Prologue. Davies's brief article is playfully provocative: it argues that we should abandon the term 'Tudor' because it 'had little purchase in its own era'. It is entirely serious, however, when it asks us to reconsider the validity of epithets so familiar that we use them almost unthinkingly. As such, it is a pertinent starting point for these opening remarks for two key reasons. First, it demands that we take time to consider what it is we mean when we talk about 'the Tudors', and thus, by extension, 'Tudor literature'. Second, it highlights the importance—and shortcomings—of labels, particularly those attached to historical periods. Indeed, contrary to Davies, what we want to suggest here is that, far from jettisoning the epithet 'Tudor', we need to embrace the implications of the term more fully. This is because the term allows us to look at English writing across a long sixteenth century rather than, as has generally be done, focusing on the later Elizabethan era—a period of literary largesse for sure, but one that should not obscure earlier riches, and which was, in any case, the product of what came before.

Who, then, are 'the Tudors'? Are they members of the royal house in whose name the country was governed between 1485 and 1603, but who—according to Davies—never perceived themselves as 'Tudors' at all? Or are the Tudors also their subjects, such as those we see on the cover of this volume, all of them enjoying—in different ways—a fete at Bermondsey, then a village south of the Thames? The appellation seems appropriate for both dynasty and nation.

Despite Davies's thought-provoking essay, it is not feasible to write history purely in terms of 'its own era': epochs need defining somehow. As C. S. Lewis wrote with regard to sixteenth-century English literature: 'though "periods" are a mischievous concept they are a methodological necessity' (1954: 64). In the particular case of sixteenth-century England, the sovereign is no bad place to start trying to define the period, even if ultimately it is the *people* labelled 'Tudor', milling around what is now London's South Bank in their holiday finery, rather than the dynasts, who interest us most.

The early modern English were, to a larger extent than now, nominally defined by their sovereign. They were required to pray for them on a regular basis; the statutes which bound them were designated by the year of the reign in which they became law; and many of the books the literate members among them read carried the stamp of royal authority—be it the phrase *cum privilegio*, frequently written out more fully as *cum privilegio regis regali* ('by privilege granted by the ruling sovereign'), or the information that they were 'seen and allowed' according to royal injunctions.

That is, even as they went about their everyday lives, the English were reminded of their status as subjects, albeit a subjecthood that was also inflected by a sense of their status as 'free' (Thomas *c*.1551: 2^r; T. Smith 1982: 57). The paradox of the English as free subjects of the monarch is reflected in the cover picture. The Tower of London (the royal prison) can be seen in the background, a reminder of royal authority and the power of the sovereign. On the other hand, the crowd of pleasure-seekers is absorbed in its own communal and apparently self-regulated activities: eating, dancing, conversing, dog-baiting. It is the spectator's critical eye which sees both at once.

We would argue that it is possible—indeed, *productive*—to talk of 'Tudor litera-ture', not least because much of that writing was composed in reaction to policies emanating from the monarch, or performed in his or her name. To be sure, labelling a period can be more damaging than productive. Lewis himself was the author of a damagingly 'mischievous' tag for the mid-Tudor decades—'the Drab Age'—which has dogged them ever since he came up with the phrase in 1954. However much he insists that he did not intend it as a 'dyslogistic term' (64), it is made precisely that by the tone of the work, the unavoidably negative connotations of the adjective (who would ever want to be called 'drab'?), and the implicitly unfavourable com-parison with Lewis's Elizabethan 'Golden Age'. Weighed down by a book he did not want to write, Lewis gets through the middle decades of the century ('an earnest, heavy-handed, commonplace age') by making wisecracks at their authors' expense— Thomas Peend and Alexander Neville are both 'very, very bad' (250, 255); George Turbervile 'is a better poet than [Arthur] Golding, but not a good one' (252). In doing so, Lewis saved later critics from having to take the writing of the period seriously, or even to read it. Instead, if ever required to engage with mid-Tudor literature, they could reach for one of his dismissive phrases.

The critical reputation of the long lines of Tudor verse (fourteeners and poulter's measure) is indicative of the corrosive effect of Lewis's quips. Subsequent scholars can scarcely write about these metres without prefixing them with an adjective like 'lumbering' or 'thudding' (Thomson 1964: 187), or lambasting the 'strange inadequacies' and 'unwield[iness]' of this 'unfortunate Tudor experiment' (Hawkes 1962: 421; A. Mortimer 2002: 15). Long lines may well thud and lumber, but they do not necessarily do so (just as iambic pentameters may or may not sound 'natural'). Compare, for example, some lines from Thomas Wyatt's 'So feeble is the thread', composed in poulter's measure in the 1530s, and iambic pentameters from Thomas Watson's *Hekatompathia* (1582). First Wyatt (whom Lewis classified a 'Drab Age' poet):

> the lyff so short so fraile that mortal men lyve here
> so gret a whaite so hevy charge the body that we bere
> that when I thinke apon the distance and the space
> that doth so ferr devid me from my dere desired face
> I know not how tattayne the wynges that I require
> to lyfft my whaite that it myght fle to folow my desyre[.]
>
> (1969, lines 21–6)

And now Watson:

> Well fare the life sometimes I ledde ere this,
> When yet no downy heare yclad my face:
> my heart devoyde of cares did bath in blisse,
> my thoughts were free in euery time & place:
> But now (alas) all's fowle, which then was faire,
> My wonted joyes are turning to despaire.
> Where then I liv'd without controule or checke,
> An other now is mistris of my minde.
>
> (1582: 1. 1–8)

Both poems consider the impact of love on the mental state of the poetic speaker. Wyatt's use of metre is subtly modulated. The lingering lines—extending the poet's description of painful separation—capture the enervating effects of the prolonged absence from the beloved, encapsulated by the almost predominantly monosyllabic fourteener (line 26), in which the poetic line, like a winged bird, fails to rise from the ground (Shrank 2008a: 388–9). This is then balanced against the speaker's yearning for contact, expressed through the frequent use of enjambment (which places yet more demands on the breath control of anyone reciting the poem aloud, making them, too, feel the strain). Watson's ten-beat, end-stopped lines, in contrast, are as thumpingly, uninspiringly regular as their clichéd evocation of love-as-bondage.

Lewis's objection to the aesthetic qualities of mid-Tudor literature highlights a key factor in its continued absence from undergraduate curriculums. Many of the things which give Tudor literature its energy also make it challenging: it is frequently of the moment, reacting to particular events or sets of concerns; it often treats of its subject obliquely; it is generally written by the intelligentsia; and it is not shy about displaying its intellectual origins and aspirations. As a rule, it needs more than a strictly 'New Critical' approach to unlock its virtues. It is consequently difficult for students, approaching it blind, to achieve the immediate rewards that they might, say, from a lyric by John Donne.

The advent of New Historicism—the most influential critical movement in early modern literary studies in the latter part of the twentieth century—did little to make the mid-century literature more accessible. The primer of New Historicism, Stephen Greenblatt's *Renaissance Self-Fashioning* (1980), showed a new generation of scholars how to perform anthropologically inflected historicist readings on pre-modern texts. However, ground-breaking though the methodology was, it was not intended to rewrite literary history. In *Renaissance Self-Fashioning*, Greenblatt leaps from Wyatt in the 1520s–1530s to Spenser in the 1580s. Subsequent practitioners tended to justify reading non-canonical material—by which they meant legal and historical texts—by showing how it shed new light on familiar, often Shakespearean, material. Rather than opening up the mid-century, New Historicism reinforced Lewis's conclusion that those decades could be skipped. Now you could be theoretically sophisticated, but you still did not have to venture beyond the well-trodden paths of the Renaissance canon. Clifford Geertz would be on the reading list, but not Barnabe Googe.

Towards the end of this Prologue, where we explain how we have divided the current volume, we revisit the problems of labels, periodization, and canonicity. But for now we want to return to the 'Tudorness' of sixteenth-century literature by looking at one of the period's many neglected but interesting and important poems: William Baldwin's *Funerals of King Edward VI*.

Baldwin wrote the *Funerals* in the interregnum between Edward's death on 6 July 1553 and his burial on 8 August, shortly after his sister Mary had routed the rival forces of John Dudley, Duke of Northumberland, and entered London as queen. Northumberland had ruled England as Lord Protector for the last two years and wished to install his daughter-in-law Lady Jane Grey as queen in Mary's place. Baldwin, however, is not interested in dynastic politics; nor, despite the title of his pamphlet, is he even concerned to describe the young king's funeral, for Baldwin tells us explicitly that he had written his book 'before his corse was buryed' (1560: A1^r).

The word 'corse' (corpse) provides the clue to Baldwin's paradoxical title. Baldwin could have waited until Edward had been interred and then have written a solemn account of his obsequies, with due attention to ceremonial details and a correctly elegiac tone. When the *Funerals* was reprinted in 1610, it was fathered—unaltered— upon Edward's tutor, Sir John Cheke, and misleadingly described as 'A royall elegie[.] Briefly describing the vertuous reigne, and happy (though immature) death of the most mightie and renowmed prince. King Edward the sixth' (A1^r). There is nothing about Edward's virtuous reign in the poem, nor is it an elegy, but—given its title and the large woodcut portrait of Edward which bookends the work (A1^r, A4^r)—that is clearly what the poem *should* have been.[1]

---

[1] The woodcut appears on the title page of Richard Jugge's edition of the New Testament in 1552 and 1553, and occupies most of *The Prayer of King Edward VI*—his deathbed prayer—issued as a single-sheet folio (July 1553).

But Baldwin resists the easy appeal of producing a properly 'funereal' image of Edward's 'corse', a marmorealized icon of royalty which would satisfy the requirements of official state discourse. Instead, in those scant passages where Baldwin ruminates directly on his dead king, he shows a strikingly well-informed interest in the physical symptoms of Edward's final illness (probably tuberculosis) combined with a curious appetite for grotesque details such as how 'The juyce congelde that in his Lounges lay rawe, | Did stop the pipes, wherthrough the breth should draw' (B2^r). Edward's royal corpse is reduced to undignified, earthy matter for Baldwin's rankly fertile imagination.

For the most part, though, Baldwin's purpose in writing the *Funerals* is not so much to praise—or even bury—the late king, as to declare 'the causers and causes of his death' (A1^r). The Tudor dynast is shouldered aside in favour of the Tudors, the unruly inhabitants of his realm. Edward was first infected with disease in order to terrify his subjects into better behaviour, as was explained at the time by several godly preachers: 'But out alas, how wer these preachers heard?' (B2^v). Careless of their sovereign's fate, the sinful English carry on as before. The poem has a specific moral intent: to attempt to succeed where the preachers had failed and to persuade the people of England to live a more godly life. Despite this apparently civic-minded purpose, however, Baldwin was unable to have the piece published under Mary; one suspects that her regime may have felt that the explosively energetic poem was rather too unruly.

The plurality of Baldwin's targets ('the causers and causes') is evident from the title page: Baldwin blames almost every one of Edward's subjects in a well-developed estates satire, which encompasses a wide range of culprits from greedy aristocrats to profiteering London wood-sellers. A poem which sets out to mourn the death of a king thus transmutes into a spirited description of disorderly quotidian life. As it does so, the poem's didactic voice starts to compete with other literary intentions, banishing the lugubrious tone to be expected from funereal verses. In this way, the poem is also a 'satire' in the old Roman sense of the *satura*: a mixed dish—a work made of various generic materials. The *Funerals* combines elements of vatic poetry, the jeremiad (calling all to repentance), dialogue (between Christ and God), a parody of epic tropes (such as the cave of the winds at the beginning of Virgil's *Aeneid*), religious allegory, the *ars moriendi* (art of dying), and—in the incorporation of detailed medical knowledge—the tendency towards secular encyclopedism found in works such as Stephen Hawes's courtly allegory of love-adventure *The Pastime of Pleasure* (c.1509).

The *Funerals* takes its point of origin in a historical event, but it does not allow that event—the King's death—to limit its poetic horizons. The actual funeral of the young monarch is the absent centre of a poem whose real and urgent concern is with a malaise at the level of the nation. The visitation of Crazy Cold— 'this fel horseman with his griesly stede' (B1^r), sent on a quasi-regicidal mission to strike down Edward as punishment for English sins—is a reminder that God may send a plague at any moment to devastate the unregenerate population of England.

Here, then, is a work which illustrates the exuberantly proliferating energies of mid-Tudor literature. But building up this picture has taken some effort. As readers, we have had to take into account the historical circumstances of its production, and then readjust our bearings when it veers away from the apparent topic in hand. We have also had to draw on knowledge of various genres, and of literature in other languages and from a range of traditions. Information about the materiality of the original text and its print history has also been brought into play, to illuminate some of its oddities and rude force. Baldwin's *Funerals* is thus indicative of some of the challenges of Tudor writing: it is often a response to a particular occurrence or process; it is wildly eclectic, in terms of both the genres and fields of knowledge which it exhibits; and it flaunts its book-learning. Bear with it, though, and you can see its vigour; an author's passionate commitment to informing, or reforming, his compatriots; and a creative tension between a subject, bound to the house of Tudor, and a citizen, who refuses to bow to the iconic pressures of kingship and often displays a sardonic awareness of the shortcomings of monarchs.[2]

The seriousness and specificity of Baldwin's purpose in the *Funerals* is typical of Tudor literature, as is the immediacy with which it addresses its readers. 'I earnestly beseche thee,' calls Baldwin in his Preface, seeking to establish a relationship between him and each individual reader through use of the familiar, second-person singular (A1ᵛ). The implied readers and audiences of sixteenth-century texts are more than a shadowy presence: they are cajoled and instructed in prefatory material, invited to set their amending hand to the printed work, even addressed mid-text. The community within and for which authors wrote is thus continually brought to mind.

That Tudor writers should display this awareness of the wider society to which they belonged, and to which their works were directed, owes much to the fact that the sixteenth century was the age of 'commonweal'. Coined during the second half the fifteenth century, the term gained rapid currency and came to dominate sociopolitical discourse in Tudor England, employed (often simultaneously) both as a synonym for 'the realm' and to denote a state in which government serves the interests of the polity as a whole. It inscribed the obligation of governors to rule for greater good, but it also imposed responsibilities on citizen–subjects to play their part.

The most frequently used metaphors of the commonweal were those of the body politic and ship of state, the continued preservation of which needed the active (if varied) involvement of all: limbs cannot survive without a body; the ship sinks with all aboard. Commonweal ties together the members of an imagined community, what Cicero describes in his famous book on duties, *De officiis*, as the *vinculum societatis humanae* ('bond of human society'; 1. 50). The ubiquity and rhetorical purchase of the idea of commonweal were sufficiently established by the early 1530s for the character representing Reginald Pole, in Thomas Starkey's *Dialogue between Pole and Lupset*, to note caustically that 'Every man speke of the commyn wele, every man hath that oft

---

[2] Baldwin was incorporated into the Stationers' Company in 1557 (*ODNB*), and was thus a 'citizen' of London by virtue of his membership of a guild.

in hys mouth that under the pretense & colour therof they may the bettur procure theyr owne' (1989: 16).

Pole might here deride the appropriation of the term, but the work in which he appears is committed to the amelioration of current social ills and the advancement of the common good. The language and ideology of commonweal infused Tudor literature. The desire to aid, inspire, or simply communicate ('common') with one's compatriots is reflected in the way in which sixteenth-century authors are recurrently drawn to 'oral' or discursive modes: dialogues, contentions, drama, answer poems, orations. And it is reflected in the way they present works to prospective audiences and patrons. When Nicholas Udall, for example, addressed Edward VI in the Preface of his translation of book 1 of Desiderius Erasmus' *Paraphrase upon the New Testament* (1548), he highlighted the way in which early modern authors (in this case, a translator) were not working in a vacuum: 'a translator travaileth not to his own private commodity, but to the behoof and public use of his country [...] to do good in the commonweal with this kind of service' (12^{r-v}). The motivation behind this is not purely selfless, however. Udall here makes a fruitless plea for state funding; if writers are not sufficiently rewarded, or compensated for their outlay of 'meat, drink, and books' when embroiled in virtuous projects, such as the translation of godly books (exactly what Udall is currently involved in), then they will simply not be able—or willing—to do the work.

Udall's comments about the 'labour' of literary production are pertinent. Writing in the period does not just happen. It was work: it took time and incurred expense. Pens needed to be sharpened at regular intervals, quills cut at a precise angle, ink mixed, (costly) paper purchased. It was not without reason that the Senecan translator Jasper Heywood described his pen as 'paynfull' (1560: *7^{v}), the meanings of which encompassed effort as well as physical discomfort.[3] So too printing was a labour-intensive process, as can be seen in Figure 1.1. Two compositors bend over their boxes, setting each piece of type by hand; another inks the set type; a fourth man removes the previously printed sheet; the large lever prominent in the right of the picture reminds us of a further task not depicted here: the manual pulling down of the heavy press.

For all the talk of how the printing press enabled the 'cheap' and 'rapid' manufacture of books, these things are relative. To produce a work was a considerable investment. The Tudor texts we read, therefore, were written because something was at stake. Authors wrote to educate their compatriots, be it how to behave, to reach salvation, or to acquire a body of knowledge. Even works of seemingly vacuous entertainment were seen to serve a purpose: allowing minds to re-create themselves, providing the rest necessary for profitable labour. Yet, for all the emphasis on the profit readers will accumulate through the offered works, there is still a satisfaction that goes beyond the allegedly utilitarian purpose of the book in hand.

Indeed, since sixteenth-century printers repeatedly advertise their wares in terms of the 'pleasure and profit' purchasers will gain, it is clear that both they and their

---

[3] 'Painful', *OED*, *adj.*, 2a. 5.

Fig. P.1 Having seen Bathsheba bathing, King David sends a messenger to her. Miles Coverdale, *Psalter* (1540), A1ᵛ.

authors believed in—or subscribed to the rhetoric of—the potential of literature of all kinds to edify their readers as well as gratify them (or alternatively, to amuse as well as instruct). Sometimes literary history loses track of pleasure. Nonetheless, delight and desire are everywhere evident in Tudor texts, even in the most unexpected places.

The example we have chosen to illustrate these unpredictable pleasures—and the varied forms they could take—is a woodcut. That mid-sixteenth-century literature is currently experiencing a critical 'renaissance' owes much to the insight of scholars working with the methodology of book history. Concentrating on the materiality of a text (in this case a visual text) brings into focus a characteristic trait of Tudor books: ambiguity that is often playful. The possibility of diverse interpretations stems, in many instances, from the variety of contexts in and for which works were produced, and the array of influences on which they draw and invoke.

The woodcut in question (Figure P.1) was first made up for the Great Bible (1539), compiled by Miles Coverdale, revising earlier translations, including his own. It illustrates the moment when King David, having seen Bathsheba bathing on the roof of the house adjoining his palace, 'sent messengers and fett [fetched] her' (46^r; 2 Samuel 11: 4). As such, the woodcut presents an image of desire which is legitimized by the fact that it illustrates Scripture; its potential lewdness is redeemed by the biblical text it depicts.

The following year, in 1540, one of the printers of the Great Bible, Richard Grafton, used the same block in his separate edition of Coverdale's translation of the psalter (A1^v). Here, removed from the parallel text of the Bible story, it assumes a more risqué character, though Coverdale presumably sanctioned the presence of the image in the 1540 volume. But now the discrepancies between the image and the biblical text for which it was apparently first designed—the sole messenger, the garden setting, the King peering from the window—assume a more disruptive aspect. Without the biblical text, the picture becomes unmoored from its authorized meaning. It resembles instead an episode from courtly romance, or the 'balettes of fylthynes' Coverdale had denounced in his *Ghostly Psalms and Spiritual Songs* (1535?, ✠1^r).

The irony of this newly liberated ambiguity is all the greater when we consider its original context. The title page of the 1539 Bible—the first English Bible to be officially endorsed by the sovereign—is an iconic representation of royal authority over the dissemination and reception of texts, a process it depicts as a 'graded hierarchy' (J. King 1982: 53). At the top, above the royal coat of arms, Henry distributes the Good Book to Archbishop Thomas Cranmer and his chief minister, Thomas Cromwell, who donate it to the clergy, who then preach it from the pulpit. In the bottom panel, Henry's subjects express their gratitude. The aristocrats cry 'vivat rex', their social standing demonstrated by their use of Latin, an elite language; the 'almost childlike' commoners use a vernacular alternative: 'God save the king' (J. King 1982: 54).

This fantasy of all-encompassing royal power often serves as the master narrative of New Historicism. The diligently politicizing critic, tracing the psalter woodcut of David and Bathsheba to its historical moment of production, might note that it was in 1540 that Henry, a notoriously concupiscent monarch, turned his attentions from his apparently somewhat dowdy queen, Anne of Cleves, to the beautiful and compliant Katherine Howard. Comparisons were frequently made between David and Henry (Halasz 1988), so it would be possible to claim that the king alludes to Henry, the scantily clad lady to Katherine. The paper which passes between the messenger and the woman now becomes a billet-doux of the kind which played an important role in the literary culture of the Henrician court (Lerer 1997).

But this reading runs up against the problem of the centrality of the figure of the messenger. Isolated from its original scriptural context, the image seems to tell the story of the young man and the lady, perhaps as an allegory of Youth and Beauty, under the watchful but indulgent eye of a relaxed Royal Majesty, resting his arms on his tasselled cushion. Psychoanalytical critics could make a good deal out of this situation, which looks remarkably like wishful thinking: the Id's pursuit of desire with the blessing of the Superego's authority. However, many sixteenth-century readers would have 'read' this image in terms of courtly romance.

One thinks here, perhaps, of the mid-Tudor compiler of Rawlinson MS C.813, which contains an adaptation of passages from Hawes's *Pastime of Pleasure*. The 1554 reprinting of the *Pastime*—quite likely supervised by Baldwin—advertised the book for its usefulness as a time-saving device: as being a quick and easy way to gain access to secular learning, 'whiche many great clarkes wythout great paynes and travayle, & long continuance of time heretofore could never obteyne nor get' (Mead 1928, p. xxxiii). The Rawlinson compiler, however, was drawn to the work not for the secular wisdom it contained, but for the passages describing the love between Grand Amour and La Belle Pucelle, which he reworked as amorous lyrics of his own fashioning (Mead 1928, p. xxxvii).

Indeed, an allegorical interpretation of the Coverdale woodcut is legitimized by an earlier version of this image, in Alexander Barclay's *Eclogues* (1530), the first three of which are courtly satires (A2^v). Again, a king, leaning on a cushion, watches from a window. This time, however, a female courtier, flanked by her attendant and a lapdog, takes the position of the messenger; rather than handing over a written message, she raises a mirror to the topless beauty, perhaps representing Venus or Pride.

When we measure this against the image in Coverdale's Psalter, the courtly-romantic acquires a more sinister hue. Venus and Pride are disruptive forces, and we might now see the king regarding the scene below him with a less benevolent aspect after all. Does he not resemble the cuckolded King Arthur, discovering the illicit, dynasty-destroying liaison of his wife and lover? And would not Arthur's Anglo-British imperial heir, Henry VIII, find himself similarly compromised by Katherine Howard's affair with the hapless Thomas Culpeper?

Playful though these suggested interpretations of the Coverdale woodcut might be, they nonetheless point to some of the ways in which the books of this period can surprise and intrigue us—and how they invite and evade different modes of enquiry. Their ability to confound our preconceptions may be due to a willingness to mix modes and registers, sometimes producing what looks—to us—like a mismatch of genre and material (a psalter and a potentially bawdy woodcut), or it may be due to a proliferation of often contradictory allusions and intertextualities. As Arthur F. Kinney writes of Holbein's famous portrait *The Ambassadors*, 'plenitude which invited multiple perspective characterized the age from its start' (2000: 7).[4]

The slipperiness and potential multiplicity of meaning was very apparent to Tudor writers; the spectre of misreading was something they both perceived as a threat, and used as a defence. With printed works in particular, writers had little control over into whose hands they came (although we witness this same anxiety with regard to private letters). One recurrent motif of prefatory addresses is the desire to shape the reception of the work, to mould readers into 'friendly' or 'gentle' ones. Chaucerian valedictions, previously made in manuscript ('Go little book'), assume an added urgency in a world of print, where copies proliferated, often provoking hostile responses, as witnessed in the period's glut of religious controversy, or the bouts of political and personal flytings, such as those produced by John Skelton in the 1510s (1983: 115–34), William

---

[4] The appearance of Holbein's *Ambassadors* on the cover of Greenblatt (1980) has also helped ensure that this portrait has become a topos of Renaissance criticism.

Gray and Thomas Smyth in 1540, or Thomas Churchyard, Thomas Camell, and others in the early 1550s (Shrank 2008*b*).

Tudor literature is in many ways characterized by such copiousness. The number of available texts increased markedly, thanks in part to concerted efforts by English humanists to allow less linguistically capable compatriots direct access to works in Latin, the vernaculars of continental Europe, or, to a lesser extent, Greek. This was also an age in which authors self-consciously worked to expand the language, borrowing words from foreign tongues, or wrenching them from one grammatical form into another (R. Jones 1953). Where it seems reasonable in the early sixteenth century to bemoan the paucity or unwieldiness of English (as in Skelton's 'Philip Sparrow' or the Preface to Wyatt's *Quiet of Mind*), clearly by the end of the century this is no longer the case (Skelton 1983, lines 774–823; Wyatt 1528: A2^r). That this was achieved is entirely due to the efforts of English writers over the course of those intervening decades.

However, we should be wary of taking the grievances of poets like Skelton at face value: as he launches into an audaciously long string of rhymes, the complaints partly serve to highlight his own poetic virtuosity, that he—despite the inadequate tools with which he works—is a master craftsman. And he is also echoing both the complaints, and bravura, of earlier poets, not least Chaucer, who objected that 'rym in English hath swich scarsitee' (1988, line 80) in a ten-line stanza dazzlingly constructed deploying only two rhymes. Tudor writers clearly delighted in linguistic profusion (*copia*) as much as they did in literary allusions. We glimpse this appreciation in flurries of rhyming prose (Boorde 1542: C3^v; Baldwin 1995: 32), or in the Tudor enthusiasm for doublets ('education and bringing up', 'carcke and care', 'flythye and sluttyshe').[5] While one role of doubling is undoubtedly pragmatic—to introduce and explain a neologism—it also serves a decorative function. In this case, while 'bringing up' elucidates the coinage 'education', the remainder—'cark', 'care', 'filthy', 'sluttish'— are all well-established synonyms, displaying and savouring the semantic variety that English already possesses (even without foreign borrowings).

The theory and discourse of *copia* goes back to Cicero, Quintilian, and other rhetoricians of classical antiquity, but the work which defined Renaissance attitudes to the concept and practice was Erasmus' *De duplici copia verborum et rerum* ('On Copiousness in Both Words and Things'), dedicated in 1512 to his friend John Colet, headmaster of St Paul's School, London. Following this textbook, Tudor schoolboys learned to vary their style, absorbing the wherewithal, and inclination, to say 'your letter has delighted me greatly' in 150 different ways; naively unthinking repetition— as opposed to rhetorically strategic *repetitio*—became anathema, in English as it was in Latin (the language in which sixteenth-century pupils would have first practised a copious style).

Copiousness maintained its hold over the Tudor imagination, and helped fashion its literary techniques, until the end of the century. The appetite for *copia rerum*— the copiousness of things, not just words—also helped re-energize a traditional

---

[5] The first example is from Elyot (1531: 15^v); the latter two from Boorde (1542: C2^v, C3^v).

encyclopedism given new vigour and new direction by the 'polymathic humanism' of the Renaissance (Pincombe 2001: 37–44). We see this in the Tudor predilection for lists of things, particular things that England possesses, as in William Harrison's *Description of England* (1577), with its roll-call of the nation's topographical features, its bridges and rivers, market towns and highways.

It was disrupting this link between *res* and *verba* which generated one of the most striking and influential styles of late sixteenth-century English prose: that devised by John Lyly in the late 1570s. Lyly was the literary heir of the Erasmian tradition of *copia*. He was the grandson of William Lily, who took over from Colet as headmaster of St Paul's in 1512, the year *De copia* was published, and who co-wrote, with Colet, 'Lily's Grammar', the standard Latin textbook taught in the Tudor schoolroom. In *Euphues: The Anatomy of Wit* (1578), Lyly produced a highly mannered style—soon branded as 'euphuism' by his critics—which made extensive use of verbal patterns which were, in the terms coined by George Puttenham in his *Art of English Poesy* (1589), 'auricular' (pleasing to the ear) and 'sensable' (pleasing to the mind). They were sometimes also 'sententious', in that they pleased both ear and mind, thus 'enlarging the whole matter besides with copious amplifications' (2007: 244; 3. 10).

While Puttenham's terms remind us of the delight that readers and audiences might derive from verbal play, Lyly's style was not universally acclaimed. It attracted the hostility of both Philip Sidney and Gabriel Harvey. What annoyed them most was Lyly's use of simile—especially similes drawn from natural history. Lyly raided Pliny's *Naturalis historia* for interesting details about animals, vegetables, and minerals, not only as material for similes, but also as models of invention. The first part of the Latin art of rhetoric, which dealt with the way speakers or writers gathered useful material, was called *inventio*, which means 'finding out'; however, Lyly's inventions are simply 'made up'. Harvey worried that Lyly's 'euphuing of Similes' (1970: 1H^v) were hard to tell from the 'real thing' found in Pliny, and that they thus devalued the currency of scholarship. Sidney castigated them as 'a most tedious prattling', complaining that 'these stories [...] come in multitudes', distracting and detracting from the real point—namely, the cleverness of 'conceits', or ideas (1973: 139).

But Tudor readers loved these multifarious fictions. As Terence Cave notes of Erasmus' approving comments on improbable fables: 'The centrifugal movement which constantly asserts and reasserts itself throughout the *De copia* and its prolific successors, that same movement of discourse towards pleasure, towards a place of celebration which is also a place of fiction, triumphs' (1979: 33). Despite Sidney's opprobrium, Lyly's readers did not always wish to distinguish between the 'idea' and the frankly ornamental simile, but, rather, relished sporting irresponsibly in the copious ocean of euphuistic prose.

For all its delight in otiose language, however, at heart *Euphues* is a didactic work—ending with a series of admonitory letters and, like Hawes's *Pastime*, laying out the ideal education of its protagonist. Both the *Pastime* and *Euphues* demonstrate the difficulties in sixteenth-century writing of separating *litterae* (book-learning) from belles-lettres (finely written literature for recreation). Rather, belles-lettres and *litterae* are intertwined, marrying 'profit' and 'pleasure'. Indeed, Sidney's own *Arcadia*, which offered a rival prose style to Lyly's euphuism, was reprocessed by Abraham Fraunce to provide English examples for his textbook on rhetorical tropes, *The Arcadian Rhetoric* (1588).[6] Fraunces's book was actually published *before* the *Arcadia* first saw print in 1590, so that Sidney's work was read by many as a technical aid before it was enjoyed as romance.

Some seventy years divide the *Pastime* from *Euphues* and *Arcadia*. Yet they are motivated by a single literary–cultural ideal with respect to this dual emphasis on learning and pleasure. The writing of this period recurrently displays certain enduring traits: copiousness; generic hybridity; a combination of playful ambiguity and political or moral seriousness; an uneasy synthesis of didactic purpose and leisurely digressiveness. Nonetheless, it cannot be perceived as a stable entity. The educational backgrounds of writers and readers changed; matters of political moment altered; and literary tastes and styles adapted accordingly.

These broad shifts are reflected in the division of this volume into four sub-periods. The first takes us to about 1530 and Henry VIII's break with Rome. The second covers *c*.1530–*c*.1560 and the turbulent period of evangelical and conservative reformation. The third and fourth parts address periods dominated by the distinctive voices of two major generations: the young writers of the Inns of Court of the 1560s (Part III) and the University Wits of the 1580s and beyond (Part IV).

The difficulties that we encountered when trying to name these parts highlight one of the key problems of periodization: labelling a period risks homogenizing it and suggests a simple diachronic plot, such as Reformation and Counter-Reformation, or the 'waning' of the Middle Ages and arrival of the 'Renaissance'. Ultimately, we decided to divide the book into chronological parts. This was not only for convenience—to break the volume into more digestible chunks—but also because these divisions reflect different literary phases of the long Tudor century. However, we declined to name these, if only to avoid suggesting that *all* works produced within these time brackets conform to the same cultural imperatives.

The year 1530 is an obvious point of transition and thus marks the start of Part II. The break from Rome begins in earnest then. And it is relatively sudden, something hardly predictable from the perspective of someone writing in the mid-1520s. After all, in 1521 the Latin *Assertio*, defending all seven sacraments against the attacks of Martin Luther, had been issued in Henry's name; had Katherine of Aragon managed to produce a son, English history might have looked rather different. Once under way, the process of Reformation had an undeniable impact on English culture and the literature it produced. Old belief systems were challenged, and institutions (religious houses, hospitals, schools, chantries) were eliminated—the abandoned buildings often scarring the urban landscape.

As James Simpson comments, in the 'envoi' to the most recent attempt to redraw the boundaries between the medieval and early modern, to try to ignore the watershed of the 1530s 'would be a misrepresentation of history' (2002: 558). The process of

---

[6] Cf. John Hoskins's *Directions for Speech and Style* (*c*.1597–8).

confessionalization after 1530—as worshippers were increasingly required to define their faith in terms of allegiance (or not) to the tenets of the Church of Rome—and the challenge posed to certain types of authority unleashes a textual energy (and frequently anger): a cacophony of voices fighting for readers' souls, attention, and social conscience. But many of the complaints (about clerical corruption, for example) are old ones, found in *Piers Plowman*, among other places. Many echo on to the present day: the young are always badly brought up (according to the older generation); the rich are always getting richer at the expense of the poor; and the bonds of community and fellow feeling are always withering.

Simpson also highlights the decline of certain genres after 1530, such as 'feminine visionary modes' and 'parabiblical invention' (559). Nevertheless, by the same token, many remain (especially dialogue, romance, interlude, love lyric, dream visions, and the 'plowman' tradition of complaint). Other continuities include the influence of Continental and classical cultures; the project to translate works into the vernacular; encyclopedism; and authors' self-consciousness about publication and the material form of books, be they in manuscript or print. Seeing everything through the lens of religious schism also disguises the friendships and allegiances that extended across the boundaries of faith and the weary desire of many for a quiet life.

The shift in tone and style from the early 1560s onwards (found in the texts and authors explored in Part III) is as discernible as that found between the literature of the 1520s and 1530s. This time, though, the reasons for that change are not event-driven, but generational, as the first swath of students educated at grammar school and the Inns of Court starts writing, choosing to model their works on classical verse and Senecan drama, rather than prose, and devoid of a need to apologize for any perceived failings of the vernacular. If they apologize, it is (usually disingenuously) for their own want of skill, rather than the weakness of the vulgar tongue.

Again, though, there are underlying continuities with the earlier periods: texts are still being translated and emulated; devotional literature is still being produced in vast quantities. Tastes have changed, however. Of the traditional triad of the great English poets, only Chaucer would be printed throughout the whole Tudor period: Gower is not printed after 1554, nor Lydgate after 1565—except for a 1590 edition of *The Serpent of Division*, which is rewritten as Elizabethan prose (Shrank forthcoming). So too other familiar medieval authors—Boethius, Langland—disappear from the Elizabethan canon (Boethius interestingly reappearing in 1609). The Elizabethan rewriting of Lydgate's *Serpent* points to their perception of their linguistic distance from medieval English. And here in many ways, as Helen Cooper discusses in her Epilogue, Spenser sounds the death knell of Tudor literature by medievalizing it, pickling it in aspic in the interests of his own 'novelty'.

Some of the differences in literary style after 1558 and the Elizabethan settlement of religion are due to the fact that writers are relieved from the pressures of Reformation and Counter-Reformation polemic. This is not to say that the Elizabethan period was a less controversial age; it is just that there is more writing overall, so that the polemical takes up a smaller amount of the market share. The consequent change in literary mood is epitomized by the shifting attitudes to *copia*, that mainstay of Tudor literature.

As noted earlier, the vogue for copiousness derived particular energy from the Tudor enthusiasm for *copia rerum*. Lists form an effective weapon in the Reformation arsenal, used to lampoon the corrupt and preposterous practices of the Roman Church. In *King Johan*, for instance, John Bale uses of a list of twenty clerical orders to denigrate the meaningless proliferation of religious offices—a roll-call which expanded to forty when revising the play. As Tom Betteridge writes: 'the poetics of confessionalization demanded two different languages—one of largely empty sentences, of windy words and misty reasons and another of short sentences, proportion and truth' (2004: 24). Compare this anxious reaction to *copia*—it almost infects Bale's own language—to the type of *copia* discussed earlier, where Lyly and his readers luxuriate in the sound of words alone.

There is, in other words, an identifiable change in gear and tone that begins in the early Elizabethan period, with the Inns of Court poets and dramatists, and intensifies in the late 1570s and early 1580s, as seen in the work of University Wits like Robert Greene, Christopher Marlowe, and Thomas Nashe (Part IV). The universities, by now much more secular than their medieval counterparts, produced large numbers of graduates, many of whom gravitated to London in search of government employment. However, by the 1580s, Richard Helgerson convincingly argues, 'the offices of state' were 'saturated [...] with men trained in good letters, leaving few openings for those who came behind' (1976: 23). As the schoolmaster Richard Mulcaster worried, many were left 'gaping for preferment' (1581: 138). At the same time, the establishment of the permanent playhouses from the late 1570s offered these highly educated and ambitious young men opportunities to make both money and a name for themselves. They brought to the public stage their classical learning and rhetorical training. In turn this mushrooming theatrical culture was hungry for new scripts, material, and ideas, a demand which this new generation of writers were able and willing to supply, honing—and no doubt relishing—their literary skills. They wrote with facility, both for the stage and for the page. As a result, there was simply more writing about, writing which was more varied and more obviously 'literary' by today's standards. That we recognize it as 'literary' is, in part, due to the fact that this is the literature which we have been brought up on, and against which other literature is measured.

In some ways, the trajectory we trace is similar to that of Lewis, in that we acknowledge that it is in the last two decades of the sixteenth century that we arrive at a period of increased literary production. Where we depart from Lewis is, first, that we do not see this as 'unpredictable' or 'startling' (1954: 1). Rather, the university-educated writers of the 1580s and 1590s follow the paths laid down by earlier generations. Secondly, unlike Lewis, we also find mid-Tudor literature abundantly satisfying. Part IV therefore takes a different tack from those which precede it (which are roughly chronological), since it deliberately pairs familiar authors of the late Elizabethan period with mid-Tudor counterparts, to illustrate how the more renowned writers are rooted in that earlier, less studied era.

As a glance down the table of Contents will reveal, the intentions of this volume are unabashedly polemical. The bulk of the chapters concentrate on the 'middle period': the years 1530–80, which are so often overlooked in university syllabuses and literary criticism. This is also a book in which Lewis's 'Golden' stars—Sidney and Spenser—receive less attention than the creative genius of writers like John Heywood or George Gascoigne, while William Shakespeare, the greatest luminary in the Tudor pantheon, receives scarcely a mention. Spenser, Sidney, and Shakespeare have every right to their hypercanonical status. But giving them their due here would, yet again, have left little space for the authors we have allowed to step into the limelight, authors whose voices have, in many cases, still to be heard. For some of our writers (such as George Cavendish, Jasper Heywood, Luke Shepherd, Nathaniel Woodes), it is the first time that they have received extensive treatment within a major collection of essays. Despite this, the volume is in no way comprehensive: Thomas Sackville, William Forrest, and Lewis's maligned Peend are regrettably absent, for instance; even Henry Howard, Earl of Surrey, has only a ghostly presence, whereas his one-time page Thomas Churchyard crops up frequently. The ambition behind the volume—and the idea behind each of the chapters—has been to give a taste of how fascinating some of these forgotten authors and their texts are, and to stimulate interest and research in this rich and fertile field. Instead of learning, in Davies's words, 'to do without the Tudors', this volume asks us to get to know even more of them.

Primary Works

Baldwin, William (1560), *The Funeralles of King Edward the Sixt*.

—— (1610), *A Royall Elegie, briefly describing the vertuous reigne, and happy (though immature) death of the most mightie and renowmed prince, King Edward the sixth*. [Repr. of *Funerals*, misattributed to John Cheke]

—— (1995), *Beware the Cat*, ed. William Ringler (Berkeley: University of California Press).

Bible (1539), *The Bible in English*. [The Great Bible]

Boorde, Andrew (1542), *A Compendyous Regyment; or, A Dyetary of Helth*.

Chaucer, Geoffrey (1988), 'The Compleynt of Venus', in *The Riverside Chaucer*, ed. F. N. Robinson (Oxford: Oxford University Press), 648.

Coverdale, Miles (1535?), *Goostly Psalmes and Spirituall Songes*.

—— (1540), *The Psalter*.

Elyot, Thomas (1531), *The Boke Named the Governour*.

Harvey, Gabriel (1970), *Pierce's Supererogation* (Menston: Scolar Press).

Heywood, Jasper (trans.) (1560), *Thyestes* by Seneca.

Mulcaster, Richard (1581), *Positions wherin those Primitive Circumstances be Examined, which are necessarie for the training up of children*.

Puttenham, George (2007), *The Art of English Poesy*, ed. Frank Whigham and Wayne A. Rebhorn (Ithaca, NY: Cornell University Press).

Sidney, Philip (1973), *An Apology for Poetry*, ed. Geoffrey Shepherd (Manchester: Manchester University Press).

SKELTON, JOHN (1983), *The Complete English Poems*, ed. John Scattergood (Harmondsworth: Penguin).

SMITH, THOMAS (1982), *De republica Anglorum*, ed. Mary Dewar (Cambridge: Cambridge University Press).

STARKEY, THOMAS (1989), *A Dialogue between Pole and Lupset*, ed. T. F. Mayer, Camden Society, 4th ser., 37.

THOMAS, WILLIAM (*c*.1551), *Jos. Barbaros Voiages to Tana and Persia*, BL, Royal MS 17.C.x.

WATSON, THOMAS (1582), *Hekatompathia*.

WYATT, THOMAS (1528), *The Quyete of Mynde*.

——(1969), 'So feble is the threde', in *Collected Poems*, ed. Kenneth Muir and Patricia Thomson (Liverpool: Liverpool University Press), 79–82.

PART I

1485–1529

CHAPTER 1

CAXTON AND
THE INVENTION
OF PRINTING

ALEXANDRA GILLESPIE

IN 1480 William Caxton, the Westminster printer, publisher, translator, and author, printed a *Doctrine to Learn French and English*.[1] The text is written in the Continental tradition of *livres des mestiers* (similar to that in Figure 1.1, in which verses by Hans Sachs accompany woodcuts of various trades and professions): it is at once a list of crafts and guilds, and a compilation of phrases and sentences for conversational use in mercantile and household settings. Among the words it has for those involved in late medieval business are some for the buyer of books:

George le librarier	George the booke sellar
A plus des livres	Hath moo bookes.
Que tout ceulx de lavile.	Then all they of the toune.
Il les achate touts	He byeth them all:
Tels quils soient	Suche as they ben
Soient embles ou enprintees	Be they stolen or enprinted
Ou aultrement pourchacies	Or othirwyse pourchaced
Il a dooctrinaulx catons	He hath doctrinals[,] catons [Cato's *Disticha*]
Heures de nostre dame	[H]oures of our lady.
Donats pars accidens	Donettis[,] parties[,] accidents [grammars]
Psaultiers bien enluminees	Sawters [psalters] well enlumined

[1] Titles, dates, and bibliographical information for Caxton's books are from Needham (1986), supplemented by STC2. Biographical details are from Painter (1976) and *ODNB*.

Loyes a fremauls dargent	Bounden with claspes of silver
Livres de medicines	Bookes of physike
Sept psalmes kalendiers	Seven salmes[,] kalenders
Encre et parcemyn	Ynke and perchemyn [parchment]
Pennes de signes.	Pennes of swannes
Pennes dauwes	Pennes of ghees [geese]
Bons breviaries	Good portoses [breviaries]
Qui valent bon argent	Whiche ben worth good money.

(Caxton 1964: 36)

The source of the *Doctrine* is a French–Flemish version, composed in Bruges, where Caxton had lived and been merchant governor of the English nation (*c*.1464–*c*.1470). Alison Hanham argues that Caxton may have written—or just acquired—a French–English translation of this sometime before 1470; internal references to currency and historical events suggest that it was further adapted for an English readership at about that time—a decade before Caxton's edition was printed. It has older and later analogues. Two Bruges manuscripts of a closely related text survive, one copied in the mid- or late fourteenth century; the other made *c*.1420. A French–Flemish *Vocabulaer*, printed in Antwerp between 1497 and 1501, seems to share a direct source with Caxton's *Doctrine* (Blake 1965; Hanham and Alison 2005).

George, the solidly English 'booksellar', gets a little lost in this textual tradition—he is 'Gorges, li librairiers' or 'Goris, de liberaris' in the late fourteenth-century French–Flemish manuscript; missing in the *c*.1420 text; 'Jorijs, die librier' in the Antwerp *Vocabulaer* (Gessler 1931: i. 16^r; iv. 30^r). What he is *not* is good evidence of the nature of the English book trade at the time of the invention of printing. This is, however, how he is known to many Tudor book historians, who encounter him in Graham Pollard's Sandars Lecture of 1959 entitled 'The English Market for Printed Books'. Pollard quotes the passage on George from the *Doctrine*, and describes the English market in terms of the bookseller's activities:

the book trade, such as it was, was almost entirely a bespoke trade. The buyer went to a stationer and ordered a book. The stationer had to find a proper text, get it copied by a text writer, rubricated by a limner, and bound by a bookbinder [...] But a stationer might also hold some books in stock, and we have Caxton's own description of what the stock of a bookseller was like [...] calendars and books of physic [...] schoolbooks and service book. Most of them were clearly second hand.   (1978: 10)

The problem with Pollard's discussion here is that George is not a pedlar of books to English folk in English towns; he is on loan—from the Low Countries; and from the sorts of French and Flemish books he peddles. Caxton's best-known biographer, George Painter, observes in a footnote that even the words 'enprintees [...] enprinted', which describe some of the books in Caxton's *Doctrine* (but not its sources, where these terms do not appear), are probably not the printer's invention so much as a re-rendering of a lost original's 'enpruntes', meaning borrowed (1976: 103). George has 'moo books' than everyone else because he has begged, 'enpruntes/borrowed' and

Fig. 1.1 'The Printer', from Hans Sachs, *Eygentliche Beschreibung Aller Stände auff Erden* (1568).

embles/stolen—or rather, this is how the *Doctrine* satirizes him. So we are not to trust him. Nor, implicitly, are we to trust the magpie–translator (or redactor) Caxton, who, by this argument, found a French–English text that sometimes mocks the noisy marketplace it describes, and then adapted this text to accommodate some books 'enprinted', and spoiled the joke about George the unscrupulous bookseller in the process. While there may have been English bookshops with shelves full of service books, grammars, and medical tracts—and while printed books may have appeared on such shelves in Caxton's time—we cannot take this text's word for it.

All this is to introduce the point that Caxton has a slightly fraught place at the beginning of a volume about Tudor literature, just as he and George the fictional bookseller have an awkward place in a discussion of 'the invention of printing' or the history of English book production. Caxton did not invent the printing press; he brought one to England. There is much that is still unknown about the manuscript book trade in England when he did this: several decades of research have added only a little to Pollard's statements about a bespoke trade and the sale of second-hand books.[2] We know more about the trade after the advent of printing: for instance, that Caxton produced only a tiny fraction of those printed books that were circulated and sold in England in his lifetime. Most English printed reading matter came from the Continent—from the presses of Bruges, Antwerp, Paris, Venice, and Cologne.[3] Nor is Caxton obviously 'Tudor': he lived much of his adult life abroad, arriving back in England at the end of the Wars of the Roses, and living for less than a decade of Henry VII's reign. He has only latterly been regarded as a writer of 'literature'. This is not just because he was a translator and adapter of Continental literary texts: after all, that is true of English authors from Chaucer to Shakespeare. Caxton has never found a secure place in the literary canon because no reader has argued that what he writes is any good. Joseph A. Dane demonstrates that even N. F. Blake, giving Caxton his first extended write-up as an author rather than a printer, quietly undercuts his subject. Caxton 'knew no Italian'; did not 'read any classical literature'; 'his own vocabulary was not very extensive'; he wrote 'rambling sentences'; and 'had no general theory as to what constitutes a work of literature' (Dane 2008: 269, citing Blake 1973: 23, 32, 37, 39, 44). In Blake's account, Caxton does have a place in scholarship—in the early Tudor period as scholars used to write about it, as a part of C. S. Lewis's 'Drab Age' (1954). It was a place posterity found for him early on. Robert Braham, praising Thomas Marsh's new edition of Lydgate's *Troy Book*, describes Caxton's *Recueil of the History of Troy* (the first book printed in English in Bruges, 1473–4) as a 'longe tedious and brayneles bablyng, tending to no ende, nor havyng any certayne begynnynge: but proceadynge therin as an ydyot in his follye' (1555: χ 2^r). Next to Caxton, even Lydgate looks good (see Machan 2006: 311–15).

But such measures of literary merit have been unfashionable for a while. Literary studies has lately redefined 'literature' as a field of cultural production, shaped by a readerly elite rather than by the merits of specific texts (Bourdieu 1993). And the heterogeneous body of scholarship that gets labelled 'New Historicism' has made the study of what is literary also the study of class, gender, sexuality, power, and any institution or concept in whose contested formation literature is found to play a role.[4] Caxton may not have been very good at Italian, Latin, or even storytelling, but he was

---

[2] Griffiths and Pearsall (1989) add some detail; cf. Christianson (1999); Blayney (2003). There is still no general history of the production and marketing of books in the century before printing.

[3] On the importation of printed books before 1500, see Needham (1999); Ford (1999).

[4] For some of the heterogeneity, and some early definitions, see Veeser (1989).

England's first printer; as a diplomat in Bruges, a translator for noble Burgundian patrons, and a London merchant specializing in the sale of vernacular texts, he was a part of the English culture of his day. In the words of William Kuskin, whose work has done much to demonstrate Caxton's historical significance, he was responsible for the 'construction of the book as a commodity and the subject as a consumer'. His work should be 'theorized as part of a larger totality of production'; it 'must derive from and be observable in the culture's social practices and intellectual statements' (2006*b*: 201; 2006*a*: 6–7). Caxton's texts, like many of the literary products of Lewis's Drab Age, may not be written out of an aesthetic definition of drabness, but the subjects that they formed make for compelling discussion. For the age shaped as 'Tudor' is anything but drab. It is the age of printing, the refashioning of English monarchy and nationhood, the rise of the commercial theatre, nascent capitalism, the spread of humanism, and the violent reformation of English religion. Its literature made for, and was made by, these changes; it continues to make them sensible to us; it deserves careful reading.

Caxton's 'George', the borrowed bookseller, is an argument of this sort in miniature. Like much of what strikes us in Tudor literature, he is Continentally derived. He is not the result of clear-eyed observation of the doings of English merchants by a writer of learning and genius, but an amalgam of civic and didactic sources arranged to meet the constraints of the *Doctrine*'s alphabetical and satirical form (L. Cooper 2005). He may not suggest precisely how the English book trade worked, but he tells us how it was imagined. In the *Doctrine*, George's books are second-hand, garnered from estates, loans gone bad, even theft. The books made by a scribe later in the *Doctrine* are, as Pollard argues they should be, bespoke; the scribe's work is entirely subject to the patron's needs:

> The parchemen is so meke;
> Hit suffreth on hit to write
> What somever men wylle.
>
> (Caxton 1964: 46)

These are useful fictions of the sort that might turn the discrete facts that scholars of medieval manuscripts collect into an engaging history—that could help us make sense of the work of a well-known fifteenth-century scribe like John Shirley in his mercantile and aristocratic milieux (Connolly 1998); or of the activities of the stationer Thomas Marleburgh and Henry IV's yeoman of the chamber Ralph Bradfield, who were taken to court in 1419 over the theft of books from the King's own collection (Stratford 1999: 261). George is one small part of what makes books—including new ones 'enprinted'—meaningful before and in the Tudor period, and still for us. In this sense, George *is* Caxton's invention, where invention is not the arrival *ex nihilo* of change, but, as Derek Attridge argues,

an otherness in the process of being translated into, while at the same time transforming, our inherited cultural norms and proclivities [...] The otherness that enters a culture through an invention [is] not a pre-existing entity somewhere outside of, and unrelated to, what is known.

Rather, it manifests itself as an event of reshaping, ranging from the major to the minuscule, brought about by an individual's or group's exploitation of a culture's contradictions, overdeterminations, marginalizations, gaps, and tensions.   (2004: 102, 136)

Caxton's George and his printed books and translated texts are inventions, legible in relation to their moment and the uses that were found for them, because they brought and continue to bring all of these—and so their 'Drab Age'—into being.

Something like this way of thinking about Caxton has made for a great part of the recent scholarship on him. Seth Lerer argues powerfully for Caxton's role in the invention of an English literary canon (1993, 1999). Kuskin describes the symbolic capital Caxton invented for the book in the early economies of printing as a part of his 'renovation' of manuscript culture and English literary tradition (2008). A range of other studies have come to complementary conclusions: Anne Coldiron describes the significance of gender and Caxton's Continental heritage to the shape of Tudor printed books; Timothy Machan considers the contribution of Caxton and those who responded to him to the development of the English language; William West thinks about Caxton and his foreman De Worde's making of the idea of an 'edition'.[5] What all such studies suggest is that there is an inventive vein in Caxton's writing and work as a maker of books—as there is in much Tudor literature—that is only just now being mined.

The discussion below will not, however, follow this line of thinking very closely. Instead, it will consider what other approaches to Caxton could contribute to our knowledge of his work and of early Tudor literary culture. One such approach is suggested by Attridge's *Singularity of Literature* (2004), cited above. I implicitly aligned Attridge's ideas about cultural invention with recent historicist work on Caxton's innovative practices—but this is to misrepresent his argument. Attridge is interested in the concern of literary studies with the literary—not, that is, with the literary institution as the construction of a literate elite, and not with literature's making of its social contexts: but with that which makes literature different from those contexts and all the other cultural objects that belong to those contexts. His work forms part of what Marjorie Levinson has described as a 'movement' across the field of literary studies. This movement, sometimes called 'new formalism', directs attention away from the historicist work that has made Caxton and many Tudor writers newly interesting to scholarship. Or at least, its adherents seek to change the weakly interdisciplinary methods that inform some of the historicist attention paid to texts: to revive New Historicism's formalism; and to rededicate literary studies to close reading—aesthetically engaged analysis of literary texts (Levinson 2007).[6]

---

[5] All appear in Kuskin (2006c). For alternative traditions of Caxton scholarship, see Blake (1969, 1991); Hellinga (1982); Sutton (1994); Fradenburg and Freccero (1996); A. Gillespie (2004).

[6] Few advocates of 'new formalism' have been able, or have tried, to divorce their work from historicism: their revival of neglected questions and techniques may or may not ultimately challenge 'New Historicism'. The same could be said for the more formal approach to book history advocated below.

Excepting W. J. B. Crotch, who praises Caxton's 'heights of eloquence' (Caxton 1928, p. cxxi), Caxton's early close readers—Blake, for instance—have not had kind words for his literary technique. When Caxton's writing has been read closely in more recent scholarship, the concern has been with its historicity and cultural significance: there has not been any argument for its aesthetic value. This chapter will not attempt such an argument at any length, but it could be interesting to do so. Consider, for instance, Theodor Adorno's insight that the aesthetic is that which resists aestheticization—that is, resists the banal affirmation of shared standards of beauty or experiences of pleasure—and in doing so allows for the new perception of the real (Kaufman 2000). Or consider Maurice Blanchot's argument (2007) that art speaks with a 'voice from elsewhere', constitutes a trace of otherness in the field of the same. Work that follows from such insights is still troubled by the difficulty of describing what is distinctive about 'literature': should the 'literary' include Romantic poetry, but not advertising jingles, as Attridge argues? Should it include Chaucer's *Canterbury Tales*, first printed by Caxton in 1476, but not Caxton's derivative French–English vocabulary for fifteenth-century merchants, as most syllabuses in English departments, implicitly, argue? Blake's claim that Caxton has no coherent sense of 'literature', and Lerer's and Kuskin's different one, that Caxton is an inventor of literary culture, might come into different focus in light of such questions.

A 'new formalist' approach might also produce new readings of Caxton's texts themselves. These have lately been treated as largely formless, still, as Braham first suggested, 'tending to no ende, nor havyng any certayne begynnynge', except to the end that they make mention of things—the economy of printing, the English language, social hierarchy—whose meaning is fully realized outside the texts that mention them. Consider again Kuskin's argument that the meaning of Caxton's work 'must derive from and be observable in the culture's social practices and intellectual statements'. It remains to consider how this imperative could be married to an account of the inventive otherness or resistant form of the work itself.

A single example may serve to illustrate these tentative points. Mark Addison Amos has argued persuasively that the violence towards women depicted in Caxton's translation of *The Knight of the Tower* (1484) figures a contemporary concern about mercantile social mobility. This argument depends upon the matrix of cultural meaning Amos discovers in sumptuary laws, guild regulations, and so on. To this familiar, broadly historicist way of describing the text, I would add: what form do these moments of violence take? *The Knight of the Tower* is a compilation of exemplary stories of misbehaving women. When the Knight's remark, 'And so her pryde | and overmuche language was cause of her death', becomes—as Amos puts it—'a frequent refrain' in the prose (2006: 78), the effects are *immediately* interesting.[7] The conjunctive adverbial form of the sentence's opening, 'And so' (for La Tour Landry's 'Et ainsi'), is at once a way of moving the narrative along, one familiar from French and English didactic and romance texts of the period, and the source of a pattern of

---

[7] Amos works from Offord's 1971 edition: the text is a translation of Geoffroy Landry's widely copied and translated French original (see Montaiglon 1854).

causation that has a particular beginning and an unavoidable end. What is 'so' is what the Knight's exemplum tells us is 'so'—it is his story that leads us to this conclusion; but it is the woman's exceptional 'pryde' and unruly 'language' that 'was cause' of what we come to know, 'and so' the language by which the Knight guides us. Her language precedes and causes his. We sense this pattern of causation in a temporal shift across the sentence, from the narrative now of 'and so' to the narrative's past in what 'was'. The repetition of such a complex structure at the end of many of the stories the Knight tells, and its generic quality, give what already seems doubly caused and so doubly inevitable a further weight of inevitability. 'And so' we already know: the fallen woman is cause of her own death; and so this is the end of every story about her. Among the Knight's exemplary narratives is, of course, that of Eve, 'notre première mère et de ses folies' ('our first mother, and of her sins'; La Tour Landry 1854: 85). In Eve's iconic example, in the text's language—in the work's literary form—just as much as in contemporary guild regulations, we perceive anew what is 'real' in the Knight's, Caxton's, Tudor, and so our own, culture.

I will not proceed further along these lines; my point is that disciplinarity—treating Caxton's texts as 'Tudor *literature*'—might reinvigorate or even challenge the historicist model developed for analysis of his œuvre. The discussion I will pursue concerns the second field to which Caxton scholarship belongs: book history. I have argued elsewhere that new formalism's dispute with literary historicism is akin to a debate within book history about the practice of bibliography—by which I mean the study of the forms of books and the variable state of the texts that they contain. The 'new formalist' charge is, in part, that New Historicist approaches have ceased to tell us very much about literary texts, or about the information that literary analysis can yield that is missed by other kinds of enquiry. Likewise, when certain bibliographers—Dane and David Vander Meulen, for instance—object to book historical studies that are about the symbolic or social meanings of books, it is largely on the grounds these studies do not treat books as complex artefacts that require close formal analysis, and that cannot always be fitted into a simple historicist (or for that matter literary) narrative.[8] This is the point of the remainder of my chapter. Recent scholarship argues that Caxton's work is important as a renovation of, reaction to, and simultaneously bringing into being of a new, Tudor, print culture: Caxton's books themselves manifest an otherness, an inventiveness, that may trouble paradigmatic explanations of this culture.[9]

Before proceeding, I wish to qualify this statement in two ways. First, I do not mean to suggest that books 'themselves' have an organic and unified meaning. It has been the business of a couple of generations of scholars to unsettle assumptions about books as repositories for fixed truths by 'socializing' study of them (see Gillespie 2008: 252–8). But the tendency of current discussions to look past physical evidence to its human significance results in a paradox: as it locates the meaning of books in a fluid

---

[8] See A. Gillespie (2008: 275–6) where I consider Dane (2003), Vander Meulen (2003–4), and similar discussions in more detail.

[9] I use the word 'book' in its medieval sense to mean a range of text-bearing objects, though this begins to change in the sixteenth century; see A. Gillespie (2008: 263, 278–9).

cultural domain, it renders them transparent; it makes them symbols for complex ideas about society. Put back at the centre of scholarly discussion, books prove less stable than this; in their inventive variety they generate new questions as well as familiar answers.

Secondly, I am aware that close reading of formal bibliographical evidence, which is the approach I am advocating here, because it makes all evidence and all possible meanings significant, even if it describes only some of these, is open to the charge of hopeless ahistoricity—a refusal to account for the work that all texts and books do to establish a dominant culture. In some ways, this is the charge that D. F. McKenzie (1999) levels against traditional bibliography: strictly formal descriptions of books do not tell us what is important about them. It is the charge that New Historicism still levels at strictly formal, New Critical, or post-structuralist literary criticism. But, as McKenzie's writing and the best historicist work shows, close, formal work is a rich basis for historical discussion. It is the capacity of books to resist categorization within established paradigms that gives them, rather like the texts they bear, their inventiveness, their capacity to continue to change what it is we *think* we know. We have come, recently, to know more about Tudor culture and Caxton's part in establishing it. What else might a single object—in this case, a copy of a pardon printed by Caxton *c*.1480—tell us about that culture?

The object I refer to is a copy, in the Lancashire Record Office at Preston, of a 1480–1 indulgence (a pardon), first recorded by R. N. Swanson (2004). The document is in fact a confessional letter—given to the devout purchaser of a pardon, in exchange for a donation, to be read before his or her confessor. Caxton printed this particular letter on behalf of John Kendale, the commissary who used it to collect donations in support of the Knights Hospitaller, then defending Rhodes against the Turks.[10] The Preston indulgence is the sort of thing that makes it tricky to talk about Caxton as a producer of a Tudor literary culture. It pre-dates the battle of Bosworth; it is not a text of Caxton's own writing; it is not literature. It does have, as did all medieval pardons, a literary life. Chaucer's fraudulent Pardoner is a layman who claims he is authorized to distribute indulgences in the form of fake relics—those that the Host feels should be enshrined in a 'hogges toord' (1987: *Canterbury Tales*, VI. 955). Perhaps the best-known scene in Langland's *Piers Plowman* involves a priest, Piers, and a pardon purchased for him by Truth. It has, like the Preston indulgence, documentary form; when Piers unfolds it, the priest finds no true forgiveness in its formula, and Piers tears it in half, as if it is not worth the parchment or paper it is copied on.[11] These are the sort of literary affiliations that make a nonsense of a periodic scheme that corrals Caxton's work for discussion of the 'Tudor' age of Sidney and Spenser, but neglects those fourteenth- and fifteenth-century traditions in which that work makes sense. The Preston indulgence, like much Tudor printing, serves the vigorously contested—but still vital—culture of the Roman, 'medieval' church

[10] STC2, 14077c.107–11—this includes various issues, including those by John Lettou of the same indulgence, discussed below. The Preston copy is RCHY 3/6/16.

[11] See Langland (1995, Prologue, 66–71, and all of Passus 7); Steiner (2003) argues that the Piers's pardon is a chirograph, and by ripping it in two he enters into a Christian compact—faith for reward.

(as argued by Duffy 1992): it has no place in a post-Reformation culture. And literary pardons and the ploughmen and pilgrims who encounter them also remind us that the term 'literature' is a poor fit for most of the texts with which ordinary folk in the medieval and Tudor period were familiar. The documents they saw and handled were not poems and plays but instruments of state and ecclesiastical bureaucracy—writs, bills, proclamations, statutes, bulls, pardons, and injunctions.

But what is problematic about a category such as 'Tudor literature' is also what may be useful about it. The great changes of the Tudor period arrange themselves inconveniently for the scholar: the first translations of Italian humanist writing and the Bible belong to the late fourteenth and not the sixteenth century. Decades pass between the advent of printing and the work of the reformers who claimed the press was God's gift to them. It is only at the very end of the Tudor period that we find the poetic and theatrical productions that are treated in most curriculums as 'Renaissance' art. The result is that we must confront, in discussions of what is emergent or just interesting in Tudor writing—its 'Protestantism' or 'Petrarchanism', for instance—evidence of stasis, stuttering and uncertain change, ruptured teleology, indebtedness, and reversal. The Preston indulgence has this effect. It requires that we think about Tudor textual culture in all its variety—about the papal bulls and pardons distributed in the same decades as printed evangelical polemic; about hundreds of monastic and 'popish' books that survived reformation, censorship, iconoclasm, and dissolution, and remained a vital part of Tudor culture (see Ross 1991).

Objects like the Preston indulgence, however, have not usually been discussed in these terms. When they feature in Caxton's story or that of the Tudor period, which is rarely, they serve as evidence of the dramatic changes wrought by printing. The sorts of argument made about them can be summarized simply as follows. Indulgence printing is evidence of the new type of capitalist investment in book production that was required by early printing, where 'capitalist' describes the capital tied up in a press and the printer's profit motive. Indulgence printing was 'jobbing', meaning that it was work undertaken by printers and paid for by others; it made use of the press's unique productive capacity—something had to keep the machines busy. The advantage was not all the printers': indulgences could be produced in documentary forms in print more rapidly than they could in oral or manuscripts forms, meaning more donations for the churches, hospitals, guilds, fraternities, and individuals who were authorized to distribute pardons for fundraising purposes.

Underlying these statements are some very familiar ideas about printing. Lucien Febvre and Henri-Jean Martin describe print in terms of mass textual production (1976); Elizabeth Eisenstein argues that this mass production made the press the most important 'agent for change'—capitalist, reformist, humanist, scientific, and democratic—in the early modern period (1979, 2002). When scholars write specifically about pardons they make their arguments within this broad framework. Paul Needham describes the importance of small print jobs to the financial success of early print houses like Caxton's; and he notes that while few copies of indulgences survive, there exist records for remarkably large print runs—200,000 pardons commissioned by the Benedictine convent in Montserrat, Catalonia, between 1498 and 1500, for instance (1986: 29–31). Alexandra Halasz proceeds to discuss more complex ideas about capitalism—the abstract notion of a book as a commodity or a book market—that emerged through the production of such ephemeral items as pardons and pamphlets (1997). David Carlson calls job printing, especially indulgence printing, one of the 'less visible components of Caxton's production', but one of special importance. The efficiency of indulgence printing, he says, was 'stunning'; a printer could keep his heavily capitalized presses busy, make a profit, and turn out pardons 'cheaply in vast numbers in a few hours, instead of hiring an expensive scribe to write more slowly one at a time' (Painter 1976: 84, cited in Carlson 2006: 40). Like Eisenstein's, Carlson's is a strong argument for technologically determined change: 'all this the machines decided', he writes (2006: 61).[12]

My argument in what follows is that the story of the Preston indulgence, if told in this way, may have become overfamiliar. It is a story that was told about printing from the first—when, for instance, the fifteenth-century humanist Nicholas Perotti writes that 'as much literature can be printed in one month by one man at this time as could otherwise scarcely be written by many men in a year' (cited in West 2006: 250–1). By force of repetition, it is a story that tends to occlude other ways of investigating early print culture. What place did George, Caxton's fictional bookseller, have in this culture, for instance? What was already known about manuscript books and medieval textual traditions that made printed books knowable? The use of printing to produce indulgences, it is suggested, was a stunningly efficient new process, which made written documents more widely available to an increasingly literate populace. But indulgences were also an old device for revenue collection, and part of a longer transition to literate practice. In England new uses of writing are evident during a tenfold increase, in the century to 1300, in the production of written records for the administration of Church and realm—the papal bulls and letters, charters, chirographs, writs, letters, cartularies, chronicles, registers, rent rolls, and yearbooks. They are evident during the development of the commercial book trade in thirteenth-century Oxford, as men like George set up shop. They are evident during the introduction of paper; and during the huge surge, where surviving books are the measure, in the production of books of vernacular literature from the reign of Richard II to Caxton's day (Edwards and Pearsall 1989; Michael 2008; Lyall 1989). These changes made writing important and legible to most members of the English estates well before the invention of printing. Legibility might not mean readability in an obvious sense: the written forms of a medieval indulgence might be recognizable through prelection and audit, or through sensory perception—seeing, touching, kissing—of the written object (Clanchy 1993). But so much is also true, as Roger Chartier has argued, for print culture in rural areas from the time of the invention of the press until educational reforms changed what literacy meant in the West (1987: 180). The case of the distribution of indulgences makes this point particularly well:

---

[12] Cf. Adrian Johns's argument that the changes effected by printing were decided by the people who worked the press, and the culture that gave their work meaning and value (1998, 2002).

printing merely intensified schemes for the mass distribution of pardons that had been invented in oral and manuscript cultures. Swanson estimates that as many as 30,000 people may have made annual, indulgenced donations to the London hospital of St Anthony of Vienne by the mid-fifteenth century. Medieval institutions authorized pardoners to distribute indulgences on their behalf; the same hospital also used 'farmers', men who leased the right to collect receipts for indulgences. Pardoners and farmers who distributed pardons worked in a variety of ways and used multiple media: they could post bills to advertise pardons; display copies of the documents that authorized their activities; and offer their pardons to parishioners at times set aside during church services. At least some donations to St Anthony were made in exchange for manuscript copies of confessional letters like those printed by Caxton: three such scribal letters survive for the period 1442–3. Another hospital, St Thomas at Rome, seems to have relied on scribal copies of confessional letters for the distribution of its pardons more routinely in the early to mid-1500s (Swanson 2008: 78, 139–40). Indulgence printing was obviously a productive development—confessional letters and bills advertising pardons could be produced more rapidly in print and perhaps distributed more widely. But the work of the press was never 'outside of' what was already known.

Other scholars—Kuskin (2008) and especially Walsham (2004)—have begun to take better account of the medieval textual culture that informed Tudor printing. It is the aim of my discussion of the Preston pardon to turn from this work, important as it is, back to the object, to books 'themselves'—and to modify well-worn arguments about early print culture in this way. I start with details from Swanson's description of the Preston indulgence: 'the bottom 18 mm of the long side [are] folded to make a sealing flap. This is pierced through both layers by two holes, through which the strings for seal have been threaded. These are of coloured silk [. . .] blue, beige, and off white. The seal itself no longer survives' (2004: 196).

The object so described is not—or not only—the product of a printing press: it has been worked on by other machines and by hand. The strings, folds, and holes tell us it was sealed. Seals on late medieval pardons—both the letters that authorized the collection of donations, and confessional letters that were sometimes given in exchange for these donations—were hung from lengths of parchment or from silk or linen cords like those on the Preston indulgence. They were double-sided impressions taken in wax, usually formed using matrices slotted into screw presses that are the direct analogue of the machine that Gutenberg invented and Caxton brought to England (Clanchy 1993: 308–17). It is normal to find the remains of a seal, or holes cut for stringing, on early printed and manuscript indulgences that have not been damaged or trimmed.[13] Such evidence is richly suggestive. The word 'enprinted', which Caxton borrows from Continental texts to describe his new kind of press, is

---

[13] See Swanson (2008: 152) on the wax sealing of manuscript confessional letters in York, 1469–70; cf. the Lettou issue of the same 1480 indulgence in BL, IA. 55405, which has a red seal on linen cord; all three surviving BL copies of Caxton's 1489 indulgence, STC2, 14077c.114 (IA. 55126–8), have holes for stringing, although only one of these was ever purchased (the other two are binder's waste); the Takamiya copy of this indulgence has its seal intact.

also borrowed from Middle English, where the word describes the old kind of press—
the seal presses used by agents of the Church, king, and great landlords to authorize
the issue of thousands of documents, indulgences among them. By Caxton's time,
writers had made the connection between the forms left by metal on wax and the
forms of words on the pages of the documents so sealed. A Middle English romance
of Troy, one of the York plays, and the Langlandian poem *Mum and the Sothsegger* all
use some form of the verb *print* to describe words pressed onto the pages of books
(*MED*, s.v. 'prenten').

This is not just interesting for what it tells us about the complex ways in which
the past is always alive in and knowable through Caxton's practice: it also troubles
assumptions about the 'stunning' efficiency of Caxton's operation, or the imaginary
space of a printing house in which indulgences are made 'cheaply in vast numbers
in a few hours, instead of [...] slowly [and by inference expensively] one at a time'.
It appears that Kendale, who collected the final receipts for the pardon printed by
Caxton for the Knights at Rhodes, had farmers at work for him. He may have given
each of them a pile of printed copies, which was how Giovanni de Giglis, another
collector, distributed an indulgence whose letters he had printed by Caxton in 1489
(STC2, 14077c.114–15; Swanson 2004: 200). Kendale may have had his pardons sealed
centrally, but that would have added enormously to the time and cost of production;
perhaps he and de Giglis just issued their agents matrices. If so, they followed established practice: seal matrices for institutions such as St Anthony of Vienne appear to
have been distributed widely to pardoners (Swanson 2008: 140).

The fact that many—perhaps all—of the indulgences that Caxton printed were
hand-sealed as well as machine-crafted does not change the fact that his press could
produce many copies of the text, where a scribe could copy only a few. But when
the strings on the Preston pardon are considered, print's efficiency seems less than
'stunning': 200,000 indulgences still represent 200,000 potential donations, but they
also represent 200,000 possible acts of stitching, a lot of mucking about with wax,
and all the complexity associated with the authorized distribution and collection of
indulgence receipts. Ideas about efficiency begin to seem insufficient if these and
other facts about the Preston copy are considered. This indulgence was printed on
parchment. Paper would have been cheaper and also easier to print on; ink did not
always take to parchment. *The Doctrine to Learn French and English* includes some
phrases for consumers irritated with their parchmeners:

> Josse the parchemyn maker
> Solde me a skyn of parchemyn
> That alle flued [ran].
>
> (Caxton 1964: 44, 13–16)

But like the wax with which it was sealed, the parchment was a familiar aspect of a
medieval document's form, and so, perhaps, a cue for a reader to recognize some part
of the text's authority. For whatever reason, Kendale did not mind the inefficiency of
parchment. Nor did he mind the inefficiency involved in employing two printers each
to produce several issues of the 1480–1 Rhodes indulgences. Both Lettou and Caxton

printed multiple versions of the indulgence, with and without the papal regnal year; with space for a single or multiple names. The variants between such copies suggest that both printers had to set and reset their type several times. Perhaps this did not seem 'inefficient'. Early Tudor English has no word for 'efficiency' (in its economic sense, it is a twentieth-century word). Modern scholars assume that the press works best when it produces 'the maximum of reading matter for the minimum of outlay' (H. Bennett 1969: 187). But Tudor book producers may have had other things in mind. Perhaps Kendale had Caxton and Lettou issue pardons in short runs, so that he and his men were not lumped with large piles of indulgences, yet to be sealed, that they might not be able to sell. Perhaps Kendale had only a few printed, and distributed these not for immediate exchange, but as exemplars for his agents, who, by the time they had strung and sealed the pardons 'slowly one at a time', might just as well have copied them. Of the handful of surviving copies of Caxton's 1480–1 Rhodes indulgences, two are in manuscript.[14] Manuscript copies survive for a great many other extant printed indulgences. Pardons continued to be conferred upon donors by oral performance of pardoners and priests, or as they recited prayers, or as they visited certain holy sites—without any sort of documentation of their actions—after the advent of printing. Like the strung and sealed Preston indulgence, such scribal and undocumented pardons require that we admit more complexity to familiar accounts of the radical changes wrought by printing. The printing of indulgences was never so 'efficient' that it replaced older ways of distributing them.

My broad argument is that, at the minute evidentiary level suggested by the strings hanging from the Preston copy of the Rhodes indulgence, seeming certainties about the invention of printing are disrupted and the printed object's capacity to invent possibilities, including new ways of thinking about Tudor culture, is restored. The two surviving manuscripts of the indulgence that Caxton printed in 1480–1 might reward similar close examination. Perhaps the hand of the scribes of these documents occurs elsewhere—in other pardons from the Tudor period, or even some of the other manuscript copies that were made of books printed by Caxton (see Blake 1989). We know, for instance, of many surviving books and documents that are the work of Westminster scribes working in Caxton's immediate ambit in the second half of the fifteenth century. It would be interesting to consider whether such scribes always worked less 'cheaply' than printers, as those who write about printing usually suggest. William Ebesham was a professional scribe and contemporary of Caxton's; records survive of his 1475–8 lease of a tenement in the Westminster Sanctuary, a short distance from Caxton's printing house. One of the books he made to order contains a copy of the *Propositio* that Caxton printed for the humanist John Russell in 1476 (Ebesham has copied texts onto the book's blank leaves) and a copy of an office for the Virgin that Caxton printed in 1480.[15] A letter from Ebesham to Sir John Paston, asking for payment for scribal copies of mostly legal texts, *c*.1469, also survives: he prices his work variously—from 1*d*. to 2*d*. per leaf (BL, Add. MS 43491, fo. 13). That would

---

[14]   NA, C270/32/13; Essex Record Office, D/DCe/Q2.
[15]   STC2, 21548 and 15848, respectively; the manuscript is Rylands Library, Manchester, Latin MS 395.

make his books more than twice the price of Caxton's, assuming that H. S. Bennett's figures for early Tudor books are about right at under 1*d*. per sheet (¹/₄*d*. or ¹/₂*d*. per quarto or folio leaf; H. Bennett 1950). But A. I. Doyle notes that Ebesham's figures for his services are muddled—positioned somewhere between hope and anxiety that he might never be paid (1957: 301). Remembering this, we might wonder again about the scribes who copied indulgenced letters for the Hospital of St Thomas of Rome in the fifteenth century: what sort of reward did they hope for? Literate servants of great lords and wealthy merchants presumably hoped for a continued place in the household or a higher annual income when they copied texts; monks did some copying as part of their regular duties; school and university scholars made copies of their own texts. The work done by these scribes was not in any simple way less efficient or more expensive than the work of the press. The Tudor populace may have found *less* use for scribal labour after the invention of printing. But recall that evidence of coterie manuscript circulation or attention to the careers of English notaries and scriveners, and secular and (until the Reformation) regular clerics, shows that scribal work still had many uses in the post-print period, and this is barely accounted for, especially for the early Tudor period.[16] The changes that came with print should not be reduced to the untested claim that the press made huge numbers of books so quickly and cheaply it finally overwhelmed less efficient ways of making books, and so 'decided' the shape of literate and literary culture.

My point here remains a methodological one. I do not want to argue that print was not the beginning of a new order of things—that it was not extremely inventive. I simply want to suggest that overmuch thinking upon familiar assumptions is a little 'stunning': it omits the complexity of, and alternatives to, dominant cultural forces. One way to invigorate discussion is to reintroduce the unfamiliar, still inventive forms of old books. Ebesham's part-manuscript, part-printed volumes, and Kendale's arrangements with two printers, some scribes, string, and sealing wax, suggest that the inventiveness of printing depended on flexible, singular, and ad hoc arrangements— just as the production and use of medieval manuscripts did. A methodology that accounts for such evidence and such arrangements, rather than one built on the claim that 'the machines decided', might be a useful way to think more broadly about Tudor print production—about the work of Grafton, Coverdale, Regnault, and Cromwell to make Henry's English Bible in the 1530s; or the work of the actors, writers, and printers who saw to the distribution of play texts in the 1590s.

Recent scholarship on Caxton has provided a much better sense of the culture in which his books were made, used, and meaningful, but there are things left to know. Linne R. Mooney is discovering more about the books made by Ebesham and other scribes in Caxton's Westminster and in early Tudor London (forthcoming). Yu-Chaio Wang has matched records to the names and hands of a remarkable number of Tudor owners of Caxton's books (2004). Dan Mosser has used watermark evidence

---

[16] Woudhuysen (1996); Marotti (1995); almost no work has been done on early Tudor clerkly scribes; there is no general study of scribal work done by the Tudor religious, though there have been many short studies of scribal activity at such centres as Syon Abbey in the period.

to identify the paper stocks on which some of Caxton's books are printed (1999). No one has yet thought systematically about second-hand books of the sort that were on the bookseller George's shelves, or about what study of them would reveal about the world in which printing was invented. But—since so many Latin and vernacular medical treatises, grammars, devotional aides, and service books survive that were made in England and on the Continent for English customers before the arrival of printing—someone could. It remains for scholars of Caxton's newly Tudor, newly print culture to consider the detailed evidence left behind by that culture—and to think again about the meanings that old books and texts are able to invent.

Primary Works

Braham, Robert (1555), 'The Pistle to the Reader', in John Lydgate, *The Auncient Historie of the Warres betwixte the Grecians and the Troyans.*

Caxton, William (1900), *Dialogues in French and English*, ed. Henry Bradley, EETS, e.s., 79.

——(1928), *The Prologues and Epilogues*, ed. W. J. B. Crotch, EETS, o.s., 176.

——(1964), *Vocabulary in French and English: A Facsimile of Caxton's Edition c.1480*, ed. L. C. Harmer and J. C. T. Oates (Cambridge: Cambridge University Press).

——(1971), *The Book of the Knight of the Tower Translated by William Caxton*, ed. M. Y. Offord, EETS, s.s., 2.

Chaucer, Geoffrey (1987), *The Riverside Chaucer*, 2nd edn, ed. Larry D. Benson (Boston: Houghton Mifflin).

Gessler, Jean (1931), *Le Livre des Mestiers de Bruges et ses dérivés: Quatre anciens manuels de conversation*, 6 vols (Bruges: Le Consortium de Maîtres Imprimeurs Brugeois).

Langland, William (1995), *The Vision of Piers Plowman: A Critical Edition of the B-Text*, ed. A. V. C. Schmidt (London: Phoenix).

La Tour Landry, Geoffroy de (1854), *Le Livre du chevalier de La Tour Landry*, ed. Anatole de Montaiglon (Paris: Jannet).

CHAPTER 2

DRAMATIC THEORY AND *LUCRES'* 'DISCRETION'

THE PLAYS OF HENRY MEDWALL

KENT CARTWRIGHT

Not only is Henry Medwall 'the first vernacular dramatist whose name survives' (Medwall 1980: 1), his early Tudor plays themselves claim an impressive number of English known firsts or near-firsts. *Fulgens and Lucres* (*c*.1491)[1]—adapted from the humanist Latin treatise *De vera nobilitate* (*c*.1428)—is the first secular, humanist play

A shortened version of this essay was presented at the 43rd International Congress of the Medieval Institute, Kalamazoo, May 2008, for which opportunity I thank Eve Salisbury. At that conference, I was privileged to see a performance of *Fulgens and Lucres*, directed by Joseph Ricke, produced by Eve Salisbury, and performed by students of Western Michigan University. This production, which treated the play largely as farce, demonstrated its theatrical vitality and high humour; it also showed how the inset Lucres story could be played in a spirit of broad comedy consistent with that of the servant figures.

[1] For the dating of *Nature* and *Fulgens and Lucres* scholars lack firm evidence. Moeslein (Medwall 1981: 6) considers them roughly contemporary. Because *Fulgens* is the more original and sophisticated, one is tempted to think of it post-dating *Nature*. For *Fulgens*, Nelson (Medwall 1980: 17–18) favours 1491/2, especially if Thomas More acted in the play as a boy, possibly in the role of A (Walker 2006: 25). Siemens (1996) favours 1496; Moeslein, 1497 (Medwall 1981: 59–69).

and the first play to be printed (*c.*1512 by John Rastell). *Nature* (*c.*1490), likewise, is the first morality play structured by humanist themes (and one of the first with scientific interests), and it became a model for subsequent plays such as Skelton's *Magnificence* (*c.*1515). *Fulgens and Lucres* and *Nature* introduce rhyme royal into drama, and *Nature*, for another first, incorporates prose. *Fulgens and Lucres* offers one of the first English plays with a fully developed sub-plot (a previous example appears in *The Second Shepherds' Play*, *c.*1450) and one of the first prominently featuring a female character (a contemporaneous instance occurs with the Digby *Mary Magdalene*). *Fulgens and Lucres* also inaugurates a dramatic question—whether true nobility derives from heredity or merit—that wends from plays such as *Gentleness and Nobility* (*c.*1527) to Christopher Marlowe's *Tamburlaine* (*c.*1590). *Fulgens and Lucres* also ranks as England's first romantic comedy; its first play to employ extensive, self-conscious meta-drama; and its first to theorize itself.

Meta-theatricality and self-consciousness appear from the outset. An unnamed personage (scripted as A) walks into an open space surrounded by a group of diners and pretends to be one of their company. Then arrives B, initially mistaken by A for an actor, who describes the plot of a play, set in ancient Rome, about to be performed. The two stand aside as a character, Fulgens, from that play enters, addresses the audience about his marriageable daughter, and converses with one of her suitors. The two Romans depart—and B decides to seek employment with the wooer. This sequence highlights the precarious boundary between fiction and reality. A presents himself as a spectator; B turns into a kind of prologue; Fulgens begins the 'formal' play. To B's decision to find office with Cornelius, A objects, 'thou wyll distroy all the play!', but B enigmatically responds, 'Nay, nay, | The play began never till now!' (1. 364, 365–6).[2] B's pun on 'play' (as both drama and game) implies that the plebeians will figure in the main plot—and, indeed, their improvisation will interject this already told tale with a countervailing sense of contingency.

In that spirit, *Fulgens and Lucres* proffers two theories of drama—which I will call the episodic and the interconnective—a bounty resulting from the coexistence of its 'main plot' and developed 'sub-plot'. In the main action, Lucres, a Roman senator's daughter, must choose between two suitors, one of noble blood but dissolute behaviour, the other of common ancestry but laudable public service. *Fulgens and Lucres'* framing sub-plot involves the antics of A and B, masterless plebeians in the household where the play is being performed, who enter its action to take employment with Lucres' suitors. In the episodic theory, A and B's comic routines have no necessary bearing on the main action, and the play can evoke different responses at different moments according to its shifting topical interests. In the interconnective theory, all the varying parts advance or complicate the play's themes, with character types collectively defining a world, and with comic material bearing upon serious themes. Although *Nature* impresses as an interconnective play, *Fulgens and Lucres* has been treated by most criticism as episodic. Scholarship has focused largely on the main action of Lucres' choice of suitors and on the implications of its heredity–merit

---

[2] All quotations from Medwall are from Nelson's 1980 edition.

debate for the politics of Henry VII's reign. What emerges, as in the contextualizing work of Olga Horner (1993), is a bracing vision of how deeply a play can be read for topical meaning. Some episodic critics do see the comedic sub-plot as relevant to the serious plot, but only to the extent that its humour defuses any potential outrage from aristocratic audience members who witness, in Lucres' choice, bloodlines playing second fiddle to good works. But perhaps the sub-plot—which consumes over 70 per cent of the play's lines (Norland 1995: 237)—functions more radically than that, in the spirit of a topsy-turvy Christmas celebration.

This chapter takes the interconnective theory as its hypothesis in order to consider the sub-plot's satire of the main plot as seriously meant. From that vantage point, the sub-plot turns the main plot's tidy, over-idealized heredity–merit debate into comic melodrama. In the medieval *Second Shepherds' Play*, Mak and Gill's sub-plot parody of Christ's nativity enlarges the circumference of meaning and allows the delight of the comedic shepherds to be folded into the wonder of the Annunciation and redemptive birth. By contrast, the sub-plot in *Fulgens and Lucres* makes its didactic truth appear forced and unreal. This difference marks a transition in drama, as messy secularity begins to nudge aside soteriology. In *Fulgens and Lucres*, the case for public service may triumph dutifully over that for ancestry, but at another level, the sub-plot makes contingent the ostensible inevitability of the main action and compromises its argument through parody. The value that emerges is the humanist value of reason, but reason modulated into an attitude, an aesthetic mode of perception and ironic delight—reason as 'discretion', best represented in Lucres' behaviour.

Medwall wrote both *Nature* and *Fulgens and Lucres* sometime in the 1490s for performance in the great hall of Lambeth Palace, John Henry Morton's residence, on the south bank of London's River Thames.[3] Medwall had been born in London in 1461 and educated at Eton and King's College, Cambridge (Medwall 1980: 3–14; 1981: 11–29). Perhaps in the late 1480s, he entered Morton's service as a legal and ecclesiastical official. Morton held the offices of Lord Chancellor, Archbishop of Canterbury, and cardinal, emerging as one of the most powerful men in England under Henry VII. Morton was celebrated for his probity, evident in his lively dinner debate, represented in Sir Thomas More's *Utopia* (1516). As a member of Morton's retinue, Medwall likely authored (and helped to stage) entertainments during the Christmas seasons (Medwall 1981: 4). He qualified as a playwright through his apparently extensive experience of drama at university. King's College, which he attended for three years in the early 1480s, was an important site for dramatic and musical entertainments, especially at Christmastide (Medwall 1980: 5–8). Although he left King's in 1483 (possibly to join Morton in a period of political instability, possibly to study law), he returned regularly to the college, and participated in its substantial holiday 'disguisings' in January 1485 during an extended residency. Likely, then, Medwall was involved in writing, producing, and perhaps acting in dramatic entertainments at Cambridge.

---

[3] On the staging of Medwall's interludes, see Medwall (1980: 18–19, 174 n.; 1981: 5, 8–10).

Both Medwall's education and his familiarity with seasonal theatrics show in his plays. His classical training is evident, for example, in his Latin tags, Latin stage directions, and allusions to Aristotle (*Nature*, 1. 57), Ovid (*Nature*, 1. 78), and possibly Macrobius (*Fulgens*, 2. 477). Medwall demonstrates comparable familiarity with English poets such as Geoffrey Chaucer and John Lydgate (A. Nelson 1980: 196 n.) and with morality-drama elements employed in plays such as *Mankind*, *The Castle of Perseverance*, and *Mary Magdalene*. The main plot of *Fulgens and Lucres* derives from Buonaccorso da Montemagno's *De vera nobilitate*, translated into English (with help from a French version) by John Tiptoft (*c*.1460) and printed by William Caxton in 1481 (Reed 1926: 97–9; Medwall 1980: 2).[4] In developing *Fulgens and Lucres* from Tiptoft's translation, Medwall seizes upon the earliest of the 'courtesy books' ('treatises on manners and courtesy either translated from Italian originals or written in imitation of them') which were then fashionable in Italy and became so in Tudor England (R. Mitchell 1938: 181). Its Italianate source notwithstanding, *Fulgens and Lucres* functions as a traditional Christmas entertainment. Thomas Pettitt places its action (which involves 'folk' elements such a mock combat, fool's wooing, singing contest, and mumming) in a 'lost tradition' of seasonal interludes: late medieval household revels that 'provided the context for a vigorous and creative interaction between a variety of popular traditions, as between traditional and academic culture' (1984: 20; cf. Medwall 1980: 2; Baskervill 1927: 425 ff.)—a dichotomy suggestive of *Fulgens*'s main and sub-plots.

Medwall's literary and dramatic sophistication shines in his versification (see Medwall 1980: 25–7; 1981: 34–8). Both *Nature* and *Fulgens and Lucres* employ two verse forms for two different sets of characters, the aristocrats and the Vices or plebeians, and for their related strains of action. These dual tracks are distinctive yet intriguingly interactive. *Nature* begins with the stately figures of Nature, Reason, Man, and others speaking in rhyme royal, the seven-line, iambic pentameter, *ababbcc*-rhymed stanza introduced by Chaucer in *Troilus and Criseyde* and later employed by Lydgate. Likewise in *Fulgens and Lucres*, main-plot characters Fulgens, Lucres, and the suitors Cornelius and Gayus speak in rhyme royal. Rhyme royal identifies its speakers as dignified and the narrative as serious. Medwall sometimes employs irregular syllabification (perhaps after Chaucer) or lengthens stanzas. Fulgens' first seven stanzas, for example, close with hexameters befitting his stateliness. Conversely, in both *Nature* and *Fulgens*, Medwall might abbreviate a stanza or distribute it between speakers.

The Vice figures in *Nature* and the comic servant figures in *Fulgens and Lucres* speak verse from a different moral realm. These characters favour tail-rhyme (also called *rime couée*, or caudate rhyme), a form identified with popular medieval romance. Medwall's tail-rhyme, compared to rhyme royal, features longer stanzas of shorter lines using a different rhyme scheme of *aaabcccb*, with the *a*- and *c*-lines typically tetrameter and the *b*-lines (the 'tail') trimeter. The effect, compared to rhyme royal, is of dynamism and speed, especially since the four-stress lines can divide symmetrically, with an accelerated tempo. Multiple speakers frequently share parts of

---

[4] For Tiptoft's translation, see R. Mitchell (1938: 213–41).

stanzas or lines, adding further energy. The tail-rhyme characters speak with a crisp, colloquial Anglo-Saxon diction, and their language, far more than that of the rhyme royal speakers, registers the experiences of sensation, sensuality, and the body—and their attendant humour. What the form forfeits in elevation it gains in capaciousness and energy. Rhyme royal and tail-rhyme stanzas establish alternate poetic and moral domains. Medwall may be influenced in this regard by Chaucer's *Canterbury Tales*, where the Prioress's sentimental martyr-tale, told in rhyme royal, is followed by the pilgrim's satiric 'Tale of Sir Topas', told in tail-rhyme, which lampoons the values and sensibility of the 'Prioress's Tale'.

Medwall's speakers can change poetic forms. Consider *Nature*, where, at a crucial moment, the Vice-like Worlde advises Man to rid himself of Innocency (1. 630–6). Man illustrates his consent and moral fall by switching from pentameter rhyme royal to a form of tail-rhyme (1. 637 ff.). When Man returns to Reason, he does so first by speaking in tetrameters but with the rhyme royal scheme, as if in transition, before moving into full pentameters (2. 1010 ff.). Here verse forms distinguish moral fields, and a speaker's stylistic shifts authenticate his life-altering decisions. In *Fulgens and Lucres*, the plebeian characters demonstrate something more, a dynamic capacity to enter into, even appropriate, the elevated rhyme royal form. When B, for example, begins to narrate the 'substaunce' of the play that the actors will present, he switches to rhyme royal (1. 68 ff.), and A and B typically use that form when speaking with the main plot's aristocratic characters. Likewise, the two are capable of employing rhyme royal but with a preponderance of four-stress lines, so that the form assumes some coloration of the plebeian verse. Gayus in his conversation with Lucres in Part 1 speaks rhyme royal, but when she departs and A and B enter the dialogue, their shortened tetrameter rhythms impose on the rhyme royal scheme (1. 575 ff.). As A and B infuse the stately verse with their humorous tones, Medwall explores the ability of the comedic form to appropriate or transform the more dignified. His sophisticated versification in *Fulgens and Lucres* should warn us against arguments that its main plot and sub-plot remain distinct from each other or that the latter is subservient to the former. It signals, rather, the interactivity of domains and the sub-plot's infectious power.

At first blush, the Lucres story might seem self-contained. *Fulgens and Lucres*, following Buonaccorso, sets out a seemingly straightforward interpretative problem: of her two suitors, Lucres will marry the nobler—but which is that? And who will decide? Publius Cornelius can claim vast wealth and exalted bloodline but self-indulgent living; Gayus Flaminius, honourable public service but inferior blood and modest fortune. Beyond its source, the conflict has analogues in literary works such as *Le Roman de la Rose* and Chaucer's 'Wife of Bath's Tale', where a knight must learn to value the beloved for her virtue (Walker 2006: 28–9). As David Bevington (1968) establishes in his foundational reading, the story's meritocratic solution mirrors contemporary court politics, as Henry VII surrounded himself not with wealthy nobles but with 'new men'. Nobles possessed geographic centres of power, were trained in chivalric arts, and maintained large retinues of armed men. Such independent feudal lords could not form the basis of a centralized nation-state. By contrast, the 'new men' were professional administrators and promising commoners or gentry promoted by Henry for their competence and loyalty to him (Guy 1988: 56). As Bevington observes, 'The man now prized at court was an eloquent speaker, canny adviser, tireless administrator of public policy, and above all well educated' (1968: 42). Gayus offers just the type of public servant of modest background that Henry VII wished to cultivate; by contrast, Cornelius represents the lavish spending noble with a personal retinue that Henry wished to contain.

Critics read *Fulgens and Lucres*, then, as a tribute to Henry's political tactics and a compliment to 'new men' such as Morton (who began his career as a lawyer). But, scholars also argue, Medwall avoids a 'defiant challenge of aristocracy by a self-made intelligentsia' by having Lucres declare that she intends to set no precedent in choosing Gayus, speaks only for herself, and considers ideal a man in whom virtue and distinguished bloodline converge (Bevington 1968: 46). The comedy of A and B assists, critics add, by framing the Roman story and distancing the audience from it emotionally through mirth and game (see, among others, Bevington 1968; Colley 1975; Norland 1995). The distancing argument addresses the fear that Lucres' devaluation of noble ancestry, left unmediated, might offend aristocratic members of the audience; thus, A and B help to keep potential outrage at bay. But this reading has limitations. The more qualified and muted the political implications, the less politically significant the play. To argue that *Fulgens and Lucres* critiques the aristocracy yet also defuses that attack makes the action potentially self-negating.

Consider alternatively that *Fulgens and Lucres* pursues two tracks of tension and conflict in the play: one concerning Lucres' negotiation of her marriage, the other concerning the function of A and B. The first conflict arises with Fulgens' preference that his daughter choose Cornelius. Thus, one problem of the play will be to overcome that obstacle and to justify her desire to wed Gayus. In the process, a central thematic value will emerge: discretion. Launching the inset play, Fulgens acknowledges his heavenly debt for his 'prosperous lyfe', lofty position, 'riche apparell', and high-status wife (1. 224, 240). Despite his self-satisfaction and his blithe likening of Lucres to himself, he avoids complete complacency by praising Lucres, first because she has 'beaute and clere understanding' and especially because she is wise and 'discrete': thus, she combines the gifts both 'of nature and of especiall grace' (1. 267, 270; see Westfall 1990: 165). Fulgens wishes Lucres well wed. When Cornelius appears and asks for Fulgens' 'gode will' in his marriage suit, the father declares that he would be glad if Cornelius obtained Lucres' favour: he promises that he will 'her advyse | To love you before other' (1. 330, 339–40). The father confirms his limits by favouring the figure most like himself in status.

Lucres possesses not only discernment, Fulgens notes, but also discretion. The two seem related. To be 'discreet' is to be 'judicious, prudent, circumspect, cautious' (*OED*, 'discreet', A1).[5] Sir Thomas Elyot offers a related understanding of discretion in *The Governor* (1531), where he characterizes it as 'Modestie', restraint, and,

---

[5] As the *OED* notes, 'discrete' (1. 267) is an alternative spelling of 'discreet', and its context in the play suggests that meaning.

interestingly, the perception of 'aptnese' (1992: 103). Discretion combines insight with a sense of fitness or proportion. This description also reasonably includes a sense of irony and humour, for in the classical view, comedy arises from what is dispropor-tionate and inapt—or, as Aristotle termed it, the 'ridiculous' (1984: 229). Discretion thus conceived will emerge as Lucres' defining quality, one both moral and aesthetic. This quality opens a cultural window, for it resembles the sensibility of moderation and ironic insight strongly associated with Erasmian humanism. Acknowledging her filial obligation to Fulgens and her respect for his counsel despite her freedom of decision, Lucres tells him that she will consent to Cornelius if he wishes. Presented with such complaisance, the father shifts course and declares that, although he 'did somewhat to [Cornelius] enclyne', he will allow Lucres free choice (1. 446). In this model of negotiation, the individual accrues rights not by insisting upon them but by displaying a willingness to resign them before authority—and authority acts reciprocally. Lucres' declaration of filial submission produces her liberty; her dis-cretion enables her will. Thus she uses her discretion instrumentally. When Fulgens gives her the reins, she takes occasion to introduce the suitor's honour test, which inevitably favours Gayus. Notwithstanding Lynn Forest-Hill's view that Lucres inter-nalizes 'masculine ideals' (2008: 48), Lucres' discretion reveals independent desire and wit.

Furthering that sense of contingency, the play must show that Lucres affects the worthier suitor. Lucres, in her 'inestimable prudence' (1. 101), asks her father for an interval to enquire into which of the two is most 'honorable' so as to establish the basis for her choice (1. 455), remarking, perhaps with playful archness, that 'Pore maydens' can 'be dissayved' by 'great dyssemblynge' (1. 475, 476). With the sudden announcement of Gayus' arrival, however, Lucres, despite her pretension to impartiality, becomes flustered. Yet when Gayus initially seems overbearing, Lucres responds disdainfully (1. 540–1). Gayus, by turning immediately deferential (1. 547–8), recovers her goodwill and encouragement. Lucres' management of the exchange asserts her strength and wit, and enforces on Gayus the value of restraint that she had demonstrated with Fulgens. Now Lucres can express to Gayus her desire for him, so that their 'affectionate relationship', as Alan Nelson observes, makes her choice 'emotionally as well as logically satisfying to the audience' (Medwall 1980: 21). (As critics highlight, Cornelius is condemned to wooing indirectly, through the father.) Medwall's dramaturgy, then, takes cognizance of the difference between an affective and a moral response. Part of the main plot's pleasure derives from the convergence of moral with emotional truth, the latter validating the former. Curiously, however, Lucres next deflects Gayus' urgency, saying that she must first her 'faders mynde assay' about his acceptability (1. 556). This sounds odd because Fulgens has previously answered that question affirmatively. Lucres anticipates a conversation that has already occurred. Her declaration may be a form of dis-creetly making assurance double-sure; alternatively, it suggests some open-endedness in the play (of which we will see more). It may also signal to the audience that the justice of Lucres' choice needs further demonstration not just verbally but theatrically.

If so, Lucres' discretion can be understood as anti-didacticism, for it insists that meanings be revealed through actions—and thus it is also aesthetic. Her restraint emerges again in her conversation with B, whom Cornelius has made his servant and, foolishly, his advocate with Lucres. B attempts to prove his bona fides to Lucres by retelling the 'token' story of how Cornelius threw her musk ball at a cuckoo nesting in the hole of an ash tree (2. 175). Lucres entertains B's ornate speech but treats it ironically, listens to B compromise his case by garbling Cornelius' anecdote into a confused and scatological tale of 'hole'-kissing, and chastises and corrects his errors (2. 285). Saying only what is needed to protect her dignity, Lucres allows B's folly and hyperbolic pleading to represent the quality of Cornelius' suit. Her indulgence of B suggests that she responds to the factor's cuckoo-like behaviour with her own controlled amusement, as if for the moment she were in comic league with the audience. Indeed, as John Scott Colley has shown, Lucres stands as an audience figure to B's garbled playlet (1975: 325–6). Her perspicacity constitutes the spectatorial value that Medwall would cultivate—especially in a play full of risible errors, as we shall see. Thus, Lucres' discretion operates aesthetically by allowing B's crudeness to symbolize Cornelius' sensibility, creating ironic pleasure and establishing a model of theatrical response.

Cornelius further illustrates the way the play's aesthetic interacts with its moral dimension. B enters midway through Part 1, now in Cornelius' service, and describes his master's extravagance. Cornelius squanders money as if 'he had not dayly remembraunce | Of tyme to come, nor makyth no store'; he is literally pre-posterous, 'For he carith not which ende goth before' (1. 704–5). He wastefully maintains numerous retainers (1. 713–16), a Tudor political issue. B's satire turns to his employer's clothing: Cornelius wears wantonly expensive silk and gold hose; a huge codpiece (his most expensive item); 'new and straunge' gowns made especially short; and fashions requiring reams of fabric that create the impression of 'whinges behind redy to flye' (1. 738, 7470), wings that foreshadow Cornelius' comparison to a cuckoo. In this caricature, Cornelius' exorbitance transforms him into something not quite human. With B's description, Medwall taps a rich vein of medieval dramatic satire of the Vice figure: Lucifer in *Wisdom* dresses as a gallant; the Vices in *Mankind* convince the hero to dress in a dandified short gown; Pryde in Medwall's *Nature* celebrates his fashionability, including his 'short gown | Wyth wyde sleves', a redundancy of fabric that links him with Cornelius (*Nature*, 1. 767–8). As Theresa Coletti argues, late medieval discussions of the gallant figure treat his material superabundance as a 'serious sin' (2004: 8). Thus, Cornelius' sartorial excess creates risible grotesqueness. Moral and social meaning becomes available through aesthetic discrimination. Cornelius' extravagance is also exaggerated by the dialogue's cues to the B actor to mimic his descriptions with burlesque gestures, as when B says deictically that Cornelius' hose 'must be strypide all *this way*' and mentions 'A codpiece before almost *thus large*' (1. 732, 743; my emphasis). Cornelius' luxuriance emerges as the aesthetic, and hence moral, opposite of Lucres' restraint and discretion.

Glimmering through this foundational humanist interlude are the nascent signs of the grand humanist vision that art has the power to effect human and social reform.

In this vision, aesthetic critique can reveal social and political truths, for aesthetic criteria—such as aptness, discretion, and proportion—are fundamentally moral. This humanist conviction radiates from Italy and works such as Castiglione's *The Courtier* (1528). In its English version, influenced by Chaucerian irony and Erasmian wise folly, it generates that humanist playfulness and delightful enigma characteristic of More's *Utopia* or the contemporary dramas of John Rastell and John Heywood (Cartwright 1999: 1–48; cf. Betteridge, Chapter 10 in this volume). The humanist aesthetic undertakes to engage readers or spectators by means of irony, sympathy, wonder, and self-recognition. Medwall's development of the capacity for audience identification with characters, argues Bob Godfrey, marks a signal historic shift in comedy (2002). In this model, the individual self-reform effected by art offers a basis for moral and political change; in the background lies a humanist vision of a commonwealth (Wakelin 2007: 160).

The sense of irony and contingency that Lucres' discretion introduces into the marriage plot is magnified by the interventional activities of A and B. Emphasizing that A and B meddle improvisationally in the action deviates from the usual critical view, noted above, that they regulate the audience, through diversion, to accept the concept of the 'new man'. The standard view fails to recognize how much the A-and-B action transforms the impression of the marriage plot, for the servants' mocking tone washes over everything and insists that the audience exercise a comedic and meta-dramatic awareness.

In an unusual commentary on the plebeians' influence, Jackson Cope argues that A 'alters the plot of the inner "*Fulgens and Lucres*" '. As evidence, he notes A's announcement of the debate plan at the end of Part 1, his breaking the play with an intermission, and his preternatural certainty about how Part 2 will unfold (1993: 104). One might contend further that A and B work against the 'inner' narrative's presumed inevitability and preordained closure. The two improvisers keep open the possibility that the Roman story might turn out differently—and aspects of the formal narrative do change as a result of A and B's intervention. Indeed, A and B illustrate—as when B attempts to explain Cornelius' 'token' to Lucres—how much a tale can be transformed in the telling. They also undercut the inner narrative's school-debate didacticism. They demonstrate that truth must be not only spoken but also shown, that things can mean differently than declared or turn out differently than expected, and that the audience must watch with its own spectatorial poetics of 'discretion', resisting preordained truths and appreciating irony and disproportion.

In that spirit, A and B meddle with the marriage narrative—B, after all, has claimed the power 'The marriage utterly to mare or to make' (1. 379). When A offers himself as Gayus' servant, he insists that he has just overheard Lucres entertaining a 'fresshe galant' on the subject of marriage (1. 586). A may be fabricating, or he may be rewriting, the conversation that he and B overheard when Lucres discussed her choice of suitors with Fulgens. From A, nonetheless, Gayus comes to understand that he has a rival, and the news provokes him nervously to assign his new servant A to follow directly after the just-departed Lucres to urge her to send a 'redy answere' to his suit (1. 677). Thus, A from the sub-plot initiates an action in the main plot.

Subsequently, when Gayus rescues A and B—who have been left trussed, sullied, and beaten by Jone—A insists that he was attacked by a band of Cornelius' men as he went on his prior errand to Lucres. Even if Gayus does not wholly believe A, that false accusation provides some cover for Gayus' claim during the suitor's debate that Cornelius maintains 'theftis and murders every day' (2. 637). A, furthermore, reports Lucres' message to Gayus that she will meet him here the next day before 'this honorable audyence' with a 'fynall answare' to his marriage offer (2. 1315, 1299). A's message introduces into the plot the public marriage-debate that will constitute much of Part 2. A's lies to Gayus have revealed a rival suitor, provoked Gayus into forcing Lucres to devise a solution, encouraged his later denunciation of Cornelius, and made the audience participate in the action of Part 2. This sequence is proving B right: the play (in both senses) never began until A and B joined in.

Through A and B (and Lucres), the ending of the Lucres story loses form. At the outset, B reports, according to the actors, that Lucres intends to marry the 'more noble of the twayne' (1. 106), but that such public disagreement will arise that the suitors' debate will be 'eschew[ed]' and the matter brought to the senate, which will judge in Gayus' favour (1. 115). We have here a 'baseline' version of the resolution. (In Tiptoft the matter is to be determined by Fulgens and the senate, but no judgment is given: our play asserts its right to revise.) A replies that he will encourage the actors to change the play's conclusion, because no 'chorles son' should be affirmed as 'more noble than a gentilman born' (1. 130, 131)—and A and B dispute, not whether the conclusion *can* be changed, but whether it *should* be. And it does change, at least in process. After the culminating debate between Cornelius and Gayus, Lucres expresses a wish for more evidence about the suitors' contentions. She will therefore enquire what 'commune fame' says about them; when she has gathered 'evidence', she will reassemble the lovers and deliver her 'sentence' (2. 726–9). But this new proceeding does not occur. Pressed by Cornelius, Lucres declares that she will go home immediately, prepare her sentence in writing, and send copies to both suitors, since, as she says, her decision really concerns them only and no one else (2. 736–44). That makes three versions of the ending so far, and it has moved from being a matter of senatorial and public importance to one exclusively private. There is more. The suitors gone, Lucres announces to the audience that she has already decided for Gayus, and asks B to deliver her decision orally to Cornelius—not in writing as she had proposed (2. 806–7). By now, however, as Lucres or any spectator should know, A and B cannot be trusted to report anything accurately, so that Lucres' request undermines her decision. Ironically, and rather delightfully, she is participating in the deconstruction of her own ending. 'Shall I do that errand?', B asks the audience (and perhaps Lucres). 'Nay, let be!' (2. 809). Lucres has made her decision, but it will never reach Cornelius. And what form would it take, coming from B? The conclusion of this play has devolved from a senatorial proclamation, to a public pronouncement, to a written private communication, to an oral message given to a servant who garbles what he hears and who refuses to deliver it anyway: how can the content of this message not disappear as the integrity of its delivery collapses? We have here perhaps a synecdoche or *mise en abyme* for the play as a whole. Certainly the Lucres story does not follow the ending promised in the 'prologue'; indeed, it may not complete itself at all. The conclusion has become increasingly contingent, and finally wholly dependent, upon a jumble-headed scallywag who refuses to cooperate.

Besides employing A and B as protagonists, *Fulgens* also emphasizes their status as stage actors. Here the two introduce another, complementary kind of contingency, the sense that the play can be misperformed or disrupted—and thus misrepresented—at any moment. The interlude emphasizes the precariousness of theatre, as when A or B tell spectators to make way for entering actors (as at 1. 193–4) or when a character invites the audience to respond to an invitation (as at 1. 354–6). A and B misspeak or forget their words at various points (1. 801, 902–4; 2. 332, 348–9), and once A even seems to lose the thread of his speech and 'go up' on his lines (2. 46). Given the muddled ending, A and B have to 'improvise' the play's conclusion (870 ff.). Indeed, when B makes a hash of the musk ball story to Lucres, we have a paradigmatic instance of the messenger–surrogate actor forgetting his lines, then becoming more flustered, and even searching frantically for a misplaced prop (the letter meant for Lucres) (2. 303–28). These acting 'errors' are woven into the texture of the play; they provide an ongoing source of comic amusement for the audience; and they redouble the sense of the moment-by-moment contingency that characterizes *Fulgens and Lucres*.

One thespian error even becomes so recurrent as to constitute a motif in the action: lateness, delay, missed entrances (and even exits)—in short, timing. The play commences with the audience silent ('still'; 1. 2) and waiting, ready for the play to start, so that the A actor, in effect, fills in for a delay. Relatedly, Fulgens asks the audience if Cornelius has arrived, and the latter rushes in overdue, apologetic, and probably breathless (1. 291–3). This problem of late entrances compounds in the play's second half. A hurries on-stage sweating and fearing that he 'sholde come to late' (2. 3), only to discover, after his introductory speech, that the rest of the acting company has not arrived either: 'I marvell gretely in my mynde | That thay tarry so long behynde' (2. 63–4). With A asking the audience to 'have pacyens', B finally arrives but is left pounding frantically at the door because he cannot get in. Once admitted, B is chastised by A 'For longe taryinge' (2. 85), and grows so annoyed himself that he threatens to leave. (Could Medwall be working into the play the delays and flared tempers of the rehearsal process?) A frets further that the contending parties have not arrived. When Cornelius finally does enter, B informs him that neither Lucres nor Gayus has appeared and advises him to depart again and make them wait for him rather than he for them, so as not to 'be theyr druge' (2. 152). Cornelius accepts that advice, and at this point the need for B to have a 'token' to authenticate himself to Lucres arises—another instance of a servant figure intervening to influence the action. Before the debate, Gayus' unaccountably late arrival becomes the occasion for Cornelius to bring on his mummers (one of whom is unable to perform), and later Cornelius encourages Lucres to dispense with preliminaries in order to speed the play along (2. 409–11). Acting miscues are structured into the dialogue and action, creating an ever-present sense that we are watching an interlude that can, and does, intermittently go off the rails, that not only the play world but also the performance itself proceeds precariously and contingently. It is no surprise then that, in what amounts to an epilogue, B apologizes for the inadequacies of the performance and, on the author's behalf, invites any audience member to rewrite the play to better effect (2. 902–19).

Besides being protagonists and actors, A and B are also audience figures. Unlike morality Vices, A might really be the confused spectator he affects. In the spirit of playgoers, A and B discuss the action, ponder the outcome, and wonder how others will take it. A insists that spectators will not believe the play's ending; no, answers B, 'the matter may be so well convayde' that everyone 'in this place' will be contented (1. 136–7). In questioning the action, venting exasperation, and expressing disbelief, A and B model spectatorial behaviour and prod the audience to respond. A begins the play wondering, 'What meane ye, syrs, to stond so still?' (1. 2): that is, why are you in the audience so quiet? A's speech sounds like a direct invitation *not* to be silent: that is, to laugh, to respond verbally, to join in the fun. Towards that end, A and B, and other characters, too, interact with the audience through direct address, gesture, and movement. Cornelius asks the 'gode felowes' of the audience if any want to be his servant (1. 354); A at the conclusion asks the women of the audience if they choose their husbands for virtue (2. 848–9). Noting the effect in *Nature* of this 'bi-focal' orientation, Godfrey suggests that Medwall innovates by making spectators feel 'implicated in the action themselves' (2002: 108), a quality that he associates with Erasmus' views of drama (on such audience intimacy, see Debax 2007: 31–3). Godfrey concludes that Medwall is the first English playwright to make the audience recognize, not the 'predigested paradigms of morality', but rather 'the immediate reality of a shared world' (108). Thus, A and B's kinship with the audience grants them affective power. Their satire acquires thereby a considerable potential to influence spectatorial responses, feelings, and judgements towards the main characters. As protagonists, actors, and audience figures, A and B orchestrate *Fulgens and Lucres*.

Accordingly, A and B's mock wooing of Jone looms as a centrally signifying action in the play. The comic wooing precedes the serious wooing, thereby preconditioning audience attitudes, as the comic version parodies precisely the serious one. Even before the mock-wooing contest proper, A and B quarrel over Jone in language so rife with sexual double entendres that their pretentions to romantic love only reveal hilariously their desire for sexual gratification. Robert Merrix examines point by point the way that the comic scene parodies the serious lovers (1977: 19–21). B stands in for his master, Cornelius, and the money-grubbing Jone treats his proposal as a financial tender. Since B can offer no wealth, he promises instead to love her 'out of measure' (1. 939), an ironic allusion to Cornelius' excessiveness. Unsuccessful, B attempts to force a kiss upon Jone; Cornelius will later define nobleness in terms of force. A interrupts their kiss and claims honourable intentions towards Jone, parodying his master, Gayus.

Urged to arbitrate the rivalry, Jone demands to see who 'can do most maystry' (1. 1095), the comic equivalent of honour. Where the serious characters combat rhetorically, the comedians do so physically. The comic suitors engage inconclusively in a singing contest and a wrestling match (although B has the edge). The broad comedy increases as A and B burlesque a knightly jousting match, here transformed into a game called 'farte pryke in cule' (1. 1169). In this game, each man has his feet bound and his hands tied in front; his knees or hands clasp a stick protruding forward (or backward) like a spear, with his opponent's buttocks as the target (Meredith 1984; Twycross 2001; the 2008 Kalamazoo production had the 'spears' sticking out behind, with the opponents hopping backwards towards each other). Jone warns the combatants to 'hold faste behynd' (1. 1181), but A, when defeated, loses bodily control, at which B recoils; 'I fele it at my nose' (1. 1212). The serious lovers' orifices of rhetoric are displaced in this combat by orifices of a different function. The projecting stick-spears constitute obvious phallic references; they recall B's remark that Cornelius' clothing features an enormous codpiece, and their size and protuberance offer a reductive interpretation of the true nature of the serious debate. Thus, as James Simpson notes, the jousting contest operates as a metaphor for buggery, the debate's 'intellectual penetration' ridiculed here as the equivalent of something anal (2002: 551). The contest culminates with Jone—who announces that she is affianced elsewhere—beating and mocking A and B. Dramatic, hilarious, and visceral, this comic wooing provides a key for the audience to decode the suitors' debate.

Thus, the 'serious' wooing contest need not be taken all that seriously. To be sure, Gayus wins the debate as the man of greater virtue. The play gives him his reward, with the outcome never in doubt. But the fun comes from elsewhere, such as in watching Cornelius' reactions to Gayus' *ad hominem* attacks. Indeed, certain of Gayus' lines seem calculated to produce laughter: 'Some of your owne meritis let se bring in, | Yf ever ye dyde ony syth ye were bore' (2. 622–3). Gayus, however, invites little spectatorial identification. He may have ardour, but he lacks colour. Mitchell finds Medwall's Gayus 'something of a prig' (1938: 184), and Bevington points out that Gayus lacks both the naval heroics and the 'Horatian' contemplativeness of Buonaccorso's Gaius (1968: 46). To the audience's amusement, Gayus is even susceptible to being duped by crafty servants (as in 1. 621–51). Gayus' attractiveness amounts largely to his freedom from Cornelius' degeneracy; he offers Lucres all the comforts of virtue, but none of romance. If Gayus is a cardboard hero, Cornelius makes a stereotypical antagonist. Announcing to Lucres that if she accepts him, 'Doubtles ye shall blesse the tyme that ever ye were bore' (2. 546), Cornelius proceeds with a speech that amounts to an index of vanity, frivolity, pomposity, and bad form. At one point, he even approaches Gayus threateningly (2. 533–5), for Lucres must intervene to remind him that she has forbid 'all maner of violence' (2. 371, 536–8). This is the kind of stuff written to provoke auditorial hisses and boos. The debate presents extreme and stereotypical characters making extreme and categorical arguments; it is less intellectual disputation than comic melodrama, and it invites the audience's meta-theatrical self-consciousness about the kind of game in which they are participating.

The 'serious' marriage contest comes in for some of its most devastating satire towards the end of the play. A and B shake their heads at Lucres' decision to marry Gayus for virtue. 'Vertue? What the devyll is that?' asks A (2. 842). With this, A and B turn to the spectators and challenge them as to whether men or women take their spouses on the grounds of virtue—for, they say, the plain evidence is that men cause their wives suffering and that women behave shrewishly (2. 848–59). To these propositions, the comic servants see agreement from the spectators: 'Therin they all agree!' (2. 859)—with some audience clamouring implied. Do men and women marry for virtue? The closing asks the question as a matter of real-world truth, and the servants and audience draw the inescapable conclusion: Cornelius, Gayus, the honour-debate, Lucres' apologia—all unrealistic and ridiculous.

In A's gulling of Gayus, B's mimcry of Cornelius' clothing, the servants' mock wooing, B's 'token' exchange with Lucres, and the plebeians' climactic dismissal of marrying for virtue—in all these, and in other moments, A and B present a relentless parody. This parody incarnates itself as wordplay, error, mimicry, slapstick, commentary, and audience interaction. Although parody as a form often attacks style, in *Fulgens and Lucres* it aims at manner, character, and the main story's central action. The displacement of the main story's action into the comedy of A and B constitutes an alternative narrative, a counter-narrative, to the inset '*Fulgens and Lucres*' and to the action that most criticism emphasizes. What kind of parody is this, and to what effect does it work? Despite B's concluding claim that the play's purpose is to call people 'to eschew | The wey of vyce and favour vertue' (2. 893–4), the parody here seems more subversive than the corrective comedy later celebrated by Sir Philip Sidney (2002: 98) and George Puttenham (1936: 31–2). A and B share with the morality play Vice certain characteristics—liminality, audience address, cynicism, forgetfulness, misspeaking, anal humour, farcicality—but they exist too much within a definable social world to be Vice figures exactly. Another perspective may help. Mikhail Bakhtin proposes a view of medieval parody as illuminating a universal 'second truth', 'a second revelation of the world', through its playful, liberating, anti-idealistic celebration of the 'lower stratum' of the human form in all its physicality and materiality (1984: 84). For Bakhtin, every act of parody is 'built as part of a whole comic world' and thus partakes of a utopian vision (88). Medwall's comedy, however, rises not from the Land of Cockaigne but from the courtly milieu. The vision behind the parody is of neither religious nor carnivalesque truth. It is, as with *Nature*, reason (Wakelin 2007)—but a certain kind of reason. This reason suspects formulaic dialectics; it thinks analogically and metaphorically; it infers wholes from parts; it scrutinizes language and tests rhetoric against observation; it appreciates embodied experience as much as ideal truth; it resists generalization; it wears a mask and delights in irony. It thinks and laughs, that is, in the manner of theatre. The habit of mind that emerges from the sub-plot, we might say, is a comic version of Lucres' discretion.

Fulgens and Lucres offers the first Tudor play to theorize drama; not surprisingly, since it makes its subject the coming-into-being of theatre. Medwall, we have said, puts forward two models, the episodic and interconnective. The episodic theory argues that drama is composed of both earnest and game. The serious 'substance' addresses those spectators who 'delytyth them in matter of sadnes', although 'toyes' that are 'impertinent | to the matter principall' must be intermingled 'to satisfye and content' those audience members who interest themselves in 'tryfles and japys' (2. 19–35). Here serious and playful elements have nothing to do with each other, as in a variety show. B repeats similar sentiments at the end, insisting that the play's intent was 'only to make folke myrth and game' and to move gentlemen to eschew vice and favour virtue (2. 890). This is the theory noted in most criticism. Its patness may hide Medwall's anxious recognition of comedy's considerable power (see 2. 887–921).

In the second theory earnest and game work together to convey the truth. This theory emerges at the beginning when A and B discuss the potential impertinence of a theatre piece that ennobles a ceorl's son. A worries that the players will be blamed, 'shent', for the offence (1. 144). B reiterates the value of the play's 'myrth and pleasure' but then adds that the drama will only disclose things that 'shall stond with treuth and reason' (1. 156, 159). When A argues that 'trouth may not be sayde alway | For somtyme it causith gruge and despite', B responds that, while that prohibition may obtain elsewhere, 'as for this parish [...]| Suche flaterye is abhorride as dedly syn' (1. 161–2, 169–70). In this dramatic theory, play enters the sphere of 'truth'; earnest and game complement each other; the reformative function of drama is subsumed within a greater representative function; and the play gives mirth and pleasure when all accords with truth and reason. This is the theory that runs through Medwall's complex versification, A and B's satire, and Lucres' discretion.

The greatness of *Fulgens and Lucres* may include its diplomatic defence of Henry's 'new men', but it also embraces Medwall's commitment to drama as an access to the social values of amused rationalism, ironic observation, and discretion, values that theatre especially embodies. Medwall engages his audience with comedy, upending the serious with the comic; he bridges the fictive and real; and draws connections between the moral and aesthetic. In *Fulgens and Lucres*, humans are both spiritual and bodily, serious and whimsical, rational and passionate. In Medwall's *Nature*, Reason stands as the principle virtue, but, by the end, man's propensity towards sensuality must be acknowledged as the source of the vitality that drives us. The character Sensuality insists that man derives from him his 'maner of felynge' and 'lyvely quyknes' (1. 192, 193). *Fulgens and Lucres* takes the complementarity of the rational and the vital deep into its heart as a structuring principle. Embedded in that humanist vision is the further implication that reform can be achieved through art—that the mediating realm of the aesthetic, affective, and ludic influences our political and moral judgements: in the very comic form of *Fulgens and Lucres*, another theatrical first is occurring.

Primary Works

Aristotle (1984), *The Rhetoric and the Poetics of Aristotle*, trans. W. Rhys Roberts and Ingram Bywater (New York: McGraw-Hill).

Chaucer, Geoffrey (1987), *The Riverside Chaucer*, 2nd edn, ed. Larry D. Benson (Boston: Houghton Mifflin).

Elyot, Thomas (1992), *The Boke Named the Governour*, ed. Donald W. Rude (New York: Garland).

MEDWALL, JOHN (1980), *The Plays*, ed. Alan Nelson (Cambridge: Brewer).

—— (1981), *The Plays*, ed. M. E. Moeslein (New York: Garland).

PUTTENHAM, GEORGE (1936), *The Arte of English Poesie*, ed. Alice Walker and Gladys Doidge Willcock (Cambridge: Cambridge University Press).

SIDNEY, PHILIP (2002), *An Apology for Poetry*, ed. Geoffrey Shepherd, rev. R. W. Maslen (Manchester: Manchester University Press).

CHAPTER 3

··

STEPHEN HAWES AND COURTLY EDUCATION

··

DANIEL WAKELIN

THE reign of Henry VII has often been seen as an 'age of transition' from 'medieval' chivalry to 'Renaissance' scholarship. It is often suggested that new conceptions of what it meant to be a gentleman emerged in the reign of Henry VII and the early reign of Henry VIII, blending bookish erudition and the consequent prudence with older arts of chivalry and courtly 'nurture' (M. Crane 1993: 4–6). It is certainly true that writers at court in the very early sixteenth century stress that those who rule should be well-read. Two 'mirrors for princes', or guidebooks in rule, presented, early in his reign, to Henry VIII, stress that 'those who judge the world should be educated', and the ubiquity of the notion is evident when both works use the same quotation from Psalm 2 in support: 'And now, O ye kings, understand: receive instruction, you that judge the earth' ('Nunc reges intelligite, erudimini qui iudicatis terram'; Baron 1990: 94; D. Carlson 1991: 35). Similarly in the reign of his father, Henry VII, there was at court some professed interest in being learned; the court employed a number of erudite French and Italian men as tutors, librarians, and poets. One of them, the official chronicler, Bernard André, reports that the King's son pursued humanist studies; whether true or not, this is clearly what people liked to hear (André 1858a: 43; see D. Carlson 1991: 255–7). Yet a specifically humanist erudition was not the only intelligence sought; writers from the court of Henry VII like to praise being clever in general. So when André describes Henry VII reforming the finances or preventing wars, he repeatedly describes these exploits as 'prudentiam' ('prudence') and describes this as the 'fons', or 'origin', of justice (1858a: 81–2, 84, 93–4).

We should, though, be wary of assuming too great a transition between 'medieval' and 'Renaissance' here. Firstly, seeing this, or any, age as the 'age of transition' would be not quite helpful: what age is not transitional between two others? More specifically, humanists were exhorting English kings and noblemen to read and be wise long before Henry VII's reign (Wakelin 2007: 23–32, 70–4). And, when they did so, chivalric and intellectual accomplishments were not mutually exclusive items in a historical sequence, 'medieval' to 'Renaissance', but simultaneous options. On the one hand, the fact that André needed to defend Henry VII's careful governance as prudence might betray some hint that there were other ways of earning the right to rule—gung-ho chivalry, rather than thoughtful bureaucracy or pacifism. After all, Henry VII seized the throne by force and, besides sponsoring scholars such as André, he also sponsored jousts and martial sports (Gunn 1990: 122–3). On the other hand, one can find hints of doubt about chivalric accomplishments in writings of the period: for example, perhaps predictably a bishop, Richard Fox, wrote to Thomas Darcy, a young courtier on the make, to warn him that jousting was not 'eny matier fittynge or convenyente', although abstention from jousting will, he says, need defending to the King (Fox 1929: 16). Even a verse report of some jousts from 1507, *The Jousts of the Month of May*, must defend jousting repeatedly against 'lewde' people who 'reprehende' it and 'reporte of gentylmen vylany' for doing it (*Jousts* 1507?: A4^{r-v}, B2^r, B4^r). He protests too much, and thus seems to betray some contemporary uncertainty about the proper accomplishments of 'gentylmen'. This uncertainty about the accomplishments befitting gentlemen or noblemen seems typical of the early Tudor period.

This uncertainty can be sensed too in the work of a writer often cited as reflecting the shift in favour of education and prudence in forming gentlemen: the poet Stephen Hawes (A. Ferguson 1960: 66–8). Like André and Skelton, Hawes presents wisdom as one essential element of a perfect gentleman. In his earliest datable poem, *The Example of Virtue* (composed 1503–4), the worth of wisdom is openly debated—and triumphs.[1] There is a lengthy debate between Nature, Fortune, Hardiness, and Wisdom over which of them is most powerful in men's lives; of them, Hardiness and Wisdom speak for longest (Hawes 1974b, lines 582–910), and thus the discussion becomes in essence one between *fortitudo* and *prudentia* or *sapientia*. (*Prudentia* and *sapientia* are not synonyms but Wisdom refers to both as her attributes; lines 729, 771.) These two virtues represent particular constituencies and activities: Hardiness is the 'captayn' of the 'chevalry', or a company of knights, and Wisdom rules over 'clerkes' (lines 169–82). Which does Hawes favour? Though Justice ends by finding all four elements essential to man's life, nevertheless it is Dame Sapience who then takes control of the action, and the 'connynge' of 'clerkes' seems indispensable to the hero's success in winning his beloved (A. Edwards 1984: 33–4, 47). *The Example of Virtue* even claims that the judgements of souls after death depend on their 'instruccyon' or 'informacyon' in life (lines 1920, 1949). In his hero's triumphs, Hawes proves what other writers in Henry VII's court proposed: cleverness is the key to success in life.

[1] For dating of *Example of Virtue* and *Pastime of Pleasure*, see A. Edwards (1984: 2–3).

Like André and Skelton, Hawes, who composed these defences of the wise and educated gentleman, was in courtly service. There is a record of him being paid by Henry VII for a 'ballett', which suggests a poem, like most of his surviving verse, in the form of rhyme royal, often called *ballade* (Hawes 1974a, p. xiii; 'ballade', *OED*, *n.*, 1a). The printed editions of his poems from 1509 onwards also presented Hawes as 'somtyme grome of the honourable chambre' of Henry VII, or a close attendant on the King. We might doubt whether the holders of these titles should be described primarily or only as courtiers; but this is how he appeared to his readers in titles and colophons. This service of the King is, although surely true, also here presented for onlookers, and for onlookers not well connected enough to know who Hawes was. Hawes crafts his persona within his poems too, most famously in *The Comfort of Lovers*, as several critics have noted (Meyer-Lee 2007: 184–9; Lerer 1997: 50–1, 55–6), and in *The Example of Virtue*, where the hero enters the service of Dame Prudence, who promises him that 'Of myn owne chaumbre ye shall be grome' (line 402). In presenting the hero of this poem as 'grome' to Prudence, there might also be flattery of Henry VII in presenting him, by analogy, as Prudence or Wisdom, although she is here, as always, female (lines 1051–1120). We might, then, view Hawes's poems as some blunt form of 'propaganda' or 'image-making' for the court to which his books claimed allegiance.

There would be some analogues for such public displays of prudence and learning. Printers in the early 1500s issued erudite Latin verses supposedly circulated at court, and other works which displayed the wisdom of courtiers, such as Caxton's printing of Christine de Pizan's *Book of Feats of Arms* (1489), or the *Eneydos*, based on Virgil's *Aeneid* with dedications to Henry VII and Prince Arthur (1490). Stephen Baron's 'mirror for princes' (*De regimine principum*), supposedly for Henry VIII on his accession, was printed by Wynkyn de Worde (after 1509); Henry VII's mother, Lady Margaret Beaufort, translated book 4 of *The Imitation of Christ*, which was printed at the back of a translation of books 1–3 by William Atkinson, and *The Mirror of Gold for the Sinful Soul*, translations which went through numerous editions between 1504 and 1526. In one of Hawes's minor poems, *The Conversion of Swearers* (1509), Wynkyn de Worde declared himself to be 'prynter unto' Lady Margaret, whatever that meant in practice (Hawes 1509: a8^r). As these works circulated, they could communicate the idea that those who ruled were learned, as Psalm 2, Skelton, and Baron demanded. The most striking demonstration of this learning is the pageants performed in London to welcome Katherine of Aragon in 1501, recorded in a report known now as *The Receipt of the Lady Katherine*. In the pageants, Katherine, like Hawes's heroes, progresses on a journey like a brief quest or romance. She travels across Salisbury Plain to London, but London resembles the dream-world of romance, with various towers and gates, each decorated and duly labelled with 'poysie in Frenche' or by people who deliver moral speeches (*Receipt* 1990: 2. 140). Often—though by no means always—the speakers declare the value of being well educated: Katherine is told that she will reach Virtue and Noblesse only after visiting Policy; 'noble' people, rather than people of 'low degre', have a special need of 'prudence' as well as virtue. When her learned ancestor Alfonso the Wise of Castile appears, he seems to endorse not only her genealogy but her wisdom. Learning is, in these pageants as in other works, for the best sort of people (2. 81–6, 117–18, 214–31). The medium of public pageantry, performed by a princess before the citizens, turns this defence of wisdom into a defence of the Princess and her betrothed, Henry VII's son Arthur, for acquiring it. The pageants make visible to the citizens the educational ideals of the court.

Yet to read, in the same way, Hawes's emphasis on education as a form of 'propaganda' for courtly culture is too simple. Early Tudor pageantry and writing such as *The Receipt* were once considered to convey subtle messages in powerful media, but recently there has been doubt about how subtle and effective such works were (Gunn 2006: 142). Furthermore, whatever we think of short propagandistic verses or pageantry on the London streets, we must think again about Hawes's poems, which are composed for a different medium, are not so readily tied to one occasion, or are greater in length and complexity. A purely historicist interpretation of his poems as works of courtly image-making does not take clear account of their form and the experience it offers to readers. A reading of Hawes's longer poems challenges an impression of their medium as one of courtly display. It complicates, too, a sense of their message, which is not as lucid a defence of book-learnt wisdom as other writers sometimes offered.[2] Even when he does write a short work of 'propaganda', his *Joyful Meditation* (1509), he exhorts the King to be 'hardy' and only hopes for him to be learned for one stanza (1974c, lines 113–19, 134–40, 163). As has been noted, in *The Example of Virtue* he debates the merits of wisdom or hardiness. And in his longest and most complex poem, *The Pastime of Pleasure* (composed 1505/6), he shows once more divided loyalties. *The Pastime of Pleasure* offers a hero who is urged to embrace 'sapyence', for if 'wysdome/ ruleth hardynes' then hardiness is 'invyncyble' (Hawes 1928, lines 2434–79). This poem does offer, then, the habitual platitudes about the importance of learning to worldly success. Yet the hero of this poem studies in both the Tower of Doctrine and the Tower of Chivalry, in both science and military pursuits; he moves from one to the other at almost exactly the middle of the poem (lines 2976–82). Furthermore, the traditions and sources of *The Pastime of Pleasure* suggest the confusedness of Hawes's interest in a literature of learning. As we shall see, the confusion is bound up with his decision in this poem to blend different genres into a curious hybrid. In particular, he draws on two genres familiar in the early Tudor period but less so now: allegories of love, in the form of visions or debates, and encyclopedic texts, with the encyclopedic poems which borrowed from them.

By modelling *The Pastime of Pleasure* on a narrative genre customarily associated with courtly leisure—the allegorical romance of love—Hawes veers away from offering instruction. *The Pastime of Pleasure*, like *The Example of Virtue* earlier, tells the story of the formation of the young narrator's character and then his quest to win his

---

[2] However, it is important not to simplify other writers either: for example, although Lady Margaret Beaufort's contribution to *The Imitation of Christ* exhorts readers to be 'doctryned and taught', it also warns that reason is secondary to faith (*Imitation* 1504: c4ᵛ–c5ʳ) and some figures in *The Receipt of the Lady Katherine* warn that religion is ultimately better than science (*Receipt* 1990: 2. 327–40, 420–33).

beloved. In the details and tone of this character's education and courtship, Hawes follows a lively series of allegories of 'courtly love' in the form of dream visions or debates of the fifteenth and early sixteenth centuries. This genre of poems presents the lover meeting allegories of various accomplishments, vices, or virtues, often represented as a troupe of elegant ladies in some court, household, or garden. So, for example, in *The Pastime of Pleasure* Hawes personifies the liberal sciences as the ladies of the Tower of Doctrine (1928: 503–11). In this, he might imitate the use of the same personifications in *The Court of Sapience* (1984, lines 1534–47), printed by Caxton and reprinted by Wynkyn de Worde in 1510 only a year after he printed Hawes's poem. Or he might imitate the tradition in general: for example, in *The Assembly of Ladies* (late fifteenth century) and *The Court of Love* (early sixteenth century) there is a lady employed as the 'ussher' or 'chamberer' who leads the narrator on his 'erand' into the presence of women with allegorical names such as Lady Loyalty, while the lady's court or garden, called something such as 'Plesaunt Regard', is described in lush detail (*Assembly* 1897, lines 89–105, 160–70, 176–81). Very similar characters and settings recur in Hawes's poem (Hawes 1928, lines 379–487), and the plot itself, an allegory of the narrator's personal maturation, has an analogue in *The Court of Love* (1897, lines 156–63). As well as this sort of allegory, a similar set of poems sees the young lover formed and helped not through meeting numerous personifications but through a debate with just one or two allegorical people, goddesses, or birds. These poems stretch from John Lydgate's *Temple of Glass* of the early fifteenth century, printed six times between 1477 and 1529, to early Tudor works such as William Walter's *Spectacle of Lovers* (1533?). In them, a lover utters his purpose, and a 'Consultor' or Venus herself advises him on achieving or alleviating his love. Debates like these, on the pains and remedies of love, unfold for much of the length of Hawes's poem too (Hawes 1928, lines 1646–1954, 2416–92, 3804–4100). He thus writes within well-established genres for describing the 'courtly' character and his desires.

However, despite choosing this genre of amorous dalliance, Hawes renders it more instructive. He turns the literature of leisure into the literature of learning. He does so by developing the allegory in this genre so that it offers not amorous counsel but moral and prudential teaching. This was no novelty within this tradition, but nor was it a given element of it. Not all such poems exploited their allegory to didactic effect: for example, although they offer tutelage in love's service or even in fashion, Lydgate's *Temple of Glass* and the anonymous *Assembly of Ladies* are reticent in moralizing; *The Court of Love* seems even to parody instruction, through lovers' 'statutes', often amoral in tenor, or in presenting amorous nuns (*Court of Love* 1897, lines 402–4, 420–34, 1149–55). Although all these poems use allegorical figures with emblematic names, so that readers need never doubt who signifies what—what is sometimes called naive allegory—the best poems handle these figures with delicacy: in *The Court of Love* personified abstractions such as Delight and Lust mingle with figures based on social types such as clerks and monks; in *The Assembly of Ladies* relatively few allegorical figures appear and they act as subtly befits their name: Diligence is solicitous and keen; 'Belchere' is in charge of entertainment in the hall (*Assembly* 1897, lines 199–203, 322).

It is fair to say that Hawes's allegory is especially transparent, for he ensures that readers can see through everything. He sometimes uses very lengthy lists of names or extravagantly long names such as 'amyte to lovers dolourous' (Hawes 1928, lines 477–83, 4865–71). Moreover, the people or things in his poem take care to explain what their action signifies or have inscriptions on them. For example, the hero enters one fine tower 'for to know what it sygnyfyed'; there he finds a painting of Fortune and Mars, and Mars within the painting somehow speaks, to interpret Fortune as a 'sygnyfycacyon' by 'moralyzacyon' of the 'trouth' of human life (lines 3022, 3207–11). Later the hero fights a three-headed giant, on whose helmets are obligingly 'wryten' not only inscriptions of the names 'falshed', 'ymagynacyon', and 'parjury', but also explanations of these vices of eleven, twelve, and twenty lines each (lines 4321–67). These inscriptions seem unfeasibly long, but the references to writing and the line 'And whan that I had seen every thynge' confirms that these are inscriptions (lines 4319–21, 4334, 4347, 4368). A seven-headed giant appears next, with several lines of writing on a flag on each of his heads; despite the fact that most of the flags warn of verbal dissimulation, the giant is very well labelled (lines 4745–94). There is similar careful labelling throughout the poem (for example, lines 84–98, 132–40, 5110–16, 5640–1) and careful signposting of the 'morall scence' in his other long poem, *The Example of Virtue* (Hawes 1974b, lines 1189–90, 1311–44, 1394–1401, 1451–71). With this explicitness, Hawes highlights the informativeness of his allegory. Thus, he strives to ensure not only that readers recognize the message but that they recognize that there *is* a message, that it is instructive.

In the woodcuts which portray these giants in the sixteenth-century editions, the flags do not have on them the texts which the poem mentions. (See, for example, Figure 3.1, which comes from the 1555 edition of *The Pastime of Pleasure*, and misrepresents the three-headed giant as a three-headed monster.) This is surprising, given that Hawes seems to have collaborated with de Worde and the woodcut artist for the earlier editions. Most likely is that the texts mentioned in the poem would be too long for the woodcut. Yet that difficulty does reveal the essentially written quality of the visuals in the poem, in which the visual spectacle is overpowered by the attempt at clear verbal allegorization and instruction.

This sort of explicitness of allegory was in fact fairly common in works read at, or written for, the early Tudor court. Among the works popular in the court—and further analogues for Hawes's poems—were some late fifteenth-century French works in prose and verse which turn the reading material of courtly leisure into a reading material of moral instruction. For example, Olivier de la Marche's *Le Chevalier délibéré* (1483) mentions the setting or props of the action and then allegorizes them instantly with a descriptive clause: 'My shield was of Good Hope' ('Mon escu fut de Bon Espoir') or 'The path that is called Delusion' ('Le sentier qu'on appelle Abuz') (La Marche 1999: 62, 128).[3] Among the works written directly for Henry VII was the blunt allegory *Les Douze Triomphes de Hercules* (1497), possibly by André.[4] It allegorizes

---

[3] This work was in the royal library by 1542 in an edition printed in 1493 (Carley 2000a, no. H2/281).
[4] David Carlson warns that the ascription to André is unproven (1998: 246).

Fig. 3.1 Grand Amour fights the three-headed beast of Falsehood, Imagination, and Perjury. Stephen Hawes, *The Pastime of Pleasure* (1555), U1ʳ.

the adventures of Hercules, a figure who reappears in the poems of Hawes (Hawes 1974*b*, lines 603–6, 631–51; Hawes 1928, lines 232–8, 1030–46) and his followers, such as Thomas Fyelde's *Controversy between a Lover and a Jay* (1527?: B3ʳ) or William Nevill's *Castle of Pleasure* (1530?: a6ʳ). On one level, the adventures are those of Henry VII, whose battles to settle the realm are compared to Hercules' labours; on a deeper level, the adventures are struggles with abstract vices and virtues: so, Hercules–Henry dresses in a lion's hide which 'is strength and prudence and wealth' ('La peau est force, et prudence, et ricesse') and saves the country 'with his bow, which I understand to be his justice' ('De son bel arc, j'entendz, de sa justice') (André 1858*b*: 136, 141, 310, 315). In another poem, *Le Temps de lannee moralize* (1510), presented to Henry VIII as a New Year's gift in the first year of his reign, André compares the ages of man to the weather of the different months, with the crudest of connections: in the spring laurels grow and 'Also the child grows' ('Aussi fait lenfant de croissance'), whereas November is stormy and 'Thus is the mood of man' ('Ainsi est homme de corage') (*Le Temps* [1510]: 4^r, 18^r). An allegorized survey of human life is found in *The Pastime of Pleasure* too, where Hawes's hero ends the poem moving from youth through marriage and age to death (Hawes 1928, lines 5299–5410). And Hawes's imitators continued to produce this sort of explicit moralizing in their verse. For example, in Nevill's *Castle of Pleasure* the narrator moves through a landscape similar to Hawes's, and his guide moralizes the landscape in a similar way: 'What call ye this hyll I pray you tell,' he asks, and is told, 'This is the mountayne of lusty courage' or 'They call this water the laver of lowlynes'; there is also a castle with 'scryptures' on it (a4^{r-v}, a5^v, a6^r). Thus, in the allegories of Hawes and his contemporaries, what seem like poems of slim courtly sentiment or flattery (André's were gifts for Henry VII and Henry VIII) deliver a universalizing moral instruction. This sort of transparency is not a hindrance to this poetry, but its very purpose: the allegory must be obvious. These works might seem like the literature of leisure, but their poets present quite explicitly their useful instructiveness.

To make *The Pastime of Pleasure* appear even more instructive, Hawes added to his courtly allegory elements from another genre: the encyclopedia. Moreover, once we identify and compare his particular encyclopedic source, we can identify exactly how much teaching he adds to *The Pastime of Pleasure*. William Edward Mead, Hawes's twentieth-century editor, suggests that he drew on a contemporary Latin encyclopedia, Gregor Reisch's *Margarita philosophica* (1503). Mead proposes that Hawes used Reisch's description of the seven sciences as the source for his own description, and that three of the woodcuts in Wynkyn de Worde's first edition of *The Pastime* were modelled on three in the first edition of Reisch's *Margarita* (Hawes 1928, pp. lxiv–lxxvii). Certainly, the three woodcuts are alike, but not enough to confirm a direct borrowing, given the frequency with which people shared, reused, or copied woodcuts (A. Edwards 1980*a*: 84; cf. Halporn 2001: 157–8). Moreover, the surveys of the seven liberal sciences in Reisch's textbook and Hawes's poem are not often close. *The Pastime of Pleasure* includes barely a fraction of the material in the enormous *Margarita* and differs in what it does cover: for example, whereas *The Pastime of Pleasure* compares music to physics (lines 1541–82), Reisch's *Margarita* does not (h4^r). When it does cover the same things, the details are not concordant—for example, the identity of the inventor of letters differs (Hawes 1928, lines 533–9; Reisch 1503: π5^v). The closest similarities are a one-sentence definition of a noun (Hawes 1928, lines 587–8; Reisch 1503: π7^r) and a longer description of *dispositio* in rhetoric (Hawes 1928, lines 841–54; Reisch 1503: e2^r). Moreover, Reisch addresses a different implied reader from Hawes's. Reisch speaks to 'Adolescentes' in formal study (π2^v), and so makes his book methodical and exhaustive, with tables of declensions or irregular nouns and illustrative musical notation (for example, I3^{r-v}, I5^v–I6^r, i3^v–i5^r); it is mostly structured as a pedagogic dialogue, as were many grammars; and, most crucially, it is in Latin, the dominant educational tongue. By contrast, when Hawes describes the seven sciences and nature, Reisch's topics, he offers only sketchy detail and in English, and he fits the description into the allegorical romance. His poem does not address readers in a conventionally educational way.

Hawes's survey of the sciences reflects not academic encyclopedism, but an interest in more casual encyclopedic instruction among English readers. English printers had issued a few encyclopedic works in the mother tongue: *The Mirror of the World* in prose printed by Caxton in 1481 and 1491; *The Court of Sapience* in verse printed by Caxton around 1483 and de Worde in 1510;[5] and *De proprietatibus rerum* in English prose printed by de Worde around 1495. When de Worde printed Hawes's *The Pastime of Pleasure* in 1509, its encyclopedic elements fitted well into this repertoire. Hawes explicitly refers to *The Court of Sapience* (1928, line 1357), wrongly attributing it to Lydgate, and to *De proprietatibus rerum* (Hawes 1974b, line 1003). Moreover, although A. S. G. Edwards has doubted the parallels (1984: 28), the discussion of the seven liberal sciences and of nature in *The Pastime of Pleasure* follows *The Mirror of the World* closely in details and their order, suggesting that it—not the *Margarita*— is the direct source (Berdan 1920: 82–3; Knowlton 1921: 201–4). There is likeness, too, between Hawes's poem and some of the encyclopedias in the decision to use illustrative woodcuts (Bartholomew 1495: 2A1^r, 2C2^r; Caxton 1913: 52–8; Reisch 1503, F6^v–F7^r). For example, Caxton took trouble over *The Mirror of the World*, the first fully illustrated English printed book, and integrated text and image well, referring to his own page layout: 'This fygure folowyng on that other side of the leef', and so on (Caxton 1913: 51, 56). Within this tradition, it is perhaps less surprising that de Worde took such trouble over the pictures for Hawes's poems (A. Edwards 1980a: 84–7). Hawes's poem and its pictures seem to offer something familiar to a wider English readership interested in encyclopedic instruction.

However, Hawes's description of the sciences is not very instructive. Unsurprisingly, no survey of the sciences in English, in *The Mirror of the World* or *The Court of Sapience*, is as thorough and precise as Reisch's academic manual. The English writers give just a few lines or stanzas to each science, and, though *The Court of Sapience* offers some precise terminology, it offers these exotic 'dyvers names' in a hectic list (1984, line 2133), as if revelling in the sounds rather than in their meaning (lines 1828–37, 1849–72, 1881–90, 2031–51, 2133–42); the poet concedes that these curious terms will 'prolong my matere' and are, therefore, not integral to it (line 1838). These English works are not really informative, and nor is Hawes's poem, which gives even less, and less specific, instruction. He often writes more lengthily than the author of *The Mirror of the World* but repeats single points from there or renders them vague. Most importantly, the description of the sciences is very short relative to the whole text: it is only one-fifth of *The Pastime of Pleasure*—an hour's reading aloud—and it is often interrupted, once for a long time, for the plot or for the poet's comments on other

---

[5] For dating, see *The Court of Sapience* (1984, pp. xiii–xiv).

things (Hawes 1928, lines 519–1295, 1408–56, 1520–82, 2556–2912). Hawes describes rhetoric well, because it underpins his own activity as a poet; and here he brings in much of his wider knowledge. But with the other sciences, he outlines what they are but little of what their students know. He ignores their practical aspects to show instead how the sciences reflect the interconnected moral order of the universe. The reflection is clear in grammar, logic, arithmetic, and music; geometry too introduces a long sequence of anaphoric stanzas on 'mesure', in moral rather than spatial terms; and astronomy leads into an account of the microcosm and how humankind is affected by the stars (lines 603–6, 617–44, 1436–42, 1541–7, 2591–2639, 2696–2905). Thus, though the hero of the poem is educated in the seven sciences, readers are not. Readers discover why these subjects matter, but in the end do not learn these subjects themselves.

Yet Hawes confesses the limitations of the instruction offered in *The Pastime of Pleasure* and does so as part of an admission of the different requirements and accomplishments of lay people, who use English books such as this, and of clerks, who use Latin. He repeatedly notes the brevity of his coverage: he cannot deal with 'all' and this is just a 'lytell werke' (line 2923). More importantly, he links the limited length and remit of what he writes to the constraints of writing in English: he will not try 'To reherse in englysshe/ more' and in his 'natyf language' he 'wyll not oppres/ More' (lines 1448, 2871–2). How should he write 'more' when his 'maternall tonge' is ignorant and one might find 'all' pleasure, by contrast, in 'the latyn tongue' (lines 2906–10) or through 'longe stody and dylygente lernynge', which suggests institutional or formal education (lines 1443–5, 2877). He contrasts his ignorance with that of university-educated users of Latin such as 'maysters' (holders of MAs) 'experte in the seven scyence' (lines 2920–1). Thus, though he tells us of some elements of the knowledge of the encyclopedia on which he draws, he does not pretend to offer us much of that knowledge himself.

Why, then, does he present heavy-handed moralizing and lengthy descriptions of the sciences within the middle of his romance, interrupting the poem? It must be conceded that he is perhaps a little incompetent in balancing essential and inessential material—a forgivable fault. Yet the taste of this period was for instructive reading. There were many conventional justifications for the sort of informative reading which the encyclopedias invite, and which Hawes seems to invite by borrowing from them. The simplest was that reading any 'bokes vertuouse' is a 'good occupacion', better than being idle, as de Worde put it in his epilogue to Bartholomew's *De proprietatibus rerum* (004^v–005^r). However, there is another more intriguing justification in Hawes's direct source, Caxton's *Mirror of the World*, which comments on who should read of the liberal sciences in the middle of its survey of them. This knowledge is presented as the preserve of 'philosophres' or 'clerkes', a 'maner of peple' distinct from others for their asceticism—they sit up all night and do not eat—and coming from Athens, Paris, Oxford, or Cambridge (Caxton 1913: 19–21, 27, 29–30). Encyclopedic learning seems at first, then, reserved to one distinct group of readers. But the distinction soon dissolves. First, there is concern that clerks nowadays merely seek to be 'called maistres' (revelling more in their reputation than in their learning), to become rich, and to own books in fine bindings (26–8). Secondly, and more pertinently, kings are exhorted to 'doo their diligence to lerne suche clergye and science' in order to ensure that they surpass these clerks in their learning and reign in heaven too (31). And *The Mirror of the World* gives further worldly reasons for studying the seven sciences later: in the past, kings, knights, and noblemen studied the sciences but prevented bondmen or even men who were 'riche' but 'of lytyl extraccion' from studying them; because only 'free and liberall' men studied them, they were known as 'liberall' sciences (41–2). This sounds like a shrewd monopoly, because apparently anybody who masters the sciences will, it is said, be believed in legal matters and be persuasive in conversation (42). *The Mirror of the World* is thus inconsistent in identifying the people interested in the seven sciences: a group of unworldly clerks, or a social elite? It is in describing this second group of readers that *The Mirror of the World* offers a clear reason for translating a survey of these sciences into English. The translation offers material well suited to the 'liberall' elite, a noble or even royal elite reading English, to help them to make friends and influence people. The instructional book, then, becomes not 'propaganda' about some already achieved wisdom of the noble elite but something even more instrumental: a tool for achieving that wisdom.

Intriguingly, Hawes skipped this section of *The Mirror of the World* when he selected the surrounding encyclopedic material for his poem, jumping from astronomy to nature (Hawes 1928, lines 2689–90, 2731–2) and substituting an account of the seven days of creation for the section on learning (Caxton 1913: jumping from 41, lines 14–15, to 43, lines 26–8). Perhaps he did not see the sciences as important in the education of the courtier: hence his woolly survey of them. Or he might have found the lines too frank about the instrumentality of his work. But he does comment candidly on the instrumentality and instructiveness of his allegory in the Prologue, and again more fully in another early section of the poem, during the description of rhetoric, before most of the allegorical fiction unfolds (Hawes 1928, lines 31–42, 50–4, 704–21, 869–72, 932–59, 981–7). Putting these comments towards the start of the work allows him to imagine the reading experience which he would like to offer and to clarify that the poem presents not only pleasure but lessons. As critics have noted, in *The Pastime of Pleasure* he defends poetic allegory as giving 'trouthe/ under cloudy fygures' or fiction with a hidden 'morall cense' (lines 720, 943; cf. A. Edwards 1984: 36–9; Ebin 1988: 137–9, 146–7, 162). There is little striking in the detail of this theory of poetry: it echoes the old defence of fiction veiling truth found in scholastic thought and in the work of earlier poets such as Robert Henryson (1981: 3). More interesting are Hawes's brief comments on why his readers might desire to learn from allegory: because to interpret allegory is instrumental, and will bring worldly success. A section with a subheading for each stanza ('Rychesse', 'Scyence', 'Pleasure', 'Example') explains the process, in reverse order (Hawes 1928, lines 960–87; A. Edwards 1984: 39–41). Poets write of 'an example/ with a mysty cloude' and 'underneth the trouthe'. This occluded truth then needs decoding, and decoding it brings pleasure:

> O what pleasure to the intellygent
> It is to knowe/ and have perceyveraunce
> Of theyr connynge [...]

By intelligently recognizing or perceiving the hidden truth in these poems, the reader will master the 'Scyence' or 'sentence':

> For by connynge/theyr arte dooth engendre
> And without connynge/ we knowe never a dele
> Of theyr sentence [...]

Mastering this 'fruytfull sentence' brings the reader from poverty to wealth ('rychesse') and helps him to dodge the blows of Lady Fortune, for:

> she can not declyne
> The noble scyence/whiche after poverte
> Maye brynge a man agayne to dygnyte.

The slight allusion to Fortune's wheel, making men rise and 'declyne', hints that this reading would be most useful for the courtiers who ride on the wheel, while the movement from poverty to dignity might also imply that this reading would be useful for other people who aspire to be courtiers. In general, just as *The Mirror of the World* sketched the usefulness of reading about the sciences, so *The Pastime of Pleasure* sketches the usefulness of reading allegory—for social climbing or, when fallen, reclimbing. By these arguments in *The Mirror of the World* and *The Pastime of Pleasure*, Hawes's poem becomes a useful one. Its difference from a propagandistic display of noble or royal learning is clear; it is now a defence of acquiring learning—an explanation, if you like, of the need for such display.

Of course, readers of *The Pastime of Pleasure* could flatter themselves that they were being informed and were displaying wisdom in merely reading the book. Although it is structured as an allegory of love, stretches of it offer the illusion of encyclopedic learning. The woodcuts redolent of Reisch's *Margarita* or of grammars, like those depicting small boys sat at Dame Grammar's feet (reproduced in Mead's edition), might make the physical book a clear prop for the social 'performance' of learning. Even the romance itself invites readers to pretend to wisdom. If, as Hawes says, decoding allegory is a sign of worldly skill, then every reader of this poem is adept, for the allegory is easy to decode, thanks to the direct labelling of it. Yet, as has been argued, the instruction in the sciences is poor, and the labelling of the allegory is clumsy. Hawes betrays—by striving too hard or by admitting his limits—the difficulty of offering a poem which is truly informative. Thus, this poem seems to express a desire for the sort of instruction, accomplishment, and prestige found or praised in other works of the time, and yet it seems to frustrate that desire. The desire is created, as is all desire, by *not* having those things; but nor does Hawes provide them. This frustration stems in part from the genre of *The Pastime of Pleasure*, built not around an encyclopedia but around an allegorical romance. Yet Hawes explicitly concedes that the desire for instruction is thwarted. It is a truism that overt writing in favour of something is a sign that the thing in question was not really in favour at the time. By this argument, Hawes's over-keen offering of instruction in *The Pastime of Pleasure* or his need to debate the merits of wisdom in *The Example of Virtue* might be evidence that such schooling was not entirely in favour in the early sixteenth century. Such anxiety about the place of education is also found in the works of Alexander Barclay (Fox 1989: 37, 39; Wakelin 2008: 474–9) or even in the defences of learning by humanists such as Richard Pace (1967: 22–3).

Hawes is open about his doubts. For example, while he makes it sound beneficial to decode instructive allegories, he also makes it sound uncommon. He puts his defence of what one might learn from allegory among some comments on people who fail to decode allegory. Like his contemporary Henry Watson in his translation of *The Ship of Fools* (Watson 1509: a2ʳ, a3ʳ), Hawes fears that the 'rude people' apparently 'byleve/ in no maner of wyse | That under a colour/ a trouthe may aryse' and will not 'moralyse/ the semelytude' (Hawes 1928, lines 792–819). He frequently rues this inability to learn from allegory, and his repeated word 'rude' suggests a lack of education (lines 806, 897, 1047). He criticizes writers, too, for 'Makynge balades' which are 'without fruytfulnes', forgetting to put something 'coverte' into their poems (lines 1389–92). He worries, then, that the sort of instruction through allegory which he would like to provide is not customary; he must defend his practice. Moreover, his comments on the failure to learn from allegory accompany comments on the failure of learning in general. People have abandoned learning because they are avaricious rather than public-spirited:

> But now a dayes/ the contrary is used
> To wynne the money/ theyr studyes be all sette
> The comyn prouffyte/ is often refused.
>
> (lines 554–6)

They are not interested in studying the 'seven scyences/theyr slouthe to eschewe | To an oders profyte' (lines 570–4), lines which could be a summary of the critique of philosophers who have abandoned their principles in Caxton's *Mirror of the World* (1913: 26–7). Contrary to any notions that the age of Henry VII esteemed instruction, Hawes suggests that the age rejected it. The attack on avarice could be a pointed comment on the shrewd financial management of Henry VII and his ministers, like the more open comment in Hawes's later poem *A Joyful Meditation* (Hawes 1974c, lines 71–4). Yet the greed which, Hawes says, prompts people to neglect study of the 'seven scyences' is in fact quite like the greed for 'Rychesse' and 'dygnyte' which, he elsewhere says, is the goal of the study of allegory (Hawes 1928, lines 960–87). His critique of self-interest here undermines his defence of reading allegory for self-interest elsewhere, by doubting how widely instructive reading is esteemed, and what its moral worth might be.

However, although this poem seems uncertain about the effectiveness of the courtly education which it relates, the poem nevertheless seems a desirable commodity—which might explain why it ran through many editions. It is clear that *The Pastime of Pleasure* renders such an education desirable by rendering it an object of readers' admiration. In fact, rather than educating readers, the poem invites them to become in some degree voyeurs on a courtly education—that of the poem's hero—gazing longingly upon it, rather than imbibing it. Given this excitation to voyeuristic reading, it is no surprise that the visuals of the poem are so extensively imagined, both in the description of visual tableaux in the poems and in the woodcuts. This vividness of Hawes's poetry has been remarked on before and it is striking (A. Edwards 1984: 24). Even the key moments of academic or moral instruction in *The Pastime of Pleasure* are staged with the sighting of an 'ymage' of some sort adorned with precise architectural and optical luxury:

> In to the besy courte/ she dyde me than lede
> Where was a fountauyne/ depured of pleasaunce
> A noble sprynge/ a ryall conduyte hede
> Made of fyne golde/ enameled with reed
> And on the toppe/ foure dragons blewe and stoute.

> (lines 387–91)

Everything looks 'fayre', 'goodly', 'noble', or 'ryall'; everything is finely coloured; many nouns are embellished with adjectives expressing the onlooker's approval; and many features are measured with precision and found impressive in number or size (for example, lines 80–4, 106–8, 127–33, 372–411). In passages such as these, *The Pastime of Pleasure* fulfils an imagined desire to gaze on education, but for its external glamour, as an object of sensory delight. Readers' experiences seem captured within the poem in a curious scene at the start, redolent of the moments of *ekphrasis* at the start of other dream visions such as *The Temple of Glass*. Here, Hawes's hero sees a 'clothe of aras/ in the rychest maner | That treted well/ of a noble story', described with a wealth of approving adjectives and adverbs ('notably', 'well', and 'mervaylous'; Hawes 1928, lines 413–74). What is odd is that the story on the arras, told at length, is the hero's own. His education thus 'well pyctured' (line 475) becomes an object of voyeuristic desire, to the character as to readers; but it becomes nothing more: the poem never more alludes to this 'aras', and its educative value is unclear. It is merely a decoration for a 'palays gloryous' (line 410) which readers can admire but not learn from.

Thus, like the 'aras', the poem is less an educative work than a decorative one. And the superficiality in this poem brings into question the depth of interest, in the reign of Henry VII, in a courtliness modelled on bookish or prudential instruction. Writers from the court in this period often advocate instruction and learning, but do they really offer it? Is their advocacy merely self-admiration and self-consciousness, like Hawes's hero gazing on the 'aras' which portrays his own education? This superficiality might suggest that Hawes was disconnected from the main educational trends and institutions of his day. After all, his idiom for describing education comes from romance and allegorical vision rather than the humanist writing then becoming common; beyond a few brief comments in favour of pursuing 'the actyfe lyfe' and the 'comyn profyte' at the opening (lines 80–112, 190–252; cf. lines 3362, 3365), the poem never demonstrates or develops humanist ideas at any length. One might, then, criticize *The Pastime of Pleasure* for being out of touch with progress. Yet it would be unfair to criticize *The Pastime of Pleasure* for not offering a humanist education. As we saw, chivalric and humanistic discourses coexisted in these years as simultaneous options, not exclusive sequential states. Moreover, in fact, many writers of humanist manifestos also praise education, with a self-consciousness like that of Hawes, but, also like Hawes, do not clearly educate readers; readers merely learn how or why to learn. For comparison, Pace's *De Fructu* defends the seven liberal arts—themselves not the core humanist curriculum—but does not really teach them; and it drifts into jokes and praise of various contemporary scholars, or of Henry VIII and Wolsey for fostering education (1967; for example, 62–3, 68–9, 96–9, 138–41). The more imaginative humanist works are not necessarily more educational; nor is Hawes's romance-based idiom for education by contrast unviable. Writers of pageantry, from *The Receipt of the Lady Katherine* onwards, and writers of fiction, from Nevill's *Castle of Pleasure* to Edmund Spenser's *Faerie Queene*, all found romance useful for describing the apotheosis of the courtier and the education and formation of the self.

Primary Works

André, Bernard (1858*a*), *Historia Regis Henrici Septimi*, ed. James Gairdner (London: Longman, Brown, Green, Longmans and Roberts).

—— (1858*b*), *Les Douze Triomphes de Henry VII*, in Bernard André, *Historia Regis Henrici Septimi*, ed. James Gairdner (London: Longman, Brown, Green, Longmans and Roberts).

Assembly (1897), *The Assembly of Ladies*, in *Supplement to the Works of Geoffrey Chaucer*, ed. Walter W. Skeat (Oxford: Oxford University Press).

Baron, Stephen (1990), *De regimine principum*, ed. P. J. Mroczkowski (New York: Peter Lang).

Bartholomew the Englishman [*c*.1495], *De proprietatibus rerum*, trans. John Trevisa.

Caxton, William (1913), *Caxton's Mirrour of the World*, ed. Oliver H. Prior, EETS, e.s., 110.

The Court of Love (1897), in *Supplement to the Works of Geoffrey Chaucer*, ed. Walter W. Skeat (Oxford: Oxford University Press).

The Court of Sapience (1984), ed. E. Ruth Harvey (Toronto: University of Toronto Press).

Fox, Richard (1929), *The Letters of Richard Fox 1486–1527*, ed. P. S. Allen and H. M. Allen (Oxford: Clarendon Press).

Fyelde, Thomas (1527?), *The Contraversye bytwene a Lover and a Jaye*.

Hawes, Stephen (1509), *The Convercyon of Swerers*.

—— (1928), *The Pastime of Pleasure*, ed. William Edward Mead, EETS, o.s., 173.

—— (1974*a*), *The Minor Poems*, ed. Florence W. Gluck and Alice B. Morgan, EETS, o.s., 271.

—— (1974*b*), *The Example of Virtue*, in *The Minor Poems*, ed. Florence W. Gluck and Alice B. Morgan, EETS, o.s., 271.

—— (1974*c*), *A Joyfull Meditacyon*, in *The Minor Poems*, ed. Florence W. Gluck and Alice B. Morgan, EETS, o.s., 271.

Henryson, Robert (1981), *Poems*, ed. Denton Fox (Oxford: Clarendon Press).

Imitation (1504), *A ful devout and gostely treatyse of the imitacyon and folowynge the blessed lyfe of our moste mercyful savyour cryste*, trans. William Atkinson and Lady Margaret Beaufort.

Jousts (1507?), *The Justes of the moneth of Maye*.

La Marche, Olivier de (1999), *Le Chevalier deliberé (The Resolute Knight)*, ed. Carleton W. Carroll, trans. Lois Hawley Wilson and Carleton W. Carroll (Tempe: Arizona Center for Medieval and Renaissance Studies).

Nevill, William (1530?), *The Castell of Pleasure*.

Pace, Richard (1967), *De fructu qui ex doctrina percipitur*, ed. and trans. Frank S. Manley and Richard Sylvester (New York: Renaissance Society of America).

Receipt (1990), *The Receyt of the Ladie Kateryne*, ed. Gordon Kipling, EETS, o.s., 296.

Reisch, Gregor (1503), *Margarita philosophica* (Freiburg).

Skelton, John (1991), *The Latin Writings*, ed. David R. Carlson, *Studies in Philology*, 88/4: 1–125.

Le Temps [1510], *Le Temps de lannee moralize*, BL, Royal MS 16.E.xi.

Walter, William (1533?), *The Spectacle of Lovers*.

Watson, Henry (trans.) (1509), 'The Prologue of the Translatour', in *The Shyppe of Fooles* by Sebastian Brant (London: Wynkyn de Worde).

CHAPTER 4

HAVING THE LAST WORD

MANUSCRIPT, PRINT, AND THE ENVOY IN THE POETRY OF JOHN SKELTON

JANE GRIFFITHS

You can't derange, or re-arrange,
your poems again. (But the Sparrows can their song.)
The words won't change again. Sad friend, you cannot change.

(Elizabeth Bishop)

JOHN SKELTON has long been a challenge to critics. His subject matter is way-ward, encompassing hawking parsons, the nine Muses, feisty ale wives, and dead sparrows. His genres range from dream vision and morality play to bawdy songs and invective. His personae include desperate court poets, humble countrymen, and irascible parrots. Many of his works are occasional: he wrote polemical poems such as *Against the Scots* to commission for Henry VIII, yet he is best known for his attacks on Henry's chief minister, Cardinal Thomas Wolsey—who subse-quently became his chief patron. Matters are further complicated by Skelton's habit of adding to and revising his poems; many exist in at least two different forms, while others show signs of having been altered twenty or thirty years after their first composition. On occasion revisions suggest an engaging view of the poem as continuous communication, revealing a desire to postpone the last word indefinitely. Yet they may also witness a determination to stifle debate by hammering the last word home. They thus manifest a pronounced tension between gestures towards a collaborative (even conspiratorial) relationship with readers, and a demand for deference.

This essay revisits Skelton's envoys—where the poet sends forth his poem—and his revisions in the light of the increasing use of print over the course of his lifetime. Born in 1463 (Brownlow 1990: 47–55), Skelton began his writing career at a time when 'publication' was more likely to be by manuscript circulation than in print. His works survive in a variety of manuscripts and early printed editions which often preserve significantly different texts, providing a basis from which to investigate assumptions about differences between print and manuscript publication. Although print used frequently to be spoken of as a medium that entails closure (Ong 2002), the printing of Skelton's *Speak Parrot* and *A Garland of Laurel* supports recent revisions of this view (Johns 1998). Like a manuscript witness, the first printed edition of *Speak Parrot* attests Skelton's habit of revision, while that of *A Garland* reveals how he exploits differences between manuscript and print in order to renegotiate his position vis-à-vis his audience. For Skelton, far from imposing a definite form on a poet's works so that he cannot (in Elizabeth Bishop's words) 'derange, or re-arrange | [his] poems again', print may serve precisely as a means of 'derangement', or rearrangement. Thus, these editions suggest that Skelton is both more engaged with his readers and more adaptable to change than has often been suggested, presenting him as a poet who is willing and able to draw on new technology both for political ends and as an aid to defining and asserting his own poetic authority.

Skelton's habit of revision is most obvious in the paratext of his poems: in the epigraphs, marginal glosses, and, above all, the envoys. These seem to represent a kind of literary *esprit d'escalier*, mediating the poem's passage into the world by establishing its social or literary credentials, making outright assertions of the poet's divinely privileged status, exhorting readers to give it a good reception, or attacking them when they fail to do so. Significantly, the majority of these envoys are in Latin rather than English, revealing Skelton's concern to frame his vernacular work at a time when the status of the vulgar tongue was still far from assured. The very presence of Latin verses in the framework of his poems functions as a guarantee of the poet's learning, and thus of his work's claim to be noticed.

Yet Latin does not serve merely as rhetorical display. For Skelton, sound knowledge of Latin and the liberal arts was a necessary qualification for a poet. Like earlier Continental writers such as Giovanni Boccaccio and Coluccio Salutati in the fourteenth century, he views poets as divinely inspired, but holds that they will not be able to receive inspiration unless they are sufficiently prepared for it; poets must always be educated. Thus, Skelton's use of Latin in the envoys and paratext of his vernacular poems demonstrates that he is worthy to be inspired. In many cases it is also a means of laying explicit claim to a privileged relationship with God, drawing on ideas that had frequently been expressed in Latin by classical authors such as Cicero as well as moderns such as Boccaccio, but which had scarcely been formulated in the vernacular until Skelton himself did so in *A Replication* (V. Gillespie 1997; Jane Griffiths 2006: 129–57). By extension, even the less polemical among the Latin envoys underwrite Skelton's position in a tradition where large claims for the poet can be made, and simultaneously demonstrate that he is himself worthy to repeat them, thus exhorting readers to take his work too on trust.

The English envoys function rather differently, aiming to influence the reception of the poem directly, rather than obliquely. They can be divided into two kinds: those designed to accompany the poem on its first foray into the world, and those added later, in reaction to reader response. The former are of the type made popular by Geoffrey Chaucer in *Troilus and Criseyde* (*c*.1385–6). Addressing the newly completed 'little book', they ostentatiously humble the author before his readers, appealing for a favourable reception, and inviting emendation in cases where the text is found wanting. The second type of envoy is more rebarbative. Far from inviting Skelton's readers to amend his poem, it attacks those who have thought fit to do so. The two types of English envoy thus propose very different relationships between the author and his readers. One cedes authority to readers; the other claws it back, claiming it has been abused.

However, the two kinds of envoy are not as incompatible as they seem; each has its origin in Skelton's view of the poet as a cornerstone of society. Early in his career, in the 1480s, Skelton translated into English the *Bibliotheca Historica of Diodorus Siculus*, a work that repeatedly expresses the idea that poets serve as the memory of their society, and thus as its moral guardian (Jane Griffiths 2006: 38–55). The same belief occurs repeatedly in Skelton's later work, influenced not only by Diodorus, but by writers closer to Skelton in time, such as Boccaccio, John Gower, and John Lydgate. It is most prominent in *A Garland of Laurel* where, as Vincent Gillespie (1981) has argued, 'Skelton Poeta' presents himself as one in a long line of poets and orators whose writing expresses concern for the good of their commonwealths. Yet it is also apparent in the intense engagement with his readers that prompts the envoys to Skelton's poems. His invitations to 'amend' his writing assume an ideal relationship between poet and readers, in which the inspired poet has a duty to use that inspiration for the good of his people, and the people recognize a respective duty to hear him. The relationship envisaged is that which is so succinctly expressed in the epigraph to *Speak Parrot*: 'Lectoribus auctor recipit opusculy huius auxesim' ('by his readers an author is granted completion of his little work'), and which has more recently been described by Anne Carson (1986: 108) as: 'an intimate collusion between writer and reader [who] compose a meaning between them by matching two halves of a text'.[1] Both Skelton and Carson presuppose a strong element of play; presenting the poem as a puzzle, the writer excites in his readers a desire to bridge the gap between them, thereby creating a meaning that is 'private and true and makes permanent, perfect sense' (Carson 1986: 99). Skelton's rebarbative envoys then record the breakdown of that ideal, when the poet's words encounter difference

---

[1] Unless otherwise specified, all quotations from Skelton's works will be taken from Skelton (1983).

of opinion or merely indifference. Taking refuge in an appeal to authority, they record Skelton's outrage at his readers' refusal to acknowledge the poet's privileged insight and exhort his readers to grant their poet the credence his divinely sanctioned knowledge deserves. As Skelton laments in the envoy to *Against the Scots*, 'Si veritatem dico, quare non creditis michi?' ('If I am telling the truth, why do you not believe me?').

Skelton's desire for reciprocity is nowhere more apparent than in the revision of and the envoys to *Speak Parrot*—this despite the fact that the work seems almost purposely to resist interpretation. Its first 228 lines are spoken in the persona of Parrot himself: an apparently vain and hedonistic bird who nonetheless has prophetic connections, but whose prophecies consist in madly mirroring what he sees and hears, refracting it through a compendium of proverbs, catchwords, foreign phrases, and the exclamations of the ladies surrounding his cage. By this means he achieves a far-reaching if elusive commentary on what he perceives as the abuses of his time, prominent among which are Wolsey's domination of foreign policy in 1519–21 (something Parrot perceives as just one facet of his immoderate ambition), and the new focus on eloquence rather than grammar in the Latin teaching of the day (Brownlow 1968, 1971; W. Nelson 1936; Walker 1989). Parrot's polyglot babble is followed by three Latin verses that (like the Latin verses concluding other of Skelton's poems) claim that he is inspired—but rather than ending with this assertion of authority, *Speak Parrot* continues (in all modern editions) with a flirtatious dialogue between Parrot and the lady Galathea, four separately dated envoys, a further series of Latin verses, the parrot's complaint at being misunderstood, a second dialogue with Galathea, and Parrot's final, outspoken attack on the abuses of the time (see Coiner 1995). As if this were not enough, a further voice in the margins provides glosses that supply all manner of historical, etymological, and stylistic diversions; rather than harnessing Parrot's speech, as glosses might be expected to, their fragmentary nature replicates it (Scattergood 1996; Jane Griffiths 2006: 101–16). The poem, then, is remarkable for its heterogeneity; it is a Babel in which the reader has to negotiate among multiple voices that potentially add up to more than the sum of their parts, but only if he is willing to participate in the construction of meaning, filling in the very obvious gaps.

It is unsurprising, then, that the poem's readers form one of Skelton's subjects. In the opening stanzas, Parrot is in constant communication with the ladies who surround him, feeding him delicacies and silencing him when he threatens to expose politically dangerous truths. It is for their benefit that he flirtatiously displays his 'blacke beard and [...] fayre grene tayle' (line 84), and for their benefit too that he makes his teasingly cryptic political pronouncements. In both respects the ladies figure the poem's extra-textual audience. Just as Parrot deploys fragments of phrases he has learnt from the ladies so as to entice them into creating a new and meaningful synthesis, he also flirts with the reader, revealing and then withholding tantalizing glimpses of his political and satirical message. In this elaborate system of mirrors, when Parrot addresses the ladies, he is by extension addressing the poem's readers too, as when he declares that:

The myrrour that I tote in, *quasi diaphonum*,
Vel quasi speculum, in enigmate,
Elencticum, or ells *enthimematicum,*[2]
For logicions to loke on, somewhat *sophistice*;
Retoricyons and oratours in freshe humanyte,
Support Parrot, I pray you, with your suffrage ornate,
Of *confuse tantum*[3] avoydynge the chekmate.

But of that supposicyon that callyd is arte,
Confuse distrybutyve,[4] as Parrot hath devysed,
Let every man after his merit take his parte;
For in this processe, Parrot nothing hath surmysed,
No matter pretendyd, nor nothyng enterprysed,
But that *metaphora, alegoria* withall,
Shall be his protectyon, his pavys and his wall.

(lines 190–203)

The shift from a first-person to a third-person speaker reveals that the two audiences are equivalent, as Parrot's voice addressing the ladies fuses seamlessly with that of Skelton addressing his readers, so that both the ladies and the extra-textual audience of 'logicions', 'retoricyons[,] and oratours' are subjected to Parrot's characteristic method of revelation and concealment simultaneously. Defining the poem as a prophetic glass, a proposition in logic, and an allegory, these lines declare ostentatiously that it contains secrets, and so excite the desire to learn what that secret is.

At the same time, they indicate the kind of reader that Skelton desires. By identifying the poem as allegory, these stanzas align it with a genre that conventionally placed high demands upon its readers; for some writers, Skelton's contemporary Stephen Hawes among them, allegory could even be said to function as a kind of litmus test, separating worthy from unworthy recipients of the poet's message (see Wakelin, Chapter 3 in this volume). Thus, by stating explicitly that *Speak Parrot* is allegorical, Skelton implies not only that there is method in Parrot's madness, but that there is a certain type of reader who will be able to discover what it is. By disclosing his working assumptions, he thus simultaneously stresses that his poem is art of the highest moral and political importance and presents it as a game. The defiant line 'Let every man after his merit take his parte' then throws down the gauntlet to those readers (past and present) who have a taste for Skelton's brand of intensely serious playfulness, daring them to rise to the challenge of unriddling Parrot's speech.

However, it is clear from the envoys to the poem that such readers were rare, and that the ladies who fail to respond to Parrot's invitation to create a shared meaning unfortunately prefigure most of the poem's readers. Skelton complains that: 'some folys say ye arre furnysshyd with knakkes, | That hang togedyr as fethyrs in the wynde' (lines 292–3). Parrot laments on a similar note: 'Som sey they cannot my

---

[2] 'Almost transparent, or like a glass, in an allegory, in the form of an elenchus, or else, an enthymeme'.
[3] 'Nothing-but-confusedly'.   [4] 'By apportioning confusedly'.

parables expresse; | Som sey I rayle att ryott recheles' (lines 386–7). In response to such misunderstandings, the gentle pointer of the epigraph is finally replaced by a challenge bordering on antagonism: 'Thus myche Parott hathe opynlye expreste; | Let se who dare make up the reste' (lines 381–2). Yet even as the poem's readers are excoriated for their failure to engage with Parrot's prophecy, Skelton still attempts to entice them into collaboration. In *Lenvoy royalle* he prays that 'lordes and ladies' and 'notable clerkes' will 'Vouchesafe to defend [his work] agayne the brawlyng scolde | Callyd Detraxion, (lines 361–2), in the evident hope of tempting at least the noble and better-educated among Parrot's readers (not to mention those who would like to be thought such) to reconstruct from Parrot's fragmentary speech a revelation of the parlous state of the nation. His patience here stands in stark contrast to the violent attacks on his detractors in earlier envoys such as the 'addicyon' to *Philip Sparrow* and the envoy to *Against the Scots*—and this is because Parrot's desire for an intimate relationship with his readers is of public importance. Their failure to engage with the poem is not a personal affront, but a failure with consequences for the whole country: Parrot's warnings against Wolsey cannot be effective unless they are understood.

It is for this reason that the stanzas concerning the Grammarians' War, which have frequently been dismissed as irrelevant to the poem's political subject matter, are in fact central to its satire. The 'war' was an acrimonious dispute, waged *c*. 1519–21, in which the grammarian Robert Whittinton attacked William Horman and William Lily of St Paul's School for teaching Latin by encouraging pupils to imitate the style of classical authors, rather than providing them with a thorough grounding in grammar (D. Carlson 1992; Jane Griffiths 2006: 79–100). It has often been claimed that Skelton's support of the conservatively inclined Whittinton proves his opposition to any form of pedagogical innovation, but in fact his objection to the new method is highly specific: he argues that the focus on eloquence comes at the expense of the students' analytical ability. In Skelton's view, then, this academic squabble has direct political consequences. Skelton's readers become figures of the students taught by the new method, who have lost the ability to reason, and thus threaten to perpetuate Wolsey's power; having lost the desire for imaginative collaboration, they are passive readers, politically as well as intellectually disabled. Considered in this light, the envoys too become an integral part of the poem, bearing witness to a failure on the part of Skelton's readers which justifies his attack on the new teaching method in the first part of the poem. And this entails a change of poetic method as well: where the first part of the poem invites readers to prove themselves the author's equals by unriddling his riddles, the envoys substitute straightforward didacticism, talking down to the poem's unresponsive audience (Walker 1989; Meyer-Lee 2007: 211–12).

This substitution is particularly interesting in light of the textual evidence. The earliest surviving witnesses to *Speak Parrot* are the manuscript version in BL Harley MS 2252 (datable to *c*.1525), and that in the first printed edition of Skelton's works, printed by Richard Lant for Henry Dab or Tab (*c*.1545), which is the source for all subsequent editions until that of Alexander Dyce (1843). These two witnesses are strikingly different. The poem as we now know it is Dyce's fusion of the two versions; in their original form, there is relatively little overlap between them. The manuscript version contains the first eight stanzas of the poem and the first line of the ninth, giving us Parrot's description of his own physical appearance, cage, and linguistic abilities, but stopping short of his satirical attack on the world around him. It resumes at the end of that attack (line 225), with Parrot's first direct appeal to readers 'to rekyn with this recule [literary compilation]', and continues with all the subsequent exchanges between Parrot and Galathea, the Latin interpolations, complaints, and envoys. (The manuscript is also the only witness to the marginal glosses and preliminary Latin epigraph.) Dab's edition, on the other hand, contains the lines numbered 1–232 and 265–77 in the standard modern edition (Skelton 1983)—which means in practice that it records the whole of Skelton's attack on Wolsey and the Grammarians' War and fragments of the exchange between Parrot and Galathea, but none of the envoys, complaints, interpolations, or subsequent dialogue.

The extreme discrepancy between the two surviving versions raises the possibility that the envoys were not merely additions to an existing poem, but were part of a much more substantial revision: that is to say that Harley and Dab represent entirely separate versions of the poem, rather than differently defective texts of the same version (Edwards 2006). However, there is no 'clean' division between the two texts: although Dab's edition does not contain the envoys, it does continue beyond the Latin verses that signal the conclusion of Parrot's speech, including a series of riddling, innuendo-laden lines concerning Parrot's relationship with Galathea and Erasmus' translation of the New Testament (lines 265–77). These lines are characteristically playful. Skelton's citation of Juvenal's line 'Concumbunt Grece. Non est hic sermo pudicus' ('They lie together in the Greek fashion. This is not a seemly manner of speaking') appears at first to reflect badly on Parrot and Galathea. Yet in the context of the Grammarians' War the word *sermo* may represent a renewal of Skelton's attack on the opposing faction. The word had recently become notorious as a result of the second edition of Erasmus' translation of the New Testament out of Greek into Latin (1519), in which he used *sermo* (speech, discourse) rather than the Vulgate's *verbum* (word) in the first line of the Gospel of St John. Erasmus was commonly associated with the kind of teaching methods advocated by Horman and Lily, and in substituting 'speech' for 'word' his translation too could be viewed as a further manifestation of his emphasis on eloquence (Boyle 1977). 'Non est hic sermo pudicus' then means 'This word *sermo* is indecent', and the unspecified 'they' who 'lie together in the Greek fashion' are Skelton's opponents in the Grammarians' War, rather than Parrot and Galathea; their sins are textual rather than sexual. However, in the version of the poem in Harley 2252, these lines are preceded by a highly flirtatious dialogue between Parrot and Galathea. This addition complicates matters by emphasizing the ambiguous nature of Galathea's relationship with her parrot. Like the absence of the envoys in Dab's edition, the absence of the first part of the dialogue between Parrot and Galathea therefore has something to tell us not only about the poem's transmission, but about the way in which Skelton revised it. Yet while the additional dialogue between Parrot and Galathea prompts mutually contradictory interpretations of their relationship, and thus furthers Skelton's games-playing with his readers, the envoys reflect a more didactic, even antagonistic, approach. Both revisions suggest that the printed edition of *Speak Parrot* witnesses an earlier version of the poem than Harley 2252. However, since the dating of individual envoys indicates that they were composed over a period of time (H. Edwards and Nelson 1938), it is possible that the poem may have circulated in various intermediary stages. The discrepancy between the kinds of addition to Harley 2252 confirms this, suggesting that the manuscript reflects not just one but several discrete stages of revision.

What then does this say either about perceived differences between print and manuscript texts, or about Skelton's negotiation of the relationship with his readers? *Speak Parrot* is fairly typical of Skelton's works in being printed posthumously. Although his *Bowge of Court* (1499) was one of the first English poems to find its way into print, few of his works were printed before the 1520s, and even of the poems written in that period, several (like *Speak Parrot*) were printed only after his death (A. Edwards 1999). It is thus tempting to consider Skelton as quintessentially a manuscript poet, and *Speak Parrot* as particularly strong evidence of his commitment to manuscript publication (Lerer 1993). In Skelton's intense focus on the reader, and his extensive rewriting, the poem displays what have been seen as characteristic features of 'manuscript culture', one of which is a tendency to view a text as subject to revision in perpetuity; in this view, print produces a 'final', authoritative version of a poem, with changes possible only from edition to edition, while in the scribal medium a work is potentially always in progress, subject to change from copy to copy (Love 1998: 52). Walter Ong makes an eloquent case for the way in which this stance privileges manuscript readers:

> The printed text is supposed to represent the words of an author in definitive or 'final' form. For print is comfortable only with finality [...] By contrast, manuscripts [...] were in dialogue with the world outside their own borders [...] The readers of manuscripts are less closed off from the author, less absent, than are the readers of those writing for print.   (2002: 130)

Clearly this is the kind of relationship posited in the first part of *Speak Parrot*, but, as we have seen, the addition of the envoys and a new dialogue between Parrot and Galathea in the Harley version of the poem provides contradictory evidence of the ways in which Skelton reconsidered it. The same applies to the omission of lines 58–224 in the manuscript. If this is held to be an authorial revision, it attests a fundamental change in Skelton's approach to his readers. Although it is unlikely that Skelton was responsible for the omission, the possibility cannot wholly be ruled out. The fact that Parrot's speech breaks off after the first line of the ninth stanza, rather than cleanly, at the end of the eighth, and that it does so in the middle of a folio (134ᵛ) suggests that the absence is due either to the loss of material from the manuscript that the scribe of Harley 2252 was using as his exemplar, or to a scribal decision made on the spur of the moment. On balance, it does not seem probable that the Harley scribe, John Colyns, was responsible for the omission. A deliberate decision to cut the lines would have been taken on grounds of either their obscurity or their political sensitivity, and it appears from the other entries in Harley 2252, Colyns's commonplace book, that he had a particular interest both in obscure prophecies and in politically sensitive material (Meale 1983). Moreover, the care with which he copied *Speak Parrot*, which is in striking contrast to the way he treated many of the other entries, and the detailed attention he gives to the complex, glossed, polyglot dialogues with Galathea, suggest that the poem was too important to him for him willingly to have omitted a large part of it. It is therefore more likely that the lines were absent from his exemplar, either because a number of folios were lost at some stage in the transmission of the poem, or because they were omitted by a scribe prior to Colyns; the fact that Colyns copies the first line of the ninth stanza and the envoy consecutively, as if unaware of any loss of text, further supports this view. It is thus just conceivable that Skelton was himself responsible for the excision, especially if F. W. Brownlow (1971: 5) is right to suggest that Colyns was copying from Skelton's holograph. Like the addition of the relatively didactic envoys, the excision would then reflect a simplification of the poem, in direct contradiction of the addition in the manuscript of the new dialogue between Parrot and Galathea and of marginal glosses that re-emphasize the writer's playful relationship with his readers. These different kinds of change, contained within a single witness, all contribute to rendering the manuscript version of the poem significantly more complex than that in Dab's edition. Thus, whether or not Skelton was himself responsible for the omission of lines 54–228, the experience of reading the two versions of the poem is radically different: the contradictory relationships between writer and reader proposed in the manuscript version in practice emphasize the need for active interpretation on the reader's part, while the printed version is relatively self-contained.

At first sight, then, the nature of the differences between the two versions of the poem seems to confirm Ong's perception that print discourages dialogue between writer and reader. Yet we should question whether they are really attributable to differences between print and manuscript. It might rather be said that the textual evidence in the case of *Speak Parrot* challenges the hypothesis that 'manuscript' and 'print' culture were (at least in the early years of print) so entirely distinct; in particular, it supports Adrian Johns's argument that 'print culture' is not an objective phenomenon, but a social construct that 'exists only inasmuch as it is recognized and acted upon by people' (Johns 1998: 19; cf. Dane 2003).

As we have seen, one notable feature of the poem's transmission is that the version in Harley 2252 (*c*.1525) represents a later text than that in Dab's edition of *c*.1545. Another is that—although there is some evidence to suggest that Dab's edition of *Speak Parrot* is materially different from its lost manuscript exemplar—the ways in which it differs are not peculiar to print, but might have occurred in manuscript transmission too. Dab's *Speak Parrot* is unglossed, yet two of the marginal glosses that appear in the Harley text of the poem recur in Dab's edition in the body of the text: the first, 'Aquinates', attributes the line 'Concumbunt Grece. Non est hic sermo pudicus' (line 269) to Juvenal; the second, the cryptic 'Cum ceteris paribus' ('With others the same'), is attached to the lines 'Amen, Amen, | And sette to a D' (lines 274–5). The layout of these lines in Harley 2252 is extremely confused and it seems likely that this confusion was replicated in Dab's copy text, so that the printer mistook the glosses for part of the text (see Figures 4.1 and 4.2). But this implies that the printer was using a glossed exemplar, and that he chose to omit those glosses that he did not

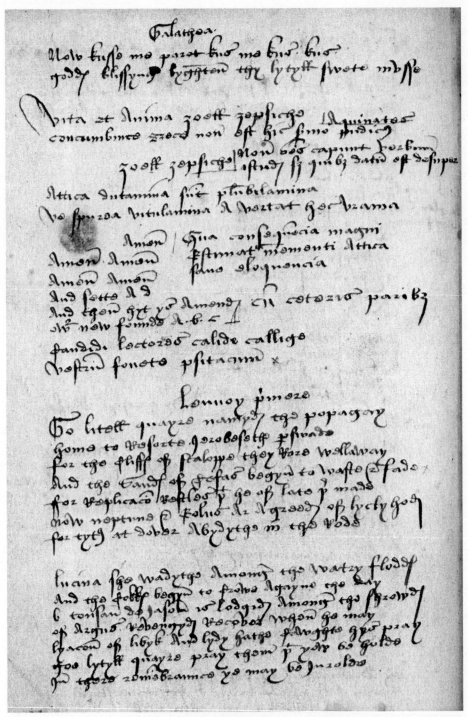

Fig. 4.1 Manuscript of John Skelton, *Speke Parrot* (c.1525), British Library, MS Harley 2252, 135ᵛ. Compare this with Figure 4.2. The gloss 'Aquinates' appears near the top on the right; 'Cum ceteris paribus' about halfway down the page, on the right.

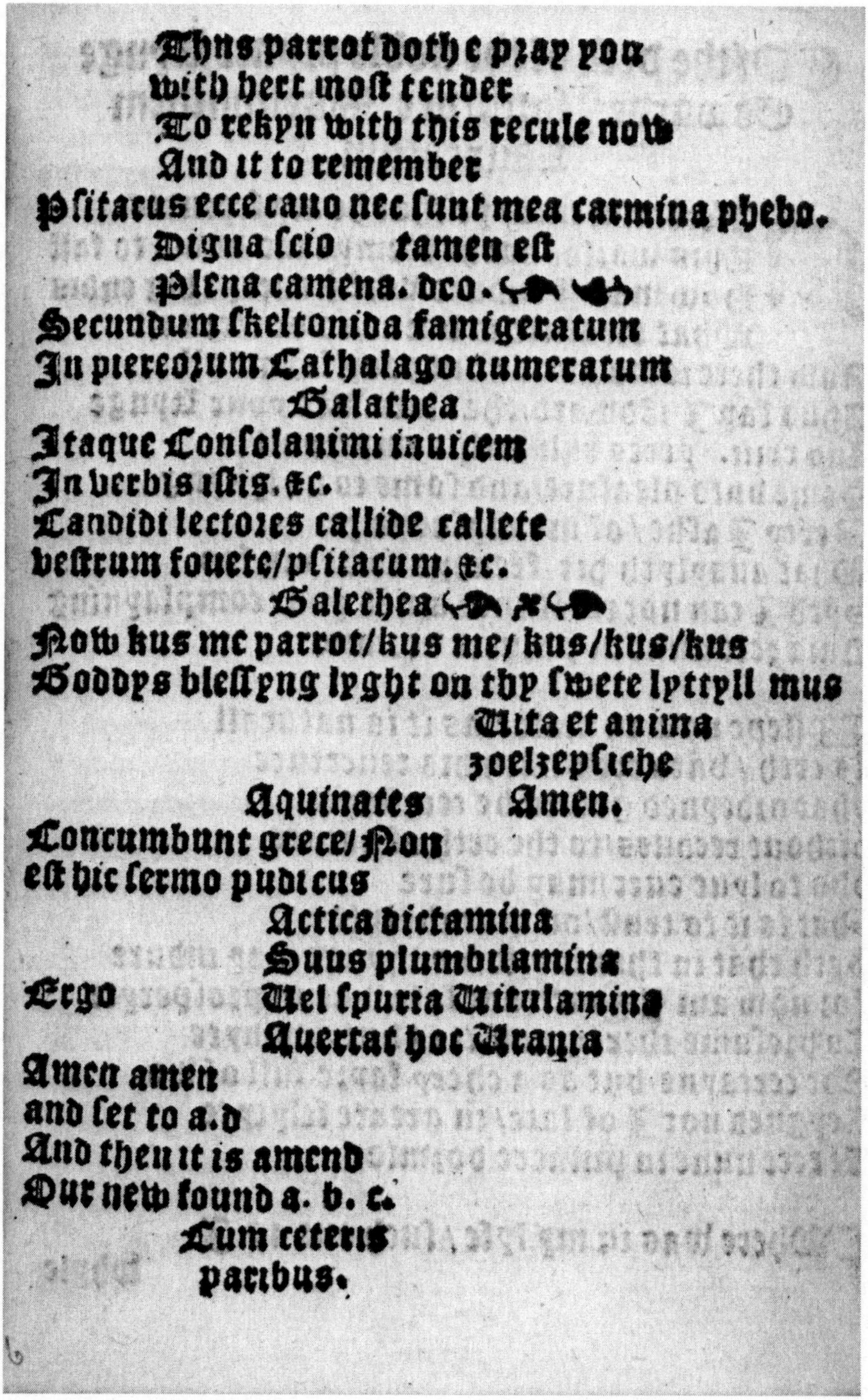

Thys parrot dothe pray you
with hert most tender
To rekyn with this recule now
And it to remember
Psitacus ecce cano nec sunt mea carmina phebo.
Digna scio   tamen est
Plena camena. dco.
Secundum skeltonida famigeratum
In ptereozum Cathalago numeratum
Galathea
Itaque Consolamini tauicem
In verbis istis. &c.
Candidi lectozes callide callete
vestrum fouete/psitacum.&c.
Galethea
Now kus me parrot/kus me/kus/kus/kus
Goddys blessyng lyght on thy swete lyttyll mus
Uita et anima
zoelzepsiche
Aquinates   Amen.
Concumbunt grece/Non
est hic sermo pudicus
Actica dictamiua
Suus plumbilamina
Ergo   Uel spuria Uitulamina
Auertat hoc Urania
Amen amen
and set to a.d
And then it is amend
Our new found a. b. c.
Cum ceteris
paribus.

Fig. 4.2 John Skelton, *Speke Parrot*, in *Certayne Bokes* (1545), A6ʳ. The printed page resembles the layout of the manuscript version (Figure 4.1). 'Aquinates' appears about halfway down the page; 'Cum ceteris paribus' at the bottom.

believe to be part of the text. The initial suspicion that arises is that he did so on grounds of the sheer technical difficulty (and therefore expense) of printing marginal notes, and thus that their absence is evidence of one way in which the use of print rather than manuscript affected textual transmission. Moreover, since the glosses are very far from providing an impersonal commentary, but rather draw attention to the text's irregularities and themselves employ widely divergent voices, their omission might also be said to have eradicated one of the means that Skelton used to stimulate readers to engage with his poem, thereby leading to a loss of immediacy, or authorial 'presence'.

If this line of argument were correct, it would be evidence if not of actual differences between 'print' and 'manuscript culture', then at least of the kind of factor that might help establish the perception of difference: particularly perhaps the assumption that print is likely to present the more monolithic, univocal text. However, both the omission of glosses and their incorporation in the body of the text had long been a feature of manuscript transmission (Echard 1998); conversely, a printed text might scrupulously replicate manuscript features, as Dab's edition itself (c.1545) does in its version of *Ware the Hawk* (c.1505). Uniquely among Skelton's posthumously printed works, this includes two decorated initials and a complex system of marginal annotation consisting of marginal hands, trefoils, and asterisks; several lines are inset and framed in a simple border of single line rules that clearly imitates an outline drawn by hand. These appear to be manuscript features, replicated so scrupulously as to suggest that Lant followed his exemplars very closely indeed, and that omitting the glosses to *Speak Parrot* may not have occurred at the point of printing at all, but in an earlier, manuscript text. This in turn suggests that the level of fidelity to a copy text depended on the individual, regardless of whether he was a printer or a scribe, and therefore that the two distinct witnesses to *Speak Parrot* confirm what David McKitterick (2003: 35) has argued: that in the early years of the sixteenth century the use of print rather than manuscript did not involve an essentially different approach to the making of books. Owing to its ready availability, Dab's edition became the basis of all other sixteenth-century editions of *Speak Parrot*, and its three reprintings in the decades after Skelton's death did effectively 'fix' one of the two different versions of the poem, privileging it over the other—yet both reflect accidents of transmission that might have occurred either in manuscript or print, and in so far as the printed copy 'fixes' the text, it does so only coincidentally. Thus, although the ultimate dominance of the printed version of *Speak Parrot* suggests that Bishop's apostrophe to Robert Lowell ('sad friend, you cannot change') might aptly be applied to Skelton too, by witnessing an earlier form of the poem than that contained in the Harley manuscript, Dab's edition in fact attests Skelton's habit of revising and circulating different versions of his poems.

At this point, it seems that examination of the textual evidence has produced largely negative findings. While it is clear that Skelton composed *Speak Parrot* over a period of time, he may or may not have intended to substitute the envoys for the cryptic attacks on Wolsey in the first part of the poem; thus, he may or may not dramatically have changed his approach to his readers. The fact that he appears to do so may well be a mere accident of transmission, while the fact that the printed editions privilege one version of the poem at the expense of another is also due to chance. Certainly there is no evidence in the case of the (posthumously published) *Speak Parrot* to suggest that Skelton was deliberately adapting his habits of composition or circulation for the advent of print. Thus, while these findings challenge the assumption that print and manuscript production involve wholly different attitudes towards texts, they also seem to confirm Seth Lerer's argument that Skelton's own primary allegiance was to manuscript. Yet editions of Skelton's works printed within his lifetime tell a strikingly different story. They reveal that Skelton did at least occasionally explore the possibility that print may function differently or (crucially) be perceived to function differently from manuscript. They suggest too that he did so precisely in order to renegotiate his relationship with his readers, using recent technology to breathe new life into the playfully serious relationship that underlies the first part of *Speak Parrot*.

This is nowhere more apparent than in *A Garland of Laurel* (1523), a dream vision published towards the end of Skelton's life which seeks to define both his own contribution to English poetry and the value of English poetry itself (V. Gillespie 1981; Brownlow 1990: 70–82). Like *Speak Parrot*, *A Garland* was subject to extensive revision. It survives in two witnesses dating from Skelton's lifetime, a defective version in BL Cotton MS Vitellius E.x and a printed edition published by Richard Faukes in 1523; there is also a later sixteenth-century edition published by John Stow in 1568 (Brownlow 1990: 17–30). What remains of the manuscript agrees with Faukes's edition in all material respects. Yet the apparently simple textual evidence conceals what is probably one of Skelton's most substantive revisions. The poem, which Skelton claims to have composed at Sheriff Hutton Castle in Yorkshire, contains a series of lyrics addressed to Lady Elizabeth Howard and her attendant ladies—and as Melvin Tucker (1969) has demonstrated, the ladies named were not in residence at Sheriff Hutton in the years immediately before its publication in 1523, but in the early 1490s. Building on Tucker's work, Brownlow (1990: 30–6) has argued that the entire poem (with the exception of the envoys and the stanzas that refer to Skelton's later works) was composed at that earlier date. This implies that the 1523 edition is a reissue, in print, of a 30-year-old poem previously circulated in manuscript, which inevitably raises questions as to why such an old poem might be relevant to Skelton's position in 1523, and why he chose print publication over renewed manuscript circulation. An exploration of the possible reasons for his decision suggests a highly inventive attempt on Skelton's part to use distinctions between the two media to establish different kinds of relationship with different readers.

The question of poetic authority is clearly a central concern in *A Garland*, in which the narrator, Poeta Skelton, dreams that he is awarded the laurel crown for his substantial poetic achievement. The historical Skelton was also laureated, by the universities of Cambridge, Oxford, and Louvain. However, the fictional Poeta Skelton receives his crown not from an institution, nor from the dubiously authoritative Queen of Fame, but from the lady of Sheriff Hutton, Elizabeth Howard, and from her ladies-in-waiting, who join forces to weave the garland for him. The ladies' support is of pronounced political significance. En route to Fame's palace (which is where he finds the Countess and her ladies) Poeta Skelton has an almost apocalyptic vision of the plight of Fame's suitors in the country named Anglia. They scrabble and backbite, showing in every possible way how unworthy of Fame's attention they are, and finally they become the target of guns fired from an unknown source, which kill at least one of them outright. Although Poeta Skelton stands safely above the mêlée, protected by his guide, Occupacyon, it has been suggested (Brownlow 1990: 69) that the vision reflects the course of Skelton's life up to 1488, with the events of 1485 as its dangerous climax, when his first patron, the Duke of Norfolk, was killed at Bosworth, and Norfolk's son Thomas imprisoned in the Tower. In this reading, just as the presence of Occupacyon implies that Skelton attributed his survival to his poetic vocation, Poeta Skelton's laureation by Skelton's real-life patron Elizabeth Howard suggests his retreat from worldly ambition to a safe haven that enables his writing—a retreat from the 'prece [press]' of court that nonetheless, paradoxically, ensures his fame.

The momentary collapse of the distinction between Fame's palace and Sheriff Hutton substitutes private worth for public display in a way that proves central to the poem. When Poeta Skelton comes before Fame to be judged, he already has the approval not only of the Sheriff Hutton ladies, but of a crowd of assembled poets and orators, the English Chaucer, Gower, and Lydgate prominent among them. As Gillespie (1981) has argued, the composition of the crowd clearly reveals that Skelton defines himself as one of a tradition of writers who had the good of their respective nations at heart—and *A Garland* explicitly contrasts this high moral authority with the trappings of courtly fame. The poem values good works and private recognition above public reward; in its first incarnation, it stands as a private token of appreciation for Skelton's patrons who liberated him from the infighting at court.

Although the focus on the poet's authority remains fundamental, in other respects the poem's publication in 1523 gives it a very different slant. The use of print, in particular, suggests a clear decision on Skelton's part to make a very public statement about his status as poet. One difference between print and manuscript that was repeatedly remarked upon by late fifteenth- and early sixteenth-century writers and readers was print's ability to produce what appeared to be vast numbers of a text for simultaneous distribution (McKitterick 2003: 135). Skelton makes the most of this perception, yet ironically he does so in order to use the startling and new publicity of print precisely as a means to convey a pointed private message to one of his readers in particular.

A Garland was published just a few months after Skelton completed *Why Come Ye Not to Court?*, the third of his satires against Wolsey, in late 1522. Skelton's abrupt abandonment of his campaign against Wolsey has frequently been viewed as a complete reversal or capitulation. His last two poems, *How the Doughty Duke* (1526) and *A Replication* (1528), show clear signs of having been commissioned by Wolsey, and Greg Walker (1988: 100–18) has argued convincingly that Skelton's failure to find patronage among Wolsey's opponents at court and among London's merchant classes necessitated his feeding from the hand that he had bitten. But although, in this reading, the supposedly 'innocuous' *Garland* might be said to mark the first stage of this rapprochement, both its envoys and the decision to print it suggest rather the reverse. The envoys are markedly heterogeneous: the first sends the book on its way into the world, requesting its readers to receive it well, and to 'amend' it where they find fault; the second dedicates the work to Henry VIII and to Wolsey; the third is a Latin celebration of the virtues of the laurel tree from which Poeta Skelton's poetic garland was woven; and the fourth consists of three versions of the same complaint about the abuses of the time, in French, Latin, and English. On the face of it, these are a curious combination, juxtaposing a humble submission to all readers and a particular submission to the two most prominent ones with an assertion of poetic independence and a lament about the injustice of the world. However, when we consider the poem in the light of Skelton's relationship with his new patron, Wolsey, the collocation is not really so strange.

One of these envoys, the dedication to Wolsey, is absent from the 1523 edition of *A Garland*. This suggests that Stow must have taken it from some other (manuscript) source, arguably a presentation copy intended for Wolsey himself. The circulation of the poem in two different versions, one including the dedication and one without, suggests that Skelton was extremely aware of the potentially very different degrees of publicity attached to manuscript and print, using one to reinforce a private agreement, the other to make a public statement. This manoeuvre could be interpreted in two quite different ways. It would be natural to suppose that Skelton circulated two distinct versions in order to keep his association with Wolsey hidden from the public, to whom he presents himself as a poet authorized by his own good works and by his association with the Howards. If so, this would of course confirm his 'capitulation' to Wolsey. Yet the opposite could also be the case. *A Garland* is by no means innocuous or apolitical. The three linked envoys that lament the absence of justice suggest that Skelton was far from abandoning his satire of Wolsey's regime. The repeated lamentation that 'Justice est morte', 'Jus [...] arripuit', 'Justyce now is dede' seems, by virtue of its repetition in three different languages, to refer to a timeless state of affairs; it can be anchored only by the context in which it appears. And although the description of the squabbling, backbiting, morally deficient courtiers was originally a description of the court of the 1480s, at the time of the poem's publication in 1523 it might easily be understood as a description of England under Wolsey, especially in view of the Queen of Fame's love for ostentatious display, which parallels that of Wolsey himself.

The presence of a dedication naming Wolsey could only serve to draw attention to those resemblances—the more so, since the dedication does not stand alone. It appears in Stow's edition in conjunction with its own, much less submissive envoy, where Skelton switches from Latin to English in order to convey what looks remarkably like a threat:

> Both worde & dede   In noblenes
> Should be agrede
> Or els & c.

(Skelton 1568: D6ᵛ)

Read together, the dedication and envoy suggest less that Skelton is offering *A Garland* to Wolsey as a conciliatory gesture, than that he is using the poem to remind Wolsey of the patronage he has already promised, and to threaten him with a resumption of his earlier satiric attacks if it is not forthcoming (Jane Griffiths 2004). Viewed in this light, the omission of the dedication from Faukes's edition of *A Garland*, juxtaposed with its inclusion in a privately circulated manuscript, threatens Wolsey with what Skelton could put into print if he chose. It thus suggests a highly sophisticated awareness both of the potential of the new medium of print to reach a wide audience, and of the opportunities that arose from the coexistence of print and manuscript as equally viable means of publication. Skelton grasps the chance to address his poem simultaneously to two different audiences in order to engage in an oddly intimate exchange with Wolsey, who becomes (potentially at least) the ideal reader posited in *Speak Parrot*: one who is able to read between the lines and understand the poet's true message, even when that message is a threat to himself.[5] Skelton's exploitation of perceived differences between print and manuscript may not be confined to this one, political instance. In particular, the incorporation of the 'addicyon' to *Phillip Sparrow* as part of Occupacyon's speech in *A Garland* suggests that Skelton may be utilizing the differences for personal reasons too. Both sixteenth-century printers and modern editors have always treated the 'addicyon' as part of *Phillip Sparrow* (and at least one reader of Stow's edition of 1568, in which both poems appear, has 'emended' his copy by cancelling the 'addicyon' where it appears in *A Garland*). However, it was as part of *A Garland* that the 'addicyon' was first printed. Here, as Lerer argues, its combative tone wholly contradicts the context in which it appears. When Occupacyon acknowledges that some readers have objected to *Phillip Sparrow*, her first response is conciliatory, employing the vocabulary of the kind of envoy that invites collaboration from the reader: 'But what of that? Hard it is to please all men: | Who list amende it, let hym set to his penne' (lines 1259–60). Yet she then promptly retracts this envoy-like invitation, launching into the 'addicyon', which begins:

> For the gyse nowadays
> Of sum jangelyng jays
> Is to discommende
> That they can not amende.
>
> (lines 1261–4)

Lerer (1993: 201) rightly calls this 'the language of the dare', presenting a challenge which the reader must inevitably fail: 'No reader has the last word here, for the *Garlande of Laurell* is itself a poem that refuses to end: a poem that continues to emend itself in different languages, meters, and styles.'

One reader who had objected to *Phillip Sparrow* was Skelton's poetic rival Alexander Barclay, who critiqued the poem in his *Ship of Fools* (Y3). Significantly, this work was itself printed in 1509, so that it seems that by printing the challenge to amend,

---

[5] Gillespie (2006: 170–2) suggests that the frontispiece to the 1523 *Garland* may function in a comparable way.

Skelton is responding to Barclay in kind, ensuring that his self-defence will circulate as widely as Barclay's attack. Yet as well as allowing Skelton to take the place of the corrective reader, the inclusion of the 'addicyon' suggests a certain enjoyment of the incongruity of incorporating a conventional *manuscript* appeal in a printed text. Although, as McKitterick (2003: 33, 101, 133–5) and Paul Saengen and Michael Heinlen (1991) have demonstrated, it was not uncommon for readers to be invited to revise a printed text with their pens, it seems possible that Skelton here plays on an emerging belief in the fixity of print, which renders ironic an appeal for emendation. Like the omission of the dedication to Wolsey from the printed text of *A Garland*, this suggests a knowing responsiveness to an emerging perception of differences between print and manuscript, irrespective of the reality of those distinctions; arguably, it witnesses the beginnings of the construction of print culture, even as it continues to entice readers into an intimate, collaborative relationship with the writer.

To what extent, then, is the quotation with which I began, Bishop's epitaph for Lowell, applicable to Skelton and his transitions into print? Clearly it would be hard to make the case that print means that a poet 'cannot change'. The transmission of *Speak Parrot*, which has come down to us in two almost wholly distinct texts, of which the printed text represents the earlier version of the poem, obviously challenges assumptions about the 'finality' of print; the disparities between the various texts of *A Garland* suggest a highly developed awareness, on Skelton's part, of both the potential and the dangers of print. Even the manuscript copy of *A Garland* repeatedly stresses the permanence of the text; Dame Pallas declares that 'wrytyng remayneth of recorde' (line 89), and Occupacyon's list of Skelton's works includes the apparently throwaway asseveration 'By Mary Gipcy | *Quod scripsi, scripsi* [What I have written, I have written]' (lines 1455–6). It is clear that for Skelton permanence is not the same as homogeneity; rather, Skelton's 'recorde' includes multiple texts of the same work, so that printing these assertions undermines the 'difference' of print even while exploring it. Thus, the very fact of difference between texts functions as the gaps in utterance of *Speak Parrot* do, providing a space for readers to engage with the work and attempt to complete its meaning. But while this might be seen simply as a perpetuation of a 'script culture' relationship between writer and readers, Skelton is not unaware of the new medium or reluctant to adjust to it. Rather, print becomes a way of making more visible the revisions, opening up the gaps for interpretation rather than closing them.

PRIMARY WORKS

Barclay, Alexander (trans.) (1509), *The Shyppe of Fooles* by Sebastian Brant.

Bishop, Elizabeth (1983), 'North Haven', in Bishop, *Complete Poems, 1927–1979* (London: Chatto & Windus).

Skelton, John (n.d.), *Garland of Laurel*, BL, Cotton MS Vitellius E.x.

—— (1499), *Bowge of Court*.

SKELTON, JOHN (*c*.1505), *Ware the Hauke*.

—— (1523), *A Ryght Delectable Traytyse upon a Goodly Garlande or Chapelet of Laurell*.

—— (*c*.1525), *Speke Parrot*, BL, Harley MS 2252.

—— (*c*.1545), *Here after Foloweth Certayne Bokes compyled by Mayster Skelton*.

—— (1568), *Pithy Pleasaunt and Profitable Workes of Maister Skelton*.

—— (1843), *The Poetical Works of John Skelton*, ed. Alexander Dyce, 2 vols (London: Thomas Rodd).

—— (1983), *John Skelton: The Complete English Poems*, ed. John Scattergood (Harmondsworth: Penguin).

CHAPTER 5

ALL FOR LOVE

LORD BERNERS AND THE ENDURING, EVOLVING ROMANCE

JOYCE BORO

JOHN BOURCHIER, Lord Berners, stands at the boundary between the medieval and early modern, his compositions hovering at their nebulous threshold. While it is recognized that *Arthur of Little Britain* (1560?) and *Huon of Bourdeaux* (*c*.1515) are written in the tradition of the medieval chivalric romance and that *Castle of Love* (1548?) reflects new, humanist trends in the genre, it is less frequently observed that these two strands of romance were both avidly read, reprinted, and adapted throughout the Tudor period. The continued appeal of romance may be explained by its ability to respond to the shifting preoccupations of diverse reading publics. For instance, as the sixteenth century progressed, *Castle* was read as both proto-feminist and misogynist, as a *speculum principis*, and as a rhetorical and amatory manual (Boro 2007). *Huon* was adapted into dramatic form and inspired William Shakespeare, Edmund Spenser, Ben Jonson, and Christopher Marlowe (Boro 2004: 239). *Arthur* was denounced as corrupting by some, while others nostalgically recalled it as favoured childhood reading (Nashe 1958: i, 11; A. Davis 2003: 30). Readers looked to romance for entertainment, education, and advice. Despised and feared by moralists, it provided children, merchants, gentlemen, women, and nobles with models of exemplary and daring behaviour, rhetorical and chivalric prowess, and political theory. Straining against the tide of continued and widespread moral condemnation, chivalric and humanist romance fiction remained popular with male and female

readers across the social spectrum (see Hutson 1994). In order to illuminate the dominance of the romance throughout the period, this chapter will provide an overview of
sixteenth-century romance production, dissemination, and readership, followed by a
closer look at Lord Berners, whose literary output reflects the evolution, enduring
popularity, and continued relevance of the genre through the Tudor period and
beyond.

5.1 ROMANCE IN TUDOR ENGLAND

'Chivalric' and 'humanist' are broad categories that serve as a convenient shorthand
for an extremely varied group of texts. As Corinne Saunders observes, 'Romance is
a genre of extraordinary fluidity: it spans mimetic and non-mimetic, actuality and
fantasy, history and legend, past and present, and is striking in its open-endedness, if
frustrating in its capacity to defy classification or resolution' (2004: 2). A romance may
contain elements of hagiography, chronicle, historical biography, tragedy, comedy,
lyric poetry, the magical and the miraculous, and amorous and chivalric adventures
in varying degrees. It can end in tragedy or reconciliation; it may narrate one discrete
episode in a knight's life or follow him and his family for generations; the hero may
be secular or saintly, a military hero or a lover; or these elements may be blended in
surprising, innovative ways (see also Wakelin, Chapter 3 in this volume).

Helen Cooper enumerates upwards of seventy medieval romances that were known
in early modern England or Scotland (2004: 409–29). The range of influence and
circulation of these romances is diverse. Two of the most popular narratives were *Guy
of Warwick* and *Bevis of Hampton*. *Guy* circulated in at least ten manuscripts, four
prints, up to four dramatizations, and six adaptations in forms ranging from broad-
side through ballad to chapbook (H. Cooper 2004: 93, 419). *Bevis* was also transmitted
in manuscript, print, and as a chapbook. In addition to its nine manuscript exemplars
and fifteen editions, *Bevis* was a formative source text for Spenser and John Bunyan.
The breadth of its readership is further suggested by the countless allusions to it by
writers of drama, verse, and prose (H. Cooper 2004: 419, 413). At the opposite end of
the spectrum to *Guy* and *Bevis* are romances such as *Amis and Amiloun* (dramatized
as *Alexander and Lodowick* in 1594) and *Gamelyn* (one source for Lodge's *Rosalynde*),
which seem only to have been known in manuscript.

The wide appeal of romance is manifested by the way it cornered the print market,
circulating in even greater numbers than any other form of fiction, including printed
drama at its zenith in the final decades of the sixteenth century (Stanivukovic 2007:
61); yet, publication records tell only part of the story. As the dissemination of *Amis
and Amiloun* and *Gamelyn* suggests, there was a vibrant scribal tradition alongside
the abundance of print. In this period when books were expensive and therefore not
dispensable, reading material encompassed older manuscripts alongside new, printed

compositions: medieval romances persisted in both formats. Over 200 medieval manuscripts containing romances still survive, and more would have circulated in the Tudor era (Guddat-Figge 1976; Hays 1985: 87–109; Seymour 1995–7). Many contain annotations in Tudor hands, indicating their continued readership. Furthermore, medieval romances continued to be transcribed: approximately twenty-six Tudor manuscripts of medieval romances are still extant. The advent of print did not forestall or slacken the production of romance manuscripts. In fact, some romances may have been copied from, or inspired by, printed editions (A. Edwards 2002: 145–6). Manuscripts could contain single romances or romance anthologies; but, in manuscript form, romances usually rubbed shoulders with all kinds of texts—secular, religious, didactic, entertaining, popular, elite, Latin, English, scientific, historical, or personal.

Whereas the continued readership of medieval romance is attested by manuscript and print circulation, textual allusions, and library inventories, the period also bore witness to new romance forms. These innovations rejuvenated the ever-thriving genre. They sustained its popularity, ensuring the romance's pertinence to new groups of readers. The chivalric romance was the most prevalent form of the genre in the medieval and early Tudor periods, but as the decades progressed it was accompanied by emerging forms, such as the humanist romance, romance collections, and dramatizations.

The chivalric romance narrates the adventures of valiant knights as they fight torturous battles, defeat mighty opponents, rescue damsels in distress, encounter supernatural elements, and overcome seemingly insurmountable odds in order to acquire or regain their inheritance, land, honourable reputation, and/or beloved lady. Despite the similar markers of success in the chivalric and humanist romance—lands, inheritance, love—the particular types of heroism depicted and the heroes' modus operandi vary: humanist romances value qualities of mental readiness rather than knightly prowess; the prudent captain replaces the errant knight as the heroic model (Hutson 1994). These new heroes are gifted with the art of eloquence. When physical prowess is required, the hero's capability is commended because it reflects his mental strength. It indicates his intellectual ability to draw on knowledge gained through reading about, or acting in, similar situations and to transform such experience into persuasive arguments and practical achievements. As the markers of success moved from battlefield to text, heroes are admired for the 'virtuoso deployments of their skill in probable argument', as they rhetorically win over unwilling ladies and other resistant forces (Hutson 1994: 99). Skill in courtship is indicative of the heroes' learning, intelligence, and value to the common weal, since their ability to persuade a woman is evidence of their capacity to find a probable argument in any situation and to convince anyone to follow their desired course of action: 'heroic masculinity, in these narratives, finds its image in the extent to which all contingency, all circumstance, has its own potential as an emotionally persuasive agent for or against a particular case' (Hutson 1994: 99). These romances place greater emphasis on the actions and emotions of female readers and female protagonists than do the chivalric romances. While this increases their appeal to women readers, as I will discuss below, the primary function of female characters is to act as a foil for the hero's discursive feats as he attempts to persuade her to follow his whims. Within this framework, humanist romances are valued for their exemplary depictions of heroic behaviour and for the rhetorical displays they offer their readers. Of particular usefulness were texts that allotted significant discursive space to persuasion of all kinds—for debates between men, political and persuasive orations, letters and pleading harangues addressed to women—that is, in texts which sought to convince and which demonstrated how probable arguments could be found and success attained in even the most seemingly desperate situations (Hutson 1994).

Consonant with the political and rhetorical pedagogical focuses of humanist romances, in these texts, through the example of the hero, readers learned how verbally and physically to manipulate any situation to their advantage. Feats of dialectical chivalry were there for readers to emulate, so that they could mirror the fictional protagonists and craft themselves as rhetorical heroes. Traces of readers in humanist romances point to audiences attuned to their didactic potential as rhetorical pedagogy. For instance, the English translations of *Arnalte y Lucenda* (1543), *Fiammetta* (1587), and *The Aethopian History* (1569?) contain printed and handwritten glosses highlighting speeches, descriptions, orations, letters, and complaints. Moreover, several Tudor rhetorical manuals borrowed letters from romances, thereby emphasizing their didacticism. The third to tenth editions of William Fulwood's letter-writing manual *The Enemy of Idleness* (1578–1621) contain model epistles derived from Aeneas Silvius Piccolomini's (Pope Pius II's) *De duobus amantibus* ('The Two Lovers', 1444) and *Amadis of Gaul* (1590?), and Thomas Paynell's handbook *The Treasury of Amadis of France* (1572?) is composed entirely of extracts from *Amadis of Gaul* and has the express purpose of epistolary instruction. This link between epistolary fiction and manuals of instruction as well as the rhetorical preoccupations visible in the marginal notations to romances suggest that these fictional works were used didactically—that their letters and other rhetorical units were to be studied and imitated by aspiring writers as they sought proficiency in highly marketable rhetoric skills.

The sentimental romance is an early manifestation of the humanist romance. Flourishing in Spain from *c*.1450 to *c*.1550, sentimental romances were translated and disseminated across Europe, gaining favour with audiences from Poland to England. These texts are generally distinguished by their focus on emotion rather than action and their interest in rhetoric, epistolarity, debate, good kingship, and women's social position. They are structured according to discrete discursive units all uttered in the first person. Diverse modes of rhetorical expression are combined, such as discursive monologues, letters, laments, challenges, and replies as the heroes argue with ladies, oppositional kinsfolk, rulers, judges, and rivals, and as these other characters argue among themselves. The heroes write letters and poems and issue long laments. Combat is rare, and when it does occur, it is dealt with summarily. The heroes face a different type of challenge from the knights of chivalric romance. While they are all trying to win the love of their ladies, in the sentimental romance the amorous conquest is rhetorical, and its success or failure is dependent on the heroes' verbal dexterity. As in humanist romance, the heroes are transformed from errant knights to talking knights, prefiguring the Renaissance humanists and courtiers who would avidly read these texts.

The esteem of the sentimental romance with English audiences is attested by the popularity of Berners's *Castle* and other English translations of works in this genre. For example, Juan de Flores's *Grisel y Mirabella* boasts three distinct English translations plus two dramatic adaptations (*Swetnam, the Woman Hater* (1620) and John Fletcher's *Women Pleased* (1647)), yielding a total of eight editions from *c*.1525–32 to 1647. Translated into English on four separate occasions, Diego de San Pedro's *Arnalte y Lucenda* exists in six editions, dating from 1543–1660. And, an important generic inspiration for these texts, Piccolomini's *De duobus amantibus* was translated on four occasions and versified, adding up to seven editions between 1515? and 1639. The adaptations, re-editions, and retranslations of sentimental-cum-humanist romances clearly indicate the popularity of these texts through the sixteenth and into the seventeenth century.

In addition to the sentimental romance, readers warmly embraced other forms of the humanist romance: the sheer amount of imprints demonstrates the extent to which the genre flourished as romance collections and Greek, pastoral, rhetorical, and *novella*-derived romances entered the literary scene. By the later decades of the sixteenth century, romance anthologies, modelled on Continental examples, appeared. The first volume of William Painter's *The Palace of Pleasure* was published three times (1566, 1569, 1575) and the second volume underwent two editions (1567, 1580?). Possibly inspired by its success, similar collections by Geoffrey Fenton (1567), George Pettie (1576), and Barnaby Rich materialized (1581). But the Anglicized Italian *novella* was only one manifestation of the popular and diverse humanist romance; a new type of romance with an intensely rhetorical style and voguish subject matter was introduced by John Lyly in *Euphues: The Anatomy of Wit* (1578). Simultaneously, Greek romance thrived. Coupled with the pastoral romance, it was formative to Philip Sidney's *Arcadia*, which was published twelve times by 1638. Greek romance, however, comes to be particularly associated with Robert Greene. Greene pairs the genre with the Italian *novella* as well as with romances by Lyly and Sidney, to produce about twenty romances, including the famed narratives of *Pandosto* (1588) and *Menophon* (1589), which underwent twelve and five editions respectively. Blending biblical, classical, medieval chivalric, Italian, French, and pastoral romances, Spenser's epic, allegorical *The Faerie Queene* (1590, 1596), extant in seven editions and reissues, represents the pinnacle of the genre. This variety of romance forms speaks to the genre's intense dynamism and fluidity. Moreover, romance's diversity and adaptability contributed to its longevity, enabled it to appeal to such a large segment of the population, and ensured that it remained one of the dominant Tudor genres.

Between 1540 and 1661 over twenty medieval romances were adapted for the stage, and if Tudor romances are included, the number doubles. These plays were central to the theatrical repertoire. They exposed audiences to familiar and much-loved romance narratives, enabling dramatists to manipulate audience expectations in powerful ways. The sheer volume of dramatizations highlights, yet again, the pre-eminence of the romance genre through the Tudor period. The drama of Berners's

Huon was a phenomenal success, taking in more on its opening night than any other play of the 1594 theatre season, beating even *Titus Andronicus* at the box office (Henslowe 2002: 20–2). *Amis and Amiloun* and *Godfrey of Boulogne* were equally beloved: *Alexander and Lodowick*, the adaptation of *Amis*, was performed an impressive fourteen times in 1597, and *Godfrey of Boulogne II* was staged twelve times in 1594–5 (Henslowe 2002: 51 ff., 22 ff.). Arthurian material inspired a host of plays (Hays 1985: 87–109). Shakespeare's *As You Like It* adapts Lodge's *Rosalynde*; his *Winter's Tale* looks to Greene's *Pandosto*; *Othello* draws on Fenton's *Certain Tragical Discourses of Bandello*; and the plots of *All's Well that Ends Well* and *Romeo and Juliet* are found in Painter's collection. In addition to these direct adaptations, Brian Gibbons demonstrates the sustained influence of the romance on heroic plays ranging from *The Shoemaker's Holiday* (1600) through *Tamburlaine* (1590) to *Mucedorus* (1598) (Gibbons 2003: 212). Moreover, the second half of the sixteenth century witnessed a proliferation of dramatic romances in the style of their chivalric counterparts, including *Patient Grisel* (1600), *Cambises* (*c*.1560), and *Clyomon and Clamides* (1599), thus further demonstrating the pervasive influence of the romance genre. In fact, about a third of all early modern plays produced or published after 1570 were based on romance materials, and the genre continued to provide playwrights with inspiration well into the seventeenth century.

The high profile of romance is further demonstrated as much by its vociferous detractors as by its appreciative readers. Moralists condemned both dramatic and non-dramatic romances. Observing that in dramatic romances 'sometime you shall see nothing but the adventures of an amorous Knight, passing from country to country for the love of his lady', who encounters monsters and relies on charms or talismans to ensure a happy ending, Steven Gosson asks, 'what schooling is this?' (1582: C6^r). Like Francis Meres, Thomas Nashe, and others, Gosson relegates the offensive texts to the domain of the uneducated, whose ignorance facilitates their moral corruption (D1^r). Virtually every sixteenth-century moralist echoes Gosson's worries. Some writers target children's reading of romance, while others stress their unsuitability for women. Still more treat romance reading as a comprehensive social and religious predicament, since the fictions, deemed papist and monastic, can corrupt all those who peruse them, especially those who are less educated or from the lower social classes (R. Adams 1959: 33–48; K. Charlton 1987: 449–71). These condemnations applied to chivalric, humanist, and dramatic romance alike. Chivalric romance generally was thought to valorize 'open man slaughter and bold bawdry' since it deems 'violente murder or murder for no cause, manhoode; and fornication and all unlawful luste, friendly love' (Ascham 1570: I3^r; Underdowne 1587: 3^r, my punctuation). Rooted in the Italian *novelle*, humanist forms were particularly suspect because of the associations of Italy with Catholicism and corruption. This link enabled the activation of religious and moral polemic against romance (R. Adams 1959; K. Charlton 1987). For instance, according to Ascham 'ten *Morte Arthures* do not in the tenth part so much harme, as one of these bookes, made in *Italie*, and translated in England' (1570: I3^v). Ascham does not name any specific texts, but his targets likely include Fenton's and Painter's beloved humanist romance anthologies. His polemic fell on deaf ears as the Italianate romance continued to flourish.

In the face of this widespread moral condemnation, it is too easy to assume an uneducated readership for romances, comprised of women and the barely literate. Yet, men and women from a range of social classes read romances for education and enjoyment. In fact, a dominant trend was to advertise and read romances as didactic manuals, capable of supplying their readers with powerful lessons. Both chivalric and humanist romances focus on young men engaged in processes of maturation. Through the successful completion of their quests the heroes become productive, valued members of their society with families and secure lands. Building on the formative work of Louis Wright, who posited romances as conduct books for ambitious young men, Goran Stanivukovic writes that 'romances imagine young men's lives as a series of cultural and personal rites of passage' (2007: 67). They 'construct narratives both of the formation of young men's lives maturing to husbands and masters of the household, and recommended models for the rhetorical strategies and actions that lead to the formation of patriarchy' (63). Classifying romances as 'an aspect of informal education in Early Modern England', Kenneth Charlton gestures towards a range of prologues and dedicatory letters in all kinds of romances which stress the texts' merit in fashioning virtuous and successful men (1987: 449). Cooper identifies one of the most common topoi of the romance as the young man leaving his home or community to achieve a personal quest. This structure has important social, political, and instructive dimensions: through their adventures, romance heroes learn to rule themselves; they therefore prove themselves worthy of returning to positions of leadership and power within their communities (H. Cooper 2004: 55–7). Moreover, 'Despite the uniqueness of the hero within each romance, the kind of learning process that both Gawain and Redcrosse undergo is designed to be exemplary so far as the reader is concerned, to offer a model of how to act and how not to act' (H. Cooper 2004: 52). By providing readers with positive models of masculinity, the romances assist male youth in their development (Hutson 1994: 88). Furthermore, attacks on romances take issue precisely with their imitative quality, thereby simultaneously recognizing and condemning the pedagogical capabilities of romance.

5.2 LORD BERNERS AND ROMANCE

Lord Berners's romance compositions mirror this didacticism as well as the larger historical developments of the genre as it widens to encompass new forms. Beginning his career with the chivalric romances of *Arthur* and *Huon*, *Castle* represents a shift towards the innovative humanist romance. By presenting Berners here as a case study and by positioning his œuvre as a microcosm for Tudor romance production, the dynamism of the romance, as it evolves to embrace a multiplicity of permutations, influences, literary developments, and sociocultural and political changes, will be further illuminated. Romance's metamorphic ability effectuates the genre's continued dominance and its popularity with a wide range of reading publics throughout the century.

Whereas *Arthur* was Berners's first romance to be written, it was the last to be printed, appearing only in 1560 and 1582.[1] Translated from the French *Artus de la Petite Bretagne*, it recounts Arthur's maturation from his birth to his preordained marriage to Florence. Each time Arthur and Florence are about to be united, Arthur's incredible adventures intervene: he fights thousands of knights; defeats lions, giants, and monsters; rescues maidens and captive knights; and overcomes supernatural challenges and automata. Only once he has neutralized all threats to Florence's empire and to his dukedom can they live happily ever after. *Arthur*'s popularity is suggested by its known readership. In his memoirs, Sir William Cornwallis fondly recalls his youthful, ennobling reading of *Arthur* (A. Davis 2003: 30). It was an important source for Spenser's *Faerie Queene*, and in *The Complaint of Scotland* (1570) a shepherd names 'Arthour of litil bertange' among the popular tales, songs, and dances then current in Scotland (Boro 2004: 239). Beloved of many, *Arthur* also came under attack by moralists. Thomas Underdowne objects to its violence and sexuality, while Nashe targets both *Arthur* and *Huon* as 'lying [...] fantasticall [...] feyned [...] foolerie' (Nashe 1958: 11).

Like *Arthur*, *Huon* is a translation of an action-packed French chivalric prose romance. Printed three or four times between *c*.1515 and 1601, with a lost dramatic adaptation performed at least three times in 1593–4 (Boro 2004: 239–40), *Huon* narrates the fantastic adventures of the eponymous character as he witnesses the marvellous and accomplishes the unexpected, often with the assistance of Oberon, the fairy king. He meets Cain, Judas Iscariot, the pope, and many fairies; overcomes and converts armies of Saracens; defeats giants, knights, pirates, Moors, and griffins; discovers rejuvenating apples of youth, magical cups, swords, horns, stones, and a magnetic island filled with marvels; rescues captives; survives a shipwreck and tempest in a rudderless boat; travels through Europe to Persia and Jerusalem; marries his beloved; has a daughter who is blessed by fairies; and, finally, defeats King Arthur, thereby succeeding Oberon as king of Fairyland. Whereas *Arthur* is a biographical romance, *Huon* is genealogical: after Huon succeeds in his quests, the romance continues to relate the equally marvellous and exciting adventures of his progeny.

The various condemnations of the romance and the range of authors it inspired indicate that numerous people eagerly read *Huon*. 'Hurtfull to youth' is the charge levelled at *Huon* by Meres (1598: Mm4[r–v]). Dering declares it to be 'full of synne and abominations [... and a] childish [...] vaine [...] wanton [...] ydle' form of 'wickednes' and 'bewytch[ing...] spiritual enchauntmentes' (1572: A2[r–v]). *Huon* was even implicated in Reformation politics: the 1539 'Declaration of the Faith' boasts that all individuals now have access to 'the Holy Bible, and *New Testament*, in their Mother Tongue, instead of the old fabulous and phantasticall Books of the *Table*

---

[1]   On the possibility of an earlier edition, see Boro (2004: 237–8).

Round, Launcelot du Lac, Huon de Bourdeux, Bevy of Hamptoun, Guy of Warwick, &c. and such other whose impure Filth and vain Fabulosity, the Light of God has abolished utterly' (A. Davis 2003: 8). Like *Arthur* and other contemporaneous fashionable romances, *Huon* is linked to the frivolous and the marvellous and opposed to Christian morals and mature understandings of honour. A varied readership is suggested by these condemnations of *Huon* as well as by its presence in the libraries of the nobility, gentry, and middle classes (Boro 2004: 239; A. Davis 2003: 30).

Both *Arthur* and *Huon* are characteristic chivalric romances, especially in the way in which knightly prowess is made to agree with Christian virtue and morality. This typicality is evident in the Prologue to *Arthur*, which polarizes its entertaining and instructive potentials, stressing the value of the 'auncient noble Hystoryes of the chyvalrous Feates and marcyall Prowesses of the vyctoryous Knyghtes of tymes paste' and their 'straunge and wonderfull adventure the whyche [...] seme in a maner to be supernaturall' (1560: 1^v). This imitative, didactic reading methodology is evoked by Berners to defend his translation of *Arthur* from charges of 'folye' (1^v), just as it is elaborated upon in *Huon*'s Preface to praise the author and encourage readers to purchase the text. In this preface the hero's deeds are extolled as the 'perfect ground of good and laudable example' that will inspire youth with 'the sparke of glorious imitation' which 'calles & invites them to the like honourable atchievements' (1601: 2^r).

When Berners turned to *Castle*, one of the first English humanist romances to be composed, the didactic potential of the genre was not forgotten. Yet, rather than focus on the hero's memorable deeds and adventures, *Castle*'s lessons are rhetorical and political in scope. This shift, as will be explored below, is entirely in keeping with the new preoccupations of the humanist romance. Although the humanist romance did not flourish until the second half of the sixteenth century, *Castle* dates to the late 1520s. Based on the Spanish *Cárcel de amor* by Diego de San Pedro and a French translation of the Spanish sentimental romance, *Castle*, printed in 1548?, 1552?, and *c*.1555, narrates the tragic love of Lereano and Laureola. Despite Lereano's eloquent persuasions in the form of epistles and orations, Laureola will not requite him. The romance progresses through a series of oral and written exchanges between the lovers and the narrator–go-between. Speech cedes to action as Lereano defeats an envious rival in judicial combat. After the battle, the king imprisons Laureola, threatening to execute her. The queen, the cardinal, and Lereano attempt to persuade the king to release her, but their efforts are in vain. When rhetoric fails, Lereano assembles a small army, and despite the overwhelming odds against them, Lereano's inspirational discourse leads them to victory and frees Laureola. These displays of verbal and physical heroism do not convince Laureola, who remains firmly resolved against love. When Lereano dies from lovesickness, Laureola is seized with regret; she loved Lereano, but could not requite him without tarnishing her reputation. The small scale of the story, the focus on the characters' emotional dilemmas, the discursive space afforded to persuasive speech, the abundance of letters, formal orations, and laments, as well as the rhetorical nature of seduction, link *Castle* to the humanist romance. The features of the humanist romance typified in *Castle* are distinctive of the sentimental romance, the immensely popular sub-genre of medieval Spanish romance to which *Castle*'s source belongs.

In keeping with the rhetorical preoccupations of the humanist romance, the poems and marginal printed notes added to the second and third editions of *Castle* indicate a reading methodology centred on rhetorical instruction. The letters exchanged by Lereano and Persio contain marginal glosses which indicate the rhetorical divisions of their epistles, thus intimating that the letters were intended to function didactically. These glosses were likely added by Andrew Spigurnell, an unknown writer who is also responsible for several poems added to *Castle*, including a new verse prologue. Spigurnell's glosses indicate different rhetorical parts of the letters in the same manner adopted in instructional treatises, such as Erasmus' *De conscribendis epistolis* (1521). These glosses show that a reader like Spigurnell could easily recognize these epistolary divisions, that he was interested enough to do so, and that he thought his annotations would appeal to his readers' interest in rhetoric and epistolary composition.

The attention to epistolarity is reinforced by one of the poems that Spigurnell adds to *Castle*. The second stanza of the poem repeats 'blyssed be' followed by terms related to epistolary composition:

> Blyssed be the hande that dyd wryte,
> Blyssed be [the] pen that made the letter,
> And blyssed be the memory that dyd indyght,
> And blyssed be the paper and the messenger.
>
> (Berners 2007: 118–19)

The poem proceeds by anaphora. The subsequent stanza follows the same model as the speaker welcomes, in successive lines, 'myrth unto my harte', 'hope that shall not departe', 'pleasure unto my syghte', and 'my comforte that dayly fyghtes' (119). The accumulation of clauses creates the effect of increasing happiness and solace from the pains of love. Two distinct but related language clusters are formed: one of positive amorous emotions, the other of epistolarity. This poem makes the specific link between the relief from the pains of love and the receipt of a letter, reflecting the importance of letters in *Castle*. The marginal note 'Note the wrytyng of leters' draws readers' attention to the letter exchange thus further highlighting the text's epistolary preoccupation (Berners 2007: 108). Moreover, Spigurnell adds 'To the good and vertuous Lady, the Lady Carewe, gretynge' to the start of the Prologue, providing it with a salutation and thereby enabling it to function as another model epistle (Berners 2007: 91).

While such instances of exemplary rhetoric position humanist romances like *Castle* as pedagogically valuable, they also highlight the author's skill at creating well-honed discourse: after all, he was the ultimate source for the hero's persuasive speech. The more convincing the hero, the more worthy the author was perceived to be. Crucially, the author's rhetorical skill did not merely indicate his linguistic proficiency; it highlighted his political value and his usefulness for the common weal as an adviser or policy-maker. Works by scholars such as Antony Grafton and Lisa Jardine (1990) have repeatedly established the link between literature and politics in the

Tudor period by focusing on the political motives leading to literary creation; by showing how individual works respond to particular concerns, circumstances, and needs at specific temporal moments; and by emphasizing how authors sought to gain preferment through their literary compositions. The firm link between politics and literature can be explained by their mutually close relationships to rhetoric, as well as by the predominant ethical component within the three disciplines. The poet and the politician were both skilled orators who relied upon rhetorical techniques to induce their audiences to follow a specific desired course of action. Literature had practical value. Like rhetoric, its form and style were exercised to persuade readers to action.[2] As a result of their shared goals, manuals of poetics and rhetoric tend to cover the same material: figures and tropes, in addition to the deliberative, judicial, and demonstrative modes of composition. Furthermore, poetry, like rhetoric, is valued for its ability to move its audience to good. These ideas were not mere theoretical abstractions; students were taught to read and compose according to this ethical and rhetorical dimension. Literary analysis accompanied the earliest grammar school lessons as texts were dissected to reveal their grammatical, rhetorical, and ethical strengths.

Moreover, in reading both fictional and non-fictional texts, 'What the contemporary reader sought and found [...] was a text that demonstrated not its own likelihood [...] but the discursive organisation that made it seem likely ("probability" in the Renaissance sense of being capable of being "proved" or developed through the techniques of dialectical argument)' (Hutson 1993: 85). Readers would not differentiate between genres, nor would history, politics, and literature be read according to different methodologies; rather, the dominant drive was the harvesting of raw materials from textual sources out of which a probable case could be made. Accordingly, the text's and author's value would depend upon the quantity and quality of probability that the work contained. Therefore, the more instances of rhetorical dexterity and exemplarity there were to be noted in the margins for readers to analyse and emulate, the more useful the text and author were deemed. In the Tudor textual landscape, strewn with men with literary talents and courtly ambitions, the use-value of texts was pragmatic and political (see Grafton and Jardine 1990). Romances and other literature functioned as pleas for advancement within a male, homosocial, humanist-educated community, wherein authors used their texts to demonstrate their utility to the common weal. Well-written texts on the theme of counsel were equivalent to presenting a curriculum vitae: such compositions offered these scholar–advisers a way of exhibiting their credentials and showing themselves to merit important political positions. Aspiring men like Berners put literature to practical uses as they composed and presented texts to their monarchs and other useful patrons as advertisements or as reminders of their talents. In these texts, the author, hero, and reader are all simultaneously cast in the role of the prudent captain, poet–courtier, scholar–policy-maker, or professional reader, all of whom dominated the political and literary scene.

[2] Cf. Sidney's influential *Apology for Poetry* (1595), in which he argues that poetry's virtue is its ability to move readers to action. It is perhaps no coincidence that the writer of this totemic specimen of early literary theory also penned the romance *The Arcadia* (1590).

Berners belonged to this class of literary scholar–politicians. He wrote to influence, gain favour, and demonstrate his value to the political regime. As a courtier during the reigns of Henry VII and VIII, he relied on the patronage of his superiors. The dedications of his works to prominent and well-connected figures such as Henry VIII, Lord Hastings, Francis Bryan, and Elizabeth Carew are revelatory of his attempts to gain advancement though his literary output. Occupying several important political, military, and diplomatic positions throughout his career, such as Chancellor of the Exchequer and Deputy of Calais, his endeavours appear to have met with success.

Not only does *Castle* function as a repository of exemplary rhetoric and debate, but its focus on the politics of counsel and good kingship position Berners as a prized adviser. The consequences of accepting bad counsel are explored in *Castle* as Laureola is unjustly imprisoned because her father, the king, heeds the unsound advice of malicious advisers. His subjects must devise a way to inform their tyrannical ruler that he is behaving unjustly and steer him back to virtue. Like so many contemporary texts, such as Berners's own translations of Jean Froissart's *Chronicles* (1523) and Antonio de Guevara's *Golden Book of Marcus Aurelius* (1535), *Castle* engages with issues of political leadership: how to give and recognize good counsel, what is tyranny, and how leaders can take responsibility for errors in judgement and still preserve their honour. In these texts, good leadership is advanced: counsel is advocated; tyranny is condemned; rulers are encouraged to place the benefit of the common weal above their own personal interest; and advisers who speak fearlessly and temperately are valorized. As such, *Castle* functions as a *speculum principis* and, like other texts of this advisory genre, as a behavioural manual more generally. Monarchs and all their subjects are taught the values of justice, mercy, honesty, and discernment, while they learn the rhetorical means necessary to persuade others to embrace those virtues. The careful handling of the political and rhetorical subject matter in *Castle* emphasizes Berners's mastery of the complexities of these twinned arts, thereby alerting prospective patrons to his suitability for political advancement. As various characters try to reform the king, the importance of counsel and the range of benefits to be gained through counsel are highlighted. From the queen's heartbreaking *planctus* through the heroine's reasoned persuasions to the cardinal's lengthy oration, counsel is urged over and again (see Berners 2007: 125, 149, 141, 134–6). The king's eventual adoption of wise counsel, which enables his final recuperation, highlights the effectiveness of their discourse and hence Berners's advisory capabilities. Moreover, the skill with which Berners unconditionally reintegrates the king as the rightful leader of a just society further demonstrates his nuanced understanding of the politics of counsel and kingship and his worthiness of courtly advancement.

Despite the unmistakable political use-value of *Castle*, Berners did not offer it to a high-ranking member of the court and it was only printed posthumously. His reasons for limiting the text to the private sphere may be explained by the rapidly changing political climate in the late 1520s, when *Castle* was finished. At that time, Cardinal Wolsey was falling from grace; it would have been inadvisable to seek preferment on the basis of a text that glorified a cardinal as a repository of wisdom and which could have so easily been linked to the disgraced politician. Moreover, a veritable dearth in literary publication marked the late 1520s to the late 1540s (Fox 1989: 126, 207). This absence of literature paralleled changes in the Henrician court as the atmosphere became more hostile and the frank expression of ideas more dangerous. The stifling environment was perpetuated by new treason and censorship legislation introduced in 1534, 1536, 1538, and 1543. John King observes that these two decades are marked by 'sub-literary rhetorical forms, including appeals to the monarch, complaints against religious and social abuses, and barely fictionalised dialogues' (1982: 4). Romances, satire, drama, and court festivities suffered imaginative declines, while royal propaganda thrived. Henry's death and the ascendancy of Edward initiated a reversal of this oppressive trend. Treason, heresy, and publishing laws were relaxed (but not completely repealed) in 1547: previously banned texts, such as works by Martin Luther, were printed; and some exiles, like John Bale, returned to England. The years 1547–50 witnessed the highest rate of printing ever seen in England, which was not surpassed until 1579 (King 1982: 88). In addition to *Castle*, these three years witnessed the publication of several earlier romances, including *Mighty Prince Ponthus of Galicia and Little Britain* (1548), *Sir Eglamour* (1550?), and *Helyas, Knight of the Swan* (1550?).

The Edwardian and Marian editions of *Castle* move the romance out of the political sphere, rooting it in a familial context, with women as its intended audience. The title page and dedicatory letter present the romance to Lady Elizabeth Carew, Berners's niece. In justifying his choice of dedicatee, Berners declares that 'the matter is very pleasante for yonge ladyes and gentle women' (Berners 2007: 91). In addressing the text to a female readership, Berners mirrors the predominance of female dedicatees for the humanist (and sentimental) romances: the French and Italian translations of *Castle* are both dedicated to women, as are numerous English romances, such as those by Pettie, Riche, Greene, and Sidney. In fact, while male readers and writers dominated the genre, by the latter half of the sixteenth century romance had achieved the status of a derided, popular, and decisively female literary form. The genre was feminized through a variety of textual and paratexual strategies including prefatory dedications and narratorial asides to female readers, the popularity of female eponymous characters, and moral attacks and satires of female readers of the genre. Comments about the genre written by and directed to men present romance reading as a sexualized experience whereby male readers can spy on a private female sphere (Newcomb 2002: 104–17; Hackett 1992: 39–67). Yet while these factors gender the genre as feminine, they do not necessarily point to an audience comprised exclusively, or even preponderantly, of women. Scholars of romance and of female reading practices have identified this association of genre and gender as a potent literary convention serving to validate male authorship at the expense of a largely imagined female readership (Newcomb 2002: 37–47, 104–17; Hackett 2002: 4–19). Whether writers attempted to avoid the stigma of print by rhetorically seducing female readers through their romances, or whether they tried to debase romance in order to point to their superior authorial skills in other genres, scholars have demonstrated that, for male romance writers and readers, the trope of the feminized romance was central to homosocial strategies of literary advancement. Despite their conventional feminization, the authoring and reading of romance were primarily masculine activities. The publication history of romance, its regular presence in library inventories, the evidence of its manuscript circulation, and the abundance of romances adapted into dramatic form suggest its continued appeal to both sexes.

Twinned with the feminization and subsequent dismissal of romance was the perception of the genre as dangerous. Reading such tales of amorous adventures could morally corrupt women, as they tended to present modes of behaviour in stark opposition to that of the ideal woman—stationary, domestic, chaste, silent, and obedient—which women were consistently encouraged to emulate. Romances often narrate the adventures of female protagonists fighting seemingly insurmountable obstacles in order to achieve emotional fulfilment. Many scholars have convincingly argued for the possibility of subversive female reading practices, in which romance was read for its prioritization of matters of the heart over the intellect, for the daring behaviour of their heroines, and as a means of mentally escaping the moral and social restrictions which governed women's lives (Krontiris 1998: 26–8; Alwes 2000: 390–4). Given the consistent aspersions cast on the morality of women who read romance, Lynette McGrath and Tina Krontiris characterize the very activity of reading them as rebellious (McGrath 2002: 116–17; Krontiris 1998: 28). Yet, however much men dominated the reading and writing of romance, it is important to recognize that women like Elizabeth Carew *did* read romances and that they may have read them subversively.

In his additions to *Castle*, Spigurnell reacts to the dangerous potential of romance; he exhibits discomfort with the prospect of women reading the text. In his Prologue to the second and third editions, he objects to Berners's decision to translate *Castle* 'for a Ladye's sake', arguing that it is 'a present moche unworthie | To be presented to a Lady or a Quene' since it recounts 'a Ladye's crueltie' (Berners 2007: 93). Female unkindness, in his opinion, contravenes women's 'naturall dispocisyon' of 'pytie mercy and grace'. But his concern is not that women will be offended, nor is he worried that the reputation of the female sex will be tarnished; rather, he fears that women may emulate Laureola's cruelty. Acknowledging that Laureola would have tarnished her reputation by heeding Lereano's requests, he concludes:

> ... pytie she shold have
> And not her lover's lyfe deprave
> For though honour before lyfe is to be preferred
> Yet another's lyfe is to be regarded.

> (93)

By ascribing more importance to her life than to her lover's, Laureola has failed to act according to her natural femininity, thereby further damaging her honour. Laureola's final despondency appeases Spigurnell, however, allowing him to concede that she may serve as an example to other merciless women who fail to understand the value of pity and the insignificance of their own lives and desires. The romance is of value:

> But to the intent that women in generall
> By theyr disdayne and lacke of pytie
> Shal note what inconvenyence mai come and fal
> To lovers that be tormented crewly.

(93–4)

Spigurnell's interpretation of the text results from his anxieties surrounding its possible reception. Not only does *Castle* contain defences of the female sex in the form of Lereano's extended deathbed recitations of the lives of exemplary women and of twenty 'reasons [...] whereby that men are bound to love women' (159), but it seriously engages with Laureola's predicament as she is forced to choose between her reputation and Lereano's life. Laureola has ample space to analyse her feelings, and her struggle is vividly and sympathetically portrayed. Moreover, her decision to remain chaste is supported by Lereano, who chooses to die rather than damage her reputation. Why Spigurnell thought the romance could incite unruly female behaviour is perfectly clear. *Castle* is dangerous: it promotes female agency and self-actualization. Spigurnell therefore uses the Prologue to transform *Castle* from a site of proto-feminism to one of repressive condemnation. The added Prologue is at odds with the romance and is equally opposed to the values Berners expresses in dedicating his work to his niece. Yet, Spigurnell's and Berners's polarized reactions to *Castle* are an accurate reflection of contemporary attitudes to female romance readers.

As the genre appealed to such diverse reading publics, romance elicited different and dichotomous responses from a broad spectrum of readers depending on their cultural and moral dispositions, their expectations, and their reasons for reading. Readers turned to romances written by Berners, his contemporaries, and his literary ancestors and descendants to satisfy professional, personal, and intellectual needs. They sought eloquence, rhetorical skills, a mastery of dialectic probability, and models of professional, personal, and amorous success. Romances like *Arthur*, *Huon*, and *Castle* fulfilled all these pedagogical functions. In reading romances, young men were exposed to positive models of masculinity in the form of exemplary language and/or action, which they could then adapt to their own lives and texts. Chivalric and humanist romances alike taught them how to be effective lovers, husbands, landowners, orators, and politicians. Through their active female protagonists and exploration of women's emotional, social, and gendered predicaments, romances ascribed value to women's feelings and experiences while exposing women to alternative modes of thought and behaviour. Authors often turned to the form for highly politicized reasons. By using their romances to showcase their rhetorical skills coupled with their nuanced understanding of political theory and current events, romance writers like Berners could present themselves as valuable advisers to prospective patrons. Yet, despite these important and varied didactic and social functions, moralists and pedagogues fearfully condemned romances because of the genre's perceived ability to corrupt its readers. The censure offers persuasive evidence of romance's ability to influence, for good or ill. Furthermore, taken as a whole, these attacks, the printing history, manuscript circulation, known ownership, and adaptations of romances, in addition to countless allusions to them, incontestably substantiate the broad appeal of this dynamic genre throughout the Tudor period and beyond. Thus, rather than think of Berners as 'the last of the great medieval translators', as C. S. Lewis labelled him for posterity (1954: 149), Berners would be more accurately remembered as one of the first great Tudor romancers: his chivalric and humanist romances anticipate and mirror important Tudor literary trends, and accordingly, they were beloved by male and female readers and theatregoers with divergent interests, expectations, reading agendas, and social backgrounds throughout the Tudor period.

PRIMARY WORKS

ASCHAM, ROGER (1570), *The Scholemaster*.

BERNERS, JOHN BOURCHIER, LORD (1560), *Arthur of Lytell Brytayne* (London).

—— (1601), *Huon of Burdeux* (London).

—— (2007), *The Castle of Love: A Critical Edition of Lord Berners's Romance*, ed. Joyce Boro, Medieval and Renaissance Texts and Studies, 336 (Tempe: Arizona Center for Medieval and Renaissance Studies).

DERING, EDWARD (1572), *A Briefe & Necessary Instruction, Verye Needefull to Bee Knowen of All Housholders*.

GOSSON, STEPHEN [1582], *Playes Confuted in Five Actions*.

HENSLOWE, PHILIP (2002), *Henslowe's Diary*, ed. R. A. Foakes (Cambridge: Cambridge University Press).

MERES, FRANCIS (1598), *Palladis Tamia; or, Wits Commonwealth*.

NASHE, THOMAS (1958), *Works*, ed. R. B. McKerrow (Oxford: Blackwell).

UNDERDOWNE, THOMAS (1587), *An Aethiopian Historie*.

PART II

1530–1559

CHAPTER 6

THOMAS MORE, WILLIAM TYNDALE, AND THE PRINTING OF RELIGIOUS PROPAGANDA

JOHN N. KING

PRINTING propaganda was essential to the progress of religious controversy during the era of Sir Thomas More and his leading antagonist, William Tyndale. Advancing competing religious agendas, printed polemics ranged from broadsheets to pamphlets—their ephemerality reflected in the fact that they frequently remained unbound—to more substantial tracts, manuals, commentaries, and treatises.[1] Written largely in the vernacular, polemics of this kind represented the chief means of engaging in doctrinal debate during different phases of the English Reformation. Even more, they articulated significant issues concerning the nature and importance of printing at a time when monarchical government attempted to control public discourse; concerning competition between unauthorized expression and official control of beliefs; concerning interrelationships among different levels of the literacy

[1] I rely throughout on Arblaster, Juhász, and Latré (2002); Daniell (1994); de Nave (1994); Trapp and Herbrüggen (1977); STC2. Silent reference is made to *OED* and *ODNB*.

hierarchy; concerning Bible translation and translation theory; and concerning the fundamentally dialogic nature of tracts based upon pro and contra argumentation.

These general lines of debate were laid down during the bitter controversy that embroiled Tyndale and some of his fellow believers (including Simon Fish, John Frith, and Robert Barnes), on the one hand, and More on the other. They clashed during the opening political phase of the Reformation (1530–8), initiated by England's schism from the Church of Rome under Henry VIII. The resulting dissolution of monastic houses fuelled vigorous propagandizing at a time when theological doctrine and ecclesiastical organization remained largely intact. Pamphlets written by More, Tyndale, and their respective co-religionists underwent republication during ensuing intervals that witnessed reversal of reform (1538–46); religious reformation under Edward VI (1547–53); a second reversal under his half-sister Mary (1553–8); and renewal of reform during the first years of the reign of their half-sibling Elizabeth I (1558–63) (Haigh 1993: 14).

The quarrel among More, Tyndale, and their associates contributed to a surge in controversial publication. Given the minute scale of the trade in English books by comparison with publication on the Continent, this increase was dwarfed by the explosion of pamphlets (*Flugschriften*) that followed Luther's posting of his ninety-five theses on the door of Castle Church in Wittenberg (31 October 1517). Nevertheless, polemical publication represented a large proportion of the books printed in English, at home and abroad. It constituted a profoundly important, if not dominant, component of the reading material available in England during this era. At its core, the More–Tyndale dispute focused on ecclesiastical organization and authority; the validity of the doctrine of transubstantiation and Roman-rite Mass; whether Christians attain salvation primarily through the operation of faith or good works; and the permissibility of publishing and reading the Bible in English. The present consideration of controversial writing by Tyndale, More, and their contemporaries will address how the production, dissemination, and material nature of printed books influenced ways in which authors, editors, printers, booksellers, and readers contributed to the diffusion and modification of both old and new ideas during an age of religious crisis.[2]

Luther's critique of late medieval theology and ritual opened a breach that remains unhealed to the present day. Not only did his pronouncements result in his excommunication by Pope Leo X, but they also triggered a battle of books. Luther's *Babylonian Captivity of the Church* (1520) articulates a revolutionary attack on the late medieval theological system by eliminating all but three sacraments—baptism, Holy Communion, and penance—and rejecting the doctrine of transubstantiation. Henry VIII entered the fray with *Assertio septem sacramentorum adversus Martinum Lutherum* (1521), which counters Luther by affirming the sanctity of all seven sacraments including ordination, marriage, and extreme unction. In all likelihood, More and John Fisher, Bishop of Rochester, assisted in the composition of this royal defence of Catholic orthodoxy. Dedicated to Leo X, this treatise secured for

---

[2] For recent thinking on the materiality of books, see J. King (forthcoming).

the King a papal title once enjoyed by his own father, Henry VII: *Defensor Fidei* (Defender of the Faith). When Luther responded with an insulting counterblast, *Contra Henricum Regem Angliae* (1522), decorum dictated that More reply on Henry's behalf with an equally crude tract, *Responsio ad Lutherum* (1523), purportedly by a Spanish scholar, Ferdinand Baravellus. Although it lacks an imprint, its official auspices are evident because it was published by Richard Pynson, the King's printer. Appearing in both Latin and English, a second rejoinder—*A Copy of the Letters, wherein Henry VIII Made Answer unto Martin Luther* (1527?)—disseminated the King's vehement rejection of Lutheran ideas to reach both a Latinate and Anglophone readership.

The English government attempted to quell the spread of Lutheran ideas by banning unauthorized importation and sale of dissident books. In 1526 Cuthbert Tunstal, Bishop of London, accordingly prohibited dissemination of heretical publications (Tournoy 1994). He also thwarted publication of a vernacular Bible because of the long-standing association between scriptural translation and Lollard heterodoxy. These strictures ran counter to the ideas of Tyndale, a Gloucestershireman educated at the University of Oxford, who responded to both Erasmus' and Luther's appeal for Bible translation. One of the best-remembered incidents in Tyndale's earliest biography recounts how he attempted to acquire the protection of an episcopal patron capable of licensing his project to translate the Bible into English. Recalling Erasmus' commendation of Tunstal's erudition, Tyndale made an overture in the bookish manner of a learned humanist by giving the Bishop a manuscript of his own translation of an oration by Isocrates. This gesture demonstrated his mastery of classical Greek. The gift failed to win Tunstal's patronage, even though he had assisted Erasmus in producing the second edition of his Greek New Testament with Latin translation (Daniell 1994: 89–90; Foxe 1570: 3D2^v).[3] This edition influenced Luther, regardless of the confessional divide between him and Erasmus. It is noteworthy that Erasmus' *Paraclesis*, an impassioned exhortation in favour of Bible translation, appeared as a preface to Erasmus' dual-language Latin edition of the New Testament, printed at roughly the same time as More's *Utopia* (1516). These landmark editions pre-dated Luther's ninety-five theses by one year.

The story about Tyndale's migration from England to the Continent in order to complete his translation is deservedly famous. Under the protection of Humphrey Monmouth, a wealthy London cloth merchant, he departed for Germany by about April 1524. Tyndale was no stranger to the printing house. In 1525 he supervised the first effort to print the English New Testament at the Cologne premises of Peter Quentell. When John Dobneck (Joannes Cochlaeus) alerted local authorities concerning Tyndale's project, they took steps to suppress it. Travelling up the Rhine valley to Worms, Tyndale and his assistant, William Roy, carried fresh quarto sheets from the disrupted Cologne printing run (Daniell 1994: 108–11). Tyndale's attention to detail is evidenced by the marginal notes and running headlines in the unique fragment of the Cologne printing (BL, G.12179). Such close involvement—for instance,

---

[3] Compare Foxe (1573: B1^v); Tyndale (1848: 396).

correcting proofs in the printing house, as Tyndale and Roy did—would have been essential when producing books printed from type set by German compositors who knew little or no English.

Printers of this period produced books in a variety of formats whose size varied according to how sheets of paper were folded and interleaved to create sewn gatherings. Format had immediate bearing on the price of books, because the cost of paper was the chief determinant of price during the hand-press era. Containing sheets folded once, folio books were typically large and expensive works of scholarship. Composed of sheets folded twice to create four-leaf (eight-page) gatherings, quartos tended to be less substantial and expensive. Comprising sheets folded three times to create eight-leaf (sixteen-page) gatherings, octavos were small, popular, cheaper, and sometimes ephemeral publications. Even more ephemeral were broadsides—single sheets of unfolded paper, typically employed for ballads and proclamations—and progressively smaller formats from duodecimo (twelve leaves), sixteenmos, and so forth (Gaskell 1972: 78–107).

When Peter Schoeffer printed Tyndale's New Testament at Worms in 1526, it was—like Tyndale's successive books—an affordable octavo whose compact size was conducive to concealment prior to sale, when merchants hid unbound sheets in the holds of vessels that plied the English Channel, and after readers had acquired it. In response to the influx of copies of Tyndale's New Testament, Bishop Tunstal banned its dissemination and organized the burning of copies at St Paul's. Tyndale's translation also spawned a stream of tracts. During the same year Schoeffer printed the translator's second extant book, *A Compendious Introduction unto the Epistle of Paul to the Romans*. The ephemerality of this anonymous paraphrase of Luther's *Praefatio in epistolam Pauli ad Romanos*, which survives in a single copy in the Bodleian Library, attests to the success of official efforts to stem the spread of Lutheran ideas in England and/or the fact that Tyndale's slender book was so popular that heavy reading wore out copies. As a general rule, one may assume that scarcity of surviving copies evidences their popularity among readers who 'read to death'.

We do not know when Tyndale arrived in Antwerp, but local printers published his books on a regular basis from 1528 to 1534. During at least part of this time he resided at the home of Thomas Poyntz, who ran the English House, an enclosed community of English merchants enjoying extraterritorial diplomatic privileges. John Rogers, the first Marian martyr, whose 1537 Matthew's Bible combined translations by Tyndale and Miles Coverdale, served as chaplain and it is likely that merchants living there smuggled Tyndale's books and New Testament into England (Daniell 1994: 155, 330, 361, *et passim*; J. King 2001: 58).

Antwerp remained the epicentre for publication of books by English Protestant exiles until 1546, when the promulgation of the Index of Prohibited Books repressed evangelical publication (Johnston and Gilmont 1998: 190–1). Until then, although the Habsburg emperors exercised control of the Duchy of Brabant (where Antwerp was located), local authorities adopted a relatively lenient policy towards dissident publication. At his establishment in Antwerp's printing quarter, the printer Martin (Merten) de Keyser (l'Empereur, Caesar) surreptitiously produced tract after tract for

Tyndale and associates such as Frith, Roy, and William Barlow.[4] To veil his identity, de Keyser employed the false imprint of Hans Luft at 'Marburg, in the Land of Hesse'.[5] The real Luft was a Wittenberg printer who gained renown, and considerable wealth, as Luther's publisher. An apology that Tyndale added to the errata for *The Parable of the Wicked Mammon* (8 May 1528) suggests that he may have had first-hand knowledge of conditions at de Keyser's establishment: 'Be not offended, most dere reader, that divers thinges are oversene thorow negligence in thys lytle treatise' (Tyndale 1528a: 63^v). Authors frequently proofread their books. It seems all the more likely that Tyndale would discharge this responsibility during the production of a book whose type was set by Flemish compositors unlikely to know English. Also issued under the title of *Treatise of the Justification by Faith Only*, this book expounds Luther's understanding of the parable of the unjust steward (Luke 16: 1–8) as a demonstration of his key doctrine of *sola fide* (justification by faith alone). Although good works represent a necessary consequence of faith, in his view, they lack validity in and of themselves.

On 2 October the same year, de Keyser printed Tyndale's most important piece of non-translation prose, *The Obedience of a Christian Man*. The original title proceeds to define the book's engagement with 'how Christen rulers ought to governe, where in also (yf thou marke diligently) thou shalt fynde eyes to perceave the crafty conveyaunce of all jugglers'. Applying the cant term *juggler* to the pope and Roman-rite priests, whose officiation at the Mass Tyndale envisions as theatrical performance and conjuration, this tract counters the widespread charge that religious reformers are revolutionary dissidents attempting to undermine the social order. Reaffirming the conservative principle that lower-ranking individuals in the social hierarchy must acknowledge their superiors' authority (children must defer to parents, wives to husbands, subjects to rulers, humans to God), he argues that it is the clerical hierarchy of the Church of Rome that challenges the authority of secular rulers. Echoing Luther's *Babylonian Captivity of the Church*, this tract employs hard-hitting, colourful, and demotic prose to disempower an ecclesiastical establishment headed by the pope:

Never the lesse this I saye/ that they have robbed all realmes/ not of Gods worde only: but also of all wealth and prosperite/ and have driven peace out of all londes & withdraune them selves from all obedience to princes [...]/ and have set up that greate ydole the whore of Babilon Antychrist of Rome whom they call Pope and have conspired agenst all commune wealthes and have made them a severall kyngedome/ wherein it is lawfull unpunesshed to worke all abhominacion.   (41^v–42^r)

Not only does he identify the pope as the antithesis of Christ and arch-enemy of godliness (see 1 John 2: 18–19), he employs the whore of Babylon astride the

---

[4] For the identification of de Keyser as the chief printer of pamphlets by Tyndale and many of his associates, see Latré (2000: 92). STC2 frequently assigns books produced by de Keyser to another Antwerp printer, Joannes Hoochstraten (see n. 5). Anthea Hume's helpful list of exilic publications in More (1963–85: viii. 1065–91), requires correction by reference to sources cited by Latré (2000).

[5] STC2, 1462.5, 2350, 3021, 10493, 11394, 24446, 24454, 24455.5, 24465. Other printers employed this facetious imprint in STC2, 17314, 17314a, 24447, and 24447.3.

seven-headed beast (see Figure 8.2) as a figure for the Church of Rome. Her fornication with worldly kings (Rev. 17: 1–5) symbolizes the dissolution of monarchical authority in the face of papal arrogation of political power during the late Middle Ages, a charge originally propounded by a Calabrian monk, Joachim de Fiore (c.1135–1202).

According to a notation in John Foxe's papers, Henry VIII's evangelically minded fiancée Anne Boleyn offered a copy of this tract to her husband-to-be. He allegedly judged it 'a book for me and all kings to read' (Mozley 1937: 143). Well he might during a time when Pope Clement VII's refusal to allow him to divorce his first wife, Katherine of Aragon, threatened his design to produce a long-sought male heir. Tyndale's charges move beyond political issues to the central allegation that the papacy has 'robbed all realmes [...] of Gods worde' (41^v). In support of his translation project, Tyndale defends the validity of English as a 'mother tongue' whose suitability for disseminating Scripture is akin to the Hebrew of the Pentateuch, koine Greek of the New Testament, and Latin of the Vulgate Bible—languages spoken by ordinary people when the texts in question came into existence.

Affirming the Lutheran principle of *sola scriptura* ('Scripture alone'), which insists upon the primacy of the Bible in spiritual affairs, Tyndale's forcefully plain and demotic language attacks Roman Catholic clerics for their ignorance of Scripture and failure to provide adequate spiritual guidance for the laity. In addition to attacking them for wantonness and ribaldry (which he associates with popular Robin Hood ballads), the translator rejects the fourfold method of literal, tropological, allegorical, and anagogical interpretation of the Bible, mocking what he terms 'chopological' (tropological) readings. Late medieval Scholasticism employed this multilevel hermeneutic method to construct esoteric readings of the Bible that Tyndale regards as mystifications of the literal sense, which he defines as the only valid textual level:

For the pope hath taken it cleane awaye and hath made it his possession. He hath partly locked it vp with the false and counterfayted keyes of his tradicions cerimonies and fayned lyes. And partly dryveth men from it with violence of swerde. For no man dare abyde by the litterall sense of the texte/ but under a protestacion/ yf it shall please the pope.   (129^{r-v})

De Keyser produced two prohibited books exported from Antwerp the following year. The first, a one-volume edition of translations of Erasmus' *Paraclesis* and Luther's commentary on 1 Corinthians 7—possibly translated by Roy, the apostate friar who assisted Tyndale in his translation project—was published on 20 June 1529 as *An Exhortation to the Diligent Study of Scripture*, enhancing Erasmus' reputation as a fellow-traveller of the German reformer. This appeared only weeks before de Keyser's publication of the second work, *An Epistle to the Christian Reader wherein are compared Christ's Acts and the Pope's* (12 July 1529), a translation of Luther's *Offenbarung des Endchrists* (1524) produced by Frith, a younger associate of Tyndale. Luther's text claims that nearly eighty deeds of Christ have undergone contradiction by papal authority and expands upon the inflammatory *Passional Christi und Antichristi* (1521), which contains thirteen pairs of antithetical woodcuts carved in the atelier of Lucas Cranach the elder, accompanied by polemical captions by Luther, Philipp Melanchthon, and others.

A third reformist English tract, Fish's *Supplication for the Beggars*, was probably printed by another Antwerp printer, Joannes Grapheus, on 2 February 1529; like de Keyser's two English publications, it was a small, affordable, readily concealed octavo. Addressed to Henry VIII in the collective persona of English mendicants, this strident complaint blames avaricious clerics for impoverishing the laity by exploiting the sale of indulgences, collection of tithes, exaction of mortuary fees, and so forth. In accordance with *The Obedience of a Christian Man*, the fictive voice of English beggars claims that the clergy live dissolute lives and undermine royal authority. According to Foxe's *Acts and Monuments*, Fish was a lawyer whose reformist sympathies led him to flee 'over the Sea unto Tindall' (1583: 1014). Foxe claims further that Anne Boleyn called this tract to Henry's attention. Little substantiation exists for a related report that Fish sold copies of Tyndale's New Testament printed by de Keyser. Merchants smuggled abundant copies of this translation into London not long before the Reformation Parliament opened session in November 1529 (Scattergood 1994).

Goaded by these reformist publications, More returned to the fray during June 1529 with *A Dialogue of Sir Thomas More*, commonly known as his *Dialogue Concerning Heresies*. He produced it under licence from Tunstal, who authorized his friend to read illicit books and publish responses to instruct the illiterati in the errors of heretical pamphlets circulating underground in England (Trapp and Herbrüggen 1977, no. 140). Although he completed it before being appointed Lord Chancellor on 25 October 1529, the title page of a second edition published by William Rastell the following year indicates that this book was 'Newly oversene by the sayd syr Thomas More chaunncellour of England'.

Publication of the *Dialogue Concerning Heresies*, like all of More's other vernacular polemics, represented a family enterprise. In this instance, More's brother-in-law John Rastell published the first edition. His premises near St Paul's were well situated at the centre of the London book trade. It is noteworthy that Rastell also composed and published in support of More's arguments a dialogue between a Christian (Comyngo) and Turk (Gyngeman), entitled *A New Book of Purgatory* (1530). Having established his own printing house on Fleet Street, at the western end of London's printing quarter, Rastell's son William published the second edition of the *Dialogue Concerning Heresies* and the remainder of More's polemics. Although Thomas Berthelet's appointment as King's printer made him the authorized publisher of official documents, John Rastell served governmental interests as a publisher of law books and other legal texts. When More replaced Cardinal Wolsey as Lord Chancellor, both father and son attained 'quasi-official' status as representatives of 'the interests of king and commonwealth' (Warner 1998: 86–8).

The Rastells' prominence as influential members of More's circle was antithetical to the obscurity of de Keyser and other Antwerp printers, whose anonymity veiled their role in disseminating dissident tracts. The format of More's *Dialogue Concerning Heresies* was similarly conspicuous. Printed in two columns on over 150 pages, its large-folio format would have impressed upon readers the establishmentarian character of a propagandistic text written by the highest-ranking civil official in the land. Rastell's employment of expansive (and expensive) folio contrasts sharply with the compact nature of the octavo pamphlets written by Tyndale and his associates, designed for concealment and smuggling into England. Rendered quite affordable by their small size and crowded textblock, Tyndale's books went into nearly fifty editions during the sixteenth century. For example, *The Obedience of a Christian Man* and *Parable of the Wicked Mammon* remain extant in eight and nine editions respectively. Reprints of Tyndale's non-translation prose swamped the publication of More's writings. The high cost of folios may have played a role in inhibiting the popularity of More's writings in defence of religious orthodoxy. Sales of his first two folio books warranted their republication, but two others were not reprinted during More's lifetime.

A further difference between the *Dialogue Concerning Heresies* and the earnest pamphlets of Tyndale and his associates, which were largely non-fictional, lies in More's construction of a fictive speaker, a messenger, as a mouthpiece for heterodox ideas. He bears a letter arguing for Bible study but against pilgrimages, praying to saints, worshipping images, and miracles. A character named 'More' defends ecclesiastical tradition and attacks Lutheran theology as heresy. This employment of pro and contra argumentation warrants comparison with the literary shape of academic disputation in general, and the dialogic structure of *Utopia* in particular. Among other arguments, More mirrors Tunstal's advocacy of burning Tyndale's English translation of the New Testament:

But now I pray you let me kno[w] your mynde concernyng the burning of the new testament in english which Tyndal lately translated/ and (as men say) right wel/ whiche makethe men mich [much] mervayl of the burnyng. It is quod I to me gret marvayll/ that any good crysten man having any drop of wyt in his hede/ wold any thyng mervell or complayn of the burning of that boke yf he knowe the mater. (129ᵛ)

More's second rejoinder, *The Supplication of Souls* (1529), attacked the *Supplication of Beggars*. The identification of More as 'chancellour of [the] duchy of Lancaster' on the title page of Rastell's edition indicates that the author had not yet assumed office as Lord Chancellor. Comprising only twelve gatherings—similar in size to a modern magazine—its word count would have more readily invited publication in quarto or octavo, rather than in folio. In place of the dialogic and quasi-fictive construction of *Dialogue Concerning Heresies*, More argues *in propria persona*, rebutting charges that Fish framed as a collective utterance of English beggars. Indeed, he cuts through the fictive structure of this dissident tract by rejecting Fish's argument that redressing the grievances of the poor would curtail clerical excess, alleviate poverty, and permit free circulation of the Bible:

And therefore this beggers proctour [proxy] or rather the proctour of hell shuld have concluded hys supplycacyon not under the maner that he hath done/ that after the clergye [are] caste out/ than shall the gospel be preched: then shall beggers and bawdys [panders] decreace: then shall ydle folk and thevys be fewer: then shall the realme encreace in rychesse [riches] and so forth. (22ʳ)

De Keyser produced a stream of dissident tracts during the ensuing years. Tyndale led the way with *The Practice of Prelates* (1530). Published the same year as de Keyser's edition of Tyndale's translation of the Pentateuch, this book must have undone any benefits gained through Anne Boleyn's intercession, if she had indeed urged Henry to read his books. Not only did Tyndale renew his attack on the Churchmen who controlled ecclesiastical affairs, he tactlessly opposed Henry's campaign to divorce Katherine on the ground that their union violated Levitical strictures against marrying your brother's widow. According to the reports of foreign ambassadors, merchants who sold copies of this book—including Tyndale's brother John—were made to parade through the city of London in humiliating attire prior to the public burning of this tract (de Nave 1994: 94).

De Keyser's prolific output of printed editions by English émigrés indicates that Reformation propaganda exerted very strong market appeal, especially when one considers that substantial disincentives militated against disseminating such books. Other books printed by de Keyser include a biblical commentary published under Tyndale's initials in September 1531: *The Exposition of the First Epistle of Saint John*. It belongs to an influential series of scriptural commentaries that he produced in addition to his biblical translations and apologetic texts. Interpretation of John's first epistle is crucial because it can be construed in opposition to the doctrine of *sola fide*. Tyndale argues, yet again, that good works, important as they may be, lack validity if they are not grounded in faith. Over and beyond his governing homiletic argument, he sinks periodically into scurrility, including his punning insult to Wolsey as 'Thomas wolfese Cardinal'. Published the same year, his translation of *The Prophet Jonas* (the book of Jonah) contains an introduction that affirms that understanding of even the most difficult scriptural texts is possible to those guided by faith.

In addition to the substantial investment required for book production in general, marketers had to absorb costs for shipping, exceeding those necessary for the domestic trade in English books. Individuals at different points in the continuum that led from production to reception incurred significant risk by flouting prohibitions against selling and reading forbidden books. Although de Keyser initially printed *The Prayer and Complaint of the Ploughman unto Christ* (1531?), the printer Thomas Godfray lowered the unit cost of copies of the second edition when he printed it in London *c*.1532. His augmentation of the text with a preface bearing the initials W.T. suggests that Tyndale's name may have had selling value. Despite the dubiousness of this attribution, bookmen such as John Bale and Foxe assigned this edition to Tyndale (J. King 2001: 79). Originally written in the late fourteenth or early fifteenth century, it employs a fictive ploughman as the mouthpiece for complaint against ecclesiastical corruption. Belonging to a genre of religious and social complaints articulated in the voice of a ploughman (see Hadfield, Chapter 32 in this volume), this book resonates with the memorable defence of Bible translation attributed to Tyndale in Foxe's *Acts and Monuments*: 'I defy the pope and all his laws [...] If God spare my life ere many years, I will cause a boy that driveth the plow shall know more of the scripture than thou dost' (1563: 2A5ᵛ).

The profitability of the risky trade in surreptitious books with even a vague association with Tyndale may be noted in the publication of a verse dialogue published under the spurious Hans Luft imprint: *A Proper Dialogue, between a Gentleman and a Husbandman* (1530). Appended to it is 'A compendious olde treatyse, shewing, howe that we ought to have the scripture in Englysshe', a recension of a Lollard appeal for Bible translation. Possibly composed by Jerome Barlow or William Roy (or even William Barlow) is *Read Me and Be Not Wroth* (1528), a scurrilous verse satire, also known as *The Burying of the Mass*, printed in Strasbourg by Johann Schott. More attacked it as 'a foolish raylyng boke against the clergy' (Trapp and Herbrüggen 1977, no. 150). Equally obscure are the circumstances of production of an edition of the heresy examinations of William Thorpe and Sir John Oldcastle, who in 1407 underwent inquisition by Thomas Arundel, Archbishop of Canterbury, a *bête noire* to Protestants because of his advocacy of burning condemned heretics alive.[6] Tyndale or a collaborator, George Constantine, may have secured de Keyser's publication of this book.

Tyndale and his associates worked with more than one evangelically minded Antwerp printer. For *An Answer unto Sir Thomas More's Dialogue* (1531), Tyndale turned to Simon Cock, who also printed Frith's attack on purgatory and *A Supplication unto Henry VIII* by Robert Barnes, an apostate friar who wavered between the old and new religion. Tyndale's sole rejoinder to More's many polemics, *An Answer* provides a bridge between More's *Dialogue Concerning Heresies* and the two parts of his *Confutation of Tyndale's Answer* (1532–3). Their duel played out against the backdrop of Henry's summoning of the Reformation Parliament and events leading to England's schism from the Church of Rome. Tyndale begins with what recent editors of this book term a 'foundational treatise', a six-part discourse that constitutes one-third of the book (Tyndale 2000, p. xxxv). It begins with Tyndale's defence of his New Testament translation before entering into analysis of scriptural authority versus ecclesiastical tradition and exposition of the theology of divine election. It continues with explorations of the alleged falsity of the Roman Church, the necessity of understanding the Bible through 'feeling faith', and the professed inadequacies of ritualistic worship. Particularly memorable is Tyndale's justification of his usage of contested terms in his New Testament translation, which provoked intense controversy because they denied the existence of scriptural warrant for the authority of ecclesiastical hierarchy and contested theological points such as the doctrine of justification by good works. In the remainder of this chapter-by-chapter reply to More's *Dialogue*, Tyndale repudiates extra-biblical traditions including veneration of saints, differentiates between 'true' and 'false' miracles, and analyses human will, faith, repentance, good works, and other subjects.

More countered with *The Confutation of Tyndale's Answer*, a prolix polemic about five times as long as Tyndale's book. Published early in 1532 and consisting of three books, the first instalment was the only controversial work that More wrote as Lord

---

[6] Like many other dissident books published in Antwerp, these examinations were assimilated into *Acts and Monuments*.

Chancellor. Printed by William Rastell after his uncle had resigned from high office, the second part of this unfinished response contains four more books directed against Tyndale and a final book confuting ecclesiastical views expounded by Barnes. Contesting Tyndale's views concerning the validity of Bible translation, More advocates burning the English New Testament on the ground that it contains Lutheran propaganda. In particular, he cites Tyndale's translation of Greek words with polemical equivalents that substitute individual *repentance* for *penitence* requiring priestly absolution and that deny the authority of the Church of Rome (*congregation* instead of *church*) and its priesthood (*senior* instead of *priest*), the doctrine of good works (*love* instead of *charity*), and key Roman Catholic practices (*idols* and *witchcraft* instead of *images* and *ceremonies*). Defending fourfold allegorical interpretations of the Bible against accusations lodged in *The Obedience of a Christian Man*, More cites Christ's use of parables and St Paul's allegorical interpretation of Deuteronomy 25 by reference to providing priests with a livelihood (1 Cor. 9).

Following More's fall from favour, William Rastell abandoned the costly folio format that he employed when completing *The Second Part of the Confutation of Tyndale's Answer* in 1533. During the same year, he made an abrupt shift to more affordable octavos when producing three additional books in which More targeted controversial views articulated by Frith and Christopher St German, who enjoyed a reputation as one of England's most learned legal scholars. More completed *A Letter Impugning the Erroneous Writing of John Frith against the Blessed Sacrament of the Altar* at his manor at Chelsea on 7 December 1532, and his nephew published it early the next year. More's briefest polemic, this slight octavo lacks the ostentatious physicality of books published before his resignation.

As Lord Chancellor, More had ordered Frith's arrest and imprisonment in the Tower of London. Prior to Frith's incarceration as a heretic, he had joined Tyndale in Antwerp, where his *Epistle to the Christian Reader* (1529) and *Disputation of Purgatory* (*c*.1531) were respectively printed by de Keyser and Cock (see above). The latter work rejects defences of purgatory by John Rastell, More, and Fisher on the ground that it is a clerical imposition that lacks scriptural warrant. According to tradition, further arguments lodged by Frith swayed Rastell away from traditional religious beliefs (de Nave 1994: 1.13). Despite his imprisonment, Frith composed the arguments against transubstantiation and validity of the Roman-rite Mass that triggered More's counter-response. Their dispute continued after Frith was burned alive as a heretic at Smithfield on 4 July 1533, when his prison writing was published posthumously in Antwerp, as *A Book Made by John Frith*.

More's quarrel with St German took on a very different complexion. Unlike Tyndale and Frith, who were isolated individuals against whom More lodged *ad hominem* arguments often framed in fictive form, St German was a learned jurist who apparently wrote under Thomas Cromwell's patronage. As Henry's chief minister, Cromwell organized a propaganda campaign against the independent power and prerogatives of the clergy that preceded the passing of the Act of Supremacy (November 1534). In declaring Henry head of the Church of England, this legislation supplanted the authority of the Roman pontiff with that of the King as an 'English pope'. Although St German's books were printed anonymously, their attribution to him is reasonably certain. The official auspices of *A Treatise Concerning the Division between the Spirituality and Temporality* (1532?) are apparent in the fact that the first edition printed by Richard Redman was followed in close succession by four more editions printed by Berthelet, the King's printer. The tight, legalistic argument of this forty-nine-page octavo succinctly outlines ways in which Church courts oppress the laity through the abuse of canon law. The ruefully dispassionate rhetorical stance of the jurist's enumeration of article after article in his case concerning clerical oppression of the laity is apparent in the opening words: 'Who may remember the state of this realme nowe in these dayes, without great hevynes and sorow of herte? For there as in tymes past hath reygned charite, mekenes, concorde and peace reygneth nowe envye, pryde, division, and stryfe' (A2^r).

Appearing close to Easter 1533, *The Apology of Sir Thomas More* followed his *Second Confutation*. True to More's habit, this lengthy treatise was more than ten times longer than St German's. Although he begins by responding to both Tyndale and Frith, More devotes most of the *Apology* to a detailed pro and contra rebuttal of St German's attack on clerical prerogatives and ecclesiastical law. True to form, he begins by belittling his antagonist's character by reference to the opening words quoted above: 'Some say that a man myght here a lytle lament this mannys wyt, that weneth yt lesse to be lamented, that debate & strife shold be bytwene prestes and religyouse persons' (1533a: 101^v). St German responded at Michaelmas (29 September) with *Salem and Bizance*, a dialogue between speakers whose names reflect the oppression of Jerusalem (Salem) by Constantinople (Bizance, i.e. the Turkish Sultan). Muslim control of the Holy Land throws into high relief contemporary divisions within Christendom. It is noteworthy that John Rastell had adopted a comparable strategy in his *New Book*, in which the courtesy with which Turk and Christian converse stands in marked contrast to the schisms within Christendom. Within about one month, More responded with yet another defence of the conduct of the clergy, *The Debellation of Salem and Bizance*. He abandoned this controversy at this point, but several more books, including *The Additions of Salem and Bizance* (1534), appear to represent further work by St German (Trapp and Hubertus Herbrüggen 1977, nos 164–7).

More produced one final polemic. Although William Rastell assigns publication of this to 1534, the colophon of *The Answer to the First Part of the Poisoned Book, Named the Supper of the Lord* indicates that he finished printing it before Christmas 1533. This rejoinder rejects views contained in a dissident tract entitled *The Supper of the Lord*, which denies that Jesus' declaration 'I am the bread of life' (John 6: 35) supports the doctrine of transubstantiation (de Nave 1994: 20).[7] Besides expounding a view of the Eucharist that reflects Zwingli's belief that it is wholly commemorative and lacks any corporeal presence of Christ, *The Supper of the Lord* satirizes More as 'Master Mocke' in a digression that defends Frith against the attack lodged in *A Letter of Sir Thomas More* (Trapp and Herbrüggen 1977, no. 157). Although the pseudonymous

---

[7] Because English bibles lacked verse divisions prior to the Geneva Bible (1560), the full title designates the text in Tyndale's New Testament by reference to an alphabetical note in the margin: 'Beginninge at the Letter C. The Fowerth Lyne before the Crosse, at These Wordis: Merely Were'.

imprint deceptively assigns publication to a Nuremberg printer named Niclas Twonson, Cock may have printed it in Antwerp. The book is anonymous, but claims have been made for Tyndale's authorship (STC2, 24468; de Nave 1994: 20). Although More sensed that Joye had written it, he declines in his *Answer* to differentiate between the heretical views of Tyndale, Joye, or some other 'yonge, unlerned fole' (More 1533*b*: 2B5^r).

Just over a year later, More was decapitated at the Tower of London (6 July 1535) after a fifteen-month incarceration for refusing to swear the oath of obedience to the Act of Succession. He had dedicated his imprisonment not to polemical writings in the manner of Frith, burned at the stake two years earlier, but to private devotion. About a year later, following a brief detention, Tyndale was also executed (at Vilvorde Castle in Brabant, for heresy). De Keyser died the same year, leaving his widow as head of his printing enterprise. Fish and Roy were long gone—the former having died of plague in 1531; the latter apparently having perished *c*.1531 in an auto-da-fé in Portugal. Barnes survived until 1540, when he was burned as a heretic at Smithfield. More's sole antagonist to live into old age, St German, died the same year of natural causes. Having returned from Continental exile during Edward VI's evangelically minded reign, when he was appointed a country parson, Joye alone among these controversialists survived Henry VIII's turbulent reign. He passed away on the cusp of the succession of Mary Tudor, who attempted to return England to the status quo prior to the schism from the Church of Rome.

Mary's commitment to restoring the old religion enabled the resurrection of More's controversial writings after a hiatus of one generation. At the outset of her reign, William Rastell returned from Louvain, where he had fled under the Edwardian regime. Although he abandoned his printing career soon after his uncle More's arrest, he laid plans in exile for an edition of the collected works of this famous relative. This project came to fruition after Rastell's return to England. Having collected, preserved, and edited More's vernacular writings, most of which he had himself published, he added a considerable amount of manuscript material that might otherwise have been lost to posterity. According to the imprint on the title page of *The Works of Sir Thomas More*, three booksellers (John Cawood, John Walley, Richard Tottel) paid the 'costes and charges' of its publication. The role of Cawood, the Queen's printer, in this project was in keeping with the establishmentarian emphases of this massive volume.

At the end of April 1557, this book went on sale at Tottel's premises at the sign of the Hand and Star in Fleet Street, within London's legal quarter close to the Inner and Middle Temples. Publication in folio was not a new development, because Rastell and his father had employed this format prior to More's fall from grace. Nevertheless, the 1,491 pages of densely packed black letter type marked a departure from both the slender folios and the compact octavos that the Rastells had produced in the early 1530s. This collection begins with a prominent dedication to Mary as 'quene of Englande, Spayne, Fraunce, both Sicilles, Jerusalem, and Ireland, defendour of the fayth, Archeduchesse of Austria, Duchesse of Burgondy, Myllayne, and Brabant, Countesse of Ha[b]spurge, Flaunders, and Tyroll'. Extolling More's writings for their 'great eloquence, excellent learninge, and morall virtue', Rastell explains that he was motivated to 'diligently collect and gather together, as many of those his workes, bokes, letters, and other writinges, printed and unprinted in the English tonge' to save them for posterity. In particular, he articulates the pious hope that this volume 'shall much helpe forward youre Majesties most godly purpose, in purging this youre realme of all wicked heresies' (2^{r-v}). Even though the editor aimed this book at a readership not literate in Latin, it does contain some Latin commendatory verse at the beginning and Latin originals of some of More's prison writings at the end. The frontmatter includes a 'table of the workes and thinges conteyned' (2nd 3^r), keyed to pages and alphabetical letters, and a 'table of many matters' (2nd 4^r) geared to helping readers locate specific ideas, such as 'Pilgrimage is a spiritual exercyse', 'the Pope is not above the generall counsayle', and 'Pore people may be releved with the goods of the church' (2nd 7^v).

The controversialists with whom More sparred won the propaganda war, at least at the level of book publication in the vernacular. The period between his execution in 1535 and Mary's death in 1558 saw only three of his books go into print other than Rastell's edition of his collected works. The absence of religious controversy in *Utopia* rendered permissible its publication in translation (1551) under Edward VI's Protestant regime; a second edition appeared in 1556; and within months of Edward's death, Tottel published Rastell's edition of a devotional work that More wrote during imprisonment, *A Dialogue of Comfort*. In contrast to this near-total eclipse, the interval between Tyndale's burning (1536) and Elizabeth I's accession witnessed the publication of nearly 150 books written or translated by Tyndale, Frith, Barnes, Roy, and Joye, the majority printed during Edward's reign. About 60 per cent were by Tyndale.[8]

When Mary's death drove William Rastell and many co-religionists into renewed exile on the Continent, Elizabeth's accession allowed the return of Protestant exiles. Among them was Foxe, who would collaborate with his publisher, John Day, on *The Whole Works of W. Tyndale, John Frith, and Doct[or] Barnes* (1573). It pays homage to these leading reformers—these 'chiefe ryngleaders' (A2^r)—in the manner of Rastell's edition of More's English works. Foxe worked with Day on this project after they had produced the first and second editions of *Acts and Monuments* (1563, 1570). While rewriting his life of Tyndale for the second edition of this influential ecclesiastical history, Foxe indicates that he builds upon Day's project of collecting Tyndale's non-translation prose:

He wrote also divers other workes under sundrye titles, among the which is that most worthy monument of hys intituled, the obedience of a Christian man [...] with dyvers other treatises: as of the wicked Mammon: the practise of Prelates, with expositions upon certayne partes of the Scripture, and other bookes also aunswering to Syr Thomas More and other adversaires of the truth, no lesse delectable, then also most fruitfull to be reade.

A shrewd businessman, Day knew that his forthcoming collection represented a highly saleable commodity. Nevertheless, he shared Rastell's imperative of rescuing

---

[8] Derived from ESTC, these figures are crude but instructive.

pious writings from oblivion, according to Foxe's notation concerning this forthcoming collection:

which partely yet beyng unknowen to many, partely also beyng almost abolished and worne out by tyme, the prynter herof intendeth (good reader) for conservyng & restoryng such singular treasures, shortly (God willing) to collecte and set forth in print the same in one generall volume all and whole together, as also the workes of Ioh. Frith, Barnes, and other, as shall seeme most speciall and profytable for thy reading. (1570: 3D2^v)

After Foxe recounts Tyndale's execution, another advertisement declares:

As concernyng the woorkes and bookes of Tyndall, whiche extende to a great number, thou wast told before (loving reader) how the Printer hereof myndeth by the Lordes leave, to collect them all in one Volume together, and put them out in print. (1570: 3D4^v)[9]

The trade in printing and, indeed, smuggling books exerted a profound influence on the course of the English Reformation. Although More, Tyndale, and other propagandists wrote and translated books in the vernacular for domestic consumption within England, it is essential to note they would have found it impossible to engage in their battle of books without relying on printers and shippers in continental Europe. The present investigation represents a tale of two cities because, to a considerable degree, London and Antwerp were the twin poles in a trade that flooded England with scriptural translations and Protestant polemics and, to a far lesser degree, More's defences of the old religion. Consideration of the publication of the important folio editions of More's works, on the one hand, and of Tyndale, Frith, and Barnes, on the other, represents a suitable terminus for the present consideration of the publication of religious controversy during the opening phase of the English Reformation. The wheel had turned full circle from the time when established London printers such as Pynson, Berthelet, and the Rastells published large-format books to disseminate august denunciations of new Lutheran ideas in the name of Henry VIII and the chief defenders of religious orthodoxy, More and Fisher. This activity coincided with the exiles of Tyndale, Frith, Barnes, Joye, and others who fled to a precarious haven in Antwerp, where marginal printers such as de Keyser courted imprisonment or execution when they produced dissident books written in a foreign language that their compositors were unlikely to understand. The employment of pseudonyms and facetious imprints and the production of readily concealed small-format books facilitated the smuggling of illicit print across the English Channel. During the brief interval when Mary returned England to the old religion, Tottel and his partners were able openly to publish writings by More that had fallen into disfavour after his execution in 1535. Her death and Elizabeth's accession then rendered it permissible, once again, for English readers to consume no-longer-heterodox books written by Tyndale and his co-religionists.

[9] For discussion of this editorial project, see J. King (2001: 64–81).

Primary Works

ARBLASTER, PAUL, GERGÉLY JUHÁSZ, and GUIDO LATRÉ, eds. (2002), *Tyndale's Testament* (Turnhout: Brepols).

ERASMUS, DESIDERIUS (1965), *Christian Humanism and the Reformation: Selected Writings*, ed. J. Olin (New York: Harper).

FOXE, JOHN (1563, 1570, 1576, 1583), *Actes and Monuments*, 1st–4th edns. [For complete transcriptions of these editions and commentary in progress, see *Foxe's Book of Martyrs Variorum Edition Online*, <http://www.hrionline.ac.uk/johnfoxe/index.html>]

—— (ed.) (1573), *The Whole Workes of W. Tyndale, John Frith, and Doct[or]. Barnes* (London: John Day).

FRITH, JOHN (1529), *An Epistle to the Christian Reader wherein are compared together Christ's Actes and Our Holy Father the Pope's* ([Antwerp]).

—— (1533), *A Boke [...] Answeringe unto M Mores Lettur* ([Antwerp]).

HENRY VIII (1521), *Assertio septem sacramentorum adversus Martinum Lutherum.*

MORE, THOMAS (1533*a*), *Apology.*

—— (1533*b*), *The Answer to the First Part of the Poisoned Book, Named the Supper of the Lord.*

—— (1963–85), *The Complete Works of St. Thomas More*, ed. Richard Sylvester et al., 15 vols (New Haven: Yale University Press).

The Praier and Complaynte of the Ploweman unto Christe (1997), ed. Douglas Parker (Toronto: University of Toronto Press).

A Proper Dyaloge, betwene a Gentillman and a Husbandman (1530) ([Antwerp]).

RASTELL, JOHN (1530), *A Newe Boke of Purgatory.*

ROY, WILLIAM (1529), *Exhortation to the Diligent Study of Scripture* ([Antwerp]).

[ST GERMAN, CHRISTOPHER?] (1532), *A Treatise Concernynge the Division betwene the Spirytualtie and Temporaltie.*

—— (1533), *Salem and Bizance.*

TYNDALE, WILLIAM (1528*a*), *The Parable of the Wycked Mammon* ([Antwerp]).

—— (1528*b*), *The Obedience of a Christen Man* ([Antwerp]).

—— (1848), *Doctrinal Treatises and Introductions to Different Portions of the Holy Scriptures*, Parker Society, 42.

—— (2000), *An Answere unto Sir Thomas Mores Dialoge*, ed. Anne M. O'Donnell and Jared Wicks (Washington: Catholic University of America Press).

—— and GEORGE JOYE (1533), *The Souper of the Lorde* ([Antwerp?]).

CHAPTER 7

RHETORIC, CONSCIENCE, AND THE PLAYFUL POSITIONS OF SIR THOMAS MORE

JAMES SIMPSON

BOOK 1 of *Utopia* (first published in 1516, in Latin) reports a debate between 'More' himself and Raphael Hythloday, a philosopher who, having returned from a visit to the island of Utopia, has a blueprint for the refoundation of western European societies. Despite his possession of this blueprint, however, Hythloday is unwilling to urge its application, since he has no faith in, and no time for, the machinations of political power. In particular, he has no time for rhetoric, since pure philosophy has a fundamental bias against rhetoric. Pure philosophy, that is, is disembodied and without place; it deals with abstract ideas, regardless of audience. Rhetoric, by contrast, is the art of persuasion: it urges the adoption of projects on specific, situated audiences, by specific, situated speakers. Rhetoric is intently focused on situation and place, whereas philosophy is utopian in the literal meaning of that word ('no-place').

In the course of the debate, which is itself very carefully situated in time and place (in the garden of the house where More stayed in Antwerp, during his embassy to Flanders in 1515), the question of rhetoric surfaces explicitly. Hythloday imagines a royal council session in which he would urge the example of the Macarians (neighbours of the Utopians): as a prophylactic against hoarding, the Macarians prohibit the King from keeping more than £1,000 in his coffers at any one time. Counsel such as this, Hythloday rightly avers, would fall on deaf ears. More agrees, but proposes in response a modified, rhetorically situated philosophical practice. Pure philosophy might be appropriate for private conversation among friends, but it has no place in the councils of power. Pure philosophy, delivered without regard to the interests and capacities of its audience, would, More argues, be no less absurd than a philosopher's appearance on stage in a comedy by Plautus. The slaves might be joking among themselves in a scene, when the philosopher suddenly, and absurdly, appears in the wrong place at the wrong time. There, even more absurdly, he declaims a philosophical passage from the pseudo-Senecan *Octavia*, about the Golden Age. Pure philosophy is almost by definition bad rhetoric, since it ignores what is perhaps the most fundamental rule of rhetoric, that of appropriateness, what rhetorical treatises called *convenientia*. A rhetorically inflected philosophy is aware of place and time. Generic decorum, and especially the decorum appropriate to theatrical performance, will be its model.

So the More figure rebuts Hythloday's purist, a-rhetorical stance by arguing that, at the councils of kings, there is 'no place' ('non est locus') for the academic philosophy that thinks that everything is suitable to every place. But there is another, more civil philosophy ('alia philosophia civilior'), more practical for statesmen, which 'knows its stage, adapts itself to the play in hand, and performs its role neatly and appropriately' ('quae suam novit scenam, eique sese accommodans, in ea fabula quae in manibus est, suas partes concinne et cum decoro tutatur'; 1965: 99).

This section of the More–Hythloday debate is, then, about rhetoric versus pure philosophy. The terms of the debate might seem merely genteel: the unworldly, unrhetorical philosopher might seem ridiculous declaiming his speech among the servants, just as the rhetorically adept councillor might seem at best ineffective and humiliated, reduced as he is to playing, however skilfully, in base comedies. The worst that might befall either is embarrassment. The stakes, however, are very much higher than this would suggest, since both positions entail huge risks, and both court violence of one kind or another. Revolutionary Hythloday's dismissal of rhetoric is correlative with his rejection of private property, since both rhetorical ap*prop*riateness and private *prop*erty respect particular jurisdictions within the commonwealth. Hythloday would, instead, appropriate all private property for the state, an inevitably violent revolution.

The life of the rhetorically proficient philosopher advising the monarch is not without its own terrors: when More imagines the philosopher's speech inappropriately declaimed in Plautus' comedy, he refers to a specific speech, the 'passage from the *Octavia* where Seneca is disputing with Nero' (99). This reference is in fact chilling, since *Octavia* is a play bathed in blood, in which Nero, who has murdered his mother and will murder his concubine, arranges for the murder of his wife. Seneca's part is nostalgically to remember the Golden Age as a time of ideal justice, just before his royal pupil Nero enters to order the heads of two 'friends'. At the heart of More's crucial argument for participation in government stands the example of the Stoic Seneca, whose suicide is the only viable response to his pupil's violence (Simpson 2002: 194).

The stakes in both 'More's' and Hytholoday's positions are high, and both positions had their historical fulfilment within half a generation of *Utopia's* composition: the English state did violently appropriate private property on a massive scale between 1536 and 1539 (the suppression of the monasteries), and More, along with a number of other councillors, was executed by the very king who appointed them. More, who was considering entry into royal service as he composed *Utopia*, knew from early on that this was a dangerous game. According to William Roper's biography of his father-in-law, *The Life of Sir Thomas More* (written *c*.1557, printed 1626), More often found himself on precarious ground from the moment he entered Henry's service in 1518. Congratulated by Roper sometime around 1525 for his familiarity with Henry, More acknowledged the King's singular favour, though also accurately predicted its distinct limits: 'For if my head could win him a castle in France [...] it should not fail to go' (Roper 1962: 208).

Rhetorical practice always implies social positioning, since rhetoric specifies the verbal rules for addressing and persuading particular groups, whether defined by age, gender, expertise, social class, religion, or any combination thereof. These social groupings produce a kind of theatricality in the speaker, whereby the orator plays certain roles for the time of the address. More, I argue in this chapter, is most at home in playing parts, exercising rhetoric from known positions to which he is certainly committed one way or another, but with which he cannot be wholly identified. He occupies positions, that is, each of which 'knows its stage, adapts itself to the play in hand, and performs its role neatly and appropriately' (More 1965: 99). He works best wearing the mask of the player. We enjoy his personality in the etymological sense of that word, which derives from the actor's mask through which the voice resounds (*per-sonare*).

As we shall see, however, the possibilities for rhetorical play consistently drain from More's position across his career. This is not so much because More himself takes on roles well outside the range of his position as secular lawyer, although he certainly does do that. It is rather because More experienced an increasingly menacing social environment, which demanded total, sincere, unequivocal, and consistent commitment to, and identification with, single positions. More was at his best in a culture of expert, shifting, rhetorical play, but found himself in a world that increasingly demanded unbending commitment. He ended up (or nearly ended up) the victim of unplayful philosophical and theological consistency under the punishing demands of 'conscience'. This chapter is, then, less about the positions More adopted than the ways in which he adopted them; it is less about philosophy or theology than about rhetoric. Before we can understand the roles More played, however, it is first necessary to have some sense of the shape of More's writing career, and the social and intellectual roles he might have been expected to play.

I

Educated at St Anthony's School, London, before proceeding to Oxford (via a period in the household of Cardinal John Morton, Archbishop of Canterbury and Lord Chancellor), More was by 1494 a student at the Inns of Court in London. Throughout his time as a law student (until *c*.1501), he learned Greek; mixed with scholars promoting humanist learning; and, from around 1500, he lived at or near the London Charterhouse, taking daily part in Carthusian spiritual exercises. By 1499 he had met the humanist scholar Desiderius Erasmus, with whom he enjoyed a warm friendship. Erasmus began his *Moriae Encomium* (*Praise of Folly/More*) while staying with More in 1509. Already in 1506 an edition of translations, from Greek into Latin, by both men had been published in Paris (More 1974). More's contribution consists of four witty dialogues translated from Lucian deflating philosophical ideals. More's interest in philosophy at this time is also evinced by his life of Pico della Mirandola in 1510, the year in which he was appointed under-sheriff of London. The life of Pico (in English) provides a model of scholarly contemplation, removed from the distractions of and engagements in the world. Offered promotion by a king, Pico replies that 'he neithir desired worship ne worldly richess but rather set them at nought that he might the more quietly give him self to studie and the service of god' (1997: 66). This period also saw More compose a panegyric, in Latin, and a series of largely political epigrams (both published in 1518). The panegyric was composed for the coronation of Henry VIII on 24 June 1509. More hails his future executioner with eulogies of many kinds, including praise for having imprisoned informers: 'Qui delator erat, vinclis constringitur arctis' (1984: 106; 'He who was an informer is bound in tight chains'). A number of the epigrams, meanwhile, express disgust for tyranny, a motif also found in More's unfinished *History of King Richard III* (1513–18), in both Latin and English. This brilliant text is a model of Tacitean annalistic narrative, syntactically terse and ethically open-eyed about the horrific and violent manipulations of Richard III (1483–5), the last pre-Tudor king.

More's examinations of power, inspired by classical models and using humanist genres (such as dialogue), continued with his Latin *Utopia*. Book 1 debates the pros and cons of intellectual service to royal administrations, whereas book 2 provides the blueprint for an 'ideal' society. In the period 12 May–24 October 1515, when book 2 was composed (before book 1),[1] More also published a letter to Martin van Dorp, a Louvain theologian who had criticized Erasmus' *Moriae Encomium*, in which More defends Erasmian satire and Christian humanism on the one hand, and rejects the arid procedures of scholastic theology on the other (More 1986). More's commitment to the ideals of Erasmian humanism is also demonstrated through the especial care he took to ensure that his three daughters were seriously educated along with his one son. The famous Holbein portrait of More's extended family, executed in 1526–7, of which only a sketch survives (Figure 7.1), portrays all but

---

[1] For the compositional order of *Utopia*, see Hexter (1952).

FAMILIA THOMÆ MORI ANGL.CANCELL.

Thomas Morus A°.50. Alicia Thomæ Mori uxor A°.57. Johannes Morus pater A°.76.Johannes Morus Thomæ filius A°.19 Anna Grisacria Johannes Mori Sponsa A°.15. Margareta Ropera Thomæ Mori filia A°.22.
Elisabeta Dauncia Thomæ Mori filia A°.21. Cecilia Heronia Thomæ Mori filia A°.20. Margareta Giga Clementis uxor Mori filiolus Conductipula et cognata A°.22.Henricus Patenfonus Thomæ Mori servus A°.40.

Fig. 7.1 *Design for More Family Group* (1526–7) by Hans Holbein the Younger.

two of the six women of the More household with books in hand (Foister 2006: 34–6).

Utopia debated the merits and demerits of royal service. Soon after its publication, More's own political career took off: by 1518 he was a member of Henry VIII's council; he was knighted in 1521 and appointed Speaker in the House of Commons in 1523. Throughout the late 1520s More served in demanding secretarial functions between Henry and the Lord Chancellor, Thomas Wolsey. After Wolsey's fall, More became Lord Chancellor himself in 1529, the first lay person to hold that office. One of the functions that he actively pursued as Lord Chancellor was persecution and prosecution of Lutheran heresy, but he had been engaged against Martin Luther and Lutheranism from the early 1520s. He may well have contributed to Henry's own theological tract against Lutheranism, the *Assertio Septem Sacramentorum* (1521), but More's *Responsio ad Lutherum* (two editions, both 1523) is his first clear contribution to the controversy, even if he sets up rather elaborate screens of alternative, fictional authorship in both versions. In the *Responsio*, after some strikingly vituperative preliminaries, More attacks Luther's understanding of the literal sense of Scripture; Lutheran ecclesiology as being without location, in 'some place and no place'

(More 1969: i. 167); Lutheran soteriology (the doctrine of salvation); and Lutheran sacramental theology.

Throughout the 1520s, following the *Responsio*, More actively pursued Lutheran heresy (see Simpson 2007, chs 2, 7). Neither Wolsey, John Fisher (Bishop of Rochester), nor Cuthbert Tunstal (Bishop of London) had pursued Lutherans with much legal rigour (D'Alton 2003). More, by contrast, was at the forefront of the fight against English Lutheranism and William Tyndale's vernacular Scriptures. High Steward of Cambridge from late 1525, More was vigorous in pursuit of Lutheranism both in that university (where Lutheran theology found the most receptive audience) and in London. In December 1525 he personally led the first of two raids on the London house of the Hanseatic merchants, seeking to enforce the ban on Lutheran books. At the subsequent ceremony at St Paul's in January 1526, four merchants were forced to abjure their heresies on pain of death; Lutheran books were burned; and Robert Barnes, who had preached a reformist sermon in Cambridge on Christmas Eve 1525, was forced to bear a faggot.

From 1526, however, the target of official repression was not only Lutheranism, but also, much more challengingly, vernacular Scripture. Itemized Lutheran opinions had been banned in England by Wolsey since 1521 (Wilkins 1737: iii. 690–3; Loades 1991: 110–11), but by 1527 specific books were officially proscribed. A list of books to be handed in under pain of excommunication in 1527 included *The New Testament of Tyndale* (1526), along with other polemical books by Tyndale and other evangelicals (Wilkins 1737: iii. 711). In 1528 the authorities relied on More for his forensic skill and, unusually for a layman, theological knowledge to answer the Lutheran challenge in English. Tunstal promulgated a licence for More to read books adjudged heretical, imported from Germany but translated into English, in order that he, More, should compose a reply for the simple and unlearned ('simplicibus et idiotis hominibus'; Wilkins: iii. 711–12). The result was More's remarkable *Dialogue Concerning Heresies* (1529), a work written less for the simple and unlearned than for the subtle and reflective. This is More's most deeply considered and carefully structured defence of orthodoxy. The text pretends to record a conversation between Chancellor More and a gifted young scholar of potentially Lutheran persuasion, in which More persuades his young interlocutor of the dangers of the new religion. Book 1 begins with a nexus of orthodox practices to which evangelicals objected (pilgrimages, images, and belief in miracles), before moving onto More's central preoccupation, the status of Scripture. Book 2 tackles Lutheran ecclesiology. Books 3 and 4 are topical, dealing with contemporary issues of heresy in England and continental Europe respectively. The book ends with a defence of the persecution of heretics past and present, even unto the stake. More's campaign against heresy continued with his moving *Supplication of Souls* (1529), a response to Simon Fish's *Supplication for the Beggars* (1528). In this text More argues as if through the voices of those in Purgatory, pleading with readers not to accept Fish's argument that Purgatory is a mere fiction.

By 1529, however, More had replaced Wolsey as Lord Chancellor. In this office, he oversaw two lists of banned books in 1530, each naming translations of the New Testament ('translatio Novi Testamenti'). The first of these also includes *The Chapters of Moses, Called Genesis*, and *The Chapters of Moses, Called Deuteronomy*, clearly Tyndale's freshly available translations from the Hebrew Scriptures, published in 1530. It was also More (as Lord Chancellor) who devised the procedure whereby heretical offenders would be tried in the secular court of Star Chamber, rather than before an ecclesiastical court. He imprisoned men for owning books, and engineered the arrest of several book handlers; six Lutherans were burned under More's chancellorship between 1529 and 1532 (*ODNB*; Simpson 2007, ch. 8).

More's chancellorship coincided with the summoning, in late 1529, of what came to be known as the Reformation Parliament. From the beginning, More's chancellorship was thus subject to buffets from administrative and ideological storms, the increasing turbulence of which was provoked by Henry VIII's marital problems. When it became obvious that the pressure of those storms was to produce Caesaro-papism in England, More resigned his chancellorship (on 16 May 1532, specifically in protest at the submission of bishops in Convocation to the King's authority). More was not, however, resigned to any failure in his polemical campaign against Lutherans for the Church's prerogatives.

Defence of those prerogatives became much more dangerous for More, precisely because royal policy was now itself one of More's potential targets, and More was one of the targets of royal policy. Nonetheless, he continued to produce quantities of polemic. In 1532 he published the first part of the huge *Confutation of Tyndale's Answer*; the second part appeared in 1533. This sprawling work attacked English Lutheranism on the following fronts: the sacraments; clerical marriage; Tyndale's translation of Scripture; unwritten traditions; the grounds of scriptural authority; ecclesiology; and councils. In December 1532 he wrote against John Frith's Zwinglian understanding of the Eucharist, in the *Letter against Frith* (published late 1533). Throughout 1533, in *The Apology* and *The Debellation of Salem and Bizance*, he devoted himself to rebutting the arguments of Christopher St German in favour of moderate ecclesiastical reform, and in favour of restrictions on the Church's jurisdiction over heresy cases. His last polemical book, also written in 1533, was *The Answer to a Poisoned Book* (published 1534), again defending what he saw as the orthodox position on the Eucharist. Throughout the time between 1529 and 1533, then, More was not only, for most of this period, occupied at the highest administrative levels. He was also staggeringly active as a writer on a very wide polemical front (Schuster 1973). More fought at first as a learned layman in defence of the status quo, and finally as a marked man in defence of what had become a treasonous position.

The fragility of More's position, especially after his resignation as Lord Chancellor, necessitated legal adroitness. In February 1534 he was implicated in the campaign against Elizabeth Barton ('the maid of Kent'), whose published visionary revelations had been critical of the King's divorce. More escaped that charge, despite the King's desire to incriminate him, but there was no escaping the Oath of Supremacy. In April 1534, by Roper's plausible account, More still saw some legal resources by which he might evade imprisonment, since, in his estimation, the oath was not consonant with the 1534 Act of Supremacy (Roper 1962: 240). This avenue of escape proved illusory, however, as Thomas Audley (More's successor as Lord Chancellor) and Thomas

Cromwell introduced a new statute for the confirmation of the oath, amplified with their additions.

On 17 April 1534, having refused to swear to the Act of Succession, More was imprisoned. Before entering prison he composed his *Treatise on the Passion*. Once in the Tower he composed two works of spiritual reflection and comfort, the *De Tristitia Christi* (*Concerning the Sadness of Christ*) and the extraordinary *Dialogue of Comfort against Tribulation*, designed to strengthen and stabilize the soul under persecution and threat of imminent death.

Despite arguments that should have exculpated More from the charges of having 'maliciously, traitorously, and diabolically' denied the King to be Supreme Head of the Church (Roper 1962: 245), he was found guilty. Once convicted, More, in Roper's account, changed discourse: he no longer appealed to secular law, but rather to ecclesiology, in denying the right of Parliament to make laws appointing the King Supreme Head of the Church. More finally abandoned argument of any kind, and instead expressed a wish. He imagines a future reconciliation between himself and his judges: just as Paul was present at the stoning of Stephen as one of his persecutors, now Paul and Stephen are saints together in heaven; so too, More says to his judges, he hopes that 'we may yet hereafter in heaven merrily all meet together' (Roper 1962: 250).

Eight letters to More's daughter Margaret—on whom he most relied for, and to whom he most gave, emotional, spiritual, and philosophical comfort while in prison—survive from his final days. In the last of these, written on 5 July 1535, the eve of his execution, More comforts his daughter by transforming brutality into a kind of part fitly played: 'For', he says, 'it is S. Thomas evin [...] and therefore to morowe longe I to goe to God, it were a daye very meete and conveniente for me.' To this idea of a part well played he suddenly adds a picture of unstudied filial affection, expressed *without* regard to appropriateness: 'I never liked your maner towarde me better then when you kissed me laste, for I love when doughterly love and deere charitie hathe no laisor to looke to worldely curtesye' (Rogers 1947: 564). More was beheaded at the Tower of London the following day.

II

More's writing career, then, falls into three distinguishable phases: a humanist phase from 1506 to 1516; a polemical, anti-Lutheran phase from 1520 to 1533; and a devotional phase from 1534 to 1535. This career was, moreover, shaped by the varying pressures of discursive novelty: in philology (for example, the return to sources and the introduction of Greek learning into England); in literature (for example, 'new' literary texts entering the current of European literary culture, translated from Greek); in philosophy (for example, active reading in Greek, especially Platonic texts); in theology (by Lutheranism); and in spirituality (by the *devotio moderna*, most persuasively expressed by Erasmian Christian humanism). More was exceptionally well read in all these disciplines, and an active contributor to the last four, despite being neither a professional poet, philosopher, theologian, nor priest (More tells us in a prefatory letter to *Utopia* that the only time he gets for study is what he 'can filch from sleep and food'; More 1965: 41). His primary professional activity was instead in law and civil service. He rarely abandoned that legal perspective in any of his writings, all of which are consistently characterized by legal acumen. As a writer, More is always acutely sensitive to the prerogatives and limits of jurisdictions (Cormack 2007); sharply conscious of the reliability of both historical and contemporary witness; and ever ready to invent arguments that unsettle established ways of looking at situations, in the manner of a brilliant legal advocate. In the *Dialogue of Comfort*, for example, More (writing from the Tower) argues his way through to a Stoic inversion of the terms 'liberty' and 'imprisonment': if the 'straightest kept' prisoner 'get the wisdom and the grace to quiet his own mind and hold himself content with that place', he is 'at his free liberty to be where he will and so is out of prison too' (1977: 268).

The pressures of these new discursive possibilities did not carry More in the same direction. On the contrary, at different points of his career, he was pushed into positions that were wholly contradictory one with the other. In *Utopia*, for example, he entertained the idea of religious toleration. Very soon after his conquest of the island King Utopus issues a decree 'that it should be lawful for every man to favor and follow what religion he would' (271). By 1529, in contrast, More actively defended the persecution of heretics. Or, to take another example of contradiction across More's career, in 1515 he defended the satire of Erasmus' delightful *Moriae Encomium* to Martin van Dorp, who had criticized it. The wicked deserve chastisement, says More, and especially so when the correction is 'more decorously and less violently [achieved] by assuming the character of Folly' (1986: 107). By the 1532 *Confutation*, More's understanding of the *Moriae Encomium* had changed utterly. In that text More broaches the contemporary force of Erasmus' text, twenty or so years after its composition. He begins by insisting on its literary quality, saying that 'Moria doth indeed but jest upon the abuses' of the Church, 'after the manner of a disour's [jester's] part in a play'. However, by the 1530s the discursive environment has changed and narrowed from when Erasmus wrote the work: given the infectious poison of heresy, 'men cannot almost now speak of such things in so much as a play, but that such evil hearers wax a great deal worse' (1973: i. 178). So More now declares himself ready to burn 'not only my darling's books [i.e. those of Erasmus], but mine own also', given the readiness of readers to read them amiss. More would 'help to burn them both with mine own hands' (1973: i. 179).

Partly as a result of these differences of position; partly because More was addressing different audiences, in different languages, in different genres across his career; and partly because More's 'positions' are in any case not always securely identifiable with the historical More: for all these reasons More's reception in cultural history has been wildly divergent. More must be the only figure in English history who has

been both hailed by the Left—for promoting the abolition of private property in
Utopia (Kautsky 1959)—and sanctified by the Roman Catholic Church (in 1935). The
deepest source of conflict in the historical reception of More is unquestionably, however, the profound divisions in English cultural history opened up by Henry VIII's
repudiation of the Roman Church. To Catholics, More is a hero; to the evangelical
tradition, his is a closed and persecutory Catholic temper. There are complicated
subsets of these positions: to champions of English liberties against tyrannical abuse
of power, More is an English hero; to many liberals, he is an illiberal censor and manic
persecutor.[2]

III

In the last section of this chapter I attempt no account whatsoever of More's 'positions', partly because that is impossible in so short a space. More to the point, looking
for stable 'positions' in More can obscure the more interesting fact that he resisted,
even if he had almost to succumb, to the very notion of taking 'positions' in the first
place. His deeper instinct was to play. In the space remaining, then, I will broach the
formal question of More's playfulness and the closing down of textual play in the
name of explicit single positions, identifiable with conscience.[3]

The play *Sir Thomas More*, written, censored, and revised by various hands including that of William Shakespeare by 1605 (though never, apparently, performed),
represents More as above all a Londoner. At one point Lord Chancellor More and
his wife entertain the Lord Mayor of London and his wife for dinner. Players offer a
choice of interlude, and More chooses one called *The Marriage of Wit and Wisdom*.
One of the players, a certain Luggins, has, however, run off to get a beard for Wit, and
is therefore missing when due to give his lines. More adroitly rescues the situation by
stepping up among the players; the role he assumes is that of Good Counsel, warning
Wit not to mistake Vanity for Wisdom:

> Wit, judge not things by the outward show:
> The eye oft mistakes, right well you do know.
> Good Counsel assures thee upon his honesty
> That this is not Wisdom, but lady Vanity.
>
> (Munday et al. 1990: 3. 3. 274–7)

This little scene is nothing if not situated advice: the play is itself giving a contentious
history lesson about the quality of More's counsel to a Tudor audience, seventy or so
years after the event. It embeds that advice in various layers of theatrical 'situatedness',

---

[2] The best recent account of More's historical and contemporary reception is Guy (2000).

[3] For More's strategic playfulness, see Greenblatt (1980: 11–73). For a broader account of the closing
down of fiction in the 1530s and 1540s, see Fox (1989).

since it is a play within a play, full of apparently ludicrous or old-fashioned absurdities. The interlude is itself one such old-fashioned 'absurdity'; just as that old, but not so old, mode is capable of bearing significant truths, however, so too does the play itself remind its audience of the contemporary significance of More's courageous and adroit counsel, theatrically delivered.

This scene in the Elizabethan *Thomas More* is evoking, no doubt deliberately, an attribute of More recorded in Roper's biography and repeated by Nicholas Harpsfield: when More served in the household of Cardinal Morton as a boy, he would, at the Christmas play, 'suddenly sometimes step in among the players, and never studying for the matter, make a part of his own there presently among them, which made the lookers-on more sport than all the players beside' (Roper 1962: 198; cf. Harpsfield 1932: 10–11). More's understanding of role-playing was not without a sense of philosophical tradition, and neither was it ignorant of the dangers of stepping too far into the brutal power-plays of the mighty. His translation of Lucian registers early on the importance of always remembering that our parts in life are only ever borrowed; we must not grumble when Fortune demands our costumes back (More 1974: 176–7). And his *History of Richard III* makes understanding of the dangers of political theatre a commonplace. After Richard III pretends not to want, but finally accepts, the crown, the bystanders disperse, wondering why he did not accept it at the first offer, when he so obviously wanted it. A shrewd though cautious popular witness explains that this is all theatre, and it is best not to break the play, for fear of having one's head broken on 'scaffolds' (meaning stages for both theatre and execution): 'And so they said these matters be Kynges games, as it were stage playes, and for the more part plaied upon scafoldes. In which pore men be but the lokers on. And thei that wise be, wil medle no farther' (1963b: 80–1). The 'overheard' voice has the luxury of not being forced onto the stage, and of willingly choosing not to step up onto the tightly constrained and dangerous performance area.

The need for discursive liberty and variety clearly preoccupied More from his earliest writings. In all the extensive humanist works (the Lucian translation, the biography of Pico, and *Utopia*), More is playing through various positions, calibrating the distance from power, and eyeing available escape routes. Lucian encourages detachment from the pretensions of power; Pico's example encourages abdication from power; and Utopia's Hythloday actively repudiates engagement in power. The very spaces of More's life also suggest a person who is most at ease in a culturally divided space: as he studied law (1494–*c*.1501), he participated in the devotional life of Carthusians, when living at or near the London Charterhouse; and his family home at Chelsea, set at a distance from both Westminster and London, was itself a divided space. The building for study and devotion was set apart from the main house (Harpsfield 1932: 65; R. W. Chambers 1935: 175–91).

For all his sensitivity to cultural thresholds, or perhaps because of that sensitivity, More stepped across such boundaries with great frequency. Above all, he played the role of theologian between 1523 and 1533. Most of the so-called 'controversialists' (apologists for Catholic orthodoxy in the fight against Lutheranism) were theologians; they wrote in Latin; and they wrote only one treatise, precisely because it was dangerous to attack Luther under a papal curia that did not support and, astonishingly, was ready to distrust those who engaged in the dispute (Bagchi 1989). In each respect, More differs from the other controversialists. He was not a theologian, nor even a priest; he wrote the majority of his works against Lutheran doctrine in the vernacular; and he wrote many more than one anti-Lutheran tract (Simpson 2007, ch. 7). In this More is forcefully putting into action a model of the 'mixed life', best formulated in English by Walter Hilton in the fourteenth century, though on a scale not envisaged by Hilton. Faced with a much more articulate laity—a laity, indeed, that had been formed by the vast programme of lay instruction initiated by the fourth Lateran Council of 1215—Hilton (1994) articulated a form of life balancing the active and contemplative, staying in the world but nevertheless making room for retirement and spiritual reflection. In all his writings against Luther, More writes as a layman stepping into ecclesiastical jurisdictions, without ever forgetting that he is a layman.

Even as More plays this role, however, he is aware that it is no game from which he can easily retire after playing his part. His brief in the *Responsio ad Lutherum* was clearly to adopt a posture of vituperation. Even as he does so, however, he feels soiled by the encounter. He is, he says, 'shamed even of this necessity, that while I clean out the fellow's shit-filled mouth I see my own fingers covered with shit' (1969: i. 313). This defilement suggests a position well beyond anything playful, a point from which it is difficult to return and to change roles. This suggestion becomes much more forceful across More's polemical career. Already in the *Responsio*, More's room for manoeuvre is narrowing, not least because, as he says in the *Responsio* itself, his enemy Luther is hostile to rhetoric, and hostile to the notion of demarcated places and functions upon which rhetorical practice depends, with its attention to the appropriateness of what is said (and how things are said) to time, place, and audience.

More had himself predicted the abolition of place in his own 'no-place' text, *Utopia*. For the fundamental assumption of the Utopian polity is that private interests are necessarily pathological, and that decisions are to be based not merely on community, but on identical interest. Apart from the absence of private property, the most obvious sign of the abolition of privacy is the indistinguishability of urban spaces and constant surveillance of all citizens. Cities may be larger or smaller, but they all observe the same plan; the fifty-four cities are each 'identical in language, traditions, customs, and laws' (1965: 113). Private houses are alike and interchanged; doors have no locks and give admittance to anyone; meals are taken in common, overseen by the magistrate and with the young set among the old, so that 'nothing can be done or said at table which escapes the notice of the old present on every side' (143).

This imagination of a polity that attempts to do away with place, and certainly to abolish demarcated spaces, is exactly what More faces as he confronts Luther's concept of the Church. More describes Luther's Church as 'somehow imperceptible and mathematical—like Platonic ideas—which is in some place and in no place' ('et in loco sit, et in nullo loco sit'; 1969: i. 167). And Luther himself actively militates against a rhetorically situated Church, arguing as he does that the Church addresses the priesthood of all believers in all places in the same way. In his *Bondage of the Will*, for example, Luther stridently dismisses a rhetorical understanding of Scripture.

He lambastes Erasmus for wishing to consider the 'times, persons, and ways in which the truth ought to be spoken' (1969: 132). By Luther's account Scripture is no respecter of persons: it speaks in the same way to all people in all places and all times. The young man with whom More argues in the *Dialogue Concerning Heresies* articulates this placeless Church: the True Church is everywhere and nowhere: 'it needeth not to assygne any place where the very chyrche and true crysten congregacyon is'. Every place is, the young man affirms, 'indyfferent' to the Church (1981: i. 196).

As More fights that placeless, anti-rhetorical concept of the Church, however, he begins to speak himself in the voice of an orthodoxy that is placeless and absolute. For in dealing with his enemies' concept of the Church, More contracts an anti-rhetorical and literalist virus from them. Not only is he reduced to quoting the works of his opponents verbatim, but, as he laboriously does so, he knows he is losing the fight against them (Headley 1969: ii. 804–10). In the *Confutation of Tyndale's Answer*, for example, More is sensitive to the charge that he has attacked the 'bad brethren' with textual partiality, 'that I do but pick out pieces at my pleasure, such as I may most easily seem to soyle [deal with, refute], and leave out what me list' (More 1969: i. 5). More denies the charge: when necessary, he cites in full, 'as of all their own words I leave not one syllable out' (i. 6). Even as he defends this procedure, the rhetorician in More recognizes that it is a lost argument: almost everyone, including his enemies, complain that his books are too long and tedious. He would have made his book much shorter, but it is easier, he says, to write a short heresy than briefly to refute one. The reader might go astray if at any one point he were not armed with all he needed to know, so 'the labour of all that length is mine own, for ease and shortening of the reader's pain' (i. 8).

More sounds remarkably like his evangelical opponents here, sinking into a painful, demanding and endless textual world as he is. Extra-textual talk for More is, now, only dangerous and negative: 'bold, erroneous talking is almost in every lewd lad's mouth' (1969: i. 11); he is surrounded by 'some say', hearsay, and its near homophone 'heresy'.[4] He is hemmed in and threatened by malicious utterances: 'these heretics be so busily walking, that in every ale house, in every tavern, in every barge, and almost every boat, as few as they be a man shall always find some, and there be they so busy with their talking' (1969: i. 159, 160). All that is left for More is to produce texts that suppress all this unregulated speech in demarcated spaces.

More, indeed, feels that talk is now a contagion. In *The Answer to a Poisoned Book*, for example, he says that the words exchanged in the treatment of heresy are themselves a way of catching the disease. If, More says in the Prologue to that book, the faithful were as loath to hear Lutheran heresy as to speak it, then they would 'hate and detest and abhor utterly the pestilent contagion of all such smoky communication' (1985: 3). In the *Answer*, the heresy problem has become primarily verbal: it is through the 'evil communication' that 'the contagion crepeth forth and corrupteth further, in

---

[4] For More's analysis and repudiation of the tactic of airing contentious issues in the voice of others, by introducing them with 'some say', see More (1979: 86–8, 94, 104).

the manner of a corrupt cancer' (4). We should therefore be very cautious in dealing with heretics, lest we succumb to the sickness, as 'the pestilence catcheth sometime the leech [doctor] that fasting cometh very near and long sitteth by the sick man busy about to cure him' (5).

The most obvious symptom of More's abandonment of a situated rhetoric is his rejection of fiction and personae in the polemical works of 1532–3. In most of More's works up to the *Confutation of Tyndale's Answer*, More adopts masks and voices. He sometimes prefaces works with an elaborate screen of fictional letters situating the written text to follow. Even where he appears in his own voice, as in *Utopia*, for example, secure identification of More with 'More' is impossible, not least because More is often ironic. Irony is itself a way of creating alternative spaces within works, and More enjoys playing with the Greek sense of *moros* (fool). He is quoted, for example, in a letter dated August 1534 to his daughter from prison: 'But I trust my Lorde rekeneth me amonge the foles, and so reken I my selfe, as my name is in Greke. And I finde, I thanke God, causes not a fewe, wherefore I so shulde in very dede' (Rogers 1947: 519).

After having abandoned fictional voices and coherent, imagined scenarios in the polemical works after the *Dialogue Concerning Heresies*, it is perhaps significant that More should be recalling the unstable possibilities embedded in his name in the Tower, since his great Tower work, the *Dialogue of Comfort*, does return to fictional voices and environments. The dialogue is set in Hungary in a very precisely imagined scene: the year is 1527–8, just before the 'permanent occupation of Buda by the Turks in the spring of 1529' (Fox 1982: 226). The parallels with the 'great Turk' and Henry VIII are unavoidable though not exhaustive, and it is also clear that the fight is lost. This work is imagined as a dialogue between Vincent and his uncle Antony. The older man gives heart and steadiness to the younger as they await the certain invasion of their fierce enemy, whose most terrifying assaults are imagined as the attacks of the 'midday devil', who can be easily seen 'with the eye of the faithful soul by his fierce, furious assault and incursion' (More 1977: 205).

Even as More finds the inner resources to confront the experience of prison and imminent death with composure, however, his situation cannot help but reveal that the spaces for which and from which he had fought so vigorously have changed completely. The very fact that the lay More writes an *ars moriendi* in the *Dialogue of Comfort*, with no priestly input, and in which the dying man offers the counsel, itself suggests the way in which orthodox late medieval spirituality has irretrievably laicized spiritual functions. Just as the lay More had written theology against Lutherans, so too he composes books of spiritual comfort as a layman. Even as More defends orthodoxy, he exposes its transformations. He reveals, that is, the effacement of boundary lines and distinct spaces. In the *Dialogue Concerning Heresies* More had disowned theological expertise: it is not for him to dispute of heresy, he says, but 'it best becometh a lay man to do in all thyngys lene and cleve to the comen fayth and byleve of crystys chyrche' (1981: i. 37). All More's polemical and devotional writings expose the hollowness of that affirmation: they all fill discursive vacuums left by ecclesiastical figures who should have been supplying them.

Even more tellingly, More's Church has abandoned him and his conscience. The Church within whose highly demarcated spaces More's conscience had been formed has now withdrawn. For More the word 'conscience' has all its etymological force, of a 'knowing together', a knowing shaped by collective experience. The conscience that he defends in prison is, however, a distinctively modern conscience, that individual moral force that is prepared to stand up against institutions. Whereas he discounts the individual standing alone against the testimony of the Church in the *Dialogue Concerning Heresies* (i. 153–62), in the Tower he finds himself in precisely this situation, defending the solitary testimony of his conscience against the decision of what had now proclaimed itself the English Church. In a very moving letter cited by his daughter Margaret, More adduces her argument that he is far outnumbered. In reply, in August 1534, More appeals not to fellow believers 'in this realme', but instead to Christendom at large, or to the community of the dead, who, he feels sure, thought as he, More, thinks. In this desolate, abandoned situation, More can appeal only to the solitary conviction of his conscience: 'But as concerninge mine owne self, for thy coumfort shall I say, Daughter, to the, that mine owne conscience in this matter (I damne none other mans) is such, as may well stand with mine owne salvacion' (Rogers 1947: 528). So far from defending the 'comen fayth and byleve of crystys chyrche', More courageously ends his life representing a distinctively modern, solitary form of conscience that closely resembles that of his courageous Lutheran enemies.[5]

Primary Works

Harpsfield, Nicholas (1932), *The Life and Death of Sir Thomas Moore, Knight, Sometime Lord High Chancellor of England*, ed. Elsie Vaughan Hitchcock, EETS, o.s. 186.

Henry VIII (1521), *Assertio septem sacramentorum adversus Martin Lutherum.*

Hilton, Walter (1994), *Epistle on the Mixed Life*, in Barry Windeatt (ed.), *English Mystics of the Middle Ages* (Cambridge: Cambridge University Press).

Luther, Martin (1969), *On the Bondage of the Will*, in E. Rupp, A. N. Gordon, Philip S. Watson, and B. Drewery (eds), *Luther and Erasmus: Free Will and Salvation* (Philadelphia: Westminster Press).

More, Thomas (1963a), *The Debellation of Salem and Bizance*, ed. John Guy, in *The Complete Works of St Thomas More*, x (New Haven: Yale University Press).

—— (1963b), *The History of King Richard III*, ed. Richard S. Sylvester, in *The Complete Works of St Thomas More*, ii (New Haven: Yale University Press).

—— (1965), *Utopia*, ed. Edward Surtz and J. H. Hexter, in *The Complete Works of St Thomas More*, iv (New Haven: Yale University Press).

—— (1969), *Responsio ad Lutherum*, ed. John M. Headley, 2 vols, in *The Complete Works of St Thomas More*, v (New Haven: Yale University Press).

[5] This brief discussion of conscience in More is indebted to two exceptionally penetrating essays: B. Cummings (2007); Strohm (forthcoming).

—— (1973), *The Confutation of Tyndale's Answer*, ed. Louis A. Schuster, Richard Marius, James P. Lusardi, and Richard J. Schoeck, 3 vols, in *The Complete Works of St Thomas More*, viii (New Haven: Yale University Press).

—— (1974), *Translations of Lucian*, ed. Craig R. Thompson, in *The Complete Works of St Thomas More*, iii/1 (New Haven: Yale University Press).

—— (1976a), *Treatise on the Passion; Treatise on the Blessed Body; Instructions and Prayers*, ed. Garry E. Haupt, in *The Complete Works of St Thomas More*, xiii (New Haven: Yale University Press).

—— (1976b), *De tristitia Christi*, ed. Clarence H. Miller, in *The Complete Works of St Thomas More*, xiv (New Haven: Yale University Press).

—— (1977), *A Dialogue of Comfort against Tribulation*, ed. Frank Manley, abr. edn (New Haven: Yale University Press).

—— (1979), *The Apology*, ed. J. B. Trapp, in *The Complete Works of St Thomas More*, ix (New Haven: Yale University Press).

—— (1981), *A Dialogue Concerning Heresies*, ed. T. M. C. Lawler, Germain Marc'hadour, and Richard Marius, 2 vols, in *The Complete Works of St Thomas More*, vi (New Haven: Yale University Press).

—— (1984), *Latin Poems*, ed. Clarence H. Miller, Leicester Bradner, Charles A. Lynch, and Revilo P. Oliver, in *The Complete Works of St Thomas More*, iii/2 (New Haven: Yale University Press).

—— (1985), *The Answer to a Poisoned Book*, ed. Stephen Merriam Foley and Clarence H. Miller, in *The Complete Works of St Thomas More*, xi (New Haven: Yale University Press).

—— (1986), *In Defense of Humanism: Letter to Martin Dorp, Letter to the University of Oxford, Letter to Edward Lee, Letter to a Monk*, ed. Daniel Kinney, in *The Complete Works of St Thomas More*, xv (New Haven: Yale University Press).

—— (1990), *Letter to Bugenhagen; Supplications of Souls; Letter against Frith*, ed. Frank Manley, Germain Marc'hadour, Richard Marius, and Clarence H. Miller, in *The Complete Works of St Thomas More*, vii (New Haven: Yale University Press).

—— (1997), *Life of Pico*, ed. A. S. G. Edwards, in *The Complete Works of St Thomas More*, i (New Haven: Yale University Press).

MUNDAY, ANTHONY, et al. (1990), *Sir Thomas More*, ed. Vittorio Gabrieli and Giorgio Melchiori (Manchester: Manchester University Press).

ROGERS, ELIZABETH FRANCES (ed.) (1947), *The Correspondence of Sir Thomas More* (Princeton: Princeton University Press).

ROPER, WILLIAM (1962), *The Life of Sir Thomas More*, in Richard S. Sylvester and Davis P. Harding (eds), *Two Early Tudor Lives* (New Haven: Yale University Press).

CHAPTER 8

JOHN BALE AND CONTROVERSY

READERS AND AUDIENCES

PETER HAPPÉ

JOHN BALE lived for almost sixty-eight years and our knowledge about his life is sufficiently detailed to allow us to be aware of its complexity. From his autobiographical writings and other sources we perceive a busy and enterprising man who experienced much in a period of intense social, political, cultural, and religious change. He was affected by these changes but he also contributed to them and I propose to examine his participation and his varied achievements by considering the many different audiences he addressed. I use the word 'audiences' because he is still well known for his dramatic works, but these are only a part of a much wider output in the pursuit of which he appealed to and addressed many readers of different types with different objectives. Moreover, the length of Bale's working life meant that changes occurred in what he needed to say to those receiving his works. It is also true that people do not always read in the same way and the nature of Bale's changing recipients proves illuminating. This approach reveals a degree of continuity and coherence in what he produced. Though his primary concern was salvation and the way to achieve it, his writings were aimed at readers of many types and they were conceived in markedly different circumstances. These aspects are reflected in the physical characteristics of his work, as we shall see, and Bale was interested in such matters as layout and illustration. We can perceive that Bale was addressing more than one target at the same time, introducing an aspect of simultaneity into the process of communication.

In order to keep track of how his written works fitted in to the many changes he experienced, I first outline the salient features of his life story. We can then review how the content of his work was directed to different recipients and consider how he sought to manage the preparation and presentation of his work by looking at the physical aspects of his books and manuscripts.

I

Born of poor parents at Cove in Suffolk in 1495, Bale was sent aged 12 to the Norwich Carmelite house. From there he went to Cambridge, where he studied for more than ten years as well as participating in the instruction of younger members of his order. During this period he travelled widely in Europe using the network of the Carmelite houses first in the Netherlands and then reaching as far south as Toulouse. Back at Cambridge he received the degree of Bachelor of Divinity in 1529, was licensed to preach in London, and began to assume positions of authority in his order as prior successively at Maldon, Ipswich, and Doncaster. In the early 1530s, the religious changes sparked by the divorce of Henry VIII led Bale to develop uncertainties about his position as a Carmelite. He turned Protestant by 1536 and his preaching began to attract official suspicion about its unorthodoxy (Fairfield 1976). The friar turned into a parish priest at Thorndon in Suffolk, marrying the 'faithful Dorothy' (Bale 1557: 703) in the following year.[1] But his conversion does not seem to have been a Pauline revelation but a rather more gradual process of change.

If we accept that Bale's conversion was complete by 1536, we must also note that he was now about 41 years old and that he had belonged to the Carmelite order for more than a quarter of a century. For many of those years he had been an active and loyal member and his first literary achievement is a series of documents which embody the progress and the fruits of a long period of studying its history. There are six surviving manuscripts, all in Latin, containing material from these years before his conversion.[2] Most of these are composite collections, individual parts of which can be dated from various kinds of internal evidence including some specific dates or references to events and the changing characteristics of Bale's handwriting over a period of up to twenty years. The majority of this work was written before his conversion and some of the collections are very large: Bodleian MS Selden supra 41 has approximately 800 pages and British Library Harley MS 3838 has 500. Sometimes they are referred to as notebooks, a description which reflects the fact that they often show a process of

---

[1] Very little is known of Dorothy, but she survived Bale by six years, living in Canterbury.
[2] Bodl., MSS Selden supra 41, supra 72, MS Bodley 73; BL, Harley MSS 1819, 3838; CUL, MS Ff.6.28.

accretion over a long period. We shall return to some of the details of these below: they have been analysed in comprehensive detail and examined for their chronology by Leslie P. Fairfield (1976; cf. W. Davies 1940: 205–7, 136–7; McCusker 1942: 97–110). They show that for many years Bale was interested in the history of the Carmelites and in many of its individual members. The contents included notes of the Carmelite past and a history of the Carmelite order as in MS Selden supra 41 (fols. 107–93). Part of this collection is much more than notes. Individual entries are rubricated, the names presented inside red circles and the items boxed in red, and marked with pilcrows, making it clear that Bale wanted a visual effect (see Figure 8.1). He included saints' lives, extracts from Carmelite authors, and catalogues of Carmelite Priors-General. His own biography appears on folio 195^r. However, his personal changes in religious orientation are also illustrated in these manuscripts. MS Harley 3838 contains two historical sketches, one about the legendary tradition of the order (fols. 118–55) and the other more factually with lives of distinguished members (fols. 156–249): both show the vigorously critical attitude towards celibacy and the monastic life which was an integral part of Bale's conversion, these sections being written later than the others.

During the 1530s as his conversion proceeded Bale's authorship became more varied. Apparently he had begun to compose plays before this change (Happé 1996: 5–6), but from about 1534 he began to write anti-Catholic plays and to take part in the performance of them. In 1537 he acknowledged support for this activity from the King's chief minister, Thomas Cromwell, who apparently saw the drama as a polemical weapon (Vanhoutte 1996: 49–77; Roberts 2002: 228). He was at one point imprisoned for his beliefs. However, his earlier industrious habits of accumulation and cataloguing, formerly devoted to the Carmelite order, now turned to another direction. The change embodied a somewhat ambivalent attitude to the monastic culture he was now castigating, for he recognized that in many of the libraries now threatened with pillage and dispersal there was untold intellectual wealth. Working in association with the antiquarian John Leland, he began to collect information about books and he continued to do so for the rest of his life in spite of the many vicissitudes he was to endure.[3]

When Cromwell fell in 1540 and a more conservative group became influential, Bale went into exile, accompanied by his wife. From the Netherlands and Germany he set out upon a polemical campaign comprising large-scale books as well as more ephemeral works. The circumstances in England had now changed radically and Bale saw himself as under threat and indeed in mortal danger and yet he continued to advocate radical Protestant ideas. He passed his fiftieth birthday in 1545 and yet he was still changing intellectually, assembling a vast array of learning and drawing also on his earlier accumulations in support of his newer polemical objectives. These show themselves in particular in the development of a Protestant view of history, discussed below in connection with *The Image of Both Churches* and *Acts of English Votaries*.

---

[3] For ideological differences between Bale and Leland, see Simpson (2002: 7–33).

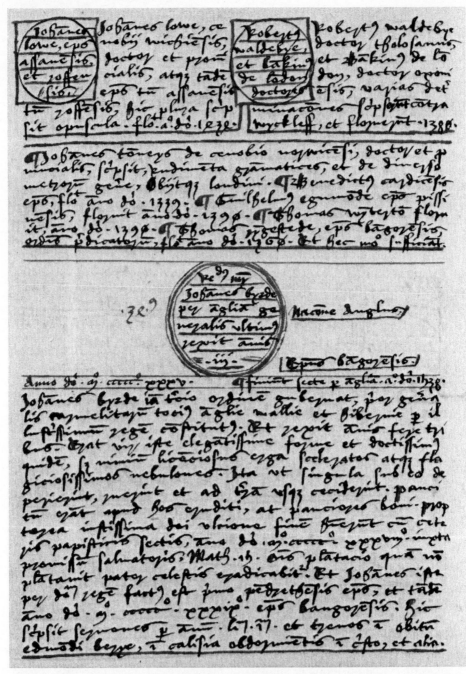

Fig. 8.1 Page from one of John Bale's 'notebooks', Bodleian Library, MS Selden supra 41, 194ᵛ.

The death of Henry VIII and the accession of Edward VI, who was Protestant in sympathy and much influenced by powerful Protestant nobles, brought in a period of hope for the exiles and Bale returned to England having achieved a remarkable quantity of publications. At Wesel four of his plays, which were now more than 10 years old, were printed and he had also brought out polemical writings, biblical commentary, and perhaps, most striking of all, in continuation of his work with Leland, he had produced the *Summarium*, an interim catalogue of British writers arranged in five centuries embodied from his newly developed Protestant view of Britain's religious history. His bibliographical work had great importance in its own right but it was also a part of his religious beliefs and the two remained closely linked thereafter. He had not finished with 'notebooks' either. Now back in England and based in the house of the Duchess of Richmond in London, he resumed his visits to libraries especially in London, Oxford, Cambridge, and Norwich. In a new, alphabetically arranged manuscript book (Bodl., MS Selden supra 64; Bale 1990) he accumulated a vast amount of information about titles, authors, incipits, and locations of copies which was eventually to be the raw material of his much larger *Catalogus* published in 1557. In 1551 he was given the living at Bishopstoke in Hampshire. He continued to publish, though on a lesser scale, and also to take part in religious activities including the production—or at least the rehearsal—of plays for performance: Bale describes the furore over rehearsals for a performance of his *Three Laws* at Bishopstoke in his *Expostulation or Complaint against the Blasphemies of a Frantic Papist of Hampshire* (1552: C2^v–C3^r).

In 1552 Bale was brought to the King's attention and appointed to the bishopric of Ossory in southern Ireland. This was more than a challenge since Protestant beliefs had not been much favoured there. Bale's confrontation of the local Catholics, lay and religious, is described in his *Vocation* (1553). This remarkable document, which is probably based on a journal, gives an often day-by-day account of his missionary activities and of the ensuing responses to it. Mary's accession in 1553 changed the political and religious climate against Bale's interests, which were already putting him in some danger. The *Vocation* gives an account of his rescue and subsequent escape from Ireland by sea and his capture by a pirate, who eventually brought him to the Netherlands in return for a ransom. Bale had been collecting books for some time and he shipped his collection with him to Ireland, but in the dangerous circumstances surrounding his escape he was unable to take them with him.

In his second exile in the Netherlands, Germany, and Switzerland, Bale continued his polemical writings but less intensively than during the first such period. Instead he seems to have concentrated upon preparing the *Catalogus* for publication by Johannes Oporinus in Basel. We should not underestimate the amount of work entailed in this two-volume folio. Comparison with the notebook he began in 1548 shows that Bale followed the pattern he had adopted for items in the *Summarium* elaborating the details enormously. He developed and enlarged the wording of the entries in many instances, as we shall see below, and he was now converting detailed notes into continuous Latin prose. The number of centuries was increased from five to fourteen. Using the chronological structure of the work he also interwove a running commentary in the form of a history of the papacy between the author entries, so that the work took on a much more formidable polemical stance. This extra material, which picked up many of the historical details he had developed in polemical writings in the 1540s, was also brought out in a separate volume as *Acta Romanorum Pontificum*, published by Oporinus in 1558.

On his return to England in 1559 following Elizabeth I's accession, Bale did not resume his see, but was given a canonry at Canterbury Cathedral. He did produce some new polemical writings and in the remaining years before his death some of his earlier works were reprinted. He also took an interest in the performance of one of his plays and there is some evidence that he was still a figure of controversy.[4] But in spite of his efforts he could not recover the many books which he had left in Ireland in 1553 (W. O'Sullivan 1996).

We can pick out a number of individuals whom Bale invoked particularly. Some of them were people of influence like Cromwell, to whom Bale wrote from prison in January 1537, in the aftermath of the Pilgrimage of Grace. This letter shows him picking his way between the complex and dangerous elements of belief (Bale 1537). In some respects this is a private document addressed only to Cromwell, Bale signing himself in a formulaic way 'your contynuall orator and bedeman'. Yet his response to his indictment for heresy has a wider public purpose, as Bale refutes article by article the charges against him over such matters as auricular confession and the English versions of the Creed, the Lord's Prayer, and the Ten Commandments which were sustained in the Six Articles of 1539 (NA, SP 1/111, 183–7; McCusker 1942: 6–13). Other individuals are John Leland, whom he praised in his introduction to the latter's *Laboryouse Journey*, which Bale edited in 1549, and Thomas Cranmer, who is eulogized in the *Catalogus*. He was also careful to praise or address three monarchs: Henry VIII, as Jehosophat, destroyer of idols, in *The Man of Sin* (1543), Edward VI, as the reformist king Josiah, in the Introduction to the *Summarium*, and Elizabeth I, as the learned Deborah, in an addition to the *Catalogus* which came out in 1559, nearly two years after its first printing (Fairfield 1976: 108; Warner 2002: 91–101).

II

In general Bale's work shows a changing perspective and one which reflects the shifting circumstances of his times. The first significant tranche of his work before his conversion shows him deeply involved in Carmelite life. He reflects in these early manuscripts the importance of the lives of saints and the intensity of belief and practices embodied in the daily life of the order. He is concerned to create a historical narrative which goes back to the earliest legends about the order's legendary derivation

---

[4] For an account of clashes with local conservative citizens in Canterbury, see Fairfield (1976: 145–9).

from Elijah. The documents are written in Latin and Bale's implied audience must have been his spiritual brothers within the order, and more probably the senior members who might respond to the persistent and meticulous detail accumulated here. Two traditional literary forms are used in particular, the saint's life and the chronicle, which in turn reflect devotion and an interest in constructing historical narrative. He showed no sign of being aware of the growing controversies and there is no direct evidence that he knew about the Protestant stirrings at Cambridge around 1518 in which his contemporaries Cranmer and Robert Barnes participated. His attention seems to have been to address only an audience within the Carmelite order, though that may, by its very intensity, have been a response to dissent. He does not write in a controversial manner: he is not concerned to defend so much as to record and perhaps thus to uphold. Nor did Bale seek to disseminate this early work beyond the confines of his order and a wider readership must remain somewhat speculative, but his efforts were so sustained that we must presume he had a distinct objective in the preservation of the interests of his brethren. Taking a longer view, we can also see that in the *Catalogus* Bale was able to make use of what he had collected and there are many details about individuals from the early documentation preserved in that work which would not have otherwise survived.

Perhaps it was through his plays that Bale first began to widen his audiences. As we have seen, these seem to have been begun in the 1530s, when Bale gradually started to move away from his earlier beliefs. There does not seem to have been any attempt to print them at this point. This is interesting because John Rastell and his son William began printing plays with a religious or political intention at this time. John was originally a Catholic who converted around the time that Skelton's *Magnificence* was printed for him by Peter Treveris *c*.1530. Shortly afterwards William, who remained a lifelong Catholic, printed a series of plays by John Heywood. It is now clear that these were an attempt to influence the religious policies of Henry VIII towards the upholding of Catholic values and affiliations (Walker 1998: 76–116; Happé 2007). We may assume that Bale was aware of this development, and indeed Cromwell encouraged the performance of Bale's plays precisely because they embodied anti-Catholic interests.[5]

It seems that Bale took part in the plays, as the later printed versions named him as the Prolocutor.[6] He also went on tour outside the capital. *Three Laws*, when it came to be published, had a doubling scheme for five actors which may suggest that it was designed for touring. Similarly *King Johan*, which survives in a complex and revised manuscript, could have been doubled by five actors (Bale 1985–6: i. 152–6). The nature of the audience is again open to some speculation but he would have performed in the open air—as the players did later at the Market Cross in Kilkenny in 1553—as well

[5] In 1534 Cromwell did question William Rastell about his printing, with the result that it stopped shortly afterwards; *LP* vii. 149.

[6] The speech prefix for the first speech is 'Baleus Prolucutor' in the printed text of four plays. See Bale (1985–6: ii. 2, 36, 53, 66). Intriguingly, in the last of these, *Three Laws*, there is also a doubling scheme which has the Prolucutor doubled with Infidelity, the Vice (ii. 121).

as finding a hearing within houses of substantial citizens sympathetic to the cause. This happened with the performance of *King Johan* in 1538 at Archbishop Cranmer's house in Canterbury. The information about this comes from the deposition of John Alforde, a youth of 18 who witnessed the performance (see Cranmer 1846: 388). The same document also mentions that Thomas Brown, a man of 50, praised the anti-papal sentiment. The social class of these men, as Paul Whitfield White points out, may be indicated by their subsequent conversation with a shipman called Henry Tote-hill in Brown's house (1993: 28–9). A further context for this is that it happened in the very city where Thomas Becket's shrine had been demolished in the same year. Indeed Cromwell paid for two performances by 'Balle and his ffellowes' at this time, one in St Stephen's Church and one at an unknown location, both in Canterbury (*LP* 14/2. 337). It has been suggested that these productions were related to the destruction of the shrine (Roberts 2002: 221–2). A passage in the play refers specifically to Becket (lines 1283–1303). Such a possibility implies that these performances at least had a multiplicity of recipients in mind: Cranmer and his guests, people of various social ranks, and the population of Canterbury in general, sensitive to the fate of the local saint.

Bale's attitude to his audience or readership is demonstrable from bibliography and textual aspects of the ways he managed his plays. Concerning the surviving manuscript of *King Johan* we derive a complex narrative.[7] The play was first written about 1534, but it exists in a manuscript which in the first instance was not in Bale's hand. There is no doubt of its existence in the 1530s as he mentions it in his list of his own plays in *Anglorum Heliades* (1536–9), one of the items in MS Harley 3838 (fol. 112^{r-v}). The main thrust of this play is King Johan's struggle with the Pope and his excommunication, brought on by the wickedness of Clergy and the weakness of Nobility, both prompted by Sedition. The subject was topical at this time when King Henry was separating his kingdom from Rome and it was suggested by at least three contemporary writers, Simon Fish, Robert Barnes, and William Tyndale (Bale 1985–6: i/14. 149–51).

But Bale revised his play, writing his changes on the manuscript with a new ending containing characters which probably did not exist in the earlier form, particularly Imperial Majesty, who become the main character once King Johan has been killed by the agents of the Pope. Possibly, but not certainly, these revisions were made in the 1540s and Bale was intending to print this play during his first exile, as he did with four of his other plays. But for some reason it never happened, and the revisions continued later as Bale added an adulatory passage greeting Elizabeth I, calling her the angel in Revelation (7:2–4; lines 2675–7). The revisions towards the end of the play became so complex that Bale added a fair copy of the last scenes. He worked intensively over the first part of the play written by the scribe. Some of these corrections, especially the shift from East Anglian linguistic forms, and the persistent marking of caesuras in nearly every line, suggest the object was printing.

---

[7] For the difficulty of dating the first composition, see Leininger (2002: 116–37).

Bale attended carefully to the printing of his four other extant plays towards the end of his first exile. He used a Dutch printer, Dirk van der Straten, who was working at Wesel, a safe German town for Protestants. They were issued in 1547–8 in matching editions.[8] *Three Laws* was included in the list in *Anglorum Heliades*, but the other three were not, suggesting that they were written at a later point when Bale set out to revise the traditional mystery cycle towards the end of the 1530s (Happé 2001a). This printing enterprise came at the end of a long period when Bale worked on an extensive series of polemical works aimed at the readership in England. Probably he foresaw the coming death of Henry and anticipated a return to his son's Protestant kingdom. His newly printed plays, attacking the papacy and Catholicism, might therefore find a congenial audience, especially at court. In the event Edward's court was very busy with plays and entertainment, but there is no evidence that Bale had any direct part in it. However, he supervised a revival of *Three Laws*, at Bishopstoke, his living in Hampshire, where he no doubt had a local role associated with his friend John Ponet, the newly consecrated Bishop of Winchester. Another revival of the three biblical plays occurred at Kilkenny in 1553, as mentioned above. The printed texts would be convenient for such a performance.

But the preparation of the plays for printing during the first exile was only a small part of Bale's approach to his readership during those years. It is apparent that he was also creating an intellectual climate for the expression of his Protestant beliefs. He thought that the English were negligent in 'the due serch of theyr auncyent hystoryes to the syngulare fame and bewtye therof' (Bale 1549: A2^r). As Paul Christianson has pointed out, he used a combination of medieval heretics like John Wyclif and John Hus, whom he presented as persecuted for their faith, and Reformation scholars like Martin Luther and Johannes Oecolampadius (1978: 14–15). The intellectual climate after Luther was one in which new approaches—in particular, ways of interpreting Scripture through individual study—had to be discovered or constructed and converts had to teach and stimulate one another. Taking account of the chronology of Bale's works, we can see that there is a process of reaction to contemporary thought and affairs and that his ideas about the new religion move in certain directions. *King Johan* and *Three Laws*, the two earliest plays, show us that Bale was concerned about the monarchy and about finding a pattern for history which reflected the operation of divine will. It was important that both these be communicated to Bale's audience which, it was assumed, contained those sympathetic to his new ideas and who needed to be instructed. For most of his life Bale promoted the duty to preach, a role which, in imitation of Christ's disciples, exposed divine teaching and which aimed to strengthen the possibility of salvation by urging repentance. This didactic function was part of his dramatic inheritance as well as now being something of contemporary importance.

---

[8] Though the original 1547–8 edition of *John Baptist's Preaching* is lost, it was printed as the first in a pairing with *The Temptation of Our Lord*, as the quire signatures reveal.

Bale's attitude to the monarchy, probably derived from Luther's promotion of the idea of the authority of kings under divine law, appears in *King Johan* (lines 101–4). It explains the interest in King Johan, who had been destroyed by the papacy working through the key villain, Sedition, and his supporter Dissimulation, apparently a Franciscan (line 641). The conspiracy between these two is in the early version of the text (lines 639–90). Monarchs also became part of Bale's audience: the *Summarium* depicts Bale presenting one of his books to Edward VI.[9] In the corpus of polemical writings between 1540 and Bale's return to England in 1548, he avoids criticism of Henry even though the royal policies were the cause of his exile. The most likely explanation for this is that it was the King whom Bale sought to persuade: he had to try to move the King in the direction he wanted him to go, towards the completing of the Protestant reformation begun in the assertion of royal authority against Rome.

For *Three Laws* Bale had adopted a pattern of history which divided it into three sections. These are communicated by means of an allegory in which the Laws of Nature, Moses, and Christ are successively undermined by a series of villains guided by Infidelity, who is one of the earliest appearances of the stage convention called 'the Vice'.[10] The situation is finally restored by Vindicta Dei (God's Vengeance). This allegory no doubt fitted the situation in the 1530s when Bale was beginning to react against what he saw as the veniality and sexual corruption of the papacy. But after 1540, in exile, it looks as though he needed a more comprehensive theoretical view of history and this he found in the book of Revelation as interpreted by a series of contemporary Protestant commentaries (Fairfield 1976: 69–75). Of these perhaps the most important was Francis Lambert's *Exegeseos in sanctam Divi Ioannis Apocalypsim libri VII* (Marburg, 1528). This linked the seven seals in Revelation with seven periods of history and this basic structure became the basis for Bale's attempt to discredit the papacy and instruct his readers towards an awareness of the expected Second Coming. In doing so Bale seems to have absorbed a considerable amount of Protestant learning and part of his preaching stance towards his readers is to instruct them in the implications of this schematization of history.

In his two major works, *The Image of Both Churches* (Antwerp, 1545), a commentary upon Revelation, and *The Acts of English Votaries* (Antwerp, 1546; London, 1551?), Bale developed a comprehensive and detailed interpretation, which also underlies the *Summarium* (1547?). He aimed to illuminate the quality of the spiritual life of the primitive Church until it became contaminated by the supremacy claimed for the see of Rome by Boniface III in the seventh century. As far as England was concerned the purer Church held out here longer than elsewhere even after the arrival of Theodore of Tarsus in 666, which completed the mission of Augustine. But Satan was loosed from his confinement in hell one thousand years after the

---

[9] Possibly this was prompted by Holbein's portrayal of Henry VIII on the title pages of the Coverdale Bible (1535) and Great Bible (1539).

[10] While some of the behaviour of the Vices in *Mankynd* anticipates 'the Vice', this stage figure did not appear until 1530s.

Ascension. One of the most significant indications of this was St Dunstan's insistence upon clerical celibacy, a constraint which went very deep with the married Bale and one to which he often returned with bitter accusation about its immoral effects. There is an earlier manifestation of this in the allegory of Sodomismus, who is the principal adversary of the Law of Nature in *Three Laws*. To bring out the quality of survival in the primitive Church Bale also dwelt upon the perennial antipathy of two churches, one virtuous, the other corrupt. This antinomy was traced back to the conflict between Abel and Cain, respectively obeying God and the Devil, and was manifest in Bale's day, but the true Church was an inward one and it had to cherish virtue within itself despite persecution. Here we touch on one of Bale's key purposes in exile in his attempt to teach his English readership how to conduct themselves under the persecution Bale perceived to be happening at home. He sustains the secret virtue of the true Church against the outwardly manifest persecution motivated by Satan.

In the *Image* Bale repeatedly addresses the 'good Christen Reader' (A2^r), urging repentance in the Preface and also offering comfort. From his position as an exile he can comment on the state of England and its present predicament: 'We wayted for tyme of helthe, and we fynde here is nothynge els but trouble' (B2^r). The emotional appeal to Bale's audience was sharpened by two further aspects. The destructive effect of the papacy was an embodiment of the Antichrist, who had been especially threatening since the millennium and whose reign would precede the Second Coming. The effect of this terrible figure is one which Bale repeatedly invokes, deriving it from Revelation. The second urgent matter was the need to create Protestant saints, but these had to be handled in such a way as to avoid the idolatry which Bale had perceived and which he dramatized in the figure of Idololatria in *Three Laws*. The bad saints offered ridiculous remedies for a catalogue of ills:

> If ye can not slepe but slumber
> Geve otes unto saynt Uncumber,
> And beanes in a serten number
> Unto saynt Blase and saynt Blythe.
>
> (lines 531–4)

In 1537, rejecting the power of the Pope to make saints in his *Answer*, Bale offered other criteria: 'But all thei whych departed hens in faith and testymonye of the wurde of God wer sayntes most lawfully canonysed or auctorysed in the blood of Crist' (McCusker 1942: 10).

But Bale needed some figures that could be more specifically Protestant than could King John, in whom Bale had found sainthood in the 1530s (Happé 1986). He was eventually able to find these in two different sources. One was in the *Fasciculi Zizaniorum*, a fourteenth-century collection of Carmelite documents against heresy which Bale acquired in Norwich about 1538 and took with him into exile. This document provides invaluable evidence of Bale's working methods. He studied it intensively, annotated it profusely, transcribed new material, and provided three indexes.

It included an account of the examination for heresy by Archbishop Arundel of Sir John Oldcastle in 1513 (Bodl., MS e Musaeo 86, fols. 90ᵛ–98ᵛ; Fairfield 1976: 211). In spite of certain rather unsavoury aspects of Oldcastle's life, including traitorously and rather inconveniently taking arms against King Henry IV, Bale saw in him admirable resistance to the orthodox doctrines of purgatory and transubstantiation. Bale needed to discourage these in his English readership, and in his *Brief Chronicle concerning the Examination and Death of the Blessed Martyr of Christ Sir John Oldcastle* (1544) he attacks them. There is also a theatricality in Oldcastle's words and actions which Bale exploits (Knott 1993: 49–52).

The second Protestant saint who figures largely in Bale's output in exile aimed at the English readership was Anne Askew. Bale apparently still had good enough connections within England to receive documents she wrote between her trial and execution in 1546. Pursuing his historical framework concerning what he believed to be the corruption of the Church, he sought to align Anne with the true martyrs from before the seventh century. Anne's account of her sufferings is extraordinarily plain in style and calm in tone, expressed in simple language. In editing her writings Bale chose the same method as he had for Revelation and Leland's 'New Year's Gift' (published by Bale as *The Laborious Journey*): to print her text with his own interpretation interwoven. His rhetoric is markedly different from Anne's plainer style. Her defence uses such matters as the rejection of transubstantiation and her trust in the Bible. Bale castigates the bishops, whom he accuses of reading 'popish portfolyoms and maskynge bokes' instead of Scripture (1996: 58). Bale had used invective to work up ridicule in the plays, and here he returned to it markedly. This feature of his approach to his audiences may well have been associated with the vigorous language of preaching. Among the rhetorical features he uses is a comparison between Anne and Christ. Both held their peace under torture. Anne's account says that she did, but Bale elaborates upon her Christ-like submission. He makes much of the clouds which appeared at her execution, expressing divine displeasure and recalling the darkness at the Crucifixion. He emphasizes the purity of her sainthood, free from the heresies of Catholic saints. Relying as he did upon the immutable truth of Scripture, he was especially concerned with the truth of the language he used (C. Bradshaw 1997: 174; Betteridge 1999: 79–88). This work on Askew was popular and it was printed four times by 1560.[11]

From exile Bale made strenuous attempts to reach his audience in England. His books were distributed in the kingdom and were ordered to be burnt. Two features suggest that he was reaching his audience successfully. Bishop Stephen Gardiner, now a conservative in religion, complained that copies of Bale's *Anne Askew* were on sale in the marketplace near his cathedral in Winchester in May 1547 (Harris 1940: 35). Secondly, the rate of publication in the years 1544–8 suggests that Bale's polemical campaign was working. Including reprints the number of his titles were: in 1544, four; in 1545, two; in 1546, four; in 1547, four; and in 1548, twelve. After

---

[11] For differences between Bale's treatment of Askew and that by Foxe which is dependent upon Bale, see Freeman and Wall (2001).

1547 several were soon reissued in England (Fairfield 1976: 165–71). But although Bale was vigorously cultivating his audience in England in these years, the appearance of the *Summarium* indicates that he had wider ambitions. He wrote it in Latin, the language of scholarship, and he attributed influence to a number of Continental scholars, some of whom he was in touch with, notably Conrad Gesner, who published his own *Bibliotheca universalis* in 1545, and Trithemius (Grabes 2005: 143; Hudson 1997: 316). He was patriotic in outlook, especially in regard to the excellence of the primitive English Church until it became corrupted, and this sentiment may well have been a spur to reaching a wider European audience and one comprising scholars especially. In spite of the polemical aspects in the *Summarium*, Bale is notably more tolerant of writers he disagreed with than he is elsewhere.

III

It has been suggested that Bale had to create a new value for books, separating himself from the past (Schwyzer 2004*a*: 111). His output comprised many different types, expressed in a variety of modes, including dialogue, autobiography, biography, translation, poetry, satire, biblical commentary, dramatization, cataloguing, and narrative. He also exercised himself over documentation, preserving the originals embedded in his books for posterity, a process which anticipates the work of his colleague John Foxe in *Acts and Monuments*, which first appeared in 1563. This also led to editorial activities in which he framed and presented the work of others. In the last part of this account of how Bale addressed his audiences I consider some of the physical characteristics of his publications. Bale used a number of printers and there are some significant decisions about how his work should appear.[12]

One of the most interesting aspects of selection is his use of illustrations in most volumes. Choices must have depended partly upon what was available in printing houses. This was certainly the case for the picture of the meek and persecuted 'English Christian' confronted by a fierce Irish papist on the title page of *Vocation*. This had been used for two other books, not by Bale, in 1539 and 1543.[13] For his book black letter labels of the two figures were added underneath the woodcut, presumably prompted by Bale. For two separate editions of *Image* by Stephen Mierdman, one in Antwerp (1545?; STC2, 1269.5) and one in London (*c*.1550; STC2, 1298), two similar but different series of about twenty illustrations for Revelation were

[12] Because of the danger he was in, Bale frequently used false imprints and places of publication, as seen in the impertinent colophon in *Vocation*: 'Imprinted in Rome before the castell of S. Angel at the sign of S. Peter'. See Fairfield (1972).

[13] The illustration, without Bale's wording, has survived in two other works printed by J. Lambrecht, Bale's printer at Wesel: *Een zu verlic boucxkin* (1543) and *Reyfreynen in vroede* (1539). See Luborsky and Ingram (1998: 52).

Fig. 8.2 John Bale, *The Image of Bothe Churches* (1545), M7ᵛ. The whore of Babylon mounted on the seven-headed beast is one of the most recurrent images in Reformation polemic. Original size: 33mm x 46mm approx.

used and reused. These were part of a tradition going back through Holbein and Cranach to Dürer (see Figure 8.2). Both sets are of remarkable quality considering that they are not much bigger than a postage stamp (Happé 2001b: 81–118). It does not seem likely that both would have been made specially to go with this text. Some of those in Mierdman's London edition were reused by T. East for his reprint (c.1570; STC2, 1300).

However, some illustrations must have been new. For Dirk van der Straten's printing of the *Summarium* there are large and small versions of a picture of Bale presenting his book to the enthroned and crowned Edward VI. In all likelihood these were made for this edition.[14] At nearly the same time (1548) a full-face portrait of Bale appeared in the same printer's *Three Laws*. Bale is dressed in academic dress and carries a book in his hand. This volume also has a magnificent woodcut as the title page, showing scenes of the Creation and Fall which are arranged around the wording of the title. I have not been able to trace this elaborate border elsewhere and it may well be that resources were available for it to be made especially along with the others. In any case, the inclusion of all these illustrations shows that Bale wanted to bring out some thematic material visually for his readers and also to stamp his work with an authoritative air.

At another level however, illustrations have a less direct bearing. Almost all of the 500 individual author entries in *Summarium* begin with a small decorated capital (21 × 21 mm). These do not form a single set but draw upon several series. It has been shown that van der Straten used some of these in other books (Steele 1909–11: 232–3), and their inclusion here is thus decorative rather than thematic. Similarly, there is a series of capitals in *Catalogus* showing scriptural scenes including Joseph and Potiphar's wife, Balaam and his ass with the angel, and David viewing Bathsheba at her bath: none of these have a discernible thematic import but they do beautify the two volumes and thus reflect upon Bale's attitude to his readership. A new portrait of Bale, perhaps more academic, showing him considerably older was created for this work. Both *Catalogus* volumes, in folio size, end with a full-page illustration of Arion on the dolphin's back. The visual impact is stunning and it may also be a reflection of humanist attitudes, which in themselves might be more appropriate to the European audience now in view. The inclusion of Latin verses, printed in italics (a humanist script), matches this.

The size of the printed volumes to some extent reveals assumptions about the audiences. Cromwell was interested in the cheap production of books aimed at the propagation of official policy. The reasons for choosing a particular page size must usually have been a matter for the convenience of printers and the requirements of the workplace. Nevertheless, we cannot rule out that choices were made in the light of the assumed needs of the market. The bulk of Bale's work appeared in octavo. The

---

[14] Another version of the presentation to Edward was made for *Votaries* in the edition printed by Abraham Vele (Bale 1551?; STC2, 1273.5), thus underlining Bale's sense of the importance of this royal connection. There is a parallel for the illustration on the title page of a translation by Princess Elizabeth of *A Godly Meditation*, edited by Bale, showing a princess kneeling with a book in hand before Christ (1548; STC2, 17320, printed by van der Straten).

plays and *Summarium* were in quarto. Exceptions are found in the first edition of *Image* (Mierdman, 1545?; STC2, 1296.5) and *A Christian Exhortation unto Customable Swearers* (Widow of C. Ruremond, 1543?; STC2, 1280) both in decimo sexto.[15] They appeared when Bale was anxious to make an impression in England and it is possible that the small size would make clandestine movement easier. Subsequent editions were switched to octavo. On the other hand the *Catalogus* appeared in folio, rich in illustrations, as I have noted, and this was clearly intended for a different market and one with a more prestigious and international readership.

The layout of Bale's books was taken seriously. Usually the title pages were carefully thought out in respect of both choice of words and general appearance even if illustrations came from elsewhere. For *Oldcastle* there is picture of an armed knight carrying a cross emblazoned with a crucifix regarded by two figures, probably Mary and St John. This is surrounded by a frame of words praising Oldcastle's valiant life and death. The type for this goes downwards on the right; it is inverted under the picture; and then goes upwards on the left side. Conventional printer's flowers and index fingers are inserted decoratively at the corners of this verbal frame. The detailed title of the book stands above the frame and there is a four-line quotation from Daniel below. The title page layout of *The First Examination of Anne Askew* is very similar, the cut showing a woman holding the Bible and trampling a dragon.

Besides close attention to illustrations in *Image*, there are other significant aspects of layout. A different size of type is used for the biblical text from Bale's interspersed commentary, which is printed in smaller type. Bale draws attention to the margins (B1^r) which are thick with references to Scripture and to a limited number of other authorities, including Francis Lambert. By the time of *Vocation* (1553) Bale had elaborated this technique enormously. He still offers references, a practice which in Protestant circles would give much cause for reflection. But now he does much more by way of giving pointers and comments. Many of the latter are indications of subject matter: 'The Temple'; 'Dublin'. But some are pointedly derogatory: 'an other Judas' (the second pirate); 'Satan' (near the mention of a bishop). These promptings to reader response may be instructional but they also reinforce the emotional response to the text. The polemical approach even appears in the preparation of the indexes. Thus in *Vocation* we find: 'Weston, a lecherouse papist'; 'Transubstantiation/ or God makinge'.

All these items suggest that Bale was deeply but ingeniously concerned to engage his audiences in a range of intellectual and emotional responses. Before his conversion he expected to please his readers by the meticulousness of his work. After it, his stance was consistently that of a preacher who engages his flock to ensure their salvation and in doing so seeks to instruct, challenge, and warn them. His robust humour and frequently abusive tone were meant to entertain but also to shame his opponents,

---

[15] The book in Bale's hand pictured in *Three Laws* is very small, and it might well have been in this size. Several German New Testaments after 1538 at Strasbourg and Zurich appeared in decimo sexto; see BL, Catalogue, s.v. 'Bible—New Testament [German]'. In the *Catalogus* portrait the hand-held book is larger.

who in their way were also part of his audience. To reach them he had learned the power of printing.

PRIMARY WORKS

BALE, JOHN (n.d.), Notebook, BL, Harley MS 3838.

—— (n.d.), Notebook, Bodl., MS Selden supra 41.

—— (n.d.), *Index*, Bodl., MS Selden supra 64.

—— (n.d.), Response to his indictment for heresy, NA SP 1/111, 183–7.

—— (1537), Letter to Cromwell, BL, Cotton MS Cleopatra E.IV.

—— (1543), *Yet a Course at the Romyshe Foxe: A Dysclosynge or Openynge of the Manne of Synne* ([Antwerp]).

—— (1543?), *A Christen Exhortacion unto Customable Swearers* ([Antwerp]).

—— (1544), *A Brefe Chronycle Concernynge the Examinacyon and Death of the Blessed Martyr of Christ Syr Johan Oldecastell* ([Antwerp]).

—— (1545), *The Image of Bothe Churches* ([Antwerp]).

—— (1546*a*), *The First Examinacyon of Anne Askewe* ([Wesel]).

—— (1546*b*), *The Actes of Englysh Votaryes* ([Antwerp]).

—— (1547), *The Lattre Examinacyon of Anne Askewe* ([Wesel]).

—— (1548), *A Comedy Concernynge Thre Lawes* ([Wesel]).

—— (1549), *The Laboryouse Journey and Serche of Johan Leylande for Englandes Antiquitiees*.

—— (1551?), *The First Two Partes of the Actes [...] of the Englysh Votaryes*.

—— (1552?), *An Expostulation or Complaynte agaynste the Blasphemyes of a Franticke Papyst of Hamshyre*.

—— (1553), *The Vocacyon* ([Wesel?]).

—— (1557), *Scriptorum illustrium Maioris Brytannie [...] Catalogus* (Basel).

—— (1558), *Acta Romanorum Pontificum* (Basel).

—— (1559), *Scriptorum illustrium Maioris Brytannie [...] Catalogus* (Basel).

—— (1985–6), *Complete Plays*, ed. Peter Happé, 2 vols (Cambridge: Brewer).

—— (1990), *Index Britanniae scriptorum: John Bale's Index of British and Other Writers*, ed. Reginald Lane Poole and Mary Bateson, introd. Caroline Brett and James P. Carley (Cambridge: Brewer). [Edition of Bodl., MS Selden supra 64]

—— (1996), *The Examinations of Anne Askew*, ed. Elaine V. Beilin (Oxford: Oxford University Press).

CRANMER, THOMAS (1846), *Miscellaneous Writings and Letters*, ed. J. E. Cox (Cambridge: Parker Society).

ELIZABETH I (trans.) (1548), *A Godly Medytacyon*, ed. John Bale ([Wesel]).

Fasciculi Zizaniorum, Bodl., MS e Musaeo 86. [Contains Archbishop Arundel's interrogation of Sir John Oldcastle]

HEYWOOD, JOHN (1991), *Plays*, ed. Richard Axton and Peter Happé (Cambridge: Brewer).

CHAPTER 9

SIR THOMAS ELYOT AND THE BONDS OF COMMUNITY

CATHY SHRANK

THE sitters for Holbein's portraits rarely smile. However, that of Sir Thomas Elyot is more sombre than most. The picture—with that of his wife, Margaret—was probably produced between 1532 and 1534 (Foister 2006: 52), after Elyot had been recalled from his post as ambassador to the Holy Roman Emperor, possibly because he failed to win adequate professions of support from Charles V regarding Henry VIII's desire to divorce Katherine of Aragon. The picture—like Elyot's dialogue *Pasquil the Plain* (1533)—was thus composed during a period in which Elyot felt that 'the Kinges opinyon [was] mynisshid towarde [him]' (Elyot 1976: 9). It is tempting to cast Elyot—the would-be counsellor sidelined after his return from the Continent—as 'something of a Pasquil figure' (D. Baker 1999: 89), a rough-tongued plain speaker eager to serve his lord, but exiled from court for his inability to curb his tongue, while the flattering Gnatho and hypocritical Harpocrates gain power and favour. Indeed, some critics have even pushed the *roman-à-clef* further, identifying Gnatho with Thomas Cromwell and Harpocrates with Thomas Cranmer, who replaced Elyot as ambassador to the Holy Roman Emperor (see Walker 2005: 185).

This biographical narrative is beguiling, as it traces a falling-off from the wide-eyed idealism of *The Governor*, printed two years earlier, in 1531. This encyclopedic work, dedicated to Henry VIII, prescribes the moral and intellectual training best suited for producing the ideal magistrate, as well as the qualities—such as affability, placability, and justice—that the ideal magistrate should nurture and display. Viewed in this light, the cynicism of *Pasquil*—which ends where it began, with Pasquil railing, unheeded, from the margins, as the corrupt courtiers return to their master—represents Elyot's disillusionment with the humanist programme outlined in his earlier work. As in the 'debate of counsel' in book 1 of Thomas More's *Utopia* (1516), which *Pasquil* replays, royal courts prove unreceptive to sound advice from the morally upright, preferring instead sycophants and self-servers.

However, this account fails to acknowledge Elyot's continued promotion of his humanist agenda. In the fourteen years between the publication of *The Governor* (1531) and Elyot's death in his mid-fifties in 1546, the King's printer Thomas Berthelet produced at least eleven more of his works.[1] All of these were steeped with a sense of public duty, and most drew on classical material, thus displaying a key characteristic of Renaissance humanism: the application of classical learning in service of the *vita activa*. This chapter examines Elyot as a humanist thinker and writer throughout his literary career, focusing on Elyot's commitment to the public role of the author, working on behalf of his compatriots. Elyot's allegiance here is to a body of people, imagined in national terms as a community of Englishmen (and, to a much lesser extent, women). Further to that, it explores Elyot's stress on the self-restraint and fellow-feeling (sometimes expressed as 'charity') necessary for community to exist at all.

Far from renouncing them or seeing their impracticality, that is, Elyot's works continued to champion the ideals expressed in *The Governor*, particularly regarding the efficacy and necessity of a humanist education for those destined to rule. Elyot's last secular work, the fictional account of the life and rule of the Roman emperor Alexander Severus in *The Image of Governance* (1541), restates—and exemplifies—the very qualities or strategies lauded in *The Governor* a decade earlier. Severus enjoys the sort of education mapped out in both Elyot's *Governor* and *Education of Children* (1533?), which advocate balancing physical training with instruction in good letters by virtuous tutors. The Emperor emerges from his schooling the model ruler, valuing scholarship—daily 'redyng som place in good authors, to augment his wysedom' (1541a: N2^r)—and following the advice laid down in *The Governor*. Severus is, for instance, affable, allowing all to approach him (1541a: A3^r). When the senator Gordian cautions him to limit access to him, Severus even recycles an argument from *The Governor* (1531: P2^{r-v}), proposing that it was Julius Caesar's approachability which allowed him to 'become so puissant', and the subsequent withholding of such contact which caused his murder (1541a: D^r). Nor does Severus indulge in the 'vaine pitie' deplored in *The Governor* (1531: Q5^r), but upholds the rigour of the law; the only times he shows mercy are in those cases which touch his own person, when he suspends the sentences of those who have conspired against him,

---

[1] *The Doctrinal of Princes* (1533?); *The Education of Children* (1533?); *Pasquil the Plain* (1533); *Of the Knowledge which Maketh a Wise Man* (1533); *A Sermon of Holy Saint Ciprian* (1534); *The Banquet of Sapience* (1534); *The Castle of Health* (1536?; two further, corrected editions in 1539 and 1540); *Dictionary* (1538; repr., rev. and expanded, as *Bibliotheca Eliotae*, 1542); *The Defence of Good Women* (1540); *The Image of Governance* (1541); *A Preservative against Death* (1545). Other potential works include *How One May Take Profit of his Enemies* (1531?); and *Dialogue between Lucian and Diogenes* (1532?).

in order to explore the causes for grievance and probe the nature and validity of their discontent (1541a: Y3^v).

Elyot's commitment to a humanist vision remains constant. Nor is he himself akin to the alienated figure of Pasquil. He might never have reached the dizzy heights of government, complaining in a letter to Cromwell that '[he] perceyve[d] other men avauncid openly to the place of Counsaylors which neither in the importance of service neither in chargis have servyd the king as [he has] done' (Elyot 1976: 9). But Elyot was no outsider, lacking a voice or role in government. Among other public duties, he served as Justice of the Peace and sheriff of Cambridgeshire and Huntingdonshire; he sat in at least one of Henry's parliaments (that of 1539, which saw the passing of the Act of Six Articles and the Act dissolving the last of the monasteries); he served at Anne Boleyn's coronation in 1533; and in 1540 he was among those appointed to receive Anne of Cleves, to whom he dedicated *The Defence of Good Women* (*ODNB*). Elyot was also a friend of Thomas Cromwell, Henry's chief minister from 1532 to 1540, a relationship stemming from the late 1520s, before Cromwell's spectacular rise to power, while he still worked for Thomas Wolsey. The affection expressed in letters from that period—where Elyot signs himself 'your Lovyng companyon' and promises Cromwell he will be made 'hartily welcome' in his 'pour house'—seems to have endured (Elyot 1976: 1). Sentiments expounded in letters written to those in high authority, particularly printed letters of dedication, are of course to be taken with a hefty pinch of salt. Nevertheless, there is a consistency to the qualities celebrated in Elyot's letters to Cromwell—printed and private—as well as the long-established nature of the friendship, born of a 'similitude of studies', which speaks to its genuineness (26). This relationship with the most powerful man at court was to be a sustaining force in Elyot's career until Cromwell's fall and execution in summer 1540, not least because the connection provided a means by which he could promote his books to Henry, as witnessed by the Preface to his *Dictionary*, in which he acknowledges the role played by Cromwell in bringing the work to the King's attention (1538: A2^v).

Indeed, *Pasquil* works not so much to lionize its bluntly spoken protagonist as to stage three negative roles: Pasquil is no more the ideal counsellor than Gnatho or Harpocrates, if measured against the strictures of both *The Governor* and Elyot's *Banquet of Sapience*, a commonplace book printed in 1534. As Elyot notes near the beginning of book 2 of *The Governor*, 'thre thinges be required to be in the oration of a man havyng autoritie; that it be compendious/ sententious/ & delectable: havyng also respecte to the tyme whan/ the place where/ and the persones to whom it is spoken' (1531: O2^v). This advice concurs with that under the heading 'bablynge' in *The Banquet*, where only he 'that can tempre his language' is deemed 'wyse' (1534: B6^r). The same dilemma found in *Pasquil*—about whether or not counsellors should speak out, particularly when correcting a fault in their monarch—is enacted in Elyot's other dialogue from 1533, *Of the Knowledge which Maketh a Wise Man*. Like *Pasquil*, the work reaches impasse. It depicts a series of conversations between two of Socrates' pupils, Plato and Aristippus, in which Plato explains why he preached about tyranny to Dionysius of Syracuse, despite the likely ineffectuality of his words and his subsequent punishment at this despot's hands. The text ostensibly endorses Plato's viewpoint. Yet the fact remains that Plato's actions have resulted—as predicted—in his banishment from court, curtailing any further possibility of influence. As his more tractable companion observes, if Plato had held his tongue and 'forborne a day, two, or thre, untill his fume had been passed [...] peradventure [his] wordes wold have ben more easely taken, and therunto [he] shuldist have founden more oportunitie' (1533a: O6ᵛ). Despite Plato's long and convoluted justification of his actions, the pleasure-inclined Aristippus remains only partially convinced that Plato has taken the right course: as he comments at their parting, their conversation has encouraged him to change only 'some what' of his 'olde opinion' (P4ʳ).

The uncompromising message of both Pasquil and 'Plato' is one, therefore, which is open to critique in Elyot's works; neither speaker can be viewed, unproblematically, as mouthpieces for Elyot himself. A measure of the open-endedness of the two dialogues can be provided by comparing them with Elyot's one other dialogue, *The Defence of Good Women* (1540), where Caninus—who begins by detracting women— is absolutely and incontrovertibly convinced by both the arguments of Criticus and the experience of meeting the exemplary Zenobia. Elyot, then, does not align himself uncritically with these marginalized and rather dogmatic figures, retreating into his books because no other channels are open to him. Instead he portrays his role in disseminating knowledge through his many and varied publications as just one facet of his public, knightly duty. The different ways in which he played his part must have been to the forefront of his mind when revising *The Castle of Health* in 1539, work which he tells us was completed while he 'attend[ed] on the parlayment [...] beynge a member of the lower house' (1539: A2ʳ). As he asks in the dedication, 'Is it any lesse the offyce of a knyghte, to preserve and defende the lyfe of his frende, than to slee his ennemyes in battayle?' And, for Elyot, saving a friend might involve doling out historical exempla, spiritual advice, or moral philosophy, as much as physic: each qualifies, in his books, as necessary 'counsel', the term used to describe all these activities. And counsel, in turn, is the greatest of gifts. So, in *The Doctrinal of Princes* (1533?), Isocrates tells King Nicocles that, by showing 'what studies desiryng, and from what workes absteining, [he] maist best order [his] roialme and citee', he brings a far more valuable present than rich garments or plate (A3ʳ).

The belief stated in *The Governor*—that 'The end of all doctrine and studie is good counsayle' (1531: 2I4ʳ)—unites all Elyot's works. Over and over, this is the motivation stressed in his prefaces and dedications. He recurrently portrays himself as 'bounden' by a desire, and duty, to communicate information and share his knowledge with his compatriots. Writing is a public duty: 'for asmuche as I am a sheriffe', he writes in the preface to his last work, *A Preservative against Death*,

I thinke my selfe the more bounden to bee thus occupied. For sens it pertaineth to myn office, and also the lawes of this realme doo compell me to punishe transgressours: Howe muche more is it my duetie, to doo the best that I can, by all studye and meanes to withdrawe men from transgressing the lawes and commaundementes of god, whiche beinge diligently and truely observed, the occasions of transgressyng of temporall lawes should be clerely excluded.   (1545: A3ʳ⁻ᵛ)

For Elyot, there is no dilemma about whether to choose *otium* or *negotium*: as he observes in *The Education of Children*, there are actually three alternatives—the 'Actife', 'contemplatife', and 'voluptuous'—although, in effect, there is no doubt about which path to follow. While the last is 'vicious' and therefore 'apperteyneth to beastis, and men of no reputation', the 'actife lyfe, lackynge philosophie, is of littell purpose [...] The contemplatife life [...] if hit be nat joyned with the active, hit is of none effecte or profite' (1533c: D2^r).

When Elyot writes, then, it is with a sense of himself as a public servant. Elyot's coat of arms (Figure 9.1) is included in the first (and usually subsequent) editions of every one of Elyot's works produced between 1534 and his death in 1546. This is particularly striking in light of the fact that printing authorial devices was not usual practice and finds no counterpart elsewhere in the output of Berthelet's press; none of the works of Elyot's peers printed by Berthelet—by Sir Anthony Cope, Sir Anthony Fitzherbert, or Sir Richard Morison—are accompanied by their heraldic signs. Perhaps this is because none of them was sufficiently prolific to merit the production of equivalent woodcuts; but the fact that Elyot was, and that he allowed his works to be so strongly identified with him as a gentleman, speaks much about his sense that in his role as author he was meeting—rather than competing with, or detracting from—his expectations of public service.

Elyot's perception of himself as participating in, and on behalf of, his community is striking. Protestation of public service—that a work was published for the common weal—is a staple trope of Tudor prefaces. Yet Elyot's pronouncements retain a sincerity, partly because the books he presents are undeniably intended to profit his compatriots in some way, be it intellectually, morally, physically, spiritually, or linguistically, through his Latin–English dictionary, or his much-stated endeavours to extend English vocabulary (according to the *Oxford English Dictionary*, we owe Elyot some 455 words, including *abdicate*, *acumen*, *commentary*, and *womanliness*). To maximize their usefulness, Elyot's works are consciously written in the vernacular, 'that thei, which do not understande greeke nor latine, shoulde not lacke the commoditee and pleasure, which maie be taken in readyng therof' (1533d: A2^v).

Elyot's sense of community also comes across in his self-presentation as an Everyman. As he imparts knowledge, it is not as an authority figure, but as someone who has himself learned from the text he now desires to share: St Cyprian's sermon, 'ones perused in redynge, [he] like[d] so well, that [he] desyred that all other persones mought understonde it' (1534b: A3^r); the 'little treatise' he has gathered 'out of holy scripture' (*The Preservative against Death*) is as much for his 'owne erudicion, as for the remembrance of other men' (1545: A3^v). The same humility is also apparent in the passages of personal experience which punctuate *The Castle of Health*. Unlike William Bullein, who emulated Elyot's works of medical and moral instruction in his own commonweal-infused dialogues in the late 1550s and early 1560s (see Withington, Chapter 27 in this volume), when Elyot intrudes into his text, it is not to display— as in Bullein's works—his talent as a physician in effecting some extraordinary cure or to present himself (martyr-like) as the victim of cruel and sustained persecution. Rather, it is to give insight into Elyot's marriage of knowledge and experience

Fig. 9.1 Thomas Elyot's coat of arms. *The Castel of Helth* (1536), A3ᵛ.

(to which I return later); but further to that, it also gives a sense of him as a man and patient, with weaknesses like the rest of us, in Elyot's case, poor digestion ('cruditie') and 'reumes fallyng out of a hotte head' (1539: U1ᵛ; 1541*b*: Y2ʳ).

That Elyot is motivated by a sense of duty to a community is also apparent from his occasional comments on his faith, which—in a time of Reformation—inevitably came under scrutiny. We see him required to defend his religious position in two letters to Cromwell in 1536. The second of these is the letter in which Elyot makes his infamously elliptical statement that the amity between him and More (executed in July 1535) extended only 'up to the altars' ('Usque ad aras'; Elyot 1976: 31). More is not actually named in the first of these letters, but the context—it is a letter in which Elyot endeavours to assert his support for the Henrician Reformation by criticizing 'the bostars and advauntars of the pompouse authoritie of the Busshop of Rome'— makes it likely that it is More and his circle to whom Elyot refers when he insists that his desire for 'a necessary reformacion' of the Church has caused 'no little contencion betwixt me and suche persones as ye have thowght that I have specially favored' (26–7).

Although 'conservative' in matters of religion—as witnessed by his will, which provides for prayers for the dead (Lehmberg 1960: 196)—Elyot, like many of his persuasion, benefited from the acquisition of former monastic land, and in 1535 served on a commission to visit the monasteries of Oxfordshire (157). He also showed himself ready to denounce most 'papist' rituals, described in a letter to Cromwell in autumn 1536 as 'vayne superstitions, superflouse Ceremonyes, sklaunderouse jong-lynges, Countrefaite Mirakles, arrogant usurpacions of men callid Spirituall' (Elyot 1976: 30). He did, however, make an exception for 'the ordre of Charity', the strength of his support for good works demonstrated by his willingness to defend them even in a letter where his own religious affiliations (and thus loyalty to Henry) were in the dock. This endorsement of the doctrine of charity is also found in *The Banquet of Sapience*, in the presence of sections entitled 'almesdeede' and 'charitie' (1534a: B4^{r-v}, B8^{r-v}), and the content of the section headed 'faythe', where seven of the eight sentences selected uphold the practice of good works, be it through injunctions to 'followe Christis lyvinge' or the statement—drawn from Romans 2: 13—that it is not 'the herers' but the 'doers of the lawe' that be 'ryghtwise' and who 'shall be iustified' (D2^r). 'Charity' was one of the flashpoints of Reformation controversy, as reformers endeavoured to uncouple its spirit from institutionalized Church prac-tices; but it was also a word which, expressing the duty owed from one human to another, was seen—by those on either side of the religious divide—as the life blood of community. It is therefore no coincidence that so communally minded a writer as Elyot should single it out for praise in his statements, or half-statements, of his faith.

Certainly in *The Governor*, Elyot puts love (*caritas*) at the core of his perception of how civilization operates and comes into being: 'Whan societie was firste ordayned of god', 'the sentence or precept came from hevyn' to 'Love thou thy neighbour as thou doest thy self' (1531: Y4^v). Without neighbourly love, civil society would be impossible. Crucially, though, this kindness depends on self-regulation, as shown in the sentence immediately preceding, where 'societie' is made antithetical to 'wilful-ness' (just as 'reason' contrasts with 'sensualitie' and 'benevolence', 'malice'). For a society to function, its participants must be made, or persuaded, to curb their own desires and inclinations (whether those instincts be towards idleness or violence and oppression). It is not just subjects who need to exercise restraint, however. Elyot's texts propound order and hierarchy, but the ruler and his ruling elite are also required to moderate their wills and rule fairly and benevolently. To some extent, Elyot's works on governance—particularly the *Governor*, *Doctrinal of Princes*, and *Banquet of Sapience*—can be seen as anti-Machiavellian treatises. Although *The Prince* was not printed until 1532, it was circulating in manuscript beforehand, and from some of Reginald Pole's correspondence, it seems that Cromwell received a copy as early as 1527 (Lehmberg 1960: 86–7; cf. Major 1964: 48). In *The Governor*, Elyot's division of injustice into two types—fraud, 'proprely of the foxe', and violence, 'of the lyon' (1531: Y8^v)—holds strong echoes with chapter 18 of *The Prince*. More important, though, is Elyot's consistent preaching against ruling by fear. 'It is more dangeour to be dred than to be despised for nedes must he feare many, whom many feareth,' he writes in *The Banquet of Sapience* (1534a: D2^v). This rejects Machiavelli's dictum that 'it is much safer to be feared than loved': rulers 'should contrive only to avoid being hated' (Machiavelli 1988: 59, 61). Written in 1534, Elyot's *Banquet* post-dates the first imprint of *The Prince*. But the sentiment is also present earlier, for example, in *The Doctrinal of Princes*, which, while as concerned as Machiavelli's treatise with the preservation of rule and maintenance of honour, promotes less cynical ways of achieving these. 'Thinke that the best and most sure garde of thy person be frendes vertous and honest, lovyng subjectes, and thine own wyll stable and circumspect,' he advises: 'for by those thynges authoritee is opteined and lengest preserved' (1533d: A8^v–B1^r). So too *The Image of Governance* produces what sounds like a direct reproof of Machiavelli: 'he moche erreth [...] that preferreth feare before love' (1541a: D3^r). Contrast Machiavelli: 'love is sustained by a bond of gratitude which, because men are excessively self interested, is broken whenever they see a chance to benefit themselves. But fear is sustained by a dread of punishment that is always effective' (1988: 59).

The motif of self-restraint—keeping 'thine own wyll stable and circumspect'—and the dire consequences of failed restraint echo throughout Elyot's works. There is something typically Elyot about the way in which *The Banquet of Sapience* begins with an entry on 'abstinence' (1534a: B1^r) and ends on the topic of 'wrath' (G7^r). To lack self-control is to be bestial because it means that you have lost sight of what distinguishes you from animals: namely, self-knowledge and the power of reason. As Plato explains to Aristippus in *Of the Knowledge which Maketh a Wise Man*:

men beinge in the state of Innocency have than the figure of man, the soule havinge the hole preeminence over the body. But after if it happen that the appetites and desyres of the body so moch do increase, that they have the hole possession of the body/ and that the affections of the soule, that is to saye/ vertues be suppressed or putte to silence/ than the lyfe becommeth beastely: than loke in what beastes the sayde appetites be mooste vehemente: he/ in whome is the semblable appetite, may be sayd hathe his soule in that best inclosed. [...] A cruel man or Tyraunt in to a tigre or lion, a glotton or drunkarde in to a wolfe or a swyne, and so furthe of other.   (1533b: D8^v–E1^r)

The trouble is that the tyrant cannot see his own beastliness: 'he perceyvethe not that he is deceived, untyll he sensibly feleth some grevous damage' (O1^v), just as in *The Image*, 'so blynded' is the 'inner eye' of the ambitious courtier Turinus 'that he could not se in hym selfe, whych he not longe before had condemned in other' (1541a: F8^r).

To avoid this moral blindness, Elyot reiterates the need for continual self-reflection, through which you know yourself. Take the advice at the start of book 2 of *The Governor*, where would-be magistrates, before accepting office, are enjoined to withdraw to 'a secrete oratorie' or 'privy chambre' to reflect upon the nature of authority: that it is a burden, not an honour; that they are answerable to God (from whom office springs); that they and their deeds are in public view; and so on (1531: N4^r). Such awareness, in Elyot's view, is the way to avoid the magisterial vices of corruption, negligence, and sensuality. Perpetual meditation on these articles is urged as a prophylactic against temptation, for which purpose Elyot recommends that they 'be delectably writen and sette in a table within [a governor's] bed chamber' (N6^v). It is not only office-holders that need to be self-aware, however; this same call for self-knowledge recurs towards the start of book 3, in a passage which extends the need for self-understanding to those bearing any kind of authority (that is, husbands or masters): 'If thou be a governour, or haste over other soverayntie, knowe thy selfe, that is to saye, knowe that thou arte verely a man compacte of soule and body, and in that all other men be equall unto the' (Y5^v–Y6^r). To 'know thy selfe' is the first step towards self-restraint, curbing the propensity towards despotism born of an overgreat sense of one's 'dignitie or autoritie'.

That Elyot places such value on self-knowledge (and arising directly from that, self-restraint) is all the more interesting when weighed against the fact that he himself—as he reveals in *The Castle of Health*—was a choleric man. (In the chapter on the diet of 'cholerike persons', for example, he talks of his own 'peynful experience'; 1539: T1^{r-v}.) Those of a choleric disposition are believed in humoral theory to be 'wrathful'; Mars, as the planet which governs choler (in Trevisa's words), 'disposeth the soule [...] to wrathe [...] and to other coleryke passions'.[2] Hence in William Shakespeare's *Taming of the Shrew* (1594), Grumio taunts Kate by offering her neat's foot, tripe, and beef and mustard, before denying her them as too 'choleric' for one of her angry disposition (4. 3. 17–25). Not insignificantly, Elyot dilutes this established connection between choler and anger. In Elyot's table of complexions, the choleric merely '*dreames* of fyre, fyghtynge, or angre' (1539: A2^v; my emphasis). Manifestations of actual anger are diverted onto those of a sanguine complexion—more usually seen as hopeful or amorous, 'Wrouhte to be lovyng' as Lydgate puts it[3]—who are said to anger 'shortly' (briefly, A2^r), and onto melancholics, whose anger is 'longe and frettynge' (A3^r). Nevertheless, despite downplaying the irascibility of choleric people, the devotion of an entire chapter to advice on how to control ire is telling—Elyot's tips for curbing rage include meditating on the sufferings of the crucified Christ, dealt with in an extended passage (R1^v–R2^r), and reciting the alphabet before you 'speake or do any thynge in anger' (R2^r). The only other mental condition treated at length is 'dolour', although much of that chapter is assigned to a discussion of ingratitude, which is acknowledged to produce anger as frequently as it does gloom (R4^r).

---

[2] 'Choleric', *OED*, *adj.*   [3] 'Sanguine', *OED*, *adj.* and *sb.*, 3a.

One thing which seems to have angered Elyot—judging by the frequency with which the complaint occurs in his prefaces—is criticism of his diction: that, in his attempts to 'augment our Englyshe tongue', whose vocabulary was seen in this period as limited, he has made his language 'derke or harde to be understande' (1533b: A3^{r-v}). Yet Elyot's prose style is a manifestation of self-restraint. Like the ideal speaker 'tempering' their language, according to when, where, and to whom they speak, Elyot is a master of different styles (Elyot 1531: O2^v). From the philosophical complexity and cautious long-windedness of Plato in *Of the Knowledge which Maketh a Wise Man* to the biblical solemnity of the Preface to *The Banquet of Sapience*, Elyot's style is tailored to the audience or subject in hand. Compare, for example, the direct concision of *The Castle of Health*—'A plover, | Is slowe of digestion, nourysheth lytell, and increaseth melancoly' (1539: H1^v)—with the gossipy, witty reversals of a private letter to Thomas Howard, Duke of Norfolk, in which he plays on the etymology of *episcopus* ('overseer'), to talk about the Bishop of Worms as both an overseer of wills and overseen, as in 'drunke' (Elyot 1976: 2–3). This attention to audience and the intended purpose of the work in hand is also manifest in the way Elyot signals the selection of material, censoring what he deems unsuitable, be it an unnamed type of evacuation (presumably abortion) in *The Castle of Health* (1539: Q8^r), or Heliogabulus' worst excesses in *The Image*, 'whiche [...] ought never to have ben wrytten for abomination therof, moch more never to have ben of any man knowen' (1541a: A8^r).

In all registers, however, Elyot strives to be clear, even when introducing neologisms; he takes pains to point out that each coining or foreign import is carefully explained, 'declared so playnly by one mean or other to a diligent reder' (1533b: A3^v). It is not for nothing that he earns the rare praise of C. S. Lewis, famously disparaging about almost every writer before Spenser. As Lewis notes: 'His sentences do not simply happen, they are built. He keeps a firm hold of his construction, he is nearly always lucid, and his rhythm is generally sound' (1954: 276). Elyot's desire for clarity extends to an anxiety about ambiguity or misnomer. Like many Henrician writers—Thomas Starkey, Thomas Wyatt—Elyot seems particularly exercised about paradiastole (misnaming).[4] 'Fraude', Elyot notes in *The Governor*, 'is at this present tyme so communely practised, that if it be but a little, it is called policie, and if it be moche and with a visage of gravitie, it is than named and accounted for wisdome' (1531: Z1^r)—a use of 'policy' suggesting that here again Elyot is pitching himself against Machiavellian *politique*. Elyot's notorious preference for the term 'public weal' (over the more usual 'common weal') would appear partly motivated by this wish for precision. Elyot readily uses 'common weal' when evoking the well-being of the whole polity ('the commune weale of theyr countrey'; 1533c: D2^r), but he distinguishes this from the word used to describe the polity itself. In doing so, he reacts against the rhetorical appropriation of the term apparent in the complaint of Pole in Starkey's *Dialogue of Pole and Lupset* (composed c.1532, contemporaneously with Elyot's early

[4]   See Wyatt (1969); Starkey (1989). For discussion of paradiastole, see Puttenham (1589: X3^v); Skinner (2008).

works). As Pole wrily observes, 'Every man speke of the commyn wele, every man hath that oft in hys mouth that under the pretense & colour therof they may the bettur procure theyr owne' (1989: 16).

The recurrent use that Elyot makes of simile and metaphor can be seen as part of this drive to elucidate. The polluting effects of idleness are thus compared in *The Image* to over-running sewers, infecting the city (1541*a*: I4^v); Plato in *Of the Knowledge which Maketh a Wise Man* justifies seeming digressions by comparing his technique to an artist, highlighting images by painting them on a dark background (1533*b*: D3^v). Elyot's enthusiasm for metaphor as an instructive tool can be seen in his extended justification of dancing as a morally, as well as physically, beneficial activity in *The Governor*, where he transforms dancing into a symbol of concord (1531: L1^r–L2^v) and an allegory for the virtue prudence; as they move, dancers will be drawn to reflect on the qualities (such as providence, industry, modesty) by which prudence is achieved (L2^v–M4^v).

Elyot's political philosophy is also underpinned by a key structural metaphor. People comprise the body politic. A healthy body politic needs healthy bodies. Physical and political health are inextricably linked, and it is no accident that Elyot's ideal governor, Severus, is well read in Galenic medicine, provides open spaces for health-giving exercise, and establishes free hospitals—reforms described at length in *The Image* (1541*a*: K3^v–M1^r). Elyot regards people's health a proper matter for state intervention: 'surfet' is a 'dungeon', into which folk are driven by the tyrannical 'spirite of gluttony', an extended metaphor which leads to a rare digression in *The Castle of Health* (for which Elyot immediately apologizes and thus draws attention to), where he laments that English laws about consumption—exempting the nobility— have targeted only the 'vayne and sumptuous expenses of the meane people', rather than the 'bodily helth' of all (1539: M1^r). Conversely, book 3 of *The Governor* includes a chapter on sobriety of diet (1531: 2F1^r–2F6^r). Good governance thus begins with good self-governance: it is therefore unsurprising, considering Elyot's belief in self-knowledge as the root of wisdom (and therefore virtue), that the title page of *The Castle of Health* should promise to provide the means 'whereby every man may knowe the state of his owne body' (1539: A1^r).

Since early modern medical theory is dominated by the notion of the four humours, such self-governance depends on restraining appetite and consuming appropriate foods to maintain the humoral balance necessary for both physical and mental well-being. Elyot's works consequently abound with images of eating. As Daniel Wakelin observes, 'metaphors from farming and gardening were [...] ubiquitous in educational writing at this time' (2007: 200). Elyot pushes these predominantly economic metaphors—concentrating on profit—into the realm of (good and bad) taste. Heliogabulus' immoderacy and the irresponsible profligacy of his rule are thus epitomized by his wasteful banqueting, feasting on only select animal parts: 'the braynes of Ostriches [...] tunges of Popingagyes, nightyngales, and other sweete syngyng byrdes, oftentymes with the myltes [spleens] of most delycate fyshes' (1541*a*: A4^v). Or we have an early objection to food miles in Elyot's disgust at Heliogabulus' insistence on 'delycate sea fyshe' only when residing 'far distaunte from the sea'. What Heliogabulus ingests is used as evidence—or is even emblematic—of his moral failings. So too Sulla's inhuman cruelty is evidenced by his perverted consumption, his outrages specifically placed in conjunction with scenes or images of eating (making concrete the cliché 'Feast your eyes'). The head of Marcus Antonius, a Roman orator, is 'brought unto hym as he sate at dyner'; or we have 'the heedes of a thousand and seven hundred of the chiefe citezins [...] brought to hym freshe bledyng and quicke, and theron [he] fedde his mooste cruell eien, which to eate his mouth naturally abhorred' (1531: P6^r). In contrast, Heliogabulus' mirror image, Severus ('a perfecte Example of Temperance'; 1541a: B4^r), dines predictably modestly, partly 'fedde' by 'learned' conversation or by reading 'good authors' while he sups (C1^v, N2^r). The body, in other words, requires intellectual as well as physical sustenance: the 'sapience' Elyot provides is arranged in a 'bankette' (1534a: A1^r); his works recurrently presented to readers and dedicatees as 'frutes' (1531: A2^v; 1533b: A7^r).

Intellectual pursuits are consequently of direct and practical use—nourishment—when it comes to governing both the self and the body politic. As Elyot notes in *The Castle of Health*, when leading someone back to 'the use of reason' and from 'the displeasure of almighty god', they need the 'counsell of a man wyse and well learned in morall philosophy' as much as they do 'the helpe of physicke corporall' (1539: Q4^v). Throughout his works, Elyot stresses the efficacy of book learning, that it is not something divorced from active life. His ideal governor, Severus, is both bookish and brawny: not a day passes without him 'exercysyng him selfe eyther in letters, or in faictis [feats] marciall' (1541a: A2^r). It is entirely apt that the motto unfurled across Elyot's coat of arms (Figure 9.1) equates *doing* with *speaking*: 'face aut tace' ('Act or be silent'). Elyot's works strive to marry knowledge (theory) and experience (practice): his medical advice, for example, explicitly takes account of his first-hand observations, refusing to rely on books alone; it is not enough, he tells us, to follow 'the sentence of authors'—even those as esteemed as Galen and Hippocrates—'whiche had never experience of Englysshe mens natures, or of the juste temperature of this realme of Englande' (1539: L3^r). Elyot writes as a man who combines scholarship with public life. As he states in the dedication to *The Governor*, in describing 'in our vulgare tunge the fourme of a juste publike weale', he has gathered material from 'noble autors' and from his 'owne experience [...] beinge continually trayned in some dayly affaires of the publike weale of this your moste noble realme all mooste from my chyldhode' (1531: A2^{r-v}). Not only does *The Governor* utilize knowledge gleaned from books and life, its effects in turn are as much practical as theoretical. It is not just a book about how ethically and intellectually sound governors might be formed. Thanks to the improving historical examples which dominate its pages, receptive readers will also, in the process of reading, be instructed in the very virtues Elyot recommends.

The use of improving historical examples in the search for a just common weal is what Elyot seems to attempt to provide in his penultimate work, *The Image*, printed exactly a decade after *The Governor*. Elyot even recommends it to readers as a suitable companion to *The Governor*, in which he had 'promised to write a boke of the forme of good governance' (1541a: a2^v). Greg Walker has highlighted the ludic nature of *The Image*, proposing that within it Elyot uses irony to suggest that, far from being an ideal ruler, Severus is in fact an irascible tyrant, ruling by fear, despite his protestations to the contrary (2005: 240–75). In doing so, he critiques Henry VIII's brutal regime, whose recent victims included Cromwell—'prince of friends' (Elyot 1976: 37)—executed the previous year, in July 1540. The framework to *The Image* certainly signals a Utopian elusiveness, mingling plausible truth with probable fiction. Elyot's Preface claims that he rediscovered the book searching for something to 'recreate his mind' while working on revisions to his 1538 dictionary, which was republished, in expanded form, as *Bibliotecha Eliotae* in 1542, the year after *The Image* (1541a: A2^r). Elyot's account of Severus purports to be a translation of a non-existent text, by 'Eucolpius'—whose name possibly means 'very windy' (Walker 2005: 241)— borrowed from an almost certainly fictitious Neopolitan gentleman, Pudericus, who most inconveniently demands the return of the work nine years after lending it, just when Elyot has embarked on the translation, 'wherby [he] was constrained to leve some part of the work untranslated' (1541a: A2^r). The reliability of this account is further undermined at the end of the work, however, when Elyot produces a rather different reason for his reliance in his conclusion on other authors, explaining that Pudericus' copy of Eucolpius lacked 'diverse quayres' (2C3^r).

Walker's argument for Elyot's use of *The Image* to satirize the late Henrician regime hinges on the portrayal of the unbending justice executed by Severus and the anger that we glimpse, bubbling under his calm exterior. 'Extortioners', for example, provoke such rage 'that he immediately wolde vomite up colar, and his face beinge as it were on a fyre, of a longe tyme mought not speake one word' (F3^r). Severus, it seems, like Elyot, was a choleric man. However, we need to be cautious about reading negatively Elyot's description of the emperor's ruthlessness. Tudor writing—including Elyot's own—is replete with endorsements of the need to be uncompromisingly rigorous in upholding the law, not least because punishment of wrongdoers serves as an example, and is therefore (in the long term) for the greater good. The epithet 'Severus' is a compliment, not a condemnation. As Elyot states, 'parte of Justyce [. . .] consysteth in execution [carrying it through]' (1541a: F3^v). He himself commends Henry VIII's conduct in trying and killing the religious radical John Lambert in the dedicatory epistle to the first edition of his *Dictionary*: Henry, presiding over Lambert's trial, is 'the perfite image of kyngely majestie' (1538: A2^r). An excursus on a condemned heretic seems unlikely material with which to introduce a Latin–English dictionary, but it is used by Elyot approvingly, as an example of monarchical power to move and inspire, just as Henry— enthused by 'maister Antony Denny', 'Wyllyam Tildisley, keper of [the royal] library', and 'lorde Crumwell'—would encourage Elyot's lexicographical project (A2^v–A3^r). And it was while revising the *Dictionary* (in which he so unflinchingly commends the judicial execution of 'the most detestable heretyke' Lambert; A2^r) that, according to the Preface to *The Image*, Elyot rediscovered his notes, 'certeyne quaires of paper [. . .] written about .ix. yeres past', on the life of Severus. Of course, rereading this eulogy in the shadow of Henry's continued bloodletting, not least of Cromwell (the very man who helped bring the dictionary to Henry's attention and whose 'vertue and cunnyng [learning]' are commemorated in the 1538 dedication; A2ᵛ), may have prompted Elyot to temper his straightforwardly eulogistic work with a more sardonic note. Yet Elyot's 1542 edition of the dictionary is dedicated to Henry, with specific praise of 'Justyce' which 'punysheth yll men under theyr deservynges' (A2ʳ). Moreover, too many of Severus' reforms—purging his household of sycophants, providing for universal education of the young, catering for public health—accord with Elyot's own views, repeatedly expressed in other works, for the portrait to be wholly negative.

For Walker, following the suggestion of Uwe Baumann (1998) that Elyot redrafted a work begun in the early 1530s, Elyot's revisions produce 'a bewildering mixture of the admirable and the seemingly grotesque presented as if it were of equal merit and virtue' (2005: 258). The difficulty of discerning what Elyot sanctions does make a reading of *The Image* reminiscent of Morus' assessment of Hythloday's description of Utopia, where we do not know what Morus approves of, what not. There is a danger, though, that we see extreme punishment through twenty-first-century eyes. Severus' Tudor reputation was for good government, not tyranny. His name is given, for instance, to George Gascoigne's stern, but just, magistrate in *The Glass of Governance* (1575). In 1586 George Whetstone published another life of Severus, dominated—like Elyot's—by reports of Severus' orations and details of his reforms and legal judgments (including the executions he ordered). Entitled *The Enemy to Unthriftiness*, Whetstone's life is presented without irony as 'a Perfect Mirrour for Majestrates' and as 'a Card or Compasse, for every yong Gentleman, honorablie and profitablie to governe his actions' (A1ʳ), that is, preaching an Elyotesque message of governance and self-governance combined.

What does distinguish Elyot's *Image* from his other works is its seeming abdication of his long-held, much-stated belief in people's capacity for self-restraint. Unlike Whetstone's work, addressing individual as well as administrative reform, the well-being of Elyot's Rome and its dominions in *The Image* is made entirely dependent—for good or ill—on the self-control, or not, of its emperor. Severus thus instigates laws regulating what people eat, for example (1541a: M2ʳ⁻ᵛ). Admittedly, Elyot dreams of such laws in *The Castle of Health* (1539: M1ʳ), but there is something peculiarly enervating about the way in which every good seems to spring from the Emperor, the laws he establishes, and the exemplary punishments suffered by those who flaunt them. This is all the more striking because *The Image* is dedicated 'To al the nobilitie of this flouryshygne royalme of Englande' (1541a: A2ʳ), the very rank who, in *The Governor*, were entrusted with the task of overseeing both themselves and the public weal. In contrast, the Roman senate seems strangely inert (and it must be remembered that Elyot sat in Parliament, England's equivalent body). The senators are described as 'vertuous and honorable' (E3ᵛ) and greet Severus' accession with joy; yet these same virtuous, honourable senators allow Heliogabulus' tyranny. There is consequently something frighteningly vulnerable about a polity whose well-being is so reliant on its ruler's moral fibre, when virtuous leaders are so obviously rare. After thirteen years of rule, Severus is assassinated by malcontent soldiers; his life (and a golden age for Rome) is thus violently and unnaturally abbreviated, like Pudericus' copy of Eucolpius' book, with its missing quires.

Perhaps, then, it is the end of *The Image*, rather than *Pasquil the Plain*, which finds Elyot stuttering into despairing silence. Both works share an anxiety about finding morally robust counsellors and what Elyot terms 'inferiour governours callid magistratis' (1531: A4^r). The roots of Elyot's disappointment with the Roman senate in *The Image* are deep-planted, and offer insight into a facet which distinguishes his humanism from that of many of his contemporaries, namely Elyot's attitude towards debate (the mode of scrutinizing policy on which Parliament, like the Roman senate, depended). Unlike other English humanists and sometime Members of Parliament, such as Thomas Smith and Thomas Norton, Elyot does not share a tendency to idealize debate as 'the best means for bolting out of the truth' (Smith 1969: 13).[5] K. J. Wilson writes of Renaissance dialogue as a 'problem-dissolving form' (1985: 100). But that is not what we see with Elyot's dialogues (*Pasquil, Of the Knowledge which Maketh a Wise Man, Defence of Good Women*). Rather than finding solutions, Elyot's dialogues reach deadlock. They expose problems—particularly the failure of rulers to heed good counsel and the inability of ethically sound counsellors to express themselves in ways which make their advice effective—but they do not resolve them. Elyot's most moral interlocutors—Pasquil, Plato, Zenobia—speak from positions of exile from which they do not hope to return. For Elyot, dialogue is a substitute for, not a means to, action. Monologic forms (orations, letters, treatises) are, for him, invested with greater agency. Elyot's ambivalence towards dialogue—discussion—is here akin to his attitude towards absolutism, which replaces a system in which members of a community freely participate and self-govern with one in which people are regulated from above, a situation which both repels and attracts him (as can be seen from his enthusiasm for dietary laws in both *The Image* and *Castle of Health*, or his assessment of Severus' reign).

There is, then, a seed of doubt (or indecision), nascent in *Pasquil*, which culminates in *The Image*, with its passive senate, helpless to prevent tyranny (be it of Heliogabulus or—less certainly—Severus). Undoubtedly, there is an unusually long pause for Elyot between this work, printed in 1541, and his next in 1545. In this subsequent book, *A Preservative against Death*, Elyot departs the temporal sphere, preparing reader (and writer) to make a good death. In Elyot's case, the work was timely: he died the following year. He left a considerable legacy: more than a dozen works, many of them extensive, testament to his commitment to a humanist belief in the need, and potential, to dovetail book learning with public life. Although Elyot is often seen as an elitist writer (owing to his ostensible focus on the proper role and education of the upper echelons of society), the form in which his books circulated belie that. Printed in the vernacular, in edition after edition, they made available to a wider reading public a classically infused literature of self-governance and self-improvement.

---

[5] Cf. Norton: 'where manie men be, there must be manie myndes, and in consultacions convenient it is to have contrary opinions, contrary reasoninges and contradiccions, thereby the rather to wrest out the best' (*Proceedings* 1981: 241).

PRIMARY WORKS

ELYOT, THOMAS (1531), *The Boke Named the Governour.*

—— (1533*a*), *Pasquil the Playne.*

—— (1533*b*), *Of the Knowledeg [sic]whiche Maketh a Wise Man.*

—— (1533*c*), *The Education [...] of Children.*

—— (1533*d*), *The Doctrinal of Princes.*

—— (1534*a*), *The Bankette of Sapience.*

—— (1534*b*), *A [...] Sermon of Holy Saynt Ciprian.*

—— (1538), *The Dictionary of Syr Thomas Eliot Knight.*

—— (1539), *The Castell of Helthe.*

—— (1540), *The Defence of Good Women.*

—— (1541*a*), *The Image of Governance.*

—— (1541*b*), *The Castel of Helth,* 2nd edn.

—— (1542), *Bibliotheca Eliotae.*

—— (1545), *A Preservative agaynste Deth.*

—— (1976), *The Letters of Sir Thomas Elyot,* ed. K. J. Wilson (Chapel Hill: University of North Carolina Press).

GASCOIGNE, GEORGE (1575), *The Glasse of Government.*

MACHIAVELLI, NICCOLÒ (1988), *The Prince,* ed. Quentin Skinner and Russell Price (Cambridge: Cambridge University Press).

MORE, THOMAS (1989), *Utopia,* ed. George M. Logan and Robert M. Adams (Cambridge: Cambridge University Press).

Proceedings (1981), *Proceedings in the Parliaments of Elizabeth I, 1558–1581,* ed. T. E. Hartley (Leicester: Leicester University Press).

PUTTENHAM, GEORGE (1589), *The Arte of English Poesie.*

SHAKESPEARE, WILLIAM (1988), *The Taming of the Shrew,* The Oxford Shakespeare, ed. Gary Taylor and Stanley Wells (Oxford: Oxford University Press).

SMITH, THOMAS (1969), *A Discourse of the Commonweal of this Realm of England,* ed. Mary Dewar (Charlottesville: University Press of Virginia).

STARKEY, THOMAS (1989), *A Dialogue between Pole and Lupset,* ed. T. F. Mayer, Camden Society, 4th ser., 37.

WHETSTONE, GEORGE (1586), *The Enemie to Unthriftinesse.*

WYATT, THOMAS (1969), 'Myne owne John Poyntz', in *Collected Poems,* ed. Kenneth Muir and Patricia Thomson (Liverpool: Liverpool University Press), 88–91.

CHAPTER 10

JOHN HEYWOOD AND COURT DRAMA

THOMAS BETTERIDGE

JOHN HEYWOOD was born about 1497 (R. Johnson 1970). By the 1520s he had established himself at the court of Henry VIII as a playwright, poet, actor, and producer. Over the next forty years until the succession of Elizabeth I, Heywood was at the centre of Tudor court culture. Despite this, his place in accounts of the literary history of the sixteenth century has invariably been small and insignificant. This is largely because his work has been traditionally placed on the margins of a teleological narrative of literary change whose broad outlines have remained unchanged since C. S. Lewis condemned the mid-Tudor period as the 'Drab Age' of literature. Indeed Lewis singled out Heywood for condemnation because not only did Heywood, in Lewis's eyes, write drab poetry: he chose to do so (1954: 145–6). This was for Lewis the ultimate crime. It is, however, not only Heywood's poetry that has been largely neglected by literary historians; Heywood's status as a dramatist has suffered owing to his place in the rather confused narrative that theatre historians tell of the development of English drama between the medieval period and the 1590s. In this narrative the debate over court drama, and the rather technical discussion of its status, have had the effect of underplaying the complexity of Heywood's Henrician drama. This chapter discusses the nature of the Henrician court and its drama before focusing in detail on a number of Heywood's plays, including *Johan Johan, The Pardoner and*

This chapter could not have been completed without support from the Arts and Humanities Research Council.

the Friar, The Four PP, and The Play of the Weather, to illustrate the sophistication—dramatic, political, and religious—of Heywoodian court drama.

10.1 THE HENRICIAN COURT

The Tudor court that Heywood worked within was a dynamic, bewildering organization. Its culture, as it developed during the early years of Henry VIII's reign, was a disturbing mixture of formality and informality, freedom and constraint, desire and frustration. This juxtaposition of oxymoronic terms affected every aspect of court, including its regulation and regulations. The Eltham Ordinance, passed in 1526, were presented in public as a serious attempt to reform the court, although it is now recognized that they also had the effect of increasing the power of Thomas Wolsey (Guy 1988: 103–4). The Ordinance is a set of rules designed to order every last detail of the court. They open with a typically Henrician claim that the reason reform is necessary is that Henry has been absent and that in his absence corruption has spread:

First, it is not unknowne how the King's Highness soon after his first assumption of his crown [...] for the defence of the church, and for sundry other great and notable respects and causes, was enforced and brought unto the wars; wherein his Grace, not for any inordinate appetite or desire, but for the weale of Christendom [...] hath much travailed and been occupied; in such wise as many officers and ministers of his household being employed and appointed to the making of provisions and other things concerning the wars, the accustomed good order of his household hath been greatly hindered and in manner subverted; which by little and little is now come more and more unto an indirect course far from the good constitutions of old times [...] his Grace is [therefore] minded and determined to see a reformation of the said errors, and establish such an order, both in this household and chamber aforesaid, as the same being duly fulfilled and observed, all said errors shall in brief time be totally removed and extinct.   (Collection 1790: 137)

It is important to remember what this passage seeks to obscure. Henry had been monarch for seventeen years when the Ordinance was issued and therefore the argument that the court had become corrupt in his absence is nothing more than a convenient fiction. The Ordinance articulates a reform programme that is utopian in scale and ambition; the entire royal household and court was to be restored and held to an absolute order right down to the management of spent candles:

Cap 27—It is ordered that the King's groom-porters and the Queen's shall fetch no wax, white lights, wood nor coals more then reasonable ought to be spent, by the oversight of the gentleman ushers; and that the said groom porters do daily bring in the remain of the torches and other wax remaining overnight, by nine of the clock in the morrow; and for lack of doing thereof to loose for every time one week's wages; the same to be overseen and executed by the clerk comptroller from time to time.   (144)

At one level the Ordinance's emphasis on controlling the remains of torches and candles reflects the extent to which in this period these were luxury items. This passage also, however, articulates a desire to order, in and through writing, every aspect of court—its organization and economy. Above all, the Ordinance is designed to impose a spatial decorum on the court. In the process, however, it conjures up two images of court: one in which everything is controlled, fixed, and managed, another marked by disorder and venality, a court teetering on the brink of a complete descent into chaos. For example, when in the Ordinance courtiers are forbidden from stealing doorknobs, tables, and cupboards, the image that is inevitably created is of a court in which it was common for people to purloin these items (145). Imagine a court in which doors can't be properly opened or closed; a court from which people pilfer large items of furniture so that one moment a space is filled with a table, the next—empty.

Not surprisingly the Ordinance sought to proscribe what kinds of people should live and work at court:

Cap. 31—And, to the intent the King's Highness may be substantially served in his chamber and household, by such personages as be both honest in their gesture and behaviour [...] considering also the great confusion, annoyance, infection, trouble, and dishonour, that enseweth by the numbers as well of sickly, impotent, inable, and unmeete persons, as of rascals and vagabonds now spread and remaining and being in all the court [...] the King's Highness therefore hath given charge unto his vice-chamberlain [...] to make view, search and report of the sufficiency, ability, demeanour, and qualities of all such persons as be officers [...] and servants in the said household and chambers.   (146)

Having servants who are honest in gesture and behaviour is an important element of the reform programme mapped out in the Ordinance. Consistently in the Ordinance morality is collapsed into transparency. Just as in More's ideal commonwealth, the perfect court imagined in the Ordinance lacks any private spaces; sin would have no place to hide in Henry's utopian court (Skinner 1987). In Heywood's court drama, however, it is precisely in performance, in the gap between the meaning of words and their enactment, that the smooth embodied surface of the Henrician courtier and servant comes apart.

The impracticality of the utopian reform programme mapped out in the Ordinance is thrown into sharp relief by the collection of poems, ballads, and prophecies that make up the Welles Anthology, a manuscript collection assembled between late 1522 and 1534. This anthology contains a bewildering range of works, including possibly the first poem written by Heywood, 'The Epitaph of Lob the King's Fool'. In particular the Welles Anthology seems caught between endorsing courtly love as the norm of courtiership and articulating a cruder version of the relationship between the sexes. For example, the poem 'O swete harte dere and most best belovyd' is a traditional courtly lover's lament:

> Love causeth me a letter to make
> the last tyme that I departyd yow froo
> That that I have done ys for your sake
> when that my harte ytt was full [of] woo

oftyn tymes full styll I goo
and yet truly Soo cryst me spede
I lett yo[u] wytt that ytt ys Soo
Your bewtye maketh my harte to blede.

(*Welles* 1991: 214)

The last line is a refrain that echoes throughout the poem, emphasizing the extent
to which the male narrator of this work is entirely and painfully in thrall to his love.
'O swete harte dere and most best belovyd' encapsulates the sense of courtly love as
a kind of exquisite masochistic game in which the male lover writes out his pain in
an act of self-abasement. The Welles Anthology, however, includes poems that depict
the relationship between the sexes in very different terms. The poem 'She that hathe
a wanton eye' is a witty misogynist text that works through numerous different types
of women to prove that all are basically the same:

She that maketh ytt strange and quoynte
and loketh as she were a seynte
and wolde be woed aman may sey
hur gentyll harte can nott say naye

...

She that hathe a wytte wandryng
and all wey hur tong clattering
and wyll abyd whysperyng yn the eyre
hur tayll shulde be lyght of the stere.

(156, 157)

Women who look like saints and those whose wits wander are basically the same
underneath.

The poems collected in the Welles Anthology create an image of the court that is
identical to that imagined in the Ordinance. At one level the court of these poems is a
highly conventional and mannered place where lovers exchange longing looks across
marbled halls, while at another it is a place awash with rampant sexual desire in which
all women are ultimately nothing more than whores on the lookout for the next man
to beguile.

Early Henrician court drama is equally split between order and disorder. In this
period the management of court drama and entertainment more generally was
becoming increasingly complex and professional, reflected in the creation of the
Revels Office in 1545 (Streitberger 1985). At the same time the records of court drama
that we possess reveal a situation in which the status of entertainments and interludes
was constantly open to negotiation. In particular, as the accounts of court events that
fill Hall's chronicle clearly demonstrate, Henry was constantly prepared to disrupt the
stately tenor of court dramas and plays with interventions whose force was predicated
on their disordered and violent status (Dillon 2002). It would, however, be a mistake
to see Henry as the only person possessing the ability or authority to create such
moments of disruption. The court depicted in Heywood's dramas is a decorous place
in which civilized debates can be staged in front of an educated audience *and* a place

in which sex and violence, wealth and poverty, good kingship and terrifying tyranny, all exist within the same space and time.

10.2 JOHN HEYWOOD AND EARLY TUDOR DRAMA

John Heywood wrote a number of plays during the 1520s and early 1530s. His place, however, in the history of the development of English literature has been obscured by a number of negative blockages. An important problem has been the question of the status of Heywood's dramas: are they plays or interludes (Craik 1958)? This is difficult to answer given that there is little evidence that Heywood's contemporaries thought in these terms. Nicholas Davis has suggested that the key distinction between interludes and plays is that while the latter were performed outside to relatively large audiences, interludes took place indoors to far fewer people (1984: 10). This distinction does have some utility. The problem is that stressing the difference between interludes and plays on the basis of performance conditions can create a misleading sense that the former are an aberration in the development of English drama from medieval morality and mystery plays to the work of Shakespeare and his contemporaries. Alternatively, interludes have been seen as providing a bridge between medieval and late Elizabethan drama and in the process have not been studied in detail in their own right. There has also been a tendency within the scholarship to assume that interludes, as courtly or aristocratic entertainments, were performed to select audiences and were intended to celebrate the magnificence of the lord of the hall in which they were performed. This in turn has fed into the assumption that court interludes are theatrically naive and politically conservative works, in contrast to 'non-metropolitan, amateur [drama], played in the street, and as critical of its own exercise of power as it is of royal and episcopal power' (Simpson 2002: 553).

None of these assumptions stands up to close analysis. Greg Walker points out that the existing interludes from the Henrician period are largely very political and often potentially critical of royal policy. He comments that:

interludes enjoyed a considerable freedom to explore political issues precisely because of their location within the great halls of the political elite. It was their *centrality*, politically if not geographically, which created its own cultural power, as it brought into being a licensed, ludic space at the very heart of the political nation, in the royal household or the courts in miniature of the provincial nobility. (1998: 62–3)

Certainly dramas like John Skelton's *Magnificence* (c.1519–20) or the anonymous *Godly Queen Hester* (c.1529) are sophisticated works of political theory that deploy the possibilities of the theatrical form in order to articulate a political critique as radical as any advanced by later dramatists. All the available evidence suggests that Henrician court entertainments and revels were elaborate and complicated affairs (Streitberger 1998). In particular, interludes created a dynamic relationship with both the audience and the space within which they took place. As Richard Southern observes, they 'must be thought of as having an oblong, central floor-space at their disposal, and as being fully prepared to make use of every inch of it' (1973: 53).

The implications of Southern's suggestion are that the relationship between audience and actors had to be constantly negotiated during the course of a performance (Carpenter 1997). Heywood's play *Johan Johan* (*c*.1526–30), a translation from a French work, is a fabliau in which Tyb, John's wife, torments her poor husband while carrying on an affair with a dissolute parish priest, Sir John. The play ends with all three fighting 'by the erys' before Tyb and Sir John 'go out of the place' leaving John alone on stage celebrating his victory over them:

> A! syrs, I have payd some of them even as I lyst;
> They have borne many a blow with my fyst.
> I thank God I have walkyd them well,
> And driven them hens. But yet can ye tell
> Whether they be go? For, by God, I fere me
> That they be gon together, he and she
> Unto his chamber, and perhappys she wyll
> Spyte of my hart, tary there styll,
> And peradventure there he and she
> Wyll make me cokold, evyn to anger me:
> And then had I a pyg in the wors panyer.
> Therefore, by God, I wyll hye me thyder
> To see yf they do me any vylany:
> And thus fare well this noble company!
>
> (1991*a*: 92)

John's speech runs through a range of registers. It opens with him pleased to have beaten both his cheating wife and her lover. Suddenly he realizes that the pair have left together and are probably even now making a cuckold of him. It is with this enraging thought that John leaves the stage and the play concludes. What this speech demonstrates is the way in which Heywood's drama occupies and transforms the space of the court or stately hall. John's sense of triumph while alone on stage in the public space of the drama is undermined by his sudden consciousness of the fact that Tyb and her lover are together somewhere in the illicit spaces that surround the public space occupied by him and the noble company. Heywood's drama stages in this moment the oxymoronic logic of the Henrician court. John thinks he has 'reformed' Tyb and Sir John; he has driven corruption from the stage and restored decorum only to realize the extent to which his reformation is undermined by the existence of the dark underbelly of the court in which Tyb and her priest are probably even now together. John is at this moment a figure for the audience who are at once part of a noble company laughing knowingly at John's naive pleasure at having driven his enemies off-stage and then sharing in the realization that like John their status is ultimately determined by what goes on behind their backs, in the hidden, twisting passages of the court.

As Heywood's drama developed through the 1520s, the sense of a violent under-current constantly intrudes into the on-stage action. In *The Pardoner and the Friar*, written in 1529, it is given an explicitly linguistic twist. Candace Lines has recently suggested that 'interpretation is at the heart of *The Pardoner and the Friar*, which centres on competitive speech and the problems of interpretation it engenders' (2000: 402). In this play Heywood's two principal characters argue over who is best equipped to preach to the audience. It would, however, be a mistake to describe the exchanges between the Pardoner and the Friar as a debate (with its connotations of rationality). It is a fight with words leading to a complete breakdown of communication: it takes only 180 lines for the two to end up in a linguistic struggle for control over the space of the play. The stage direction at this point of the play reads: 'Now shall the Frere begyn his sermon, and evyn at the same tyme the Pardoner begynneth also to shew and speke of his bullys, and auctorytes from Rome' (1991*b*: 98). The following dialogue stages the effect of this simultaneous speaking.

FRERE Good devout people, this place of scrypture
PARDONER Worshypfull maysters, ye shall understand
FRERE Is to you that have no literature
PARDONER That Pope Leo the tenth hath granted with his hand,
FRERE Is to say in our englysshe tonge—
PARDONER And by his bulles confyrmed under lede,
FRERE As 'departe your goodes the poorefolke amonge'
PARDONER To all maner people, bothe qucyke and dede,
FRERE And God shall than gyve unto you agayne:
PARDONER Ten thousande yeres and as many lentes of pardon
FRERE This in the gospel so is wryten playne.   (98–9)

The Pardoner and the Friar was written in the same year (1529) that saw the publication of Simon Fish's violent anticlerical tract *A Supplication for the Beggars*. And it is possible to see Heywood's work as anticlerical. After all, it presents two members of the clergy as rogues who fill the space of the stage, which it later transpires is a church, with violent and meaningless dispute. Heywood, however, is a more sophisticated writer and thinker than Fish. In the exchange above there are three versions running currently. On the one hand, there is the suspiciously Protestant-sounding Friar with his consistent references to Scripture. On the other, there is the Pardoner with his equally insistent and problematic invocations of papal authority. There is also, however, their combined speech, which, read as a single speech pro-duces a scriptural defence of traditional penitential teaching. The Pardoner and the Friar, however, remain completely unaware that their combined speech produces religious teaching that is far more persuasive then their individual doctrinal pos-tions. Instead they continue to dispute until the Parson enters and orders them to stop their wrangling in his church (107). When the Parson finds he cannot control them on his own, he asks a neighbour, Prat, for help. At the end of the play, however, the Pardoner and the Friar remain obstinately unreformed, and the play ends with an image of real violence as the Parson and Prat fight with the Pardoner and the Friar:

PARSON Helpe, helpe, neybour Prat, neybour Prat!
      In the worshyp of God, helpe me somewhat!
PRAT Nay, deale as thou canst with that elfe!
      For why? I have inoughe to do my selfe.
      Alas, for payn I am almoste dede!
      The reede blood so ronneth downe my hede.
      Nay, and thou canst, I pray the helpe me!
PARSON Nay, by the mas, felowe, it wyll not be—
      I have more tow on my dystaffe than I can well spyn.
      The cursed frere dothe the upper hande wyn!
FRERE Wyll ye leve than, and let us in peace departe?
PARSON & PRAT Ye, by Our Lady, even with all our harte.
FRERE & PARDONER Then adew, to the devyll, tyll we come agayn!
PARSON & PRAT And a myschefe go with you bothe twayn!   (109)

There is a palpable sense of threat. The Friar and the Pardoner have left the church–stage, but they clearly intend to return. The combination of the Parson and Prat, parish priest and neighbour, has proved incapable of finally defeating them and indeed in many ways at the end of the play they are left in a worse state than their opponents.

It is a critical commonplace to locate Heywood's plays within humanism and to describe then as staged debates (Walker 2000: 434). In *The Pardoner and the Friar* Heywood is undoubtedly drawing on humanist ideas, but he is also criticizing them. The Pardoner and the Friar do produce, in the quotation above from the opening of their intertwined sermons, good orthodox teaching; however, this is entirely coincidental to their own teaching. What *The Pardoner and the Friar* illustrates above all is not the power of debate, but its limitations. In particular, Heywood argues in this play that any debate predicated on a division between scriptural and papal authority will lead to violence. The truth that emerges in the exchange between the Pardoner and the Friar is produced not by their conflicting intellectual claims to authority but by the act of performance, the way in which the dramatic form forces their two voices to share the same space.

At the end of the play the Pardoner and the Friar, despite their profound differences, are united against the forces of moderate religion and neighbourliness, personified in the Parson and Prat. This conclusion, however, does not simply reflect Heywood's conservatism. It also marks his commitment to an Erasmian rejection of, in Brendan Bradshaw's arresting phrase, 'the fideist dichotomy between reason and revelation' (1982: 416). Heywood portrays his Pardoner and Friar not simply as corrupt teachers, with the latter's over-reliance on papal authority and the former's constant emphasis on Scripture suggesting strongly a papist Pardoner and a Protestant Friar, but more generally as representations of ignorance and vice. Ultimately what their competing sermons show is that, under their displays of intellectual wit and skill, these two men are purely driven by their desire for earthly wealth. It is as figures of human frailty and arrogance that the Pardoner and the Friar threaten the world of the Parson and Prat, and as such they can never be finally or conclusively defeated. The best one can hope for is their temporary expulsion from the world of the stage, but they will always be lurking in the wings waiting for a chance to re-emerge and fill the world with the noise of their boasting and corrupt teaching.

At the centre of Heywood's Henrician drama is a critique of what can most usefully be described as authorship, not in the modern sense as referring to the writer of a text but more generally in relation to the idea that individuals can or should claim authority through the production of individual coherent texts. In *The Four PP* (*c*.1531) Heywood again stages the limitations of debate as a method for solving disputes. The play focuses on an argument between a Pardoner and a Palmer (pilgrim) over who is best able to guide souls to heaven. The debate between these two characters is interrupted by the entrance of a Potycary (apothecary), who claims to be much better than either at sending souls to their Maker. At this point the final P enters, a Pedlar, who is persuaded to adjudicate and who suggests a lying competition as the most appropriate task for the three other Ps. The Potycary tells a bawdy story based on his ability to cure a young woman of epilepsy. He claims to have used a suppository, which, when the young woman farted it out, flew 10 miles and levelled a castle. The Pardoner tells his tale next. This is a wonderful account of his journey into purgatory and hell in search of a woman with whom he was 'friendly' on earth. Failing to find his friend in purgatory and knowing that she was no saint, the Pardoner travels to the gates of hell, where he meets an old friend:

> And fyrst the devyll that kepte the gate
> I came, and spake after this rate:
> 'All hayle, syr devyll', and made lowe curtesy.
> 'Welcome', quoth he, thys smillyngly,
> He knew me well and I at laste
> Remembered hym syns longe tyme paste.
> For as good happe wolde have it chaunce,
> Thys devyll and I were of olde acqueyntaunce
> For oft in the play of Corpus Christi
> He hath played the Devyll at Coventry.

> (2000*a*: 448)

The courtesy of this infernal meeting between the Pardoner and Hell's Gatekeeper is maintained through the former's journey through hell. Before embarking on this voyage, the Pardoner has to wait at hell's gate for a warrant to be issued by Lucifer granting him safe passage. When this arrives, it sounds suspiciously like the kind of warrant that an earthly king might issue. Indeed Heywood's whole portrayal of hell, and in particular Lucifer's court, is replete with echoes of the Tudor court. When the Pardoner finally enters Lucifer's presence, he is confronted with a figure of majestic power that is impressive, dangerous, and slightly comic:

> Then to Lucyfer, low as I coude,
> I knelyd, whiche he so well alowde
> That thus he beckte, and, by Saynt Antony,
> He smyled on me well favoredly,
> Bendynge hys browes as brode as barne durres,
> Shakynge hys eares as ruged as burres
> Rolynge hys yes as rounde as two bushels,
> Flastynge the fyre out of his nose thryls,
> Gnashynge hys teeth so vayngloro[u]sely
> That me thought tyme to fall to flattery.

> (98–9)

The Pardoner flatters Lucifer so well that he is given permission to rescue his friend from hell. The nature of her sin, and indeed their relationship, is confirmed when the Pardoner finds her in the kitchens turning the spit, since the implication is that it was her spit-turning on earth, in other words her sexual wantonness ('spit' being slang for penis), that led to her dispatch to hell in the first place. The Pardoner ends his story by telling his listeners that if they wish to find the woman, they can find her at Newmarket (450), the location of Devil's Dyke, allegedly an entrance to hell. The Pardoner's tale ends with a mocking reference to a popular superstition that further emphasizes the tale's fictional nature (450).

At the end of his story the Pardoner seems almost to forget that he is meant to be telling a lie. This echoes the similar failure of generic decorum that runs through Geoffrey Chaucer's 'Pardoner's Tale'. It also, however, reflects Heywood's meta-theatrical argument in this play, which is that fiction and fictionality are in the eyes, and perhaps ears, of the spectators. As the courtly audience listens to the Pardoner's incredible tale, they are transported into a hellish court ruled over by a figure whose mere presence induces the Pardoner to fall to flattery. Clearly this is a potentially disturbing moment for Heywood's court audience since it reproduces, albeit in parodic form, norms of Tudor courtship. The radicalism of this collapse between the world of Heywood's play and that of the Tudor court is, however, kept safe by the clearly fictional status of the Pardoner's story.

It is, however, important to note that although the Pardoner is telling a lie, and Heywood stresses its fictional status, the motifs and themes that comprise the Pardoner's tale are drawn directly from a tradition of medieval stories focusing on journeys to hell and purgatory. Eamon Duffy has discussed in detail medieval beliefs about purgatory; one of the key points he makes is that kinship and friendship were 'recurrent notions in the cult of Purgatory' (1992: 349). He goes on to discuss theological problems caused by popular beliefs in the ability of specific prayers and masses to influence the fate of individual souls in purgatory. Duffy comments that these beliefs are 'indicative of the tendency of lay practice, in search of supernatural solace and certainty to stray beyond the strict bounds of orthodoxy' (273). The Pardoner's story is located on the edge of orthodoxy. It occupies a liminal space between mainstream teaching on purgatory and reformist attacks on the whole doctrine of pardons and indulgences. On the one hand, the Pardoner's story appears designed to supply support for critics of purgatory. It is completely unbelievable. The Pardoner does act out of a friendship, but one of which the Church would certainly have disapproved. At the same time, the intense and self-conscious fictionality of the Pardoner's story, its status as part of a lying competition, not only has the effect of drawing the sting of its potential endorsement of criticisms of purgatory, it also works to suggest that to believe such criticism would be to be so naive as to be unable to separate fact from fiction. It is the very self-conscious hyper-fictionality of the Pardoner's story that protects orthodox teaching on purgatory. Indeed one can go further than this and argue that what Heywood does in *The Four PP* is place in the centre of the court a ludicrously extreme story about purgatory that only a fool would believe and in the process suggests that similarly extreme stories, clerical and anticlerical, should be treated with equal scorn.

The lying competition in *The Four PP* ends when the Palmer wins by simply stating that he has never seen a woman lose her temper. In effect the play privileges simple, direct, non-authored wisdom over the lies of the Pardoner and the Potycary. The play concludes with the Palmer 'Besechyng Our Lorde to prosper you all | In the fayth of Hys churche universall' (2000a: 462). The relatively optimistic ending belies the unresolved tensions of the play. It is almost as if Heywood's conclusion is itself an act of faith, that in a world in which who has the ability to send the most souls to heaven is settled by a lying competition, faith in the universal Church is the only place of stability and certainty. The Potycary is left peddling his lethal cures, and more worryingly the Pardoner's lies are left unchallenged if not ultimately endorsed since the play suggests that they are relatively less untruthful than the Palmer's claim never to have seen a woman lose her temper. There is a reductive logic at work within the play in that what it ultimately suggests is that in a fallen world all that can really be distinguished is degrees of untruthfulness. *The Four PP* undermines any possibility of reform by suggesting that lies and enormities as gross as the Pardoner's are only relatively bad and are in any case part of the normal fallen nature of humanity.

The Play of the Weather (c.1533) builds on this insight.[1] In this play Heywood mounts a sustained attack on Henrician politics. He mocks the language of the royal supremacy and creates a paradoxical image of Henry as an omnipotent but passive monarch. Lurking within this play, however, are images of violence and tyranny which constantly endanger the drama's apparently smooth surface. As so often, the basic plot is simple, verging on non-existent. The play opens with Jupiter telling the audience that, having restored peace in the heavens, he is intent on creating similar

---

[1] On 10 May 2007 I was Principal Investigator on an AHRC-funded workshop in the Great Hall at Hampton Court, which staged the opening scene and the scene with the gentlewoman; Greg Thompson directed; the actors were Cara Kelly, Richard Heap, David Fielder, Peter Kenny, and Marin Ware. Their creative responses to Heywood's text have informed and transformed my reading of the play.

harmony on earth: to this end he decides to appoint a messenger to ask every estate to elect a representative to come before him and plead for the weather that they most desire. At the end of this process, he tells the audience he will decide what the weather should be and this in turn will restore harmony between the estates. Perhaps not surprisingly, what Heywood's play illustrates is the impossibility, indeed the hubris, of this desire since the impossibility of satisfying everyone becomes quickly apparent. The demands of the Water Myller and Wind Myller can never be reconciled, nor can those of the Gentlewoman and the Laundress. What makes the achievement of agreement even more problematic is Jupiter's initial decision to appoint a character called Merry Report as his messenger and representative on earth. Merry Report's suitability for this role is at best dubious and he performs it with such partiality that it is clear that Heywood is commenting critically on the management of access to Jupiter–Henry.

The Play of the Weather opens with an extended speech by Jupiter which sets the scene for the following action. Jupiter's speech, however, is not of a disinterested partial chorus, although at times this is what it appears the god is seeking to suggest. Jupiter presents his speech as a simple account of what has happened and his own position as lord of the gods:

> Ryght farre to longe as now were to recite
> The auncyent estate wherin our selfe hath reyned,
> What honour, what laude gyven us of very ryght,
> What glory we have had dewly unfayned
> Of eche creature whych dewty hath constrayned,
> For above all goddess, syns our fathers fale
> We Jupiter were ever pryncypale.
>
> (2000*b*: 457)

This speech is typical of Heywood's Jupiter in the way it combines assertions with facts that appear to undermine what is being affirmed. For example, Jupiter concludes this section of his speech by stating that he has been 'ever pryncypale', but the proceeding line suggests a time in the past when Jupiter's father ruled. It clearly would have been more accurate for Jupiter to claim precedence since his father's fall, but to do so would evoke a time when his power was not complete or total. This desire to close down the possibility, any moment, time, or space, when his rule was incomplete affects all aspects of Jupiter's speech including the syntax. This becomes particularly noticeable, as Walker has recently pointed out (2005: 106), when Jupiter attempts to explain away the moment when the gods, gathered in parliament, surrender their powers to determine the weather to him:

> [The gods] have in conclusyon holly surrendryd
> Into our hands (as much as concernynge
> All maner of wethers by them engendryd)
> The full of theyr powrs for terme everlastynge,
> To set suche order as standyth wyth our pleasynge,

> Whyche thynge, as of our parte, no parte required
> But of all theyr partys ryght humbly desyred.
>
> (458)

In performance this speech is almost impossible to deliver while retaining the dignity required to play Jupiter. The twisted logic of Jupiter's opening speech, as Walker has brilliantly shown, reproduces exactly that of the official justifications of the Henrician Reformation, and perhaps specifically the Act in Restraint of Appeals. Walker comments that 'the terms of Jupiter's speech betray Heywood's acute ear for the cadences and tropes of Henrician public utterances', in particular in its 'piling up of syntactically tortuous, sense deferring clauses in search of a full-stop and [its] gathering together of at times near synonymous words and phrases without drawing any obvious distinctions between them' (2005: 116). Jupiter sounds like Henry, or rather he sounds like a personification of the official language of the Henrician Reformation. This does not mean, however, that Heywood was in any sense republican or even directly opposed to Henry's policy in the 1530s. *The Play of the Weather* clearly suggests that it is appropriate and necessary for a monarch to have absolute power over his subjects since what it stages is the complete inability of the people who petition Jupiter to think beyond their immediate class interests. This is vividly illustrated by the example of the first petitioner, the Gentleman, who comes to request weather conducive to hunting, the preferred leisure activity of his caste:

> And fyrst for us nobles and gentylman
> I doute not, in his [Jupiter's] wysedome to provyde
> Suche wether as in our hunting, now and then,
> We may tense and receive on every syde.
>
> Whyche thynge, ones had, for our seid recreacyon
> Shall greatly prevayle you in preferrynge our helth,
> For what thynge more nedefull then our preservacyon,
> Beynge the weale and heddes of all comen welth?
>
> (462)

These verses are fundamentally contradictory since, although they conclude with a reference to the gentry's role in maintaining the commonwealth, in practice the Gentleman is advancing a very specific class agenda which effectively places the preferred recreation of his estate above everyone else's needs. This is a constant refrain throughout the play, with each estate being shown to be quite incapable of seeing beyond its own narrow interests. The one thing that distinguishes the Gentleman's petition is his bare-faced attempt to deploy the discourse of commonwealth in its support.

It is Merry Report who presides over the competing suitors and controls their access to Jupiter. At the same time, and disturbingly, Merry Report is a Vice, playing with the audience and mocking the other characters. As Richard Axton and Peter Happé comment, the Vice's part is 'notably large' and 'the theatrical space takes on the highly charged and politically sensitive atmosphere of the "haut-pace at the king's chamber door" ' (1991: 26). Heywood's decision to place a Vice at the centre of a play whose main concern is the exercise of reforming royal power is potentially profoundly critical of Henry's rule. Jupiter desires to create harmony between his squabbling subjects and his agenda fails for two key reasons: it is impossible to satisfy all their demands and the person that he places in control of the process is a selfish, incompetent Vice. It would, however, be more accurate to argue that Merry Report's role is not so much to undermine Jupiter's reformist agenda as to show its impracticality to the God, and the king. This is not to suggest that Merry Report can be seen as a simple representative of common sense. There is something slightly demonic about many of his speeches, and in particular there are times when his bawdy seems to be in danger of slipping completely out of control, not only destroying his place in the play, but also undermining any possibility of humanist-inspired reform. For example, after his encounter with the Gentlewoman, Merry Report directly addresses the audience.

> Oft tyme yt is sene both in court and towne
> Longe be women a bryngyng up and sone brought down.
> So fete yt is, so nete yt is, so nyse yt is,
> So trycke yt is, so quycke yt is, so wyse yt is.

This passage refers at once to the Gentlewoman, women in general, and the penis. All are at once tricky, quick, and wise. In this speech Merry Report is being typically sexist and bawdy while at the same time suggesting an equivalence between his own quick wits and those of women. The punning work that 'yt' is required to do in this passage, coupled with the lack of specificity in terms of what it refers to, who or what each 'yt' is, and how all the 'yts' relate, reflects Heywood's scepticism concerning the reforming potential of language. What kind of reform could one expect from a court filled with Merry Report's 'yts'?

Merry Report personifies the dual focuses of the Henrician court as reflected in the Eltham Ordinance and the Welles Anthology. At once a source of humour, wit, and courtly play, he can suddenly become a far more violent and lascivious figure. This tendency is especially pronounced in terms of the politics of *The Play of the Weather*, where Merry Report consistently skirts dangerously close to contemporary politics. When the Gentlewoman wishes to see Jupiter but is repulsed, Merry Report explains her rejection in a speech loaded with political allusions:

> By my fayth, for his lordship is ryght besy
> Wyth a pece of work that nedes must be done.
> Even now is he makynge of a new moone:
> He sayth your old moones be so farre tasted
> That all the goodness of them is wasted;
> Whyche of the great wete hath ben moste mater,
> For olde moones be leake, they can holde no water.
> But for this new mone, I durst lay my gowne

Except a few droppes at her goynge downe,
Ye get no rayne tyll her arysynge
Without yt nede, and then no mans devysynge
Coulde wyshe the fashion of rayne to be so good:
Not gushynge out lyke gutters of Noyes flood,
But smale droppes sprynklyng softly on the grounde:
Though they fell on a sponge they wold gyve no sounde.
This new moone shal make a thing spryng more in this while
Than an old moon shal while a mile may go a mile.

(471)

When I worked on this speech with Greg Walker, David Fielder, and Greg Thompson, it became apparent that it was so potentially politically dangerous that it had to be played entirely straight. If one marked the fact that Merry Report's new moon refers to Anne Boleyn and the old to Katherine of Aragon, then this speech fills the space of the court with bawdy jokes not only about the 'tightness' of the new moon compared with the leakiness of the old, but also with references to Katherine's miscarriages (the old moon cannot contain its water but instead lets it gush out in too great quantities and before its time) and to Henry's sexual prowess (the new moon will make a 'thing' 'spring').

The Play of the Weather was quite possibly the last play that Heywood wrote for the Henrician court, although it is possible that the *Play of Love*, another debate play whose language is in places almost impenetrably obscure, may have followed it (Axton and Happé 1991: 21–4). Heywood's drama was not simply written to entertain the Henrician court; it participated in the emergence of a specifically Tudor court idiom and culture. *The Play of the Weather* on the surface is a simple piece of courtly wit mocking the courtiers, and Henry himself, in its portrayal of selfish petitioners and, in the figure of Merry Report, those who controlled access to the King. Underneath this surface, however, is a play fully conscious of the dark side of court life; of a world in which politics, reform, violence, and desire jostled each other in a dangerous and potentially explosive mix.

10.3 CONCLUSION

In one of the last works that he wrote, *A Treatise on the Passion* (*c*.1534), Thomas More used a theatrical metaphor to defend orthodox teaching on the Mass, asking his readers,

if ther were but even in a playe or an enterlude, the personages of ii or iii knowen princes represented, if one of them now liked for his pleasure to playe his own part himselfe, dyd he not there his owne persone under the fourme of a player, represent his owne persone in fourme of his own estate?'   (1976: 157)

Just as the bread is at once a symbol and the reality of Christ's body, so a king playing himself in an interlude would at once be himself and the theatrical representation of himself. It is impossible to know to what extent Henry viewed himself as Jupiter; indeed it cannot be conclusively proved that *The Play of the Weather* was performed at court. It is, however, difficult to imagine that the play was not intended for a courtly audience. Heywood's dramas consistently attack not one party or faction but more generally a form of debate, a desire for reform, predicated upon absolutes both negative and positive. Jupiter cannot see the Gentlewoman because he is making a new moon; as the speech progresses it seems to become apparent that the new moon refers at one level to Anne Boleyn. It may, however, have a more scatological meaning and be intended to suggest that Jupiter is in the toilet. There is, however, one other possible meaning, which is that the new moon Heywood refers to is that of the island of Utopia, which More described as shaped like a new moon. In this context making a new moon means being involved in a pointless fantasy of reform. Heywood's principled rejection of utopian politics and Reformation polemics has left him without a place in literary histories of the sixteenth century; as Walker comments, 'unlike More's texts, Heywood's dramas argue, not that heresy should be suppressed, but that contention itself should be eliminated' (Walker 1998: 110). Mary Thomas Crane has pointed out that Heywood's later work, much of which took the form of collections of epigrams, also mocked the presentations of reformers, Protestant and humanist. Crane argues that Heywood deliberately wrote epigrams that were anti-authoritarian in a rough, vernacular verse form to stress the extent to which they were brief concrete sayings from everyday life (1986: 178). Heywood has no place in literary histories of the sixteenth century because he held to a clear and explicit aesthetic throughout his career as a writer, one that is not conducive to the fantasies and desires of humanist reformers and literary critics, for whom displays of textual pyrotechnics and authorial prowess are all.

PRIMARY WORKS

CHAUCER, GEOFFREY (1988), 'The Pardoner's Tale', in *The Riverside Chaucer*, ed. F. N. Robinson (Oxford: Oxford University Press).

Collection (1790), *A Collection of Ordinances and Regulations for the Government of the Royal Household*.

FISH, SIMON (1529), *A Supplicacyon for the Beggers* ([Antwerp]).

HEYWOOD, JOHN (1991*a*), *Johan Johan*, in *Plays*, ed. Richard Axton and Peter Happé (Cambridge: Brewer).

—— (1991*b*), *The Pardoner and the Friar*, in *Plays*, ed. Richard Axton and Peter Happé (Cambridge: Brewer).

—— (2000a), *The Four PP*, in *Plays*, ed. Richard Axton and Peter Happé (Cambridge: Brewer).

—— (2000b), *The Play of the Weather*, ed. Greg Walker (Oxford: Blackwell).

MORE, THOMAS (1976), *A Treatise on the Passion*, ed. G. E. Haupt, in *The Complete Works of St. Thomas More*, xiii (New Haven: Yale University Press).

WALKER, GREG (ed.) (2000), *Medieval Drama* (Oxford: Blackwell).

Welles (1991), *The Welles Anthology: MS Rawlinson C.813: A Critical Edition*, ed. Sharon L. Jansen and Kathleen H. Jordan (New York: Medieval and Renaissance Texts and Studies).

CHAPTER 11

··

THOMAS WYATT AND FRANCIS BRYAN

PLAINNESS AND DISSIMULATION

··

JASON POWELL

SIR THOMAS WYATT's third satire, 'A spending hand', is dedicated to Sir Francis Bryan, a man 'who knows how great a grace | In writing is to cownsell man the right' (BL, Egerton MS 2711, fo. 56^r).[1] As a diplomat and courtier, Bryan was known for his love of sententious wisdom, and for telling the unvarnished truth to Henry VIII. But in the Egerton manuscript of Wyatt's poetry, these lines end with a question mark. The punctuation was probably inserted after Wyatt's death by an aspiring mid-Tudor editor. Nevertheless, it seems to encompass much of the relationship between the two men, as well as the satire's ambiguous pose. Bryan, known at court as Henry's 'Vicar of Hell' for his dissolute advice and lifestyle, certainly had very public experience in delivering moral counsel. But to 'cownsell man the right'? That is a question indeed.

[1] Quotations from Wyatt's poems and fatherly letters come from BL, Egerton MS 2711, except for quotations from 'Mine own John Poyntz', taken from a more complete version in Corpus Christi College, Cambridge, Parker Library, MS 168. Citing the poetry, I have expanded abbreviations and represented original punctuation as can best be determined. I have modernized punctuation in the letters. I am grateful for the support of the National Endowment for the Humanities, the Huntington Library, and the British Academy towards work from which this chapter proceeds.

In the sixteenth century, both Wyatt and Bryan were elevated as models of one or another virtue. Wyatt was canonized by Henry Howard, Earl of Surrey, and by the antiquary John Leland in elegies printed by John Herford (1542?) and Reyner Wolfe (1542), respectively. Surrey praised him as a model of a new kind of poetic honour (Sessions 1994). The Elizabethan commentator George Puttenham later named Wyatt, with Surrey, one of a 'new company of courtly makers' (Thomson 1974: 34). Bryan was also credited with poetic excellence: Michael Drayton called him a 'sweet-tongued' poet, one of the 'best makers' of the era and an anonymous contributor in Tottel's *Miscellany*. In republishing Bryan's translation of *A Dispraise of the Life of a Courtier* in 1575, the printer Thomas Thynne described Bryan as a Xenophon—after the Greek soldier and historian famous for collecting Socratic aphorisms—who shaped his countrymen, sword in one hand, pen in the other (Kinsman 1979: 279).

The characterizations of both men were flawed. Wyatt was perhaps the country's most important poet since Chaucer, but he was not quite the figure of honour that Surrey portrayed. Bryan was hardly a poet at all: his one known piece of extant verse is clumsy and derivative even by the standards of early Tudor imitation, and there is little evidence that he authored any of the anonymous poems in Tottel's *Miscellany*. Nevertheless, Tudor commentators got one thing right: as writers, Wyatt and Bryan epitomized two models of early Tudor 'virtue' in an age of profoundly shifting ethical value systems. These two models play out most dramatically in the shifting, ironic voices of Wyatt's third satire.

I

William Sessions has argued that Surrey's elegy 'Wyatt resteth here' was designed to promote a new conception of honour and nobility centred on the poet and his communal role (1994: 169). The poem sets Wyatt as a model of unappreciated—even martyred—virtue amid the rampant vice of court. The Egerton manuscript—in which Wyatt collected, corrected, or even composed much of his known verse—suggests that Wyatt had a similarly acute sense of his own role as poet. Moreover, by the late 1530s, Wyatt was sealing his letters with the imprint of an ivy leaf, on which was embedded a 'V' for the Latin form of his name (Viat). As Petrarch himself indicated while receiving a garland on the Capitol steps in 1341, ivy was a well-known classical symbol of poetic achievement (Powell 2007). When Surrey promoted Wyatt as a poet, he probably followed Wyatt's own self-promotion.

Surrey's version of honour and poetic nobility would prove particularly compelling for Elizabethan poets and critics, but it was not one that Wyatt shared. Like Bryan, Wyatt portrayed himself in his writings as a plain and honest man, and the concept of honesty Wyatt promoted was no less complex (or classically inflected) than Surrey's idea of honour. William Empson (1951) was perhaps among the first to note the incredible breadth of the word 'honesty' in this period. The modern conception of honesty as 'not lying, not cheating, not stealing' predominated only by the end of the sixteenth century. Before that, the word was more often associated with a nebulous bundle of moral qualities linked to honour (including chastity for women). Most importantly, the concept of 'honour' could not yet be separated from reputation. Conceptions of 'honesty' were thus tied to a moral system that was implicitly external, based on the perception of other 'honest' men. At the same time, a number of ironic and casual uses persisted. One could refer to drunkards or hard-working peasants as 'honest', using the term in 'general praise among friends, on a good fellow basis' (Empson 1951: 186). Such uses may have contained a vestigial irony, since the drunken 'good fellow' was not truly honourable. He was 'honest' in the sense of 'simple'—perhaps because he was not crafty enough to be truly deceptive, or because any deception was true to his base nature. Neither Wyatt nor Bryan could claim this particular kind of simplicity; neither was low-born, and neither eschewed the comforts of a privileged life. Yet both claimed to speak with his own particular version of honesty—plain, transparent, and, crucially, at odds with the environment at court.

Wyatt's two extant letters to his son Thomas, written from France and Spain in 1537, present a clearer conception of his own sense of honesty, one he repeatedly and explicitly defines against other uses of the term, as here in the second letter:

I have nothing to crye and cal apon you for but honestye, honestye. It may be diversly namid, but alway it tendith to one end. [...] I meane not that honestye that the comen sort callith an honist man. Trust me that honist man is as comen a name as the name of a good felow—that is to say, a dronkerd, a taverne hanter, a riotter, a gamer, a waster—so are among the comen sort al men honist men that are not knowin for manifest naughtye knaves.

(BL, Egerton MS 2711, fo. 72^v)

Wyatt deliberately excludes Empson's uses of 'general praise' in favour of a less common moral designation. In a previous letter, written from Paris on 14 April the same year, he advances a clearer positive definition of his 'honesty':

And here I call not honestye that men comenly cal honestye, as reputation for riches, for authorite, or some like thing, but that honestye that I dare well say your granfather (whos soule God pardon) had rather left to me then all the lands he did leave me—that was wisdome, gentlenes, sobrenes, disire to do good, frendliness to get the love of manye, and trougth above all the rest.   (fo. 71^r)

The 'granfather' mentioned here is Sir Henry Wyatt, the author's father, who had died on 10 November 1536. Henry Wyatt was a Yorkshireman and a creation of the Tudors. He supported Henry Tudor against Richard III, and gradually ascended over the next five decades to wealth and high office, as a Privy Counsellor under Henry VII, and as master of the jewels, treasurer of the chamber, and sheriff of Kent under Henry VIII. He was wealthy enough to purchase Allington Castle in Kent in 1492 (ODNB). His success epitomizes social changes that are concealed here beneath the mention of a landed legacy ('the lands he did leave me'). This legacy implies that Wyatt is referring to the oldest sense of 'honesty', from its original relationship to honour. But here 'honesty' is opposed to the physical inheritance; Wyatt begins to exclude social perceptions, a task he continues in the second letter, where he asks his son to 'Seke not [...] that honesty which aperith and is not indead' (fo. 72^v). This concept of honesty is no longer contained by the standard notion of honour because it deliberately excludes reputation.

Wyatt has been called a 'bookish' author (Scattergood 2006), so we should not be surprised to find humanist sources behind Wyatt's letters as we do behind his poetry. The courtesy literature of the period drew upon a wide variety of classical and medieval sources, including the sayings of Isocrates, the distichs attributed to Cato, and the proverbs collected in John Lydgate's *Fall of Princes* (*c*. 1439). However, Tudor writers who discussed honesty, and particularly the relationship between honesty and profit, typically enlisted Cicero's *De officiis* ('Of Duties'). Like Wyatt's advice letters, *De officiis* was written by a father for a son, in this case by Cicero for his son Marcus during the political struggle following Caesar's assassination in 44 BC. It focuses on the apparently contradictory principles of morality (*honestas*) and profit (*utilitas*). Crucially, Cicero altered the Stoic values he found in Panaetius' *Peri tou kathekontos* ('On Duties') to fit his own conception of politics (Dyck 1996), as Marcia Colish notes in her comparison of Cicero and Machiavelli:

Had [Cicero] used his terms in a Stoic sense he would have defined *honestum* as the *summum et unicum bonum* and the *utile* as a synonym of the Stoic preferables, or *adiaphora*, conducive to virtue under certain circumstances but, taken by themselves, as morally neutral en bloc. The reconciliation of the *honestum* and the *utile* would be achieved simply by asserting that the *honestum*, being intrinsically good and an end in itself, should be the changeless criterion by which the admissability of the *utile* should be judged. However, this is not the argument which Cicero in fact puts forth in the *De officiis*. Instead, he elevates the *utile* to the level of an ethical criterion in its own right, making it the norm of the *honestum*. He also redefines the *honestum* itself, treating it not as Stoic virtue, which he sees as inhuman and unattainable in practice, but as the *medium officium*, the intermediate duty of the public man, which can be achieved in the real world and which pertains to the *usus vitae*, the needs of daily life.   (1978: 86–7)

Cicero's honesty (as *honestas* was most frequently translated in the sixteenth century) consisted of four virtues—wisdom, justice, courage (or fortitude), and decorum (or temperance)—and these were often pragmatically applied. Cicero repeatedly claims that what 'is honest, is profitable'.[2] But his 'honesty' is clearly public honesty—a moral value to be sure, but one defined principally by the good of the state. When he examines specific cases, he finds that 'promises also, many times, ar not to be perfourmed', particularly if they interfere with the interests of the nation or community (1990: 3. 1362–72). As Jennifer Richards notes, 'Cicero's idea of decorum proves rather slippery' for early modern writers, since it implies that 'it is sometimes also "honest" *not* to tell the truth' (2003: 28, 27, 26).

---

[2] Cicero (1990: 3. 451; cf. 3. 654–8, 867–9, 1073–7, 1116–19, 1166–70, 1194–6, 1231–5, 1456–67, 1607–9, 1698–1701).

Wyatt claimed with Cicero that profit would ensue from honesty: 'Glorye and honest name' will follow honesty 'as light folowth fire, though it wer kindled for warmth' (fo. 71ʳ). His distinction between seeming and being was a common classical idea, known from the writings of both Cicero and Sallust. Wyatt describes his own father as an example of honesty, listing his qualities to match those virtues associated with Cicero's philosophers. He does not fail to mention that 'both the kings his masters noted [...] greatly' these qualities (fo. 71ᵛ). He even suggests his son maintain virtue through a community of honest men: 'Think and ymagine alwais that you are in presens of some honist man that you know, as Sir Jhon Russel, your father in law, your unkle, parson, or some other such, and ye shal, if at ony time ye find a plesur in naughtye touchis, remember what shame it wer afore thes men to doo naughtily' (fo. 71ʳ). But although an 'honist name is goodly', and should be 'be kept, preservid and defendid' (fo. 72ᵛ), glory and reputation are not the 'very ends wherefore' (fo. 71ʳ) honesty should be sought. These letters never eschew profit, but *utilitas* has none of the moral value it acquires in Cicero's treatment.

Instead, the moral values Wyatt espouses are essentially Stoic. He recommends Seneca and Epictetus for his son's reading, and writes in the plain style of Seneca's letters—a mode Wyatt repeatedly used to develop his ethos as a plain and honest man. This use of a Stoic honesty, and particularly the separation of honesty from reputation, suggests that Wyatt was beginning to use Stoic thought in a new ways. Wyatt depicts his 'honesty' as the inheritance from a bygone world, but he re-envisions the concept within a newer, particularly humanist, intellectual context. This may be one way of understanding 'honesty' and its evolution as a word in Tudor England: Stoicism, along with the powerful interiority of Protestantism, forced a private ethic upon the public face of Ciceronian eloquence.

Students of the Elizabethan period, who are likely to remember the fatherly authority projected by Cecil's commanding *Ten Precepts* (Burghley et al. 1962), or the irony of the long-winded Polonius advising Laertes to 'Give thy thoughts no tongue' (Shakespeare 1997: 1. 3. 59), may be surprised by the utter self-consciousness of Wyatt's fatherly voice. Far from promoting himself as an implied model of perfection or even authority, Wyatt accepts his failures, naming himself 'a nere example' of 'foly and unthriftnes' that brought him as he 'wel deservid [...] into a thousand dangers and hazardes, enmyties, hatreds, prisonments, despits and indignations' (fo. 71ᵛ). Some of these failures were blatantly obvious to Wyatt's young son, who had seen his father imprisoned in the Tower with the alleged lovers of Anne Boleyn only a year before. In such circumstances, humility may be a rhetorical necessity. But these letters are conversational in the true Erasmian sense of the humanist epistle—so much so that the speaking voice can project moments of apparently unguarded vulnerability. This vulnerability, like the plainness of Wyatt's persona, is belied by the complicated 'bookishness' of his writing. Herein lies the paradox of Tudor plainness: as language shifted beneath complex and contested understandings of morality, real plainness became either reductive or rhetorical. One sought plainness only by ignoring inconvenient complexities, or by constructing an elaborate framework for recognizing that complexity, in which case the plainness was lost.

Wyatt's fatherly letters, as much as his poetry, are crucial to understanding Wyatt's satire for Bryan. This is not to underestimate the difference between a father writing to a son and a poet writing to a fellow courtier, but rather to acknowledge that Wyatt's satires and letters are embedded in the same generic traditions of the epistle and early modern conduct literature, that they both engage with the relationship between honesty and profit in a rapidly changing world of royal service.

Among the principal virtues of Wyatt's 'honesty' was the term 'trouth', identified by Thomas Greene as 'the Chaucerian word that organizes Wyatt's moral code'. Greene suggests that Wyatt builds 'his poems consciously around words whose meanings are pointedly debased', and that Wyatt's poems record 'the ungrounding of *trouth*, a property of human relations that is also a property of language'. Like 'honesty', the word 'trouth' divides and changes in the century; 'trouth' became 'truth' as 'faithfulness' ceded ground to the indication of 'accuracy' or 'agreement with reality'. It is also a word without equivalent in Wyatt's Petrarchan sources (Greene 1982: 254–5). But the insufficiency of 'trouth' for Wyatt lay not in the word's lack of meaning, but in the confusing multitude of potentially conflicting meanings. What happens when the 'reality' signified by this word is no longer 'true'?

Some of Wyatt's better-known lyrics remain his most problematic for critics and editors. Among these, 'The long love' metaphorically figures love as a partial construct of male relationships—in this case between the speaker and love, a militant Cupid portrayed as a feudal lord. The focus of Wyatt's Petrarchan source (*Rima* 140) lies on desire and restraint. But Wyatt converts this into a commentary on the more general tragedy of political 'trouth'. The 'lord' of the poem misbehaves from the beginning, offending the woman and embarrassing the speaker by inciting his forwardness. The sestet depicts love's flight 'with payn and cry' to the forest, where he 'hideth and not appereth'. How then can Wyatt's loyalty end in 'the feld', when his master appears to remain in the 'forrest'? The question assumes continuity between the two tercets. But unlike both Petrarch and Surrey, who adapted the same sonnet, Wyatt fails to name love in the final tercet, referring to it only as 'my maister'. One effect of this omission—combined with the strange figurative return to the field—is to generalize the poem's final statement. It is no longer so much about restraint *in love* as about the complexities of fidelity to a master who lacks all restraint:

> What may I do when my maister ferethp
> but in the feld with him to lyve and dye
> for goode is the liff ending faithfully.
>
> (BL, Egerton MS 2711, fo. 5^{r-v})

For both Petrarch and Surrey, the death is sweet because the love is sweet (perhaps with a pun on 'death' as 'orgasm'). For Wyatt, death is good because faithfulness is good, even if the 'maister' is not. But the kind of faithfulness Wyatt's speaker professes is not always any more possible for the speaker than for the objects of his affection. The confusion between 'feld' and 'forrest' at the poem's close may represent a moral confusion at its core. If the speaker retreats with 'love', he can maintain a Petrarchan faithfulness to both Cupid and the woman's instructions. But if the lord returns to the field (and thus into 'bold pretence' towards her), the speaker remains faithful to 'love', but not to the woman who taught him to suffer. However much the speaker tries to achieve closure, the question on which the poem closes implies that one kind of faithfulness will violate another.

We begin 'The long love' with a clear conception of love as a subject and the woman as an object of that love. But the woman fades from view by the end, when the speaker reframes steadfastness more assuredly as faithfulness to an idea instead of a person. In 'What vaileth trouth', we begin the poem without a clear sense of love as a topic, only to discover in line 13 that we had been discussing love all along:

> What vaileth trouth or by it to take payn
> to stryve by stedfastnes for to attayne
> to be juste and true and fle from dowblenes
> sythens all alike where rueleth craftines
> rewarded is boeth fals and plain
> sonest he spedeth that moost can fain
> true meanyng hert is had in disdayn
> against deceipt and dowblenes
> What vaileth trouth
>
> Deceved is he by crafty trayn
> that meaneth no gile and doeth remayn
> with in the trapp withoute redresse
> but for to love lo suche a maisteres
> whose crueltie nothing can refrayn
> What vaileth trouth.

(fo. 4^{r-v})

The poem's effect comes from its irregular rhythm. A caesura separates the first four syllables of the first line from the last six syllables. The second line reverses the syllable count around the caesura, creating an awkward emphasis on 'stedfastness' in the midst of a rhythmic shift. The third line begins with an anapaestic foot, followed by two iambs split across another caesura. But rather than close with an another anapaest, creating the metrical mirror Wyatt often employs in broken-backed lines, this line refuses such 'dowblenes'. Lines 10–12 are arguably in iambic tetrameter (assuming a two-syllable pronunciation of 'Deceved', a silent 'eth' on 'meaneth', and a one-syllable 'doeth'), a rhythm as simple as the beguiled person. Meanwhile, the 'trapp' of the caesura remains, growing stronger as these three lines progress. Then comes line 13—'but for to love lo suche a maisteres'—where 'lo' is emphasized by interrupting the caesura. The final line ends the poem with a rhythm (assuming two syllables for 'crueltie'[3]) again as plain as its truth. Walker (2005) and Hannen (1974)

---

[3] Wyatt sometimes corrects the spelling of this scribe to clarify the rhythm of the poems, converting an 'eth' ending into 's', or 'ed' into 't', and vice versa. See, for instance, BL, Egerton MS 2711, fo. 29^{v}, where he corrects the scribe's 'pricked' in line 5 of 'Who hath herd' with 'prykt', a change which more obviously indicates the one-syllable reading necessary for his decasyllabic line. In the first line of the same poem, Wyatt also changes the scribe's 'tyranny' to 'crueltye' (fo. 86^{r}), replacing a three-syllable word with another three-syllable word. This might suggest that Wyatt always read 'crueltie' with three syllables. However, in line 4 of the holograph version of his Penitential Psalms (fo. 86^{r}), Wyatt clearly uses

both note the speaker's apparent confusion, as if the poem is less a commonplace lament than an honest request: what does trouth avail, and how might one avoid this trap? But, as so often happens in Wyatt's verse, the canny purposefulness of the poem's shifting rhythms belies the diction that creates such an impression: this is 'honesty' by art, its confusion carefully crafted.

By contrast, Wyatt's epistolary satire 'Mine own John Poyntz' seems anything but an 'honest' request. It almost certainly derived from a period of 'house arrest' after his release from the Tower in 1536, just months before he wrote the two letters to his son (Powell 2004). Here, Wyatt essentially outlines his conception of 'honesty' without ever stating the word. Like the second letter to his son, the poem defines by a succession of negations what the speaker cannot do: that is, to 'frame my tonge to fayne', as required by courtly service. The satire also poses an artfully implied collapse of the relationship between landed wealth and independence in the 'clogg' that 'yet doth hang at my hele'. In the midst of pastoral liberty, in which 'no man dothe marke wher to I ryde or goo', the clog recalls the fact that Wyatt's withdrawal was enforced by the king (Parker Library, MS 168, fo. 200ᵛ).[4] In his poetic practice, this 'honesty' is often less a moral success than a failure of effective dissimulation (implied here by the repeated use of 'cannot' rather than 'will not'). This attitude is no less self-aggrandizing: for what honest man would be a good liar? But it is clear in his poems, as in the fatherly persona Wyatt presents to his son, that the speaker cannot sustain the stance of honesty. In a world of newfangledness, the person cannot match the ideal, however much he must strive towards it.

II

Despite Drayton's claims, only one known poem bears a relatively certain sixteenth-century ascription to Bryan,[5] 'The proverbes of Salmon' (Huntington Library, MS 183), comprising twenty-three stanzas (184 lines) in *ottava rima*. The first stanza of Bryan's poem gives a fairly representative sample of his poetic technique:

'cruelly' as a two-syllable word, suggesting that 'crueltie' in the final line of 'What vaileth trouth' might also be a two-syllable word. See also Trinity College, Dublin, MS D.2.7, fo. 119ʳ, where 'decevyd' has two syllables in line 7 of 'Longer to troo ye' (though this poem is less certainly Wyatt's, and is not in his hand). Wyatt did not correct the Egerton scribe for rhythm in 'What vaileth trouth', so that we can only make informed guesses about the syllable count for 'doeth' and other words with 'eth' endings.

⁴ Parker MS 168 contains no modern foliation; I cite an inconsistent pencilled numbering in the MS. Harrier (1975) estimates this as fo. 110ᵛ.

⁵ Another possible ascription is a thirty-line prayer in rhyming couplets—more self-consciously Protestant than Bryan's known writings—composed for Edward VI (Surrey History Centre, Loseley MS 1085/18/2). Though the leaf is endorsed 'wrytt by Bryan', the online catalogue suggests this may be the work of a recusant priest, Alexander Bryant. I am grateful to Steven May for bringing this poem to my attention.

> The proverbes of Salmon do playnly declare
> That wysdome ys the vessell that longest will endure;
> She calles children from childhod and byddes them beware
> Of a covytuus mynde, whiche ys a hard cure;
> Who cares not for wysdome falles ofte into care;
> The braunches of that frute ys tryed hole and sure,
> For powre without wysdome ys a feble foundacion:
> Wyse councell well ordered ys a Realmes presservacion.

> (Kinsman 1979: 284)

Bryan sets the initial praise of wisdom in the context of Solomon's proverbs from the Old Testament. The second and third lines recall the traditional connection between Solomon and Sapience, and the ninth chapter of Proverbs, in which—having built her house—Wisdom calls out to children (301). But the introduction, in line 6, of the metaphor of Wisdom as a tree springs awkwardly from the previous metaphor of the 'vessell' (whether a ship or a bowl is left unclear).[6] If the mention of 'falles' in the previous line is designed to introduce the tree, it does so only by inverting the concept, since no brittle branches are mentioned alongside the sure ones of wisdom. Wisdom's branches then quickly become a foundation in the next line, not in this case for the children's lives, but for the 'Realmes presservacion', a topic only distantly implicit in Solomon's role as a king. Bryan employs the feminine rhyme with which Wyatt was also experimenting, as well as the fashionable form of *ottava rima*, but the irregular rhythm less often reflects the meaning.[7]

Only after the discovery of Bryan's source can we understand the background to his rapidly clashing metaphors. He based much of the poem on the prose *florilegia* collected in Sir Thomas Elyot's *Banquet of Sapience* (to which 'Solomon' was a chief contributor, according to Elyot's marginal attributions), which may have been first printed in a lost edition of 1534. Robert Kinsman calculates that more than half the lines after the first stanza of 'Proverbes' derive directly from Elyot's *Banquet* (Kinsman 1979: 307). Many of the remaining lines are expanded paraphrases of concepts Elyot introduces. So pervasive was Bryan's dependence on Elyot that he even inserts Elyot's introductory dedication into his first stanza. *Banquet* begins with the figure of Sapience building her house and calling out to the inhabitants of the city:

[Sapience] calleth out abrode in the stretes, & in the chiefe assembly of people, and at the gates of the cytie she speketh with a loude voice: Ye babies how long wil ye delyte in your childyshnes? [...] Come on & eate ye mi brede & drinke my wyne [...] By me kynges do reign, & makers of lawes do determyne those thynges that be ryghtwyse. By me pryncis do governe,

---

[6] Kinsman notes the use of 'fruit' to mean 'tree' here. See 'fruit', *OED*, *n.*, 3.

[7] Though Bryan's lines usually have four stresses, the positions of these vary widely, just as the syllable count in each line varies from eight to twelve without a particular pattern of variance. This extremely uneven rhythm is one reason I doubt Drayton's claims that Bryan authored poems in Tottel's *Miscellany*, where the insistent regularization into iambic pentameter of the poems required at least rhythmic regularity in the initial text. On Wyatt's use of feminine rhyme, see for instance the first stanza of 'Mine old dear en'my'. Helen Cooper first drew my attention to Wyatt's unusual experimentation with feminine rhyme in this poem.

& in autorite do give sentence accordyng to justice [...] my fruyte doth excell gold & stones precious, and my branches are better than fyne tryed silver.   (1539: A4^v)

Here, the metaphors that clash so rapidly in Bryan's poem are slowly and logically drawn into order—the plain declaration of Solomon instead of Sapience, and her call in the streets, the tree and branch metaphor, and the apparently sudden turn at the end of Bryan's first stanza towards the issue of governance. Even Bryan's 'foundacion' and 'vessell' are suggested by the house and banquet Sapience offers.

Recent scholarship has portrayed *Banquet* as a highly political work, and describes Elyot's introductory discussion of Sapience as 'a bold and compelling voice' which allowed him to 'speak to kings' in a 'voice of authority' to argue for moderation (Walker 2005: 231). If so, then Bryan's 'Proverbes' effaces any such potential. Though he consistently returns to the subject of 'Highe auctoryte' and 'The strenghe of a Realme' (Kinsman 1979), even where no *Banquet* source exists, Bryan's platitudes have little particular resonance with early Tudor politics.

Whatever its poetic limitations, such a collection of sententious advice seems designed to convey the impression of a sober, thoughtful, literate author, one perfectly educated for royal service. Bryan was known by 1547 as a patron of 'good and vertuous workes most necessary to the knowledge of morall wysedome whereof ensueth the avauncement of common welthes' (Whittington 1547; Kinsman 1979: 309). In the early 1530s, he asked his uncle John Bourchier, Lord Berners, to translate Antonio de Guevara's *Golden Book of Marcus Aurelius*, and he later translated Guevara's *Dispraise of the Life of a Courtier* himself (Kinsman 1979).[8]

The impression such works convey clashes with the well-known details of Bryan's life. Bryan had been a favourite of Henry VIII since his appointment to the newly created post of Gentleman of the Privy Chamber in September 1518. Less than a year later, he was purged from the chamber and expelled from court along with Nicholas Carew, Henry Norris, and several others who 'not regarding [the King's] estate nor degree, were so familier and homely with hym, and plaied such light touches with hym, that they forgat themselves'. Bryan and the others were blamed for the King's 'incessant gambling' and for their own dissolute 'French' manners, acquired in autumn 1518 when Bryan and Carew rode 'daily disguysed' through Paris with Francis I, 'throwyng Egges, stones and other foolishe trifles at the people' (Walker 1989: 10, 2, 14). Despite the purge, Bryan was back at court six months later and attended Henry at the Field of the Cloth of Gold in 1520 (*ODNB*).

From 1527 Bryan was increasingly engaged in English diplomacy, first accompanying Cardinal Thomas Wolsey in his meeting with Francis I. During the crucial diplomatic negotiations over the 'Great Matter' of Henry VIII's divorce from Katherine of Aragon in 1528 and 1529, Bryan was Henry's trusted representative to Rome and Paris. The 'Bryan' of Wyatt's satire is the consummate royal servant, who 'trottes still

---

[8] The colophon to *Golden Book*, published posthumously in 1535, claims that the translation was undertaken 'at the instant desyre of his nevewe syr Francis Bryan knyght' (Kinsman 1979). Bryan's translation from Guevara was published in 1548. Bates (1993: 256 n.) notes another translation of Guevara's *Aviso de privados*, entitled *The Larum of Court*, attributed to 'Fr. Br. gent', copied into one seventeenth-century manuscript (Houghton Library, Harvard College Library).

up and downe | And never restes: but runnyng day and nyght | From Reaulme to
Reaulme, from cite, strete and towne' (BL, Egerton MS 2711, fo. 56ʳ). The real Bryan
would be the veteran of a dozen embassies, and, at least until 1538 (when he finally
lost the King's confidence), he was a far better ambassador than a poet. Men of the
privy chamber were sent abroad precisely for their closeness to Henry. But few if any
considered themselves close enough to him to dispense with careful circumlocution
of diplomatic language. Wyatt, also a member of Henry's privy chamber, was capable
of displaying proverbial wit and colourful narration. But he never dared to write
so directly as Bryan, whose diplomatic missives are extraordinary studies in the
rhetorical role of the honest royal servant.

In the world that Bryan reports to Henry, no one speaks the truth to him but Bryan,
who exposes the fraud of false counsellors and merit of faithful servants. 'Who so
ever', Bryan writes to Henry on 21 April 1529, 'hath made Your Grace beleve, that He
[the Pope] wold doo for You in thys cause [of the divorce], hath not, as I thynke,
doone Your Grace the best service.' Bryan knew well who had made Henry believe
the Pope: Wolsey, soon to fall for this failure. The Pope, he continued, offered 'fayre
wordys, and fayre wrytynges' but no 'dedys', and though there 'ys no man lyvyng
more soryer to wryte this newys to You', Bryan would nevertheless do his 'deytye'. The
letter begins, as all but three of the twelve paragraphs in it, not with the customary
opening (such as 'Yt may plese Your Grace to be advertysyd'), but with a plain and
simple address—'Sir'—as if Bryan had taken the King aside in the privy chamber
(*State Papers* 1830–52: vii. 166–9).

This pose of orality helps create a sense of intimacy in reports that were anything but private. Bryan's conversational style in letters to his friends maintains
such a posture, but with an 'honesty' more plainly dissolute than true. From Marseilles during a special embassy to France in 1533, Bryan writes to his friend Lord
Lisle, Deputy of Calais, that he would soon be dispatched home through Calais,
and that 'I, Sir Francis Bryan, desire you to make more ready for me a soft bed
than an hard harlot' (Byrne 1981: 66)—this in a letter also signed by the bishop
Stephen Gardiner and John Wallop. After Lisle's response, Bryan writes playfully
that

Sir, whereas in your ^last^ letter I perceive that in Calais ye have sufficient of courtezans to
furnish and accomplish my desires, I do thank you of your good provision, but this shall be to
advertise you that since my coming hither I have called to my remembrance the misliving that
ye and such other hath brought me to; for the which, being repented, have had absolution of
the Pope. And because ye be my friend, I would advertise you in likewise to be sorry of that
ye have done, and ask my lady your wife forgiveness, and that forgiveness obtained, to come
in all diligence hither to be absolved of the Pope, who I think will not tarry here much longer
than Hallowmas.   (Byrne 1981, no. 66a)

Bryan's joking 'absolution' from the Pope (who was at Marseilles at the same time) did
nothing to stem his drinking and gambling. Both of these letters and several others
from Bryan remark on the quality of the wine in Marseilles, compared to 'the feble
strengh of your thre halfpenye bere/that ye byb off there' (no. 66a). The point is

not that Bryan's actual life accorded to the jokes he distributed in letters to friends (though there is ample evidence that it did), but rather that the clash between Bryan's persona of 'honesty'· in his epistolary conversations with Henry VIII and his poetry sits uneasily with the demonstrative role as the 'Vicar of Hell' for Henry and his friends.

If 'Proverbes' was part of Bryan's attempt to refashion his public image on the model of the sober, learned counsellor, he was far from unique. A century later, Elizabeth I's old favourite Sir Walter Ralegh would, from his Jacobean cell in the Tower, remake himself with the rectitude of a Cecil or Henry Sidney by writing a set of ten precepts for his own son and collecting an ambitious history of the world. While Elizabethans such as Drayton fell for Bryan's refashioned public image—an image of 'honesty' in the sense of uprightness and reputation—'A spending hand' seems to suggest in part that Wyatt and Bryan's friends never would.[9]

III

Wyatt's verse epistle integrates the entire range of Bryan's fractured public persona: proverbial language and poetry, but also a 'conversation' in letters that playfully stretches the famous Erasmian notion of the humanist letter as 'a conversation between absent friends' (Erasmus 1974: 50). It is no coincidence that Wyatt turns to one of Horace's satires for his model. Colin Burrow has shown how Renaissance editors of Horace frequently noted the similarity between the Roman writer's *Satires* and *Epistles*, both of which had an addressee. As one Horatian commentator notes in 1511, 'Epistolis enim absentibus loquimur, sermone praesentibus' ('We speak in epistles to absent people, in conversation to those present'; Burrow 1993*b*: 33).

Horace's Sermo 2. 5 comprises an imagined conversation between the Homeric characters Tiresias and Odysseus in the underworld. In Homer's epic, Odysseus has come on Circe's instruction to learn about his voyage home. The prophet Tiresias warns him about harming the cattle of the sun, and about his own death. Horace's dialogue is an insertion of sorts into Homer's text, designed in part to mock legacy-hunting. The classicist Niall Rudd suggests that it comes after Odysseus' reply to an extended speech by the prophet: 'No doubt, Tiresias, the gods themselves have spun these threads; but come, tell me this as well, and tell me true' (Rudd 2007: 228). Horace, however, ignores the subsequent discussion about the shade of Odysseus' mother, and continues his Sermo with 'quibus amissas reparare queam res artibus atque modis' ('By what ways and means can I recover my lost fortune?'; Horace 1978: 199). Tiresias' response provides a litany of ways to earn legacies by flattering rich old men and pandering to their wives.

---

[9]   For another poem Wyatt addressed to Bryan, see 'Sighs are my food' (BL, Harley MS 78, fo. 27[r]).

Wyatt's satire begins instead with the proverbs for which Bryan was perhaps already known, including his 'rolling stone' that 'dothe never gather mosse' (Kinsman 1979), called here the 'stone' where 'groweth no mosse'. But rather than overhearing a conversation, as in Horace, we glimpse a letter: 'I thowght forthwith to write Bryan to the.' Wyatt proceeds to question Bryan's royal service:

> to the therefore that trottes still up and downe,
> and never restes but runnyng day and nyght
> ffrom Reaulme to Reaulme from cite strete and towne
> why doest thou were thy body to the bones,
> and myghtst at home slepe in thy bed of downe
> And drynk goode ale so noppy for the noyns,
> fede thy self fat and hepe up pownd by pownd
> lykist thou not this?

(BL, Egerton MS 2711, fo. 56^r)

Until this point, the 'epistle' respects its generic confines, being conversational only in the classical sense of *familiar*. But then Bryan intrudes quickly with a 'No' (fo. 56^r), as if to defend his 'honest name' (fo. 57^v). As a dialogue begins, the language changes temper, from written idiom to common oral phrasing ('By god well sayde'; fo. 56^r). The recipient need not wait on a post horse; the 'absent' friend in Wyatt's letter is present indeed.

Such moments are perhaps anticipated in satires by Horace, Juvenal, and Persius. However, the conversational responses in classical satires are most often overtly imagined, in which the respondent 'speaks' as an exercise. This is generally made explicit by subsequent phrases such as 'you would say'. By contrast, Wyatt's 'Bryan' is never revealed as being ventriloquized. Instead, the letter seems to become an actual conversation. This modest violation of generic convention—or extension of a generic fiction ('conversation') to its impossible conclusion—initiates a larger pattern in which figurative concepts are taken literally. Critics consistently note the contradictions that suffuse the poem and its portrayal of the historical Bryan. Elizabeth Heale, following Diane Ross, notes how Wyatt's ' "rolling stone" proverb, like the other proverbs his speaker invokes as "sure" and enduring, "quickly becomes a subject of debate" ', so that the 'mossy stone has the mineral equivalent of the good life—safe, rested, protected' (Heale 1997: 428). Others have noted that despite 'Bryan's' rejection of the speaker's advice to 'seke to plese' and to dote on rich old men (fos 56^v, 57^r), the real Bryan had already accepted such a life:

he had married one wealthy widow and was to marry another; his two sisters had made stunning matches (both with future Gentlemen of the Privy Chamber) that had been the foundation of Bryan's own career; while as Gentleman of the Privy Chamber he had performed—ex officio—the vilest of services for one old or oldish man, Henry VIII.   (Starkey 1982: 236–7)

Wyatt's Horatian source provides a further layer of satire, since the unnamed speaker here (often assumed to be 'Wyatt') borrows his essential pose from a famous classical prophet. Most of what this Henrician 'Tiresias' advises has *already* come true.

'Wyatt' advises 'Bryan' to 'ffle therefore trueth' (fo. 56^v), claiming that 'trowght shall but offend'. The historical Bryan, if not a model of virtue, was nevertheless 'honest' in one sense: he spoke his mind. 'A spending hand' is most plausibly dated to the period after Wyatt's first imprisonment in the Tower in 1536 (Powell 2004: 280). Both Wyatt and Bryan were sent abroad as ambassadors the next year, and Bryan was charged with the secret apprehension of an attainted English recusant, Cardinal Reginald Pole. But far from performing this service, Bryan may instead have helped advertise the plot to the Cardinal's friends: Wyatt's mistress Elizabeth Darrell let slip under examination that a 'familiar' of Bryan at the French court had warned Pole (Starkey 1982). Wyatt, too, was under suspicion, and later faced the charge that he had sent members of his embassy to meet the Cardinal. In such circumstances, Bryan's 'trueth' may have indeed offended his own king.

The character of 'Bryan' here is not the historical character, but rather the image that much of his writing seems to project: the learned collector of wisdom, the poet, the royal servant, and, most importantly, the 'honest' man, speaker of truths. The 'Bryan' of Wyatt's satire is Sir Francis Bryan's self-fashioned persona taken literally. Just as the fiction of epistolary 'conversation' is taken literally, 'A spending hand' accepts the 'Solomon' Bryan at his word.

This is a crucial trope of satirical writing—by elaborating the impossible, writers can expose the underlying absurdity of a perceived reality. But here, Wyatt's impossible is honesty itself, which is consistently contingent, relative, and various in the poem. The kind of honesty that 'Bryan' epitomizes is not the Stoic virtue described in Wyatt's letters: 'Bryan' holds it 'next godly things to have an honest *name*' (fo. 57^v; my emphasis). However lacking in virtue his advice may be, 'Wyatt' too is honest, both in telling 'true' (as did Horace's Tiresias) how Bryan might repair his fortune, and in the sense of exposing, however guardedly, the reality of court. The advice to 'slepe in thy bed of downe | And drynke goode ale [... and] fede thy self fat' (fo. 56^r) suggests another common sense of honesty in the simplicity of the common man. Contesting concepts of honesty here seem designed to undermine the impossibility not only of the 'Bryan' Wyatt depicts, but also of the capacity for poetry, letters, or 'conversation' to arrive at any meaningful and unified kind of truth.

Discussing Wyatt's uses of trouth in the satires, Christopher Hobson (1997) has argued for dismantling the polarities between new historicist depictions of a self that lacked any stable core and older critical approaches that tended to accept rhetorical self-portrayals without sufficient scepticism. As this methodological work proceeds, we may also begin to understand the larger context within which Tudor conceptions of 'trouth' and 'honesty' evolved. Greg Walker has recently argued that the humanist refashioning of English poetry by Wyatt and Surrey was a direct response to Henry VIII's 'tyranny', that these poets created 'a new literary polity, a public sphere that could sustain and justify public writing outside the conventions of courtly counsel, and beyond the direct gaze of the monarch who had hitherto been the ultimate patron and arbiter of literary activity' (2005: 415). Henry has been considered a tyrant by everyone from the Victorians to the early New Historicists (Greenblatt famously remarked that 'conversation with the king must have been like small talk with Stalin';

1980: 136–7). One lasting element of G. R. Elton's achievement was to highlight the complexities of the term 'tyranny' while instilling some doubt about the ease with which it was applied to Henry. Walker, however, revives the charge, claiming that the remarkable poetry of the period was generated in direct response to tyranny. This is a powerful argument, but it requires us to view English poetry in isolation from similar literary movements on the Continent, and to simplify Wyatt's manifold purposes as a poet and prose-writer. Nevertheless, however we define the reign of this king or the concept of tyranny, it is clear that Henrician reformations went beyond religious policy. Among these, Henry established the College of Arms and rewrote his own coronation oath to claim that 'honour now sprang from the king himself' rather than from the independent traditions of the nobility (Sessions 1999: 15; H. Miller 1986). The meaning of words such as 'honour' and 'honesty' could be highly freighted in an age after the 1534 Treason Act equated words with deeds. The concept of honour and the ethical system which attended it now required a wholesale redefinition.

Similarly, Richards has persuasively argued that sixteenth-century courtesy literature employs 'a sophisticated interpretation of Cicero's rhetorical values and political philosophy' which 'enabled the humanists to explore and debate the interplay between self-interest and social duty in personal relationships as well as within local and national government'. She opposes this to the hierarchical values expressed in 'medieval "estates satire"' and a descendent form of the genre, revived by reformers in the 1550s and allied with a hierarchical conception of society (2003: 28, 168, 169). Such dichotomies may tend to obscure the contours of a larger ethical crisis in Tudor society: the 'civil conversation' of courtesy books and interiority of Stoic casuistry were part of a more general humanist project, one triggered in part by the Reformation and the humanist obsession with eloquence as the keystone of a civil society. Wyatt's 'honesty', Surrey's 'honour', Bryan's 'Solomon', and the 'civil conversation' Richards so aptly illuminates were all part of the process by which early modern humanists sought to create or recover a value system independent from either the whims of an individual monarch or the reputation upon which honour depended.

Wyatt was hardly indifferent to the honesty rooted in public perception. Rather, his success as a poet is best demonstrated in the space between these two competing definitions of the word, and in the complexities of the plainness that sought to encompass both. As Wyatt's fatherly letters suggest, 'private', or Stoic, honesty could only be formed and maintained from the combination of the internal (conscience) and external (the community of honest men and honest ideas, or 'good opinions'; BL, Egerton MS 2711, fo. 73^r). It thence became public by the very act of its creation, and, once public, it became inevitably rhetorical. Wyatt's poetry, like much of his prose, depended upon his ability to deconstruct the honesties of others—whether a 'Bryan', a lover, an accuser, or even a king. But the success of his best poetry hinges on the self-consciousness that exposes the failures of such rhetoric, a self-consciousness that constantly threatens to reveal plainness and all kinds of honesty as a farce. This intense self-consciousness was precisely what Bryan lacked, and what Wyatt's satire momentarily exposes.

Primary Works

Burghley, William Cecil, Lord, Sir Walter Raleigh, and Francis Osborne (1962), *Advice to a Son: Precepts of Lord Burghley, Sir Walter Raleigh, and Francis Osborne*, ed. Louis B. Wright (Ithaca, NY: Cornell University Press).

Byrne, Muriel St Clare (ed.) (1981), *The Lisle Letters* (Chicago: University of Chicago Press).

Cicero (1990), *Marcus Tullius Ciceroes Thre Bokes of Duties*, trans. Nicholas Grimald, ed. G. O'Gorman (Washington: Folger Shakespeare Library).

Elyot, Thomas (1539), *The Bankette of Sapience*.

Erasmus, Desiderius (1974), *Collected Works of Erasmus*, xxv, ed. J. K. Sowards (Toronto: University of Toronto Press).

Horace (1978), *Satires, Epistles and Ars Poetica*, ed. H. R. Fairclough (Cambridge, MA: Harvard University Press).

Howard, Henry (1542?), *An Excellent Epitaffe of Syr Thomas Wyat*.

Kinsman, Robert (1979), ' "The proverbes of Salmon do playnly declare": A Sententious Poem on Wisdom and Governance, Ascribed to Sir Francis Bryan', *HLQ* 42: 279–312.

Leland, John (1542), *Naeniae in mortem Thomae Viati equitis incomparabilis*.

Muir, Kenneth (1963), *Life and Letters of Sir Thomas Wyatt* (Liverpool: Liverpool University Press).

Puttenham, George (1589), *The Arte of English Poesie*.

Shakespeare, William (1997), *Hamlet*, in *The Norton Shakespeare*, ed. Stephen Greenblatt et al. (New York: W. W. Norton).

State Papers (1830–52), *State Papers of the Reign of Henry VIII*, 11 vols (London: Eyre and Spottiswoode).

Tottel's Miscellany (1928–9), ed. Hyder Rollins, 2 vols (Cambridge, MA: Harvard University Press).

Whittington, Robert (1547), *The Myrrour [...] of Maners and Wysedome*.

Wyatt, Thomas (n.d.), BL, Egerton MS 2711. [Poems and letters]

—— (n.d.), 'Longer to troo ye', Trinity College, Dublin, MS D.2.7.

—— (n.d.), 'Myne owne John Poyntz', Corpus Christi College, Cambridge, Parker Library, MS 168.

—— (1969), *Collected Poems*, ed. Kenneth Muir and Patricia Thomson (Liverpool: Liverpool University Press).

CHAPTER 12

PIETY AND POETRY

ENGLISH PSALMS FROM MILES COVERDALE TO MARY SIDNEY

HANNIBAL HAMLIN

HENRY VIII had himself painted as King David the Psalmist; Edward VI had psalms sung to him as he relaxed in his chamber; Elizabeth I attached her own version of Psalm 14 to her translation of Marguerite de Navarre; and Lady Jane Grey recited Psalm 51 before her execution. On roughly the same spot almost twenty years earlier, Thomas More recited the same psalm before he went to the block. Philip Sidney ranked David chief among poets, and Henry Howard, Earl of Surrey, compared Thomas Wyatt's Penitential Psalms to Homer's epics. The 'Hebrew Psalter' was among the magic books of Christopher Marlowe's Doctor Faustus, and William Shakespeare's Falstaff died with Psalm 23—'and 'a babbled of green fields'—on his lips in *Henry V*. The Psalms were simply the most popular poems in sixteenth-century England,[1] known to the literate and illiterate, from reading and singing in church, at home, or at informal gatherings that sprang up after English translations became available.

Psalm-translating was also among the most popular exercises for English writers, in verse and prose. Metrical psalms, cast into English (or classical) metres, rhyme

---

[1] In early modern England, the Hebrew psalms were seen as poems. Their form is based on syntactic and semantic parallelism, however, rather than metre or rhyme, so when translated into English they resemble prose. To make English psalms seem more like English poetry, many Tudor translators cast them into metrical verse.

schemes, and stanza forms, were one of the most important literary 'kinds' in sixteenth-century England, no less than Petrarchan love lyrics. Both genres were imported from other languages, both depended upon translation, and the English history of both begins in the same decade (1530s), and includes some of the same poets, not least among them Wyatt, Surrey, George Gascoigne, and Edmund Spenser.[2] Complete psalters in verse were also produced for public worship and private devotional singing by Robert Crowley and the contributors to 'Sternhold and Hopkins'. Prose translations were written by George Joye, Arthur Golding, and Miles Coverdale.

It is often possible to distinguish versions sung communally or read in church or domestic worship from those written as private devotional exercises (which often survive in manuscript),[3] and both of these from versions written primarily as literary works—as poems. One can also distinguish more broadly between singing psalms, provided with tunes for use in church and at home, and psalms intended to be read, silently or aloud (Quitslund 2005). Yet, it is also true that such categories overlap the more closely one looks at specific writers and translations. For example, church psalms were sometimes translated into English with the intention of capturing the literary greatness of the Hebrew originals, while the writing of even the most 'literary' of translations may yet have involved some measure of devotion. Furthermore, sung psalms were also read in private, while some translations intended for reading were later set to music. Nevertheless, keeping in mind such limitations, this chapter describes sixteenth-century psalms in roughly these categories, which developed more or less chronologically: Tudor psalm translation began with efforts to produce English versions for public worship; devout Protestants then began producing metrical translations for personal use; increasingly, throughout the century, accomplished poets wrote psalm translations in their endeavours to produce an English literature matching both Continental rivals and classical models.

12.1 PHASE ONE: PUBLIC WORSHIP

Although there were many English translations of the Bible, no single biblical book was so frequently translated as Psalms. Why? First, there was an ancient tradition that the Bible was the sum of all knowledge, and Psalms was the sum of the Bible. Richard Hooker asked, for instance, 'What is there for man to know that the Psalmes are not able to teach?', repeating St Basil's question from the fourth century (1977: ii. 150). Secondly, Psalms, uniquely among biblical books, consists of direct utterances

---

[2] Spenser's 'seven Psalmes' do not survive; William Ponsonby lists them in the introduction to Spenser's *Complaints* (1591), among works he wanted to publish.

[3] John Croke, for instance, a Chancery clerk during Henry VIII's reign, translated thirteen psalms into common metre, apparently as a gift for his wife, Prudentia (Croke 1844).

of believers to their Creator. These utterances are so various in tone and style, and reflect such a variety of human situations, that, as John Calvin wrote, they represent an 'Anatomy of all the partes of the Soule' (Golding 1571: *6^v). Similarly, John Donne preached that Psalms is the 'Manna of the Church', since, just 'as Manna tasted to every man like that that he liked best, so doe the Psalmes minister Instruction, and satisfaction, to every man, in every emergency and occasion' (1971: 91). Thirdly, since the earliest history of Israel, Psalms was central to public worship, and if reformed worship was to be conducted in the vernacular, such practice demanded a vernacular psalter.

Thus, the first English psalter precedes by half a decade the first complete English Bible, the Coverdale Bible of 1535. In 1530 George Joye, a Cambridge fellow who had fled persecution, published in Antwerp *The Psalter of David*, based on the Latin Psalms commentary of the Strasbourg reformer Martin Bucer. Joye's psalter provided the Psalms in English prose, each preceded by a brief summary. Joye's Preface declared that his reader must not 'mesure and Juge' his psalms 'after the commen text': 'For the trowth of the Psalmes must be fetched more nyghe the Ebrue verite in the which tonge David with the other singers of the Psalmes first sunge them' (A1^v). The 'commen text' is the Latin Vulgate, which Joye claims to supersede on the basis of the 'Ebrue [Hebrew] verite', to which he had at least second-hand access through Bucer's scholarship (Hobbs 1994). The desire to produce a version even closer to the Hebrew continued to motivate psalm translators, including Joye, who in 1534 published a new translation of David's Psalter, based on Ulrich Zwingli's Latin version (1533). Joye's translation from Bucer was also reprinted that same year, in London, and again c.1544. Despite these reprints, both of Joye's psalters were soon eclipsed by Miles Coverdale's translation, which became the most widely known prose version.

Coverdale, another Cambridge scholar and, like Luther, a former Augustinian friar, was a follower of William Tyndale. For the 1539 Great Bible, commissioned by Henry VIII (at Thomas Cromwell's instigation), Coverdale revised his 1535 prose translation.[4] From Edward VI's reign on, this version was included in the Book of Common Prayer. As a result, it is still perhaps the best-known English version of Psalms, used in services and read privately for over 400 years. Coverdale was a creative wordsmith, and it is to him, according to the *OED*, that we owe words such as 'blood-thirsty' (Ps. 25: 9), 'day-time' (Ps. 21: 2), 'bloodguiltiness' (Ps. 51: 14), 'loving-kindness' (Ps. 25: 6), 'slippery' (Ps. 34: 6), and 'well-tuned' (Ps. 150: 5). One of Coverdale's greatest gifts was his ear for the rhythms of English prose and (like Tyndale) for plain yet affecting English idioms. This explains why Coverdale's Psalm 121, to mention only one of many examples, was taken virtually verbatim into the King James Version (1611): 'I will lyft up myne eyes unto the hilles, from whence commeth my helpe? | My helpe commeth even from the Lorde, which hath made heaven and earth' (Coverdale 1911). Psalm 102 exemplifies Coverdale's ability to capture the Psalmist's complaint in homely English diction:

---

[4] The Great Bible was a revision of the Matthew Bible (1537), which John Rogers had compiled and revised from earlier translations by Coverdale and Tyndale.

For my dayes are consumed awaye lyke smoke, and my bones are brent up, as it were with a fyre brande. My hert is smitten downe and withered lyke grasse, so that I forget to eat my bred. For the voice of my gronynge, my bones wyll scarse cleve to my flesh. I am become lyke a Pellycane of the wilderness, and lyke an owl that is in the deserte.   (3–6)

Though he knew no Hebrew, Coverdale was an accomplished Latinist, yet only three words ('consumed', 'Pellycane', 'deserte') in these four verses are Latinate; the rest are plain, often monosyllabic, Anglo-Saxon.

Coverdale also had an instinctual sense of parallelism, the basic formal structure of Hebrew poetry that was not articulated until Robert Lowth's seminal lectures (1753). Hebrew poetry is arranged in pairs (occasionally triplets) of parallel clauses, the second of which rephrases, elaborates, intensifies, or qualifies the first, while maintaining a similar syntax (Alter 1985; Kugel 1981). Any translation based on the original (even at second or third hand) is likely to achieve something of this form, but Coverdale's knack for compact, balanced phrases was acute:

When Israel came out of Egypt, and the house of Jacob from among the strange people.
Juda was hys Sanctuary, and Israell his domynion.
The sea sawe that and fled, Iordan was driven backe.   (Ps. 114: 1–3)

Joye (1530), by comparison, despite the medial colons, spins out the second half of each verse, diffusing the rhythmic compactness and weakening the parallelism:

When Israhel came oute of Aegipte: the house of Jacob frome the people of a straunge tonge:
Juda was goddis holy people: and Israhel was the folke over whom he wolde have rule.
The see sawe the hoste of god come and she gave backe: Jordane fled and gave place.

Protestant church services required two kinds of psalm translation: prose versions of the complete Bibles, read aloud by priests and deacons; and metrical versions set to music—'singing psalms'—sung by the entire congregation. Luther had recognized from the start that songs were an effective means of spreading Reformation doctrine, and shortly after publishing his 1522 New Testament he wrote the first of his many metrical versions of Psalms. These he cast into regular metre and rhyme and set to tunes borrowed from secular songs, harmonized by Johann Walter. They were extremely popular, sung in churches, homes, and at work, fulfilling Erasmus' famous wish: 'I wold to god/the plowman wold singe a texte of the scripture at his plowbeme/And that the weaver at his lowme/with this wold drive away the tediousnes of tyme' (1529: $\pi6^r$). Similar metrical psalms soon appeared in France (translated by Calvin, Théodore de Bèze (Beza), and Clément Marot) and in the Netherlands (the anonymous translations of the 1540 *Souterliedekens*), but the first English collection of singing psalms was yet another translation by Coverdale, *Ghostly Psalms and Spiritual Songs* (1535?), many of which were translations of Luther's German. Coverdale's book was condemned as heretical, publicly burned in 1546, and never reprinted. It was known to a few readers, however, since John Foxe mentions it in his *Acts and Monuments*, and it had a demonstrable influence on the metrical psalms of the Scottish poet John Wedderburn (Leaver 1991: 65, 84–6).

But the most popular English metrical psalms, for a century and a half, comprised the collection of singing psalms known popularly as 'Sternhold and Hopkins'. In 1549 *Certain Psalms* was translated by Thomas Sternhold, Groom of the Robes to Henry VIII and Edward VI, and his small collection of nineteen psalms was dedicated to the latter, who, according to Sternhold, took 'pleasure to heare them song sumtimes of me' (A3^r). The dedication proceeds to state that the printed psalms were intended for Edward's continued pleasure, whether in his own reading or in having them sung to him by courtiers like Sternhold himself. Oddly, then (though this resistance to categorization is typical of psalm translations), what eventually became the standard metrical psalter for congregational singing in English churches began as a set of psalms to be read or sung privately at court. Sternhold cast his psalms into ballad or common metre (essentially fourteeners—iambic heptameters—broken into lines of eight and six syllables, rhymed *abcb*). Sternhold was praised as a poet by John Bale (Zim 1987: 143, 295 n.128), among others, but reading his thumpingly regular verses today is a tedious, though occasionally amusing, business:

> O Lorde I call to the for helpe,
> and yf thou me forsake,
> I shall be lykened unto them,
> that fall into the lake.
>
> (Ps. 28, lines 1–4)

The idea of casting Psalms into common—or 'Sternhold's'—metre, did not actually originate with Sternhold, since in the same year (a boom year for psalm translations) Robert Crowley had published his *Psalter of David*, translated into common metre from the Latin of Leo Jud, a Swiss reformer and colleague of Zwingli. Crowley was a friend of Foxe and a fierce writer of reformist tracts, as well as the first editor of William Langland's *Piers Plowman* (printed first in 1550). In his psalter, Crowley provided only a single four-part musical setting to which all his psalms could be sung interchangeably. He made clear his purpose in the long title, which announced that the Psalms were 'newely translated into Englysh metre in such sort that it maye the more decently, and with more delyte of the mynde, be reade and songe of al men'. However, Crowley's psalter was never reprinted, perhaps because, with its lone tune and rhythmically awkward texts, it was not 'delightful' enough. Metrical psalmody was becoming a competitive field.

John Hopkins, an otherwise obscure clergyman, was the first to add psalms to Sternhold's limited selection—seven of Hopkins's own verse translations plus seventeen new ones by Sternhold that Hopkins somehow acquired after Sternhold's death in 1549. The collection was later expanded by English Protestant exiles in Geneva and elsewhere, including William Kethe (whose 'All people that on earth do dwell' is still famous as the 'Old 100th'), Thomas Norton (co-author of *Gorboduc* and translator of Seneca and Calvin), Thomas Churchyard (soldier and poet, contributor to the *Mirror for Magistrates*), and William Whittingham (a leader of the English congregation in Geneva and chief translator of the Geneva Bible), until the psalter was eventually completed. *The Whole Book of Psalms* was published in London in 1562 and republished in over 700 editions by 1696. Popular to a degree neither Sternhold nor Hopkins could have imagined, the collection was part of the daily lives of English men and women of all social ranks, for singing in church and at home, or for reading as private devotion and consolation (Hamlin 2004: 19–50).

Numerous metrical singing psalters were subsequently penned in attempts to oust 'Sternhold and Hopkins' from its hegemonic position, but none was successful until *A New Version of the Psalms* by Nahum Tate and Nicholas Brady (1696). Indeed, although a number of Church leaders (like Archbishop Matthew Parker, whose *Whole Psalter* was published in 1567 with tunes by Thomas Tallis), rival psalm translators (like George Wither), or poets (like Donne) grumbled about its inaccuracy and/or bad verse, most English Christians in the sixteenth century (and beyond) seemed happy with their familiar 'Sternhold and Hopkins'.

12.2 PHASE TWO: PRIVATE DEVOTION AND PERSONAL COMPLAINT

Psalms were also translated for personal reasons, and often by those in prison on political or religious charges. In 1549 (for example), in addition to the metrical psalms of Crowley and Sternhold, *Certain Chapters of the Proverbs of Solomon Drawn into Metre by Thomas Sternhold* was published by William Seres (publisher of Tyndale and Bale). It actually had no connection to Sternhold but contained metrical translations from the Bible, including several psalms by Surrey, composed while a prisoner in the Tower of London. Surrey was dead by 1549, the last man executed in Henry VIII's reign (in 1547). *Certain Chapters* was no doubt an attempt by Seres to exploit the popularity of metrical psalms, especially Sternhold's; not only were Surrey's translations misattributed, but the book's title clearly mimicked Sternhold's. Surrey was among the great innovators in English poetry, committed to the improvement and promotion of a national literature. This was a matter of both patriotic and family pride, part of his project to rehabilitate the English nobility, with himself at its head (Sessions 1999).

Though his writing was highly 'original', Surrey was a translator and imitator of ancient and Continental writers. However, it is crucial to note that early modern literature was not expected to be 'original' in our modern sense of the word; it was expected to be good. 'Good' often involved openly imitating or 'translating' works of known excellence; imitations were not judged derivative but admired as achievements in their own right. For instance, Golding's translation of Ovid, Norton's of Plutarch, and George Chapman's of Homer were among the acknowledged literary masterpieces of their day. Surrey himself translated Petrarch's sonnets and four books of the *Aeneid* (see Tudeau-Clayton, Chapter 23 in this volume). He also translated

Psalms 8, 73, and 88 into poulter's measure (alternating lines of twelve and fourteen syllables, rhymed in couplets). Though the metre has since been judged awkward and amateurish (much like Sternhold's 'eight and six'), for Surrey it was something new, since it seems to have been recently invented by his friend Wyatt. Surrey may also have seen it as an English approximation of classical metres, such as the elegiac, with its alternating hexameters and pentameters. Surrey's Psalm 55, his last poem, was written in unrhymed hexameters, a similarly experimental metre and one which perhaps originated in English with this poem (Sessions 1996).

Surrey's choice of psalms reflected his own condition: they address the kind of political intrigue and betrayal that were his downfall. Surrey's Psalm 88, moreover, includes lines that he significantly altered from the 'original' verse 8 (verse 7 of the Vulgate), in which God himself, rather than unfaithful friends, is the agent of the Psalmist's isolation:

> The faithfull frendes are fledd/and banisht from my sight
> and suche as I have held full deare/have sett my frendshipp light.

> (*Arundel Harington MS* 1960: i. 127)

Longe fecisti notos meos a me; posuerunt me abominationem sibi. (Thou hast made my familiars far from me: they have put me abomination to themselves.)

> (Biblia sacra, Ps. 87: 7, Catholic numbering)

His final psalm (55) calls on God to 'breake that coniured league' and complains,

> It was a frendlye foe/by shadow of good will
> myne olde feere and deare frend, my guyde that trapped me
> wheare I was wont to fetche, the cure, of all my care
> and in his bosome hyde, my secreat zeale to god.

> (*Arundel Harington MS* 1960: i. 131)

Surrey does not greatly depart from his source here, but many readers have taken the 'frendlye foe' as a reference to Richard Southwell, Surrey's former friend who gave evidence against him (Sessions 1999: 375–7; Brigden 1994). Such personal application of Psalms was traditional. In the fourth century, for instance, Athanasius made a table of psalms to turn to in various situations of distress or elation. Applying Athanasius' principles, in 1546 the Protestant martyr Anne Askew translated into common metre Psalm 54, which held particular resonance for her situation. The biblical headnote identifies the psalm's context as David's betrayal by the Ziphites, among whom he was hiding (1 Sam. 23); Askew was similarly betrayed by a neighbour (Askew 1996, p. xxxvi). But Surrey's Tower psalms go further in subtly adapting the biblical texts. Askew translates the psalm faithfully, but reads it in her own voice; Surrey also reads his own voice into the psalm, but boldly adapts it to make the identification stronger.

Surrey's psalm translations set a precedent for later Tower prisoners. For instance, Thomas Smith, a humanist scholar and later Secretary of State, was imprisoned after the fall of Protector Somerset in 1549; while in the Tower, he translated a number of psalms into metre, including Psalm 55. Like Surrey, he was no doubt attracted to its call for vengeance on 'bloud thrustye and disceatfull men' (Coverdale). Similarly, after the abortive attempt to place Lady Jane Grey on the throne, most of the Dudley family was imprisoned in the Tower, where two of them, John, Earl of Warwick, and Robert, later Earl of Leicester, produced metrical psalms.[5] Robert translated Psalm 94, another psalm of vengeance, which he adapted to his own situation:

> ffor lorde yf thow forbeare/and suffer suche to raigne
> How longe shall then those hawltie men/so lordlye us disdayne?
>
> (*Arundel Harington MS* 1960: i. 340)

Coverdale's version reads simply,

Lorde how longe shall the ungodly, how longe shall the ungodlye triumph?
How long shall all wicked doers speake so dysdaynfull, & make soch proude boasting?'

(1911: 94: 3–4)

Robert turns the ungodly into 'hawltie' and 'lordlye' men and even those who 'raigne' wickedly (like the current sovereign, Mary). John produced a version of Psalm 55, adapting it, as Surrey had, to courtly intrigues, cursing those,

> Whoe with faire Clokes of truce/and fawninge lowlye bowes
> Have trait'rouslye conspired my death/and falst their solemne vowes
> All Soothinge sugred speache/eke past their flyringe lypps.
>
> (*Arundel Harington MS* 1960: i. 339)

Neither Coverdale nor the Vulgate have the courtly images of 'faire Clokes' or 'fawnlye lowlye bowes'.

The Dudleys' psalms and Surrey's survive in the same manuscript, known now as Arundel Harington, alongside more Tower poetry and Wyatt's psalms, including his translation of Psalm 37. In its personal topicality, Wyatt's Psalm 37 is more like Surrey's than Wyatt's other psalms (his Penitential Psalms, discussed below). Wyatt's psalm begins in the mode of courtly complaint so familiar from other Tower poems:

> Althoughe thow see th'owtragious clime alofte
> Envye not thow his blynde prosperytie
> The wealthe of wretches thoughe it seemythe softe
> Move not thie harte by their felicitie
> They shall be fownde lyke grasse turnd into haye
> And as the hearbes that wither sodeinlye.
>
> (*Arundel Harington MS* 1960: i. 206)

Wyatt, like Surrey and the Dudleys, adapted the psalm (which in Coverdale begins less specifically: 'Fret not thy self because of the ungodly') to his own condition,

---

[5] Jane Grey also turned to Psalms in the Tower, incorporating phrases from them into her private prayers, published posthumously, including her final prayer (Foxe 1563: 919).

transforming it into the scriptural equivalent of his translation of Seneca: 'Stond who so list upon the Slipper toppe | of courtes estates' (*Arundel Harington MS* 1960: i. 356).

John Harington the elder, who compiled much of the Arundel Harington manuscript, was in the Tower with the Dudleys in 1554, suspected of conspiracy in the rebellion of Thomas Wyatt the younger, the poet's son. Moreover, the elder Wyatt's poems may themselves have been written in the Tower when he was imprisoned in 1536 or in 1541. The world of Tudor England was a small one, but for those in the Tower it was smaller still. All these psalms may have been circulating among the same small group of Protestant-leaning nobles; certainly during this period metrical psalm translation was a conventional pastime for the imprisoned and persecuted.

12.3 PHASE THREE: LITERARY COMPOSITION

While Surrey's psalms, and even Crowley's and Sternhold's, had literary ambitions, psalm translations aiming at poetic sophistication became increasingly common during Elizabeth's reign. Again, international competition played an important role in stimulating literary psalm translation, as it did in non-biblical poetry. For example, Donne lamented that

> these Psalmes are become
> So well attyr'd abroad, so ill at home,
> So well in Chambers, in thy Church so ill,
> As I can scarce call that reform'd until
> This be reform'd [...]
> And shall our Church, unto our spouse and King
> More hoarse, more harsh than any other, sing?[6]

(1978: 34–5)

The 'ill' psalms that Donne critiques are undoubtedly those of 'Sternhold and Hopkins', which held sway for many decades yet. There are several possible candidates for the 'well attyr'd' psalms abroad; most likely are Marot's and Beza's French psalms. Marot began translating psalms in the 1530s. There was a vogue for psalms at the French court, where nobles often adopted particular psalms as personal mottoes, or *imprese* (Pidoux 1962, vol. ii, pp. viii–ix). Marot's psalms also appealed to Calvin, who later gave the exiled poet shelter in Geneva, where the French Huguenot psalter was ultimately completed by Beza, Calvin's successor in Geneva. These French metrical psalms were, like Luther's and Sternhold's, set to vigorous tunes. But they were metrically more sophisticated than their German and English counterparts: Marot translated content relatively freely and employed a wide variety of metres and

---

[6] By 'that' and 'this', Donne refers to the English Church and English Psalms.

stanza forms, a formal ingenuity that appealed to poets like Donne and the Sidneys. The French melded effectively two traditions of psalmody that remained relatively separate in England: singing psalms, best exemplified by 'Sternhold and Hopkins', and literary psalms, later exemplified by the Sidneys (discussed below). By contrast, Marot's psalms could be admired at court and in literary circles while also being sung by Calvinist congregations and Huguenot armies marching into battle. Italian poets similarly translated Psalms into sophisticated verse, and Italian examples particularly influenced Wyatt (Reid 1971; Zim 1987: 43–79).

Wyatt's psalms are normally cited in histories of English psalm poetry, as they should be, but his Penitential Psalms (published as *Certain Psalms* in the *annus mirabilis* of Psalms translations, 1549) stand out in significant ways from the later practice of metrical psalmody, which developed only after his death. Though long dismissed in favour of his secular lyrics, especially his Petrarchan imitations, Wyatt's Penitential Psalms is beginning to be recognized as a complex and powerful work— and as a single long poem, rather than a collection of selected psalms like those of Surrey or Smith. Wyatt takes his narrative form from Pietro Aretino's *I sette salmi de la Penitentia di David* (1534). Both Aretino and Wyatt link the traditional seven penitential psalms (6, 32, 38, 51, 102, 130, 142) by interpolating original poetical material to create a continuous narrative about David's penitence over his adulterous affair with Bathsheba and his effective murder of her husband, Uriah (2 Sam. 11). The Penitential Psalms had long been associated with this episode (the headnote to Psalm 51 makes the context explicit), but the detailed narrative created by the interpolations was Aretino's invention. Although Wyatt translates Aretino, his poem becomes increasingly free of Aretino as it progresses, borrowing from other sources like Joannes Campensis, Joye's translation of Zwingli, the Vulgate, and Tyndale's commentaries, before finally departing from sources entirely. Also unlike Aretino, whose *salmi* ends with a pious lesson by the narrator, Wyatt's poem ends with David's own voice in Psalm 142. This lack of closure in his narrative frame, combined with the ambiguous characters of both David and the anonymous narrator, makes Wyatt's poem difficult to pinpoint. Some critics interpret Wyatt's David as a figure for Henry VIII, and the poem as a covert satire on the King's abuses—as already noted, Henry liked to represent himself as David (Greenblatt 1980; Halasz 1988; Walker 2005; Tudor-Craig 1989). This might align Wyatt's psalms with Surrey's, as political or even personal complaint (Wyatt could be seen as a Uriah figure, if indeed he was sent to the Tower by Henry for an affair with Anne Boleyn; Greenblatt 1980: 121). Others argue that the poem is not topical but theological, exploring the nature of penitence in terms more Protestant than Catholic (Mason 1959; Heale 1996). The close of Wyatt's Psalm 51, for instance, has been cited as describing a specifically Protestant theology, emphasizing not outward works but inner faith:

> The sacrifice, that the lord lyketh moste
>   Is spirite contryte; lowe harte in humble wyse
> Thou doeste accepte, o God, for pleasaunt hoste.
>   Make Syon, Lorde, accordynge to thy wyll,

> Inward Syon, the Syon of the [gost]:
> Of hartes Jerusalem strengthe the walls still.

(1549: C8^v)[7]

Rhyming 'hoste' and 'gost' may also implicitly critique the Catholic theology of transubstantiation, in which the 'host', or Eucharistic bread, is not only inhabited by Christ's 'gost', or spirit, but becomes his actual body. Yet the complexity of the poem and its elusiveness (is the narrator to be equated with Wyatt or not? is David meant to be sympathetic or not?) resists interpretative closure in a way that suggests that its ambiguity, like that of poems by Shakespeare and Donne, is intentional and one of its notable strengths.

Like Surrey's psalms, Wyatt's Penitential Psalms was also innovative metrically. Aretino's *salmi* were in prose; imitating Luigi Alammani's translation of the Penitential Psalms (1532), Wyatt writes *terza rima*, of which only one previous example in English, by Chaucer, is extant. Wyatt's interest in this stanza form is evident, since he also used it for his Psalm 37 and his satires (a fact that raises questions about the relationship between these two groups of poems, usually considered separately owing to the modern preference for keeping apart the sacred and secular).

After Wyatt and Surrey came a steady increase in English translations with self-consciously literary aspirations. John Hall, for instance, a Kentish surgeon, published metrical psalms in two volumes. The first, printed in 1550, claimed authorship of some of the paraphrases spuriously attributed by Seres to Sternhold in *Certain Chapters*—the same collection that included misattributed psalms by Surrey (see above). Fifteen years later, in 1565, after his earlier *Certain Chapters* (its title reappropriating that of Seres's 1549 publication) had been reprinted several times, Hall published *The Court of Virtue*, a collection of 'many holy or spretuall songes Sonettes psalms ballettes short sentences as well of holy scriptures as others' (Arber 1875–94). Hall's purpose seems to have been to compete with *The Court of Venus*, a 1538 collection of love poems (including some by Wyatt). This was a literary if also an evangelical endeavour, as was Sternhold's, who wrote that the 'tender and Godly zeale' of Edward VI did 'more delyghte in the holye songes of veritie than in anye fayned rimes of vanitie' (1549? A3^r).

Yet, most psalm translators did not write to combat 'bokes of lecherous ballades' (Hall 1550: A5^v). Anne Vaughan Lock was primarily concerned with religious instruction, translating Calvin's sermons on the song of Hezekiah (Isaiah 38) for English evangelical readers.[8] Yet Lock should also be included among literary psalmists, since her extended paraphrase of Psalm 51 seems to be the first instance of an English sonnet sequence. This underscores the relationship between Petrarchan sonnets and metrical psalms (in terms of their sophisticated narrative and poetic structures, their representation of complex psychological states, their sudden shifts in voice and argument), which has yet to be fully explored in the sonnet sequences of Sidney, Spenser,

---

[7] 'Gost' (from Arundel–Harington) is substituted for the printed 'hoste', which is surely erroneous.

[8] R. Smith (2005: 13–38) argues for *Meditation*'s political intent, admonishing Elizabeth I to follow Hezekiah and David.

Shakespeare, and others.[9] Greatly admired by her close friend John Knox, Lock was a remarkable woman, leaving her husband behind in England late in Mary's reign to flee with her children to Geneva. Lock's *Sermons of John Calvin*, composed in Geneva, was published in London in 1560, after her return. Appended to this was *A Meditation of a Penitent Sinner: Written in Manner of a Paraphrase upon the 51st Psalm of David*. A note by Lock states that this sequence of twenty-six sonnets was 'delivered me by my frend', but scholarly consensus is that the work is probably hers (Lock 1999, pp. liii–liv). Critics have argued that psalm translation was one of the few accepted literary outlets for early modern women, but apparently in 1560 even this godly genre was considered risky enough by Lock to warrant a narrative veil.

Lock's formal choice is intriguing, since her *Meditation* long pre-dates the English vogue for sonnet sequences (Thomas Watson's *Hekatompathia* did not appear until 1582). As an educated woman who had lived on the Continent, Lock may have read Petrarch or other Italian or French sonnets, but no clear formal precedent for *Meditation* has been established. Lock's poem begins with a preface of five sonnets, but unlike Wyatt's interpolations, Lock's preface employs the same narrative voice as the body of the poem. Lock's treatment of the English sonnet form (following Surrey) is as uncomplicated as her treatment of narrative voice. Nevertheless, she handles metre and rhyme competently, and the sequence has a cumulative intensity and some memorable effects, like the apparent play on her name in sonnet 11:

> Loke on me, Lord: though trembling I beknowe,
> That sight of sinne so sore offendeth thee,
> That sight of sinne, how it doth overflowe
> My whelmed soule, thou canst not loke on me,
> But with disdaine, with horror and despite.
> Loke on me, Lord: but loke not on my sinne.
> Not that I hope to hyde it from thy sight,
> Which seest me all without and eke within.
> But so remove it from thy wrathfull eye,
> And from the justice of thyne angry face,
> That thou impute it not. Looke not how I
> Am foule by sinne: but make me by thy grace
> Pure in thy mercies sight, and, Lord, I pray,
> That hatest sinne, wipe all my sinnes away.
>
> (1999, lines 227–40)

This poem, with its five instances of 'loke/looke', anticipates Shakespeare's punning on his own name, Will, in Sonnet 135, or Donne's on his surname in 'Hymn to God the Father' ('When thou hast done, thou hast not done'). Lock also achieves some fine relations between sound and sense, as in the enjambment which mirrors the 'overflow' of emotion between lines 3 and 4, and in the caesura of line 11 that forces readers to pause, emphasizing the theologically critical point about imputed righteousness (here expressed negatively, as a desire not to be imputed sinful).

---

[9] An exception is Kaske (2004).

Lock's combination of educational and literary motives is also found in Golding's psalms. More famous today as the translator of *Metamorphoses*, Golding wrote a powerful prose translation of the complete psalter to accompany his influential translation of Calvin's Psalms commentaries (1571). Golding states that Calvin's book 'beareth the Bel, bothe for varietie of matter, substantialnes of doctrine, depth of iudgement, and perfectnesse of penning' (*5ʳ). But Golding's accompanying translation of Psalms must share some of this praise, with Golding's Psalm 45 deemed by Donald Davie the best in English at capturing the psalm's 'barbaric and erotic occasion' (1996: 48):

My heart is boyling of a good woord. The woork that I endite shal bee of the King. My tung is the pen of a swift wryter. [...]
The kinges Daughter is altogether glorious within, hir rayment is of cloth of Tissew.
She shalbe brought to the King in raiment of needle work; hir maidens that are nexte about hir shalbe brought unto thee.   (Ps. 45: 1, 14–15)

With quite different motives (though these are hard to determine with this shifty poet), Gascoigne included a translation of Psalm 130, the famous 'De profundis' from the Penitential group, in his *Hundred Sundry Flowers* (1573) and again in *Posies* (1575). The poem inserts itself into the tradition of devotional psalm translation playfully; the verse preface describes it as Gascoigne's meditation on his 'conscience of muche time misspent' (2000: 290). But, as many critics have noted (F. Hughes 1997; Hamlin 2004: 112–18), *Posies* is full of poses as well as poesy; the preface may be ironic, no more trustworthy than the ludic narrative frame of Gascoigne's *Adventures of Master F.J.* The psalm itself is a virtuoso poetic performance, full of rhetorical devices like alliteration, internal rhyme, and anaphora (Hamlin 2004: 112–18):

> From depth of doole wherein my soule doth dwell,
> From heavy heart which harbours in my brest,
> From troubled sprite which sildome taketh rest,
> From hope of heaven, from dreade of darkesome hell.
> O gracious God, to thee I crye and yell.
>
> (2000: 290)

Gascoigne's devotion to apparently antiquated poetic schemes like alliteration might seem a throwback, but literary history is not neatly progressive. For instance, though Langland wrote in the fourteenth century, the printing of *Piers Plowman* in 1550 was part of a sixteenth-century Chaucerian revival, which may have drawn poets to experiment with older metres and styles. It may also be that the preoccupation of psalm poets like Gascoigne with schemes rather than tropes—with enjambment, for instance, or sonic effects like alliteration, assonance, and rhyme—was because in this area they were free to invent; they had to accept the content of Psalms, its subjects, images, metaphors, as (largely) already written.

Other alliteratively inclined psalmists include William Hunnis, gentleman of the Chapel Royal under Edward and Elizabeth and from 1566 Master of the Children of the Chapel, and Richard Stanyhurst, the Irish Catholic whose history of Ireland was incorporated into Holinshed's *Chronicles* (1577). Hunnis's *Seven Sobs of a Sorrowful*

Soul for Sin (1583) is a considerably expanded paraphrase of the Penitential Psalms into common metre, and it was popular, reprinted six times before 1600 and many times in the next century. Hunnis's book begins with the standard tropes of inadequacy and humility; this evinces not his lack of literary ambitions, but rather his chosen literary mode—the Protestant plain style: he praises his own book for being 'More rich [...] in thred-bare cote, | than some in silken gowne' (a3ᵛ). Stanyhurst's experiments aimed at writing English verse in classical metres, which involved creating a new system of spelling to accommodate strict Graeco-Roman rules of quantity.[10] He also attempted several psalms, shaping them into iambics, elegiacs, asclepiads, and Sapphics. Stanyhurst was lambasted for his alliterative excesses by Thomas Nashe, quoting lines from Stanyhurst's 1582 translation of *Aeneid*: 'Then did he make heavens vault to rebounde, with rounce robble hobble | Of ruffe raffe roaring, with thwick thwack thurley bouncing' (Nashe 1996: 89). By contrast, modern readers may find these effects delightful and original. Stanyhurst's style suits Psalm 2's distress at the ferocity of heathen nations:

> Wyth franticque madnesse why frets thee multitude heathen?
> And to vayn attemptings what furye sturs the pepil?
> All thee worldlye Regents, in clustred coompanye, crowded,
> For too tread and trample Christ with his holye godhead.

> (Stanyhurst 1880: 127)

Nashe was a biased reader, committed to what C. S. Lewis famously called the 'golden' poetry of Sidney, Spenser, and Shakespeare that defined the literary mainstream (Lewis 1954: 318–535). The quantitative movement (not to mention the Elizabethan alliterative revival or Stanyhurst's spelling reforms) was ultimately a dead end, but it did not seem so at the time, and it produced some fine poems, by Sidney as well as Stanyhurst. Yet even Stanyhurst felt that his psalms experiments were not wholly successful. Regarding Psalm 1, he writes, 'Too my seeming [...] the Iambical quantitye relisheth soom what unsavorlye in oure language' (1880: 126–7).

The motive of the English quantitative poets in translating psalms was to enrich English culture with infusions from both the Hellenic and Hebraic, attempting to syncretize classical and biblical cultures, based on the widespread notion that the Old Testament was the literary source from which classical poetry had sprung, a misguided idea derived from Jerome. The biblical precedent was also a powerful justification for the poetic vocation, at a time when writing poetry (especially in the vernacular) still carried some stigma. Another of these syncretists, Abraham Fraunce, included psalms in quantitative hexameters in his *Countess of Pembroke's Emmanuel* (1591; Figure 12.1), perhaps because the volume's dedicatee, Mary Sidney Herbert, Countess of Pembroke, wrote psalms in classical metres. Fraunce's psalms are little known and seldom anthologized, but contain some effective lines, like these from Psalm 104:

[10] In classical prosody, 'long' and 'short' syllables were determined purely by sight and involved counting consecutive consonants and vowels (Hamlin 2004: 88–92).

Fig. 12.1 Abraham Fraunce, *The Countess of Pembroke's Emanuel* (1591), title page, A1ʳ. David with his harp is depicted on the left; Moses, with the stone tablets, on the right

> Stil-springing fountaines distil fro the rocks to the ryvers,
> And christall rivers flow over along by the mountaines:
> There will wylde asses theyr scorched mouthes be refreshing,
> And field-feeding beasts theyr thirst with water abating.
>   There by the wel-welling waters, by the sylver-abounding
> Brookes, fayre-flying fowels on flowring bancks be abiding,
> There shall sweete-beckt byrds theyr bowres in bows be a building,
> And to the waters fall theyr warbling voice be a tuning.

$$(E3^r)$$

Fraunce creates some fine alliterative effects, as in the lapping 'w's of 'wel-welling waters' or the flowing 'l's and 'r's that mimic the 'christall rivers' of line 2 (and return in the final one, as the birds mimic the rivers). He is also a master of assonance and internal rhyme, as in the linked vowels of 'field-feeding beasts', 'bowres in bows', and 'fowels on flowring'.

The psalter of Fraunce's patron and her more famous brother Philip Sidney (the Dudleys' niece and nephew) is the greatest literary achievement in sixteenth-century psalms, saving perhaps Coverdale's distinctly different prose versions. Philip Sidney began translating Psalms into English metre in the 1580s, and had completed the first forty-three before his early death in 1586. Mary, married to Henry Herbert, second Earl of Pembroke, wrote the remaining 107 psalms and revised many of her brother's versions, completing the work by 1594 (Brennan 1982). Copies of the Sidney psalter survive with manuscript annotations suggesting devotional or even liturgical use (in private chapels), and some of their psalms were set to music in the seventeenth century.[11] Yet these are clearly translations not originally intended for church singing. Any but the most through-composed of musical settings would obscure the complexity of their prosodic and rhetorical effects. Such settings were common in the later seventeenth century, but not in 1590 (Jorgens 1982).[12] Thus, these were psalms to be relished largely for literary accomplishments. The Sidney psalter circulated widely in manuscript, and was greatly admired by Donne, George Herbert, and John Milton (Rienstra and Kinnamon 2002). It explores, in addition to classical metres, a multitude of verse forms, with all but one psalm set in a unique metre and verse form, including different kinds of sonnet, *terza* and *ottava rima*, rhyme royal, acrostics, and even common metre. The result is a tour de force demonstration of the potential of English verse, expressing the literary ideals of its two authors.

Sidney's psalms are occasionally less accomplished than his sister's (for example, his use of 'Sternhold's metre' results in a rather thumping version of Psalm 19). But then, his premature death left his project incomplete and unrevised. On the other hand, his Psalm 39 manipulates the verse line to effect a naturalness new to English psalms, by alternating iambic and trochaic feet and breaking the regularity of the tightly rhyming couplets with enjambment and medial caesuras:

---

[11]   One such annotated manuscript is BL, Add. MS 12047. For song settings, see Herbert (1998: i. 47–8).
[12]   For different views, see Brennan (2002) and M. White (2005).

> Thus did I think: I well will mark my way,
>   Least by my tongue I hap to stray;
> I mussle will my mouth while in the sight
>   I do abide of wicked wight.
> And so I nothing said, I muët stood,
>   I silence kept ev'n in the good.

(1962: 329, lines 1–6)

Sidney also uses alliteration with considerable subtlety. Though the repeated 'w's and 'm's in his first five lines are obvious, perhaps even harkening back to the structural alliteration of Langland, Sidney's choice of consonants that require closed or nearly closed lips is suited to the psalm's subject of remaining 'muët' and 'mussled'. When the psalmist finally bursts into speech, the consonants shift to fricatives and plosives: 'The fire took fire and forcibly out brake' (line 11).

Mary took her brother's language of psychological distress even further, effectively representing interior thought processes in a manner usually associated with Shakespeare's later soliloquies. For example, the opening of her Psalm 73 is so halting in its syntax, so full of parenthetical qualifications and clarifications, that readers practically need the end-rhymes to recognize it as verse:

> It is most true that god to Israell,
>   I meane to men of undefiled hartes,
>   is only good, and nought but good impartes.
> Most true, I see, albe, almost I fell
>   from right conceit into a crooked mynd;
>   and from this truth with straying stepps declin'd.

(Herbert 1998, lines 1–6)

Pembroke also anticipates Milton in her mastery of enjambment, as in the falling off in 'fell | from right conceit' (see Hamlin 2005: 144–57).

Rightly, several of the Countess's most powerful psalms, including 52 and 139, are now regularly anthologized. In Psalm 52, the short lines reflect the Psalmist's righteous anger:

> Tyrant whie swel'st thou thus,
>   of mischief vanting?
> since helpe from god to us,
>   is never wanting?

(lines 1–4)

Her Psalm 139 anticipates seventeenth-century metaphysical poets in its extended conceits for God's formation of the child in the womb, drawn from architecture and feminine domestic crafts:

> Thou, how my back was beam-wise laid,
>   and raftring of my ribs dost know:
>   know'st ever'y point
>   of bone and joint,

> how to this whole these partes did grow,
> in brave embrodry faire araid,
>   though wrought in shop both dark and low.

(lines 50–6)

Many of Pembroke's other psalms are equally effective: her psalms in classical metres (89, 120–7, variant 122), for instance, are among the most successful quantitative experiments, adhering to classical rules but also accommodating the natural rhythms of English (Attridge 1974: 204–5; Hamlin 2004: 92–9). They deserve to stand alongside her brother's more famous quantitative poems in his *Arcadia*.

The rapidly growing body of criticism on the Sidney psalms addresses their formal complexity and relationship to both biblical and secular poetics, commitment to Protestant theology, inclusion of political theory (on monarchy, for instance), and also, in the Countess's psalms, their interest in women's writing and social roles (Hamlin 2005; Quitslund 2005; Hannay 2001; M. White 2005; Zim 1987: 152–202). It is sometimes difficult to separate English translators' contributions from those of the Hebrew original; but this is part of the interest of translations that aim not just at mechanical transmission of the original content but at creating something 'original', as in 'new'. Sixteenth- and seventeenth-century readers of the Sidney psalms were aware of this complexity. It is telling that the Sidneys had a profound impact on later metrical psalms (by Phineas Fletcher, Francis Davison, George Sandys, Thomas Carew, and Milton, among others; Hamlin 2005). They also influenced seventeenth-century religious lyrics, providing the most important model for Herbert's *Temple* (which includes a metrical translation of Psalm 23). Herbert's work subsequently influenced collections like Henry Vaughan's *Silex Scintillans* (1650), which includes three fine psalm translations, and Christopher Harvey's *Synagogue* (1640). Most early modern English poets would agree with Milton, who wrote that psalms were incomparable 'over all other kinds of Lyrick poesy' (1957: 669), but it was the Sidneys who made the best case for that argument in Tudor literature.

PRIMARY WORKS

ARBER, EDWARD (1875–94), *A Transcript of the Registers of the Company of Stationers of London, 1554–1640* (London: privately printed).

Arundel Harington MS (1960), *The Arundel Harington Manuscript of Tudor Poetry*, ed. Ruth Hughey, 2 vols (Columbus: Ohio State University Press).

ASKEW, ANNE (1996), *The Examinations of Anne Askew*, ed. Elaine V. Beilin (Oxford: Oxford University Press).

Certayne Chapters of the Proverbes of Salomon (1549).

COVERDALE, MILES (1535?), *Goostly Psalmes and Spirituall Songes*.

——(1911), 'Great Bible Psalms', in William Aldus Wright (ed.), *The Hexaplar Psalter* (Cambridge: Cambridge University Press).

CROKE, JOHN (1844), *Thirteen Psalms*, Percy Society, 11.

CROWLEY, ROBERT (1549), *The Psalter of David*.

DONNE, JOHN (1971), *Prebend Sermons*, ed. Janel M. Mueller (Cambridge, MA: Harvard University Press).

—— (1978), 'Upon the Translation of the Psalmes by Sir Philip Sydney, and the Countesse of Pembroke', in Donne, *Divine Poems*, ed. Helen Gardner (Oxford: Clarendon Press).

ERASMUS, DESIDERIUS (1529), *An Exhortation to the Diligent Studye of Scripture* ([Antwerp]).

FOXE, JOHN (1563), *Actes and Monuments*.

FRAUNCE, ABRAHAM (1591), *The Countesse of Pembrokes Emanuel*.

GASCOIGNE, GEORGE (2000), *A Hundreth Sundrie Flowres*, ed. G. W. Pigman III (Oxford: Clarendon Press).

GOLDING, ARTHUR (1571), *The Psalmes of David*.

HALL, JOHN (1550), *Certayn Chapters taken out of the Proverbes of Salomon*.

—— (1565), *The Courte of Virtue*.

HERBERT, MARY SIDNEY, COUNTESS OF PEMBROKE (1998), *The Collected Works*, ed. Margaret P. Hannay, Noel J. Kinnamon, and Michael G. Brennan, 2 vols (Oxford: Clarendon Press).

HOOKER, RICHARD (1977), *Works*, ed. W. Speed Hill, 2 vols (Cambridge, MA: Belknap Press).

HOPKINS, JOHN, THOMAS STERNHOLD, et al. (1562), *The Whole Booke of Psalmes*.

HUNNIS, WILLIAM (1583), *Seven Sobs of a Sorrowfull Soule for Sinne*.

JOYE, GEORGE (1530), *The Psalter of David* ([Antwerp]).

LOCK, ANNE VAUGHAN (1999), *Collected Works*, ed. Susan M. Felch (Tempe: Arizona Center for Medieval and Renaissance Studies).

MILTON, JOHN (1957), *Complete Poems and Major Prose*, ed. Merritt Y. Hughes (New York: Odyssey Press).

NASHE, THOMAS (1996), 'To the Gentlemen Students of Both Universities', Preface to Robert Greene, *Menaphon*, ed. Brenda Cantar (Ottawa: Dovehouse Editions).

SIDNEY, PHILIP (1962), *Poems*, ed. William A. Ringler (Oxford: Clarendon Press).

STANYHURST, RICHARD (1880), *The First Four Books of the Æneid of Virgil: With Other Poetical Devices thereto Annexed* (1582), ed. Edward Arber (London).

STERNHOLD, THOMAS (1549?), *Certayne Psalmes*.

WYATT, THOMAS (1549), *Certayne Psalmes*.

CHAPTER 13

···

KATHERINE PARR AND HER CIRCLE

···

JANEL MUELLER

SOMETIME in 1543–4, Francis Goldsmith, who joined Queen Katherine's household as her attorney, saluted her in a letter in florid Latin—assuming and affirming Katherine's learning—praising the atmosphere that she had created at court:

Truly the most great and greatest God set your mind towards piety [...] Days that were seldom such are now truly Sundays [...] By your example, most noble of women surrendered to Christ, in your company they will be able to understand how much and in what way.

(Goldsmith 1547, fo. 43)[1]

This chapter explores the character of the 'pious studies' Katherine promoted: both through her own work, as translator and author; and through sponsoring translations by members of her household. It traces Katherine's movement from a traditional spirituality—associated with the girlish verses addressed to her uncle William Parr that she inscribed in her father's Latin primer[2]—through a transitional phase to her self-signalled positioning as a reformer. In its devotional orientation, Katherine's work shows affinities to the spiritual and intellectual outlook of John Fisher, whose blend of scripturalism, Scholasticism, and humanism found expression in a theology—balanced between reform and traditionalism—centred on Christ's passion, repentance, and the dynamics of salvation (Rex 1991: 84, 97).

The intermediary for this model may well have been George Day, Bishop of Chichester, the Queen's almoner, who seems to have served her as a religious and literary mentor. While Day accepted the royal supremacy, he was intrinsically conservative,

---

[1] All translations from Latin are my own.
[2] *Horae ad usum Sarum*, CUL, Inc. 4.J.1.2 (3570), C4ʳ.

one of a group of fellows of St John's, Cambridge, under the spiritual and intellectual influence of Fisher, then the university's Chancellor; younger members of the group included Day's protégé Roger Ascham and Thomas Cranmer during his student years (MacCulloch 1996: 16–24). Day's name figures prominently in a bill dated 12 May 1544, submitted by Thomas Berthelet, the King's printer. The bill records as 'delivered to my Lord of Chichester for the Queen's Grace' six 'gorgeously bound and gilt' copies of 'the Psalm prayers' and fourteen more copies of the same work 'gorgeously bound and gilt on the leather' (Rose-Troup 1911: 41). The work, published by Berthelet in April of that year, is *Psalms or Prayers taken out of Holy Scripture*, a translation of Fisher's Latin Psalms. Katherine can be identified as translator by the inclusion at the end of the volume of two of her original compositions, prayers 'for the King' and 'for men to say entering into battle', as well as her personal order of specially bound presentation copies.[3] The routing of these copies by way of Day pointedly implies that it was he—a long-time admirer of Fisher and more recent intimate of the royal household—who prompted Katherine to this particular spiritual and literary exercise in the first year of her marriage to Henry.

Fisher's *Psalmi seu precationes* is a finely wrought assemblage of dozens of phrases excerpted from Vulgate versions of the Psalms, prophetic books, and Gospels; shorn of source references, these clauses are freely recombined into fifteen new compositions entitled 'Psalms'. Appended paraphrases of the Vulgate texts of Psalm 21 (recast as Christ's complaint on the Cross) and Psalm 99 (creation's thanksgiving to its Creator) conclude the volume. Katherine's translation is highly accurate and closely consonant with the Latin. Her translation also demonstrates her extensive recognition of the exact location of Fisher's Vulgate excerpts, for her English renderings frequently reproduce the wording of corresponding phrases in the Coverdale Psalter or Great Bible that Henry VIII authorized for publication in 1538–9. By any standard, the familiarity with Scripture manifested in *Psalms or Prayers* is profound. Fisher's eclectic selection and recombination of Vulgate fragments also appear to have fired Katherine's literary imagination, for she employed the same compositional procedures in two of her subsequent works: *Prayers or Meditations* and her personal prayerbook.

Fisher's fifteen psalms divide thematically into near-equal halves. An initial group of seven, dominated by the speaker's extreme self-abasement and remorse for sins committed, modulates into pleading that God will impart wisdom, hear the sinful speaker, and give direction for good living (Psalms 5–7). Psalm 1 powerfully intensifies the reprehension of sin with an extended meditation on the sufferings of the crucified Christ. A second group of eight, dominated by the speaker's obsessive yearnings to be delivered from persecutors, likewise modulates into professions of trust in God, patience (with an extended meditation on Christ's patience), and thanksgiving for God's goodness in confounding enemies (Psalms 11–15). Hindsight reveals how characteristic of Katherine's spirituality and writing this conjunction of abjectly confessed

---

[3] Further indication of Katherine's authorship of these two prayers appears in the title of the second edition of her *Prayers or Meditations*, published by Berthelet (colophon 2 June 1545), which became known as 'The Queen's Prayers' in subsequent editions.

sinfulness and affective meditation on Christ's passion would become. At this point, it is already evident that she never develops this key conjunction in the direction of mystical transport or Eucharistic adoration. True to Fisher's precedent, her conjunctions remain grounded in biblical phrases and images. It is further indicative of Katherine's religious positioning at this time that she renders the Vulgate's characterization of John the Baptist's preaching ('poenitentiam remissionis peccatorum') as 'forgiveness of sins to them that do penance'. Her terminology of penance rather than repentance bespeaks a conservative orientation, since penance in the English context was always understood as entailing oral confession to a priest. Equally notably here, she signals her conformity with Henry VIII's declared view in *The King's Book* (1543) that the sacrament of penance joins with faith to prepare sinners to receive God's redeeming grace (MacCulloch 1996: 344–5).

With regard to Fisher's other dominant theme, the marked attraction in Katherine's spirituality to Psalm passages of anguished brooding and lamenting hostility finds more obvious sources of explanation in her later experiences—Stephen Gardiner's and Thomas Wriothesley's nearly successful plot to discredit her with Henry, her bitter competition for precedence with her former lady-in-waiting, the Duchess of Somerset, the Lord Protector's wife, in Edward VI's reign—than in her experiences during her first year of marriage to Henry. Yet she and her two stepchildren by her second husband, Lord Latimer, had been in serious danger when rebel troops, infuriated by his manoeuvrings during the Pilgrimage of Grace, took him hostage on one occasion, and on another ransacked the Latimer residence, threatening Katherine and the children (S. James 1999: 78–84). More insidiously, hence less demonstrably, Katherine's role as Henry's sixth queen and the associations of Hampton Court with her unfortunate predecessors Anne Boleyn and Katherine Howard, whose violent ends resulted from the machinations of enemies, may have sensitized her to give this theme the special prominence it holds in *Prayers or Meditations* and her personal prayerbook.

Psalms or Prayers made a designedly local impact in Katherine's household. She certainly gave Henry a copy, not least because the work in its multiple later printings acquired the informal title of 'The King's Prayers'. Other likely recipients are the ladies who crowded into the Queen's closet at Hampton Court to attend Henry's and Katherine's wedding, all of whom were, or became, Katherine's intimates: these included her sister Anne Parr Herbert; Princesses Mary and Elizabeth; and Katherine Willoughby, Duchess of Suffolk. Further likely recipients are other members of the Queen's inner circle (S. James 1999: 153–4): her cousin and close childhood friend Maud, Lady Lane; a more distant cousin and developing friend, Elizabeth Tyrwhit; and Mary Wotton, Lady Carew. Copies were also probably given to Francis Mallet, her personal chaplain, another Cambridge graduate who had formerly served Cranmer and Henry VIII; Walter Bucler, her personal secretary; and Anthony Cope, her chamberlain.

A compact book (about five by seven inches), the format of *Psalms or Prayers* is that of a pocket-sized prayerbook, suggesting that Katherine intended it for personal use as an adjunct to the household prayers at which Mallet officiated. That *Psalms or*

Prayers had some such purpose in the Queen's household seems likely in view of the later compilation published by her lady-in-waiting Elizabeth Tyrwhit, whose *Morning and Evening Prayers* (1574), printed in girdle-book format, provides a rich surround of private devotions to complement morning and evening prayer in the Book of Common Prayer. However, a distinctly public implication arises from Katherine's two original compositions which conclude the volume, the prayers for the King and for men to say entering battle. The stately cadences of the latter invoke God to grant victory and unity to the English:

Our cause now being just, and being enforced to enter into war and battle, we most humbly beseech Thee, O Lord God of hosts, so to turn the hearts of our enemies to the desire of peace, that no Christian blood be spilt: or else grant, O Lord, that with small effusion of blood, and to the little hurt and damage of innocents, we may to Thy glory obtain victory: and that the wars being soon ended, we may all with one heart and mind, knit together in concord and unity, laud and praise Thee, Which livest and reignest, world without end.   (1544: M1^r)

Such phrasing sounded highly seasonable notes. On 27 May 1544 Archbishop Thomas Cranmer published the first service book in English for public use. Henry authorized it because he was persuaded that praying the litany in English would unite his subjects in support of his impending invasion of France. The Queen's two original prayers and the Archbishop's introduction of a royally sanctioned vernacular service book display a shared objective of augmenting the role of the people in worship.

In other matters of public importance, Katherine was making heady discoveries regarding the extent of her influence with Henry. She is credited with assembling his children for Christmas celebrations in 1543, and with advocating the restoration of Mary and Elizabeth in the line of succession, officially decreed by King and Parliament on 14 January 1544. Katherine is also attributed with proposing the appointments of two Cambridge scholars, Richard Cox and John Cheke, another of Day's protégés, as tutors to Prince Edward in his newly instituted household, created by King and Privy Council on 7 July 1544. Providing for Edward's household and education was part of Henry's larger intent in arranging the interim exercise of royal authority while he was absent on his French campaign; another part was his appointment of Katherine as regent-general of England.

Katherine acted in Henry's stead for three months, from July to late September 1544. This exercise of sovereign authority in consultation with a select subset of the Privy Council, notably Cranmer—who attended her daily—was demonstrably catalytic for her spiritual and literary activity; it was also instructive for the 11-year-old Elizabeth to observe the kingdom in a queen's charge (James 1999: 186). During and after her regency, Katherine evidently came to regard translating spiritually valuable works as an activity that she would no longer undertake, but would instead energetically promote. The earliest ramifications of this decision appear within the Queen's inner circle: Elizabeth translated Marguerite of Navarre's poem *Miroir de l'âme pécheresse* into English prose as *The Glass of the Sinful Soul* as a New Year's gift for the Queen in 1545. Like Katherine's translation of Fisher, Elizabeth's translation of Marguerite closely traces the spirituality of a prominent contemporary expressed in copious self-abasement for sin and exaltation of Christ as Redeemer, and presented in a thickly textured weave of biblical quotations and allusions (Prescott 1985; Shell 1993; Elizabeth I 2009).

While she was regent-general, Katherine decided to sponsor a considerably more ambitious translation project: English versions of the Latin paraphrases of the Gospels and Acts of the Apostles in Erasmus' *Paraphrases in Novum Testamentum*, first published by Frobenius at Basel in 1524 (Devereux 1968–9). The conception of this project illuminates the Queen's own spiritual and literary proclivities in 1544–5—her attraction to artfully composed works with a markedly biblical tenor, written by eminent contemporaries, that mingle Christ-centred piety with moral urgency—but it also reveals new concerns and a new sense of a public role that bespeak Cranmer's influence. As patron of the English *Paraphrases*, Katherine committed herself to advancing the people's understanding of scripture and, with it, their capacity to attend to and answer for the state of their own souls—thus exercising, by indirect means, functions parallel to a pastor's. This notable extension on her prior activity was clearly recognized by Nicholas Udall, whom the Queen commissioned to serve as general editor and to translate Erasmus' paraphrases on Luke and Acts. In a fulsome letter to her dated 30 September 1545, Udall hails Katherine's expansion of her activity from 'Psalms and contemplative meditations [...] which ye have set forth as well to the incomparable good example of all noble women' to commissioning the selected paraphrases:

By this means doth your Highness right well declare that all your delight, all your study, and all your endeavour is by all possible means employed to the public commodity of all good English people, the King's most loving and obedient subjects, to be nuzzled and trained in the reading of God's Word, and in the meditation of His most holy Gospel [...] that all English people may to their health and ghostly consolation be abundantly replenished with the fruit thereof.   (Udall et al. 1548: A2ᵛ–A3ʳ)[4]

Katherine's Paraphrases project had repercussions in her household. Thomas Key, the Oxford scholar appointed to say daily prayers in her oratory, described in his letter prefacing the Mark paraphrase how he had been 'moved' by the royal physician George Owen to volunteer as a translator (Udall et al. 1548: a2ʳ). More intriguingly, Udall's letter to Katherine prefacing the John paraphrase singles out, among the learned and virtuous ladies of the day, 'the most studious' Princess Mary, 'for taking such great study and travail in translating this paraphrase [...] at your Highness' special contemplation'; he then commends Mary for persisting through 'a grievous and long sickeness' until compelled by ill health to relinquish the translation to the Queen's chaplain, Mallet, 'to be finished and made complete'. 'What could be a more evident proof of her will and desire to do good to all her father's most dear beloved subjects,' exclaims Udall, 'what could be a more plain declaration of her most constant purpose to promote God's Word, and the free grace of His Gospel, than so effectually to prosecute the work of translating which she had begun' (3A2ʳ). Mary's unexpected

---

[4] All quotations from *Paraphrases* are from STC2, 2854.5 (Folger copy); the volumes are separately paginated.

involvement in this project is confirmed by a Latin letter to her from the Queen, which oddly survives as a text in Elizabeth's handwriting. Katherine asks affectionately after Mary's health and probes her inclination regarding the public attribution of her translation (Parr 1545?: 37ʳ).

In the event, it would not be Katherine deftly inducing Henry to authorize publication of the English Paraphrases, as Udall had imagined in his prefatory letters, but Edward whose reign saw the completion of this project. The project also fell short of its envisaged homiletic benefits, as English readers demonstrated their preference for the plain vernacular New Testament over the copious rewordings to which Erasmus had subjected the text (Devereux 1968–9: 367). Yet Katherine's patronage of the project assured her recognition as a major advocate of making Scripture and aids for understanding it available to all in English. It evinces, on the one hand, her deepening realization of the nature of the Gospel message; on the other, a heightened awareness of what deviated from Scripture in the Church and society of her day. Udall clearly recognized this. As he enthuses, in particular, over the Queen's assignment of the Luke paraphrase to him, he notes his own earlier resolve to translate it, since—of all the Gospels—Luke is most theologically sound, the 'most earnest and full in the justification of faith, and most pithy against the justification of works', therefore the most effective in exposing the 'Romish abomination' of 'all things [...] contrary to Christ'. A colourful catalogue counterposes New Testament simplicity with the papal 'fond ceremonies' then in the process of being reformed (A3ᵛ–A4ᵛ). Udall's emphases in this letter tally with Cranmer's known convictions at this date (MacCulloch 1996: 209–12, 342–3). They further indicate that the Archbishop's influence with Katherine was undergoing reinforcement from another quarter.

In the aftermath of her regency Katherine claimed for her own use the redacting functions that Fisher performed in his *Psalmi seu precationes* and Cranmer in his English litany: selecting, adapting, and freely recombining source materials to produce an original work. She published *Prayers or Meditations* (1545) under her name, reprinting her two original prayers from *Psalms or Prayers*. The source for *Prayers or Meditations* is the third book of *The Following of Christ* (F. Hoffman 1959: 354), an English translation (1531?) of Thomas à Kempis's *Imitatio Christi* by the Bridgettine monk Richard Whitford.[5] Again, this choice of source aligns with the strain of spirituality manifested in Fisher (as well as Marguerite of Navarre): an intense absorption in Scripture that yields an acutely personalized sense of sin and an equally personalized affectivity centred on Christ, lovingly evoked as a near presence imparting comfort and joy. While Fisher, Marguerite, and à Kempis are tradition-bound in conceiving of the Church and its authority, their spirituality melds with Reformation tendencies in its scripturalism, its personalism, and its emphasis on sin and salvation as ultimate concerns for which individual souls are answerable.

In *Prayers or Meditations* Katherine revises à Kempis's text in some distinctly reformist directions. Entirely dismantling the monastic framework and affiliated

---

[5] For a discussion of Parr's adaptation of the *Imitatio*, see Mueller (1990).

terms of reference, she excises the dialogue between a gender-marked pair of intimates identified as 'Jesu', 'Lord', 'sir', 'sire', on the one hand, and 'my son', on the other. Eliminating this dialogue also dispenses with a dynamic in which the monk of the source is brought, by instruction and exhortation, through stages of moral and spiritual proficiency to mystical rapture in a relation of ever closer male bonding. Katherine replaces dialogue with monologue: the 'I', 'me', and 'my' of a soul whose psychology is specified only in terms of the shared human faculties of heart, mind, and will. From the densely scriptural weave of the *Imitatio* she consistently selects lyrical and affective verses couched in the first person or restyles them in this form. The result is to centre her abridgement of Whitford's version on a degendered human speaker who yields self to God in a posture of total dependency in utterances drawn from God's Word. The salient features of Katherine's speaker reflect an emphasis characteristic of Henrician reformers, particularly as found in Cranmer's Litany: the as yet unproblematic presumption of the spiritual equality of all before God. Degendering from explicit masculinist norms in the direction of a fresh univer-salizing of the Gospel thus appears to be the chief design and effect of the first attributed work by an Englishwoman written for print circulation and produced for a historically specific context. What Cranmer's litany purported to be as a text for the English Church understood as the English people, Katherine's *Prayers or Meditations* proposes to be for English men or women aspiring to worship rightly in private.

Katherine's systematic selections and alterations wrench the spirituality expressed in the *Imitatio* from traditionally Catholic connotations to those of an emergent Protestantism. While her source text recurrently limits the term 'grace' to the pref-erential divine favour accorded the contemplative, grace figures, for Katherine, as the vital empowerment by which God opens in the sin-marred human psyche the only means to a positive relation between himself and humankind. The Queen adopts the Reformation sense given to 'grace' by Luther (Bornkamm 1965: 16–44; Gerrish 1962). Her reworking of a notable apposition in Whitford–à Kempis registers the force of the divergent apprehensions. 'Gather my wits and powers of my soul together in Thee,' implores the soul in chapter 53 of the *Imitatio*; 'grant me to cast away and wholly to despise all fantasies of sin' (Whitford 1531?: 126^{r-v}). The soul in Katherine's text, however, confides its yearnings for psychic wholeness and moral strength to the workings of grace: 'Gather, O Lord, my wits and the powers of my soul together in Thee, and make me [...] by Thy grace strongly to resist and overcome all motions and occasions of sin' (1545: C2^v).

Because the theology and psychology of spiritual effort remain fundamental to the *Imitatio*, Whitford's translation inscribes a harsh late medieval dualism, in which heaven is to be embraced and this world renounced; only the spirit freed of the flesh can achieve goodness. Katherine's redaction insistently rejects such dualisms, especially those which privilege cloistered recluses as the true 'religious'. Thus, where Whitford's text proposes to 'witness the apostles' as chief examples of Christ's elect, they figure as 'princes of all the world which nevertheless were conversant among the people without complaining' (1531?: 92^{r-v}). Katherine reworks this along discernibly

Cranmerian lines to model a clergy busy among the people in preaching and visitation: 'Witness be the blessed apostles, whom Thou madest chief pastors and spiritual governors of thy flock' (1545: B1^v).

The other key stylistic tendency (besides explicit degendering) is Katherine's consistent heightening of deference and dependency in her vocabulary of self-reference. This emphasis provides the work with unity of theme and tone, as can be seen in respective quotations from its opening and its close:

Lord, Thou knowest what thing is most profitable and most expedient for me. Give me therefore what Thou wilt, as much as Thou wilt, and when Thou wilt. Do with me what Thou wilt, as it shall please Thee, and as shall be most to Thy honour.   (A2^r)

Teach me, Lord, to fulfill Thy will, to live meekly and worthily before Thee, for Thou art all my wisdom and cunning; Thou art He, that knowest me as I am, that knewest me before the world was made, and before I was born or brought into this life: to Thee, O Lord, be honour, glory, and praise for ever and ever.   (D1^r)

The dominance accorded to a lyrical posture of utter subjection, the forfeiting of personal will to an all-powerful and all-knowing Lord, bespeaks immediate personal experience: Henry chose Katherine for his queen; there was no resisting. Yet there were, as well, counterbalances and compensations, among them opportunities for influence, leadership, and authorship. Katherine seems to have thought that *Prayers or Meditations* carried particular expressiveness as a gift from her, for she made in her own hand a miniature (incomplete) copy in the format of a girdle prayerbook (now preserved in Kendal Town Hall, Cumbria), illuminated in red, blue, and gilt, to present to a daughter of Sir Brian Tuke, treasurer of the chamber in the household of her brother William Parr, Earl of Essex.

After Henry returned from his French campaign in October 1544, the compounded effects of the regency with which he had entrusted her continued to work upon Katherine. Daily consultations with Cranmer and contact with Udall had fostered overtly reformist tendencies in her spiritual and literary activity. It is probable that, about this time, Katherine began to compile an English prayerbook for herself (BL, Harley MS 2342; Mueller forthcoming).[6] This diminutive volume, written entirely in her hand and illuminated in red, blue, and gilt, comprises a sequence of prayers, meditations, and portions of Scripture taken with few or no changes from devotional books issued by English Lutheran redactors and printers, including George Joye's *Garden of the Soul* (1530), Thomas Godfray's *Fountain or Well of Life* (1534?), William Marshall's *A Primer in English* (1534)—which Cranmer used in compiling his English Litany (MacCulloch 1996: 328)—and Robert Redman's *Prayers of the Bible* (1535?) (Butterworth 1953). It also, however, contains excerpts from the prayers that Fisher and Thomas More had composed as prisoners in the Tower of London while awaiting execution for declining to swear the Oath of Supremacy.

Katherine sustained as well her lively interest in Elizabeth's and Edward's developing capacities, promoting in them her own reformist tendencies. The impetus

[6] The manuscript has been known as 'Lady Jane Grey's Prayerbook', which it did become, probably when Jane attended Katherine as she lay dying.

to translate Marguerite's *Miroir* that Katherine gave Elizabeth in 1544 also inspired Elizabeth's New Year's gifts in 1546: the Queen received an English translation of chapter 1 of the first French version of Calvin's *Institution de la réligion chrestienne* (1541), with its source prudently left unidentified; the King, a trilingual (Latin, French, Italian) translation of Katherine's *Prayers or Meditations*. The Queen's interests in education also brought others of a reformist bent under her patronage. After transferring Mallet to serve as Mary's chaplain and collaborator in translating the John paraphrase, she appointed as her new chaplain John Parkhurst, a graduate of Magdalen College, Oxford, who had written a commendatory Latin epigram on Katherine that alludes to her role as regent-general of the realm, pronouncing her virtues greater than those of Penelope, Ulysses' faithful wife (Parkhurst 1573: 10–11). In 1544–5 Parkhurst was chaplain to Charles Brandon, Duke of Suffolk, whose wife, Katherine, one of the Queen's inner circle, displayed reformist sympathies more overtly in tandem with Katherine's own.

In autumn 1545 Reformation and realpolitik converged as Parliament sought to relieve royal finances severely depleted by Henry's French campaign. Acts passed on 23 and 24 November directed the further dissolution of specified religious foundations, including chantries and colleges, and the transfer of their assets to the Crown. The motive for dissolving colleges involved the felt lack of need to train priests to offer masses for souls of the dead, but where colleges served genuine needs for preaching and other forms of pastoral care, exemptions were to be made. Following these acts, acute alarm took hold in Cambridge University. Ascham, writing for the university as its orator, and Thomas Smith, former university Vice-Chancellor and current Clerk of the Privy Council, signalled the public recognition of the leadership Katherine had demonstrated during her regency as well as the reputation she had gained as a promoter of sound learning in determining Edward's education and sponsoring the Paraphrases project. Ascham and Smith appealed to her to exercise her influence with Henry on behalf of the Cambridge colleges. Katherine's self-assured response is dated 26 February 1546:

I gently exhort you to study and apply those doctrines as means and apt degrees to the attaining and setting forth the better: Christ's reverend and most sacred doctrine. For this Latin lesson I am taught to say of St. Paul, *Non me pudet evangelii,*[7] [to] the sincere setting forth whereof I trust universally in all your vocations and ministries you will apply and conform your sundry gifts, arts, and studies, to such end and sort that Cambridge may be accounted rather a university of divine philosophy than of natural or moral, as Athens was [...] I according to your desire attempted my lord, the King's Majesty, for the stay of your possessions.

(Parr 1546: 11^r; *LP* xxi, no. 279)

The revelations in Katherine's letter are manifold. Her words resonate with the concern for rightly propagating the Gospel that informed her Paraphrases project. She also re-echoes a provision in the Act for the Dissolution of Colleges, that those found to be training ministers soundly would be exempt from its effects. But there are distinctly imperious notes too. Katherine declares, as a condition to be met,

---

[7] 'I am not ashamed of the Gospel.'

her desire that Cambridge become 'rather a university of divine philosophy than of natural or moral'—'divine philosophy' being a phrase frequently used by Erasmus in the Paraphrases to refer to Christ's teachings and example. To ensure the university's compliance with her wish, she continues to inform it that, on the strength of her persuasions, Henry, 'being such a patron to good learning', has resolved not to dissolve the colleges and confiscate their properties, but, further, to erect and endow a new college, 'so that learning may hereafter ascribe her very original, whole conformation, and sure stay to our sovereign lord, her only defender and worthy ornament'. (Trinity College was duly founded by Henry in 1546.) The Queen effectively promotes herself as an instrument of supreme royal authority exercising itself to advance the highest knowledge, which she equates with the religion of Christ and St Paul.

This same imperiousness was almost her undoing. As John Foxe relates, 'being indeed become very zealous toward the gospel and the professors thereof', she was emboldened 'frankly to debate with the king touching religion'. The King's smouldering irritation—exacerbated by a downturn in his health and increased pain in his phlebitic leg—provided Gardiner and Wriothesley, religiously conservative members of Henry's privy chamber and Privy Council, with an opportunity to plot Katherine's downfall, secretly searching her rooms for heretical writings. Since none were found, loyal members of her household must have removed incriminating volumes—among them, the Lutheran primers being used by Katherine to compile her personal prayerbook—in the nick of time. The conspiracy, recounted in *Acts and Monuments* (Foxe 1843–9: v. 553–60), was almost successful: Katherine only escaped death by prevaricating about her beliefs. In the voice of a generic Christian soul with immediate access to Christ and with personal accountability for the state of that soul, her *Prayers or Meditations* envisaged gender equality. Her Paraphrases project and letter to Cambridge University bore witness to the priority she placed on knowing Christ—faith in salvation through him, familiarity with his teachings and example—to animate English people to genuinely Christlike living. But Katherine was forced to pretend to Henry that her deepest convictions were mere experiments or pretexts for diverting conversation. Setting the record straight by expressing her real beliefs must consequently have been a dominant preoccupation in late summer and autumn 1546, when Katherine probably composed the fluid three-part sequence of reflections that comprise her wholly original work, *The Lamentation of a Sinner*, although it remained in manuscript until almost a year after Henry's death.

Lamentation's opening section is an emotively charged first-person account of a soul in abjection, full of self-reproach, where the shocks of recognition registered in the showdown with Henry (Foxe 1843–9: v. 558–60) have been entirely assimilated to the speaker's apprehension of great distance and utter difference from God. 'I am', writes Katherine, 'forced and constrained with my heart and words, to confess and declare to the world, how ingrate, negligent, unkind, and stubborn, I have been to God my Creator; and how beneficial, merciful, and gentle He hath been always to me His creature, being such a miserable, wretched sinner' (1548: A1^r). This initial section offers an account of her conversion experience which is at once highly analytical and yet devoid of autobiographical specificity. As in *Prayers or Meditations*, moralized commonplaces of faculty psychology—blind reason, wayward will, vain imaginations—lend a generic cast to Katherine's evocation of her own subjectivity. In this female-authored discourse, the genderlessness of the self-presentation bespeaks neither cowardice nor co-optation by male norms. Instead, the combination of universalism and personalism that energized early reformers—the conviction that all souls are equal before God and that every soul is individually accountable to God—empowers Katherine to conceive herself as a subject for discourse on these common grounds. In a new recasting of the binary emphasis on the sinful self and redeeming Christ found prominently in *Psalms or Prayers* and *Prayers or Meditations*, Katherine confesses her guiltiness. Next she evokes her struggles with justification by faith, which she finally came to understand through a personal apprehension of the theology of the Passion.

The middle section of *Lamentation* expatiates on this theology, which is central to her religious outlook. Katherine daringly appropriates devotional terminology for doctrinal purposes as she focuses on what she calls 'the book of the crucifix'. She makes clear that her 'crucifix' is not a physical object liable to idolatry. Rather, it is a lively image that the inward eye of the Christian is enabled to see through knowledge of the Gospel as characterized by Paul in 1 Corinthians 2: 2: 'I determined not to know anything among you, save Jesus Christ, and Him crucified.' Echoing the optimism of Erasmus and early reformers regarding Bible-reading by the laity, Katherine outgoes Paul in her reiterated 'book' metaphor, her means for impressing upon her reader the accessibility of this knowledge of Christ. But, unlike Erasmus, she ultimately returns her emphasis to Paul and the specifically affective experience of faith without which, in her view as in Cranmer's, even Scripture will remain a dead letter (Mueller 1997*b*).

The final section of *Lamentation* extends the lessons of the 'book of the crucifix' into the domain of communal Christian behaviour and daily social life—the enterprise of reforming England that elicited such imperious notes from Katherine in addressing Cambridge University and her husband. She sustains her agenda of putting her most deeply held beliefs on record, but she carefully modulates her tonalities. Taking cues from Udall's Preface to the Luke paraphrase, which compared Henry to the biblical King David, who as a youth destroyed the heathen giant Goliath, and to King Hezekiah, who destroyed idols erected for the Hebrews to worship, Katherine offers her own encomium:

Our Moses, and most godly, wise governor and king, hath delivered us out of the captivity and bondage of Pharaoh. I mean by this Moses, King Henry the eight, my most sovereign, favourable lord and husband [...] And I mean by this Pharaoh the bishop of Rome, who hath been and is a greater persecutor of all true Christians than ever was Pharaoh, of the children of Israel. For he is a persecutor of the Gospel, and grace, a setter forth of all superstition, and counterfeit holiness, bringing many souls to hell [...] And this lesson I would all men had of him, that when they begin to mislike his doing, then only begin they to like God.

(1548: D6^{r-v})

The final gradation here from censure to charitable forbearance is a new tonality for Katherine. Zeal blends with fellow-feeling, and the imperative mood has no place in this final section.

The Queen's overview of the English commonwealth in her concluding section reflects the optimism that characterizes English reformers generally until the accession of Mary: the polity itself is sound, but occupants of specific positions within it require moral renewal and a livelier sense of responsibility for the welfare of fellow subjects and souls. Two categories of persons attract reprehension, but Katherine interestingly does not specify social positions for them: they are denominated only as 'weaklings' and 'carnal gospellers', both of whom impede the establishment of true religion. This final section ends with urgent exhortations to a general amendment of life, reinforced with a sobering, heavily scriptural evocation of the Last Judgement.

As the King's health declined markedly in December 1546, he was certainly not 'friends as before' (the words Foxe reports he said when reconciling with Katherine); she probably saw Henry for the last time shortly before Christmas (S. James 1999: 286). Thereafter he sequestered himself with his Privy Council and excluded female companionship. The male dominance to which the Katherine of Foxe's narrative had paid lip-service in Henry's presence was enacted as political fact in the weeks preceding his death on 28 January 1547 and the days immediately following. Henry's demise was kept secret for three days, during which time Edward Seymour engineered control of government as the newly elevated Duke of Somerset and Lord Protector of his nephew the boy king Edward VI. Other powerful counsellors negotiated major appointments in this new, energetically Protestant regime. No place was made for Katherine. A handful of documents dating shortly after Henry's death, signed 'Kateryn the Quene Regent, KP'—a significant variation on her standard signature 'Kateryn the Quene KP'—attest her short-lived expectation that she would resume the powers, including, apparently, guardianship of Edward, with which Henry had entrusted her in July 1544. In the event, not only these would be denied her, but also possessions that were manifestly hers, such as the new jewels given her by Henry in August 1546, and at least one of her dower properties (S. James 1999: 288, 305). Katherine's change in status—to dowager queen, excluded from formal political agency—reduced her household from a full royal complement of ladies-in-waiting and other attendants, but did not affect her core group of retainers or intimate circle. She was an extremely wealthy noblewoman of exalted standing who retained the use and income of extensive Crown holdings for the duration of her life.

After her fourth and final marriage to Lord Admiral Thomas Seymour sometime in the spring of 1547, Katherine's household continued as the locus of her spiritual and literary activities. Against the backdrop of the emphatically professed Protestantism of the Seymours and their allies, who now controlled court and government, she had more latitude than ever to maintain the daily devotions and Bible study that were the hallmarks of her household. Her extended roles as patron of the Paraphrases project and advocate for the Cambridge colleges also received fresh confirmation. Anthony Cope, a member of Katherine's household while she was queen, paid tribute in dedicating to her *A Godly Meditation upon XX Select Psalms of David* (1547) as proof of his 'loyal and obedient heart toward [her]' and her own 'gracious intent and godly purpose in the reading and study of Holy Scripture, and the advancement of the true Word of God' (A3^{r-v}). In November 1547, when colleges again faced possible Crown confiscation of their properties, Ascham as Cambridge University orator wrote an appeal in Latin addressed 'To our Most Serene Lady, Queen Katherine, Most Illustrious Ruler of Virtue, Nobility, and Learning'. He hailed her for possessing 'that universal glory of learning [...] shared with great sweetness of mutual society with Lady Elizabeth alone' and implored her to exert what influence she could on the university's behalf during the current session of Parliament (Ascham 1865: i/1. 111–12; my translation). But despite the success of her efforts with Henry in November 1545, Ascham did not rely exclusively on Katherine's good offices now. He also wrote Latin letters to Edward VI, to Cheke, Edward's tutor, and to Katherine's brother William.

Ascham's strategic decision to solicit advocates other than Katherine is explicable. On the same day that Parliament convened, 5 November 1547, her *Lamentation* appeared in print. The fuller title states that the work was 'set forth and put in print at the instant desire of the right gracious lady, Katherine, Duchess of Suffolk, and the earnest request of the right honourable lord, William Parr, Marquess of Northampton'—Katherine's most steadfast friend of her post-Henry years, and her own brother, newly advanced in rank and prestige. The decision to publish *Lamentation* must have been difficult: on the one hand, it was her most complete and forthright statement of her spiritual beliefs; on the other, its point of departure was a ruthlessly degrading self-study of her sinful soul. Nothing remotely similar to her self-abasement as a Christian queen had been presented to English readers, although within a year, John Bale would publish Marguerite de Navarre's extremes of self-denigration in his edition of Elizabeth's translation of the *Miroir* as *A Godly Meditation of the Christian Soul* (1548). Sir William Cecil, then the Lord Protector's master of requests and soon after his secretary, furnished *Lamentation* with a prefatory letter that alludes to her metaphor of a 'book' of essential reading. Cecil defends her bold self-exposure as requisite for making a powerful reformist impact on her readers:

The fruit of this treatise, good reader, is thy amendment; this only had, the writer is satisfied. This good lady thought no shame to detect her sin to obtain remission; no vileness to become nothing, to be a member of Him, which is all things in all; no folly to forget the wisdom of the world to learn the simplicity of the Gospel; at the last, no displeasantness to submit herself to the school of the Cross, the learning of the crucifix, the book of our redemption, the very absolute library of God's mercy and wisdom. This way thought she her honour increased, and her state permanent, to make her earthly honour heavenly, and neglect the transitory for the everlasting. Of this I would thee [be] warned, that the profit may ensue [...] See and learn hereby what she hath done. ($\pi 4^{v}$–5^{r})

It requires little imagination to project the range of reactions that contemporary readers could have had to this dowager queen, who, having newly buried Henry

VIII, rushed into the arms of Edward VI's sexually attractive uncle, and now publicly confessed herself a great sinner.

The end of the same month saw the publication of the first volume of the English *Paraphrases*, the title page dated 'the last day of January [...] 1548'. Udall's letter to 'the most virtuous Lady, Queen Katherine Dowager, late wife to the most noble and most victorious King Henry the Eight' follows those to Edward VI and to 'the gentle Christian reader'. This letter sustains Udall's earlier vein of fulsome praise, but its reflections are noticeably retrospective. He commends Katherine's commissioning the translation in the perfect tense, as action now completed, belonging to the past: 'Ye have therein, most gracious Lady, right well declared both how much ye tender God's honour, and also how earnestly ye mind the benefit of your country' (1548: B8^r). Likewise, Udall's prefatory letters to John and Acts, also addressed to 'Queen Katherine Dowager', respectively affirm her reputation among other learned ladies and, now, as the third-ranking 'public benefactor', after Edward and 'his most dear uncle Edward, Duke of Somerset', having 'set others in hand with writing or translating, to the fruitful exercise of the learned, to the wholesome instruction of English readers, and to the effectual edifying of the simple, ignorant multitude' (Acts, 3A1^{r-v}). Udall cites 'divers most godly Psalms and meditations of your own penning and setting forth' to bolster Katherine's status as 'chief patroness [...] next unto these two', but he makes no mention of her *Lamentation* (3A1^{r-v}). Judging from Cecil's exculpatory letter and Udall's carefully circumscribed praises,[8] the dowager queen's influence had become both disputable and diminished since her remarriage. Ramifications were felt even in her household. When Elizabeth's tutor, William Grindal, died in January 1548, Katherine and Seymour urged that Francis Goldsmith replace him; Elizabeth, however, held out for Ascham, and she prevailed.

By January 1548, Katherine knew that she was pregnant—a development not known to have occurred in her previous marriages—and the confines of her household gradually set the limits of her activity. Her friendship with Katherine, Duchess of Suffolk, deepened as the two supported each other's advancing reformist proclivities in the domestic sphere. Probably at the Duchess's suggestion, Katherine appointed Miles Coverdale as her almoner on his return from Germany in March 1548. Seymour seems to have had no interest in the godly edification of the household which Katherine cultivated. This, at least, is what Hugh Latimer asserted in a sermon preached before King and court in Lent 1549, after Katherine had died and Seymour had been executed as a traitor: 'I have heard say when that good queen that is gone had ordained in her house daily prayer both before noon and after noon, the Admiral gets him out of the way, like a mole digging in the earth' (Latimer 1968: 127–8). In spring 1548, however, Seymour's political ambition enhanced the quotient of godliness in Katherine's household, when he secured the wardship of the ardently reformist Lady Jane Grey from her father, the Marquess of Dorset, on the promise that he would arrange her marriage to Edward. Conversely, in June 1548 Elizabeth left the household

---

[8] Cf. Ascham's Latin letter to Cecil (1865: i/1. 111–12).

after Seymour's over-familiar behaviour was recognized for the grave dangers it posed to her person and reputation.

In mid-June 1548 Seymour escorted his wife, now six months pregnant, and his young ward, Lady Jane, to his newly acquired property, Sudeley Castle in Gloucestershire, for the baby's safe delivery far from plague-ridden London. Katherine was attended by her long-time friend and doctor Robert Huick; her almoner, Coverdale; her chaplain, Parkhurst; her intimate friend the Duchess of Suffolk; and long-serving attendants such as Elizabeth Tyrwhit. Katherine gave birth to a daughter, Mary, on 30 August, but died of puerperal fever on 5 September. Elizabeth Tyrwhit recorded her observations of Katherine's fevered delirium and Seymour's attempts to soothe her. His extreme grief must account for his absence from Katherine's funeral, held in the castle chapel, with Lady Jane as chief mourner, her newest possession the personal prayerbook written in Katherine's hand. Coverdale's funeral sermon included a reformist explanation of the candles surrounding the dowager queen's body: they were lit to honour her, not as accessories to prayers for the fate of her soul, which would not be said (S. James 1999: 331–3). Parkhurst composed and eventually (as Bishop of Norwich) published a poignant Latin epitaph: 'In this urn lies Katherine, lately Queen of England, women's greatest glory. She died in giving birth. After bringing forth an infant girl, lo, at daylight's seventh shining, she breathed her spirit forth' (1573: 153).

What became of Katherine's daughter Mary has been a long-standing mystery; the series of legal and financial documents relating to her ends in September 1550, shortly after her second birthday (S. James 1999: 339). But, in a final demonstration of the spiritual and literary activity generated by and around Katherine in her household circle, Parkhurst composed and published a set of short-lined Latin verses in which, appropriately for an orphan, the baby daughter pronounces her own epitaph:

With what great travail, and at her life's expense, my mother the Queen gave birth; a wayfarer, I, her infant girl, sleep beneath this marble stone. If cruel death had given me a longer while to live, those virtues of that best of mothers—propriety, modesty, restraint, both heavenly and manly—would have lived again as my own nature. Now, whoever you are, farewell; and because I say no more, you will excuse this by my infancy.   (Parkhurst 1573: 154)

Parkhurst's pun on '*infans*' (infant, one unable to speak) evokes a very young daughter on the threshold of speech, who crosses it briefly, inspired by her dead mother's surpassing virtues to extol them, before lapsing into the speechlessness of death. But the rest is not silence. A rich legacy of expressiveness survives in the four spiritual and literary works left to us by Katherine Parr, the first Englishwoman to publish her works in print, and by members of her circle who were moved to emulate her example.[9]

---

[9] Thomas Bentley recognized the spiritual and literary legacy of Katherine and her circle in assembling what he calls 'Lamp' ii of *The Monument of Matrons* (1582), containing Elizabeth's translation of Marguerite's *Miroir*; Katherine's *Lamentation*, preceded by Cecil's letter; Katherine's *Prayers or Meditations*; Jane Grey's *Prayers* and *Exhortation*; and Elizabeth Tyrwhit's *Morning and Evening Prayers*.

Primary Works

Ascham, Roger (1578), *Familiarium epistolarum libri tres.*

—— (1865), *Whole Works*, ed. Revd Dr Giles, 3 vols in 4 (London: John Russell Smith).

BL, Harley MS 2342. [Katherine's prayerbook]

Cope, Anthony (1547), *A Godly Meditacion upon .XX. Select Psalmes of David.*

Elizabeth I (2009), *Translations, 1544–1589*, ed. Janel Mueller and Joshua Scodel (Chicago: University of Chicago Press).

Fisher, John (1544), *Psalmi seu precationes.*

Foxe, John (1843–9), *Acts and Monuments*, 8 vols (London: T. Allman).

Goldsmith, Francis (1547), Letter to Katherine, 1543–4, BL, Lansdowne MS 97.

Latimer, Hugh (1968), *Selected Sermons*, ed. A. G. Chester (Charlottesville: University of Virginia Press).

Parkhurst, John (1573), *Ludicra.*

Parr, Katherine (1544), *Psalmes or Prayers taken out of Holye Scripture.*

—— (1545), *Prayers or Medytacions.*

—— (1545?), Letter to Mary, 20 Sept., BL, Cotton MS Vespasian F.III, art. 35.

—— (1546), Letter to Cambridge University, 26 Feb., BL, Lansdowne MS 1236, art. 8.

—— (1548), *The Lamentation of a Sinner.*

—— (forthcoming), *Complete Works and Correspondence*, ed. Janel Mueller.

Tyrwhit, Elizabeth (1574), *Morning and Evening Prayers.*

Udall, Nicholas, et al. (1548), *The First Tome [...] of the Paraphrases of Erasmus upon the Newe Testament.*

Whitford, Richard (1531?), *The Folowyng of Christ.*

CHAPTER 14

....

JOHN LELAND AND HIS HEIRS

THE TOPOGRAPHY
OF ENGLAND

....

PHILIP SCHWYZER

JOHN LELAND was among the most innovative and influential scholar–patriots of the English Renaissance. He has been credited with founding or pioneering the modern disciplines of English bibliography, topography, and local studies. Leland's work can be said to lie at the roots of modern discursive phenomena ranging from the guide-book and travelogue to the literary canon itself (Ross 1991; Simpson 2002). Yet for all that, he remains an elusive figure, curiously difficult to capture in focus. This is in part because he was able to publish only a small proportion of what he accomplished—and, undoubtedly, accomplished a still smaller proportion of what he projected. Succumbing in 1547, in his early forties, to a serious mental illness from which he never recovered, Leland died in 1552, leaving behind a clutch of printed Latin poems, some on topographical themes; polemical tracts including a defence of King Arthur and an attack on the Pope; and, crucially for later scholars, 'A New Year's Gift for King Henry VIII' (1546), in which he outlined a remarkable range of unfinished projects bearing on the literary history and physical topography of England and Britain. He also left a mass of notes and unfinished manuscripts relating to various projects, which more fortunate scholars would mine and adapt for their own purposes.

Leland very swiftly acquired a range of self-appointed collaborators and heirs, who claimed to understand his intentions and to be in a position to fulfil them. Among the first of these was the vehemently Protestant cleric and scholar John Bale, who endeavoured to yoke Leland's scholarship more closely to the project of religious reform. It was Bale who published the 'New Year's Gift', with his own copious commentary, as *The Laborious Journey of John Leland* (1549). In the field of topography, the most significant of Leland's 'heirs' was undoubtedly William Camden, who has been credited with making Leland's dream of a complete topographical survey of Britain a reality (Levy 1967: 158).

A number of recent studies have set out to rescue Leland from his rescuers. James Simpson (2002) has questioned the compatibility of Bale's ideological agenda with the more scholarly Leland's goals and methods. Similarly, Jennifer Summit (2007) has counselled against reading Leland's aims as a topographer backwards from the achievements of his celebrated successors. Indeed, it is worth noting that suspicions regarding the real relationship between Camden's work and Leland's were raised even in the Tudor era. In 1599 a disgruntled herald, Ralph Brooke, penned a cleverly spiteful poem in which Leland's ghost accuses Camden of suppressing and plagiarizing his achievement. Recalling how Leland spent his 'travayle, witts and health [...] to doe his cuntrie pleasure', Brooke laments that 'such rare fruits of his laboriouse penn | Came to be drownd in such a thankles *Denn*' (1596, final page).[1] Camden's ('Came [...] *Denn*') *Britannia* is here refigured as a sinister, dark hole comparable to 'Errour's Den' in Spenser's *Faerie Queene*, in which the light of Leland's achievement has been obscured.

There is little to substantiate Brooke's charge that Camden attempted to conceal his debt to Leland. Camden in fact makes frequent respectful references to 'Leland our Countriman', citing both his topographical poetry and his speculations on the etymology of place-names (1610: 343, 497, 607). Yet the charge that the Elizabethan 'discovery of England' spearheaded by Camden and his collaborators involved a distortion of Leland's work—or at any rate of his intentions—may not be entirely empty (see Helgerson 1992: 107–47). Focusing on the circumstances that led Leland to topography and the purpose with which he undertook his travels, I argue that Leland's understanding of national space was markedly distinct from that of his successors. Ironically, the very problems and paradoxes that impeded Leland's own projects came to characterize—even to be celebrated in—the topographical triumphs of the Elizabethans.

An initial aim of this chapter is to disentangle Leland's projects and personality from his would-be collaborators and inheritors. As a means to this end, I situate his career alongside that of a seventeenth-century writer whose name has rarely been mentioned with his. There is a curious and potentially instructive resemblance in the lives and deeds of Leland and John Milton, both of whom were born in London in the first decade of their respective centuries (Leland between 1503 and 1506). Coincidentally, they attended the same London school (St Paul's) and the same Cambridge

---

[1] The lament of Leland's 'Supposed Ghost' loses a good deal of force and becomes unintentionally comic when Brooke—a stickler in theology as in heraldry—admits in conclusion that it is not a real ghost after all: 'I am deceav'd, for Leylands ghost doth rest | From plaints and cryes with soules of blessed men.'

college (Christ's, from which Leland graduated BA in 1522). More revealingly, both promising young scholars seem to have been torn between an eagerness to win praise for their considerable talents and contempt for the conservative academic and clerical establishment from which that praise might be expected to flow. Both would find a temporary solution to this dilemma by travelling abroad, where they composed Latin poetry and cultivated the acquaintance of poets and humanists; thus, Leland, denouncing English academics as 'noisy sophists', decamped to Paris and Guillaume Budé's circle in the late 1520s. Their Continental travels brought home to both of them the piteous state of English letters, and both conceived the career-defining ambition of rescuing their native land from literary obscurity. For Leland, as for Milton, this meant laying claim to the mantle of the English Virgil. As Leland wrote confidently in praise of himself and his homeland: 'Mantua bore Virgil; Verona, Catullus | The city of London is my noble birthplace' ('Mantua Virgilium genuit, Verona Catullum. | Patria Londinum est urbs generosa mihi'; Leland 1589).

Like Milton in 1539, Leland in 1529 or thereabouts returned to a homeland on the brink of unprecedented upheaval; as the English Revolution occupied Milton's time and pen throughout his thirties and forties, so the English Reformation had a determining impact on Leland's career at roughly the same life-stage. Leland indeed shared something of Milton's gift for religious polemic: his *Antiphilarchia* is an attack on papal supremacy (CUL, MS Ee.v.14). Immersed in the struggles of the day, neither man forgot his larger ambition: to leave an indelible mark on English literature. But while Milton lost his sight not long after his fortieth birthday, Leland at the same age lost his mind. For him there would be no final phase of retirement in which the great task, long planned and long delayed, might be at last fulfilled.

Leland was granted neither Milton's share of talent nor his comparatively good fortune. Yet their personalities present similar paradoxes: selfless patriotism alongside unrestrained egoism, careful scholarship wedded to a talent for caustic polemic. Above all they appear united by an overriding specific ambition—the determination, in an era of national turmoil, to celebrate and vindicate the English nation through an unprecedented literary endeavour. The form of Leland's venture was a product of his time, as Milton's would be. Writing before Camoens and Tasso, it probably never crossed Leland's mind that England might be celebrated in epic poetry in the English vernacular. Rather, he proposed to dignify the nation through compendious works of bibliographical and topographical description: his chief aim, as he informed Henry VIII, was 'to describe your moste noble realme' (Leland and Bale 1549: C2ʳ). If Leland's projects strike us as more prosaic than Milton's, they nonetheless played a role in making Milton's epic ambitions imaginable. The young Milton's decision to write epic verse in English is bound up with a patriotic vision of national topography:

although I be forever unknown and utterly without fame in the world outside, if only yellow haired Usa reads my poems, and he who drinks from the Alan, and Humber, full of whirling eddies, and every grove of Trent, and above all my native Thames, and the Tamar, stained with metals, and if the Orkneys among their distant waves will learn my song [...]   (1997: 285)

This vision of the native landscape as audience is based in an understanding of national space enabled and inaugurated by Leland.

By his own account, Leland began his travels around England and Wales in 1533. The initial motive for his journeying was not geographical discovery, but bibliographical recovery (Carley 2000). As he attests in the 'New Year's Gift', Leland had received a commission from the King:

to peruse and dylygentlye to search all the lybraryes of Monasteryes and collegies of thys your noble realme, to the entent that the monumentes of auncyent wryters, as wel of other nacyons as of your owne provynce, myghte be brought out of deadly darkenesse to lyvelye light.   (B8ʳ)

The bringing of books out of darkness into light can be read as a semi-literal description of Leland's activity. The phrase conjures an image of the scholar, candle in hand, prying into dusky libraries where volumes languish like hopeless prisoners: 'tyed up in cheanes, and hydden undre dust', as Bale put it.[2] But for Leland the idea of bringing to light had a deeper and more encompassing significance. Images of brilliant illumination—described by Cathy Shrank as a 'vocabulary of approbatory luminosity' (2004b: 90)—pervade his writing, and seem central to his understanding of his age, his king, and his career. Today, 'enlightenment' as a term for intellectual progress is a thoroughly dead metaphor, making it difficult to grasp how powerfully attractive the image of scholar as light-bearer must have seemed to Leland. If there are echoes of Petrarch in Leland's luminous lexicon, there are echoes too of Scripture. (God, in the English Bible of 1539, calls his people 'out of darcknes into hys mervelous lighte'; 1 Pet. 2: 9.) Light for Leland, then, is associated with scholarship, spiritual reform, and the present historical moment; darkness with ignorance, monastic superstition, and the past.

The dissolution of the monasteries in 1536–40 had drastic consequences for the pace and nature of Leland's labours. Whatever commission they had given Leland earlier in the decade, Henry VIII and his ministers spared little thought for the contents of monastic libraries. A harsher light than that of Leland's candle now greeted the fragile volumes, as the very walls that sheltered them were torn away. Like his friend Bale, Leland could not help regretting the heedlessness with which the libraries were dispersed, even as he applauded the royal reforms (Lawton 2001; Simpson 2002; Schwyzer 2004b). Commentators on Leland have found it hard to resist associating his madness with the divided and perhaps guilty conscience engendered by the Henrician bibliocaust (Simpson 2002). What is clear is that Leland's quest to serve his country by reviving its lost literary heritage was now severely curtailed. Whatever he might now succeed in bringing to light would be but a shadow of the complete literary history of Britain he had thought awaited him when he set out in 1533.

---

[2] Leland was particularly outraged by the state of the Franciscan library at Oxford: 'Dust, cobwebs, moths, cockroaches, mould, and filth' (Kendrick 1950: 52).

Faced with this disaster, Leland abandoned neither his goal of describing the realm, nor the cherished image of national illumination. Instead, he transposed his grand project from a bibliographical to a topographical key. Summer 1539 saw him traversing the north-eastern counties of England on a new mission, not to visit the last beleaguered religious houses, but to take stock of the land and its inhabitants. He seems to have undertaken a similar journey every summer for the next six years, though records of some of these tours have been lost.[3] By 1546 he was able to report to his king that

I have so traveled in your domynions both by the see coastes and the myddle partes, sparynge neyther labour nor costes by the space of these vi yeares past, that there is almost neyther cape nor baye, haven, creke or pere, ryver or confluence of ryvers, breches, washes, lakes, meres, fenny waters, mountaynes, valleys, mores, hethes, forestes, woodes, cyties, burges, castels, pryncypall manor places, monasteryes, and colleges, but I have seane them.

(Leland and Bale 1549: D4^{r-v})

Accounts of Leland's career can give the impression that his topographical project grew organically out of his library work, with the travel entailed in visiting monasteries prompting a natural interest in the places seen along the way. Leland himself gives a somewhat different account of the connection between his historical and topographical researches, though one that similarly involves the natural emergence of the latter from the former. He claims that reading the 'honest and profytable studyes' of medieval historians 'totallye enflamed [him] wyth a love, to se throughlye all those partes of thys your opulent and ample realme, that I hadde redde of in the aforsayd wryters' (D4^{r}). Leland's account of how reading history engenders the desire to travel is intriguing not least because it precisely reverses a more conventional view of history, namely that it serves as a substitute for travel with its attendant dangers. As William Caxton observes in his Preface to Higden's *Polycronicon*,

He is and ever hath ben reputed the wysest whiche by the experyence of adverse fortune hath byholden and seen the noble Cytees maners and variaunt condycions of the people of many dyverse Regyons [...] yet he is more fortunat and may be reputed as wyse [... that] syttynge in his chambre or studye maye rede knowe and understande the polytyke and noble actes of alle the worlde as of one Cyte [...] in suche wyse as he had ben and seen them.   (1482: a2^{v})

But what Leland studiously avoids explaining or even hinting at is surely the most fundamental factor: he began travelling for its own sake because there were no more monastic libraries left. His 'discovery' of the land was in some degree a substitute for the loss of the books; space was called upon to stand in for history.[4]

The shift from 'monumentes of auncyent writers' to 'mountaynes, valleys, mores' may seem drastic, but it allowed Leland to remain true to his ultimate goal, 'to describe your moste noble realme'. Prior to the shock of the dissolution, Leland

---

[3] The most thorough attempt to reconstruct the content and sequence of Leland's journeys is Chandler (1993).

[4] Scattergood (2000) sees Leland's nationalism as itself a response to the dissolution (61).

seems to have conceived of that realm primarily in historical terms, as a sequence of events; England and Englishness were crystallized in 'the excellente actes of [Henry VIII's] progenytours' (Leland and Bale 1549: C2ᵛ). His understanding of the nation as a temporal entity constituted in historical time was one he shared with the medieval chroniclers he cherished, as well as contemporaries such as Bale. If shifting from bibliography to topography saved the project of national description, it nonetheless necessitated a radical shift in the way the nation was imagined. In place of the nation understood as immanent in history, Leland proffered the nation embodied in geographical space; in place of a temporal England extending from its origins into the present, he gestured to an undiscovered country stretching from Berwick to Land's End. This is not to say that Leland was ever prepared or able to dispense with history in favour of a purely spatial conception of England and Eng-lishness. Rather, the more he struggles to let geography do the work of chronol-ogy, the more space itself becomes paradoxically imbued with time. As Summit concludes, for Leland 'places are always in time, and time is always sedimented in place' (2007: 163). Yet throughout Leland's works there are also tensions and internal contradictions that testify to the uneasiness of this marriage of time and space.

By 1545 Leland had undertaken a string of journeys and compiled a mass of descrip-tive 'itineraries' and assorted notes on the natural and human landscapes of England and Wales. The most coherent passages offer a close account of his progress through a region, with particular attention to features including bridges, fortifications, crops, and tombs of local worthies. Here he is in the North Riding of Yorkshire:

Mougreve [Mulgrave] castle stondith on apon a craggy hille: and on eche side of it is an hille far higher then that whereon the castelle stondith on. The north hille on the toppe of it hath certen stones communely caullid Waddes Grave, whom the people there say to have been a gigant and owner of Mougreve. There is by these stones a bekyn [...]
From Malton to Shirburne villag about an 8 miles by champain ground, fruteful of grass and corne, but litle or no wood. The Erle of Saresbyri was lord of Shirburn: and King Richard had it by Anne his wife.
From Shirburne by hilles on the right hond and low ground with carres on the lift hond a v. miles to Semar, a great uplandisch towne [...] I saw yn the quire of the mean paroch chirch there a playn marble stone yn the quire, with an epitaphi yn French, wher were buried John Percy and Johan de Aton.   (1906–10: i/1. 58)

In this brief passage, Leland ranges from legendary giants to recent dynastic history, from fertile fields to stone tombs. His account draws on local knowledge, first-hand observation, and matters of public record. Yet however rich the content, the style is undeniably, almost defiantly flat. There is none of the literary embellishment we might expect from England's self-nominated Virgil. The bland prose reminds us that these are notes made for personal use. Although there is precedent in William Worcester's late medieval *Itinerarium*, Leland never intended to publish his *Itinerary* in anything like its surviving form. Rather, his declared intention was to dissem-inate his topographical research in three very different forms: a wonderful silver 'table', a book on British topography (*Liber de topographia Britanniae primae*), and a massive county-by-county antiquarian history of England and Wales (*De antiquitate Britannica*).

By Leland's own account, the first fruit of his topographical labours was to consist in a grand gift to Henry VIII:

Thus instructed, I trust shortly to se the tyme, that like as Carolus Magnus had among his treasures thre large and notable tables of sylver, rychely enameled, one of the syte and descripcion of Constantynople, an other of the site and figure of the magnificent citie of Rome, and the third of the descripcion of the worlde. So shall your Maiestie have thys your worlde and impery of Englande so sett fourthe in a quadrate table of sylver, yf God sende me lyfe to accomplyshe my beginning, that your grace shall have ready knowledge at the fyrst sighte of many right delectable, fruteful, and necessary pleasures, by contemplacion therof, as often as occasyon shall move yow to the syghte of it.   (D5^r)

Nothing like the 'table' described in the 'New Year's Gift' survives, nor is there any record of its existence. In all likelihood, Henry's death in 1547 and Leland's own mental decline conspired to prevent its construction. Leland's extraordinary proposal has not received the attention it merits, partly because the object was never created (and perhaps could not have been), and partly because the plan seems so obviously at odds with what we consider the thrust of Leland's work. His *Itinerary*, which contains far too much detailed local information ever to be compressed into such a limited visual space, is lacking in the very kind of detail required for making maps (Summit 2007: 163).[5] Yet although Leland did propose to produce a book of British topography to accompany the silver 'table', this was not intended as a repository for the mass of unrepresentable detail. Rather, it would provide precisely the same kind of detail, thereby serving as a guide for the production of similar tables throughout the country: 'such a descripcion [...] of your realme in wryttinge, that it shall be no mastery after, for the graver or painter to make the lyke by a perfect example'.

Difficult as it is to imagine how Leland ever hoped to represent the England he discovered on the ground within such limited confines, the 'quadrate table of sylver' is an idea he could not do without. The unrealized, impossible object represents the pinnacle of his topographical ambitions. Its superiority in Leland's mind to any attempt at written description rests on two qualities in particular. First, it literally shines. A fitting gift for the King Leland names as 'the day starre' (D1^r); it reflects and seems to give forth light. In its preciousness and purity, the 'table' can be thought of as symbolically cleansing and ennobling what was in practice a

---

[5] There has been general agreement that Leland is promising 'a map' (Kendrick 1950: 48; Mottram 2008; Scattergood 2000: 62; Shrank 2004*b*: 98–9). Living before the great Elizabethan advances in cartography, Leland might have had other ideas on how to represent the nation visually. Charlemagne's silver tables which Leland cites as his model would certainly not have featured maps in any modern sense, but more probably depictions of walls and major buildings, or female personifications of Constantinople and Rome (Deliyannis 2003). Leland may indeed be thinking of a more distant model, Homer's Shield of Achilles, with its depiction in metalwork of emblematic landscapes. Whether he had in mind an actual table or (more probably) a large tablet, Leland almost certainly imagined his 'quadrate table' as a companion to the Arthurian 'round table' he saw at Winchester (see Biddle 2000).

'laboryouse'—and muddy—journey. Secondly, it sums up the nation in a small and regular space, allowing the whole of Britain to be apprehended in a single, unified gaze. Although the 'table' will offer variety in the form of 'many right delectable, fruteful, and necessary pleasures', these are imagined as being available simultaneously, 'at the fyrst sighte'. In this respect it is superior to a topographical text, in which the discovery of the landscape is progressive and, at any given moment, inevitably partial. In the silver 'table' and only there will Henry be able to see his realm clearly, and to see it whole.

As the luminous sheen of the 'table' suggests, Leland is determined that topography, no less than history, should be an enterprise of enlightenment. Yet it is far from immediately obvious how the metaphor of illumination can be translated into topographical terms. Unlike the books mouldering in monastic libraries, the land Leland endeavours to record was already visible, bathed in the light of day. Rhetoric aside, one cannot in fact 'discover' England, at least not in the sense that one might discover a lost manuscript—nor even in the debatable sense in which Europeans might discover America. Leland succeeds in retaining the illumination metaphor only by, in effect, inverting it, reversing the relationship between scholar and his subject, the present and past:

Yea, and to wade further in thys matter, where as now almost no man can wele gesse at the shaddow of the auncyent names of havens, ryvers, promontories, hilles, woodes, cities, townes, castelles, and varyete of kyndes of people, that Cesar, Livi, Strabo Diodorus, Fabius Pictor, Pomponius Mela, Plinius, Cornelius Tacitus Ptolomeus, Sextus Rufus, Ammianus, Marcellinus, Solinus, Antoninus, and dyverse other make mencyon of. I trust so to open this wyndow, that the lyght shal be seane, so long, that is to say, by the space of a whole thousand yeares stopped up, & the old glory of your renoumed Britaine to reflorish through the worlde.

(D7ᵛ)

Whereas previously for Leland the source of illumination lay in the scholarly present and shone on the obscure past, now the light must be understood to shine from the distant past to illuminate the present.[6] The need for illumination in the present is explained through the stopping up of the light source 'by the space of a whole thousand yeares'. The past, then, contains a form of brilliant illumination, but also an obstacle, which prevents light from reaching the present, except in the form of puzzling shadows. It is by opening an aperture to that ancient source of illumination that the land in the present can be made known. To discover Britain on the ground Leland must first discover—or disclose—Britain's lost antiquity.

The specification of 'a whole thousand yeares' as the period lying between the darkened present and the source of national illumination is meant more or less literally. In the passage quoted above, Leland names Roman authors from the first century BC to the fourth century AD as authorities on Britain; as Shrank argues, it is vital for Leland that Britain be imagined as not only glorious but classical

---

[6] Shrank discusses a similar association of ancient place-names with illumination in *Cygnea cantio* (2004*b*: 89).

and Latinate. Yet the millennial measure points more specifically to the early sixth century, which is to say the age of Arthur. As T. D. Kendrick put it, and as Leland's other writings bear out, 'The land where King Henry VIII reigned was for Leland the land where King Arthur had lived, and ancient Britain and modern England were not only equally dear to him, but each was for him incomplete without the other' (1950: 56). It is in Arthur's Romano-British milieu that 'the old glory' and essential character of 'renoumed Britaine' are to be located. It was to this era that Henry VIII and his advisers turned for evidence that his realm was legally an empire, exempt from papal jurisdiction. Likewise, English reformers looked for the true origins of the Church of England in the British Church of late antiquity, before the Anglo-Saxons fell under the sway of Roman Catholicism at the close of the sixth century (Kidd 1999; Schwyzer 2004b). The light shining from Arthurian Britain mingles an imperial radiance with the pure glow of apostolic religion.

It is an odd but compelling notion that a nation might have an essential time or era, a point on the historical timeline at which its true character, place-names, and internal and external borders become fixed, once and for all. For much of Leland's career, this idea lay close to the heart of government policy (Schwyzer 2004b). Aiming to rationalize the political map and enhance the authority of the centre, policy-makers claimed to be restoring the state to its authentic and original condition. In abolishing anomalous entities ranging from the Marcher lordships on the Welsh border to the palatinate bishopric of Durham, they were cleansing the political map of medieval corruption, much as reformers were simultaneously cleansing the Church. There can be no doubt than an ideological narrative emerging out of the pressures of the 1530s had a profound influence on Leland's topographical endeavours in the 1540s. As Shrank argues (2004b: 86), in topographical poems like *Genethliacon* (1543) and *Cygnea cantio* (1545) Leland both classicizes the British landscape and homogenizes it. Cultural differences between Wales, England, and Cornwall are erased; all seem equally close to the royal centre, and of course equally loyal.

Yet when one turns from poetic fictions to the first-hand observations of the *Itinerary*, the problems involved in the idea that the national essence is rooted in the sixth century become immediately apparent. Keen as Leland is to emphasize sites with classical or Arthurian associations, he cannot avoid acknowledging that the majority of the places he visits (as well as the majority of noble families and honourable institutions) not only bear the mark of the millennium of corruption and obscurity, but have their origin within it. The recently dissolved monasteries, which still loom so large in urban and rural landscapes, provide the most powerful case in point. If their dissolution is supposed to mark a return to the purity of the ancient British Church, the buildings themselves remain, sometimes as unsightly ruins, sometimes turned to new uses which nonetheless serve as reminders of historical complexity, permutation, and loss. As Summit argues, 'Leland's *Itinerary* is a record of the residual' (2007: 168), constantly testifying, in a manner that is beyond if not against the author's will, to the ineradicable presence of the past.

In his vision of the silver 'table', Leland sought a means of making national topography conform to the classical unities—a nation belonging to one time, represented in one space, and offering a single (glorious) spectacle. If there is a point in his notes where Leland seems to discover the objective correlative of this idealized England, it is at Bewdley in Worcestershire:

The towne of Bewdeley is set on the syd of an hill, soe coningly that a man cannot wishe to set a towne bettar. It riseth from Severne banke by est upon the hill by west; so that a man standinge on the hill trans pontem [across the bridge] by est may descrive almost every howse in the towne, and at the rysynge of the sunne from este the hole towne gliterithe, being all of new buyldinge, as it were of gold.   (1906–10: ii/5. 87–8)

Bewdley is charged with all the qualities Leland hoped to discover and reveal in the nation. It is luminous, prosperous, and—from the right angle—apprehensible in a unified gaze. It is also, perhaps significantly, 'a very newe towne'; granted its charter by Edward IV, Bewdley has known little of the corruption and compromise characteristic of the dark centuries. Bewdley 'gliterithe' because it is new, because it is not medieval. For Leland, there is a sense in which being 'newe' is the closest thing to being a thousand years old.

If Bewdley contains all that is best and truest in Britain, it can stand for the larger nation only emblematically or synecdochally. It is also one among myriad parts, more than can ever be captured or perceived in a unified gaze. Leaving Bewdley, Leland swiftly descends into a mass of irreducible and sometimes puzzling particulars: 'From Bewdley to Mitton village about a 4. miles by woody ground, and some corne in enclosures. Here dothe Stoure ryver breke into 2. or 3. armelets, and servyth milles [...]'. He passes Hertlebury Castle ('ther is a park with deere, and a waren for conyes; but the soile about this castle is baren'); notes a stone bridge over a brook flowing down from Droitwich 'where the salt is made'; and passes on to Ombersley ('a goodly lordship of 180 l. by the yere, lately longing to the abbay of Evesham'), before arriving at the next major town: 'I reken Worcester to be a 14. miles from Beudeley, thowghe it be communely countyd of sum to be but 12. miles' (89).

What binds these particulars together in the *Itinerary* is ultimately nothing more than the mobile figure of Leland himself. The *Itinerary* does not describe places so much as trajectories: it is, in a rudimentary way, a narrative. Chronology overlays topography not only in the presence of the past, but also in the way that land is presented as a sequence of personally experienced events. ('I cam [...] I left [...] I lernid [...] I hard [...] I markid [...] I saw'). In this regard, it seems significant that Leland pays more attention to bridges than to the sources of rivers, the latter being a more conventional subject of interest (Summit 2007). It is true that Leland does not cut a very memorable or prominent figure, yet his movements endow landscapes with pattern and form, making them graspable. 'I travelled from Bewdeley to Worcester by way of Mitton' may not make for a gripping story, but it arranges these places in a web of meaningful coherence. Toiling forward on his laborious journey, Leland himself provides the relationships between endless local particulars. The *Itinerary* does not so much discover a unified nation already present on the ground as, through the figure of the itinerant, bring one into being.

As we know, Leland did not intend to publish his *Itinerary*. His two strictly topographical projects, the silver 'table' and the accompanying volume, could never have contained more than a tiny fraction of the material recorded in his notebooks. The larger mass of notes was intended for his third project:

I have matter at plenty, already prepared [...] to wryte an hystorie, to the whiche I entende to adscribe this title *de Antiquitate Britannica*, or els *Civilis historia*. And this worke I entende to dyvyde into so many bokes, as ther be shires in Englande, and shyres & great dominions in wales. So that I esteme that thys volume wyl enclude a fyfty bokes, wherof eche one severally shall conteyne the beginninges, encreases, and memorable actes of the chiefe townes, and castelles of the province allotted to it.   (D8ᵛ–E1ʳ)

It is hard not to read the turn to history in *De antiquitate Britannica* as a retreat from the challenge posed by the nation-in-space. Leland's determination to reduce the variegated British landscape to a significant pattern is further evident in the division of his massive study into precisely fifty books, as many 'as ther be shires in Englande, and shyres & great dominions in wales'. Fifty is a round and richly suggestive number, implying a rational and above all meaningful structure, and hence a national body greater than the sum of its parts. Tellingly, Leland got his arithmetic wrong here: it would in fact require fifty-two volumes to represent the shires of England and Wales as they existed in the 1540s (thirty-nine for England and thirteen for Wales). His plan for getting round this problem seems to have been to count certain of the old Welsh Marcher lordships ('great dominions'), abolished by the Acts of Union in the 1530s, rather than the five new Welsh counties created in their place. Ironically, Leland can arrive at the significant number only by selective reference to an outmoded map of Wales, one moreover which could be said to embody medieval corruption, and only by ignoring the Henrician statute which claimed to restore Wales to its true and original form.

It is to the grandly conceived *De antiquitate Britannica* that later scholars refer when they describe Camden's *Britannia* as 'the book Leland might have written' (Levy 1967: 158). Leland does indeed anticipate Camden's shire-by-shire format. But the relationship between Leland's work and that of his Elizabethan 'heirs' is complex and problematic. While topographers like Camden, John Stow, and many others made extensive use of Leland's notes, they often developed them in the opposite direction from what Leland seems to have intended, minimizing rather than enhancing the elements of pattern and overarching structure. Thus, Stow painstakingly transcribed Leland's manuscripts with little alteration other than to excise many of the first-person narratorial references, thereby producing something more approximate to a direct description of places in themselves (Leland 1906–10, vol. i, p. xxiv). If the Elizabethans saw themselves as fulfilling Leland's project, their achievements were based in strong misreadings of that project. The very things that impeded Leland's effort to capture the nation as luminous and unified—the thick layering of the past, the diversity of regions and individual places—became the central focuses of Elizabethan topography.

Of the major Elizabethan topographers, it is probably William Lambarde who draws nearest to Leland in spirit. Lambarde shared much of Leland's Protestant zeal and fascination with royal authority; more importantly, he also began with the aim of capturing and codifying English topography within a unifying framework. By 1567 he was at work on an ambitious *Alphabetical Description of the Chief Places of England and Wales*. This was, as the title implies, a kind of historical dictionary:

BOSWORTH A plaine neare Tamworth, wheare the Usurper *Rich*. III received his Desert at the Handes of *Hen*. VII, the lawfull Enheritour of the Red Rose. The Name of the Place wheare the Overthrow was given, is called *Ambyam* Hill.

BLACKHEATH A Playne between Grenewiche and Shooter's Hyll, called blacke of the Coulour of the Soyle, which by reason of the Sonne above, and the hote Sand and Gravel beneath, is parched like a Coale. It hath borne thre severall rebellious Assemblyes.   (1730: 32–3)

This curious document can be understood as a textual approximation of the never-constructed silver 'table'. If Lambarde could not make the nation and its history apprehensible in a single gaze, he could at least subdue his information to a regular and methodical format, one which, importantly, is calculated to minimize and even deny regional difference. A document in which Bosworth abuts Blackheath, and Newcastle (225) lies in close proximity to the New Forest (227), is one whose very form privileges the nation as unifying factor and denies the significance of regional and local identities.

Lambarde never finished his *Alphabetical Description*, however. This was in part because he recognized that his project had been superseded by Camden's research, but more because he became absorbed in the extended description of a single county, his native Kent. In the *Perambulation of Kent* (1576), the towns and natural features of the region are organized with respect to geographical rather than alphabetical contiguity; the survey is organized along the lines of a walking tour, though Lambarde the perambulator does not intrude into the text as an agent of narrative in the way Leland does in his *Itinerary*. Here Lambarde reveals an unanticipated fascination with particularity and difference. In a revealing passage, he enthuses over the little village of Tenham (now Teynham), nestled among cherry and apple orchards, as 'not onely the most dainty piece of all our Shyre, but such a Singularitie as the whole Brittish Iland is not able to patterne' (1596: 246). The tone here is very different from Leland's praise of Bewdley—Tenham is not praised for its potential to emblematize the best of Britishness, but rather for its uniqueness, its resistance to incorporation within any larger 'patterne'. Likewise, in his treatment of the county at large, Lambarde singles out as of particular interest not those features which bind it to the rest of England, but those that set it apart. Kent's distinctive legal traditions and forms of land tenure (gavelkind) are testimony that this county, unlike all others, 'was never vanquished by the Conquerour, but yielded it selfe by composition' (14).

Many of the great achievements of Elizabethan topography—Lambarde's *Perambulation*, Richard Carew's *Survey of Cornwall* (1602), George Owen's *Description of Pembrokeshire* (1602–3)—exemplify a mode of topographical inquiry that is antiquarian and regional in its emphases. Although these writers profess patriotism, all choose to view the nation from its spatial and temporal margins. Thus, while Carew claims to find the Cornish most admirable when they conform to broader national models—forsaking his primitive domestic furnishings, 'the Cornish husbandman conformeth himselfe with better supplied civilities to the Easterne patterne' (66)—he clearly finds them most interesting and appealing where they do not. As Richard Helgerson observes, in a study like the *Survey of Cornwall*, the 'marking of difference [...] becomes the chief justification for writing' (1992: 135).

The relationship of the regional part to the national whole is a matter of explicit interest in Owen's study of Pembrokeshire, a county which—as he regularly reminds readers—is known as 'Little England beyond Wales'. Owen's concern to demonstrate the 'worthiness of Pembrokeshire' is such that, he insists, he would rather repeat himself than fail to specify any particular: 'rather had I herein be taxed with the fault of tautology in too often repeating one thing than found obscurely to use the figure of synecdoche in laying down the part for the whole' (1994: 198). Just as Owen refuses to let the part stand for the whole within his description of a single county, so he declines to let his 'Little England' stand for the larger nation of which it is a part.

Owen was no Pembrokeshire nationalist (though he does complain repeatedly that Pembroke bears too large a burden in conscription). Likewise, Lambarde and Carew do not see their love of county as being in any way at odds with national pride. These topographers simply fail to share Leland's anxiety that acknowledgement of difference and particularity could undermine national unity. Rather, their work suggests an understanding of Englishness (or Britishness) as rooted in and emerging from the locality. Implicitly, they remind us that the gaze that captures the nation in a single unifying perspective (as Leland sought to achieve with his silver 'table') must itself be located somewhere outside the nation. The Elizabethan 'Surveys', by contrast, reflect a perspective rooted within a particular corner of the national landscape.

In the eyes of his learned contemporaries (dissenters like Brooke excepted) and of posterity, Camden's *Britannia* (1586) fulfilled and set the seal on the Elizabethan historico-topographical project. For Lambarde, Camden was the 'most lightsome Antiquarie of this age' (1596: 9); for Spenser in 'The Ruines of Time', 'the nourice of all antiquity' (1912, line 169). *Britannia*, which appeared in a succession of expanded editions until it was at last translated into English by Philemon Holland in 1610, undertakes a county-by-county survey of England, Wales, Scotland, and Ireland, with their surrounding islands. Like Leland, Camden locates the essential geography of Britain in the Roman period: 'The most antient division of Britaine [...] is that, which is found in Ptolomee' (1610: 155). Deeper than the counties themselves run the borders of the old Romano-British tribes with their obscure yet resonant names: Iceni, Belgae, Attrebatii, and so on. The running header on every verso page serves as a reminder that Gloucestershire and Oxfordshire (for instance) will forever constitute the domain of the Dobuni.

Yet whereas Leland's love of ancient place-names was tied to a narrative of apocalyptic national redemption, Camden's topological conservatism is more recogniz-
ably antiquarian. For Leland's belief in national antiquity as a source of undying
illumination—a light that can illuminate the present, if only we would open the
window—Camden substitutes the rather different image of time as a river:

> For I am not ignorant that the first originalls of nations are obscure by reason of their
> profound antiquitie, as things which are seene very deepe and farre remote: like as the courses,
> the reaches, the confluents, and the out-lets of great rivers are well knowne, yet their first
> fountaines and heads lie commonly unknowne.   (1610, 'The Author to the Reader')

The hidden wellsprings of the nation can with much labour be discovered and
made known, but the river cannot return to its source. Rather, each passing year
bears Britain further from its origins. The difference between Camden's and Leland's
understandings of nation-time are nowhere more evident than in their approach
to the dissolution of the monasteries, which for Camden represents not a defeat of
darkness by light, but rather the river of history in uncontrolled flood:

> about the xxxvj yeere of the reigne of the said Henrie the Eight, a sudden floud (as it were)
> breaking thorow the banks with a maine streame, fell upon the Ecclesiasticall State of England,
> which while the world stood amazed, and England groned thereat, bare downe and utterly
> overthrew the greatest part of the Clergie, together with their most goodly and beautifull
> houses.   (163)

Camden here sounds less like Leland than like an early modern Walter Benjamin,
for whom history is a 'catastrophe which keeps piling wreckage upon wreckage'
(1999: 249).

A word may be said in conclusion about a sub-genre that links Leland to several
Elizabethans, including Camden, and which sheds an odd but revealing light on the
Tudor topographical mind. This is the poem tracing the course of an English river, or
celebrating the marriage of two such rivers. In *Cygnea cantio* (1545), a Latin poem with
copious prose commentary, Leland imagined the dying journey of a swan down the
Thames from Oxford to Deptford, the voyage providing the occasion for the laudatory description of royal palaces and other landmarks testifying to England's glory.
The poem found a sequel in William Vallans's *Tale of Two Swans* (1590), describing a
similar progress down the Lea. Camden wrote verses on the marriage of Tame and Isis,
which he published in segments in *Britannia*. William Harrison in his *Description of
Britain* did not venture into verse, yet he described his tracing of the routes of rivers as
a 'poeticall voyage' (Holinshed 1587: 65). As Andrew McRae has observed, rivers in the
works of topographers like Harrison and Camden serve 'as structural devices, ways
of translating spatial description into narrative' (forthcoming).[7] Like the first-person
narrative of the itinerant Leland, following the course of a river provides a means of
making landscape unfold as a sequence of events.

Edmund Spenser above all grasped the full potential of this peculiar form. Spenser
may never have written his potentially massive *Epithalamion Thamesis*, in which he

---

[7] On the genre, see Oruch (1967); Sanford (2002: 27–52).

proposed to 'shewe his first beginning, and offspring, and all the Countery, that [Thames] passeth thorough, and also describe all the Rivers throughout Englande, whyche came to this Wedding, and their righte names, and right passage, &c' (1912: 612). He did, however, describe the marriage festivities of the Thames and Medway in *The Faerie Queene* (book 4, canto 11); he also, in *Colin Clout's Come Home Again*, described the courtship and illicit union of two Irish rivers, the 'Mulla' (Awbeg) and Bregog. Unlike other river poets, such as Leland, Camden, and Vallans, where 'geography is subservient to history' (McRae), Spenser does not use the form to describe the human and historical landscape through which the rivers pass. Rather, his river-marriages supplant history with landscape, making the rivers themselves the source of narrative. Thus, Spenser takes geographical fact—the near-meeting of the Thames and Medway near Gravesend, their drawing apart to take different courses round the Hoo peninsula, before falling together into the sea—and transforms it into a tale of extended fluvial courtship:

> Long had the *Thames* (as we in records reed)
> Before that day her wooed to his bed;
> But the proud Nymph would for no worldly meed,
> Nor no entreatie to his love be led;
> Till now at last relenting, she to him was wed.

(4. 11. 8)

The story of Thames and Medway is part of the story of England. It is a story with a happy ending, yet one which seems to take place outside the flow of historical time. Turning from the poem to the map, we find that every part of the narrative is happening simultaneously: Thames is always drawing near to Medway; she is always drawing back; they are always meeting in marriage. There is thus no potential for disjunction between the present and the past: this is consummation without loss. History as we understand it is almost entirely banished from Spenser's river poetry.[8] In its place we discover landscape as event, history that can be located not only on the map but *in* it. No passage in Tudor literature comes closer to reconciling the nation-in-time with the nation-in-space. Perhaps it is Spenser, after all, who can best lay claim to the disputed title of Leland's Elizabethan heir.

PRIMARY WORKS

ANON. (1539), *The Byble in Englyshe*.
BROOKE, RALPH (1596), *A Discoverie of Certaine Errours Published in Print in the Much Commended Britannia, 1594*.
CAMDEN, WILLIAM (1610), *Britain*, trans. Philemon Holland.

---

[8] It is not quite banished, the most disturbing intrusion being in the mention of the Irish river Oure, 'late staind with English blood'; see Fitzpatrick (2004).

CAREW, RICHARD (2004), *The Survey of Cornwall*, ed. John Chynoweth, Nicholas Orme, and Alexandra Walsham (Exeter: Devon and Cornwall Record Society).

CAXTON, WILLIAM (1482), 'Preface' to Ranulf Higden, *The Polycronycon*.

HOLINSHED, RAPHAEL (1587), *The First and Second Volumes of Chronicles*.

LAMBARDE, WILLIAM (1596), *A Perambulation of Kent*, 2nd edn.

—— (1730), *Dictionarium Angliae topographicum & historicum: An Alphabetical Description of the Chief Places in England and Wales*.

LELAND, JOHN (1543), *Genethliacon illustrissimi Eäduerdi Principis Cambriae*.

—— (1545), *Cygnea cantio*.

—— (1589), *Principum, ac illustrium aliquot & eruditorum in Anglia virorum, encomia, trophaea, genethliaca, & epithalamia*.

—— (1906–10), *The Itinerary of John Leland the Antiquary*, ed. Lucy Toulmin Smith, 5 vols (London: Bell).

—— and JOHN BALE (1549), *The Laboryouse Journey and Serche of Johan Leylande*.

MILTON, JOHN (1997), *Complete Shorter Poems of John Milton*, ed. John Carey (Harlow: Longman).

OWEN, GEORGE (1994), *The Description of Pembrokeshire* (Llandysul: Gomer Press).

SPENSER, EDMUND (1912), *The Poetical Works*, ed. J. C. Smith and E. de Selincourt (Oxford: Oxford University Press).

VALLANS, WILLIAM (1590), *A Tale of Two Swannes*.

CHAPTER 15

BIBLICAL ALLUSION AND ARGUMENT IN LUKE SHEPHERD'S VERSE SATIRES

MARK RANKIN

LUKE SHEPHERD'S verse satires rank among the most important produced in England between the writings of Henry Howard, Earl of Surrey, whose lyrics circulated under Henry VIII, and Gascoigne, whose verse collection *A Hundred Sundry Flowers* appeared in 1573. Although he is not widely known as a satirist, Surrey could give vent to satirical ire in verse. 'Th' Assyrians' king, in peace with foul desire', for example, possibly contains a thinly veiled allegation against Henry VIII, who appears in the guise of Sardanapalus, the legendary decadent Assyrian king. Another of his satires, 'London, hast thow accused me', describes the city as a latter-day Babylon, the prototypical biblical city of apocalyptic judgement. Surrey's target here are those

> prowd people that drede no fall,
> Clothed with falshed and unright
> Bred in the closures of thy wall.

George Gascoigne, who spent much of his career in search of patronage, is the most important Elizabethan poet active before Sidney and Spenser. *Sundry Flowers* disguises itself as a poetic anthology produced in the milieu of the royal court, but it offended the authorities and was suppressed (see Maslen and Pugh, Chapters 17 and 34 in this volume). Other mid-century verse satirists include Miles Hogarde, who affords virtually the only example of a popular Catholic propagandist under Mary I. John Heywood's *The Spider and the Fly* (1556), an estates debate written in rhyme royal, also occupies a prominent place (see Hunt, Chapter 20 in this volume). Among these writers, Shepherd remains remarkably accessible and dynamic.[1]

Shepherd employs a vigorous, Skeltonic style and a series of complex, shifting narrative personas in order to deliver vituperative critique against traditional religious beliefs and practice. Janice Devereux, Shepherd's modern editor, proposes 1547 as the date for some of his poems, all of which had certainly appeared by 1548.[2] The skilful use of macaronic diction (burlesque, mixed English–Latin verse) expands the possibilities of the Skeltonic mode in these poems. His satires afford outstanding examples of the native verse complaint, written in the tradition of *Piers Plowman*, which was co-opted as Protestant propaganda (see Hadfield, Chapter 32 in this volume). Shepherd moved in reformist circles during the opening years of Edward's reign, where he would have gained familiarity with writings by William Tyndale, John Bale, and other evangelicals. The wide-ranging targets of his critique include the practice of clerical celibacy, the failure of Catholic clergy to prioritize learned ministry over the ale pot, the feast of Corpus Christi, and above all the ritual of the Mass, which became illegal in England following the promulgation of Archbishop Thomas Cranmer's Order of Communion in 1548 (MacCulloch 1996: 384–6). Both Corpus Christi and the Mass rite came under attack for their central emphasis on the doctrine of transubstantiation, in which worshippers venerated the Eucharistic host as the literal body of Christ. Protestant reformers rejected this tenet on grounds that it promoted idolatry, and in 1548 they banned the Corpus Christi celebration. Cranmer's 1548 communion service anticipates the radical reversal prescribed in the 1549 and especially the 1552 Book of Common Prayer, which emphasize the Eucharist merely as a commemorative event. These years witnessed thoroughgoing Protestant reform under Protector Somerset and the explosion of propaganda that coincided with the repeal of Henrician censorship legislation under the new regime (J. King 1999: 165–6).

The importation of Italianate modes of versification during the Elizabethan period, however, ushered Shepherd into long-standing neglect, from which he is still emerging.[3] Even though his biographical details are obscure, Shepherd enjoyed a lively

---

[1] Howard (1966: 85–7, lines 45–7). For an overview of Gascoigne's career, see Ronald Johnson (1972). On Hogarde and Heywood, see J. Martin (1981); Holstun (2004).

[2] Shepherd (2001: 103). Shepherd's eight verse satires include: *Antipus, Comparison between the Antipus and the Antigraph, Doctor Double-Ale, John Bon and Mast Person, Pathos, Philologamus, A Poor Help*, and *The Upcheering of the Mass*. Two prose works are also attributed to him: *Cautels Preservatory* (STC2, 4877.2), edited in Shepherd (2001); and *A Godly and Wholesome Preservative against Desperation* (STC2, 20203.5), conjecturally assigned to Shepherd by STC2.

[3] Shepherd receives no mention in Lewis (1954). He receives negative treatment in Simpson (2002: 342, 382).

reputation during his own day. His satires, all of which are printed anonymously,[4] tended to appear as inexpensive chapbooks printed in octavo format, in which each sheet of paper is folded three times to form gatherings. The low survival rate of most of his works points to these treatises simply being read to pieces. Substantive references to contemporary figures and events in these poems possibly indicate the poet's intent to address a learned audience, which would have been familiar with developments at court and is known to have read and collected cheaply printed texts during this period (Watt 1991: 1–2). At least one Shepherd satire was definitely read at court. Shepherd's printer John Day was summoned before the Lord Mayor of London, Sir John Gresham, after printing *John Bon and Mast Person*, which had been reported as seditious. The courtier Edward Underhill defended the work on grounds that it was popular at court. He also gave Gresham a copy, who 'reade a litle off [i.e. of] it, and laughed theratt, as it was bothe pythye and mery' (Foxe 1859: 172; Evenden 2008: 12–13). Shepherd's prose builds upon the satirical tone of his verse, in his scathing prose commentary concerning strategies for preserving the consecrated Eucharistic host from decay (*Cautels Preservatory*).[5]

Far from offering merely 'puerile anti-Catholic railings',[6] Shepherd's verse satires require complex engagement on the part of readers, particularly in terms of their treatment of scriptural sources. Like many of his contemporaries, he enjoys invoking the ideal of a learned, Bible-reading laity. This ideal finds expression in Desiderius Erasmus, who recommends vernacular Bible-reading among commoners in his 'Paraclesis', the preface to his 1516 Greek–Latin edition of the Bible. 'I would that even the lowliest women read the Gospels and the Pauline Epistles,' Erasmus writes:

And I would that they were translated into all languages so that they could be read and understood not only by Scots and Irish but also by Turks and Saracens [...] Would that, as a result, the farmer sing some portion of them at the plow, the weaver hum some parts of them to the movement of his shuttle, the traveller lighten the weariness of the journey with stories of this kind!   (1965: 97)

The figure of the learned ploughman undergoes expansion in Tyndale's famous purported claim that his scriptural translation would enable the unlearned plough-boy to know more Scripture than a cleric (Foxe 1563: 2A5^v). Shepherd incorporates the personified version of this Bible reader as a vehicle for anti-Catholic satire. In his attack on clerical ignorance and drunkenness, *Doctor Double-Ale*, for example, the title character, who represents Henry George, curate of St Sepulchre's parish, performs divine service so badly that 'yet could a cobblers boy him tell, | That he red a wrong gospell' (lines 171–2). 'Ye shuld fynde I am afrayde', the anonymous narrator continues,

---

[4] Authorship of the Shepherd canon is confirmed by Bale (1902: 283) and by various internal and bibliographical evidence.

[5] Details drawn from J. King (1982: 252–70); Shepherd (2001, pp. ix–xii, 103, 115–17). All quotations from Shepherd's works will come from this edition and appear parenthetically.

[6] Simpson (2002: 382).

That the boy were worthy
For his reading and sobrietie
and judgement in the veritie
Among honest folke to be
A curate rather then he.

(lines 199–204)

George was a former Augustinian canon who persisted in offering Latin Mass even after its annulment; Shepherd identifies him by name in *A Poor Help* (lines 382–5).[7] *John Bon and Mast Person*, a forceful dialogue against the feast of Corpus Christi, likewise pits a self-righteous cleric against a witty ploughman, who questions the doctrine of transubstantiation on grounds that it is not reasonable.[8] Satirical attack against this clerical interlocutor is compounded by the printer's inclusion of a title page woodcut showing a Corpus Christi procession in progress (Figure 15.1). This woodcut had earlier appeared in a Richard Pynson imprint titled *Here Beginneth the Rule of Saint Benet* (Shepherd 2001: 109), but in Shepherd's tract the illustration acquires new meaning. An accompanying poem, which vilifies the processors as 'poore fooles' who 'beare a great God, which ye yourselfes made', accents Shepherd's views. Elsewhere, the anonymous narrator of *The Upcheering of the Mass* describes 'plowmen smythes & cartars' (line 28) as those who reject the Mass because it lacks apostolic authority. The lack of learning never prevents the humble artisans who occupy Shepherd's poems from challenging their clerical antagonists over the orthodox interpretation of the Bible.

Shepherd's reading of Scripture underpins his complex innovations to modes of biblical argument and satire throughout his verse. In this chapter, I wish to demonstrate how these poems enjoin particular strategies of Bible-reading in order to support Shepherd's rejection of allegedly offensive doctrine. This approach challenges existing theories concerning the relationship between propagandists and the religious establishment during Edward's reign. It is tempting to equate the radical gospelling literature published during these years with the anti-Catholic bias of the government. Indeed, Shepherd's agenda for religious and social reform places him among the so-called 'commonwealth' writers of social complaint, including Robert Crowley, Hugh Latimer, and Thomas Lever. The extent to which these men formed a 'party', or even shared a consistent programme, however, has been seriously challenged (Elton 1979; cf. Loach 1999: 62). Both Latimer and Lever preached before the King, and internal evidence may suggest that Shepherd wrote some of his work in conjunction with Cranmer's abolition of the Mass. Nevertheless, allusion to biblical narrative in the satires does not always align Shepherd, the radical, with the Edwardian government's anti-papal position. At a time when some commentators hailed the young king as a latter-day David who would purge the nation of corrupt practices in the manner of his Old Testament royal prototype, Shepherd offers distinctive critique of traditionalism while refusing to conform wholly to the royal line. Comparison to Hugh Latimer's

---

[7] For further details concerning George, see Shepherd (2001: 13–14 and n.); Bridgen (1989: 440).
[8] 'Mast' is abbreviation for 'Master'.

Fig. 15.1 Title page of Luke Shepherd's *John Bon and Mast Person* (1548?), showing a traditional Corpus Christi procession. The clergy carry a pyx; the dignity of the procession is undercut by Shepherd's mocking verse beneath.

sermons is instructive in illuminating Shepherd's position. In his first extant sermon preached before Edward, on 8 March 1549, Latimer argues that preachers possess spiritual authority that licenses them to instruct kings. Nevertheless, he defers to the royal will, provided that Edward conform himself to his 'godly' predecessors. 'Let us learn to frame our lives after the noble King David,' he enjoins. 'Let us follow David [...] Let us pray for his good state, that he live long among us' (1968: 56–7). In other orations before the King, Latimer voices the official position against clerical idleness and absenteeism and in favour of viewing the Eucharist as a commemorative event.[9] Shepherd takes similar positions to these in his poems, but he is also unafraid to criticize the government and its representatives in print. Attention to Shepherd's use of scriptural argument in his satires sheds light on how he represented and responded to changes in official policy. The Protestant belief in *sola scriptura*—that the Bible is the only source of doctrine—becomes for Shepherd a point of departure for addressing the establishment concerning its stewardship of the opportunity to realign religious belief and practice.[10] In this way, Shepherd's verse provides a window onto mid-Tudor literary composition and ironic method.

The attribution of the printing of seven of Shepherd's ten surviving works to John Day (working alone or in partnership) provides essential context for analysing his deployment of scriptural argument. Day was a pre-eminent printer of vernacular Bibles; he also brought out works by prominent reformers such as Tyndale and Latimer. Although Shepherd's patronage connections are unknown, Day enjoyed patronage from both Katherine Brandon, Duchess of Suffolk, and William Cecil, the future Lord Burghley (Evenden 2008: 9–10, 17–18). Day and William Seres together printed Shepherd's *Upcheering of the Mass* and its companion piece, *Pathos; or, An Inward Passion of the Pope for the Loss of his Daughter the Mass*. The complex narrative structure of these works lodges heavily ironic critique of the Catholic Mass rite, in which a cleric and the Pope successively (and inadvertently) condemn the ritual while apparently attempting to defend it. Day and Seres also printed *John Bon and Mast Person*. Its ingenious use of humour and clever employment of dialogue render it Shepherd's most accessible tract. Day printed *Antipus* single-handedly as a highly affordable single-sheet folio. It brings forward various paradoxes from Scripture as analogues to the doctrine of transubstantiation. Day also produced Shepherd's compendium entitled *The Comparison between the Antipus and the Antigraph*, which reprints the *Antipus* and an antagonistic reply, the *Antigraphium*, followed by Shepherd's counter-reply, entitled *Apologia Antipi*. Shepherd may have written this apologia in response to Sir John Mason, a member of Edward's Privy Council (Wheat 1951: 64–8). Day's final Shepherd imprint is the prose satire *Cautels Preservatory Concerning the Preservation of the Gods which are Kept in the Pyx*.[11]

Shepherd's satires form a centrepiece of the Protestant propaganda campaign that flourished during the late 1540s. They frequently employ radical tropes characteristic of Protestant interpretation of Scripture. Shepherd's name itself appears to emerge

---

[9] See the sixth and seventh royal sermons in Latimer (1968).

[10] On the challenges presented by *sola scriptura* in practice, see Betteridge (1999: 88–98).

[11] 'Pyx': vessel or box for keeping the consecrated Eucharistic bread.

from a scriptural source. It is likely a pseudonymous combination of St Luke, the gospel writer and physician, and the figure of Christ as the Good Shepherd. We know that Shepherd was a London physician, but his choice of pseudonym further aligns him with the voices of rural labourers who occupy his poems (J. King 2002: 191). In scriptural allusions within the works themselves, he often follows John Bale's commentary on the book of Revelation, *The Image of Both Churches* (c. 1545), in describing the Mass rite as the personification of the whore of Babylon, a prototypical scriptural figure of wickedness. Protestants frequently interpreted her as a persona of the papal Antichrist. The speaker of *The Upcheering of the Mass* asks,

> What did I call hir pore?
> Naye some wyl cal hir whore
> And stireth a great uprore
> Some cal hir popes daughter.

> (lines 143–6)

Genealogical descent of the Mass from the Pope recalls Bale's proto-nationalist history play *King Johan*, where the Vice Sedition describes his own descent from his papal ancestor, via his father, Privy Treason, and his grandfather Infidelity. Paradoxically, Sedition both descends from and also upholds the papacy (Bale 1985, lines 212, 673–8). Shepherd may or may not have known Bale's play, but his *Pathos* makes the Mass's familial heritage a central organizing principle of the satire. Discomfited by the advance of Protestant doctrine in England, the papal narrator, who appears as the Mass's own father, seeks aid from a variety of non-Christian sources, including Greek and Roman deities, Muhammad, and other Islamic thinkers. For Shepherd, the Mass's descent from the Pope accompanies an equally inauspicious allusion to Cain, who first committed fratricide in the Old Testament (Gen. 4: 1–8). As a prototype for the Mass, Cain is responsible for the violence she provokes: 'Some sayes she made manslaughter' (*Upcheering*, line 147). The Mass also descends from her grandfather Pluto, who affords a sardonic analogue for Satan (*Pathose*, lines 726–7).

Shepherd regularly develops satirical content from a scriptural source and subsequently departs from that source in a tendentious manner. Indeed, Shepherd's treatment of the Bible defines the extent to which the poems function as propaganda. Ironically, those who defend the Mass proclaim its falsity:

> For lowdly do they sounde
> That missa is not founde
> Within the byble boke.

> (*Upcheering*, lines 195–7)

The failure of Catholic clerics to explain the scriptural origin of Mass doctrine obviously constitutes a major complaint of early Protestantism. Shepherd, however, expands and modifies existing approaches with a more complex exegetical method. In his prose treatise *The Obedience of a Christian Man* (1528), Tyndale had advocated the abandonment of the fourfold method of biblical interpretation employed by medieval scholastic theologians, which comprised comparative analysis of the literal, tropological, allegorical, and anagogical senses of the text. Tyndale instead enjoins readers to embrace only the literal sense (2000: 158–62). Shepherd and other early Protestant commentators, who followed Tyndale in emphasizing the primacy of a literal reading of the Bible, unsurprisingly based their rejection of the Mass upon its failure literally to appear within Scripture. Nevertheless, they constructed allegorical readings in which the Mass appears manifested in the figure of the whore of Babylon. For Tyndale, 'the literal sense [rather than the allegorical sense] prove[s] the allegory and bear[s] it, as the foundation beareth the house' (Tyndale 2000: 159). Protestant interpretation of Christ's words of consecration, 'Hoc est corpus meum', fundamentally denied that this was Christ's actual body and diverged from traditional Catholic doctrine in the process. These commentators denied the literal sense on this crucial point while broadly celebrating its primacy elsewhere. Shepherd's views concerning the non-scriptural foundation of the Mass in *Upcheering* therefore take on considerable complexity when read against contemporary models of Protestant exegesis. They provide evidence of complex, nuanced differences among early Protestants concerning methods of Bible-reading and commentary. The poem explicitly tells how readers will search the Scriptures in vain for evidence concerning the Mass. Instead, they will discover the narrative concerning Meshach, one of three Hebrew youths who refused during the Babylonian captivity to worship the image of gold made by King Nebuchadnezzar (line 201; see Daniel 3). Meshach's defiance typologically anticipates the resistance of Shepherd and others to the Catholic Mass rite. The approach to Scripture in *The Upcheering of the Mass* reminds us that early Protestantism in England was a fluid phenomenon characterized by evolving allegiances.

Pathos, one of Shepherd's most vindictive satires, comprises the sequel to *Upcheering* and expands its use of Scripture as a vehicle for criticism. The earlier poem concludes when its anonymous clerical narrator concedes victory and the Mass is sequestered to hell with other Babylonians ('In regno plutonico |[...]|| Cum cetu babilonico'; lines 378–80). The reference to Babylon as a type of banishment is common throughout Tudor religious literature.[12] In Shepherd's sequel, the Pope, who is literally based in hell, seeks help to restore the ailing Mass. He does so within an explicitly scriptural framework. The Pope's appeal to Jupiter and other deities echoes Old Testament appeals for divine aid.

> To you I call and crye
> That are the goddes on hie
> That ye will all applie
> To send some remedye,
>
> (lines 108–11)

he pleads. The Pope is sure that they will answer his prayer following his offer of divine sacrifice:

---

[12] Another noteworthy example appears in Harpsfield (1878: 185).

> I offer here therfore
> Of oxen thre scoore
> Of Ramys as many more
> And gots no small store.
> With pige and sowe and bore
> Of every birde a brode
> And washe them in their bloude
> To mytygate your moode.
>
> (lines 120–7)

In this passage Shepherd sarcastically reverses Deuteronomic instructions for worship at the Mosaic Tabernacle in order disparagingly to associate the Mass with outdated Old Testament ritual. The papal prayer blasphemes by offering up pig, boar, and bird—creatures deemed unfit for sacrifice in Levitical law (see Lev. 1 and 11). The narrator's subsequent appeal to Ceres, Roman goddess of the harvest, encapsulates the Protestant attack on transubstantiation as idolatry, since this papal spokesman explicitly describes the Mass as offered in her honour (lines 141–4). Similarly, Bacchus, the Roman god of wine, receives the Pope's open idolatry:

> Thou myghtest well behold
> How willingly we woulde
> The[e] worship as we shoulde
> Wyth wyne in cuppes of golde.
>
> (lines 160–3)

In addition to delivering biting critique against clerical drunkenness, this passage recalls the Old Testament narrative concerning the Babylonian king Belshazzar (Daniel 5), who brought out the gold articles taken from the Hebrew Temple and offered them to deities of gold, silver, and iron. Shepherd shares with Bale the tendency to employ an explicit scriptural backdrop in order to personify the Pope as an open conspirator.

The papal narrator misreads the Bible in *Pathos*, with far-reaching consequences. In a derisive allusion to the doctrine of transubstantiation, the Pope tells of his habit of literally beating up Christ in the act of consecration. 'Betwene my holy fistis', he declaims,

> I can not be debarde
> To handle hym softe or harde
> But if he be frowarde
> He shall fynde me waywarde.
>
> (lines 179–83)

Papal loyalty to Christianity depends in this case upon Christ's unlikely willingness to accommodate the Pope's non-scriptural practices. The papal narrator characteristically misinterprets Christ's entry into Jerusalem in anticipation of his crucifixion:

> Howe porely dide he ride
> Upon a pore asse
> Was he a lorde, alasse
> On that fation to passe
> Into a noble cytie?
>
> (lines 200–4)

Shepherd's narrative source (Luke 19: 28–40) emphasizes Christ's humility, but here the Pope amplifies his own pride. Given the Mass's debilitating illness in *Pathos*, the Pope is no longer able to manipulate Scripture to cloak his deception, as he did when the Mass was new (lines 619–25). This portrayal of 'false' religion as wilful deception rather than merely misguided devotion represents a popular motif in mid-Tudor religious literature.

Shepherd's activity as a propagandist and biblical exegete at this moment of fervid literary activity, then, acquires layered meanings when closely examined. He is neither a writer of bald propaganda nor a maverick independent, but rather a spokesperson for competing perspectives within a broadly defined Protestant position. Internal references in the poems to the Edwardian injunctions of 1547, the dissemination of Cranmer's Order of Communion (8 March 1548) and Catechism (June 1548), and the imprisonment of Bishop Stephen Gardiner[13] provide clues to the dating of Shepherd's works (see *The Comparison between the Antipus and the Antigraph*, lines 156–7; *John Bon and Mast Person*, lines 143–5; *Doctor Double-Ale*, lines 61, 326–30; *A Poor Help*, line 183; and *Upcheering*, lines 316–19; cf. Shepherd 2001: 114). *John Bon and Mast Person* must have been current among members of the establishment, given its readership at court (mentioned above). *Pathos* also would have best been understood by a learned readership, since it contains a lengthy catalogue of Protestant reformers and their Catholic antagonists (lines 500–41), who are obscure in many cases. Nevertheless, a shared opinion on these matters between Shepherd and his superiors does not necessarily indicate Shepherd's complete support of current policy. This slight discrepancy is overlooked in existing accounts of radical religious change under Edward and the Protestant propagandists who emerged, we are told, to support the changes (see, for example, Duffy 1992: 460). Available data suggest how Shepherd might have appealed to the Protestant intelligentsia, but intellectual agreement in principle does not preclude the possibility of subtle differentiation between positions. Shepherd's commitment to purity of worship grounded in Scripture diverges from the official position, for example. Cranmer had already produced an English litany under Henry VIII, and he would follow with a vernacular communion service in the 1549 Book of Common Prayer. Shepherd, though, banishes collects to hell along with other liturgical components of the Mass rite in *Pathos* (lines 747–8), despite the fact that these prayers would form a centrepiece of the new liturgy in Cranmer's formulation (Rosendale 2007: 30–1, 209). When the Pope abandons the Mass at the conclusion of *Pathos* in order to

---

[13] Gardiner was incarcerated in the Fleet Prison from 25 September 1547 until 8 January 1548. His imprisonment in the Tower began on 30 June 1548.

> Shewe myne obedience
> To the prince infernal
> In derknes eternal,
>
> (lines 790–2)

Shepherd may glance critically against blind acceptance of the royal supremacy. To some degree, Shepherd's satires reveal the relationship between Crown and propagandist to be defined as much by nuance and negotiation as by polemic. This trend is ongoing from the previous reign, when the use of the press to disseminate propaganda responded to evolving policy (King and Rankin 2008: 54–5).

Shepherd's satires do not specifically depart from a Cranmerian approach to divine service, but they do display ambivalence towards the changes. Cranmer released his translation of the Lutheran Nuremberg catechism, *Cathechismus: A Short Instruction into Christian Religion*, in June 1548. This work prompted Gardiner to question whether Cranmer's views had become more conservative. 'Bishop Gardiner, in his book against the Archbishop,' writes Strype,

takes advantage of two things in this Catechism against him, as though he himself, when he put it forth, was of the opinion of the corporal presence. The one was a picture that stood before the book, where was an altar with candles lighted, and the priest appareled after the old sort, putting the wafer into the communicant's mouth.   (1822: i. 227)

Cranmer insisted that the printer had obtained the woodcut from 'the Dutch edition of the book' and 'afterwards caused the popish picture to be altered into a picture representing Christ eating his last supper with his disciples' (Strype 1822: i. 227–8). Cranmer and Gardiner addressed both learned and unlearned readers by publishing their Eucharistic polemics in both Latin and English (Wilson 1990: 8–14), but Shepherd's *John Bon and Mast Person* anticipates the failure of official opposition toward the Mass in a distinctly popular voice:

> But now the blessed messe is hated in every border
> And railed on & reviled, with wordes most blasphemous
> But I trust it wylbe better with the help of Catechismus
> For thoughe it came forth but even that other day
> Yet hath it tourned many to ther olde waye
> And where they hated messe and had it in disdayne
> There have they messe and matins in latyne tonge againe.
>
> (lines 141–7)

These lines take on considerable irony, since Shepherd, speaking through John Bon, has already ridiculed the cleric's illogical defence of Corpus Christi. This cleric's spiritual blindness prevents him from realizing that Cranmer's catechism is designed to bolster the Protestant position, not undermine it. At the same time, the vigorous opposition to the Mass in Shepherd's critiques betrays his fear that official efforts towards reform may be inadequate. Such satire depends for its effect on the prevalence in society of the subject being satirized, at least from the perspective of the author. Shepherd's layered verse refuses to serve as unqualified propaganda.

As a self-appointed spokesman for radical change in religion, Shepherd claims poetic authority to speak on his own behalf from a perspective grounded in his view of Scripture and Protestant worship.[14] That view is considerably playful and occasionally mocking. In *Antipus*, he delineates a scheme for Bible-reading within the specific confines of royal ecclesiastical authority, as he defines it on his own terms. From the viewpoint of the anonymous narrator, its nine scriptural paradoxes and the dubious doctrine of transubstantiation all lack reliability. Indeed, only the 'kings commission' can overcome the seditious preaching of thieves and robbers who would likely promulgate such fictions. This attack (lines 23, 29–30) constitutes *ad hominem* critique against William Layton ('Leighton'), a prebendary of St Paul's Cathedral who refused to conform to government injunctions to denounce the Mass from the pulpit (*Chronicle* 1852: 56). Recourse to royal authority constitutes a *deus ex machina* that restores order to biblical interpretation. Shepherd anticipates his contemporary Robert Crowley, who worked as a bookseller and propagandist from Ely Rents in Holborn. Crowley's *Philargyrie of Great Britain* (1551) describes the predation of rapacious Protestant and Catholic landlords who impoverish the country (see Warley, Chapter 16 in this volume). It concludes with explicit deliverance arriving from the King, who

> For fear gan spring
> Unto the Bible book,
> And by and by
> Right reverently
> That sword in hand he took.
>
> (2004, lines 1380–4)

The Bible as a symbol of royal authority constitutes a prominent theme elsewhere in contemporary Protestant literature, appearing, for example, on the title pages of vernacular Bibles published during the reign of Henry VIII (J. King 1989: 54–6). In addition to appearing in *Antipus*, this trope of clerical misuse of royal authority emerges in *Doctor Double-Ale*, where the title character 'to sum mens thinking | Doth stay hym muche upon the kyng' by extorting illegal ecclesiastical payments (lines 140–50).

After reminding readers of the royal authority under which his polemic circulates unimpeded, Shepherd makes his case against transubstantiation in *Antipus* through a series of absurd interpretations of Scripture. They accord with the etymology of this poem's title, which indicates oppositional polemic.[15] In a series of deliberate ironies, the anonymous narrator reverses the narrative trajectory of his scriptural sources in order paradoxically to affirm biblical 'truth'. This complex process requires readers to recognize the purported falsity of the stated interpretations; to identify

---

[14] In this he follows the model of poetic accomplishment set by Skelton, although to vastly different effect. See Jane Griffiths (2006: 4–6).

[15] 'Antipus' = 'anti' (opposite) + 'pus' (Latinized Greek *pus*, i.e. foot); literally 'the other foot' (i.e. an opposing stance). The title may also pun on either 'antipape' (i.e. antipope) or Herod Antipas, the biblical tyrant. I am indebted to Shepherd (2001: 143) for these associations.

those interpretations with Shepherd's satirical target, the Catholic Church; and to reassert the contrary interpretation based on the Bible's literal sense. 'As verely as Adam created firste his God | So verely he tasted not, the fruite that was forbod,' the narrator begins. 'As verely as Abell, dyd kyll hys brother Kayn | So verely the shyppe made Noye this is playne' (lines 1–4). The contradictions continue in similar fashion at the level of misread narrative. Just as Isaac supposedly begat Abraham, Sodom remains unburned; just as the Hebrews allegedly oppressed the Egyptians, Moses delivered the divine law to God; just as the lion slew Samson, Goliath purportedly killed David; and so forth. Roman Catholic Eucharistic doctrine joins these accounts as purportedly false. Readers have been trained to recognize the narrator's decision to discard his ironic persona by the earlier manipulation of source texts. 'As verely as bread doeth make and bake the baker,' readers learn, 'So verely these thefes the prestes can make their maker' (lines 21–2).

Antipus provoked debate over the function of scriptural argument in Eucharistic polemic. This controversy reveals how Shepherd utilizes Scripture to define his position and demonstrates the potentially fraught nature of biblical exegesis among mid-Tudor Protestants. The reply to *Antipus*, the *Antigraphium*, survives only in Day's compilation *The Comparison between the Antipus and the Antigraph or Answer thereunto, with An Apology or Defence of the Same Antipus. And Reprehen[sion] of the Antigraph*. The response to *Antipus* is apparently the work of Sir John Mason, a diplomat and member of the Privy Council. Evidence for attributing this poem to Mason appears in a pseudonymous reference to 'Mason' in Shepherd's *Apologia Antipi*, the third item in the compilation (line 215), as well as in a passage from Shepherd's *Philogamus*, which responds to another, lost work by Mason.[16] Along with other mid-Tudor courtier–poets and dramatists, including John Heywood and William Forrest, Mason was a political survivor who endured shifts in religious policy under Henry VIII and his successors. He entered into controversy with Edmund Bonner during the 1530s over his alleged connections to Cardinal Reginald Pole, who antagonized Henry concerning the royal divorce. Mason may have carried a public reputation for conservatism, for he expressed sorrow over the execution of Sir Thomas More and John Fisher in 1535. Like many of the scholar–intellectuals who worked for the government during the 1530s, his precise beliefs are difficult to pinpoint: besides his apparent conservatism, Mason enjoyed the patronage of Thomas Cromwell, who oversaw many of the Henrician evangelical reforms of the 1530s (*ODNB*). His background makes him an interesting respondent to Shepherd. Their exchange supplies additional evidence of Shepherd's influence within the government, in that a Privy Counsellor chose to respond to such an occasional piece as *Antipus*. This disagreement reveals the potential for diverse reactions among the 'establishment' to Edwardian religious changes.

In an attempt to reassert ownership over 'proper' exegetical method, Mason's *Antigraphium* reverses Shepherd's ironic biblical inversions from *Antipus* in line-by-line fashion. Significantly, the text invites readers to encounter the literal sense of

---

[16] See *Philogamus*, lines 25–6. For an alternative interpretation of these lines, see J. King (1982: 260–1).

the scriptural source, even though Shepherd's verse had surreptitiously affirmed the very same sense. 'As verely as Adam was create[d] by God | So verely he tasted the fruite was forbode,' its anonymous narrator reports. 'As verely as Abel was killed of Cayn | So verely made Noy the ship, this is plaine' (*Comparison*, lines 32–5). The *Antigraphium* accurately reprises seven of Shepherd's dicta, but, at the same time, it departs significantly from the pattern of *Antipus* in its interpretation of particular scriptural texts. In one of his nonsensical sentences, for example, Shepherd refers to Simon Magus, who attempted to purchase divine power from St Peter: 'As verely as Simon Magus the Apostels dyd confute | So verely the Apostels dyd princes persecute' (*Antipus*, lines 15–16; Acts 8: 9–24). Mason ignores this item altogether, possibly because under its logical reversal, the notion of princes persecuting Apostles could be construed as providing ideological grounds to the reformers' stance against 'false' religion. Shepherd's ninth point concerns papal authority, and here the *Antigraphium* avoids the scriptural source entirely. In response to Shepherd's original claim, 'As verely as the devyll hath perfecte love and hope | So verely goddes worde doth constitute the pope' (*Antipus*, lines 17–18), the rebuttal declares, 'As verely as the devel hath not perfecte love and hope | So verely consente not I to the falsenes of the pope' (*Comparison*, lines 46–7). The logical correction to this contrived mis-statement by Shepherd would admit that the Bible provides no evidence for papal primacy. Both Shepherd and Mason thus assert the literal sense while simultaneously taking its interpretation in conflicting directions. The *Antigraphium* cannot avoid a kind of interpretative incoherence, because the first seven corrections it makes to the *Antipus* ask readers to interpret the self-evident literal sense, and the eighth does not. Mason defends transubstantiation explicitly from the Bible on the basis of Shepherd's avoidance of this subject: 'verely by gods worde we consecrate our maker', he writes (*Comparison*, line 51). However, the anonymous narrator of *Antipus* supplies apparently contradictory readings of biblical narratives in order to argue that the self-evident literal sense disproves those inconsistencies in the same way that it exposes the falsity of Catholic Eucharistic doctrine. These two texts shed light on the diverse interpretative possibilities provided by competing claims of ownership of the literal sense.

Approaching this controversy as a disagreement over scriptural argument sheds considerable light upon the relationship of literature to the government's evangelical project. Protector Somerset and other patrons certainly employed satirists in their service (J. King 1982: 106–13), but the *Antigraphium* explicitly confounds Shepherd's profession of loyalty to the Crown, which he lodged in *Antipus*. Not only is Layton 'A man well regardynge oure soveraignes commission' (*Comparison*, line 63). Mason explicitly denounces radical propagandists like Shepherd, whose ironies threaten to redefine orthodox Bible-reading:

> And you that call you Gospellers that in Ire do swell
> You are as fare frome the Gospell as heaven is from hell
> Amende your lives and folowe charitie
> Leave your presumptuouse and folishe vanitye

> The misteries of God ye knowe thys is playne
> Ye cannot conceyve in your fantasticall brayne
> Commite your selfes to God, and the Kynge
> And folowe holy churche to your endynge
> For unto these three I wyll sticke
> And never regarde no false hereticke.
>
> (*Comparison*, lines 64–73)

The *Antigraphium* here lodges its appeal that the teachings of 'holy churche' (the Church of Rome) be equated conceptually with both divine will and royal policy. In Mason's formulation, the biblical texts underpin this triad of God, King, and Church. Shepherd, of course, disagrees. In his response, the *Apologia Antipi*, he criticizes Mason by alluding to the Parable of the Two Houses: 'Without lyne or level, foundacion ye laide | Wherfore it apereth, your worke muste decaye' (*Comparison*, lines 90–1). In rejecting Mason's exegesis as metaphorically lacking a solid foundation, Shepherd accuses him of misreading his source: 'the trade of your trechery, shall sone be confounde', his anonymous narrator declares. 'To maynteyn your errours, the scriptures ye frame | So that ye muste be overthrowe with the same' (*Comparison*, lines 95, 98–9). Although these passages lack manifest irony, Shepherd is being facetious in much of the *Antigraphium* by ignoring Mason's reliance on the literal sense. Shepherd himself, in fact, has framed his scriptural sources in *Antipus* to make this very point. Much of the *Apologia Antipi* constitutes instruction in the proper reading of the Pauline epistles, Christ's words of consecration, and other biblical proof texts.

After attempting to undermine Mason's use of scriptural sources, Shepherd resorts to typological argument in order fully to dismiss him. Punning on his antagonist's name, Shepherd associates him with the builders of the Tower of Babel, which Protestants interpreted as a type of the Church of Rome. By linking Mason with Nimrod, the legendary founder of Babylon, and Tubal-Cain, the prototypical craftsman, Shepherd again subjects his scriptural sources to his advantage:

> The Mason first at Babilon began,
> Byldyng of the towre that men cal Babel,
> Though he be a Babilonite, Nemprothes [Nimrod's] owne man.
> That nowe raineth in Rome, it is no great marvaile
> Thubalkaim [Tubal-Cain] the first smyth, and graver of metell,
> For antiquitie and frendshyp, must nedes stande hym by
> To forge him his toles, to buylde Idolatrie.
>
> (*Comparison*, lines 215–21)

Nimrod's association with the papacy emerges clearly enough in Shepherd's account. Tubal-Cain, however, appears during the antediluvian period, whereas Nimrod and the Babel story post-date the Noachian deluge (Gen. 4: 22; 10: 8–10; 11: 1–9). The narratives are genealogically distinct, but Shepherd unites them. These prototypes appear to reveal the pointless loquacity of his opponent, whom Shepherd abandons

In knavery.
In heresy.
In baudry.
In popery.
Etcetera.

> (*Comparison*, lines 236–40)

Nevertheless, the exchange has revealed both writers employing similar exegetical tactics. Shepherd frequently satirizes the Mass ritual even after the Edwardian regime proscribed it. The intensity of his distaste for this religious rite need not derive exclusively from his fear that conservative devotion maintained a stronghold in London. His concern could attend equally to the proliferation of competing methods of scriptural reading among Protestants.

Repeated recourse to methods of Bible-reading emphasizes this theme as a driving force in all of Shepherd's verse. He accuses Richard Smith, for example, of fabricating pseudo-scriptural justification for 'false' doctrine. Smith, a defender of transubstantiation, held appointment as Regius Professor of Divinity at Oxford under Henry VIII and would preach at the burning of bishops Latimer and Nicholas Ridley in October 1555. In a fine instance of Skeltonics, Shepherd accuses him of having

caught at large
More then he could dyscharge
Or fynde in text or Marge
Concernyng Consecratyon
And Transubstanciation
Or all oure Transmutacion
And Substaunce Alteracion
Deniyng Veneracion
And also Adoration
In tyme of Ministration.

> (lines 424–33)

Shepherd gravitates in this example towards Smith's reliance upon printed marginal annotation as integral to reading. The passage appears in *Philogamus*, a biting and sarcastic refutation of a work of Mason's against clerical marriage that does not survive. Smith emerges as one of Mason's alleged associates and joins him in suppressing legitimate Bible-reading in churches. Accounts survive from this period concerning the disruptive reading aloud from the vernacular Scripture during Mass.[17] Shepherd's anonymous narrator rebukes Mason for interrupting these readings and

Endevouryng to dryve oute
The reader in our queare
That draweth to hym here
Men commyng farre and neare.

> (lines 415–18)

---

[17] For one such narrative, see Shields and Forse (2002).

This apparently alludes to Mason's tenure as royal visitor for Rochester for the enforcement of the government's injunctions in 1547 (Shepherd 2001: 167). If people flock to hear this unnamed reader of the unadorned text, Smith supplements both text and printed marginal note to suit his purposes. Reading only the bare Scripture is the preferred method of access for Shepherd, whose views towards the literal text continue to take him away from interpretations laid down by opponents. The poet reprints twenty lines of ungracious Latin that may derive from Mason's original text. Here the hypothetical narrator addresses married priests as a 'Genera Viperarum' (line 122), or a 'race of vipers', thereby echoing Christ's rebuke of the Pharisees in the same terms (Matt. 3: 7). Shepherd employs the exact scriptural trope in his response. He subdivides his rebuttal into segments that include 'A Latten Clubbe, or Hurle Batte', a sixty-line derisive reply, also in inelegant Latin, to the earlier Latin excerpt. Here, the unmarried Catholic priests receive contempt as a 'Viperarum Genus' who are 'Dediti Incestibus' ('given to incest') (lines 355–6). Shepherd echoes charges lodged by Bale in his *Acts of English Votaries* (1546) that Catholic clerics practised sexual deviancy. Within Shepherd's satirical method in *Philogamus*, then, he establishes two models of Bible-reading (approaching the literal sense before appropriating it for satire) that help guide appropriate and inappropriate interpretation.

Shepherd's most memorable satire, *Doctor Double-Ale*, relies upon similarly conflicting epistemological and exegetical patterns. The title character's surname refers to the doubly strong beer that he regularly consumes. Shepherd's anonymous narrator uses his subject as an occasion to criticize the entire clergy, who share in his naivety. England suffers when such clerics

> bring them to the gates
> Of hell and utter derkenes
> And all by stubborne starkenes
> Putting their full trust
> In thinges that rot and rust.
>
> (lines 49–53)

Shepherd incorporates passages from the Sermon on the Mount to characterize the clergy as Pharisaical legalists who pay insufficient attention to spiritual things. He invokes divine instructions concerning avoiding the wide gate that leads to destruction and the injunction not to invest in temporary riches that decay rather than in spiritual riches. The passage applies these source texts as fuel for satire, since the scriptural writer concludes this section of Shepherd's source with a report of Christ's hearers praising his ability to speak with more authority than their own religious leaders (Matt. 7: 13; 6: 19–20; 7: 28–9). Shepherd's narrator identifies Double-Ale and his fellows with the Hebrew Pharisees, those teachers whom Christ regularly chides for neglecting spiritual duties. For Shepherd, this particular kind of bad teacher carries more damaging connotations than the simple figure of a drunken priest.

Scriptural argument underpins Shepherd's satire here as well as elsewhere. The anonymous narrator adopts a persona in mockery of the drunken cleric and delivers a mock-Latin diatribe in the cleric's voice that serves as a sardonic apologia for priestly drunkenness. In a dismissive allusion to the doctrine of transubstantiation, the narrator-persona praises ale over Eucharistic wine and invites his hearer to drink with him (lines 400–3). In justification of his rebuke he quotes from the 'De profundis', one of the seven Penitential Psalms: 'Quia apud | Te propiciacio' (lines 405–6).[18] The 'satisfaction' or 'propitiation' that the Psalmist experiences through divine meditation ironically comes to this cleric over a pint. The passage may allude to evangelical complaints against priests who recite parts of the Latin liturgy by rote but understand little scriptural meaning. The narrator sarcastically affirms that this cleric cannot work the miracle of consecration, and so his audience should beware his fraudulent abilities. According to the mock clerical monologue, this audience should shun Bible-reading in favour of traditional devotion.

> Tu non potes facio
> Tot quam ego
> Quam librum tu lego,
> Cave de me,

the narrator-persona opines ('you cannot make as much as I can [referring to the consecration of Eucharistic elements], whatever book you read. Beware me'; lines 407–10). This audience's hypothetical book points towards the Bible, but it ought not to persuade hearers to abandon clerical instruction. Of course, Shepherd has already destroyed this cleric's credibility as a reliable teacher, so these lines take on a double irony. They appear near the conclusion of the poem to offer counterpoint to the 'right' reading of Scripture by members of the laity modelled near the opening of the work.

Shepherd's primary concern in his verse satires is twofold. He refuses to endorse unthinkingly the evangelical reforms of the Edwardian government. Instead, he employs scriptural argument within a broadly Protestant framework in order to champion the ideal of a learned laity while simultaneously cautioning authorities not to abuse the opportunity for reform or fail to take the Reformation to its con-clusion. Perhaps more fundamentally, the satires provide a blueprint for 'true' and 'false' readings of the Bible. Shepherd insists that Scripture in its vernacular form should anchor any reformed commonwealth. He also reveals the damaging effects of irresponsible or even incorrect exegesis, in terms of both doctrine and devotion. These interpretative concerns help define Shepherd's satirical project. They take on a defining role in his employment of the full range of literary devices and modes throughout his work, including *ad hominem* attack, Skeltonics, the use of layered narration, and the sheer energy of the verse. Shepherd's biblical arguments help clarify the flexible interaction between this radical Protestant writer and the equally, but not identically, radical Protestant regime under which he worked. Shepherd makes his source texts into malleable forms that they were not, at least in terms of contemporary Protestant discourse concerning the 'immutable' divine word. If Protestants accused

---

[18] See Psalm 129: 4 (Vulgate): 'Quia apud te propitiatio est: et propter legem tuam sustinui te, Domine' ('For with thee is merciful forgiveness: and because of thy law, I have waited for thee, O Lord').

Catholic writers of distorting Scripture in defence of 'unwritten verities', Shepherd parodies both accuser and accused. In the process, he generates, legitimizes, and sustains his own unique voice and attempts to persuade his readers to adopt his positions.

PRIMARY WORKS

BALE, JOHN (1902), *Index Britanniae scriptorum*, ed. Reginald L. Poole and Mary Bateson (Oxford: Clarendon Press).

—— (1985), *King Johan*, in *The Complete Plays of John Bale*, ed. Peter Happé, i (Cambridge: Brewer).

Chronicle (1852), *Chronicle of the Grey Friars of London*, ed. John Gough Nichols, Camden Society, o.s., 53.

CROWLEY, ROBERT (2004), *Philargyrie of Great Britain*, in John N. King (ed.), *Voices of the English Reformation: A Sourcebook* (Philadelphia: University of Pennsylvania Press).

ERASMUS, DESIDERIUS (1965), 'Paraclesis', in John C. Olin (ed.), *Christian Humanism and the Reformation: Selected Writings* (New York: Harper & Row).

FOXE, JOHN (1563), *Actes and Monuments*.

—— (1859), *Narratives of the Days of the Reformation, Chiefly from the Manuscripts of John Foxe the Martyrologist*, ed. John Gough Nichols, Camden Society, o.s., 77.

HARPSFIELD, NICHOLAS (1878), *A Treatise on the Pretended Divorce between Henry VIII and Catherine of Aragon*, ed. Nicholas Pocock, Camden Society, n.s., 21.

HOWARD, HENRY (1966), *The Poems of Henry Howard, Earl of Surrey*, ed. Frederick Morgan Padelford (New York: Haskell House).

LATIMER, HUGH (1968), *Selected Sermons of Hugh Latimer*, ed. Allan G. Chester (Charlottesville: University Press of Virginia).

SHEPHERD, LUKE (2001), *An Edition of Luke Shepherd's Satires*, ed. Janice Devereux (Tempe: Arizona Center for Medieval and Renaissance Studies and the Renaissance English Text Society).

STRYPE, JOHN (1822), *Memorials of the Most Reverend Father in God Thomas Cranmer*, i (Oxford: Clarendon Press).

TYNDALE, WILLIAM (2000), *The Obedience of a Christian Man*, ed. David Daniell (London: Penguin).

CHAPTER 16

REFORMING THE REFORMERS

ROBERT CROWLEY AND NICHOLAS UDALL

CHRISTOPHER WARLEY

IN Act 3 scene 3 of *Respublica*, a 'merye entrelude' performed first in 1553 and probably written by Nicholas Udall, the character People enters with the unforgettable first line 'whares Rice puddingcake? I praie god she bee in heale' (Udall 1952, line 636). '[W]ho? Rice puddingcake?' responds a baffled Adulation, a Vice figure disguised as Honesty. It is hard not to have a little sympathy for Adulation. What exactly does 'Rice pud-dingcake' mean? Who is 'she'? '[Y]ea alese dicts [*alias dict*, also called] comonweale', People explains in his nearly impenetrable accent (line 637).[1]'Rice puddingcake' is People's pronunciation of 'Respublica', and where the 'widowed' Respublica might be—figuratively, what is wrong with her—is the central question of the play. It is also one of the central questions of the period. The voluminous complaint literature of the Tudor period, notes Lawrence Manley, focuses particularly on 'England's condition' by attempting 'to establish new priorities of communal life, to refashion the corporate identity of what was coming to be called the "common weal" or "commonwealth"' (1995: 63). People begins his part in this refashioning by supplying a detailed list of things wrong in this *respublica*:

---

[1] Key features of this accent include use of 'v' for 'f', 'z' for 's'.

ther falleth of corne *and* cattall/ wull, shepe
woode, leade, tynne, Iron *and* other metall,
And of all [th]ing*es*, enoughe vor goode and badde
[...] as er we hadde.   (lines 666–9)

'[A]nd yet', he exclaims, 'the price of everye thing is zo dere | as thoughe the grounde
dyd bring vorth no suche thing no where' (lines 670–1). 'In dede', chimes in Respublica
in her usual flat, monotonous tone (she has, in fact, been on stage all along, but Adu-
lation works to keep People away from her), 'I have enoughe if yt be well ordered, |
but fewe folke the better yf I bee misordered' (lines 672–3). What is the cause of
Respublica's misorder? Where, so to speak, is the common weal, the good of all? Or, as
Adulation puts it to People, 'who hathe wrought to youe suche extremytee?' 'Naie to
tell how zo [so], passeth our captyvytee', People responds (lines 653–4). 'Captyvytee'
is People's malapropism for 'capacity' or 'imagination', but in some respects 'captivity'
is a better word. Though he can detail the ills befalling him, he cannot explain them.
Despite his suspicion of Adulation, People cannot finally say with certainty why
prices are so high when there appear to be plenty of commodities. Something besides
Adulation and other Vices holds People captive.

   That something nowadays is usually called 'history'. Caught in a matrix of forces
he cannot understand, People exists in a social world whose broad structures he
can never quite comprehend. In this sense People might be seen as representative
of mid-Tudor literature generally. This literature has been typically neglected in large
part because it seems to speak with such an impenetrable accent, seems incapable
of understanding the grand historical shifts it sits inside, and seems (at best) like
a momentary amusement that quickly grows tedious the longer one has to keep
sorting out what it is saying. '[I]n literature as in politics', remarks David Norbrook,
'the age promised more than it performed' (1984: 49). Stuck in the middle of the
transition from feudalism to capitalism, from medieval to Renaissance, from Catholic
to Protestant, from community to individualism, the literature of the period is unable,
by and large, adequately to name the sources that shaped it.

   Udall's *Respublica* (1553) and Robert Crowley's *Philargyrie* (1551) are two of the
more notable literary texts in mid-century England. Of the two, *Respublica* has been
more studied, largely as part of the prehistory of Shakespearean drama (see Marcus
2000; Walker 1998; Blank 1996; Bevington 1968). While *Philargyrie* gets regularly
mentioned in surveys of Tudor literature, it has been closely considered very little;
the card included in the copy at the Beinecke Library at Yale is representative of
how the poem is generally treated: 'Of this important poem attributed to Crowley
and attacking excessive love of money only one other copy has been traced. It was
printed at London in 1551.' Why it is important, what exactly 'excessive love of money'
might mean, or what the conditions of its printing were have only relatively recently
become the subject of scrutiny (see J. King 1982; Graham 2005). One reason for this
neglect is, no doubt, an inevitable nagging question: why should anyone read these
poems at all? Are they anything more than curiosities from a tumultuous era, literary
marking points recording the gradual move from medieval allegory to the emerging

'modernism' of Spenser and Shakespeare? The answer is not clear, at least to me, and recovering a literature that has been unjustly neglected runs the complementary risk of overstressing its importance.

However, if we take seriously the idea that poems are interesting because they help to divulge things that are otherwise invisible in the society in which they are made, that they are ideologemes that reveal the constitutive contradictions that create social structures, then perhaps there is some work for the literary critic as well as the literary historian.[2]Such an approach needs to be differentiated from a strictly historical reading—historical in the sense of the self-conscious debates in which people in the era participated. As far as I can tell, what Crowley and Udall thought is not especially unique. Though both *Philargyrie* and *Respublica* make relatively transparent criticisms of the Reformation (see Graham 2005; Walker 1998), most of the political and intellectual debates of the period are more subtly articulated in *A Discourse of the Common Weale* (1549), probably written by Sir Thomas Smith (Skinner 1978: i. 225; W. Jones 1970: 3). Instead, it seems to me that we need another justification for reading these works: that they are valuable as literature. They are valuable not because they are literary masterpieces (I certainly do not think they are), but because, as literary writing, they make available issues that are largely invisible to other sorts of writing (political, religious, and so on). As a result, I close-read these two works to get a grip on some of the elusive and odd social transformations that mark mid-Tudor existence, and in particular the vexing question of social relations. Crowley's poem quotes Mark 4: 11 after the preface 'To the Reader': 'Unto suche as be yet wythoute | All thyngis shalbe spoken in | Parables' (1980, lines 28–30). Both these texts remain, so to speak, 'yet wythoute'. The truth they speak is never entirely clear. When, like People, they cannot explain the causes of their captivity, however, we get to the heart of the social transformations in which they exist.

I

Respublica and *Philargyrie* hit upon a single figure to try to explain the source of the social unrest they depict. Both these allegorical works make an Avarice character the prime mover of evil. In *Respublica*, Avarice is the clear leader of the other Vices, who act as self-interested courtier–counsellors to the widowed and somewhat feeble Respublica. 'What enie of us getteth' from Respublica, Oppression assures Avarice, he 'haste the chiefe price' (326). Crowley's poem labours even more intently to imagine economic greed as the root and producer of pretty much everything, quoting 1 Timothy 6: 10 on the bottom of the title page: 'The rote of al mischife that ever dyd spring | Is carefull Covetise, & gredy Gathering' (1980: 46; see Figure 16.1). Though

---

[2] Two paradigmatic accounts of this critical position are Jameson (1981) and Adorno (1991).

Philargyrie (Lover of Silver) insatiably eats money, the vice stressed in the text is greed, not gluttony (see J. King 1982: 351). This focus on avarice is not unusual in the period. 'Covetousness is the root of all; every man scratcheth and pilleth from other; every man would suck the blood of other,' writes Bernard Gilpin (Manley 1995: 92). Probably the most famous instance of such emphasis on greed is Hythloday's complaint in book 2 of More's *Utopia* (1516): 'When I consider and turn over in my mind the various commonwealths flourishing today, so help me God, I can see in them nothing but a conspiracy of the rich, who are advancing their own interests under the name and title of the commonwealth' (1989: 105). Complaining about greed may be as old as humanity, but the intensity of the focus of Tudor writers on avarice as the key to social problems is conspicuous.

Yet it is not always clear what these Tudor writers mean by avarice, and it certainly is not clear in *Philargyrie* or *Respublica*. The full title of Crowley's poem is 'Philargyrie of Great Britain', and the poem cannot decide what exactly 'of' means here: is the poem demonstrating the greed of the nation as a whole? Or is Philargyrie merely an individual agent in Great Britain? Is the poem about Great Britain's love of silver, or is it about isolated instances of love of silver in Great Britain? The poem begins as a tale of a giant who comes and oppresses people. Philargyrie

> was so stronge
> That none emonge
> That brutyshe nation
> Durst take in hande
> Him to wythstande
> In any station.
>
> (lines 41–6)

Yet much of the information about him is unclear from the start. The headnote to the section called 'The Fable' declares that Philargyrie is '[th]e great Gigant | of great Britain', but seven lines in, the trickiness of 'of' becomes explicit:

> Sometyme certayne
> Into Britayne
> A lande full of plentie
> A Gyaunte greate
> Came to seke meate.
>
> (lines 35–9)

Is Philargyrie native or an invader? Are the traits he allegorically embodies integral to 'great Britain' ('That brutyshe nation') or are they a foreign influence that ruins a 'lande full of plentie'?

Upon arrival, Philargyrie immediately sets up a sort of protection racket whereby anyone who brings him gold will be made 'Free for to take | All thyngis that he can fynde' (lines 69–70):

Fig. 16.1 The silver-loving giant (Philargyrie) shovels coins into his sack with the help of a Bible. Robert Crowley, *Philargyrie* (1551), title page.

So that he bryng
To me some thynge
I wyll defend him styll
None so hardye
Him to deny
Or to saye he doeth Ill.

(lines 77–82)

As soon as this offer is known,

A Legion
Were redy at hys wyl
To do all thynge
At his byddynge
Whether it were good or Ill.

(lines 90–4)

But the poem never becomes the story of Philargyrie's gang of thugs, for despite this lingering threat, there is almost no violence. The giant turns out to be more rhetorician than heavy. The first section ends not with a violent monster but with a careful orator:

Then forth he stode
Wyth full mylde mode
Desyrynge them silence
Tyll he had tolde
All that he wolde
Unto that Audience.

(lines 95–100)

The oration that follows sounds a bit like the sort of thing the economist Milton Friedman might say. 'Your busynes', says Philargyrie succinctly, is 'To get rychesse' (lines 218–19). While this giant briefly mentions outright theft and threats of 'force' (line 121), most of the oration is an exhortation to find ways of driving up prices: acquire goods such as metal, leather, or yarn cheaply and then export them out of the country ('Convey awaye | These thyngis beyond the fome'; lines 168–9), or by hoarding foodstuffs. Even 'Draffe', garbage, insists Philargyrie, can be a profitable commodity if it is properly handled:

The tyme hath byn
That men coulde wynne
By smoke and by Uryne
And why shoulde nat
Gayne ryse of that
Wher with me[n] fede their swine?

(lines 203–8)

The speech thus does what it says: it persuades its audience not by threat but by rhetorical flourish, just as it advises increasing prices not by force but by manipulation. Indeed, Philargyrie is more fun and eloquent than most giants from the outset:

> Good syrs (quoth he)
> Full well I se
> That ye have ben opprest
> Long tyme wyth lawes
> Not worth two strawes
> But that shalbe redreste.
>
> (lines 101–6)

He comes as a jolly liberator, not an oppressor, and he will free 'ye' from laws measured not by their justness or divine sanction but by their economic value: they are 'Not worth two strawes'. '[W]here you spye | Commoditie', he insists, 'Ther plant your dwelling place' (lines 139–40).

The tempering of any physical coercion gets extended in his remarkable claim, not mentioned in any of the prefatory material, that Philargyrie is in fact not only a giant but a god 'That can not dye' (line 228); that is, Philargyrie appears not only as an abomination or mutation of nature (a giant) but also as a supernatural force. The tension in these two characteristics appears when we discover that, while Philargyrie is a god, he still has to eat:

> A God am I
> That can not dye
> Wherefore I muste be fed
> Wyth golde most pure
> That wyll endure
> And not wyth bryckle breade.
>
> (lines 227–32)

What exactly does 'wherefore' mean here? The poem seems to wish to make a distinction in the sort of food Philargyrie requires—as a god, he must eat gold, not bread. But it does not quite explain why he has to eat at all, or why, in the next section, he demands to be fed three times a day, 'That I do not decaye' (line 298). At an allegorical level, the point would seem to be that Philargyrie can only exist as long as the greed of men continues to feed him, but the poem does not quite feel that way: gods may like it when people serve them, but service is not strictly necessary. Philargyrie's appetite seems to be a remnant of his status as a giant, not a god. As a result, as a character he hovers between an irresistible force and a force that could be resisted (and killed off) with a little self-control.

The inconsistency of Philargyrie's character expresses a more general sense that what used to be called greed increasingly appears to be a different problem—though what exactly to call this different problem is, in some sense, the problem that keeps reappearing in the poem. Crowley's recourse to the traditional figure of avarice sets in motion 'the disruptive influence of forces as yet too new and obscure to be named' (Manley 1995: 74). These forces are, in retrospect, probably best termed 'capitalism'. Yet the term 'capitalism', vague and misunderstood, always threatens to turn into a modern synonym for avarice—as nothing more than greed and the commercialism it prefers.[3] But Philargyrie is more specific than a general lament about greed. Besides a depiction of a timeless vice, the poem is also a history 'of greate Britayne' as well. It begins by claiming to narrate 'Thyngs done long tyme before' (line 34)—as a fable, it exists once upon a time—but the poem is also quite clearly a chronicle of historical events, particularly though not exclusively the Reformation. Philargyrie gains control; Hypocrisy invents Catholicism (and founds 'Nodnoll', London; line 511) to maintain Philargyrie's control; Philaute, or Self-Love, invents Protestantism to wrest control back to Philargyrie after Hypocrisy double-crosses him (his name is Hypocrisy, after all). And finally, 'all thyngs were well' (line 1414) when the king listens to 'Trueth' and drives 'that wycked sort oute of his realme' (line 1379). The history that *Philargyrie* narrates, then, is the history of the power of 'that wycked sort'.

So who are 'that wycked sort'? What is the particular historical configuration ('*that* wycked sort') getting articulated in the poem? Or as Adulation puts it in *Respublica*, 'who hathe wrought to youe suche extremytee?' (line 653). Part of *Respublica's* answer to that question is that 'suche extremytee' arises from moral lapses represented by Adulation, Insolence, Oppression, and above all Avarice. By having Adulation ask People in 3. 3 who has 'wrought' these ills, the play tacitly suggests one answer: there must be a who, not a what. Times are bad because greedy people (Philargyrie, Avarice) are in charge, an explanation reinforced by the fact that it is Adulation, one of the Vice figures of this allegorical play, who is suggesting it. As Respublica remarks in her first speech,

> by all experience thus muche is well seen
> That in Comon weales while goode governors have been
> All thing hath prospered, and where suche men dooe lacke
> Comon weales decaye, and all thinges do goe backe.
>
> (lines 453–6)

Respublica echoes the vast humanist advice-to-princes literature that places a premium on counsel and that consequently places the working of history in the hands of particular men.

Despite the stress on 'that wycked sort', however, *Philargyrie* not only never represents any good counsellors; the poem practically never represents anyone except the 'wycked' sort. It is likewise not entirely clear that *Respublica* ever represents any good governors either. In Crowley's poem, the difficulty of specifying who the wicked and greedy are emerges in tandem with the difficulty of saying precisely who Philargyrie is. To drive them out of the realm would mean imagining Philargyrie

---

[3] On the transition to capitalism, see Aston and Philpin (1985); Brenner (1989); Manley (1995: 63–76); E. Wood (2002); DuPlessis (1997).

as a foreign, imperial giant, rather than a native; that is, it would require imagining avarice as something external to the commonwealth rather than an inherent part of it. Instead, within the poem, everyone is part of 'that wycked sort'. In 'Hypocrisy's Oration', for example, Philargyrie is enthusiastically received by 'all' 'Wyth full assent' (line 489), not by some with misgivings. In a poem filled with promises of hoarding, stealing, theft, and economic (if not physical) subjection, there is not a single scene of anyone suffering or crying. In fact there is no representation of anyone resisting Philargyrie's arguments (except Hypocrisy, who double-crosses him). Even the one hint of political trouble reiterates the obscurity of Philargyrie's victims. Among the other things (London, monasteries, almshouses) that Hypocrisy builds are

> Bulwarkis also
> A thousande moe
> Then any man can tell
> To beate them downe
> That ware the crowne
> If they dyd once rebell.
>
> (lines 533–8)

Rather than a clear antagonist, a person or group, the opposition to Philargyrie is reduced to 'them [...] That ware the crowne' who might 'rebell'. Who is 'them'? What crown? Only kings, or is there a hint of popular rebellion here as well? The point, again, is that these things are not clear, and they are not clear in large part because the poem does not decide who or what, exactly, Philargyrie is and what the stakes of his rule are.

The society that Philargyrie controls is thus strangely undifferentiated; everyone is part of 'that wycked sort', and there seems little possibility of any other sort existing at all. Most of the horror and anxiety of the poem, consequently, is directed less at Philargyrie (who is, after all, quite entertaining) than at those who accept him. Indeed, lurking behind the poem's cry against greed is a sneaking hatred of people in general, who seem so happy to be duped by whatever ideology (Catholicism, Protestantism) comes along. The subject of the poem, in this sense, is less avarice than the social configuration in which avarice thrives. Consider, for example, the section titled 'How the People of Britaine Became Subject to Philargyrie':

> Then wyth one voyce
> All dyd rejoyce
> And clapt theyr handes apase
> And after that
> They fell all flatte
> Prostrate before his face.
>
> (lines 269–74)

The prostrate idolatry offered to Philargyrie contrasts with the rewards he promises:

> him that can
> Best playe the man
> In gettynge golde and fe
> I wyl promote
> And set aflote
> In wealth and hygh degree.

(lines 251–6)

Strictly speaking, it is not greed that gets people to obey Philargyrie. Instead, his followers want the promotion to the crucially vague 'wealth and hygh degree': they want monetary wealth because it leads to the well-being associated with social advancement. The precariousness of this arrangement lingers in the word 'aflote'. '[H]ygh degree' always has a possibility of sinking. And yet in this sea of social mobility, the lack of a differentiated people who are oppressed points to a lack of 'degree' generally; if anyone can acquire 'hygh degree', there is no God-given difference between people: everyone is greedy. *Philargyrie*, then, has as much trouble locating 'commonwealth' (the good of all) as Udall's interlude. If everyone is greedy, the commonwealth is made up of undifferentiated individuals, not stable social groups. As Respublica laments in her opening speech,

> Lorde what yearethlye thinge is permanent or stable,
> or what is all this worlde but a lumpe mutable?
> who woulde have thowght that I from so florent estate
> coulde have been browght so base as I am made of Late?
> But as the waving seas, doe flowe and ebbe by course,
> So all thinges els doe chaunge to better and to wurse.

(lines 439–44)

The perennial lament that the only thing constant in the world is change is made historically specific when it is Respublica herself making the complaint. It is less 'all this worlde' that is a 'lumpe mutable' than it is the commonwealth and its people. The sea of Udall's play and Crowley's poem is a world lacking clearly defined sorts of people, of a commonwealth 'misorded' not (or not just) economically but socially. Blaming avarice as the source of all problems is consequently a symptom of the more general failure at social differentiation in the texts.

Throughout his writings, Crowley is consistently adamant about decrying social mobility *tout court*. 'The Beggar's Lesson' in *The Voice of the Last Trumpet* insists that

> If God have layede hys hande on the,
> And made the lowe in al mens syght
> Content thiselfe with that degree.

(Crowley 1975, lines 9–11)

The disruption of social degree is the disruption of God's plan. As C. S. L. Davies remarks about Crowley's fellow (and more famous) reformer Hugh Latimer, 'There was nothing revolutionary' about their writings decrying greed because 'There was no question of social equality' (1977: 272). What Crowley 'envisioned', stresses John King, was 'a theocratic monarchy' (Crowley 1980: 48). Yet this devotion to monarchy and loathing of social mobility always sits uneasily with Crowley's championing of the poor. His various publications, and especially his publishing of the first edition of *Piers Plowman*, made him, Latimer, and Thomas Lever the 'social conscience of Edwardine England', in Patrick Collinson's opinion (1990: 49). Owing to the work of A. F. Pollard (1900) and R. H. Tawney (1938), it was once commonly thought that Crowley, Latimer, and Lever formed the core of a political party known as the Commonwealth Men who sought to advise Somerset and promote progressive reform. The existence of such a party was largely discredited by G. R. Elton (1979), who persuasively argued that these men did not form a distinct political party nor had much in the way of political influence. Elton instead saw Crowley and Latimer less as political actors than as moralizers nostalgic for an imaginary past (see Skinner 1978: i. 224–8; Holstun 2004). We need not completely follow Elton in discounting the volatility of these texts, however, just because Crowley was a bit of a crank rather than a programmatic thinker like Smith.[4] Though Crowley could not escape nostalgic delusions that a strong monarchy would solve all the social crises of the age, his poem opens up the issue of social differentiation in broader ways by helping us move our focus away from particular groups and self-conscious individuals and towards the murky issue of social differentiation more generally. What Davies calls the 'degree of novelty in the urgency' of decrying social ills manifests itself not in a political programme but in the form of the poem, the paradoxical reverberations of the desire to blame a particular group or attitude that the poem can never quite isolate (1977: 272).

We might in this light qualify Quentin Skinner's eloquent summary of mid-century reformers like Crowley who sought 'the protection of the common good against the encroachments of an uncaring individualism'. 'The basic aim of these moralists', emphasizes Skinner, 'is [...] to identify and denounce the various social groups responsible for undermining this traditional concept of the public good' (1978: i. 226). What is interesting about *Philargyrie*, and to a certain extent *Respublica* as well, is its inability to 'identify' the 'various social groups' responsible. The poems end up specifying not a coherent class of people but the general unease in the period about how social distinctions could be made at all. If everyone is subject to avarice, and if avarice is the root of all mischief, how is anyone different from anyone else? Rather than simply decrying the encroachment of individualism, the poem helps a new, socially destabilizing individualism to creep along.

There are, at least at first glance, more clearly defined groups in *Respublica*. People is effectively the antagonist of the four Vice characters in *Respublica*. He is suspicious of them from the beginning, delineates with great precision the ills they are perpetuating, and attempts to convince Respublica herself not to believe them. In response, the Vices taunt and physically beat People at the end of Act 4, shaking

---

[4] Manley similarly critiques the failure of historians 'to see any historical significance in the literary myths and structures by which the discourse of Tudor social criticism was mediated' (1995: 73).

him up sufficiently that People disappears for seven scenes and only agrees to remain on stage after Respublica assures him, 'They shall not doe the harme the value of a poincte' (line 1605). Part of the clear opposition between People and Avarice is an effect of genre: People is Everyman set up against Vice, and the sympathy People gets from the play (even as it makes fun of his accent) is a remnant of what Erich Auerbach called the Middle Ages' willingness to imagine Everyman as sublimely tragic (1968: 314). The antagonism, though, is not only part of the generic tradition of the play, for the occasion of the play's performance made the perennial confrontation between an Everyman and a Vice figure more topical. According to the title page, *Respublica* seems to have been 'made' in 1553 and performed at the court of Queen Mary over Christmas. As Greg Walker remarks, the 'play's sustained focus upon the failures of policy and abuses of power allegedly perpetrated by Edward's courtiers and ministers would [...] have made acutely uncomfortable viewing for many among its initial audience' because many of the courtiers watching this play were also part of the Edwardian court (1998: 183). The Vices were not only on stage; they were apparently in the audience as well.

As the blurring of its political allegory suggests, the problems of social differentiation so conspicuous in *Philargyrie* also appear in *Respublica*. The lines between good and evil, common and elite, People and Vices, as Leah Marcus notes, become 'genuinely perplexed' (2000: 146). Whose side is People on? Paula Blank points out that the relation between People and Respublica

is described throughout as an intimate one; he is alternately her 'man' or agent, her child or a beloved friend. Their interests, particularly where economics and religion are concerned, are the same. In fact, the relationship between Respublica and People is one of near identity, a relationship spelled out in the etymological derivations of their names; 'People' is very nearly the English equivalent of the Latin 'Respublica'.   (1996: 86)

But etymological kinship does not always transform itself into a political allegiance: people and commonwealth are not always the same thing. For Blank, 'despite its sincere support for popular causes', the play 'ultimately refuses to translate' the distinction between 'the English "People" and the Latin "Respublica"'. For Walker this linguistic difference marks a real political tension: 'When People stands up before Respublica and complains about the lot of the nation's poor [...] he not only voices a righteous cry for justice, but also presents a dire warning of the consequences of further mismanagement and abuse' (1998: 178). People's complaint ineluctably recalls the social revolts of 1549. When he catalogues his suffering, People is not only searching for the true Respublica but threatening to make a different commonwealth: *respublica*, 'alese dicts' ('also called') people. People enters looking for Respublica, and it is not entirely clear that he has, metaphorically speaking, found her by the end of the play.

Even the opposition between People and the Vices is less sharp than it initially appears. When Veritie comes from heaven at the end of the play to denounce the Vices, Nemesis hands Avarice over to People so that Avarice

maie bee pressed, as men doo presse a spounge
that he maie droppe ought teverye man hys lotte,
to the utmooste ferthing that he hath falslie gotte.

(lines 1903–5)

If there is ironic justice in People squeezing money out of Avarice, People also here acts like Avarice. 'An ye bydde mee chill [I'll] squease hym as drie as A kyxe', says People, and Avarice responds, 'I shall then die of the flixe' (lines 1906–7). There is no squeezing Avarice dry as a 'kyxe', or dried stalk; he will die instead of the 'flixe', that is, flux, or diarrhoea. Avarice, it seems, is endlessly productive, and perhaps this latent power is one reason that Nemesis immediately qualifies the authority she gives to People: 'Naie, thowe shalte deliver hym to the hedd Officer | which hathe Authoritee Justice to mynister' (lines 1908–9). People and Avarice could prove a potent team.

There has already been another identification between People and the Vices. Like People, Adulation too is an inveterate misnamer. In 1. 4 Avarice changes the names of the Vice figures to conceal their true identities (a sort of paradiastole): Avarice becomes Policy, Insolence becomes Authority, Oppression becomes Reformation, and Adulation becomes Honesty. But Adulation has a lot of trouble keeping the new names straight. First he keeps calling his fellow Vices by their original names, and then has trouble remembering the new names:

AVAR Well than for this tyme thy name shalbe *Honestie*.
ADUL I thanke youe Avaryce. *Honestie, Honestie*.
AVAR Avaryce ye whooresone? Policye I tell the.
ADUL I thanke youe Polycye. Honestie, Honestie.
      How saie youe Insolence? I am nowe *Honestie.*.
AVAR We shall att length have a knave of youe *Honestie*
      Sayde not I he sholde be called mounsier Authoritye?
ADUL Oh frende Oppression, *Honestie, Honestie*
AVAR Oppresion? hah? is the devyll in thye brayne?
      Take hede, or in faithe ye are flatterye againe.
      Policie, Reformacion, *Authoritie*.
ADUL *Hipocrysie*, Diffamacion, *Authorytie*
AVAR Hipopcrisye, hah? Hipocrisie, ye dull asse?
ADUL Thowe namedste Hipocrisie even nowe by the masse.
AVAR Polycye I saide, policye knave polycye.
      Nowe saye as I sayd.
ADUL Policie knave policie
AVAR And what callest thowe hym here?
ADUL Dyffamacion.
AVAR I tolde the he shoulde be called Reformacion.
ADUL Veraye well.
AVAR What ys he nowe?
ADUL Deformacion.   (lines 389–407)

Avarice eventually has to resort to forcing Adulation to sing as a mnemonic device:

AVAR Come on, ye shall Learne to solfe: Reformacion.
    Sing on nowe. Re.
ADUL Re.
AVAR Refor.
ADUL Reformacion.   (lines 410–11)

The joke, playing to the newly Catholic court, is that from the point of view of official Marian England, the Reformation is a 'Dyffamacion' and a 'Deformacion', and the Vices are the embodiments of the hypocrisy of Protestant reformers; the play goes out of its way, in fact, to draw parallels between the Vices and the six years of the Edwardian Protectorate. But the fluidity of language in *Respublica* is analogous to the fluidity of greed in *Philargyrie*. In both cases, it becomes increasingly difficult to make sharp distinctions between sorts of people. If 'rice puddingcake' and 'comonweale' are synonyms for People, the play is less than reassuring about equating the weal of the government and the weal of the people.

II

These slippages are supposed to end, in both texts, with the actions of a monarch. In *Philargyrie*, the king, who—King notes—has been 'strangely absent', appears to drive out the 'wycked sort' with the help of men, sent by God, 'bent | Oppression to expell' (lines 1410–11); that is, the violence that is largely muted in Philargyrie's takeover of the nation appears quite conspicuously when the sovereign expels Philargyrie (J. King 1982: 347). In *Respublica*, the Prologue tells us that Queen Mary is 'oure most wise/ and most worthie Nemesis' (line 53) who finally passes judgement on the Vice figures. Yet in neither text is monarchical power unequivocal. In *Respublica*, the resolution offered by Nemesis as (according to the dramatis personae) 'the goddes of redresse and correction', aided by nothing less than Misericordia, Veritas, Justica, and Pax (the four opposites of the Vice figures), is constantly undermined. Marcus notes that if Mary is Nemesis, it is at the same time 'almost impossible not to identify Mary with Respublica' (2000: 146). The monarch is always here both the figure of strength and the figure of weakness. If *Respublica* celebrates the power of Mary as Nemesis to impose order, it also records the power of Avarice and People to create their own order.

This dynamic is especially apparent at the end of *Philargyrie*. The poem ends with an appeal to the king to save his 'flocke' (line 1354): 'Thy people are | So full of care | That nowe to god they cal' (lines 1346–8):

> Wyth that the Kynge
> For feare gan sprynge
> Unto the Bible boke
> And by and by.
> Ryght reverently
> That swerde in hand he toke
> . . .
> Then fell he downe
> And cast his crowne
> And diademe asyde
> And lokyng on hye
> Up to the skye
> To God aloude he cryed
>   Lorde God, quoth he
> Thou hast chosen me
> Over thy flocke to raygne
> Make me of myght
> All wrongis to ryght
> And make all well agayne
>   Then God him sent
> Men that were bent
> Oppression to expell
> Whoe chased oute
> This gygante stoute
> And then all thyngs were well.

(lines 1379–1414)

The appeal to 'the Bible boke' no doubt aligns with Crowley's own revised Protestant politics, where the Bible 'is the model for good government' (J. King 1982: 355). But here the poem is more interesting than an expression of Crowley's lumbering politics. What emerges in the text is the last in a series of ideological supersessions. The poem structurally stages one ideology after another taking over Great Britain: greed, Catholicism, feudalism, Protestantism. The king thus seems like the latest in a line of rhetorically persuasive arguments that have, at their heart, self-interest—the world the way the king wants it. Because of the way the poem has set it up, the king's declamation at the conclusion sounds as hollow as Hypocrisy or Philaute. Casting aside the crown becomes a more effective way of claiming it. If the poem obviously wishes to endorse monarchical power at the conclusion, the structure of the poem undermines that promise by exposing monarchy as itself another ideology. More than just a means of separating the divine right of the king from any earthly legitimacy, the poem registers something similar to the double status of Mary as both Respublica and Nemesis. At the very moment that the legitimate power of monarchy is celebrated, it is also made impotent.

King notes that, at the close of the poem, 'Crowley so universalizes the action that readers could apply it with equal validity to every monarch from Henry VIII to James II' (J. King 1982: 355). This universalization exposes the more general contradiction of monarchy in the period: the power of the monarch simultaneously becomes the model for other forms of individual power antagonistic to the monarch. This closing figure sounds not merely like a Protestant monarch; he sounds an awful lot like the poet who claims (not so tacitly) that

> God hath me set
> Such thyngis to let
> And all wrongis to redresse.
>
> (lines 1388–90)

The poem itself becomes the voice of 'Trueth' telling 'all' to the king: its critique of religion and, especially, of economic greed. This claim is quite explicit in the introductory lines 'To the Reader', where the poem displays a high degree of self-consciousness, and perhaps unease, with its authority:

> If poetes maye prove and trye theyr owne wytte
> In feyneyng of Fables greate Vices to blame:
> And if they be blamelesse although they do hytt
> The Trueth in theyre Treatyse under a straynge name
> Then maye I by ryght (me thyncke) do the same
> Wherefore though I touth the take it in good parte,
> For I wyll the none Ill as God knoweth myne herte.
>   I graunte I have feyned and written a lye,
> And yet not so lowde as I woulde it were,
> For truely thys Gigant greate Philargyrie
> Is present in greate Brytayne even every where.
>
> (lines 1–11)

In a work whose broad political thrust never hesitates ('al thynge that good was is nowe made tobad'; line 28), the hand-wringing here—'maye I by ryght (me thyncke) do the same'—is conspicuous. The repetition of 'blame' and 'blamelesse' begins to identify poets with the very 'greate Vices' they satirize. Using feigning and lies to attack feigning and lies is a famously slippery slope. Crowley's speaker is nervous about embracing the implications of his own argument. Those implications, clearly, are that the speaker of the poem ends up resembling the king he would subordinate himself to and the Vice he would denounce: the poem too tries to take in hand the sword of the 'Bible boke'.

If the poem here ends up sounding like the king who will save the land from vice, it also ends up sounding like Philargyrie, the greedy individual it would denounce. By exposing 'greate Vices' to tell 'The Trueth [...] under a straynge name', the poem too sounds greedy. Its power emerges from its ability to harness a variety of phenomena under a single 'great Gigant of great Brytayne'. Crowley's poem fanatically traces nearly everything to a common cause: Catholicism, Protestantism, feudalism, dearth, nationalism, urbanization—all these things are supposed somehow to be traceable to greed. This urge, of course, makes so much of the poem tiresome: the dull claims that 'The Hypocrites had gotten into theyr owne hands | All placis of Pleasure' (lines 15–16), that 'The Hypocritis were Ill but worsse is selfe love' (line 22), sound a lot like a sixteenth-century caller into a talk radio programme, trying to reduce complex things into a straightforward morality tale. Yet the harder the poem tries to blame social ills on the traditional problem of vice, the more the poem sounds individualistic. Indeed, the poem serves as a reminder that despite his insistence on social subordination, Crowley's ability to publish his own propaganda places him among the very new type of Renaissance individual he would denounce; as a publisher of his own propaganda, Crowley's works 'paid their own way, since he had no known patron' (J. Martin 1983: 88). After all, when he speaks, Philargyrie sounds like a poet in his urge to control through rhetoric, not force, and he too compulsively traces everything to 'commoditie' (line 138). A poem that wishes to denounce greedy individualism ends up emphasizing its own individual power.

Truth, Foucault never ceased stressing, is a thing of this world, a function not of God or the universe but of the discourses and systems that nominate some things as true and others as false (Foucault 1984). It is an idea about truth that both *Respublica* and *Philargyrie* struggle with. What is interesting about the mid-Tudor period generally is that there does not seem to be a single 'regime of truth' maintaining a monopoly, no Tudor world-picture that comfortably orders the responses of people of the time. Instead, the period is marked by an epistemic clash, a misorder of things, that expresses itself in the formal contradictions of these works. At its root, if I can put it that way, this epistemic crisis consists of a crisis of social differentiation, a profound uncertainty about how society can or should be ordered. Both these texts labour to answer Adulation's question—'who hathe wrought to youe suche extremytee?'—but they end up contributing to the very extremity they would resolve: the denunciation of individualism creates individualism; the denunciation of social displacement is socially disruptive. *Philargyrie* and *Respublica* are relatively minor players in the great transformations of their time, but both participate in the general 'serious interest in trying to explain the social and economic dislocations of [the] age' (Skinner 1978: i. 223). The interest of these texts, I think, though, does not lie in their answers—their explicit critiques, their moments of political calling out, their religious convictions. Crowley is often enough a simple-minded zealot, and Udall, at least in *Respublica*, does not seem to have much in the way of political commitments—indeed, according to Matthew Steggle, under Edward VI he was a Protestant, not Catholic, 'propagandist' (*ODNB*). Instead, what is 'serious' about these texts is their formal misorder, their ability to register the momentous shifts in an age that did not have terms to explain them. If we do continue to read them, surely this will be one reason why.

Primary Works

Crowley, Robert (1975), *The Select Works of Robert Crowley*, ed. J. M. Cowper (Millwood, NY: Kraus Reprint Co.); first pub. in EETS, e.s., 15 (1872).
—— (1980), *Philargyrie of Greate Britayne*, ed. John N. King, *ELR* 10: 46–75.

MORE, THOMAS (1989), *Utopia*, ed. George M. Logan and Robert M. Adams (Cambridge: Cambridge University Press).

SMITH, THOMAS (1969), A *Discourse of the Commonweal of this Realm of England*, ed. Mary Dewar (Charlottesville: University Press of Virginia).

UDALL, NICHOLAS (1952), *Respublica: An Interlude for Christmas 1553*, ed. W. W. Greg, EETS, o.s., 226.

CHAPTER 17

WILLIAM BALDWIN AND THE TUDOR IMAGINATION

R. W. MASLEN

Who was William Baldwin? The question is unusually hard to answer. His personality is rendered less accessible, not more so, by his habit of writing in the first person, since many of his narrators stand at several removes from himself. The pompous pseudo-scholar Gregory Streamer in his 'novel' *Beware the Cat* (1553); the Roman talking statue Pasquillus (P. Esquillus) in his scabrous anti-Catholic satire *Wonderful News of the Death of Paul III* (*c.* 1552);[1] the bumbling editor of *The Mirror for Magistrates* (1559), 'William Baldwin', who struggles to organize his collection of historical poems in the face of censorship, unreliable contributors, and onsets of somnolence;[2] *Mirror*'s parade of garrulous ghosts; none throws much light on the printer–writer who presents their narratives to the public.[3]

Moreover, in all his works the narrator's voice gets lost in a cacophony of rival voices, clamouring for the reader's attention. 'Baldwin' is only one of a group of friends who meet to assemble the *Mirror*, each of whom has strong opinions on the merits of each contribution. Streamer is one of a bewildering succession of first-person narrators in *Cat*, ranging from his amanuensis G[uillelmus] B[aldwin]

This chapter is indebted to participants at the Baldwin workshop (Newcastle, June 2008). Especial thanks are due to Tom Betteridge, Scott Lucas, Anne Overell, and Mike Pincombe.

[1] For the Roman statue Pasquillo–Pasquino and eponymous satires, see Nashe (1904: i. 57, line 4 n.); 'pasquin', 'pasquinade', *OED*.

[2] For the history of *Mirror*'s composition, see Baldwin et al. (1960, introd.).

[3] For Baldwin's life and career, see Gutierrez (1993).

to the cat Mouseslayer; while *The Canticles or Ballads of Solomon* (1549) is a dialogue between Christ, the Church, and the 'younglings' (ordinary Christians), a discussion of the past and present state of the English Church from which the book's editor ('Baldwin') humbly absents himself. Among all these voices, identifying the 'authentic' voice of the man who has come to be recognized as the most significant mid-Tudor author must be impossible. Baldwin's playful practices effectively erase him from his writings—an erasure he may have considered prudent in an age of religious conflict, when you never quite knew what faction might control the English government at any given time.

Furthermore, many of Baldwin's first-person narratives pose as translations (Maslen 1999). His most successful book, a collection of sayings called *A Treatise of Moral Philosophy* (1547), attaches the names of ancient philosophers to all its citations, although many of these attributions are patently false (Starnes 1933). *Ballads of Solomon* masquerades as a version of the apocryphal Song of Songs, although its complex experiments with metre and versification go well beyond the remit of simple translation. *Wonderful News* comes from the vitriolic Latin of the Italian reformer Pier Paolo Vergerio (Overell 2000). Even *Cat* presents itself as a translation—from the language of cats, accomplished by a master linguist, Streamer, aided by magical headphones that open his ears to the speech of birds and beasts. His first experience with the headphones encapsulates the experience of reading Baldwin's work as a whole. His ears opened, Streamer finds himself assailed by noises from every quarter of the city, and is staggered by the phonic mayhem. For Baldwin, Reformation Europe is locked in a titanic Battle of the Bands, where antagonistic voices compete for possession of bewildered believers' hearts and minds. And the magic potion deployed by the antagonists—the headphones by whose means they hope to occupy the senses of Europe's citizens—is the medium by which Baldwin earned his living: print.

Print is no respecter of authorship. Baldwin learned this the hard way in 1555, when Thomas Palfreyman published an expanded edition of Baldwin's *Treatise* without his permission (Maslen 2000*b*). Baldwin responded with his own revised edition, in which he attacked Palfreyman for the liberties taken with his text. But by 1555 Baldwin had already played astonishingly sophisticated games with the concept of authorship in *Beware the Cat*. His ascription of the text to a fictional 'source', Streamer, was so successful that when it finally saw print in 1570, an anonymous pamphlet, *A Short Answer to Beware the Cat*, denounced Baldwin for his 'false fabels' and 'loude lyes' about the virtuous scholar–priest—despite the fact that Baldwin had died in 1563, and Streamer probably never existed.[4] Early modern print generates a plethora of fictions in its endless quest for new material; and some of the most elaborate fictions, as Baldwin knew, concern the authorship of its more controversial products.

It should come as no surprise, then, to learn that the canon of Baldwin's works has yet to be established. Granted, his fame is assured thanks to his editorship

---

[4] Although a Gregory Streamer attended Oxford University, 1529–31 (Baldwin 1988: 58 n.).

of the *Mirror*, the most influential English poetry collection of the sixteenth century, and his authorship of *Beware the Cat*, the most brilliant work of Tudor prose fiction. But he has also been credited with another 'novel', *The Image of Idleness* (1556), and two substantial poems, published *c*. 1551 under the pseudonym 'Western Will'.[5] I made a detailed case for his authorship of *Image* in another work (Maslen 2000*b*). In this chapter, I would have liked to argue with equal conviction for his authorship of the Western Will poems—except that in their 1560 reprinting (*The Contention betwixt Churchyard and Camell*) they were 'signed' by another writer, William Waterman (G1ʳ), now known only as the translator of Johannes Boemus' *Omnium gentium mores, leges, et ritus* (1520), published as *The Fardle of Fashions* in 1555.

Yet these two poems throw a good deal of light on the world that shaped Baldwin. He would have known them, since they were written in defence of a poet he admired, Thomas Churchyard, and were popular enough to be reprinted in 1560.[6] Indeed, given Baldwin's attitude to authorship—which makes it secondary to the need to furnish copy for the press and to advance the cause of social and religious reformation—perhaps it does not really *matter* if he wrote them. They spring from the commercial, intellectual, and imaginative milieu in which he worked, and reading them alongside Baldwin's work subtly modifies the way we read it. In this chapter, then, I hurl Waterman's poems into the critical pot with *Beware the Cat*, to see what magic potion results. With luck, the exercise may help us hear Baldwin's voice more clearly, just as Streamer's potion opened his ears to the language of feline orators on the London rooftops.

I

In *Wonderful News*, the satirist 'P. Esquillus' dispatches a scurrilous bulletin from hell concerning the reception of Paul III's spirit by a committee of devils and damned souls. The report is of course fictional, as Baldwin admits in his translator's preface, but the facts it conveys are genuine:

All this he fayneth properly, but lyeth not I am afrayde [...] for I believe that al whiche is here written of the Popes actes, and of others, be true, and that because I knowe no man would have ben so shameles so to make reporte, excepte he were assured of them.   (A2ʳ⁻ᵛ)

Truth emerges with difficulty in the mid-Tudor world. The crimes here attributed to Paul III are so appalling (parricide, incest, treachery, rape) they bring shame and

---

[5] STC2 attributes to him 'Western Will, upon the debate betwixt Churchyard and Camell', which implies his authorship of its sequel, 'Western Will to Camel'.

[6] For Baldwin's admiration of Churchyard, see comments following the tragedy of Shore's Wife (Baldwin et al. 1960: 387).

danger to those that expose them, making it necessary to 'declare and publishe' them in indirect or fabulous form (A1^v). A year after translating this satire, Baldwin wrote one of his own: *The Funerals of King Edward the Sixth* (*c*. 1553), which blames Edward's premature death on the deep-seated corruption of the English ruling classes. Unsurprisingly, Baldwin found the poem impossible to print in Mary Tudor's censorious reign, and its publication was delayed until 1560. But even under Edward VI, when the English authorities showed extraordinary tolerance for radical Protestant polemics, direct or fabulous intervention in the cause of social and religious reform carried risks (J. King 1982). And these risks could impart tremendous energy to publications in which they were incurred.

Baldwin may have learned about this energy from a literary episode antedating both *Mirror* and *Beware the Cat*: the squabble over Churchyard's modest verse satire *Davy Diker's Dream* (*c*. 1551).[7] The *Dream* critiques Edwardian society by a device also used by the Fool in *Lear* (Shakespeare 1997: 3. 2. 80–94): a metrical list of desiderata, each beginning with the word 'when', and each implicitly absent from the realm at the time of writing ('When Justice joynes to truth, and law lookes not to meede, | And bribes help not to build fair bowres, nor giftes gret glotons fede'; A1^r). Once all these desiderata are achieved, 'dredfull dayes' will cease (A1^v), and the English will finally live free from oppression and factional infighting. Churchyard's poem is written in the persona of a labourer who has experienced a dream vision like that of Piers Plowman (the name 'Davy Diker' comes from Langland's famous allegory, printed by Robert Crowley in 1550; see S. Lucas 2007*b*). The *Dream* immediately provoked a sharp retort in verse from one Thomas Camell, who thought that Diker should stop meddling in state affairs. For Camell, there was scriptural precedent for the view that rulers should be revered as gods by their subjects: 'It grees not, it cordes not, nor orderly fyttes | That men should fynd fault, with Gods and theyr wyttes' (A1^v). Camell's argument prompted an indignant reply from Churchyard; and the quarrel quickly escalated to involve other controversialists, some of whom were clearly the original combatants under new names ('Geoffrey Chapel' and 'Stephen Steeple' sound like pseudonyms of Churchyard).

Viewing the quarrel between Churchyard and Camell from the 1570s, George Gascoigne saw it as a spectacular instance of comic misreading. A 'blockheaded reader', he tells us, thought the controversy arose from a dispute between two neighbours, 'Of whom that one having a Camell in keping, and that other having charge of the Churchyard, it was supposed they had grown to debate, bicause the Camell came into the Churchyarde' (2000: 266). But this risible misunderstanding has serious implications for every Tudor author of imaginative texts. A similar misreading, Gascoigne claims, led to false suppositions about his own miscellany of fictions, *A Hundred Sundry Flowers* (1573), judged 'offensive' by certain readers for its apparent references to real-life intrigues among the Elizabethan aristocracy (2000: 359). Gascoigne's allusion to the Churchyard–Camell controversy occurs in the Preface to a revised edition of the *Flowers*, rechristened *The Posies of George Gascoigne Esquire*

---

[7] All references to *Dream* and its responses are from Churchyard et al. (1560).

(1575). The new title hints punningly at the fictional nature of its contents: 'Posies' may be read either as 'Poesies' or as an abbreviation of 'Supposes'—that is, fictions (suppositions) or texts vulnerable to misreading (*supposed* to be about one thing when they are about another). *Posies'* prefatory matter claims both that Gascoigne's texts have been cleaned up to render them less scandalous (361), and that his intentions in publishing them were always instructive—aimed at deterring young men from his own 'youthfull imperfections' (366). Despite these assurances, *Posies* fell foul of the Elizabethan censors, and was withdrawn from circulation by the High Commission (see Pugh, Chapter 34 in this volume). Gascoigne's passing reference to the Churchyard–Camell controversy suggests that he may have anticipated just such a fate for the collection, since Churchyard too riled the authorities at the start of his career.

An early text by Churchyard provoked 'the displeasure of the Privy Council', a potentially lethal situation from which he was rescued by the personal intervention of Protector Somerset (Shrank 2008b: 111; S. Lucas 2002). The offending text may or may not have been the *Dream*; but Camell, at least, found the *Dream* seditious, and Churchyard thought Camell had attacked him in order to curry favour with certain aristocrats who bore him a grudge—perhaps the Privy Council.[8] The quarrel initially raged on a largely *ad hominem* basis, with much play on Camell's bestial name and Churchyard's asinine qualities. Then Waterman (writing as Western Will) put his oar in, and the dispute abruptly changed its tone.

Like all Baldwin's works, Waterman's contribution to the Diker debate shows intense awareness of the material conditions of the printer's trade. 'Western Will, upon the Debate betwixt Churchyard and Camell' describes how three mariners visit a London printer, seeking something new to carry home to Malden. The printer shows them the *Dream* and the controversy it spawned, assuring them that 'A merier jest ye can not finde, a boord with you to beare' (C4ʳ). The sailors are skilled in reading wind and compass but otherwise unlettered; so they ask the printer to read the *Dream* aloud before they buy it. He complies, and despite their illiteracy, they prove adept at interpreting its provenance and purpose. One pronounces Diker 'no fole', but a serious thinker about 'the worldes change' (D2ʳ). Another insists that the poem is too orderly to record a real dream, and sees it instead as a serious appeal for social reform, disguised as fiction. The printer concurs, likening the dream to Plato's *Republic*, which urges its readers to 'bringe our stat as nyghe' to its recommendations 'as mans devyce can ma[t]che' (D2ᵛ). The last mariner states that the *Dream* echoes things he has heard from the pulpit, and guesses it was written by someone better educated than a 'sely [foolish] swaene'. He too is right, says the printer; it was penned by one of Diker's childhood friends, a courtier. So the satire has a courtly provenance, which makes nonsense of Camell's outrage at its intrusion into high politics.

---

[8] 'Your words ye frame and set, | To creepe into some noble hertes, a credit for to get' (Churchyard et al. 1560: B4ᵛ).

In fact, the ease with which the mariners understand the satire renders *all* Camell's objections absurd, and exposes his ignorance of the function of fiction itself. As one sailor notes, 'a Dreame is but a Dreame, a fansye of thee heade'; Diker never meant his text to be taken as 'gospell', but as 'a sweven or fantasie' which hurts nobody, but urges the redress of the abuses catalogued (D3ᵛ). Camell's disgust, he concludes, suggests that he is either opposed to social reform or has a hidden agenda (his writing 'smelles of craft').⁹ This counter-accusation accords Camell the very qualities of secretiveness and treachery he assigned Churchyard. And Waterman aligns himself with the mariners' viewpoint. Having overheard the conversation, he sets down their 'sporte', not verbatim, but in 'such wordes as I [...] lyst to fantasy' (D4ʳ). Waterman, then, sees no harm in imaginative invention; and he ridicules Camell's resistance to it by printing the mariners' critique of his position as part of the pamphlet series Camell condemns.

In doing so, he makes it inevitable that Camell must respond in order to restore his damaged reputation as a critic. The response ('Camelles conclusion, and last farewell then, | To Churchyarde and those, that defende his when'; E2ᵛ) considerably raised the stakes of the controversy. Exonerating himself, Camell drops clues to Western Will's identity which suggest he thought he was Baldwin. Will, he declares, is a 'fyner freke' than Churchyard, and 'I have his workes wel reade' (E3ᵛ)—implying that, unlike Waterman, Will has published enough good writing by the early 1550s to merit the description 'works' (as opposed, say, to 'pamphlets'). This is certainly true of Baldwin, whose *Treatise* was the best-selling book of the 1540s, and whose *Ballads of Solomon* proclaims its author's high ambitions through its dedication to Edward VI. Camell adds that he knows where 'wyse men might hym seche' (E3ᵛ); this sounds like an allusion to Baldwin's career as a purveyor of printed 'wisdom', first in the quasi-philosophical *Treatise*, then in his poetic variations on the verses of Solomon, the wisest of men. A third clue comes when Camell says Will has appointed himself 'judge' of Camell's verses, thus assuming Solomon's mantle in another capacity for which the biblical king was famous, that of adjudicator in legal disputes. But Will does not share Solomon's unerring discrimination; he 'judgeth me amysse', Camell claims (E3ᵛ). Camell therefore invites impartial 'wyse men' to 'judge atwene Dicar and me' in Will's place (E4ᵛ); an invitation which might be taken as an appeal to professional judges, either in the law courts or in the Privy Council, to make a belated intervention in his dispute with Churchyard.¹⁰ This, and the aggressive tone of the rest of Camell's text, may have made Baldwin (the putative Will) as well as Waterman (the real one) sit up and take notice.

Camell proceeds to strengthen his case against Churchyard through a close reading of the *Dream*. Each line of the poem, he stresses, begins with the relative pronoun

---

⁹ Camell's opposition to social reform is implied by the mariners' statement that he would not have attacked Diker 'Excepte he ware one of those sortes, that [it] wolde have redrest' (D3ᵛ)—that is, unless he were one of those corrupt subjects it aims to redress. The 1560 *Contention* omits the crucial word 'it', supplied from 'Westerne Wyll' (*c*. 1552: [7]).

¹⁰ This reading is supported by Camell's referring the case to 'those whom it dothe touche' (Churchyard et al. 1560: E4ᵛ), i.e. England's rulers.

'when', invoking 'future tyme to comme' (E4^v), a grammatical detail that bothers Camell. He particularly dislikes the phrase 'when justice joynes to truthe'; couched in the future tense, this suggests that justice and truth are presently divorced in England. Camell vehemently repudiates this implication, urging Churchyard and his supporters to name one judge they would accuse of divorcing justice from truth in his legal practices (F1^r). More seriously, he objects to the phrase 'when Rex dothe reigne and rule the roste', which implies that Edward VI is powerless (F1^r). The *Dream*, then, is not 'false' as harmless fiction is—a literary conceit with moral purpose— but defamatory, even treasonous. Camell reinforces this accusation by objecting to Churchyard's final claim that Edwardian England is plunged in 'stryfe', which he refutes by invoking the 'rule and order' of his home town (F1^v). He closes with a threat, repeated from the beginning of the poem: Western Will must expect shipwreck if his mariners guide their vessel as ineptly as he and Churchyard have conducted their arguments (E3^v, F2^r). Shipwreck implies disaster or personal ruin; and it is as a man threatened with personal ruin that Waterman shapes his answer, 'Western Will to Camell and for himself alone' (F2^r).

The title suggests a poet in a panic. Keen to disengage himself from the other writers with whom Camell has bracketed him—Churchyard, his defenders, and maybe Baldwin—Waterman insists that he speaks only for himself; and he underlines the point by signing off with his own name, 'W. Watreman' (G1^r). He clearly feels that the Churchyard–Camell debate has got out of hand, and is fearful of being implicated in a situation more serious than anything he could have foreseen. Fiction has turned nasty owing to Camell's perverse misreading, and Waterman seeks to escape from the 'suspecte' or suspicion Camell has cast over the *Dream*. At the same time he takes revenge on Camell by subjecting his words to an equally malicious misreading, doing so with an ingenuity that may have tickled Baldwin's fancy, as a man who delighted in literary cleverness.

'Western Will to Camell' begins dramatically, deploying the metaphor of a storm that assails the light verse 'boat' commanded by Waterman. Faced with this emergency, the writer shoulders aside the three mariners used as a front in his earlier poem and takes the helm himself (F2^{r-v}). The reason for this, Waterman explains, is that he now finds himself exposed to very different conditions from the 'calme' that reigned when he entered the *Dream* controversy (F2^v). He intervened in the spirit of an 'ydle man' who observes 'the plaiers game | where parte hym self, hathe none', and who decides to divulge his impartial 'fansie' on the proceedings. But Camell hates the kind of open discussion represented by Will's intervention ('But ye no lookers on, in no wyse can abyde | To say their fansyes free'). Camell therefore reacted with unwarranted hostility, and Waterman feels constrained to respond with equal aggression. First, he identifies Camell as a labourer like Davy— a shit-shoveller, who 'busieth hymself' digging up dirt on other writers. This ugly busy-ness Camell conceals by posing as a 'symple man | That nothing meanes but right, to further as he can' (F3^r). But his true intentions are far from simple. After all, if the *Dream* were as bad as he claims, instead of printing his complaints, he would have complained to the authorities (F3^{r-v}). His failure to do so proves he has no legal case against Churchyard. Camell found, in fact, the merest 'sparke' of a fault in Churchyard's satire, which needed much puffing on his part to ignite it (F3ᵛ). His accusations are libellous, a damaging fiction which could have had dreadful consequences for the writers at whom it was directed. Water-man proceeds to give Camell a taste of his own medicine. Since Camell 'so well can racke, the mening of ones mynde', Waterman will now 'racke' Camell's mean-ing, stretching his words beyond their proper significance until they start to sound treasonous (F4ʳ).

The term he chooses to 'racke' is Camell's most flattering metaphor for the English government, 'the word wherin you sieme to triomphe most': that is, 'gods', a term lifted from Psalm 82 for his own sycophantic purposes. In the psalm, the powerful men described as 'gods' are also corrupt judges: 'How long will ye judge unjustly, and accept the persons of the wicked?' (82: 2). Waterman easily transforms Camell's com-pliment into a libel on England's rulers. Since Christians acknowledge only one god, he argues, Camell must be comparing England's rulers to pagan gods, those 'fansyes of ydolatres' (F4ᵛ). Even the briefest scrutiny of these gods' behaviour compounds the insult. Should Waterman choose to persuade his readers that Camell's 'entente' was to insult the English government, 'I coulde make some beleve ye ware to be suspecte'. But he refrains from discussing the 'rable' of ancient gods further, for fear 'That people in my rithmes suche thinges unfytt would riede'. Digging for dirt is easy; extricating oneself from the fallout of malicious misreading is more problematic, for both victim and perpetrator.

Clearly, both Camell and Waterman see the *Dream* controversy as a debate about fiction. Waterman highlights this when he invokes Plato's *Republic*: once directly, when the printer compares the *Dream* to the celebrated dialogue; once implicitly, when Waterman recalls the pornographic stories of the ancient gods. In the *Republic* Plato accuses poets of inventing these stories; it was for spreading these damaging fictions that he barred them from his ideal commonwealth. Like Sidney, however, Waterman reminds his readers that the *Republic* is itself a fiction, a tale containing 'many thynges that [Plato] wolde have [...] That never yet in earthe ware founde' (D2ᵛ). Mentioning the dialogue invokes two contrasting attitudes to imaginative writ-ing. On the one hand, it is irresponsible frippery, undermining divine and worldly authority; on the other, it provides space for serious political or philosophical debate. Camell sees the *Dream* as flippant; but his use of metaphor shows that he also recognizes fiction as a useful tool in shaping rational arguments. Waterman's response shows that Camell's fictions, too, can be read in contrasting ways: either as dangerous frivolity, or as serious contributions to a debate over free speech (in which case he should read others' writings with the courtesy owed his own).

In the Diker controversy, then, Tudor England is full of fictions, some legitimate, some illegitimate, some supporting rational debate, some arising from irrational hostility. Waterman's interventions expose his sensitivity both to the wide range of political and religious inventions that spread across England in the 1550s, and to the dangers courted by purveyors of such inventions. One danger in particular stands out. When one of Waterman's mariners says that Camell should not take Diker's dream 'for gospelle' (D3^v), he links the poem with the religious strife ravaging Europe, where questions about what constitutes 'truth' or 'fiction' might destroy the questioner, and where mischievous misreadings of printed texts could lead writers and printers to the gallows. Two years later, Baldwin locates *Beware the Cat* in the same European context. Its topic is the proliferation of fiction in an age of religious struggle, and its narrative unfolds in the shadow of the dismembered corpses of executed traitors, suspended on poles outside the window of the house where it is set. The novel makes a major contribution to the history of the early modern imagination; and like Western Will's poems, it identifies imagination as one of the major ideological battlegrounds of the mid-sixteenth century.

II

As its name informs us, *A Marvellous History Entitled Beware the Cat* tells of impossible wonders, which compete for readers' attention with the factual narratives purveyed in chronicles, or 'true histories'. Set at Christmastime, when fictions rule, the narrative begins at Edward VI's court, where Baldwin's friend George Ferrers has been appointed Lord of Misrule and given official licence to entertain the monarch. Its setting, in a real place at a precise historical moment, lends it authority on several fronts.[11] Its basis in 'fact' is attested by the living witnesses it invokes—Ferrers, Master Willot, the rhetorician Richard Sherry[12]—while the fictions it contains are authorized by their courtly provenance (much as the printer's claim that Diker's *Dream* was transcribed by a courtier lent weight to its inventions). The book's contents, then, should be taken no more seriously than any other Yuletide game—they are, as Western Will would say, 'fancies of the head'; yet they have been approved by no less a person than the King. Their setting emphasizes, too, the extent to which imagination impinges on the material realities of Tudor life, especially at certain times and places—at Hallowe'en and Midsummer Night, for instance, when spirits mingle with mortals in graveyards, woods, and bedchambers.

Like the setting, the narrative techniques are designed to blur boundaries between fancy and reality, true and false, matter and spirit. The dedication, for example, stresses the unusual mimetic skill with which the story has been constructed. The first-person narrative gives readers the illusion of being present at the events it describes: its editor, G.B., has, he claims, 'so nearly used both the order and words of him that spake them [...] that I doubt not but that [Master Ferrers] and Master Willot shall in the reading think they hear Master Streamer speak, and he himself in the like action shall doubt whether he speaketh or readeth' (1988: 3). If, as seems likely, Streamer is as fictional as Raphael Hythloday in More's *Utopia* (translated into

---

[11] For the setting's significance, see Betteridge (2004: 113–20).
[12] For identification of Sherry, see Baldwin (1988: 62 n.).

English in 1551), this claim of accuracy demonstrates how easily the imaginary can be made real through language. The illusion of authenticity can be conjured by the deft deployment of a range of verbal tricks described in *A Treatise of Schemes and Tropes* (1550)—written by Richard Sherry, one of the characters in *Cat*—-and readers must remain constantly alert to the possibility that they are being hoodwinked into an inappropriate and possibly perilous suspension of disbelief.

The dedication highlights, too, the *form* of the book that follows (Bonahue and Edward 1994). 'I have divided [Streamer's] oration', G.B. explains, 'into three parts, and set the argument before them and an instruction after them, with such notes as might be gathered thereof, so making it book-like' (3). The text is 'book-like' in that it physically resembles a serious work of scholarship, with summary, marginal comments, and didactic conclusion—like Baldwin's *Ballads of Solomon*. A superficial glance would therefore fail to distinguish it from a historical or religious tract, intervening in the period's ferocious political and religious debates. At the same time, the title page carries a caution: the injunction to 'beware the cat' warns readers to treat the text as a witty game of cat-and-mouse, and to watch for signs that they are letting their minds be seduced into imaginative complicity with customs and moral imperatives they should reject. The caution resembles the printer's warning to Western Will's mariners, when he tells them to 'ware thee Camell', since this is a tricksier beast (being both man and critic) than its name suggests (D3^r). Fiction is dangerous territory, and habitually produces repercussions well beyond its purported remit.

The tendency of fantasies to proliferate beyond their licensed limits in time and space is made obvious in the 'argument' following the dedication. In the intimate setting of Ferrers's bedchamber, a group of men learn their parts for 'certain interludes' devised 'for the King's recreation' (5). As they prepare for sleep, they relax into conversation, beginning with a discussion of the art of fiction, which rapidly widens to embrace philosophical and even theological considerations. G.B. objects to plays that feature talking animals, since it is unreasonable to expect audiences to accept the *sight* of 'speechless things' speaking 'reasonably', even if *reading* about them works well enough (as in Aesop's fables). G.B.'s objection pertains to the different constraints governing fantasy on stage and on the page; but his bedfellow Streamer claims that talking animals are no fantasy. Beasts and fowls, he asserts, possess reason, 'as much as men, yea, and in some points more', and he has first-hand proof of this, having heard them speak 'as well as I hear and understand you' (6). This makes Ferrers laugh; after all, it defies the 'grave and learned' authorities cited by G.B. Offended, Streamer offers to describe his encounters with articulate animals, on condition that there are no more interruptions: for 'as soon as any man curiously interrupteth me, I will leave off and not speak one word more' (6–7). His resistance here to both laughter and dialogue contravenes the Christmas spirit in which the narrative began. He launches us into a different mode of discourse, that of the proto-scientist, or 'Divine'; unwary readers might thus be tempted to take his ensuing narrative seriously. But it is governed throughout by its provenance in the bedchamber of a Lord of Misrule—a hotbed of comic invention. So Streamer's successive ventures into antiquarianism, translation, astronomy, alchemy, and divinity infect all these branches of learning with the twin viruses of laughter and fiction. Mid-Tudor culture is a bewildering fusion of the serious and risible, real and imagined, and every detail of *Beware the Cat* alerts us to the consequences of this fusion.

Streamer, who delivers the rest of the narrative as an 'oration' (a term that again stresses its rhetorical, as against rational, construction), has an identity as multiple as the narrative he offers. He is a 'Divine' (5), but serves a Lord of Misrule, and seems more preoccupied with beasts than people. He is closely involved in the print industry, especially the dissemination of learning through print; his adventures occur in a printer's house, where he sometimes stays to oversee the printing of 'Greek alphabets' (9); yet in the story his learning is used only to eavesdrop on feline gossip, enabled by spells cribbed from the work of a medieval magician, whose instructions he fails to follow. His name is as slippery as his personality. The forename Gregory allies him with several popes, strengthening readers' growing sense that he is a clandestine Catholic; while his surname evokes a flag or pennon (he 'like a streamer waves | In ghostly good'; 55), suggesting that he changes direction with the wind—that he is a turncoat. 'Streamer' rhymes, too, with 'Dreamer', the title Camell gives Churchyard. If this suggests that *Cat* is a satire like the *Dream*, then the name may also invoke the notion that the satire is strictly limited in its application—that it is to some extent self-censoring. Western Will uses the term 'stream' to dissociate himself from any controversial elements in the *Dream*: such things, he says, 'be without my streame', and should be attributed to Churchyard, not him (F3ᵛ). And in one of Baldwin's probable contributions to *The Mirror*, the ghost of the poet Collingbourne—executed by Richard III for writing a satire on tyranny—warns fellow poets 'not to passe the bankes | Of Hellicon, but kepe them in the *streames*' (Baldwin et al. 1960: 358; my emphasis): an injunction to political restraint that preserves poets' 'freedome' while protecting them from the excruciating 'extreames' to which tyrants might subject them if they took free speech too far (see Hadfield 1994: 102–7). Streamer, then, could be said to embody the unrestrained stream of eloquent free speech; but speech that keeps itself within certain confines, as a well-regulated river keeps within its banks.

Yet at times Streamer's oration seems far from restrained, incapable of sticking to its subject (see Gutierrez 1989). It begins in the most solidly material setting evoked by any sixteenth-century narrative: John Day's Aldersgate printing house, with its capacious fireplace, its garden overlooking St Anne's steeple, and its window viewing the grisly remains of traitors displayed on poles (9–10). But this location is also linked with conjecture and myth, as Streamer shows when he gives several incompatible etymologies for the place-name Aldersgate at the start of his oration (9). And the solid setting quickly gives way to a series of speculative anecdotes concerning cats— ranging topographically from Staffordshire to Ireland, and chronologically from the present to forty years before—which furnish material for increasingly extravagant speculation as storytelling gives place to philosophical enquiry.

Worse still—given that Streamer cites them as proof of feline intelligence— these anecdotes depend on unreliable reporters. They are narrated at the fireside, a traditional breeding ground of fairy tales and ghost stories, by travellers and servants, two social groups notorious for spreading rumours and gossip. The first story describes just such a rumour—a word-of-mouth message sent from Ireland to western England concerning the death of the cat Grimalkin—originally told to the servant storyteller by his mother, who 'knew both the man and the woman which [owned] the cat that the message was sent unto' (11). The second anecdote relates how Grimalkin was killed in Ireland by Patrick Apore, a murderous robber, later killed in his turn by a vengeful kitten. This tale derives from a farmer, on evidence provided, presumably, by the sole witness of Patrick's death: the victim's wife (14). Both stories, then, are old wives' tales, and thus proverbially unreliable. Yet the second storyteller claims that he 'never told [...] a more likely tale' (12); and he lends it authenticity by the insertion of telling cultural details: Irish words and phrases, cooking practices, and garments (see Hadfield 1998: 141–7; Maslen 1999). In entering Streamer's company, then, we enter a world where knowledge of history, geography, and local custom springs from the convoluted grapevine of 40-year-old gossip; and where such gossip is adopted as the basis of serious religious, scientific, and cultural analysis. Streamer's oration, that is, furnishes evidence not of feline intelligence but of the dominance of fictions in Edwardian England, and of the complex means by which these fictions flourish once implanted in the minds of gullible recipients.

The story of Grimalkin's death leads to a philosophical discussion among Streamer and his companions. This discussion starts with conjectures concerning feline culture, which the speakers assume is organized along the lines of the Catholic Church hierarchy (15). It goes on to consider how a cat could eat a sheep, a cow, and a man, as Grimalkin did, despite her diminutive stature (15–16). And it embraces another set of old wives' tales concerning the notion that witches can transform themselves and others into cats and wolves. One speaker compares belief in such transformations to the Catholic belief in transubstantiation, whereby Christ's body is plucked from Heaven and 'thrust [...] into a piece of bread' (17): a doctrine he thinks absurd. Instead he proposes that witches cannot change shape, but instead project their souls into new bodies, or give the illusion of shape-shifting 'by deluding the sight and fantasies of the seers' through tricks or magic ointments. As the debate unfolds, then, it traces a direct path from fancy, superstition, and illusion-working to religious orthodoxy. Witches and Catholic priests are both held in 'high reverence' for fear of their malicious powers (17, 20). Both strengthen their hold on popular imagination by spreading irrational beliefs based on deceit. And both adhere to traditions transmitted from generation to generation, in defiance of reason and evidence. In Western Will's poems, a harmless collection of printed pamphlets was transported from London to Malden by a crew of cheerful English sailors. In Cat, a different set of imaginative narratives—concerning witchcraft, superstition, and casual violence inflicted by robbers, beasts, and religious fanatics—gets carried from Ireland to England by ship's cats. Baldwin seems to be confirming Camell's fears concerning the subversive potential of irresponsible fictions. Such fictions, he implies, are already widespread, disseminated not by good Protestants like himself but by an unholy alliance between witches, their familiars, and clandestine Catholics, using as their medium not print but the incessant working of loose tongues.

Baldwin also shows how these specifically Catholic oral fictions combine popular superstition with the paraphernalia of esoteric knowledge. The discussion in Day's printing house freely mixes fairy tales with learned allusions, as when Streamer compares the actions of witches to the practices of Apollo's Delphic priestesses (16), or invokes the English goblin Robin Goodfellow alongside 'telchines' (classical craftsmen); other speakers combine references to Socrates and Pythagoras (17, 21) with legends of magic pigs and werewolves. Superstition even touches England's elite academic institutions: one speaker supports his claims about shape-shifting witches with the testimony of a 'credible clerk of Oxford' (20). The dire consequences of mixing learning and superstition are woven into Streamer's oration, as he casually observes that one of his principal informants (called Thomas) 'died afterwards of a disease which he took in Newgate, where he lay long for suspicion of magic because he desired a prisoner to promise him his soul after he was hanged' (9). Streamer's reliance on Thomas for his conversion to a belief in feline intelligence, and later for certain ingredients of the magic recipe giving him access to the speech of cats, taints his narrative with the 'suspicion of magic' of a peculiarly noxious kind.

Part two of Streamer's oration shows how easily the superstitions of part one may translate into ill-advised action. Obsessed by the debate over feline intelligence— so that he can no longer concentrate on books (22)—Streamer supplants his usual studies with prolonged surveillance of the cats outside his window. Afterwards he turns to a text by the medieval magician Albertus Magnus to find a spell for learning their language. But his inability to read books (including, presumably, the Bible— hence his willingness to seek knowledge elsewhere) renders him incapable of following Albertus' instructions, as if infected with the same proneness to misreading as Camell, who failed utterly to understand the *Dream*. Where Albertus identifies the exact time and place for collecting a precise list of ingredients, Streamer's eagerness for instant results prompts him to gather random items on the wrong date, in the wrong location. So when he claims to have concocted a medicine enabling him to comprehend the speech of birds and beasts, we should treat the claim with scepticism. The term 'imagination' occurs repeatedly in this part of the oration, stressing the fanciful nature of Streamer's assertion. The disastrous effects of his imaginings are repeatedly highlighted by references to the Devil—from Streamer's use of the Irish word *diabhal* (devil) in his spells, to the terror felt when his hearing becomes attuned to every urban noise, which 'came with such a rumble into mine ear that I thought all the devils in Hell had broken loose and were come about me' (32–3; see Maslen 1999: 19 n. 22). As Streamer's magical–medical preparation nears completion, a marginal note observes that 'A man may die only by *imagination* of harm' (33; my emphasis); and this confirms what we already know from the fate of Thomas: over-reliance on fantasies may lead to spiritual as well as bodily destruction.

Part three of Streamer's oration narrates the stories he hears with the help of his magical preparations. They are told by a cat called Mouseslayer as she defends herself at an impromptu trial, rather as Churchyard defended himself against a trumped-up charge of sedition in the *Dream* controversy. Her tales expose the malpractices of clandestine Catholics, whose love of deceit extends from making exaggerated claims for the miraculous efficacy of the Host (37 ff.) to tricking naive young wives into deceiving their husbands (40 ff.). Besides the raunchily Chaucerian pleasure afforded readers, these stories reinforce the moral of Baldwin's book as signalled in its title. Tudor citizens, states G.B. in his closing 'Exhortation', must 'beware the cat' because those observant pets 'understand us and mark our secret doings, and so declare them among themselves', and because 'through help of the medicines by him described any man may, as he did, understand them' (54). Clandestine breaches of human and divine law will be exposed at last, whether by feline means or human, by cats or mariners. If not exposed on earth, these hidden crimes will be noted by the greatest spies of all, God and his angels, who 'see, mark, and behold all men's closest doings' (54). Baldwin's fictitious cats are instruments of truth, and through them Baldwin draws readers' attention to God's all-seeing eyes, spying out truths we seek to disguise.

This process of exposure is neatly summarized by the way the stories expose their narrator's hypocrisy. Twice at least Streamer gets implicated in his tales of Catholic malfeasances. In one, a group of Catholics is filled with abject terror by the glow of a cat's eyes in the dark, and in their fear they repeat a phrase first shrieked by Streamer when startled by a crow in part two: 'The Devil, the Devil, the Devil!' (33, 48). More damningly, in another story a forged love letter—written to persuade a virtuous wife to adultery—is signed with Streamer's initials, G.S., identifying him as an accomplice in the plot to corrupt a young woman (44). Streamer thus has much in common with the Catholic bawd in the letter story, who is 'taken for as honest as any in the city' (41) but whose devotion to Our Lady's image is more than matched by the imaginative deviousness with which she plies her illicit trade. Similarly, Streamer's disapproval of the practices of clandestine English Catholics is no fiercer than his desire to sniff them out and display them to the voyeuristic gaze of his Protestant countrymen.

But despite his association with hypocrisy, devilishness, superstition, and manifest folly, Streamer is a vehicle of truth—an Erasmian mock philosopher. G.B. signals this in the dedication, when he says that if *Cat* is well received, 'I will hereafter, as Plato did by Socrates, pen out such things of the rest of our Christmas communications as shall be to [Streamer's] great glory, and no less pleasure to all them that desire such kinds of knowledge' (3–4). Streamer's association with Socrates is strengthened in part one, where 'Master Sherry' says it is Streamer's custom 'always to make men believe that you be not so well learned as you be', in the manner of the great Greek thinker (17). Socrates' ugly appearance concealed great wisdom; Streamer's concealment of his 'wisdom', by contrast, only reveals his folly.[13] Yet this folly may also conceal certain 'kinds of knowledge' if properly used. Those who object to Streamer's stories convict themselves of no less folly, as Camell convicted himself of folly for his

---

[13] Erasmus discusses Socrates' ugliness at length in *Adagia* (1967: 77–97).

disapproval of Diker. Conversely, accepting Streamer's fictions is a sign of acuity, since they expose a range of hidden realities: the machinations of clandestine Catholics; the conflict between old and new religion and the different generations that practise them; the various misreadings to which texts and events are subject; the superstitions that pervade mid-Tudor England. Streamer's folly, then, accidentally enlightens, like Folly in Erasmus' *Encomium Moriae* (translated by Baldwin's friend Thomas Chaloner in 1549).[14] And the disjunction between the scholar–priest's ridiculous verbal 'surface'—his prose style—and the knowledge it conveys, makes him not so very different from the deceptively blunt and unattractive philosopher–narrator of Plato's *Republic*.

This link with Socrates—which recalls the *Dream*'s link with the *Republic*—identifies *Beware the Cat* as vulnerable to censorship, since Socrates was drastically silenced by his enemies through forced suicide. Given its date of composition—when the ailing Edward VI was about to secede the throne to his Catholic sister—*Cat*'s author could hardly have expected to publish it without a struggle. Indeed, as a printer's assistant he knew that publication at the wrong time and place would be an act of Socratic self-destruction. Even casting it as a serio-comic fable cannot banish the shadows cast by the limbs of executed traitors which so unnerve Streamer—just as Waterman was unnerved by the accusation of treachery that greeted his light-hearted response to Camell, only one or two years before the writing of *Cat*.

Nevertheless, reading Baldwin's text alongside the *Dream* reveals it as an eloquent plea for freedom of speech, directly opposing Camell's equally eloquent case for shutting speech down. Where Camell insists on the suppression of oppositional voices, Baldwin urges the unleashing of all the voices in the land, whatever their creed or faction, so that their din may noisily expose the multiplicity of devilry and superstition competing for the attention of Tudor subjects. As we have seen, Streamer's eavesdropping on cats leads to the public humiliation of Catholic priests, pimps, and adulterers, and the revelation of illegal goings-on in secret chambers, behind locked doors and decorative wall-hangings. His nonsensical reasoning demonstrates the state of mind—particularly of the imaginative faculty—that leads his compatriots to embrace superstition. His mingling of the popular and academic shows how easily the former can disrupt the order of the latter. Suppress the voices of Streamer, Diker, or Western Will, and you lose the opportunity for such revelations. Substitute for their fictional voices the 'authentic' voices of their authors, and you rob those revelations of the Borgesian subtlety to which they aspire. If, however, we attend closely to that subtlety, we shall find that the products of the mid-Tudor imagination are as dazzlingly complex as anything produced in Shakespeare's lifetime. And *that* would be a literary revelation worth talking about on the voyage home to Malden.

---

[14] As Thomas Betteridge implies, further study of links between *Cat* and *Praise of Folly* would prove fruitful (2004: 120), as would examination of Baldwin's debt to *Utopia*.

Primary Works

A Shorte Answere to the Boke called Beware the Cat (1570).

BALDWIN, WILLIAM (1988), *Beware the Cat*, ed. William A. Ringler and Michael Flachmann (San Marino, CA: Huntington Library).

——et al. (1960), *The Mirror for Magistrates*, ed. Lily B. Campbell (1938; Cambridge: Cambridge University Press).

CHURCHYARD, THOMAS, et al. (1560), *The Contention bettwyxte Churchyeard and Camell, upon David Dycers Dreame*.

ERASMUS, DESIDERIUS (1967), *Erasmus on his Times: A Shortened Version of The Adages of Erasmus*, ed. Margaret Mann Phillips (Cambridge: Cambridge University Press).

GASCOIGNE, GEORGE (2000), *A Hundreth Sundrie Flowres*, ed. G. W. Pigman III (Oxford: Clarendon Press).

NASHE, THOMAS (1904), *Works*, ed. Ronald B. McKerrow, 5 vols (London: Bullen).

SHAKESPEARE, WILLIAM (1997), *King Lear*, in *The Norton Shakespeare*, ed. Stephen Greenblatt et al. (New York: W. W. Norton).

Westerne Wyll (*c*. 1552), *Westerne Wyll, upon the Debate betwyxte Churchyarde and Camell*.

CHAPTER 18

DIRECTIONS FOR ENGLISH

THOMAS WILSON'S *ART OF RHETORIC*, GEORGE PUTTENHAM'S *ART OF ENGLISH POESY*, AND THE SEARCH FOR VERNACULAR ELOQUENCE

WOLFGANG G. MÜLLER

THOMAS WILSON'S *Art of Rhetoric* (1553), a comprehensive humanist attempt to make English readers acquainted with rhetoric in the tradition of Cicero, and George Puttenham's *Art of English Poesy* (1589), a rhetorical poetics and conduct book designed for the English courtier in his role as a poet, are both concerned with eloquence or persuasive speech as an essential element of social and cultural life. These two pioneering works, which self-confidently extol the function of eloquence in different social milieux, have to be seen in the context of the rise of English vernacular as a medium of public and literary expression. This context will be briefly characterized before the discussion of the two texts. The vernacularization, which took place in the sixteenth century, is a central process in a fascinating construction of national identity to be observed in all areas of cultural production, for instance in descriptive works from William Caxton's *The Description of England* (1498) to William Harrison's *Description of England* (1575) and William Camden's *Britannia* (1586), in history-writing from Thomas More's *History of King Richard III* to Edward Hall and Raphael Holinshed, or in political literature from Sir John Fortescue's *The Governance of England* (1471–6) to Thomas Starkey, *A Dialogue between Reginald Pole and Thomas Lupset* (1536–8), Sir Thomas Smith, *De republica Anglorum* (first published in 1583), and Fulke Greville's *A Treatise of Monarchy* (1600).

The decisive historical event in the emergence of an English national identity in the Tudor Age is the Reformation, as much a political as a religious phenomenon which affected the whole country. It caused a separation of England from Rome, effected by a number of parliamentary Acts between 1533 and 1536, and contributed essentially to laying the basis for the development of a sense of a national identity (Shrank 2004*b*: 10). A national consciousness, a concern for the nation involving national self-esteem, finds expression in what Cathy Shrank calls 'a rhetoric of English nationhood' (2004*b*: 2), which emerges in almost all types of Tudor discourse. Without this development Gaunt's speech in Shakespeare's *Richard II*—'This royall Throne of Kings, this sceptred Isle' (2. 1. 40)—would not have been imaginable.

One area which conspicuously reveals the process of nation-building in sixteenth-century England is the vernacular, which underwent an astonishing change as far as vocabulary, style, and rhetoric are concerned and which, after heated controversies, gained considerable national prestige. Earlier Tudor writers tended to complain about the rudeness and lack of diversity and expressive resources of English, although their criticism should be taken with caution. Thomas Wyatt, for instance, finds it 'tedious' to 'make' Petrarch's prose text 'of the remedy of yll fortune [...] into our englyssh' for the lack of 'diversyte in our tong', on account of which it 'shulde want a greate deale of the grace' (440), when in actual fact his translations and adaptations of Petrarch's poems reveal, despite some metrical problems, remarkable artistry. Another example is John Skelton's poem *Philip Sparrow*, in which Jane Scrope refers to 'our naturall tong' as 'rude', 'rusty', 'cankered', and 'dull' (Skelton 1983: 774–9), while the poet himself exhibits—despite his inclination to display his erudition and insert Latinisms into his texts—a rhetorical virtuosity, and even writes after his laureation in 'The Garlande of Laurell' 1,600 lines in honour of himself as *English* poet.

A controversial topic in sixteenth-century discussions on the English language is its restricted lexicon, which comes up in Jane Scrope's complaint that she lacks words ('Termes') 'To wryte ornatly' (781–3). The question is whether gaps should be filled by neologisms and whether the influx of words from Latin and the Romance languages should be prevented, or tolerated, or hailed. John Cheke, a purist and in this respect akin with Thomas Wilson, believes 'that our own tung shold be written cleane and pure, unmixt and unmangeled with borrowing of other tunges'. However, he is also aware that, English being imperfect, gaps may have to be closed with borrowed words, yet with such discretion that it may appear that 'the mould of our own tung could serve us to fascion a woord of our own' (Cheke 1994: 12–13). As another option his advice is to look 'if the old denisoned wordes could content and ease this neede'.

Despite such warnings and the widespread polemics against 'inkhorn terms' (learned or bookish words of Latin or Romance origin), the process of expanding the English lexicon was unstoppable. Its most obvious manifestation was the doublings and triplings cultivated by writers such as Andrew Boorde and Thomas Elyot, a famous example occurring in the title of book 1, chapter 4, of the latter's *The Book Named the Governor*, 'The Education or Form of Bringing Up'. Such doublings used to be interpretative or explanatory in that to a foreign word or a word of foreign origin they added a plain English equivalent or synonym. Their function is to increase the readers' knowledge of their language, but such a narrow didactic intention was soon transcended in that writers desired to give their texts verbal variety and richness and thus to display the resourcefulness and expressive potential of the English language, vocabulary-building becoming an aspect of nation-building. In the course of this development the English language, which, in the early Tudor age, tended to be regarded as rude and imperfect, became a national asset and the medium for the greatest poetical achievements.

A decisive point in the rehabilitation of the English language as a national treasure is reached with the educationalist Richard Mulcaster. In the 'Peroration' of his *Elementary* (1582) he makes a powerful plea for the value and virtues of English. His famous triad—whose incisive style foreshadows Brutus' forum speech in Shakespeare's *Julius Caesar*—cannot be quoted too often: 'I love *Rome*, but *London* better, I favor *Italie*, but England more, I honor the Latin, but I worship the *English*' (Mulcaster 1582: 254). In this anaphoric structure, which represents a kind of national trinity of capital, country, and language, language takes the last, climactic position. The crucial role language plays in the construction of national identity is here expressed more emphatically than anywhere else. Mulcaster believes that English can compete with all other languages: 'I do not think that anie language, be it whatsoever, is better able to utter all arguments, either with more pith or greater pla[i]nesse, then our *English* tung is' (258). The use of foreign terms is no longer a problem: 'And tho we use & must use manie foren terms [...] we do not anie more then the bravest tungs do' (274). In prophetic words (256) he imagines the international expansion of English which was to be witnessed in the course of the twentieth century.

Thomas Wilson's *Art of Rhetoric* (1553), the first text to be discussed in this chapter, is an important document in the process of vernacularizing the English culture of the Renaissance. It is the first large-scale treatment of rhetoric in English, which demonstrates the uses of eloquence in law, politics, church service, and on numerous social occasions (see Plett 2004: 25). With its many orations in different styles, illustrating the use and abuse of rhetoric, and with its anecdotal richness and humour, it is a landmark in the history of English prose. Entertaining and yet with a clear didactic aim and written for the practical purpose of giving readers assistance in the production of written and spoken discourse, it was an Elizabethan best-seller, which saw a total of eight editions between 1553 and 1585. The text exists in two versions. When Wilson had returned from exile in Italy in 1560, the publication of a new, revised edition was proposed to him and, and as he reports in the 'Prologue to the Reader', he was asked to 'amende it, where I thought meete'. He refused to do so— 'let the booke firste amende it self, and make me amendes'—and almost renounced it, because it had brought him only trouble, persecution as a heretic in England under Queen Mary and even during exile in Rome: 'For surely I have no cause, to acknowledge it for my boke, because I have so smarted for it' (1560: A5^r). Note the liturgical style of the triad in which he states his renunciation: 'I will none of this booke from henceforthe [...] As it was, so it is, and so be it still hereafter for me' (A5^{r-v}). His amazement that 'thinges doen in Englande seven yeres before, and the same universallie forgiven, should afterwardes be laied to a mannes charge in *Roome*' (A4^v) may explain his refusal to revise his book. Its unaltered republication implies, as Andrew Hadfield comments (1994: 112), a coincidence of the experience of self and nation. It is a symbol of personal and national triumph. At the end of the Prologue to *The Art of Rhetoric* Wilson writes accordingly: 'GOD be praised, and thankes be given to him onely, that not onelie hath delivered me, out of the Lions mouth: but also hath brought Englande, my deare Countrie, out of greate thraldome and forrein bondage.'

A kind of sequel to his treatise on logic *The Rule of Reason*, which he had published two years before, in 1551, *The Art of Rhetoric* must be seen as part of a project of vernacularizing two of the *artes liberales*: 'the Preceptes of Rhetorique, sette foorthe by me in Englishe, as I had erste doen the rules of Logique' (A3^r). For Wilson the gifts of 'speache and reason' belong together, 'Arte and eloquence' persuading men of what has been 'ful oft found out by reason'. As distinct from Leonard Cox's *The Art or Craft of Rhetoric* (*c*. 1535), largely a translation of Melanchthon's *De rhetorica*, limited to invention, Wilson's *Rhetoric* is a genuinely English work of its author's own making. Although it is based on Cicero and Quintilian, it dispenses almost entirely with Latin, let alone Greek, terms. Wilson uses Anglicized versions of his precursors' terms, for which he then gives purely English equivalents or periphrases. Latin or Greek terms are relegated to the margin as a paratext. To give examples, Greek *enargeia* and Latin *evidentia*, a vivid description which places something before the hearer's eye, is rendered in the title of a chapter as 'An evident, or plain settyng forthe of a thing as though it were presently doen' (91^r). Or 'insinuation' is by graphic metaphors named 'a privie twining, or close creping in' (51^r). 'Hyperbole' is called 'Mountyng above the truthe' (93^v). There are numerous instances in which not even an Anglicized version of a classical term is quoted in the main text, e.g. 'Reasonyng a matter with our selfes' (*dialogismos*; 105^v), 'Wordes loose' (*oratio soluta, asyndeton*; 104^v), 'Oft using of one worde in diverse places' (*polyptoton*; 104^v).

To appreciate the innovative quality of Wilson's vernacularization of the terminology of rhetoric, a glance at other early rhetorical handbooks may be useful. The entries in Richard Sherry's *Treatise of Schemes and Tropes* (1550) regularly start with the Greek term, then add the Latin term, and finally an Anglicized version of the Latin term, as in 'APORIA. *Dubitatio*, dubitacion, when wee doute of two thynges, or of many' (D3^r). A comparable procedure is to be noticed in Peacham's *The Garden of Eloquence* (1577), which has an intention similar to that of Wilson, namely that of supplementing extant 'bookes of Philosophy and preceptes of wyse-dome, set forth in english' by a treatment of 'Eloquence' (A2^v). It is astonishing that Peacham's exposition of elocution in the English language does not affect rhetorical terminology. He does not Anglicize classical terms or look for English equivalents. Greek or Latin terms invariably form the title of an entry. They are repeated at the beginning of the entry and then explained in English, as in the following example: '*Antiphrasis*. Antiphrasis, when a word is understoode by the contrary' (C4^v).

Compared to contemporary rhetoric books, Wilson seems to have deliberately made his book look as English as may be. His avoidance of difficult terms of Greek, Latin, and French origin in the main text ties in with the criticism with which he treats 'inkhorn terms' in his section on style ('elocution'). The first lesson that should be learned is 'that wee never affecte any straunge ynkehorne termes, but so speake as is commonly received' (82^v). The idea of a standard of English emerges in expressions such as 'one maner of language' (83^v) and 'mother tonge' and even 'the kinges Eng-lishe' (82^v). Also he believes that 'The Shire or Toune helpeth somewhat, towardes the encrease of honour'. To 'Lincolne', where Wilson was born, he opposes the capital, London, where 'the ayre is better, the people more civill, and the wealth muche greater, and the menne for the moste parte more wise' (7^r). He does not explicitly refer to language here, but what he means is obvious: 'The standards of "civility" and proper speech approved by Wilson are those of London and the South-East' (Shrank 2004*b*: 192). Wonderful parodies are the texts which he presents as examples of a style overladen with Latinate diction, for instance the letter of a Lincolnshire clergyman seeking preferment (83^{r-v}), or a request for financial help abounding with malapropisms. The petitioner speaks of 'contrarie Bishops', 'revives', and 'Southsides to the king', when what he wants to say is 'contributions', 'relief', and 'subsidies to the king' (84^r). In the many model speeches and epistles with which Wilson enriches his text he evinces stylistic skill, wit, and sense of humour.

The examples and the numerous anecdotes which the book provides as illustration of the author's exposition of the theory and practice of rhetoric reveal an affinity with the genre of the jest-book, but political implications are unmistakable. Here are two examples which belong to Wilson's treatment of abuses in the logic of talking. First, the story of an 'old grandamme', who was kneeling before 'the ymage of our Ladye'. Upon being asked why she did so she replied, 'I praye to our Ladye, that she maye praye to her Sonne for me.' When her interlocutor laughed at her ignorance, she corrected herself, 'I praye to Christe in heaven, that he will praie for me to this good Ladie here' (73^{r-v}). This is more than ridicule of the Roman Church's veneration of the Virgin Mary. Wilson pinpoints the decisive theological issue, the Roman Catholic belief that the saints have to be prayed to as intermediaries between the believer and God, while the Protestants are expected to seek the direct address to God. In Archbishop Cranmer's version of the Litany of 1544, the number of invocations to the saints had been reduced drastically and the successive versions entirely dispensed with them. As funny as it may be, the story of the old woman's confusion about whom to pray to reflects a current theological debate and indicates an anti-papist position which runs through the whole book.

The second example concerns the roundabout ways a man may take in his thinking and talking:

> Would not a man thinke hym madde, that havyng an earneste errande from London to Dover, would take it the next waie, to ride first into Northfolke, nexte into Essex, and last into Kent? And yet assuredly, many an unlearned and witlesse man, hath straied in his talke moche farther a great deale, yea truely as farre, as hens to Rome gates.   (45^r)

The characterization of not taking the straight way as 'mad' and the reference to going as far as Rome imply a mockery of the vagaries of those whose thinking and talking are influenced by the Roman Church. Shrank (2004b: 185–6) observes that in the context of such passages references to England tend to appear. The rejection of Rome coincides with an espousal of England.

Another fine example of Wilson's technique of integrating political statements into his explication of rhetoric is to be found in his commentary on *Digression; or, Swaruyng from the Matter.*

> We swarve sometimes from the matter, upon juste consideracions, makyng the same to serve for our purpose, as well as if we had kept the matter still. As in making an invective againste rebelles, and largelie setting out the filthe of their office [offences], I might declare by the waie of digression, what a noble countrey Englande is, howe great commodities it hath, what traffique here is used, and how moche more nede other Realmes have of us, then we have nede of them.   (92^v)

The proper argument, or 'matter', proposed in this example is an 'invective' against hateful rebels such as Straw and Kett, who in Wilson's eyes represent political disorder and chaos. Into this argument a digression is inserted which praises England as a counter-image of chaos, a place of order and model for other nations, which brings to mind Mulcaster's proud assertions. The explanation and illustration of a rhetorical figure is here used again to make a political statement, in this case a laudatory remark on England.

The concept of rhetoric on which *The Art of Rhetoric* is based can be related to Wilson's political convictions, but we should not forget that Wilson was a humanist and that his understanding of eloquence is, at least in his early works up to *The Art of Rhetoric*, indebted to classical authors, notably Cicero and Quintilian. From these he borrowed, as Plett says (2004: 419), the concept of 'the unity of ethical and rhetorical perfection' as the origin of human civilization, and a morally based understanding of the orator as a *vir bonus dicendi peritus* ('a good man being capable of speaking'). Accordingly, Wilson paraphrases in the Preface to *The Art* the *locus classicus* of this concept, the first chapter of Cicero's early rhetorical work *De inventione*:

> And althoughe at firste, the rude coulde hardelye learne, and either for straungenes of the thing, would not gladlie receive the offer, or ells for lacke of knowledg could not perceive the

goodnes: yet being some what drawen and delighted with the pleasauntnes of reason, and the swetenes of utteraunce: after a certaine space, they became throughe nurture and good advisement, of wilde, sober: of cruel, gentle: of foles, wise: and of beastes, men: Soche force hathe the tongue and soche is the power of eloquence and reason, that most men are forced even to yelde in that, whiche most standeth againste their will. (A2ᵛ)

This passage shows that reason must be combined with rhetoric to turn men into social beings. It is the unity of *sapientia* and *eloquentia* which engenders social harmony. Using Wilson's term, Plett calls this type of eloquence 'the rhetoric of "good order"', a characterization which requires clarification with regard to Wilson. Basically the kind of rhetoric referred to in *The Art of Rhetoric* is determined by its affective power, a power to move people which is stronger than that of military force, 'with a woorde to win Citees, and whole Countries', as Wilson says in the dedicatory epistle. The idea of avoiding 'bloodshed' which here emerges may have a humanist ring, it is true, but Wilson's hyperbolic formulation 'without bloodshed achive to a conqueste' seems problematic. In yoking together discrepant notions it is less a paradox than a contradiction in terms. The statement following in the epistle that an orator may cause a crowd to be 'ravished and drawen, whiche waie him liketh beste to have theim' (A2ᵛ), i.e. to move them against their wills, comes disquietingly close to demagoguery. It implies a dominance of the affective function (*pathos*) over reason (*logos*) and ethics (*ethos*), which seems to be at variance with humanism.

But we must be careful, for the word 'reason' appears significantly in Wilson's commentary on a mythological representation of this affective type of rhetoric in the Preface to *The Art*, the image of the Gallic Hercules (Figure 18.1), an old man who has lost his physical strength, but, leading men whose ears are chained to his mouth, achieves the greatest triumph through the gift of eloquence:

Hercules being a man of greate wisedome, had all men lincked together by the eares in a chaine, to draw them and leade them even as he lusted. For his witte was so greate, his tongue so eloquent, and his experience soch, that no one man was able to withstande his reason, but every one was rather driven to do that whiche he woulde, and to will that whiche he did: agreyng to his advise bothe in word & worke, in all that ever they were able.

Neither can I see that menne coulde have been brought, by anye other meanes to lyve together in fellowshyppe of life, to mayntayne Cities, to deale trulye, and willyngelye to obeye one an other, if menne at the firste had not by Arte and eloquence perswaded that, which they ful oft found out by reason. (A2ᵛ–A3ʳ)

There is again a certain contradiction to be noticed. Reason is almost forced into Hercules' hearers by the power of rhetoric. The addressees of his eloquence appear as a kind of rhetorical chain gang with no choice but to listen and accept the wisdom which the orator instils into them. Wilson believes that persuasion must be applied analogous to physical force to make people law-abiding citizens. Rhetoric is here actually conceived as 'an instrument of control' (Shrank 2004b: 195) meant 'to perswad with reason, all men to societye' (Wilson 1560: A2ᵛ). The people who are in need of rhetorical competence and for whom Wilson wrote his book are those who 'beare

Fig. 18.1 The Gallic Hercules draws behind him a crowd of listeners, chained by the ears by his eloquence. Aulus Gellius, *Noctium Atticarum libri* (1519), title page.

rule over many, or must have to doe with matters of Realme'—the governing elite of the country.

Wilson's presentation of rhetoric, its system, principles, and prescriptions, is pervaded by more or less explicit references to a view of society based on order, hierarchy, and obedience. A characteristic example of his integration of political philosophy into the teaching of rhetoric is to be found in a passage which explains 'disposition and apt ordering of things':

And now, next and immediatly after invention, I thinke meete to speake of framyng, and placyng an Oration in order, that the matter beeyng aptely satelde [settled], and couched together: might better please the hearers, and with more ease be learned of al men. And the rather I am earnest in this behaulfe, because I knowe that al thinges stande by order, and without order nothyng can be. For by an order we are borne, by an order wee lyve, and by an order wee make our end. By an order one ruleth as head, and other obey as members. By an order Realmes stande, and lawes take force.   (80^r)

Disposition in rhetoric is, by the author who is 'earnest in this behaulfe', related to order as a fundamental principle ruling life, society, and the whole world. As to society, its hierarchical structure is in this passage emphasized by the traditional metaphor of the body politic, with the 'head' ruling the 'members'.

An aspect which cannot be passed over is that Wilson's concept of order also makes a distinction in rank between man and woman. Order understood in a narrower sense—as a rhetorical figure concerning the arrangement of the parts of a sequence in a semantically ascending or descending scale—is illustrated by the following example: 'the one [sort of order] is, when the worthier is preferred, and set before. As a man is sette before a woman' (106^r). Immediately after the above-quoted passage in which Wilson articulates the idea of London as a place of exemplary civility, where 'the menne' are 'for the moste parte more wise', he makes a distinction between the sexes strongly in disfavour of the female sex: 'To bee borne a manchilde, declares a courage, gravitie, and constancie. To be borne a woman, declares weakenes of spirite, neshenes [softness] of body, and fickilnesse of mynde' (7^r). Women are excluded from the sphere of the male elite, which needs the knowledge and competence of rhetoric to rule the country and manage the state.

Whether the type of rhetoric required in the political context envisioned in *The Art of Rhetoric* can justly be called a 'rhetoric of *good* order' remains questionable. Of the three aims of rhetoric—moving (*pathos*), teaching (*logos*), appeal to moral sense (*ethos*)—the text is almost silent with regard to the latter function. It is interesting that, referring to Cicero's *De oratore*, Wilson replaces this traditional triad by that of 'To teache. To delight. And to perswade' (I^v; see Cicero 1951: 2. 28. 121). Wilson has no vision of an all-embracing common good for society. In this context it is symptomatic that the above-mentioned ideal of the rhetor as a good man (*vir bonus*) almost seems a *corpus alienum* in his text. It is perfunctorily referred to in the rather abrupt ending of the book: 'the good will not speake evill: and the wicked can not speake well' (113^r). Wilson seems to have 'a divided mind on the issue of the ethical justification of his subject' (Derrick 1982, p. lxxii). However authoritarian

Wilson's political attitude seems and actually is, one should hesitate to put his *Art of Rhetoric* together with the homilies into the category of contemporary 'obedience literature' and impute to it a law-and-order ideology. For such a characterization the work is on the whole influenced too much by humanism and shows a free wit and a strong sense of humour which transcend narrow-minded political orthodoxy.

One may finally ask in which way Wilson's *Art of Rhetoric* is innovative as far as the theory and system of rhetoric is concerned. Its organization is traditional in that after a general discussion of the principles, methods, and aims of rhetoric it deals with the five parts of the process of composition, invention, disposition, style, memory, and delivery. The treatment of invention is remarkably innovative for the sixteenth century. This holds true in particular for the discussion of the methods of finding arguments (topics) which Wilson tends to relate to the oration as a whole, and to the extensive examination of the role of amplification and humour in relation to invention. His discussion of elocution (style) is less extensive, but it abounds with good examples frequently of his own making and not simply taken from Cicero or Quintilian. Elocution receives due praise as the *officium* which gives shape to the intellectual content of a speech. It is elocution which makes the orator 'compt halfe a God among men' (82^r). In Wilson's concept of rhetoric, *res* and *verba*, matter and style, form an inseparable unity, as distinct from the Ramist theory of Pierre de La Ramée and Omer Talon, which separates invention and disposition from rhetoric, assigning the former two disciplines to logic–dialectic and reducing the latter—rhetoric—to style, delivery, and memory. Peter Medine, who finds 'the most significant of Wilson's innovations' in his treatment of invention, emphasizes that, unlike traditional discussions of invention, *The Art of Rhetoric* refers to judicial *and* deliberative and demonstrative rhetoric and to the sermon in the part dealing with invention. This is true, but on the whole 'legal issues and instances dominate Wilson's work' (Medine 1994: 15). Thus, demonstrative rhetoric is illustrated by an oration 'in commendacion of Justice' (12^r), towards whose end the authority of the king and of justice are related: 'What maketh wicked men (which els would not) acknowledge the King as their soverein lorde, but the power of a lawe, and the practise of justice for evill doers?' (14^r). This is again an instance of Wilson's characteristic technique of using examples and illustrations of rhetorical forms and devices to express his rather authoritarian political convictions.

The second text to be examined, *The Art of Poesy* (1589), published anonymously but ascribed to George Puttenham by scholarly assent, is a courtly poetics and a conduct book designed to enable the English courtier, who is conceived as a *poeta orator*, to stand his ground at the court as an ambience with various social forces at work and a strict code of conduct.[1] It is his intention 'to make this Art [poesie] vulgar for all English mens use' (19), and, more specifically, to teach 'Ladies and young Gentlewomen, or idle Courtiers, desirous to become skilful in their owne mother tongue [...] *beau* semblant, the chiefe profession as well of Courting as of

---

[1] The following discussion is indebted to Plett (2004: 164–73).

poesie' (132). The book is dedicated to Queen Elizabeth—'tending to the most worthy prayses of her Majesties most excellent name' (2)—and the frontispiece shows her portrait with the *imprese* 'A colei Che se stessa rassomiglia, & non altrui' ('For the one who cannot be compared to others'). This double homage exemplifies Puttenham's ideal of courtly discourse, which privileges the epideictic–demonstrative genre. The shift from the judicial genre to the epideictic one is here fully realized. In accordance with the dominance of epideictic rhetoric in his conception of eloquence—'the Poets being in deede the trumpetters of all praise and also of slaunder' (28)—Puttenham's innovative classification of the literary genres, which makes an important part of his book, uses praise and blame as defining criteria. The political significance of epideictic rhetoric is revealed at the end of the book, when Puttenham renews his praise of the Queen, asking for preferment: 'I presume so much upon your Majesties most milde and gracious judgement howsoever you conceive of myne abilitie to any better or greater service' (258). The reference in this context to 'these great aspiring mynds and ambitious heads of the world seriously searching to deale in matters of state' (258; see Whigham 1984) gives us a glimpse of the court as a world of patronage, rivalry, and ambition.

Before looking at details of Puttenham's poetics, it is necessary to place his work in the above-mentioned context of the vernacularization which took place in England in the course of the sixteenth century. In the third part of *The Art of English Poesy*, which deals with 'Ornament', there is a chapter on language, which describes the genesis of a national language: 'But after a speach is fully fashioned to the common understanding, & accepted by the consent of a whole countrey & nation, it is called a language.' The language in which 'our maker or Poet' ought to write is to be 'naturall, pure, and the most usuall of all his countrey'. He rejects, among other things, the language of the 'Universities where Schollers use much peevish affectation of words' and the language of 'poore rusticall or uncivill people' in remote regions (120). He admits that the language north of the Trent is 'the purer English Saxon at this day, yet it is not so Courtly nor so currant as our Southerne English'. The poet's yardstick is thus to be 'the usual speach of the Court, and that of London and the shires lying about London within lx. myles, and not much above' (121). Wilson's plea for a norm or standard of English is here reiterated, albeit with greater regard to the court as the centre of the country's culture. Standardization seems to have progressed considerably since Wilson's time, as Puttenham refers to the fact that 'we are already ruled by th'English Dictionaries and other bookes written by learned men'. Yet he follows his forerunner in warning 'our maker' against 'inkhorne termes so ill affected brought in by men of learning as preachers and schoolemasters' (145). He draws up, though, a long list of 'usurped Latine and French words' which he would not like to miss (147).

Puttenham not only proposes a standard language as the basis for the endeavours of English poets; he also seems to be aware that there is something like an English national literature. In the first book of his poetics, 'Of Poets and Poesy', there is a chapter entitled 'The Most Commended Writers in our English Poesie', which is in fact a little history of English literature from Chaucer to the present. Puttenham is grateful to authors who 'so much beautified our English tong [...] as at this day it will be found our nation is in nothing inferiour to the French or Italian for copie [richness] of language, subtiltie of device, good method and proportion in any forme of poeme'. Praise is given to Chaucer, and also to Thomas Wyatt and Henry Howard, Earl of Surrey—who 'greatly pollished our rude & homely maner of vulgar Poesie' (48) as 'the two chief lanternes of light to all others that have since employed their pennes upon English Poesie' (50)—and to contemporary poets who excelled in various genres such as tragedy, comedy, interludes, eclogues, and elegies. *The Art of English Poesy* evinces a consciousness that English poetry had found its identity among its Continental neighbours and that it had had after 'rude' and 'homely' beginnings a triumphant history. Puttenham's pride can be related to Richard Carew's *The Excellency of the English Tongue* (*c*. 1596), which glories in the fact that English poets match or surpass their classical precursors: 'Will yow reade Virgill? take the *Earll of Surrey*: Catullus? *Shakespheare*, and *Marlowes* fragment: *Ovid? Daniell: Lucane? Spencer: Martiall?* Sir *John Davis* and others. Will yow have all in all for prose and verse? Take the miracle of our age Sir *Philip Sidney*' (293).

It is curious that Puttenham should at the end of his survey of English poets praise 'the Queene our soveraigne Lady, whose learned, delicate, noble Muse, easily surmounteth all the rest that have written before her time or since, for sence, sweetnesse and subtillitie, be it in Ode, Elegie, Epigram, or any other kinde of poeme Heroick or Lyricke'. There is no historical evidence that Elizabeth actually wrote poetry and in doing so exceeded 'all the rest of her most humble vassals' (63). It is, though, hardly plausible that Puttenham is here deliberately lying. The truth may be that his strong predilection for the epideictic led him into creating a fiction. Psychologically this may be understood as a projection: the Queen is the centre of the court, the incarnation of courtly culture, so it may come natural to Puttenham to idealize her as union of sovereign and poet. In Puttenham's text there emerges the ideal of a statesman–poet, when he speaks of 'poets who have skill not only in the subtilties of their arte', but also in 'all maner of functions civill and martiall' (13). Of '*Julius Caesar* the first Emperour' he says that he 'was not onely the most eloquent Orator of his time, but also a very good Poet, though none of his doings therein be now extant' (13).

Another aspect of the vernacularization is Puttenham's attempt to find English equivalents for classical terms. In doing so, he refers to precursors like 'Master Secretary *Wilson*', who gave logic the name '*Witcraft*' (191). His procedure is unique in that it reveals the socio-aesthetic basis of his theory of style. In his translation of Greek and Latin names of figures and particularly tropes he tends to use *nomina agentis*, which refer to social role behaviour. Thus, he calls hyperbole 'the Over reacher' or 'loud lyer' (159), *sententia* 'the Sage sayer' (197), *liptote* 'the Moderatour' (153), meiosis 'the Disabler', and *tapinosis* 'the Abbaser' (154). The most conspicuous name is given to allegory, the trope to which he accords the highest rank in his courtly poetics, 'the Courtier or figure of faire semblant' (251). Rhetoric and the courtier are by this translation identified. The social dynamics of courtly life are here seen to infiltrate the very nomenclature of rhetorical devices, which elsewhere tend to look abstract and bloodless.

The Art of English Poesy consists of three parts: Part 1 ('Of Poets and Poesy') is a general discussion of the name and nature of the poet and poetry and of the genres and history of poetry, including a survey of English literature. Part 2 ('Of Proportion Poetical') deals with prosody, particularly with the *carmen figuratum* ('pattern poem') and the emblem. Part 3 ('Of Ornament') treats 'Ornament Poeticall' on the basis of elocution and thus shows the connection of Puttenham's poetics with rhetoric. The rhetorical conception of his work concerns its very substance. For Puttenham poetry is a higher form of rhetorical eloquence, a 'form of super-rhetoric', as Brian Vickers calls it (1983: 418), a *rhétorique seconde* in the words of French poets of the time. Poetry is distinguished by an incomparable persuasiveness which surpasses even that of rhetoric: 'So as the Poets were also from the beginning the best perswaders and their eloquence the first Rethoricke of the world' (6). This statement implies a genetic connection between rhetoric and poetry, which is also expressed by William Webbe, who says that 'Poetry' and 'Rhetoricall *Eloquution*' are 'by byrth Twyns' (1904: 228). Puttenham also takes up the problem of the relative persuasiveness of prose and verse. More strongly than other Renaissance authors does he argue that 'speech by meeter' is

more eloquent and rhetoricall then ordinarie prose [...] because it is decked and set out with all maner of fresh colours and figures, which maketh that it sooner invegleth the judgement of man, and carieth his opinion this way and that, whither soever the hearte by impression of the eare shalbe most affectionatly bent and directed.   (5)

A literary analogue is the forum scene in Shakespeare's *Julius Caesar*, in which the verse of Antony triumphs over the prose of Brutus.

The decisive criterion in Puttenham's discussion of figures and tropes is their capacity to move men, to elicit emotional response. According to him, it is the use of figures and tropes which creates the greatest effect. That is why in his treatment of ornament he inserts a digression referring to conspicuous examples of the power of rhetoric, for instance the story of the orator Hegesias, 'who inveyed so much against the incommodities of this transitory life & so highly commended death the dispatcher all evils' that 'a great number of his hearers destroyed themselves' (118). He also refers to the Gallic Hercules as an outstanding example of forceful persuasion, but as distinct from Wilson he is aware of the danger of such rhetoric. With this emphasis on the criterion of effect Puttenham's poetics can be related to other poetological writings of the Renaissance, for instance to Sir Philip Sidney's *An Apology for Poetry* (written *c*. 1580), which applies the triad of *docere*, *delectare*, and *movere* to poetry and thus equates, as far as effect is concerned, rhetoric and poetry. Sidney argues that poetry is in this respect superior to all other disciplines: 'Nowe therein of all Sciences [...] is our Poet the Monarch. For he dooth not only show the way [*docere*], but giveth so sweete a prospect into the way [*delectare*], as will intice any man to enter into it [*movere*]' (Sidney 1595: 172).

Sidney here stands in a tradition of Renaissance poetics, which is most concisely expressed in Minturno's demand to the tragedian that he should prove, entertain, and move: 'ut probet, ut delectet, ut moveat' (Minturno 1970: 179–80). This formulation, derived from Cicero's 'ut probet, ut delectet, ut flectat', which, as we have seen, also influenced Wilson's *Art of Rhetoric*. As far as Sidney is concerned, 'mooving is of a higher degree then teaching' (171). As to the high position of the aim of moving (*movere*), Sidney's understanding of poetic persuasion accords with the great importance of the appeal to the emotions in Wilson's *Rhetoric* and in Puttenham's *Arte*. If we are dealing with rhetoric as a shaping force in Renaissance poetry, we have to be aware of the fact that theorists and poets of the period believed that poetry has *sui generis* an eminently rhetorical character. The rhetorical concept of poetry emerges most clearly in the rhetorical–allegorical interpretations of the myth of Orpheus, which follow the example of Horace's *Ars poetica* (5. 391–3). Thus, in *The Garden of Eloquence* (1593), Henry Peacham interprets the passage from Horace in such a way that the tigers and lions which Orpheus charmed with his song have to be understood as primitive, barbarous men who had become through the power of wise eloquence civilized humans: 'which notwithstanding by the mightie power of wisdome, and prudent art of perswasion were converted from that most brutish condition of life, to the love of humanitie & pollitique government' (AB3ᵛ (sic); for the rhetorical interpretation of Orpheus, see Plett 2004: 396–410). Peacham interprets the 'poet' as an 'orator'. The characteristic union of poet and orator, the ideal of the *poeta–orator*, appears in Peacham in a humanist context, while in Puttenham it is adapted to the conditions of courtly culture.

Puttenham's theory of style, undoubtedly the most original part of his poetics, proceeds from language to style, and ornament. Language as the poet's material is, as discussed above, the standard of London and the court. Style belongs to a higher level. It is the habitual use of oral and written speech—'a constant & continuall phrase or tenour of speaking and writing' (123)—which reveals a man's individual character, the 'matter and disposition of the writers minde'. The definition of style as 'the image of man (*mentis character*)' (124) belongs to a rich and ancient tradition, and it is important to realize that this time-honoured concept of style as an image of man is in Puttenham related not to poetic discourse, but to everyday language (see Müller 1981: 136). It postulates a general analogy between style and a man's disposition: 'For if the man be grave, his speech and stile is grave: if light-headed, his stile and language also light' (124). From this individualistic concept of style Puttenham soon proceeds to a normative position, which defines style with regard to the nature of the subject, that is, as a matter of *aptum* or *decorum*: 'But generally to have the stile decent & comely it behooveth the maker or Poet to follow the nature of his subject' (124).

Compared to style, which Puttenham understands as non-poetic, a man's individual manner of speaking and writing, ornament is in his theory situated on a higher linguistic level. It is 'the good or rather bewtifull habite of language and stile' (119). He distinguishes between two kinds of ornament in terms of their effect, 'one to satisfie & delight the'eare onely by a goodly outward shew set upon the matter with wordes', the other characterized 'by certaine intendments or sence of such wordes & and speaches inwardly working a stirre to the mynde' (119). To the first type he applies the Greek term *enargeia*, to the second the term *energeia* (see Plett 2004: 195–6). By *enargia* he means the outward decoration of the text which produces aesthetic pleasure and by *energeia* the effect words have on the mind. Accordingly, his classification of rhetorical figures observes primarily their sensuous and emotional effect. His approach is innovative in that he classifies the figures 'according to receptive rather than formal criteria' (Plett 2004: 196). Figures are categorized with respect to their appeal to the ear, the intellect, or both: 'auricular figures', 'sensable figures', 'sententious figures' (133–4). Expressions such as 'pleasant and agreable to the eare' (134) indicate that the language of poetry is regarded as a source of aesthetic sensualism. This holds true also for Puttenham's description of prosody in the second part, where the visual dimension is added to the auditory in the discussion of pattern poems and emblems.

The socio-aesthetic basis of Puttenham's concept of ornament is shown in the application of the metaphor of dress to style. In a long passage he argues that just as 'these great Madames of honour' gain acceptable beauty only by their 'courtly habillements', so can poetry 'shew it selfe either gallant or gorgious' only by 'ornament', i.e. by 'figures and figurative speaches, which be the flowers as it were and colours that a Poet setteth upon his language by arte, as the embroderer doth his stone and perle, or passements of gold upon the stuffe of a Princely garment' (114–15). He understands his poetics as a 'science', which 'teacheth *beau* semblant, the chiefe profession aswell of Courting as of poesie' (132). In connection with the discussion of the tropes, the idea of dissimulation, the concealment of the proper term, emerges constantly. Thus, Puttenham characterizes allegory as 'a duplicitie of meaning or dissimulation under covert and darke intendments' (128) or elsewhere as 'the figure of [*false semblant*, or dissimulation]' (155). Of periphrasis he says that it holds 'somewhat of the dissembler' (161).

The idea that figures of speech, especially tropes, have a dissimulatory character is linked to Puttenham's concept of *dissimulatio artis*, the concealment of art, which in turn can be related to *l'artifice caché* of the Pléiade poets in France and to Castiglione's concept of *sprezzatura*, i.e. the capacity to make art appear as the result of unstudied grace (see Javitch 1978). Puttenham is aware of the ambiguity of the concept of dissimulation, the fact that *beau semblant* and *false semblant*—both terms are applied to allegory and to the conduct of the courtier in general—cannot always be separated strictly. That is why he says that 'we allow our Courtly Poet to be a dissembler only in the subtilties of his arte' (253). The danger for the courtier to degenerate into a hypocrite and the court to be invaded by Machiavellianism is ever-present.

To conclude, Wilson's *Art of Rhetoric* and Puttenham's *Art of English Poesy* are landmarks in the development of English from a language which in the first decades of the sixteenth century many humanists felt to be rude and limited in its resources to one which was capable of sustaining a literary and intellectual culture. In adapting Ciceronian oratory to the conditions of Reformation England, Wilson creates a rhetoric for the English as a significant contribution to the growth of national identity. Wilson's 'rhetoric of order' articulates its rather authoritarian political position explicitly in the paratext (dedicatory epistle, Prologue to the Reader, Preface) and interwoven in the teaching of rhetoric in the main text. While Wilson provides rhetorical instruction for the practical needs mainly of the ruling male elite, it is Puttenham's intention to make poetry 'vulgar for all English mens use' and, more specifically, to teach ladies and courtiers the art of poetic eloquence. He makes available to English poets a classification of literary genres which they could cultivate and instructs them in questions of metre and particularly in the use of stylistic ornament which for him is the heart of courtly discourse. It is significant that at a time when the English language was coming into its own and English literature was ready to rise to unmatched eminence, Wilson and Puttenham should publish ground-breaking handbooks on eloquence in rhetorical and poetic discourse.

Primary Works

CAREW, RICHARD (1904), *The Excellency of the English Tongue*, in G. Gregory Smith (ed.), *Elizabethan Critical Essays* (London: Oxford University Press).

CHEKE, JOHN (1994), 'Letter to Thomas Hoby', in Baldassare Castiglione, *The Book of the Courtier*, trans. Sir Thomas Hoby, ed. Virginia Cox (London: Dent; Rutland, VT: Tuttle), 10–11.

CICERO (1951), *Ciceronis De oratore libri tres* (Hildesheim: Olms).

MINTURNO, A. S. (1970), *De poeta* (Munich: Fink).

MULCASTER, RICHARD (1582), *The First Part of the Elementarie*.

PEACHAM, HENRY (1593), *The Garden of Eloquence*, 2nd edn.

PUTTENHAM, GEORGE (1936), *The Arte of English Poesie*, ed. Gladys Doidge Willcock and Alice Walker (Cambridge: Cambridge University Press).

SHAKESPEARE, WILLIAM (1968), *The First Folio of Shakespeare*, ed. Charlton Hinman (London: Hamlyn).

SHERRY, RICHARD (1550), *A Treatise of Schemes and Tropes*.

SIDNEY, PHILIP (1595), *An Apologie for Poetrie*.

SKELTON, JOHN (1983), *Phyllyp Sparowe*, in *The Complete English Poems*, ed. John Scattergood (Harmondsworth: Penguin).

WEBBE, WILLIAM (1904), *A Discourse of English Poetry*, in G. Gregory Smith (ed.), *Elizabethan Critical Essays* (London: Oxford University Press).

WILSON, THOMAS (1560), *The Arte of Rhetorique*.

WYATT, THOMAS (1969), *The Quyete of Mynde*, in *Collected Poems*, ed. Kenneth Muir and Patricia Thomson (Liverpool: Liverpool University Press).

CHAPTER 19

ORDER AND DISORDER

JOHN PROCTOR'S *HISTORY OF WYATT'S REBELLION* (1554)

ALAN BRYSON

THE reign of Mary I crystallized debates about whether or not it could ever be justified to overthrow a monarch. This chapter examines John Proctor's literary response to conspiracies and uprisings against the Queen, *The History of Wyatt's Rebellion* (1554). That book comprises a chronicle–history and two anti-sedition tracts and is a detailed condemnation of the rebellion of Sir Thomas Wyatt the younger in 1554, showing how it was bound to fail (as insurrections always do) and contrasting his disobedience and the disorder it creates with Mary's good government. It is part of the mid-Tudor reaction to rebellion epitomized by the flurry of obedience tracts produced during crisis years for the English polity (1536, 1549, and 1569).[1]

I am grateful to Sylvia Adamson, Tom Charlton, Liz Evenden, Tom Freeman, Ian Gadd, Steve Gunn, John Guy, Beverley Matthews, Steve May, Tony Moore, Mike Pincombe, Alec Ryrie, Fred Schurink, Cathy Shrank, and Tracey Sowerby for their helpful advice.

[1] For example, see Richard Morison, *A Lamentation in which is Showed what Ruin and Destruction Cometh of Seditious Rebellion* (1536), *A Remedy for Sedition* (1536), *An Invective against Treason* (1539); John Cheke, *The Hurt of Sedition* (1549, 1569); Thomas Norton, *To the Queen's Majesty's Poor Deceived Subjects* (1569), *A Warning against the Dangerous Practises of Papists* (1569).

With its use of 'original' documents, *Wyatt's Rebellion* gestures towards the growing influence of antiquarianism on Tudor history-writing. John Bale, Edward Hall, Richard Grafton, and above all John Foxe made use of documentary evidence to authenticate their accounts of fifteenth- and early sixteenth-century England and of the Protestant martyrs; Proctor responded in kind for the Marian Counter-Reformation (Freeman and Wall 2001; Betteridge 1999). *Wyatt's Rebellion*—like Bale's *Latter Examination of Anne Askew* (1547) and its expanded reprints, Hall and Grafton's *Union of the Two Noble and Illustrate Families of Lancaster and York* (1548), and the various editions of Foxe's *Acts and Monuments* (1563–83)—consolidated a new approach to history-writing in the closing decades of the chronicle tradition. Chronicles record events and facts in order, often failing to discriminate over how important or relevant these are. The new history-writing, on the other hand, focused on interpreting significant cultural, political, and religious changes, shaping them into a narrative (and often an argument). The overlap between these two genres during the mid-sixteenth century makes it possible to compare and contrast how Proctor and the chroniclers gather and shape their material. In Proctor's case, documentary evidence and eyewitness status reinforces the truthfulness of his version of what occurred.

The final, related, themes examined here are ones that prompted *Wyatt's Rebellion* in the first place: loyalty and obedience. This chapter looks at Proctor's role as historian; and his use of the recent past in the service of the Counter-Reformation in his first and last books. We begin with his background and education, studying how these shaped his early development as a Counter-Reformation writer and thinker in his first polemical work, *The Fall of the Late Arian* (1549).

Aged 16 years and 9 months, John Proctor (1520–58) matriculated at Corpus Christi College, Oxford, in January 1537. He was admitted BA on 20 October 1540, elected Fellow of All Souls College that year, and proceeded MA on 9 February 1545. At some point he was canon and prebendary of King Henry VIII College (Christ Church), alongside John Cheke and John Leland, and probably lived off his pension of £26 13s. 4d. after its dissolution in 1545. In 1547 he vacated his fellowship (Bindoff 1982: iii. 159–60; Emden 1974; *LP* xxi/1. 643, fo. 24). Mid-Tudor Oxford was more conservative in religion than Cambridge, and Corpus Christi—under its President, John Morwen—was no exception (Reginald Pole was a student there in the 1520s and the conservative theologian Dr Richard Smyth was a Fellow at Merton College, next door). Morwen and other college fellows were sent to the Fleet Prison in June 1551 on suspicion of observing Corpus Christi Day ceremonies (banned under the 1547 royal injunctions); and in 1556 Morwen was appointed to the legatine visitation of the university charged by Pole with enforcing the Counter-Reformation. All Souls was perhaps different: its Protestant Warden, John Warner, was deprived under Mary. However, Proctor's education was shaped fundamentally by his time at Corpus Christi, then a centre for English humanism with one of Oxford's best libraries of Latin, Greek, and Hebrew books. Therefore, he was very much part of Cheke and Leland's intellectual world but shared little of their enthusiastic Protestantism (Fowler 1893: 79–102; McConica 1986).

Nothing is heard of Proctor again until he became rector of Old Romney in Kent on 6 July 1549. His first book, *The Fall of the Late Arian*, was printed on 9 December. It was written against 'this oure late Arrian', who had recently 'denyed Christ devinitie and equalitie [...] with God the father' (D5^r), for which he was brought before the Privy Council.[2] Taking the form of a dialogue between Proctor and the 'Arian', the book refutes the latter's heretical opinions line by line, and is dedicated to Princess Mary, comparing her to the Virgin Mary. Although not named, the 'Arian' was probably the priest John Ashton, who was tried for heresy by Thomas Cranmer, Archbishop of Canterbury, late in 1548 (MacCulloch 1999: 116–18 n. 30; Ryrie forthcoming). As he would do later in *Wyatt's Rebellion*, Proctor strengthens his argument by foregrounding his role as a witness. Ashton's depositions 'came into divers mens handes' (D5^v), including one of Proctor's friends, who asked what he thought of them. Proctor felt 'that so blasphemous & perilous opinion shuld be confuted by some man, and that with speedye expedicion', especially because people were too readily swayed by newfangled ideas and might be taken in by this Arianism. These depositions form the basis of Ashton's parts within the dialogue, although—lacking the originals—we cannot now tell whether Proctor reshaped them to fit his own didactic purpose.

The Fall is also a sly critique of the Protestant reformation, particularly through its equation of Arianism, Anabaptism, and other heresies with the new Church of England. How had Proctor managed to get it printed? In mid-August 1549 'an ordre was taken that from hensforth no prenter sholde prente or putt to vente any Englisshe booke butt suche as sholde first be examined by' Sir William Petre, Sir Thomas Smith, and William Cecil. This latest effort at print regulation in England should have made the content of *The Fall* subject to censorship (*APC* 1890–1964: ii. 311–12; Gadd 2008). However, following the October coup against Edward, Duke of Somerset, the religious direction of the realm was uncertain, giving Proctor his opportunity. While he attacks Somerset for his arrogance and ungodliness, and the political and social instability he created, he praises the men who had toppled him and implies that he expects a change in religious policy (Bryson 2001: 166–74). He is also ambivalent about the Church of Rome, describing how the English had been 'bewytched, by that Romysh man, the pevysh Pope' (B2^v), who had usurped ecclesiastical authority in the realm. This is remarkable, considering Proctor's place in the canon of English Counter-Reformation writers. There was a range of opinion among mid-Tudor Catholics, however Proctor 'was not a simple Catholic apologist'. Alec Ryrie (forthcoming) describes him during Edward VI's reign as a 'latter-day Henrician', who feared that the Reformation was now spinning out of control. Proctor attacks the mechanical and unthinking nature of pre-Reformation Catholicism but finds new, Protestant innovations even more distasteful. While he agrees that the Bible should be available for all to read, many people do so only to find justification for their own misinterpretations. 'Forget not that it is a hygher matter then the booke of Robynhoode' (C4^v), he admonishes, because misreadings lead to heresy and schism.

---

[2] Arius (d. 336) did not believe in the Trinity of God the Father, Son, and Holy Ghost.

The Fall employs the idiom then current among such Protestant and commonweal writers as Robert Crowley and Luke Shepherd, expressing similar concerns about inequality, high fines, increased rents, and lack of charity and hospitality among the gentry (Betteridge 2004: 87–129). Here we see that style (in this case documentary) and even voice (commonweal writing) are not necessarily drawn up along confessional lines; this is also true of *Wyatt's Rebellion*, particularly regarding use of evidence to 'prove' the veracity of the author's politics and Catholic faith. In *The Fall*, he perhaps first borrows these commonweal clothes in order to get printed. *The Fall* also demonstrates Proctor's learning, especially his grasp of the Bible, Church Fathers, classical writers, ancient history, and mythology. His frequent quotations in Latin from all these sources is interesting because he almost always takes care to translate them plainly but elegantly into English for the benefit of the majority of his readers, who presumably were expected to know only the vernacular. This makes sense because one of his stated aims was to instruct his countrymen in the dangers of heresy through explication from the Bible, something he did out of a sense of patriotic duty. The ability to quote and translate the Bible was, of course, also vital to Proctor's claims to theological expertise. *The Fall* is long and at first stilted, but grows in confidence and fluency as the dialogue unfolds, foreshadowing *Wyatt's Rebellion* in ambition and style, especially in its detail and the cleverness and complexity of its argument.

Proctor is not heard of again for several years. In May 1553 Sir Andrew Judde obtained letters patent to found a free school in his native Tonbridge in Kent, with the Skinners' Company as trustees. He wanted Latin, Greek, and Hebrew taught there and this must have been a factor in Proctor's appointment as its first Master (he certainly knew the first two languages). Another was perhaps his time as a Fellow of All Souls, which had been founded by Judde's ancestor Henry Chichele, Archbishop of Canterbury (Rivington 1925: 18–22, 94–104, 125–7; Orchard 1991: 8–11; Jordan 1961). It is unknown exactly when Proctor was appointed Master, but it was certainly by the time Wyatt's rebellion broke out because the Sheriff of Kent, Sir Robert Southwell, describes him as 'skolmaister of tunbridge' in a letter to the Privy Council on 24 February 1554 (Southwell 1554: 80^r–81^v). Work on building the school began immediately and it was complete and endowed with property worth £60 3s. 8d. a year by the time Judde died in September 1558. Judde's own religious sympathies are unknown: while he signed the letters patent for the limitation of the Crown to Lady Jane Grey on 21 June 1553, the London aldermen had been browbeaten into this by John, Duke of Northumberland, and the Privy Council; and his will opened with a fairly unambiguous Catholic soul bequest (Rivington 1925: 94; Judde 1558: 58^r). Also, he might have expected the author of *The Fall* to be unsympathetic to the Edwardian religious reforms. Tonbridge School was not a Catholic preserve, however. Protestantism had made greater inroads in Kent than almost anywhere else in England, albeit the Catholic majority managed to live peaceably with their Protestant neighbours until the Marian persecutions began.

It was at the forefront of the local Counter-Reformation, having adjusted his religious views from those expressed in *The Fall* back to Roman Catholicism, that

Proctor found himself writing in the 1550s (Clark 1977; Zell 2000; Collinson 2006; Ryrie forthcoming). His first foray was a work of Catholic piety, *The Way Home to Christ and Truth Leading from Antichrist and Error*, printed by Robert Caly on 22 October 1554. Again dedicated to Mary, it was a translation of St Vincent of Lérins's Latin *Liber de Catholicae fidei antiquitate*. Its purpose was to provide 'a perfect table' for those who stray into error and heresy, 'wherin our home is lyvelye set furth, and the waye also thither. Our home I cal the catholike church, the true spousesse of Christ, our most lovinge mother' (1554a: A3ᵛ). This subject is developed further in *Wyatt's Rebellion*.

Wyatt's Rebellion was granted a royal licence and printed in octavo in London on 22 December 1554 by Robert Caly, who had a good eye for what would sell. This was a pretty rapid response in print to the rebellion and proved sufficiently popular to be reissued by him in January 1556, but there were no subsequent editions until the end of the nineteenth century (Loach 1986a). Proctor dedicated his work to Mary, provocatively including the titles she acquired as consort to Philip of Spain, whom she had married at Winchester Cathedral on 25 July 1554 (Proctor 1554b: a2ʳ). Fear of this marriage had been one of the principal motivations for Wyatt's rebellion. The book offers three things: 'The historie of wyates rebellion, with the order and maner of resisting the same' (A1ʳ–K8ʳ); 'An earnest conference with the degenerates and seditious, for the search of the cause of their greate disorder' (L1ʳ–M3ʳ); and 'A Prosopey [Prosopopoeia] of Englande unto the degenerat Englishe' (M3ʳ–N2ʳ).

In the dedicatory epistle and the address 'To the Lovyng Reader' (a2ʳ–a8ʳ) Proctor lists his reasons for undertaking *Wyatt's Rebellion*, stating that it is a

Necessary policie of all ages, as stories do wytnes, that the flagicious enterprises for the wicked [...] with trayterous force to subvert or alter the publike state of their countries, as also the wise and vertuous policies of the good, practised to preserve the common weale, and to repell the enemies of the same, shuld by writing be committed to eternal memorye.   (a2ʳ⁻ᵛ)

His aim was partly to remind England of the consequences had Wyatt's rebellion succeeded, but mainly to confront the traitors with the enormity of what they had done. It was also a warning to future rebels of the futility of their actions, as all sedition is bound to fail.

On-site in Kent as it unfolded, Proctor gathered information about the rebellion, which he deemed 'litle inferior to the most daungerous reported in any historie, either for desperate courage of the authour, or for the monstruous end purposed by [him]' (a3ᵛ), namely regicide. He conducted an 'earnest and diligent investigation' at this time and in the immediate aftermath, with the intention of recording these events for posterity rather than of publishing them himself (a4ʳ). However, inaccurate accounts of the rebellion were circulating widely, 'facioned from the speakers to advaunce or deprave as they fantased the partes'—that is, purportedly factual versions of what happened that were actually not based on evidence or eyewitness testimony. These were giving Kent a bad name, with people saying that the whole county supported Wyatt. Many 'to mine owne knowledge' (a4ʳ) proved loyal. Key facts 'either of hast or of purpose were omitted in a printed booke late sette furth at Canterbury' (a4ᵛ).

As with *The Fall*, Proctor now felt compelled to put his own work into print for truth's sake.

Scholars have wondered what this 'printed booke' that Proctor criticized could be, their interest sparked in part because few works were published outside London during the sixteenth century. It was not until the 1960s that it was identified as an anonymous continuation of the *Breviat Chronicle* issued before 25 March 1554 by John Mitchell (Wiatt 1962). The rapidity with which this short account came out seemed to justify Proctor's charge that it was inaccurate, populist, and slight, but it is testament to the immediate local and national interest and anxiety that Wyatt's rebellion sparked. Also, the *Breviat Chronicle* continuation contains information not present in *Wyatt's Rebellion* and the two works agree on most of the facts, for example that Wyatt rebelled because he was a heretic.

'The safe & sure recordation of paynes and peryls past, hath present delectacion (sayeth Tullye),' notes Proctor (1554b: a6ʳ). To set the facts straight, but also to entertain, Proctor 'contrive[d] the late rebellion practised by Wyat, in forme of a chronicle' (a6ʳ⁻ᵛ) and got it printed. Chronicle as a genre presents exemplars of loyalty and perfidy, virtue and vice: Proctor did likewise by recounting the activities of the loyal nobility, gentry, and commons of Kent and of the rebels, including illustrating the latter's fate. Readers should emulate the virtuous behaviour of his heroes, while Wyatt should act as a warning. The author claims to be a dispassionate chronicler, who feels no malice towards the rebels and faithfully notes their actions and words, ascribing motives to them based on understanding their aims and characters. Wyatt, 'although he was [initially]utterly unknowen unto me, yet for the sundrie and singular giftes, wherwith he was largelye endued, I had him in great admiration' (a7ᵛ). However, these virtues 'were abused in the service of cursed heresie'. Proctor considers himself beyond reproach in terms of how he handles his subject matter or the content of his book, 'the one havynge sufficient perspicuitie, and plaines, thother ful trueth' (a8ʳ).

Proctor was certain that the cause of Wyatt's rebellion was heresy and that this was the universal origin of all such risings, as evident from the recent histories of Bohemia and Germany with their Hussites and Lutherans. His attitude contrasts with that expressed five years previously in *The Fall*, where he praises certain Continental reformers; but this reflects changed times in religion. 'What a restlesse evil heresie is,' he comments in *Wyatt's Rebellion*: 'with what waies of craft and subteltie she dilateth her dominion, & finally howe of course she toyleth to be supported by faction, sedition & rebellion' (A1ʳ). Contemporaries believed that ruptures in the body politic were caused by faction, which was itself viewed as endemic to government and politics; although, in fact, faction was more of an aberration than the norm in Tudor England (S. Adams 2002: 13–23; Bryson forthcoming). Proctor states that Wyatt was brought up a heretic and could not stomach the accession of a Catholic, fearing renewed persecution as a result. However, Wyatt 'labored by false persuasion otherwise to have coulored it' (A1ᵛ); that is, to hide the fact that heresy was the real grounds for rebellion. This has created confusion ever since, with scholars like David Loades (1965) taking him at his word and arguing that his motivation was fear of Habsburg dominion rather than of revived Catholicism. Malcolm Thorp (1978) emphasized the religious causes, but his article did not have the impact it deserved. Proctor reports that Wyatt recognized that religion would not be a 'plausible' cause for most people to rebel (and knew that fellow Protestants would support him anyway). Therefore, he decided 'to speake no worde of religion, but to make the colour of hys commotion, only to withstand straungers, and to avaunce libertie' (A3ᵛ). To further his point, Proctor recounts how, as the rebellion broke out at Maidstone in Kent, one bystander told Wyatt that 'I trust [...] you wyll restore the right religion again? [...] Whiste quod Wyat, you may not so much as name religion, for that wil withdraw from us the heartes of manye' (A5ᵛ). Wyatt did secretly admit, though, that 'we mynde only the restitution of Gods word'. It is impossible to confirm whether this incident actually occurred or was invented by Proctor to strengthen his case, because he referred to this bystander only as 'one other of good wealthe'. What is clear is that Wyatt's efforts to conceal his true motives for recruitment purposes have distorted our perceptions of one of the two main causes of his rebellion: religion.

Proctor then narrates the unfolding of events in great detail. As a result, *Wyatt's Rebellion* has become one of the primary sources for Mary's reign. The book opens with Wyatt leaving his accomplices recruiting to his cause in Kent while he heads for London to 'stirre the duke of Suffolk & his brethren, with others of power in further countries, whom he knewe to be like affected to heresies, and consequently to burne in semblable desire for continuance of the same' (A2ʳ). However, he lost the element of surprise when a fellow conspirator from Kent was arrested and he himself was summoned before the Privy Council. This precipitated his appearance at Maidstone market cross a mile and a half south of his home (Allington Castle) with his armed followers on 25 January 1554, where 'by proclamation in writyng, [he] published his devillishe pretence' and sparked off the rebellion (A3ʳ).

Based in Tonbridge, only 11 miles south-west of Maidstone, Proctor was in close proximity to events as they unfolded. Vicinage is a key theme of *Wyatt's Rebellion*, with Proctor recording neighbouring occurrences carefully and foregrounding the close social relationship between the protagonists; he also gives a strong, specific sense of place by naming each village, locating it geographically (particularly while the narrative takes place in Kent) to enhance the authenticity of his account. He similarly uses documentary evidence to strengthen both his narrative and his argument, employing it in the service of 'truth' and 'virtue'. Yet he also shapes this material in order to ensure that the 'true' version is a pro-Catholic one. Sometimes this editing is transparent, as in his version of Southwell's 'exhortation' made at West Malling in Kent on 27 January, a copy of which he probably received directly from the author. 'I shall report the same in substance truelye,' he tells us: 'how be it not fully in the same forme & maner, as I founde it, & as it was penned & pronounced by the shireffe. Who in thutteraunce & settinge furth therof, spared not to speake plainly & touch sharply as then the present tyme and case imployed vehement occasion' (C1ʳ).[3] At other times,

---

[3] Proctor probably edited the exhortation to maintain the anonymity of as many rebels as possible, partly because of the royal pardon issued to them, partly to discourage vendettas.

though, the selection, adaptation, and omission of material is done silently, to shape a version of the rebellion designed to depict Wyatt as a man who deceived his followers and manipulated popular support to achieve his own ends. It is these twin themes—of deception and popular politics—that the subsequent account of *Wyatt's Rebellion* traces.

In his proclamation at Maidstone, Wyatt claimed to act from loyalty to the Queen and with the support of the Privy Council, nobility, and gentry; his aim, to oppose Mary's marriage to Philip and to repel the Spanish. To win over his neighbours, he even named some of the most prominent men in the county as his supporters (Henry, sixth Lord Abergavenny; the Lord Warden of the Cinque Ports, Sir Thomas Cheyne; and Sir Robert Southwell) and suppressed any reference to religion. Another clever move on his part was to invoke the language of the common weal before the gathered crowd of his neighbours, claiming for his followers the consultative role of natural counsellors. He asked the commons 'to assemble & determine what may be best for the advauncement of libertie and common wealth in this behalfe' (B1ᵛ). Other gentlemen raised rebellion elsewhere in the county, including as far away as Ashford and Milton Regis, and Proctor notes as many of these incidents as possible, including the seizure of the Catholic Christopher Roper of Lynsted for preventing the proclamation being issued there and calling Wyatt traitor. The author here implies that loyal Catholics were targeted deliberately by the rebels (Bindoff 1982: iii. 213–17).

Wyatt's appeal to the common weal gave the rebellion the momentum it needed, cowing efforts by the local gentry to check its progress. To counter this, on 27 January Southwell issued his 'exhortation' against him, refuting Wyatt's claims that Abergavenny and he had joined him and proclaiming him a rebel. One Barham, a servant to Abergavenny, reiterated the commonplace 'you maye not so muche as lyfte your finger against your kinge or quene' (D1ᵛ), words perhaps put in his mouth by Proctor to emphasize this theme of obedience. The defeat by Abergavenny of a rebel contingent at Blacksole Field near Wrotham in Kent on the night of 27–8 January drove Wyatt to employ popular politics and 'to drawe the careles multitude unto him'—although his end result could only be 'spoyle and raven [plunder]' according to Proctor (E4ʳ).[4]

Proctor then relates one of the most famous incidents, the desertion to Wyatt at Strood in Kent on 30 January of the London Whitecoats under the command of Thomas, third Duke of Norfolk, and Sir Henry Jerningham. The Whitecoats greeted the rebels before going over to them with cries of 'we are all Englishe men, we are al Englishemen' (E6ᵛ). This incident exposes the tension at the heart of *Wyatt's Rebellion*: Proctor's reaction to the religious changes of Edward's reign was ambivalent and in his book he cannot entirely disguise the unease he felt subsequently at the popularity of Protestantism or the widespread support the 'patriotic' Wyatt received (Betteridge 1999: 144–50). At first, Proctor obfuscates, attacking the 'neuters', local men who stood on the sidelines watching how things played out (although nobody is

---

[4] For popular politics, see Shagan (1999, 2003); Hoyle (2001); A. Wood (2002).

named). A way round this problem was to argue that the common rebels became disillusioned with their gentry leaders, who prevented them from having any contact with the government (including hearing the Herald's proclamation at Rochester on 27 January) or who lied outright, for example by saying that Abergavenny was hanging people summarily (which Southwell, in fact, was). As a result, Proctor claimed that 'the common people being with [Wyatt . . .] began to rise against him' (G2^v). Proctor even implies that Wyatt's closest supporters 'sought as many waies as thei could to be rid of him' (G3^r), thus confirming the truism that all rebellion turns on itself because of its monstrous nature. He also argues here that this popular politics was not genuinely participatory but a way for Wyatt to exploit the people for his own purposes.

The Whitecoats' desertion marks a turning point in the narrative. After 'a great and solemne counsel' (F5^v) at Rochester, during which Proctor ascribes nefarious intentions to the rebels, they march on London, moving the action to a wider geographical and political stage. This broader scale diminishes the focus, as Proctor describes things at an ever further remove from his locality. He stops being an eyewitness, nor can he gather as reliable or as much testimony from strangers as he did from his neighbours. His grasp of the chronology breaks down as the rebels near London, and the subsequent events he describes are usually a day out.

As related by Proctor, Mary's response to the rebellion was a political master stroke and also hinged on her own appeal to popular sentiment. Knowing the importance of retaining the support of London, she went to the Guildhall on 1 February to justify her monarchy and emphasize that the Privy Council backed her marriage— condescending to talk of matters that Elizabeth I would later define as *arcana imperii*, 'mysteries of state' not to be debated by her subjects (Guy 1997: 94–5; Mears 2005). 'I am alreadie maried to this common weale, and the faythful membres of the same, the spousall rynge whereof I have on my fynger, which never hitherto was nor shal hereafter be leaft of' (G6^r), she tells them, holding up her hand and showing them the coronation ring to confirm her legitimate succession from Henry VIII. Also, she promises to remain in London, despite the danger. Proctor describes how the streets thronged with the citizens, cheering her all the way back to Whitehall.

Wyatt found the gates to London Bridge unexpectedly barred when he arrived in Southwark on 4 February. He remained there for two days debating with his men what to do next. Proctor claims that mistrust grew among them and that Wyatt was for flight, again confirming one of the book's themes, that rebellion always tends to its own decay. Here, too, we see Wyatt's reliance on (illegitimate) popular politics redound upon him. They decided to cross the Thames 10 miles upstream and at 9 a.m. on 8 February, 4,000 of them reached Hyde Park in Middlesex, only to find a large royal army barring their way. Wyatt's immediate company ran down underneath the park wall adjoining St James's Palace and into Charing Cross, where they encountered the royal household and fierce fighting broke out. He managed to slip through to The Strand and Fleet Street, passing as far as Ludgate, before 'the queenes true subjectes' (I6^v) prevented his entry into the city. Finding himself trapped, he surrendered.

Proctor had been drawn into Wyatt's rebellion by his proximity to its point of origin in Maidstone; this must have prompted his desire to continue witnessing events by travelling up to London for their conclusion. He is therefore an eyewitness to Wyatt's trial in Westminster Hall on 15 March. He describes hearing clearly what Wyatt said under cross-examination, when he pleaded for his life 'not by plee of hys matter, or justifying of him self, but by earnest suite in humble submission for the queenes mercye' (K3^v). 'It semeth not amisse here to make reporte of suche special wordes as by him were uttred at his arrainement, whiche I my selfe hearde standinge not tenne fote from him at that time,' he comments (K3^v). *Wyatt's Rebellion* is fairly close here to parts of the trial record in the *Baga de secretis* and other accounts, but Proctor shapes his material in interesting ways by focusing only on Wyatt's performance as the contrite subject admitting error. Such a role was commonplace following disgrace. Wyatt was executed at Tower Hill on 11 April after making the customary penitent scaffold speech. All rebellions have ended thus: 'peruse the Cronicles', we are instructed by Wyatt himself (K4^r).

The second and third parts of *Wyatt's Rebellion* take the form of anti-sedition tracts, although ones written after the fact. The first is 'An earnest conference with the degenerates and seditious, for the searche of the cause of their greate disorder' (L1^r–M3^r). Here, Proctor reprimands the commons for their uprising. First, 'God alwayes defendethe his chosen and electe vessell' (L1^v), the monarch, and rebellion inevitably ends in confusion, dissension, and failure, particularly when it is led by the wicked for evil ends (and Wyatt could only mean to harm Mary). In the present case, the fault is all with the commons and not with the Queen, who has shown herself the ideal 'princelye Magistrate' (L2^v) and not even prosecuted heresy: God 'by sundrie tokens and dayly experimentes declareth him selfe to delite' in her (L5^v). Turning to the question of the marriage, the purported reason for the rising, Proctor points out that it is Mary's right to choose her own husband and that the Privy Council supports this match. He repeats his claim that Wyatt's true motive was to maintain heresy, although at his trial Proctor has Wyatt declare that it was fear of Habsburg domination. Protestantism leads inevitably to political and social disorder, licentiousness, and oppression; in fact, rebellion and this heresy are indistinguishable in the author's mind. As evidence, he points out that the Reformation could only be maintained through 'tyrannye' during Henry and Edward's reigns and by open 'rebellion [and] treason' in 1553 (M1^v).

The second anti-sedition tract, 'A Prosopey [Prosopopoeia] of Englande unto the degenerat Englishe' (M3^r–N2^r), develops the ideas present in the first, particularly that Protestantism is synonymous with sedition and rebellion and that there is a community of interest vested in the idea of common weal. Therefore, the rebels are assailing not only Mary but also England and every subject of the realm. Prosopopoeia is a rhetorical figure that lets a concept (such as England) 'speak', and this is what happens here. England attacks the rebels for subverting and trying to overthrow the polity, leaving her prey to invasion, despite the fact that she bore and nurtured them, a commonplace of anti-sedition tracts. Because of the Reformation the realm has become a shocking example of disorder and decay, which Mary is now restoring. Despite this, certain people will not be returned to Catholicism and obedience, but rather 'wyll beleve what that most vile and develishe rable of Antichristes ministers by their pestilent bokes teache you in corners, as that by gods law ye maye rebell against youre head' (M8^{r-v}). As a result, God punishes the innocent as well as the guilty (because England is one common weal) with dearth and disease. Proctor concludes with his final reason for writing: to make his pro-Catholic, pro-Mary point of view explicit. He then reiterates, so that there can be no doubt: why the rebels are wrong and were bound to fail; that this is a universal precept; and links rebellion and sedition again inextricably with Protestantism.

How and why does Proctor's narrative differ from other contemporary histories? The London chronicles are generally less detailed, although they often provide infor-mation absent from his work (Metzger 1996). The *Grey Friars Chronicle*, for example, states that during Mary's Guildhall speech she carried the 'cepter in hare [her] honde in tokyn of love and pes' (*Chronicle* 1852: 86)—a striking image that would have fitted well with Proctor's themes of concord, loyalty, and good government. Both authors usually agree on the facts, however. The Windsor Herald Charles Wriothesley was also well placed to observe the final, critical stages of the rebellion in London, providing a fuller, more accurate account than the Grey Friars Chronicler. He is also more reliable than Proctor over dating once the rebels reach the environs of the city, and has new material about the Guildhall speech (1875–7: vol. i, pp. i–xlviii; ii. 107–15). The Grey Friars Chronicler and Wriothesley write within the chronicle tradition, providing little commentary on what was happening, nor documentary evidence. Henry Machyn is slightly different. He was a merchant tailor, who in 1550 began recording city events, making him perhaps the most contemporary narrative source. A Catholic, he was unsympathetic to the rebellion, and cites the Spanish match as the cause. He gives us new facts, including describing the Mayor and Common Council's mistrust of the London citizens—something *Wyatt's Rebellion* would never admit. Unlike Proctor, Machyn dates events in the city correctly. Although misrepresented as a diary by his modern editor, Machyn's work is still very much a chronicle, giving it more in common with the Grey Friars Chronicler and Wriothesley than with Proctor (I. Mortimer and Anthony 2002). All three chronicles provide as full a report as they can within the constraints of their generic tradition and how much news they can garner, whereas Proctor clearly shapes his narrative to suit his didactic purpose, omitting anything unpalatable.

The Chronicle of Queen Jane and Two Years of Queen Mary is the fullest, and one of the most even-handed, to record the rebellion, exposing Proctor's agenda in contrast. Like the other three chroniclers, its author was a Londoner, who most probably served in the Tower Mint. He gives opposition to the Spanish marriage and the removal of evil counsel as Wyatt's motivations, again omitting religion. There is a long passage on the incident at Rochester, and here Proctor can be seen to have misrepresented Wyatt's dealings with the Herald, who was in fact permitted into the camp and allowed to issue his proclamation. Proctor's reason for leaving this out is clear: 'but the same [proclamation] being ended, eche man cryed they had don nothing wherfor they shold nede eny pardon, and that quarrell which they toke they wold dye and lyve yn it' (*Jane and Mary* 1850: 38). The rebels had *not* been hoodwinked by their gentry leaders, and knew exactly what they were doing: protesting on behalf of the common weal against what they regarded as royal tyranny. Also absent from Proctor is the long speech by the Whitecoats' Captain, Alexander Brett, exhorting his men to change sides, and the fact that 'parte of the garde' went over, along with three-quarters of Norfolk and Jerningham's own retinues (39); Jerningham and Norfolk both fled, 'being abashed' (39). This raises serious questions about the loyalty of Mary's household servants, something Machyn also noticed (1848: 55; Tighe 1987; Braddock 1987). Other inconsistencies in *Wyatt's Rebellion* are shown up by the *Jane and Mary* Chronicler, like Mary's ambivalence over whether to remain steadfast at Whitehall or to remove to the Tower of London once the enemy approached St James's. The rebels are, in fact, portrayed by the Chronicler as articulate, conscientious, resolute, brave, and a highly organized and well-led army—none of which Proctor admits. The long passage covering the rebels' final stand parallels *Wyatt's Rebellion* closely, although it is fuller and provides new details. The *Jane and Mary* Chronicler concludes with the whole of Wyatt's execution speech ('or moche-like words in effecte'), which is not present in Proctor. Here, Wyatt thanks the Queen for her forgiveness and admonishes others against rebelling (very much in the mould of Proctor's penitent) before proceeding to deny that Elizabeth and Edward, first Earl of Devon, were involved. At this point, his confessor, Dr Hugh Weston, contradicts him by saying that he has already implicated them, and cuts him short. It was perhaps dangerous to critique Elizabeth in print in 1554 (she was the heir to the throne), and this could explain the silence here and elsewhere in *Wyatt's Rebellion* over her role.

While the *Jane and Mary Chronicle* is better on events in London, this source does show how well informed Proctor was about what happened there (most likely based on eyewitness testimony gathered when he came to the trials of the rebels). The *Jane and Mary* Chronicler is a step up from the other London chroniclers because—like Proctor—he discriminates over the relative importance of what he records more carefully, and interprets its significance. He is Proctor's mirror image in terms of detail. Like him, he provides a copious (and therefore convincing) account, backed where possible by eyewitness testimony (often his own) and documentary evidence. However, unlike Proctor, he does not appear to have shaped his narrative to fit a didactic and confessional purpose. As a result, he is our most reliable contemporary narrative source.

Wyatt's Rebellion, in contrast, is a direct response to recent history and a thanksgiving for the providential deliverance of English Catholicism from rebellion and its companion heresy. Whereas the rebellion itself forms only part of the London chronicles: it is Proctor's entire subject. Yet this does not make *Wyatt's Rebellion* the reliable narrative that historians generally assume. One of the book's most remarkable achievements is how it employs the same methods as its Protestant rivals so successfully and its precocity in defence of Counter-Reformation England (misgivings notwithstanding), especially as Pole was only just getting the official propaganda campaign under way in 1554. Proctor shapes his story carefully in order to emphasize his key themes, often as opposites. These include obedience and disobedience, which he relates to Catholicism and heresy; documented truth; and the common weal. Other themes brought out are royal mercy, popularity, and vicinage—that by making his depiction of Kent so detailed and vivid, his account is somehow more truthful. *Wyatt's Rebellion* is an anti-sedition tract too and can be read as a riposte to the early anti-Marian literature, works like John Knox's *Admonition or Warning*, printed in London in May 1554. Proctor also shapes his text through omission, omission caused in part by the uncomfortable popularity of Protestantism: awkward facts, particularly widespread support for Wyatt and apathy towards Mary, are either passed over briefly or ignored altogether. This is clearly seen over his coyness about singling out by name more rebels or any of the 'neuters'. Yet, these perplexing details often remain embedded in the text.

Finally, we return to the question raised earlier in this essay: what prompted Proctor to write *Wyatt's Rebellion*? On the one hand, the answer is obvious: loyalty and obedience to the Marian regime. It is important to remember that Proctor is not just an eyewitness: he is a participant in the events he describes, spying on the rebels and reporting to the government. For example, on 23 February he gave to Southwell a copy of Wyatt's second proclamation, issued at Tonbridge, Sevenoaks, and elsewhere in the Weald (NA, SP 11/3/32, 80^r–81^v; NA, SP 11/3/32(i), 82^{r-v}). This proclamation is printed verbatim in *Wyatt's Rebellion*, and shows the rebels trying to manipulate popular feeling, and 'alienate the peoples heartes' from Abergavenny, Southwell, and George Clarke, who were approaching with forces loyal to Mary (B5^v).

But we must also record that Proctor stood to gain from pressing home the themes of loyalty and obedience. He has to deal with the fact that rebellion broke out in his own county and with the ambivalent behaviour of some of his neighbours. He draws attention to the ways in which many local nobles and gentry proved loyal and opposed Wyatt, for example Christopher Roper, Thomas Monde, John Tooke, George Darrell of Calehill, Sir Henry Sidney, and Sir Thomas Cheyne. In relating the government victory at Blacksole Field on 27–8 January, the author not only paints a vivid scene but also enumerates twenty-five loyal Kentish gentry who participated in defeating and scattering the rebels. This is one of the most geographically specific descriptions of people's movements in the entire book, as if Proctor wishes to root his protagonists firmly in the Kent he knows well. He is also keen to stress that this skirmish somehow hobbled the rebellion, that 'Gods secret hand was greatly felt' (D8^v). Proctor was, in fact, probably encouraged by the Kentish gentry to produce this apology, *Wyatt's Rebellion*, 'proving' their loyalty to the Marian regime.

And Proctor was, indeed, rewarded for his own loyalty, becoming MP for Chippenham in Wiltshire in the November 1554 Parliament and JP for Kent by spring 1555, as part of the Queen's drive to purge local government for political and religious reasons (NA, SP 11/5/6, 37^r–38^r; Clark 1977: 98–107, 131–2). By 23 October 1558 he had fallen ill, however, and died a few days later, numbering himself among 'faithfull & catholicke mene [men]', and was buried on 3 November in the Chancel of St Peter and St Paul's in Tonbridge, 'dyrectly where I use to sytt'. He bequeathed to this church his crucifix, vestments, 'and a fayre corporas case [a Eucharistic vestment]' (Proctor 1558). Mary and Proctor died within weeks of each other; their Counter-Reformation died with them. History is written by the victors, and *Wyatt's Rebellion* would not be reprinted until the end of the nineteenth century.

Primary Works

APC (1890–1964), *Acts of the Privy Council of England*, ed. J. R. Dasent et al., n.s., 46 vols. (London: HMSO).

Baga de secretis, NA, KB 8/26, mm. 1^r–36^v; KB 8/27, mm. 1^r–9^v; KB 8/32, mm. 1^r–17^v.

BL, Add. Charters 76667–76670.

Chronicle (1852), *The Chronicle of the Grey Friars of London*, ed. John Gough Nichols, Camden Society, 1st ser., 53.

HUGHES, P. L., and J. F. LARKIN (eds.) (1964–9), *Tudor Royal Proclamations*, 3 vols. (New Haven: Yale University Press).

Jane and Mary (1850), *The Chronicle of Queen Jane and Two Years of Queen Mary, and Especially of the Rebellion of Sir Thomas Wyat*, ed. John Gough Nichols, Camden Society, 1st ser., 48.

JUDDE, SIR ANDREW (1558), will, NA, PROB 11/42A.

MACHYN, HENRY (1848), *The Diary of Henry Machyn, Citizen and Merchant-Taylor of London, from 1550–1563*, ed. John Gough Nichols, Camden Society, 1st ser., 42.

NA, SP 11/5/6; 11/3/32; 11/3/32 (i).

PROCTOR, JOHN (1549), *The Fal of the Late Arrian*.

—— (1554a), *The Waie Home to Christ*.

—— (1554b), *The Historie of Wyates Rebellion*.

—— (1558), will, Centre for Kentish Studies, DRb/Pwr 12, 328^v–329^v.

SOUTHWELL, SIR ROBERT (1554), Letter to the Privy Council, 24 Feb., NA, SP 11/3/32, NA, SP 11/3/32(i).

WRIOTHESLEY, CHARLES (1875–7), *A Chronicle of England during the Reigns of the Tudors from, 1485 to 1559*, ed. W. D. Hamilton, 2 vols., Camden Society, 2nd ser., 11, 20.

CHAPTER 20

MARIAN POLITICAL ALLEGORY

JOHN HEYWOOD'S *THE SPIDER AND THE FLY*

ALICE HUNT

IT seems entirely appropriate that John Heywood's *The Spider and the Fly* forms the subject of a chapter entitled 'Marian Political Allegory'. Published in 1556, three years into Mary I's reign and two years after her marriage to Philip II of Spain, this 400-plus-page poem draws attention to its allegorical status in its opening lines. Heywood's Preface tells us of his poem's doubleness, of its ability to say one thing and mean another: 'Parable is properly one thing | That of another doth conceiving bring' (1966a: 3). We therefore begin to read expecting the poem's characters and plot to reflect real people and a real situation.

The parable consists of a protracted debate between a spider and a fly who has become entangled in the spider's web by flying through a hole in a window's latticing. The author and master of the house, Heywood, observes the episode and the consequent legal arguments between the fly and the spider regarding the fate of the former: should the fly be pardoned and released or sentenced to death? After twenty-seven (of ninety-eight) chapters of unresolved debate about ownership and rights to holes in windows, the spider and the fly decide to summon arbitrators: the spider chooses 'a cousin of mine | Pierce pismire called Antony Ant', the fly his 'grandsire

Bartilmew butterfly' (133). But, after another twenty-odd chapters, neither Antony nor Bartilmew can reach a resolution. War breaks out, thousands of rebel flies die but only hundreds of spiders, and Antony Ant is taken prisoner. Finally, the spider grants the flies half the holes (which comprise only a small fraction of the entire window area) but still claims the right to kill the fly. Just as the spider is about to pierce the fly's head (387), the maid comes in and knocks down the web with her broom. The fly is released, but the spider is crushed underfoot by the maid. In his conclusion, Heywood identifies the maid as England's new queen, Mary I.

The Spider and the Fly follows in the medieval tradition of allegory, written in seven-line rhyme royal. As John Berdan points out, it recalls other animal works such as *Reynard the Fox* (1920: 104), but *The Spider and the Fly* is remarkable in that Heywood himself seems to point to his poem working as both moral and political allegory, the insects and the maid representing real people rather than virtues or vices. We want to identify specific characters with contemporary political figures, and more generally—and possibly thanks to the success of Marian historiography, which has largely focused on the reign's Catholicism and hostility to reform—it seems appropriate to interpret the opposition between the spiders and flies as that between Protestants and Catholics. Heywood's known commitment to the Catholic faith only endorses such a reading, and thus the whole poem can be, and has been, cast as an example of Counter-Reformation literature and Marian panegyric that is unequivocal in its support for England's new, Catholic queen.[1] Indeed, such an interpretation is offered by Heywood, who adds 'a few words' by way of the poem's conclusion. It is as if the 'proper' meaning suddenly emerges, bright and clear—it 'Lighteth in the lap of imagination':

> Wherewith, as this parable here taketh end,
> So I (with a few words therein) an end intend.
> Of this last piece plain interpretation,
> Lighteth in the lap of imagination.
> Which, of force, in weighing the sense literal,
> Clearly conveyeth the sense allegorical
> To our sovereign Lady, Queen Mary, and maid.
> At God's bringing whom to her crown, may be laid
> Our like strife risen, and more than like to rise
> Than showeth here risen between spiders and flies.
> Whose sword, like a broom that sweepeth out
> Not a sword that filleth the house by bloody mean,
> This merciful maiden took in hand to sweep
> Her window, this realm, not to kill, but to keep
> All in quiet, on her bringing us thereto,
> As that maid all spiders and flies showeth to do.

> (426–7)

---

[1] See, for instance, Axton and Happé (1991). But as Axton and Happé also point out here, Heywood's religious beliefs can be overemphasized: he was one of those Tudor literary men associated with the court who successfully straddled Henry's, Edward's, Mary's, and Elizabeth's reigns, suggesting that 'his status as a literary man of wit was of far greater importance than his religious leanings' (7).

The poem's ending, then, seems to instruct us how to unlock the fable. Tom Betteridge, for example, reads *The Spider and the Fly* as 'an allegorical poetic history of the Edwardian Reformation' which strikes a 'completely new note' at its end when, with the identification of the maid as Mary, 'it is made clear that the chief spider is a figure for a leading Protestant, probably Northumberland but possibly Cranmer' (2004: 143). Indeed, he reads the story's 'convoluted and frustrating detail' as 'the poem's most eloquent criticism of the Henrician and Edwardian Reformations', in that the debate between the spiders and the flies is, ultimately, sterile (148). John N. King also reads *The Spider and the Fly* as an allegorical attack on the Reformation. He writes,

Ever since the dissolution of the abbeys, [Heywood] had worked in manuscript on this attack on the Reformation. Only after the reconciliation with Rome was it safe to drop his allegorical veil and identify Queen Mary as the maid who ends the protracted conflict between the Protestant spider and the Catholic fly by killing off the predator and sweeping England's house clean of cobwebs and debris.   (1982: 252)

But, prior to its conclusion, *The Spider and the Fly* is a much stranger text than this interpretation allows. The initial experience of reading page after page of powerful if irresolvable debate is such a rich and disorientating one that for the poem's 'meaning' to be unequivocal praise of Mary and the restoration of Catholicism feels oddly unsatisfying. The poem is not consistent in its support for the supposedly Catholic rebel flies, and doctrinal issues are hardly mentioned at all. Neither, as this essay will consider, is the poem uncritical of monarchical rule, and this problematizes Heywood's praise for Mary. James Holstun, for example, has argued that it is impossible to read the entire poem as 'unalloyed encomium to Mary' and sees it rather as 'bold loyalist counsel'. He goes on:

Far from celebrating Mary's accession, the poem appeared two to three years into her reign; and the Maid's late appearance in the poem suggests Mary's tardiness in pursuing a program of commonwealth reforms. The Maid seems to have been somewhat lax in her housework, allowing the spiders to usurp upon the middle of the windows, until the resistance of the flies attracts her attention.   (2004: 78)

To read the poem as a straightforward attack on the Reformation falls in with history's predominant interpretation of Mary. This has tended to see Mary and her reign in religious terms, casting her as unprogressive and hostile to reform of all kinds— determined to crush all Edwardian spiders. We would do well to think instead about continuities across the reigns which challenge the primacy of doctrinal differences. Holstun places *The Spider and the Fly* within the development of commonwealth thought that continued across Henry's, Edward's, Mary's, and Elizabeth's reigns. 'Heywood produces', Holstun writes, 'a remarkable continuation of the early Tudor estates debates and the radical commonwealth writing of the Edwardian gospellers' (2004: 55). To read *The Spider and the Fly* as a wholesale attack on the Protestant reformation, then, only raises the question: Which bits of the Reformation? Heywood's known religious conservatism does not have to imply a similar political conservatism.

At the same time, though, despite the conclusion, Heywood warns against too historically specific an interpretation of his poem. Indeed, 'right reading' would seem to entail moral instruction, and we should be looking to see ourselves:

> Thus wishing wishingly, in reading this,
> Readers to read and scan all sentences
> As we first mark and mend ourselves, and then
> To mark, to mend, the faults of other men,
> Without more scanning here.

> (6)

Invoking the popular analogy of the book as a mirror, Heywood invites us to look into *The Spider and the Fly*, to 'spie' (a favourite word of Heywood's that nicely echoes both 'spider' and 'flie') faults in ourselves first, before seeking out the faults of others. But although Heywood, perhaps teasingly, invites us to root out the meaning behind the parable and to amend our ways, *The Spider and the Fly* is notoriously difficult to 'spie' into. In addition to its length, which is off-putting enough to try most readers' patience, *The Spider and the Fly* seems wilfully impenetrable. William Harrison, in his *Description of England*, blames Heywood's style and complains that he 'dealeth so profoundly and beyond all measure of skill that neither he himself that made it, neither anyone that readeth it, can reach unto the meaning thereof' (Berdan 1920: 104). It is true that *The Spider and the Fly* has, regrettably, been largely ignored, both at the time of its publication and since. Judith Rice Henderson describes it as 'one of the least appreciated of many neglected poems of mid-Tudor England' (1999: 243). After it was published in 1556 it was not reprinted again until 1894, and there are currently only two editions available—both over one hundred years old.[2] Leaving aside Harrison's barbed comment about Heywood's style, there are a number of factors which frustrate the 'right reading' and diligent scanning that Heywood demands. First, and particularly problematic for critics intent on the allegory, is the poem's long period of composition. In the conclusion, Heywood claims that the poem—the 'thing'—was first begun over twenty years prior to its publication, thus in 1536 at the latest (423). The references to Mary and Philip were added later, just before the poem's eventual publication, as was the explicit identification of the maid with Mary. Why did Heywood think that in 1556 his work was suddenly ripe for publication, without (apparently) any substantial revision? What about the character of the maid? Was she always in the poem, or added later?[3] The conclusion pulls the parable of the spider and the fly into Mary's reign, but the claim that the poem was started in Henry's reign undermines the specific Marian interpretation that Heywood provides. Richard Axton and Peter Happé describe the poem as 'an allegory of legal intrigue in Westminster' that was then cannily redirected to Mary on her accession (1991: 9), elaborating that 'Possibly this began as the story of how John Rastell was caught in Cromwell's web and altered to how Heywood himself was caught in Cranmer's web'. It seems impossible to settle on a historically nuanced reading when we cannot

---

[2] John S. Farmer's 1966 edition is a facsimile of the Early English Drama Society's 1908 edition.
[3] Henderson (1999) argues that the maid always featured in the poem.

settle on a historical context, and we oscillate between reading generally—for moral correction, say—and topically, for political relevance.

For some readers, the key is the poem's claimed starting point in the mid-1530s. The spider, for example, has been identified as Thomas Wolsey (which pushes the poem's genesis back to the mid-1520s and the crisis over financing Henry's wars with France), Henry VIII, and Thomas Cromwell. Meanwhile, Buz, the fly, has been identified with Thomas More, John Rastell, and even, as quoted above, with Heywood himself (the spider in this interpretation being Thomas Cranmer).[4] Such specific interpretations perhaps say more about our expectations of allegory than they help with making sense of this wonderful tale. These critics select one specific date and context from the twenty or so years that Heywood gives as the poem's possible gestation period but choose to ignore other possible contexts and inconsistencies. The various interpretations only prove how slippery the poem is as a religious allegory, with both the spider and the fly being able to represent Protestant and Catholic figures. Readings that focus on an earlier and particular date are unable to accommodate the important Marian spin granted by the conclusion, and hence the remarkable role of the maid. As Holstun points out, her entrance contravenes the genre of the insect debate because she is human (2004: 58, 71). The poem's debates about ownership, property and rights, the hangings and threat of executions, the trials and spirit of rebellion, can certainly be argued to allude to real moments of political unrest in mid-sixteenth-century England, but it is most likely that the poem collapses several debates, policies, rebellions (such as Kett's in 1549), and real-life trials and executions (such as Northumberland's in 1553 and Cranmer's in 1556), making it impossible for one scenario—or one religious view—to prevail.[5]

Since we cannot be sure about the poem's process of composition—what Heywood may have added, deleted, or amended—readings that root the poem in its Marian context are most persuasive, particularly Holstun's argument that the poem *continues* debates about tenure and commoners' rights that began in Henry's reign, persisted throughout Edward's, and remained relevant in the 1550s. The spider and the fly debate long and hard about their respective rights to the window, rights that are dependent on their different class. The fly refers to himself as a 'yeoman' and spiders as 'gentlemen' (199), and the spider and the fly address each other according to this awareness. The fly calls the spider 'sir' while the spider employs the familiar pronoun 'thee': 'Fly', says the spider to the fly, 'I [...] grant to hear thee speak' (46). Their division is social, not religious, and it is important to be reminded that their debate, along with many other real debates of the mid-Tudor period, need not be a confessional one. It would seem that *The Spider and the Fly*, like other texts and events of its time, has been hampered by overly religious readings that ultimately just do not fit. Like Holstun, Henderson has argued convincingly for the poem as Marian political

---

[4] On Wolsey as chief spider, see Haber (1900); Berdan (1920). For the spider as Henry and the fly as Heywood's father-in-law, More, see Bolwell (1921); Berdan (1920); cf. Reed (1926) on More, Holstun (2004: 60) on Henry. For the spider as Cromwell, see R. Johnson (1970). Bolwell (1921) argues for the spider representing Cranmer.

[5] On the spider representing Northumberland, see Berdan (1920); Ward (1967, introd.).

counsel. She argues that it was always directed to Mary, first as a princess (before she was made illegitimate) and then as queen, as an allegory of effective female rule. 'I suggest that Heywood began writing his insect fable', she writes, 'to help prepare the teenage princess to rule her nation'; he abandoned it in the 1530s following the births of Elizabeth and then Edward (1999: 242). But while Henderson is no doubt right to emphasize the importance of the maid in this aspect, she does not fully explore what exactly the poem advocates as effective—or indeed legitimate—female rule. It is the problematic nature of authority, and specifically female monarchical authority, embedded in *The Spider and the Fly* that this essay explores. It does so alongside another kind of authority that the poem similarly problematizes: that of the author and his book.

Heywood ends *The Spider and the Fly* by arguing for its Marian context; we should therefore use it as our beginning. We can only take Heywood at his word that he did indeed begin his poem over twenty years before, spent a year writing it, and then left it until just before its publication. Even if, as is most likely, he did amend and revise his text quite substantially at several points during this twenty-year period, he wants his readers to tie the poem to its Marian times. By telling his readers that it has only recently become 'ripe', Heywood draws attention to a particular understanding of his role as author, and to his authority over his text. He associates his poem with the ripening and enriching effects of time, and its eventual publication with fate. By seemingly dissociating himself from his work, as if he does not have final control over it, he simultaneously heightens the poem's purpose and hints at the prophet-like role of the poet. It is as if the poem's meaning would only become clear in time, which, like Mary's motto, 'Veritas temporis filia' ('Truth is the daughter of Time'), would eventually bring truth to light. Suddenly, with Mary's accession, the work can flourish, and end. Heywood writes:

> I have, good readers, this parable here penned,
> After old beginning newly brought to end.
> The thing, years more than twenty since it begun,
> To the thing years more than nineteen, nothing done.
> The fruit was green; I durst not gather it then,
> For fear of rotting before riping began.

> (423)

It is as if the poem began in spite of itself, when it did not know what it was allegorizing or what its correct interpretation could be: only time would reveal its 'proper' meaning. Of course, it is shrewd and convenient to make an old piece suit its new times—and a new monarch—but Heywood nonetheless points to poetry's ability to teach beyond itself.

But Heywood's role as an author, and his relationship with his text, is contradictory. At the same time as distancing himself from his creation, as a fruit which he 'durst' not pick too early, Heywood turns himself—or at least the figure of an author—into a prominent character in this drama. There is an intrusive narrative voice in *The Spider and the Fly* and the owner of that voice is represented throughout in many of the accompanying woodcuts which are integral to the experience of reading this poem. Each of the ninety-eight chapters is prefaced by an illustration, some full-page (such as the maid crushing the spider) and some double-page spreads (such as the battle scene). When the maid is 'at point to tread the spider to death' in chapter 90 (388), we spy the author observing the scene from the other side of the window, striking a decidedly judgemental pose. He is there again, outside the window, in the illustration that depicts the maid actually killing the spider (once she has listened to his tale) at the beginning of chapter 94 (Figure 20.1). He is, of course, also the master of the house, and thus served by the maid. As he watches the maid about to stamp on the spider, he describes how she was emboldened in her behaviour by her master's absence:

> The maid, by mine absence to be the more bold
> To work her will, as she came in, I went out,
> And looked in at the window, her to behold.
> She swept down the cobweb; the fly flew about
> The parlour round, never more lusty nor stout;
> The spider on the ground, under the maid's foot,
> To tread him to death, and was about to do't.

(389)

Looking in at this scene from the outside, the author also reflects us as readers–observers, and makes us conscious of our own engagement with the tale, and our role as interpreters and even judges. The woodcuts that show the author in this way are not purely illustrative of the poem's story; they also encapsulate the poem's preoccupation with competing types of authority: the spider's, the maid's, the master's, the author's, and the reader's. The animals' wrangle about correct political authority is, I suggest, mirrored by the poem's play with literary authority, and such play with literary authority was a political matter in Marian England.

Authority, and its correct deployment, is one of the key problems debated by the spider and the fly, and was one of the most contested terms of the Reformation period. In Nicholas Udall's 1553 play *Respublica*, 'Authoritie' is a corrupt character and an alias for 'Insolence'. Monarchical and religious reforms entailed the clarification and reinterpretation of the nature of the authority of people, Parliament, law, traditions, customs, and conscience. Debates about the correct extent of monarchical authority in a commonwealth accelerated in Henry's reign with the supremacy, persisted throughout Edward's reign and the terms of the Protectorate, and were exacerbated by the accession of England's first queen regnant in 1553, and by her subsequent marriage to the Spanish Philip II in 1554. In chapter 38 of *The Spider and the Fly*, the debate hinges on whether the spider or the fly is more honest, and therefore more credible, but as each can be argued to be honest and therefore credible—'as every spider or fly is honest, so is he credible' (167)—their relative positions of authority are invoked as the final arbiter of their case. As one of the spiders argues:

> Grant here's a spider of honesty no whit,
> To whom admit a fly of great honesty,

Fig. 20.1 The author observes the maid crushing a spider. John Heywood, *The Spider and the Flie* (1556), 2Q^v.

> The spider (not the fly) to authority knit;
> Is not that spider, in authorised degree,
> More worshipful and credible taken to be
> Than that inferior fly?

(170)

To which a fly responds, noting the injustice:

> Last, authority ye bring in assistance,
> Th'unhonest and authorised thereby t'ensue,
> In worship and credence.

(170)

The spider continues:

> As honour, or worship, and credence do depend
> Upon all that are honest, by honesty,
> So worship and credence in like case too bend
> On all in authority, by authority.
> Nay (quoth the fly) (quoth the spider) friend, tell me,
> Is not authority to be worshipped?
> Yes, master (quoth the fly), or else God forbid.

(171)

But authority cannot, as the fly points out, be bowed to for its own sake. There is a critical difference between authority—namely, God—and those who are authorized. The former should be worshipped for what it is, but the latter only if they correctly use the authority they have been given. The spider, however, points out how many 'authorised' persons are reverenced, regardless of how good or 'ill' they are, to which the fly responds that there is a difference between reverencing the *person*, and reverencing the higher authority that has authorized his or her position:

> That curtsey (quoth the fly) rightly directed,
> Runneth to th'authority in the authorised,
> Not the authorised person, respected;
> Th'authority in the person here reverenced.
> Th'authority for the person, not worshipped,
> Nor the person for himself, lacking honesty,
> Because he lacketh honest use of authority.

(171)

Trying to determine the honest use of authority, however, will prove exceedingly difficult, but the fly concludes that

> Spiders using authority honestly
> For place and person both where case so ensues,
> Flies to spiders humble reverence must use.

(173)

The misuse of authority is played out later in the poem, towards the end, where the spider and the fly swap places, as the prefatory note to chapter 83 explains, to 'imagine and set forth other's part the best they can' (356). It is an exercise in role reversal and the dangerous theatricality of power. The fly moves so that he is 'solemnly set in the spider's chair' and the spider 'to the fly's base place did repair' (358). A woodcut shows the fly sitting in the spider's throne-like chair—a 'stately place' (359)—and the spider crouched below. The author is delighted by this piece of theatre, and notes the characters' new demeanours as they find their new roles:

> The fly being once set in the spider's place,
> Advanced himself, setting hands under his side.
> The spider crouched, in countenance mild and base,
> Looking pale and wan, as though he should have died.
> Which change (upon this sudden) when I espied,
> It printed in me a wonderful wonder,
> To see parties (from their parts) so asunder.
>
> (359–60)

In his new stately position, the fly assumes the authority, power, and wealth of that position to such an extent that he becomes 'spiderlike' and rules against the flies. He 'With spiderlike spiteful words' (360) declares that spiders 'own all windows':

> He was from the fly's part so carried away,
> By being suddenly there thus elevate,
> That all claim laid by the spider there that day
> The fly ruled for right of most lawful right rate.
> So farforth he forgat where and how he sate,
> That upon the chair-boll hard beating his fist,
> Spiders own all windows, he sware by gods blist.
>
> (360)

The fly falls from the dizzy heights of power by falling out of the chair. There is of course a lesson here in the dangers of pride and ambition—the fly himself acknowledges how altered and 'puffed up' (362) he was by his position of power and prosperity.

The problem is the wrongful assumption of power, of illegitimate and unprecedented power, and the poem offers as a solution that it is the established hierarchy of rule and stability of custom that should be obeyed. The poem's refrain is that the spider and the fly will resolve their dilemma according to 'reason, law, custom, and conscience' (373, and throughout). Ultimately, it is custom that prevails and trumps the other three principles, leading the spider to pass judgement on the fly and sentence him to death:

> Custom, one chief post principal (as erst said)
> Declareth, and hath declared, this six thousand year,
> All flies (or any fly) in cobwebs (or cobweb)
> However they come there, if they there appear

> No reason in reason and law alleged here
> Could discharge them thence, but straight there cometh amain
> A spider, who slayeth him and sucketh out his brain.
>
> (366)

Custom here is brutal, and it is mirrored by the entrance of the maid, whose sudden appearance prevents the fly's brain from being sucked out. But the maid, also calling on the precedence of custom, proceeds to crush the spider to death. Custom seems worryingly tyrannous, and the maid herself alludes to the burden of custom when she tells the spider: 'ye finally burdenously | Burdened the fly with custom, thereby to die' (391). She goes on:

> And as thou madest custom thy sheet-anchor chief
> (Conjoining thereto reason, law, and conscience),
> Of the fly's death (by right) to make perfect preef
> From first age of the world had in consequence;
> So bring I custom, fetched like far time from hence.
> Custom is thy warrant to suck the fly's brain,
> Whereto mark how custom warranteth me again.
>
> (394)

Despite the spider's, and then the maid's, seemingly legitimate enforcement of custom, the dangerous abuse of power lurks throughout this poem. It lies behind the fly's masquerade as the spider, and in the ambivalent stance the poem takes towards custom. In both the episode of the fly's near death, and that of the spider's actual death, the custom used to enforce order is violent, and exacerbated as such by Heywood's graphic detail and the accompanying woodcuts. Indeed, when the maid crushes the spider it seems to be against her will, and nature:

> The water ran down the cheeks of them both two;
> The maid, pitying both, wept as fast they;
> But for that she must do more than she would do,
> The spider had been forgiven, and gone his way.
> But they gone weeping away, without delay,
> The spider lying prostrate, she thereupon,
> Setting her foot on him, he was forthwith gone.
>
> (410)

The maid's maidenliness and mildness is appealed to in the poem: the spider, from under the maid's foot, lifts 'his hands high' and beseeches her 'of mild maidenly pity' (389). But the manner of the spider's eventual crushing is not mild, and it needs to be remembered that our maid was about to kill the spider immediately, without letting him plead his case, and that she, like the fly when he assumes the stately seat of the spider, was temporarily—and illegitimately—emboldened by her position of power (388).

After the spider's death, the maid addresses the twelve spiders and twelve flies—as if addressing a monarch's council—and tells them of her duty to serve her master and mistress and restore order as if according to a natural hierarchy where each has his correct and accustomed place:

> But leave this, and take that, mine order erst told;
> Keep you your places, and let me keep mine,
> As nature and custom willeth you of old,
> While reason and custom do me clear incline
> My master's and mistress's will to work in fine;
> As I under them, and you under me,
> May lovely live (I say) each in due degree.
>
> (415–16)

Restoring 'This ancient order' (414) wins. Mary I, like the maid, is described in the conclusion as having similarly restored order: 'Pointing us our places (and paths) of old known' (428). This is the correcting power of the absolute monarch, like that of the goddess Nemesis in Udall's *Respublica*, who is sent down to redress political and social disorder and who is also explicitly identified with Mary. The conundrum of authority in *The Spider and the Fly* should be resolved by the entrance of the maid, and consolidated by Heywood in his conclusion. It seems that the lesson is obedience to the natural hierarchy in a kingdom. The ultimate authority is God, and Mary, like a maid, serves her master—God, Christ—and her mistress, the 'mother holy church catholical' (428), and 'with that one stroke of her broom' purges disobedience and rebellion and restores custom ('accustomed state', 'right rate', 'our places (and paths) of old known'):

> And as that one maid, with that one stroke of her broom,
> Cleansed her window clear in every room,
> Setting flies at liberty in their right rate,
> Placing spiders likewise in accustomed state,
> Pointing both parties path of direct direction
> To trace and tread in as wealth's protection;
> So this one maid [Mary], with this one stroke of her sword,
> From long thrall thraldom hath set us clear a board,
> Pointing us our places (and paths) of old known,
> Great guides both to ghostly and worldly wealth grown.
>
> (428)

But how comfortable is this poem's analogy between a maid and a queen? It is an analogy for female power that stresses servitude and duty rather than monarchical prowess. Maids obey rather than are obeyed, and Mary is invoked as serving God and the Church, but also as serving—rather than ruling—her kingdom. It is an image of monarchical rule that privileges the interests of her commonwealth and challenges absolute authority.[6] Furthermore, Mary is represented by a maid whose maidenliness is emphasized, by the time of the poem's publication even though Mary was married. The poem also illustrates on several occasions the importance of a council and the need for those in power to seek counsel. The preface to chapter 92, for example,

---

[6] *Respublica* similarly critiques absolute rule and privileges the commonwealth (Hunt 2007).

describes how the spider, before his death, speaks to his son and twelve counsellors to give 'his best advice for most quiet and best governance' (397). In this confessional and repentant speech the spider advises that his heir seek 'wise' and 'expert' counsel, and to the counsellors he stresses the importance of the commonwealth, the body politic:

> Thy counsel choose, in these conditions bent,—
> Few, wise, secret, expert, temperate, and true,
> Satisfied with sufficiency, and diligent
> All sale of justice and all offers t'eschew
> That shall to thee or commonwealth hindrance brew
> . . .
> Now to you of his counsel, mark what I devise.
> In you, lieth the putting in ure of all this;
> You are his hands, his feet, his ears, and his eyes;
> Hearing, feeling, or seeing, in him small is
> To walk or to work with, you working amiss.
> You are the mirrors that all lookers look in;
> As you work, they work, but you must first begin.
>
> (404)

The poem also explicitly expresses its doubts about the virtues of a monarchy when, quite early on, the spider and the fly digress to discuss various types of rule (chapter 27). They compare 'three kinds of commonwealth' (125): government by a monarch, by the aristocracy, and by the commons. But as in all of this poem's debates, they are unable to reach a resolution. No form of government is found to be ideal, and we are left with the contradiction inherent in the spider's claim that 'tyranny is worst' and 'Rule or reign of a king is best', but that it is in 'rule of a king' that 'tyranny may blow blast' (126), despite a king being 'God's anointed' and therefore 'above the rest appointed' (125).

The conclusion of *The Spider and the Fly* asks for the readers' obedience to Mary, as God's appointed:

> To this maid, as spiders and flies to that maid,
> Let our banners of obedience be displayed
> Of love, the badge of rejoicing, the right root,
> And of our own wealth the right and full boot.
> Love we her, and obey we her, as we ought,
> And also our sovereign Lord Philip, to her brought
> By God, as God brought her to us.
> Conjoined one in matrimonial train,
> But one also in authority regal,
> These two thus made one both one here we call,
> Which two thus one, rejoice we every one.
>
> (428–9)

But, again, this appeal to Mary's sovereignty is not as straightforward as might first appear. As England's first queen regnant, Mary's regal authority needed defining—not just because of her gender, but because there was simply no precedent for her rule—no 'custom'. As Judith Richards has written, 'the concept of a female monarch was sufficiently problematic for clarifying legislation to be needed' (1997*a*: 903; cf. 1997*b*). While notorious texts such as Thomas Becon's *An Humble Supplication unto God for the Restoring of His Holy Word unto the Church of God* (1554) and John Knox's *First Blast of the Trumpet against the Monstrous Regiment of Women* (1558) should not be assumed to represent the general attitude towards female rule—inflected as they are by hostility to Catholic rulers—it was certainly true that the lack of precedent caused some anxiety. It was not simply that female authority per se was problematic, but that female authority needed definition: what exactly would constitute the power of a queen (McLaren 1999)? At the time of her accession, Mary reassured her Privy Council that she would rule according to her male predecessors—that is, not as a female tyrant—and that she would heed their counsel. A few days before her coronation in October 1553, she summoned her Privy Councillors to the Tower and, sinking to her knees before them, pledged her intention to rule 'to the public good and all the subjects' benefit', telling them that she 'entrusted her affairs and person [...] to them'. Her Councillors were reportedly moved to tears by this unprecedented action: 'amazed as they were', the ambassadors report, 'by this humble and lowly discourse, so unlike anything ever heard before in England' (*CSP Spanish* 1916: 259–60). Mary's marriage to Philip complicated further the anomaly of a queen's authority since a marriage would make her a wife and thus subservient, by the established laws of marriage, to her husband. Property and inheritance laws—as *The Spider and the Fly* also makes clear—would mean that, should Mary die, her crown would pass to her husband. The matter of Philip's authority also needed clarifying, not least because he too was prince of his own country.

Heywood's closing lines from *The Spider and the Fly* quoted above refer to Mary's marriage, and to Philip's authority as husband to the Queen of England. Philip had sought to be made king on his marriage, but the idea of a Spanish Catholic being crowned King of England was extremely unpopular (Loades 1991: 170). The marriage treaty and published royal proclamation of January 1554 sought to reassure the English that Mary's regal power would not be compromised. She could act as both queen, and wife, and Philip would 'aid' her, but would not assume monarchical power, especially in the event of Mary's death (Richards 1997*a*: 908; P. Hughes and Larkin 1964–9: ii. 21–6). Further legislation later in 1554 addressed the matter of Mary's authority, as a female monarch and wife. In April 1554 what has become known as the Act for Regal Power was passed by Parliament. It declared that 'the Regall power of thys realme is in the Quenes Majestie as fully and absolutely as ever it was in anye her mooste noble progenytours kynges of thys Realme'. Parliament confirmed that Mary's authority as queen was 'fully and absolutely' equivalent to that of an English king—which included both the extent and limitations of that authority:

Be it declared and enacted by the authority of this parliament that the law of this realm is, and ever hath been and ought to be understood that the kingly or regal office of the realm, and all dignities prerogative royal power preeminences privileges authorities and jurisdictions thereunto annexed united or belonging being invested either in male or female are and be and ought to be as fully, wholly, absolutely, and entirely deemed, judged, accepted, invested and taken in the one as in the other; so that what or whensoever Statute or Law doth limit and appoint that the King of this Realm may or shall have execute and do any thing as King [...] the same the Queen may by the same authority and power.

(Statutes of the Realm 1810–24: 1 Mary, st. 3, c. 1)

This Parliament also sought to define and clarify further Mary's authority in relation to her impending marriage to Philip (they would marry that July). This statute stressed Mary's 'sole' power despite her marriage:

we your faithful loving and obedient subjects do most humbly beseech your highness, that it may be provided, enacted and established by the authority of this present parliament that your majesty as our only queen, shall and may solely and as a sole queen use, have, and enjoy the Crown and sovereignty of and over your realms, dominions, and subjects.

(Statutes of the Realm 1810–24: 1 Mary, st. 3, c. 2)

What, then, does Heywood mean when he seemingly innocuously refers to Philip as 'one also in authority regal'? Is he assuring readers of the fullness of Mary's authority, that is, that Philip has the *same* regal authority, not that Mary has less? Or is he appealing to their joint authority (possibly as flattery to Mary) and thus granting Philip the regal authority that was so contested by some? Mary is known to have acknowledged the equality of their authority and her obedience to Philip (Richards 1997*a*). Entangled in the conclusion is the problem of authority that Mary and her marriage caused. It is reflected in Heywood's convoluted lines about oneness, which seem to gesture towards equality:

> These two thus made one both one here we call
> Which two thus one, rejoice we every one.
> And these two thus one, obey all as one.
>
> (428–9)

This is not the 'oneness' of Mary's authority as articulated by the statute. Following the spiders' and the flies' protracted debates about different aspects of authority, and then the embodiment of female monarchical authority in the figure of a maid, we have a conclusion that draws attention to the hot issue of Mary's authority as a married queen regnant. Taken together, this poem ultimately shows authority to be disputable, negotiable, non-absolute, and definable by law.

Heywood's conclusion should resolve many of the poem's debates. But *The Spider and the Fly* does not feel resolved. The 400 pages of debate have raised issues which cannot be swept away with a broom, as is implicit in the narrator's telling parenthetical phrase 'for the time': 'The spiders and flies (for the time) being gone' (419). The persona of the author—who can be safely identified with Heywood himself, principally owing to the similarity between the figure depicted in the poem's woodcuts and the frontispiece 'portrait' of Heywood—interjects in the maid's part in the drama in a way that becomes problematic when the maid is identified as England's queen. In the drama the author is, of course, the maid's master, and attention is explicitly drawn to this in the episode of the spider's judgement and death. We have already seen how the author watches the maid's entrance from outside the window, and tells how his absence emboldens the maid to begin crushing the spider to death without hearing his tale. Then, once the spider has been killed and the offending webs swept away, the author re-enters to inspect the maid's 'workmanship': 'Out went she, | And in came I, her workmanship there to see' (421). Satisfied with her work, he 'went from the window, to the board to dinner' (422). It is the author's approval that brings the parable to an end.

In a poem where the correct ordering of authority, from the spider's to the maid's, is shown to be problematic and in need of confirmation, it is all the more striking that this is a poem that plays consciously with the authority of the author—both the tale's persona of the author and Heywood himself. The poem is book-ended and punctuated throughout by the author. He presides over the tale, and we are continually reminded, visually and verbally, of his mediating and authoritative role: it is his tale. He is represented first as a figure with book in hand, looking for an imaginative escape:

> Whereas (anon) a book I took in hand
> Something to read, to fode forth fantasy,
> And stepping to a window, there to stand,
> In at a lattice hole, right suddenly,
> Even at a fling, fast flew there in a fly
> That sang as shrill and freshly in my mind
> As any bird could do, bred of that kind.
>
> (27)

The 'fantasy' the figure is looking for becomes his own work: the episode of the fly flying into the cobweb is transformed by his imagination. The woodcuts that proliferate throughout the poem serve to remind us of the process of writing, and of the fanciful and artificial nature of the tale by showing the author at his desk, with his books open, gazing at the window, quill in hand (Figure 20.2), or temporarily resting on the table—as if an author seeking, and finding, material for inspiration. The poem's woodcuts illustrate less the events than the *nature* of the tale; those images which do not depict the author seem suggestive of what is taking place in the author's imagination. Invention and wit are highlighted. The fly's opening words buzz with humour and hyperbole, as one might expect of a playwright such as Heywood:

> Alas, alas, alas and wellaway!
> To cry aloud, alas! what cause have I!
> Alas (I say) that ever I saw this day!
> My whole estate, in twinkling of an eye,
> Is here transformed from mirth to misery;
> For froward fortune hath led my mishap
> To lay and lock me in mine enemy's lap.
>
> (29)

Within the fabric of the tale, further tales are told—by the spider, fly, ant, butterfly, maid. As the spider says to the maid in chapter 91, 'That's a false tale' (393), and

Fig. 20.2 The author at his desk, watching the fly caught in the cobweb. John Heywood, *The Spider and the Flie* (1556), B2ᵛ.

Antony Ant goes home to tell his family and other ants the tale of 'all his trouble' in chapter 78 (334), which ostensibly means retelling the tale of *The Spider and the Fly*. Like the spiders' webs, tales are spun and respun, signalling the possibilities for differing interpretations, and the varying authority of those tales. Tellers become listeners and judges, and listeners become tellers and interpreters. The reader's act of engagement in the tale is matched by that of the author—who is also a reader and interpreter—and of the animal characters who listen and react to the tales of others.[7]

The Spider and the Fly's debate about authority and its correct uses and figureheads is enmeshed with a debate about the authority of writing. Both types of authority are subject to the vagaries and possibilities of interpretation and can—indeed should— be questioned and challenged. Tom Betteridge has argued that the interpretability, and openness, of texts is a particular feature of Marian literature. He writes that 'Marian culture emphasized the need to withdraw the self from the reading process and privileged the social realm as an arena for textual interpretation. This meant that smashing the text to find its kernel or pawing over it to penetrate its secrets were rejected as proper or useful models of interpretation' (Betteridge 2004: 135). The problem of politics is also the problem of poetry; they are inextricable, as so often is the case with Tudor literature. Reading is both private and public, reflecting private follies and public debates. The figure of the author is shown in a private, domestic situation, beginning with a walk in the garden and ending with his retirement to dinner, but the parable is stretched to address a reigning monarch and the public sphere. The poem is simultaneously a private work of imagination, and something of far larger consequence, that took over twenty years to write but, as already mentioned, was waiting to come to fruition in Mary's reign, as if this was somehow out of the author's control. In this context it is useful to remember Heywood the author of proverbs and epigrams. In their attempt to pin down cultural truths, epigrams depend on the accepted authority of their author. Heywood clearly saw himself as able to wield such authority, while remaining all too aware of the potential elusiveness of the authority of the word. In 'To the Reader' of his *First Hundred of Epigrams*, he writes:

> Ere ye full reject these trifles following here,
> Perceive, (I pray you), of the words th'intents clear.
> In which, (may ye like to look), ye shall espy
> Some words show one sense, another to disclose;
> Some words, themselves sundry senses signify;
> Some words, somewhat from common sense, I dispose
> To seem one sense in text, another in glose.
> These words in this work, thus wrought your working tool
> May work me to seem, (at least), the less a fool.

(1966b: 107)

---

[7] Betteridge (Ch. 10 in this volume) and Happé (2008) both discuss the importance of rhetoric and the performativity (and open-endedness) of debate in Heywood's work, attributing it to his humanism. I am grateful to Peter Happé for letting me read an advance copy of his essay.

The Spider and the Fly is a text whose 'sense allegorical' (426) is at once clear (as Heywood proposes in his arguably playful conclusion) and made deliberately ambiguous (by Heywood's drawing attention to the poem's long period of composition). But delight should be taken from this poem's spinning possibilities and struggle for sense, for it is in this wrangling that the poem's real struggle lies: for the correct and appropriate use of political authority.

PRIMARY WORKS

CSP Spanish (1916), Calendar of Letters, Despatches, and State Papers, relating to the Negotiations between England and Spain, 13 vols in 20 (London: HMSO, 1862–1954), xi.

HEYWOOD, JOHN (1894), The Spider and the Flie, ed. A. W. Ward (Manchester: Manchester University Press; repr. New York: Burt Franklin, 1967).

—— (1966a), The Spider and the Fly together with an Attributed Interlude Entitled Gentleness and Nobility, ed. John S. Farmer (New York: Barnes & Noble).

—— (1966b), The Proverbs, Epigrams, and Miscellanies, ed. John S. Farmer (Guildford: Charles W. Traylen).

—— (1991), Plays, ed. Richard Axton and Peter Happé (Cambridge: Brewer).

Statutes of the Realm (1810–24), ed. A. Luders et al., 11 vols in 12.

UDALL, NICHOLAS (1952), Respublica: An Interlude for Christmas 1553, ed. W. W. Greg, EETS, o.s., 226.

CHAPTER 21

HALL'S CHRONICLE AND THE *MIRROR FOR MAGISTRATES*

HISTORY AND THE TRAGIC PATTERN

SCOTT LUCAS

EDWARD HALL's chronicle, *The Union of the Two Noble and Illustre Families of Lancaster and York* (1548), and the historical verse tragedy compilation *A Mirror for Magistrates* (various editions from 1554) are two of the Tudor period's most remarkable literary success stories. Neither work enjoyed an auspicious beginning: the chronicler Hall died with much of his massive history left incomplete, while government officials suppressed the earliest version of *A Mirror for Magistrates* and forbade publication of it for the first five years of its life. Despite these early obstacles, however, both texts found their way into print and, over the long life of their material, exerted a profound influence upon the historical, poetic, and dramatic literature of the Tudor and early Stuart periods. These two works are linked by more than their early difficulties and later success. Hall's chronicle served as a chief inspiration for the authors of *A Mirror for Magistrates*, who employed it not only as a primary source of information for their own historical verse narratives but also as a model for understanding the most important political tragedies (both actual and feared) of their own time, tragedies which they dared to confront and to protest by means of the allusive material and topically applicable exemplary narratives included in many of their poems. In great measure, Hall's chronicle set the tragic pattern for interpreting and representing English politics adopted by the *Mirror* authors for their collection. In turn, the compelling nature of both Hall's approach to English history and the emotionally powerful *de casibus* tragedy form of the *Mirror* ensured that this pattern would remain influential upon later generations of English poets and playwrights as they created new literary engagements with England's past.

21.1 HALL'S CHRONICLE: PLANTAGENET TRAGEDY AND TUDOR TRIUMPH

Edward Hall's *Union of the Two Noble and Illustre Families of Lancaster and York*, better known even in its own time as 'Hall's chronicle', stands as a seminal text in English historiography. Hall's sharp focus on a single period of the English past (1399–1546), his zeal to identify historical causes and to trace the unfolding progress of historical developments, his interest in the character of those he discusses, and his highly rhetorical, ornate prose style, all helped to usher in important changes in vernacular English history-writing. Hall's text not only inspired generations of subsequent chroniclers, who modelled their own historiographical practice upon Hall's (and often borrowed from him wholesale); it also exerted a profound influence upon numerous Tudor and Stuart literary authors, who filled their plays, poems, and prose works with material and metaphors mined from Hall's text.

Edward Hall (or Halle) was the son of a prominent London grocer. Born in 1497, he was educated at Cambridge University and Gray's Inn. While his lifelong occupation was that of a lawyer, Hall also pursued a lengthy public career, serving in at least four of Henry VIII's parliaments and in a number of posts in London, including under-sheriff for the city (from 1535 to his death in 1547). Hall's fervent devotion to Henry VIII earned the King's favour: it was Henry himself who helped Hall to his most prestigious London offices and who commended Hall as 'our well-beloved subject' (Bindoff 1982: ii. 279–82).

It is not known when Hall determined to compose his English chronicle, although he may have begun collecting material for his account of Henry VIII's reign in the late 1520s. It is certain, however, that Hall did not actually begin to write the bulk of *The Union* (the material covering the years 1399 to 1509) until 1534 or after, for it was only in that year that Polydore Vergil published his Latin history of England, *Anglica historia*, the work that served as the foundation of Hall's narrative. The Italian cleric Vergil had published *Anglica historia* in Basel, intending his history not for English readers but for Europeans who needed an introduction to the island nation in which Vergil had spent much of his life. Hall seized upon Vergil's work and used it both as his primary source for *The Union* and as a model for much of his own additions to Vergil's text (Kelly 1970: 109–37). Only in two places does Hall depart substantially from Vergil's narrative, namely, in his accounts of Henry VIII's rule (which Vergil's published volume did not handle) and of Edward V's and the first part of Richard III's reigns, which Hall took nearly verbatim from a manuscript narrative composed by Sir Thomas More (More's *History of Richard III*, 1513–18). While Vergil and More supplied most of his fifteenth-century matter, Hall nevertheless added to their accounts a large amount of historical material of his own, information he gleaned from medieval and early Tudor English chronicles, primary political and legal documents, French and Burgundian histories, contemporary pamphlets, and, it seems likely, private family traditions and eyewitness accounts (Kingsford 1913: 261–5).

Hall was shrewd in grounding his chronicle upon the work of the humanist-influenced Vergil and More. From Vergil, Hall gained a focused, streamlined model of historical composition, one that allowed him to replace the baggy, annalistic, and often scattershot approach of previous English chronicles with a relatively tight and uncluttered narrative form. Vergil's example also prodded Hall to seek out the long-term causes of the historical events he records, a practice alien to most other English historical writers of the time. Unlike many earlier Tudor chronicles, Hall's work was no mere gathering of dates, kings, and notable events. Rather, it announced in its very title a desire to trace the development of a single historical problem, the dissension that grew among members of the fifteenth-century nobility out of two competing claims to the English throne. Although not averse to including unrelated matter in his volume, Hall nevertheless strove to keep his announced subject at the forefront of much of his work, a move that made his *Union* all but unique among the printed vernacular histories of its time.

More's highly dramatic account of Richard III's rise to power, in turn, inspired Hall to embellish his own chronicle with literary and quasi-literary elements, including rhetorically sophisticated set speeches, engagingly dramatic descriptive scenes, and a prose style heavy with metaphor, analogy, alliteration, and emotional personal asides. Following More (who derived his own lively approach from the classical tradition), Hall chose to place a number of fictitious orations into the mouths of his historical subjects. While this practice undermines the strict historical accuracy of Hall's text, it adds to the excitement of its narrative, as history seems to come alive before readers' eyes. For instance, Hall not only reports to readers Henry Bolingbroke's decision to return to England to challenge Richard II, but he also leads them to experience vicariously the events that led up to Henry's fateful decision, most notably the effect of the Archbishop of Canterbury's long, pleading speech that (Hall claims) sealed Henry in his decision to challenge his monarch. Similarly, Hall does not merely record the horror of propertied Englishmen and -women at the prospect of the so-called Amicable Grant of 1525; instead, he illustrates their shock through a number of dramatic scenes and descriptions, including the Mayor of London's first anguished reaction to news of the grant, Chancellor Thomas Wolsey's several mendacious and self-serving orations designed to gain Londoners' wealth, and the alleged dialogue between an elderly commoner and the Duke of Norfolk that won the Duke to the aggrieved people's side. Passages such as these endow Hall's *Union* with an excitement and emotional depth only rarely seen in previous printed English chronicles.

Hall's decision to focus on one relatively brief section of English history allowed him to pursue three chief projects in his text. The first of these is the subject announced so prominently on his chronicle's title page, an account of the origin, development, and final healing of the 'discension for the croune' that flared between the two 'famelies' of Lancaster and York. Hall presents the most visible event associated with this struggle, the War of the Roses, as but one part of a much longer conflict that began with Henry of Lancaster's deposition of Richard II. In his accounts of Henry IV's and Henry V's rule, Hall describes the conspiracies these kings faced in terms of their relation to the rival claim to the throne first held by Richard II's heir Edmund Mortimer and eventually conveyed to the Yorkist branch of the Plantagenet family. Unlike many of the medieval chroniclers upon whom he draws, Hall is even-handed in assessing the merits of the two warring sides; rather than offer wholesale support to members of either faction, Hall assesses each historical figure upon his or her own actions and not upon his or her political allegiance. Hall is thus willing to defend and to indict members of both 'houses' in his text, and often he provides both praise and blame for the very same person under consideration. For example, Hall leads readers to recognize the manifest failings of the deposed Richard II, but he also defends Richard by ascribing his faults not to an evil disposition but to his untrained youth (1550, 'Henry IV', 6^{v}).[1] In a similar manner, he celebrates Henry VI as a man of virtue, even as he condemns him for his failures as a monarch ('Henry VI', 68^{v}). Hall even admits that his personal *bête noire*, Wolsey, was 'a good Philosopher' and an eloquent man, before he excoriates Wolsey for his pride, rapaciousness, and lust for power ('Henry VIII', 46^{r}). Few of the chief actors in Hall's narrative appear as figures of pure good or evil; rather, Hall often strives to compose surprisingly complex and well-rounded portraits of those he handles. By contrast, Hall is unequivocal in his hatred for civil war and his sorrow over the numerous tragedies experienced by English nobles and commoners alike during the bloody decades of the fifteenth century, a period so terrible in its brutality and its 'unnaturall devision' between countrymen, Hall exclaims, that 'my witte cannot comprehende, nor my toung declare, neither yet my penne fully set [it] furth' (Introduction, 1^{r}).

For Hall, it was the marriage of the Lancastrian Henry Tudor (Henry VII) to Elizabeth of York that brought about the 'union of the two houses' and an end to their contention (Preface, A2^{v}). For years, scholars have claimed that in guiding readers to this event Hall follows a simplistic providential outline, one created to bolster the 'Tudor myth' of divine sanction for the new regime. More recent work has shown, however, that there is little to suggest that Hall understood the collapse of the Plantagenet dynasty and the accession of Henry VII as elements of a grand providential scheme. Instead of fitting historical developments into a

---

[1] Since the 1550 edition of Hall's chronicle commences a new foliation at the opening of each monarch's reign, I cite passages in Hall's *Union* by section name (e.g. 'Henry IV') and folio number. I cite Hall's unfoliated Preface by signature.

single cosmic plan, Hall usually leads readers to find the causes of the events he records in the strengths and failings of individuals, men and women whose varying degrees of foresight, pragmatism, wisdom, folly, ambition, weakness, and greed created the conditions that brought alternately great glory or terrible catastrophe to the realm.

Hall's second chief project in *The Union* is the preservation for future generations of the glorious and inspiring deeds of prominent figures of England's past. Hall begins his chronicle with a lament for the numerous British and early English leaders whose stirring achievements have been lost for ever to 'Oblivion, the cancard enemie of Fame and [...] the defacer of all conquestes and notable actes'. Only history-writing, Hall continues, ensures that the admirable deeds of great men (and the shameful practices of villains) may live on after them, providing undying glory for the good and educative examples, both positive and negative, for future readers (Preface, A2^{r-v}). It is Hall's deep love for 'notable actes'—by which he means primarily those of chivalry and foreign conquest—that moves him so often to depart from the domestic concerns of his announced historical project to focus upon England's martial adventures in Scotland and France. Hall dwells at length in the earliest sections of his chronicle upon the great successes of warriors such as Henry V and Thomas Montague, Earl of Salisbury, and he later describes in detail the blunders and betrayals of those under Henry VI who lost France for England. In a similar manner, Hall presents Henry VIII's several French invasions as the very high points of the King's reign, and he often records even minor sixteenth-century border skirmishes to preserve the names and doings of those who took part in them. While modern scholars have dismissed Henry VIII's French and Scottish adventures as futile, wasteful endeavours, Hall celebrates them for the opportunities they offered Henry and his nobles to perform the sort of martial feats that earn glory for themselves and for their country.

The last of Hall's great projects is the one that lay nearest to his heart: a celebration of his own monarch, Henry VIII, and of the King's assumption of control over the English Church. Unfortunately, Hall died before he could bring his Henry VIII section to completion; it was 'perfited [perfected] and writt', according to Hall's printer, Richard Grafton, only up to or including the twenty-fourth year of the King's reign (May 1532–May 1533) (Ellis 1809, p. vii). Hall left the rest of his text only in the form of scattered 'pamphletes and papers', a body of writing that Grafton edited, augmented with his own material (though he initially denied doing so), and printed as the last and largest single section of Hall's *Union*.[2]

Hall composed his completed sections of the Henry VIII narrative as a celebration of his monarch, as an assertion of his prince's power over the English Church, and as an attack on the wealth, arrogance, and alleged misdeeds of the pre-Reformation English clergy. In the earliest sections of his Henry VIII narrative, Hall presents the young King Henry as nothing less than an early modern celebrity, a man more

---

[2] For an analysis of Grafton's conflicting claims concerning his additions to Hall's chronicle, see Devereux (1990: 39–41). That Grafton added to Hall's text is undeniable: the chronicle's account of the cruelties of the Act of the Six Articles, for instance, refers to the repeal of this Act, an event that occurred after Hall's death.

fascinating for his elegance and recreations than for his role in the day-to-day guidance of the nation. In Hall's telling, the Henry VIII of the 1510s was a proud, fierce, yet cheerfully insouciant young man whose chief benefit to the nation lay in the glory that his sumptuous entertainments and his victorious martial adventures bestowed upon the realm.[3] Hall treats Henry as the embodiment of English pride, and he carefully ascribes nearly all of the setbacks and troubles of the first half of Henry's reign not to the King himself but to foreigners (such as the fickle European allies who thwarted continuing English martial success abroad) and to the Roman Catholic clergy and its nefarious English leader, Wolsey. Hall was a fiercely anticlerical Erastian (believing in the subordination of ecclesiastical to secular authority), who consequently zealously championed the royal supremacy and who served in the 1540s on several commissions designed to enforce Henry's religious strictures. While his support for the dissemination of the Bible in English certainly exceeded that of his monarch, Hall does not appear to have been a particularly radical reformer. The passages in the last section of Hall's work that attack the religiously conservative Act of the Six Articles (an Act which Hall himself helped to pass and to enforce) and that express sympathy for evangelical dissenters from Henry's Church were almost certainly added by Grafton—whose reformist tendencies were much stronger than Hall's—during the period of relatively free speech for evangelicals that followed Henry's (and Hall's) death.[4]

Grafton printed Hall's *Union* twice in Edward VI's reign, first in 1548 and again, with indexes added to help readers locate specific names, in 1550. In 1555 Mary I's Catholic government ordered all copies of Hall's work destroyed, owing to its Protestant content and its strong attack on the validity of Henry VIII's marriage to Mary's mother, Katherine of Aragon. Hall's chronicle was published once more at the opening of Elizabeth's reign (1560); however, by the last decades of that queen's rule much of its material had already been incorporated (often verbatim and at length) into newer histories by authors such as John Stow, Raphael Holinshed, and even Hall's own printer, Grafton. Elizabethan chroniclers were not the only later authors to borrow from Hall's text for their writings. In Mary's reign, Wolsey's former servant George Cavendish drew upon Hall for his biographical 'Life and Death of Cardinal Wolsey' (1554–8), mining Hall's text for factual information about his subject while muting Hall's fierce hostility to his former master (May 1975; cf. Pincombe, Chapter 22 in this volume). Later, in James I's reign, Sir Francis Bacon employed Hall's decades-old chronicle as a chief source for his celebrated *History of King Henry VII* (1622). Given the highly rhetorical and often dramatic nature of Hall's narrative, it is not surprising that numerous literary authors also turned to Hall (either to *The Union* directly or to the edited versions found in later histories) for both historical details and rhetorical inspiration. Most famously, William Shakespeare made Hall's work (both in the original and in the redacted form offered in Holinshed's *Chronicles*) his richest source for his historical dramas. It was Hall, for instance, who gave to

---

[3] For a meticulously annotated edition of the Henrician spectacles in Hall's text, see Dillon (2002).

[4] I thank Thomas Freeman for sharing with me his thoughts on Hall's religious beliefs.

Shakespeare his condemnatory portrait of Joan of Arc (in *1 Henry VI*), his story of Prince Hal's striking of the chief justice (told in *2 Henry IV*), his idea for Richard III's and Richmond's speeches before Bosworth (*Richard III*), and the bulk of the historical material out of which he constructed his three *Henry VI* plays. Hall's aureate language and striking turns of phrase, furthermore, inspired Shakespeare in the creation of many of the brilliant speeches, metaphors, and images with which he filled his histories (Zeeveld 1936; Goy-Blanquet 2003). Despite its own relatively short life as a printed text, Hall's work and its historiographic model served as a spur for later English historians to embrace the new humanist-influenced style of vernacular history-writing that flowered in the late Elizabethan and early Jacobean periods, a style whose emphasis upon narrative, character development, historical analysis, and the critical use of sources owes an enormous debt to Hall and his chronicle.

21.2 *A MIRROR FOR MAGISTRATES*: HISTORICAL TRAGEDY AND CONTEMPORARY POLITICS

Outside of Shakespeare's dramas, the most important literary work to draw directly upon Hall's *Union* was the historical verse tragedy collection *A Mirror for Magistrates*. Few works of Tudor literature were as long-lived and influential in early modern England as the *Mirror*, which between 1559 and 1621 remained almost constantly before the public, appearing in new, ever-expanding editions in 1559, 1563, 1571, 1574, 1578, 1587, and 1610, and in the form of reissues of earlier editions in 1575, 1619, 1620, and 1621. During its long life, the *Mirror* earned copious praise from Sir Philip Sidney and others, it influenced the work of celebrated authors such as Shakespeare and Michael Drayton, and it created a decades-long vogue for historical *de casibus* tragedies that spanned the Elizabethan and Jacobean periods. Several of its admirers added historical *de casibus* tragedies of their own to the original text, swelling the size of the collection to over three times its initial length by the time of its last edition (see below).

Hall's chronicle exerted a far-reaching influence over the content and themes of *A Mirror for Magistrates*. While the formal model for the *Mirror* was John Lydgate's century-old poetic collection of *de casibus* tragedies, *The Fall of Princes* (*c*.1431–9), it was Hall's *Union* rather than Lydgate's text that substantially guided the *Mirror* authors both in their understanding of their poems' chief subject matter, late medieval English history, and in their interpretation of the unfolding political events of their own time. Hall's portrait of fifteenth-century England's rapid descent into weakness abroad and civil war at home as a result of political infighting, ruthless ambition, and misrule provided the authors with a pattern by which to interpret the often bloody conflicts that had plagued the tumultuous seven years between the death of Hall's hero Henry VIII (1547) and the composition of the original *Mirror* poems (1554). What Hall proclaimed to be the happy end to the bloody conflicts of the fifteenth century, namely the 'triumphant' reigns of kings Henry VII and Henry VIII, the *Mirror* authors understood to be merely a break in the tragic action, as first the rule of a minor king (Edward VI) and then the accession of a monarch many believed to be bent on tyranny (Mary) seemed to invite a new round of just the sort of internecine conflict and monarchical oppression that Hall decried at length in his chronicle.

To understand fully the original poems of *A Mirror for Magistrates*, one must place them in the precise period of their production. Although scholars usually treat it as an Elizabethan work, *A Mirror for Magistrates* actually began its life in the reign of Mary, when it was compiled and printed under the title *A Memorial of such Princes, as since the Time of King Richard the Second, have been Unfortunate in the Realm of England*. The printer who commissioned the work, John Wayland, conceived of the *Memorial* as a continuation of Lydgate's *Fall of Princes*. In the manner of Lydgate's *Fall*, the *Memorial* would present to readers exemplary narratives of famous historical figures who suffered untimely deaths. In a departure from Lydgate, however, each tragic figure of the *Memorial* would be British in origin, each would recount his tragic narrative in his own voice, and each poem would be followed by a prose passage representing the *Memorial* authors responding to the tragedy just presented and the various issues (whether political, moral, aesthetic, or even editorial) that it raised. Wayland assigned the task of creating this text to his print shop employee William Baldwin, a leading light of mid-Tudor letters (see Maslen, Chapter 17 in this volume). Baldwin accepted Wayland's project and gathered seven other men to assist him in composing nineteen tragedies spanning from the last decades of Richard II's reign to the end of Edward IV's (*c.* 1387–1483).[5] With one exception ('Humfrey Duke of Gloucester'), these tragedies and prose links would later compose the contents of *A Mirror for Magistrates* (1559).[6]

Only two of those whom Baldwin recruited for the *Memorial* project have been identified with certainty, George Ferrers and Sir Thomas Chaloner.[7] Ferrers was a lawyer and parliament man who came to literary prominence through the elaborate Christmas entertainments he devised for Edward VI's court. Chaloner was a humanist, parliamentarian, and diplomat who had penned the first English translation of Erasmus' *Praise of Folly* (1549). Like Baldwin, Ferrers and Chaloner were

[5] Baldwin concluded his collection with a twentieth tragedy cast in the voice of Edward IV, a work posthumously ascribed to John Skelton by sixteenth-century editors but whose authorship many modern scholars now deem uncertain.

[6] For evidence that the 1559 *Mirror* is a lightly edited version of the 1554 *Memorial*, see Lucas (2009: 237–41).

[7] A third figure, Thomas Phaer, is often grouped with the original circle of *Memorial* authors; however, there is no reliable evidence to link Phaer with any specific *Memorial* poem. Although the anonymous editor of the 1578 *Mirror* ascribes to Phaer the tragedy 'Owen Glendower', the poem is not Phaer's but Baldwin's, as the surviving leaf of the *Memorial* and all other Elizabethan editions of the *Mirror* make clear. See *Mirror* (1938: 119–20).

both Protestants who had thrived under Edward VI's evangelical government and who had suffered both mentally and materially under the new rule of the religiously conservative Queen Mary.

Evidence suggests that Baldwin initially sought to fulfil Wayland's request for an uncontroversial literary–moral compilation in the manner of Lydgate's *Fall*. A number of *Memorial–Mirror* poems meet Wayland's vision, offering chiefly versified renderings of chronicle history joined with moral admonitions. At some point, however, Baldwin and several other *Memorial* authors turned their hands to a different sort of tragedy, one exemplary in form, topically evocative in content, and politically interventionary in purpose. The poems of this type may be divided into two groups. The first sort targets Marian magistrates, presenting them with admonitory exempla designed to dissuade them from current courses of political action to which the *Memorial* authors were opposed. In this first type, the *Memorial* authors created their tragedies of political admonition in response to the fears of incipient tyranny that gripped many in the spring and summer of 1554. In the period following the failure of Sir Thomas Wyatt the younger's uprising (January–February 1554), an angry Queen Mary and her chief officers moved to strengthen their power over the realm and to punish those whom the Queen held to be her enemies. In the first months of 1554, Mary and her Privy Counsellors ordered the execution of the widely revered Protestant Lady Jane Grey and incarcerated a number of prominent members of the nobility and gentry, including the Queen's own sister Elizabeth, not for any recent crimes but simply because they had raised Mary's suspicion or ire. These actions, coming in the wake of earlier illegal moves against English evangelicals, led Protestants in particular to conclude that the Queen's chief officers were increasingly willing to subvert English law to satisfy the personal desires of their monarch. Fears of growing oppression were only exacerbated by the knowledge of Mary's imminent marriage to Philip of Spain, a zealous Roman Catholic whom many Englishmen and -women saw as a cruel tyrant. Oppositional pamphlets, placards, and even open comments in Parliament suggested that once in power Philip and Mary would simply abrogate all English laws and liberties and govern as absolute rulers (Loach 1986b: 96–7, 184–90).

Such were the concerns that prompted the *Memorial* authors to compose historical tragedies warning against current actions that they believed would lead the realm into tyranny. As Annabel Patterson first noted (1994: 160), Ferrers opens the *Memorial–Mirror* volume with one such work, 'Sir Robert Tresilian', a topically allusive exemplum spoken in the voice of Richard II's corrupt Chief Justice. In crafting this poem, Ferrers radically rewrites the details of his protagonist's life story to make Tresilian's crimes on Richard's behalf precisely mirror those committed by Mary's chief justices on their own queen's behalf in the notorious treason trial of the evangelical Sir Nicholas Throckmorton (April 1554). In Ferrers's telling, it was the very same practice of wilful misinterpretation of statute law employed by Throckmorton's judges that led in Richard II's time to oppression of the people, a violent uprising, and, finally, to Tresilian's own execution. Similar misery, Ferrers's poem insists, awaits contemporary England unless its legal officers immediately eschew the corrupt practices of Tresilian (and Throckmorton's judges) and resist the ever-present temptation to abuse the law to satisfy their prince's whims (*Mirror* 1938: 80; Lucas 2009: 172–201).

The second sort of topical tragedy included in the *Memorial* addresses itself to those Marian Protestants who had celebrated the rule of the charismatic evangelical military hero and political leader Edward Seymour, Duke of Somerset, Protector of the realm in the early years of Edward VI, and who continued to suffer from the bewildering manner in which Somerset's career and life had ended. In 1547 English evangelicals had hailed the accession of the 9-year-old Edward and the rule of his uncle Protector Somerset as manifest evidence of God's favour for the evangelical cause. Their celebrations turned to horror, however, when Somerset first fell disgraced from office in 1549 and then was executed in 1552. Somerset's deposition from the protectorship, which was justified at the time by numerous charges of malfeasance and incompetence, deeply wounded his followers, who had placed great trust in Somerset and his 'godly' policies of religious and social reform at home and imperialistic expansionism abroad. It was to lead suffering evangelicals to comforting understandings of the recent past that several *Memorial* authors composed seemingly historical tragedies designed to put readers in mind of Somerset's time in power. In 'Humfrey Duke of Gloucester', for example, Ferrers shapes his poem's protagonist Humphrey Plantagenet, Henry VI's protector of the realm, to evoke memories of Somerset, Edward VI's Lord Protector. Ferrers then uses his tale of Humphrey's persecution and death (reshaped from Hall's account) as an exemplary guide for understanding Somerset's own suffering, leading readers to blame not Somerset for the failure of his rule but a conspiratorial cabal of envious opponents who undermined his virtuous government for their own ambitious ends. Another, anonymous poet crafts 'Thomas Earl of Salisbury' as a guide for reinterpreting Somerset's failure to achieve the great foreign policy initiative of his rule, his bid to bring Scotland under English (and Protestant) control. The poet endows his hero, the mighty fifteenth-century military leader Thomas Montague, with attributes specific only to Somerset, bestowing upon him, among other things, an unhistorical period of service in Somerset's office of Protector and the unique combination of 'loving' overtures and brutal violence that Somerset so famously employed in his dealings with the Scots. The poet does so in order to move readers to understand Somerset's failure to attain his goals in Scotland in the manner they do Salisbury's failure to take France in the poem, as the result of unlooked-for misfortune (in Somerset's case, his deposition) brought about by forces outside his control (Lucas 2009: 67–105, 135–48). Poems such as these seek to induce readers to understand the once-revered Somerset's time in power not as one of villainy and failure (as the dominant voices of Mary's regime would have it) but as one of righteousness and tragically unfulfilled promise.

Writing under the strictures of Marian censorship, the authors adopted historical verse tragedy as a relatively safe and inoffensive, yet powerfully effective—because affective—medium for communicating their controversial views. The authors' bid to avoid censorship, however, did not succeed. Soon after the *Memorial* went to the press, Lord Chancellor Stephen Gardiner caught wind of the project and forbade its publication. The printed pages of the *Memorial* were scrapped, and its contents were not allowed to come before the public until after Mary's death.

Only upon Elizabeth I's accession was Baldwin finally able to bring his long-prohibited *Memorial* into print in a lightly edited form under the title *A Mirror for Magistrates* (1559). Baldwin bestowed upon the collection a new dedicatory epistle addressed 'to the nobylitie and all other in office', in which he presented the work as a volume of urgent political counsel. In this dedication, Baldwin urges English officers to see themselves first and foremost as servants not of the Crown but of God, and he insists that each of them holds a divinely appointed duty to make the well-being of the people his overriding concern. When he speaks of the monarch, Baldwin characterizes England's ruler not as a person superior in nature to those under him or her but as one more officer enjoined by God to labour on behalf of others and to ensure justice in the realm. Finally, he warns of great harm, both practical and providential, for any governor who dares to act unjustly towards the people (*Mirror* 1938: 64–5). His dedication's identification of princes and magistrates alike as endowed with a sacred charge to strive on behalf of all those placed under them, joined with the *Memorial–Mirror* poems' calls for magistrates to resist monarchical misbehaviour with force if necessary, made the *Mirror* one of the chief repositories for elements of Edwardian commonwealth thought and Marian resistance theory in the Elizabethan and Jacobean periods (Lucas 2007*a*).

While evidence suggests that the first edition of the *Mirror* found immediate favour among early Elizabethan readers, the decades-long popularity of the collection was probably only assured by its second edition, which appended to the original gathering a collection of previously unpublished Marian and Elizabethan pieces titled *The Second Part of the Mirror for Magistrates* (1563). *The Second Part* comprised eight new tragedies by seven different authors cast chiefly in the voices of figures from Edward V's and Richard III's reigns (*Mirror* 1938: 11–15). It included as well the poem that would become the most famous *Mirror* contribution of all, Thomas Sackville's 'Induction'. The 'Induction', which Sackville had originally composed to open a single-author *Mirror*-style volume of his own, leads readers on a journey through a Virgilian underworld filled with vividly described allegorical figures and fallen men and women of the ancient world (*Mirror* 1938: 297). With its flowing lines, striking images, stately language, and copious classical allusions, the 'Induction' is a poetic tour de force, and it remains to this day the single most celebrated poem of the *Mirror* and, indeed, of the entire period between Surrey's death in 1547 and Spenser's *Shepheardes Calender* (1579). The *Second Part* also included Thomas Churchyard's 'Shore's Wife', the first *Mirror* tragedy to be composed in a woman's voice. 'Shore's Wife' offers readers a fascinating glimpse into the psychology of Edward IV's famous mistress Elizabeth (or Jane) Shore. Shore's lengthy, anguished description of her mental suffering in the poem forces readers to balance their impulse to condemn Shore for her adultery with their sympathy for her as a woman whose tragic beauty led her first into sin and then into cruel affliction. The emotional fervour and compelling moral complexity of Churchyard's poem inspired a host of later poets to try their hands at similar verse complaints in the voices of suffering women, and it helped to make Shore one of the most familiar fifteenth-century characters in Elizabethan and Jacobean literature (Schmitz 1990; M. Scott 2005).

Baldwin died in 1563, most likely before his *Second Part* appeared in print. Those who followed Baldwin as editors of the *Mirror* abandoned Baldwin's politically interventionary project in favour of a new focus (anticipated in the prose links of the 1563 *Second Part*) on the aesthetics of the collection. The mostly anonymous editors of subsequent *Mirror*s rewrote numerous rough or unclear lines in the original tragedies, and in several places they laboured to dampen rather than to amplify the contentious political content of the work. These editors were prescient in their practice, for it was through its poetic qualities that the *Mirror* left its most lasting mark on Elizabethan and Jacobean culture. Successive generations of Tudor and Stuart authors venerated Baldwin's text for its high moral tone, moving characterizations, didactic purpose, and thought-provoking political messages, and they used it as a nearly inexhaustible source of inspiration for their own endeavours in drama, poetry, and prose.[8] Baldwin's *Mirror* began its life as a work of topical political intervention, designed in great part not for all time but for an age. Nevertheless, the quality of its thought, its themes, and the best of its poetry ensured it a lifespan and an influence nearly unprecedented in early modern England.

So admired was Baldwin's collection in Tudor and Stuart England that several authors sought not merely to compose individual poems in its style but to create whole multi-tragedy sequels. Each of these continuations was eventually joined to the text of the *Mirror* itself; today, scholars refer to them as the 'parts added to *A Mirror for Magistrates*'.[9] The first author to compose a *Mirror* continuation was John Higgins, an Oxford graduate and friend of Churchyard. A deep admiration for the 'finely pende' lines of Baldwin's collection inspired Higgins to try his hand at his own set of historical *de casibus* tragedies (*Parts Added* 1946: 36, 40). For his subject matter, Higgins turned to the tales of early British history constructed by the twelfth-century author Geoffrey of Monmouth, which had been passed down as truth (with varying degrees of scepticism and augmentation) by generations of English chroniclers. Higgins's first two pieces in the *Mirror* style won such praise from his friends that he quickly created fourteen more, each presenting a figure from Britain's pseudo-historical past who lived between the time of Brutus' entrance into Britain and the birth of Christ. Titling his work *The First Part of the Mirror for Magistrates*, Higgins offered his collection to the *Mirror* publisher Thomas Marshe, who released it in 1574 as a companion volume to Baldwin's *Mirror*. Such was the popularity of Higgins's work that Marshe brought out a second edition in 1575 (with one new tragedy added) and, in 1587, Marshe's assign Henry Marshe printed a third edition of Higgins's text, uniting it with Baldwin's collection and adding to it twenty-three new tragedies by Higgins, one new work by Churchyard ('Thomas Wolsey'), and two

---

[8] For the *Mirror*'s influence on later poetry, see Craun (1971); Zocca (1950: 36–93); Nearing (1945: 1–84). For its influence upon early modern drama, see Winston (2006a); Budra (2000: 73–93).

[9] The name derives from Lily B. Campbell's edition (1946) of Higgins's and Blenerhasset's *Mirror* additions.

early sixteenth-century poems by Francis Dingley that had been supplied to Higgins by the chronicler Raphael Holinshed.

Higgins admits in his text that he undertook the *First Part* as an 'exercise' in literary imitation, and his work is best read with that purpose in mind (*Parts Added* 1946: 35). In constructing his collection, Higgins borrowed extensively from other writers. From Baldwin, Higgins took the title of his collection, the form of its dedicatory epistle, and its focus on fallen rulers of Britain's past. From Sir Thomas Elyot, he took both the language of his volume's Preface (often borrowing from Elyot's 1531 *Governor* verbatim) and his identification of temperance (rather than Baldwin's justice) as the pre-eminent political virtue (Starnes 1927: 37–8; see also Shrank, Chapter 9 in this volume). From Sackville, Higgins borrowed the form of the poetic induction that begins his tragedies as well as his penchant for displays of classical learning. From Lydgate, Higgins derived the practice of joining his tragedies with poetic 'envoys' and, less happily, a tendency to allow the details of his protagonists' biographies to obscure a sharp presentation of the morals their lives were supposed to teach.

Among Higgins's most successful creations are his several poems inspired by Churchyard's 'Shore's Wife'. In the successive tragedies 'Locrinus', 'Elstride', and 'Sabrine', for instance, Higgins handles the life and death of Elstride, the captured Hungarian queen who fell from high estate and who, like Churchyard's Mistress Shore, became a royal concubine and suffered as a result. In his account of Elstride's travails, Higgins strives for the same sort of moral complexity and emotional force that Churchyard achieved in recounting Shore's life. Higgins thus has Elstride confess her sins of pride and adultery, but he then moves readers to dwell not on her admitted faults but on the pain of her emotional and physical suffering at the hands of the vengeful Queen Gwendoline. In a similar manner, Higgins has Cordila (Shakespeare's Cordelia) acknowledge herself a suicide who died in despair; however, Higgins leads readers to forgive Cordila her last moments of weakness by emphasizing her virtuous life, the unjust nature of her afflictions, and the terrible privations she underwent in the period before her suicide. In poems such as these, Higgins expands upon the generally monologic model of earlier *Mirror* tragedies by introducing multivocal and often dramatic elements into the *de casibus* tragedy form. Thus, many of Higgins's speakers not only tell their own stories but also communicate material such as long set speeches by other characters, dramatic exchanges of dialogue, impassioned private prayers, and even the contents of verse epistles. Higgins's tragedies in the voices of fallen women, together with his patriotic poems such as 'Albanact' and 'Nennius' celebrating exemplary British warriors, are some of the most accomplished pieces of verse of the 1570s. Like the poems of Baldwin's work, their popularity helped inspire such later authors as Drayton and Thomas Middleton to produce increasingly sophisticated *de casibus* tragedies and verse complaints in the late Elizabethan and early Stuart periods.

Unfortunately, most of Higgins's tragedies fall far short of the artistry of his best work. The bulk of Higgins's poetry is inspired not by Baldwin's *Mirror* but by Lydgate's *Fall of Princes*. These pieces have few of Lydgate's strengths and many of his weaknesses; in general, they tend to be uniform, unengaging, and often very brief.

While many of these works handle the falls of immoral rulers, Higgins evinces in them little interest in carrying on Baldwin's project of providing sharply focused warnings against particular acts of political misbehaviour. Instead, Higgins is usually content to denounce misrule only in the broadest terms, and he often rehearses the life of a fallen tyrant chiefly to inveigh against universal rather than specifically political vices. In the tragedy of 'Morindus', for instance, Higgins describes at length the oppression his royal protagonist visited upon his subjects; however, when he comes to moralize Morindus' death (swallowed by a sea monster that he had rashly decided to battle single-handedly), Higgins uses it solely to warn readers against the dangers of making hasty decisions (*Parts Added* 1946: 189). Indeed, at times Higgins seems to forget by the end of a tragedy just what he had set out to teach within it. At the beginning of 'Mempricius', the fratricide and tyrant Mempricius urges readers to learn the wages of a vicious life by observing the nature of his fall. However, when he comes to narrating Mempricius' death (devoured by wolves), Higgins surprisingly claims that Mempricius met his end only by 'chaunce' (*Parts Added* 1946: 127).

Higgins allows himself such a cavalier approach to the content of many of his tragedies precisely because his overriding concern in composing them was neither narratorial coherence nor moral admonition but formal poetic experimentation. In all three editions of his collection, Higgins includes tragedies written in a wide variety of stanzaic and metrical forms, ranging from the brief and choppy tetrameter quatrains of 'Bladud' (1574) to the cumbersome octaves of hexameters followed by a single fourteener line in which he casts 'Londricus' (1587). Few critics have found Higgins's prosodic experiments successful, and even Higgins himself acknowledges in the *First Part* that many readers will find fault with his verse (*Parts Added* 1946: 129–31). It may be, however, that Higgins's zeal for poetic innovation provided inspiration to contemporaries such as Spenser and Sidney as they pursued their own investigations into new forms and metres for English poetry. Further, it is certain that several important authors of the late Elizabethan and early Stuart period admired Higgins's best pieces enough to draw upon them as sources for their own compositions. Most notably, Shakespeare and Spenser used matter from Higgins's 'Cordila' for *King Lear* and *The Faerie Queene*, while the anonymous author of the drama *Locrine* (1595) kept Higgins's *First Part* nearby as he created his own account of King Locrinus' troubled career (*Parts Added* 1946: 27–8; Farnham 1926).

The next poet to pen a continuation of Baldwin's *Mirror* was Thomas Blenerhasset (or Blener Hasset), a Cambridge scholar turned soldier who was an admirer of both Baldwin's and Higgins's poetry. In 1578 Richard Webster published Blenerhasset's *Second Part of the Mirror for Magistrates*, a volume that presented fallen British and Anglo-Saxon figures from the time of Rome's occupation of Britain until the entrance of William the Conqueror.

Blenerhasset's strongly Puritan sympathies led him to compose tragedies chiefly admonishing readers to eschew moral rather than solely political vices.[10] While he

---

[10] Blenerhasset's claims that he had no chronicles with him when he composed his tragedies and that he did not mean for his poems to be circulated among a wide audience both appear to be disingenuous. For Blenerhasset's chronicle sources, see Lämmerhirt (1909). For evidence that Blenerhasset composed

warns against a host of ethical failings in his collection, it is the sin of lust that exercises Blenerhasset most greatly. Blenerhasset's revulsion for lechery leads him several times to depart from his chronicle sources to compose matter that insists upon the numerous miseries awaiting those who indulge in wantonness. Thus, in recounting the life of King Alured (better known as Alfred the Great), Blenerhasset dutifully praises Alured's learning and victories over invading Danes. However, so eager is Blenerhasset to dissuade men from sins of the flesh that he ends his poem with the entirely unhistorical claims that Alured spent his last years engaged in sensual indulgence and that such behaviour resulted in an agonizing death from a sexually transmitted disease. In a similar manner, Blenerhasset has Uter Pendragon blame his lust for the wife of Duke Garelus (Gorlois) for the loss of his kingdom, an assertion found in none of Blenerhasset's sources. The tragic result of Uter's fall into temptation, which Uter attributes to the deplorable British custom of allowing women to appear publicly without veils, allows Blenerhasset an opportunity to inveigh against the habits of contemporary Englishwomen, who, he claims, are so brazenly bedecked with 'fylthy furnitures' and so bold in their sexual enticements that even Roman courtesans would look upon them with disgust. His ideal of feminine virtue is Lady Ebbe, the Saxon nun who convinced the members of her convent to mutilate their faces to protect their virginity from lecherous Viking invaders (*Parts Added* 1946: 469, 440, 465–8).

Blenerhasset's *Second Part* did not have the influence upon later writers that Baldwin's and Higgins's collections were to enjoy, and it was not reprinted until Richard Niccols's omnibus edition of the *Mirror* in 1610. If Blenerhasset's poetry has not stood the test of time, however, the *Second Part* remains interesting as an example of early Elizabethan Puritan literature. Blenerhasset's strong expression of Calvinist beliefs and 'godly' moral values, the surprisingly bold defence of English Presbyterians included in the collection, and his barely disguised satirical condemnation of the vices of English churchmen in the tragedy 'Cadwallader', all offer important glimpses into the nascent literary culture of separatist English Puritanism.

Niccols's Jacobean edition of the *Mirror* was to be last of the early modern period. For his volume, Niccols gathered together most of the poems of Baldwin's, Higgins's, and Blenerhasset's editions, deleting their prose and poetic links, rearranging their order, editing their lines, and adding to them several poems of his own, including an induction, ten new tragedies, and a lengthy paean to Elizabeth and her rule titled 'England's Eliza'.[11] A study of Niccols's Jacobean *Mirror* tragedies lies beyond the scope of this Handbook; it is enough to say that Niccols's smoothly flowing lines, so indebted to the late Elizabethan verse of Spenser and Drayton, highlights how far English metrics had come from the rough, plain, and by now old-fashioned prosody of the original *Mirror* authors. Though its model would continue to inspire writers

his tragedies with a popular audience in mind, see E. Miller (1959: 144–5). Lämmerhirt's list of Blenerhasset's sources may be augmented by the addition of Polydore Vergil's *Anglica historia* (for the early stanzas of 'Guidericus') and John Stow's *Summary of English Chronicles* (for 'Lady Ebbe' and 'Alurede').

[11] Niccols also included Drayton's previously published *de casibus* tragedy 'Thomas Cromwell'.

well into Charles I's reign, the text that began its life in 1554 finally ran its course with the last reissue of Niccols's edition in 1621. Like Hall's chronicle, however, the *Mirror* did so only after rendering a profound and lasting influence upon the literary culture of Tudor and early Stuart England.[12]

PRIMARY WORKS

ELLIS, HENRY (ed.) (1809), *Hall's Chronicle* (London: G. Woodfall).

HALL, EDWARD (1550), *The Union of the Two Noble and Illustre Famelies of Lancastre & Yorke* (London: Richard Grafton).

Mirror (1938), *The Mirror for Magistrates*, ed. Lily B. Campbell (Cambridge: Cambridge University Press).

Parts Added (1946), *Parts Added to The Mirror for Magistrates*, ed. Lily B. Campbell (Cambridge: Cambridge University Press).

---

[12] For comments on Higgins's and Blenerhasset's *Mirror* contributions, see Budra (2000); for Niccols's additions to the text, see Nearing (1945: 44–55).

CHAPTER 22

A PLACE IN THE SHADE

GEORGE CAVENDISH AND *DE CASIBUS* TRAGEDY

MIKE PINCOMBE

GEORGE CAVENDISH is one of the great forgotten figures of mid-Tudor poetry. His so-called *Metrical Visions* is a long visionary poem containing a sequence of tragic complaints spoken by the phantasmal apparitions of a series of mid-Tudor personages from Cardinal Wolsey (d. 1530) to Lady Jane Grey (d. 1554).[1] Cavendish probably wrote the main sequence of the poem between 1552 and 1554, when he started work on his *Life of Wolsey*, and he wrote out a fair copy of the two works, together with a final epitaph on Mary, in a single manuscript (BL, Egerton MS 2402), dated 24 June 1558. Since then, the fortunes of the two works could hardly have been more different. The *Life* was copied many times in the early modern period; it supplied the Elizabethan chroniclers with material for their histories; and it found print as early as 1641. But the *Metrical Visions* had to wait until 1825 before it was printed, and hardly anybody— perhaps nobody—seems to have consulted the manuscript before that date. Why have the *Metrical Visions* been overlooked for so long? They surely provide one of the most

---

[1] Cavendish's orthography is not easy to read, so I have modernized it, as I have quotations from all other Tudor texts.

fascinating texts for scholars and critics interested in 'poetry and politics', and easy and reliable access to the text was made possible as long ago as 1980 by A. G. S. Edwards. Yet this chapter may be the first to give serious attention to the *Visions* as well as to the relatively familiar *Life of Wolsey*.

It is especially surprising that the current revival of interest in *A Mirror for Magistrates* has not led to the rediscovery of the *Metrical Visions*. After all, many scholars are attracted to the *Mirror* because its tragedies, especially those which appear to have been written around 1554 for the first version of the text, known as the 'Memorial', seem to offer an allegorical commentary on recent historical events. So, for example, Scott Lucas (2003) has recently deciphered George Ferrers's tragedy of the fifteenth-century Duke of Somerset, Edward Beaufort, as a covert allusion to the fall of his sixteenth-century counterpart: Edward Seymour, Duke of Somerset, and Lord Protector in the early years of the reign of Edward VI. Lucas is particularly interested in the way Ferrers's poem may seek to explain to Somerset's Protestant supporters how the 'good duke' had fallen because that was his destiny, rather than because God wished to punish him for his complicity in the political murder of his brother Thomas, the Lord Admiral. All this, he ingeniously argues, is set forth allegorically in Somerset's tragedy in the *Mirror* (see also Lucas, Chapter 21 in this volume). But Cavendish's Somerset *openly* laments his rise and fall in the *Metrical Visions*, as does his brother—indeed, as do all the other phantasmal speakers who tell their stories to Cavendish in his vision.

It is quite possible that the team of poets working on the 'Memorial' were at least aware of the existence of the *Metrical Visions* and the basic form of the poem. The 1559 and 1563 editions of the *Mirror* were 'sponsored' by the bookish minor nobleman Henry, Lord Stafford, who was a neighbour, friend, and colleague of George's younger brother William Cavendish (A. Anderson 1963: 233). If the connection goes back to the 1554 'Memorial', as seems to me very likely, given Stafford's almost proprietorial interest in the *Mirror*, then the probability of influence is even stronger (his friendship with William Cavendish dates to the 1540s). The compiler of the *Mirror*, William Baldwin, on the other hand, tells his readers that there was not 'any alive that meddled with like argument' (*Mirror* 1938: 69)—but this coy denial may hide a modicum of knowledge of the very similar work that Cavendish was finishing off even as the 'Memorial' team sat down to their own project in 1554.

One feels that a great resource for historically-minded critics of Tudor literature lies unappreciated between the pages of Edwards's edition of Cavendish's poem. However, my aim in this chapter is not to illustrate how the *Metrical Visions* open up a rich field of topical allusion to mid-Tudor political history, but, rather, to explore certain elements of the formal structure of Cavendish's poem in the light of the English *de casibus* tradition. The main current of this literary genre—or, rather, genre complex— was transmitted to Tudor readers and writers by John Lydgate's *The Fall of Princes*, a verse 'translation' (via a French intermediary) of Giovanni Boccaccio's *De casibus virorum illustrium*. Cavendish is likely to have read the poem in the most recent edition, which was printed by Richard Pynson in 1527, when Cavendish was still in the service of Cardinal Wolsey. He certainly knew the poem well: 'Nearly two hundred lines in the *Metrical Visions* are borrowed from Lydgate' (A. Edwards 1980*b*: 10). And he also used his material intelligently.

For example, Cavendish's tragedies of the two Seymour brothers borrow largely from the tragedies of Thyestes and Atreus in the first book of the *Fall*.[2] The fratricidal context makes the comparison obvious enough; but Cavendish's poetical instincts allow him to appreciate the special quality of this episode in Lydgate's vast poem. Very few of the phantasms who appear to Boccaccio, or 'Bochas', as he sits among his books in his study, are permitted to tell their own stories; Bochas prefers to tell them all himself—which means that he merely rewrites the stories as he finds them written in his histories and chronicles. The three or four who do speak are betrayed by their own accounts as partial and unreliable witnesses, and roundly berated by Bochas for their mendacity. But for the modern reader of Tudor literature, *de casibus* tragedy is marked precisely by the fact that it takes the form of a complaint spoken in the first person, as in *A Mirror for Magistrates*. It was Cavendish who introduced this innovation, not Baldwin and his co-writers.

Moreover, the *Mirror*, for all its excellent qualities, is less true to the *de casibus* tradition than the *Visions*. Although the title of Cavendish's poem is not his own, but the invention of its early nineteenth-century editor, it very neatly captures the two elements that matter most in our appreciation of the poem. Sadly, Cavendish does not score highly as a versifier, and the little criticism of his poetry that does exist—all negative, nearly all worthless (see A. Edwards 1980*b*: 11–12)—has focused on this deficiency (it is motivated by same spirit of trivial and tiresome critical malice that makes jest of the fourteener and poulters' measure). But as a visionary poet, Cavendish was a long way ahead of William Baldwin and his colleagues on the original Marian version of *A Mirror for Magistrates*. Baldwin, the compiler, abandons all pretence to the visionary framework that supported the earlier examples of *de casibus* tragedy from Boccaccio onwards. There is only one dream in the entire original sequence, the rest of the tragedies being performed by their composers as a kind of charade in the 1559 version, or simply read out by Baldwin in the additions made in the 1563 version. But when Thomas Sackville attempted to take over the project in the early 1560s, and when John Higgins added new poems to the sequence in 1574, both men reverted to the visionary framework in which a solitary narrator is privileged to 'see'—and hear—what really happened to the fallen princes of Anglo-British history.

Cavendish's contribution to *de casibus* tragedy, then, was to defy Bochas and his impatiently authoritarian attitude towards the act of individual memorial witness. For Bochas, to tell one's own story is tantamount to lying; but Cavendish listens patiently and sympathetically to all those who come and make their moan to him. After Thyestes and Atreus have spoken to Bochas, he tires of their endless dispute, and 'Put up his pen, and wrote not more a word, | Of their fury, ne of their false

---

[2] The information on Cavendish's imitation of Lydgate comes from Edwards's edition (see also A. Edwards 1971).

discord' (Lydgate 1924–7: 22ᵛ; 1. 4212–14).[3] But Cavendish records the complaints of Thomas and Edward Seymour with equanimity, allowing them to deny being guilty of the crimes for which they were sentenced and executed—he even agrees that Somerset was abused 'most shamefully with cruelty' (line 1749). He piously concludes: 'God's works, which be known to none, | For his judgements be secret, till they be past and gone' (lines 1751–2).

Despite his privileged access to the voices of the recently deceased, then, Cavendish does not claim to penetrate the secret world of divine providence. He sees God's hand at work in the lives of the Seymours, but he does not know exactly what it means. Thus, though he may as a visionary poet see things that other men have not been permitted to see, he does not present himself as a fully fledged *vates*, or 'prophet'. Prophetic poetry was a crucial complex of genres in the Edwardian period, when the Roman Catholic Cavendish, former servant of a despised cardinal, was writing his tragedies.[4] Generally speaking, Protestant prophet–poets presented the rise of their own Church as a fulfilment of the book of Revelation, as the final instalment of universal history. Cavendish was hardly likely to have time for such a view; but he does not reject prophecy outright, and it is my purpose in the pages that follow to give an account of his work—both the *Metrical Visions* and the slightly later *Life of Wolsey*— in the light of a particular prophecy, uttered by Wolsey on his deathbed, to which only Cavendish and one or two others were privy. In the momentous final episode of his modest public career, on 6 December 1530, Cavendish denied all knowledge of this prophecy before Henry VIII and his council. But later, as Wolsey's prophecy seemed to be coming true, his conscience urged him to write—and this is what made him a poet.

I

Cavendish was a young man, probably about 25, when he entered Wolsey's service as a gentleman usher around 1520; but despite the detail with which he tells the story of his master's life in the 1520s, Cavendish seems to have left very little trace of his own activities in these years.[5] It is only after he left public life in 1530, and returned to his home county of Suffolk, to manage the estate left to him on the death of his father in 1524, that the name of George Cavendish starts to appear with unexceptional regularity in legal documents, mainly relating to the transfer of property, until

---

[3] In references to Lydgate's *Fall*, the first element refers by folio to the 1527 edition by Richard Pynson, which is the one I think Cavendish probably read; and the second by book and line to Bergen's standard edition of the Bodl. MS Bodley 263 copy of the poem.

[4] For the composition of prophecies, see J. King (1982: 209–70); for their interpretation, see *ODNB* 'John Foxe'.

[5] For Cavendish's life, see Sylvester (1959, pp. xiii–xxvi) and *ODNB* 'George Cavendish', which gives a new and apparently firm date of birth as 1494 (though without producing new evidence).

Fig. 22.1 Two-faced Fortune shows Bochas (on the right) the fate of Cardinal Wolsey. John Lydgate, *The Fall of Prynces* (1527), 2D1ʳ.

his death around 1562. Paradoxically, then, Cavendish only becomes visible after he leaves the limelight of the early Henrician political scene; and, even so, he is only obscurely visible—and we will have more to say on this in the conclusion of this chapter.

We need not go into the detail of Cavendish's biography of Wolsey here; it will be enough to say that Cavendish does shape his material into a *de casibus* narrative of rise and fall, with plenty of allusions to Fortune at key moments, and with some sense of a master narrative which leads us through the minutiae of the book.[6] If, as seems likely, Cavendish used the most recent edition of Lydgate's *Fall of Princes*, the one printed by Richard Pynson in 1527, he would have seen there a woodcut which had been especially redesigned to show his master—'Fat-faced and flat-hatted' (A. Gillespie 2006: 173)—at the top of Fortune's wheel, ready to begin his descent (Figure 22.1). In any case, after describing Wolsey's rise to wealth and power, Cavendish notes that 'Fortune [...] began to wax something wroth with his prosperous estate' (1962: 30). She therefore 'procured Venus, the insatiate goddess', to make Henry fall in love with Anne Boleyn, whom he 'fantasied [doted on] so much [...] that almost everything began to grow out of frame and good order' (31). Anne was in love with Henry Percy, heir to the Earl of Northumberland; and Wolsey was the King's instrument in prising

---

[6] Sylvester (1960) gives a very good analysis of the *Life* as a *de casibus* tragedy.

her loose from this attachment—to his own eventual ruin. Cavendish exclaims: 'O Lord, what a God art thou, that workest thy secrets so wondrously? Which be not perceived until they be brought to pass and finished' (37). Note the similarity between the comment on divine providence here and in his coda to the tragedy of Somerset in the *Metrical Visions*—and the difference. Writing soon after the Duke's death in 1552, Cavendish will not speculate on what it may mean; but writing a quarter-century after the Cardinal's death, Cavendish allows himself to see the workings of God's will—*in retrospect*.

Anne Boleyn never forgave Wolsey's interference in her *amour*, and she plotted, says Cavendish, to eliminate his master, finally succeeding in turning the King against him in the late 1520s. Cavendish presents this tragic sequence of events as a personal conflict between Wolsey and Anne Boleyn as rivals for the King's trust and affection; he says hardly anything of their religious differences, yet Wolsey was a papal officer of the highest order and Anne was a committed supporter of the evangelical movement. Cavendish knew this, because in his tragedy of Anne Boleyn in the *Metrical Visions*, he makes the Queen compare herself (in a borrowing from Lydgate's *Fall*) to 'Gatholia', namely, the Hebrew queen Athaliah, who 'Spared not the blood, by cruel vengeance, | Of Gods' prophets' (Cavendish 1980, lines 563–4; cf. Lydgate 1924–7: 52^r; 2. 1884–90). She explains that she caused laws to be made against those who spoke against her, and thus 'with great oaths […] found out the trade [practice] | To burden men's conscience' and to 'danger the innocent' (Cavendish 1980, lines 569–71). It is not clear to which specific acts of legislation he refers here, but the point is made that Anne put innocent men's souls at risk by making them keep quiet or even to swear oaths against their conscience.

The confessional antipathy between Wolsey and Boleyn which lies hidden behind their personal animosity in Cavendish's biography only once seems to find relatively direct expression—and, even so, not very direct. When Wolsey died in Leicester Abbey on 30 November 1530, only two men were present at his bedside: Cavendish himself, and Sir William Kingston, a loyal and experienced servant of the Crown whom Henry had sent to fetch Wolsey back from York to London. Wolsey urged Kingston to advise the King that he should 'depress [repress] this new perverse sect of the Lutherans, that it do not increase within his dominions through his negligence' (Cavendish 1962: 184).[7] Anne was not exactly a Lutheran, but she was strongly committed to evangelical reform; and, in any case, Wolsey would simply have regarded both her own group and the Lutherans as 'heretics'. He reminds Kingston of the popular commotions associated with 'Wycliffe's seditious opinions' (185) in the time of Richard II, and the resistance shown to Henry V by 'that traitorous heretic, Sir John Oldcastle'. His argument is that once a sovereign prince allows heresy to spread through the commons by his 'negligence', he is paving the way for challenges to the authority of the Church and his own 'regaly': the royal prerogative (181). He concludes: 'And then will ensue mischief upon mischief, inconvenience upon

---

[7] Cavendish spells 'Lutherans' as 'lutaryaunce', miscorrected to 'lutarnaunce'. It is as if he cannot bring himself to write the name of heresy.

inconvenience, barrenness and scarcity of all things for lack of good order in the commonwealth, to the utter destruction and desolation of this noble realm—from which mischief God for His tender mercy defend us' (185–6). The message could hardly be plainer: Stamp out heresy or England will go to ruin. However, Kingston—wisely—did not pass this message on to Henry and his council. Though rumour of a prophecy had somehow leaked out through the yeoman of the guard, Kingston denied any knowledge of it, and advised Cavendish to do the same: 'if you should tell them the truth [...] what he said, you should undo yourself, for in any wise they would not hear of it' (189–90). Cavendish does as he is told. The remarkable part of the story is that Cavendish remained silent for so long; it was nearly thirty years after the event that he finally divulged the prophecy in his *Life of Wolsey*—and even then only to the privileged few who might have access to his manuscript.

Cavendish's long silence can best be explained, I think, by the operations of conscience. He may well have feared for his own 'convenience' if he should have told his story while Henry was still alive. Then, when Somerset and his party established a Protestant regime in England under Edward VI, it must have seemed that Wolsey's prophecy had come true, especially after the popular revolts of 1549, which were particularly vehement in Cavendish's own local area. In the *Metrical Visions*, Somerset does not mention his religious reforms, but he does confess that he was a rabble-rouser:

> I maintained the commons to make insurrections,
> I thought in the commons to have sure aid,
> But at my most need, I was of them denied.
>
> (1980, lines 1702–4)

By the early 1550s, Cavendish's conscience may well have troubled him. Although he must have known in 1530 that revealing the prophecy to Henry would not have made much difference to his policy, Cavendish did not bear true witness to his master.

Cavendish's remaining silent about Wolsey's prophecy is not quite on the level of Peter's denial of Christ in the Gospels (but see Sylvester 1960: 68); still, he may have felt that he had been tried and found wanting. Cavendish explains that he has written the *Life* in order to set the record straight about Wolsey's life against the malicious misreports 'set forth in divers printed books' (1962: 3). Cavendish repeatedly refers to Wolsey's 'enemies' in the *Life*, and he explains that he felt threatened by them himself:

Since his [Wolsey's] death, I have heard divers sundry surmises and imagined tales made of his proceedings and doings, which I myself have perfectly known to be most untrue. Unto the which I could have sufficiently answered according to the truth; but as me seemeth then, it was much better for me to suffer and dissimull [dissemble] the matter, and the same to remain still as lies, than to reply against their untruth, of whom I might for my boldness sooner have kindled a great flame of displeasures than to quench one spark of their malicious untruth.   (4)

Cavendish felt he could not speak the truth and he suffered. More precisely, he preferred to suffer the indignity of dissembling what he knew and felt in order to avoid the greater pains hinted at by the imagery of combustion in the 'great flame of displeasures'. Plenty of 'heretics' were burned for their faith under Henry VIII.

Cavendish's need to placate his conscience is evident, I think, in the ambiguously worded final stanza addressed to him by Wolsey's phantasm in the *Metrical Visions*:

> This is my last complaint, I can say you no more,
> But farewell my servant, that faithful hath be [been].
> Note well these words, quod he, I pray thee therefore,
> And write them thus plain as I have told them thee,
> All which is true, thou knowest it full well, pardee.
> Thou failedst me not, until that I died.
> And now I must depart, I may no lenger [longer] bide.

(1980, lines 253–9)

Does the sixth line of this stanza mean that Cavendish never failed Wolsey while the Cardinal lived—or that he failed him after his death by refusing to reveal the prophecy as he was required? In either case, Wolsey gives Cavendish a second chance to tell his story truly. He returns from the dead to instruct his old servant, now a poet, to note his words and to write them down for posterity. The *Metrical Visions* were no more intended for general circulation than the *Life of Wolsey*; but Cavendish knew that he was writing for himself, for Wolsey, and for God. He concludes the prologue to the *Life*, as follows: 'Therefore, I commit the truth to Him that knoweth all truth' (1962: 4).[8]

II

Cavendish's *Life* is not an autobiography in the strict sense, but, as Elizabeth Heale demonstrates in Chapter 36 in this volume, recent developments in the study of life-writing which have widened the scope of the genre might indeed open up an autobiographical perspective on this fascinatingly personal account of the great Cardinal (see also Skura 2008). In the *Metrical Visions*, however, the first-person narrator is

---

[8] We only have Cavendish's word for it, of course, that Wolsey really did make the prophecy, and Britnell is right to note that it provides 'a description of the Reformation period seen from the standpoint of a religious conservative who valued a quiet life' (1997: 273–4). No doubt, it was indeed coloured by Cavendish's own perspective; but Britnell also argues that the external corroboration of other details in Cavendish's account of the final episode of the *Life* makes it 'probable and acceptable' (280).

far more elusive, even though he is thrust to the foreground of our attention by the generic dynamics of the text far more assertively than he is in the *Life*, for all its similarity to a personal memoir. This is mainly because Cavendish is much more consciously artistic in the *Visions*; he is following a complex and various tradition of visionary poetry, and he inserts his 'self' into its formal structures with conscientious effort. In this section, I want to examine the ways in which Cavendish explores the author position of the 'witness' in the *Metrical Visions* by looking particularly at the 'dream within a dream' in which Cavendish accompanies Morpheus to the deathbed of Henry VIII, where he sees the King expire and hears—and this time reports—his last words.

Cavendish has just been listening to the complaint of Henry Howard, Earl of Surrey; he has written down what Surrey said, moralized a little in an envoy, and resolved to end his task. Then he trembles to hear a trump; it is Dame Fame, who tells him that 'Dead is that royal prince, the late eighth Harry' (1980, line 1227).[9] Cavendish sits down to lament him, but as he leans back in his chair, he falls asleep. At this point, his vision turns into a dream in which he is led by Morpheus and Fancy to a candlelit chamber where a mighty prince lies dying, surrounded by his servants, but also by the three Fates: Clotho, Lachesis, and Atropos.[10] The prince persuades Atropos to hold her shears, while he confesses—in terms borrowed largely from Lydgate's tragedy of Hercules in *The Fall of Princes*—that he has 'darked [his] honour, spotted fame and glory' (line 1334) by breaking the bond of marriage

> for the love and fond affection
> Of a simple woman [...]
> By means whereof this realm is brought in ruin.
>
> (lines 1313–14, 1317)

The allusion is to Henry's divorce of Katherine of Aragon and marriage with Anne Boleyn, and the ruin that befell England as it was predicted by the dying Wolsey in Cavendish's *Life*. Cavendish thus makes Henry confirm the prophecy which he himself had suppressed and would not fully divulge until the closing pages of his biography of the Cardinal.

Cavendish watches the King die, then wakes up weeping, and Morpheus leaves him. Fancy, however, stays with him, and, reminding him of all the tragedies he has written on other fallen princes, urges him to write at least an epitaph. This turns out to be a

---

[9] Henry died only ten days after he had had Surrey executed on 19 January 1547.

[10] The pairing of Morpheus and Fancy is also found in William Neville's *Castle of Pleasure* (1530). This is one of several books which Cavendish may have read as a young man at court. The rare word 'umber' (see p.385), used by Cavendish of an oak tree in the second line of the *Visions*, also appears in the Prologue to Guillaume Alexis's *Argument betwixt Man and Woman* (1525), where the poet–dreamer sits down one hot summer's day 'Under the umber of a tree' (A2ʳ). A. Edwards (1980*b*: 151) notes that Cavendish must also have read the Prologue to John Skelton's *Garland of Laurel*, first printed in 1523, in which the poet–dreamer also sits under an oak. Works such as these provide a non-tragic context for the *Visions*, in addition—perhaps even in opposition—to the *de casibus* theme.

rather mechanical affair in which Henry's virtues are compared to those of a long list of ancient gods and heroes:

> A Jupiter of providence,
> A strength of Hercules,
> A Mars of excellence
>
> (lines 1438–40)

—and so on for another thirty lines, including the following pair:

> An holy Phocion,
> A continent Fabricius.
>
> (lines 1458–9)

It is startling to find Henry praised for continence after his own confessions of concupiscence; and Cavendish seems to disown the allusion by making a deliberate mistake. Fabricius was known not for his continence but for his incorruptibility: 'Fabricius was a noble man of Rome whom no man could make to possess riches or receive gifts or to use craft or fraud against his enemies in time of mortal war' (Erasmus 1533: M2ᵛ). This is a sidenote to a passage in Erasmus' *The Manual of the Christian Knight*. Cavendish probably took Fabricius from this extremely popular text because Erasmus mentions Phocion and Fabricius in the same breath, noting 'the holiness of Phocion, [and] poverty of Fabricius'. This item is thus strikingly out of line with all the other correctly commonplace comparisons. It allows the reader to 'deconstruct' the epitaph as a eulogy written specifically for public consumption—propaganda, in fact. Conversely, the description of the scene of Henry's death, which Cavendish is privileged to witness thanks to Morpheus and especially to Fancy, assumes a greater air of authority—it speaks to the truth of poetry.

I have already noted that critics in search of a well-turned verse will find plenty of poor lines in Cavendish to whet their wits on; but this is a superficial approach to poetry, and it has kept back a genuine appreciation of the imaginative power of the *Metrical Visions*. In his prologue, Cavendish makes the usual apologetic gestures in a stanza which displays not only artistry but also his imitation of Lydgate's general prologue to *The Fall of Princes*. He lacks 'cunning exercise' in writing tragedy (line 53), but he knows that 'A woeful plaint must have a woeful style' (line 63):

> To whom, therefore, for help shall I now call?
> Alas, Calliope my calling will utterly refuse,
> For mourning ditties and woe of fortune's fall
> Calliope did never in her ditties use,
> Wherefore to her I might myself abuse;
> Also the Muses that on Parnassus sing,
> Such warbling dole did never temper string.
>
> (lines 64–70)

This stanza is a close and artful reworking of two passages in Lydgate's general prologue to *The Fall of Princes* (1924–7: A2ʳ, A3ᵛ; 1. 239–42, 456–7); but his acceptance of the traditional idea that Calliope and the Muses do not deal with tragedy (it was generally left to the Furies) sits oddly with the invocation of his epitaph for Queen Mary at the end of the manuscript: 'Descend from heaven, O muse Melpomene, | Thou mournful goddess, with thy sisters all' (lines 2279–80). Cavendish could, therefore, have 'corrected' Lydgate, had he been more pedantically inclined. But he follows his master because these references to Calliope are a way of signalling to his reader that he is writing tragedy in the traditional vernacular manner.[11]

In the end, however, Cavendish calls not on Calliope and the Muses, but on 'that lord whose power is celestial' (line 71). As in the *Life of Wolsey*, Cavendish produces an author position in which he acknowledges the role of God as the superior author who sanctions his mortal servant's poetry and prose inasmuch as Cavendish tells the truth as he knows it. In his own prologue, Lydgate explains that his patron, Humphrey, Duke of Gloucester, instructed him to 'be not partial' (1924–7: A3^v; 1. 445]); and Cavendish follows suit, but with God as his guide to the impartial truth:

> Now by thy help, this history I will begin,
> And from the effect vary nothing at all;
> For if I should, it were to me a great sin
> To take upon me a matter so substantial,
> So weighty, so necessary of fame perpetual.
>
> (lines 78–82)

The word 'effect' here probably resonates with the Latin sense of *effectus*: 'something completed' (cf. 'effect', *OED*, *n*., 5). We have returned to Cavendish's interest in prophecy, then, and its emphasis on retrospective confirmation rather than prospective speculation. Cavendish takes his role as a poet seriously, but he will not claim the full prophetic status of the *vates*. History is the 'effect' of divine providence: the relatively clearly stated record of 'God's works, which be known to none, | For his judgements be secret, till they be past and gone' (lines 1751–2). It is Cavendish's task to report these judgements, now declared by history, without varying from their expression—*as he sees it*.

There is always a problem of interpretation when we deal with enigmatic utterances. In the *Life of Wolsey*, Cavendish reports on the 'Dun Cow' prophecy, which states: 'when this cow rideth the bull, then priest beware thy skull' (1962: 131). He tells us how he and Wolsey discussed it, but neither understood 'the effect of this prophecy'; and it was not until later that 'all men' came to believe the prophecy had been fulfilled when Anne Boleyn mastered Henry VIII and brought about the downfall not only of Wolsey but of many other priests, 'both religious and secular' (132). But this only became evident *after the event*, and Cavendish goes on to attack the use of such 'dark and obscure riddles and prophecies' as a rationale for political action: 'Let prophecies alone, a God's name!' (128–9). God disposes such prophecies

---

[11] Sackville does exactly the same in the manuscript additions to his tragedy of Buckingham, where he writes a memo to himself to 'Look in the prologue of Bochas, fol. 64' (*Mirror* 1938: 546), and then duly works up the relevant stanza about Calliope, Parnassus, and the Muses from Lydgate's *Fall* (1527, fo. 64; 1924–7: iii. 8–14).

not in order that men may foresee the future, but that they may look back and see that history is a record of divine providence—or 'foresight' (from the Latin *pro* and *videre*). But even retrospective judgement still requires an act of interpretation, and Cavendish cannot be cleared from the charge of disingenuousness on this point.

However, although Cavendish plainly favours interpretations of prophecies which are in accord with his own political and religious conservatism, he is, at least, remarkably restrained in his application of his prejudices to the various complaints which make up the *Metrical Visions*. For example, you would hardly know that there had been an attempt at reformation in Tudor England from reading these poems; there is no mention of gospellers or the English Prayer Book or even direct reference to the dissolution of the religious houses. Only in the epitaph to Mary, written four years after the completion of the main sequence of tragedies, does Cavendish at last openly declare his confessional allegiance, when he fearfully recalls how Mary rescued England from the defacement of altars, the burning of altars, the general apostasy and spoliation into which the realm had fallen: 'This chaos confuse, this heap of horror' (1980, line 2361)—in other words: hell.[12] But in the rest of the poem, Cavendish keeps his peace.

This is not to say that his poetry is politically anodyne. There is a remarkable moment in Henry's speech to Atropos in which he admits that he does not know his posthumous destination: 'To weal or woe I shall once rise again' (line 1298). 'Weal' means heaven, and 'woe' means hell—or at least the torments of purgatory. In the public voice of the epitaph, Cavendish announces Henry's stellification:

> Whose honour to magnify
> The mighty power divine
> Hath chosen him forthy [therefore]
> Above the stars to shine.
>
> (lines 1470–3)

But behind the confident assertions of the epitaph, and the official literary culture of 'fame perpetual' which Cavendish mentions in his prologue (82), there is this private moment of doubt, a 'secret' which Cavendish has been privileged to witness and which he now shares with his reader. Likewise, the discretion with which Cavendish has Henry disclose his tyranny also takes on the character of a 'secret history'. Henry admits that, to satisfy his lust, he has

> constrained by mortal violence
> So many to die, my purpose to attain,
> That now more grievous surely is my pain.
>
> (lines 1340–2)

---

[12] Cavendish's phrasing clearly recalls that of the Vulgate Latin version of Job, where we hear of 'the shadowy land, hidden by the gloom of death, the land of misery and the shadows of death, where there is no order (*nullus ordo*) and where eternal horror dwells (*horror inhabitans*)' (Job 10: 21–2).

Cavendish makes Henry suffer from a guilty conscience, then, but he may also allow himself the satisfaction of hinting that the King knows he may be punished for his sins in hell or purgatory.

It is a remarkable fact that *de casibus* tragedy from Boccaccio to the *Mirror for Magistrates* is very reluctant to specify where the souls of the fallen princes have ended up after their deaths. Boccaccio identifies hell as the destination of one or two (but not all) of the most notorious persecutors of the early Christians, such as Galerius: 'Horrible death first did [him] here confound, | With furies infernal [he] lieth in hell bound] (Lydgate 1924–7: 172^r; 8. 1021–2); and Richard III is to be imagined 'tormented [...] in the deep pit of hell' (*Mirror* 1938: 359). It is only in the case of individuals whose fate is deemed uncontroversial that *de casibus* poets will take it upon themselves to declare God's final judgement on their princes. In the case of Cavendish's Henry, however, the point is that the King's own doubts about his spiritual future, like his frank confession of his egotistical concupiscence, contradict the confident fatuities of the epitaph manufactured for public consumption as the official record of Henry's 'fame perpetual'.

III

Cavendish took himself seriously as a tragic poet, even if—perhaps precisely because—he did not claim the vatic status of a 'seer'. For him, tragedy was a species of historical writing, and he calls his poem both 'this tragedy' (1980, line 49) and 'this history' (line 78)—with apparent indifference. It was his self-imposed task to give an accurate and impartial survey of the 'effect' of the lives of his subjects, that is, not so much the detailed account one might expect from a biographical study, but rather evidence of the way in which their lives and deaths seemed to shadow forth the workings of divine providence. The world called up by Cavendish's phantasmal speakers is thus devoid of the almost gossipy particularity of the *Life of Wolsey*. In fact, it seems as vague and portentous as the visionary framework of the poem itself, with its gloomy but indistinct location and the usual sense of a time that has slowed down or even stopped. Only once, at the very start of the poem, do light and clarity seem to shine in the poem, and in this section I want to look a little more closely at the curious *mise-en-scène* of the *Metrical Visions*, once more to bring our attention back to the 'retro-prophetic' character of its inflection of *de casibus* tragedy.

It is difficult to establish with any certainty a *terminus a quo* for the *Visions*, but we may assume that Cavendish did not start writing until after the death of Henry VIII in 1547 (see A. Edwards 1974). I have suggested above that Cavendish may have been motivated to write the poem partly as a means of satisfying his conscience after having remained silent about Wolsey's prophecy for so long. He may also have been provoked by the appearance in 1548 of Edward Hall's chronicle, which is very hostile to Wolsey, and which some critics have argued stirred Cavendish into writing his *Life* as a defence of his old master in 1554 (see May 1975). But I would argue that the key event was probably the rebellions of 1549, in which conservative resistance to the evangelical innovations introduced by the Duke of Somerset and his supporters flared up all across southern England. The towns and villages a few miles to the east of Cavendish's manor of Cavendish Overhall were a traditional hot-spot of riot and unrest, and they flared up once again in 1549.[13]

The 1549 rebellions produced a good deal of literary activity, especially on the part of the government and its supporters, who were shaken by the scale and purposefulness of the resistance to their policies (see Betteridge 2004: 89–113). I think the *Metrical Visions* probably has its origins in Cavendish's own experience of the period, which he considered retrospectively as a confirmation of Wolsey's prophecy that toleration of 'Lutherans' would lead to popular insurrection. The next step, according to Wolsey, would be 'the utter destruction and desolation of this noble realm' (Cavendish 1962: 186). This is the tragic drama lurking behind the sunny *mise-en-scène* of Cavendish's prologue, which begins with a very familiar image: 'In the month of June, I, lying sole alone | Under the umber [shade] of an oak with boughs pendant' (1980, lines 1–2). Indeed, these two lines would have been instantly recognizable to any educated reader as an imitation of one of the most famous lines of Western literature: the opening line of the first of the ten eclogues which make up Virgil's *Bucolics*. This reads: 'Tityre, tu patulae recubans sub tegmine fagi', or, 'Tityrus, lying under the spreading cover of the beech-tree'. This line was so famous—Helen Cooper notes that it 'haunted almost every writer of eclogues for centuries' (1977: 19)—that it was usually varied in a gesture of *imitatio*; hence one reason for the substitution of an oak for the beech. Moreover, it was not just pastoralists who were haunted by this line. Thanks to the key position of Virgil's *Bucolics* on the grammar school curriculum, the first words of the line were shorthand for the whole volume. In his famous *Letter* (1575), Robert Langham recalls how, as a schoolboy in the fifth form of St Anthony's School in London, probably about the time that Cavendish was writing the *Visions*, he 'began with [his] Virgil, *Tityre tu patulae*' (86).[14] We may be pretty sure that Cavendish knew it, then, and that he expected his readers to know it as well.

But the substitution of the oak for the beech also signifies a generic negotiation between pastoral and tragedy. A few lines after greeting Tityrus in this celebrated first line, Meliboeus, on his way into exile with his family and flocks, recounts how he has lost a pair of lambs, as had been predicted, he realizes now too late, by certain 'oaks touched by heaven' (line 17). But it is not merely for the sake of these lambs that the oaks were blasted as a sign of imminent disaster; the whole land is in uproar: 'there is trouble (*turbatur*) everywhere, in all the countryside (*totis agris*)' (lines 11–12). Meliboeus cries: 'See how civil discord (*discordia civis*) has brought forth wretches

---

[13] Cavendish's first wife was Agnes Spring (Sylvester 1959, p. xviii), who was a scion of the family upon whose enterprise was built the wealth of the 'prodigy cloth town' Lavenham—a town which was also a tinderbox of revolt (MacCulloch 1986: 296).

[14] In the following century, the word 'Tityre-tu' was used to refer to 'One of an association of well-to-do "roughs" who infested London streets' (*OED*).

[such as us]' (lines 71–2). Allegorically, the *discordia civis* refers to the civil war which followed the assassination of Julius Caesar in 44 BC. The victorious Octavian seized the property of many of Virgil's former neighbours in his native province of Northern Italy to reward his veterans. But the important point here is what this scene meant not to Virgil, but to Cavendish, and I want to argue that the oaks that are blasted by lightning thus tell—or foretell—the same story as Wolsey's prophecy: 'the utter destruction and desolation of this noble realm'.

Cavendish's substitution of the oak for Virgil's beech thus has a deep symbolic value for the English writer—for the oak, of course, is the English tree par excellence.[15] In terms of Virgilian pastoral, it suggests a recuperation of the tragic ruin signified by the blasted oaks of the first eclogue, in that the oak now provides the poet with shade and rest. But in Cavendish's poem, I suggest, the oak is a symbol not so much of pastoral ease, nor its shade a symbol of patronage, as of a mythical 'England', one which is imagined as being capable of resisting any change that is imposed on it—even apparent ruin.[16] Cavendish's oak represents the perdurability of a pre-Reformation England in the face of what he regarded—in accordance with Wolsey's prophecy—as the long decline which sets in after the break with Rome, and which reaches its nadir in the commotions of 1549. But we need not see this in specifically confessional terms, though Cavendish was definitely a Roman Catholic, and in his epitaph on Mary he asks for prayers for her soul to be spoken by the Pope and his cardinals (lines 2342–4). Rather, it is an essentially *conservative* vision.

We have seen how Cavendish makes very little—perhaps no—direct reference to confessional conflict in the *Metrical Visions*; and this in itself may be regarded as a conservative position. Anglophone critics of sixteenth-century literature have always tended to be mesmerized by the reformers and their works; it is no doubt a legacy of the Reformation itself. Consequently, we have lost sight of so many Tudor writers for whom the violence of fundamentalist belief and practice—on both sides of the confessional divide—was either too abhorrent or simply too dull or stupid to engage their attention. Cavendish is one of these writers, I think, still quietly dozing beneath his oak tree, but ready to be woken up by a revival of critical interest in the literary culture of the moderate writers of the period. The present hegemony of Reformation topics in the study of mid-Tudor literature is no doubt benign, but it does mean that certain writers tend to get overlooked—and this is probably the main answer to the question I raised at the outset of this chapter. In fact, Cavendish *should* be part of this new literary history, for though I have argued that he hardly ever deals directly with the momentous changes to Church and religion that occurred during his lifetime, he nevertheless does think about them—but represses these thoughts. It is as if by denying the scale of these changes, he could pretend they could be reversed, that the blasted English oak could be restored to health and vigour. He is therefore a good example, I suggest, of a writer whose deeply felt concerns may indeed be registered

[15] The 'Oak of Reformation' under which the Norfolk rebels held court on Mousehold Heath in 1549 comes to mind here, but not as a model for Cavendish's oak!

[16] For shady oaks as symbols for various English patrons, including the Duke of Somerset in a poem called 'The Hospitable Oak' by John Harington, see A. Patterson (1987: 53–6) and J. King (1982: 240–1).

by the absence of their expression. However, I wish to end this chapter with a final brief reflection on the first element of its title as a literary–generic topos, literally a 'place'—a place in the shade.

IV

When we talk of '*de casibus* tragedy', we tend to forget the second part of Boccaccio's original title, in which it is specified that those who fall are 'illustrious men' (not quite the 'princes' that we are used to from Lydgate's title). The word *illustris* means 'in the light'; and Boccaccio clearly imagines that for the illustrious man the *casus* is a fall not merely into wretchedness, but also into *obscurity*. But that is exactly the path which Cavendish willingly takes at the end of the *Life of Wolsey*. When Henry VIII proposes to take him into royal service, Cavendish contrives to refuse the unrefusable offer and quietly slips away back home to Suffolk: 'and so I returned into my country' (1962: 192). After that, as we have seen, he continued to live obscurely and ever more reclusively, so that we do not know for sure where or when he died. Cavendish renounced the tragic world of the court and of public life in general and retired, as far as we can see, to the life of a country gentleman.[17]

The 'umber' in which Cavendish lies at the start of the *Metrical Visions* is the comfortable obscurity of the rural *vita contemplativa*, the dream of many a tired public servant even to this day, a dream kept alive by a perennially conservative notion of 'Old England'. One thinks particularly of John Buchan's Peter Pentecost in his historical novel *The Blanket of the Dark* (1931). Pentecost is the lost noble champion of the conservative reaction to Henrician reform, who saves his adversary, the King, when he could have let him drown and so take the throne of England for himself. He finally disappears—around 1530, the year in which Cavendish left the court—into 'a world of which there has never been a chronicle, the heaths and forests of old England' (1961: 279).[18] His charismatic Gypsy mentor observes: 'It appears our new king is to rule not in England but in the greenwood'; and the poet of the company, Pierce the Piper, agrees: 'My lord here is one that dreams dreams and sees visions' (276).[19] And, indeed, when we first meet Peter Pentecost, one fine summer's day, he has been making verses

[17] Cavendish may be compared with Sir Thomas Wyatt, who was rusticated in 1536, after the show trial and execution of Anne Boleyn, and spent a short while kicking his heels at his father's home in Kent. Wyatt was all too aware of the tragedy of court life, as we can see from such poems as 'Who list his ease and wealth retain' and 'The pillar perished is'. But unlike Cavendish, Wyatt returned to court—and back into the history of English literature.

[18] In fact, Peter is the 'lost' son of the Duke of Buckingham, executed in 1521. This distinction was enjoyed—in historical fact—by Henry, Lord Stafford, whom I have proposed as the sponsor of the *Mirror*.

[19] Crewe (1990: 101–17) argues that Cavendish really wished to emulate the magnificent Wolsey, but I think he is closer to Buchan's Pentecost.

'in the shadow of the great oaks which had been trees when Domesday Book was written' (9–10).

It is tempting to view the Reformation as an epochal moment in English history which generates a complementary moment of refusal and revolt, in which the pre-Reformation world of medieval Catholicism provides an imaginative refuge from the trials of modernity; and we should remember that the author of *The Blanket of the Dark* (the title, taken from *Macbeth*, is a not-so-coded allusion to the Henrician Reformation) was himself a Calvinist. As Raymond Williams says in connection with another famous English oak tree—William Cowper's poem 'Yardley Oak' (1791): 'What is at issue, really, is a dialectic of change' (1985: 71). In this case, Cavendish, by deliberately disappearing from public view and dreaming in obscurity, would stand out as one of the great founding fathers of such a 'dissident tradition'.

PRIMARY WORKS

ALEXIS, GUILLAUME (1525), *An Argument betwixt Man and Woman*.

BUCHAN, JOHN (1961), *The Blanket of the Dark* (1931; Harmondsworth: Penguin).

CAVENDISH, GEORGE (1962), *The Life and Death of Cardinal Wolsey*, ed. Richard S. Sylvester and Davis P. Harding (New Haven: Yale University Press).

——(1980), *Metrical Visions*, ed. A. S. G. Edwards (Columbia: University of South Carolina Press for the Newberry Library).

ERASMUS, DESIDERIUS (1533), *The Manual of the Christian Knight*.

LANGHAM, ROBERT (1575), *A Letter*.

LYDGATE, JOHN (1924–7), *The Fall of Princes*, ed. Henry Bergen, 4 vols, EETS, e.s. 121.

Mirror (1938), *The Mirror for Magistrates*, ed. Lily B. Campbell (Cambridge: Cambridge University Press).

NEVILLE, WILLIAM (1530), *The Castle of Pleasure*.

VIRGIL (1900), *Bucolica*, in *Opera*, ed. Friedrich Artur Hirtzel (Oxford: Clarendon Press).

CHAPTER 23

···

WHAT IS MY NATION? LANGUAGE, VERSE, AND POLITICS IN TUDOR TRANSLATIONS OF VIRGIL'S *AENEID*

···

MARGARET TUDEAU-CLAYTON

TUDOR England saw the publication of four, arguably five, translations of Virgil's *Aeneid*, all within a thirty-year period between 1553 and 1584. In 1553 William Copland printed the translation by Gavin Douglas (completed in 1513) of Virgil's twelve books and a thirteenth book, the *Supplementum* (1471), by the Italian Renaissance poet Maffeo Vegio; in the next year, 1554, John Day printed Henry Howard's translation of book 4, and in 1557 Richard Tottel printed this again together with the translation of book 2 (both completed at an unknown date before Howard's death in 1547); John Kingston immediately followed this up in 1558 by printing Thomas Phaer's translation of the first seven books (completed by Phaer in 1557); then, in 1562, Rowland Hall printed the nine books completed by Phaer before his death in 1560; and, in 1573, William How printed the Phaer translation as completed by Thomas Twyne, an 'entirely different version' according to Steven Lally (Phaer 1987, p. xlviii); Twyne's translation of Vegio's thirteenth book was added in another edition printed by How in 1584; finally, in 1582, John Pates in Leiden printed the one translation produced outside England, a translation of the first four books by the Anglo-Irish Catholic exile Richard Stanyhurst, which was printed for a second time the following year in London by Henry Bynneman. What was the cultural and political importance of these translations for the Tudor era?

At stake for printers and translators alike was a capital of cultural authority that printers could bank on to generate sales, especially given the demand created in this period by the expansion of a formal education apparatus to which Virgil was central (Tudeau-Clayton 1998: 31, 44–77). The success of the Phaer–Twyne translation, which by 1620 had been printed four more times, was doubtless due in part to its capture of this market, itself an outcome of the advertised consensus established by the end of the sixteenth century, after published skirmishes over the merits of the perceived principal rival version by Richard Stanyhurst, that it was 'without doubt the best' (Webbe 1971: 243; see Phaer 1987, pp. xxii–xxiii).

As cultural and literary historians have often remarked, this was an epic age of translation when to translate carried significant sociopolitical and ideological stakes. Translation of Virgil's epic, however, carried particularly high stakes. For if national identity is arguably always at stake in translation, this was especially the case for the text that furnished a source as well as model for founding myths of national origin in western Europe, including the legend of Brute, putative eponymous founder of Britain. With such cultural authority at stake, translation of Virgil's *Aeneid* undoubt-edly offered translators an occasion for self-promotion, as Colin Burrow has argued (1997). Still more important, however, if linked to self-promotion, was the occasion it offered for the promotion of cultural forms, notably verse forms and forms of diction, as national equivalents to the unifying model furnished for the Roman people by the 'columen linguae latinae' ('the pillar of the Latin language'), as Virgil was described in one of the biographies in circulation (Tudeau-Clayton 1999: 510). In this respect the Tudor translations are striking in their diversity. Indeed, diversity is highlighted by the title pages. These consistently advertise the verse form which is invariably described in national terms. This advertised specificity suggests how the high ground of Virgilian cultural authority constituted at once the object and site of competition between verse forms as between the authorial translators that promote them. Centrifugal rather then centripetal in its effects, this competition is specifically in tension with the shared aspiration to 'defence', as Thomas Phaer puts it, 'of my countrey language' against its denigration as 'barbarous' (1987: 296), the defence, that is, of a national as well as linguistic totality—'my' language and so 'my' country—in its differential relations to the surrounding nations of Europe, specifically with respect to the crucial ideological oppositional hierarchy of 'civilized' and 'barbarous'. It is a competition that turns precisely around the possessive pronouns 'my' and 'our': whose forms, whose language, will gain the cultural high ground of national equivalent to the Virgilian model? What is at stake, in short, is the question voiced at the centre of *Henry V*, the Shakespearean play that most nearly approaches a national epic for the end of the Tudor era: 'What ish my nation?' (1997a: 3. 3. 62). Addressed by the figure of an Irishman to the figure of a Welshman in the presence of the figure of a Scot in a scene of centrifugal, multivocal Englishes that ironize the centripetal rhetoric of Henry's immediately preceding speech to those he addresses as 'noblest English' (3. 1. 37), the question embraces each and all of the four nations gathered round the English king under the flag of St George. It is this question, then, that is at stake in the different and diverging Tudor translations of the Virgilian epic. Indeed, three of the translations were done respectively by a Scot (Douglas), an Englishman who lived in Wales (Phaer), and an Anglo-Irish exile (Stanyhurst). It is, moreover, the translation done by an Englishman (Howard) who lived particularly, indeed dangerously, close to the geopolitical and cultural centre of the Tudor court that hit upon the verse form that would ultimately, if not immediately, 'become the standard' (Sessions 2006: 256), that would, that is, survive as the fittest form of a national equivalent to Virgil, in part, at least, precisely because it was best adapted to the speech rhythms of an emerging standard of English: first advertised as 'strange metre' by John Day, then as 'English meter' by Richard Tottel, subsequently dubbed 'blank verse', Howard's third way between traditional, accentual rhymed forms (Douglas and Phaer) and unrhymed classical 'quantitative' forms (Stanyhurst) succeeded in constituting itself as the national verse form—*the* 'English meter'—first for a self-conscious national drama and subsequently (with Milton) for an equally self-conscious national epic.

I

It is to the occasion of their printing that Donna B. Hamilton (2000) turns in a reconsideration of the religious politics of the Tudor translations of the *Aeneid*, arguing from the evidence of dedications that the printing of this culturally and ideologically loaded text was instrumentalized by both sides, notably during the Marian regime (1553–8), when no fewer than three of the translations—by Douglas, Howard, and Phaer—were issued. Religious politics were not, however, the only, nor even the primary, motivation in every instance, as the two editions of Howard's translation illustrate. For if Tottel may well have been motivated by religious politics—from various evidence including his publication of the works of Thomas More in the same year as Howard's translation (1557) he appears to have been a Catholic—Day almost certainly was not, since he was arrested for his Protestant activism shortly after printing Howard's translation (1554). It was, as Sessions suggests, rather 'financial advantages' that appear to have motivated Day (1999: 270); and national cultural politics also played their part, as we shall see. Similarly, it is a 'factional' cultural politics that motivated the printing of a second edition of the Twyne–Phaer translation rather than (or as well as) the Protestant religious politics implied in the dedication, as Hamilton suggests. Like the occasion of translation, the occasion of printing is, finally, a complex, over-determined event that requires that practices and declared purposes as well as the circumstantial evidence of lives and dedications be taken into account.

This is borne out by what is the most interesting instance of printerly intervention—Copland's publication in 1553 in London of 'The xiii Bukes of Eneados of the Famose Poete Virgill Translatet out of Latyne verses into Scottish metir, bi the Reverend Father in God, Mayster Gawin Douglas Bishop of Dunkel and unkil to the Erle of Angus'. Undoubtedly this title page seeks to advertise the prominent place enjoyed by Douglas in the structure of the Catholic Church, as well as his close ties with the Tudor dynasty as uncle to the second husband of Margaret Tudor, sister to Henry VIII. Yet, as David Coldwell has argued, this edition is also 'remarkable for [...] its Protestantism', notably in the consistent substitution of Christ for Mary as the figure of divine intercessor and muse in the prologues to books 1 and 3 (Douglas 1957–64: i. 101–2; cf. J. Bennett 1946). A Protestant orientation is, moreover, consistent with Copland's religious publications, which include Ulrich Zwingli's *Detection of Blasphemies* (1548) and William Tyndale's *Obedience of a Christian Man* (c.1550, 1561; see Duff et al. 1913: iv. 3, 5–6). On the other hand, the 'conversion' of Douglas's text is only partial: as Coldwell again points out, references to purgatory remain, as does one explicit use of the word 'Catholyk' interchangeably with 'Cristyn' in the prologue to book 6 (Douglas 1957–64: iii. 4, lines 105–6). Together with the title page, this partial 'conversion' suggests either that Copland was divided in his religious sympathies, like so many at this moment, or that he was hedging his bets, or both. Indeed, his preparation of the edition must have begun before the accession of Mary Tudor in July 1553, during the highly volatile period of jostling for power among dynastic 'princes' which preceded it. Hence the poignancy of an appeal inserted in a comment between the sixth and seventh books when Copland takes up the Renaissance human-ist interpretation of Aeneas as a 'myroure to all Prynces' that Douglas himself had highlighted, and applies it to 'the Prynces of our dayis', who are called upon to follow the example of the 'nobyl, and princly verteous [virtues]' furnished by Aeneas, for the very pragmatic reason that 'Thare Impyr. [imperial] Kyngdomes, and posterityes, schalbe the mair durabyll' (Douglas 1957–64: iii. 300–1).[1] Still more telling than this testimony to the ambient political instability of 1552–3 is Copland's insistence (not in Douglas) on the specific virtue of 'clemency' exhibited by Aeneas in time of war. This exemplary clemency manifests itself in Aeneas' treatment of 'these quhom he had subdewit in war', 'wan [...] to be hys veray frendys' 'with his grete gentylnes', an illustration of clemency that again carries a self-interested pragmatic thrust. In the practice of such pragmatic 'virtue' princes work for the good of 'commoun welthys' which thrive under such virtuous (and 'durable') princes. Turning the mirror of the Virgilian model on the contemporary moment, Copland's edition calls then for a pragmatic politics of reconciliation across the religious divide in the interests of political stability and the prevention of conflict. It is a politics that at the same time is practised in what might be described as a pragmatically two-faced edition that looks to make friends on both sides of the religious divide, or, at least, not to make any enemies.

---

[1] The comment has actually been inserted, presumably for reasons of space, after the prologue to the seventh book.

The edition is also directed towards reconciliation across another divide—between the Scots and the English, enemies of long standing who expressed their mutual hostility in recurring border skirmishes when not in outright war. In this respect, Copland follows Douglas, who was as pro-English in his active politics as in his translation (see Tudeau-Clayton 1999: 515–16).[2] Like Thomas Phaer and Richard Stanyhurst after him, Douglas expresses the aspiration to a Virgilian eloquence in 'our langage', that, like Phaer, he recognizes is reputedly barbarous ('a barbour tong') (1957–64: ii. 3–17, lines 40, 21). The terms of the constituency of ownership—the 'our'—shift, however, if not at the level of estate—Douglas, like the other translators, addresses an elite readership—then at the level of region. For if 'our langage' is first defined as 'the langage of Scottis natioun' (line 103), differentiated from the 'Inglys gross' used in the prose redaction of 1490 by William Caxton 'of Inglis natioun' (lines 138–9), this differential definition is then revised as a difference between 'our awyn langage' and 'sudron' (line 111), a modification that carries the suggestion of regionally differentiated varieties—northern and southern. This is borne out in what follows when Douglas acknowledges that he has in fact made use of southern forms in what he calls a neighbourly fashion ('as nyghtbouris doys'; line 114), just as he has made use of Latin, French, or English where Scots was lacking (lines 117–18). Representing the language of his translation as drawn from proximate and related vernaculars with permeable and shifting boundaries, Douglas specifically offers a view of (the) Scots and (the) English as neighbours rather than nations, their respective languages not so much distinct national vernaculars as varieties or 'dialectes' of 'ane [one] nation', as the Scot Alexander Hume puts it a century later in the tellingly titled *Of the Orthography and Congruity of the Britain Tongue* (1619; cited in Blank 1996: 155). Exemplifying the point made by sociolinguists that the distinction between national languages and varieties is often made not on linguistic grounds but for political and ideological reasons, Hume works to promote James I's aspiration to the political union of 'Britan', a totality that Douglas calls Albion—'the most ancient name of this ile [...] that conteineth England and Scotland' (Cooper 1584, s.v. 'Albion')—in his expressed ambition to a broad transnational readership: 'Throw owt the ile yclepit Albyon | Red sall I be' (Douglas 1957–64: iv. 187, lines 11–12). His linguistic practices in translation are precisely in conformity with this ambition; recurrently using Anglicisms as well as 'Southern verb forms', Douglas practises what Coldwell calls a 'kind of English', or what we might call a variety of Scots, that 'did not prevent Londoners from reading him' (Douglas 1957–64: i. 111, 127). Indeed, in his translation as in his politics, Douglas looked towards London, where, appropriately enough, he spent the last days of his life, and where he is buried.

It is in London, then, that the translator's political project is taken up by Copland, who may well have been of northern origin himself, to judge from his family name, which is of Scottish and northern English provenance, and from a line in a poem by

---

[2] The temptation has, of course, been to see a Scots nationalist agenda, as, for example, Canitz (1996).

his brother (or father) Robert to the effect that he is 'of the north' (Francis 1961: 9). If Copland (like Douglas) initially advertises the 'Scottish' character of the translation on his title page, he proceeds to work against the distinction by Anglicizing the language still further for a broad readership across the national divide. More strikingly still, he edits out the specifying adjective 'Inglis', which Douglas uses three times in his virulent critique of Caxton's prose redaction, a revision for which there were professional as well as political reasons. For, professionally speaking, Copland stood in a direct line of descent from England's first printer, who is reverently described as 'my mayster' by Robert Copland (*ODNB*).[3] In seeking to foster good relations between English and Scots, northerners and southerners, Copland may have had his eye on the imminent accession of Mary Tudor, when the two nations would once again share a common Catholic religious ground. His aspirations would not have been entirely unjustified: 'relations between the English and Scots government were initially cordial', and in December 1553, as Claire Kellar comments, 'the young Scottish queen [...] wrote to Mary Tudor' expressing the hope that they might be joined in inviolate friendship as they were in blood and lineage (2003: 142–3). But, as Kellar points out, attempts to forge an alliance between the English and the Scots could not resist the stronger ties of 'conflicting foreign affiliations', specifically the 'old alliance' between the Scots and the French. It is, indeed, against this old alliance that Douglas had worked in his political life as in his first prologue, where he expresses overt anti-French sentiment, again in the critique of Caxton, who is damned finally not so much because he is English as because he sounds like a Frenchman and so is not to be trusted: 'under coullour of sum strange Franch wycht' he 'So Franchly leys [lies like a Frenchman]', that scarcely 'twa wordis gais rycht' (Douglas 1957–64: ii. 10, lines 269–70).[4] Addressing a non-regionally differentiated elite of 'gentill redaris' (line 263) and 'worthy noblys' (line 267)—the constituency addressed by all the translators including Caxton himself (see Tudeau-Clayton 1999: 513–17)—Douglas seeks to persuade them to prefer a variety of English coloured by Scots to a variety coloured by French as 'their' native equivalent of Virgilian eloquence. Fifty years later, Copland reiterates the offer with an eye on its contemporary political implications.

When, in the following year, John Day brings out Howard's fourth book, it is to reassert the divide that Copland's edition seeks to cross, through a pointed advertisement of it as 'translated into English'. No doubt for commercial as well as for these political reasons, Day highlights the difference between the two, despite—or probably rather because of—the lexical debt that Howard owes Douglas, whose translation he read in manuscript.[5] Tottel goes one step further, working to reduce

---

[3] It is clearly out of respect for the profession's founding father that Copland has revised two lines in the first prologue which excuse the faults of the prose redaction on the grounds of Caxton's failure to understand Virgil's language, where Douglas merely sends his work to the Devil (Douglas 1957–64: ii. 10, lines 259–60; for Copland's 'correction', see ii. 243).

[4] Copland edits out the first use of 'French' here, but the damning second line remains with the form 'frenschly', which underscores that it is the French that are intended here (see Douglas 1957–64: ii. 243).

[5] The debt has never been questioned, only its extent. The case for very extensive debt is given by Ridley (Howard 1963: 13–29) and qualified in Austin (1965).

this debt either by editing out likenesses or by choosing a version of book 4 with less of them (Howard 1963: 20). Nation, indeed, takes priority over novelty for Tottel, who, on his title page, turns Day's 'strange metre' into 'English meter', marking the contrast with Douglas's 'Scottish metir', advertised by Copland even as he erases the possible suggestion of a foreign (specifically Italian) model (Hardison 1989: 131). He thus claims for Howard's verse the status of a defining English form. It is this truly English version that both printers set against the 'Scottish' version it so resembles, an aspiration to differentiation along national lines that carried a particular edge given the lingering collective memory of the Howard family's prominent service in northern military campaigns against the Scots throughout the first half of the sixteenth century, notably during Douglas's lifetime under Henry VIII (see Sadler 2005: 438, 446).

If motivated by these national politics, the printing of Howard's translation was conditional on the rehabilitation of the family under Mary Tudor. This condition underlines the intimacy between the two dynasties, an intimacy that Howard himself had portrayed in an image drawn from one of the books of the *Aeneid* he was to translate. Out of favour (and in prison in Windsor) in 1537, he remembers an earlier time of favour spent in the company of Henry VIII's illegitimate son the Duke of Richmond, in the place he finds himself now:

> prowde Wyndsour, where I in lust and joye
> With a kinges soon [son] my childishe yeres did passe,
> In greater feast then Priams sonnes of Troye;
>
> (Howard 1964: 25, lines 2–4)

Associating the closely connected Howards and Tudors with the ruling dynasty of Troy as if they were one, Howard remembers an irrecoverable time of carefree intimacy, a memory over which the imminent destruction of Troy and the end of Priam's rule casts its shadow, as if to suggest that in the fall of the Howards is implied the fall of the Tudors. It is of course this tale of destruction—the collapse of a dynasty and the end of an empire—that is told in book 2 of the *Aeneid*, told, moreover, in retrospect by Aeneas for whom the recollection is as painful as Howard's recollection of his earlier happiness. Though usually dated later, it may be that Howard started his translation of book 2 where he had the leisure to do so as he reflected on his own life in Windsor prison. Certainly, the act of translation required that he identify with the subject position of Aeneas as teller as well as witness of the end of the dynastic empire of Priam, 'That royal prince of Asie, which of late | Reignd over so many peoples and realmes' (Howard 1963: 88, lines 726–7). There are, moreover, moments of recognition, as when Laocoön's warning to the Trojans not to accept the gift of the horse is rendered: 'I dred the Grekes, yea when they offer gyftes' (line 66). The colloquial immediacy of 'yea' here is heavy with ironic recognition of lived experience on the part of a translating I–eye familiar with the treacherous world of international as well as national Tudor politics. It was this sense of recognition perhaps that led Howard subsequently to book 4, which tells again of deceit and destruction. Indeed, his attention would have been drawn to the likeness between the two books by Douglas, for whom both exemplify the precariousness of human happiness; the last line of his prologue to the second book, 'erdly glaidness fynysith with wo' (Douglas 1957–64: ii. 65, line 21), is echoed by 'Temporal joy endis wyth wo and pane' in his prologue to the fourth (ii. 153, line 221). More particularly, the end is again of empire, since the death of Dido, 'Danter [subduer] of Affryk, queyn foundar of Cartage', implies not only the loss of her 'realmys' and 'conquest', but the very fall of Carthage (lines 226, 260).[6] Virgil's epic may have furnished a model and source for founding myths of an imperial dynasty and nation, but the books singled out by Howard for translation point up rather the political instability he sees around him.

It was perhaps to furnish affirmation of the imperial dimension, as well as competition for the status of English rival to Douglas, that Thomas Phaer did not wait to complete his translation of the twelve books, but persuaded John Kingston to publish the year after Tottel's edition of Howard's translation 'The seven first bookes of the *Eneidos* of *Virgill*, converted in Englishe meter' (a title page that recalls both Copland's Douglas and Tottel's Howard) with a fulsome dedication to Mary Tudor that precisely highlights her dynastic imperial claims as 'Quene of England, Spaine, Fraunce, both Scicills, Hierusalem and Irelande [...] Archduchesse of Austriche, Duchess of Burgundie, Millain and Brabant, Countess of Ha[b]spurg, Flanders and Tyroll' (1558: A2^r). It is, moreover, as a poet of empire that Phaer is represented in an epitaph written after his death in 1560 by Barnabe Googe, who claims that in Phaer's translation 'Britain great' has a greater wonder than Virgil was to imperial Rome (Googe 1989: 82, lines 9–10). To confirm this pre-eminence, Googe proceeds to name Phaer's predecessors, Howard and Douglas, describing their relations explicitly in terms of a competitive sport in which 'Douglas won the ball' (line 22) until the arrival of Phaer, who outdid both. This is to render explicit what is suggested by the translators themselves, who are self-consciously engaged—together with their collaborators, the printers—in a cultural competition for the coveted 'ball'—the status of national equivalent for an elite readership of the model of cultural authority that Virgil's *Aeneid* represents. It is, moreover, Phaer (with Twyne) who, by the end of the sixteenth century, is generally recognized as winner of the ball after the brief attempt in the 1580s to snatch it for Stanyhurst and the cultural faction he supported.

II

In the aspiration to find and found equivalent, defining national forms printers, then, were crucial agents. This is effectively recognized by Richard Stanyhurst when he lays claim to recognition as pioneer and founder in the virgin territory of an equivalent

---

[6] The fall of Carthage is evoked by Virgil himself, who likens the lamentation at Dido's death to lamentation over the city; see Quint (1993: 378).

verse form, describing his translation into quantitative hexameters as 'thee mayden-hed of al wurcks, that hath beene beefore this tyme, *in print*, too my knowledge, divulged in this kind of verse' (1933: 56; my emphasis). Tending to bestow at once prominence, and, as Benedict Anderson has argued in relation to language varieties, privileged normative status (2006: 43–6), print was indispensable to occupation of the cultural high ground. Most strikingly illustrated by Douglas's and Howard's translations, which both owe their survival in Tudor culture to printers, as we have seen, printerly agency is apparent too in the 1573 edition of the combined translation by Phaer and Twyne. For, as Lally has shown, the printer William How actively collaborated with Twyne, exploiting the possibilities of print technology to introduce quantity into Phaer's rhyming fourteeners through a system of metrical typography. Far, then, from exhibiting the invisibility of mediating agents—printers as well as translators—that, as Lawrence Venuti argues (1995), characterizes translation in the modern era, these translations all tend to foreground them. At the threshold of the modern era, the cultural authority that made the Virgilian text an object of competing aspirations indeed allowed more rather than less scope for printerly as well as authorial innovation and display.

For the social historian Christopher Hill, the coalition of translators and printers that produced the wave of translations during the Tudor period—starting crucially with the vernacular Bible printed and widely circulated for the first time under Henry VIII—carried 'democratic implications' and so constituted one of the intellectual origins of the Protestant and bourgeois English Revolution (1997: 27–31). Since for Hill these implications lie in the dissemination of discourses that are recognizable today as scientific knowledge (such as medicine and mathematics), he does not mention translations of Virgil. Yet prior to the emergence of the discourses of 'modern science' in the seventeenth century, Virgil's poems, especially the *Georgics*, but also the *Aeneid*, were treated as repositories of natural-philosophical knowledge. Called 'secretes of *Nature*' by Richard Stanyhurst, in his dedicatory address (1933: 53), these are described as 'misticall secretes' by Thomas Phaer, in a brief address to readers appended to his translation of nine books (1987: 296). Though elsewhere advocating and working for the dissemination of 'scientific', especially medical, knowledge through translation, Phaer here invokes these secrets only to acknowledge their absence from his trans-lation, which has as its declared object rather 'defence of my countrey language' through the production and dissemination of Virgilian eloquence—'innumerable sorts of most beautifull flowers, figures, and phrases'—among those to whom the translation is explicitly addressed—'you the Nobilitie, Gentlemen and Ladies that studie no Latine'. As this signals, Phaer is no more 'democratic' in his declared object to disseminate Virgilian eloquence than he is in his refusal to divulge the secrets of Virgilian knowledge. Indeed, like all the translators, who, either explicitly (Douglas, Stanyhurst) or implicitly (Howard), share Phaer's aspiration to raise the vernacular to 'civilized' status through their Virgilian forms of eloquence, Phaer seeks to confine these forms to what Richard Bailey calls a 'linguistic gentry' (1992: 37), a limited constituency within the sociopolitical elite whose ownership of these linguis-tic resources would serve to advertise their own 'civilized' status together with that of

398   MARGARET TUDEAU-CLAYTON

'their' country. These translators do not, then, seek democratically to spread Virgilian eloquence so much as to elicit support for their version of this eloquence from an elite readership that in return will receive a cultural and linguistic capital confirming their own 'civilized' status as well as that of their nation. Sponsorship by the elite is, indeed, second only to print in importance for occupation of the cultural high ground.

Richard Stanyhurst consciously evokes the 'democratic implications' of print culture even as he seeks to circumvent them through exclusionary strategies. At the same time he also recognizes the importance of print to his project. Print was all the more crucial in his case because of the geographical distance that separated him as an Anglo-Irish Catholic exile in Leiden from the specific circle in England to whom his project is principally addressed. The translation thus furnishes a particularly striking illustration of the possibilities afforded by the relatively new technology for long-distance negotiation of cultural sponsorship as well as sociopolitical relations. Advertising first religious and dynastic affiliations by addressing a dedication to his Irish Catholic brother-in-law, 'thee Lord Baron of Dunsanye' (1933: 53), Stanyhurst proceeds to claim a very specific sociocultural alliance by placing his translation under the sign of Roger Ascham's *Schoolmaster* (1570). Something of a cultural manifesto that, as Richard Helgerson has argued, 'spoke with the unmistakable voice of cultural authority' in the last decades of the Tudor era (1992: 28), Ascham's *Schoolmaster* was crucial to the inauguration of what has been called the 'quantitative movement' (Attridge 1974, *passim*): the movement to find and found a national verse form equivalent to the quantitative classical hexameter, 'English heroical verse' as it is advertised on the title page to Stanyhurst's translation. Claiming that he undertook the translation in response to the expressed will of 'mayster *Askam*' that 'Universitie students [...] applie theyre wittes in bewtifying oure English language with heroical verses', Stanyhurst declares that his purpose was to raise the cultural value of a shared national vernacular—'oure English language'—through his Virgilian forms. The implied constituency of ownership—the 'our'—is, however, restricted to those few within the sociopolitical elite equipped and motivated to produce unrhymed quantitative verse in English. Described as a 'faction' by one of its members, Edmund Spenser (89), this small circle of self-appointed cultural legislators, who styled themselves an Areopagus after the place of assembly of the Athenian lawgivers, sought expressly to oust 'balde Rymers' and their accentual, rhymed verse and to take over the cultural centre. In what we may take as a particular instantiation of this faction's aspirations, Stanyhurst seeks to oust the translation into 'English rythme [rhyme]' by his predecessor Phaer. It is, indeed, as much with this factional cultural politics that Stanyhurst is engaged as he is with the 'democratic implications' of print, although the two are connected.

Anticipating the argument of 'ignorant' critics that the groundwork has been done by Phaer, Stanyhurst makes this a pretext to assert the pioneering character of his translation, not only in its verse form, but also in its diction. His diction is, he claims, consistently different, except where he could find no satisfactory alternative, in which case Phaer is to be considered as neither the 'first fou[n]der' nor 'thee only owner of such termes' (54). If his ostensible purpose is 'the honoure of thee English' (language and nation), this is belied by his language here, which suggests, rather, a will to install his own forms and himself in the place of a 'founder' and occupier of the cultural centre. His will to difference expressed itself in a remarkable lexical inventiveness, which in turn drew immediate fierce public attacks from Thomas Nashe and Joseph Hall, who condemned the 'new coyne of words' as outside the pale of 'English', not, that is, at the centre but, on the contrary, as 'eccentric', which is, ironically, where the translation came subsequently to be more or less permanently located together with the movement to which it was allied (see Stanyhurst 1933: 8–22; D. Crane 1984).

More important still for Stanyhurst than the differences in diction and verse form is the difference in relation to Virgilian knowledge of nature. Phaer's neglect of Virgilian secrets of nature is a failure which allows Stanyhurst to advertise again the superiority of his translation: 'in some poinctes of greatest price, where thee matter, as it were, doth bleede, I was mooved too shun M. Phaer his enterpretation, and clinge more neere to thee meaning of mine authoure' (54). To illustrate the precious vital matter that has been lost in Phaer's translation, Stanyhurst gives two examples: Virgil's description of Mercury in Aeneid 4, and his use of the epithet 'Saturnia' of Juno throughout. These examples reveal that the discourse of Virgilian knowledge to which Stanyhurst refers is the 'pre-modern' discourse of alchemy, a discourse to which he was actively committed, as an unpublished treatise in defence of his practices written in Spain in 1593 and dedicated to the Spanish king testifies (ODNB). Were it not for these examples, however, this discourse of knowledge would not be apparent in the translation itself except for those readers already predisposed and equipped to see it. Stanyhurst, that is, adopts a strategy of minimal indication in translation which effectively circumvents any 'democratic implications' it might carry by preserving the knowledge of nature as secret together with a hierarchical structure of authority between insiders and outsiders, like the hierarchy between priesthood and laity in the institution of the Catholic Church to which Stanyhurst, a friend and associate of the Jesuit martyr Edmund Campion, was as actively committed as he was to alchemy. Indeed, while in Spain in the 1590s, he worked closely with English Catholic activists for Spanish military intervention in England and Ireland to restore Catholicism. His translation might then be described as 'Catholic', as, more specifically, it might be compared with the English Catholic New Testament, published in the same year as the translation (1582), and likewise produced abroad, by the English Roman Catholic college at Rheims. Explicitly denouncing the dispersal of the 'blessed booke of Christ' 'into the handes of every man'—a distribution impossible 'before printing was invented'—this translation circumvents the democratic implications of print it recognizes through strategies which tend to the preservation of a hierarchy of authority, notably the use of 'sacred wordes' which seem 'strange' and which require an insider's explanatory gloss (Görlach 1993: 265–8).

It is as an exclusionary, esoteric, and inherited form of knowledge possessed by a priesthood of 'learned' insiders that the 'true making of verses' is represented in an energetic conclusion when Stanyhurst returns to and reiterates Ascham's appeal that 'thee learned [...] applye theym selves' to such verses 'as thee *Greekes* and *Latins*, thee fathers of knowledge, have doone' (1933: 57). Stanyhurst here evokes a 'pre-modern' view of the quantitative form of classical verse as (like alchemy) a received, esoteric form of knowledge, specifically of the 'reason of Numbers' underpinning the order of the universe (see Tudeau-Clayton 1998: 101–7). The hierarchy of authority between the 'learned' and the 'ignorant' created by the production of this form of knowledge is, moreover, expressly called for as a means to circumvent what Stanyhurst describes as the 'frye' of '*wooden rythmours* [rhymers]' who 'swarme' in 'stacioners shops', a vivid evocation of the democratic implications for producers as well as for consumers of the marketplace of print culture. Whether or not other members of the 'faction' shared his view of quantitative verse as a form of knowledge, Stanyhurst's representation of it in these terms suggests how their movement, which, as Helgerson points out, was associated with absolutist politics (1992: 33–9), aspired to the production of a hierarchy of authority like the hierarchy of the Catholic Church, for which it may have been something of a secular substitute that served to counter the 'democratic' forces unleashed by the coalition of Protestantism and print. More specifically, it may have offered the prospect of a compensatory form of (cultural) power to men whose aspirations to political power had been frustrated. Certainly this helps to explain the movement's appeal to the Catholic exile, whose intervention from abroad on behalf of this 'faction' bears comparison with his later attempts at more directly political interventions from Spain on behalf of the Catholic cause or 'faction' in England.

If his alliance with this movement is asserted at the outset through explicit reference to one of its founding fathers, it is reiterated at the close through a verbal echo which carries a more personal appeal for sponsorship from one of its key figures. For in his description of the 'rude rythming and balducktoom ballads' that will be ousted by the 'true making of verses', Stanyhurst echoes Gabriel Harvey's description of 'our new famous enterprise for the Exchanging of Barbarous and Balductum Rymes with Artificial Verses' (1971: 101), in the 'familiar letters' between himself and Edmund Spenser published in 1580, another manifesto that served again to promote the movement. This echo is followed by an explicit invocation of the authority of '*M. Gabriel Harvye* (if I mistake not thee gentleman his name) [...] in [...] his familiar letters' in the address to 'thee learned reader' which follows the dedication, and which lays out Stanyhurst's formal principles for English quantitative verse (58–61). The parenthesis deferentially acknowledges the absence of a 'familiar' relation with Harvey that at the same time it solicits through the medium of print. This solicitation met with some success inasmuch as, if the two men do not appear to have met, Harvey took on the public promotion of Stanyhurst's translation in England as Thomas Nashe mockingly pointed out (Stanyhurst 1933: 9). It was, moreover, doubtless thanks to Harvey that Henry Bynneman, who had published the 'familiar letters' in 1580, agreed to take on the (commercially risky) job of printing a second edition of the translation in London in 1583.

This publication in turn surely motivated Twyne to bring out in the following year a second edition of his completed version of Phaer's translation, advertised on its title page as 'now the second time newly set forth for the delite of such as are studious in Poetrie'. As this signals, the edition was specifically revised for a sociocultural elite, in other words serious competition for the attention of the 'faction' addressed by Stanyhurst. This is borne out by the revisions in which, as Steven Lally has shown, Twyne worked with the printer William How to draw his own translation still further away from Phaer's rhymed fourteeners and native, archaic (medieval and Anglo-Saxon) diction—the forms denigrated by this faction as 'barbarous'—and towards its preferred forms of quantitative verse and Latinate diction (for instance, replacing his earlier 'hill' with 'mount' as a translation of 'mons'; Phaer 1987, p. xxxix). These revisionary moves carried, moreover, not only a factional, but also a regional, cultural politics. This is foregrounded by Twyne, who follows Phaer's practice of identifying the time and place of the completion of each book on the last page. Thus, while Phaer's nine books are located in the Forest of Kilgerran in Wales during a period from 1555 to 1558, the remaining books done by Twyne are located in London during a period from May to June 1573. This points up Twyne's geographical as well as temporal distance from Phaer, who is identified with an older generation (Twyne is thirty years his junior) at a 'barbaric' moment before the advent of the quantitative movement and in a place far from the centre that is London. This advertised distance furnishes implicit justification for the revisions which bring the translation up to date and draw it towards the geopolitical and perceived cultural centre. In these aspirations Twyne achieved a measure of immediate success, for in 1586 William Webbe claimed for this translation the achievement of the 'right Heroicall verse' (1971: 256).[7] Its more lasting success, however, especially in the grammar schools, was probably despite rather than because of Twyne's revisionary work, since, once the quantitative movement failed to gain hold, notably in the political centre at court, the more radical experiments such as Stanyhurst's were marginalized as 'eccentric'. The less radical experiment by Twyne, who, after all, left intact Phaer's rhyming fourteeners, even as he marked them for syllabic quantities, survived, precisely because it was something of a compromise between tradition and radical innovation.

It is, however, Howard's rather than, or perhaps as well as, Phaer's translation that is remembered in a self-consciously staged scene of translation that marks the end of the century and the Tudor era: the player's performance of 'Aeneas' tale to Dido' in Shakespeare's *Hamlet* (1997b: 2. 2. 426–98). Burrow has suggested that the archaic diction of the player's speech together with its heavy alliteration evoke Phaer's translation (1997: 24). Yet, in 1600, Howard's translation would have sounded as archaic as Phaer's (which, incidentally, draws on both Douglas and Howard for diction). More importantly, the speech is in 'blank verse', as Hamlet anticipates in his initial welcome of the news of the players' arrival (2. 2. 313). It is, however, a blank verse that is sometimes clumsy, and certainly without the suppleness of the

---

[7] It should be added that if he mentions Twyne (Webbe 1971: 243), Webbe refers rather to Phaer, and the passages he quotes are not from the 1584 edition. But, a supporter himself of the quantitative movement, he recognizes Twyne's aspiration to a 'heroical' (i.e. quantitative) verse form.

blank verse of the play within which the player's speech is performed. Recalling the awkwardness of the innovative 'strange metre'—famously described by C. S. Lewis as 'Virgil in corsets' (1954: 234)—used by the form's founding father in his translation of 'Aeneas' tale to Dido', the speech marks the passage of time between this inaugural monument and the present, as its archaic diction marks the passage of time in language. Language and verse forms are thus shown to be subject, like and with empires, to the 'strumpet Fortune' against which the player rails (2. 2. 473–7). If 'un-Vergilian', as Robert Miola has pointed out (1988: 284), the image of Fortune's turning wheel is associated by Douglas with the Virgilian narrative, notably with the two books translated by Howard. Indeed, for Howard, as for Douglas's printer Copland, Virgil illustrates not so much the founding of empires as their vulnerability and violent end. It is, moreover, in this that Virgil holds a mirror up to the age—the highly volatile age of the Tudors—that in 1600 is about to come to the end anticipated by Howard sixty years earlier. Consciously announcing the end of a dynastic empire, *Hamlet* is preoccupied with 'the stuff of history—the fall of states, kingdoms and empires', nowhere more evidently than in the player's speech (de Grazia 2007: 48). Reflecting on the end of dynastic empire, the speech points to the attendant issues not only of political succession but of the cultural succession bound up with it, both subject to the arbitrary turns of Fortune's wheel. At the same time, it anticipates the ultimate triumph of Henry Howard's 'strange metre' as the defining national verse form. Indeed, when Hamlet announces, in anticipation of the players' performance, that 'the Lady shall say her mind *freely*, or the blank verse shall halt for it' (2. 2. 112–13; my emphasis), he foresees how the form, emancipated through the medium of a popular drama, will come to represent, as for Milton it will do, a specifically English form of '*liberty*' (my emphasis).[8] It is here, then, finally, that the democratic implications of the Tudor translations of Virgil's *Aeneid* lie.

PRIMARY WORKS

COOPER, THOMAS (1584), *Thesaurus linguae Romanae et Britannicae*.

DOUGLAS, GAVIN (trans.) (1957–64), *Aeneid*, ed. D. F. C. Coldwell, 4 vols (Edinburgh: Blackwood).

GOOGE, BARNABE (1989), *Eclogues, Epitaphs, and Sonnets*, ed. Judith M. Kennedy (Toronto: University of Toronto Press).

---

[8] 'The measure is English heroic verse without rhyme [...] an example set [...] of ancient liberty recovered to heroic poem from the troublesome and modern bondage of rhyming' (Milton 1968: 38–9). The Restoration of the monarchy sees, of course, the return of rhyme in the heroic couplet, and with this a revival in the fortunes of Gavin Douglas's translation, which is described in the *Athenian Mercury* of 1693 as 'the best' of the available translations (Douglas 1957–64: i. 126). The translations by the royalist sympathizers John Denham and John Ogilby (1649, 1654) revert to this form in anticipation of the Restoration (see Burrow 1997: 26–7).

HARVEY, GABRIEL (1971), 'Letter IV', in G. Gregory Smith (ed.), *Elizabethan Critical Essays* (Oxford: Oxford University Press), i. 101–22.

HOWARD, HENRY (trans.) (1963), *Aeneid*, ed. Florence H. Ridley (Berkeley: University of California Press).

—— (1964), *Poems*, ed. Emrys Jones (Oxford: Clarendon Press).

MILTON, JOHN (1968), *Paradise Lost*, ed. Alastair Fowler (London: Longman).

PHAER, THOMAS (trans.) (1558), *The Seven First Bookes of the Eneidos.*

—— (trans.) (1987), *The Aeneid of Thomas Phaer and Thomas Twyne*, ed. Steven Lally (New York: Garland).

SHAKESPEARE, WILLIAM (1997a), *Henry V*, in *The Norton Shakespeare*, ed. Stephen Greenblatt et al. (New York: W. W. Norton).

—— (1997b), *Hamlet*, in *The Norton Shakespeare*, ed. Stephen Greenblatt et al. (New York: W. W. Norton).

SPENSER, EDMUND (1971), 'Letter I', in G. Gregory Smith (ed.), *Elizabethan Critical Essays* (Oxford: Oxford University Press), i. 87–92.

STANYHURST, RICHARD (trans.) (1933), *Aeneis*, ed. D. van der Haar (Amsterdam: Paris).

WEBBE, WILLIAM (1971), *A Discourse of English Poetrie*, in G. Gregory Smith (ed.), *Elizabethan Critical Essays* (Oxford: Oxford University Press).

CHAPTER 24

THOMAS HOBY, WILLIAM THOMAS, AND MID-TUDOR TRAVEL TO ITALY

JONATHAN WOOLFSON

THOMAS HOBY and William Thomas come upon us as if by surprise. In their enthusiasm for foreign cultures, in their commitment to their own national culture and its development, in their facility at directing their learning to broad contemporary interests and ends, there had been nobody quite like them among previous generations of British travellers to Italy. In this they seem to define a quite special mid-Tudor moment.

Of course the British fascination with Italy was not new, and previous generations of travellers had exploited the resources of that country in significant ways, contributing to the enrichment of Tudor culture under kings Henry VII and Henry VIII. One might remember John Colet's encounters, literary but possibly also face to face, with the Italian thinkers Marsilio Ficino and Pico della Mirandola in the 1490s; or Reginald Pole's studies with the philosopher Niccolò Leonico Tomeo at Padua in the 1520s; or Thomas Starkey's and Richard Morison's studies in Padua and in Venice in the 1520s and 1530s; or John Caius' tour of Italy to examine manuscripts of Galen in the early 1540s. The travels of each of these had significant, clearly documented consequences for English culture. And these are the mere 'headline' figures, each of whom now belongs to a fairly well-defined historiography.[1] Behind them are networks of

[1] See Jayne (1963); Gleason (1989); Trapp (1991); Woolfson (1998); Mayer (1990); Nutton (1979, 1987).

obscurer men whose chance mention in fragmentary evidence should nevertheless be sufficient to convince us that educational travel in various forms was, by the beginning of the sixteenth century, already an established phenomenon. Although it has not always received due recognition in mainstream accounts of Tudor cultural and intellectual history, it was largely responsible for creating the climate in which the later Tudor engagement with Italian culture, in all its richness and ambivalence, took place.

Yet against this backdrop Hoby and Thomas may still surprise us in two broad and related areas. First, their understanding of the relationship between Italy's past and present, and of the consequences of that relationship for English language and culture, is unprecedented. It anticipates uncannily some major themes of the literary culture of the age of Elizabeth I, such as its concern with the interaction between language on the one hand, and religion, national identity, civility, and courtliness on the other. Secondly, thanks to extant evidence about their journeys, Thomas and especially Hoby serve to illustrate a kind of intersection between reading, travel, and literary production which seems new for British travellers in the sixteenth century.

Thomas Hoby was in Italy from 1548 to 1550 and again from 1554 to 1555, whereas William Thomas was there from 1545 to 1548.[2] But like their predecessors they formed part of a larger group of English travellers. This group was rendered coherent not only by their own and Italians' perceptions of their Englishness, but also by their gentle-manly status and family and educational ties, with Cambridge University in general, and St John's College in particular, playing notable roles. Besides Edmund Harvel, the semi-official English ambassador in Venice, we know that William Thomas had con-tact with several other English travellers in Italy, including John Tamworth, Thomas Wrothe, John Cheke, and Anthony Cooke, as well as Thomas Hoby himself and his brother Philip Hoby. Thomas Hoby's diary of his travels is a fascinating document and a key source for mid-Tudor travel to Italy.[3] It names numerous Englishmen—over forty across his two Italian periods—whom he encountered and with whom he journeyed. Indeed so ubiquitous was their presence in the Italian peninsula that on one occasion he struggled to get away from them (Hoby 1902: 37–8).

Some of Hoby's and Thomas's acquaintances were or came to be broadly engaged in the kind of cultural and linguistic activities for which they themselves became famous. For example, the Marian exile John Astley was encountered by Hoby in Padua in 1554. He was later praised by Roger Ascham for his facility in Italian and, according to Gabriel Harvey, was proposed by the Italian exile Pietro Bizzarri as 'a perfect Patterne of Castilio's Courtier'. He wrote *The Art of Riding*, published in 1584. Drawing extensively on the leading Italian authority on horsemanship, the Neapolitan Federico Grisone, the book reveals an interest in this subject which must have been stimulated by observing the famed riding masters of Italy (*ODNB*; Ryan 1963: 103–4; Harvey 1593: 51). Peter Whitehorne, whom Hoby encountered in Siena in 1549 and with whom

---

[2] For work on Thomas, see *ODNB*; Adair (1924); Laven (1954); Rossi (1966); Shrank (2004*b*: 104–42).

[3] BL, Egerton MS 2148. All quotations are from Edgar Powell's 1902 edition. A more recent edition is included in Masello (1979).

he travelled to Rome, was, like William Thomas, an enthusiast for Machiavelli, and produced an accomplished English version of Machiavelli's *Arte della guerra* (first printed in 1560 and subsequently in 1573 and 1588). Whitehorne also translated into English Fabio Cotta's Italian translation of Onosander's *General Captain* (printed in 1563); both works were in fact completed long before their printing (see Anglo 2005: 188–92). Though he is absent from Hoby's diary, mention must also be made of John Shute, sent to Italy by Sir Robert Dudley in 1550. His *First and Chief Grounds of Architecture*, published in 1563, draws both on Vitruvius and on Sebastiano Serlio's *Regole generali di architettura* (1537), as well as, according to the Preface, 'my owne experience and practise, gathered by the sight of Monumentes in Italie' (*ODNB*). Also missing from Hoby's diary but present in Italy at the same time as him is the musician Thomas Whithorne; his books of songs were published in 1570 and 1590, drawing on what he had learnt of the madrigal in that country (*ODNB*; Heale 2003: 41–56; Whithorne 1961).

Some of these travellers may be linked even more closely to Hoby's and Thomas's literary activities. John Tamworth, for example, whom Hoby would encounter in Padua in 1554 together with the sons of Anthony Denny, had requested that Thomas write his *Italian Grammar* (first printed in 1550) probably as an aid to his own study of the language or that of his students.[4] John Cheke, who must already have known Hoby from Cambridge in the 1540s, travelled around Italy with him and his brother in 1554 and 1555. His commendatory letter appended to Hoby's translation of Baldassare Castiglione's *Cortegiano* supports Hoby's commitment to a version of English 'written cleane and pure, unmixt and unmangeled with borowing of other tunges' (Hoby 1561: 2Z5^r).[5] Hoby's *Courtier*, first printed in 1561 with subsequent editions in 1577, 1588, and 1603, represents his major achievement as a mediator of Italian culture. Cheke's prestigious endorsement of vernacular purism in this work— a purism, incidentally, which was not entirely shared by Castiglione himself in the *Cortegiano*—comes from the former Regius Professor of Greek at Cambridge, the leading classical scholar of mid-Tudor England, one of the men who taught Edward VI to read the ancient tongues. It is thus particularly striking and surely exemplifies a more general reorientation of values in the light of Edwardian religious reform and social and political unrest, which must have emphasized for England's governing class the importance of communicating with ordinary people in a language which they could understand.[6] At Padua as a Marian exile Cheke held readings to English students on Demosthenes' *Three Orations*, which inspired another member of this group and one of his former students, Thomas Wilson, to translate the *Orations* into English (printed in 1570). Wilson too, in his *Art of Rhetoric*, first printed in 1553 but revised in subsequent editions in the light of his experience in Italy, contributed to the project of both synthesizing ancient and Renaissance learning in the

---

[4] On Thomas's *Italian Grammar*, see Gamberini (1970: 60–9); Wyatt (2005: 211–12).

[5] On Hoby's translation more generally, see Avila (1992).

[6] In 1549 Cheke had published *The Hurt of Sedition*. Between 1551 and 1553 he began translating the New Testament into English from the Greek originals on principles consonant with his advocacy of vernacular purism in his letter in the *Courtier*. On Cheke, see *ODNB*.

vernacular and at the same time championing a version of the English language which avoids imported 'inkhorne' terms and bases itself, as much as possible, on common usage.[7]

William Barker's experience in Italy suggests that one particular site of Italian literary activity, the Florentine Academy, may have been of special importance for the development of Hoby's and Thomas's ideas on language.[8] A St John's alumnus who was later condemned as 'ane Italianfyd Inglyschemane' by Thomas Howard, fourth Duke of Norfolk,[9] Barker travelled from Siena to Rome with Thomas Hoby, Peter Whitehorne, and others in 1549. In 1566 he published a collection of Latin funerary epitaphs and inscriptions, *Epitaphia et inscriptiones lugubres*, that he had seen during his extensive travels in Italy. This was an interest closely shared with Hoby, whose diary of his visit to Italy is full of such inscriptions. Indeed Barker may even have made use of his friend's material (Bartlett 2006: 127). South of Siena, Barker must have visited the famous baths at Petriolo, which would subsequently serve as the setting for his (very free) translation of Lodovico Domenichi's dialogue *La nobiltà delle donne* (originally set in Milan and published in 1549; Barker's version, dedicated to Elizabeth I in 1559, was probably written in 1553 or 1554 but was not printed until 1904–5).[10] Barker also translated Giambattista Gelli's *I capricci del bottaio* (1546, reprinted 1548), a serio-comic dialogue between a cooper and his soul, first published in English in 1568 as *The Fearful Fancies of the Florentine Cooper*. Domenichi and Gelli were leading figures in what Barker calls 'the vulgar universitie of Florence' (1568: A3^r), that is, the Accademia Fiorentina, which was organized to serve as a cultural vehicle for Duke Cosimo I de' Medici's authoritarian politics.[11] Domenichi, originally from Piacenza, was a poet and editor who worked for the press of Lorenzo Torrentino in Florence, the official printer for the Academy.[12] Gelli was a founding member of the Academy and was famous for his artisan status as a hosier.[13] His presence established something of the egalitarian and anti-aristocratic tone of the Academy, which existed for the promotion of literature and science in the Florentine vernacular, in contrast to the elitist Latin learning of the universities. *The Fearful Fancies* emphasizes at length the capacity of the 'vulgar tongue' to transmit knowledge and virtue as effectively as Latin and Greek (39^r–43^r). Gelli was part of a commission established by Cosimo I to reform the Florentine tongue in 1550. This resulted in his *Ragionamento sopra la difficultà di mettere in regole la nostra lingua* (printed in 1551), in which he argues that the Florentine language is a living organism that cannot be reduced to codification. The key event in the Academy's calendar was a weekly lecture open to all citizens. William Thomas witnessed just such a lecture and writes

---

[7] On Wilson, see *ODNB*.

[8] But cf. Woolfson (1998), where I emphasized rather the role of the opponents of the Florentine Academy, the Paduan Accademia degli Infiammati (126–7).

[9] See Howard's letter to Elizabeth I, 23 Jan. 1572, in *State Papers* (1740–59: ii. 170).

[10] The original manuscript is in private ownership. See Hosington (2006).

[11] On the Florentine Academy, see Zanré (2004); Plaisance (1995, 2004); Sherberg (2003).

[12] On Domenichi, see Piscini (1991).   [13] On Gelli, see Piscini (1999).

admiringly of it in his *History of Italy* (1549: 239^{r-v}).[14] Indeed he stayed while in Florence with a prominent member of the Academy, Bartolomeo Panciatichi (238^{v}). Thomas Hoby, meanwhile, names Gelli among the illustrious vernacular writers of Italy in his dedicatory letter to *The Courtier* (1561: A3^{v}). It is also noteworthy that some members of this Academy—including Gelli (whose *Capricci* contains clearly Protestant sentiment[15] and whose works were placed on the Papal Index of Prohibited Books), Panciatichi, and Domenichi (who were both imprisoned on charges of heresy in the early 1550s)—held distinctly heterodox religious views. As in the case of their interest in the satirist and letter-writer Pietro Aretino (the most famous vernacular writer of sixteenth-century Italy), Hoby and Thomas may well have been drawn to this environment because of its reformist and anticlerical tendencies.[16] As such these literary encounters, which surely served to inspire Hoby and Thomas in the promotion of their own vernacular tongue, may also be regarded as one aspect of a broader exchange of religious ideas between England and Italy in the Edwardian period which involved the visits to England of a significant number of prominent Italian reformers (Overell 2002). It is significant that John Cheke played a key role in facilitating the English sojourns of several of these visitors.

Finally, we should not ignore links between Hoby and Thomas themselves. During their travels their paths crossed several times. They saw each other in Strasbourg in 1548, at the court in England in 1550, and on embassy in 1553 and again in 1554. They had friends in common, including, most significantly, Sir Walter Mildmay (the brother-in-law of John Tamworth, who organized the printing of Thomas's *Italian Grammar*) and the Parr family (Partridge 2007: 777–9). Mary Partridge's recent study, indeed, suggests that Thomas may himself have been working on a translation of Castiglione which never saw the light of day because of his premature death, executed for treason in the wake of Wyatt's rebellion in 1554. It was only after this that Hoby decided to add the other three books to his already completed translation of book 3. The suggestion underlines the importance of acknowledging the collective dimension of Hoby's and Thomas's project. The harvest of cultural production emerging from the group of mid-century travellers of which they formed a part—and my account of it is far from complete—is considerable.

In contrast to that of many of their predecessors in Italy, this project is determinedly contemporary and has the acquisition of modern Italian at its core. It reflects changing approaches to the classical and the contemporary both in Italy and in England. Compare Hoby and Thomas, for example, with their illustrious predecessor Thomas Linacre, perhaps the most accomplished classical scholar of the entire Tudor

[14] The lecture was probably held in the Sala del Papa in the cloister of the Church of Santa Maria Novella (Sherberg 2003: 28).

[15] See esp. Barker (1568: 53^{r}–73^{r}).

[16] Hoby cites Aretino as one of the illustrious writers of Italy in his Preface to *The Courtier*. His brother Philip corresponded with Aretino (Landoni and Vanzolini 1873–5: i. 244). Thomas's dedicatory letter to *Peregrine* is addressed to Aretino (Shrank 2004*b*: 109–10). Aretino, who was relatively well known in England, was also a correspondent of Bartolomeo Panciatichi (Landoni and Vanzolini 1873–5: ii, nos 47–8; Aretino 1997–2002: ii, nos 110, 167). On Barker generally, see *ODNB* and Parks (1957); Parks's bibliographical study is essential, but no longer completely accurate.

age, and one whose Italian period, being unusually well documented, clearly reveals its impact on his formation and work as a medical humanist innovator (see Schmitt 1977: 36–75).

Some time between 1487 and 1490, while in Florence, Linacre studied Latin and Greek with two of the leading humanistic lights of Italy, Demetrius Chalcondy-las and Angelo Poliziano. While reading in the Vatican Library in Rome between 1490 and 1492, he seems to have met yet another major humanist figure, Ermolao Barbaro, and subsequently, in 1496, he acquired a medical degree from the University of Padua. He completed this wide-ranging, not to say exhaustive, engagement with Italian scholarship at its very highest levels by working on the Aldine *editio princeps* of the Greek Aristotle in Venice (1495–8) and by translating from Greek into Latin pseudo-Proclus' *De sphaera* (1499). In the Preface to this work, the head of the press, Aldo Manuzio, celebrates Linacre's contribution as vanquishing the English late medieval scholastic tradition:

I hope that one day [Linacre] will give us [...] other useful books of philosophy and medicine, so that from that same Britain, from where barbarous and uncultivated learning once advanced on us, overran Italy, and still occupies its strongholds, we may welcome a truly polished and Latin learning. With these British helpers, barbarity will be put to flight, we will recover our strongholds, and the wound will be healed by the very spear that inflicted it.[17]

Back in England, Linacre fulfilled his promise by publishing Latin grammatical works and Latin translations of Galen. He also became a royal physician, donor of medical lectureships to Oxford and Cambridge, and, most famously, founder of the London College of Physicians.

There is little of the antiquarian in Linacre. On the contrary, his highly directed studies of the ancient languages and of a brand of medical learning—the most prestigious and innovative of its time—that required access to ancient Greek medical writings in their original language suggest a focused, programmatic attitude to his studies in Italy. His Italian period helped him reach the highest positions in the Eng-lish medical establishment and gave him the ability to innovate on Italian lines with extraordinary success: the foundation statutes of the London College of Physicians explains that the college is to be modelled on Italian medical colleges directly. This last example demonstrates that Linacre was not so steeped in his books that he was incapable of drawing a lesson from contemporary Italian social and medical practice (Whitteridge 1977). Nevertheless, what Italy seems to have offered him above all was an extraordinarily developed intellectual culture predicated on deep familiarity with the languages and writings of the ancient world.

Hoby and Thomas might as well come from a different planet and might leave us astonished at the rapidity of the cultural changes involved. The premiss of their travels in Italy is completely different. Though they are not entirely averse to Latin and Greek scholarship, what for them seems new and exciting in Italy is communicated in the Italian vernacular. Though Hoby attended some university lectures, on the whole they

---

[17] This English translation draws on that provided in Lowry (1979: 259). For the Latin original, see Manuzio (1976, no. xvii).

both eschew the narrowly academic and the acquisition of degrees.[18] Italy was not for them the springboard for a future career, though we should not underestimate their awareness of the benefits of this kind of tour for work in public, especially diplomatic, service: after all, both enjoyed extraordinary if short-lived career successes after their returns to England. Still, the link is indirect: first and foremost they were in Italy for observation, discovery, and experience. Perhaps by Linacre's standards they may seem hopelessly superficial and touristic, valuing breadth over depth in everything they did. But as a result they saw a great deal more than their predecessors and produced remarkably open-minded accounts of a culture that they recognized as one of the most powerful of their times.

Naturally their encounter with Italy is informed by the classical heritage as they had absorbed it in their educations at home. Just as Linacre had studied Pliny's *Natural History* with Angelo Poliziano, so Hoby's travel diary demonstrates his familiarity with this work, and his copy of the 1548 Venice edition, translated into Italian by the reformer Antonio Brucioli, is extant in Durham University Library.[19] Other of Hoby's named ancient sources include Livy, Martial, Strabo, Plutarch, Horace, Virgil, Ovid, and Cicero. Although it is not clear how many of these represent later additions to his diary, one senses his pleasure in recognizing places mentioned in these works, with which he or his potential readership (probably his family) would already have been familiar. Hoby also notes ancient ruins and other sites important to ancient history and culture, such as the birthplace of Virgil, and is struck by the remains of the classical past in Rome.

Likewise William Thomas reveals deep familiarity with ancient sources. The dedicatory letters to the *Italian Grammar* and to *Peregrine*, his dialogue set in Bologna in defence of Henry VIII, both pay due reverence to the eloquence of Cicero, in characteristic Renaissance style, as 'the flowre of eloquence' (1550: $\pi 2^v$; cf. Thomas 1861: 9).[20] *An Argument, wherein the Apparel of Women is both Reproved and Defended*, Thomas's treatise on women's clothing, printed in 1551, is more or less a direct translation into English of a section of Livy's *Ab urbe condita* (A. Carlson 1993). In the early pages of *The History of Italy* Thomas sets out a table comparing ancient place-names with modern ones, aware, presumably, that this will be a major point of reference for many of his readers. His description of Rome is profoundly influenced by the contrast he sees between the glories of the ancient past and its present ruined state, and he describes some of the antiquities he sees in great detail, referring frequently to what was known about them from ancient sources. Take, for example, his description of the Colosseum:

the Amphitheatre, now called Coliseo, is yet standyng, one of the perfectest to be seen amongeste all the antiquities of Rome, and may in deede be accompted one of the wonders

---

[18] See e.g. Hoby (1902: 8).

[19] *Historia naturale di C. Plinio Secondo. Nuovamente tradotta di latino in vulgare toscano. Per Antonio Brucioli* (Venice, 1548), Durham University Library, Winterbottom J35.

[20] On *Peregrine* generally, see Wyatt (2005: 70–2); I. Martin (1997). Martin argues convincingly that the only edition of this work printed in the sixteenth century, in 1552 in Italian, was not translated by Thomas.

of the worlde. For though part of it be alreadie fallen downe, and the reste decaiyng daily, yet is it not so defaced, but that you maie see perfectelie, what it hath been, aswell for the mervaylouse height, great circuite, and fayre stone: as also for the excellent workemanship and proporcion. It is rounde bothe without and within, from the grounde within upwardes, it ryseth uniformely one steppe above an other staierwise to a very great height: so that to beholde the shewe in the bottome, whiche I thynke is above .300. yardes in compasse, there myght sitte an hundred thousande persons at theyr ease. And because they used to gravell the grounde, whan any great pastyme shoulde be, therfore in the latine tounge some aucthours have called it Arena: notwithstandyng they have knowen the name to be Amphitheatrum, whiche signifieth two Theatres joygned togethers, and after moste opinions this Amphitheatre was builded by Vespasian and his sonne Titus.   (1549: 30^r–31^r)

Once again Pliny the Elder appears to have been a principal source of ancient lore for Thomas, but he also draws heavily on Livy, while citing many other authors such as Varro, Cicero, Frontinus, Cassiodorus, Virgil, and Ovid.

However, modern authors are just as in evidence. For Rome, Thomas makes much use of Flavio Biondo's mid-fifteenth-century *Roma instaurata* and *Roma triumphans*, and Andrea Fulvio's *Antiquitates urbis* of 1527. He also cites Lorenzo Valla (on the Donation of Constantine), Platina (on the history of the papacy), Pandolfo Collenuccio (on the history of Naples), Castiglione (on Urbino), and, most notably, that other admirer of Livy, Machiavelli.[21] For it is clear that, in Machiavellian spirit—and in spite of the title of his work—Thomas is primarily interested in Italy's past inasmuch as it informs Italy's present and may afford practical lessons for his own time. (As the adviser to Edward VI, Thomas would subsequently mobilize his Machiavellian learning more directly, offering the young king advice and maxims on current affairs drawn from the Florentine author.[22]) *The History of Italy* is in fact equally concerned with the present state of Italy, which is described at length and directly, sometimes in the first person so as to lend a sense of immediacy to the text. The work is premised on the value of direct observation: since, in the words of his dedicatory letter, Italy seems to 'flourishe in civilitee moste of all other at this dai' (A2^r), its history serves numerous lessons in how that came to be.

The result is both history and a brilliant work of travel-writing—perhaps derivative or shallow in parts, but also extraordinarily clear, intelligent, well informed, as well as humorous, worldly, and humane. Thomas is not universally positive about Italy, carrying forward an already well-established Protestant tradition of negative stereotypes. He is particularly critical of what he sees as moral degradation. He claims that 'wheras temperance, modestie, and other civile virtues excell in the numbre of the Italian nobilitee, more than in the nobilitee of any other nacion that I knowe: so undoubtedly the fleshely appetite with unnaturall heate and other thynges in theim that be viciouse, dooe passe all the termes of reason or honestie' (4^v). Even the Venetians, whom Thomas admires more than any other Italian people, are criticized for their licentiousness: by the age of 20 the average Venetian nobleman's son 'knoweth as muche lewdnesse as is possible to be imagined'; 'common women' and

[21] On Thomas and Machiavelli, see Donaldson (1988: 41–4); Anglo (2005: 102–9); Khoury (2006).

[22] BL, Vespasian MS D.xviii, fos 1–48, printed in Thomas (1774: 131–94). See Shrank (2004b: 129–34).

'Courtisanes' proliferate in Venice because younger brothers remain unmarried so as not to dissipate the family inheritance (84^v–85^r).[23] Thomas is scathing about the Pope, who is always referred to as the Bishop of Rome, for his authoritarianism, and for his and the Church's pomp and vainglory, as witnessed by Thomas first hand in a Roman procession in 1547 (37^r–39^r). He links the corruption of the clergy to the presence in Rome of numerous courtesans and prostitutes, reporting an estimate of 40,000 'harlots' in the city, mostly maintained by the clergy (39^r). The picture of the papacy is rounded off by the claim that Pope Paul III is so old that he 'is nourished with the sucke of a womans breast: and to helpe his colde nature, hath two younge girles to lie by hym in his bedde a night' (72^v).[24] The spirit of such observations is far from unique. In spite of the usually neutral or enthusiastic tone of his journal, Thomas Hoby is not beyond mocking what he calls the 'fond folishnes' of Catholic superstition, whether at Mount Etna, where he casts doubt on the local belief that the relics of St Agatha protect the inhabitants from volcanic eruptions (1902: 47), or in Rome, where he comments as follows on indulgences during the Jubilee year of 1550:

> Whooever will receave the full indulgence of this Jubilie must visit the vii principall churches of Roome all in on daie (which he shall have inough to do) a foote. With these and like fond traditions is the papall seate cheeflie maintained, to call menn owt of all places of christendome to lighten their purses here, at pardons, indulgencs, and jubileis to stocks and stones. But suche fond folishnes was never better spied owt then it is now, nor less observed in all places, thowghe manie perforce bee kept blinde still. And especiallie in Roome itself where they have bine so used to yt, that they are wearie of yt a great number.   (60–1)

It is important, then, not to lump Thomas and Hoby together in some 'pro-Italy' party, to be set irreconcilably against, for example, Roger Ascham, who famously and influentially warned in *The Schoolmaster* of 1570 against Italian travel:

> If some yet do not well understand, what is an English man Italianated, I will plainlie tell him. He, that by living, & traveling in Italie, bringeth home into England out of Italie, the Religion, the learning, the policie, the experience, the maners of Italie. That is to say, for Religion, Papistrie or worse: for learnyng, lesse commonly that they caried out with them: for pollicie, a factious hart, a discoursing head, a mynd to medle in all mens matters: for experience, plentie of new mischieves never knowne in England before: for maners, varietie of vanities, and chaunge of filthy lyving. These be the inchantementes of Circes, brought out of Italie, to marre mens maners in England.   (26^v)

Ascham recommends instead the sober reading of Hoby's Castiglione at home (20^v); his comments may have had the effect both of limiting the extent of mid-Elizabethan travel to Italy and of helping the success of Hoby's *Courtier*.[25] A student of Cheke,

[23] Cf. comments on the Genoese, 362^r.

[24] On Thomas's negative images of Italy, see Shrank (2004b: 111–16).

[25] For discussion of changing patters of travel to Italy in the mid-Elizabethan period, see the various positions of Warneke (1995); Woolfson (1998: 119–35); and Wyatt (2005: 159–63). Hoby's *Courtier* ran to four Elizabethan editions and, though by no means the only way in which Castiglione was accessed in later Tudor England (for example, Bartholomew Clerke's Latin edition of 1571 ran to more editions), clearly had a considerable influence.

Ascham formed part of the very circle of Cambridge 'Athenians' of which Hoby was a young member. Even if, in *The Schoolmaster*, his concerns about English travel in Italy develop into a wholesale attack on Italian cultural influences in general, his motivation is self-evidently anti-Catholic, a position on which Hoby and Thomas are more or less in line with him. The difference is one of degree and not of kind, and the critical note may partly be explained by the revisions of his book which Ascham undertook in the later 1560s prior to having it printed, in a political and religious context that was drifting towards hardline confessionalization (Parks 1937–8). After all, as Sara Warneke points out, in 1551 Ascham wrote that the value of learning languages abroad was worth ten fellowships at St John's (1995: 54 n. 60; 52–8). And even in *The Schoolmaster* he praises Italian as his third favourite language after Latin and Greek (1570: 23^r).

Much earlier, one of the key mentors of this group could also be deeply critical of Italy. Writing from Padua to Sir William Petre in July 1554, Cheke was clearly unimpressed:

I am hear in a contree, much estemed in opinion, in deade not such as a man wold have gessed it, I am yet unskilfull thearof, and thearfor can not judge certainlie without rashnes, else to judge at the first sight I wold sai that nether for private order, nor yet comune behaviour, it is anie thing to be compared to our barbarouse supposed countree. Cortizans in honour, haunting of evil houses noble, breaking of mariage a sport, murdre in a gentilman magnanimitee, robbrie finesse it be clean conveid, for the spieng [spying] is judged the faut, and not the stealing, religion to be best, that best agreeth with aristotel de anima, the commun tennant though not in kinde tenancie, marvelouslie kept bare, the gentilman never the lesse yet barer that kepeth him so, in speche corteise in deade skarse, more liberall in asking then in giving. thei sai the forder we go into Italie the worse, which when I have seen, I will unfainedlie write unto you thearof.[26]

Despite all of this, William Thomas himself did ultimately convey a positive image of contemporary Italy to his compatriots and there is evidence that his work had a significant influence on their perceptions. *The History of Italy* was reprinted in 1561, and one avid Elizabethan reader, Gabriel Harvey, commended it for containing 'Excellent Histories, and notable Discourses for every politician, pragmatician, negotiatour, or anie skillfull man' (Stern 1979: 237).[27]

As for Thomas Hoby, his diary is a first-person account of what he saw and did while abroad, with particular attention to southern Italy and Sicily, areas much less familiar to Englishmen—indeed almost completely unknown—when compared to the north. The diary is thoroughly 'presentist' in approach. It includes accounts of Hoby's encounters with English gentlemen and with Italian aristocratic society, as well as his own original descriptions, supplemented after the event with sections translated out of Leandro Alberti's *Descrizione di tutta l'Italia*. As in the case of Thomas, Hoby uses the past for present ends: the past is a key to understanding the present. It is indeed encompassed in the present, not unlike the way in which

[26] *CSP Foreign* (1861), no. 240; printed in full in Baskerville (1967: 99).
[27] For other responses to Thomas, see e.g. Bartlett (1991: 144); Yeames (1914: 106).

the writings of Cicero are both encompassed in but also absorbed by Castiglione: in the dedicatory letter to his translation of the *Cortegiano*, Hoby acknowledges Castiglione's debt to Cicero but, in comparing them, also presents Castiglione as the new Cicero, the Cicero for Hoby's time (1561: A4ʳ). The *Cortegiano* may nostalgically evoke the lost world of early cinquecento Urbino, but for its English readership it is 'live' in its combining of performative entertainment, scholarship, wisdom, skills, and practical models and advice. Above all, in its famous teaching on *sprezzatura*, it persuades its readers of the irresistible, elusive possibility that spontaneity can be learnt. Something of the playfulness and role-playing element of the *Cortegiano* is perhaps captured in the way Hoby chose to inscribe his name in his copy of Dante's *Divine Comedy*, now in St John's College, Cambridge: 'Thomaso Hoby Inglese' (*La comedia di Dante Aligieri*, Venice, 1544, Gg.8.38).

To talk of Castiglione's *Cortegiano* today is to evoke a text that has become one of the icons of sixteenth-century elite European culture, with its unique mixture of refinement, courtesy, learning, deference, artifice, and dissimulation (Burke 1995). But the emerging story of the making of Hoby's *Courtier* suggests that the cultural programme of which it forms a part developed only gradually.

Thomas Hoby's first formal exercise in translation was from Latin of Martin Bucer's *Gratulation unto the Churche in Englande*, an evangelical response to Stephen Gardiner's defence of clerical celibacy which Hoby undertook in 1548 while staying with Bucer in Strasbourg. It was published in the following year in England (Hoby 1902: 8–9). The very first activity that Hoby mentions in his diary on his arrival in Italy is 'to obtain the italian tung' (8). Facility in the language remained one of his most urgent priorities. Writing of 1549 he comments: 'After I had taried a yere sometime in Padoa and somtime in Venice, and obtayened some understanding in the tung, I thowght yt behovffull to travaile into the middes of Italye, as well as to have a better knowleg in the tung, as to see the countrey of Tuscane, so much renowmed in all places.'

He was motivated to travel to Sicily 'both to have a sight of the countrey and also to absent my self for a while owt of Englishemenne's companie for the tung's sake' (37–8). This direct engagement with spoken Italian—though one may wonder how much sense Hoby was able to make of what he heard in Sicily—was supplemented by the acquisition of Italian books. Besides the Pliny and Dante already mentioned, extant works revealing his ownership include Ariosto's *Orlando furioso* (Venice, 1554), Torello Saraina's *De origine et amplitudine civitatis Veronae* (Verona, 1540), Fernando de Rojas's *Celestina* (Venice, 1535), and Giovan Battista Pigna's *Il duello* (Venice, 1554).[28] Hoby may possibly have made a first start on the *Cortegiano* as early as 1550 while in Siena with William Barker and Henry Parker, the son of the translator of Boccaccio, Henry Paker, Lord Morley (61). He more clearly first translated the third book of the *Cortegiano* after his first Italian period, while staying in Paris in 1552. He did so while writing an 'epitome of the Italian tung' at the request of Henry Sidney

---

[28]   See Hesketh & Ward, *Continental Books*, catalogue no. 34 (London, Dec. 2003), 4–6. The first two works are in private ownership while the last two are in the Folger Shakespeare Library.

(78). The third book of the *Cortegiano* was undertaken at the request of Elizabeth Parr, the Marchioness of Northampton, wife of William Parr, whose embassy to France in the previous year was attended by Thomas Hoby (Partridge 2007: 774). Partridge convincingly argues that Hoby completed the translation in 1556–7, but because of its anticlerical content and secular attitudes, the book was considered too risqué for printing during the era of Catholic restoration under Mary I so did not see the light of day until 1561 (784).

This does not exhaust Hoby's activities as a translator. In 1550 while in Augsburg he translated *Libero arbitrio* by the Italian reformer Francesco Negri, dedicating the work to William Parr (Bartlett 2006: 128).[29] More significantly, Hoby's journal needs to be seen as part of his activity as a translator, because large unacknowledged chunks, including accounts of travels before 1550, are translated out of the encyclopedic and hugely popular *Descrizione di tutta l'Italia* of Leandro Alberti, first printed in 1550. Some passages are translated literally and directly, some are fused together, others are used as a basis for broader elaboration. It had already been clear to Hoby's editor Edgar Powell in 1902 that the diary as we have it was a version mainly written after the journeys it describes, before Maria Grazia Padovan's discovery of the crucial role of Alberti's *Descrizione* in a study of 1982. Powell convincingly suggested on the basis of internal evidence that events from 1547 to 1554 were written up at Padua during the winter of 1554–5, and later entries were added piecemeal. The additional material from Alberti suggests that the rewriting was undertaken mainly for family consumption, to explain and give depth to the bare account of Hoby's travels. (The absence of comments on Italy's sexual decadence, so frequent among Hoby's peers, may point to the same conclusion: that the diary was intended for his family.) And indeed we find Hoby's son Edward making annotations in the manuscript which, excepting one brief hiatus, remained at the family seat of Bisham Abbey until the end of the eighteenth century (Hoby 1902, pp. vi, vii, 8, 37; see also Bartlett 2006; Chaney 2000: 63; Padovan 1982).

Examining retrospectively the printed and manuscript works of Thomas Hoby and William Thomas, we have what amounts to a cultural programme consisting of the transmission of contemporary Italian literature and culture in both Italian and English for the furtherance of English civilization. This programme is underscored by a sense of English pride but also inadequacy. Both Thomas and Hoby complain about the slowness of Englishmen to catch up with their Continental counterparts by developing a literature in the vernacular. As Thomas writes in the dedicatory letter to his English translation of Johannes Sacrobosco's *De sphaera*, 'if our nation desier to triumphe in Civile knoledge, as other nations do, the meane must be that eche man first covett to florishe in his owne naturall tongue, withoute the whiche he shall have much ado to be excellent in any other tongue' (Woolfson 1998: 125–7).

They share—and in different ways attempt to combat—a long-standing Italian Renaissance perception of British barbarism which originates with the early human-ists' contempt for 'barbari Britanni', those Oxford Scholastics and logicians who

---

[29] Hoby's translation is no longer extant.

had made headway in the Italian universities in the fourteenth century and beyond (Courtenay 1982; Garin 1960; Hay 1971). The trope of British barbarism was made famous by a letter of Petrarch's that compares the Oxford dialecticians with the Cyclopes of Sicily (1975–85: 1. 7). As indicated above, it was still alive and well during Thomas Linacre's time in Italy (Boitani 2007; Woolfson 1997: 896). Thanks to the humanist equation of language and civilization, the trope tended, in the case of England, to condemn both. It is this perception of England that Thomas attempts to counter in *Peregrine*, defending not only the schismatic Henry VIII but also the country as a whole against his Italian interlocutors' perception that the British are notoriously barbarous. While his clear admiration for Italy is countered by criticism of its moral laxity in *The History of Italy*, his descriptions of Tana and Persia, translated from Josephat Barbaro's account, function to throw into relief England's perceived barbarism as against the actual barbarism of other peoples (Shrank 2004b: 112–13).

In the case of Thomas Hoby the links between national pride, civilization, and language emerge forcefully from his prefatory letter to *The Courtier*. Castiglione, he writes, is already well known in Italy, France, and Spain; 'In this point I knowe not by what destinye Englishemen are much inferior to well most all other Nations,' for 'Where the Sciences are most tourned into the vulgar tunge, there are best learned men.' But the *Cortegiano* is at last 'beecome an Englishman', a work of transformation that Hoby has undertaken for the 'commune benefite', with the aim that 'we alone of the worlde maye not bee styll counted barbarous in our tunge, as in time out of minde we have bene in our maners' (1561: A4^r–B2^r).

The *Cortegiano* 'is beecome an Englishman'. The Italian adventures of William Thomas and Thomas Hoby, so formative in their different ways for later Tudor literature, should serve to remind us of the imitative origins of the English Renaissance. In convincing generations of readers of the naturalness of their language through eschewing 'inkhorne' terms, Elizabethan writers show themselves to have brilliantly absorbed Castiglione's key teaching 'To shon Affectation or curiosity above al things in al things' ('fuggir quanto piú si po [...] la affettazione').[30] In doing so they decisively shook off England's reputation for barbarism and created a Renaissance that was itself an extraordinary performance in 'Recklesnesse to cover art', or *sprezzatura*.

Primary Works

ARETINO, PIETRO (1997–2002), *Lettere*, ed. Paolo Procaccioli, 4 vols (Rome: Salerno).
ASCHAM, ROGER (1570), *The Scholemaster*.
BARKER, WILLIAM (1568), *The Fearfull Fansies of the Florentine Couper*.
——(1904–5), *The Nobility of Women by William Barker, 1559*, ed. R. W. Bond (London: Roxburgh Club).
CASTIGLIONE, BALDASSARE (1947), *Il libro del cortegiano*, ed. Vittorio Cian (Florence: Sansoni).

---

[30] Hoby (1561: E2^r); Castiglione (1947: 155).

CSP Foreign (1861), *Calendar of State Papers, Foreign Series, of the Reign of Mary, 1553–1558*, ed. William B. Turnbull (London: HMSO).

HARVEY, GABRIEL (1593), *Pierce's Supererogation; or, A New Praise of the Old Ass.*

HOBY, THOMAS (trans.) (1561), *The Courtyer of Count Baldessar Castilio.*

—— (1902), 'The Travels and Life of Sir Thomas Hoby of Bisham Abbey, Written by Himself, 1547–1564', ed. Edgar Powell, *Camden Miscellany*, 10, Camden Society, 3rd ser., 4.

LANDONI, TEODORICO, and GIULIANO VANZOLINI (eds) (1873–5), *Lettere scritte a Pietro Aretino*, 2 vols (Bologna: Gaetano Romagnoli).

MANUZIO, ALDO (1976), *Aldo Manuzio editore, dediche, prefazioni, note ai testi*, ed. Giovanni Orlandi (Milan: Edizioni Il polifilo).

PETRARCH, FRANCESCO (1975–85), *Rerum familiarum libri*, trans. Aldo S. Bernardo (New York: State University of New York Press).

State Papers (1740–59), *A Collection of State Papers*, ed. S. Haynes (London).

THOMAS, WILLIAM (1549), *The Historie of Italie.*

—— (1550), *Principal Rules of the Italian Grammer.*

—— (1551), *An Argument, wherein the Apparaile of Women is both Reproved and Defended.*

—— (1774), *The Works of William Thomas*, ed. A. D'Aubant.

—— (1861), *The Pilgrim: A Dialogue on the Life and Actions of King Henry the Eighth*, ed. J. A. Froude (London: Parker, Son, and Bourn).

WHYTHORNE, THOMAS (1961), *The Autobiography of Thomas Whythorne*, ed. J. M. Osborn (Oxford: Clarendon Press).

CHAPTER 25

POPULARIZING COURTLY POETRY

TOTTEL'S MISCELLANY AND ITS PROGENY

STEVEN W. MAY

RICHARD TOTTEL clearly had no idea in June of 1557 what a best-seller he would find on his hands when there issued from his press *Songs and Sonnets*, better known by its publisher's name as Tottel's Miscellany.[1] That same summer he issued two revised reprintings of the work, both dated 31 July, testifying to the unexpectedly brisk sales of the first edition. With a total of eleven editions by 1587, Tottel's Miscellany is the most popular printed anthology of secular Tudor verse. For a number of reasons, however, the appearance of this kind of book from Tottel's press at this time was an improbability. It is not improbable that a London printer could obtain copies of so much 'coterie' verse of courtly origin—as we shall see, these works were in far more plentiful supply than is ordinarily supposed. The mystery is why Tottel risked such expense to publish these poems, and why the book sold so well. We would, of course, like to know Tottel's immediate source manuscripts for *Songs and Sonnets*. There is also the long-standing question of who, if anyone, edited these poems for the press, since comparison of these printed texts with those in contemporary manuscripts shows that Tottel's versions were substantially revised before publication. Finally, the Miscellany's influence on later poetry and poets deserves recognition, but recognition

---

[1] Tottel et al. (1965). References to this edition are by poem numbers, or by page and line numbers.

tempered by an understanding of the multiple influences that shaped middle and late Elizabethan verse.

A significant deterrent to publication of the Miscellany was the fact that such a volume of courtier and other verse dominated by love lyrics had been for some time decidedly out of step with the prevailing atmosphere at court, if not in the country at large. Henrician court culture, the milieu that had nurtured the poetry of Sir Thomas Wyatt and Henry Howard, Earl of Surrey, vanished abruptly upon Henry VIII's death in 1547. His son Edward VI was a boy-king whose household was dominated first by Protector Somerset and later by John Dudley, Earl of Northumberland: it was no fit environment for courtly dalliance. Although some of the love poetry that appeared in *Songs and Sonnets* was composed during Edward's reign, none of it can be traced to the pens of Edwardian courtiers. Queen Mary, his half-sister and successor in 1553, presided over a court that, at least early on, should have elicited the kinds of verse we consider 'courtly'. During her first year on the throne she was, like Elizabeth after her, an adult maiden queen fully immersed in the social life of her court. Tottel's marketing strategy, it has been argued, catered to the concerns of the Marian court, where Surrey's son Thomas was highly regarded. He served as one of seven gentlemen of the chamber to Mary's husband, Philip of Spain, and succeeded his father as fourth Duke of Norfolk in August 1554 (Sessions 2002: 231). Accordingly, the title page of *Songs and Sonnets* mentions only one poet, 'the ryght honorable Lorde Henry Haward late Earle of Surrey' (N. Williams 1964: 31; Sessions 2002: 231).

But if Mary's courtiers snapped up copies of the Miscellany in summer 1557, what they read neither harmonized with the poetry circulating at court nor inspired imitation in court society. The Marian court, especially after the Queen's marriage to Philip, developed an increasingly dour and sterile atmosphere fuelled by resentment of the Spanish influence on the royal household and by the persecution and burning of English Protestants that had begun after the rebellion led by Sir Thomas Wyatt the younger (the poet's son) in 1554. William Forrest, a pious Catholic versifier, emerged as the foremost Marian court poet. If her courtiers produced a body of vernacular poetry modelled on the precedent set by Wyatt, Surrey, and their followers, all trace of it has disappeared.[2] As John N. King observes, under Mary 'literary creativity dried up as the London book trade reverted to the noncontroversial publication that had characterized Henry VIII's reign' (1982: 413).

Perhaps Tottel targeted, instead, an out-of-court audience for his Miscellany. Seth Lerer has argued that *Songs and Sonnets* appealed primarily to court outsiders who now gained access to the restricted world of their social betters. Lerer contends that Tottel gave ordinary citizens 'a glimpse into the workings of aristocratic manuscript assembly and, in printed form, provided such readers with a model for their own construction of the personal anthology and their own writing of courtly verse' (1997: 31–2). In 'The Printer to the Reader' Tottel does congratulate purchasers of the

---

[2] The poet Thomas, second Baron Vaux, was present at Mary's coronation (*ODNB*), but is not known to have written verse during her reign. Another Catholic poet, Henry Parker, Lord Morley, prepared at least one translation as a New Year's gift for Mary after she became queen, but also appears not to have written English verse during her reign (Carley 2000*b*: 34–6, 44–5).

Miscellany for acquiring works denied them by 'the ungentle horders up of such treasure' (1965: A1ᵛ). But he also sets forth a number of other reasons why educated, discriminating buyers should purchase the book. His overarching defence of the work is patriotic: given that 'divers Latines, Italians, and other' have written well in verse, the English poetry in this volume proves, he affirmed, 'That our tong is able in that kynde to do as praiseworthely as the rest'. For those who would study 'Englishe eloquence', Tottel presents the Miscellany as a rare collection of lyrics to serve as models for their own writing. Buyers of *Songs and Sonnets* were encouraged to imitate its lyrics to keep English verse on a competitive footing with its classical and Continental predecessors and rivals. These or other aspects of the collections may account for its popularity but, in fact, we have no idea who bought these inaugural editions of the Miscellany or why.

The selfish 'horders' of the Miscellany's poems were, presumably, privileged members of coteries who circulated manuscript copies of the poems in snobbishly restricted circles. This understanding of the nature of Tudor manuscript culture has long governed suppositions about how Tottel acquired the texts for his Miscellany. Richard Harrier, for example, argues from textual evidence that the Arundel Harington manuscript was Tottel's principal source for Wyatt's poems at least. A. S. G. Edwards supports this view by noting that Arundel Harington and another Harington family anthology, BL Add. MS 36529, are the only manuscripts that assemble poems by both Surrey and Wyatt 'in significant numbers' (2004: 286). John Harington the elder would thus be the principal unselfish anthologist who shared his coterie treasures with Tottel and, through him, the reading public at large.

But was the elder Harington—court musician under Henry VIII, servant to Lord Admiral Thomas Seymour, and adherent of Princess Elizabeth during Mary's reign—a likely collaborator with Tottel? He had spent most of 1554 in prison for his suspected involvement with the Wyatt conspirators. As a known Protestant and retainer of Elizabeth, Harington remained under suspicion; he kept a prudently low profile during the rest of Mary's reign. In contrast, Tottel published several works the year after Mary's accession that reveal his Catholic sympathies.[3] His law book monopoly— granted near the end of Edward VI's reign—was reconfirmed by the Crown in 1556. His name then appears on the list of those pardoned by Elizabeth I at the time of her coronation, and in Tottel's case the pardon no doubt relates to his support of the Marian regime. Moreover, the renewal of his patent to publish law books specifies that it is granted '(so long as he shall behave well)' (*ODNB*; *CPR Elizabeth I* 1939–86, i. 62–3). In both religion and politics, then, Harington and Tottel belonged to opposing parties, making their collaboration on *Songs and Sonnets* unlikely.[4]

---

[3] In 1554 Tottel published a translation of the 'Commonitorum' of St Vincent of Lérin entitled *A Book Written against Certain Heretics*. This fifth-century tract proposed ways to distinguish heresy from Catholic doctrine. In a similar vein, the same year Tottel printed Richard Smith's *A Buckler of the Catholic Faith of Christ's Church* (*ODNB*).

[4] For different reasons, Ruth Hughey, editor of the Arundel Harington manuscript, doubts that Harington involved himself in Tottel's project (Harington 1971: 52).

Beyond these personal differences between the publisher and his possible source, evidence from contemporary manuscripts casts doubt on the Harington hypothesis. More than enough manuscript verse circulated at the time to supply Tottel's needs. Arundel Harington is one witness to this abundance, but not the only one. Omitting the manuscripts directly associated with the elder Harington, seventy-six texts of poems published in *Songs and Sonnets* crop up in nineteen other manuscripts transcribed before or within a year of the publication of Tottel's Miscellany.[5] The printing history of both Wyatt's and Surrey's verse likewise indicates that manuscript collections of their work circulated widely enough that five different printers had obtained and published some of their canon before 1557. Two collections of Wyatt's lyrics had reached print before Tottel's Miscellany: *The Court of Venus* (1538?) and the *Book of Ballettes* [*Ballads*] (*c*.1549). Both imprints are known only from fragments, yet it seems likely that they included at least five canonical works by Wyatt and three possible poems.[6] Moreover, an edition of Wyatt's paraphrase of the seven Penitential Psalms was published in 1549 under the title *Certain Psalms Drawn into English Metre by Sir Thomas Wyatt*. Surrey's lyrics also saw ample circulation in manuscript. One of his verse epitaphs for Wyatt was published anonymously about 1544 in *An Excellent Epitaph of Sir Thomas Wyatt*. In 1547 William Baldwin published a version of Surrey's sonnet beginning 'Martiall, the thinges that do attayn' (Tottel et al. 1965, no. 27) in the first edition of his *Treatise of Moral Philosophy* (Q1ᵛ). Both poems were reprinted from other manuscript sources in *Songs and Sonnets*. In 1554 William Owen published Howard's blank-verse translation of the fourth book of Virgil's *Aeneid*; as Edwards (2004) notes, its Preface sheds considerable light on the availability of Surrey's works at the time.

The Preface, also a dedication to the Earl's son Thomas, explains that, initially, Owen 'coulde understand of no man that had a copy [of Surrey's translation of Virgil . . .] but he was more wyllyng the same should be kept as a private treasure in the handes of a fewe, then publyshed to the common profyt and delectacion of many' (Howard 1933: *1ᵛ). Owen implies here that he had identified more than one owner of the text but without obtaining permission to publish it. Next, however, he secured a copy that 'although it were taken of one, wrytten wyth the authors owne hande, was not yet so certeine, that it myghte be thought of itselfe sufficient to be publyshed'. He solved this problem by 'gettyng two other copies also, written out by other men'. He then 'caused myne to be conferred [compared] with them both', and in this way he established the printed text. In all, Owen located at least six copies of the poem: two or more that he was forbidden to use, the author's holograph, a copy taken from it that he was allowed to use, and two other transcriptions of the text which he collated with that one. While several of these manuscripts were locked up in classic coterie fashion, Owen availed himself of three more copies in order to set forth a dependable text for his readers.

---

[5] These manuscript texts can be traced in Ringler (1992).

[6] Chaucer et al. (1955: 33–5). For the argument that none of the texts in these anthologies is by Wyatt, see Huttar (1966: 193–5).

Not only were texts of Surrey's poem readily available to this London tradesman, his testimony further deflates the notion of exclusive coterie circulation of the work when we consider that not one of these sources is known to have survived. The only extant manuscript of Surrey's translation of *Aeneid* 4 is found in BL Hargrave MS 205, compiled *c*.1568. Similarly, Surrey's translation of *Aeneid* 2, published with book 4 by Tottel in the same month he printed *Songs and Sonnets*, survives in neither an early Tudor nor a later manuscript—the loss rate is 100 per cent. My point here is that most of the manuscripts available to bourgeois publishers such as Owen and Tottel have long since disappeared—their absence should not be misinterpreted as evidence that only a few such texts circulated four and a half centuries ago or that they circulated only among the socially elite. The fact that more than a score of pre-Elizabethan manuscripts that do preserve texts found in *Songs and Sonnets* have survived argues that these texts saw wide circulation in the sixteenth century. A balance, then, needs to be struck between the notion (supported in both Owen's and Tottel's prefaces) that elite manuscript verse was detained by private owners, and the equally valid conclusion that even the Miscellany's most aristocratic lyrics were available in manuscript to an audience far too numerous and unconnected to fit the received understanding of a coterie. Accordingly, Harington might have supplied Tottel with some of the texts that ended up in *Songs and Sonnets*, but neither the textual evidence nor the nature of mid-Tudor manuscript culture leads us inevitably to that conclusion. Many copyists in addition to Harington no doubt had access to substantial collections of verse by Wyatt, Surrey, and other poets represented in the Miscellany. Indeed, given Harington's modest social standing and lack of direct personal ties with either poet, it would be inexplicable that he was the only contemporary who gained access to their works. Rather, we should be grateful that this one collector and his descendants preserved these copies so that their witness can shed light on the kinds of verse that circulated widely in manuscript at mid-century.

The oddity regarding *Songs and Sonnets*, accordingly, is not that Tottel gained access to so much court-related poetry—so had four other publishers before him. The mystery remains why he chose to publish these works after obtaining them. Not only were such poems out of step with the climate at court, but English printing had as yet established no market for such anthologies. The fragmentary *Court of Venus* and *Book of Ballettes* sparked little interest; by 1557 they had apparently seen only a single edition each. Indeed, the same is true for Wyatt's *Psalms* and Surrey's *Aeneid* (except that Tottel himself reprinted the latter work). Although French printers were at the time making good money producing anthologies of secular French lyric poetry, by 1557 English printers had good reason to decline such risky ventures (Boffey 1991: 25–6).

The most likely source for at least some of the poetic texts Tottel published in *Songs and Sonnets* would be the person or persons who secured his monopoly on printing law books. The fact that this privilege was issued during Edward VI's reign and renewed under both Mary and Elizabeth suggests that Tottel was the client of an influential and politically nimble patron. Without knowing the identity of this person (perhaps, persons), we can nevertheless characterize the kinds of manuscript Tottel had assembled when he began to set type for the Miscellany. One component of these materials was of Henrician origin, the forty poems attributed to Surrey plus the ninety-seven attributed to Wyatt, although Tottel need not have obtained the works of both poets from the same source or in a single manuscript. The Surrey material may well have been a distinct collection that included his translation of the *Aeneid*. This Tottel differentiated from the Earl's lyric verse and published separately in the same month that he brought out *Songs and Sonnets*. Moreover, he drew on at least two sources for his Wyatt and Surrey canon, for after printing the final gathering of the first edition, he added three more leaves to append four 'Other Songes and Sonettes written by the earle of Surrey', plus six poems 'written by sir Thomas Wiat the elder' (2C3^v, 2D2^r). These were obviously lyrics that had come to hand while the book was in press, and they provide further testimony to the wide circulation of Wyatt's and Surrey's poetry.

The ninety-four poems attributed to 'Uncertain auctours' in the first edition probably derive as well from multiple sources. Among the identifiable poets in this group, John Harington, John Heywood, and William Gray were court servants, while Sir Anthony St Leger, and Thomas, Lord Vaux, were at some point connected with one or more of the early Tudor courts. In contrast to these elite contributors, we can identify the work of professional, out-of-court poets in the two poems published by the balladeer John Canand (Tottel et al. 1965: ii. 262–4), and two more that had been printed in 1549 in John Hall's *Proverbs of Solomon* (Tottel et al. 1965: ii. 334). Adding to the diversity is poem 238, Chaucer's 'Trouth' (beginning 'Flee from the presse'), a lyric that anthologists might have copied from either manuscript or printed sources. The diverse media and social origins these poems represent suggest that Tottel drew the texts of his 'Uncertain auctours' from more than one level of contemporary manuscript circulation. This becomes even more likely considering that he added thirty-nine new poems to the second edition of *Songs and Sonnets*, surely from a newly obtained manuscript or manuscripts.

Another manuscript that Tottel certainly acquired in time to include in the first edition contained the forty poems attributed there to Nicholas Grimald. Only the year before Tottel had published Grimald's translation of Cicero's *De officiis* as *Cicero's Three Books of Duties*. Through this association he apparently obtained a manuscript of poems assembled by Grimald. These were presented in *Songs and Sonnets* with considerable respect for their author, who was a licensed preacher, recognized scholar, and lecturer at Christ Church, Oxford. Surrey's poems bear no heading beyond the title page; the series is subscribed with a blunt 'SURREY' (Tottel et al. 1965: i. 31). Wyatt's poems follow Surrey's without any heading at all, and conclude with the subscription 'T. WYATE the elder' (i. 92). At the top of the next page, however, Grimald's contribution is introduced with the title 'Songes written by Nicolas Grimald'. His section ends with the subscription 'N.G.' (i. 120). A further distinction occurs in the running head to the pages dedicated to Grimald's verse. For the rest of the volume, the running head echoes the book's title page, reading 'Songes' at the top of versos, 'and Sonettes' on rectos. Whatever the word 'sonnet' meant at this time, it was here considered too trivial to describe the work of an Oxford don and cleric, many of whose poems were learned translations of Latin originals. Yet among Grimald's 'Songes' are three perfectly regular Surreyan sonnets ('Concerning Virgils Eneids', Tottel et al. 1965, no. 138; 'To. m.D.A.', no. 146; and the 'Epitaph of Sir James Wilford', no. 156), plus another fourteen-line poem in couplets ('The Lover to his Dear', no. 129). 'Songes' alone, however, is the running head throughout Grimald's portion of the Miscellany, with no mention of 'Sonettes' here or in the opening title to his part of the book.

The preferential treatment accorded Grimald and his poetry in *Songs and Sonnets* was of short duration, however. Thirty of his poems in the first edition disappeared from the reprints of July 1557, to be replaced by thirty-nine new poems among the 'Uncertain auctors'. H. J. Byrom interpreted the cut as evidence for Grimald's editorship not only of the first edition but also for his ongoing supervision of the anthology's contents. With thirty-nine new poems at hand, Byrom argues, Tottel risked producing an overly bulky volume, so Grimald sacrificed a group of his own poems roughly equivalent in their number of lines to the added lyrics (1932: 132–3). Grimald's role as editor is also suggested by his widespread literary activities, prior involvement with Tottel's printing house, and the fact that the regularization of metres in the Miscellany's poems, in contrast with versions of the same works in manuscript, resembles Grimald's own metrical practice.

These arguments are not persuasive, however. In fact, Grimald's thirty deleted poems total only 613 lines, less than half the 1,459 lines of verse that replaced them in the second edition. Moreover, it seems unlikely that Tottel would have flinched at expanding the reprints of his best-seller by another quire or two, and even less likely that he would have altered its successful formula by voluntarily omitting some of its poems. The careful bracketing of Grimald's section of the work with the author's name and initials, along with the change in the running head, may indicate that Tottel, as editor, knew that he risked offending Grimald by publishing these poems. Strangely too, several of the poems in Grimald's section are clearly attributed by their initials to other poets (Tottel et al. 1965, nos 131, 132). It is hard to imagine that Grimald as editor would have allowed this to happen (granted that it is something of an awkward oversight whoever edited the volume). On balance, I think that Grimald probably shared with Tottel a collection of manuscript verse, most but not all of it his own. Some of these poems, such as the epitaph for his mother, were of a quite personal nature. Tottel presumed to add this collection to *Songs and Sonnets*, then withdrew most of its poems, including the most personal ones, when Grimald objected to their appearance in print.

If not Grimald then, who did edit *Songs and Sonnets* for the press? Both Harington and Thomas Churchyard have also been nominated as the Miscellany's editors; their relatively weak claims have been countered by Rollins (Tottel et al. 1965: ii. 92) and by Harington's biographer and editor Ruth Hughey (1971: 52–3). Without pursuing these arguments further, however, I want to present additional evidence that Tottel himself, as Rollins proposed, was the most likely editor of *Songs and Sonnets* (Tottel et al. 1965: ii. 93).

The regularizing of metres in *Songs and Sonnets*, above all in Wyatt's poetry, is the main evidence that its lyrics were substantially revised for publication. Rollins termed the editing of its texts a 'modernizing process, which runs throughout the miscellany' (Tottel et al. 1965: ii. 95). For the most part, this was accomplished by inserting, deleting, or transposing words and phrases. Presumably, Tottel the publisher of prosaic law books lacked the cultural sophistication to align these poems with the cutting-edge accentual-syllabic standards that were gradually replacing the rough accentual metres that had dominated English verse for at least a century.[7] Yet literary and specifically poetic works had been and would continue to be a prominent sideline of Tottel's output before and after *Songs and Sonnets*.

Although the publication of law books, especially editions of statutes of the realm, was the mainstay of Tottel's business throughout his career, *Songs and Sonnets* was by no means his first venture into literary publishing. Several of his other 1557 imprints were largely in verse if not entirely literary. They include the first edition of Thomas Tusser's *Hundred Points of Good Husbandry*, a versified guide to estate management and agricultural pursuits interspersed with poems on a number of other subjects. Tottel's 1557 reprint of William Baldwin's *A Treatise of Moral Philosophy* (as revised by Thomas Palfreyman) contains 103 poems. Of a wholly literary bent was his edition that same year of Surrey's *Aeneid*. In 1555 he had published Stephen Hawes's narrative poem *The Pastime of Pleasure*. Later in his career he would bring out Arthur Brooke's *Romeus and Juliet* (1562, the source for Shakespeare's play), William Painter's *Palace of Pleasure* (1566, 1567), and Thomas North's *Dial of Princes* (1568). As further testimony to his personal interest in verse, two English couplets appear quite gratuitously and unexpectedly in a dry legal treatise Tottel assembled and published in 1572, entitled *A Collection of the Laws & Statutes of this Realm concerning Liveries of Companies and Retainers*; since Tottel explained his personal role in assembling this compilation in the Preface to the Reader (A2^v), the distichs—translated from Claudianus (B3^r) and Horace (C2^r)—may well be Tottel's own work. Tottel also had ample opportunity to learn how to distinguish accentual-syllabic verse from the mishmash of stressed rhythms that typified early Tudor poetry. Grimald could have discussed the matter with him while having Tottel prepare his translation of Cicero for the press. In addition, Tottel would have heard regular metres at their most relentless in 1554 when he issued the forty-four psalms of the Sternhold and Hopkins psalter.[8] His decision to publish this work is also curious, for under Mary the English metrical psalter was suppressed in favour of the traditional Latin psalter. Tottel's interest in the new poetics may have caused him to publish a work that otherwise conflicted with his overall support of Mary's Catholic reforms.

In addition, *Songs and Sonnets* was not the first book of poetry to issue from Tottel's press with its metrics significantly regularized. In the same year he published the metrical psalms, Tottel printed the third edition of John Lydgate's *Fall of Princes*,

[7] The arhythmic confusion in English verse during the fifteenth and early sixteenth centuries is outlined in Woods (1984, ch. 2); cf. Raffel (1992); Young (1928, chs 10, 11).

[8] This is STC2, 426.5, a unique and now unlocated copy that reprinted the same forty-four psalms that appeared in its predecessors, STC2, 2420 (1549), and STC2, 2425 (1553). See STC2, i. 101, 103.

a fifteenth-century translation into English verse of Boccaccio's *De casibus virorum illustrium*. Until signature C3, Tottel's is a page-by-page reprint of Richard Pynson's 1527 edition, woodcuts and all. But where we would expect a derivative text wholly dependent on the earlier imprint, we find instead a thoroughly revised edition. Tottel proclaims on his title page that his reprint has been 'corrected, and augmented out of diverse and sundry olde writen copies in parchment'. This is no idle boast, for not only did he augment Pynson's text with Lydgate's 'Daunce of Machabree' ('Dance of Death'), he altered hundreds of readings in the 1527 version of the *Fall of Princes*. Tottel's is a meticulously revised edition of that work, and it is striking how many of the alterations transform its rhythms from the often irregular beat of Pynson's version into regular iambic pentameter. The following examples are typical of the changes in 1554 that regularize the metres of 1527:

Signature	Pynson	Signature	Tottel
A4^v	Eyther for helpe or encrease of peyne	A4^v	Eyther for helpe, or for encrease of payne
A5^v	In bareyne erthe to seke his batayle	A5^v	In barraine earth to seken his vitayle
H1^r	Though god above/full oft them respyte	H1^r	Though god above ful oft them doth respite
N3^r	With wepyng eyen/there dyd apere	N2^v	With weping eyen to hym there dydappere
Q4^v	After these mighty princes twayne	Q4^v	After these noble mightie princes tweine

Someone went to a great deal of trouble here to present readers with a wholly revised text of Lydgate's poem. Perhaps Tottel paid someone to make the verse he printed conform to cutting-edge metrical standards, yet the simplest explanation is that Tottel edited this poetry himself. His Preface to *Songs and Sonnets* expressed his pride in English poetic achievement; to encourage it, he risked financial loss in publishing the Miscellany. The other verse he published throughout his career, in literary works and otherwise, testifies to his personal interest in poetry. The intensive though erratic metrical 'smoothing' of his 1554 Lydgate served, I believe, as something of a dress rehearsal for Tottel's systematic regularizing of metres in his Miscellany three years later.

The atmosphere at court changed again, and significantly so, with Elizabeth's accession. Music, dancing, plays, and masques were once again typical of court life, yet the new regime also inspired, in place of dread, uncertainty. After 1559 Elizabeth's subjects could only wonder if her religious settlement, confirmed by Parliament, would end decades of violent persecution by one faction or the other, and whether or not their unmarried and childless sovereign would ensure political stability by marrying and giving birth to an heir. The nature of Renaissance courtliness during the first decade of Elizabeth's reign was, however, like that at her father's court, something of a veneer. Love was in the air as royal suitors were proposed and disposed of, yet most of the poetry demonstrably produced at court from 1559 to about 1570 was moral, academic, and as likely to be in neo-Latin as English (May 1991, ch. 2). Ironically, *Songs and Sonnets* may have continued its appeal to an elite readership, a courtier class now readjusting to a court where the environment was still not quite right for the sort of love lyrics elicited by the much harsher court culture of the 1530s and 1540s.

Songs and Sonnets maintained its popularity, again, without regard to the climate at court: five more editions appeared between 1559 and 1570. The book's runaway success should have spawned a host of imitations, but there is no evidence that it did. Rollins cites the lost 1566 edition of Clement Robinson's *A Handful of Pleasant Delights* as the earliest competitive printed miscellany (Tottel et al. 1965: ii. 108), yet Robinson's collection differs radically from *Songs and Sonnets*. Instead of drawing its contents from the work of courtiers and other amateur poets whose verse circulated in manuscript, the *Handful* primarily recycled ballads that had been composed and published by professional writers (Robinson 1965, p. viii). It featured lyrics that readers could sing to designated tunes, and its subject matter was far more heavily weighted towards amorous verse than *Songs and Sonnets*. Accordingly, instead of looking back to Tottel for its inspiration, Robinson's miscellany actually looks forward to the second true anthology of previously published Elizabethan verse, *England's Helicon* (1600). For nearly two decades *Songs and Sonnets* chalked up a handsome profit for its publisher, yielding nine separate printings between 1557 and 1574, without a single comparable rival. The first similar miscellany, the *Paradise of Dainty Devices*, did not challenge Tottel's market niche until 1576.

Songs and Sonnets did, nonetheless, significantly influence early Elizabethan verse. Its most important positive influence on the future of English poetry concerns the model it provided for how to compose regular iambic metres. Granted, that model was not restricted to the Miscellany. The most widely read, and heard, accentual-syllabic poetry of the time was undoubtedly that of the Sternhold and Hopkins psalter, which saw more than ninety editions between 1557 and 1587 (see Hamlin, Chapter 12 in this volume). Other examples of regular rhythms in English verse included the popular *Mirror for Magistrates*, with five editions from 1559 to 1578, and Thomas Phaer's translation of the *Aeneid* (completed by Thomas Twyne) with six editions between 1558 and 1600 (see Lucas and Tudeau-Clayton, Chapters 21 and 23 in this volume). Yet *Songs and Sonnets*, as a specifically *literary* collection of lyric verse, was best suited to influence aspiring poets. Necessarily, the iambic rhythm was most pronounced, and thus most easily heard, in the long-line metres (poulter's measure and fourteener couplets) employed by Wyatt, Surrey, Grimald, and many other contributors to the anthology. The national Muse had to hear that heavy, monotonous beat, had to practise it even to excess, before it could move on to attempt substitute feet and the modulation of stressed and unstressed syllables that creates the varied rhythms of technically sophisticated poetry. The cost of this emphasis on metre was a consequent (and chronic) failure to cultivate new poetic forms. *Songs and Sonnets* had introduced a number of new forms to English verse including the Italian, or Petrarchan, and Surreyan (English) forms of the sonnet, *terza rima, ottava rima*, plus an array of other complex short-line stanzas, some with refrains. All suffered relative neglect during the first two decades of the Miscellany's ascendancy as the premier printed anthology of English verse. Yet a number of these other Miscellany forms held far more potential for creating a lasting poetic heritage than the long-line couplets so popular during the 1560s and 1570s.

A second way in which *Songs and Sonnets* influenced early Elizabethan poets concerns the style exemplified by most but not all the poems in the Miscellany. This verse exemplified a largely rhetorical art anchored in rhythmic expression and rhyme.[9] The peculiar effect of this distinctive mid-century style resulted from its dependence on a limited range of schemes and tropes. For its larger effects, poetic themes and even entire poems were developed through the trope of *amplificatio*, the copious listing of examples to illustrate a point. Surrey's vivid line-by-line images in 'The soote season' (Tottel et al. 1965, no. 2) show off this technique at its best:

> The nightingale with fethers new she singes:
> The turtle to her make hath tolde her tale:
> Somer is come, for every spray nowe springes,
> The hart hath hong his olde hed on the pale.

After a dozen such examples, the sonnet concludes with this epigrammatic reversal of the pattern they establish: 'And thus I see among these pleasant thinges | Eche care decayes, and yet my sorow springes.' Lesser poets, however, merely piled up examples with unimaginative monotony (e.g. Tottel et al. 1965, nos 197, 251, 261). The examples sometimes took the form of similes ('As fish that swalow up the hoke'; no. 255, line 30), or allusions to the Bible, or to classical mythology and history ('In sober wit a Salomon, yet one of Hectors sede', no. 160, line 9; 'That Paris would have Helene left', no. 254, line 26). Surrey's lines, meanwhile, illustrate another characteristic of mid-century verse: its alliterative phrasing (see Hamlin, Chapter 12 in this volume). A broad range of stock alliterative tags were soon in widespread circulation, fit to express almost any general theme. Love laments, for example, are overrun with a host of 'wofull wight[s]' who seek 'soveraigne salves for sondry sores' to bring their 'trickling tears' and 'secret·sighes' to an end (no. 209, line 34; no. 175, line 23; no. 204, line 33; no. 220, line 11). Other aspects of this style—anaphora, isocolon, and the weaving of proverbial expressions into verse—all find precedent in Miscellany poems. But again, there is much more in the anthology's rhetoric that later poets might have borrowed. Instead, they cultivated this narrow range of stylistic devices that, with the sing-song iambic rhythms of long-line verse, dominated English poetry well into the 1580s and remained one of its prominent modes for decades thereafter.

Tottel's immediate and foremost imitators were neither courtiers nor rival printers but individual writers who followed his exhortation 'to learne to be more skilfull' by modelling their verse on the examples he set forth 'to the honor of the

---

[9] Lewis termed the mid-century style 'drab' with the caveat that this was 'not a pejorative term' (1954: 227). Peterson analysed its characteristics as 'plain style' (1967, ch. 2); for its development by later Elizabethan poets, see May (2004: 227–30).

Englishe tong, and for profit of the studious of Englishe eloquence' (Tottel et al. 1965: A1ᵛ). Instead of publishing anthologies of works by many writers, however, these poets set forth their own poetry in what were essentially single-author collections. The earliest such anthology was Barnabe Googe's *Eclogues, Epitaphs, and Sonnets* (1563), followed by George Turbervile's *Epitaphs, Epigrams, Songs and Sonnets* (1567), and Thomas Howell's *The Arbour of Amity* (1568). Howell followed up this volume with his *New Sonnets, and Pretty Pamphlets* (c.1570). His last work, *H. his Devices* (1581), was among the last of the Tottel-inspired anthologies, preceded during the 1570s by George Gascoigne's *A Hundred Sundry Flowers* (1573, revised and reissued in 1575 as *The Posies of George Gascoigne*), George Whetstone's *Rock of Regard* (1576), J.C.'s *A Poor Knight his Palace of Private Pleasures* (1579), and H.C.'s *Forest of Fancy* (1579).

Tottel's followers, particularly those poets who published collections of their verse in the 1560s, cultivated mid-century poetics in their technical forms and rhetoric. In addition, they were equally selective in the subjects of their poems relative to the wide variety of genres represented in *Songs and Sonnets*. These poets minimized the amorous themes that dominate the Wyatt–Surrey canon and comprise about two-thirds of the Miscellany's overall content. As Cathy Shrank (2007) has shown, individual poets inspired by the Miscellany favoured instead moral admonitions, elegies, celebrations of male friendship, and warnings about the dangers of love and women's wiles. Granted that the single-author anthologies appearing in the 1570s are more heavily weighted towards love lyrics than those of the 1560s, all of them are significantly fraught with poems on moral themes that make up a large part, but only part, of the range of subjects treated in *Songs and Sonnets*.

If we accept love poetry as the hallmark (if by no means the sole genre) of Tudor courtier verse, the poets who followed in Tottel's wake made no effort to revive the Henrician courtly aesthetic. This does not mean that they lacked courtier ambitions. Googe was from his youth a trusted retainer of Secretary Sir William Cecil, while Howell served in the household of Henry, second Earl of Pembroke (R. Barnett 1969: 66–7; *ODNB*). Perhaps their restricted choice of non-amorous topics reflected their understanding that, at least during the 1560s, love poetry was out of fashion at court. By concentrating in their poems on the most moral and respectable topics from the broad spectrum of serious and light subject matter in *Songs and Sonnets*, Googe, Turbervile, Howell, and their followers stayed in step with their times. In doing so, they insulated themselves from the ubiquitous, pious accusations that poems were ungodly 'toys' that led others into idleness, temptation, or worse (Fraser 1970: 4–6).

Tottel's Miscellany did not stand alone in spreading regular metrics and the enjoyment of poetic rhetoric to English poetry, but it did introduce one unique feature that was also widely imitated by publishing poets. They learned from Tottel to give their poems titles that provided contexts, however general, for what followed. Every poem in *Songs and Sonnets* bears a title. As a typical example, Tottel supplied a context for Wyatt's 'In fayth I wot not what to say' (Tottel et al. 1965, no. 60), with the prose title 'The lover rejoyseth against fortune that by hindering his sute had happily made him forsake his folly'. Such titles are not characteristic of the manuscript tradition in which these poems originally circulated. *Songs and Sonnets'* titles seldom offer insight into the motives or contexts of composition, but instead usually summarize what can be deduced from reading each poem; they no doubt represent one more aspect of Tottel's editing of the collection. Nothing this systematic appears in the works of Stephen Hawes, *The Court of Venus,* or *Book of Ballettes,* but it is picked up wholesale by Googe, Turbervile, Howell, and their followers. This borrowing from Tottel culminated during the early Elizabethan period in the contextual titles devised by Gascoigne and his stepson Nicholas Breton. The titles they give their poems are sometimes more complex and psychologically interesting than the ensuing verses. Gascoigne's prose fiction narrative *The Adventures of Master F. J.* (1573) stands as the ultimate extension of this trend. His poignant tale of a young man's first experience with love is introduced not as a story, but merely as the context—an extended title—for understanding the fourteen poems which, in fact, merely punctuate the narrative.

Thomas Whithorne's handwritten *Autobiography* (Bodl., MS Eng. Misc. c.330) owes something to Tottel with regard to both its title and the titles prefixed to some of its poems. Whithorne entitled his manuscript 'A Book of Songs and Sonnets'. Like Gascoigne's *Master F.J.,* Whithorne's narrative is interspersed with (several hundred) poems, and those in the last dozen folios appear with such titles as 'Of Clemency', 'Of Untamed Will', and 'The Good Estate of a Happy Life'. Whithorne's captions, however, tend only to categorize the ensuing verses, whereas the Miscellany's titles attempt to summarize the ensuing poem. Whithorne's model is less *Songs and Sonnets* than John Heywood's epigrams, first published in his 1562 *Works.* Whithorne served Heywood as a young man and regarded him as a mentor who had trained him as a musician and poet, and given him full access to his own poetry (1961, pp. xix–xx). Accordingly, the titles to Whithorne's poems imitate those of Heywood's epigrams— 'Of Few Words', 'Of Books and Cheese', 'The Woodcocke and the Daw'—as opposed to Tottel's more discursive practice: 'The complaint of a lover with sute to his love for pitye', or 'The lover blameth his love for renting [rending] of the letter he sent her'. Sir Nicholas Bacon also supplied titles for his poems in *The Recreations of his Age,* a work that survives in two manuscript copies, but again, his style follows Heywood, not Tottel. Despite Lerer's supposition that *Songs and Sonnets* taught its readers how to set forth their own manuscript anthologies (1997: 32), titles were employed chiefly by publishing poets, not the compilers of Elizabethan manuscript anthologies of verse.

When *The Paradise of Dainty Devices* at last offered a well-defined rival to *Songs and Sonnets* in 1576, its format was only superficially different. Most of its poems bore titles modelled more or less after Tottel. Where the Miscellany advertised on its title page a collection of poems by 'the late Earle of Surrey, and other', Henry Disle, printer and probable editor of *The Paradise,* described it as primarily the work of Richard Edwards. Yet Disle's title page lists by name eight other contributors to the anthology including Lord Vaux, Edward de Vere (Earl of Oxford), and William Hunnis. In addition, and unlike *Songs and Sonnets,* the *Paradise* texts are all attributed by either name or initials. Most different of all, fewer than half the lyrics in the volume concern love (forty-six of 109 poems). Its emphasis on sage advice, moral admonition, and godly exhortation signal the victory of Turbervile and the poets of his generation who made these subjects, not love poems, the dominant themes of their works.

In subsequent Elizabethan anthologies, Tottel's influence becomes more difficult to trace once we question the assumption that his example was the model for these collections. *A Gorgeous Gallery of Gallant Inventions* (1578) reveals by its alliterative title as well as the titles and genres of its poems its self-conscious attempt to cash in on the popularity of *The Paradise* (a work that entered its third edition in the same year *Gallery*'s sole edition appeared). Tottel's influence was indirect at best. Perhaps Thomas Proctor, the *Gallery*'s only 'title' poet, lacked the status and reputation to carry the work, or it may have been simply upstaged by its well-established rivals. At any rate, the regular reprintings of *Songs and Sonnets* and *Paradise* during the 1570s and 1580s seem to have effectively stifled the competition until the last decade of Elizabeth's reign. *Britton's Bower of Delights* (1591, 1597) was clearly set forth as a one-man production in the manner of Googe, Turbervile, and Howell some two decades earlier. The fact that it really was an anthology by at least five other poets, and that Nicholas Breton protested in print his lack of responsibility for all but a few of its entries, cannot overshadow the fact that it bore no overt resemblance to *Songs and Sonnets*. *The Arbour of Amorous Devices* (1597), like the *Bower*, used an alliterative title that evoked its literary rather than moral or rhetorical intentions—but like the *Bower*, it failed to attract a wide readership. *The Phoenix Nest*, however, amounted to an attractive version of Tottel's Miscellany updated for the styles and tastes of the 1590s. Tottel had played up the fame of the Earl of Surrey, a deceased but widely admired nobleman and military leader. *The Phoenix Nest* billed itself as a tribute to another national hero, Sir Philip Sidney. Sidney's career at court and in the field, cut short by his early death in 1586, paralleled Surrey's in many key respects. Yet Sidney's far greater public reputation and renown should have endowed *The Phoenix Nest* with even greater marketability. The volume included, as well, a significant number of poems that were, like so many poems from *Songs and Sonnets*, available otherwise only in manuscript. Moreover, *The Phoenix Nest* contained a number of poems that were written, and quite likely commissioned, expressly for this anthology. In format, however, it departed from the Miscellany (and its Elizabethan predecessors) by failing to provide titles for most of its poems. Yet this alone can hardly explain why *The Phoenix Nest*, despite all its virtues in common with *Songs and Sonnets*, saw only one edition. The last Elizabethan anthology, Francis Davison's *Poetical Rhapsody* (1602), was more successful, though less so than either the Miscellany or *Paradise*. Davison aligned his collection with the Sidney–Herbert families by dedicating it to William Herbert, third Earl of Pembroke, and including in it two heretofore unpublished poems by Sidney and one by his sister the Countess of Pembroke. This anthology also offered poems by many authors on a wide variety of subjects—and most of its entries bore titles. *A Poetical Rhapsody* saw four editions by 1621.

Tottel's Miscellany reached its eleventh and last Renaissance edition in 1587. In the same year the final edition of Gascoigne's poetry appeared as *The Whole Works of George Gascoigne Esquire*. By this time, however, the collections of original verse published by Googe, Turbervile, and Howell were long out of print. A new English poetics had begun to emerge during the 1580s, one that would displace the mid-century style epitomized by *Songs and Sonnets*. Sidney's verse, for example, circulated widely in manuscript even before his death in 1586. His lyrics and those of other 'golden' poets shortly reached print in such works as William Byrd's earliest song books and the two editions of Nicholas Yonge's *Musica transalpina*.[10] The new style did not rediscover neglected virtues in *Songs and Sonnets* so much as it redirected how poetry was to be read and enjoyed. The mid-century emphasis on style for its own sake shifted to an increasing concern with the emotional and aesthetic effects that have been associated with poetry ever since. True, in his *Defence of Poetry*, Sidney had noted 'in the Earl of Surrey's lyrics many things tasting of a noble birth, and worthy of a noble mind' (1973: 112). And early in his career Sidney wrote a score of sonnets in the Surreyan (English) rhyme scheme, while his later sonnets favoured the Italian form introduced by Wyatt (Sidney 1962, pp. lviii–lix). Yet it is difficult to trace a more direct influence from Tottel on Sidney, the sonneteers who imitated him, or late Elizabethan verse in general. If the new poetics ultimately owed its 'mature' rhythms to the regular metres of such mid-century models as *Songs and Sonnets*, these later poets varied those rhythms to produce effects unknown to their predecessors. They also broadened the rhetorical resources of mid-century verse while experimenting with forms and genres that lacked any precedent in the Miscellany. By the mid-1590s, the poetic style of *Songs and Sonnets* was as out of fashion as the codpiece. Shakespeare satirized such outdated verse in *The Merry Wives of Windsor* with Master Slender's longing for 'my book of songs and sonnets'; his allusion to Tottel's anthology helps characterize Slender as a hopelessly unfit suitor for 'sweet Ann Page' (1997: 1. 1. 206). The *Songs and Sonnets* had made its contribution to English letters.

Primary Works

Bacon, Sir Nicholas (1919), *The Recreations of his Age*, ed. C. H. O. Daniel (Oxford: privately printed).

Baldwin, William (1547), *A Treatise of Morall Phylosophie*.

Breton, Nicholas (1957), *The Arbor of Amorous Devices, 1597*, ed. Hyder E. Rollins (repr. of 1936 edn; New York: Russell & Russell).

Byrd, William (1588), *Psalmes, Sonnets, & Songs*.

—— (1589), *Songes of Sundrie Natures*.

Chaucer, Geoffrey, et al. (1955), *The Court of Venus*, ed. Russell A. Fraser (Durham, NC: Duke University Press).

A Collection of the Lawes & Statutes of this Realm concerning Liveries of Companies and Reteynours (1572).

[10] Lewis termed the new poetics of the late Elizabethan age 'golden', but with the qualification that it 'is not used here in the eulogistic sense' (1954: 318). For the widespread dispersal of Sidney's poems, see Woudhuysen (1996, chs 9, 10); Byrd (1588, 1589); Yonge (1588).

CPR Elizabeth I (1939–86), ed. Simon R. Neal et al., 9 vols (London: HMSO).

CPR Philip and Mary (1937–9), ed. A. E. Stamp et al., 4 vols (London: HMSO).

HEYWOOD, JOHN (1562), *Woorkes*.

HOWARD, HENRY (1933), *Surrey's Fourth Boke of Virgill*, facs. ed. Herbert Hartman (Purchase, NY: Carl H. Pforzheimer).

ROBINSON, CLEMENT (1965), *A Handful of Pleasant Delights*, ed. Hyder E. Rollins (New York: Dover).

SHAKESPEARE, WILLIAM (1997), *The Riverside Shakespeare*, ed. G. Blakemore Evans, 2nd edn (Boston: Houghton Mifflin).

SIDNEY, PHILIP (1962), *The Poems of Sir Philip Sidney*, ed. William A. Ringler (Oxford: Clarendon Press).

—— (1973), *Miscellaneous Prose of Sir Philip Sidney*, ed. Katherine Duncan-Jones and Jan van Dorsten (Oxford: Clarendon Press).

TOTTEL, RICHARD, et al. (1965), *Tottel's Miscellany (1557–1587)*, rev. Hyder E. Rollins, 2 vols (Cambridge, MA: Harvard University Press).

WHYTHORNE, THOMAS (1961), *The Autobiography of Thomas Whythorne*, ed. James M. Osborn (Oxford: Clarendon Press).

YONGE, NICHOLAS (1588), *Musica transalpina*.

PART III

1560–1579

CHAPTER 26

MINERVA'S MEN

HORIZONTAL NATIONHOOD AND THE LITERARY PRODUCTION OF GOOGE, TURBERVILE, AND GASCOIGNE

LAURIE SHANNON

INVOCATIONS of the Muses are especially associated with a quest for inspiration in a poetic mode. Lyric poets in Elizabeth's early years invoked them liberally, and so they are commonly described as participants in a 'cult of the Muses'. The phrase is apt, especially given its synergies with Petrarchism and the 'cult of Elizabeth', which likewise depend on vertically aspirational forms of address and self-presentation. But considering the breadth of textual and intellectual work then under way—from prodigious efforts translating classical and contemporary materials, to experiments in both lyric and prose, to theorizations of literature itself—we see a range of practices perhaps more precisely considered to be in the jurisdiction of Minerva, Roman goddess of wisdom and of arts and sciences. Certainly this is what Seneca's translator Jasper Heywood means when he urges Seneca's visiting ghost to seek out those producing 'woorks of waight' and to

> goe where Minervaes men,
> And finest witts do swarme: whom she
> hath taught to passe with pen.

The place to find them, Heywood continues, is

> In Lyncolnes Inne and Temples twayne,
> Grayes Inne and other moe,

where men labour with 'paynfull pen' (102).[1] Conceiving these hard workers to have been born, as Minerva was, 'Of mightie Jove his brayne' (102–3), Heywood directs Seneca's ghost to the buzzing mid-century hive of the Inns of Court and their affiliated Chancery Inns as the collective factory of contemporary textual and intellectual activity.

As Heywood's directions suggest, the Inns were the hub of new, sixteenth-century intellectual networks of textual production and exchange—networks that this chapter argues had not only literary effects, but also broadly constitutional consequences. This is to stress the implications of the fact that these men and their texts addressed (and were often literally addressed to) one another and also to complicate the role of the monarch and court culture in emerging paradigms of nationhood. In the expansive cultural moment of Elizabeth's early reign, trajectories of textual address *among* 'Minerva's men' traced a horizontal mode of English nationhood, a new web of (relatively) lateral relations among individuals who were not otherwise related by blood, land, or more formal patronage arrangements.[2] Very frequently, classical friendship discourses provide this community of not always 'equal' but nevertheless 'proximate' gentlemen with terms by which to describe and extend itself.[3]

When prefaces, dedications, and other cross-referencings then displayed such relations through the relay of print for readers' consumption, they publicly mapped new social networks for the broader early modern political imaginary. While a rising 'republic of letters' has been situated in the eighteenth century, and the urban cultures of the coffee house and newspaper develop only in the seventeenth century in England, the culture anchored in the sixteenth-century Inns may claim a part in the history of 'public' culture.[4] The Inns fostered mutual

---

[1] Admitted to Gray's Inn in 1561, Heywood displays the ethical dimension of the work under way. While the Inns are often associated with dilettantism and amatory verse (especially in later decades), 'Minerva's men' are producing what Mike Pincombe calls 'serious works which any magistrate might usefully read' (2000: 112–32, 118–20).

[2] Insisting on the significance of social circulation, Arthur Marotti's account of the waning of vertical patronage focuses on its displacement by a new form: the anonymous reader or buyer in the marketplace. This general address, Marotti notes, sometimes itself took up friendship tropes (1991: 2). My effort here reads socially horizontal modes of address, beyond the disappearing noble patron and despite an emerging general reader.

[3] On friendship's experimental politics, see Shannon (2002); on likeness ideals among unequal yet 'proximate gentlemen', see Shannon (2004).

[4] On the legal culture of the Inns, I am in debt to Paul Raffield's comprehensive study (2004) of sixteenth-century constructions of the 'Ancient' Constitution, the political investments of the common law and common lawyers, and the role of physical spaces and institutional practices as the utopian microcosm of a contractarian and constitutional English state at odds with more monarchical visions.

address by individuals brought together under the new professional, economic, and cosmopolitan circumstances of urban life. The new modes of literary production developed there reflected and enacted these relatively horizontal forms of political relation.

This chapter concerns three members of this community: Barnabe Googe, George Turbervile, and George Gascoigne. Their ranging textual work has mainly been measured by its lyric component; their lyrics, in turn, have been heavily judged or faintly praised. George Saintsbury's comments, for a sample, concede the generation contained 'some individual, and in their way, original writers who, though in no case of any merit at all equal to that of Wyatt, Surrey, and Sackville, yet deserve to be singled from the crowd'. He includes Googe, Turbervile, and Gascoigne among them. Gascoigne he rates highest ('always tolerable if never first-rate'), while the other two, though worthy, serve to demonstrate grounds for a larger dismissal of their historical moment: the 'tentative character of the time, together with its absence of original genius, and the constant symptoms of not having "found its way", are also very noteworthy in [...] Turberville and [...] Googe [...] friends and verse writers of not dissimilar character' (Saintsbury 1887: 15–20).[5] Stemming from their reputation for 'stiff imitations of Virgil and Mantuan' (E. Chambers 1969, p. xix), lamentations of their passion for 'Englishing' foreign texts,[6] and complaints about alliterative excess or the fourteener line they often favoured, Turbervile and Googe have met with particular neglect. They figure well the general disregard accorded the literary productions of Elizabeth's early reign, notoriously burdened by C. S. Lewis's having dubbed it 'a Drab Age' (1954: 64).[7] This aesthetic judgement has blunted our sense not only of the literary-historical, but also of the constitutional import of the activities of this company of writers and their friends.

Recent historicizations of the post-Romantic limits of aesthetic judgements like these (especially assessments of the regimes of authorship and originality that underwrite them) have vastly enlarged our scope for reading these writers. Before turning to the larger question, however, of what a broader cultural and political reading of this trio of 'Minerva's men' can tell us, one major exception to the chorus of aesthetic condemnation deserves closer attention. In 1939 Yvor Winters challenged the dominion of Petrarchan poetics—in both the sixteenth century and our accounts of it. Proposing a detailed counter-canon, he stressed a separate lyric genealogy that made Sidney and Spenser operatively ornamental to the engines of literary history. Instead, Googe, Turbervile, and Gascoigne anchor this lineage, along with selected poems of Wyatt,

---

[5] Beyond these, Saintsbury notes 'many shadowy names might be added if the catalogue were of any use [...] they seem to have been [...] personally acquainted with one another [...] most of those who devoted themselves to literature came into contact and formed [...] a clique' (1887: 19–20). I consider this 'clique' in more consequentially political terms.

[6] Saintsbury describes them as 'all studiously and rather indiscriminately given to translation' (1887: 20). For an effective counter-argument in favour of the scholarly seriousness of these translation activities, see Winston (2006b: 29–58, 30–2). Analysing the reception of Seneca, Winston explores 'the social function of translation' (32).

[7] The continuing hold of 'orthodox aestheticism' is anatomized in Shrank (2004b: 11).

Surrey, Ralegh, and Nashe. Winters ranks Gascoigne 'among the six or seven greatest lyric poets of the century, and perhaps higher', calling 'Gascoigne's Woodmanship' 'unsurpassed in the century except by a few of the sonnets of Shakespeare' (1939: 266, 269). For Winters, enthusiasms for Sidney and Spenser have obscured this 'school of poets, greater as poets and more important if one is to have a clear idea of the history of poetic development in the century' (259). He highlights their poetic ethos, which favoured simple, even proverbial, themes, handled in verse where both the affect and the rhetoric are 'restrained to the minimum required by the subject' (262). In this, the school is anti-Petrarchan, embracing directness and economy over what Winters terms 'the pleasures of rhetoric for its own sake' (262). He celebrates here, of course, the English 'plain style'.

Winters is certainly right that casting about for 'imperfect Sidneys' is historically and intellectually in error for these years. Despite the ideological freight of its anti-rhetoricism, Winters's bracing aesthetic reorientation of the century supports an evaluation of these writers on broader cultural grounds. By expanding the domain of their impact beyond lyric, this chapter takes a wider view of the literary production of Googe, Turbervile, and Gascoigne; the cultural networks that this form of literary production—as a kind of textual traffic among 'friends'—traced, reinforced, and sometimes forged; and, lastly, the consequences of establishing that network, in terms of an English constitutional imaginary. Textual networks of address and exchange, with the Inns as their social and intellectual home, not only served to produce a literary tradition for an emerging nationality; they operated as an experimental, quasi-corporate form of alternative polity—what we might even venture to call a 'republic-in-waiting'.

26.1 THE INNS: 'WHERE MINERVAES MEN, AND FINEST WITTS DO SWARME'

Barnabe Googe was born in 1540 in Kent; in 1555 he matriculated at Christ's College, Cambridge, but did not complete a degree, and at 17 he became a ward of the court (Kennedy 1989: 4). George Turbervile was born c.1544 to an ancient Dorset family; he attended Winchester and New College, Oxford, but likewise left without taking a degree (Panofsky 1977, p. v). George Gascoigne followed a similar course: born around 1534 to an old Bedfordshire family, he is believed to have studied at Trinity College, Cambridge (under Steven Nevynson), but took no degree (Pigman 2000, p. xxv). Each came from established provincial gentry; each incompletely pursued a university education. Most consequentially here, each then entered the London universe of the Inns, which in Tudor contexts was dubbed 'the Third University of England' (see J. Baker 1990). Googe entered Staples Inn (a Chancery Inn associated with Gray's Inn, rather than one of the four Inns of Court per se) by 1559. Turbervile's Inn is not known specifically, but he was studying law in London by 1561–2. Gascoigne entered Gray's Inn as a student in 1555 (and returned in 1565). In this, each followed the 'standard educational pattern' for men of their class (Kennedy 1989: 4).

Scholars offer mixed perspectives on the Inns' social meaning, a mixture justified by their hybrid function. John Fortescue indicated a divided function as early as the late fifteenth century, noting that 'Knights, Barons, and the Greatest Nobility of the Kingdom, often Place their Children in those Inns of Court, not so much to make the Law their Study, much less to live by the Profession [...] but to form their Manners and to preserve them from the Contagion of Vice' (1737: 112). According to legal historian Wilfred Prest, by Elizabeth's reign, 'the law had virtually replaced the church as the career [by] which able young men could climb to power' (and the rate of admissions to the Inns skyrocketed after 1540); even so, there were separate spheres within the Inns and 'young gentlemen' persistently distinguished themselves from serious common law students and lawyers. 'Hence the aggressive insistence on their own gentility [...] hence also the competitive aping of court modes in dress and taste, the cult of wit, the incessant versifying' (Prest 1972: 41).[8] Clearly the Inns served diverse purposes for different groups. More recently, however, Paul Raffield's bracingly comprehensive account of early modern legal culture outlines a potentially more integrated arrangement, one where the constitutional models propagated within the common law ideology that was then emerging professionally at the Inns would surely have engaged the interests of landed gentlemen resident there, given their investments in disseminated power rather than centralized forms of political organization.[9]

In addition to this constitutional dimension, for the generation of textual producers connected to the Inns in Elizabeth's early reign—Thomas Norton, Thomas Sackville, Thomas North, Jasper Heywood, Arthur Hall, Francis Kinwelmersh, George Whetstone, Arthur Brook, Thomas Phaer, Alexander Neville, Laurence Blundeston, Richard Edwards, Arthur Golding, and many others—the further sense of a new cultural imperative to stock or 'store' the English language was palpable. Justifying publication as a public service was certainly a vital strategy to combat 'the stigma of print',[10] but such claims are so persistent that we should also consider their arguments against 'hoarding' knowledge seriously. To take an example from Googe, prefatory matter from Laurence Blundeston (the agent of publication whom Googe calls 'a very friend of mine') claims to show 'goodwill' by condemning 'hord[ing] up [...] treasure'; he proposes that a good reception might persuade other poem-hoarding writers, 'who yet doubting thy unthankful receipt niggardly keep them to

---

[8] Finkelpearl characterizes the Inns as a 'finishing school' (1969: 16).

[9] Raffield argues that Inns of Court revels in particular must be understood not as licensed misrule and repressive tolerance, but as an experiment with an alternative constitutional settlement based on disseminated power rather than royally centred governance (2004: 84–123).

[10] See J. Saunders (1951). For a thorough analysis of this issue and its associated gendering, see Wall (1993). Marotti (1995: 35–7) discusses manuscript culture at the Inns.

their own use and private commodity, whereas being assured of the contrary by thy friendly report of other men's travails, they could perhaps be easily entreated freely to lend them abroad to thy greater avail and furtherance' (Googe 1989: 39–40).[11] Similarly in Gascoigne, in prefatory matter to *The Adventures of Master F.J.*, we see a virtual scrum of participants involved in relaying the text to publication (including a 'G.T.' some speculate may refer to Turbervile), one of whom pronounces that he 'thought better to please a number by common commoditie than to feede the humor of any private parson by nedelesse singularitie' (2000: 142). The socially utilitarian dimension of these arguments favouring circulation, of course, prefigures eighteenth-century rationales for a 'republic of letters', and they also support the public dissemination of both verse 'inventions' and the translation of texts otherwise not available to English readers. In light of this imperative to assemble a storehouse of and for English, it is no surprise that the energies of the age scored any number of literary high water marks.

With Tottel's Miscellany (1557) as only a partial precedent, Googe is credited with the first English lyric collection by a single author, with his *Eclogues, Epitaphs, and Sonnets* published in 1563 under his own name—and with his permission.[12] Turbervile published the second of these lyric experiments, his *Epitaphs, Epigrams, Songs and Sonnets*, in 1567. Gascoigne rather famously put a twist on this question of authorial signature, first publishing his gathered works (with many items from the 1560s) as a *false* miscellany of 'sundrie authors' (*A Hundred Sundry Flowers*) in 1573, only to republish that material under his own signature as *The Posies* in 1575. While 1616 publications by Ben Jonson and James I often stand as the first 'complete works' by living authors, *The Posies* sets a far earlier mark. Although Gascoigne's volumes contained enormous generic variety, these publishing breakthroughs tend to be read in a lyric frame. For purposes of analysing this trio, however, we also need to read the (not very Petrarchan) lyric strand *within* a generically kaleidoscopic braid of socially networked textual activities.[13]

For new modes of literary production also included original drama (with the collaborative *Gorboduc*, the first blank-verse drama, performed during the Christmas Revels at the Inner Temple in 1561), as well as prose, long poems, travel accounts, literary theory, and numerous translations of both classical and contemporary material. In the remaining pages, I consider the contributions of Googe,

---

[11] In justifying publication, Blundeston suggests he found himself barren of poetry, and having 'a paper bunch [...] | Of filéd work of Googe's flowing head', the solution was simply to publish his friend's verse (in Googe 1989: 39–43).

[12] Kennedy (1989: 19–20) details Googe's compliance with Blundeston's 'unauthorized' steps. Continental Reformation precedents by Clément Marot and Théodore de Bèze are important; some of their poems appeared in Tottel's Miscellany (1557), but the formal influence of the Continental volumes (grouping poems by type) appears in Googe.

[13] Turbervile's answer poem to Googe on Petrarchism is dismissive. To Googe's 'Twoo lynes shall tell the griefe | that I by love sustaine: | I burne, I flame, I faint, I freeze, | Of Hell I feele the paine', 'Turberviles aunswere' replies, 'Twoo lynes shall teach you how | to purchase ease anewe: | Let reason rule where Love did raigne, | and ydle thoughts eschewe' (both in Turbervile 1977: 46).

Turbervile, and Gascoigne in terms of an intersubjective, quasi-corporate practice of textuality, offering a narrative that traces the friendship dimension of this new political imaginary.[14] These contributions traverse categories of translation (itself a form of textual conversation), lyric (especially answer poems and the communitarianism of pastoral), and other textual forms like verse letters and literary theory that are, at once, forms of friendly address and exchange. These writers' efforts reflect new social modes of production, in which a lateral community of the 'studious' addressed one another and marked each other's achievements. If the imperative of their generation was to stock English letters as a service to the newly 'national' project of culture, these authors fulfilled it very substantially—by means of addressing each other in the quasi-corporate form of a literary company.

26.2 THE WORK OF TRANSLATION: 'THE FAMILIAR CONFERENCE OF STUDIOUS FRIENDS'

Googe is now best known for his 1563 lyric collection. But, with strong Protestant leanings and encouraged by no less a friend than John Bale, he had already made a name for himself with a translation of three books of Palingenius' *The Zodiac of Life* (dedicated to his grandmother) in 1560, and then six more books (dedicated to William Cecil, his kinsman, a member of Gray's Inn admitted in 1540, and, among other offices, secretary to the Queen) in 1561.[15] When Heywood refers Seneca to the Inns, Googe appears with North, Sackville, Norton, Christopher Yelverton, William Baldwin, Thomas Blundeville, and William Bavande. 'There Googe a gratefull gaynes hath gotte,' and report 'runneth ryfe' about his translation of *The Zodiac of Life* (Heywood 1913: 102–3). This poem was immensely popular, and Googe's translation went through many editions.

In the first edition, Googe portrays a debate among the Muses about what he should translate. Calliope wins, arguing for Palingenius' 1543 *Zodiacus vitae*, while the Googe figure nervously insists that

> in England here a hundred heads
>   more able now there be
> This same to do,

[14] This collaborative mode around the Inns suggestively connects to the collaborative norms of later Elizabethan dramatic production elaborated by Master (1997).

[15] The final twelve books were also dedicated to Cecil. Indeed, another way to assess period intellectual culture would be to analyse a 'cult of Cecil'; his importance as a patron of learning should not be overshadowed by his political attainments. Numerous admissions to Gray's Inn seem to have been effected on his word, as evident in the register of admissions to Gray's Inn (see Foster 1889: 66).

but he then complies,

> Commanded thus to english here
> this famous Poet's book.
>
> (1989: 129–30)[16]

In later editions, Googe extends his commendations of this Italian author, who was lionized in the Reformation for having been posthumously deemed heretical. 'I could not find out a Poete more meete for the teaching of a Christian life […] than this […] famous Italion […] neither ye unquietness of his time […] ne yet the furious tyranny of the Antichristian Prelate […] could […] amase the Muse, or hinder the zealous […] spirit of so Christian a Souldier' (1565, Epistle Dedicatory). The translation redresses circumstances in which 'so Christian a writer' should 'lie hyd and unknowen to the ignoraunt sorte'. Googe's first publication, then, is a translation, and it is offered as a public-spirited contribution to the national store of godly models.

In ensuing editions, Googe expands his commentary to the godliness of verse and the importance of vernacular, while reflecting the communal terms of textual production. He urges that 'auncient fathers and holy Prophetes' highly esteemed 'this kinde of wryting in verse' and enters into a defence of English: 'Be not so straight of judgement', he urges, as not to 'abyde to reade anything written in Englishe verse, which is nowe so plenteously enriched wyth a numbre of eloquent writers, that in my fansy it is lyttle inferiour to […] the auncient Romaines.' Concerning the enriched state of contemporary eloquence, he stresses that before proceeding with his translation, he made 'dilligente inquirie' to ensure that no one else was attempting 'to english the same'. Googe worries about the busy conditions under which the *Zodiac* was completed (due to his simultaneous labours for Cecil), noting his corresponding absence from 'the familiar conference of any studious friends whereby in some doubtes I might better have bene resolved' (1565, Epistle Dedicatory). The picture is one of a larger community of textual production, especially regarding the flurry of translations under way; Googe is committed to avoiding redundancy and competition, while solicitous of a circle of learned and friendly readers to support this work.[17]

In the same context of this broad translation effort, Gascoigne translated Ariosto's play *I suppositi* in 1566; that year he and Francis Kinwelmersh (also of Gray's Inn, admitted in 1557) collaboratively translated Euripides' tragedy, producing the first

---

[16] Likewise, Turbervile recounts a dream in which the Muses sort jurisdictions, redirecting him away from Lucan's 'civill broyles' (better allotted to Sackville) and towards Boccaccio instead (Turbervile 1977: 342, 336).

[17] Further testimony to the larger sense of a communal project appears in Arthur Hall's dedication of his *Ten Books of Homer's Iliades* (1581). He tallies 'the ripe wits of this age, and […] the diverse works so exquisitely done […] by our own Nation, as the travail of […] Barnabe Googe in Palingenius, the learned and painful translation of part of Seneca by […] Jasper Heywood, the excellent and laudable labor of […] Arthur Golding […] the worthy works of that noble gentleman my L. of Buckhurst [Sackville], the pretty and pithy conceits of […] George Gascoigne, and others in great numbers' (Kennedy 1989: 13).

vernacular English version of Greek drama with *Jocasta*.[18] Like Heywood's Senecan translations, *Jocasta* was much influenced by the event of *Gorboduc*'s production at the Inner Temple. The expansive subtitle Gascoigne gave *Supposes* in 1573 describes a comedy 'Englished by George Gascoygne of Grayes Inne Esquire, and there presented'; likewise, *Jocasta*'s subtitle stresses location, describing the play as 'translated and digested into Acte by George Gascoigne, and Francis Kinwelmershe of Grayes Inn, and there by them presented'. Here we see the productive work of 'Englishing' again closely associated with friendly collaboration and the communal forms—not only of festivity, but also of constitutional comment—harboured in the Inns' social spaces.

For *Jocasta* refracts key political concerns raised by Sackville and Norton in *Gorboduc*. Gorboduc, as king, swerves from the 'Ancient' Constitution (a concept then very actively being elaborated at the Inns) by invoking an unconstitutional prerogative to divide the realm between two sons, thereby inciting the murderous ambitions and reprisals that leave the kingdom bereft of rulers. Raffield's account of the Inner Temple performance stresses that, though we may see proto-republican sentiments, the text primarily attempts to realign the 'conventional [...] jursiprudence of the king's two bodies [...] *within the framework of a sovereign common law*' (2004: 125–6; my emphasis). Thus, in its portrayal of a succession crisis and resulting chaos, *Gorboduc* manifested an 'Inns' perspective on both Elizabeth's marriage possibilities and the larger relation between the monarch and common law.

So, too, does *Jocasta*. It concerns a dilemma more patently unstable than dividing the kingdom: Oedipus' sons inherit a right to rule in alternating years, with predictably disastrous results. Against strife between brothers, the translators stress images of equality and the strength of 'concord'. One brother is urged, for example, to

> drive from [his] doubtfull brest
> This monstrous mate [vaine ambition], in steade whereof embrace
> Equalitie [...] true and trustie knots
> Of friendly faith which never can be broke;

as the emblem of one 'dumbe shew' is glossed, 'hereby was noted the incomparable force of concord betweene brethren' (Gascoigne 2000: 110–11). In its intense focus on constitutional stability, *Jocasta* relates not only to *Gorboduc*, but also to Baldwin's *A Mirror for Magistrates* (1559) and the 1576 blank-verse satire *The Steele Glas*, 'compiled by George Gascoigne, *Esquiere*' with a prefatory commendation from 'Walter Rawelie of the Middle Temple'. These literary productions comprise a persistent Inns of Court viewpoint, warning monarchs against mistaking royal prerogative for personal right and underscoring accountability to an Ancient Constitution. That constitution, of course, depended on an interpretation of the common law; that interpretation, in turn, was arguably a professional monopoly of the Inns and its 'familiar conference of studious friends'.

[18] See *ODNB* 'Kinwelmersh, Francis'. Translated from Italian rather than Greek, *Jocasta* is the sole extant Gascoigne manuscript (see Pigman 2000, pp. xlvi–xlvii). Christopher Yelverton, also of Gray's Inn (and later Speaker of the House in the 1597 Parliament), wrote the Epilogue.

26.3 PASTORAL COMMUNITY: 'THE FOLLOWING OF MY FRIENDS' PERSUASIONS'

Like Googe, Turbervile is mainly known for his lyric collection *Epitaphs, Epigrams, Songs and Sonnets* (1567).[19] That same year, however, he also published translations of Ovid's *Heroides* and the *Eclogues* of Mantuan. Like Palingenius, Mantuan's eclogues figured prominently in grammar schools (Baldwin 1944: i. 624). Mantuan, an Italian humanist who became a Carmelite in 1463, was (again like Palingenius) celebrated in Reformation England for his criticism of Church corruption. He makes a comic appearance in *Love's Labour's Lost*, when the pedant Holofernes reflects the school-text life of Mantuan by exclaiming, 'Ah, good old Mantuan' (4. 2. 93–9)—after garbling the first Latin line of his eclogues. The curricular centrality of Mantuan's eclogues ensured a powerful relay for Virgilian pastoral, and Turbervile's popular translation further disseminated Virgilian themes in the vernacular, with the implicitly 'Reformation' credential that Mantuan supplied. The repeatedly imagined pastoral community of friendly poet–shepherds in the eclogues of Googe and Turbervile, as an emblem of poetic conversation, resonates directly with friendship's horizontal politics in and around the Inns.

In the ostensible 'elsewhere' of the eclogues' pastoral context, verse stories are exchanged by poet–shepherds in dialogues. The pastoral transactions these narratives represent usually begin with a request or invitation from one shepherd for the performance of a poetic tale (normally about the tribulations of love, sometimes about town or weather events). Here we see a likeness of the larger traffic in texts going on between friends in and around the Inns. In Turbervile's translation of Mantuan, the opening phrase of the first speaker, Fortunatus, apostrophizes his 'Frend Faustus' (the fourth use of 'friend' in thirteen lines) and calls for poetry:

> since our flock
> in shade and pleasaunt vale
> Doth chewe the cudde: of auncient love
> let us begin to tale.
>
> (1567: 1^r)

Friendship is textually generative.

Heterosexual love receives little endorsement. Faustus tells how 'cloyd with cares and Cupids coales yfreat' for the duration of his passion; love not only 'blynds the senses sore', but it also 'reaves the freedome from the minde | of man in monstrous wyse' (3^{r-v}). Once the protagonist is married, the tale collapses—'What neede so many words?' (8^r)—ending with a lament on the transience of pleasure (9^r). By contrast, the sustaining affect of the eclogues is persistently homosocial friendship. Friendly forms of like-kind exchange drive the pastoral poetic economy. Thus,

---

[19] Turbervile expands the use of narrative headings in the lyric collection. There may have been an earlier version, since the title page calls it 'newly corrected, with additions' (Panofsky 1977, p. vi).

Turbervile's second eclogue is offered as a requital of the first; one shepherd's tale is repaid by his auditor's poetic recompense:

> His Faustus tale to quite,
>   here Fortunatus gan:
> And after to recite
>   the fonde affects of man.
>
> (9ᵛ)

This story more vociferously opposes love than the first. Fuelled by full-bore misogyny ('No countrey is so barbarous, | is none so savage seckte, | As doth not hate the womans love | and fansies fonde rejecte'), it uses terms of political submission to describe mankind's succumbing to tyrannies of passion. Fancies lead to 'broiling warre & strife', and this disastrously causes 'Lawes and sacred Bookes' to be 'in yron chaines ybound' (15ᵛ). Mankind

> first was free, but to his necke
>   him selfe did frame the yoke:
> In servile chaine him selfe he bounde,
>   and bands of freedome broke.
>
> (15ʳ)

The distinction offered here, quite familiarly of concern in Elizabethan legal culture, concerns lawful authority and obedience ('Lawes and sacred Bookes') and the 'chains' of tyrannical compulsion. The image of the 'Lawes' in chains cannot possibly be limited to an emblem of private love.

Googe's 'Egloga prima' starts with a similar exchange to those in Turbervile's Mantuan. It takes place between the shepherds Daphnes and Amintas, who open the volume with the hortatory

> Let shepherds us yield also tales,
>   as best becomes the time:
> . . .
> Begin to sing, Amintas.
>
> (1989: 45)

In a surprising detail, a woodcut illustrates the collection (Figure 26.1). By reference to the names in the caption, it portrays the two shepherds of the first eclogue. The probably recycled image, however, shows what are more likely to be scholars (or perhaps pilgrims) in Renaissance rather than shepherding garb.[20] The figures engage in energetic conversation, posed in forms of rhetorical disputation as one gesticulates with a roll of paper (suggesting modes of writing and not just the poetic sonorities of pastoral vocalization). The woodcut, then, illustrates not so much two rustic shepherds as a more urbane conversational encounter or debate, perhaps between 'studious friends'. Indeed, the image faces not the eclogue in which its captioned characters appear, but Blundeston's prefatory address 'to the Reader'.

[20] I am grateful to Ann Rosalind Jones for her helpful consultation on this image.

Fig. 26.1 The friends Daphnes and Amintas in conversation. Barnabe Googe, *Eclogues, Epitaphes, and Sonettes* (1563), D4ʳ.

The prefatory matter to Googe's volume situates it squarely in the milieu of the Inns and frames its sociability through the languages of friendship. Blundeston—the Googe volume's 'true begetter' in a practical sense—was admitted to Gray's Inn in 1561 (Foster 1889: 30). After a verse by Alexander Neville celebrating the poetic honours due him, Googe dedicates the volume to 'William Lovelace, Esquire, Reader of Gray's Inn'.[21] Gascoigne refers to Lovelace too, in 'Dulce bellum inexpertis', remembering 'all the rest | Of good Grayes Inn' and 'Sergeant Lovelace, many ways my friend'.[22] For his part, Googe says publication resulted from 'the following of my friends' persuasions', calling Blundeston 'a very friend of mine' and showering Lovelace, too, with the language of friendship's unmathematical reciprocities. He offers his book 'to the perfect view of [Lovelace's] friendly mind', counting himself bound by 'the numbered heaps of sundry friendships' Lovelace extended him, and yet desiring 'for recompense the friendly receiving of [his] slender gift' (1989: 38–9). While Lovelace has clearly attained a position of authority at the Inns, the address marks the relative proximities of 'friendship', compared to a more distant approach to an inaccessible noble or royal patron, and records the sense of a quotidian traffic in probably minor but materially helpful transactions.

In grammatical terms, the core dynamic of exchange is embodied in the swapping of question and answer. The question–answer format of disputation, of course, was instilled by Tudor grammar schools and developed intensively in the legal environment of the Inns. The address and response verse exchanges we have seen dramatized in Googe's pastoral eclogues and in Turbervile's translations manifest an intersubjective, friendly dynamic. At the broadest theoretical level all literary production is collaborative in this sense. But a particular verse form arising in these contexts, greatly practised by Googe and Turbervile, concretizes these actions: the 'answer poem'. As Marotti has suggested, 'given the socially dialogic context of manuscript miscellanies and poetry anthologies [...] it is no surprise to discover [...] various forms of verse exchange, including large numbers of answer poems' (1995: 159–60).[23] According to Richard Panofsky, the answer poem draws its energy from 'the school exercise called *thesis*, the writing on a given issue either favoring or denying a given position' and manifests school 'ideals of using poetic composition as a means of social exchange carried over into the writerly creations of the young men of a literary circle' (1975: 159–60 n.). Some of the earlier examples are those between Googe and friends and between Turbervile and Googe. The later poems exchanged between Christopher Marlowe and Walter Ralegh—debating, *pro et contra*, the *carpe diem* theme—are the best known of this genre.

---

[21] A skilled Latinist and translator of Seneca's *Oedipus*, Neville (like Turbervile) does not appear in official Inns of Court admissions records; perhaps he, too, was in a Chancery Inn. He is associated with Gray's Inn, however, by his involvement in 'Gascoigne's Memory', which Gascoigne's friends exacted from him as a mock precondition for his return into their 'fellowship' there.

[22] Here Gascoigne recalls the Inn 'where honest Yelverton [author of the Epilogue to *Jocasta*], | And *I Per se* sometimes yfeere did rest, | When amitie first in our brests begonne' (2000: 437).

[23] E. F. Hart's classic essay (1956) concerns a later, seventeenth-century vogue.

Earlier verse exchanges between friends, however, tend to engage moral issues, the labours of writing, and warnings against various temptations. Neville's reply, for example, to a lyric Googe addressed to him exemplifies this:

> O happy, then, that man account,
>   whose well directed life
> Can fly those ills which fancy stirs,
>   and live from bondage free.

Blundeston offers a similar perspective:

> Both wise and happy, Googe, he may be hight,
> Whom God gives grace to rule affections right.
>
> (Googe 1989: 88, 87)

Such exchanges usually confer about the 'well-directed life'; they thus embody the acts of counsel enshrined in discourses of 'sovereign' friendship.[24] As is typical of these writers, the languages of self-regulation, reciprocal governance, and political authority share the same idiom.

Googe wrote a number of 'sonnets' to male friends, including Alexander Nowell, John Bale, Edward Cobham, and Richard Edwards, and several each to Blundeston and Neville (whose replies are quoted above). Of special interest are two pairs of answer poems. Each involves a poem published by Googe to which Turbervile responds in his 1567 volume. The first involves a friendly refutation of Googe's well-known phrasing of the proverb 'Out of sight, out of mind'. In 'Oculi augent dolorem', Googe argues that since the presence of a beloved object incites lust, pain, and sadness, her 'absence, therefore, like I best' (Googe 1989: 97). Echoing this poem's rhetorical structure exactly, but to the opposite conclusion, Turbervile's 'To Maister Googe, his sonet out of sight out of thought' argues that nearness, rather than absence, gives less pain ('The lesse I see, the more my teene [distress]') (Turbervile 1977: 277–8). The grammatical symmetry frames the exchange as one between equals.

The second pair of verses, important for their friendship theme, includes Googe's ironic 'Of Money', and Turbervile's reply, 'To Maister Googes Fancie that begins, give monie mee, take friendship who so list'. They explore the economic dimensions of the conventional wisdom that friends are few when needed, but plentiful when in need themselves. Googe's 'fancie' entertains a conceit that, since 'Fair face show friends, when riches do abound, | Come time of proof, farewell they must away,' gold should be preferred since it 'never starts aside, but in distress | Finds ways enough to ease thine heaviness' (Googe 1989: 100). Turbervile's spirited rejoinder urges 'Friend Googe' to 'choose the Friend and let the Monie lie', since 'Thy coine will cause a thousand cares to grow,' but 'Thy Friend no care but comfort will procure' (Turbervile 1977: 259–60). Indeed, he urges, 'The faithfull Friend will never start

---

[24] The mutual rebuke that became a litmus for true friendship represents an opening chapter in the political history of modern 'freedom of speech' (see Shannon 2002, ch. 6).

aside, | But take his share of all that shall betide,' that is, of both good and bad.[25] At stake is a friendly quibble between Turbervile and 'Friend Googe' on the true versus the false friend; only adversity reveals the difference. The dialogic exchange enacted in these poems embodies the friendship principle of common property, even as it performs the 'office' of friendship as an exchange of moral advice or commentary.

The highest achievement in this mode, however, comes from Gascoigne in 1565, and it structurally enacts the blurry economics of friendly poetic exchange. The occasional 'Gascoigne's Memory' stems from five of Gascoigne's Inns of Court friends' agreement to welcome him back to Gray's Inn—on one condition. As Gascoigne's headnote explains, 'Being required by five sundrie gentlemen to wrighte in verse somewhat worthy to be remembered, before he entred into their felowship, he compiled these five sundry sortes of metre uppon five sundry theames which they delivered unto him' (Gascoigne 2000: 274). The five friends (Francis Kinwelmersh, Gascoigne's collaborator in *Jocasta*; his brother Anthony; Neville; John Vaughan, and Richard Courtrop) dictated five paradoxical 'theames' of the sort used for classroom dilation, and Gascoigne embarked on a brilliant development of each, including one—'In Haste Post Haste' (278–81)—that is arguably the first corona sequence published in English. A tour de force, this mock contract for poetic production between friends records the textual dynamic around the Inns: the fact of its community of proximate gentlemen engendered the production of literary texts in the 1560s. Gascoigne's 'payment' for his return to the 'felowship' of the Inns reflects how much this 'studious' community indexed a distinct institutionality with resonance as a utopian political form. Collaborative or intersubjective practices figured an alternative economy, an elsewhere to the prevailing orders of both capitalist greed and court corruption. The poetic transaction memorializes and situates friendship as the Inns' notional alternative regime.

26.4 FRIENDLY LETTERS: 'THUS ABSENT FRIENDS SPEAK'

The answer poem enacts the dynamics of the poetic epistle, itself a highly friendship-oriented form. If the letter from John Donne (admitted to Thavies Inn in 1591 and proceeding to Lincoln's Inn in 1592) to Henry Wotton (admitted to the Middle Temple in 1595) beginning 'Sir, more than kisses', is its grandest instance, the history of

---

[25] See also Turbervile's 'That it is Hurtful to Conceal Secrets from Our Friends' (1977: 221–4). In a later publication, Turbervile echoes the friendly debt language, offering *Tragical Tales* to 'his verie friend Ro. Baynes' and opening with the claim that 'My worde, thy wish, my det, and thy desire, | I meane my booke (my Baynes) lo here I send | To thee at last, as friendship doth require' (1977: 330).

epistolary verse practice reveals how earlier writers had already embraced the form. In Donne, a critique of the terms of court, city, *and* country life is juxtaposed to ideals of self-governance inherent in friendship's values. Many of Googe's sonnets addressed to friends can well be read as verse epistles, given their use of direct apostrophe and second-person address. Turbervile perhaps goes further in this vein, one with precursors like Wyatt's 'Mine own John Poyntz'.

In his 'To his Friend Francis Th: Leading his Life in the Countrie at his Desire', Turbervile argues—just as Donne does to Wotton—that 'The Towne is but a toyle, and wearie lyfe' (1977: 188–9). Donne's letter ends with an elaborate pun on the mutual self-rule of bound friends ('If myself I'have won | To know my rules, I have, and you have—Donne', but Turbervile's 'To Browne of Light Beliefe' on the risks of 'fained friendship' ends with a similar claim:

> So that it is a matter harde
>   their double drifts to flee:
> But yet thou shalt avoyde the wurst
>   if thou be rulde by mee. ([quoth]) G.T.
>
> (1977: 164–6)

Both of these verse letters end with a vision of friendship as a form of rule offering a better alternative to existing forms. Indeed, when Turbervile goes later to Moscow (in the company of the Elizabethan ambassador Thomas Randolph in 1568–9), he writes epistles to friends on the subject of 'the Moscovites maners'. Even in contexts of a diplomatic mission abroad, he uses London friendship to frame his view back to England. Writing to 'his especiall frende' Edward Dancy and longing for his 'native soyle', Turbervile laments,

> My Dancie deere, when I
>   recount within my brest:
> My London frends and wonted mates
>   and thee above the rest,
> I feele a thousand fittes
>   of deepe and deadly woe.
>
> (424)

The sense that 'London frends' can stand in for—or as—'native soyle' suggests how much friendship figures operate to alter and extend the constitutional imaginary.

In this chapter's consideration of a lateral matrix for envisioning a horizontal national constitution, one linking rough equals in a network of textual exchange, the Inns of Court (and of Chancery) and the friendship languages they harboured performed indispensable enabling work. As a last matter, this synchronic horizontal formation connects to the building of a diachronic literary-historical tradition for the emerging nation, a tradition forged in tandem with the new production of the Ancient Constitution at the Inns. A landmark in this tradition occurred when Gascoigne published the first treatise on English prosody in 1575: 'Certayne notes of Instruction concerning the making of verse or ryme in English' (in *The Posies*).

It seems only fitting to recall here that 'Certain Notes' is written as a letter to a friend.

In 'Certain notes' Gascoigne responds to a request from Edouardo Donati for an account of English verse-making, and he begins with an apostrophe: 'Signor Edouardo, since promise is debt, and you, (by the lawe of friendship) do burden me with a promise that I shoulde lende you instructions [...] I will assaye to discharge the same' (454). The 'few poynts following' must surely have appealed to Winters. Gascoigne stresses a 'good and fine devise, shewing [...] quicke capacitie', which he terms *aliquid salis* ('a pinch of salt'); that being found, 'pleasant woordes will follow well inough and fast inough' (454–5). 'Beware', he warns, 'of rime without reason' (458). Offering a comparative lesson in the accenting of English, he famously claims that 'the more monasyllables that you use, the truer Englishman you shall seeme, and the lesse you shall smell of the Inkehorne' (458). In this, we have clearly moved from a mere defence of the vernacular to an almost regulatory refinement of it.

It is Gascoigne's configuration of 'tradition', however, that speaks to the social forms of national and literary community. The retrospective constitution of a tradition in George Puttenham's account has been much noted. At the end of Henry VIII's reign, he writes, there 'sprong up a new company of courtly makers, of whom [...] Wyat [...] & [...] Surrey were the two chieftaines [...] And in her Majesties time that now is are sprong up an other crew [...] who have written excellently well' (48–9). Many of the Elizabethans he lists served the Queen or Cecil, but virtually all were members of the Inns. Sackville and Edward Dyer were members of the Inner Temple; Philip Sidney was a member of Gray's Inn, like Gascoigne; Fulke Greville belonged to the Middle Temple and then Gray's Inn; Walter Ralegh belonged to the Middle Temple; and Nicholas Breton, like Turbervile, escapes record, but he appears in a 1595 list of writers associated with the Inns (Ellis and Jim 2001: 303 n.). In this vision of literary history, Puttenham's cohort of 'courtly makers' can also be seen as a group springing specifically from the cultures of the Inns. His use of the terms 'company' and 'crew' captures the corporate and communal nature of literary exchange, echoing the 'swarme' Heywood had described.

Gascoigne, however, makes rich use of the term 'tradition'. When he refers to 'tradition' in 'Certain Notes', it is worth attending to the legal and exchange valences of the term: '1. The action of handing over (something material) to another; delivery, transfer. (Chiefly in *Law*.)' (*OED*). By invoking this term, Gascoigne makes his letter of instruction an action of delivery; his sense of tradition is a personal and intersubjective transaction. 'I covet rather to satisfie you particularly', he writes, 'than to undertake a generall tradition' (455), and though he admits that he follows 'a preposterous order in [his] traditions', he is content to leave them casual and disordered since, in the treatise's last line, 'I know that I write to my freende, and affying myself thereupon, I make an ende' (462). To 'affy' oneself is to invoke the languages of trust and espousal or affiliation. With the Inns as a politically defined separate space of communal textual production and with the discourse of friendship to describe it, an extended network of quasi-corporate authorship arose in the 1560s and beyond. Early Elizabethan writers modelled a horizontal social form for a new English constitutional imaginary. These writers were a crew not only—or even predominantly—of '*courtly* makers', but also a company of 'studious friends'.

PRIMARY WORKS

DONNE, JOHN (1985), 'To Sir Henry Wotton', in *The Complete English Poems*, ed. C. A. Patrides (London: Dent), 159–62.

FORTESCUE, JOHN (1737), *De laudibus legum Angliae*, ed. John Selden.

FOSTER, JOSEPH (ed.) (1889), *Register of Admissions to Gray's Inn, 1521–1889* (London: Hansard Publishing Union).

GASCOIGNE, GEORGE (2000), *A Hundreth Sundrie Flowres*, ed. G. W. Pigman III (Oxford: Clarendon Press).

GOOGE, BARNABE (trans.) (1565), *The Zodiake of Life* by Marcellus Palingenius.

——(1989), *Eclogues, Epitaphs, and Sonnets*, ed. J. A. Kennedy (Toronto: University of Toronto Press).

HALL, ARTHUR (trans.) (1581), *Ten Books of Homer's Iliades*.

HEYWOOD, JASPER (1913), *Jasper Heywood and his Translations of Seneca's Troas, Thyestes, and Hercules Furens*, ed. H. de Vocht (Louvain: A. Uystpruyst).

PUTTENHAM, GEORGE (1589), *The Arte of English Poesie* (London: Richard Field).

SHAKESPEARE, WILLIAM (2005), *Love's Labour's Lost*, in *The Norton Shakespeare*, ed. Stephen Greenblatt et al. (New York: W. W. Norton).

TURBERVILE, GEORGE (trans.) (1567), *The Eglogs of the Poet B. Mantuan Carmelitan*.

——(1977), *Epitaphes, Epigrams, Songs and Sonets*, ed. Richard Panofsky (New York: Scholar's Facsimiles).

CHAPTER 27

'FOR THIS IS TRUE OR ELS I DO LYE'

THOMAS SMITH, WILLIAM BULLEIN, AND MID-TUDOR DIALOGUE

PHIL WITHINGTON

THE early 1560s were a difficult time for Sir Thomas Smith and William Bullein, the most accomplished dialogue writers of their generation. Their difficulties, it must be said, were different in kind. A pensioner of the Crown during the Marian regime, Smith's political rehabilitation after Elizabeth's accession had been frustratingly slow for a man so invested in public service. Although elected a parliamentary burgess for Liverpool, his estrangement from his erstwhile friend and patron William Cecil meant he lacked a court position, and it was not until September 1562 that he secured public office: the embassy in Paris (Dewar 1964; *ODNB*). Bullein faced problems less grand but altogether more pressing. Since 1554, when he resigned the Sussex rectory of Blaxhall on ideological grounds, he had served as physician in the household of the Durham gentleman Sir Thomas Hilton. Sir Thomas's death in 1559—and Bullein's marriage to Sir Thomas's widow and executor, Agnes—brought Bullein into direct conflict with the younger brother, William Hilton, who accused Bullein of poisoning his brother; successfully sued the newly-weds for 350 marks that Hilton claimed Sir Thomas owed him; and refused to repay a bond of £50 that Agnes maintained he owed Sir Thomas's estate. In the meantime Bullein endured violent intimidation, a loss of reputation, and the protracted and expensive litigation that feuds of this kind entailed (NA, C3/13/91, *Bulleyn* v. *Hylton*). The pressures were such that by 1562 Bullein and Agnes had left the north-east for the London parish of St Giles, Cripplegate, where he practised physic until his death in 1576 (*ODNB*).

Although Smith and Bullein contended with different circumstances during the early years of Elizabeth's reign, their responses were similar in at least one respect: they wrote. More precisely, they wrote dialogues. It was during his exclusion from office that Smith penned *A Communication or Discourse of the Queen's Highness's Marriage*, 'one of the most widely copied tracts in Elizabethan England' (Dewar 1964: 4).[1] It was not the first time he had resorted to this course of action. During his more serious political exile after Somerset's fall in 1549, Smith composed *A Discourse of the Commonweal of the Realm of England*, a manuscript dialogue quite as incisive and topical as the *Communication*.[2] More strikingly, Bullein published his entire corpus during his period of domestic and professional turbulence. His first dialogue, *The Government of Health*, was printed in 1559 (in time to be dedicated to Sir Thomas Hilton); his second dialogue, *Bullein's Bulwark of Defence Against All Sickness*, was written in the eye of the conflict with William Hilton and appeared in 1562, the same year he published *A Comfortable Regiment Against the Pleurisy* (his only non-dialogic work); his final and most ambitious work, *A Dialogue Against the Fever Pestilence*, followed in 1564. As this suggests, a key difference between Smith and Bullein is that while Smith wrote for a network of manuscript readers, Bullein purposefully—and successfully—embraced the commercial world of print (Slack 1979: 250, 259). Indeed Bullein's unhappy experiences in the hands of Hilton's lawyers and the busi-ness of establishing a London household no doubt encouraged him to publish as intensively as he did. That is not to say that Smith wrote without any anticipation of what he would have termed 'profit', though in his case it was cultural, social, and political capital that he sought. Within the influential reading community in which he participated, his dialogues sought to disseminate his ideas, inform public policy, demonstrate his learning, and renew his prospect of office. Nor is it to claim that Bullein, as a printed author, was without ideological intent. Just as Smith used the dialogic form to serve various personal ends, so the minister-cum-physician was clearly committed to reforming the practice of healing by publicizing a particular tradition of knowledge—Hippocratic medicine—for as wide a readership as possible (Wear 2000: 44, 60).

The contrast between the technologies and audiences of Smith and Bullein are significant and clearly influenced the content and form of their dialogues. However, there are also important similarities between the two that at once provide a context for these differences and point to the place of Smith and Bullein within—and their contribution to—the literary culture of the period. Both men were humanists and moralists, who used dialogue in innovative and stylistically striking ways. They were also proponents of 'commonwealth' who (among other things) examined the limits

---

[1] The text used here is BL, Add. MS 48047, compiled by Robert Beale.

[2] The text was revised and published posthumously as *A Compendious or Brief Examination of Certain Ordinary Complaints of Divers of Our Countrymen in These Days* (1581).

and possibilities of 'counsel' in their respective fields of expertise. Furthermore, while Smith affirmed the potential of 'discourse' and 'counsel' to resolve dissension and establish an acceptable truth among self-interested parties, Bullein came to suggest the opposite: that eloquence and knowledge were dangerous tools to be manipulated for private interest and profit. In this way their work illustrates the contrasting scribal and commercial audiences to which dialogues could be directed as well as the different kinds of knowledge the form could bear. Perhaps most importantly, they suggest two trajectories of the English humanist project as it had developed by 1560: the idealistic faith in the power of rhetoric to identify and serve the public good; and the more pessimistic intimation that not only was the 'new learning' socially ineffectual, but in the wrong hands it actively corroded commonwealth.

I

Smith and Bullein were almost exact contemporaries. Born into comparable upper-yeoman/lower-gentry families, they spent their formative years in small boroughs situated in neighbouring south-eastern counties (Saffron Walden in Essex; the Isle of Ely in Cambridgeshire) and are testimony to the educational possibilities this environment afforded men of their 'sort'. Smith's biography—the archetypal Tudor success story—is well known. A precocious child, he was moved to Cambridge aged 11 and became the 'flower' of the university: a prominent scholar and celebrated humanist; university and ecclesiastical office-holder; royal counsellor and statesman. That of Bullein is less researched, though perhaps more typical of 'learned' Englishmen at the time. He claimed to have attended university (there is no record of his attendance) and may have studied abroad. His subsequent livelihood depended on Church livings, noble patronage, and, after moving to London, his ability to establish a professional reputation and sell himself as a healer and writer. His reliance on the market rather than the corporate powers and privileges of the London College of Physicians is notable; it remains to be explained why Bullein chose to remain a 'non-collegiate' physician rather than become an incorporated Fellow of the College (Pelling 2000: 39–42).

In their different ways, then, Smith and Bullein were 'public' men of early Elizabethan London. While Smith operated in the rarefied offices of public power, Bullein was a popular physician and author whose epitaph read 'he always had medicines which he gave to rich and poor alike' (*ODNB*). Moreover, he publicized his second dialogue, *Bullein's Bulwark*, by including his own name in the title, which suggests he actively sought to engender authorial recognition and repute. Certainly Thomas Nashe, the great experimentalist and self-publicist of late Tudor literature, took inspiration from Bullein. Nashe acknowledged that *Have With You to Saffron Walden* was written 'in the nature of a Dialogue, much like Bullen' (1596: D^r); *Nashe's Lenten Stuff* (1599) used the same type of self-advertising title as *Bullein's Bulwark*; and (as we shall see) the experiments in pastiche and elusiveness for which Nashe is now credited can also be found in Bullein's later work. In all these respects it is difficult to see why Nashe rather than a writer like Bullein should be regarded as the first exponent of the new 'market in print' (Scott-Warren 2005: 98). Smith has recently received a degree of insightful critical attention (Richards 2003; Shrank 2000, 2004*b*). Bullein remains, however, largely ignored by literary scholars. This lack of recognition is perhaps unsurprising given that dialogue itself is not usually highlighted as an important literary genre of the period: it goes unmentioned, for example, in Jason Scott-Warren's recent survey of early modern literature. This neglect ignores a powerful tradition of Tudor writing that dates from Thomas More's *Utopia* (a text against which both Smith and Bullein position themselves) and which obscures continuities with the more familiar post-1580 literary scene and beyond (see D. Baker 1999).

Dialogue can be defined as the written representation of a conversation between two or more interlocutors. Such conversations could be real or fictional or both: indeed it was the genre's blurring of these categories that made well-executed examples of the form—most famously *Utopia*—so beguiling. The genre was deeply rooted in classical culture: just as the origins of the dialogic tradition were conceived by early moderns to be Greek, so it was in the language of international discourse, Latin, that More wrote, circulated, and eventually published *Utopia* (although readers needed working knowledge of Greek to understand the jokes). However, just as *Utopia* was translated into English in the 1550s—Ralph Robinson provided Edwardian and Marian editions—so the genre as a whole lent itself to vernacularization; and the dialogues of Smith and Bullein nicely reflect the advanced state of that process by the second half of the sixteenth century. As far as Smith was concerned, dialogue facilitated reason: 'that kind of reasoning seems to me best for bolting out the truth which is used by way of dialogue or colloquy, where reasons be made to and fro as well for the matter intended as against it' (1969: 13). For Bullein it was pedagogic tool: a complex body of knowledge like Hippocratic medicine could be 'Reduced into the form of a Dialogue, for the better understanding of the unlearned' (1559: A1^r). In what follows I want to consider two dialogues that Smith wrote while removed from court, the *Discourse* and *Communication*, before discussing in more detail Bullein's less familiar dialogues.

II

Smith's *Discourse* involves an anonymous author describing for the reader (in the form of a letter) a five-way conversation related to him by one of the interlocutors, the Knight. From the outset, there is a plurality of voices and perspectives. This diversity is further accentuated by the social background of the characters: the Knight is joined in 'company' (1969: 11) by a Merchant, Husbandman, Capper, and Doctor to consider 'the manifold complaints of men touching the decay of the Commonweal that we be in' (15). This unusually complicated dialogic structure affirms the Preface's premiss that discourse about commonwealth should involve all its participants. As a marginal note posits: 'No man is a stranger to the commonweal he is in' (11). This is presented not so much as a point of democratic principle as discursive common sense. As Smith notes, 'The gifts of wit be so divers. Some excel in memory, some in invention, some in judgement, some at the first sight ready, and some after long consideration.' It is because men's wit is so varied that 'Of many heads is gathered a perfect counsel.' These diverse natural abilities are in turn distributed socially, men excelling in many different occupations and 'arts'; and it is on this basis that he 'would not only have learned men (whose judgement I would wish to be chiefly esteemed herein) but also merchantman, husbandman, and artificers (which in their calling are taken wise) freely suffered, yea and provoked, to tell their advice in this matter' (12).

The matter in question was an economic paradox. Smith's characters note that 'though there be scarcity of nothing', England was nevertheless experiencing 'dearth [i.e. costliness] in all things [...] desolation of counties by enclosures, desolation of towns for lack of occupation and crafts, and divisions of opinion in matters of religion'. Why should this be and, more pressingly, what should be done about it? The cumulative answer provided by the *Discourse* is notable in at least two respects. First, Smith breaks with conventional wisdom articulated by other commonwealth writers over the preceding decade and accepts 'the widespread reality of self-interested economic behaviour' (Wrightson 2000: 154). Furthermore, he actively encourages pursuit of legitimate personal profit as the most effective means of countering current problems and benefiting the commonwealth. Rather than perceiving all self-interest as covetous and socially damaging, he suggests that well-regulated and responsible pursuit of gain is a fillip to the common good. Secondly, developing this position, Smith redefines normative conceptions of sociability and commerce according to the Ciceronian concept of *honestas*, or civility: 'the self-restraint of potentially domineering speakers' (Richards 2003: 2). This mode of civility required individuals to develop qualities requisite of self-possession and control—discretion, wisdom, decorum—enabling sociability, or 'civil conversation', between people of contrasting perspectives, conflicting interests, and unequal wealth and status. As Jennifer Richards has argued, the *Discourse* propagated this mode of civility in at least two ways: it represented 'civil conversation' in action; and the kind of socio-economic behaviour it recommended as normative was itself imbued with the values of *honestas* (101–6). In this way 'the most brilliant and most enduring' work of sixteenth-century political economy owed at least some of its prescience to the vernacularization of a classically inspired literary form (Smith 1969, p. ix).

As such the *Discourse* is by no means as socially inclusive as its Preface and dramatis personae might imply. The participants are all 'creditable' representatives of their crafts and callings who have already cultivated qualities necessary for civil conversation. In this way, they engage in structured discourse and so transform their personal 'opinion' into a shared 'knowledge of the truth' (134). Nor do they do this unaided. Rather the Doctor (a cipher for Smith) dominates: he manages the conversation; the company's conclusions are his; and the final part of the dialogue—'wherein are devised the remedies for the said griefs'—consists almost entirely of him answering questions asked by the Knight (the only other character represented in this crucial section is the Merchant, who interjects twice). The *Communication*, written twelve years later, retains this faith in dialogue to establish truth. However, it does so through the talk of five learned 'friends' rather than different estates, and without a presiding figure like the Doctor. Indeed the most authoritative interlocutor, who coordinates the discussion and gives each speaker a nickname, is a stutterer (styled 'Godfather') whose 'tongue will not follow' (1561: 104^r). Likewise, Smith's character neither advances an argument himself nor passes judgement on what has been said: he merely describes the conversation to his 'friend' and neighbour 'F.W.' (97^v). The effect is to place even more trust on the ability of the dialogic process—and the characters and audience involved in that process—to deliver and recognize a rational conclusion.

The matter discussed in the *Communication* is whether or not Elizabeth should marry; and, if so, whether her husband should be a 'subject' or 'stranger' (98^v). The cumulative argument, while open-ended, is carefully structured. Spitewed's reasons against marriage are successfully refuted by Lovealien, who then makes the case for a foreign match. Homefriend compliments the first part of Lovealien's argument but attacks the second, advocating instead marriage to an English nobleman. This position goes unanswered as the conversation is terminated by dinner (a technique also deployed in *Utopia*): this invites the final arbitration of readers' discretion and the possibility of Elizabeth's intervention. Each of the speakers is eloquent; the narrator gushes at the outset that 'me thinke I am in *Platoes Acadamie* or *Ciceroes Tusculano*' (98^r). The self-consciousness of the work's rhetorical display is nicely captured by Lovealien, analysing Spitewed's oration:

Nowe your seconde part was so well handled and so finelie you entered into your matter and so well ye shadowed it with your histories and examples of such things as hath been done before that I assure you if I had not [...] tied my self to my maste as Ulisses did to passe by the Sirens I had been caught as a fish with a hook and ye had led me by the eares whether ye had woulde.   (106^r)

Lovealien is fully conscious of the power of words which, in the mouth of a talker as skilful as Spitewed, make him 'tremble' and 'afraide as children be made afraid of bearebugges and bulbeggers'. It is only through careful reflection that he 'began to laugh at my self' for being so affected (108^r).

Cathy Shrank has argued that this sensitivity to language demonstrated by each character—and so the manner in which 'the text exposes the mechanics of rhetoric' rather than simply presenting plausible reasons for and against marriage—amounts to a 'policy of evasion' on Smith's part (2004b: 160). Such a 'policy' is certainly understandable given Smith's personal circumstances and the problematic nature of the issue disputed. However, Smith's concern for the 'mechanics' as well as the content of the discourse also points to another, perhaps more telling, feature of a text that sketches a moment in which eloquence between equals attempts to convert 'opinion' into 'truth'. As Spitewed's words reveal, he and his interlocutors are engaged in a mutual endeavour. He notes that he will be 'at a great disadvantage' in talking before 'so good confutors' (whose abilities he has witnessed in Parliament): 'whatsoever I shall saie they can with words make that it shall appeare quite overthrown'. Nonetheless, Spitewed agrees to speak 'because I my self would gladlie learn whither I be in a right opinion or no and heare either mine owne opinion so weakened or thether so strengthened with good reasons that I may by comparing thone to thither knowe mine errors which I could never yet Doe'. All he requests is that his fellow orators 'sustaine your indulginece of me until ye have hearde all my reasons which moveth me to take this parte'. In this respect the speakers' skill and knowingness neither impede the establishment of reason nor reduce the conversation to a series of technical and self-interested manoeuvres. Rather they are crucial to the discursive process, allowing the characters at once to speak and, as importantly, to listen and deconstruct the words of others. As such, the silences which follow each oration do not, as Shrank suggests, signify the speakers' reluctance to engage with so politically sensitive an issue. Rather they establish the conversational decorum appropriate—indeed necessary—for a disputation of this quality. As the narrator observes after Spitewed's surprisingly powerful initial salvo: 'And none of thither were hartie to answere whether it were because they did meditate and recorde with themselves what he had said [...] or how they should confute or no I know not But I perceive they looked not for such an oration (104^r).

It is left to Lovealien, the main dismantler of Spitewed's argument, to establish how the *Communication* serves as a template for the kind of conversation closest to Smith's heart—namely, counsel. Lovealien explains that just as friends can disagree over royal policy, so 'wherefore be counsellors but because they be not always of the same affecon that the prince is, Indeed it is by this dissenting is the beste waie founde'. The process is akin to digging for gold: counsellors sift through 'an heape of sand' and wash and test what 'glisterethe and appeareth gaie' (110^r–111^v). Difference is crucial: 'where wise persons dissent the one from thither there having opportunitie thene to conferre with thither the truth appeareth and the best waie is chosen' (111^v). In this way Smith locates his *Communication*, like the *Discourse* before it, within a humanist tradition that had long regarded counsel as the centrepiece of governance (see Walker 2005: 141–8). What distinguishes his dialogue between equals from royal counsel is the potentially distorting effect of monarchical authority on the conversation—authority which can easily transform counsellors into flatterers. Whereas Morus in *Utopia* urges Hythloday to overcome such problems through circumspection and compromise, Lovealien proposes boldness: 'Happie is that prince that hath so wise a counsellor that can see what is beste but more happie is he that hath one so bolde that dare tell it to him and so beloved of him that he will heare it at his hands and beare it well' (111^v; cf. More 1998: 35–6). However, Lovealien is here talking of no average counsellor; he is outlining the advantages of a (foreign) husband, who can provide conciliar government at the heart of the royal household. Whether lesser-placed courtiers could realistically prefer Smith's boldness to More's circumspection is less clear. Certainly Dewar suggests that it was precisely Smith's tendency to speak 'plainly' rather than circumspectly that hampered his courtly career (1964: 57, 115).

Recent historical research (Withington 2001) suggests that the kind of diverse, dissenting, discreet, and bold counsel Smith promotes was much more likely to be found outside than inside the Tudor court—within the commonwealth at large. This might be the kind of informal conversations represented in the *Discourse* and *Communication* (hierarchical conversations in the former, talk among equals in the latter). It might also be in the corporate and civic locations that structured local political participation—and demanded civility on the part of participants—during the later sixteenth and early seventeenth centuries (Withington 2007; Barry 2000). Such sites included the governing councils of university and ecclesiastical 'commonwealths' as well as the common councils that increasingly governed the corporate institutions of English boroughs and cities in the century after 1540.[3] As a leading humanist and statesman of his generation, Smith was fully attuned to this corporate culture; and his conciliar vision is never better demonstrated than by his template for the settlement of Ulster during the 1570s. This ill-fated venture has been noted for its appropriation of Roman models of colonization (Morgan 1985; Canny 1998). That the constitutional arrangements envisaged by Smith also closely resembled contemporary urban governance in England has gone unacknowledged. These arrangements centred on 'the counsel and advice of the gravest and Fathers of the Colony': that is, the 'common counsel of the Towne'. Drawn from the 'adventurers' who first settled the colony, the common council was to be equal in power to the Deputy Colonel (who controlled the colony's garrison), responsible for making and abrogating laws, choosing and expelling office-holders, charging and collecting subsidies, 'and genrall in all weightie affairs' (Smith's Family Papers). It was a conception of governance that nicely reflected Smith's investment in counsel and his faith in civil discourse. It would also have been instantly familiar to the 'better sort' of householder across England (and indeed the Irish pale)—William Bullein included.

III

Smith had an overarching concern with reasoned and reflective discourse based on classical precedents: he conflated such discourse with contemporary permutations of counsel; he prescribed it as a normative mode of political sociability in both his dialogic and constitutional writing; and he did so more often in the vernacular

[3] See Slack (1999, ch. 1); Tittler (1991, ch. 5; 1998, ch. 9); Withington (2005, chs. 2, 5).

than in Latin. He was, in short, an upholder of the humanist project insofar as it had developed in England by the second half of the sixteenth century. Bullein's less well-known dialogues, although ostensibly very different from Smith's *Discourse* and *Communication*, nevertheless engage with this project in important respects. On the face of it this should not be surprising given the influence of what historians describe as 'medical humanism' on both the theory and practice of medicine in the sixteenth century—in particular their excavation of original Greek texts, their retranslation into Latin, and the further promulgation of this knowledge through vernacular treatises and textbooks (Siraisi 1990: 192–3; Maclean 2002, ch. 1). Bullein was very much involved in this process, and in this respect his printed dialogues can be regarded as exercises in medical humanism just as Smith's manuscripts were part of a larger programme of political reform based on humanist principles. However, Bullein's contribution to mid-Tudor humanism extends further than the convenient but (in this instance) misleading distinction between medical and commonwealth writing. This is suggested simply by the fact that Bullein is the only sixteenth-century writer of vernacular medical tracts to present his material dialogically: major influences like Thomas Elyot and Andrew Boorde eschewed the form in their medical writings; and other popular writers like Thomas Moulton, Jean Gœurot, Thomas Cogan, and Pierre Drouet preferred tabular formats (Wilson 1976: 53). Bullein was also notable for systematically representing the precepts and practice of physic according to the language of counsel. It was not unusual to characterize physic in these terms. In *The Castle of Health* (1541) Elyot establishes the close relationship between the health of the natural body and the body politic, and Andrew Boorde explicitly labels the physicians' advice as counsel (1541: A2^{r-v}; Boorde 1542: A1^r, B2^v, B3^r; cf. Drouet 1578). However, it is Bullein who builds the idiom into a set of normative values by which medical theory and practice should be judged—an aspect of his writing that becomes clear if his dialogues are approached as a kind of trilogy.

Viewed as a corpus, the texts, while certainly outlining Hippocratic principles, also engage with the same issues as Smith. Moreover, reading them together allows us to trace Bullein's changing attitude to the mid-Tudor commonwealth. This shift in perspective brings the relationship between dialogic form and content into sharp focus. Turning from hopeful humanist to popular satirist, Bullein the author also transforms—even transcends—the dialogic form with which he increasingly skilfully works. *The Government of Health* adheres to a simple though well-wrought format of question–answer between a physician and prospective patient. *Bullein's Bulwark* supplements this structure by detailing a series of conversations between different characters and engaging in political digression and autobiographical anecdote. *A Dialogue Against the Fever Pestilence* is a polyvalent, multi-narrative, generically hybrid, five-act 'entertainment' that anticipates the theatrical and pamphleteering riches of the late Elizabethan era. The progressive acquisition of authorial skill that this suggests can usefully be understood by regarding Bullein's publishing career as a kind of six-year apprenticeship that culminated, as craft apprenticeships did, with the presentation of his 'masterpiece'. Certainly he recurrently expresses respect for 'honest handicraft men' and asks the 'gentle reader [...] to accept me amonge the fellowship of botchers [*sic*]' rather than the College of Physicians (1564: 3).

That is not to say that Bullein's public persona is unlearned. Just as his authority as an author is inextricable from his relationship to the ancients, so his conception of counsel is classically based. Smith appropriates a Ciceronian tradition of *honestas* as the ideal basis for civil conversation and counsel. Bullein, as a physician educated in a particular epistemological tradition, drew in the first instance on *cautelae*—a corpus of advice literature for physicians that prescribed the appropriate rules not simply for diagnosis and doctor–patient relationships but also decorous behaviour in general (Maclean 2002: 96–8; French 2000). Early modern exponents of *cautelae*, like Gabriele de Zerbi, were concerned with protecting the institutional status of university-educated physicians in the healing 'market' of fifteenth-century Italy, envisaging the ideal of the 'canonical physician' as a means to secure the trust and business of the populace (French 2000: 96). However, Bullein was without institutional affiliation; indeed his explicit agenda in publishing his dialogues was to circumvent vested institutional interests like the College and promulgate proper medical practice to literate laypeople. The concept of counsel—a term that, as we have seen, was very much of the cultural moment—was not only familiar to readers but also offered a useful way of justifying and legitimizing this enterprise: it valorized the work of both physician and dialogist.

The result in *The Government of Health* (1559) is the construction of not so much the canonical physician as the counsellor–physician. The tone is set in Bullein's dedication (to Sir Thomas Hilton) with a story about Alexander the Great and Phillip the Physician which 'declare[s] the great trust in the one, and the fidelitie in the other' (A3^v). The 'gentle reader' is then assured that 'when men dooe decaye through sicknesse, then the counsel of the Phisicion, and the virtue of medicine, is not to be refused, but most lovingly to be embraced as a chief friend in the tyme of adversitie' (A7^{r-v}). The idiom continues into the main text through a conversation between a young man, John, and a physician, Humphrey. Before Humphrey can begin to impart his knowledge he must persuade John to engage in conversation and treat his knowledge as authoritative: that is, as counsel. Their opening exchange quickly establishes scene and character and directly addresses doubts readers might have about the authoritativeness of the medical information that follows. John tells Humphrey, 'I require not your counsel, I pray you be your own carver, and geve me leve to serve my fantasy. I will not charge you, you are very ancient and grave, and I am but yonge, we be no match' (C1^r). In response, Humphrey warns John that 'Good counsel is a treasure to wyse men, but a very trifle to a foole, if thou haddest sene those things [plagues] which I have seen, I know, thou wouldest not be such a man, nor thus spend thy time [in merrymaking].' John probes further the epistemological basis of physic, repeating 'a report that men of great estimacion say: what nedeth physicke, it is but an invention only for money' and asking 'why is phisicke of such great authority' (C3^v). Humphrey suggests that physicians are appointed by God to use nature for the benefit of man (physic is a 'calling' and 'gift'), and also alludes to the ancient learned traditions upon which physic is based. It is this last answer—the appeal to the ancients, and in particular the Greeks—that most impresses John, who assures Humphrey that 'If thou canst bringe in any reverent fathers that loved phisick: I will not despise, but greatly esteeme it, and desire counsell in demanding of a few questions.' Humphrey then regales John with the names of the ancients 'to prove phisicke to be of great authoritie among old fathers' (C3^r) and is quick to 'counsel thee John to love wel Hippocrates the prince of Phisicions, whiche began the best maner to geve rules to all the lovers of phisicke' (F7^v). John is now willing to participate in counsel with Humphrey. Indeed so successful is Humphrey in establishing his credentials that their conversation becomes straightforwardly didactic: when Humphrey says midway through the dialogue, 'Now marke well this lesson following, for thyne urine,' John replies, 'That shall I gladly, reade but softly and I wyll wryte thy words' (49^v).

Here Bullein deftly uses characterization and dialogue to insist that the physician's craft should be a consultative process encompassing an assimilation of principles and procedures learnt from classical knowledge and personal experience. The ancients communicate like the living: just as 'Hippocrates geveth counsaile that men should not mingle medicins with meat' so 'Galen geveth counsail in his regiment of helth, saying: a good aire which is pure and holsome is that, whiche is not troubled in standing waters, pooles' (31^r, 41^r). Knowledge is then implemented—as counsel—according to the skill, wisdom, sobriety, and discretion of the counsellor–physician. The skills and qualities required of counsellors are very similar to those prescribed by Smith: not only do Bullein and Smith invest in the same concept, but they also define it in similar ways. However, Bullein disseminates the concept far beyond the institutional boundaries of court and city (or indeed university and College): by joining 'the company of this my little book'—itself a sociable act—readers become equipped to judge physicians according to specific criteria and even act as physicians (or counsellors) in their own right (A7^r). Smith's humanism seeps into a whole new set of relationships and spaces. Of course, the counsel valorized by Bullein was not intended to consider issues of political economy or courtly politics. However, the deliberate use of the same concept to describe medical and political discourse encourages a degree of interplay between them. In particular it conflates the discursive processes through which ailments of both physiological and political bodies should be addressed; and it prescribes for both types of counsellor the same characteristics. In these ways Bullein can be seen as uniting two of Elyot's prevailing concerns: physic and politics (and the importance of counsel to the latter).

Counsel is replaced in 1562 with an altogether more violent and brooding idiom. As in *The Government of Health*, Bullein uses the paratext of *Bullein's Bulwark* to establish his prevailing metaphor. The frontispiece advertises what follows as a 'defence against all sicknesse, sores, and woundes, that doe daily assaulte mankind, which bulwarke is kept with Hillarius the Gardiner, Health the Physician, with their Chyrugion, to helpe the wounded souldiers'. The point is reiterated in the dedication to Henry Carey and his 'salutation' to the 'good reader'. The dialogue is no longer an act of counsel so much as a fortification; the ancients are not counsellors but 'captains' and 'soldiers'

The booke of the vse of sicke men, and medicens.

Surfeite, age, and sickenes, are enemies all to health,
Medicines to mende the bodie, excelleth worldly wealth:
Phisicke shall florishe, and in daunger will giue cure,
Till death vnknit the liuely knot, no longer we indure.

Fig. 27.1 Internal title page of William Bullein's *The Booke of the Use of Sicke Men, and Medicens*, in *Bulleins Bulwarke* (1562), 18ʳ.

(see also the defensive idiom of the verse on the internal title page to *The Book of the Use of Sick Men, and Medicines*, Figure 27.1). Moreover, from the initial justification for writing the book a concern for commonwealth is ever present:

And I being a childe of the commonwealthe, am bounde unto my mother, that is, the lande, in whom I am borne: to pleasure it, with any good gift, that it hath pleased God to bestowe upon me, not to this ende, to instructe the learned, but to helpe the ignoraunt, that thei may resort to this Little *Bulwarke*.   (C2ʳ⁻ᵛ)

The first part of the dialogue recycles material from 1559—it is the explicitly political additions, glosses, and digressions that are new. For example, when Hillarius (the equivalent to Humphrey in *The Government of Health*) revisits the subject of bees, the passage is extended to include their association with classical and biblical figures as well as their capacity for work, for society, and for their refusal to allow 'no filthiness to be amongst them, nor strangers to dwell within their citie or common wealth'. Talk of bees allows the political and discursive authority of the ancients to be implied—'about Athens is the best honey in the world'—and a subject's political duty highlighted: 'Yea rather would to God that idle people would take bees for an example to labour, and subjects to obey' (4^v).

A striking new stylistic feature is Bullein's embedding sociopolitical criticism in passages ostensibly outlining the medicinal value of plants. In this way elements of the natural world signify the social uses to which they are put. Hemp, also known as 'gallowgrasse' and 'Neckeweede', precipitates a warning against 'yonge wantons':

if there be any swashbuckler, common theefe, ruffen, or murtherer past grace the nexte remedie is this Lace or Corde. For them which never loved concorde, peace nor honestie, this will end all the mischief, this is a purger, not of Melancholy, but a finall banisher of al them that be not fit to live in a common wealth.   (28^v)

Malt signals a call 'to amend the market' that allows export of goods 'in the time of our extreme nede' (29^v). Milk allows a blistering attack on Bullein's nemesis, William Hilton, and mistletoe initiates a long lament for the decline of the 'ancient Parkes' and traditional values (neighbourliness, friendship, hospitality) of the Suffolk gentry (84^{r-v}, 53^v–54^v). Peas and beans link a series of vignettes that lurch from Anglo-Saxon elections to the names of Roman patrician families to modern popes to the social value of horses (29^v–30^v).

These examples indicate that Bullein's moral framework is removed from Smith's *honestas* (with its reciprocity of public and private interest): instead there are familiar complaints against covetousness, strangers, markets, and the corrosion of traditional bonds and values that is reminiscent of Protestant polemic from the early 1540s. Bullein's conservatism is interspersed with details from his difficult recent past. Indeed just as he notes in the dedication that he writes for the commonwealth, so he apologizes to readers in advance for what at times might appear 'a storie or Tradige [i.e. tragedy] [...] in the place of Phisicke' (C3^v). There seems little doubt that Bullein and Agnes genuinely suffered at Hilton's hands: certainly the move to London via debtors' prison was traumatic (C3^v), travails which were fully incorporated into the structure of the dialogue. Whereas Smith's voice is either consistently developed in one character (the Doctor in the *Discourse*) or clearly demarcated as the narrator (in the *Communication*), Bullein appears unexpectedly in his *Bulwark*, reinforcing both the sense of authorial possession indicated by the title as well as the deeply felt nature of the moralizing digressions. The sense of embattlement so engendered combines a sense of inner psychological disarray with the perceived malaise of the external world, of the commonwealth itself. This existential and social crisis—Bullein's subjective turmoil reflected in the degradation of commonwealth—makes it all the more essential that people with the appropriate skills and authority fulfil their social and intellectual responsibilities. As Bullein puts it, there are 'three kinds of callynges in this world' that enable men 'to walke truely, obediently and charitable in the sight of God and man': the Church, law, and medicine (61^v).

Dialogue Against the Fever Pestilence demonstrates, among other things, why medicine and law—or rather physicians and lawyers—are not up to the challenge outlined in the *Bulwark*. Written against the backdrop of plague, the dialogue promises 'consolation and comfort against death'. Such consolation is provided in two ways. First is the form of the dialogue itself. Bullein notes in his dedication that in a book about so 'mournful' a subject, 'the diversitee or varietee of pleasaunt colours, doe grace and beautifie the same, through the settyng foorthe of sondrie shapes: and as it were, to compel the comers in, to beholde the whole worke' (A2ᵛ). What follows is an accomplished bricolage of genres, voices, and images that describes how two London inhabitants—Civis, an English citizen, and Antonius, an Italian merchant—cope with the pestilence overtaking the metropolis. Transcending the question–answer format of his earlier dialogues, Bullein introduces a range of diverse and untrustworthy characters in dramatic situations. He also deploys a good deal of visual imagery— for example, characters describing paintings in ways that invoke reading practices associated with popular ballads (61ᵛ–71ʳ; see Watt 1993). Indeed, the medical advice on the plague is limited to a mere one-sixth of the text (23ᵛ–39ᵛ). That this is delivered by a corrupt and atheistic physician, Medicus, as he defrauds the dying Antonius, leaves the physician's words utterly discredited, despite the theoretical and empirical accuracy of his account. Instead of learning the practical physic available, readers instead follow a dazzling sequence of scenes that see the rich but godless Antonius put his faith in parasitic physicians and lawyers—opportunists who use their particular brands of knowledge to exploit the fearful and desperate. His fate is intertwined with that of Civis, an Everyman figure who experiences a number of confused and confusing conversations as he seeks counsel on the best way to escape the plague with his wife and servant. His journey culminates with his death and words that he (and readers) can finally trust. These are spoken by the Protestant cleric Theologus, whose concluding monologue can be understood as an answer to the questions raised in the previous dialogues and which represents the final 'comfort' in a dangerous and cacophonic world.

Two conversations nicely illustrate how Bullein undermines the ideal of counsel to which he contributed five years earlier. The first is the exchange between Medicus and Crispin—the physician's apothecary and accomplice-in-crime—following Medicus' exposition of the Aristotelian basis of physic for the dying Antonius. In return for the useless diagnosis Antonius gifts Medicus a new mule, gown, and golden cloth; Medicus then celebrates with Crispin, observing that during the plague 'I shall have more worke then I can put my hande unto. It is now a golden worlde with me, and with you also.' Crispin concurs: 'God continue the same: I would thousands were sicke, but I would have none dedde, but the beggars that doe trouble the world, and have no money to pai.' He then asks Medicus, 'what thinke you of Maister Antonious shall he escape it or no?' Medicus replies: 'I have his plentifull rewarde, and money for you also [...] But to bee plain with you, I thinke never to se hym again alive. He was paste cure of I came to hym [...]'. With delicious irony Bullein has Crispin note, 'I perceive your talke was unprofitable to him, yet I wrote it in a little page booke in my hande,' hinting that the pair might double their money by publishing Medicus' speech as an advice book (which is of course what Bullein, in printing the dialogue, has effectively done). Readers are left in no doubt that Medicus is no counsellor, his 'long talk' no counsel. As he concludes: 'He loved me as I loved him:

He me for healthe, and I hym for money' (39^{r-v}). Medicine has become a financial transaction.

The second conversation is a complicated exchange involving Civis, his wife, Uxor, his apprentice Roger, and a self-styled traveller called Mendax, who regales them with tales from beyond the seas. The discourse engages with issues of eloquence, truth, and honesty in a number of ways. The very content of Mendax's speech, which describes worlds that no one else has seen, demands either scepticism or credulity on his audience's part—responses which readers in turn evaluate in the wider context of the dialogue. Mendax asserts on a number of occasions the veracity of his words; and it transpires that the most gullible listener is Civis, the only remotely sympathetic character in the entire dialogue (and even he is later shown to be a covetous landlord) (80^r, 88^r). His initial response to Mendax is 'You speake like a wiseman, I perceive by your behaviour, you have been welle brougth up'; he parts by remarking, 'Gentleman fare you well, I doe give credit to your tale' (75^v, 88^v). It is left for Roger, already himself revealed as loquacious and opportunistic, to recognize a liar. When Mendax finally concludes 'And thus fare you well, for this is true or els I do lye,' the apprentice responds: 'I will sweare upon a Booke thy last words are true, and all the rest are lies' (87^r). This scepticism is reinforced by Bullein's marginalia, which maintains a sardonic commentary throughout. 'No lye, no lye' accompanies one anecdote (that clearly is a lie) and 'Mendax wyl sonner saye the truth' another (76^v, 87^v).

In these respects this 'grave company' continue the predominant theme of the dialogue: that just as people (physicians included) are self-interested manipulators, inventing or obscuring the truth for their own ends, so eloquence is their primary weapon. However, this particular scene takes the point further by some astute inter-textual allusions. While the descriptions of 'Terra Florida' and beyond invoke the fantastical conceits of cosmographical writing, they conclude with a longer description of a distant commonwealth—featuring 'the best reformed Citie of this worlde'—that has a different textual referent in mind (79^r, 82^v, 83^v). This is, of course, *Utopia*, the foundation text of English humanism—and Tudor dialogue—as well as the most insightful sixteenth-century exposition of counsel. Mendax describes his version of Utopia ('Taerg Natrib') as a commonwealth of astonishing godliness in which the Sabbath is enforced, ministers are 'wise, sober, honeste and learned', and 'the idle are sette to worke, or sore punished for slothe' (83^r, 84^v, 85^v). It is also a land that inverts the moral basis of More's fiction in important respects. Most obviously Mendax—meaning 'Liar'—is a degraded Hythloday ('peddler of nonsense'): a charlatan who lacks any of Hythloday's classical learning or integrity and who speaks to impress rather than inform.[4] The same is true for Nodnol, capital of Taerg Natrib, which bears no resemblance to the cities of the 'Barbarous Grekes': the place Mendax outlines is not simply without classical associations—Utopia's prevailing feature—but is anti-classical in nature (83^r–84^v). It transpires that its remarkable godliness is enforced through external compulsion: drunkards are starved in prison; adulterers, felons,

---

[4] I am here indebted to Cathy Shrank's forthcoming work on English dialogue; cf. her entry on Bullein's *Dialogue*, <http://www.hrionline.ac.uk/origins/frame.html>.

murderers, and disobedient youths are executed; 'jugglers' (tricksters) lose their eyes, 'common swearers their tongues' (85^r). This is in sharp contrast to Utopia, where the populace behave well and for the common good because of a natural inclination that is inculcated and improved through their upbringing and learning (More 1998: 65–6). It is on the basis of these personal qualities that Utopians are able to govern themselves through a system of household democracy and counsel devolved throughout society. As Hythloday recalls: 'all matters which are considered important are first laid before the assembly of syphogrants. They talk the matter over with the households they represent, debate it with one another, then report their recommendation to the senate' (48). Mendax describes, in contrast, a system of docile subjects policed by 'judges and worthie lawyers [...] whiche hath great stipends of the prince and take no fees of the people' (1564: 87^v). This state-salaried judiciary holds monopoly of the discursive and rational abilities idealized by More and Smith. It is only by centralizing counsel and its requisite virtues that the conflict and self-interest inherent to any commonwealth can be transcended. Mendax portrays, in effect, a populace who cannot be trusted to talk.

The bleak playfulness with which Bullein subverts More's text is indicative of both his aptitude as a writer and his disillusionment with the investment that humanism placed in the civilizing power of classically informed discourse. A Dialogue Against the Fever Pestilence demonstrates that eloquence is much more diverse, heterogeneous, and dangerous than writers like Smith and perhaps Bullein himself would like to think. In this sense he endorses the dystopianism found in Thomas Wilson's 1572 Discourse upon Usury (see Shrank 2004b: 205–19). Certainly Roger's attempt to undermine Uxor's counsel to Civis nicely demonstrates not only his own discursive skill but also the range of unauthorized places that people could learn the persuasive arts: 'I thinke you learned your Rhetorike in the universitie of Bridewell: you were never well wormed, when you were young' (46^v). As they dramatize the multiplicity of rhetorical practice, Bullein's dialogues display an interesting tension. The more stylistically complex—and so literary—the work, the more traditional and straightforward the cumulative moral message becomes: indeed the polemical power of Bullein's climactic work rests on the artful juxtaposition of form and content. His masterpiece demonstrates that it is precisely because language and its uses are so bewildering— and the establishment of truth through counsel so unlikely—that the recovery of the moral certainties expounded by commonwealth writers of the 1540s is required. This is, of course, the opposite conclusion to Smith, who retains faith in people's ability to speak for the common good in a rational and self-profitable fashion: to communicate in ways which transcend rather than consolidate particular interests. Looking forward, these contrasting perspectives on discourse had a significant legacy. They were inherited and developed by the next generation of writers—most obviously Smith's protégé Gabriel Harvey and Bullein's admirer Nashe (see Richards 2003: 114–22; Scott-Warren 2005: 93). They fed into the subsequent tension between 'old' and 'new' humanism (see Tuck 1993, ch. 2). And it could well be argued that they have continued—albeit in new forms and guises—to the present day (see Ashenden and Owen 1999).

Primary Works

BOORDE, ANDREW (1542), *A Compendyous Regyment; or, A Dyetary of Helth.*

BULLEIN, WILLIAM (1559), *The Governement of Healthe.*

—— (1562), *Bullein's Bulwarke of Defence.*

—— (1564), *A Dialogue Against the Fever Pestilence.*

DROUET, PIERRE (1578), *A New Counsell Against the Pestilence.*

ELYOT, THOMAS (1541), *The Castel of Helth.*

MORE, THOMAS (1998), *Utopia*, ed. G. M. Logan and R. M. Adams (Cambridge: Cambridge University Press).

NASHE, THOMAS (1596), *Have With You to Saffron-Walden.*

SMITH, THOMAS (1561), *A Communication or Discourse of the Queen's Highness's Marriage*, BL, Add. MS 48047.

—— (1583), *De republica Anglorum.*

—— (1969), *A Discourse of the Commonweal of this Realm of England*, ed. Mary Dewar (Charlottesville: University Press of Virginia).

Smith Family Papers, Essex Record Office, D/DSh/01/7.

CHAPTER 28

ENGLISH SENECA

HEYWOOD TO *HAMLET*

JESSICA WINSTON

In the Preface to his translation of Seneca's *Thyestes* (1560), Jasper Heywood presents a dream in which the ancient Roman tragedian asks him to translate the play. The Preface works to authorize the translator: Seneca confirms Heywood's pre-eminent linguistic and literary talents when he handpicks him to 'revive' the tragedies, making them accessible for a new country and age (Heywood 1982: 40). Reading through the bobbing fourteeners of the Preface and the translation itself, a modern reader might be tempted to conclude that Heywood was an ambitious writer who was overly confident in his abilities. Yet the early reception of *Thyestes*, as well as Heywood's translations of other tragedies by Seneca—*Troas* (1559) and *Hercules furens* (1561)—suggests that he had good reason to be hopeful about the impact of his work. His edition of *Troas* was printed four times between 1559 and 1581, and *Thyestes* and *Hercules furens* twice each in the same period.[1] Contemporaries praised Heywood for his 'learned and painefull translation' (Hall 1581: A2ᵛ) as well as his 'perfect verse', 'smouth and fyled style', and ability to make 'even Seneca hym selfe to speke in englysh' (Studley 1566a: ¶8ᵛ, A3ᵛ–A4ʳ). Indeed, his translations helped to renew interest in Seneca, so much so that the Roman tragedies became one of the most important influences on the drama of late sixteenth- and early seventeenth-century England.

Prior to 1560, only a few of Seneca's works appeared in manuscript and print. But beginning with Heywood, considerable interest developed in the tragedies, mainly

---

[1] *Troas* appeared twice in 1559, once in 1562, and again, along with reprints of *Thyestes* and *Hercules furens* in Newton's collection of *Senecas His Ten Tragedies* in 1581.

among students at the universities and early English law schools, the Inns of Court, where in just a few years nearly all of Seneca's tragedies were translated into English.[2] Students also put on performances of Seneca and wrote plays, such as *Gorboduc* (1562) and *Gismond of Salerne* (1568), which adapted some characteristic features of Senecan tragedy (the five-act structure, revenge-driven plots, lengthy deliberative speeches, quick verbal exchanges, and common characters, such as a chorus, messengers, nurses, and ghosts).[3] Moreover, Seneca's tragedies remained popular later in the century. In 1581 Thomas Newton compiled the *Tenne Tragedies*, the first complete edition of Seneca's plays in England. In 1601 Sir William Cornwallis published *Discourses upon Seneca the Tragedian*, a commentary on political advice inherent in the tragedies. And throughout the 1580s and 1590s playwrights such as Thomas Kyd, Christopher Marlowe, John Marston, and Shakespeare adapted elements of Seneca's drama in their works.

A considerable number of studies have illustrated the importance of Seneca for Renaissance drama (H. Charlton 1946; Braden 1985; Miola 1992), so the fact of such influence need not be documented here.[4] Suffice it to say that dramatists in the period imitated and alluded to the plots, characters, rhetorical devices, and lines from Seneca so frequently that one Elizabethan author complained that English playwrights were actually killing Seneca. Contemporary dramatists 'let blood' from the classical author, copying his words 'line by line and page by page', until he 'at length' came to 'die to our stage' (Nashe 1966: 316).

To be sure, Heywood started something important, helping to develop interest in Seneca's works by making them accessible for a new generation of readers and writers; however, he was not wholly responsible for the ancient tragedian's growing popularity. How, then, can we explain the increasing interest in and importance of Senecan drama in the latter half of the sixteenth-century? This chapter addresses this question, making special reference to *Thyestes*, 'the most influential of all the tragedies on Elizabethan theatre' (Fantham 1986: 436). As we shall see, Seneca's plays were especially popular in the 1560s and the 1580s and 1590s, that is, at the start and end of Elizabeth's reign (1558–1603). At these times, two related issues, the succession and the potential for monarchic tyranny, were topics of widespread concern. Seneca's plays develop portraits of kings and nobles as they become tyrants and despots. Such works provided a genre and source that Elizabethan authors could allude to and imitate in order to register their and their audiences' apprehension about the autarchic potential of the monarch at a time of political uncertainty.

---

[2] In addition to Heywood's translations, Alexander Neville translated *Oedipus* (1563). John Studley translated *Agamemnon* (1566), *Medea* (1566), *Hercules on Oeta* (1566), and *Hippolytus*, also known as *Phaedra* (1567). Thomas Nuce translated *Octavia* (1566). The final tragedy attributed to Seneca in the period, *Thebais* (now more commonly known by the title *The Phoenician Women*), was translated and published in 1581 by Thomas Newton in the *Ten Tragedies*.

[3] For more details on Seneca in print and performance from 1500 to 1570, see Winston (2006b: 30–1).

[4] H. Baker and Howard (1939) and Hunter (1967, 1974) caution us not to overly emphasize Seneca's influence on Renaissance dramatists, but the fact that his works inspired many of the plots, techniques, lines, and characters in a huge number of Renaissance plays is not in dispute.

Several critics have noticed the political relevance of Seneca's works in Renaissance England, and this chapter is especially influenced by Gordon Braden's *Renaissance Tragedy and the Senecan Tradition* (1985), which explores the significance of Seneca's views on tyranny for Renaissance authors. Still, most studies, including Braden's, focus only on the later Elizabethan reception of the tragedies, and this chapter contributes to this topic by distinguishing between the early and later phases (the 1560s and the 1580s–1590s). Doing so allows us to address some of the similarities and differences in the character and political orientation of the translations and adaptations of Seneca in each one. As we shall see, the political interests of earlier and later translators and adapters of Seneca differed, depending on their backgrounds and intended audiences. In the most general terms, while authors in the earlier phase were drawn to Seneca's representation of tyrants, later ones were interested in his depictions of the way such rulers affect their subjects. Still, in order to appreciate such differences, we must first look into two topics, Seneca's tragedies in their own time and views of Seneca in the Elizabethan period, subjects that will provide the background we need to appreciate the politics of Seneca in early and later Elizabethan England.

28.1 Seneca's Tragedies in Nero's Rome

For many Elizabethan translators and dramatists, the attraction of Seneca's plays grew out of their understanding of the role such works played in Seneca's life and political career. It will be helpful first, then, to review some important aspects of Seneca's biography and its relation to the tragedies.

Seneca was a philosopher, tragedian, and political adviser in first-century Rome. He was born sometime around or before 1 BCE in the Roman colony of Corduba in Spain (modern Córdoba). When he was very young, he was brought to Rome, where he was educated to be an orator, philosopher, and lawyer. He was successful in these fields and became a politician, holding a magistracy about CE 33 and eventually entering the senate. Despite such accomplishments, Seneca suffered several reversals of fortune. In the reign of Claudius (41–54), he was accused of having an affair with a member of the royal family and was exiled to the island of Corsica for eight years (41–9). When he was recalled, he became a tutor to the future emperor Nero, who came to power in 54. Seneca became his close political adviser. Nero was an erratic ruler, but during the early years of his reign, the empire was governed relatively well, largely through the influence of Seneca and another adviser, Burrus (Fitch 2002–4: 11). In 62, when Burrus died, Seneca's influence waned and Nero became an increasingly unpredictable ruler. For example, in the year Burrus died, against the objections of Seneca and other advisers, he divorced his wife, Octavia, and married Poppea, prompting a popular revolt. In addition, after the great fire of Rome in 64, he squandered public funds building a vast new imperial palace, the Domus Aurea (Golden House). Faced with these changes, Seneca withdrew from public life. In 65, when he was implicated in a conspiracy to assassinate Nero, he committed suicide. (Whether he took part in the plot is unclear.)

Sometime during this career, Seneca wrote the plays, although their total number and dating are matters of debate. Critics generally agree that he wrote eight tragedies, the earliest of which are *Agamemnon*, *Phaedra* (also titled *Hippolytus*), and *Oedipus*. These are followed by a middle group, consisting of *Medea*, *The Trojan Women* (also titled *Troades* and *Troas*), and *Hercules* (also called *Hercules furens*), and a last group, dating from after 62 CE, comprising *Phoenician Women* (also titled *Thebaid* and *Thebais*) and *Thyestes* (Fitch 2002–4: 12; P. Davis 2003: 15). Two other plays attributed to Seneca in the sixteenth century, *Hercules on Oeta* and *Octavia*, most likely were written by later Roman imitators of his work.

One of the most vexing critical questions about the tragedies concerns their relationship to other aspects of Seneca's life. Seneca's Stoic philosophy encourages indifference to things 'external to the self—wealth, position, friendship, even health' and supreme control of the emotions (Fitch 2002–4: 24). Yet he was very much a man of the world, one of the richest and most powerful men in Rome. His plays, moreover, present characters who are wholly overcome by emotion: Phaedra, who attempts to seduce her son-in-law Hippolytus; Medea, who kills her children in a jealous rage; Hercules, who slaughters his family in a fury; and Atreus, who murders his nephews, bakes them in a pie, and serves them to his brother at a banquet. Emily Wilson summarizes attempts to make sense of these apparent incongruities: in one view, the violent, angry, passionate characters of the plays are 'moral lessons, examples of all the nasty things which happen to you if you let your passions get out of control'. In another, the tragedies allow Seneca to express 'the dark fears and possibilities which are repressed in his prose writings' (2004: 4–5). Whichever (or whatever else) may be the case, it seems clear that the plays reflect Seneca's life in the imperial court, dealing as they do with acts he experienced or witnessed over his career: despotism, revenge, assassination, murder, incest, adultery, and sudden reversals of fortune (Herington 1966: 430; Sullivan 1985: 157). Yet, as Fitch observes, 'we should [not] expect a one-to-one correspondence between the events of the dramas and the events of the court' (2002–4: 13). For the mythological subject matter 'provided an opportunity for [...] distancing the ideas from actual circumstances and personal elements' (Henry and Walker 1963: 10).

With this background, we can look at *Thyestes* for an example of how Seneca's experiences influenced his drama. While the play does not comment on a specific event, it seems to address Nero's despotism in a general way, illustrating the psychology of a tyrant and the difficulty of recognizing and limiting the power of an increasingly tyrannical ruler.

Knowing the mythological background for the play is crucial. The two main characters, Thyestes and his brother Atreus, are descendants of a royal family doomed to repeat the crimes of murder, cannibalism, and adultery. This fate originates with their grandfather Tantalus, who sought to trick the gods by killing his son Pelops and serving him to them at a banquet. Discovering the deception, the gods restored Pelops to life and severely punished Tantalus, placing him in Hades to be tormented by perpetual hunger and thirst. When Pelops died, his sons Atreus and Thyestes battled over the kingdom. Atreus gained the crown, but Thyestes seduced Atreus' wife and stole a golden fleece, which would secure the throne for him.

Seneca's *Thyestes* begins at this point. Recalling this back story, Act 1 presents the ghost of Tantalus, who is forced by a Fury to curse Atreus and Thyestes to repeat his crimes. The next acts illustrate the effects of this curse. Atreus vows revenge, deciding that he will lure Thyestes and his children to the palace by pretending to want peace. Following in his grandfather's footsteps, he tricks Thyestes, luring the children to a dungeon, where he kills and bakes them. He then feeds them to Thyestes at the feast. Atreus achieves what he set out to do, which is to dominate Thyestes completely. Unlike the gods with Tantalus and Pelops, Thyestes recognizes too late what Atreus has done and, demonstrating his powerlessness, begs the gods to punish his brother, who gloats in triumph.

The Tantalus family myth was one of the most popular sources for ancient drama, having been told in at least fifteen Greek and Roman plays before Seneca (Tarrant 1985: 40–3). Seneca's version emphasizes a central theme, the legacy of crime in the house of Tantalus. Even so, he shapes the story to reflect his personal experiences, his attempts to understand and work with Nero, tailoring the plot to bring out a double perspective on tyranny. On the one hand, in Atreus the drama lays bare the psychology of the tyrant; on the other, in the Chorus it displays the difficulty of making sense of, and therefore reacting to, the increasingly bizarre actions of such a ruler. These two perspectives need to be understood, since (as we shall see) they subtly inform the political orientation of early and later Elizabethan adaptations of the plays.

When compared with their Greek precursors, Seneca's tragedies, according to John Fitch, 'have a greater inwardness, a greater focus on the individual and the psychology of the self' (2002–4: 5). *Thyestes*, in particular, explores the psychology of the tyrant, showing his need and 'capacity to enforce his will upon his victims' (Mader 1988: 37). Such psychology, as Gottfried Mader shows, is especially evident in a famous scene in Act 2 in which Atreus discusses his plans for revenge with an Assistant, who in turn urges the king to reconsider. In the end, Atreus prevails (there is never any sense that he will not), and the Assistant vows to remain silent. Under threat from Atreus, he promises to keep the plans secret:

Haud sum monendus: ista nostro in pectore
fides timorque, sed magis claudet fides.

(I need no warning. Loyalty and fear will hide it in my heart—but chiefly loyalty.)
(Seneca ii. 258–9)[5]

---

[5] References to tragedies by Seneca (as opposed to the early Elizabethan translations of them) will be to volume and page numbers in John G. Fitch's edition, *Seneca's Tragedies* (2002–4), referred to throughout as Seneca.

The Assistant's assertion, Mader writes, 'is just a shade too vocal to be taken at face value, and the perceptible accent on *fides* [loyalty] perforce redirects the reader/auditor to the *timor* [fear] which it ostensibly disclaims' (1988: 33). Such redirection underscores the import of the line, which is that the Assistant submits against his will. The line reveals the psychology of a tyrant, like Atreus, for whom 'obedience is not enough' (38). He needs to see the servant submit against his own good judgement. As Atreus says earlier in the scene: The 'greatest value of kingship: that the people are compelled to praise as well as endure their master's actions' (ii. 247). He must see the moment when his subjects are compelled to endure and even support him, confirming that he has 'destroy[ed] their psychological autonomy and integrity' (Mader 1988: 37). The rest of the play develops this idea, repeating moments of tyrannical domination, beginning with the submission of Tantalus to the petty tyrant the Fury, and closing with the submission of Thyestes.

Seneca displays a deep concern about the psychology of the tyrant, but shows as well the difficulties of those around the tyrant, who must make sense of his motives and actions, a theme that Seneca develops in the Chorus. As in most classical tragedies, Seneca divides the acts of *Thyestes* with a chorus, speeches by a group of citizens who are anxious about the welfare of their country. As P. J. Davis (1989, 2003: 61–9) argues, throughout the play this group has difficulty understanding and responding to events. For instance, in Act 1 Tantalus curses his heirs, and the audience knows that, based on the mythology, his crimes will infect later generations. Yet, at the end of the act, the Chorus prays that the family strife will cease. The Chorus is obviously ignorant of the myth. In later acts such ignorance turns into misunderstanding. Davis observes that, at the end of Act 2, the Chorus describes the ideal king, noting especially that the ideal is 'rid of fear' and not influenced by the 'shifting favour of the hasty mob' (Seneca ii. 261; P. Davis 2003: 66). In doing so, they unwittingly describe Atreus, who is likewise not influenced by the favour of the people. As he says earlier in the play, 'Righteousness, goodness, and loyalty are private values: kings should go where they please' (ii. 247). Kings are not bound by conventions (as private citizens are) and can do what they want. As Davis comments (2003: 66), the Chorus's discussion of the nature of kingship is unwittingly inaccurate, making it possible for Atreus to meet their criteria. To be sure, through the play, the Chorus routinely displays its ignorance, creating instances of dramatic irony in which we know something that the citizens do not. Even so, such moments point to a larger issue, which is that their ignorance 'is not limited to mere unawareness of facts but [...] extends to a more general and profound lack of understanding of the way in which the world they inhabit works' (P. Davis 1989: 434).

Ultimately, *Thyestes* illustrates the situation faced by those subject to tyranny: the tyrant ignores conventional ideas ('righteousness, goodness, loyalty'), seeking instead to impose his will on the people, who themselves ineffectually appeal to traditional values in order to make sense of events. In this way, *Thyestes* is typical of Seneca's tragedies, which show (to varying degrees) the psychology of rulers (mainly kings, but also queens) who desire to dominate others completely, and the misunderstanding of those who are forced to submit to such domination. In *Thyestes*, Atreus is consumed by anger; in *Hercules furens*, the tyrant Lycus is merciless, and in *Thebais*, Eteocles, one of the feuding sons of King Oedipus, his 'lust for rule', is 'willing to sacrifice his native land, his household gods, even his wife' (Armstrong 1948: 20). At the same time, we see each king's subjects' corresponding inability to deal with such situations: the Chorus misunderstands Atreus' motives; Hercules, mistakenly and against the petitions of his father, kills his own family, thinking them the family of Lycus; Jocasta in vain urges her warring sons Eteocles and Polynices to see reason.

Thus, overall, in his tragedies, Seneca analyses the psychology of tyrants and their subjects. One can see that anyone living under or concerned about a corrupt or even autarchic government might find his works especially relevant and intriguing. Renaissance authors were concerned about such issues, but did Seneca matter to them because of his analysis of tyranny?

28.2 SENECA IN ELIZABETHAN ENGLAND

The answer is yes, and two kinds of evidence from the period allow us to arrive at this conclusion. The first is direct, consisting of comments explicitly about Seneca and the import of his works. The second is circumstantial, that is, evidence that indirectly suggests knowledge of and attitudes about the ancient writer. Both sorts show that Seneca's plays were important for a number of reasons. Elizabethan translators and dramatists were drawn to Seneca's style and the morally improving nature of the tragedies, but they also found the political situations in the tragedies compelling.

Contemporary comments on Seneca's works tend to focus on two main qualities: his writing style and the morally improving character of his treatises and plays. To be sure, in 1565 Thomas Cooper lumped Seneca together with his father, describing them both only vaguely as 'two great learned men' (P6^r). Yet most comments are far more specific, praising Seneca especially for his style and morality. In his translation of *Troas*, Heywood describes Seneca as 'the flowre of all writers' and 'so excellent a writer' (1559: A3^v–A4^r), and in the Preface to *Thyestes*, he notes that Seneca has a 'woondrous wit and regall stile' (1560: *5^v). John Studley, in his translation of *Medea*, describes Seneca as 'pearlesse Poet' (1566*b*: A1^v), and Thomas Newton refers to Seneca's 'peerelesse sublimity and loftinesse of style' (A3^v).

According to contemporary writers, Seneca's style facilitates his ultimate goal, which is to inculcate virtue. Thus, Arthur Golding observes of Seneca's *De beneficiis* (1578): 'His sentences are short, quick, and full of matter; his wordes sharpe, pithie, and unaffected; his whole order of writyng grave, deepe, and severe; fitted altogether to the reforming of mennes myndes, and not too the delyghting of their eares' (*2^v). The tragedies, in particular, teach virtue. Alexander Neville tells readers to observe 'what is ment by the whole course of the Historie [i.e. the tragedy]: and frame thy lyfe free from suche mischiefs, wherwith the worlde at this present is universally overwhelmed'. He continues: 'Onely wysh I all men by this Tragicall Historie (for to that entent was it written) to beware of Synne: the ende wherof is shamefull and myserable' (A5ʳ–6ʳ). Likewise, W. Parker writes of *Agamemnon*:

> This tragedy of worthy Seneca,
> Whose sawes profound (who so theron do loke)
> To vertues race do shew a ready way.
>
> (Studley 1566a: ¶8ʳ)

Some readers must have thought that Seneca's subjects (incest, murder, cannibalism) did not inculcate virtue, but Thomas Newton argues that the tragedies must be read correctly:

I doubt whether there bee any amonge all the Catalogue of Heathen wryters, that with more gravity of Philosophicall sentences, more waightynes of sappy words, or greater authority of sound matter beateth down sinne, loose lyfe, dissolute dealinge, and unbrydled sensuality: or that more sensibly, pithily, and bytingly layeth downe the guerdon of filthy lust, cloaked dissimulation and odious treachery; which is the dryft, wherunto he leveeth the whole yssue of ech one of his Tragedies. (A3ᵛ–A4ʳ)

Seneca's tragedies inculcate virtue in those who read them, encouraging them, in Newton's words, to 'beat down sin, loose life, and dissolute dealing'. Yet Renaissance authors were well aware of the political aspects of Seneca's career as well as his works. Later writers likely knew his biography from the Tacitus' *Annals*, a history of the reigns of the emperors Tiberius, Caligula, Claudius, and Nero, written *c*.116 and first published in England in 1598. Thus, in his *Advancement of Learning* (1605), Francis Bacon refers to his biography, describing the counsellor who 'after he had consecrated that *Quinquennium Neronis* [the five years of Nero's minority] to the eternall glorie of learned Governors, held on his honest and loyall course of good and free Counsell, after his Maister grew extreamely corrupt in his government' (2000: 18). Earlier authors may have known Tacitus from manuscript sources or by reputation, but even if they did not, they were aware of Seneca's career. Arthur Golding describes him as a 'somtyme Courtyer, and also a Counseller of the greatest state in the worlde' (1578: *2ʳ). Such awareness came from works like *Octavia*, a play by a later Roman imitator of the tragedies, which was published in a translation by Thomas Nuce in 1566. The plot concerns Nero's divorce from Octavia and stars Seneca himself as an oppositional counsellor to the emperor. Critical of Nero, the play clearly associates Seneca's career with his drama. For this reason, Elizabethan authors—who thought *Octavia* was by Seneca—may well have taken the play as a signal that this and the other tragedies should be read as forms of political observation and admonition.

At least one author explicitly read Seneca's tragedies in just this way. In 1601 Sir William Cornwallis published *Discourses upon Seneca the Tragedian*, a commentary on the political guidance implicit in lines from the plays. To give just one example, the first quotation in *Discourses* comes from Act 3 of *Oedipus*. Echoing the sentiment of Atreus in *Thyestes*, Oedipus says to Creon:

Odia qui nimium timet regnare nescit: regna custodit metus. (A1^r)

(One unduly afraid of being hated is incapable of ruling; a throne is safeguarded by fear.)

(Seneca ii. 78–9)

Commenting on this line, Cornwallis argues that rulers of necessity inculcate fear in their subjects, since 'out of subjects feare groweth Princes saftie' (A1^r). Even so, how the prince creates fear leads either to tyranny or to good government (A1^v–A2^r).

For Cornwallis, Seneca's plays offer advice to princes and magistrates. It is likely that early translators and dramatists read the tragedies in a similar way. For instance, early Elizabethan translators dedicated their plays to Elizabeth or members of her Privy Council.[6] To be sure, authors frequently dedicated their works to members of the nobility. That said, that the tragedies were dedicated exclusively to the most powerful people in England suggests that the translators viewed the plays as relevant in some way to the political situations encountered by such figures. The first Senecan-style drama in English, Thomas Sackville and Thomas Norton's *Gorboduc*, reinforces this view. *Gorboduc* tells a story from ancient British history in order to urge Elizabeth and Parliament to resolve the succession question, the debate over who should next inherit the throne.[7] That Sackville and Norton would have used both ancient history and Senecan forms for this purpose suggests that they were copying a link they associated with the Seneca's tragedies, the use of stories from the distant or mythological past to address contemporary political issues.

All told, Elizabethan translators and dramatists appreciated Seneca's style and moral sensibilities, but they knew the political nature of Seneca's plays and, as we shall see in more detail below, used him as a model to write their own works that, like Seneca's, could address contemporary political concerns. It is worth asking why writers were so explicit about their appreciation of Seneca's style and morality but said so little about his politics. It is possible that Seneca's plots and themes were so obvious or so provocative that authors were deliberately circumspect about this aspect of his works. Whatever the reason for such silence, Elizabethans found the political situations depicted in the tragedies relevant to their own day.

Yet beyond such general claims about the writers' interest in Seneca's style, morality, and politics, it is difficult to be more specific about Elizabethan attitudes, since the extent and character of the engagement with the drama altered over time. As we have seen, there was considerable interest in his tragedies in the 1560s and the

---

[6] C. H. Conley (1927: 18–33, 129–54) discusses the literary community at the Inns of Court in the 1560s and illustrates the tendency of writers, and specifically translators, to dedicate their works to the nation's leaders, especially members of the Privy Council.

[7] For a list of some main articles that make this point, see Winston (2005: 28).

1580s and 1590s, while in the 1570s little attention was paid to his work.[8] In addition, the two phases of active interest in Seneca were different in a number of ways. In the 1560s the translation and adaptation of Seneca was confined to a relatively elite group, students at the universities and Inns of Court. Moreover, these men tended to rework Seneca in an extensive way, producing complete translations or extended imitations of his works. In the 1580s and 1590s, on the other hand, the interest in Seneca was more popular, developing among the dramatists for the private and public stage. Yet such dramatists engaged with the tragedian's work in a less comprehensive way, tending as they did to imitate or adapt only specific lines, scenes, or characters in their plays.

In a way, the waxing and waning of interest in Seneca is readily explained. As Gordon Braden has argued, his plays represent a certain autarchic style of selfhood (characterized by its will, self-sufficiency, and ambition), and it was this style of selfhood that Renaissance authors found compelling, since they too faced the possibility of absolute rule. Under Elizabeth, such fears were most intense in the early and later years of her reign, when earlier her marriage policy and later her old age heightened concerns about the succession. At these times, the Queen's refusal to settle the issue, despite the urgings of her counsellors and subjects, raised the spectre of autocracy, of a ruler who, like Atreus or Nero, refuses to take counsel. In such periods, the issues in the tragedies and in Seneca's life were relevant indeed.

Nevertheless, in order to understand other changes in the reception of Seneca, we must look at each phase on its own. The authors and dramatists in each phase had different aims and, in general, wrote for different sorts of audience; the way such writers engaged with Seneca's works changed accordingly. As we shall see, one of the most significant differences concerns the aspect of Seneca that writers found most intriguing, those parts that focused on the rulers or those that focused on the ruled. As we saw earlier, *Thyestes* is indicative of Seneca's tragedies in the way that it develops two perspectives on kingship. The early and later Elizabethans each developed one of these perspectives. While there are exceptions, early Elizabethans tended to address the psychology of rulers, and the later Elizabethan dramatists tended to deal with the dilemmas of those around a king cum tyrant, people who must try to understand and respond to a corrupt leader.

28.3 THE 1560s

In the 1560s Seneca's plays were popular among a circle of poets, translators, and playwrights associated with the Inns of Court and universities. That Seneca was

[8] In this decade, Seneca's tragedies were not translated, published, or performed. Excerpts from some of his letters appeared in a translation of Philip de Mornay, *The Defence of Death* (1576).

popular among such writers makes sense. As H. B. Charlton observes, it was the 'natural bias of law students looking to state services for their future' (1946: 163). For this circle consisted of ambitious young men who wanted to obtain positions in the government as secretaries, ambassadors, and Members of Parliament. Such men shared their writing with each other and with national leaders in order to form social and professional connections with one another and potential patrons. Their work with Seneca illustrates the social function of their creative activities. Such translations and adaptations helped authors to connect with other participants in this literary and social community, and to address issues that were important to them in contemporary political affairs.

Prefaces to two of the translations indicate how such works helped such authors to form literary and social connections. The clearest instance is the Preface to *Thyestes*, in the dream vision in which Seneca visits Heywood to ask him to translate the play. Initially, in response to this request, Heywood refuses, telling the tragedian to look for a translator among the writers at the Inns of Court, where he says, 'Minerva's men and finest wits do swarm'. He then praises numerous authors, who are associated with the Inns: Thomas North, Thomas Sackville, Thomas Norton, Christopher Yelverton, William Baldwin, Thomas Bludeville, William Bavand, Barnabe Googe, and a 'great number more' whom he does not have space to name (1982: 81–104). As we saw above, the Preface authorizes Heywood, and this passage does so especially. Later in the Preface, at the insistence of Seneca, Heywood agrees to translate the play. This passage helps to validate that decision, suggesting that Heywood is a better translator than even those authors whom he praises here. At the same time, the passage facilitates social networking. When he translated *Thyestes*, Heywood was a fellow at All Souls College, Oxford, but he was about to become a member of Gray's Inn, one of the Inns of Court. The Preface uses flattery to develop links with the social group that he was about to join.[9]

Although not written by him, the prefatory matter in John Studley's *Agamemnon* functions in a similar way. The translation begins with poems by fellow Senecan translators Thomas Newton and Thomas Nuce, as well as other writers, who praise Studley and compare his translation with the work of contemporary authors, including Heywood, Thomas Phaer, Barnabe Googe, Arthur Golding, and Richard Edwards (1566a: ¶8ᵛ–A1ʳ). Like Heywood's Preface, the poems link Studley to the current literary scene at the schools, which included Studley's friends, who commend him in their verses, as well as those other contemporary translators, poets, and dramatists to whom he is compared in the poems themselves.

Even as such works established literary and social connections, they also gave authors an opportunity to develop their interests in contemporary political affairs,

---

[9] Heywood joined Gray's Inn in 1561, although he stayed only briefly before leaving to become a Jesuit priest in Rome. Still, Heywood probably had ties to the Inns before he joined. At least one of the works mentioned in the Preface, Plutarch's 'Fruit of Foes', was published after *Thyestes*, while others were published in the same year. Heywood likely received at least one work, and probably the others as well, in manuscript, which would suggest that he was already part of the relatively tightly knit social circle of manuscript production and circulation at the Inns of Court.

providing stories which allowed them to consider and comment on those general political questions raised by Seneca concerning tyranny and kingship. Thus, for example, Heywood uses *Troas* as a form of ambiguous political commentary. The play details the fates of Hecuba and other women of Troy in the aftermath of the Trojan war. Heywood made several changes to the play in order to enhance the presentation of the Trojan queen as a victim of fortune, for instance by adding a chorus at the end of Act 1 on the ephemeral nature of power (B2ᵛ–B3ᵛ). Such changes enhance the theme of the transience of political authority in the play. Yet he then dedicated the play to Elizabeth, who had just come to the throne, possibly in order to urge the new queen to be merciful and just by reminding her of her own susceptibility to reversals of fortune (Winston 2006b: 46).

In addition to translating Seneca, contemporary authors also produced original plays which incorporated Senecan elements. These include Sackville and Norton's *Gorboduc* (1562), Richard Edwards's *Damon and Pithias* (c.1565), and the multi-authored *Gismund of Salerne* (1568). Such plays also facilitated the political thinking and involvement of those who wrote and watched them. *Gorboduc* provides an especially striking example of this pattern, since it raises general questions about governance (specifically about tyranny and the role of counsel) and, unusually for the drama of the period, also comments explicitly on the specific issue of the succession.

Performed at the Inner Temple, one of the Inns of Court, and later for the Queen at court, *Gorboduc* is the story of an ancient British king who divides his realm between his two sons, Ferrex and Porrex. The decision ignites a disastrous civil war, which ends with the deaths of Gorboduc, his queen, Videna, and both Ferrex and Porrex. As they wrote, Sackville and Norton drew on a number of literary traditions, including medieval drama (a source for the dumb shows between acts) and *de casibus* poetry, which depicts the falls of kings and nobles (a source for the Chorus's speech on Gorboduc as a mirror, or lesson, for rulers). Seneca was an important influence too, inspiring the five-act structure, the use of a chorus between acts, and the long declamatory speeches. The tragedies also seem to influence particular moments: Queen Videna's opening speech recalls Octavia's at the opening of *Octavia*, and Gorboduc's speech on the fate of the Trojans and their descendants recalls one by Hecuba in *Troas* (P. Davis 2003: 89).

Critics have long agreed that the play addresses the succession. The topic is raised implicitly in the opening act, where Gorboduc overrides primogeniture, establishing a new principle of succession, divided rule. But the play comments explicitly on the topic in a famous speech at the end in which Gorboduc's adviser Eubulus (a name meaning 'wise counsellor') describes the best way to deal with succession: the monarch and parliament should work together to establish a legitimate line to the throne, and 'set the state in quiet stay' (Norton and Sackville 1971: 5. 2. 71). The comment was unambiguously relevant to the succession question, since much of the controversy concerned how much individual or joint power the Queen, her Privy Council, or her Parliament had to decide the issue. Moreover, we know that the play was viewed as a comment on the topic, since a viewer of the first performance noted in his journal that 'many thinges were saied for the Succession to putt thinges in certenty'

(Winston 2005: 25). Sackville and Norton clearly picked up on the combination of drama and political commentary in Seneca, using the tragedies as a precedent for offering political admonition in their play.

Perhaps the most subtle and striking aspect of the influence of Seneca on the works of the 1560s has less to do with their form or content than with their political orientation. In general, the translators and dramatists are concerned with the tribulations of rulers (as opposed to their subjects), that is, with the attitudes and dilemmas of leaders, like Atreus (as opposed to the concerns and reactions of their people, like the Chorus). One telling example of this orientation comes from a non-dramatic work from the period, a version of the *Thyestes* story that appears in Thomas Cooper's mythological appendix to his dictionary of 1565. The story emphasizes Atreus' perspective: Thyestes, 'aspyrynge' to be king, 'committed adu-outrie [adultery] with the wife of his elder brother Atreus, who therefore slue the children of Thyestes, and causynge them to be rosted, made his brother to eate them unwares' (1565: S4^v). Cooper portrays only the point of view of Atreus, not that of Thyestes. Atreus' acts are revenge, the consequence of Thyestes' violation of familial bonds.

While never so explicit, the tendency of plays in the period to focus on rulers (rather than subjects) is evident in subtle and pervasive ways, for instance, in the tendency to dedicate the translations to the Queen and members of her Privy Council, as though the plays are especially relevant to the nation's leaders. But this orientation is also evident in subject matter, which focuses on the concerns of rulers and their counsellors—their susceptibility to fortune, their problems with succession, and the like. Thus, *Damon and Pithias* presents a tyrant who is transformed into a good king when he witnesses the friendship of Damon and Pithias. *Gismond of Salerne* presents the turmoil of a king who forbids his daughter to marry. We even see this orientation in plays like Thomas Preston's *Cambises* (*c*.1560), George Gascoigne's *Jocasta* (1566), and Thomas Pickering's *Horestes* (1567), where the influence of Seneca is considerably less apparent. Even these plays seem to display an interest in rulers, in the transformation of a good king into a tyrant (*Cambises*), in the circumstances in which one can depose a king, and specifically in the scandal over the deposing of Mary, Queen of Scots, following her suspected affair with the Earl of Bothwell and the murder of Henry Darnley (*Horestes*), and in the psychological trauma of a deposed and disgraced king (*Jocasta*).[10] Such an orientation towards rulers is fitting. For the most part, the writers in this period were educated men who were concerned about and, in many cases, sought to obtain places at court and in the government. They used their plays to demonstrate their critical engagement with and sympathy for the concerns of the ruling elite. This orientation is all the more notable since the dramatists of the later Elizabethan period are drawn far more (albeit not exclusively) to the other set of issues raised by Seneca, the way that the actions of rulers affect their subjects.

---

[10] For a discussion of *Horestes* and Mary, Queen of Scots, see Philips (1955) and K. Robertson (1990).

28.4 THE 1580S AND 1590S

Writing in the late 1580s, Thomas Nashe complained that too many playwrights were copying Seneca's plays. Referring to English editions of the tragedies and the now lost drama *Hamlet*, he grumbles: 'English *Seneca* read by candle light yeelds many good sentences, as *Blood is a begger*, and so forth; and if you intreate him faire in a frostie morning, he will affoord you whole Hamlets, I should say handfuls of Tragical speeches' (1966: 315). Nashe exaggerates the extent to which Elizabethan dramatists copied Seneca's 'sentences' and 'speeches', but it is true that there are lots of allusions to the tragedies in the drama of the latter part of the sixteenth century, most commonly in paraphrases of his lines and adaptations of his speeches, especially in the popular revenge tragedies like Thomas Kyd's *The Spanish Tragedy* (late 1580s), Christopher Marlowe's *Jew of Malta* (1589–90), Shakespeare and Peele's *Titus Andronicus* (1592), Shakespeare's *Hamlet* (*c*.1601), and John Marston's *Antonio's Revenge* (1602). Indeed, underscoring this influence, at least two revengers, Hieronimo in *The Spanish Tragedy* (Act 3, scene 13) and Antonio in *Antonio's Revenge* (Act 2, scene 2) carry copies of Seneca with them on stage (P. Davis 2003: 93, 106).Yet the influence of Seneca in these two decades differs from that of the 1560s. In the main, dramatists allude to and imitate the tragedies in less extensive, more sporadic, more tactical ways, using specific lines and speeches to develop characters or situations. Thus, in *The Spanish Tragedy*, as Hieronimo contemplates the need to revenge the murder of his son, he repeatedly quotes Latin lines from Seneca's plays, citing Clytemnestra in *Agamemnon*, Andromache in *The Trojan Women*, and Oedipus in *Oedipus* (P. Davis 2003: 93–5). Such quotes help to convey changes in his character, suggesting that he is trying to become as emotionally overwrought as the figures in Seneca's plays.

More importantly, the plays of the late 1580s and 1590s have a different political orientation. Certainly some tragedies, such as Marlowe's *Tamburlaine* (*c*.1587) or Shakespeare's *Richard III* (*c*.1593), portray Atreus-like figures who rise quickly to power and focus on the psychology, as well as the daring schemes and gloating triumphs, of tyrants. Many more plays, however, appear more concerned with those people who, like the Chorus in *Thyestes*, must react to and negotiate a world dominated by corrupt leaders. This is again especially true of the revenge tragedies and figures like Hieronimo in Kyd's *The Spanish Tragedy*, who revenges the murder of his son when he feels that the legal system, which he helps to administer, will not help him; or Barabas in *The Jew of Malta*, who begins a vengeful killing spree when he is treated unjustly by the rulers of Malta; or Hamlet in the play of that name, who contemplates revenge when he discovers that his deceptive uncle Claudius has secured the throne by murdering the former king. Indeed, Andrew Hadfield argues that Shakespeare likely wrote *Hamlet* with the histories of ancient Rome and 'their representations of the tyranny and cruelty of imperial Rome very much in the forefront of [his] mind' (2003: 571).

Such differences from the 1560s are understandable. The playwrights of this period wrote for the public and private stage, in other words, in a competitive market that catered to larger and more varied audiences than those at the universities, the Inns, and the court in the 1560s. In this market, dramatists looked to Seneca for inspiration, for lines, speeches, characters, and plots that would draw audiences to their plays. More importantly, these dramatists were not amateur authors, but professional writers who aimed to entertain playgoers, a group of people who in the main suffered from the decisions of the powerful but did not have much say in political decisions. Such playwrights and audiences, therefore, were more likely to be interested in figures like Hieronimo, Hamlet, or Antonio who have to make sense of and respond to the corrupt regimes in which they find themselves, often at the cost of becoming mad themselves.

To be sure, when he translated *Thyestes*, aiming to 'revive' Seneca's reputation, Heywood could not have predicted how important the tragedies would become. But the plays obviously spoke to a range of authors, readers, and audiences across the period. As Emily Wilson writes of the current resurgence of interest in Seneca among classicists: 'He is a writer for uncertain and violent times, who forces us to think about the differences between compromise and hypocrisy, and about how, if at all, a person can be good, calm or happy in a corrupt society under constant threat of death' (2004: 4). Just as now, in the Elizabethan period Seneca filled a need among readers and audiences across the social spectrum: the need for a fictional space in which to consider in a general way important political questions about kingship, counsel, tyranny, and subjugation. His tragedies resonated with Elizabethans since they offered what seemed a gripping analysis of autocracy. It is a form of rule that is so personal, so opposite to convention, that rulers who govern this way are successful, at least at first and because their eccentric behaviour bewilders, confounds, and even maddens their subjects.

PRIMARY WORKS

BACON, FRANCIS (2000), *The Advancement of Learning*, ed. M. Kiernan (Oxford: Clarendon Press).

COOPER, THOMAS (1565), *Thesaurus linguae Romanae et Britannicae*.

CORNWALLIS, WILLIAM (1601), *Discourses upon Seneca the Tragedian*.

GOLDING, ARTHUR (trans.) (1578), *Concerning Benefyting [De beneficiis]* by Seneca.

HALL, ARTHUR (trans.) (1581), *Homer's Iliades*.

HEYWOOD, JASPER (trans.) (1559), *Troas* by Seneca.

——(trans.) (1560), *Thyestes* by Seneca.

——(trans.) (1561), *Hercules furens* by Seneca.

——(trans.) (1982), *Thyestes* by Seneca, ed. Joost Daalder (New York: Norton).

NASHE, THOMAS (1966), 'To the Gentlemen Students of Both Universities', in *The Works of Thomas Nashe*, ed. R. B. McKerrow, rev. F. P. Wilson, 5 vols (New York: Barnes and Noble), iii. 300–26.

NEWTON, THOMAS (ed.) (1581), *Seneca his Tenne Tragedies*.

NORTON, THOMAS, and THOMAS SACKVILLE (1971), *Gorboduc; or, Ferrex and Porrex*, ed. Irby B. Cauthen (Lincoln: University of Nebraska Press).

SENECA (2002–4), *Tragedies*, ed. and trans. John G. Fitch, 2 vols (Cambridge, MA: Harvard University Press).

STUDLEY, JOHN (trans.) (1566a), *Agamemnon* by Seneca.

—— (trans.) (1566b), *Medea* by Seneca.

....

CHAPTER 29

POLITICAL TRAGEDY IN THE 1560S

CAMBISES AND *GORBODUC*

....

DERMOT CAVANAGH

'How did the tragic theater of Shakespeare and his colleagues', asks Norman Rabkin, 'climb with such lightning rapidity out of the unpromising slime of mid-sixteenth-century tragedy?' (Rabkin 1985: 28). This contrast between exhilarating ascendancy and obstinately earthbound matter is far from uncommon when the development of Renaissance tragedy is considered, even for an otherwise subtle reader of earlier drama like Rabkin. Yet the attempt to examine the relationship between mid-sixteenth-century works and the later canonical theatre is a useful one because it is so often neglected. A recent survey of Renaissance tragedy is not untypical in dismissing the precursors of Kyd and Shakespeare: 'The early Tudor tragedies generally strike modern audiences as dull or crude or both, often labouring along in the verse form known as "fourteeners" [...] with predictable didactic morals and psychologically unbelievable characters' (Watson 2003: 307). In fact, such plays are performed rarely, and when they are the result is not as drearily predictable as this judgement assumes (E. Hill 1992: 432). At the end of this chapter I would like to reconsider how Elizabethan tragic drama can be understood across the breadth of the period rather than simply at its end. Rabkin's interpretation offers, unintentionally, a place to begin.

Rabkin's thesis is that the artistic ineptitude of plays such as *Cambises* and *Gorboduc* is, paradoxically, their greatest strength. The dramatists of the early 1560s may attempt to compose genuinely edifying works but they are also inventive enough to explore some independent dramatic possibilities; these keep outwitting their best intentions. They become fascinated, for example, by the appeal of the immorality they should condemn or they grant equal weight to the role of destiny and individual choices in the onset of catastrophe. Consequently, these plays keep producing contradictions as well as problems of interpretation. Unwittingly, Rabkin suggests, such works made a truly tragic theatre possible, one that could range far beyond the scope of doctrinal teaching to explore more profound and irresolvable ethical problems and political conflicts. These rudimentary works demonstrated to more self-conscious and sophisticated tragedians that 'there is no single and simple right answer to the problems' tragic drama could explore and this brings them 'prophetically close to the ethos of later Elizabethan tragedy' (Rabkin 1985: 31).

The assumption in this reading that canonical plays realize their intentions whereas earlier ones only manifest their confusions is one that this chapter will contest. However, it has one important consequence: it breaks away from reading these works as theatrically animated homilies. In such accounts, *Cambises* is interpreted as a 'dramatic illustration of the current Anglican doctrine of passive obedience' (Armstrong 1955: 295) and the authors of *Gorboduc* as 'working with generally accepted principles that were thoroughly orthodox', in particular 'the necessity for good counsel and for a single sovereign power in an undivided realm' (Talbert 1967: 93, 109). In contrast, Rabkin stresses that it is the play's failure to teach such lessons clearly that is the key to their potential success as tragedies; this is a suggestion worth pursuing. We can follow it by considering the teaching offered by both plays and then by exploring how their tragic aspirations lead to a more unsettling understanding of political experience and, especially, of political sovereignty.

29.1 POLITICAL TEACHING

What kind of political lesson might an early Elizabethan audience expect from tragic theatre? One clue to this can be derived from the principal source for one of our plays, Thomas Preston's *Cambises*, first performed at the Elizabethan court during the Christmas season of 1560–1 (E. Chambers 1923: iv. 79). The events it depicts are drawn indirectly from Herodotus' *Histories*, but the play relies upon their retelling by the Henrician humanist Richard Taverner in his *The Garden of Wisdom*, first printed in two parts in 1539 (Baskervill 1932: 154–5; Farnham 1936: 263–4; Armstrong 1950). This collection of exemplary historical anecdotes and sayings, drawn largely from Erasmus and reinforced by Taverner's own extensive commentary, displays the humanity and wisdom of a range of monarchs, philosophers, and statesmen from antiquity (Starnes

1956). Instances of corrupt rule are rare, but the outstanding example is Cambises. *The Garden of Wisdom* is usually deemed to be the 'doctrinaire creation' of a Henrician loyalist (Armstrong 1955: 294), but this judgement is questionable in ways that are significant for Preston's play. Still, its political orthodoxy should not be underplayed, and tyrants such as Cambises allow Taverner to augment the distinction between those monarchs who embody in person and in practice an ideal standard of kingship and those who disgrace their office. The latter contrast sharply with Henry VIII, who is so assured of his subjects' love that he dispenses with a personal guard:

> Lord god wyth what inward joy, with what hartie love and reverence do al his liege subjectes imbrace the majestye of his graces person, and not only his liege subjectes, but also even the very ranke traytours, whiche intended nothyng elles but sedicion, yet the incomparable majestie of his owne person they coulde not, but have in wonderous reverence [...] his grace beareth hym so benignely, so gentilly, so lovyngly to all his subjectes, that he may very well be called *pater patriae*, the father of the countrye [...] the noursynge father.
>
> (Taverner 1539: A2^r–A3^v)

Admittedly this passage acknowledges that 'ranke traytours' have defied Henry's sovereign presence, but even these succumb in the end to the universal recognition of his 'incomparable majestie'. In this account, the only conflict that arises in relation to political sovereignty is between those, like Henry VIII, who honour the obligations of their divinely endowed office as a 'noursynge father' and those whose ungoverned appetites lead them to violate these solemn duties.

The tragic effect of both *Cambises* and *Gorboduc* can be understood in this moralized way: they teach by negative example. They depict monarchs who fail to govern their own wills and who fall into immorality or show drastically poor judgement, thereby destroying the moral or material basis of their sovereignty. The power of such works also derives from their playing upon the apprehensions and anxieties generated by the great political question of the day: the resolution of the Elizabethan succession (Levine 1966). In *Cambises* supreme power is invested in an evil incumbent who abandons all the values that should make him a fitting object of loyalty; in *Gorboduc* the sovereign's use of his prerogative to decide the succession results in catastrophe and the king loses his power of command. Both plays project nightmarish outcomes to the question of succession for admonitory effect: to deepen gratitude for the benefit deriving from Elizabeth's accession and to stress the importance of ensuring its continuity. If we follow the ramifications of this lesson in both plays, we can evaluate more clearly whether this tragic method of instruction is their sole rationale.

The great contemporary interest in the succession does help to explain why Preston found such a sensational story from *The Garden of Wisdom* so compelling and apparently edifying. The play describes how Cambises succeeds to the imperial throne of Persia and his attempt to follow the glorious example of his father, Cyrus. His first action is to launch a military campaign against Egypt. During his absence, he appoints the judge Sisamnes as his deputy; the latter proves to be corrupt, and in his one just if grisly deed, Cambises has this unruly magistrate beheaded and then flayed in front of Sisamnes' son (Figure 29.1). However, the king is himself in need of correction, most notably in his increasing drunkenness. When advised against this vice, Cambises shoots his counsellor's son in a ghastly demonstration of prowess, cutting out the child's heart as a trophy. Meanwhile, the play invents its own narrative concerning the Vice Ambidexter, an unprincipled hypocrite and mischief-maker. He moves between scenes of rough comedy and the world of the Persian court, leading the innocent and the guilty towards their destruction and advancing the corruption of those in authority. He incites Sisamnes to new excesses and cultivates a murderous jealousy within Cambises towards his guiltless brother. The king concludes his tyrannous career consumed by an incestuous passion for his cousin, whose life he swiftly dispenses with after their marriage. Cambises dies providentially, or perhaps merely accidentally, impaled by his own sword as he mounts his horse.

The political meaning of this shocking narrative, featuring 'an outrageously cruel protagonist stalking through a succession of bloody crimes to a bloody doom' (Farnham 1936: 268), is made evident from the outset when the play specifies its concern with the duties of a sovereign. It begins with a battery of *sententiae* that advise kings on how they should understand their powers and responsibilities, especially the imperative to 'rule with laws, eke justice' and to be 'himself a plain and speaking law' (Preston 1974, Prologue, 4, 9). Cyrus understood this, yet his son fails to recollect any of the wisdom bestowed upon him: 'He in his youth was trainèd up, by trace of virtue's lore; | Yet (being king) did clean forget his perfect race before' (19–20). Succession can result in a monarch who derogates from all the great responsibilities of the office. Consequently, the play intensifies appreciation of the good government practised by our 'noble Queen' and 'honourable council' in comparison to the 'tragical history of this wicked king' (Epilogue, 15–16, 2).

Norton and Sackville's *Gorboduc* is also deeply concerned with the difference between virtuous and irresponsible monarchy and, especially, with the importance of a well-ordered succession. It was performed a year after Preston's play, on 18 January 1562, and it too featured as part of the Christmas festivities held at court having been produced a month earlier at the Inner Temple, of which both authors were members. There are certainly striking formal differences between the two works, but both are dedicated to imbuing tragic and sorrowful events with a didactic political meaning. Norton and Sackville derive the events of their play from the ancient 'British' past as recounted in Geoffrey of Monmouth's *History of Britain*. From this material they weave a revenge drama in the Senecan mode, replete with machination, plot, and counter-plot, and culminating in national as well as royal catastrophe. At the core of this is the issue of succession. King Gorboduc abdicates from the throne and divides the kingdom between his two sons. Subsequently, the two brothers resort to armed conflict over the right to supreme sovereignty and the younger kills his elder. Their mother, Queen Videna, has been appalled throughout at the loss inflicted upon her elder son by Gorboduc's decision and in revenge for his death murders her youngest child. This atrocity provokes a popular revolt in which both Videna and Gorboduc are slaughtered and the royal line of Brutus is destroyed: 'No ruler rests within the

The description

Of Iustice.

The signification.

SHe which sitteth hauing in one hande a sworde, and in the other a paire of balance, is iustice, also hauyng but one eye in the midst of her forehed, signifieth vpright iudgement, not exteining the person, the balance equitie, to vse no parcialitie, nether for loue nor fauour, the sword to cut of all rebellious persons and offenders, the other are signified in the chapter.

Fig. 29.1 An allegorical representation of Justice, with her eyes closed. The corrupt judge is on the left, with the flayed skin of Sisamnes hanging over the lectern. Stephen Batman, *The Christall Glasse* (1569), P1ᵛ.

regal seat' (Norton and Sackville 1974: 5. 2. 184). Once this rebellion is quelled, the nobility fall into further armed conflict over the succession. Each act of the play is preceded by a Dumb Show and then concluded by a Chorus so that the audience is left in no doubt over the implications of what it witnesses. The former insists 'that a state knit in unity doth continue strong against all force, but being divided, is easily destroyed' (Dumb Show 1) and the latter confirms:

> And this great king that doth divide his land,
> And change the course of his descending crown,
> And yields the reign into his children's hand,
> From blissful state of joy and great renown
> A mirror shall become to princes all,
> To learn to shun the cause of such a fall.
>
> (Chorus 1: 388–93)

If Gorboduc had settled the succession in the traditional way and preserved the unity of the kingdom, none of the desperate events which follow would have occurred.

Interpreting *Cambises* and *Gorboduc* as admonitory political homilies on the succession is one answer to the question of what political tragedy meant in the 1560s: both plays deepen the audience's appreciation of the political stability it enjoys, and that can prove so fragile, as well as underlining the obligation of the monarch to preserve this. Yet Rabkin was correct to identify an excess within each play that makes their doctrinal message seem far from comprehensive. Although the problem of Cambises' succession is evident, it is less easy to know what to do about it. After all, he is a legitimate monarch whose succession is uncontested; the consequences of this, it seems, can only be endured. Perhaps that it is the lesson. One critic asserts that 'discerning members of Preston's audience' would agree with the play's voluble condemnation of those who complain against the king's tyrannical actions as traitors and with its commendation of the passive obedience that is urged upon Cambises' persecuted brother (and later, in similar terms, his queen): 'Let him alone, of his deeds do not talk [...]| live quietly, do not with him deal' (636, 640; Armstrong 1955: 295–6). Yet this advice is proposed by Ambidexter, the play's opportunistic intriguer and hypocrite. Some commentators suggest that this displacement of sober discourses is far from accidental and that it reveals the play's unregenerate delight in acting and spectacle for its own sake. On this view, the play's shameless indulgence of Ambidexter and, more generally, of comedic and parodic material results in a pointed mockery of homiletic theatre. Consequently, the play is shaped primarily for theatrical pleasure rather than solemn instruction (Bushnell 1990: 80–2; Cartwright 1999: 102–8).

Equally, the didactic assurance of *Gorboduc* is incomplete. The judgements offered by the Chorus do not always address the scale of the tragedy unfolded by the play. The king should have ensured an uncontested succession after his death by allowing the throne to pass to his elder son, Ferrex, yet the latter proves to be unreliable. In the second act of the play, he is consumed by violent resentment towards his younger brother, and one of his advisers urges Ferrex to set aside scruple and to seize full sovereign powers. The fittest candidate should rule, he argues, and even the principle of succession by primogeniture is not sacrosanct:

> If Nature and the Gods had pinchèd so
> Their flowing bounty and their noble gifts
> Of princely qualities from you, my lord,
> And pour'd them all at once in wasteful wise
> Upon your father's younger son alone,
> Perhaps there be, that in your prejudice
> Would say that birth should yield to worthiness.

> (2. 1. 81–7)

Now the speaker here is Hermon, a cynical counsellor who is attempting to incite Ferrex to destroy his brother; it would be foolish to trust anything he says. Yet as this example shows, it is difficult to turn aside all the implications of his argument. In Taverner's *Second Book of the Garden of Wisdom*, for example, Cambises' predecessor, the admirable Cyrus the Elder, makes a powerful case that 'it is not the byrth of man' but personal excellence that should distinguish a prince (Taverner 1539: B4^r). This was an argument which other Tudor humanists had explored (Starkey 1989: 68–76). As *Cambises* shows, trusting to succession simply on the grounds of primogeniture can indeed result in catastrophe. Some commentators feel *Gorboduc* is also composed in a sophistic rather than a didactic mode. It explores many different sides of an issue in a playful, explorative way to provoke continuous reflection in the viewer (or reader). This encourages multiple ways of seeing the issue at stake so that the full complexity of the problem is grasped rather than the solution to it (see Altman 1978: 249–9; Herman 2001).

This chapter will propose another reason why both plays present a less coherent lesson about political sovereignty than first appears. This depends upon emphasizing the tragic aspirations of these dramatists. Those critics who observe a playful or sceptical disposition in these works make an important contribution because they stress that although each play may elaborate a political moral they are not political moralities. In the latter tradition of drama, in plays such as Skelton's *Magnificence* (*c*.1520–2; printed 1530) or Sir David Lindsay's *Satire of the Three Estates* (1554; printed 1602), it appears that the sovereign is potentially redeemable and sovereignty can be reformed and reconstituted on a more equitable basis. In *Cambises* and *Gorboduc* the lawless or misguided sovereign is not capable of moral recuperation (cf. Bushnell 1990: 96). These plays present a much bleaker form of tragic narrative where irredeemable consequences follow from the embodiment of sovereignty in a single person. The latter point is crucial because it helps to foreground the implications of another constitutive aspect of tragic experience in these plays: their insistent representation of suffering and lament. Readings which emphasize the playful or intellectual qualities of these dramas can grant less weight to this. However, in both works, mourning and lament have an unusual degree of prominence and provide a primary means by which the exercise of sovereign power is comprehended and endured.

Gorboduc and *Cambises* grasp the issue of sovereignty in tragic as well as homiletic terms and there is a tension between these two categories. As tragedies, both plays imagine conditions of emergency where the sovereign ruptures the standards, institutions, and processes by which a state should be governed. This is a much more alarming experience than depicting an erring but redeemable monarch because the very existence of the state and of monarchy itself is jeopardized. What would one do then? Some crucial questions follow from this: what kind of authority abandons just governance or renders it impossible? What happens to a society under the sway of inequitable rule? What should subjects do about it? What limits are there to the powers of the Crown? How should they be enforced? What alternatives are there to monarchical sovereignty? *Cambises* and *Gorboduc* establish tragedy as a medium in which these enduring questions could be considered.

29.2 POLITICAL TRAGEDY: *CAMBISES*

In its depiction of how succession can lead to tyranny, Thomas Preston's *Cambises* contains scenes of tremendous pathos and suffering: the public execution of the corrupt deputy Sisamnes witnessed by his son; the grotesque killing of the counsellor Praxaspes' son by the king and the lament for this child by his mother; the murder of Cambises' brother; and, perhaps most emotive of all, the encircling of the queen by Cruelty and Murder as she sings a psalm of forgiveness at the point of her death. It is this tragic potential that Preston developed from his source: the creation of a luminous sequence of moments where death is confronted, endured, and lamented. There is also a significant causal pattern at work in this inasmuch as all this suffering and loss is the responsibility of the sovereign who acts outside both positive and natural law. In this account, sovereignty is indeed 'a power that having its origin *in itself*, is thereby released from any control' (Moretti 1988: 45). The theatrical elaboration of this bears further scrutiny as the prerogative of sovereignty begin to disclose their tragic potential.

It is important to remember that, at the outset, Cambises is not simply the 'other' face of sovereignty, cruel and pitiless. Indeed, the succession, to begin with, is a successful one. The king upholds a monarchical system where supreme authority does not belong to him alone but to the king and his council, an assumption, according to John Guy, that remained central to the period's understanding of sovereignty (Guy 1995: 292–3). Cambises fulfils expectations in this respect by seeking advice from his 'counsel grave and sapient' on his determination to invade Egypt: 'Extend your counsel unto me in that I ask of you' (line 14). The decision to appoint the judge Sisamnes as his substitute is a collective one reached after mature deliberation. Yet in the moment of delegating supreme power, *Cambises* lets us see how easily the regulation of monarchical will can lapse as Sisamnes realizes: 'Now may I abrogate the law, as I shall think it good; | If any one me now offend, I may demand his blood' (117–18). In this way, the play begins to tell a more fateful story concerning the powers of majesty and to concentrate attention on the quality of the decisions made by Sisamnes as he descends, with the encouragement of Ambidexter, into the iniquitous exploitation of his office.

Yet the play also presents the exercise of sovereign prerogative that brings this corrupt official to account in an equally unsettling way. We have already been warned that Cambises now imitates the 'tiger's kind' (346), yet his decision to execute Sisamnes is not unjust. Its excess leads, however, to the first of the play's great scenes of tragic spectacle. Sisamnes' son offers his own life for his father's; instead, the king insists he witness his father's death. The fearful punishment that follows marks a crucial shift in the play's balance of sympathies. Cambises' instruction after the decapitation is carried out is savage, as is the subsequent stage direction: 'Pull his skin over his ears to make his death more vile [...] *Flay him with a false skin*' (463, 464 s.d.). As importantly, this action provokes a moving lament from Sisamnes' son on the consequences of the king's retribution; this reduces both himself and his father to tears as they realize 'the king hath no remorse' (446). The laments shared between Sisamnes and his son make it far less easy to answer Cambises' question 'Have not I done a gracious deed?' (477).

This qualification of sympathy is intensified as this pitiable scene moves immediately into the king's sadistic killing of his counsellor Praxaspes' son and the cutting out of his heart. This gruesome action is again accompanied by striking passages of public mourning and lament; these disclose the human devastation caused by the king's insensate will. Praxaspes' 'sweet child' and 'only joy' (517) is killed because of his father's wise advice concerning the king's drunkenness, and the atrocity that results from this shatters the conciliar system, revealing Cambises to be completely lawless. The counsellor asks, 'Is this the gain now from the king for giving counsel good'? (543), as he witnesses the horror of his child's death and evisceration. From Cambises' perspective and that of his sycophants this spectacle is indeed relative, an occasion for triumphant hilarity, but it is weighed against the experience of Praxaspes, the 'woeful man' (570), and his wife. Their laments for their dead child freeze the fast-flowing action of the play, and the inconsolable mother recollects in moving terms the physical presence of her lost child and the destruction of her political faith: 'O king, of tiger's brood! | O tiger's whelp, hadst thou the heart to see this child's heart-blood?' (593–4). These sustained passages of lament are as integral to the play as its equally energetic depiction of immoral intrigue and action, and they call this latter form of theatrical pleasure to account. The sharing of sorrow over these tragic events also involves the dissolution of political trust, and it implies 'that the institution of absolute monarchy itself may encourage the unnatural and unkind behavior that the play portrays' (Vanhoutte 2000: 231).

This way of considering *Cambises* draws upon some of the emphases Walter Benjamin discerned in his study of the baroque *Trauerspiel*, or 'mourning play'. Benjamin's work has not been central to recent interpretation of Renaissance tragedy, although there is now a revival of interest in its far-reaching implications (Strohm 2006). The detail of his argument lies beyond the scope of this chapter; however, some of its key elements are of exceptional interest because they illuminate how tragedy may share political preoccupations and theatrical effects across a broad sweep of time. Principally, this derives from Benjamin's interest not only in the mood of mourning aroused by tragic theatre but in its political implications. At the centre of the mourning play is the suffering human body, and this affects, in turn, understanding of the nature and imperatives of sovereignty. These works stress the violent and arbitrary capacity of sovereign power, and, in the drastic situations this produces, subjects degrade into sycophancy or they become powerless victims to be dispatched according to the imperatives of lawless will. In the same way, a country or a 'kingdom' is succeeded to as a personal possession to be disposed of according to peremptory desires.

In this respect, there was also an important principle of dramatic form that characterized mourning plays, and this, as much as their forbidding content, allowed consideration of how states of emergency also reveal foundational problems. The theatrical mode they adopt involves a constant principle of interruption, whereby dramatic episodes interpose and disconcert each other. This does not preclude the comic; indeed, 'the comic interior of the Trauerspiel', Benjamin insists (1998: 128), is integral to its effect. As we see in *Cambises*, the power of decision also belongs to an intriguer like Ambidexter, or to the goddess Venus, who engineers the king's erotic obsession with his cousin; these figures are equally substantive authors of the plot. In the scenes where they dominate, the autonomy of the sovereign is demeaned, although the plots of these intriguers also fail in the end as they are unravelled by their own method of dissimulation and reversal. For Benjamin, such actions typify the mourning play as it claims its own theatrical authority to punctuate and scrutinize the exercise of sovereign will. Ultimately, the latter also pursues its own undoing as its motives and decisions are subject to an irregular dramatic rhythm of sudden change that reveals its limitations and illusions. This constant shifting of focus and perspective exposes the myth of sovereign self-sufficiency both to the audience and, ultimately, to the sovereign within the play who has to confront his or her own finitude. Crucial to this are scenes of tragic consequence, of mourning and lament.

Even in this brief account, the tenor of Benjamin's suggestions about the attractions of tragic form as a way of thinking about sovereignty can be noted. For example, it allows a reconsideration of what might appear to be merely playful in *Cambises*. Ambidexter interprets the play in a mischievous spirit and he debunks lament, mocking Praxaspes' wife for mourning her son and taking delight in the fate of Sisamnes at the hands of 'this tyrant Cambises' (616). Similarly, he indulges in mock lament after the highly charged killings of Cambises' brother—'With sorrowful lamentations I am in such a heat! (741)—and his queen: 'Very grief so torments me that scarce I can speak' (1130). In one sense, this is an expected part of Ambidexter's carnivalesque antagonism to all serious forms of discourse as mere posturing:

> But, Lord! So the ladies mourn, crying 'Alack!'
> Nothing is worn now but only black:
> I believe all the cloth in Watling Street to make gowns would not serve.
>
> (1133–5)

Yet his disdain for this community of female mourning is continuous with his failed endeavour to domineer over women such as Marian May-be-good and Meretrix in the play's comic sequences. These are also attempts to diminish the political force of lament by a figure whose only interest is domination.

Other figures in the play break through into new kinds of insight very different in temper from Ambidexter's. For instance, Cambises' brother Smerdis disapproves of the king but accepts the Vice's counsel to be quiescent and to adopt a public language of obedience and fidelity. Yet once Cambises has fallen prey to Ambidexter's false accusations concerning his brother's ambitions, he orders his assassination. It is only when Smerdis confronts his annihilation at the hands of this violent and capricious king that he is able to reach a new understanding of his brother by naming him: 'tyrant tyrannious |[…] all his doings be damnable and pernicious' (724–5). Later, Cambises' new queen remembers this shocking act of fratricide. When the king tells the cruel story of setting one of two weak 'whelps' to fight a young lion and how his 'brother whelp' came to his assistance, 'Which thing to see before mine eyes did glad the heart of prince' (1018–29), the queen's response is very different: 'At this tale told, let the Queen weep' (1029 s.d.). She recollects, 'to shame of royal king', the killing of the king's brother Smerdis: 'faithful love was more in dog than it was in your grace' (1034, 1040). It is this tragic sympathy that provokes Cambises to commit his final outrage: the killing of the queen as she sings a psalm while being surrounded by Cruelty and Murder. This is one of the most powerful ways of perceiving and judging sovereign power in *Cambises*: from the viewpoint of the suffering body it has ostracized and condemned.

What kind of political lesson is to be drawn from the play? Its own conclusion is an unremarkable one that returns us to the simple polarities of gratitude for Tudor beneficence in contrast to 'oriental' tyranny. No resistance is ever countenanced against this monstrous tyrant, whom, it appears, providence disposes of in a suitably arbitrary manner. Yet, as Eugene D. Hill suggests in a fine essay, the Protestant subjects of Elizabeth had just emerged from a period of persecution under Mary that had produced a range of dissentient arguments concerning the powers and capacities of sovereigns and subjects (Hill 1992). Could literary and theatrical representations of tyranny also produce reflection in this mode? We have a fascinating and neglected piece of evidence from Preston's source, *The Second Book of the Garden of Wisdom*, that this was possible. In this work, the significance of Cambises' reign is debated after his death by the chief Persian lords as they consider who should now be elected king or whether they should have a king at all. The latter view is put forcibly:

no more kynges shulde be chosen, but that by leage and sure confederacie made betwene them, all the lordes myght rule alyke, so shuld libertie be maynteyned and kept on every syde and every man at libertie, for before, it was wel proved by examples that where one man is lorde of so many and so great thynges, he maye easyly be to proude and hawtie, and sone growe out of kynde and degendre unto tyrannye, even as now of late it was seen of Cambyses.

(Taverner 1539: C6^{r-v})

This is not the only lesson to be drawn from Cambises' reign in Taverner's text and it is opposed successfully; monarchy is restored under Darius. Yet the latter's ascendancy is achieved by trickery and Taverner's attitude to Darius remains ambivalent; a few pages later, the Persian monarchy lapses again into tyranny under Xerxes. What conclusion is to be drawn from this is left open, and this is also part of the unpredictable effect of the play's concentration on the sorrow produced by sovereign power. One implication of this is that succession under absolute sovereignty does indeed appear to be a tragedy waiting to happen.

29.3 POLITICAL TRAGEDY: *GORBODUC*

A long tradition of criticism has established *Gorboduc* as 'the first Elizabethan succession tract' (Levine 1966: 30), a theatrical tragedy intended to circumvent historical tragedy. One of its speakers condenses its message concerning the succession into a simple imperative: 'keep out [...]| Unnatural thraldom of [a] stranger's reign' (5. 2. 176–7). Indeed, an important piece of eyewitness testimony has been recovered in which exactly this understanding of the play is deduced, reading it as dissuading Elizabeth from foreign suitors and promoting a native-born candidate, Robert, Lord Dudley, created Earl of Leicester in 1564 (H. James and Walker 1995). In this interpretation, the play presents both a diagnosis of the problem of succession and a cure for it by supporting Leicester. It should also be noted that Elizabeth's response to such advice 'stressed the limits of [Parliament's] authority to counsel a prince' so as to 'insulate her sovereignty' (Guy 1995: 302). The Queen's response to a parliamentary petition on this issue presented in 1566 is explicit: 'I will deal therein for your safety, and offer it unto you as your Prince and head, without request; for it is monstrous that the feet should direct the head' (Levine 1966: 185).

The neoclassical decorum of the play can also be seen to reinforce its message, and, in this, it contrasts strikingly with *Cambises*. *Gorboduc* uses blank verse for the first time as its principal dramatic medium and it adopts Senecan conventions throughout. The play also moves away from affective spectacle, which emphasized the physical presence of the suffering body, towards affective rhetoric in which such suffering was only described; comedic or parodic episodes are also omitted. If Norton and Sackville were aware at all of Preston's play, their own work might be understood as a learned rebuke to its predecessor. Understood in this way, *Cambises* exemplifies the potentially undisciplined energy of the native theatrical tradition that *Gorboduc* refines and concentrates into a new kind of tragic experience.

Yet the play's tragic elements, especially its extensive use of lament, complicates its political teaching and ensures that *Gorboduc* probes deeper into the question of sovereignty. Even the presentation of the core issue of abdication and division is far from straightforward despite the testimony of the Dumb Show and the Chorus. In the second scene, the king's counsellors discuss his proposal in a self-reflexive mode by citing tragic examples in a manner very similar in kind to the play that is now unfolding. For Eubulus, the king's determination will lead to disaster and the moral is simple: 'Within one land, one single rule is best' (1. 2. 259) because 'faith and justice, and all kindly love, | Do yield unto desire of sovereignty' (265–6). Nothing should be done to provoke the fearful consequences of the latter, and Eubulus reminds the king of some ancient history. 'Brute, first prince of all this land' (270), divided the kingdom between his three sons and the result was tragic: bloodshed, treachery, civil war, and the loss of sovereignty (269–82). Eubulus' bleak moral realism proves to be accurate, and his understanding of the lesson taught by tragic history is correct. Yet, it is not the only conclusion to be derived from a lamentable tale in this scene. Philander also opposes the king's decision to abdicate but agrees with him on the issue of division, otherwise political ambitions will be inflamed, not extinguished (148–246). If the kingdom becomes Ferrex's alone, Philander imagines a tragic future which will be the subject for lament, one deriving from the 'unkindly wrong' done to the subjected younger son who 'Gapes' for the elder's death and who will embark on vengeance (183, 194). Experience discloses other and equally tragic instances of the 'famous stocks of royal blood destroy'd' (191) by botching the succession in this way.

Events show Philander to be mistaken, but he is not corrupt or flagrantly irresponsible. In fact, his tragic insight is not without credibility: Gorboduc's younger son is moved easily to act against his brother when he possesses half the kingdom (2. 2. 38–66). It may be that his sudden change of fortune has provoked him, but his mother suspects from the outset his 'growing pride' (1. 1. 31). Would the sole succession of Ferrex have prevented this? Perhaps so, and the division is the catalyst for all that follows. Eubulus may well be the more serious student of tragic history because he considers what has happened, as well as the prudential action needed to avoid its reoccurrence, rather than imagining possible futures. Yet the presentation of the issue elicits questions and conjectures; it is, at least, debatable, and seriously so because different and opposing moral lessons can be deduced in good faith from tragic examples. Philander's argument is a moving one and driven equally by his care for the commonwealth. In this way, the experience of division is also a problem of understanding or response; even the 'right' decision in this case might not have avoided catastrophe. For Norton and Sackville, tragedy is not the place where conventional moral or political judgements are easily vindicated. More daringly, *Gorboduc* suggests that the crisis would not simply be averted by the sovereign making the 'correct' decision; it is not simply a matter of his or her personal virtues or faults. It results rather from one individual possessing the authority to decide the succession and to determine which body (or bodies) should be invested with this supreme power. Even the outrageous Cambises appeared to take the practice of counsel very seriously at the start of his reign; in contrast, it is implied that Gorboduc has already made his decision and that this debate, with its tragic speculations pro and contra, is largely superfluous (see 1. 1. 45–50).

The use of tragic examples in this scene of counsel is one example of how *Gorboduc* releases the power of lament to sweep away assurance and to stimulate thinking about fundamental questions of power and prerogative. In its fourth act, for example, the catastrophe that follows from Gorboduc's division of the realm is intensifying: the younger son, Porrex, has invaded his brother's land and killed him. The act opens with Videna, Gorboduc's queen, and her lament for her 'belovèd son! O my sweet child!' (4. 1. 23). In this extensive speech of mourning, Videna disowns her treacherous younger child: 'Ruthless, unkind, monster of nature's work' (71). His inherited entitlements are rendered meaningless as Videna places him outside the familial and human community as an animal who can be slaughtered. Yet the Porrex we see immediately after this, appealing to his father for pity, is remote from this unfeeling monster (4. 2. 35–134). He too draws upon lament, appealing to be seen as a 'woeful man' with a 'mournful case': his elder brother planned to assassinate him and Porrex moved against him only to preserve his own life (43, 45). The act ends with another extensive female lament, the servant Marcella's piteous account of Porrex's killing by his mother. The 'peerless prince, | Son to a king, and in the flower of youth' cried to his mother for aid not realizing she was his assassin (200–1).

In the fourth act of *Gorboduc*, mourning deepens problems of judgement and demands that rival claims are considered critically. Porrex is condemned by his mother and father, but then presents a full and convincing account of his tragic dilemma; finally, his death elicits such eloquent pathos that it endows him with a heroic presence. As Kent Cartwright has shown, Norton and Sackville deploy a subtle management of retrospect throughout the play to show 'that meaning can be provisional' (1999: 112–21). Lament is crucial to this process, and although it gives great power to all of its speakers, it bestows none of them with the credibility to make a definitive judgement or decision. Gorboduc mourns the passage of events, but he remains mystified by them and can only blame 'cruel destiny' and 'froward fate'; he is unable to grasp his own responsibility (4. 2. 142–8). Benjamin stressed the importance of this aspect of the mourning play: as successive scenes and speeches qualify and counter each other, the argument of the play becomes more unfathomable. Within *Gorboduc*, no one can find a solution that will resolve the tragic crisis.

This openness of the play to speculation about motives and judgements also grants it a remarkable range of reflections on the nature of sovereignty, and it subjects the true purposes of the latter to constant redefinition. Gorboduc perceives his own office in a perfectly orthodox manner, despite his disastrous exercise of prerogative. He believes the monarch's primary duty is to

> preserve the common peace,
> The cause that first began and still maintains
> The lineal course of kings' inheritance.

> (1. 2. 22–4)

The piety of these reflections is soon challenged, however, when the king signally fails to fulfil this obligation. In the counter-case, put by the inflammatory adviser Hermon, the sovereign's only duty is to maximize the scope of his or her powers regardless of moral scruple. Monarchs may adopt a moralized discourse to justify themselves, but when reality is exposed by a state of emergency we grasp a very different truth: power seeks to perpetuate and augment itself. Hermon urges Ferrex to understand this and to dismiss illusions such as the 'fear of gods' or 'nature's law' (2. 1. 140–1):

> Know ye, that lust of kingdoms hath no law.
> The gods do bear and well allow in kings
> The things [that] they abhor in rascal routs.
> Murders and violent thefts in private men
> . . .
> Are heinous crimes, and full of foul reproach;
> Yet none offence, but deck'd with glorious name
> Of noble conquests in the hands of kings.
>
> (2. 1. 143–5, 152–5)

Hermon insists that 'reason of state' should be the sovereign's pre-eminent concern: the necessity to maintain and, where possible, enlarge their dominion (see Viroli 1992). Yet even those who oppose such an unprincipled view provoke a competing question about sovereignty: where is it best located? Who or what possesses the quality that demands loyalty and in whose defence we might surrender our lives? Lament is again crucial to the formulation of these questions because it also allows a new object to come into view as the locus of sovereignty: 'Britain land, the mother of ye all', 'your mother land' (5. 2. 115–79, 135, 179). It is the country, in the last instance, that demands protection and constitutes the foundation of loyalty; the concluding imperative is 'To save your realm, and in this realm yourselves' (119; cf. Vanhoutte 2000). Admittedly, the definition of the nation here is an exclusive one based on an aristocratic sense of custodianship: the 'ancient honour of your ancestors' (143). Yet it does allow another sovereign institution to become significant because it is only 'by common counsel of you all | In parliament' (157–8) that the succession can be decided and 'the regal diadem | Be set in certain place of governance' (158–9). In his concluding lament, Eubulus despairs over whether parliamentary agreement could now be reached in this matter and foresees only further catastrophe (180–279). He does not dispute, however, that this was the solution missed earlier and that a decision of the king-in-parliament would have had a truly distinctive power rather than simply the king's alone. Such a lawful solution is now far too late and the crown will be seized and lost by force.

If *Gorboduc* teaches a lesson about sovereignty, it also considers questions about its nature. In this respect, Stephen Alford is right to note how the play addresses 'the controversial issue of the location of power in the English polity in the 1560s' (1998: 103). *Cambises* too opens up onto a speculative situation where the premises and limits of allegiance are tested during a crisis. Lament is the principal way in which this situation is addressed, experienced, and challenged, and it constitutes a place where some of the play's most exacting thinking is done on political problems. This identifies one crucial point of contact between earlier and later instances of Elizabethan tragic theatre. Robert Y. Turner has suggested that the creation of pathos was the common motivation of tragedians from the 1560s until the 1590s. Understanding the experience of tragedy involves grasping 'the playwrights' practical concern for expressing sorrow and suffering and for moving their audiences', especially on the part of 'those who have been deprived of some loved one' (1961–2: 98, 110). However, these episodes of personal loss are always connected to broader issues of governance in the ethos of the mourning play. Tragedy is a medium in which the period's enduring political concern with the responsibilities of sovereigns and subjects is addressed in ways that extend far beyond homiletic conventions: this is what drew audiences and dramatists to the form. It is in this respect that we can begin to re-examine the relationships between early and late forms of Elizabethan tragic theatre. When the grief-stricken Hieronimo in Kyd's *The Spanish Tragedy* (*c*.1582–92; printed 1592) imagines the power of his lament for his butchered son Horatio, he describes it as disrobing nature and penetrating hell itself (Kyd 1974: 3. 7. 1–18). Yet when his lament reaches 'the brightest heavens', his words 'find the place impregnable; and they | Resist my woes, and give my words no way' (13, 17–18). Hieronimo must endure and act in this world; there is no higher court of appeal he can resort to beyond confronting those worldly powers that are the origin of rather than the solution to political crisis. It is to this scene that Elizabethan tragedy returns repeatedly and one of its most compelling qualities lies in portraying how the failures and excesses of sovereignty leave it open to question.

PRIMARY WORKS

KYD, THOMAS (1974), *The Spanish Tragedy*, in T. W. Craik (ed.), *Minor Elizabethan Tragedies* (London: Dent).

NORTON, THOMAS, and THOMAS SACKVILLE (1974), *Gorboduc*, in T. W. Craik (ed.), *Minor Elizabethan Tragedies* (London: Dent).

PRESTON, THOMAS (1974), *Cambises*, in T. W. Craik (ed.), *Minor Elizabethan Tragedies* (London: Dent).

STARKEY, THOMAS (1989), *A Dialogue between Pole and Lupset*, ed. T. F. Mayer, Camden Society, 4th ser., 37.

TAVERNER, RICHARD (1539), *The Garden of Wysdome and The Second Booke of the Garden of Wysdome*.

CHAPTER 30

....

JOHN FOXE'S *ACTS AND MONUMENTS*, 1563–1583

ANTIQUITY AND THE AFFECT OF HISTORY

....

ANDREW ESCOBEDO

JOHN Foxe produced a great deal of non-narrative writing throughout his lifetime, much of which influenced or was shaped by his massive narrative *Acts and Monuments*, popularly known by readers, then and now, as *The Book of Martyrs*. He translated (into Latin and English) sermons and treatises by Martin Luther, Urbanus Regius, Edmund Grindal, Thomas Cranmer, and others. He organized and wrote introductions for editions of works by several writers, including William Tyndale, John Frith, and Robert Barnes. He authored (in whole or in part) sermons, two manuals on memory improvement, a theological tract about the Eucharist, two treatises on Church discipline, several anti-Catholic polemics, and a commentary, unfinished at his death, on the book of Revelation. He was also a successful and charismatic London preacher. Nearly all this material is relevant to (and some of it reprinted in) *Acts and Monuments*, which has an aggressive religious and political agenda. Yet in this introduction to Foxe I will consider this agenda in terms of his book's narrative operations. In *Acts and Monuments*, at least, Foxe is a storyteller first and foremost; he regularly refers to the polemical or theological sections of his book as 'digressions' from his narrative. This chapter, then, will focus on two central narrative concerns in

Foxe's book: the attempt to reconstruct the ancient past of his nation, and the effort to fine-tune the presentation of pain suffered by martyrs in his own time. But first, because the material shape of his book is so bound up with its content, we will start with the printing history of the martyrology.[1]

30.1 THE BOOK, THE STORY, AND THE AUTHOR(S)

The prehistory of the first English edition of *Acts and Monuments* includes two Latin editions, printed in 1554 and 1559, of a martyrology that Foxe wrote while in exile on the Continent during Mary I's reign. Fellow exile Edmund Grindal, who was in contact with Foxe as he worked on the second Latin edition, seems to have promoted a concentration solely on the Marian persecutions, but the book Foxe actually wrote began far earlier. The 1559 version, about 750 folio pages divided into six books, started with the life of John Wyclif, the famous fourteenth-century dissenting cleric, proceeded through the martyrdoms during the reign of Henry VIII, and stopped at 1556 with the Marian burnings. The teachings of Wyclif thus offered a starting point for English religious reformation, and the martyrs' perseverance at the fires of Smithfield represented a culmination. That he resisted the advice of the influential Grindal is an early indication of Foxe's commitment to a comprehensive history of what he and his fellow reformers called 'the true church', a narrative that in later years he would repeatedly hail as 'a full and complete history' (*3^v). Nonetheless, Foxe profited enormously from the research on the Marian burnings that Grindal and his colleagues had undertaken, as well as from information about earlier periods gleaned from John Bale's *Catalogus* (1557–9), a massive bibliography of medieval texts, and Edward Hall's chronicle (1548, 1550).

The first English edition of the martyrology was published in 1563 by the Protestant printer John Day, four years after Foxe had returned to England. *Acts and Monuments* was a double-columned folio of 1,800 pages, expensively prepared with more

---

[1] Until recently many scholars relied on the AMS Press reprint of the edition of *Acts and Monuments* published by Stephen Reed Cattley between 1837 and 1841. This edition is convenient for modern readers, but rather indiscriminately mixes together material that remained distinct in Tudor editions of the book. On the many disadvantages and risks of using this edition for scholarship, see Thomas Freeman (1999). For this chapter I cite primarily from the first four editions of *Acts and Monuments* (1563, 1570, 1576, and 1583) held at the Rare Books and Manuscripts Library at Ohio State University (with the gracious assistance of the library's staff). I also made use of the digital facsimiles of these editions available through Early English Books Online (EEBO). Finally, I found immensely useful the transcriptions of the first four editions provided by the *Foxe's Book of Martyrs Variorum Edition Online* (<http://www. hrionline.ac.uk/johnfoxe/index.html>). In the passages quoted in this essay, I have modernized the spelling and have cited references parenthetically in the text to the 1583 edition, unless otherwise noted. I cite by page number, except with prefatory materials that lack pagination, in which case I cite by signature.

than fifty woodcuts illustrating scenes described in the text, and employing multiple fonts to distinguish reprinted primary documents from Foxe's own commentary and summary. The disparate audiences identified in the prefatory material reveal Foxe's and presumably Day's expectation of a wide readership and, in some cases, of hostile response (J. King 2005). In the years preceding the book's publication Foxe drew further on English and Continental historical sources, and, unlike its Latin predecessors, the English edition reprinted tremendous amounts of domestic archival material: church records from the diocese of Norwich, episcopal registers for Coventry, Lichfield, and London, and written accounts sent to Foxe by eyewitnesses.[2] Foxe contextualized this local, archival evidence with a vision of cosmic history considerably expanded from that of the earlier Latin editions. After the prefatory sections, the book was divided into six 'parts'. Part 1 begins not with Wyclif but with the release of Satan in c.CE 1000, according to Foxe's reading of the millennium mentioned in Revelation 20. This apocalyptic threshold coincided with the rise to power of Pope Sylvester II, who, Foxe assures us, 'was a Sorcerer' (1563: 11). Foxe can thus begin his story with an example of how wicked popes began to interfere in domestic English affairs as the visible Church slid into corruption (see Figure 30.1). Parts 2 through 6 stretch from Wyclif's burning to 'the most flourishing reign of Queen Elizabeth' (1720, misnumbered as 1708). Part 5, describing at length the martyrdoms under Mary I, represents the heart of the story and its most explicit anti-Roman propaganda: the other five parts range in length between thirty and 300 pages, but part 5 is over 800 pages long.

The second edition (1570), at 2,300 pages and about 150 woodcuts, expanded the story's historical scope and fundamentally revised earlier material. Foxe dramatically increased the evidence base of archival sources, consulting diocesan registers and church records from Canterbury, Hereford, Lincoln, Rochester, Bath, Durham, and York; he likewise made copious use of interviews with eyewitnesses to the Marian burnings. In the rewritten prefatory material, Foxe repeatedly mentions the attacks on the 1563 edition from his Catholic adversaries, both in England and abroad. Yet it is clear there were also complaints from Protestants: the Calendar of Martyrs is gone, presumably owing to Puritan objections about its resemblance to Catholic calendars of saints. Difficult as it is to generalize about the tone of such a large volume, we can cautiously say that the second edition is more polemical and, in some places, more vitriolic and shrill than the first, betraying Foxe's awareness that the reformed Church in England had achieved far less than complete triumph (Betteridge 1999: 161–206). At the same time, the book projects far grander historical ambitions than the earlier edition, beginning with the birth of Christ and tracing subsequent ecclesiastical history with tremendous archival detail. The third (1576) and fourth (1583) editions both maintain these qualities from the second, as well as its basic organization. The third adds some material, but is about 300 pages shorter than the second, a reduction achieved by using at times minuscule font. This may speak to a desire to produce

---

[2] Freeman (*ODNB*) suggests that 'the great difference between this book and Foxe's previous martyrologies was its reprinting of archival material'.

Fig. 30.1 King John's supplication to the Pope. John Foxe, *Actes and Monuments* (1583), Y2^r.

a more compact and convenient volume, but may have also resulted from an effort to reduce costs. The fourth edition swelled again to about 2,200 pages, making the typescript a bit less compressed, and it also prominently reinserts the Calendar of martyrs that the 1563 edition had included.

The later editions begin with a lengthy exordium that considers 'the state of the primitive church compared with this latter church of Rome', initiating the pattern of good sliding into bad that inflects the subsequent narrative. Then book 1, starting with the birth of Christ, considers the first ten persecutions of the early Church; it concludes with the emperor Constantine's godly reign in the fourth century. After this the story returns to its English lens, and book 2 backs up slightly, treating the early Church among the Britons and Saxons, from CE 180 to around 800. Books 3 and 4 extend the story from the early English Church among the Saxons and Danes through the Anglo-Normans and stops at the fourteenth century. Foxe was able to expand his account of the early medieval Church so thoroughly owing in large part to the massive manuscript collection of Archbishop Matthew Parker, an avid antiquarian and Anglo-Saxonist. From there, book 5 presents the story of Wyclif in detail, and, significantly, Foxe redates the millennial release of Satan to about 1360, a revision that gives Wyclif's life an apocalyptic prominence it did not possess in the first edition. Books 5 and 6 go on to describe martyrdoms from the reign of Henry IV through Henry VII, concluding with a lengthy account of the Turks as enemies of the true Church. Book 7 likewise reveals Foxe's interest in international as well as national history: he interrupts the account of martyrdoms under Henry VIII in England at 1521, shifting to the story of Martin Luther and his Continental followers, and then describing martyrdoms in Germany, France, Spain, and Italy up to 1561. Book 8 returns to and finishes the martyrdoms under Henry VIII, while book 9 describes the brief historical respite under Edward VI before Mary I's reign of terror, described at dizzying length in books 10, 11, and part of 12. The eyewitness accounts that Foxe gathered in the 1560s play an especially prominent role in these books, not surprisingly. Book 12 finishes with 'the miraculous preservation' of notable English Protestants, including 'the Lady Elizabeth, now Queen of England'.

Telling a history of such scope and in such detail required an unprecedented printing effort on the part of John Day and his assistants. Andrew Pettegree (*ODNB*) estimates that to do the job Day had to operate three presses simultaneous for over a year, and that the cost of press maintenance, labour, ink, and paper would have reached close to £1,000, a staggering amount staked by Day prior to any profit. *Acts and Monuments* sold well, but the financial risk of taking on such a project was considerable, even with the pecuniary protection of lucrative printing monopolies (the ABC, Catechism, and *The Whole Book of Psalms*) that the Crown granted Day (Evenden and Freeman 2002). Here we see the crucial role that entrepreneurial printers like Day played in the dissemination of Protestant literature and propaganda. Foxe even devotes several sections of his book to discussions about the 'divine and miraculous invention of printing', by which 'tongues are known, knowledge groweth, judgment increaseth, books are dispersed, the Scripture is seen, the Doctors be read, stories be opened, times compared, truth discerned, falsehood detected' (707).[3] Yet it is important to note that print served the Catholic opposition with equal force— Patrick Collinson (2002: 378) has observed that for a time during the Elizabethan period the Protestant book trade actually fell behind its Catholic counterpart— and Foxe knew this. Already in the 1563 Preface about the 'utility and profit of this history', Foxe had wearily noted of printed books that 'nowadays the world is pestered not only with a superfluous plenty thereof, but of all other treatises, so that books may rather seem to lack readers, than readers to lack books' (B4ᵛ). It is perhaps not a far cry from this complaint to Edmund Spenser's supremely unsettling account of dangerous books, in *The Faerie Queene*, where the serpent Error vomits out

---

[3] J. King (2001) has further suggested that Foxe, starting in the 1570 edition of his book, deliberately revised his earlier account of William Tyndale's life so as to exaggerate the coincidences between biblical translation, martyrdom, Reformation, and printing.

bookes and papers [...]
With loathly frogs and toades, which eyes did lacke,
And creeping sought way in the weedy gras [...]

(1. 1. 20)

Here, print gushes from theological error rather than suppressing it.

This printing history of *Acts and Monuments* likewise raises the question of authorship. Foxe did the research, gathered the data, wrote the summaries, and crafted the commentary. But the book also reprints vast amounts of primary material. Furthermore, we know that Day's staff would receive new martyrdom accounts during the lengthy process of printing and paste them onto already printed pages: how much control could Foxe have had over the selection and placement of this material? John N. King (2006: 23–5) has suggested that such circumstances oblige us to call Foxe an 'author–compiler' rather than an author. If we resist this suggestion, we may do so out of desire to have a text accountable to a single person, one more available for close reading. On the other hand, Foxe does sometimes lavish attention on his prose, revising it subtly and deliberately from edition to edition. One of my favourite examples comes early in the 1570 edition, when Foxe, replying to the Catholic criticism that the Reformers have blasphemously preferred innovation to English tradition, explains that if earlier generations of Englishmen 'held any thing which receded from the faith and rule of Christ, therein we now remove ourselves from them, because we would not with them remove from the rule of Christ's doctrine' (1570: 3). Clear enough: God's truth trumps even venerable tradition. Yet Foxe's anxiety about the antiquity of the reformed Church (which we will discuss below) compels him to revise this bold statement of historical difference in the 1576 edition, rewriting the above sentence to read, 'we now remove ourselves *not because we would differ* from them, but because we would not with them remove from the rule of Christ's doctrine' (1576: 3; my emphasis). Foxe here tellingly softens his earlier stance, placing the rejection of wanton innovation precisely between the terms of present and past, 'us' and 'them'. The tiny detail resonates with the overriding preoccupation of the story. This kind of attention, at least, is the work of what we think of as an author.

30.2 ANTIQUITY: FROM BRITONS TO SAXONS

'Not because we would differ from them' expresses in brief the challenge confronting Tudor Protestant historical writers. Protestant apologists never thought to defend their Church as an innovation that simply broke from a corrupt past, as rhetorically convenient as such a claim might have been. 'Innovation' was, by and large, a term of abuse. They insisted, instead, that the reformed Church restored elements of the pristine, or 'primitive', Church, which for them meant *primus*, the first. Historical and antiquarian writers such as Foxe, John Bale, John Leland, and Matthew Parker knew that the battle for the true Church was also a battle for antiquity. As Foxe observed pointedly, 'if the things which be first (after the rule of Tertullian) are to be preferred before those that be latter, then is the reading of histories much necessary in the church, to know what went before, and what followed after' (*3ʳ). If Foxe shared with his fellow reformers the wish to demonstrate the priority of the true Church, he also wanted even more than most of them to demonstrate its continuity, to reveal 'the continual descent of the church till this present time' (*5ʳ−v). The reformed Church represented not simply a restoration of the truth for Foxe, but also the triumphant culmination of a long-beleaguered (but always extant) tradition. This sense of continuity spoke to Foxe's skills as a storyteller. The medieval martyrs transform, under his pen, from a heretical minority in history to the heroic representatives of Christ's unbroken community.

The Tudor reformers' search for anteriority and continuity included the question of early Christianity among the Britons and Saxons. On this front they faced an uphill struggle. The 'English' Church had been Catholic for centuries, as English Catholics loved to point out. Thomas Stapleton, a Catholic theologian who left England soon after the accession of Elizabeth, could in his popular *A Fortress of the Faith* (1565) confidently link English identity with the presence of the Roman faith on the island, 'well near a thousand years old, even so old as the faith of us Englishmen', far older than 'the upstart news of Protestants' (1565a: 10ᵛ, 109ᵛ). Catholic anteriority wins out not only in history but also in historiography: in his 1565 English translation of Bede, Stapleton insisted that readers could trust early Catholic historians like Bede, who 'writeth the history of things done [...] in his life time, or in few years before, the memory of them being yet fresh and new', in a way that they could not trust latecomer Protestant historians, who 'report things passed many hundred years before their days' (1565b: A2ᵛ, A3ʳ). Thus, when John Bale wrote in *The New Year's Gift* (1546) that in his nation's medieval period, 'the more part of writers were wholly given to serve Antichrist's affects in the perilous ages of the Church' (1993: 2), the statement was partly defensive and partly concessive. The true Church was hard to find in English history because historians in the past had failed to write about it.

It is significant, then, that of the completely new material in the 1570 edition of *Acts and Monuments* (and in the editions of 1576 and 1583), Foxe included, after book 1's account of the ten persecutions, a brief history of his island from CE 180 to about 800. He did so despite the fact that documentary evidence about this period—the kind of historiography that Foxe loved—was quite scanty, as he himself confessed. Yet Foxe needed to include this segment of national history because it confirmed the completeness of his story and it made the Protestant case for a native Christianity independent of the Church of Rome. The demands of polemical origin made Foxe especially sensitive to the historical transition from Britons to Saxons on the island. By 1570, ecclesiastical historians had already staked out certain partialities: the Protestants liked the Britons, who were mostly gone from the island before the Church of Rome began to exert its pernicious influence, and the Catholics liked the Saxons, who were converted by Roman missionaries (Curran 2002; Kidd 1999: 99–122). Yet Foxe offers a more complicated view of the matter, and his account of this early history provides a telling illustration of his inclinations as a historian and storyteller. He favours, on the one hand, the beleaguered Christian Britons afflicted by pagan and later Romanized Saxons, yet, on the other hand, he cannot locate a firm national origin with the Britons, who are unreliable Christians themselves and whose history is riddled with fable. In other words, he acknowledges the otherness of the past, even when it would suit his polemic purposes to insist on its familiarity.

Foxe starts with the basic question of origin: did England receive the Gospels first from the Church of Rome or from the Greek Church? Initially, Foxe declares that readers need not take precedent as the criterion of validity: even if British Christianity first came from Rome, 'it little availeth the purpose of them which would so have it [...] that we must therefore fetch our Religion from thence still, as from the chief wellhead and fountain of all godliness' (106). For a moment Foxe, hypothetically granting the Catholic claim to antiquity, seems willing to subordinate precedent to well-meaning change. Yet immediately after making this striking statement, he shows it to be irrelevant, since he confidently denies 'that our Christian faith was first derived from Rome, which I may prove by 6 or 7 good conjectural reasons'. And, indeed, after considering these reasons, Foxe concludes: 'By all which conjectures, it may stand probably to be thought, that the Britains, were taught first by the Grecians of the East Church, rather then by the Romans' (106). In effect, Foxe says: even if the Catholics have antiquity on their side, it doesn't matter; though, in fact, we probably have it on our side. We ought to take Foxe's rhetoric in these passages as a microcosm of the Tudor Protestant attitude towards tradition: a theoretical willingness to suspend it that is almost always trumped by a deeper conviction that tradition—what Foxe calls 'the wellhead and fountain'—ultimately holds the truth.

To a considerable extent, Foxe tries to align his nation's well-head with the Britons, especially to the degree that he can distinguish the original Celtic inhabitants from the pagan or Romanized Saxons. In one of his prefatory addresses he says that for 'about the space of four hundred years, Religion remained in Britain uncorrupt, and the word of Christ truly preached, till about the coming of Austen [the missionary Augustine] and of his companions from Rome, many of the said Britain preachers were slain by the Saxons' (*4^r). This 400 years of British Christianity protract into what Foxe elsewhere describes as the second apocalyptic age, or the 'flourishing time of the church' (1). He here conflates the subsequent Saxon invasion with the invasion of Roman missionaries, which cut short this British period of religious peace and purity. In his account of the ten persecutions of the early Church, Foxe again makes a point of highlighting British exceptionalism: 'Where, by the way, is to be noted that this realm of Britain being so christened before, yet never was touched with any other of the nine persecutions, before this tenth persecution of Diocletian and Maximinian' (89). When he reaches the Britons' story proper, in book 2, Foxe repeatedly solicits his readers' sympathy for their sufferings: 'poor Britain, being left naked and destitute on every side' (108); 'the miserable Britains thus were bereaved of their land by the cruel subtlety of the Saxons' (112); 'here began the state of miserable Britain daily more and more to decay, while the idolatrous Saxons prevailed in number and strength against the Christian Britains' (113).

'Idolatrous Saxons' responds, in 1570 and after, to the kind of Catholic historiography we saw with Thomas Stapleton in the 1560s, which took the Saxons as the starting point of England's religious and racial identity.[4] Foxe insists, to the contrary, that the Saxons sought to destroy true religion in a manner that anticipated the damage done by Catholic misinformation. When he describes the depredations of the German invaders, he emphasizes their seemingly deliberate attack on the Britons' Christian institutions: 'they begin to make spoil and havoc of the Britain nation, destroying the Citizens, plucking down Churches, killing up the Priests, burning the Books of the holy Scripture, leaving nothing undone that tyranny could work' (113). Foxe surely intends the Saxons' Bible-burning to recall the efforts of Tudor Catholics in his own time to destroy English translations of the Bible by Protestants such as William Tyndale. The Saxons are, as it were, proto-papists.

It is thus less surprising that Foxe suspends his usual distaste for fable and tells at length the legendary murder of the British lords by Hengist and his Saxon followers, who tricked the British king Vortigern to attend a meeting under the guise of a truce:

This wicked act of the Saxons was done at Almesbury, or at a place called Stonehenge, by the monument of which stones there hanging, it seemeth that the noble Britons there were buried. The fabulous Story of the Welshmen, of bringing these stones from Ireland by Merlin, I pass over. Some stories record that they were slain being bid to a banquet, other do say that it was done at a talk or assembly, where the Saxons came with privy knives contrary to promise made, with the which knives they giving a privy watchword, in their Saxons speech (*neme your sexes*) slew the Britons unarmed: and thus far concerning the history of the Britons.   (108)

This act of treachery marks the transition from Britons to Saxons, from first to second, and, implicitly, from true religion to false. The mention of Anglo-Saxon language here seems to emphasize the foreign quality of Hengist's followers, as invaders from the outside, rather than recalling a native English linguistic heritage. Although Foxe tries to minimize the more outlandish elements of the story ('fabulous story of the Welshmen'), he does allow Stonehenge to stand as a kind of burial place of the British past. Shortly after narrating the massacre, Foxe proceeds to list, with commentary, the Saxon rulers who dominated the island for the next 500 years (110–12). 'And thus far concerning the history of the Britons': the transition seems complete.

But it is not complete. After the list of Saxon kings, Foxe unexpectedly returns to the Britons, reminding us that they were 'not so driven out or expulsed, but that a certain kingdom remained among them [...] The said Britons, moreover, through the valiant acts of their kings, sometimes reigned also in other countries, displacing the Saxons and recovering again their own' (112). This is certainly true, as far as Foxe's

[4] On the effort of Tudor Protestants, including Foxe, to combat the Catholic use of Saxon history, as well as their efforts to co-opt that history, see Robinson (2002).

historical sources go, but it seems an awkward way of organizing his history: first Foxe describes the Britons' defeat, then the Saxons' rule, and then he backs up again to describe the last bit of British resistance. Most surprisingly, Foxe retells the entire story of the Stonehenge massacre, providing all the details of the first telling, including, in the margin, that notorious Saxon watchword 'neme your sexes' (113). Why this odd repetition? In part, it signals Foxe's fascination with this originary crime on British soil, the fall from purity to corruption that marks so much of his history of the true Church. Yet it also signals his inclination to flesh out and complicate the effect of the first version, primarily by adding details that inculpate the Britons in their own destruction. In this second telling, the British king Vortigern's marriage to Rowena, Hengist's daughter, offers an 'example to all ages and countries what it is, first, to let in foreign nations into their dominion, but especially what it is for Princes to join in marriage with infidels' (113). Foxe had briefly mentioned this marriage before (108), but now it represents 'the mother of all this mischief, giving to the Saxons not only strength but also occasion and courage to attempt that which they did'. As Foxe explains it, Hengist uses Vortigern's affection for Rowena to seduce him and the other Britons foolishly to attend the fateful meeting. They are the instruments of their own destruction.

There is not a radical change of tone in this second version: Hengist's men are still 'infidel Saxons' who persecute the 'Christian Britons' (113). But the second telling blurs the clear contrast between good and bad. It reinforces the negative qualities of the Britons, such as residual paganism and barbarism, that Foxe has up to now only briefly mentioned, qualities that plagued other Protestant attempts to forge a native Christianity out of British material (Curran 2002). Foxe had earlier conceded that among the Britons 'the civil governors for the time were then dissolute and careless [...] and so at length they were subdued by the Saxons' (*4^r). He asserts British culpability much more pointedly when he later observes that the Britons ignored the criticisms of their own most famous cleric, Gildas, who 'was laughed to scorn and taken for a false prophet, and a malicious preacher. The Britons with lusty courages, whorish faces, and unrepentant hearts, went forth to sin, and to offend the Lord their God. What followed? God sent in their enemies on every side, and destroyed them, and gave the land to other nations' (32). The Britons never come off quite so badly in Foxe's account of them in book 2, but 'lusty' and 'whorish' participate in the same mix of flawed ethnic character that makes King Vortigern susceptible to the charms of Rowena. Similarly, concerning the Saxons, Foxe follows up an earlier concession—that after the Britons' defeat 'began Christian faith to enter and spring among the Saxons, after a certain Romish sort, yet notwithstanding some what more tolerable, than were the times which after followed' (*4^r)—with admiring accounts of the efforts of the kings Oswald and Edmund to maintain true religion among the Saxons (114). The transition from Briton to Saxon was not quite the slide from purity to corruption that Foxe earlier indicated.

Foxe similarly complicates a crucial moment of violent contact between the two peoples when he describes the notorious Saxon massacre of the British monks at Bangor. Bede (1979, bk 2, ch. 2) related that these monks received a visit from the

Roman missionary Augustine around CE 609, that they were unwilling to comply with his suggested revisions of their devotional practices, and that shortly afterwards a Saxon leader named Æthelfrith (Aedilfrid in Latin) slaughtered them. Augustine was a hot point of religious contention: for Catholics he represented one of the original sources of Roman Christianity on the island, whereas for Protestants he represented the kind of violence the Roman Church would commit against the island's already extant native Christianity. The Protestant apologist John Jewel (1845–50: iv. 779) and his Catholic opponent John Harding had in the 1560s argued in print about the details of the events in Bangor, with Jewel implicating Augustine in the massacre whereas Harding insisted that Augustine had already died before the massacre occurred. In his English translation of Bede, Stapleton (1565b: N3^r) likewise reported Augustine's death prior to the massacre, although Jewel objected that this merely represented creative Catholic editing practices.[5]

In his account, Foxe certainly has no love for the Catholic missionary: he denies that Augustine was dead (119), and he pointedly computes the duration of true Christian faith in early Britain by starting with the death of King Lucius in CE 180 and ending with Augustine's mission (115). The pious monks of Bangor 'all did live with the sweat of their brows and labour of their own hands', whereas Augustine in his initial visit to Bangor comports himself haughtily, 'after the Romish manner' (119). Foxe also explicitly turns the monks into witnesses of the true Church, insisting that when Æthelfrith ordered his men to attack 'the silly unarmed Monks [...] he slew at the same time, *or rather martyred*, 1100' (119; my emphasis). Yet whereas other Protestant historians describe the Roman missionary encouraging Æthelfrith to murder the Bangor monks, Foxe refrains from saying so. Instead, he suggests a shared responsibility:

Of both these parties, the reader may judge what he pleaseth: I can not see but both together were to be blamed [...] First, Austen in this matter can in no wise be excused, who being a monk before, and therefore a scholar and professor of humility, showed so little humility in this assembly [...] Again the Britons were much, or more to blame, who so much neglected their spiritual duty in revenging their temporal injury, that they denied to join unto their helping labour to turn the Idolatrous Saxons to the way of life and salvation.   (119)

Foxe here reconceptualizes the relationship between Britons and Saxons from an opposition between true and false to one of evangelistic duty. The Britons' superior faith obliges them to try to pass on this faith to the as yet unconverted, securing 'the continual descent of the church till this present time', as he put it in one of his prefaces (*5^r–v). Their failure to do this explains Foxe's harsh judgement on their actions here.

The sense of mixed culpability, spiritual backsliding, and Catholic devotionality makes it hard for Foxe to locate the origin of the English Church with either the Britons or the Saxons. He begins book 2, as we saw, by arguing that British

---

[5] 'These last words of Beda, concerning the death of Augustine, are manifestly forged, and have been violently thrust into the text by a guileful parenthesis, by them that since have been ashamed of his cruelty [...]' (Jewel 1845–50: iv. 779).

Christianity came from the Eastern Church, not the Church of Rome, and in this opening he calls the British cleric Gildas 'our countryman' (106). Yet throughout the rest of the book he almost never refers to either the Britons or the Saxons as 'we' or 'us'. When Foxe refers to his island as 'this land (which now we Englishmen call England)' (107), he does not so much insist on the authenticity of the British originals as he acknowledges that authentic origins for the English Church are hard to come by. This distance from the past that Foxe implies in book 2 obliges us to re-evaluate D. R. Woolf's characterization of Foxe as 'a historian preoccupied with sameness and resemblance', for whom the many martyrdoms throughout the ages resolve into the same pattern of persecution (1995: 264). Undeniably, Foxe refuses to entertain the idea that the reformed Church amounts to an innovation, and he believes that the spiritual meaning of all martyrdoms remains the same because the spiritual nature of Christ's Church never changes. But this provides little evidence about Foxe's distinct sensibilities as a historical writer: all Christian martyrologists, at all times, believe likewise. Yet even martyrologists can feel, despite Christ's spiritual continuity through time, the effects of historical change that make it difficult to tell a story from beginning to present. The Britons' failings do serve as an analogy for modern English failings, yet they are still not quite 'us', and Foxe is looking for precisely 'us' in his account of the early history of his island. He has a hard time finding it. Attempting to impose continuity over historical difference, Foxe concedes the challenge of matching then up to now, of finding a historical well-head and fountain for the English Church.

30.3 THE AFFECT OF HISTORY

Whatever his ambivalence about the link between the ancient Britons and modern England, Foxe does seek to enlist them as members of the true Church when he calls them 'martyrs'. Their status as witnesses to Christ's dispensation confirms the visible presence of this Church throughout history. In the early parts of his book Foxe seeks to secure antiquity for the Church; in the later parts he seeks to demonstrate its presence in contemporary times through the elaborate descriptions of the martyrs' suffering. The intensity of this suffering, ostensibly guaranteed by eyewitnesses, is crucial to Foxe's demonstration. The Elizabethans were accustomed to seeing public exhibitions of pain. Officials would have the bodies of criminals cut open with knives. Thieves, when hanged, did not usually die of a broken neck but slowly suffocated before a crowd of onlookers. Nonetheless, English people did experience horror at the sight of bodies burned to death. The accounts in *Acts and Monuments* of the spectators' expressions of revulsion can be partly corroborated by other sources; they are not purely the propagandistic invention of Foxe, even if he uses the revulsion for rhetorical purposes. The affective power of the suffering could even reach across the religious divide: a letter by a Catholic man named 'J.A.' expresses admiration for Thomas Cranmer's stoicism at the fire, calling him an 'Image of sorrow'—though J.A. laments that the former archbishop died for a 'pernicious error' (Monta 2005: 9). The Jesuit Robert Southwell's *Epistle of Comfort* (1587) likewise acknowledges the emotional pull of the Marian martyrs, but ascribes it to despair, which makes the heretics seem as if they possessed 'bodies of steel, that felt no pain or torment' (184^v).

Of course, such a claim speaks directly to the anxiety, for both Protestants and Catholics, that the painful public execution of their enemies might win converts to their enemies' religious persuasion. Better, then, to refer to heretical or papist bodies as *steel*, which has no feelings, so one cannot identify with its pain. This raises one of the central questions for *Acts and Monuments*: what does pain *mean*? Modern theories of suffering and torture have not proved very useful: in Foxe, the public exhibition of pain does not, *pace* Michel Foucault (1979), affirm the early modern power of governing authorities (quite the contrary), and the act of torture does not, *pace* Elaine Scarry (1985), dismantle the martyrs' sense of self. Foxe scholars have thus tried to account for pain in terms of the book's historical context and relevant religious traditions.[6] Yet pain, by its phenomenological nature, remains difficult to interpret with certainty. This is why Ludwig Wittgenstein selected pain as his favourite example of the disjunction between language and sensation: 'Misleading parallel: the expression of pain is a cry—the expression of thought, a proposition [...] I have seen a person in a discussion on this subject strike himself on the breast and say: "But surely another person can't have *this* pain!"' (1958: §§317, 253). The seemingly private nature of pain makes it hard to identify a logically consistent public consensus about the sensation. At the same time, Wittgenstein is careful to concede the obviousness of pain: 'Yet we go on wanting to say: "Pain is pain—whether *he* has it, or *I* have it" [...] Just try—in a real case—to doubt someone else's fear or pain' (§§351, 303).

This is certainly not the only way to think about pain, but the Wittgensteinian account—which makes pain phenomenologically obvious and semiotically elusive—has important affinities with the Tudor representation of the suffering of martyrs, on both the Protestant and the Catholic side. Foxe wrote his martyrology, as Susannah Brietz Monta (2005) has ably demonstrated, with a keen awareness of what his Catholic opponents were saying about *their* martyrs. This polemical scenario meant that, to a degree unprecedented in the history of Christian martyrology, the resolve to die for the sake of Christ's Church could just as easily be taken as apostate despair. The meaning of pain was not self-evident: it needed interpretation, which is to say that for Foxe pain became a question of *literary* convention. Once again, polemical exigencies called upon Foxe's skills as a storyteller.

These skills appear throughout the various segments of the martyr stories, which generally follow a three-part structure: investigation by Catholic authorities leading to arrest; interrogation in prison; and, finally, agonizing death by fire. Foxe is usually

---

[6] See in particular Collinson (1983); Knott (1996); Mueller (1997*a*); Marshall (2002: 85–105).

faithful to the archival or eyewitness record, such as he has; indeed, the 1570 edition reins in some of the more egregious anti-Catholic abuse found in the 1563 edition in order to approximate a tone of neutral, accurate reporting. Yet even in the later editions he does not scruple to employ what John N. King has called an 'artful literary hand' (1997: 14) in his organization of information (see also Collinson 1997). In the case of the private conversation between bishops Ridley and Latimer before their executions, Foxe uses the lack of information to convey a sense of poignant intimacy: 'What they said, I can learn of no man' (1769). Such novelistic moments also sometimes occur when the narrative suggests an ambiguity about how a martyr *manages* the experience of pain. In the course of describing the especially horrific burning of John Hooper—three separate fires were started before he finally died—Foxe emphasizes the former bishop's calm stoicism: 'he prayed, saying mildly and not very loud (but as one without pains), O Jesus the son of David have mercy upon me, and receive my soul'. But, as the ordeal wears on, Foxe lets Hooper register the agony: 'After the second [fire] was spent, he did wipe both his eyes with his hands, and beholding the people, he said with an indifferent loud voice: For God's love (good people) let me have more fire. And all this while his nether parts did burn' (1511, misnumbered as 1577). The shift in volume from 'not very loud' to 'indifferent loud' reveal Foxe's effort to calibrate a response somewhere between stone-like insensitivity and irresolute susceptibility to pain.

Yet Foxe faces his greatest challenge in registering the *meaning* of pain as he describes the *fact* of pain suffered by his martyrs. The fisherman Rawlins White, preparing to be burned in Wales in 1555, confides to a friend that he is not confident about weathering the agony of the fire, and so asks this friend, 'therefore I pray you when you see me any thing tempted, hold your finger up to me, and I trust I shall remember myself' (1558). 'Remembering oneself' is precisely what the pain of the fire threatens to prevent: it represents the risk that physical agony will drown out the purpose of martyrdom, which is to demonstrate a deliberate sacrifice for the sake of Christ's true Church. Wild screams of agony are hard to distinguish from the despair of the reprobate—precisely the point of Catholic commentators—whereas complete indifference to the fire suggests an anti-dramatic insensitivity, akin to the steel bodies of which Southwell complained. How can Foxe make this pain signify, by contrast, the deliberate resolve of the faithful in the face of persecution? He does so by adding to (or at least emphasizing within) many of the death scenes what we might call the 'visible seal' of martyrdom. The visible seal takes many forms: a gesture of a martyr at the stake, an unexpected utterance, or a supernatural sign from God. This seal surfaces in addition to or even despite the tortured suffering of the martyr, and as such concedes that naked pain remains partly opaque: it requires literary convention to make it signify in the way Foxe wishes.

Perhaps the most common example of the visible seal is the moment when the martyr, assumed dead and gone by the crowd, suddenly claps his hands or shouts a final praise to Jesus. Such gestures confirm that pain has not trumped purpose: suffering remains merely instrumental to what the martyr intended to demonstrate, namely, that burning to death is a small price to pay for membership among Christ's elect—indeed, such a death may be a positive privilege. This is precisely the issue about which Thomas Haukes's friends, on the occasion of his burning, want assurance:

the same again, being feared with the sharpness of the punishment which he was going to, privily desired that in the middest of the flame he would show them some token, if he could, whereby they might be more certain whether the pain of such burning were so great, that a man might not therein keep his mind quiet and patient. Which thing he promised them to do, and so secretly between them it was agreed, that if the rage of the pain were tolerable and might be suffered, then he should lift up his hands above his head toward heaven before he gave up the ghost.   (1592)

In effect, Haukes's friends face a Wittgensteinian problem: 'If one has to imagine someone else's pain on the model of one's own, this is none too easy a thing to do: for I have to imagine pain which I *do not feel* on the model of the pain which I *do feel*' (1958: §302). In Foxe, the 'token' that will ideally make possible qualitative comparisons of pain is determined 'secretly between them': those in the know can interpret pain in a way that others cannot, although these others will have some apprehension of what transpires. Such is the effect of Haukes's final death gesture:

so that now all men thought certainly he had been gone, suddenly and contrary to all expectation, the blessed servant of God, being mindful of his promise afore made, reached up his hands burning on a light fire (which was marvellous to behold) over his head to the living God, and with great rejoicing, as seemed, struck or clapped them three times together. At the sight whereof there followed such applause and outcry of the people, and especially of them which understood the matter.   (1592–3)

Haukes remains 'mindful' of his promise to show his friends a token—much as Rawlins White had hoped to 'remember' himself—and so assures that pain evinces rather than overwhelms the resolve of the martyr. Everyone in the crowd can see this, but especially Haukes's friends, a group that possesses special knowledge about the meaning of suffering.[7] *Acts and Monuments* invites its sympathetic readers to join this group.

Haukes claps his hands 'suddenly and contrary to all expectation'. It is precisely the surprise of the gesture, surprising no matter how many times it happens in the narrative, that testifies to the genuine nature of the cause. With this gesture, the martyr steps out of the somatic script of physical agony and enacts extemporaneous authenticity. When the crowd at George Marsh's burning had 'supposed no less but he had been dead, notwithstanding suddenly he spread abroad his arms, saying: father of heaven have mercy upon me [...] Upon this, many of the people said that he was a martyr, and died marvellous patiently and godly' (1576). The clerk Robert Smith, 'being well nigh half burnt, and all black with fire, clustered together as in a lump like a black coal, all men thinking him for dead, suddenly rose up right before the people, lifting up the stumps of his arms, and clapping the same together, declaring a rejoicing heart unto them' (1701). The same with the tailor, William Coberley, who

---

[7] On this point, see the excellent discussion in Monta (2005: 60).

'when all they thought he had been dead, suddenly he rose right up with his body again' (1895), and the schoolmaster Julins Palmer, whom the crowd 'judged already to have given up the ghost', when 'suddenly Palmer, as a man waked out of sleep, moved his tongue and jaws, and was heard to pronounce this word Jesu' (1940). These death gestures are not neutral: they signify the directing presence of God that makes the victim seem like a martyr rather than an oblivious carcass. Foxe at times explicitly argues that such visible seals are indisputable, even to hostile viewers. When the fire leaves the crisped body of linen weaver Christopher Wade with arms held up as if in prayer, Foxe comments, 'this sign did God show upon him, whereby his very enemies might perceive, that God had according to his prayer, showed such a token upon him, even to their shame and confusion' (1680).

Even when the visible seal takes the form of shouts and gestures, then, Foxe implies that such moments of agency come from the inspiration of God. In other cases Foxe reports the occurrence of explicitly supernatural signs, not scrupling to employ the kind of miraculous visitation that he elsewhere criticizes in Catholic martyrology. He reported at length the 1555 burning of the preacher Robert Samuel in the 1563 edition of *Acts and Monuments*, but in subsequent editions he added this: 'The report goeth among some that were there present, and saw him burn, that his body in burning did shine as bright and white as new tried silver in the eyes of them that stood by: as I am informed by some which were there, and did behold the sight' (1704). In some places, God grants a visible seal at the request of the martyrs themselves, to ensure that their deaths be interpreted properly, as Foxe instances in the 1563 edition:

Here is to be noted by the way amongst these that suffered at Bainford, one there was of the said company, who at their burning desired of God some token to be given, where by the people might know that they died in the right. After coming to the place of execution, and being in the fire, there appeared in him that so prayed, in his breast, a marvellous white cross, as white as the paper, the breadth whereof extended from the one shoulder to the other, the length being as much as the breadth. The compass thereof in every place was a broad as a hand. This cross appeared so long, till he fell down flat to the fire.   (1682, misnumbered as 1670)

This Bainford martyr reveals his desire to die a good death, but also reveals his awareness of the polemical milieu that renders his suffering open to interpretation. The visible seal works to control such interpretation among the spectators at Bainford and the readers of Foxe's book. Yet such seals also risk rhetorical overreaching: in 1566 the Catholic controversialist Nicholas Harpsfield harshly attacked this scene in the narrative as an improbable fabrication (962), and Foxe dropped it in subsequent editions of *Acts and Monuments*. The visible seal confirms belief in the authenticity of the martyrdom, but in order to do so the seal must itself be believable.

Foxe knows that literary devices such as visible seals will only persuade so far. They face the same limitation that Philip Sidney assigns to tragedy, which has the capacity to move to tears a tyrant like Alexander Pheraeus, 'who without all pity had murdered infinite numbers', but which cannot mitigate his tyranny, only compel him to leave the theatre before the play 'might mollify his hardened heart' (1985: 46). Foxe writes with an awareness that his book has audiences who will stop reading before their hearts are mollified, who will always interpret death agony as despair rather than as spiritual witnessing. The best Foxe can do is to register that pain requires literary coding because otherwise it remains either too obscure or too susceptible to hostile interpretation. He tries to prevent the martyrs' pain from slipping into these extremes, attempting to manifest the invisible Church of the saints within the visible Church through a carefully calibrated presentation of human suffering.

Primary Works

Bale, John (1993), *The New Year's Gift*, in *John Leland's Itinerary*, ed. J. Chandler (Dover, NH: Sutton).

Bede (1979), *Historia Ecclesiastica gentis Anglorum*, ed. and trans. J. E. King (Cambridge, MA: Harvard University Press).

Foxe, John (1563), *Actes and Monuments*.

—— (1570), *Actes and Monuments*.

—— (1576), *Actes and Monuments*.

—— (1583), *Actes and Monuments*.

Harpsfield, Nicholas (1566), *Dialogi sex contra summi pontificatus, monastica vitae, sanctorum sacrarum imaginum oppugnatores et pseudomartyrs* (Antwerp).

Jewel, John (1845–50), *Works of John Jewel*, ed. J. Ayre, Parker Society Publications, 23–6, 4 vols (Cambridge: Cambridge University Press for the Parker Society).

Sidney, Philip (1985), *An Apology for Poetry*, ed. F. G. Robinson (New York: Macmillan).

Southwell, Robert (1587), *Epistle of Comfort*.

Spenser, Edmund (2001), *The Faerie Queene*, ed. A. C. Hamilton (New York: Longman).

Stapleton, Thomas (1565a), *A Fortress of the Faith* (Antwerp).

—— (1565b), *The History of the Church of England* (Antwerp).

Wittgenstein, Ludwig (1958), *Philosophical Investigations*, trans. G. E. M. Anscombe (New York: Macmillan).

CHAPTER 31

TRAGICAL HISTORIES, TRAGICAL TALES

JONATHAN GIBSON

In Tudor literature, 'tragical' events come in a variety of shapes and sizes. The words 'tragical', 'tragic', and 'tragedy' were often employed quite loosely (much as in casual modern usage) to refer simply to grim events involving such things as extreme violence and sudden death.[1] The early part of the reign of Elizabeth I saw the publication of two very important collections of 'tragical' narratives, each dealing with a different type of event squarely planted in the public realm of religious and political change. Foxe's *Book of Martyrs* (1563), in prose, chronicled the deaths of martyrs for the Protestant faith, while *A Mirror for Magistrates* (1559), in verse, narrated the downfall of 'unfortunate princes'. The 'tragical histories' described in this chapter involve events of a third type: not martyrdoms, not political tragedy on the model of Boccaccio's *De casibus virorum illustrium*. The lurid happenings they narrate are overwhelmingly motivated by sexual desire: rapes; suicides of rape victims; accidental deaths of young lovers; murders of love rivals—or of people wrongly perceived to be love rivals; murders of unfaithful lovers—or of lovers erroneously thought to be unfaithful; violent revenges for sexual assaults; violence against sexually promiscuous family members; murders undertaken to keep illicit relationships secret.

---

[1] There seems to have been an expectation that 'tragedies' on stage should involve people of high status brought low by terrible events (see Doran 1954: 101–11). This was, however, far less of a requirement for non-dramatic 'tragedies' or 'tragical tales': rarely is it suggested that a 'tragical' event outside a play should necessarily have cosmic resonance or tick any of the Aristotelian boxes that some post-Enlightenment uses of the word 'tragic' seem to require.

Stories of this type can be found in a variety of literary contexts. The genre of—or, more precisely perhaps, the 'generic space' opened up by—the early Elizabethan 'tragical history' was hospitable to the valuable material provided, for example, by Ovid's *Metamorphoses* and Livy's *Histories*; Plutarch, Heliodorus, and Seneca were also frequently mined classical sources. It was built more substantively, however, out of one particular element in the late medieval genre of the Italian *novella*.[2] Many collections of *novelle* (short, usually fairly realistic prose narratives) appeared in the sixteenth century, distant descendants of the genre's originary classic, Giovanni Boccaccio's *Decameron* (1353). Italian *novelle* are of many different types: some are simple joky stories; some are bawdy, like medieval *fabliaux*. Others are romantic escapades; still others satirize clerical abuses and pomposity. The basis for the Elizabethan tragical history was a different type of narrative that took its cue from the stories of the *Decameron*'s fourth day: tales about people whose love affairs ended in disaster. Other texts by Boccaccio provided models too: the master of ceremonies for the fourth day, for example, Filostrato ('the man struck down by love'), shares his name with Boccaccio's tragical story of a faithless woman *Il filostrato* (1341). In turn, *Il filostrato* inspired Chaucer's late fourteenth-century masterpiece *Troilus and Criseyde*, a key influence on the early Elizabethan tragical history.

But tales of sexual violence were particularly strongly associated with the work of Matteo Bandello (1480–1562), an Italian Dominican friar whose *Novelle* were published in four volumes (the first three in 1554, the fourth in 1573).[3] England in the 1560s saw a flurry of tragical tales of this type indebted both to Bandello and to other sources, including, as well as the *Decameron*, more recent works in the *novella* tradition such as the Italian *Hecatomitthi* (1565) of Giovambattista Giraldi (generally known as Cinthio) and the French *Heptaméron* of Marguerite de Navarre.[4] Part of a wider pattern of translations of Italian secular literature, these texts excited considerable hostility. Lurid 'Italianate' stories were perceived as morally debilitating, with their foreign, Catholic provenance at the heart of the problem. The best-known attack was mounted by Roger Ascham in his educational treatise *The Schoolmaster* (1570). Ascham denounced certain 'fond books, of late translated out of Italian into English' as 'enticing men to ill-living'—and popery (1967: 67).

The main objects of Ascham's fury were two substantial story collections, each of which had provided English readers of the 1560s with violent and lascivious tales, many of them derived ultimately from Bandello: William Painter's *Palace of Pleasure* and Geoffrey Fenton's *Certain Tragical Discourses*. An irony underlies the anti-Italian moral panic of writers such as Ascham, however, as Painter's and Fenton's books were not as 'Italianate' as they appeared. The versions of Bandello's tragical tales offered by both writers were not translated directly from the Italian, but filtered through the

---

[2] For a colourful survey of the genre and its deployment in English literature, see Kirkpatrick (1995, ch. 6).

[3] For an Italian text, see Bandello (1966). English translations of most of the *novelle* can be found in Bandello (1890).

[4] Previous translations of Italian *novelle* and similar narratives, by, for example, Chaucer, Lydgate, and William Walter, had focused primarily on Boccaccio.

very considerable revisions made to Bandello's work by his French translators. Not only that—the very impression that Bandello's narratives predominantly consisted of lurid tales of sexual violence seems to have been the creation of Bandello's first French translator, Pierre Boiastuau, who published his versions of six tales of this sort under the influential title *Histoires tragiques* in 1559.[5] Further, broadly similar, selections of stories translated from Bandello were produced by Boiastuau's successor François Belleforest. Belleforest co-opted Boiastuau's title in a series of volumes, beginning with a first instalment which appeared, like Boiastuau's, in 1559.[6] Not all of Boiastuau's and Belleforest's stories seem 'tragic' to a modern reader: indeed, the first and last stories in the first volume of the *Histoires tragiques* have happy endings. The common thread seems to be not so much 'tragic' denouements as the occurrence at some point in the narrative of extreme events excited by sexual passion.[7]

Bandello's stories are blunt and straightforward; they are also, Bandello insists, true. Each narrative is introduced by a letter addressed by Bandello to a personal acquaintance—usually a writer, a courtier, or an aristocrat—reminiscing about the milieu (usually courtly) in which Bandello first heard the tale that he is now writing down. Bandello led a peripatetic life, so the locations conjured up in his dedicatory letters range across a wide variety of courts and households in Italy and France. Each story is given by Bandello in the voice of the supposed original teller, complete with local references and asides to the original listeners (sometimes including Bandello himself). This structure differs from that of many other *novella* collections, from the *Decameron* onwards, which often framed their stories within an overarching narrative (a *cornice*: 'frame') involving debates and conversations among a single group of people.

Critics sometimes describe Bandello's stories as 'amoral'. This does not seem quite accurate. Most of Bandello's *novelle* are set in the context of a moral discussion of some sort, if, often as not, very brief: opinions about the morality of the action of the story are offered both in the dedicatory letters and in the narrative itself. The moral framework, however—unlike that in most other *novella* collections—is discontinuous: it changes with every new *novella*. Each new story brings with it a new occasion, a new narrator, a new set of moral issues. The fact that the morals of some stories seem to contradict those of others thus does not seem too disturbing to a modern reader. Bandello's French translators, though, were clearly troubled by such relativism. They removed the Italian text's discontinuous *cornici*, establishing in their place no overarching narrative framework outside the translators' own moral certainties. The dedicatory epistles are removed and each story introduced instead by a short consideration (or *sommaire*) of the moral principles supposedly at issue in it. The stories thus become *exempla* of moral positions laid down by Boiastuau

[5] René Pruvost makes the point that Bandello's collection contained many other types of story (1937: 24).

[6] For the complicated textual history, see Belleforest (1948: 46–50).

[7] Boiastuau himself is aware of this anomaly, and casually dismisses it (1977: 7).

and Belleforest, rather than descriptions of free-standing events about which various people can have various opinions.

Strikingly, the French writers retain Bandello's emphasis on the factual basis of the stories ('histoires' in the title of their collections does not simply mean 'narratives'), though with a very different emphasis. Boiastuau's and Belleforest's prefatory materials make it clear that they are treating their Bandellian source material as moralized history: factually grounded and ethically valuable texts that will provide their readers with examples of good behaviour to emulate and bad behaviour to avoid.[8] Both translators are clearly operating within what D. R. Woolf has called 'the 'Ciceronian tradition' of history as a morally educative 'light of truth" (1990: 10). This was an approach which did not stint at interpolating, for ethically productive effect, newly minted speeches into 'historical' narrative, or at altering its events.[9] Accordingly, first Boiastuau, and later (and more thoroughgoingly) Belleforest, insert newly written speeches, letters, and other forms of text in the voice of the stories' principal characters.[10] They also freely add moral commentary and alter the events originally described by Bandello. In describing his practice in this regard, Belleforest is almost gleeful: he is delighted to have planted his conquering flag on the 'somewhat coarse' texts of his original, in a process he stresses is one of 'embellishment' rather than 'translation'.[11]

Painter's and Fenton's English translations from Boiastuau and Belleforest appeared chronologically very close together. The first volume of Painter's Palace of Pleasure was printed in 1566. Hot on its heels, the following year, came Fenton's Certain Tragical Discourses, alongside the second volume of Painter's Palace. Painter translated tales of many different types from many different sources, both ancient and modern, Boiastuau and Belleforest among them—sixty tales in his first volume; thirty-four in the second; five more in the augmented edition of the first volume that appeared in 1575.[12] Fenton translated just thirteen tales, all from Belleforest (five from Belleforest's first volume and eight from the second), but at much greater length. His choice of texts—Belleforest rather than Boiastuau—was presumably influenced by the fact that

---

[8] Thus, in his first volume of translations, Belleforest states that he finds Bandello's original worthwhile for 'the truth of the story' and 'the fruit it yields'. He says he has selected the stories which seem 'more truthful' and which can most help 'the education of the youth of today' (Boiastuau and Belleforest 1578: T8^r).

[9] 'When the historian spoke of the "truth" of histories, he meant their moral as much as their factual verity; he never had in mind the kind of precise, literal truth denoted in the ninenteenth century by Ranke's famous phrase "the past as it actually happened" ' (Woolf 1990: 12). For a discussion of these issues in relation to Elizabethan fiction, see W. Nelson (1973).

[10] Demonstrating thereby their culture's obsession with matching off-the-peg rhetorical set pieces to specific occasions. Hutson's important analysis of this process—focusing on Painter and Fenton rather than their French sources—relates it to a 'humanistic textualisation of social agency' (1994: 135), which she sees as entailing anxiety about the power of rhetoric to deform human relationships. The speech-acts Belleforest added to his Histoires tragiques were siphoned off as models for imitation in a 'treasury' published in Paris in 1581.

[11] Boiastuau and Belleforest (1578: T8^r). Belleforest has, he says, 'enriched [Bandello's originals] with maxims and stories, speeches, and letters, as the situation seemed to me to demand'.

[12] For Painter's sources, see Painter (1566: 3¶2^v; 1567: 3*2^v) and Bush (1924).

Painter had already, in his first volume, published all but one of the stories translated by Boiastuau. On the other hand, Painter's second volume contains four tales that overlap with Fenton.[13]

The approach Painter and Fenton take to their material is the same as Boiastuau's and Belleforest's. There is no overarching frame narrative in either collection, and the emphasis in Painter's and Fenton's prefatory materials, as in the French texts, is on the stories' value as morally uplifting history. Although customarily discussed by modern critics under the rubric 'Elizabethan Prose Fiction', both Fenton and Painter stress that their works are emphatically *not* fictional. The prefatory materials to their collections attempt to situate them in broadly the same context as Foxe's *Book of Martyrs* and *A Mirror for Magistrates*: as factual and morally valuable 'history'. Their (unsuccessful) aim is clearly to pre-empt attacks such as Ascham's. Both translators distinguish their historical material from 'feigned' or fictitious material: 'fained fables' (Painter 1566: 3¶2ʳ), or 'the fained tales of Poets' (Fenton 1567: *3ʳ). Painter, he claims in the dedication of his first volume to Ambrose Dudley, Earl of Warwick, had originally intended to write a work entirely consisting of translations from the Roman historian Livy: the decision to include translations of modern works was taken at a later stage (Fenton 1567: *2ᵛ–*3ʳ). Fenton's dedication to Mary Sidney, *née* Dudley (Philip Sidney's mother), meanwhile, praises history as constituting 'the onely and true tables, wheron are drawne in perfect colours, the vertues and vices of every condition of man'. Both translators attempt to give a systematized account of the lessons to be learnt from their fiction. In both of his volumes, Painter provides a long list of tales with appended morals (1566: 2¶3ᵛ–3¶1ʳ; 1567: 3*1ʳ–3*2ʳ). Fenton, meanwhile, rattles through every calling of life, allocating each moral lessons from his stories (*2ᵛ). Painter claims that his stories are 'profitable' because they show 'what glorie, honor, and preferment ech man attayneth by good desert' and 'the tragicall endes of them that unhappily doe attempt practises vicious and horrible' (2¶3ᵛ).

The programme laid out by all four writers—Boiastuau, Belleforest, Painter, and Fenton—seems coherent. It is possible to imagine stories—even 'tragical histories' involving extreme violence—that might plausibly carry moral lessons of the sort the translators claim they are purveying. Yet throughout these story collections there is no sense of moral stability: instead, chaos reigns. This is largely the result of a confused approach to 'love', the motive force behind the plot of most tragical histories. As R. W. Maslen writes, in connection specifically with Fenton's *Tragical Discourses*, 'all Fenton's stories without exception take love as the central topic, and the one certain conclusion they reach is that love always and everywhere resists the rigid moral controls imposed on it by the responsible historian' (1997: 92). Love is said sometimes to be good (akin to a refining, Platonic force); sometimes to be bad. The extent to which lust is bad is uncertain. The basis for the distinction between the two different types seems to be that good love involves the wish to get married, while bad love is

---

[13] For chapter and verse, see Pruvost (1937: 1–2). Pruvost's book, the standard treatment of Bandello and English literature, is an indispensable—and under-cited—work of scholarship.

more opportunistic and short-term. When a man woos someone lower in the social scale than himself, it generally means his intentions are not honourable. Often the narrator will assert that love should be resisted; but equally often he suggests that a particular heroine is so beautiful that anyone—a saint, for example—would have fallen in love with her.

These sorts of inconsistency originate in Bandello's *Novelle*. There, however, they can be contained within the discontinuous *cornici* created by Bandello's dedicatory epistles—the specific contexts in which individual stories were supposedly originally told. Boiastuau's and Belleforest's attempts to flatten out these discontinuities into a single moral landscape (and, following them, Painter's and Fenton's) simply make the different and complex moral implications of different stories more salient and awkward.

Boiastuau's and Belleforest's additions to their Bandellian sources make matters worse. Interpolated speeches tend to follow quite stereotyped patterns: complaints by male and female lovers; love letters; laments on parting; speeches of accusation and suicide. The problem is that the interpolated speech-acts tend to be cut from similar cloth, whatever the detailed circumstances of the story. A vicious would-be rapist will thus protest his love in identical terms to a timid young lover dreaming of marriage. Both might, for example, point to their physical suffering as a pressing reason for a lady to take pity on them and relent; both might offer service implicitly or explicitly demanding reward, appealing to their lady's better nature; both might use mediators and write letters. The rhetoric of love used by good and evil characters is identical. The frequent moralizing comments added by Boiastuau and Belleforest to their source material do not help either, as these moral points are generally tied to specific moments in the text and often do not combine together into a coherent single point of view. (Sometimes, indeed, they reflect the divergent opinions of different individuals in Bandello's original.) It is a striking feature of these Bandellian narratives, too, that the speech-acts interpolated by Boiastuau and Belleforest often seem nugatory or beside the point. Most of them either fail in their attempt at persuasion or are not intended to persuade in the first place, being isolated, self-defeating complaints.

Painter and Fenton approached their bizarre inheritance from Boiastuau and Belleforest in distinct ways. While Painter experimented with giving relative autonomy to female agency and sexuality, Fenton took the opposite course, in a story collection that emphasizes repression and control.

Painter's work is marked by a particular interest in power relationships. In his first volume, a major theme is resistance to tyranny, inflected by his project's starting point in the writings of the republican historian Livy.[14] The 'cruell actes and tiranny' of 'great princes' (Painter 1566: *3^v) narrated by Painter often involve sexual violence against women: the stories of Lucrece and of Appius and Virginia are both from Livy (see Hackett 2000: 34). Painter's first volume also contains six stories translated from

---

[14]   See Hadfield (1998: 147–62). Hadfield goes on to hypothesize that Painter's *novella* translations were 'designed to dilute and disguise [Painter's] original [republican] purposes' (154).

Boiastuau's and Belleforest's reworkings of Bandello. Three involve cruel punishments inflicted on wives by husbands, and another concerns the savage murder of a faithless lover by his mistress. Following these tales—and uniquely in his collection—Painter comments that, after so much gloom, the reader needs a break, and promises his next tales will involve 'pleasaunt devises and disportes' (1566: 3V2ᵛ). Not all of the stories that follow are 'pleasaunte', particularly those in the penultimate section of the book, taken from Marguerite de Navarre's *Heptaméron*, where, for example, two of the stories describe vicious punishments of women taken in adultery.

Painter, whose second book opens with a section on the Amazons (1567: A1ʳ–B1ʳ) and contains a plethora of heroic female figures, is sometimes thought by critics to be particularly sympathetic to women.[15] His proto-feminism does not, however, extend as far as censoring the patriarchal adjustments made by Bandello's French translators to stories which in Italian had valorized female independence. The story of the Duchess of Malfi, for example, opens in its Bandellian form (Bandello 1966: i, story 26) with a number of comments sympathetic to the plight of the Duchess, killed at her family's orders for marrying a servant. There are attacks on the brutality with which men punish women for doing as they please, and on the double standard which, objecting to the Duchess's marriage, sees nothing wrong with marriages between noblemen and social inferiors. In Belleforest (1948: 130–55), by contrast, and also in Painter (1567, story 23), all this material is replaced by a passage highlighting the need for those of high rank—in particular, women—to behave modestly.[16] That Painter could have translated directly from Bandello is shown by the fact that five of his stories set in ancient Greece and Rome were taken from Bandello's versions, in Italian.[17]

Fenton interpolates into his stories one particular type of aside, about which he is very self-conscious: an address to parents, highlighting the importance of keeping daughters under lock and key. This practice—close to being a nervous tic—is symptomatic of him, as his book is shot through with what seems to be an almost hysterical need to keep in check the tricksiness of his tragical histories—and, in particular, female sexuality. The need to raise barriers against immorality perhaps also explains Fenton's verbosity. His book contains only thirteen stories—yet they are spun out to immense length, Fenton adding—in much the same way as Boiastuau and Belleforest—new speech-acts, passages of heavy moralization, and short extra phrases and images. He will often provide an exordium to open a speech consisting in Belleforest of a simple generalization on a moral theme. And, throughout, his fervent Protestantism is on view in plentiful religious additions. What is striking about all these interventions is their fundamentally static nature. Rather than extending or complicating the meaning of Belleforest's sentences, Fenton's additions have a habit of simply fitting in with them—acts of politeness or keeping in keeping rather than active supplementation.

[15] See C. Lucas (1989: 40). Cf. Kirkpatrick's account (1995: 243) of Painter's sensitive response to Boccaccio's Ghismonda.

[16] For more detail, see Kirkpatrick (1995: 249–50).

[17] Stories 4, 5, 7, 9, and 10 in Painter (1567).

The contrast between Fenton's tangled and clotted sentences and Painter's swiftly moving and lucid prose—barely deviating from its source material—is striking.

At the centre of Fenton's book—seventh out of thirteen stories—like a malevolent spider, is Blanche Maria, the Countess of Celant, heroine of a story also found, in a rendering much closer to Belleforest's, in Painter. Kept chastely within his house in Milan by her first husband, Ermes, Blanche Maria runs riot after his death. Two men court her simultaneously; in the end, she marries the Count of Celant, who promises her greater liberty than she enjoyed in her first marriage. When the Count reneges on his promise, the Countess runs off to Pavia, where she takes many lovers, including Ardizzino Valperga, Earl of Massino, usurped in the Countess's affections by his friend Roberto Sanseverino, Earl of Gaiazzo. When the rejected Valperga slanders the Countess, she attempts, without success, to persuade Gaiazzo to murder his friend. Gaiazzo in turn having been rejected, the Countess takes up again with Valperga—and promptly reverses her plot, asking Valperga to kill Gaiazzo. She is again unsuccessful, and when Valperga leaves (telling all to Gaiazzo), she moves to Pavia and takes as her new lover a naive Spanish captain, Don Pietro. Don Pietro agrees to undertake the assassination of both Valperga and Gaiazzo and, with the help of twenty of his men, manages to kill Valperga. He is, however, captured before he can kill Gaiazzo and implicates Blanche Maria. The Countess ends her life on the headsman's block.

Many of the changes Fenton makes to his French source can be read as vain attempts either to keep Blanche Maria under restraint, or to emphasize her depravity. Fenton is supersensitive to the physical details of Blanche Maria's seductions. His added material sharpens the focus of the narrative on her 'filthy' behaviour. Much of it involves the elaboration of descriptions of the Countess's self-display—an obvious way of highlighting the need to keep her in check. Fenton imagines with some vividness the places in which the Countess's libidinous behaviour has taken place. For example, in material added to Belleforest's text, he visualizes her returning to 'Casalia' (Casale) after her marriage and setting out her stall: 'glauncing uppon every one oute of the windowe, kepinge privat banquettes in the nighte with a haunte of masquers with covered face, and on the daye, sittinge at her gate as a stale, to allure a staye of suche as passed by the stretes' (S5^r). The Countess's physical appearance is also important to Fenton—he sees it as more instrumental in Blanche Maria's depravities than do either Belleforest or Painter. Blanche Maria is described as 'quite pretty but wanton, alert and rather too lively' by Belleforest (289) and, in a close translation, 'indifferent fair, but in behavior lively and pleasant' by Painter (3D1^r). Fenton, unlike Painter and Belleforest, sets up morality and beauty in a binary opposition, removing vivacity altogether: his Blanche Maria is 'more faire, then vertuouse, lesse honest then was necessarie, and worse disposed, then well given any waye' (S3^r).

Fenton also seems anxious about Blanche Maria's failure to respond to reasoned argument. He adds a lengthy gloss to a stern attempt made by her second husband to instil into her a sense of wifely duty. Fenton praises the Count for attempting to 'reform the abuses in his wife' with words rather than 'cruelty or constraint'. Elephants and tigers, for example, are tamed by kind behaviour. Yet Fenton is forced to conclude that none of this applies to the wicked Countess: 'neither gentle perswacions colde allure her, nor feare nor force reduce her to reconcilement, or amendement of life, but accordynge to the stone of *Scylicia*, uppon whom, the more you beate, to bruse or breake yt in peces, the greater hardnes is dryven into it, so the greater indevor therle used to persuade his wyfe, eyther by allurement or offer of correction, the more perversative he founde in her, with lesse hope of amendement' (T3^r).

To what extent were Painter and Fenton aware of the ethical morass opened up in their texts? It is possible, as Helen Hackett has suggested (2000: 41–2), that, rather than grappling unconvincingly but in good faith with intractable moral problems, both writers were working hypocritically—promoting as ethically valuable narratives they knew to be lascivious and amoral in their implications.[18] The other key text in the creation of the genre of the Elizabethan 'tragical history', published a few years earlier than Painter and Fenton, is more openly contradictory in its ethical position-ing. Arthur Brooke's *Romeus and Juliet* (1562), a verse adaptation via Boiastuau of Bandello's *novella* (and the main source for Shakespeare's *Romeo and Juliet*), starts with a sternly moralistic prose epistle.[19] The spin Brooke gives in this Preface is very different from the broadly sympathetic view of the lovers taken both by Boiastuau and by Painter in the version which appeared in the second volume of the *Palace* (1567, story 25). Brooke writes of Romeus and Juliet as

thralling themselves to unhonest desire, neglecting the authoritie and advise of parents and frendes, conferring their principall counsels with dronken gossyppes, and superstitious friers (the naturally fitte instrumentes of unchastitie) attemptyng all adventures of peryll, for that-taynyng of their wished lust, usyng auriculer confession (the kay of whoredome, and treason) for furtheraunce of theyr purpose, abusyng the honorable name of lawefull mariage, to cloke the shame of stolne contractes, finallye, by all meanes of unhonest lyfe, hastyng to most unhappye deathe.   (1562: ¶2^v–3^r)

In the text of the poem, however, Brooke is lavish in his praise of Friar Lawrence and the lovers. Indeed, the effect of his major additions to Boaistuau's story is largely to heighten sympathy for Romeus and Juliet.

Many of the additions to Boiastuau involve cadenzas on the emotional status of the principals—for example, the conclusion that, prior to Romeus' appearance at Juliet's house, Juliet was more woeful than Romeus (B6^r). Throughout, both lovers express their emotions more physically than in Boiastuau's text: they weep and wring their hands more often, and Romeus ends one of his speeches with 'an othe' (B7^r). Throughout, Brooke's narrator, in extensive material added to the French source, is tremblingly sympathetic to the lovers' plight. At the beginning of his story, his pen

---

[18] Meanwhile, Maslen (1997: 96–7) draws parallels between duplicity in Painter's and Fenton's fictions and duplicity in their lives: Painter, clerk to the Ordnance Office, confessed to embezzlement; Fenton, in his later career, worked as an informer in Ireland.

[19] For modern English translations of Italian and French analogues, see Salernitano et al. (2000). Brooke says in his prefatory material that he has seen the story as a play (¶3^r), so some of what seems to be original to him—and is discussed below as such—might in fact derive from the stage version.

shakes with emotion (A1^v). In a striking personal interjection, on the occasion of the consummation of the lovers' marriage, the narrator reveals his own lack of sexual experience:

> I graunt that I envie
>   the blisse they lived in:
> Oh that I might have found the like.
> I wish it for no sin.
>
>   (D2^r)

Elsewhere, Romeus' youth (implicitly, it seems, in parallel to the narrator's own) is emphasized: we learn that Romeus lacks a beard (A2^r) and is younger than Tybalt, the man he kills (K3^r).

J. J. Munro (1908: 147–63) attributes the tentativeness of Brooke's narrator, as well as many other features of *Romeus and Juliet*, to the influence of Chaucer's *Troilus and Criseyde*, the *locus classicus* for unhappy young love throughout the early Elizabethan period. Munro shows that Chaucer's poem is behind some of Brooke's most extensive alterations to Boiastuau's story—in particular, the development of two confidant figures, one for Romeus (Friar Lawrence) and one for Juliet (the nurse). Each of these characters owes something to Chaucer's Pandarus—in the case of the nurse, her bawdiness and broadly comic qualities; in Friar Lawrence's, the robustness of the advice he offers to his young male friend. The roles of these two characters, both present in Boiastuau, are substantially enlarged by Brooke. The nurse barely speaks in Boiastuau; in Brooke, by contrast, she is comically garrulous. While Friar Lawrence is important in Boiastuau's narrative, Brooke gives him a long extra speech (deriving much of its material from *Troilus and Criseyde*) counselling Romeus after he has heard he is to be banished (E6^v–F2^r). This whole scene—including Brooke's appealing evocation of the Friar's cosy, hidden-away cell (E4^r) and Romeus' despairing complaint against the universe (E5^r–E6^r)—is original to Brooke. Against Romeus' 'womanly' melancholia, Friar Lawrence sets a Stoic ideal: reason, patience, a 'constant mind' (E7^v).

Brooke explicitly mentions the parallelism between the nurse and Friar Lawrence: 'Young Romeus powreth foorth | his hap and his mishap', he points out, 'Into the friers brest.' So 'where | shall Juliet unwrap | The secretes of her hart?' (C2^r). It is tempting to read the care Brooke takes to balance the conversations of the two confidants as a side-effect writ large of the metrical form he uses: poulter's measure. Poulter's measure consists of a sequence of long-line couplets, often laid out, as in the 1562 printing of *Romeus and Juliet*, as four short lines per couplet. The first line of each couplet comprises twelve syllables, the second fourteen. The bumpy inequality in line-length means that there is a tendency for each couplet to skid to an independent conclusion rather than shift on fluently to the next line of the poem. Brooke repeatedly exploits this bittiness by bouncing off the meaning of the first long line of a couplet (or, as laid out on the page, the first two short lines) against the meaning of the second long line (or the final two short lines), as a parallelism or an opposition. Frequently, the short lines within each long line are balanced against each other too. These binary, intra-couplet structures often form part of wider oppositions or parallelisms added by Brooke to the story: day becoming night and vice versa within the perceptions of the lovers (F8^v–G1^r); Romeus' double life (happy in public, sad by himself) at Mantua (G1^r–G2^r); the dolorous metamorphosis of a wedding into a funeral (I6^v).

In much of his poem, though, Brooke is able to resist over-easy phrasal–metrical parallelism of this sort. Indeed, the assiduity with which he translates Boaistuau's unpicking of the lovers' emotional meanderings aptly reflects the claim of his Chaucerian narrator to be deeply moved by the story. Some of his additions too, like this restrained *aubade*, are appealingly lucid and sensitive. Romeus, aware of the approaching dawn, prepares to take his leave:

> As yet, he saw no day:
>   ne could he call it night,
> With equall force, decreasing darke,
>   fought with increasing light.
> Then Romeus in armes
>   his lady gan to folde,
> With frendly kisse: and ruthfully
>   she gan her knight beholde.
> With solemne othe they both:
>   theyr sorowfull leave do take,
> They sweare no stormy troubles shall
>   theyr steady frendship shake.
>
> (F8^v)

The binary structures encouraged by poulter's measure are present here, of course (most obviously in the light–dark opposition which opens the passage) but Brooke exploits them skilfully.

The nurse is considered far more critically by Brooke than Friar Lawrence. Clustering around her are some of the most striking features of *Romeus and Juliet*—those moments in which Brooke, in general so sympathetic to the lovers, adds to Boiastuau tentative indications that there might be something ethically suspect about Romeus' and Juliet's behaviour. Brooke does not accentuate these moments by moralizing sternly on them (as Fenton would have done): his comments are much gentler—he seems content to let doubts begin to grow in the readers' minds while keeping his narrator apparently as sympathetic as ever to the lovers. When the nurse first meets Romeus, for example, she chats at length about the audacity with which Romeus and Juliet are planning to deceive Juliet's mother (by trumping up a specious reason to visit the friar). Later, speaking to Juliet, the nurse offers support to Juliet's independence of her parents' wishes by saying that she herself would have liked to have lost her virginity earlier than she did (C4^r). This conversation, like the nurse's earlier banter with Romeus (C2^v–C3^r), is also very largely concerned with the deception of Juliet's mother (C4^v). The nurse is delighted at Juliet's engagement to Paris: if Romeus ever returns from banishment, she says, Juliet will have two husbands, one legal, the other covert (H8^v–I1^r). All of this suggests that Brooke is using the nurse as a way of writing something of the sexual unreliability of Juliet's faithless precursor Criseyde—picking up on the skill with which Juliet can deceive people—into a tale with an apparently exemplary, faithful heroine.

One point at which the narrator comes close to criticizing Juliet openly is his comment on the mercantile nature of the skill with which Juliet, putting her goods cynically on display (H7^v–H8^r), pretends to like Paris. Another, also original with Brooke, is Juliet's deception of the nurse during the wedding preparations:

> Juliet the whilst her thoughts
>   within her brest did locke.
> Even from the trusty nurce,
>   whose secretnes was tryde,
> The secret counsell of her hart
>   the nurce childe seekes to hide.
> For sith to mocke her dame [i.e. her mother]
>   she dyd not sticke to lye,
> She thought no sinne with shew of truth,
>   to bleare her nurces eye.
> In chamber secretly
>   the tale she gan renew,
> That at the doore she tolde her dame
>   as though it had been trew.
>
>   (H8^v)

Munro shows that Brooke was indebted to *Troilus and Criseyde* for the mythological apparatus which decorates his poem: a lightweight and predictable use of features associated with classical epic: extended similes; mythological sunrises; references to the classical pantheon and other mythological figures, in particular Cupid and Venus (1908: 147–63). All this makes *Romeus and Juliet* seem a rather more 'literary' sort of text than Painter's and Fenton's story collections. Though the book describes itself on its title page as a 'tragicall historye' (¶1^r), Brooke's prose epistle 'To the Reader', in a swerve away from Painter and Fenton, does not stress the basis of the story in fact. This contrasts strongly, too, with Boiastuau's insistence in the *sommaire* with which he precedes his version of the story that despite its extraordinary nature the tale of 'Rhomeo' and 'Juliette' is based in reality. Early on in Brooke's version, moreover, in a passage added by Brooke, worrying that Romeus might have impure intentions, Juliet thinks of her plight in terms of literary precedents. She mentions Dido and Theseus but knows of many more, however:

> A thousand stories more,
>   to teache me to beware:
> In Boccace, and in Ovids bookes
>   too playnely written are.
>
>   (B3^v)

In writing a suicide note to his father explaining the circumstances of his death, Romeus is, Brooke says, composing 'his tragedy' (I1^r). Another 'Tragedy' (L1^v: the word is, again, added by Brooke) narrated by Friar Lawrence in the speech, on an 'open stage' (K7^r), is the means by which he saves himself from execution at the end of the story, a startling addition of Boiastuau's to Bandello's tale.

Brooke's *Romeus and Juliet* sets up an opposition between, on the one side, its literary and melancholic lovers and their empathetic, inexperienced narrator and, on the other, the stern moralism of the prose 'To the Reader' which opens the volume. Not only that: its tale of doomed youth is garnished with quasi-epic flourishes. That the concoction was appealing to Elizabethans is signalled both by the number of editions of *Romeus and Juliet* that were printed and by the frequency with which later books alluded to the story (1908, pp. xx–xxi, lxi). The fact that Brooke died young, in a shipwreck (Munro 1908: 165–7), would have added piquancy—particularly since one of the most noticeable elements in Brooke's poem is the recurring comparison he makes, expanding on Boiastuau with the help of Chaucer, between the vagaries of Fortune and a storm-tossed sea.

Brooke's publisher, Richard Tottel (also the publisher of Painter's first collection), followed up on the success of *Romeus and Juliet* with Bernard Garter's poem *The Tragical and True History Which Happened between Two English Lovers* (1565), a tale supposedly based on fact. For most of its course, Garter's piece reads like a transposition of *Romeus and Juliet* into a major key. There are two (unnamed) young lovers and each has a friend to talk to—for her, a nurse; for him, a doctor. However, while Romeus and Juliet manage to get together without much help from anyone else—and then only need help from their confidants when the situation gets nasty—Garter's lovers are too timid to approach each other and need their friends' help from the first. Their parents play as important a part in their coming together as the doctor and the nurse, and the lovers marry without a hitch. It is like a sunny rewriting of Brooke's story until the closing pages, when the male lead is suddenly killed in a duel. In his opening 'To the Reader', Garter expresses bafflement at God's judgement (A3^r): did the lovers sin in lusting after each other too early in their relationship? Garter constantly shies away from engaging with his lovers' (particularly his heroine's) feelings, preferring to pile up physical details instead, including constant references to food and drink. Rather than the heroine telling someone about her feelings, her nurse rushes to the doctor with a urine sample (B5^v). Garter's lists—one physical detail after another—are, like Brooke's parallelism, in part a function of the metre he has chosen. Garter uses fourteeners, long-line couplets (like Brooke's poulter's measure) but with an equal number of syllables (fourteen, as one would imagine) in each line. Couplets (and the short lines of which they consist) thus combine much more easily into long, symmetrical lists than do bumpier poulter's measure. Even these lists emphasize reluctance on the part of Garter's narrator, as many of them are examples of the rhetorical trope *occupatio* (the description of something a writer says is not going to be described). Some of his narrator's tentativeness Garter has presumably caught from Brooke (who in turn took it from Chaucer): in Garter, though, the psychological light and shade of this technique has been lost and the effect is one of mere cluelessness.

Brooke and Garter were followed by a mini-boom of tragical verse narratives. Texts included *The Pitiful History of Two Loving Italians: Galfrido and Barnardo le Vain* (1570) by John Drout (a tale of male friendship); and William Averell's *Charles and Julia: Two British, or rather, Welsh Lovers* (1581); as well as a number of similar works with happier endings. Thomas Achelley's vivid *Didaco and Violenta* (1576) stands out from the rest, partly by virtue of the extreme violence of its action. Another text in the same genre is William Hubbard's pithy *Ceyx and Alycone* (1569), an adaptation from Ovid, a key source for tragical narratives. Hubbard's work was part of a wave of Ovid translations in this period, the best known today being Golding's *Metamorphoses* (1567). Interest in Bandellian tragical histories clearly overlapped with the interest in Ovid. There was a further overlap with the contemporaneous craze for translations of Seneca's bloody tragedies. James Sanford's prose translation of the sensationalist stories in *The Amorous and Tragical Tales of Plutarch* (1567), meanwhile, belongs more obviously alongside Painter and Fenton.

Many other types of tragical history appeared in the years following the publications of Painter, Fenton, and Brooke. The overall trend is a movement towards something that looks like fiction and away from the insistence on historicity (and morality) so characteristic of Painter and Fenton—a shift, in effect, from tragical histories to tragical tales.

This was not an easy or straightforward movement. Fiction remained an ethically problematic form, and some fictional narratives still masqueraded as fact, at the same time as evolving a range of complex devices to help 'authorize' the production of lurid fiction. While Robert Smythe's *Strange, Lamentable and Tragical Histories* (1577) is a straightforward collection of four prose narratives, translated from Belleforest, other appearances of this type of story in the literature of the 1570s were framed in more elaborate ways. Collections of *novella*-type narratives, such as Barnaby Rich's *Dialogue between Mercury and an English Soldier* (1574) and George Whetstone's *Heptameron of Civil Discourses* (1582), began to feature *cornici* in which two or more people come together to exchange stories. The use of this device signals a greater readiness in English writers to bat about the issues arising from *novelle*—a lessening of the anxiety about fiction itself and the ethical pressures on storytelling that had formed such a powerful element in the publications of the 1560s. Meanwhile, in his *Defence of Poetry* (c.1579), Philip Sidney argued that fiction could be more morally efficacious than history.

Two strategies used in narratives of this period can be traced back to germs in Painter, Fenton, and Brooke. The first—the alacrity with which writers assert that their *novelle* have been written with a female readership in view—seems indebted to the asides to unknown, imaginary female readers concocted by Painter and Fenton at second hand from Bandello's historically grounded narrators. Implying that one is writing a text purely to entertain women seems to have had the effect of easing the pressure on the writer, lowering the stakes.[20] A second device popular with writers of the last quarter of the century echoes the disjunction in *Romeus and Juliet* between moralistic prose epistle and irresponsible poetic text: this is the frequently made claim in prefatory material that the literary work following is a reprehensible product of the author's youth now spurned by the author himself in the act of publication. Writers who use this device—in Richard Helgerson's phrase, 'Elizabethan Prodigals' (1976)— include George Whetstone in his *Rock of Regard* (1576). Like other works of the 1570s, Whetstone's book combines strategies and mixes genres. The author disavows the amorality of the second section of his book, 'The Garden of Unthriftinesse', a collection of love poems (¶2^r). His opening section, meanwhile, frames Italianate narratives with a stern moralism. One of the pieces in this section recasts the story of the Countess of Celant in first-person, *de casibus* form: like Jane Shore, the subject of Thomas Churchyard's very popular *Mirror for Magistrates* piece 'Shore's Wife' (1563), Whetstone's Countess condemns herself out of her own mouth—as she signally does not in other versions of her story (A1^r–B1^r). Meanwhile, George Turbervile's verse *Tragical Tales* (1587—but also printed earlier, see Pruvost 1937: 77), echoes a self-deprecatory strategy in Painter's first volume. As Painter claimed to have originally meant his collection of stories to contain only tales culled from Livy, so Turbervile tells us in a prefatory poem that his first plan had been to translate the Roman poet Lucan's *Pharsalia*, an epic retelling of the civil war between Caesar and Pompey (A6^v–B3^v). The project would, Turbervile claims, have been of considerable benefit to the commonwealth. Melpomene, however, advises Turbervile that he is being too ambitious, and Turbervile, in a melancholic frame of mind, turns to translate tragical *novelle* instead, renouncing high seriousness.

Tragical tales continue to feature in the narrative texts which appeared towards the end of Elizabeth's reign, but their deployment is complex, largely because by that point prose fiction had emerged as more of a fully fledged genre in itself, and had accumulated an impressive array of newly introduced generic templates to work with. Stories stopped being translated from Bandello or his French adapters: writers preferred to make them up. The kaleidoscopic welter of narrative genres at this time—represented in little in the variety of Robert Greene's output—plays host to the tragical tale, as to many other forms, but in many different ways. Elements of the tragical tale can be found in all sorts of different places—for example, speckled throughout *The Faerie Queene* (1590, 1596) and *The New Arcadia* (*c*.1584), and in the Cutwolfe strand in Nashe's *Unfortunate Traveller* (1594). The abandonment of the idea that these tales were 'historical', meanwhile, seems to have opened up a gap in the Elizabethan generic economy that was filled, in time, by the genre of the crime pamphlet—grittier than the Italianate *novella* and underpinned by a different type of moral frame: the faith that providence would bring hidden crimes to light. Tragical

---

[20] Famous examples include George Pettie's *Petite Palace* (1576) and Barnaby Rich's *Farewell to Military Profession* (1581). For one of many recent discussions of this phenomenon, see Hackett (2000).

tales did hold their own as free-standing narratives, however, in one place: on the stage. Throughout the Elizabethan and Jacobean period, Bandellian narratives were mined by dramatists, in a complex process that created some of the best-known cultural artefacts of the English Renaissance.[21] By contrast, Painter, Fenton, Brooke, and their non-dramatic progeny are very odd beasts, stuffed full with sex and rhetoric, violence and moral panic—but nonetheless worth anatomizing for that.

PRIMARY WORKS

ASCHAM, ROGER (1967), *The Schoolmaster*, ed. Laurence V. Ryan (Charlottesville: University Press of Virginia for the Folger Shakespeare Library).

BANDELLO, MATTEO (1890), *The Novels of Matteo Bandello*, trans. J. Payne, 6 vols (London: Villon Society).

—— (1966), *Tutte le opere di Matteo Bandello*, ed. F. Flora, 2 vols (Verona: Mondadori).

BELLEFOREST, FRANÇOIS DE (1948), *The French Bandello: A Selection. The Original Text of Four of Belleforest's Histoires Tragiques*, ed. F. S. Hook, University of Missouri Studies, 21/1 (Columbia: University of Missouri).

BOIASTUAU, PIERRE (1977), *Histoires tragiques*, ed. R. A. Carr (Paris: Champion).

—— and FRANÇOIS DE BELLEFOREST (1578), *XVIII. Histoires tragiques* (Lyon).

BROOKE, ARTHUR (1562), *The Tragicall Historye of Romeus and Juliet*.

FENTON, GEOFFREY (1567), *Certaine Tragicall Discourses*.

GARTER, BERNARD (1563), *The Tragical and True History Which Happened betwene Two English Lovers*.

PAINTER, WILLIAM (1566), *The Palace of Pleasure*.

—— (1567), *The Second Tome of the Palace of Pleasure*.

—— (1890), *Palace of Pleasure*, ed. Joseph Jacobs, 2 vols (London: Nutt).

SALERNITANO, MASUCCIO, LUIGI DA PORTO, MATTEO BANDELLO, and PIERRE BOAISTUAU (2000), *Romeo and Juliet before Shakespeare: Four Early Stories of Star-Crossed Love*, ed. Nicole Prunster (Toronto: Centre for Reformation and Renaissance Studies).

TURBERVILE, GEORGE (1587), *Tragicall Tales*.

WHETSTONE, GEORGE (1576), *The Rocke of Regard*.

[21] *Romeo and Juliet*, *Hamlet*, and *The Duchess of Malfi*, to name just three. See Doran (1954: 128–42); Kirkpatrick (1995: 246–53) on Webster; Levenson (1984) on *Romeo and Juliet*.

CHAPTER 32

FORESTERS, PLOUGHMEN, AND SHEPHERDS

VERSIONS OF TUDOR PASTORAL

ANDREW HADFIELD

THAT representations of hardy and vigorous rural workers feature prominently in much Tudor literature should not surprise us. In 1485 Tudor life and economy were almost exclusively rural, wealth based on the acquisition and maintenance of land and property. The only substantial city in England was London, which did indeed grow significantly during the reign of the Tudors. Its population was just under 50,000 when Henry VII claimed the throne, relatively small compared to Venice, Milan, Naples, and Paris. When Elizabeth died, it had nearly tripled in size to more than 120,000 inhabitants, making it one of the largest cities in Europe (Rappaport 1989: 61). Given that the population also expanded rapidly in this period, estimated at 2.8 million in England and Wales in 1545 and 3.75 million in 1603, we get a clear sense of the pace of change in a society that was still predominantly focused on the countryside (Coleman 1977: 12–13). By the end of the sixteenth century most writers either lived in or had access to London, where the major printing presses were housed (the only exceptions being the university presses in Oxford and Cambridge). The rural labourer, who had once been an organic part of everyday life, assumed the status of a figure under threat who needed protection, the authentic link to a past that was disappearing before everyone's eyes.

Any study of this period needs to consider what was published as well as what was actually written during the period. Many of the old Lollard texts were actually printed and more widely disseminated in the sixteenth century than they had been as manuscripts in the fifteenth century. They were co-opted as evidence of a Protestant tradition that pre-dated the Reformation as a means of answering the Catholic taunt 'Where was your church before Luther?' (S. Barnett 1999: 14–41). William Langland's late fourteenth-century alliterative poem *Piers Plowman* spawned an influential genre in the late Middle Ages, especially among Lollards and other critics of the Church, establishing the exploited rural labourer as the privileged voice of dissent. Near the end of the 'Vita', the first part of the poem, in which the characters seek truth, imagining they can establish a fair society on earth, Piers is briefly persuaded to lay down his tools, plunging Langland's fictional England into chaos:

> 'I shall cessen of [abandon] my sowing,' quod Piers, 'and swynke [work] noght so harde,
> Ne aboute my bely joye [enjoyment of food] so bisy be na moore:
> Of preieres and of penaunce my plough shal ben herafter,
> And wepen whan I sholde slepe, though whete breed me faille.
>
> (Langland 1978, Passus VII, lines 117–21)

Langland's point is that the world has its demands too, and the belief that everyone can find an identical route to truth and spirituality will have catastrophic effects. Labourers need to work, and if Piers abandons his plough then everyone will go hungry because there will be no bread. Penance and abstinence will turn directly into widespread famine. It is not surprising that one chronicler of the Peasants' Revolt of 1381 thought that one of the leaders was actually called Piers Plowman, illustrating the close connections between radical and literary traditions (Hilton 1977: 178). The rural labourer, often but not always a ploughman, became the central figure of Lollard and Wycliffite ecclesiastical satire. A late fourteenth-century prose satire, the apocalyptic *Jack Upland*, imitates the alliterative style of *Piers Plowman* (although the alliteration is an embellishment rather than a structural principle—which, in fact, emphasizes the link between the texts) as well as the contrast between the simple Christian virtues of good earnest labourers and the lazy, parasitic lifestyle of their rulers as the world hurtled towards its end:

To the comoun people hath Anticrist govun leve to leve her trewe laboure and bicome idil men ful of discretis to bigile eche othere, as summe bicome men of crafte and marchauntis professed to falsnes, and summe men of lawe to distroye Goddis lawe and love amonge neighboris, and summe crepen into feyned ordis and clepen hem religious, to lyve idilli bi ipocrisie and disceive alle the statis ordeyned bi God. And thus bi Anticrist and hise clerkis ben vertues transported to vicis—as mekenes to cowardice, felnes [cruelty] and pride to wisdom and talnes, wraththe to manhode, envye to justification of wrong, slouthe to lordlynes, coveytis to wisdom and wise purveyaunce, glotonye to largynes, leccherie to kindeli solace, mildenes to schepissenesse, holines to ipocrisie, heresye to pleyne sadness of feyth and oolde usage, and Holy Chirche to synagogue of Satanas.   (*Jack Upland* 1991: 120)

The anonymous text situates itself as a continuation of Langland's dream vision, which ended with the forces of Antichrist assaulting Holy Church as a prelude to the Apocalypse. In *Piers Plowman*, the magnificent allegorical moment of Will's vision of Piers Plowman riding into Jerusalem as Christ in Passus XVIII, a moment when salvation and truth are finally united, dissolves into further chaos and the need to find the humble ploughman to set matters right:

> 'By Crist!' quod Conscience tho, 'I wole bicome a pilgrim,
> And walken as wide as the world lasteth,
> To seken Piers the Plowman, that Pryde myghte destruye,
> And that freres hadde a fyndyng, that for need flateren
> And counterpledeth me, Conscience. Now Kynde me avenge,
> And sende me hap and heele [luck and health] til I have Piers the Plowman!'
> And siththe he gradde [cried out] after Grace, til I gan awake.

(1978, Passus XX, lines 381–7)

Piers Plowman concludes with the quest for Piers continuing, manifestly unfinished and encouraging others to add, expand, and adapt the text according to the current state of the world, exactly what did happen. *Jack Upland* is a good example of the potency and ubiquity of the tradition, which requires very few generic markers: alliterative style, criticisms of Church and society, and a name. We know nothing about Jack apart from his name, yet it is clear that he is a rural labourer. 'Jack' makes him a quintessentially English figure; 'Upland' suggests that he is a freeholder, someone with a stake in the land, not one of the most impoverished labourers, but undoubtedly struggling to make a living from the soil. This name alone indicates that he is akin to a ploughman, an honest and trustworthy figure whose word is to be taken at face value.

More definitive still was another anonymous Lollard poem, *The Plowman's Tale*, also known as *The Complaint of the Plowman*, which was written *c.*1400. Whereas *Jack Upland* continued Langland's vision, *The Plowman's Tale* co-opted Chaucer into the same tradition. The text is a straightforward imitation of a Chaucerian tale, prefaced by a Prologue in which the Plowman, deciding that his work is done for the summer, joins the pilgrimage to Canterbury, where Harry Bailly asks the Plowman to tell a tale to the assembled pilgrims. In the tale the Plowman sets out to establish who is falser, a dichotomy that will be familiar to all readers:

> That one side is, that I of tell,
> Popes, cardinals, and prelates,
> Parsons, abbouttes of great estates.
> Of hevyn and hell they kepe the Yates,
> And Peters successours they ben all.
> This is demed by olde dates,
>   But falshed, foule mought it befall!
> The other side ben poore and pale,
> And people put out of prease [favour];
> And seme catyffes sore a-cale [painfully frozen],
> And ever in one without encrease,

> I-cleped lollers and londlese [the lazy and the landless].
> Who toteth [looks] on hem, they bene untall [short, i.e. weak];
> They ben arrayed all for the peace;
>   But falshed, foule mote it befall!
>
> (*Plowman's Tale* 1991, lines 61–76)

It is hard to imagine a reader who will not already have worked out the answer to the Plowman's dilemma. He encounters two creatures, a griffin, who sides with the Pope, and a pelican, who takes the part of the poor Lollards. The Griffin speaks very little throughout the text, which cannot be classified as a genuine debate poem like *The Owl and the Nightingale*, and serves as a straw figure designed to enable his opponent to make his case. When the Griffin argues that the Church needs a strong leader, the Pelican counters that Christ is their leader and they do not need an earthly figurehead. In the final part the Griffin and the Pelican fight, the Griffin aided by a cohort of birds, 'foules fele [fierce] | Ravens, rokes, crowes, and pye' (lines 1333–4), the Pelican by the Phoenix (symbolizing Christ). The Pelican and Phoenix triumph and the Plowman narrator asks readers to decide the meaning of the fable as he surrenders to the judgement of Holy Church.

The most significant feature of this tale is probably the representation of the Plowman in the Prologue. He contrasts his own valuable labour with the indolence of the clergy, a defining feature of the Piers Plowman tradition:

> Our Host him axed, 'What man art thou?'
> 'Sir,' quod he, 'I am an hyne [servant, worker],
> For I am wont to go to the plow
> And erne my mete [food] yer that I dyne.
> To swete and swinke I make avow [promise],
> My wife and children therwith to fynde,
> And serve God, and I wist how;
> But we leude [simple, uneducated] men bene fully blynde.
>
> For clerkes say we shullen be fayne
> For hir lyvelod to swet and swinke,
> And they right nought us give agayne,
> Neyther to eate yet to drinke.
> They mowe by lawe, as they sayne,
> Us curse and dampen to hell brinke.
> Thus they putten us to payne,
> With candles queynt [extinguished] and belles clinke.
>
> (lines 25–40)

A pointed contrast is established between the simple workers who serve God properly and those who profit from their labour and so abuse God while claiming that they are his true representatives on earth. The opposition is structured around radically divergent relationships to food. The Plowman can only eat after he has finished his work, whereas the priests can demand food produced by the labourers, threatening to excommunicate them if they fail to deliver. A whole host of prominent biblical verses are being ignored and violated, including 'the labourer is worthy of his hire' (Luke 10: 7), and, most importantly, Christ's declaration that he is the bread of life: 'the bread of God is he which commeth down from heaven, and giveth life unto the world' (John 6: 33). The Church should nourish the people spiritually, and each section of society should provide for another, but the priests' livelihoods are actually a tax on the work of ordinary men and women, an abuse of the Church's authority that cannot be tolerated. The labourers either know their Bible better than the ignorant priests, or the priests are hiding the Bible from the people. Either way, the allegation is the cornerstone of radical anticlerical satire, one that eventually led to the rallying cry taken from the sermon of the rebel priest John Ball, 'Whan Adam dalf [delved] and Eve span, wo was thane a gentilman' (Hilton 1977: 211). The work required to produce the basic sustenance of life cannot be separated from issues of justice and spirituality.

The Piers Plowman tradition continued well into the sixteenth century as Protestant writers co-opted Langland's goodly Christian worker as a rare voice of sense and proper values in the largely (as they perceived it) godless world that preceded them (Barr 1993; J. King 1982: 11–12, 339–47). Both *The Plowman's Tale* and *Jack Upland* were published in John Foxe's *Acts and Monuments* in 1570, as part of the Chaucer canon (J. King 1990: 24). Chaucer was seen in terms that went beyond his subsequent reputation as a satirist of clerical excesses. For many Protestant readers he was a reformer who would have challenged the authority of the Pope had he lived in a later age (Miskimin 1975: 18, *passim*). Chaucer was being read in terms of Langland, the favourite medieval poet of radical Protestants, despite the obvious political, social, and theological differences between the two writers, a position easier to maintain given the works that were added to published editions of Chaucer.[1]

Piers Plowman itself was ignored by the major English printers in the early sixteenth century—William Caxton, Wynkyn de Worde, and Richard Pynson—perhaps because of its radical reputation, as they saw many other medieval works into print, including Chaucer, Gower, and Malory. It was finally published in three editions based on the B-text in 1550 by the poet and printer Robert Crowley.[2] Crowley added a series of glosses that situate the poem within an enfolding Protestant history. He was the author of a number of works within the Piers Plowman tradition, including *Philargyrie of Great Britain* (1551), a satire of the excesses of the Protestant State–Church, as the woodcut on the title page 'depicting the "great Gigant" Philargyrie as a fur-clad Protestant aristocrat who rakes gold coins into a sack with the Bible' indicates (see Figure 16.1; J. King 1982: 346; but see also Warley, Chapter 16 in this volume). Crowley was clearly able to take advantage of the liberal attitude to censorship that existed at Edward VI's court in order to publish both his own poems of far-reaching social critique and Langland's masterpiece, though in the wake of the Western Rebellion of 1549 he may have been taking a serious risk (J. King 1982: 85–90; Jordan 1971, ch. 4). Crowley equates Langland and Wyclif as reformers, seeing them as a key feature of

---

[1] For discussion of Chaucer's and Langland's politics, see Aers (1990); Simons (1990); on sixteenth-century editions of Chaucer, see Walker (2005, pt 1); J. King (1982: 50–2).

[2] For analysis of this edition, see M. Johnson (2006). This paragraph is indebted to this article.

the English past who need to be co-opted into a Protestant tradition. As Crowley comments,

We may surely connject therfor, [that] it [*Piers Plowman*] was firste written about two hundre yeres paste, in the time of Kinge Edwarde the thirde. In whose time it pleased God to open the eyes of many to se his truth, giving them boldnenes of herte, to open their mouthes and crye oute againste the worckes of darckenes, as did John Wycklefe.   (M. Johnson 2006: 52)

As the above analysis makes clear, while one reason for the importance of representations of rural work was the nature and significance of country life, this was reinforced by a biblical tradition that placed great emphasis on the dissemination of religion through similar metaphors. Images of ploughmen—unsurprisingly—have produced some of the most memorable passages in the Bible, the liturgy, and Christian tradition. Hugh Latimer, the radical Protestant Bishop of Worcester, whose star rose spectacularly during the short reign of Edward VI, preached a series of sermons on the plough in the first year of the young king's reign. The subject matter and style of the sermons were part of an attempt to seize the religious agenda for the reformers' cause, a project that had profound effects for writers of literary as well as religious texts (J. King 1982; 1990: 22–3). Latimer is clear that he is working within the Piers Plowman tradition, making what was once radical official policy, replacing the forces of ecclesiastical tradition and reaction:

I liken preaching to a ploughman's labour, and a prelate to a ploughman. But now you will ask me, whom I call to a prelate? A prelate is that man, whatsoever he be, that hath a flock to be taught of him; whosoever hath any spiritual charge in the faithful congregation, and whosoever he be that hath cure of souls. And well may the preacher and the ploughman be likened together: first, for their labour of all seasons of the year; for there is no time of the year in which the ploughman hath not some special work to do: as in my country in Leicestershire the ploughman hath a time to set forth, and to assay the plough, and other times for other necessary works to be done. And then they also may be likened together for the diversity of works and variety of offices that they have to do. For as the ploughman first setteth forth his plough, and then tilleth his land, and breaketh it in furrows, and sometimes ridgeth it up again; and at another time harroweth it and clotteth it and weedeth it, purgeth and maketh it clean: so the prelate, the preacher, hath many diverse offices to do.   (1906: 55–6)

Latimer's words are decisive and provocative. He establishes that there can be no straightforward separation between the different estates in society, so that those employed by the Church are not of a different order from those who perform humbler tasks. In fact, Latimer emphasizes the similarity of the work of the rural labourer and the churchman, placing the role of the ploughman before that of the prelate, establishing the offices of the worker as a point of comparison for those of the cleric, and not vice versa. The prelate's offices are to be thought of in terms of the hard grind of rural labour: ploughing, tilling, furrowing, ridging, harrowing, weeding, and so on, the very English vocabulary assuming precedence over the Latin vocabulary of the Church's offices. Latimer had fought a series of battles with more conservative clerics such as Stephen Gardiner in the final years of Henry VIII's reign and was only released from prison with the accession of Edward, when he was able to resume what Susan Wabuda calls his 'stellar career as a preacher' (*ODNB*). In establishing the figure of the ploughman as the key to understanding the working of the Church, Latimer was making sure that official religious policy and radical traditions were fused. Had Edward not succumbed to consumption in 1553, the future of both the English national Church and English literary history would undoubtedly have looked very different. And Latimer would not have been burned at the stake on 16 October 1555, becoming one of Foxe's most significant martyrs, defining an English Protestant tradition through his spectacular death (J. King 2004: 279–85).

Writers in Edward VI's reign did indeed produce a substantial amount of radical Protestant literature, much of it centred on the figure of the ploughman. A telling and representative example is Thomas Churchyard's short poem 'Davy Dyker's Dream' (*c*.1551),[3] perhaps the first work of a long, not always distinguished, career (*ODNB*). Churchyard's poem is an imitation of Langland's alliterative verse presumably written in an understanding that such literature was likely to gain him favour at court, especially given his subsequent attempts to generate publicity and fashion a literary identity for himself in the middle years of the century. The title is taken from the ending of Passus VI in Crowley's recently published *Piers Plowman*, which warns the idle and the industrious alike of an imminent famine:

> Ac I warne yow werkmen—wynneth [obtain (food)] whil ye mowe [can],
> For Hunger hiderward hasteth hym faste!
> He shal awake thorough water, wastours to chaste,
> Thorough flodes and thorough foule wedres, fruytes [crops] shal faille—
> And so seith Saturne and sent yow to warne;
> Whan ye se the [mo]ne amys and two monkes heddes,
> And a mayde have the maistre, and multiplie by eighte,
> Thanne shal deeth withdrawe and derthe be justice,
> And Dawe the Dykere deye for hunger—
> But if God of his goodnesse graunte us a trewe [truce].
>
> (Langland 1978, Passus VI, lines 320–30)

While the famine is a punishment from God, Davy represents the poor, defenceless, and lowest class of worker who needs protection from the rest of Christian society. Churchyard imitates Langland's style in the form of a prophecy to outline the hopes and dreams that Davy might have, and to provide a damning analysis of contemporary society in the style of Crowley's own poetry:

> When faith in frendes beare fruit, and folysh fancyes fade,
> & crafty catchers cum to nought, & hate gret love hath made
> Whan fraid flieth far from towne, & lewterers [loiterers] leave the fielde,
> And rude shall runne a rightfull race, and all men be well wude [mad?]:
> When gropers after gayne, shall carpe for comen welth,
> And wyly workers shall disdayne, to fugge [fight] and lyve by stelth:

---

[3] The ESTC dating of 1552? is incorrect: Churchyard states in 1599 that he was saved by the intercession of the Duke of Somerset when he was in trouble with the Privy Council for 'some of [his] first verses'; this poem must then have been written before Somerset's arrest, charged with high treason, in October 1551. See S. Lucas (2002).

When wisdome walks a loft, and folly syts full low,
And virtue vanquish pampered vice, and greate begins to grow.
When Justice joynes to truth, and law lookes not to meede [gain, reward] [4]
& bribes help not to build fair bowres, nor gifts gret glotons feede
. . .
Then balefull barnes [children] be blythe, that here in England wonne [live],
Your strife shal steynte I undertake, your dreadful daies are done.

(lines 1–10, 27–8)

Churchyard's poem also belongs to a wider tradition of prophecy, much of it derived from Geoffrey of Monmouth's twelfth-century *Historia regum Britanniae* (Dobin 1990). More specifically, the list of impossible and improbable happenings dreamed of by the suffering working class recalls the prophecy of the Land of Cockaigne, the mythical place where work was impossible because not only did ripe fruit fall within the easy reach of every man and woman, but roast pigs ran around with carving knives stuck in their sides crying, 'Eat me! Eat me!' (Morton 1952, ch. 1). Davy Dyker looks forward to a time when justice will exist for all and the nation's goods will be evenly and fairly distributed, in the full understanding that this will probably never happen. Such political prophecy provides the means of social critique without the need for specificity and with the proviso that life has always been like this so things may never change. The Davy Dykers of this world will always be with us and always dreaming impossible dreams.

Churchyard's poem is only twenty-eight lines long, but it generated a much longer text with the publication of *The Contention betwixt Churchyard and Camel, upon David Dyker's Dream*, which reprinted the poem, along with a compilation of responses, in 1560 and again in 1565. Churchyard's arguments with Thomas Camel are published side by side, along with contributions from William Waterman, Geoffrey Chapel, and Steven Steeple, most—if not all—of which were undoubtedly written by Churchyard himself, given the Langlandesque names. Much of the text adopts the nature of a 'flyting match', a predominantly Scottish tradition in which poets insulted each other in inventive, metrical ways.[5] Churchyard refers to his opponent as 'a curre dogge [...] a beast [...]| A Camel, A Capon a Curre sure by kynde' (Churchyard 1560: A3^{r-v}). The debate is one that became much more familiar later in the century, whether English verse should adhere to a native tradition, as represented by Churchyard's poem, or adopt a more Latinate style, as Camel favoured (Vickers 1999). But, as all the poems are written in the style of the original poem, it is hard not to see which way the argument is weighted, and to suspect that, given the similarity of their style, and the fact that no trace of Thomas Camel survives outside this controversy, one author may have produced them all. The debate is also, in line with the Plowman tradition, 'concerned with defining who has the right to voice opinions about the commonweal', as Cathy Shrank has argued in an important essay on the uses of popular print culture in mid-sixteenth-century England (Shrank 2008*b*).

[4] The word deliberately recalls Langland's personification, Lady Meed.
[5] The best-known example is probably William Dunbar's 'The Flyting of Dunbar and Kennedy' (1970: 5–20).

While Langland's ploughman became the main radical voice of Protestant dissent, it is important that we heed other voices. The legend of Robin Hood appeared in a number of ballads dating from the late Middle Ages, but existed most importantly in one major text, *A Merry Jest of Robin Hood, and of his Life*, which had been printed at least six times by the middle of the sixteenth century.[6] In the opening lines of the ballad, Robin issues clear instructions to his companions John, Scarlock, and Much when they are in Barnsdale that reveal how closely related the poem is to the figure of the radical ploughman, as he sends them out to find an unwilling guest to buy them all dinner:

> look you doe no husbandman harme
> That tilleth with the plough,
> Nomore you shall no good yeoman
> That walketh by greene wod shaw:
> Ne no knight, ne no Squire
> That would be a good fellow.
> Bishops and these Archbishops
> ye shall them beate and binde,
> the high Sherrife of Nottingham
> hung hold in your minde.

(1560: A2r)

The rich are fair game, but the poor workers must not be exploited. As in the Plowman tradition there is a symbiotic relationship between rural workers and the land that must not be severed. Those who do not support this fundamental bond are cast as enemies of the people.

Robin's confederates find a knight and ask him to dine with them, ready to present him with the bill. Little John greets him courteously, 'Welcome be thou to greene-wood | hend knight and free' (A2v), but the sarcasm of this introduction is transformed when the knight reveals that he has no money and is heavily in debt to the monks of St Mary's Abbey, York, to the tune of £400, as he was forced to mortgage his lands after his son killed a knight and squire. The knight thus emerges as a victim of social forces and the connivance of the unscrupulous ruling class, one of the dispossessed, who has had to surrender his lands and has been deracinated. As Robin's men work to make free the knight from his debt and reclaim his lands, the forest becomes a site for upholding justice and liberty, the nearest place that dreamers like Davy Dyker will ever be able to obtain their desires.

The ballad is a mixture of the radical and the reactionary, characteristic of the populist Robin Hood tradition. On the one hand, it extols the virtues of the outlaw, attacks the clergy, and argues that all men should be free to enjoy the land on which they toil. On the other, it carefully limits its critique so that the king is seen to be in tune with the thinking of the outlaws and only the classes in between the ruler and the populace are at odds with a comforting native tradition of loyalty. Robin's fidelity to

---

[6] In 1500, 1506, 1509, 1515, 1560, and 1590. I have used *A Mery Geste of Robyn Hoode and of hys Lyfe* (1560). For a discussion of the ballad, see Stephen Knight (1994: 70–81).

the king is balanced by that of his own men to him, and in this way strict hierarchies are preserved, not challenged. The knight is seen to act as he has to in order to preserve what is rightfully his, and in the last fit his lands are restored and everything returns to normal. We never learn what Robin does in his twenty-two remaining years (between the restoration of the knight's land and Robin's death, tricked by a local prioress and bled to death). The implication is that the outlaws correct problems and redistribute wealth properly when their enemies overstep the bounds of justice. But there is an implicit utopian edge to the ballad, represented by Robin's eagerness to return from royal service to the life of the forester, a feat he manages with as little disloyalty to the king as he can. Whereas the life of the ploughman is invariably seen as painful and laborious, that of the forester is represented as more desirable than the expensive and restricted life of a courtier. The king's desire to have Robin and the outlaws at court is not just born out of admiration for their obvious qualities, but is also a form of vicarious envy for the lives they lead and the ancient English freedoms they can enjoy, a theme taken up later by Shakespeare in *As You Like It*. The forest, more than the field, is the site of English liberty, hunting the sport that unites kings and commoners:

> Foorthe he had our comely king
> full faire by the hand,
> Many a Deere there was slaine
> and full was fast dight and:
> Robin tooke a full great horne
> and loud he gan it blowe,
> Seaven score of wight yeomen
> came running on a rowe.
> All they kneeled on their knee
> full faire before Robin,
> The king said himselfe until
> and swore by Saint Austin,
> here is wonder seemely sight
> me thinketh by Gods pine
> His men are more at his bidding
> then my men be at mine.
>
> (F4^v–G1^r)

The king sees Robin's authority and the ideal nature of his society, regarding them with more than a little envy. But, as is obvious enough, the life of the outlaw in the forest cannot be for everyone and Robin's parallel authority to that of the king functions as a doppelgänger. He rules a utopian society in which problems are solved, justice works properly, there are no disputes over property because no one has any, and everyone is happy, one that could never work in the real world outside the forest.

Another more obviously literary tradition, which was written in a similar ballad metre, relies on this broad tradition of rural discontent even though it is clearly rooted in city life. John Skelton's truth-telling persona Colin Clout, who exposes the greed and corruption in the Wolsey-dominated England of the early 1520s, is part of a related tradition of anticlerical satire (Walker 1988, ch. 4; Fox 1989, ch. 10). Skelton's persona is an outsider who expects his coarse poetry to offend the delicate sensitivities of refined city folk:

> My name is Collyn Cloute.
> I purpose to shake oute
> All my connynge bagge,
> Like a clerkely hagge.
> For though my ryme be ragged,
> Tattered and jagged,
> Rudely rayne-beaten,
> Rusty and mothe-eaten,
> Yf ye take well therwith
> It hath in it some pyth.

> (1983, lines 49–58)

It is clear from these lines that Colin's poetry is that of the rustic labourer who toils outside at the mercy of the elements (his verse is 'rayne-beaten'). His poetry is rough and amateurish, lacking the sophisticated politeness of court poetry (of course, this is a carefully constructed fiction that the audience would have recognized, a staple feature of pastoral poetry, which pretended that the urban and rural could be separated this simply; see Alpers 1997, ch. 5). Nevertheless, as a dutiful citizen he has risked everything and come to London to remind the powerful of their responsibilities towards those they govern. In insisting on the need to punish an over-powerful cleric, Colin show that he knows the life of the city as well as that of the rural poor, a significant extension of the Piers Plowman tradition. Colin demands that the main author of everyone's ills—clearly Wolsey and other corrupt clergy—be forced to confront the reality of the city he knows so little:

> Take him, wardeyn of the Flete,
> Set hym fast by the fete!
> I say, lieutenaunt of the Toure,
> Make this lurdeyne [vagabond] for to loure [feel afraid]
> Lodge hym with beanes and pease!
> The Kynges benche or Marshalsy,
> Have hym thyder by and by!
> The vyllayne precheth openly
> And declareth vyllany;
> And of our fee symplenes [unrestricted possessions, a legal term]
> He sayes that we are rechles [careless]
> And full of wylfulnes,
> Shameles, and mercyles,
> Incorrigible and insaciate;
> And after this rate
> Agaynst us dothe prate.
> At Poules Crosse, or elsewhere,
> Openly at Westmynstere,

> And Saynt Mary Spytell
> They set nat us a shyttell [shuttlecock]
> And at the Austen Fryars
> They count us for lyars;
> And at Saint Thomas of Akers
> They carpe of us lyke crakers.
>
> (lines 1165–89)

The sharp-eyed rural critic is able to enter the city and explain what is wrong to the country's complacent and ignorant rulers. Here Skelton shows how the plain-speaking 'man of the people' comes from a rural setting but immediately adapts to an urban one, exploring the key locations of the city so that he can discover what needs to be known. The litany of place-names detailing the central areas of Tudor London does more cultural work than is apparent on a first reading. Colin lists the four principal prisons (Tower of London, Fleet, Marshalsea, King's Bench), suggesting that the accused be housed in 'Lytell Ease', a small cell in the Tower where important political prisoners were kept; the main central hospitals (St Mary of Bethlehem in Bishopsgate, St Thomas of Acre in Cheapside); and the principal inner-city churches (St Paul's Cross, where outdoor sermons were preached on Sunday mornings to huge crowds, and Austin Friars in Broad Street). The self-proclaimed country bumpkin shows that he has adapted quickly to city life, suggesting the range and dynamic nature of Tudor pastoral poetry and its characters.

It is a measure of the importance of this tradition of rural dissent that Edmund Spenser—the most important non-dramatic poet of Elizabeth's reign and the first major writer to plot a literary career in print—employed Skelton's most famous persona in his first published poem and made significant references to the character at key points in his writing (Helgerson 1983; Bernard 1989; N. Hoffman 1977). *The Shepheardes Calender* (1579) is a literary watershed in Tudor poetry for a number of reasons. It shows immense ambition and realizes the full potential of what a writer could achieve using the resources of print, imitating a humanist edition of a classical text with elaborate prefaces, glosses, and notes, many of which are fake and deliberately misleading, and using a variety of fonts and woodcuts (McCanles 1982). Moreover, it seized the tradition of rural dissent and using a combination of classical, European, and English influences—Virgil, Clement Marot, Chaucer, Skelton—and elements of popular culture—almanacs (especially *The Calendar of Shepherds*), religious writings—forged a new tradition of pastoral poetry that effectively sidelined that of earlier Tudor writers.[7] The Plowman tradition was probably moribund by the middle of the Elizabethan period, having become the marginalized voice of the radical Protestant after a brief period of hegemony during Edward VI's brief reign. It also appeared repetitive and old-fashioned for a generation eager to experiment with new verse forms and styles and not committed to an English tradition alone.[8]

---

[7] On the materials that Spenser used, see Norhnberg (1976); J. King (1990, ch. 1). On the longevity of this tradition, see O'Callaghan (2000).

[8] See, for an account of one series of experiments (in classical metres), Attridge (1974).

Sir Philip Sidney found little to celebrate in English poetry apart from Chaucer, *A Mirror for Magistrates*, and *The Shepheardes Calender*, and, perhaps significantly, he makes no mention of any ploughman verse (2002: 110). Spenser saw the chance to seize the agenda and transform English literature, revitalizing a genre that must have seemed extinct to most readers. In the first eclogue Colin, despairing of his failed suit for Rosalind, breaks his pipe:

> I love thilke lasse, (alas why doe I love?)
> And am forlorne, (alas why am I lorne?),
> Shee deignes not my good will, but doth reprove,
> And of my rurall musick holdeth scorne.
> Shepheardes devise she hateth as the snake,
>   And laughes the songs, that *Colin Clout* doth make.
> Wherefore my pype, albee rude *Pan* thou please,
> Yet for thou pleasest not, where most I would:
> And thou unlucky Muse, that wontst to ease
> My musing mynd, yet canst not, when thou should:
> Both pype and Muse, shall sore the while abye.
> So broke his oaten pype, and downed dyd lye.
>
> (1999, 'January', lines 61–72)

Colin breaks his pipe because Rosalind laughs at his rural songs, which she hates and holds in contempt. The implication is that they are too crude and unsophisticated for her urban taste; the accompanying woodcut (Figure 32.1) shows a forlorn Colin with his broken pipes looking back at a grand city in the background. The passage abounds with the ironies that Spenser practised throughout his career. This is the first eclogue and eleven follow it, so it is clear that Colin is not silenced by his actions. Colin duly reappears in the June eclogue debating the continued failure of his suit with Hobbinol, and again in the November eclogue to compose elegies on the death of Dido with Thenot. And, as the first note by E.K. makes clear, Colin is Spenser, an English identity derived from Skelton that the author has adopted in imitation of Virgil:

COLIN Cloute) is a name not greatly used, and yet have I sene a Poesie of M. Skeltons under that title. But indeede the word Colin is Frenche, and used of the French Poete Marot (if he be worthy of the name of a Poete) in a certain Æglogue. Under which name this Poete secretly shadoweth himself, as sometime did Virgil under the name of Tityrus, thinking it much fitter, then such Latine names, for the great unliklihoode of the language.   (1999: 38)

The note appears vague and careless, almost colloquial in its style, as if these were opinions hastily conceived and immediately reproduced. But this is a deliberate illusion. The note mentions English (Skelton), French (Marot), and classical (Virgil) authors, alerting wary readers to the complex and carefully crafted work that they are reading. Moreover, the style in which the opening sentence is cast makes it appear more like an annotation than a considered note by a scholar, which in such a carefully produced book should alert us to the fact that all is not what it seems.

Ægloga prima.

ARGVMENT.

IN this fyrst Æglogue Colin cloute *a shepheardes boy complaineth him of his vnfortunate loue, being but newly (as semeth) enamoured of a countrie lasse called* Rosalinde: *with which strong affection being very sore traueled, he compareth his carefull case to the sadde season of the yeare, to the frostie ground, to the frosen trees, and to his owne winterbeaten flocke. And lastlye, fynding himselfe robbed of all former pleasaunce and delights, hee breaketh his Pipe in peeces, and casteth him selfe to the ground.*

COLIN Cloute.

Shepheards boye (no better doe him call)
when Winters wastful spight was almost spent,
All in a sunneshine day, as did befall,
Led forth his flock, that had bene long ypent.
So faynt they woxe, and feeble in the folde,
That now vnnethes their feete could them vphold,

All as the Sheepe, such was the shepheards looke,
For pale and wanne he was, (alas the while,)
May seeme he lovd, or els some care he tooke:
Well couth he tune his pipe, and frame his stile,
A.I.   Tho

Fig. 32.1 Colin Clout looks back at a grand city, in the 'January' woodcut, Edmund Spenser, *The Shepheardes Calender* (1579), A1^r. The pipe here is a bagpipe, not a flute.

The breaking of the pipe should be read as an attack on other poetry rather than that in *The Shepherdes Calender*. The songs that Rosalind scorns are not contained in the text but pre-date it. The symbol of the broken pipe shows that Spenser means to use an ostensibly primitive tradition to transform the nature of English poetry, discarding the past and forging a new range of styles that will represent the maturation of English poetry so that it can take its place at the forefront of contemporary writing. Colin is not announcing his silence—far from it, as his subsequent career in *The Faerie Queene* (1590, 1596) and *Colin Clouts Come Home Again* (1591) demonstrates—but the end of an old, dying verse tradition (see also Cooper, in the Epilogue to this volume).

The Shepheardes Calender shows off a variety of poetic styles, forms, and subjects, the diction ranging from the popular to the courtly. It contains elegy, debate poetry, Virgilian pastoral, erotic verse, epideictic poetry, satire, in a range of metres and verse forms. The text includes ecclesiastical satire, absorbing and adapting the tradition of rural dissent. The May eclogue, the first of the ecclesiastical eclogues in the poem, is a debate between the two shepherds, Piers and Palinode, about the nature of the shepherd's life. The real subject, as becomes clear as the poem progresses, is the duty and responsibility of the Church to the people, Piers, as the headnote states, being the Protestant, and Palinode, the Catholic. Piers makes a case that readers of the Plowman tradition would recognize, claiming that contemporary clerics are complacent and appropriate too much of the land's resources for themselves when they should really live an ascetic and austere life, as they did in the past:

> The time was once, and may againe retorne,
> (For ought may happen, that hath bene beforne)
> When shepheardes had none inheritaunce,
> Ne of land, nor fee in sufferaunce:
> But what might arise of the bare sheepe,
> (Were it more or lesse) which they did keepe.
> Well ywis was it with shepheards thoe:
> Nought having, nought feared they to forgoe.
> For *Pan* himself was their inheritaunce,
> . . .
>
> And little hem served for their mayntenaunce
> Tho under colour of shepheardes, somewhile
> There crept in Wolves, ful of fraude and guile,
> That often devored their owne sheepe,
> And often the shepheardes, that did hem keepe.
> This was the first sourse of shepheardes sorrowe,
> That nil be quitt with baile, nor borrowe.
>
> ('May', lines 103–12, 126–31)

Piers's argument that the Church is being undermined by Catholic infiltrators, through the stock Protestant image of wolves in sheep's clothing, is countered by Palinode:

> Thou findest faulte, where nys to be found,
> And buildest strong warke upon a weake ground:

Aprill.   *fol.* 16

returneth all the thanck of hys laboure to the excellencie of her Maiestie.
VVhen Damsins] A base revvard of a clovvnish giuer,
Yblent] Y, is a poeticall addition.blent blinded.

Embleme.

This Poesye is taken out of Virgile, and there of him vsed in the person of Æneas to his
    mother Venus, appearing to him in likenesse of one of Dianaes damosells: be-
    ing there most diuinely set forth. To vvhich similitude of diuinitie Hobbinoll
    comparing the excelency of Elisa, and being through the worthynes of Colins
    song, as it were, ouercome with the hugenesse of his imagination, brusteth out
    in great admiration, (O quam te memoré virgo?) being otherwise vnhable, then
    by soddein silence, to expresse the vvorthinesse of his conceipt. VVhom Thenot
    answereth vvith another part of the like verse, as confirming by his graunt and
    approuaunce, that Elisa is novvhit inferiour to the Maiestie of her, of vvhome
    that Poete so boldly pronounced, O dea certe.

Maye.

Ægloga Quinta

ARGVMENT.

In this firste Æglogue, vnder the persons of two shepheards Piers & Pa-
linodie, be represented two formes of pastoures or Ministers, or the prote-
stant and the Catholique: whose chiefe talke standeth in reasoning, whether
the life of the one must be like the other. with whom hauing shewed, that it
is daungerous to mainteine any felowship, or giue too much credit to their co
                                                                        lourable

Fig. 32.2 The May festival, depicted in the 'May' woodcut, Edmund Spenser, *The Shepheardes Calender* (1579), A7ᵛ.

> Thou raylest on right withouten reason,
> And blamest hem much, for small encheason.
> How shoulden shepheardes live, if not so?
> What? Should they pynen in payne and woe?
> Nay sayd I thereto, by my deare borrowe,
> If I may rest, I nill live in sorrowe.

(lines 144–51)

In the Plowman tradition it is clear that Piers's argument would triumph, and there has been a wealth of support from critics who have read the eclogue in this context (Hume 1969; J. King 1982: 33–44). However, Spenser's text is probably more nuanced than this straightforward choice would imply (Heninger 1990: 647–8), and articulating two opposed positions in itself indicates that there is an argument that needs to be made either way. Moreover, the woodcut represents the May festival that Palinode describes (lines 19–36) and shows the shepherds arguing in the background (Figure 32.2), which also suggests that the right answer is not as easy to determine as the reader might assume. We might also bear in mind that Spenser does not always appear to side with the 'hotter Protestants' in his writings: for example, the Blatant Beast's destruction of the monasteries in *The Faerie Queene* (6. 12. 23–5) inspired Ben Jonson to inform William Drummond that 'by the Blating beast the Puritans were understood' (Spenser 2001: 686). It is indeed likely that Piers has the better of the argument, given his topical comments on the problems surrounding the projected Alençon match (Hadfield 1994: 117, 186–7). However, *The Shepheardes Calender* is also a reminder to the reader that poetry matters as well as politics and we need to read it as a work of literature as well as critique. The tradition of rural anticlerical writing was not yet over, but, for ambitious Elizabethan writers, it had become something to be absorbed, challenged, and confronted, not simply adopted.

PRIMARY WORKS

CHURCHYARD, THOMAS (1551), *Davy Dycars Dreame*.
—— et al. (1560), *The Contention bettwyxte Churchyeard and Camell, upon David Dycers Dreame*.
CROWLEY, ROBERT (1980), *Philargyrie of Greate Britaine*, ed. John N. King, *ELR* 10: 47–75.
DUNBAR, WILLIAM (1970), *The Poems of William Dunbar*, ed. W. Mackay Mackenzie (repr. of 1932 edn; London: Faber).
Jack Upland (1991), in *Six Ecclesiastical Satires*, ed. James Dean (Kalamazoo: Medieval Institute Publications).
LANGLAND, WILLIAM (1978), *The Vision of Piers Plowman: A Complete Edition of the B-Text*, ed. A. V. C. Schmidt (London: Dent).
LATIMER, HUGH (1906), 'A Sermon of the Plough, Preached in the Shroud at Paul's Church in London, on the Eighteenth Day of January, 1548', in *Sermons*, ed. Canon Beeching (London: Everyman), 54–71.

A Mery Geste of Robyn Hoode and of hys Lyfe, wyth a newe playe for to be played in Maye games very pleasaunt and full of pastime (1560).

The Plowman's Tale (1991), in *Six Ecclesiastical Satires*, ed. James Dean (Kalamazoo: Medieval Institute Publications).

SIDNEY, PHILIP (2002), *An Apology for Poetry*, ed. Geoffrey Shepherd, rev. and expanded by Robert Maslen (Manchester: Manchester University Press).

SKELTON, JOHN (1983), *Collyn Clout*, in *The Complete English Poems*, ed. John Scattergood (Harmondsworth: Penguin).

SPENSER, EDMUND (1999), *The Shepheardes Calender*, in *The Shorter Poems*, ed. R. A. McCabe (Harmondsworth: Penguin).

—— (2001), *The Faerie Queene*, ed. A. C. Hamilton, 2nd edn (Harlow: Longman).

VICKERS, BRIAN (ed.) (1999), *English Renaissance Literary Criticism* (Oxford: Oxford University Press).

CHAPTER 33

INTERLUDES, ECONOMICS, AND THE ELIZABETHAN STAGE

PAUL WHITFIELD WHITE

AMONG the most staunchly Protestant plays of the early Elizabethan period is the Norwich Grocers' *Pageant of Paradise* (1566), which uses the story of the Fall to teach a lesson about divine election and salvation by faith. At the same time, the surviving documentation concerning the play's final performance on a pageant wagon in the Norwich city centre in 1566 reveals that it also was a clever piece of commercial opportunism. For the array of exotic fruits—'Orenges, fyges, allmondes dates Reysens, preunis, & aples'—which decorated the Tree of Knowledge and gave splendid colour and appeal to the staged paradise were precisely those imported goods which the Grocers' Guild sold to the townspeople watching the play (Galloway 1984: 43; *Norwich* 11–18; Pound 1988: 57). And it was the trafficking in these pricey wares that made the Grocers among the richest and most prestigious trades in Norwich. However, this was more than a brilliant marketing ploy tacked on to a religious play. The Grocers had a reputation for piety as well as prosperity that dated back to the early Tudor period, and the play implicitly links the guild's commercial success to Protestant religious zeal (P. White 2008: 77–88).

The Grocers' *Pageant of Paradise* shows all the features of an early Elizabethan Protestant interlude, though it is rarely, if ever, identified as such (for more on these features, see below). And yet no other surviving interlude of the same time period, to my knowledge, positively conjoins economic prosperity with godliness. At least among guild plays, there must have been others like it in this respect, especially now that Ann Lancashire has firmly established that many of the greater and lesser trade companies of London (including the Grocers) during the Reformation era featured plays in their feast-day entertainments (Lancashire 2002). Moreover, the notion that God materially rewards those who combine diligence with righteousness, and indeed signifies his favour through prosperity, is traceable to the earliest of extant Protestant plays in England: John Bale's *Three Laws*. By the late sixteenth century, England's mercantile prowess is celebrated as evidence of God's providential favour in a number of plays, notably first in Robert Wilson's *The Three Lords and Three Ladies of London* (1590), about which more will be said later.

And yet, during the period in between, and especially in the decades immediately following Elizabeth's accession when London in particular experienced unprecedented growth and rapid expansion of trade, the preponderance of extant Protestant religious drama is deeply distrustful of commercial practices. Representative of this highly critical attitude towards commerce is a series of printed plays that specifically target economic issues. They are *The Cruel Debtor* (1565), *The Trial of Treasure* (1567), *Like Will to Like* (1568), *Enough Is as Good as a Feast* (1570), *The Tide Tarrieth No Man* (1577), and *All for Money* (1578). Identified today as 'moral interludes' (and indeed four of the six are called such on their title pages), these plays are essentially religious in purpose, present characters who are part allegorical abstraction and part social type, and appeal to popular audiences. As I will argue, they were written in response to what early Elizabethan preachers and play-makers saw as the widespread practice of fraud, oppression, and injustice arising from a surge in the growth of commerce and wealth. Emphasizing the spiritual implications of economic ill-doing, these interludes were part of a print propaganda campaign led by the advanced Protestant wing to outlaw usury and to reduce rent-racking and other forms of economic exploitation. Indeed, it was not that long ago that scholars assumed that these plays were *merely* print propaganda, that they never made it onto the stage. However, as the discussion below will reveal, they are quite sophisticated and entertaining 'performance texts'.

33.1 INTERLUDES, COMMERCE, AND SOCIAL ILLS IN EARLY ELIZABETHAN ENGLAND

Early Elizabethan Protestant commentators did not condemn capitalism; indeed, they depended on the patronage of the merchants and financiers, as well as the aristocracy, to support the reformed cause. Moreover, they approved of modest profits from commercial practice, and many did not object to moneylending at a moderate rate of interest. However, as the moral interludes examined here amply illustrate, they were generally distrustful of the mercantile community and held it responsible for a host of social evils: the acquisitive drive for wealth, fraudulent sale of goods, usurious moneylending, racking of rents, oppression of the poor, and profligate spending habits and the crippling debt they engendered (see Bevington 1968: 133–7). For the urban middle class, to whom these criticisms appear to have been addressed, the early years of Elizabeth's reign promised great prosperity and economic growth. The recoinage of 1562 restored confidence in English currency on the international market following the disastrous debasements of the Henrician and Edwardian governments, and the Statute of Artificers the following year provided a labour code and settled disputes over wage-earning. Then in 1567 perhaps the single most important event in the economic history of Elizabeth's reign took place: the opening in Cornhill of the 'Great and Goodly Bourse', renamed the Royal Exchange four years later (Wheeler 1949: 206–7). That same year, the founder of the Royal Exchange, Sir Thomas Gresham, persuaded Queen Elizabeth to pass new legislation permitting interest up to 10 per cent (the Usury Act of 1571).

Despite the growth of wealth and the strengthening of the economy, however, the central government remained conservative in its views of economic practice and suspicious of the more adventurous proposals of the rich merchants, with some administrators, namely Leicester and possibly also Sir Christopher Hatton, supporting the anti-usury campaign led by Thomas Wilson, Thomas Rogers, Robert Crowley, and others (Rosenberg 1957: 145–6). The economic interludes voice the opinion of these moralists and their patrons that the advancement of commerce did little to alleviate the suffering of the poor and dispossessed, and it only compounded social and economic problems by promoting greed and exploitation in the areas of trade and housing. Commercial success was in part responsible for the thousands of provincial labourers and foreign emigrants (the latter welcomed by the Crown in the early 1560s) who flooded into London and the larger towns looking for work, which in turn contributed to overcrowding and squalid living conditions. When the demand outstripped supply, rents for housing to let rose to unaffordable rates for poor commoners, many of whom were evicted to make room for the much-resented foreign tradesmen from France and the Low Countries. Food prices similarly rose as grain production failed to keep up with the population growth, so that it was widely believed that merchants, like landlords, used the price-rising trends to profiteer even further. And London was not the only urban centre with rapid population growth and accompanying economic woes. Norwich, for example, doubled in size between 1560 and 1580, largely as a result of a huge influx of Dutch and Walloon immigrants during the early years of Elizabeth's reign—with an increase in poverty, too (Pound 1988: 125–6; N. Jones 1993: 254–5).

The authors of the Elizabethan economic interludes, like most commentators of the time, seem to have had little grasp of the complex interplay of forces causing price inflation, high unemployment, and other economic realities of the day. The playwrights *did* take the government to task for contributing to the current situation, openly challenging its legalization of interest in the Usury Act of 1571, its lax immigration policy, which encouraged foreign labourers to work in England, and the 1559 parliamentary bill authorizing the Crown's seizure of bishops' lands, which impoverished many parish clergy. Yet they were generally sceptical that 'policy' could change social conditions. Like the so-called commonwealth men of Edward VI's reign, they perceived covetousness, ambition, and oppression ultimately as 'spiritual' evils, responsibility for which resided with individual sinners, not with the 'system'.

For George Wapull's *The Tide Tarrieth No Man*, commercial abuses and disorders had their origins in the base drives and desires of corrupt human nature, signified by the play's Vice, Courage. Courage's assistants, named Hurtful Help, Feigned Furtherance, and Painted Profit, are financial brokers and middlemen who illustrate the dangers of a cash nexus economy in which individual identity is increasingly defined in monetary terms (see Crow 1980: 316–17). Among the predatory rogues deceived by Courage and his henchmen are Greediness, a usurious moneylender and double-dealing merchant, and No-Good-Neighbourhood, a wealthy immigrant and landlord who is equally unscrupulous. Those most victimized by such economic conditions are the virtuous and the poor, exemplified in the persons of Tenant and Debtor, who get caught up in the network of intrigue engineered by Courage.

The strong sense of individual responsibility for economic conduct in these interludes and corresponding sermon literature derived in part from the Calvinist doctrine of the calling, which taught that the manner by which people pursue their divinely appointed vocations in the social order is a direct reflection of their spiritual condition. The Elizabethan preacher William Perkins, whose *Treatise of Vocations, or Callings of Men* (1599) was the culmination of English Calvinist ideas on the calling, distinguished between worldly and spiritual callings but concluded: 'if thou wouldst have signes and tokens of thy election and salvation, thou must fetch them from the constant practise of thy two cal[l]ings joyntly together' (1608: i. 734). Calvinist notions of calling and divine vocation have generated much debate among economic historians since the publication of Max Weber's *Protestant Ethic and the Spirit of Capitalism* in 1904, in which Weber famously asserted:

the religious valuation of restless, continuous systematic work in a worldly calling, as the highest means of asceticism, and at the same time the surest and most evident proof of rebirth and genuine faith, must have been the most powerful conceivable lever for the expansion of that attitude toward life which we have here called the spirit of capitalism.   (Weber 1930: 172)

Rationalizing the profit motive in religious terms and linking economic success to divine favour were, without question, present among the Protestant middle classes from the beginning, as I asserted at the outset of this discussion.[1]

---

[1] Weber's thesis is slightly modified in Tawney. For the history and essential articles of the Weber controversy, see Green (1959).

However, we now know the situation was more complicated. Indeed, Elizabethan Calvinist notions about calling and stewardship in the Elizabethan interludes do not challenge but reinforce traditional political opinion about social order and economic relations. Thus, in *Enough Is as Good as a Feast* and *The Trial of Treasure*, the ruling class are exhorted to fulfil God's will in the important vocations to which they have been called, the 'poor men & commons' to 'walke well in your vocation', banishing greed and ambition in the pursuit of heavenly treasure (Wager 1920: B2^v; *Trial* 1908: D2^v). *All for Money* likewise teaches that the poor labouring class should accept its lowly station, even if it means a life of poverty, and that the wealthy and privileged have an obligation to practise charity towards the poor and sick (Lupton 1910: C3^r). Within this scheme of things, the rapid social advancement of ambitious merchants and middle-class landlords are perceived as a threat to social stability. In *The Tide Tarrieth No Man*, the courtier Willing-To-Win-Worship becomes a victim of the acquisitive rogues Hurtful Help and Feigned Furtherance, who lend him money at an exorbitant rate of interest and seize his property when he is unable to pay it. Only in a society where wealth is valued above principles of morality and order can an upstart merchant advance to the level of a gentleman while the gentleman, landless and broke, descends to the lowly station of a pauper.

The chief vice which leads men to abuse their callings and jeopardize their own souls is covetousness, 'the Londoners sinne', as the Calvinist preacher Henry Smith describes it (1599: A2^r). To the covetous merchant, what constitutes 'enough' changes from day to day. Smith comments: 'whe[n] we had nothing we thought it *enough* if we might obtain lesse then we have: when we came to more, we thought of an other *enough*, so *enough* is alwaies to come, though too much be there already'. Covetousness, and the restless, acquisitive need to possess more, even though one has 'enough', is the focus of Wager's *Enough Is as Good as a Feast*. Thinking only in terms of his welfare in this lifetime, the greed-driven landlord Worldly Man justifies his accumulation of wealth on the grounds that misfortune may strike at any time and therefore one must prepare for old age by storing up riches now (A3^r). This leads him to embrace the most presumptuous argument of all: he ought to be in the business of making money because it is his divinely appointed vocation (D3^r). The suffering and oppression caused by his covetous practices are dramatized by three tableaux figures who recall Wapull's lowly victims noted earlier. Tenant complains that his rent has been doubled owing to Worldly Man's greed and to the influx of foreigners who cause prices to rise. He is joined by Servant, who complains that he is treated more like a slave than a servant, being deprived of basic needs. A third victim, Hireling, claims that Worldly Man has cheated him out of a half-year's wages. When the three request to have their grievances redressed, they are callously turned away by the landlord and his steward. Through this behaviour, Worldly Man manifests his spiritual reprobation. Failing to respond to the sermon of the Prophet, he is visited by God's Plague and dies impenitent and damned. If Worldly Man's restless drive for wealth brought him to damnation, Wager implies that the government must be in some measure responsible for encouraging such behaviour through his condoning of usury. Wager's alignment with the anti-usury campaign is voiced through a speech by Satan, who enters to carry off the reprobate's corpse to hell:

> How cunningly put he his mony to usury:
> Yea, and that without offense of any law.
> . . .
> All you worldly men, that in your riches doo trust,
> Be merry and jocund, build Palaces and make lust cheer:
> Put your money to usury, let it not lye and rust,
> Occupye your selves in my lawes while ye be heer.
>
> (G2ᵛ)

As a remedy for the restless drive for gain and status, these interludes urge every man in his calling to restrain his affection from the world, to trust in divine providence, and to practise contentation (see also Perkins 1608: i. 745; Smith 1599: C1ʳ). Wager conveys this alternative lifestyle through the example of Worldly Man's elect counterpart, Heavenly Man. Heavenly Man accepts his social station with providential resignation, and regards the temptations and adversities of this world as means of strengthening his faith. In contrast to Worldly Man's deserved damnation, he is visited with Rest, who brings him joys 'prepared for the heavenly from the beginning: | And given unto them for a rewarde of their godly living' (Wager 1920: G3ᵛ). This last quotation, implying that Heavenly Man's salvation is foreordained, draws attention to the most anomalous feature of Reformation religious drama as a whole. At the same time as it attempts to evangelize, to press for changes within the Church and within society, it also insists on an Augustinian view of predestination. If Heavenly Man's salvation is predested, 'the worldly man will needs be a worldly man still', we are told, since 'it will not out of the flesh that is bred in the bone verily' (D4ᵛ).

The sense of determinism is no less pronounced in *The Trial of Treasure*, *The Tide Tarrieth No Man*, *All for Money*, and *Like Will to Like*. In these interludes, the majority in society are perceived to be hopelessly depraved and fixed in their evil ways. Their reprobation is depicted largely in economic terms. On the other hand, only the Faithful Few practise virtue and attain salvation. The authors apparently did not see any inconsistency between the notion of predestination and their proselytizing aims. Thus, the assumption is that those who respond to the message are imbued with the necessary grace to do so, and therefore must have been elect in the first place. As Godly Admonition states at the conclusion of *All for Money*:

> Here have you had [seen] inordinate love
> Which man hath to money although it worke his wo:
> But such as have any grace, this will them stirre and move
> To cast their love from money and other pleasures also
> For feare they dwell with the devill, their cruell and mortal foe.
>
> (Lupton 1910: G3ᵛ; my emphasis)

33.2 Economic Interludes and Print Propaganda

We owe the survival of all early Elizabethan interludes to the London book market. Most were entered into the Stationers' Register and subsequently printed in at least one edition between 1560 and 1580. Their printers were familiar figures, most of them setting up their trade and bookstalls in St Paul's churchyard and nearby Paternoster Row, where Londoners could find moral interludes on shelves alongside prose tracts and sermons addressing the same economic abuses (H. Bennett 1965: 256). While intended for a reading audience, they do not appear to have sold particularly well, with only *Like Will to Like* going into more than one edition (Grantley 2004: 196). Indeed, plays made up a very small fraction of Elizabethan published writings. The previous section of this essay indicates the extent to which their subject matter and tone correspond with those in homiletic and devotional works which dwell on the spiritual consequences of economic wrongdoing.

All of the known authors of these interludes appear to have been clergymen with some connection with the book trade, either as prose-writers or otherwise. Ulpian Fulwell and Thomas Lupton both wrote works of Protestant religious propaganda, while George Wapull is the first known clerk of the Stationers' Company, and William Wager was a warden for the Stationers' in 1589.[2] These playwrights were supported, perhaps directly sponsored, by prominent Protestant patrons, notably the Earl of Leicester and Lord Burghley (P. White 1993: 70–1). Wager was a popular London preacher who also served as master on Barnet Grammar School, itself linked to Leicester. Fulwell may have been a West Country member of Burghley's circle. While rector of St Andrew's parish in Naunton, Gloucestershire, Fulwell dedicated *The Flower of Fame* and *Ars adulandi; or, The Art of Flattery* to Burghley and to his wife, Lady Mildred, respectively. It is now well known that both Leicester and Burghley were involved in protecting and patronizing advanced Protestants. At the very least, then, these plays fit within the Protestant print culture of the period and promoted the same aims as non-dramatic religious writing.

Until the 1950s, most scholars dismissed these moral interludes as closet plays, operating on the assumption that their Puritan sympathies were incompatible with any tolerance for theatrical performance. However, we now know that even the more moderate Presbyterians were supportive of plays, with, indeed, *The Tide Tarrieth No Man* adopting an anti-episcopal stance (P. White 1993: 93–4). More importantly, these interludes were written for the stage. On their title page they are advertised as suitable for acting troupes of anywhere between four and seven actors (Bevington 1962: 68–85). It is generally assumed that professional troupes were targeted because of the interludes' meticulous approach to doubling of roles, making them attractive to touring troupes, but the plays were likely performed by various acting groups, amateur as well as professional.

---

[2] For details, see Kathman (2004); *ODNB* 'Lupton, Thomas'; Eccles (1981: 258–62); Happé (2008).

33.3 DRAMATURGY AND STAGING

As 'literature', the scripts of Elizabethan Protestant interludes make for fairly dull reading, but when studied as performance texts, or indeed observed in performance, they exhibit the complexity and appeal associated more frequently with major Renaissance drama. We need to imagine the stage inhabited not by mere personified abstractions but by merchants, landlords, courtiers, and their servants and tenants; they are often colourfully dressed, as when Money in *All for Money* appears wearing a coat sewn all over with glittering gold coins, or the devil figures and agents of retribution are shown in terrifying masks. Stage pictures, pageantry, processions, and action sequences involving fencing, wrestling, and comic buffoonery abound, as do musical set pieces, consisting mainly of 'impromptu' songs delivered in multi-part harmony and probably with instrumental accompaniment. The interlude playwrights appear to have been, for the most part, skilled craftsmen with hands-on experience of the theatre. David Bevington has recently argued, for example, that Wager's approach to casting and doubling of parts in *Enough Is as Good as a Feast* and *The Longer Thou Livest* is virtually flawless (Bevington 2007: 370).

In performance, the death scene in *Enough* is a tour de force. It develops with mounting intensity, the conscience-stricken and now debt-laden Worldly Man awaiting the arrival of his creditors, terrified by the voice of God's Plague offstage, and mocked by the grotesque laughter of his former confidant, Covetous. Physician offers him no relief from the sickness with which he is suddenly afflicted, and Ghostly Ignorance, a corrupt and sinister popish priest, provides no spiritual comfort. Prostrate on stage, attempting to write his will, he dies alone, impenitent, and stricken with fear. Those of us who staged and witnessed the play in performance a few years ago were struck by how powerful the final sequence turned out to be, and appreciated how much Marlowe drew on the dramaturgy of his immediate predecessors when staging the final hour of Doctor Faustus. Wager uses a story of overreaching greed and exploitation to forge a tragedy of damnation.

These interludes are diverse in terms of dramaturgy and structure. The so-called 'psychomachia' plot of the medieval moral play, featuring Humanum Genus being alternately exhorted to goodness by personified virtues and tempted into evil by personified vices (in disguise as virtues), survives in many post-Reformation interludes. Among the economic interludes of the 1560s and 1570s, it is most fully developed in *Enough Is as Good as a Feast*. The hero of this play, Worldly Man, starts off boasting to the audience of his wealth and property but, through the influence of Enough and Contentation, converts to godliness. In typical morality play fashion, this spiritual about-face spurs the Vices into action, led by Covetous, the steward to Worldly Man's estates, whose sumptuous gown, gold chain, and cap are the proverbial dress of the usurious moneylender. With Covetous disguised as Policy, and with his companions Inconsideration, Precipitation, and Temerity posing as Reason, Ready Wit, and Agility, the Vices win back Worldly Man by convincing him that his parsimonious lifestyle prevents him from being generous towards the poor and needy. Where Wager departs from the traditional morality play pattern, however, is in supplanting the old 'comic' conclusion of repentance and forgiveness on the hero's part with a 'tragic' one of persisting impenitence and damnation. The Calvinist doctrine of predestination goes a long way towards explaining this modification of the old narrative sequence, as does the new theology's emphasis on divine justice rather than mercy, and the homiletic notion that fear of divine judgement is an effective inducement to repentance (the 'fire and brimstone' approach to homiletics) contributed to modifications of this pattern. Moreover, *Enough*'s juxtaposition of Worldly Man with Heavenly Man, his 'elect' counterpart, illustrates a splitting of Humanum Genus into elect and reprobate heroes which Wager deploys in his other interlude, *The Trial of Treasure*, where the godly Just never seriously wavers into sin, while his reprobate counterpart, Lust, is in thrall to the Vice Natural Inclination throughout the action.

At the centre of most economic interludes of the 1560s and 1570s is the Vice, operating as a kind of evil intelligence. The Vice provides some continuity with the medieval morality, but in other respects this figure is quite different dramaturgically. Plays such as *Like Will to Like* and *The Tide Tarrieth No Man* are less concerned with individual religious experience and its theological components than they are with the spiritual condition of the society as a whole. They therefore resort to a structure demanded by this subject matter, one presenting a series of episodes in which the Vice propels various social types into acts of treachery and deceit, and usually concluding with the punishment of that Vice in the final scene. The interlude *All for Money* is stylistically perhaps the most experimental of the interludes, showing little in common with the traditional Humanum Genus formula. Rather than presenting a continuous sequence of scenes, *All for Money* features six independent episodes, each with its own distinct set of characters and logic of presentation, which are interrelated by their thematic concern with money, its power, and its corrupting influence in a society devoid of spiritual values.

Jean-Paul Debax has recently argued that the Vice is not really a character at all, or at least not a mimetic one within the fictional world of the play. He points to a parish record from Bungay, Norfolk, where a payment is made 'To Kelsay the vyce, for his pastime before the plaie, and after the playe' (Debax 2007: 34; Galloway and Wasson 1980: 142). But the interlude owes its development at least as much to the households of the elite as to the popular tradition, as Debax himself observes, and the Vice's role can be traced to the lord of misrule appointed to oversee revels during Christmas and Shrovetide. The Vice spends a good deal of his time on stage working the audience, charming and amusing them with his wit and physical comedy, taunting and surprising them with audacious questions and insults, rebuking them for the same sins and shortcomings observable in the play's extortionists, bawds, and spendthrifts. The lord of misrule's licensed anarchy is for entertainment only, but in the interlude Vice's constant interaction with the audience has a homiletic end—it keeps them actively engaged with what's happening on stage and it creates a greater sense of immediacy between the real world they occupy and the stage world of the play. That homiletic end, however, may not always be achieved. As with Nichol Newfangle in *Like Will to Like*, the Vice's rhetorical dexterity and sophistication is potentially subversive (Hayes 2004: 45–56). He is above all a highly ambivalent character whose capacity for generating sympathetic laughter and directing audience response in other highly entertaining ways can interfere with the proselytizing intentions of the play's author and organizers. The Vice's dominance is no better illustrated than in *The Tide Tarrieth No Man*, where the action is largely structured by a series of soliloquys (eleven in all) delivered by the Vice, Courage, in which he becomes increasingly more intimate with the spectators. Courage spends his time during these soliloquys gloating over his success in cozening the dupes who appear before him on stage, assisted by his accomplices in the marketplace, Hurtful Help, Painted Profit, and Feigned Furtherance. The victims include the usurious merchant and landowner Greediness and the investor who covets his property, No-Good-Neighborhood, the courtier Willing-to-Win-Worship, who is driven into debt, a couple of young spendthrifts, Wantonness and Wastefulness, who end up in beggary, and Debtor, who is arrested and imprisoned.

Courage's role as soliloquizing commentator is taken over about two-thirds of the way through the action by a pair of Virtues named Christianity and Faithful Few. They attempt to reverse the damage done by Courage, but only with limited success. Greediness is indifferent to their reasoning, and Wastefulness, in despair, dies in a state of damnation. However, they direct the audience's response to the play's central moral: spectators must abandon their pursuit of material pleasures and possessions and place their trust in God's Word and the treasures that await the faithful in the next life. Moreover, the Virtues achieve this as much through pageantry as through preaching. The stage directions prescribe that Christianity 'must enter with a sword, with a title of pollicy, but on the other syde of the tytle, must be written gods word, also a shield, wheron must be written riches, but on the other syde of the Shield must be Fayth' (Wapull 1910: F3^r). Thus, Christianity enters with the worldly labels visible: the sword of 'pollicy' and the shield of 'riches'. In his opening speech to the audience, he says:

> … I beare this deformed sword and shield,
> Which I may be ashamed to hold in my hand,
> But the Lord deliver me from their thraldome and
>   band,
> For if the enemy assayle me, then am I in thrall:
> Because I lack such Armoure, as is taught by S. Paule,
> For in steade of Gods word, and the shield of fayth,
> I am deformed with pollicy, and riches vayne.   (F3^r)

The rhetoric here is unmistakably Puritan and contains a lightly veiled attack on the infiltration of greed and corruption within the national Church as well as the public marketplace.

Stage pictures and pageants are staple features of the homiletic method in the economic interludes. The central stage image of *The Trial of Treasure* is a horse's bridle. The elect hero, Just, struggles to shackle the Vice Natural Inclination, and only succeeds with the assistance of his old counsellor, Sapience. After Just and

Sapience depart the stage and Inclination delivers a long soliloquy explaining the significance of the bridle, Lust enters to free him. In the concluding scene, Just manages to bridle the Vice a second time. When Natural Inclination neighs like a horse, Just's response drives home the moral: 'Even so may all men learn of me again, | Thy beastly desires to bridle and restrain.' Another remarkable instance of an argument being conveyed by a series of stage pictures occurs in scene 2 of *All for Money*, where the playwright's purpose is to show how love of money leads eventually to damnation. To achieve this, he gives dramatic expression to a familiar literary trope: the genealogy of evil. The action centres around a chair and begins with the seated Money 'giving birth' to Pleasure, who in turn sits down to deliver Sin into the world; Sin then engages in the same stage business to bring forth Damnation. The stage directions make clear that in each incident the 'newborn' is to appear from beneath the chair by means of 'some fine conveyaunce'. This need not call for a trap door, but probably only required the seated actor to be dressed in a long skirted gown, with the 'child' emerging from between his legs and through the skirt (Southern 1973: 473).

A variation of this same device is to introduce a series of figures, one after another in pageant-like fashion, to dramatize a spiritual process, as in the concluding scene of *Like Will to Like*, where Virtuous Life leads in Honour, who are then accompanied by Good Fame in the final prayer and chorus. In some plays the spiritual process, whether it be a conversion to grace or a backsliding into unregeneracy, is dramatized by having figures represent the conflicting impulses, desires, beliefs, in the acting space, usually with them standing behind or on one side or another of the central character as he undergoes change. In *Enough Is as Good as a Feast*, Worldly Man's conversion is visualized by his embracing Enough and Contentation, with whom he leaves the stage walking hand in hand. Another feature that gave the stage an advantage over the press and the pulpit as an instrument of propaganda was its manipulation of the relationship between word and image. In *Enough*, for example, Covetous's appearance before Worldly Man wearing the cloak of office and a gold chain gave him an air of respectability that concealed his covetousness, although it is worth noting that the fur-trimmed robe and gold chain later came to be identified with the usurious moneylender. The same device is deployed in *All for Money*, where Money shows up as a Judge. Since the days of John Bale, Protestant playwrights were adept at using drama to expose the deception of appearances, the most frequent instance of this being the outward sanctity conveyed through the Catholic clergy's vestments.

To a modern audience raised on naturalistic theatre, the disjuncture between actor as expositor commenting on and critically detached from the action and actor as the impersonator of a 'character' (whether social type or distinct individual) may be unsettling, although it is a common feature of some modern stagecraft, in Brecht for example. To Tudor spectators, however, rooted in the notion of drama as 'game' imparting 'earnest', the shifting modes of presentation are accepted as a convention. The disjuncture, however, is perhaps not as pronounced as might be thought initially, for frequently a character will demonstrate through his actions the quality he represents. On the level of psychological allegory, for example, the Vice Covetous in *Enough Is as Good as a Feast* is a outward projection of Worldly Man's acquisitive nature, but as the steward of his estate who at times engages in realistic conversation with him, he also stands for the type of companion who both practises covetousness and encourages such behaviour in an individual who struggles with his good and evil impulses. This brings up one last point about characters in the economic interludes indicated earlier but worth emphasizing. In most instances, the audiences would have clearly recognized themselves and other familiar persons represented in the acting space. Popish priests, Genevan evangelists, courtiers, merchants, landlords, lawyers, city apprentices, prostitutes, common labourers, and servants, fill the dramatis personae of these plays and enable the playwright to add an additional layer of topical meaning. This topical dimension is also helpful in locating the play's action within particular time and place.

33.4 AUDIENCES AND PERFORMANCE SPACES

Who made up the audiences of these interludes? Where were they performed, and by whom? They surely would have appealed to ordinary playgoers in London. Since the action of *The Tide Tarrieth No Man* takes place in the city, we can reasonably assume that it was performed there, although a touring company might have staged it elsewhere. When Courage catches up with Greediness, he asks him where he is going. 'Towardes Powles Crosse' is the merchant's reply; he is on his way there to track down 'my ill debtors' who frequent the place to hear sermons, and indeed at St Paul's Cross Debtor is arrested by the Sergeant. *The Cruel Debtor* mentions London as if the action is partly set there and suggests that the Clink prison is close by. In *Enough Is as Good as a Feast*, Covetous's fellow Vices are familiar with London prisons; they have searched for their master in the Marshalsea, Newgate, and the King's Bench. The play makes references to other locations in and around London, such as Blackheath, Tyburn, and St Paul's (which dominates the panorama of London, Figure 33.1). *Enough*'s author, William Wager, must have known London very well. He was born there and served as rector of St Benet Gracechurch from 1567, around the time his interludes were published in the city. Other London connections indicate that he resided there most, if not all, of his life. His parish church of St Benet's was walking distance to what appears to have been a theatre district developing in the vicinity. Gracechurch Street was the location of two of London's most popular play-producing inns, the Cross Keys and the Bell; a third inn, the Bull in Bishopsgate, was just a few streets away. These inns, as well as several nearby halls, the Merchant Taylors' Hall, Leadenhall (also on Gracechurch Street), and the Drapers' Hall, were connected with dramatic performances during the early decades of Elizabeth's reign or before (Wickham 1963: 185–6). The registry of St Benet Gracechurch, moreover,

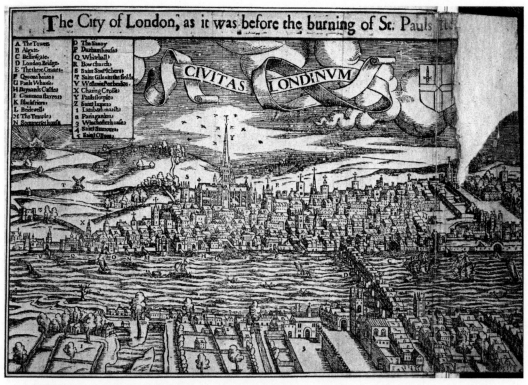

Fig. 33.1 Panorama. *The City of London, as it was before the burning of St. Pauls ste[eple]* (1565). The spire was destroyed by lightning in 1561.

yields the first known Elizabethan reference to a named professional actor, 'Robert Burger, a common player' (Bentley 1929: 370). It seems to me entirely plausible that interludes such as Wager's own *Enough Is as Good as a Feast*, *The Trial of Treasure*, and *The Cruel Debtor* would have been popular fare at both the public halls and the inns in London during these years. *The Trial* may have been intended for one of the Gracechurch Street inns across from Wager's parish, for in a scene where Lust meets Lady Treasure, Natural Inclination calls out, 'Drawer, let us have a pynte of white wyne & borage' (Wager 1920: D3^r); a drawer is a barman who draws wine or ale from a barrel. This would indicate, I think, indoor inn performance, rather than staging in the yard. At the same time, 'yard' playhouses began to appear in the vicinity of London as early as 1567, with the Red Lion in operation at least from that year, and of course the better-known public playhouses of the Theatre and the Curtain opening in 1576–7 and Blackfriars (where the boys' productions took place) around the same time.

It is generally assumed that these interludes were written for professional troupes on tour. As David Bevington (1962) has shown, they all require extensive and intricately worked-out doubling of parts by actors skilled in changing roles quickly (in as few as ten lines) and musical ability, particularly singing. And there is no question that aristocratic troupes performed them, as the eyewitness report of 'The Cradle of Security' by a noblemen's troupe in Gloucester Guildhall in about 1575 proves (Douglas and Greenfield 1986: 362–4). Moreover, as I have argued elsewhere, aristocratic patrons who actively promoted the religious and economic ideas promoted in the interludes discussed above (the earls of Leicester and Warwick, the Duchess of Suffolk) patronized such companies and presumably used them also for propaganda purposes (P. White 1993: 62–6). But we should definitely not rule out amateur playing, either of the highly skilled variety at the boys' schools or of a more occasional nature, especially now that it is known that doubling was also used by amateur playing troupes, and that such troupes might have found that practice advantageous when they made short 'tours'. John Wasson has identified an amateur group who used extensive doubling in their parish play in Yorkshire during James I's reign, and another known parish troupe in Stanton, Oxfordshire, who took their Christmas play on a short tour is also known to have doubled roles (Wasson 1994: 151–2; P. White 2008: 196–7). Indeed, I would suggest that the casting requirements advertised on the title pages of these plays were targeting local churchwardens as well as professional actors. Among them appear to have been the previously identified wardens of Bungay Holy Trinity, who, in 1558, evidently purchased one printed playbook for 4*d*., and then turned it over to a scribe for copying out individual acting parts. The Elizabethan clergyman Samuel Harsnet surely has moral interludes in mind when recalling in 1603 'the old church plays, when the nimble Vice would skip up nimbly like a Jack an Apes into the devil's neck, and ride the devil a course' (114–15). It is worth adding that *Like Will to Like*, which concludes with the Vice riding off on Satan's back, may have been written by Fulwell for his parish church of St Andrew's in Naunton, Gloucestershire. Having said that, clearly the appeal of these economic interludes with their concern with rack-renting, usurious moneylending, and other abuses would have been to urban communities in the provinces as well as in London.

33.5 THE POST-1575 LEGACY

By 1580 the exploding commercial scene in London created careers for professional authors, who thereafter dominated playwriting for the popular stage. As already observed, the extant homiletic interludes on economic issues of the previous two decades had been written largely by Protestant clergymen. That some of these preacher–playwrights now lost faith or interest in the stage is illustrated by Stephen Gosson, who forsook writing plays in favour of penning polemical tracts against them and settling into a parochial ministry. Moreover, the Queen's Men acting company, formed in 1583, ushered in the age of the large-cast play. Where groups of four to seven actors were typically involved in staging the early Elizabethan interludes, plays now called for as many as eighteen actors, making it possible to present thirty or more characters engaged in more complex plot lines (MacLean and McMillin 1998). If these changes brought an end to those plays we now call interludes, their extended critique of economic issues, as well as the sophisticated dramaturgy developed to explore those issues theatrically, survived in countless city comedies. It is beyond the scope of this chapter to examine the post-interlude tradition, but let me close my discussion with reference to a pair of plays by the Elizabethan actor–playwright Robert Wilson, *The Three Ladies of London* (*c*.1581) and *The Three Lords and Ladies of London* (*c*.1589), which most faithfully extend the aims and methods of the economic interludes of the early Elizabethan period, and which represent a transitional phase between the moral interludes and the later 'money plays' of Marlowe, Shakespeare, Heywood, Jonson, and Massinger.

In *The Three Ladies of London*, which Wilson probably penned as a member of Leicester's Men in the early 1580s, the city is seduced by Lady Lucre through her corrupt servants Dissimulation (a farmer), Fraud (a ruffian), Simony (a churchman), and Usury (a merchant). The other ladies, Love and Conscience, are evicted from their homes by Usury; the former becomes a monster with two faces, while Conscience, reduced to selling brooms for a living, is further humiliated when Lucre spots her face with ink from 'the boxe of all abhomination' (Wilson 1592: E1^r). Faring no better are the virtuous countryman Simplicity, who is whipped by Fraud (a respectable burgess), and his penniless cousin Sincerity, a godly minister, who ends up in the parish of St Nihil (Nothing) because he cannot bribe Simony (read bishop). Wilson comes down hard on foreign immigrants, who crowd into port cities and cause housing rents to soar, and whose poor-quality goods sold at cheap prices put skilled English craftsmen out of business. Imported luxuries (the very goods the Norwich Grocers' traffic in) should be restricted. Wilson is both daring and specific in his attack on the economic abuses of the powerful in *Three Ladies*: Usury has been 'seene at the Exchange very lately'; Simony 'seene walking in Paules, having conference & very great familiaritie with some of the Cleargie' (F3^v). However, he moderates his position somewhat in his post-Armada sequel, *Three Lords and Ladies of London* (1590), a Queen's Men play. In celebrating London's success in the wake of victory over Spain, the city's commercial prowess is treated favourably in this play. Lady Lucre, the villain of the previous play, bans her former suitors (who now flourish in Catholic countries) and, at the play's conclusion, marries Lord Pomp, himself abandoning his former usurious ways. By 1590, this more favourable Protestant view of the commercial world receives increased attention.

Precisely because they intersect with important developments in late Tudor drama, print culture, and religion, the early Elizabethan interludes on economic reform merit further study. Clearly, most of the plays we have examined here reflect the profound anxiety with which many English reformers greeted the rapid expansion of commercialism in early modern England, particularly in London. In pamphlet after pamphlet, sermon after sermon, the reformers decried the social injustice and spiritual dangers of commercial practice and protested government policy on usury. By way of the interludes, the theatre provided them with the ideal vehicle through which to convey the duplicity, deception, and social destructiveness they associated with the culture of the marketplace. At the same time, plays such as the Norwich

Pageant of Paradise and *The Three Lords and Ladies of London* embody that spirit of capitalism that Weber and Tawney linked directly to Protestantism; how many other plays reflected this generally sympathetic view of urban commerce and its positive link to religion in early Elizabethan England is impossible to say, since so few of them are extant. *The Three Lords and Three Ladies* in particular looks ahead to Thomas Heywood's extended panegyric to Sir Thomas Gresham and the opening of the Royal Exchange in 1569, *If You Know Not Me You Know Nobody II* (*c*.1603), which celebrates England's mercantile strength as a sign of providential favour. At the opposite end of the spectrum (and drawing extensively on the dramaturgy and ethos of the earlier interludes) is Christopher Marlowe's *The Jew of Malta*, which condemns this conflation of religious sentiment with commercial gain by having Barabas justify his massive accumulation of riches as 'the blessings' due to Abraham and his offspring. Even if Barabas, in his role as Vice, or villain, eventually dismisses this belief and all religion, there is enough correspondence between it and the conviction that English prosperity is a clear manifestation of England's 'elect nation' status for audiences at the Rose playhouse to have grasped Marlowe's point.

PRIMARY WORKS

BALE, JOHN (1986), *The Complete Plays of John Bale*, ed. Peter Happé, 2 vols (Cambridge: Brewer).

CALVIN, JEAN (1582), *The Institution of the Christian Religion*, trans. Thomas Norton.

FULWELL, ULPIAN (1909), *Like Will to Like*, ed. J. S. Farmer (London: Jack).

HARSNET, SAMUEL (1603), *A Declaration of Egregious Popish Impostures*.

LUPTON, THOMAS (1910), *All for Money*, ed. J. S. Farmer (London: Jack).

MARLOWE, CHRISTOPHER (1997), *The Jew of Malta*, ed. David Bevington (Manchester: Manchester University Press).

Norwich (1970), *The Norwich Grocers' Play*, in N. Davis (ed.), *Non-Cycle Plays and Fragments*, EETS, s.s., 1.

PERKINS, WILLIAM (1608), *Workes*, 3 vols.

SMITH, HENRY (1599), *Three Sermons Made by Maister Henry Smith*.

STOW, JOHN (1908), *A Survey of London*, ed. C. L. Kingsford, 2 vols (Oxford: Clarendon Press).

Trial (1908), *The Trial of Treasure*, ed. J. S. Farmer (London: Jack).

WAGER, WILLIAM (1566), *The Cruell Debtter*.

—— (1920), *Enough Is as Good as a Feast*, ed. S. de Ricci (New York: Huntington Library).

WAPULL, GEORGE (1910), *The Tide Tarrieth No Man*, ed. J. S. Farmer (London: Jack).

WILSON, ROBERT (1590), *The Three Lordes and Three Ladies of London*.

—— (1592), *The Three Ladies of London*.

WILSON, THOMAS (1584), *A Discourse upon Usurie*.

CHAPTER 34

OVIDIAN REFLECTIONS IN GASCOIGNE'S *STEEL GLASS*

SYRITHE PUGH

A fascination with Ovid is one of the distinctive features of later Elizabethan literature. But reading and imitating Ovid was central to the humanist education in English grammar schools throughout the century (Baldwin 1944), and the impact of this on English poetry begins to be felt early in Elizabeth's reign. The 1560s saw a spate of translations: Arthur Golding's complete *Metamorphoses* (1567), individual tales in T.H.'s *Fable of Ovid Treating of Narcissus* (1560) and Thomas Peend's *Pleasant Fable of Hermaphroditus and Salmacis* (1565), George Turberville's translation of the *Heroides* (1567), and Thomas Underdowne's of *Ibis* (1569); Thomas Churchyard's translation of *Tristia*, books 1–3, followed in 1572. But the first substantial original work to make prominent use of Ovid in the period is George Gascoigne's *The Steel Glass with The Complaint of Philomene* (1575). It is especially interesting and unusual because, as later poets would do (Pugh 2005; Heather James 2005), it uses Ovid for political ends (Maslen 2000*a*). Indeed, it couples Ovid with Lucilius, the outspoken Republican satirist, as its twin classical inspirations.

Gascoigne's volume has been neglected because it does not fit comfortably into the usual narrative about changing ways of reading Ovid in the Renaissance. The 1560s translations from the *Metamorphoses* are strongly affected by the moralizing tradition, which dominated the medieval reception of Ovid and still figured in the commentaries in sixteenth-century editions. Peend and T.H. devote as much or more space to moralizing and allegorical interpretations as to their chosen tales. Yet there are signs that this moralization is starting to be seen as an optional extra that readers may ignore (Lyne 2001). Both poems divide into two distinct sections, the moralization clearly separated from the narrative, which is told 'straight'. In Golding too, though prefatory poems insist on the 'secret meanings' and moral usefulness of Ovid's tales, the translation itself is uncluttered by such material. The later Elizabethan epyllion is usually seen as having completed this detachment, jettisoning accretions of moral commentary to rediscover the amoral, erotic Ovid beneath. Gascoigne, however, does not discard the moralizing, but uses it in the service of qualities we appreciate today: purposeful ambiguity, complexity, and a ludic irony enabling him to criticize authority while evading censorship. All this makes it deeply Ovidian in ways which reach far beyond the translations of the 1560s and yet which are quite different from later Elizabethan epyllia.

34.1 'My lusting dayes are done': The Penitence of Gascoigne and Ovid

To understand Gascoigne's political use of Ovid in *The Steel Glass*, we must first understand its autobiographical aspect. The story of Philomel—which structures *The Steel Glass* and its accompanying *Complaint of Philomene*—revolves around sexual desire and censorship, dominant themes in the careers of Gascoigne and Ovid alike: both began by writing poetry about adulterous love, and both had their work banned as a result. This is the foundation of Gascoigne's imitation of Ovid in *The Steel Glass*, but it is a resemblance he recognized earlier.

Gascoigne's first publication, *A Hundred Sundry Flowers* (1573), may have attracted the censors' attention: this is at least the impression given by Gascoigne in a revised edition, retitled *The Posies* (1575).[1] Here an apologetic letter 'To the reverende Divines' (apparently the High Commission, the ecclesiastical body responsible for censorship) defends Gascoigne against supposed charges that the 1573 volume contained 'wanton speeches and lascivious phrases' and an exposé of an actual adulterous affair, 'written to the scandalizing of some worthie personages', in its prose narrative *The Adventures of Master F.J.* (Gascoigne 2000: 359, 362–3). The present edition, he avows, is 'clensed from all unclenly wordes', and is supposed to demonstrate 'the reformation of [his] minde' (363). The apparent attempt to placate the censors was not successful, however, and *The Posies* (we know for sure) was recalled in 1576 (Greg and Boswell 1930: 86–7).

---

[1] Prouty (1942) assumes that the 1573 volume must have been banned; Clegg is more cautious (1997: 103–22).

Gascoigne was to repeat this claim of moral reformation in later publications, including the epistle to Leicester in *The Steel Glass*. In fact it is a note he had already struck in the middle of the 1573 volume ('Gascoigne's Recantation', Gascoigne 2000: 273–4), and is better seen as a stance periodically adopted for rhetorical purposes than as evidence of actual change. Nevertheless, it has had a strong influence on Gascoigne's modern critics, and it is widely held that after the *Posies* he 'cranked out works which were either grimly moralistic or insipidly occasional', in an effort to comply with the censorious outlook of his betters and thereby gain employment (McCoy 1985: 32). But this supposed conformism has been greatly exaggerated. Felicity Hughes has demonstrated that 'the "revised" and supposedly expurgated volume of 1575 is no "cleaner" than the first', concluding 'that it represents an attempt to brazen it out with the censors rather than to placate them' (1997: 1). His other professions of penitence ring hollow, too: *The Steel Glass*, in particular, is far from compliant, rather mounting a devastating counter-attack on his enemies.

In its broad outlines, Gascoigne's encounter with censorship echoes Ovid's. Ovid's first publication, the *Amores*, is a poetic collection about an apparently adulterous affair, with a loosely narrative shape. Though written in the first person, these poems are often regarded as employing an ironic persona, as Gascoigne's love poetry repeatedly does (Cahoon 1988; Stephens 1986). He proceeded to reduce the sophisticated stratagems of the lovers in the *Amores* to a set of teachable principles in a mock-didactic treatise, the *Ars amatoria*. Again, though it claims to be concerned only with courtesans and not respectable married women, there are hints that the love in question is adulterous. Ovid was thus rather openly flouting Augustus' laws on sexual morality; a few years later the *Ars* was the reason given publicly for his 'relegation' to Tomis, an imperial outpost on the Black Sea, where he remained until his death, writing verse epistles to friends, family, and people of influence for publication back in Rome. These two collections, the *Tristia* and *Ex ponto*, protest his repentance for having written wanton verse, but his innocence of actual crime; they complain bitterly about the miseries of exile, and plead for their author to be recalled. Like Gascoigne's late work, they have usually been thought dull and insipid, with the poet's former liveliness and originality replaced by abject grovelling for a pragmatic end. Yet behind the cover of the penitent persona Ovid launches a sustained attack on Augustus' despotism and the venality of contemporary society.

Gascoigne certainly draws analogies between his own career and Ovid's in the 1575 *Posies*. A prefatory verse urges any reader offended by his work to

> reade but others workes, and marke if that they finde,
> No toyes therein which may dislike, some modest readers minde?
> Reade *Virgills Pryapus*, or *Ovids* wanton verse,
> Which he about *Corinnaes* couche, so clerkly can rehearse.

> (2000: 385)

As well as comparing his writing to Ovid's, Gascoigne follows Ovid's own defence against charges of scurrility levelled at the *Ars*. In *Tristia* 2, Ovid asserts that the most respectable literature contains 'the theme of love' and 'much that is frivolous' ('materia amoris', 'multa jocosa'; 1959, lines 382, 422): even Virgil has 'played' with the theme of love in his *Eclogues* and *Aeneid* 4 (lines 533–8).[2] Gascoigne's epistle 'To the Divines' also mentions Ovid, interestingly associating him with the idea of censorship as castration which figures largely in *The Steel Glass*. Gascoigne defends his decision to republish his 'wanton' work:

I have seene dyverse Authours, (both learned and well learned) which after they have both reformed their lives, and converted their studies, have not yet disdeyned to read the Poems which they let passe their pennes in youth [...] I neither take example of wanton Ovid, doting Nigidius, nor foolish Samocratius. But I delight to thinke that the reverend father Theodore Beza, whose life is worthily become a lanterne to the whole worlde, did not yet disdaine too suffer the continued publication of such Poemes as he wrote in youth. And as he termed them at last *Poëmata castrata*, So shal your reverend judgements beholde in this seconde edition, my Poemes gelded from all filthie phrases.   (2000: 361)

While mentioning Ovid as an example of a penitent love poet who did not altogether repudiate his early erotic work, Gascoigne understandably finds Beza, the Protestant theologian who had published amatory poetry in his youth, a more suitable role model to advertise 'to the Divines'. Yet Beza does not seem ever to have used this expression, 'Poëmata castrata', and Gascoigne could have found the idea, and a model for the hermaphroditic persona adopted in *The Steel Glass*, in Ovid's exile poetry.

In *Ex ponto* 1. 1, Ovid begs admittance to Rome for his 'chaste verses' ('casti versus'; 1959, line 8). He promises that they contain nothing amorous (line 14), but only 'praise of the gods' ('laudes [...] deorum'; line 29), that is, of Augustus—and those who come to praise the gods are not driven away:

Who would be so bold as to drive away from the threshold one who shakes the jangling Egyptian sistra in his hand? When the piper plays on the curved horn before the mother of the gods, who refuses him his meagre fee?

(ecquis ita est audax, ut limine cogat abire iactantem Pharia tinnula sistra manu? ante deum Matrem cornu tibicen adunco cum canit, exiguae quis stipis aera negat?)   (lines 37–40)

Ovid here likens himself to a priest of Isis and to a *gallus*, one of the eunuch priests of Cybele. As he explains in *Fasti* 4, the castrating of the *galli* commemorates Attis, a devotee of Cybele who broke his vow of chastity. The angry goddess killed his beloved, and Attis, maddened, emasculated himself, declaring, 'Let the parts which harmed me die!' ('pereant partes, quae nocuere mihi'; lines 239–40). Ovid's self-comparison to a *gallus* is laden with memories of this story, both in his own account and in Catullus' *Carmina* 63; these resonances reflect badly on the Augustus he ostensibly tries to appease. Like Attis, Ovid has incurred the wrath of a vengeful god by transgressing a strict code of sexual morality; Catullus' Attis also laments his exile, making his plight even closer to Ovid's. These echoes imply a parallel between Augustus and

---

[2] All translations from Latin to English are my own.

Cybele, which gives an unflattering twist to the rhetoric of deification through which Ovid expresses his supposedly zealous loyalty to Augustus and Augustan values. Attis' story illustrates the extremity of Cybele's wrath, far from the image of sober Roman rationality and clemency Augustus wanted to cultivate.

This is typical of Ovid's approach in the exile poetry: behind the penitent façade is a sustained exposé of Augustus' unreasonable ferocity, exemplified by Ovid's unjust punishment. The apparently abject and helpless poet launches an oblique but devastating counter-attack; out of seemingly harmless laments comes a real power to harm. When Gascoigne imitated these methods in *The Steel Glass*, he may also have had another example in mind. In *Tristia* 5. 1, after another assurance that he has abandoned wanton verse, Ovid claims that he now only writes 'to lighten misfortune with words', which is 'why Procne and Alcyone make their complaint' ('est aliquid, fatale malum per verba levare: | hoc querulam Procnen Halcyonenque facit'; lines 59–60). Alcyone may be a convincing example of harmless plangency, but Procne, Philomel's sister, is another matter: her complaint ends in bloody revenge. Here, then, is another hint of the threat concealed beneath the surface of Ovid's lamenting. Poets have at least the power to make their enemies infamous: as he warns an anonymous enemy in *Tristia* 4. 9, 'if I should have no opportunity for revenge, the Muses will give me power and their weapons' ('denique vindictae si sit mihi nulla facultas, | Pierides vires et sua tela dabunt'; lines 15–16).

In *The Steel Glass* Gascoigne too applies the myth of Philomel and Procne to his own experience of censorship, and running through this volume—published the same year as his 'gelded' *Posies*—is a similar ambiguity over the power of song. On one hand, the poet's art is associated, through the lament of the nightingale Philomel, with the supposed helplessness of women, 'whose force is not to force' and whose 'words', mere 'blasts of blustring winde', are no compensation for their physical weakness (1575: Q4^r). On the other, Procne and Philomel are hardly examples of feminine helplessness, and while Procne is presented as making an unfeminine choice of vengeful *action*, the whole process of their revenge is initiated by Philomel's creation of a narrative of her victimization. Gascoigne's text is equivalent to Philomel's tapestry, and by reproving vice in the high places of society it has the same ability to exact vengeance, whether merely by shaming his enemies, as Ovid threatens in *Tristia* 4. 9, or, like her, by rousing others to action, for 'right revenge doth rayse rebellion' where 'crueltie [and] tyrannie [...] raigne' (C3^r).

34.2 REPROVING THE REPROVERS: OVID AND SATIRE IN *THE STEEL GLASS*

Ovid's story of Philomel, the maiden raped and mutilated by her brother-in-law Tereus and finally transformed into a nightingale, frames Gascoigne's volume. *The*

Fig. 34.1 Tereus cuts out Philomel's tongue. Ovid, *Metamorphoseon* (1582), Q6ʳ.

Steel Glass begins by invoking the nightingale, who, like Gascoigne, sings for lovers, and who teaches him to defy his enemies:

> This worthy bird, hath taught my weary Muze,
> To sing a song, in spight of their despight,
> Which worke my woe, withouten cause or crime.
>
> (B1ʳ)

Those enemies, Gascoigne explains, are in fact descendants of Philomel's persecutor Tereus, who 'did carve hir pleasant tong, | To cover so, his owne foule filthy fault' (Figure 34.1). Gascoigne draws a clear parallel between Philomel's mutilation and the censorship of his earlier volumes, implying that his censors were motivated by a desire to hide their own 'foule fault'. The suggestion is that the bishops of the High Commission—or someone behind them—are guilty of the kind of sexual escapades recounted in the *Hundred Sundry Flowers*. Though Gascoigne asks Philomene to help him tell 'A tale [...] which may content the mindes | Of learned men, and grave Philosophers' (B1ᵛ), it is already apparent that this morally unexceptionable satire attacks precisely those 'learned men' who censored his work.

Before we come to the main body of *The Steel Glass*'s satire, we encounter an elaborate adaptation of Philomel's story, which teases out these implications. It opens by springing a very surprising persona on us:

> I am not he whom slaunderous tongues have tolde,
> (False tongues in dede, and craftie subtile braines)
> To be the man, which ment a common spoyle
> Of loving dames, whose eares wold heare my words
> Or trust the tales devised by my pen.
> I n'am a man, as some do thinke I am,
> (Laugh not good Lord) I am in dede a dame,
> Or at the least, a right *Hermaphrodite*.
>
> (B2ʳ)

This hermaphrodite introduces herself as Satyra, daughter to Plain Dealing and Simplicity, sister to Poesy. She relates how the nobleman Vain Delight, attended by followers including False Semblant and Flearing Flattery, married Poesy and took her to live at court. Years later, Vain Delight fetches Satyra to visit her sister; on the return voyage, 'enflamde' by Satyra's song, he ravishes her 'to please his wanton minde' (B3ᵛ). Fearing that she will 'disclose | His incest', he sends Slander to accuse her of enticing him 'to love and luste'. Finally, they imprison her 'in cage of Miserie' and 'Cut out [her] tong, with *Raysor of Restraynte*, | Least [she] should wraye, this bloudy deed of his' (B4ʳ). This is Ovid's tale of Philomel, with the characters replaced by allegorical personifications. Indeed, Satyra ends by comparing herself to Philomel explicitly, because they are both permitted by the gods to continue singing despite their mutilated tongues.

Gascoigne's main thrust is obvious. Those who censored his work first used it 'to please [their] wanton mind': they enjoyed reading the naughty bits. Indeed, the act of censorship, as in the Philomel story, is intended to conceal the censors' own crimes. That Gascoigne's persona is called Satyra contributes to this, implying that the censored work was intended satirically, as indeed the *Posies* claimed: after the comparisons to Ovid and 'Virgil' quoted above, the prefatory poem continues:

> *Lucilius* ledde the daunce, and *Horace* made the lawe,
> That poetes by Aucthoritie, may cal (A dawe) *A Dawe*,
> And eke (a hore) *A hore*, but yet in cleanly wordes,
> So that the vice may be rebukt.
>
> (Gascoigne 2000: 385–6)

If Gascoigne described lewd behaviour, in other words, he did so in the spirit of the satirists Lucilius and Horace, to punish vice by exposing it to public ridicule. Even when it appeared wanton, his poetry was merely holding a mirror to society.

This is also the point of Gascoigne's main addition to the Philomel story in *The Steel Glass*, Slander's accusation that Satyra 'entist *Delight*'. This alludes to the charge that the *Hundred Sundry Flowers* tried to 'seduce' young readers, against which Gascoigne argues, in the epistle 'To al yong Gentlemen' in the *Posies*, that the reader is responsible for the moral effect of reading:

as the industrious Bee may gather honie out of the most stinking weede, so the malicious Spider may also gather poyson out of the fayrest floure that growes [...] To speake English it is your using (my lustie Gallants) or misusing of these Posies that may make me praysed or dispraysed for publishing of the same. For if you (where you may learn to avoyd the subtile sandes of wanton desire) will runne upon the rockes of unlawfull lust, then great is your folly, and greater will growe my rebuke.   (2000: 366–7)

Again, the position could be derived from Ovid's defence of the *Ars* in *Tristia* 2, where he posits that if readers are viciously inclined, whatever they touch will instruct them in it: even Ennius and Lucretius will prompt thoughts about illicit sex. Verse read in an honest frame of mind, meanwhile, can harm no one. By translating this into the fable of Slander's attack on Satyra, Gascoigne claims that the author of erotica is as innocent as a rape victim, and the charge that it corrupts the young an undeserved slur on the helpless and abused.

Gascoigne's adoption of the hermaphroditic persona works to similar ends, as jocular reassurance that this is the work of a chaste and innocent Gascoigne, not the reputed sexual predator of the earlier volumes. It implicitly reprises the image of the 'Poëmata castrata' in the epistle 'To the Divines': hermaphroditism was considered, not a combination of sexual attributes, but a deficiency of masculinity and equivalent to castration. Like Ovid using the image of his own castration to compare Augustus' treatment of him to the excessive rage of Cybele against Attis, Gascoigne deploys it to align his censors with that other Ovidian figure of tyranny and censorship Tereus. The figurative castration is gradually elided with the glossectomy which Satyra tells us has made her 'Not as I seemd, a man sometimes of might, | But womanlike, whose teares must venge hir harms' (B4^r).

The emasculated persona is evidently intended to imply that the current work is not only sexually innocent, but altogether innocuous. Like the passive text imagined in the epistle 'To al yong Gentlemen', powerless to influence how its readers use or abuse it, Gascoigne suggests that Satyra's, Philomene's, and his own 'mournefull' plaints are devoid of any manly 'might' to act on the world, and merely afford the same relief as 'teares'. It evokes Ovid's claim in *Tristia* 5. 1 that his exile poetry is written only as therapy, like Alycone's or Procne's songs, and it is just as disingenuous. Gascoigne's imitation of the fable of Philomel ends with Satyra's mutilation and imprisonment, but here, just at the point where he ceases to pursue Ovid's narrative, a marginal gloss directs us to it: 'note now and compare this allegory to the story of Progne and Philomele'. Gascoigne thus points us to Ovid's conclusion, where Philomel is far from helpless. 'Teares' are certainly not the only recourse for Ovid's sisters, who do not lack the 'might' to take vengeance. If Gascoigne resembles these women, his enemies should beware. While superficially Satyra elides that vengeance, comparing her song to the 'pleasant note' of the nightingale in its aftermath, her description of that song makes it resemble another part of Ovid's tale:

> That with the stumps of my reproved tong,
> I may sometimes, *Reprovers* deedes reprove,
> And sing a verse, to make them see themselves.
>
> (B4ʳ)

What reveals and reproves Tereus' deeds in Ovid's story is Philomel's tapestry, which prompts the sisters' hideous revenge. Beneath the surface, then, it is this potent and dangerous writing to which Gascoigne compares his own.

Given the way in which Satyra's glossectomy is elided, as noted above, with the figurative castration of Gascoigne and his *Posies*, the two anatomical extremities becoming blurred into one another, the image of Satyra continuing to sing 'with the stumps of her reproved tong' might also prompt us to wonder whether Gascoigne's continuing to write proves that his 'castration' has not been entirely successful—particularly if we remember the frequent puns on pens and penises in *The Adventures of Master F.J.* Satyra's song, after all, will be *The Steel Glass*, Gascoigne's satirical attack on the corruption and injustice of his society, demonstrating an aggressive potency far from the innocuous, therapeutic lamenting which the femininity of his persona is intended to convey. The unusual spelling of Satyra's name carries a similar implication, recalling the widespread but false etymology which derived 'satire' from 'satyr': as well as representing the literary genre, Satyra is also a feminized version of the notoriously lustful mythological beast. A priapic and unreformed Gascoigne peeps through the modest female dress.

The fable of Satyra also makes more general points about the role of poetry in society and about how Ovid should be read. It is strongly reminiscent of an interpretation of Philomel's story in Sabinus' well-known commentary, but differs in pointed and significant ways. According to Sabinus, Procne and Philomel

are to be understood as Oratory and Poetry, which are nearly sisters [...] because one wants to live in roofs and cities, the other in groves and woods, signifying that the swallow is like the eloquence of the city, and those who practise eloquence in houses, in the senate and in the forum. The nightingale is truly like the eloquence of the grove and of poets, who love woods and solitudes, and places haunted by Muses and by gods, not by men, and who handle matters as different from legal disputes as can be imagined.

(intellexisse Oratoriam & Poeticam, quae prope sorores sint [...] quod in altera sit mira libido tecta & urbes incolendi, in altera arbusta & sylvas: significantes hirundinem similem esse urbanae eloquentiae, & illis qui in domibus, in senatu, in foro, suam facundiam exercent; Philomelam vero similem eloquentie nemorali & Poetarum, qui sylvas & solitudines, & loca non ab hominibus, sed a Musis & a diis celebrata, amant: & materias a forensibus controversiis remotissimas tractant.)   (1584: 245)

While rhetoric is involved in the social and political, poetry confines itself to a purely aesthetic realm, transcending mundane concerns. For Gascoigne, however, it is Poetry which, as the Procne figure, is taken to the abode of men—here not a city, where political and legal questions are openly debated, but rather the court, home to Vain Delight, Flearing Flattery, Detraction, and Deceit, a place where language is abused to pervert truth and justice. Gascoigne's Philomel figure is Satyra–satire, and she keeps her distance from populous abodes not because she is unconcerned with worldly affairs, but because the false values of court are antipathetic to her. Her 'simple mynde' cannot be won 'from tracke of trustie truth' by courtiers' 'guiles'; in turn her honest speech is not tolerated, but deemed 'medling' and suppressed with the 'Raysor of Restraynte' (B3ᵛ). Gascoigne implies that, in the transition from the Roman-style mixed constitution evoked by Sabinus' image of the city, with its senate and forums, to the centralized power of the early modern court, there is no longer any place for oratory's openness. Poetry takes its place, because its artifice and indirection are more assimilable to the deceptive forms of speech current, and necessary, at court (Ahl 1984; Javitch 1978). Yet this represents not a depoliticization of discourse, but its opposite: the alternative to poetry's courtiership is not aesthetic transcendence but the critical distance from the centre of power now symbolized by Satyra's remote dwelling.

Gascoigne's adaptation reads Ovid's tale as political satire *about* satire and freedom of speech (an appropriately self-reflexive gesture for a poem calling itself a mirror). Though his use of allegory may seem quaint, his interpretation is not far-fetched. Within Ovid's *Metamorphoses*, Philomel's tapestry reminds us of another victimized weaver earlier in the same book. Arachne's depiction of male gods transforming themselves into animals to commit rape resembles Ovid's own poem and includes some of the same tales. She is punished by an envious Juno, who transforms her into a spider. It is hard not to see a pattern, in which Ovid aligns himself with artists subjugated because they reveal the crimes of tyrants. That the artist in the later Philomel episode achieves revenge suggests that in Ovid, as in Gascoigne, oppression turns art into an oblique political weapon.

34.3 MISLEADING READINGS: MORALIZING *THE COMPLAINT OF PHILOMENE*

The Steel Glass is followed by Gascoigne's translation of Ovid's fable, presented as a dream vision in a frame offering ironically conflicting interpretations. Gascoigne recounts how he falls asleep listening to a nightingale, wishing 'To understand, what hir swete notes might meane' (K3ᵛ). In his dream 'a dame of heavenly kinde', bearing a scourge and a bridle, comes to him.[3] She later identifies herself as Nemesis, but here we have only a clue: her demeanour is said to signify 'That *Just revenge*, is *Prest for every chance*' (K3ᵛ). She tells him the gods have sent her to answer his prayer, and proceeds to recount Philomel's story in a fairly close translation of Ovid's tale. Oddly for a divine messenger, she defers to Ovid as an authority: 'For he that wel, *Dan Nasoes*

---

[3] The scourge and bridle are attributes of Nemesis in later emblem books, but Gascoigne seems to have been the first to devise this emblem.

verses notes, | Shall finde my words to be no fained thing' (K4^r). This ironic moment anticipates the tussle at the end of the poem over who has authority to assign meaning to a text, reprising the earlier themes of satire, censorship, and interpretation. The *Complaint* ends with quite different interpretations of the fable from Nemesis and the dreamer. Both are moralizing in tendency and thus, superficially, conformist. But both are riven by irony, the dreamer's especially undoing itself by internal confusions, self-parody, and most of all by contradicting Nemesis's supposedly authoritative reading. The way in which these orthodox readings trip each other up neutralizes their attempt to overrule the political interpretation of Ovid's fable implied throughout Gascoigne's volume. But it also implicitly asserts that interpretation is arbitrary, and that therefore authors cannot be held responsible for the kind of incendiary meaning we saw hinted at above.

The translation itself highlights what we might call the gender politics of the tale, but for the most part avoids making explicit its wider political implications. Yet our reading is necessarily coloured by Gascoigne's earlier allegorical reworking of Ovid's tale in the fable of Satyra, with its strong political and autobiographical overtones, and the *Complaint* goes beyond that fable by including the terrible revenge of Philomel and Procne, which was there elided. If Gascoigne's adoption of the female persona Satyra at the beginning of the volume presented him as a harmless victim, to be pitied and not suspected of posing any further threat to the authorities, the conclusion of Ovid's tale reveals the disingenuousness of that argument. The poet and satirist may rely on women's proverbial weapon, words, but these are far from the innocuous last resort of the powerless. Philomel's narrative of her rape, woven into the tapestry she sends to her sister, instigates the violence and bloodshed that follows, as the sisters murder Tereus' son and feed him to his father. The women who provide the archetype for 'textual' composition in their weaving are indeed a fit analogy for the poet, but one which implies dangerous power, not innocence and vulnerability. The Muses offer the poet weapons, just as a woman's weapon is her tongue, and these weapons are anything but weak.

The political interpretation of Philomel's tale reaches what could be seen as its climax, though a veiled one, with an intratextual echo at the moment when Procne resolves to suppress her 'womanlike' pity and take her terrible revenge. Here Gascoigne adds a stanza more self-justifying in tone than anything in the original:

> You should degenerate,
> If right revenge you slake,
> More right revenge can never bee,
> Than this revenge to make.

> (O2^v)

The repeated phrase 'right revenge' strikes a chord across the volume. At the beginning of *The Steel Glass*, Gascoigne saw in his glass 'a world, of worthy government', where 'No crueltie nor tyrannie can raigne, | No right revenge, doth rayse rebellion' (C3^r). This ideal commonwealth, we soon realize, is an inversion, not a reflection, of contemporary reality. Gascoigne implies that his own age, perhaps his own society, is tyrannical. He certainly indicates that rebellion against tyranny is justifiable, a far from orthodox view. The official position was that tyrants are placed in power by God to punish our sins, so that to resist them is to earn 'everlasting damnation' (*Certain Sermons* 1559: S2^r). Protestants responding to religious persecutions sometimes thought differently, however: that same Beza to whom Gascoigne compared himself in the *Posies*, for instance, argued for the right to depose tyrants in *De jure magistratum* (1574), written in response to the St Barthlomew's Day massacre in 1572. Gascoigne's intratextual echo places Procne's tyrannicide in the context of sixteenth-century resistance theory. If her act also represents the poet's power to strike back at the authorities who condemn him, one cannot imagine a more dramatic overturning of Gascoigne's supposedly conformist and penitent stance.

Nemesis attempts to efface these radical political implications with her moralizing reading, and to reinforce this reading she intrudes the ultimate image of authority into the conclusion of the tale, as 'the heavenly benche' (to which she belongs) metamorphoses Tereus, Philomel, and Procne to break the cycle of violence and as punishment for their crimes. There is no suggestion of divine intervention in Ovid. Like the Christianizing commentaries, the addition suggests that the *Metamorphoses* reflects a Christian providential world-view, but here the idea serves a political end. Well into Nemesis's commentary, after the expected denunciation of Tereus, we realize that she embodies not Philomel's and Procne's vengeance on Tereus, nor divine vengeance on him through them as agents, but divine vengeance on all three characters: it is only at this point that Nemesis names herself. The sisters are culpable because 'men must leave revenge to Gods, | What wrong soever raigne' (P3^v). The use of 'raigne' indicates that this prohibition covers not only private revenge, but also tyrannicide, contradicting the reference to 'right revenge' at the beginning of *The Steel Glass* and adopting the position of the 'Homily on Obedience'.

This 'paraphrase' is Nemesis's last word, but our earlier impressions regarding her remain strong, and these tend to identify her—as a powerful female figure, embodying revenge—with Philomel and Procne, implicitly endorsing their actions. The initial description of her demeanour—'by this it may appeare, | That *Just revenge*, is *Prest for every chance*'—chimes with the description of Philomel's opportunism,

> womans witte,
> Which sodainly in queintest chance,
> Can best it selfe acquit.

> (N2^v)

Moreover, the very image of 'the heavenly bench', which seems to lend authority to Nemesis's reactionary moralization, actually throws it into doubt. An intrusion in Ovid's tale, it is nevertheless not extra-Ovidian: rather, it is remembered from Arachne's story. In her weaving contest with Arachne, Juno depicts the pantheon, an imposing image of divine authority intended to overawe her mortal opponent. If it asserts the orderliness and justice of the gods' reign, however, its lesson is soon undermined. Unable to fault Arachne's work, Juno assaults her and then transforms her into a spider, memorably demonstrating the irrational spite of Ovid's gods. Shadowily evoked by Gascoigne, this hints at the unreliability of Nemesis's commentary on the fable.

At least Nemesis's interpretation addresses the theme of justified resistance, though reversing Gascoigne's earlier position. Before she vanishes, however, Nemesis tells the dreamer to make of her words 'a metaphore' for 'profite and pastime', and the volume concludes with his moralization, a mini-sermon against lust, taking the fable of Philomel for its text. 'O whoredom, whoredom, hope for no good happe', he preaches, promising 'everlasting fire' for those 'which still in sinne do sinke' (Q3^{r-v}). The dreamer thus displays a reductive and distorting obsession with sex, to the exclusion of other moral issues the tale raises. It becomes increasingly clear that it parodies the puritanical attitude to sex which made the High Commission censor Gascoigne's earlier work. The first interesting thing about this as a reflection of the divines' fixation is that it bears so little relation to the real concerns of the gods: Nemesis, their messenger, mentions lust only in passing, concentrating on violence and the ethics of revenge. Secondly, it results in an absurd injustice. After admonishing lustful men, the dreamer turns to women:

> Yea bravest dames, (if they amisse once tredde)
> Finde bitter sauce for al their pleasant feasts.
> They must in fine condemned be to dwell
> In thickes unseene, in mewes for minyons made,
> Until at last, (if they can bryde it wel)
> They may chop chalke, and take some better trade.
>
> (Q4^{v})

The focus on living 'in thickes unseene' makes it clear he is thinking of Philomel, who as a nightingale leads 'covertly | A cloister life' in 'thickes' (O4^{v}). It outrageously implies that rape was a 'pleasant feast' for Philomel's lascivious appetite, for which she now pays. Yet more perversely, her life as nightingale is interpreted as prostitution. The 'thickes unseene' in which Philomel is condemned to dwell are 'mewes for minyons made': as well as a cage for a moulting bird, a 'mew' was any place of confinement; one made for 'minyons' implies a brothel, and the profession awaiting the fallen woman.[4] This implication is reinforced by the hope that such women might one day change 'trade' 'if they can *bryde it wel*', implying a prostitute's tricking a client into wedlock ('bryde' punning on bird and bride, both in the familiar sense of a woman at her marriage and the now obsolete meaning 'to mince, practise affectedly').[5]

This perverse moralization resembles Slander's accusation in the *The Steel Glass* that Satyra 'entist' her attacker (B3^{v}). Slander conspired with the Tereus figure, Vain Delight, to oppress and silence Satyra: the dreamer's slanderous aspersions on Philomel likewise align him, and the censorious divines he parodies, with Tereus. His interpretation transforms the thickets where the metamorphosed Philomel hides for safety into the equivalent of the sheepcote where Tereus raped and imprisoned her—that was also a 'mew' for a 'minyon', a prison where a woman was kept for sexual

---

[4] 'Minion', *OED*, I. 1. b, 'man or woman kept for sexual favours'.   [5] 'Bride', *OED*, *n.*, 1a; *v.*, 2.

favours. (Gascoigne may here be building on a latent, though probably anachronistic, possibility in Ovid's text itself. The word Ovid uses to describe the place of Philomel's confinement is *stabula*, which Gascoigne correctly translates as 'sheepcote' in the body of the *Complaint*. But he might well have been familiar also with its use by later poets including Martial to signify 'brothel'.) The dreamer's 'metaphor', then, repeats Tereus' crime on a figurative level. Once again moralistic reading, whether for the sake of censorship or in the production of a moralizing commentary, is conflated with sexual misconduct, to suggest the hypocrisy of the high commissioners.

A final twist has the same effect. Nemesis moralized Tereus' transformation into a lapwing with observations on lapwing behaviour, asserting that the female flees the male, her chicks flee her, and the father seeks his son with frantic cries. The dreamer gives this a new spin:

> the sonnes of such rash sinning sires,
> Are seldome sene to runne a ruly race.
> But plagude (be like) by fathers foule desires
> Do gadde a broade, and lacke the guide of grace
> Then (Lapwinglike) the father flies about,
> And howles and cries to see his children stray,
> Where he him selfe (and no man better) mought
> Have taught his bratts to take a better way.
>
> (Q4^{r-v})

In this context, the lapwing howling at his children's errancy resembles a sermonizing elder decrying the sins of youth. The censorious divines are again compared to Tereus. But now there is an added barb: wayward youths like Gascoigne have actually learned their wantonness by imitating those same disapproving but hypocritical elders. The bishops offer the youth of society only an example of 'foule desires', not, as they should, 'the guide of grace', and are therefore themselves responsible for the sins of others as well as for their own.

Thanks to the stance struck in this mock sermon, however, Gascoigne also compares himself to Tereus. He too berates youthful errors in this moralizing conclusion, and he, of course, has by his own account (and the divines') been guilty of 'wantonnesse'—so his own example seems almost to prove his accusation against them. This unbalances the reader, accustomed to linking Gascoigne with Tereus' innocent victim throughout the volume. But it is not entirely new: rather it takes us back to the initial description of Gascoigne in *The Steel Glass*, just before Satyra announces her hermaphroditism:

> I am not he whom slaunderous tongues have tolde
> . . .
> To be the man, which ment a common spoyle
> Of loving dames.
>
> (B2^{r})

This predatory male is not so unlike Tereus, and though Gascoigne denies the truth of such 'slander', it is in order to deny that he is a man at all: his disowning of the reputation is no more serious than his humorous adoption of the hermaphroditic persona. We might remember too that Procne considers castrating Tereus:

> Or let me carve with knife,
> The wicked Instrument,
> Wherewith he, thee, and me abusde.
>
> (O1^r)

Gascoigne's figurative castration at the hands of the censors thus also ties him to Tereus as well as to the mutilated Philomel. Of course, this would also confusingly imply that Procne herself is comparable to the censors. When we try to pin down the meaning of this elusive work, it slips away with another ironic twist—which is of course only to say that, thanks to Gascoigne's Ovidian wit, his text contains nothing actionable.

Gascoigne bows out with an invitation to the reader to turn the satire against the author. The 'metaphor', and the volume, end with a direct address to Leicester:

> Then if you see, that (Lapwinglike) I chaunce,
> To leape againe, beyond my lawful reache,
> (I take hard taske) or but to give a glaunce,
> At bewties blase: for such a wilful breache,
> Of promise made, my Lord shal do no wrong,
> To say (*George*) thinke on *Philomelâes* song.
>
> (Q4^v–[R]1^r)

As the hypocrisy of the sermonizing elders he parodies might already suggest, his reform is a precarious thing and unlikely to last. It is not entirely clear, though, what kind of 'wilful breache' he foresees. His metaphor has just explained that hypocritical moralistic preaching, as well as 'lechery', can be called 'Lapwinglike'. His future offence, then, might take the form of orthodox moral didacticism, or another mock sermon, satirizing the authorities. The imagined warning from Leicester would be an appropriate response, reminding the songster of the threat of censorship symbolized in Philomel's mutilation. This ambiguous air of irresponsibility is in keeping with the rest of the work. Even as the last line of the poem names Gascoigne for the first time as himself ('*George*'), apparently putting aside ironic masks in a disarmingly frank relationship with its primary reader, it cedes authority and its very voice. A reader literally has the last word, and Gascoigne retreats to the shadows like a naughty boy whose father knows he is up to something but will never be sure quite what.

The central conceit of the mirror in *The Steel Glass* evokes the long tradition of speculum literature, of which the *Mirror for Magistrates* is a familiar contemporary example. But where the mirror in that tradition offers stable and authoritative moral didacticism, Gascoigne's reminds us that reflections in mirrors are apt to change or vanish as the beholder's viewpoint shifts. The layers of self-reflexive irony in

Gascoigne's volume make it a veritable hall of mirrors. Amid the confusion and ambiguity he passes responsibility for the dangerously satirical implications of his text onto the reader. Interpretation is arbitrary, readers create meaning freely in their reception of the text, and the author cannot be held responsible for it. But even this has a bold political significance. If authors cannot control interpretations put upon their texts by readers, neither can the political authorities. Who is to stop the reader from finding in Gascoigne's text, or in Ovid's, a call for vengeance against tyrants, and from answering it? The reader's responsibility is also the reader's power.

Primary Works

Certain Sermons (1559), *Certayne Sermons appoynted by the Quenes Majestie.*

Gascoigne, George (1575), *The Steele Glas* [. . .] *togither with The Complainte of Phylomene.*

—— (2000), *A Hundreth Sundrie Flowres*, ed. G. W. Pigman III (Oxford: Clarendon Press).

Ovid (1959), *Tristia; Ex ponto*, ed. Arthur Leslie Wheeler, Loeb Classical Library (1924; London: Heinemann).

—— (1984), *The Metamorphoses*, ed. G. P. Goold, Loeb Classical Library, 3rd edn (London: Heinemann).

Sabinus, Georg (ed.) (1584), *Fabularum Ovidii interpretatio, ethica, physica, et historica* (Cambridge).

CHAPTER 35

THE ART OF WAR

MARTIAL POETICS FROM HENRY HOWARD TO PHILIP SIDNEY

D. J. B. TRIM

THE 'art of war' was the subject of a voluminous and wide-ranging literature in Tudor England. Warfare in the sixteenth century underwent dramatic technological and conceptual changes: the former were the fruit of new techniques in metallurgy and of the European discovery and then development of gunpowder weapons; the latter were the fruit of the mindshift associated with the Renaissance. The result was that the art of war itself—the way in which soldiers conducted themselves and were controlled on campaign and in combat—went through a period of significant change. As an English military commentator wrote late in Elizabeth's reign: 'Then was then, and now is now; the wars are much altered since the fierie weapons first came up' (Barret 1598: 2). Mastering the art of war was more complicated and challenging, yet at the same time it was more dependent on system, order, and mathematical principles; the art of war was therefore receptive to systematization and theorization to an extent probably unmatched since classical antiquity—and systematized and theorized it most certainly was, in a voluminous technical and theoretical literature, such as that illustrated here (Figure 35.1), Thomas Styward's *Pathway to Martial Discipline*, deemed 'verie necessarie for young souldiers, or for all such as loveth the profession of armes' (1581: A1^r).

One consequence was that soldiers, more than at any time since antiquity, were also authors, but authors of more than technical and didactic works. This chapter deals

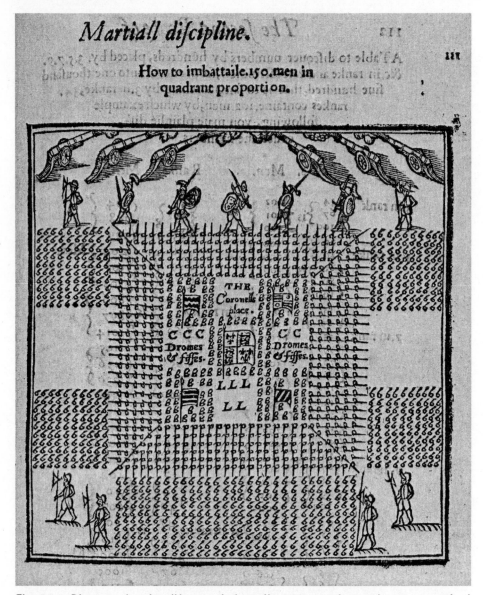

Fig. 35.1 Diagram showing 'How to imbattaile 150 men in quadrant proportion'. Thomas Styward, *Pathwaie to Martiall Discipline* (1581), P4[r]. The 150 men are represented symbolically.

with 'poetry' by military men, or 'martialists', but it takes the view of poetry expressed by Sir Philip Sidney, soldier, general, and poet, who in his influential *Defence of Poesy* includes history as one of the subjects of the poet, and observes: 'One may be a Poet without versing, and a versefier without Poetrie' (1595: F3[v]). Thus, 'martial poetics' includes more than verse. It is writing that, even when factual rather than fictional, in prose rather than in verse, is also reflective and experiential—writing that recounts the author's own history: his experience of encountering, and attempting to engage in, the transformed art of war; and that often reflects on the impact that encounter had on the author's life, whether for good or ill.

It is writing of this sort that is examined in this chapter. However, it is essential to understand the wider context of military literature, because soldier–poets usually wrote in different styles, and martial poetics emerges from (and is sometimes to be found within examples of) general military literature.

I

Another consequence of the changes in warfare in the sixteenth century was that works dealing with various aspects of warfare proliferated. The very term 'art of war' itself comes from an early theoretical treatise, Machiavelli's *Libro della arte della guerra* (1521), which was regularly reprinted and hugely influential (Cockle 1978: 135, 9–10). Writing on war naturally circulated in manuscript, but in England, as on the Continent, it also became a staple of the printing industry (see Eltis 1991: 8, 26–7, 356–7; Hale 1983: 232–3).

Depending on the definition used, from seventy to 147 'military books' were printed in English during the rule of the Tudors—the figure is 'almost two hundred if one includes reprints, enlarged editions, and military newsbooks' (Webb 1965: 170).[1] This figure includes translations of classical works and contemporary foreign books, but not books published in other languages, many of which also circulated in Tudor England. Not only were there many different titles, but they could also sell well (Donagan 1995: 80).

In subject matter these 'military books' are very diverse. As D. A. Eltis points out, there are treatises on the overall 'nature of war on land' and its conduct, intended to influence government policy; histories, 'whether classical or more recent'; military regulations; instructional manuals for artillery and personal weapons; polemical treatises on the relative worth of weapons, especially the longbow and firearm; didactic and informative literature on duelling, swordsmanship, horsemanship, and military medicine; 'exhortatory works without a detailed factual basis'; 'works of largely religious or moral content' (Eltis 1991: 7–9); there are also instructional treatises on skills that, while not solely military, were of value to the soldier, such as geometry and 'Arithmetike', which mathematicians like John Dee, as well as soldiers, recognized 'to be one of [the soldier's] chief Counsaylors, directors and aiders' (Dee 1570: *4ᵛ). In addition, there was a new sub-genre of self-help manuals for the inexperienced,

---

[1] See the bibliographies (overlapping but not identical) in Cockle (1978: 2–59); Webb (1965: 223–32); Langsam (1951: 199–203); on the total number of titles, cf. Eltis (1991: 7).

part-time officers of the militia's 'trained bands', on which, rather than a standing army, England relied for national defence, thanks to the safeguard of the sea.

There was thus from the middle of the sixteenth century onwards a large body of readily accessible printed material on military and related subjects. Many were not written by soldiers and were instead based on 'reportes, historyes, & Chronicles written of warres', especially works by Greek and Roman authors, knowledge of which many commentators held to be chiefly (or only) 'requisite & needeful unto a good Captaine' (Proctor 1587: ¶4^v). However, from the middle decades of the sixteenth century, an increasing number of pamphlets and books were published by martialists— based on their experiences and declaring the value of practical knowledge. There were many literate and educated soldiers of gentle or noble birth, among both the rank and file and the officers of English military contingents (whether in English or foreign armies). In addition to contributing to the technical literature on the art of war, they also produced 'poetry', in both verse and prose.

Soldier poetry has been little studied by modern scholars. It is totally ignored, along with most military activity before 1585 and most soldier–poets, by otherwise excellent recent overviews of the English Renaissance (e.g. Fox 1997; Hadfield 2001). This is perhaps partly because martial poetics is elusive. It might be better described as a genre complex than a genre, for it emerged out of epic, romance, lyric, panegyric, reportage, and life-writing, and at times resembles these literary forms. Yet it is distinctive and deserves attention. It is recognizable because it conveys the attitudes and values of veteran martialists—frequently in their own words; occasionally articulated by writers from their circle of friends. It repays reading precisely because in it we hear the voices of men who have made soldiering their career and learned by doing, not just by reading the other types of military literature—and, as Elizabeth Heale argues, their writing therefore claims the moral authority of experience (Heale 2008).

What, then, are the characteristics of martial 'poesy'? Fundamental to the nature of martial poetics is the social context in which its texts were produced. Soldier–poets were all members of the social elite: the *nobilitas*, which in England (unlike the rest of Europe) was divided into the nobility (the peerage), or *nobilitas major*, and the gentry, or *nobilitas minor*, and which it is therefore convenient to characterize as 'aristocratic' (Trim 2002: 49–51). The social origins of martial poetics are reflected in the most significant of its distinctive traits.

These are, first, a certainty that soldiering was properly the vocation of the upper orders; and, second, a series of convictions about the nature of honour, the paramount virtue of society. These, in turn, were that honour was performative, rather than passive, and that it particularly required active participation in *war*; that honour was chiefly derived from personal courage and deeds of prowess in combat; and, in sum, that masculinity and aristocratic privilege were alike vindicated by honourable military activity, so that experience of at least one campaign was desirable, if not essential, for those who aspired to honour. Whatever else the noble or gentle man might be, he must first of all be skilled at arms and willing to endure pain and privation. Only thus could he prove himself a true aristocrat— and, it is clear, a true man. Thus, although there is also in some soldier poetry an uneasy tension between the notional values of chivalry and the actual experience of the realities of 'modern' warfare, martial poetics generally expresses and endorses the traditional heroic values of the chivalric ethos, which, contrary to the arguments of much recent scholarship, was still extremely influential in early modern England. Indeed, soldier poetry was to some extent inspired by, and contributed to, the revival of heroic, chivalric literature that followed the printing of Malory's *Morte d'Arthur* (1485) and Lord Berners's English translation of Froissart in 1523 (see Gunn 1987: 34; Heale 1998: 25). The soldier–poets of the sixteenth century worked on existing popular themes; they did so in their own style, often in forms that were new to English poesy, but in support of an ethos with which their readers already sympathized.

II

Soldier–poets endorse and promote the notion that soldiering was properly the vocation of a limited section of the population: the aristocracy, both the title-holding nobility and the gentry. Sidney reported approvingly the view of an Italian soldier that 'souldiers were the noblest estate of mankind' (1595: B^{r-v}). When Thomas Churchyard, who made a living both from the pen and from the sword and served in English and foreign armies over a fifty-year period, wanted to show 'how Gentilitie begane, and where and in what sorte honour was first gotten and maintained', he pointed to 'the lives of noble Soldiours' (1579: M1^r). Writing near the end of his life, Barnaby Rich—like Churchyard, both a professional writer and a career soldier—was sure that war 'is the Theatre where on Nobilitie was borne to shew himselfe' (1609: B^r).

Soldier–poets assumed that the martial life was naturally congenial to the gentleman. To the playwright and satirist Ulpian Fulwell, who wrote a narrative of the siege of Haddington (1547) in prose and verse at the request of (and based on information from) 'certaine Capitaines that had served in king Henries warres, & in king Edwardes, and eversince', it was obvious that 'The noble harte for honour fyghtes' (1575: 49^r, 56^r). Walter Morgan, a soldier sprung from the minor Welsh gentry, who served in the Netherlands for thirty years, began a memoir of his first service there in 1572–3 with this reflection on his youth: 'the employe wherein I conceavyd moste felicitie in all of my youthe too the contentacion of mynde [was] in the disipline of marciall afaeyrs' (Codrington MS 129: 1^r).

The identification of military qualities with aristocratic birth was reinforced by the presumption that the common man or plebeian was innately an unreliable soldier. Surrey classed the man 'that hath no hart to fight' as a 'wretch' (Howard 1964: 33). Churchyard scorned 'common hirelyng[s]' as not 'fit to be registered, or honoured among the renouned sort of warlike people' (1579: M2^v). This contrast, and the view that commoners were naturally unfit for the martial disciplines, are elaborated in an epitaph for Lord Sheffield, slain by the plebeian rebels of Norfolk during Ket's rebellion in 1549. It was composed sometime in the following dozen years by Barnabe Googe, a government administrator and professional writer who associated with and admired soldiers, before serving himself in the military garrison in Ireland in 1574 and 1582–5. It both derides and laments the 'brutish broil and rage of war' which 'in clownish hearts began', and the tragedy that:

> The noble Sheffield, Lord by birth
> and of a courage good,
> By clubbish hands of crabbèd clowns
> there spent his noble blood.
> His noble birth availèd not,
> his honour all was vain,
> Amid the press of masty curs
> the valiant Lord was slain.
> After such a sort (O ruth!)
> that who can tears suppress?
> To think that dunghill dogs should daunt
> the flower of worthiness.
>
> (1989: 79)

In martial poetics there is also a strong sense that, while honour and the martial aptitude that was naturally associated with it were the innate inheritance of gentle or noble birth, those of aristocratic blood nevertheless had to *demonstrate* that those virtues were in them, by soldiering.

The tone was set for the Tudor period by Henry Howard, Earl of Surrey. As his most recent biographer observes, he consciously 'assumed the role of guardian of honour and defender of true nobility' and sought 'to make his life an image of his honour' (*ODNB*). Nearly a quarter-century after his death, Sidney found 'in the Earle of Surreis Lirickes, manie thinges tasting of a Noble birth, and worthie of a Noble minde' (1595: H3ᵛ). But to Surrey, honour was demonstrated above all by how a man behaved in time of war. And because honour was naturally an aristocratic quality, if a man of gentle—indeed even of royal—birth was ineffective in combat, it probably reflected a lack of honourable qualities. Hence, in Surrey's celebrated sonnet on the Assyrian king (Howard 1964: 29), the king (possibly a figure of Henry VIII) cannot wage war effectively because he lacks courage, fortitude, and magnanimity—all traits associated with aristocratic honour (Greaves 1964: 17–25, 112).

However, the virtues that were an aristocratic birthright would be lost if left unused. Genetic inheritance alone did not guarantee honourable behaviour. As Walter Morgan later asserted: 'hit ys not mans byrthe entitulyd wythe seremonis of honor that ys too stande an armie in effecte [...] but his industrus spiritte of knowledge and value in Judgement' (Codrington MS 129: 21ʳ), which come by experience. Similarly, Barnaby Rich described in a prose romance a fictional duke whose victories in battle in effect confirm both his 'greate policie and experience in Marciall affaires', which are learned abilities, and 'his owne magnanimitie and valiaunce' (1959: 24), or innate virtues. The two went hand in hand—and when men acted, it vindicated their claim to gentility.

For example, Surrey buried his squire, Thomas Clere, who died on active service, in the Howard family chapel and justified this extraordinary act in a Virgilian epitaph. He praised Clere precisely because he had shown himself, on the field of battle and in sieges, to be Surrey's devoted comrade-in-arms:

> Tracing whose steps thou sawest Kelsall blaze,
> Laundersey burnt, and battered Bullen render.
> . . .
>
> At Muttrell gates, [where] hopeless of all recure,
> Thine Earl halfe dead gave in thy hand his Will;
> Which cause did thee this pining death procure.
>
> (Howard 1964: 32)

Clere was of a gentry family, so was presumed to have honourable qualities; but what made him, in effect, an honorary member of England's premier noble family? It was that he had proved himself, by his faithfulness and courage in combat from Scotland to France, and by his death on active service, Surrey's equal in worth and honour (see Zitner 1985: 106–15). Honourable military service confirmed Clere as a true, worthy member of the *nobilitas minor*, and even attested that he had the qualities of one of the *nobilitas major*. Likewise, when William Blandy, a veteran of the Dutch Revolt, praises his fellow English and Welshmen in the Netherlands for their good conduct, he declares they have 'become peerlesse, noble, and magnificent' (1581: 25^v).

III

We have seen, then, that in martial poetics there is a presumption that a man's gentility or nobility must be demonstrated in war. But as is partly apparent in the Clere epitaph, not just any kind of involvement in war was valued. It had to be active participation. A fame that lasts was thus the product of acting and doing—it was generated actively, not passively.

This emerges clearly in soldiers' writing. In an epitaph on the Earl of Pembroke, an experienced soldier and general, Churchyard praises the Earl's deeds, which make him comparable to Hector and the ancient Trojans (1570); elsewhere he lauds Henry Champernowne, an English captain in the Huguenot army, who served in France 'as one desirous of renowne, and greedie of glorie gotten by service [...] where lively fame was to be wonne' (1579: K2^v); and he praises the English and Huguenot soldiers who captured Belle-Île in 1573 for their performance in 'hotte skirmishe, and many more matters worthie memorie' (L4^v). He also avows that 'fame and reputation is the marke that men shoote at' (M2^v), that 'honour and reputation accompanies the soldiours' (N2^v), and that 'noble behaviour of Soldiours [...] maie not bee forgotten, nor left bare and naked from the roebes of renoune, and remembraunce of the worlde' (T1^v–T2^r). William Blandy, who (1576) translated an influential Continental work on the characteristics of nobility, and in 1580 served in the Netherlands, published in 1581 a book that begins as a treatise on military policy, but ends as an extended reflection on his experiences as a soldier; he is explicit that it is 'by their desartes' that men 'wonne fame and glorye' (1581: H3^r). Both Blandy and George Pettie (another veteran of the Netherlands and translator of Continental works into English) specifically praised John Norreys, the English general in the Netherlands, because 'by his valiant actes' and 'renowned deedes' he had 'proved himselfe [...] a fountayne of fame, a welspring of vertue' (Blandy 1581: 25^v; Pettie 1581: *^{r}). As Rich declared, it was by 'the Militarie profession [that] menne were advaunced to the greatest renowne' (1959: 12).

Because of the belief that honour, although intrinsically aristocratic, was performative, soldier poetry also tends to privilege particular *types* of action. By performing notable deeds in combat, the soldier demonstrated his skill at arms; by undertaking dangerous actions, he displayed his bravery, élan, fortitude, and sangfroid. As a result, being 'forward' in combat, literally at the hard edge, whether in attack or desperate defence, was the ideal.

Again, these were traditional, chivalric values, but they predominate in Tudor martial poetics. In 1579, looking back to the 1540s, in which he first saw military service, Churchyard recalled: 'He was thought happest and moste valiaunt, that sought credite by the exercises of Armes, and dissipline of warre. Whiche did so animate the noble mindes of men, that in a maner he was counted no bodie, that had not been knowen to bee at some valiaunte enterprice' (1579: A1^r). Writing of the same period, Ulpian Fulwell asserted: 'At point of harde distresse | a hardie man is knowne' (1575: 56^r).

Similar values are very evident in verse and prose describing the wars of Elizabeth I. Churchyard published a string of books in the five years from 1575 on the experiences of soldiers—some in prose, some in a mix of verse and prose. In them he praises English troops in Scotland for their bold 'forwardness', and commends those in the Netherlands for frequently engaging the Spanish in 'divers hote skirmishes, & couragious rencontre', noting that they 'deserved much praise for their forwardnesse', and that they have won praise from their Spanish besiegers for their 'great and noble valliauncie and courage' (1575: 5^v, 39^r, 40^r, 99^r; 1578: 54; 1580c: C4^v; 1579: K3^r). Blandy describes how, after a Spanish assault on an English force in the Netherlands, a counter-attack was made in case 'the enemy might thinke their Larum to have any maner wayes touched us with a shiver of feare'. He then comments: 'Behold here true value comming from a courage, most stedfastly setled in resolute mindes.' He goes on to praise several of those who were killed in this skirmish for 'value, fiercenese, and courage laudable', for being 'stout and couragious', and for their 'prowes and stoutnesse' (1576: 22^v, 23^v). The officers who led a subsequent charge are similarly praised for 'value, courage and fury' and 'vertue and stoutnesse'; Blandy concludes that all who were forward in the fight 'deserve highly to be praysed' (25^r).

Nor were these values promoted only in narratives of England's recent wars. George Pettie, veteran of the Netherlands, puts them in the mouths of the heroes in the prose romances gathered in his immensely popular *Petite Palace of Pettie his Pleasure*. The historical Roman figure Germanicus is praised for 'valiant exploytes atchived in warre' (1576: 9). The fictitious aristocrat Synorix is anxious that the woman he admires should not 'count mee in the number of these cowardly Souldiours, which at the first Canon that roareth, give over the siege of the citie they assaulted, for [...] the more harde the fight is, the more haughtie is the conquest, and the more doubtfull the battayle, the more doubtie the victory' (11). Churchyard, in a passage of near-philosophical contemplation, rather than descriptive purple prose, reflects that the desire for glory 'pricketh' a man 'so fast forward', that he will ignore 'the multitude of enemies' (1579: M2^r).

Even death was a small price to pay for honour. In his epitaph for Lord Sheffield, Barnabe Googe emphasizes that Sheffield 'didst not fear to die' (1989: 80), which lent his death a heroic aspect that overcame its ignominious circumstances. Similar values are even more evident in the epitaph Googe composed in the 1560s for Edward Shelley, slain in 1547 at the great battle of Pinkie in Scotland. In Googe's epitaph, Shelley defies the fear inspired by the (alleged) numerical advantage of the Scottish army, which momentarily left many of his countrymen 'aghast', and by the knowledge that 'who should first the onset give | was sure therein to die' (1989: 80–1). He rebukes and rouses his compatriots with a bold speech, then finally inspires them by his deeds:

> forth before them he sprang,
>   as one no whit dismayed.
> With chargèd staff on foaming horse
>   his spurs with heels he strikes,
> And forward runs with swifty race
>   among the mortal pikes.

Although it ends in death, to Googe it is 'this race with famous end'. In giving his mortality, Shelley had won immortality.

The same was true of Henry Champernowne, acclaimed by Churchyard because, whereas some English volunteers serving the Huguenots returned home after their defeat at Jarnac (1569), Champernowne,

desirous of renowne, and greedie of glorie gotten by service, remained till his death [...] and served so nobly and so gallantly, as the whole Campe where he was in, sounded of his valliantnesse, and [...] to this daie his deedes [...] are moste noblie spoken of, greatly to the honour of all our Englishe Nation.   (1579: K2^v)

And Churchyard was moved 'to give others their due praise: that served in Fraunce and Flaunders, in these perillous tymes, and daies of no little daunger' (ibid.).

Elsewhere he commends English troops in Scotland who 'desired to do a dayes service, to venter his lyfe, to shed his bloud' (1575: 39ʳ) and who, 'For true renowne [...] troedg and toyill a main | Whear danger dwels and heapps of hazards aer' (99ʳ); he lauds Sidney because 'He feared no death' (1586: A4ᵛ). Death was not to be treated lightly, but fear of dying must not govern a man's living: in a romance by Pettie, one of the protagonists, Amphiaraus, having certain foreknowledge of his death if he goes to war, 'covertly hid himselfe in his owne house' (1576: 73), but even though his king, Admetus, knows of the prophecy, he is enraged and condemns Amphiaraus as a coward who brings disrepute on the kingdom. Churchyard's reflections on this issue in general are striking. So powerful are 'greedinesse of glorie and ambitio[n] [...] that neither the man lookes uppon the multitude of enemies: Nor regardes the daunger of death'; he 'doeth combate like a Lyon, and either conquers like a man, or dieth like a conquerour'— all 'so he maie bee eternised, and live in the good opinion of the [...] people' (1579: M2ᵛ).

Contrast with this Elis Gruffudd's recollection of combat in northern France in the mid-1540s. Gruffudd, a soldier for forty years, usually served in the ranks but was drawn from the minor gentry, and completed around 1552 a history of the world, which included his experiences in Tudor armies in France. He records his disdain for those 'Welshmen and Englishmen' who, when 'the French would come to the field to offer battle', would 'suddenly [...] turn back either to the shelter of the town or of the hedges and ditches', because in the skirmishes 'every day [...] some of each side were left on the ground but most often the English'. Such men, unnerved by the risk of death, are characterized as not merely 'unventuresome' but also 'badhearted' (1949: 71). Churchyard agreed, dismissing 'common' soldiers who never 'tarrie long in the feelde' and who make 'many shiftes [...] to putte of[f] any paine and hazard' (1579: M2ᵛ). Thus, overcoming fear of death was an instance of true gentility or nobility, in contrast to what was expected of the plebeian; as George Gascoigne, who fought in the Netherlands during 1572–4, declares in his long poem 'The Fruits of War': 'Noble mindes their honour more esteem | Than worldly wights, or wealth, or life can deem' (2000: 434).

IV

To reiterate, then, in the poetry of soldiers and their circle, it was deeds, not words, that counted—style was not as important as substance. After all, as Googe observed in 1569, even women could be 'With scarfes and feathers like to souldiers drest' (2001: 11).

Even those who thought that, by venturing themselves in a joust, they had truly experienced war and thereby demonstrated true prowess were disparaged. Gascoigne expressed his scorn for the 'vain avail' of men whose triumphs were won only in the tiltyard, mockingly urging that it

> Should not allure thy flytting mynd to feeld
> Where sturdie Steedes in depth of daungers roon
> With guts wel gnawen by clappes that Cannons yeeld.
>
> (2000: 219)

Churchyard likewise contrasts those who only ride in tournament and those who additionally, like Sidney, go into real combat:

> Though manhood runnes in Armor gay
> where great exployts have bin.
> Yet courage casts more men away
> then all the world can win.
>
> (1586: A4^r)

He makes it clear that what counts is the field of battle, not the tiltyard, the experience of a soldier, not a tourneyer:

Shall not a man that hath coped with Champions, buckled with Conquerors, and abidden the hazard of the Cannon, stande on his Pantoffelles, and loke to the steppes he hath passed. Yes sure, and suche a member of the state [...] ought to be made of, deserveth place and pre-eminence, and is no companion for punies, nor Milksoppes, whose manhoode and maners differs, as farre from the grave Soldiour, as a [...] kite in courage and ambition, differs from a Jerfauco[n].   (1579: M2^r)

There can surely be little doubt that such considerations were what motivated Surrey to risk-taking on the battlefield in the 1540s—and motivated Sidney, serving in the Netherlands in 1586, to take greater risks than contemporaries thought were strictly necessary, and so lose his life.

There is also, however, little doubt that the terms in which soldier–poets expressed their disdain of counterfeiting martial deeds present a gendered view of skill-at-arms and of courage—these are distinctly masculine traits, while their reverse are feminine. This view is present more widely in, indeed is characteristic of, martial poetics and is frequently not just implicit, but explicit. Masculinity and martial prowess were clearly bound up together. In an epitaph on Sir Hugh Paulet, Churchyard praises his subject:

> Brought up in armes and Marciall feats,
> a maister of that arte:
> Whiche oft in feeld and countreis cause,
> did plaie a manly parte.
>
> (1580a: A2^r)

Elsewhere he waxes nostalgic for the days of 'that noble prince Kyng Henry the eight', in which 'manhoode [was] so much esteemed', that men 'sought credite by the exercises of Armes, and dissipline of warre' (1579: A1ʳ); and describes a joint attack by English and Huguenot troops on a French island fortress, 'In whiche service [...] manhoode, and diligence of manne was throughlie tried: And the Englishe nation did shewe their accustomed courage' (L4ᵛ). Fulwell, in praising the captains who fought at Haddington, commends one who 'manfully [...] did in the quarrel stande' (1575: 57ʳ), while Gascoigne is proud of the 'bolde attempts' by which his troops in the Netherlands 'shew[ed] their force like worthie English men' (2000: 417). To another veteran of the Netherlands, George Pettie, 'renowned deed[s]', 'valour', 'valiancie', and 'manly prowesse' were associated aspects of the successful, honourable soldier (1581: *ʳ⁻ᵛ).

Those who lacked manly physical attributes could not be expected to have soldierly qualities. Elis Gruffudd was scornful of those 'too wretched in body [...] to be soldiers' and of the 'feckless boys' sent to 'become auditors rather than soldiers, and learn by the hardships of wind and rain, heat and cold and frost, to be ready early and late to serve and achieve honour and glory' (1950: 27). William Blandy praises an English captain in the Netherlands for his 'manlynesse' and a junior officer 'for his manlynes and activitye, for his strength and knowledge in every weapon that belonges to a tall and expert Souldiar' (1581: 23ᵛ), and 'many more, whose prowes I commend to those, the whome theyr proper names and peculiar natures are knowne as well, as to us theyr singular manhood and rare vertue' (26ʳ bis).

The association in soldier poetry of masculinity with martial, chivalric values is heightened by a marked tendency to associate femininity with lack of skill at arms and aptitude for war, and with ignoble characteristics. For example, in Surrey's meditation on the cowardice of the Assyrian king, he attributes it not merely to a craven spirit. A 'filthy lust [...] stained his regal heart', and

> In war, that should set princely hearts afire,
> Vanquished did yield for want of martial art.
> The dint of swords from kisses seemèd strange,
> And harder than his lady's side, his targe [shield];
> From glutton feasts to a soldier's fare, a change,
> His helmet, far above a garland's charge.
> Who scarce the name of manhood did retain,
> Drenchèd in sloth and womanish delight,
> Feeble of sprite, unpatient of pain,
> [...] he [...] lost his honor and his right.
>
> (Howard 1964: 29)

Churchyard is acerbic about the qualities that might fit one for the company of ladies: 'Where Cannon roard, and Dromme did sounde, | I did not learne, to daunce a rounde' (1580b: 7).

Barnaby Rich was particularly fond of this theme. In 1574 he contrasted the 'womanlike mynded men' who could never 'injoy their delightes' quietly, with 'the noble Souldier [...] who is the very Wal and only Bulwark to defend them' (1574: M3^v–M4^r). In 1581 he lamented that men in London had started to carry fans: 'it is as fonde a sight to see a manne with suche a bable in his hande, as to see a woman ride through the streate with a launce in hers' (1959: 11). In one of his prose romances he portrays the confusion of a great captain in wartime, who, in peacetime, cuts a sorry figure in a society now enamoured of womanish fashions and accoutrements:

His bodie most ineured to weare a coate of steele, could not be brought in fashion with this queint and nice araie. His [...] fingers commonlie practised to graspe the sworde or launce, could not bee brought in frame to strike the Virginall or Lute: His voice served hym better to cheare his Souldiers in the feeld, then either to faine or syng ditties in a ladies Chamber: His tongue had more used to speake simplie and plaine, then to dissemble with his freend, or flatter with his foe: His legges had better skill to marche [...] then to mince [...]   (24–5)

Twenty years after, his opinion had not changed: 'The Souldiour, who in the time of warre savoreth of sweat, (the true testimony of exercise and labour) in the time of Peace, is all to bee spiced with perfumes (the witnes of effeminate and womanish nicite)' (1609: B^v).

The innate interconnections of aristocracy, martial aptitude, and masculinity, and of cowardice, weakness, and femininity, were obvious even to those gentlemen who, at least initially, made a living as scholars rather than soldiers. In Googe's epitaph on Edward Shelley's glorious death in battle in 1547, Googe (writing sixteen years later) praises Shelley's forwardness and courage, which was in his sources, but he goes beyond them, inventing a speech, put in Shelley's mouth, which brings out Googe's view of aristocratic, martial virtue. The hero chides his countrymen, not merely as 'cowards all', but as 'maidly men, of courage faint and weak', and scornfully asks, 'is this your manhood gone [...]?' At last, 'all inflamed with heat [...] of valiant mind', he concludes:

> No cowards we, nor maidly men,
>   ne yet of dastards' kind
> I would you wist did ever come,
>   but dare be bold to try
> Our manhood here, though nought appear
>   but death to all men's eye.
>
> (1989: 81)

Googe makes it clear that the way for male aristocrats to prove they were not 'girly men' (to use the more recent terminology of the Austrian-American film actor and politician Arnold Schwarzenegger) was to be 'bold' and forward in battle and to disregard danger—as he wrote elsewhere, only the 'fearefull hart refuseth [to take the] painefull way' (2001: 5).

V

However, first-person writing by soldiers also sometimes reveals a degree of disenchantment with the ills of war and a sense that its realities were at odds both with the image of it in traditional literature and with the value system associated with that literature.

Recalling his experiences in and around Boulogne in the 1540s, Elis Gruffudd wrote bitterly that most of the captains 'set more store by their own advantage than by doing a harporth of good to the common soldiers' (1949: 56). He was particularly unimpressed by the Earl of Surrey's craving for opportunities to perform deeds of prowess, at least if it overrode military common sense. On one occasion, for example, Gruffudd notes disapprovingly that, having attacked the French with insufficient strength, for pride's sake, Surrey then when battle was joined acted 'in the pride of his folly'. The result was defeat for the English, which Gruffudd caustically attributes to 'the Earl their leader, whose head and heart were swollen with pride, arrogance and empty confidence in his own unreasoning bravery' (1950: 39–42). Yet it would be mistaken to overdraw Gruffudd's antipathy to the ethos of chivalry, for personal courtesy and courage when combat was joined were supposed to complement—and in many soldiers' eyes could not compensate for—careful preparations for and capable disposition of soldiers in combat. Gruffudd was far from the only soldier to believe that the latter, as well as the former, were chivalrous qualities. His disappointment with those who did not live up to the chivalric ethos signals clearly that he himself subscribed to it. For example, he observes of some captains of the 1540s whom he regards as dishonourable that 'it is hardly fitting to talk about the deeds of those who preferred honour and glory and the affection of the weak and the strong to worldly wealth when the so-called chieftains of this time [put self-interest above honour]' (27).

In Gascoigne's verse, in particular, a clear sense of cynicism, even bitterness, about the traditional aristocratic attitudes to war and soldiering appears to be present. It seems to be the consequence of going to war with lofty ideals, derived from heroic romance (and perhaps from the soldier poetry of Surrey's generation), which are shattered by the actuality of war. Elizabeth Heale's recent sensitive and textured analysis of 'The Fruits of War' concludes that, in contrast to Churchyard and Rich, in whose texts 'the plain and virtuous' soldier inhabits a 'relatively clear moral universe', Gascoigne's long poem presents 'a landscape in which moral certainties are increasingly hard to find' (Heale 2008). For example, he scorns the man who 'hunts (nought else) but honor for to get' (Gascoigne 2000: 406) and bitterly observes that 'those love to live in warre, | When (God he knows) they wote not what it meanes' (413).

The same sense of cynicism or disillusionment seems evident elsewhere in Gascoigne's verse. In 'Gascoigne's Woodmanship', he represents himself discovering that the ideal that manliness and courage will bring fame and fortune—ubiquitous in heroic martial literature and, as we have seen, common in soldier poetry—is at odds with the real:

> But now behold what marke the man doth find,
> He shootes to be a souldier in his age,
> Mistrusting all the vertues of the minde,
> He trusts the power of his personage.
> As though long limmes led by a lusty hart,
> Might yet suffice to make him rich againe,
> But flussing [Flushing] fraies have taught him such a parte,
> That now he thinks the warres yeld no such gaine.
>
> (314)

There thus may seem to be little doubt about the mature Gascoigne's attitudes to war and the traditional chivalric values of the warrior.

Yet this is not the end of the story. Elsewhere in Gascoigne's verse he endorses these values. In addition to examples quoted in earlier sections, it is notable that, in 'The Fruits of War', he is proud of the deeds of prowess done by English soldiers in the Netherlands and assumes they will win lasting fame as a result:

> Our English bloudes did there full many a deede,
> Which may be Chronicled in every coaste,
> For bolde attempts.
>
> (417)

He is concerned for his own honour: his soldiers' 'faults so plucke his honour downe', that it is unlikely that he 'climes [...] to renowne' (418). And in the concluding 'L'Envoie' he 'coumpts him selfe to bee' one of those men who wait 'till drummes do draw them out':

> for sure withouten doubt,
> If drummes once sounde a lustie march in deede,
> Then farewell bookes, for he will trudge with speede.
>
> (438–9)

The apparent cynic seems really to be merely waiting the call to do deeds of prowess once more. Furthermore, this is in accord with what we know about Gascoigne himself; whatever he may have written or thought about the aristocratic value system, he personally embodied it, at least at times. During a battle near Flushing in 1572, with English and Spanish troops locked at push of pike, Gascoigne was one of a small band of gentlemen armed with sword and shield who made a heroic charge and thereby helped secure an English victory. It was a deed of both courage and personal prowess at arms, one that won him acclaim both by his fellow soldiers and back in England, where it was reported (Devereux 2: 7^v).[2]

---

[2] The Devereux Papers are cited by permission of the Marquess of Bath.

What are we to make of these contradictions? The problem with Gascoigne's œuvre is that it is very difficult to generalize accurately about it. His style is richly layered; he adopts and shifts between multiple personae; and he is partial to collapsing concepts that he has, as it appears, previously established. It is in consequence often far from clear whether we are supposed to agree with views expressed at any given point; Gascoigne's own views remain elusive and obscure. Ultimately, as Heale concludes, 'Gascoigne the soldier', as presented in his verse on his own experience of war, is 'riven between a desire to portray the soldier's life as one of travail and bitterness, unrewarded by a thankless nation, and a desire to represent himself as a man of courage and enterprise, ready and eager to follow when the drum beats' (see Heale 2008; 2003: 73, 75–6).

To sum up: ambiguity about chivalric values certainly is present in some soldier poetry; but those values are much more often affirmed than queried and are never truly undermined.

VI

In addition to being in accord with the values of traditional chivalric culture, martial poetics often consciously evokes the literature of chivalry, especially romance and epic. At times it does so in extremely specific terms. Sidney in his *Defence of Poesy* emphasizes that 'heretofore, Poets have in England also flourished: and which is to be noted, even in those times when the trumpet of Mars did sonnd lowdest'—that war, in other words, was a midwife to good poetry; and that, by implication, war could be encountered and was celebrated in poetry (1595: H2^v). He also avows that 'Poetrie is the Companion of Camps' and that 'Orlando Furioso, or honest king Arthure, will never displease a souldier' (G3^r). This may be a hint that he had enjoyed a preview of Spenser's *Faerie Queene* in draft, but regardless, what is clear is his positive attitude towards the traditional heroic literature of chivalric society.

Sidney was certainly not the only consumer of chivalric literature, whether heroic poetry or historical prose. The translation of Froissart by Lord Berners (Surrey's half-uncle) went through four editions from 1523 to 1563 (and two more early in the seventeenth century); its known owners include the Duke of Somerset, Lord Protector during the early part of Edward VI's regency, and Shelley's commander-in-chief at Pinkie. Gruffudd was keenly aware of great martial feats of the past and believed his fellow gentlemen soldiers aspired to 'achieve honour and glory [...] as the captains of old' (1950: 27). Churchyard was confident that soldiers were aware of 'the former fame of our auncient predecessors and countreymen' and desired to emulate the deeds 'many great Kynges and Capitaines have doen, whose ensamples a long while agoe, as yet remaines freashelie in memorie' (1579: K4^r, M2^v). Moreover,

Sidney consciously modelled much of his poetic output on late medieval romance. David Norbrook observes that the 'revised version of the "Arcadia" became a heroic romance, a celebration of Protestant magnanimity. Sidney added lengthy descriptions of chivalric combats' (Norbrook 1984: 104), in defiance of early sixteenth-century humanists' tendency to ridicule romance.

However, even while evoking and to some extent utilizing the heroic literature of the past, the mid- and late Tudor soldier–poets introduced new elements, reflecting the changes that had taken place in the art of war. This is not always immediately apparent—both close reading of the text and knowledge of the historical context is required.

In *Astrophil and Stella* Sidney conveys a disparaging image of gunpowder weaponry, when Astrophil at one point declares (with some exaggeration):

> Flie, fly, my friends, I have my death wound; fly,
> See there that boy, that murthring boy I say,
> Who like a theefe, hid in darke bush doth ly,
> Til bloudie bullet get him wrongfull pray.
>
> (1962, no. 20)

Sidney seems to despise the capability a firearm gives to a commoner, who may have no personal physical or martial prowess (in this case a 'boy'), without even engaging in personal combat ('like a theefe, hid in darke bush'), to 'murder' a knightly paragon.

The conclusion that Sidney detested firearms because they threatened the chivalric ethos of individual heroism is especially tempting because we know that he himself was mortally wounded at the battle of Zutphen (1586)—charging mounted, in full armour, in every sense like a knight of heroic literature—by a musket bullet. The contrast seems so poetic that it is easy to read more into it than is warranted. Sidney's death was lamented in verse by, among many, the poet Matthew Roydon, who pictures Mars taking aim at him with:

> An iron cane wherein he put,
> The thunder that in cloudes do breede,
> The flame and bolt togither shut.
> With privie force burst out againe,
> And so our *Astrophill* was slaine.
>
> (1593: 6)

One prominent Sidney scholar calls this 'a means to lend epic tone to the doubtful arquebus' (Baker-Smith 1990, p. ix). In fact, from the early fifteenth century, medieval warriors, including those who consumed contemporary chivalric literature and were praised by it, embraced gunpowder weaponry and were often expert in its use (Trim 2004: 82–3). In the sixteenth century, the short firearm or pistol, and the two forms of long firearm—the arquebus (or hackbut) in the first half of the century, to which was added the heavier musket in the second half—were widely and unhesitatingly utilized by the aristocracy.

To return to *Astrophil and Stella*, as Alistair Fox points out: 'From the outset, Astrophil is depicted as immature.' The poses Sidney makes him adopt, including that quoted above, are 'exaggeratedly histrionic' (Fox 1997: 70). Elsewhere in his poetry Sidney endorses the idea that the knightly warrior must 'not leave the care of necessary furniture' to others and should be 'the best armed' (Sidney 1973: 289; Gouws 1986: 69–70). Sidney himself in the Netherlands was not only the captain of a company of armoured knights but also the colonel of a regiment of infantry, comprising musketeers and pikemen (Trim 2002, app. 5). Far from revealing ambivalence about firearms, Roydon's verse actually demonstrates how readily gunpowder weapons were integrated into the traditional value system espoused in epic and in martial poetics, even by one who was not a soldier. Thomas Wyatt made use forty years before Sidney of the imagery of gunpowder combustion for poetic effect: 'The furious gun in his raging ire' provides Wyatt with an effective analogy to his breaking heart. Rather than demonstrating suspicion of the arquebus and other gunpowder weapons, it demonstrates detailed knowledge:

> When that bowl is rammed in too sore
> And that the flame cannot part from the fire,
> Cracketh in sunder, and in the air doth roar
> The shivered pieces. Right so my desire [...]
>
> (1975: 52)

Wyatt, a one-time High Marshal of Calais, was familiar with the weaknesses of gunpowder weaponry and could count on his aristocratic readers knowing them as well. In the 1570s Gascoigne also incorporated musketry into his poetry, in terms that cast it in positive terms: 'The Devil so must we overthrow, | With gunshot of belief' (2000: 287).

All in all, then, Astrophil's attitudes to the sniper (who had not actually given him a death wound) and to his weapon are not those of the author nor of other soldier–poets.

VII

This brings out a wider point. In embracing traditional, chivalric values, English soldier–poets were not rejecting the harsh realities of modern warfare by burying themselves in a nostalgic past, as some scholars have assumed. Changes in the art of war did not alter the prevailing aristocratic assumption that it was in war that a man's nobility or gentility and his masculinity were put to the ultimate test. Most Tudor soldier–poets saw the traditional values as perfectly compatible with the new realities of sixteenth-century warfare—and this is reflected in much of Tudor martial poetics.

Primary Works

Barret, Richard (1598), *The Theorike and Practike of Moderne Warres*.

Blandy, William (trans.) (1576), *The Five Bookes of Hieronimus Osorius, contayning a discourse of Civill and Christian Nobilitie*.

—— (1581), *The Castle or Picture of Pollicy*.

Churchyard, Thomas (1570), *The Epitaphe of the Honorable Earle of Penbroke*.

—— (1575), *The Firste Parte of Churchyardes Chippes*.

—— (1578), *A Lamentable and Pitifull Description of the Wofull Warres in Flaunders*.

—— (1579), *Churchyardes Choice*.

—— (1580a), *Churchyards Chance*.

—— (1580b), *Churchyards Charge*.

—— (1580c), *The Takyng of Macklin*.

—— (1586), *The Epitaph of Sir Philip Sidney*.

Codrington MS 129, Walter Morgan, Memoir, 1572, All Souls College, Oxford, Codrington Library, MS 129.

Dee, J. (1570), 'Mathematicall Praeface' to *The Elements of Geometrie* by Euclid, trans. Henry Billingsley.

Devereux 2, Longleat House, Warminster, Wiltshire, Devereux Papers, MS 2.

Fulwell, Ulpian (1575), *The Flower of Fame*.

Gascoigne, George (2000), *A Hundreth Sundrie Flowres*, ed. G. W. Pigman III (Oxford: Clarendon Press).

Googe, Barnaby (1989), *Eclogues, Epitaphs, and Sonnets*, ed. Judith M. Kennedy (Toronto: University of Toronto Press).

—— (2001), *The Shippe of Safegarde* (1569), ed. Simon McKeown and William E. Sheidley (Tempe, AZ: Center for Medieval and Renaissance Studies).

Gruffydd, Elis (1949), 'The "Enterprises" of Paris and Boulogne', ed. and trans. M. B. Davies, *Bulletin of the Faculty of Arts: Fouad I University*, 11: 37–95.

—— (1950), 'Boulogne and Calais from 1545 to 1550', ed. and trans. M. B. Davies, *Bulletin of the Faculty of Arts: Fouad I University*, 12: 1–90.

Howard, Henry, Earl of Surrey (1964), *Poems*, ed. Emrys Jones (Oxford: Clarendon Press).

Pettie, George (1576), *A Petite Pallace of Pettie his Pleasure*.

—— (trans.) (1581), *The Civile Conversation of M. Steeven Guazzo*.

Proctor, Thomas (1578), *Of the Knowledge and Conducte of Warres*.

Rich, Barnaby (1574), *A Dialogue between Mercury and an English Souldier*.

—— (1609), *Roome for a Gentleman*.

—— (1959), *Riche's Farewell to Military Profession*, ed. Thomas M. Cranfill (Austin: University of Texas Press).

Roydon, Matthew (1593), 'An Elegie, or Friend's Passion for his Astrophill', in *The Phoenix Nest*, ed. R.S.

Sidney, Philip (1595), *The Defence of Poesie* (STC2, 22535).

—— (1962), *Astrophil and Stella*, in *The Poems of Sir Philip Sidney*, ed. William A. Ringler, Jun. (Oxford: Clarendon Press).

—— (1973), *The Countess of Pembroke's Arcadia (The Old Arcadia)*, ed. Jean Robertson (Oxford: Clarendon Press).

Styward, Thomas (1581), *The Pathwaie to Martiall Discipline*.

Wyatt, Thomas (1975), *Collected Poems*, ed. Joost Daalder (London: Oxford University Press).

....

THOMAS WHITHORNE AND FIRST-PERSON LIFE-WRITING IN THE SIXTEENTH CENTURY

....

ELIZABETH HEALE

THE texts studied in this chapter, examples of sixteenth-century first-person writing that claim to record or express personal experience, have no easily available label. The term 'life-writing', used in the title of this chapter, is flexible enough to include the variety of forms in which first-person writing occurs in the sixteenth century, for example, memoirs, chronicles, travel accounts, diaries, and verse, but it also covers biographies of subjects other than the author.[1] The more familiar term 'autobiography', a nineteenth-century coinage, is misleading because it implies a prose narrative of the whole or a large part of the author's life, figuring the self as introspective and individualistic (see Gusdorf 1980; Burke 1977; L. Davis 2006).[2] Sixteenth-century

---

[1] For an account of the wide variety of autobiographical forms used by early modern 'artisans', see Amelang (1998, ch. 2). I am particularly indebted to this very stimulating study throughout my discussion.

[2] For some of the difficulties of trying to fit sixteenth-century life-writing into the conventional autobiographical genre, see Osborn (1959). While 'autobiography' as a genre presents problems to a

life-writing presents us with a far more fragmented and heterodox array of texts, some of which show little interest in producing a coherent or sustained narrative of the self, while in others, vivid versions of authorial selves are produced, often engaged in a complex process of self-definition. The voices and purposes of first-person subjects in sixteenth-century writing vary as the kinds of texts in which they are produced vary, from eyewitness testimony to intimate complaint. It is, no doubt, only from a modern individualist perspective, fascinated by early presentations of the self and personal experience, that the texts studied in this chapter can be seen as part of a related phenomenon at all. This retrospective perspective, however, does seem to bring into focus a striking body of work in which first-person experience and witness are of central importance. Jacob Burckhardt's famous claim that it was not until the Renaissance in Italy that 'man became a spiritual individual, and recognized himself as such' has long, rightly, been rejected as a gross oversimplification (Burckhardt 1944: 81; see L. Patterson 1990; Aers 1992). Nevertheless, for reasons no doubt having much to do with the growth in literacy, personal life-writing began to proliferate throughout Europe in the sixteenth century (Amelang 1998: 190; Burke 1977: 21).[3] Although often taking strange and unfamiliar forms, the texts studied in this chapter suggest a widespread interest, particularly in the middle decades of the century, in formulating first-person voices and developing genres for the writing of personal experience.

Recent studies of autobiographical writing have stressed the contingency of the self as subject (Greenblatt 1980, esp. introd. and con.; Sprinker 1980; Porter 1997: 1–16). Following their lead, my discussion takes for granted that the sixteenth-century selves we meet in texts are the products of language, subject to the ideological discourses and generic constraints that shape the text and define what can be thought and said about the self. However lively, idiosyncratic, and persuasive they may seem, the subjects of sixteenth-century personal writing are products of their specific time and place, voicing, as we shall see, concerns and perspectives that share much in common with each other. Sixteenth-century subjects may also often seem discontinuous, undeveloped, and at times conspicuously artful to modern readers, more used to the introspective continuous narratives of much modern autobiography. But while the unfamiliar genres in which first-person writing of personal experience is found in the sixteenth century, from eyewitness chronicles to occasional verse, undoubtedly help to shape and define the authorial subject who writes, genre is itself subject to shifts in ideology that create new discursive possibilities. As cultural codes and systems of belief and practice change, old forms and genres become distorted and are recombined to produce new and distinctive voices. The subjects of much first-person writing in the sixteenth century find expression in unexpected forms, often in older

student of sixteenth-century literature, the adjective 'autobiographical' to describe writing about the authorial self remains useful and does service throughout this chapter.

[3] Incomplete lists of sixteenth-century diaries can be found in Matthews (1950), and of life narratives in Matthews (1955); see also Houlbrooke (1988).

genres pressed to new uses.[4] Old formats were adapted and changed to voice new understandings of the self and the significance of experience.

James Amelang observed of early modern artisan literature that 'one can properly refer to it as a literature of displacement, in various senses of the term' (Amelang 1998: 124, 190; see also Greenblatt 1980: 7–8; Delaney 1969: 19). Displacement, often in the literal form of travel, but also expressing a sense of detachment from, or disillusionment with, existing social structures is a recurring theme in English first-person life-writing in the sixteenth century. For the linguist Émile Benveniste difference is structurally necessary for the production of subjectivity: 'consciousness of self is only possible if it is experienced by contrast' (Benveniste 1971: 224; Silverman 1995: 45). A sense of difference has indeed been hailed as the defining mark of autobiography, linking the genre to an emergent sense of individualism (Masuch 1997). Felicity Nussbaum, writing on autobiography and ideologies of freedom and enterprise in eighteenth-century texts, suggests that 'autobiographical writing encouraged a consciousness of a more particular sense of uniqueness from others in the species, and allowed the definition of that uniqueness as requiring realization through self-interested pursuit' (1995: 53). While a sense of difference is implicit in the very act of writing in the first person, the sixteenth-century first-person subject is rarely presented as unique or concerned with individual self-realization (Amelang 1998: 233–4; Harari 2004: 45–63).

In many respects the apotheosis of sixteenth-century personal life-writing is Thomas Whithorne's extraordinary autobiographical manuscript 'The Book of Songs and Sonnets'. Whithorne's manuscript records his poems, both secular and religious, contextualizing them with long prose narratives which present a life that strives to achieve social and professional success at the same time as conforming to approved standards of virtue. This text, however, shares a great deal in common with, and can only be properly understood as an example of, first-person writing more generally in the sixteenth century, particularly its concern with finding a stable and acceptable social identity, and its use of verse to produce rhetorically heightened versions of the self. In the next three sections of this chapter I will thus review a range of sixteenth-century first-person writing, including career narratives, chronicles, accounts of experience abroad, and versions of the self in verse, before turning in the final section to a more detailed discussion of Whithorne's manuscript.

36.1 LIVES AND CAREERS

Whithorne's account of his life and career is exceptionally full and detailed, and no straightforward analogues survive. Nevertheless, there are a number of career

---

[4] Skura (2008) is particularly concerned with the relation of individual voices to genre conventions. Her book appeared too late for me to be able to use in writing this chapter.

narratives from the period that recount lives of social fluidity and struggle produced in both verse and prose. A striking example is the life-writing of the astrologer and physician Simon Forman. Forman's sense of anxiety about his social status, and the sense of grievance that he repeatedly articulates against an establishment that fails to recognize and support him, are themes that are repeated over and over in the first-person writing of the period. Forman kept an annual diary that covers the years 1564 to 1602, composed two fascinating and circumstantial autobiographical poems in the form of psalms (one of them designed to be sung aloud) in thanksgiving after periods of local persecution and imprisonment in 1576 and 1579, and wrote, in 1600, an unfinished prose narrative of his life from his birth in 1552 to 1573.[5] The unfinished prose narrative rehearses the first stages of a rags-to-riches story, told from the perspective of later commercial success with a lucrative London practice. In Forman's prose life, God's hand is clearly visible, enabling the authorial subject to triumph over threatening disaster. Describing a persistent childhood dream of overcoming great odds, Forman writes:

These visions God did show him in his youth to signify unto him his troubles in his riper years [...] Yet God, the only defender of all that be his, would never let him to be overthrown, but continually gave him always in the end the victory of all his enemies. And he overpassed all with credit, by the help of God, to whom be praise for evermore! Amen.   (1947: 269)

Forman's troubles included imprisonment and persistent opposition from more orthodox physicians who objected to his lack of formal education and unconventional methods (Traister 2001; Kassell 2005).

Forman's lack of an established social identity is characteristic of sixteenth-century life-writers, but his writing is unusual in its sense of personal triumph and confidence. More typical are a series of career narratives, written in verse and printed in the middle years of the sixteenth century, in which the threatening failure and disgrace that lurk implicitly in Forman's narrative overwhelm the authorial subject. In these narratives, virtue, effort, and enterprise bring no rewards. Thomas Tusser's popular versified manual *Five Hundred Points of Good Husbandry* (1557) takes as its fundamental rationale the idea that virtuous effort and a willingness to learn will bring success, but the inexorably downward trajectory of the author's own life, first appended to the third edition in 1573, tells a very different tale. Shifting from place to place, from employment to employment, Tusser's resigned reflection on his own career contradicts the self-help ethos of his manual: 'in world is set, ynough to get, | But where and whan, that scarsely can, the wisest tell' (1984: 210).

George Gascoigne echoes the same theme in his poem 'Gascoigne's Woodmanship', printed in *A Hundred Sundry Flowers* (1573). He moves from job to job, serially inept as courtier, soldier, and lawyer. The tone of his poem shifts between a comic presentation of his own incompetence and a sense of being the victim of recurring

---

[5] Forman (1947) contains a transcription of Bodl., MS Ashmole 208, fos 136^r–142^r, 11^v–67^r—the diary and the life. The personal psalms are in MS Ashmole 802, fos 121^r–125^r. There is also a psalm on Forman's troubles with the College of Physicians in MS Ashmole 240, fos 25^r–27^v, continued in MS Ashmole 802, fos 131^r–133^v. See the discussions by Traister (2001: 3–30) and Kassell (2005: 19–30).

bad luck. Self-justification finally predominates, with Gascoigne, referring to himself in the third person, claiming to choose integrity over corrupt self-advancement:

> He cannot climbe as other catchers can,
> To leade a charge before himselfe be led,
> He cannot spoile the simple sakeles man,
> Which is content to feede him with his bread.
> He cannot pinch the painefull souldiers pay,
> And sheare him out his share in ragged sheetes.
>
> (2000: 314)

Tusser and Gascoigne present themselves as men without a fixed place in society, unrewarded in spite of effort and virtue. Lack of reward and recognition also keeps Thomas Churchyard continually on the move as a soldier in two poems that construct a narrative around events in his own life, 'A Tragical Discourse of the Unhappy Man's Life' in *Churchyard's Chips* (1575) and 'A Story Translated out of the French' in *A Light Bundle of Lively Discourses* (1580). Churchyard's life story is one of privation and imprisonment on continual campaigns, in Scotland, Ireland, France, Flanders, then back to France, only to find no home or recognition in England: 'With labours long, in vaine we beat the ayre |[...] Small hoep [hope] in those, that sits in Golden chayre' (1973: 63ᵛ).

Tusser, Gascoigne, and Churchyard present themselves artfully in verse to a print audience, and to the patrons, actual and potential, to whom the poems are also addressed, as deserving, active, and enterprising but unfortunate.[6] They claim to be resigned to God's dispensation, although social criticism makes itself clearly heard in Churchyard's texts. The selves produced by these texts are typically socially unfixed, claiming to be gentlemen on the title pages of their books, but without a recognized place and calling to give them a stable identity or status. Such personae may well have exerted a powerful appeal to a literate, but socially fluid, London print market of young men and women trying to make their way in the world. In the cases of Forman and, as we shall see, Whithorne, writing in manuscript, there is the intriguing possibility that the ideal addressees are the authors themselves.[7] For Forman and Whithorne, both of whom took a pleasure in having their portraits painted, the fashioning of a desired self is a lifelong work of art and effort, perhaps primarily for their own scrutiny and assessment.[8]

---

[6] 'Gascoigne's Woodmanship' is addressed to Lord Grey of Wilton. Churchyard alludes to his fear of offending a patron: 'In mouth I have a gegg' (1973: 67ʳ).

[7] The evidence is very ambiguous in both cases. Forman had married but as yet had no legitimate children when in 1600 he began his prose narrative of his life. Traister (2001: 132) argues that some of Forman's writings do hint at having been written for posterity. Whithorne was not married and had no children when he wrote, though his manuscript frequently addresses an unnamed friend.

[8] For Forman's portrait, see Traister (2001: 21). For Whithorne's portraits, see Whythorne (1961, app. 5). This is a complete edition using the original orthography.

36.2 THE SELF AS EYEWITNESS

In English first-person writing, as in Amelang's Continental first-person texts, the experience of displacement is often, literally, an experience of travel. To leave England and venture abroad is to experience cultural dislocation and disturbance and to expose familiar values and settled identities to the disturbing effects of otherness (Bedford and Kelly 2007: 63). In a number of first-person accounts of experience abroad by those serving as soldiers on campaigns, or aboard ship, writers not only confront their stay-at-home readers with glimpses of disturbing strangeness and disorder, but, more disturbingly, call into question the stability of familiar behaviours and values once removed from home. The forms in which these accounts are written include personal chronicle, travel account, and narrative verse. The primary function of the self in these texts is often that of authenticating eyewitnesses of events and actions, but the authorial self intrudes into the text to at least some, and often to a very great, degree. What all the texts have in common is a sense of the way dislocation challenges familiar and accepted identities and conventional narratives.

The manuscripts of the soldier–chroniclers Elis Gruffudd, describing in Welsh English campaigns in France from the 1520s to the 1550s, and William Farmer, describing campaigns in Ireland at the end of the century, erase, to a greater or lesser degree, the authorial self in order to focus on the historical events they witness. In each case, nevertheless, the authors' own perspectives and judgements shape the accounts. The Welshman Gruffudd casts himself as an experienced and sceptical onlooker, with disillusioned views about the behaviour of his fellow soldiers. War is a place where honour and glory are in short supply, especially among the gentlemen and aristocrats charged with leadership.[9] William Farmer, less explicitly present in his own text, constructs in the face of Irish otherness a determined version of the English as compassionate, orderly, and civilized. Only occasionally do the fissures in this ideal become visible, as in an episode where Irish children found cannibalizing their mother turn out to have been robbed of all other form of sustenance by the English themselves (1907: 129–30).

War and its power to throw assumed values and familiar categories into disorder is vividly evident in Gascoigne's verse account of his own service in the Netherlands in the early 1570s, 'The Fruits of War', printed in *Posies* (1575). Gascoigne figures himself at first as a disinterested intellectual without first-hand knowledge of war, but that persona is abandoned in the second half of the poem, in which Gascoigne invokes his own experience as a soldier to depict a military chaos caused by English incompetence and Dutch veniality. The experience of war, it seems, is quite different from bookish definitions. In the upside-down world of the Netherlands depicted in this poem, land is water, sailors lead soldiers, and Gascoigne's own heroic efforts are misinterpreted as cowardice and betrayal. No doubt the poem's printing aims to

---

[9] For two examples among many of Gruffudd's criticism of leaders and captains, see Gruffydd (1949: 67; 1950: 27).

right that misapprehension, but the poem in fact deprives the reader of stable values and perspectives. Not only is the authorial Gascoigne presented as contradictory and unreliable, but England, the 'Peroratio' hints, may be contaminated by the same veniality and lack of integrity that has so undermined the Netherlands (435–8; see Heale 2008).

Miles Philips spent fourteen years as a captive of the Spanish in Mexico (Philips 1965).[10] His narrative begins as an account of what happened to some of the 114 sailors put ashore in the Gulf of Mexico by Hawkins in 1568 but in its final section focuses on the experience of Philips himself. The collective 'we' of the early part of the narrative gives place to the first person as Philips is separated from his companions when they come under the scrutiny of the Spanish Inquisition (Helgerson 2003). Philips's shift into the rhetoric of first-person testimony ('And then was I Miles Philips') suggests not only the Inquisitorial process he underwent in Mexico, but that Philips's narrative may be in some sense conceived of as a legal testimony before actual or anticipated English inquisitors. He may have felt his relatively lenient treatment by the Inquisition, compared to most of his companions, and his often admiring and sympathetic account of Spanish life in Mexico, needed some justification.[11] Philips asserts his loyalty:

For mine owne part I could never throughly settle my selfe to marrie in that countrey, although many faire offers were made unto mee of such as were of great abilitie and wealth, but I could have no liking to live in that place, where I must every where see and know such horrible idolatrie committed, and durst not once for my life speake against it.   (1965: 575)

The prose in this passage, as repeatedly elsewhere in his narrative, registers the seductions and attractions of the settled civil life of Spanish Mexico, even as it asserts the purity of his Protestant English identity.

Another traveller, Robert Baker, found the certainties of his own English identity less impervious to the disintegrative effects of the other. In two poems, part epic, part traveller's account, Baker presents himself as a second Orpheus braving the dangers of a hellish Africa and its devilish inhabitants on voyages in 1562 and 1563. In the second poem, in which Baker is cast adrift with nine companions in a small boat off the 'Guinie' coast of Africa, the epic machinery of Roman gods and the underworld gives way to a discourse of dependence on divine grace. The 'black devils' prove kinder and more hospitable than the Portuguese Christians. Finally, Baker and his surviving companions lose all marks of racial difference, living naked and digging in the ground for roots like the 'black devils' they had previously mocked, and, but for the grace of God, coming close to cannibalism (1965: 132–42; see Heale 2003: 80–5).

In these tales of deracination and confrontation with a godless and savage foreignness, settled identities and established values seem to come under threat. In

[10] Philips's account was printed in the first edition of *Principal Navigations* in 1589, but Hakluyt records, in his *Discourse of Western Planting* (1584), that the Queen was presented with a copy of Philips's text just after his return to England in 1582.

[11] Fuchs (2002: 55–68) argues that Philips's narrative asserts his English Protestant identity for an English audience, a reading contested by Helgerson (2003: 577).

the journals of Richard Madox, a chaplain on the 'troublesome' voyage of Captain Edward Fenton in 1582, it is the familiar and seemingly civil that proves savage and godless (Bedford and Kelly 2007: 85–91). The Oxford-educated clergyman records, with fearful secrecy, his horror as he finds that his own assumptions about the English officers, commissioned by the Crown, are misplaced. Far from exemplifying the ideals of gentlemen, and pursuing the 'public good', they turn out to be pirates, hypocrites, and cowards (Madox 1959: 182). Madox's journal fervently asserts his own virtue, but his enforced participation in a collective enterprise of dishonour compromises his reputation and undermines the ideals of English enterprise that inspired his participation in the voyage. John Bale's *Vocation* (1553) should have been a triumphant account of his calling by God and the King to evangelize the Irish in the bishopric of Ossory. Instead it turns into a tale of persecution, kidnap, and the disintegration of all stability. In Ireland, Bale finds himself isolated in the face of attacks by his landowning neighbours, and the outrageous ignorance, hypocrisy, and corruption of his fellow priests, not least 'that great Epicure' the Archbishop of Dublin. Attempting to return home to England, he is taken for ransom at sea. The disorder Bale experiences abroad and on the water mirrors the overthrow of order at home as the reign of the godly Edward VI turns into the reign of the godless Mary I. The experience confirms for Bale that deracination in this world is a sign of homecoming in the next: 'For no chosen chylde receyveth he to enherytaunce | without muche correction' (1990: 52, 79).[12]

In such first-person narratives of experience abroad, the authors figure themselves as eyewitnesses of events and societies that call into question established assumptions about identities and callings, and in some cases challenge a sense of the civil English self as different from or better than barbarous or idolatrous others. In much of the travel-writing, as in the career and life narratives considered in the previous section, finding and maintaining a desirable identity in the face of disorder and instability is a central concern and a source of considerable anxiety and effort.

36.3 VERSIONS OF THE SELF IN VERSE

Many of the life-writers we have considered use verse to produce heightened, overtly artful, personae fashioned in print for a public readership.[13] The use of the self and allusions to the author's own life story in complaints, love sequences, and other forms of occasional verse became a distinctive feature of single-author volumes of verse printed in the 1560s and 1570s. The cue for many of these publications is *Tottel's Miscellany* (1557), which made public the coterie compositions of courtly poets such

---

[12] For discussions of the *Vocation*, see especially Fairfield (1971) and Happé (2000).

[13] McCabe has described such 'auto-biographical' writing as 'a peculiar form of rhetorical discourse, as valuable for what it occludes as for what it reveals' (2006: 185).

as Sir Thomas Wyatt and the Earl of Surrey. Suggesting their own gentlemanly participation in the exchange of occasional verse, the poets of mid-century single-author miscellanies present themselves in print as unfortunate but virtuous subjects, of gentle birth but uncertain prospects, thus promoting themselves to potential wealthy patrons at the same time as appealing to a London readership eager to find models for their own social aspiration.

If the loss, or at least a sense of the fragility, of seemingly stable identities and values characterizes the first-person narratives of the previous section, themes of social, as well as geographical, displacement are characteristic of autobiographical mid-century miscellany verse. Thomas Howell prefaces his verse collection *New Sonnets and Pretty Pamphlets* (1570) with an autobiographical complaint about a change of fortune that has destroyed his prospects, reducing him to a 'mean estate' that is quite unlike the middling estate idealized as a place of contentment by more courtly writers.[14] He compares his loss of freedom to that of a caged bird:

> that flew hir timely flight,
> Throughout the groves and fertile fielde, in joyes and great delight,
> Which shall no sooner feele hir selfe, to be restrainede,
> From hir such wonted libertie, as some time she retained,
> But foorth withal she doth, such inwarde thought conceave,
> That yelding up hir pleasures past, hir life therewith doth leave.

> (1879: 119)

Other verses in the same collection, in the form of an exchange of verses with a friend, make it clear that Howell's status has been reduced from free gentleman to gentleman servant (153).

George Turbervile in *Epitaphs and Sonnets* (1574/6?) recalls his own travels in the entourage of Thomas Randolph, Elizabeth's representative, on a mission to Russia in 1568–9 as the setting for a series of first-person poems. In a prefatory poem addressed to 'a mother Cosin', the journey abroad is presented both as evidence of the poet's active enterprise, and as a sign of the failure of England to provide a proper role and place for a son:

> I must no longer stay
> advantage is but vile
> The cruel lady fortune on
> your sonne will never smile
> My countrey coast where I
> my Nurses milke did sucke,
> Would never yet in all my life
> allowe me one good lucke.

> (1977: 348)

---

[14] M. Crane comments that it is 'one thing for Wyatt or another courtier to praise the mean and sure estate, and another thing for a grocer to read about it' (1993: 170).

In a series of three verse epistles written from Russia and dated 1568, appended to the collection, he longs for home, feeling contaminated, as the travel-writers Philips and Baker had felt, by the strange outlandishness of his hosts. Russia is also used, in an innovative sequence of first-person love poems, as a place whose distance from home and whose unwelcoming climate and landscape figure an emotional experience of exile and rejection (353–78).[15] Turbervile's verses in *Epitaphs and Sonnets* use themes similar to those of the autobiographical poems in Howell's pamphlet and Gascoigne's collections to construct a version of the authorial self as subject to misfortune and displaced, geographically, socially, and emotionally.

Perhaps the most fascinating and inventively artful use of the self to articulate themes of social displacement and a sense of uncertain social identity is Isabella Whitney's collection of verse *A Sweet Nosegay* (1573). This volume adapts many of the characteristics of the mid-century single-authored miscellanies to suit a female perspective and experience. Whitney observes gender decorum by presenting herself as a humble editor and versifier of the aphorisms of Hugh Plat, and this material occupies the first half of her collection. However, unannounced in the prefatory material, the book then adds a section of personal poems in the form of verse letters exchanged with family members and friends, concluding with an extraordinary 'Wyll and Testament' written on the author's departure from London. Like the male miscellanists, Whitney presents herself as taking part in a manuscript exchange of verse among a coterie group, but in her case, this exchange maintains the family network with epistles of solicitude and advice, a number of which contain counsel from male friends and family members, in a way that, superficially at least, maintains gender decorum.[16]

Like her male counterparts, Whitney presents herself as someone on the margins of society without a fixed and recognized social role or place. She describes herself as 'serviceless' and 'subject unto sickness' in the prefatory poem 'The Author to the Reader' (1582: A5^v). Her lack of health and place are referred to throughout her epistles:

> For why I least,
> Of fortunes favours fynd:
> No yeldyng yeare she me allowes,
> Nor goods hath me assind.

(C6^r)

Her lack of a fixed place and role are described, however, more ambiguously in a letter to a married sister, 'Mistress A.B.':

> I know that you to huswyery intend,
>   though I to writing fall.
>
>   . . .

[15] The poems on these pages explicitly refer to absence and Russia, but the sequence may continue with less specific allusions.

[16] For actual letter-writers maintaining such family networks, see Daybell (2006: 182–4, 195–9). For his interesting discussion of women's letter-writing and autobiography, see pp. 165–74.

> Had I husband, or a house,
>   and all that longes therto
> My selfe could frame about to rouse,
>   as other women doo:
> But til some houshold cares mee tye,
>   my bookes and Pen I wyll apply.

$$(D2^r)$$

The tone of these lines is difficult to gauge. Is the lack of a husband and a house a misfortune or an opportunity? On the one hand, Whitney presents herself, as do most mid-century poets who write about themselves, as marginalized and unfortunate, but on the other hand, as Whitney in particular makes clear, these authors are empowered by their writing, presenting distinctive and sympathetic images of themselves to the public at large.[17]

Whitney's pleasure in reading, and especially her self-presentation as writer, figure significantly in the final poem in the volume, which extends the theme of sickness that has run throughout: 'The Aucthour (though loth to leave the Citie) upon her Friendes procurement, is constrained to departe: wherfore (she fayneth as she would die) and maketh her WYLL and Testament, as foloweth: With large legacies of such Goods and riches which she most abundantly hath left behind her' (E2^r). Where male writers such as Turbervile, Gascoigne, and Churchyard vaunted their own active service and enterprise as signs of their worth, Whitney presents herself as helpless in the face of misfortune, her fate, and her subjection to others, those 'friendes', almost certainly male kindred who make the crucial decisions about her life.[18] Whitney does, however, possess one unusual means (for a woman) of enterprise and self-assertion: her ability to read and write. Her will and testament paradoxically asserts her will and a very distinctive voice even as she figures herself as socially insignificant and powerless (Wall 1993: 296–310).

In the course of an imaginary survey of London that takes in shambles and bakehouses, luxury shops and brothels, prisons and playhouses, Whitney 'aboundantly' bequeaths to the city its own 'Goods and riches' because she cannot afford to take any of them with her: 'For there it is: I little brought | but nothing from thee tooke' (E5^r). Whitney is a ghost-like presence in the vital city she depicts, listing but never possessing its cornucopia of goods: 'french ruffes, high Purles, Gorgets and Sleeves' (E4^r). She also imagines some unusual redistribution of wealth to counter the disorders and injustices she sees all around her (Howard 2006: 228–30):

> And wealthy Widdowes wil I leave
> To help yong Gentylmen:
> Which when you have, in any case
> Be courteous to them then:
> And see their Plate and Jewells eake
> May not be mard with rust.

---

[17] For discussions of Whitney's work, see e.g. Beilin (1987: 94–101); Hutson (1994: 116–28); Howard (2006).

[18] OED, n., A. 3, 'A kinsman or near relation'.

> Nor let their Bags too long be full,
> For feare that they doo burst.

(E6ᵛ)

There is an unexpectedly lewd innuendo to these lines that suggests that if widows are fleeced of their goods to improve the prospects of penniless young gentlemen, they at least receive sexual compensation. The real London is not so kind. For all that she has 'a fixed fancy set' (E2ᵛ) on the town and is 'loth to leave', it is cruel and unjust to Whitney, as to all of its inhabitants who fail to thrive or who struggle to make a living:

> And now hath time me put in mind,
>   of thy great cruelness:
> That never once a help wold finde,
>   to ease me in distress.
> Thou never yet, woldst credit geve
>   to boord me for a yeare.

(E2ᵛ)

Only among the booksellers at St Paul's does Whitney have more than an imaginary impact on the city: 'Amongst them all, my Printer must, | have somewhat to his share' (E6ᵛ). The term 'my Printer' calls attention to the printed book in which we read Whitney's self-effacing poem about her own marginality. At the end of the poem, even as she asks to be forgotten, 'in oblivion bury mee | and never more mee name' (E7ᵛ), she describes the solitary process of writing, witnessed only by 'Paper, Pen and Standish [inkstand]' (E8ᵛ), tools of her craft, and signs of the enterprise that ensure her poem is read, her marginalized perspective asserted, and her name known four centuries later.

36.4 THOMAS WHITHORNE'S 'BOOK OF SONGS AND SONNETS'

A possible purchaser of such pamphlets as Whitney's and, certainly, Gascoigne's from the printers at St Paul's was Thomas Whithorne, whose manuscript of ninety folio leaves relating his life, achievements, and thoughts from his birth in 1528 to the probable date of writing in 1576, was entitled, by Whithorne himself, 'A book of songs and sonnets, with long discourses set with them of the child's life, together with a young man's life, and entering into the old man's life' (1962, manuscript title page). The manuscript is addressed ostensibly to a friend in order to provide context for the verses 'not only to show you the cause why I wrote them, but also to open my secret meaning in divers of them' (1). This explanation echoes a statement by the fictional editor of Gascoigne's *A Hundred Sundry Flowers*, who claims to have gathered and ordered the poems of acquaintances with a rehearsal of 'the very proper occasion whereuppon [each] was written' (2000: 145). The most sustained example of such prose contextualizing of verses and explanation of their secrets in *A Hundred Sundry Flowers* is 'The Adventures of Master F.J.', which narrates in a titillating manner an amorous affair between F.J. and Lady Elinor.[19]

Whithorne started his career in the 1540s as an amanuensis and apprentice of the court poet and musician John Heywood, helping him to transcribe, and possibly set, the poems of Sir Thomas Wyatt and the Earl of Surrey. The device used by Tottel, and later Gascoigne, of providing their verses with titles that imply specific occasions clearly provides Whithorne with one potent model for the narration of aspects of his life. Whithorne was a music master and superior household servant to a series of wealthy women, with many of whom he describes himself conducting amorous dalliances, involving the writing and the exchange or singing of verses, whose occasions and coded allusions Whithorne meticulously explains: 'I made this song somewhat dark and doubtful of sense, because I knew not certainly how she would take it, nor to whose hands it might comen after that she had read it' (1962: 31).

Whithorne's pleasure and evident pride in his own elegance and mastery of a coded language of courting is, however, persistently juxtaposed to passages of anxiety about his reputation, his moral integrity, and his dignity—anxiety that leads to an almost obsessive sifting and explaining of his intentions and probity:

This lo! did touch me somewhat nigh and brought me in great perplexity. For one while the suggestions and motions of my ghostly enemy would provoke my flesh to rebel against the spirit; and another while God's grace working in me (His name be praised for it) would put into my mind and remembrance those of the Ten Commandments which do say 'Thou shalt not commit adultery' [...] So that upon the consideration hereof, I was thoroughly determined that, whatsoever came of it, I would by God's grace never defile her wedlock bed.   (87)

Here the language of coded courting is overtaken by the language of self-justification and moral integrity that were also central to Bale's and Forman's presentations of their lives.

While narratives of courting and intimate secrets provide a powerful model for Whithorne, his manuscript is also a career narrative which shares much in common with the failed career narratives of Tusser or Gascoigne, but also with Forman's hubristic celebration of his own achievements. Whithorne's many employments included music tutor to wealthy women, a 'chief waiting-man', a 'schoolmaster and tutor' to a Cambridge undergraduate, the London agent of a man of affairs, and, at the apex of his career, Master of Music to the Archbishop of Canterbury. This is in many respects a successful career, but there are repeated moments when

---

[19] For two articles considering Whithorne's debts to Gascoigne and the mid-century miscellanies, see Shore (1981, 1982). For discussions of Whithorne's manuscript, see Mousley (1990) and Heale (2003, ch. 2).

Whithorne describes his despondency at yet another new start after his hopes have been disappointed:

it rather gave me cause to call to my remembrance the whole discourse of all my former life. And then, considering of everything that I had passed, how I had been many times in hope of prosperity, and then presently out of security; and then tossed from post to pillar, now up, now down, by the illusions of flattering and fickle fortune, who would never suffer me to be in quiet when I was well and in prosperity.   (138–9)

Whithorne belongs to the same uncertain social class as many of the mid-century writers, and shares their fluid and vulnerable social identity. This is particularly evident in his repeated insistence on his social and professional status. He is dismayed, early in his career, to be employed, like the equally mortified Thomas Howell, as 'a serving-creature or servingman, it was so like the life of a water-spaniel' (28). Later on, he repeatedly insists on his social status in the face of challenges from others, asserting his equality with a Cambridge tutor (101–2) and his dignity as a teacher of music, 'one of the seven sciences liberall' (46, 193), and reflecting bitterly on his enforced deference at the tables of his social superiors:

when I called to my remembrance how, when as heretofore at sundry times I had been in the companies of those who be worshipful, right worshipful, and also honourable, and saw the meaner sort (in comparison of their estates) were driven to put up quietly some injuries at their hands; also how such things, which the inferior sort either said or did in the presence of their greaters or betters, was but allowed of as it pleased their superiors to take it [...] [it] learned me that I should not keep company with my greaters.   (138)

Mary Thomas Crane has described the importance of aphorisms and commonplace books in 'framing' young men in accordance with approved models: 'Framing, then, implies the construction of the self in accordance with a pre-existing rule, both grammatical and ethical,' providing 'a kind of fortification for the mind' (1993: 73). Just such a use of aphorisms and proverbs to construct an approved self and fortify the mind is everywhere evident in Whithorne's manuscript. One of its functions appears to be as a commonplace book, a place for Whithorne to store and apply lists of proverbial precepts. Before embarking on his career as a music tutor to rich women, Whithorne arms himself by listing as many misogynist proverbs and anecdotes as he can remember, concluding his collection with the confident assertion that he will henceforth 'give no heed to the allurements, enticements and snares of women' (21), a statement which his subsequent narratives largely support, with a significant wobble or two. The process by which he frames and fortifies himself is particularly evident at his lowest point, when his hopes of wealth and employment as a London agent are shattered by the death of his employer and his own health is threatened by the plague in London. Faced with such a crisis, Whithorne copies into his manuscript, and often versifies, pages of bracing precepts: 'I now again, as my leisure served me, gave myself to the reading godly and grave books, out of the which I took certain notes and counsels for me to have in mind at this time' (121).

A major framework for Whithorne's narrative of his life is the idea of the ages of man (see Dove 1986; Bedford and Kelly 2007: 15–20). Whithorne repeatedly assesses his own progress within this paradigm. In the 'age named adolescency, which continueth [from fifteen] until twenty and five' (11), Whithorne arms himself against women because he has heard 'that in this age Cupid and Venus were and would be very busy to trouble the quiet minds of young folk' (12). Later on, finding himself some three or four years into 'the juventute, the which is from the twenty-fifth until forty years of age', he is not surprised to find himself easily choleric because that humour chiefly reigns 'in the second and last part of the young man's age' (66). Whithorne not only assessed his behaviour and progress according to this detailed paradigm of a man's life, he had at least four paintings made of himself at different stages in his life, scrutinizing his images, as superior mirrors, for appropriate signs of his stage in life (12, 38, 116). When preparing for the printing of a selection of his *Songs* in 1571, he takes great care over the image of himself that will be presented to the public, deciding to preface the volume with an engraved portrait, his coat of arms, and a motto that puns elaborately on his name:

Seeing the books with the music in them should be as my children, because they contained that which my head brought forth [...] also because they should bear my name, I could do no less than set in every one of them their father's picture or counterfeit, to represent unto those who should use the children the form and favour of the parent.   (175)

Whithorne is presented by his narrative as a man anxious to conform to the best approved models, but for whom such conformity is a continual effort of self-creation and self-fashioning, using the forms and models available to him. Barbara Traister has written of Simon Forman that he had an obsession with writing, of turning 'himself into text' and that he used 'his books [...] to shape and present himself and to make orderly and comprehensible a world that might otherwise have seemed merely chaotic' (2001, pp. xii, 144). The observation is suggestive for Whithorne. His manuscript strives to present, in prose and verse, versions of himself to parallel the self-portraits which he hung in his room and which gave him such pleasure. Even the technical process of writing is carefully and idiosyncratically fashioned; Whithorne uses a 'new Orthografy', a spelling system involving special letters that was culled from what he considered the best authorities, but which he makes distinctly his own, by altering and adapting and selecting from among his approved models, painfully inventing a new and perfected form for his written English (1961: 4–6). Similarly, Whithorne's life is constructed out of the multiple forms and paradigms available to him, but it is neither commonplace nor second-hand. His manuscript is an extraordinary, poignant, and in many ways a triumphant document which, like his 'new Orthografy' manages to produce out of available materials something entirely new in the sixteenth century: an extended account of a middling kind of life, contradictory and muddled, and rich in introspective reflection. It is a life and voice that seems in some respects strikingly familiar to us now in the twenty-first century.[20]

[20] Amelang makes some interesting comments on the frequency with which 'artists of all sorts' were autobiographers, suggesting they were the members of society most likely to employ a new language of 'talent, effort and achievement' (1998: 191). Whithorne's manuscript is contemporary with, although he could not have read, the artist autobiographies in Italy by Cardano and Cellini.

Although unique, Whithorne's manuscript shares much with other examples of sixteenth-century life-writing in English. What characterizes the majority of such texts is a sense of displacement, actual or threatened, from settled roles and identities, and a desire to construct narratives that make sense of, or justify, unsettling experience. Travellers' tales and accounts of military campaigns more fundamentally call into question the stability of a system of differences in which English selves, defined as honourable, civilized, and virtuous, can be easily distinguished from disturbing others. Characteristically, in sixteenth-century English life-writing, the narratives are told by those who place themselves precariously on the social margins, geographically and socially, figuring themselves as excluded by ill fortune or a hard-hearted establishment from social recognition and reward. Sixteenth-century personal life-writing is abundant, but it is found in unfamiliar forms and genres. The selves that are articulated by such writing, socially fluid, unsettled, and fragmented, were a new phenomenon in the sixteenth century, articulating new selves and perspectives out of the available materials.

Primary Works

Baker, Richard (1965), 'The Firste, and Second Voyages to Guinie', in *The Principall Navigations, Voyages and Discoveries of the English Nation*, ed. R. Hakluyt, repr. and ed. D. B. Quinn and R. A. Skelton (Cambridge, MA: Harvard University Press), 130–42.

Bale, John (1990), *The Vocacyon of Johan Bale*, ed. P. Happé and J. N. King (Binghampton, NY: Medieval and Renaissance Texts and Studies).

Churchyard, Thomas (1580), *A Light Bondell of Livly Discourses*.

—— (1973), *The Firste Parte of Churchyardes Chippes* (Menston: Scolar Press).

Farmer, William (1907), 'William Farmer's Chronicles of Ireland from 1594 to 1613', ed. C. L. Falkiner, *EHR* 22: 104–30, 527–52.

Forman, Simon (n.d.), Autobiographical Psalms, Bodl., MSS Ashmole 240, 802.

—— (1947), 'Autobiography' and 'Diary', in A. L. Rowse, *Simon Forman: Sex and Society in Shakespeare's Age* (London: Weidenfeld and Nicolson), 267–99.

Gascoigne, George (2000), *A Hundreth Sundrie Flowres*, ed. G. W. Pigman III (Oxford: Clarendon Press).

Gruffydd, Elias (1949), 'The "Enterprises" of Paris and Boulogne', ed. and trans. M. B. Davies, *Bulletin of the Faculty of Arts: Fouad I University*, 11: 37–95.

—— (1950), 'Boulogne and Calais from 1545 to 1550', ed. and trans. M. B. Davies, *Bulletin of the Faculty of Arts: Fouad I University*, 12: 1–90.

Hakluyt, Richard (1993), *A Particular Discourse Concerninge the Greate Necessitie and Manifolde Commodyties that Are Like to Growe to this Realme of Englande by the Westerne Discoveries Lately Attempted, written in the yere 1584*, ed. David B. Quinn and Alison M. Quinn (London: Hakluyt Society).

Howell, Thomas (1879), *The Poems of Thomas Howell (1568–1581)*, ed. A. B. Grosart.

Madox, Richard (1959), 'Private Diary', in *The Troublesome Voyage of Captain Edward Fenton, 1582–1583*, ed. E. G. R. Taylor, Hakluyt Society, 2nd ser., 113 (Cambridge: Cambridge University Press), 150–98.

PHILIPS, MILES (1965), 'A Discourse Written by One Miles Philips Englishman', in R. Hakluyt (ed.), *The Principal Navigations, Voyages, Traffiques & Discoveries*, repr. and ed. D. B. Quinn and R. A. Skelton (Cambridge, MA: Harvard University Press), 562–80.

TURBERVILLE, GEORGE (1977), *Epitaphes, Epigrams, Songs and Sonets and Epitaphes and Sonnettes*, ed. R. J. Panofsky (Delmar: Scholars' Facsimiles and Reprints).

TUSSER, THOMAS (1984), *Five Hundred Points of Good Husbandry*, ed. Geoffrey Grigson (Oxford: Oxford University Press).

WHITNEY, ISABELLA (1982), *A Sweet Nosgay* (London: R. Jones, 1573), repr. in *The Floures of Philosophie* by Hugh Plat (1572); and Whitney, *A Sweet Nosgay* (1573) and *The Copy of a Letter* (1567); all ed. R. J. Panofsky (Delmar: Scholars Facsimiles and Reprints).

WHITHORNE, THOMAS (1961), *The Autobiography of Thomas Whythorne*, ed. J. M. Osborn (Oxford: Clarendon Press).

—— (1962), *The Autobiography of Thomas Whythorne: Modern-Spelling Edition*, ed. J. M. Osborn (London: Oxford University Press).

CHAPTER 37

PAGEANTS AND PROPAGANDA

ROBERT LANGHAM'S *LETTER* AND GEORGE GASCOIGNE'S *PRINCELY PLEASURES AT KENILWORTH*

JANETTE DILLON

QUEEN ELIZABETH'S summer progresses provided a regular occasion for ceremonial and entertainment. They presented an opportunity for the Queen to interact publicly with her subjects, from the chosen host, his household, and the travelling court to the wider public who might attend or participate in certain elements of the entertainment; and the publication of pamphlets recounting the events was a way of representing that interaction to an even wider public. The visit to the Earl of Leicester at Kenilworth on the summer progress of 1575, however, was unusual in two ways. First, its extended duration and magnificence (lasting nineteen days, at an estimated cost to Leicester, according to some reports, of £1,000 per day, not to mention the costs of embellishing Kenilworth over a period of years before 1575) were unmatched by any of Elizabeth's progresses before or after it; and secondly, two printed accounts of it are extant, a situation which allows comparison between two different ways of representing the progress to different audiences.[1]

The more straightforward of the two accounts (in the sense that its author and purpose are fairly easily identified) was written by George Gascoigne and printed as *The Princely Pleasures at the Court at Kenilworth* in 1576.[2] Gascoigne was one of several authors employed to write and perform in the entertainments for the Queen, and his printed account identifies William Hunnis, John Badger, George Ferrers, Richard Mulcaster, William Patten, and Harry Goldingham as the authors of others for this occasion. He had fought in the Netherlands in 1572–3, supporting the Dutch revolt against the Spanish, an affiliation he shared with the Earl of Leicester, whose Puritan leanings made him a strong supporter of the Dutch. Commissioned by Leicester, then, to help write the entertainments, and politically aligned with him, Gascoigne's printed text was probably also commissioned by Leicester and likely to reflect Leicester's interests.

The second account, whose full title is *A Letter: Wherein, part of the entertainment unto the Queen's Majesty, at Kenilworth Castle, in Warwickshire, in this summer's progress, 1575, is signified: from a friend officer attendant in court, unto his friend a citizen, and merchant of London*, was published anonymously, with no publisher's name or date, in 1575, but names its author within the text by variants of the formulae R.L. and Robert Langham, or Laneham. Its authorship and purpose are considerably more problematic. Though the most recent editor of the *Letter*, R. J. P. Kuin, remains convinced that it is indeed the work of Robert Langham (a London mercer and Keeper of the Council Chamber), other scholars have argued that it was written by William Patten, named by Gascoigne as a co-writer of the entertainments.[3] A private letter written by William Patten to Lord Burghley, dated 10 September 1575, a few weeks after the Kenilworth events, makes reference to an order 'hoow the book waz too be supprest for that Langham hath complaynd upon it. and ootherwize for that the honorabl enterteinment be not turned intoo a jest'; and this has been read, in tandem with other evidence (such as the characteristic spelling of the *Letter*), as indicative that the *Letter* was in fact written by Patten as a joke against Langham. If so, however, it seems to have been a joke that Patten expected Langham to share, since he himself had directed Thomas Wilson to give Langham a copy, and in his letter to Burghley he professes himself 'sory [...] that he [Langham] takez it so noow'.[4]

[1] Kenilworth is the first progress for which we have two surviving accounts, and Holinshed's *Chronicle* mentions a third, now lost (see Smuts 2000). It was not, however, to remain unique in this respect for long. The Queen's visit to Norwich in 1578 was recorded in two printed narratives. Smuts further notes that printed records of progresses scarcely existed before the 1570s, while Gabriel Heaton (2007: 232–3) points out that manuscript accounts of Elizabeth's progresses throughout the reign outnumbered printed pamphlets, and that the cluster of printed descriptions in the latter half of the 1570s was unrepresentative.

[2] This edition is now lost, and is known only through the reprint in Gascoigne's *Whole Works*, printed in 1587, and through a transcript in *Kenilworth Illustrated* (1821).

[3] The case for Patten's authorship is made by O'Kill (1977) and D. Scott (1977). Scott quotes Patten's letter in full (301), and quotations from the letter below are taken from this source.

[4] Shortly before this chapter went to press, I was fortunate to have the opportunity of reading in proof Elizabeth Goldring's very full discussion of the authorship question, which brings new archival evidence to bear in arguing the case for Langham's authorship. The case against him, she argues, has

Kuin is right, however, to indicate that 'of the work's original eighty-six pages, by far the greater number is in fact perfectly straightforward, with no great attempt at humour', and it is perhaps impossible to resolve the intention of the *Letter* at this distance in time. What is clear, however, is that it differs in tone and target audience from Gascoigne's text. While not consistently satirical, it is certainly more colloquial, witty, and knowing in tone than Gascoigne's rather literary, text-based, and carefully attributed record. It also records parts of the entertainment that Gascoigne dismisses as 'countrie shews [...] and the merry marriage, the which were so plaine as needeth no further explication' (Gascoigne 1788:69).

In addition to these two full printed accounts by Gascoigne and Langham, there is also a third and passing reference to the Kenilworth entertainment, addressed to a very different and specific target audience, Gabriel de Zayas, the Spanish Secretary of State. This occurs in a letter written by the resident Spanish ambassador in England, Antonio de Guaras, and provides a strikingly different perspective. The bulk of the letter, written on 18 July, reports on two matters of state before turning briefly to the Kenilworth festivities: first, preparations for arming and inspecting English ships and further rumours which lead de Guaras to believe that the English may soon send aid to the Netherlands in their continuing attempts to resist Spanish domination; and secondly, a Scottish armed raid that had captured or killed over 600 Englishmen. People at court are discussing both these matters, de Guaras indicates, while the Queen, he continues,

now at a castle belonging to Lord Leicester, called Kenilworth, has been entertained with much rejoicing there, and it is said that whilst she was going hunting on one of the days, a traitor shot a cross-bow at her. He was immediately taken, although other people assert that the man was only shooting at the deer, and meant no harm. The bolt passed near the Queen but did her no harm, thank God!   (*CSP Spanish* 1892–9: ii. 498)

Neither Gascoigne's *Princely Pleasures* nor Langham's *Letter* mentions this attempted assassination of the Queen, and de Guaras himself, in a subsequent letter of 25 July, writes that 'There is nothing more said about the prisoner that they took at Court, as I mentioned before, and no one dares to mention the matter, which, indeed, few people can understand' (*CSP Spanish* 1892–9: ii. 500).[5]

---

largely been based on the belief that the (auto)biographical detail in it is implausible and that the writing style is 'suspiciously worldly and learned' for a mercer (Goldring 2008: 5). Goldring demonstrates not only that most of the detail can be corroborated, but that some of it would have been known only to Langham. She also shows that the mercers generally, and Langham and his father in particular, had close connections with the Earl of Leicester. Patten's role, she argues, may have been that of putting the letter into print, perhaps with some alterations and probably against Langham's will. The case for regarding Langham as the author of the original manuscript letter, if not in quite the same form as the printed version that remains extant, is a good one, and, though authorship is not germane to the concerns of this chapter, I will assume Langham as the name of the author on the basis of Goldring's case. Kuin takes the target audience of the *Letter* to be a 'wider' market (1983: 11), but the colloquial tone could designate a more exclusive address to a peer or peer group. It fits well with Goldring's argument that this is one mercer writing to another with shared interests, anticipating that the recipient may show it to a few mutual friends.

[5] Kuin suggests (1983: 91) that this may have been an elaboration of the Savage Man incident discussed below, when a horse was startled by a falling tree close to the Queen.

There is, then, a 'competition for representation' between these three texts, each selecting and omitting aspects of the Kenilworth progress for their own very different purposes, which this chapter will explore in more detail.[6] But it is worth pausing at this point to notice how powerfully the idea of competition may shape this and other progresses or indeed court performances of any kind. The Queen understood and expected that entertainments staged for her would perform more than mere entertainment. She knew that there was always an agenda. As she famously remarked to an earlier Spanish ambassador at an entertainment laid on by the Earl of Leicester in 1565, presenting a play about marriage: 'This is all against me'; and though she did not intervene to change anything on that evening, she did the next day, when the Dean of St Paul's, Dr Alexander Nowell, turned his sermon to abuse Catholic writings and use of images. 'Do not talk about that,' she interjected as soon as he began; and when he continued, apparently not hearing her, she raised her voice to tell him: 'Leave that, it has nothing to do with your subject, and the matter is now threadbare.' The occasion ended in confusion as the preacher came to a swift close, the Queen left in anger, and many of the Protestants among the audience wept, while the Catholics rejoiced (*CSP Spanish* 1892–9: i. 404–5). All present understood that any public performance might have a political agenda, and patrons and performers had to tread a dangerous line between making their views and counsel evident in an acceptable way and overstepping the mark.

There was competition, not only between those who represented the performance after the event in writing, but also between those who commissioned it, performed it, and witnessed it. In reading accounts of the Kenilworth progress more than four centuries after the event, we must try to read between and across them as well as in and through them; and we must try to supplement that complex reading of written texts with an awareness of place, images, and persons derived from other written and pictorial records too. Place, as any Elizabethan spectator knew, was as much a maker of meaning as scripted performance; and part of the struggle for representation is played out through the opposition or complementarity between the performed content and its space. But Kenilworth itself, as Elizabeth Woodhouse notes, has hitherto been the neglected performer in scholarly examination of the Kenilworth entertainments (1999: 127). The uncertainty as to whether there really was an attempt on the Queen's life hinges on the different agendas of the reporters, and in turn on the tension between the places they occupy: the court, a place of diplomatic interaction, rumour, and intrigue, and Kenilworth, a beautiful park constructed on the occasion of the Queen's visit as a *locus amoenus*, a refuge from the daily events of political life (though it tacitly also seeks to convey a carefully constructed political agenda, one which, as we shall see, is prevented from going ahead as planned). If there was an attempt on the Queen's life within the bounds of such a pleasurable place, that event

[6] Frye (1993) uses the phrase 'the competition for representation' to explore a sequence of moments in Elizabeth's reign in terms of her struggle to control their iconography. Her chapter on Kenilworth is full of suggestive and illuminating readings of events, though it perhaps over-reads the relevance of Elizabeth's imprisonment in 1554–5 to these events of twenty years later.

would have constituted an equally carefully constructed disruption of a supposedly protected and idealized environment.

Even before the Queen reached Kenilworth, the tone was carefully set. Leicester had a spectacular tent constructed at Long Itchington, 7 miles outside Kenilworth, where Elizabeth dined on Saturday 9 July, before arriving at Kenilworth itself later that evening. According to William Dugdale's *Antiquities of Warwickshire* (first published in 1656), 'the Earl of Leicester gave the Queen a glorious entertainment here [...] erecting a tent of extraordinary largeness for that purpose, the pins belonging whereto amounted to seven cart-loads; by which the magnificence thereof may be guessed at' (Furnivall 1907: 5). The word 'tent', however, has misleading connotations for modern readers. Tudor traditions of temporary building, including royal building, routinely used canvas structures for some of the most extraordinarily rich banqueting halls, and Leicester's Long Itchington building was evidently in this tradition. The *Letter* calls it 'a Tabernacl indeed for the number and shyft of large and goodly roomz [...] that justly for dignitee may be comparabl with a beautifull Pallais, and for greatnes and quantitee with a proper Tooun, or rather a Citadell' (1983: 75).[7] Dining in such a place before even arriving at Kenilworth was intended to give the Queen a foretaste of the scale of the entertainments that awaited her.

Leicester had spent considerable time and money (£60,000 according to Dugdale) rebuilding and adding to the house at Kenilworth and enhancing the natural beauty of the park, so that the estate as a whole became one great theatre waiting to receive the Queen as chief spectator, and in a sense also chief performer.[8] Just as Jacobean masques found their centre (literally) in the monarch's throne, placed at the single point from which the perspective stage could be totally and perfectly viewed, so the Elizabethan great house and garden came fully into being only when the Queen stepped into them. Both Burghley and Sir Christopher Hatton built Theobalds and Holdenby respectively with a view to hosting the Queen there. Hatton openly copied Theobalds, and spoke of Holdenby as a 'shrine' dedicated to Elizabeth, although in fact she never stayed there (Cole 1999: 67).

Besides constructing one of the first Italianate gardens in England, Leicester incorporated further architectural features such as the bridge, the arbours, and the first recorded grass terrace in England specifically as viewing platforms for both the scripted shows and the estate itself (see Woodhouse 1999). Yet, as Leicester constructed all this to impress and win favour from his queen, the estate itself was at the same time a source of competition between them. Besides showcasing the park and gardens by using them as locations for spectacular shows (the Lady of the Lake being borne across the lake, fireworks erupting out of the fountain, strange music emerging from an arbour), the scripts called attention to the host as provider of such rich entertainment, and the park and gardens everywhere displayed the personal emblems of Leicester. Elizabeth lost no time in reminding Leicester whose property Kenilworth ultimately was. When, on the evening of her arrival, the Lady

---

[7] For an extensive account of such a building, see, for example, Hall's account of the temporary palace built for Henry VIII at the Field of the Cloth of Gold, in Dillon (2002: 73–6).

[8] Simon Adams (2002: 326) revises Dugdale's estimate down to £40,000.

of the Lake floated towards the Queen 'upon a moovabl Iland, bright blazing with torches', uttering verses that recounted the castle's history down to its present 'owner' and, with seeming courtesy, offered her 'The Lake, the Lodge, the Lord [...] to command', the Queen responded with acerbity: 'we had thought indeed the Lake had been oours, and doo you call it yourz noow? Well we wyll heerin common more with yoo hereafter' (Langham 1983: 40–1; cf. Gascoigne 1788: 61).

The distribution of the quotations here between the two texts is indicative: Gascoigne gives the full text of the Lady's verse and tells us that 'M. Ferrers, sometime Lord of Misrule in the Court', penned them; only Langham records the Queen's somewhat testy response. Thus, as Elizabeth and Leicester play out a contest for the ownership of Kenilworth, Langham and Gascoigne play out a contest for the 'ownership' of the entertainment, setting different representations of its nature and achievement against each other. Gascoigne likes to maintain the appearance of a relatively smooth and unruffled performance of homage and receptivity between Leicester and his queen, recording in full even performances that did not take place and giving clear priority to the ideal scripted drama. The *Letter*, by contrast, more readily incorporates moments where performance deviated from the script to let failures, revisions, and possible clashes of interest show through (though Langham avoids reporting certain kinds of politically inflected clashes, as we shall see). Thus, for example, Gascoigne's account of the pageant of the Savage Man, like his account of the Lady of the Lake, prints in full the verse dialogue between Echo and the Savage Man, ending by noting that these verses were written by Gascoigne himself, while the *Letter*, after summarizing the verses, tells us of how spectacularly this show actually went wrong in the performance:

But shall I tell yoo maister Martyn by the mass of a mad aventure? az this Savage for the more submission brake his tree asunder, kest the top from him, it had allmost light upon her highnes hors hed: whereat he startld and the gentlman mooch dismayd See the benignitee of the Prins, az the footmen lookt well too the hors, and he of generositee soon callmd of him self, no hurt no hurt quoth her highnes Which woords I promis yoo we wear all glad too heer, and took them too be the best part of the play.   (46)

Some degree of spontaneity, on the other hand, was frequently built into the genre of the progress entertainment, since the Queen as performer was scripted personally to complete some of the shows in the same way as her presence completed the estate that hosted her. Potential competition, even conflict, always lurked within such shows. Elizabeth, as scholars have often noted, was an adept performer, as she demonstrated from the inception of her reign, when, being handed a copy of the English Bible by the figure of Truth on her coronation progress, she 'kissed it, and with both hir hands held up the same, and so laid it upon her brest, with great thanks to the citie therefore' (Holinshed 1807–8: iv. 168). Her graciousness in dealing with the Savage Man's mishap is as notable as was her sharpness with the Lady of the Lake. But the point is that the tension was always present. Even without the kind of random bad luck that poor Gascoigne (who himself played the Savage Man) was subject to, the potential for offence sat alongside the potential for flattery (see Gascoigne 1788: 65).

Fig. 37.1 A knight brings home a wild man captured in the woods. Henry Watson, *Valentyne and Orson* (1555), L2^v.

Progress entertainments were risky affairs, subject to changes in the weather, to the failures or loss of confidence to which amateur actors are prey, or to the Queen's own refusal to play her expected role or to allow the entertainments to go ahead as planned.[9]

Sometimes 'failures' of one kind or another could give unexpected pleasures, as did one spontaneous moment not reported by either Gascoigne or Langham:

There was a Spectacle presented to queen Elizabeth upon the water, and amongst others Harry Goldingham was to represent Arion upon the Dolphins backe, but finding his voice to be very hoarse and unpleasant, when he came to performe it, he teares of[f] his Disguise, and sweares he was none of Arion not he, but eene [even] honest Harry Goldingham; which blunt discoverie pleasd the Queene better, then if it had gone thorough in the right way; yet he could order his voice to an instrument exceeding well.[10]

[9] The question of whether Leicester's Men took any part in the entertainments remains unanswered. It is evident from Gascoigne's text as well as this manuscript that he and other amateurs took speaking parts in the quasi-spontaneous entertainments in the grounds, and it seems to me likely within this context that Leicester's Men, if they participated at all in these, took the lesser rather than the major roles. They may have had separate opportunities to display their talents, as in the play 'set foorth by [...] Actoourz' within the house after the day's other entertainments on 17 July (Langham 1983: 55).

[10] Note from a manuscript collection of 'Merry Passages and Jests' in BL, Harley MS 6395 (cited in Kuin 1983: 100).

Langham, but not Gascoigne, reports some of the other less scripted and controlled entertainments included in the sequence of events. Though not scripted specifically for the progress, events such as the bride-ale and the Coventry Hock Tuesday play must at the very least have been allowed, if not invited, into the grounds by the Earl of Leicester, but Gascoigne clearly considers them too rustic to be worth including in his account of events. He dismisses them in a sentence as too 'plain' to need further description (69), moving straight on instead to a show of his own composition.

Langham, by contrast, greatly enjoys recounting at length the rural eccentricities and failures of courtliness, as he sees it, of the popular offerings. He mocks the appearance of both bride and groom, openly insulting the bride as 'ill smellyng [...] ugly fooul ill favord' and foolishly keen to dance before the Queen, and dwelling in mock-heroic detail on the rough and unpolished performance of the groom in running at the quintain. He is less scornful about the Coventry play, which he calls 'good pastime', but notes the poor timing of both, being presented too soon beneath the chamber window, while the Queen was still watching 'delectabl dauncing' within (55). This mistiming, however, demonstrates the risk and the potential for both good and bad outcomes inherent in this kind of performance: whereas the bride-ale, obviously, is unrepeatable and simply has to go ahead without the Queen's attention, the Coventry men are treated with great grace to compensate them for their wasted effort: the Queen rewards them with both money and an invitation to repeat their performance the following Tuesday, on which second occasion she takes care to pay attention and laugh (presumably appropriately). By contrast, the show that Gascoigne moves swiftly on to describe, after dismissing the popular entertainments, is one that did not even take place. Gascoigne devotes about a third of his total text to giving the full text of this show, which focuses on Diana's loss of her nymph Zabeta (a deliberately transparent variation on Elizabeth) and culminates in Iris' advice to Zabeta to marry. Gascoigne's explanation as to why this show was not performed sounds somewhat faux-naive in context: 'being prepared and redy (every Actor in his garment) two or three days together, yet never came to execution. The cause whereof I cannot attribute to any other thing, than to lack of opportunity and seasonable weather' (80). If extended rain or cold were really the issue, we might expect him to report them specifically. Instead, the curious vagueness of phrasing and indirectness ('two or three days', 'cannot attribute to any other thing than', 'lack of opportunity') suggests awkwardness, as does the fact that this incident is immediately followed in Gascoigne's text by the Queen's 'hasting her departure' (80).

The *Letter* makes clear that this entertainment was to have taken place at Wedgenall (Wedgenock Park), 3 miles west of Kenilworth. Langham also writes of 'weather not to cleerly dispozed', but is strangely disinclined to report the content of the cancelled entertainment: 'least like the boongling carpentar, by missorting the peecez, I mar a good frame in the bad setting up, or by my fond tempring afore hand embleamish the beauty, when it shold be reard up indeede' (59).[11] He also notes that on this

---

[11] Kuin hovers over what point in the *Letter* to equate with the cancelled mask, and first links it to Langham's account of the first full day of the Queen's visit, Sunday 10 July, when Langham notes the cancellation of a mask 'of an incredibl cost', and attributes its cancellation to the lateness of the hour: 'the tyme so far spent and very late in the night noow, waz cauz that it cam not foorth too the sheaw'

same day there was also 'such earnest tallk and appointment of remooving that I gave over my notyng, and harkened after my hors' (59). He is, however, quite willing to spend the next several pages of his letter describing another unperformed entertainment centring on an ancient minstrel. It seems likely, then, that the content of the cancelled marriage mask gave offence. The topic of marriage was certainly one that had offended Elizabeth on more than occasion before, and one long associated with Leicester. There is no real consensus about how seriously Leicester might still have proffered a marriage proposal to Elizabeth. It was perhaps by this time a set of expected courtly moves aimed to please and flatter a female monarch long accustomed to such behaviours; certainly the question of producing an heir and ensuring the succession was no longer a live issue. On the other hand, Elizabeth Goldring has recently shown that Leicester commissioned four portraits especially for the visit of 1575, consisting of two sets of paired portraits of himself and the Queen that may seem to suggest Leicester as 'consort *manqué*' (2007: 174).

Susan Frye argues that the offence lay in the mask's representation of Elizabeth's imprisonment prior to the start of her reign, in that it emphasized her vulnerability and helplessness and showed her marriageability, rather than her courage or self-possession, as the key factor in her delivery. But this would be to highlight matters almost twenty years before, which scarcely makes sense unless the immediate context renders such matters still relevant; and their relevance may have been to Leicester's present feeling about his prolonged courtship of the Queen and her rejection of him, together with her expectation that he maintain a continuing posture of abject devotion. Henry Sidney, writing nine years earlier, in 1566, reported Leicester's response to the Duke of Norfolk's advice to abandon his suit as follows: 'he [Leicester] would do as he [Norfolk] advised if it could be so arranged that the Queen should not be led to think that he relinquished his suit out of distaste for it and so turn her regard into anger and enmity against him which might cause her, womanlike, to undo him' (*CSP Spanish* 1892–9: i. 518).[12] Though Leicester may have accepted the position that he would never marry the Queen, and may not have been pressing the advice to marry in any expectation that she might still marry him, he may have relished the opportunity to remind her of what she had lost and of his long-serving devotion to her. Alternatively, or perhaps at the same time, he may have wished to give her a final opportunity to confirm her rejection of his suit before taking the radical step of marrying another woman, as he was to do in 1578, at which point the Queen was indeed furious. Leicester had been involved with Lady Douglas Sheffield since 1570 or 1571, and this mistress had borne him a son in 1574. He had been refusing to marry Sheffield for some time, being quite clear in his mind that 'yf I shuld marry I am seure never to have favor of them that I had rather yet never have wyfe than lose

(Langham 1983: 56). As Kuin himself notes, however, this was clearly an indoor mask, and the show Gascoigne scripted was equally clearly an outdoor entertainment and surely to be equated with the cancelled 'devise of Goddessez and Nymphes' scheduled for Wednesday 20 July (Langham 1983: 59).

[12] McCoy (1989: 42–3) discusses the question of when Leicester abandoned his suit, noting the Spanish ambassador's report some months after this that 'It is easy to see that he has not abandoned his pretensions' (*CSP Spanish* 1892–9: i. 575).

them'; yet, as he went on to assert, there was 'nothing in the world next that favor that I wold not gyve to be in hope of leaving some childern behind me, being nowe the last of our howse' (*ODNB*). The birth of his son the previous year may have helped to move him closer to the view that he must risk losing the Queen's favour in order to sire a legitimate heir. Besides the liaison with Sheffield, rumour also linked Leicester with Lettice Knowles, Countess of Essex, from 1575, so that when her husband died in 1576 the story circulated that Leicester had poisoned him. In any event, it was Lettice Knowles whom Leicester secretly married in 1578, thereby incurring the very fury he had anticipated from Elizabeth when the marriage was revealed.

Whatever the offence of this Kenilworth mask, if offence there was (and there is no clear evidence that censorship rather than the weather was responsible for the cancellation of this entertainment), the fact that it was one of at least two cancelled entertainments heightens the probability of censorship. The other cancellation is differently dealt with in the two texts, but provides much clearer evidence of intervention. Since a show did take place on this occasion, Langham is able simply to describe it without mentioning any alterations to the script. In his text it is a graceful compliment to the Queen, whose presence delivers the Lady of the Lake from thraldom to Sir Bruce sans Pity (57). Gascoigne, however, while recounting the same event (noting the detail of Merlin's prophecy that the Lady of the Lake 'coulde never be delivered but by the presence of a better maide than herselfe'), closes by remarking at some length on the wonders of the show as first devised:

surely, if it had bene executed according to the first invention, it had been a gallant shewe; for it was first devised, that (two dayes before the Ladie of the Lake's deliverie) a captaine with twentie or thyrtie shotte shoulde have bene sent from the Hearon-house (which represented the Lady of the Lake's Castell) upon heapes of bulrushes: and that Syr Bruse, shewing a great power upon the land, should have sent out as many or moe shot to surprise the sayde Captayne; and so they should have skirmished upon the waters in such sort, that no man could perceive but that they went upon the waves: at last (Syr Bruse and his men being put to flight) the Captaine should have come to her Majestie at the castell-window, and have declared more plainly the distresse of his Mistresse, and the cause that she came not to the Court, according to duetie and promise, to give hyr attendance: and that therupon he should have besought hyr Majestie to succour his Mistresse [...] This had not onely bene a more apt introduction to her deliverie, but also the skirmish by night woulde have bene both very strange and gallant; and thereupon her Majesty might have taken good occasion to have gone in barge upon the water, for the better execution of her deliverie. (69)

The length of this digression reveals some degree of investment in its content on the part of either Leicester or Gascoigne or both. And on this occasion Gascoigne offers no explanation for the omission of the skirmish and makes no reference to the weather. The reason here is clearer, since the potential allegory at stake is self-evident, given the political moment. Leicester's active concern to do more to protect the Protestant Netherlands against their Spanish overlords was well known, but Elizabeth's approach was more cautious, and she was unwilling to commit herself openly against Spain. Events were at a crucial point over that summer, and the fear that England might take decisive military action is evident in the Spanish ambassador's letters. In the same letter of 18 July in which de Guaras recounts the rumoured assassination attempt at Kenilworth, he also notes the fitting out of two ships at Plymouth and warns: 'When least expected they will carry the business through, and I have been told that [. . .] by St Bartholomew's Day [24 August] a great service would be done' (*CSP Spanish* 1892–9: ii. 498). In his next letter, written on 25 July, he notes that the two armed ships have immediately put out to sea and repeats the warning: 'It will be found that support will reach them in this enterprise by land and sea as soon as they begin it, and the sending of these two ships with such wonderful diligence is a sign that the day for the attempt is not far distant, and no doubt the day will be St Bartholomew's' (*CSP Spanish* 1892–9: ii. 499). Though the Netherlands are nowhere explicitly mentioned, the letter is between two people who both know what they are talking about, and the reference to St Bartholomew's Day, the date of the Huguenot massacre in Paris three years earlier and, as a Catholic atrocity, an obvious moment to intervene against Spain on behalf of the Netherlands, leaves the subject in no doubt.

In this context it becomes evident that the scheduled entertainment at Kenilworth was an allegory in which the distressed lady was the Netherlands and the powerful Sir Bruce, Spain. The Captain's plea to the Queen was to have been the Earl of Leicester's platform to plead directly for England's active military intervention on behalf of the Netherlands against Spain. Gascoigne includes it in his text fairly fully, while Langham omits all mention of it. Gascoigne retains the unperformed text, probably at Leicester's behest, though as an ex-soldier in the Netherlands himself and an ex-prisoner of the Spanish, he presumably shared his patron's dedication to the Dutch Protestant cause. Since pamphlets recounting entertainments were normally published very soon after the event, Leicester may have seen publication as an opportunity, substituting for the lost opportunity of performance, to influence public sympathy, if not the Queen, towards his political point of view.[13]

What this discrepancy between performance and printed text generally reveals, a point which has received very little attention in accounts of progress entertainments, is that there must have been a routine pre-vetting of the texts for performance carried out on the Queen's behalf. The system that came into place for public theatres, whereby the master of the revels vetted all scripts for performance, was a natural extension of the role played by earlier masters of the revels and lord chamberlains in choosing performances for the court. Shakespeare famously shows Philostrate performing this office at the start of *A Midsummer Night's Dream*. It should come as no surprise to find that performances before the Queen outside her own palaces should also have been subject to inspection prior to performance.

The cancelling of an entertainment and the substitution of another one in its place must have entailed not only someone reading or hearing the intended show before it was performed, but subsequent negotiations about what would substitute and speedy revision or new writing at very short notice. Writing about the Savage Man entertainment, somewhat disingenuously and without offering any indication as to cause,

[13] The printer's Preface to *The Princely Pleasures* is dated 26 March 1576, at which point the Netherlands question was still a burning one, but Leicester may have expected it to be published within a few weeks or months of the events themselves, as was often the case with such topical pamphlets.

Gascoigne notes: 'These verses were devised, penned, and pronounced by master Gascoyne: and that (as I have heard credibly reported) upon a very great sudden' (65).

On the same day as the revised Sir Bruce entertainment went ahead, the Queen also knighted five men and 'cured' nine people by touching for 'the peynfull and daungeroous diseaz, called the kings evell' (Langham 1983: 58). It would be interesting to know how much of this performance of sovereign, quasi-divine power was pre-planned or how far it was part of a last-minute alternative performance put together to fill the gap left by an entertainment now curtailed in revision or, as Susan Frye argues, to pit the Queen's agenda against the Earl's (Frye 1993: 62). It must be borne in mind, however, that, quite aside from the particular competitive valencies operating on a progress hosted by the Earl of Leicester, Elizabeth's long-time favourite and suitor, the Queen's performance of her own presence was as much a part of any progress as the performances played before her. A progress may have been conceived by the host as an opportunity to please and perhaps advance himself with the monarch, besides displaying his own estate to best advantage to the most elite possible audience (as well as to all those on and around the estate itself); but it was conceived by the monarch not merely as an opportunity for a rural holiday, an escape from the dangers of plague in London, and a way of rewarding a loyal subject, but also as an opportunity to make herself available to public and popular view in the best possible light. And for most of the spectators, especially those resident in the area visited, the Queen, not the entertainment, was the primary object of attention. As those designing the layout of Christ Church Hall, Oxford, for a visit by King James had to be reminded by visiting court officials in 1605, the question of how much of the play the King could see was considerably less important than the question of how well he himself could be seen.

The Queen's performance, however, despite its centrality to the event as a whole, can disappear from view in records of the event. Ironically, this is made even clearer by the existence of two printed records of the Kenilworth progress. We have seen how one text may record an intervention by the Queen which is omitted by the other; but both texts become notably coy about the last stretch of the Queen's visit, to the point where it is impossible to decipher quite what happened, when, or why. As noted above, both Gascoigne and Langham indicate a problem with the cancelled Wedgenall entertainment, the mask of goddesses advising Elizabeth to marry. Gascoigne, without explicitly linking them together as cause and effect, simply begins the paragraph after his possibly arch speculation on the cause of cancellation thus: 'The Quuenes Majestie hasting her departure from thence, the Earle commanded master Gascoigne to devise some farewel worth the presenting; whereupon he him-selfe clad like unto Sylvanus, God of the woods, and meeting her as she went on hunting, spake *ex tempore*, as followeth' (80). What follows is at first not a farewell speech at all but an extended plea for the Queen to reconsider her departure plans and stay. The Queen is obviously proceeding on horseback while Gascoigne delivers this speech (perhaps literally making her way out of the grounds of Kenilworth?) and Gascoigne records how her performance changes from continuing to proceed to kindly staying her horse 'to favour Sylvanus, fearing least he should be driven out of breath by following her horse so fast' (82).

Gascoigne–Sylvanus continues his speech, which has up to this point been an elaborately complimentary allegory centring on the lamentation of the gods at the Queen's proposed departure and beseeching her to remain. As Gascoigne resumes, however, his speech becomes progressively bolder in its tone, turning from lament first to rebuke and then to mischievous obscenity. Gascoigne speaks of the Queen as having 'so obstinatly and cruelly rejected' some suitors for grace that he sighs 'to thinke of some their mishaps'. While allowing the justice of her behaviour towards some, he can scarcely 'declare the distresses wherein some of them doe presently remayne' (83–4). A new allegory of two suitors named Deepedesire and Dewedesert, who are turned respectively to a laurel bush and a holly tree by the cruel Zabeta, allows Gascoigne to turn the allegory into a sly mockery of Elizabeth's unmarried state, which seems both impudent and scarcely plausible as part of a plea for her to forgive and forget any offence taken by the cancelled marriage mask. 'There are two kinds of Holly,' says Sylvanus, 'He-Holly, and She-Holly. Now some will say, that She-Holly hath no prickes; but thereof I intermeddle not' (85). To reduce the Virgin Queen to a hollybush with no pricks seems more like a dangerously bad joke than an attempt to revoke her decision to leave. Or could it be that none of this is as serious as it seems? Was Leicester really close enough to the Queen to risk this kind of joke and get away with it? Much depends on whether the planned Wedgenall mask really gave offence or was genuinely cancelled because of bad weather.

The closing moments of Sylvanus' 'farewell' (which now does begin to look more like a teasing farewell than a genuine attempt to persuade Elizabeth to stay) bring her to a hollybush, which masquerades as the transformed Deepedesire, who speaks as the Queen approaches, begging her to remain and 'to commaund againe | This Castle and the Knight, which keepes the same for you' (86). Was this part actually taken by Leicester himself, who is so clearly represented by Deepedesire? Gascoigne does not tell us, but Deepedesire sings a song of farewell and lament (indicating of course that Elizabeth's departure was never in doubt, and that the plea to her to stay was a mere conceit of the entertainment). Silvanus concludes with a prayer that Deepedesire 'may be restored to his prystinate estate' (87), suggesting that Leicester really has offended the Queen and wishes to be restored to favour; and Gascoigne concludes his account of events at this point, ending with the motto he adopted following his service in the Netherlands: 'Tam Marti, quam Mercurio'.

Gascoigne's account thus makes it impossible to tell when the Queen departed or how long a gap there was between the cancelled Wedgenall mask and her departure, though its sequence suggests that the one followed hot on the heels of the other. The *Letter* therefore comes as a surprise, since it states that, although there was 'such earnest tallk and appointment of remooving' on the day of the cancelled Wedgenall mask, dated to Wednesday 20 July, the Queen in fact stayed until the following Wednesday, 27 July; 'for which seaven daiz, perceyving my notez so slenderly aunswering: I took it less blame, too ceas and thearof too write yoo nothing at al, then in such matterz to write nothing likely'.[14] The *Letter* makes no mention of the

---

[14] Kuin, however, notes (1983: 105) that if this date is correct, the Queen must have left before the Council, since they met at Kenilworth on 28 July. The date of her departure thus remains unclear.

farewell entertainment that Gascoigne describes, and at this point moves away from the description of entertainments altogether to a more generalizing meditation on their contents. What is going on here? What happened in these remaining seven days? When did the farewell entertainment take place, if it did, and did the Queen stay on at all beyond it? Why is the *Letter* silent about the events of that week (or the absence of them)? Did the farewell entertainment take place (as Gascoigne's detail about the Queen staying her horse implies it did), and, if so, why does the *Letter* make no mention of it?

While having two texts of the same progress is in some ways so revealing, in other ways what it reveals most emphatically is the limit to what can be known from the extant records. Evidently, in addition to whatever censorship of performance may have taken place at the time of the events themselves, there is a further degree of self-censorship (and perhaps even external censorship) operating over the printed records. The silences indicate points where the texts do not wish to focus attention; but they do not, and cannot by definition, give us clarity about why that focus is unwelcome.

Progress performances, we have seen, offer a characteristic mix of script, spontaneity, and scripted pseudo-spontaneity. They show us the monarch and her subjects both on show and at play, and feigning play even as they are most on show. Records of these performances operate by a similar mechanism, describing what was not performed as well as what was, omitting some of what was performed and feigning all the time a full and frank representation of events. Where two or more records exist, one does not merely supplement the other, but rather contests and exposes it. In the contest and the exposure lies some indication of the potential gap between performance and its records.

Primary Works

CSP Spanish (1892–9), *Calendar of State Papers, Spanish, Elizabeth I*, ed. M. A. S. Hume, 4 vols (London: HMSO).

Gascoigne, George (1788), *The Princely Pleasures at Kenelworth Castle*, in John Nichols (ed.), *The Progresses, and Public Processions, of Queen Elizabeth*, Eighteenth Century Collections Online, ii. 57–89.

Holinshed, Raphael (1807–8), *Holinshed's Chronicles of England, Scotland and Ireland*, ed. H. Ellis, 6 vols (London: Johnson).

Langham, Robert (1983), *A Letter*, ed. R. J. P. Kuin, Medieval and Renaissance Texts, 2 (Leiden: Brill).

CHAPTER 38

SIR PHILIP SIDNEY AND THE *ARCADIAS*

HELEN MOORE

That perfect-unperfect *Arcadia* [...]

THIS comment by John Florio (R3ʳ) on Sidney's *Arcadia* describes the composite edition of 1593, in which Sidney's revised, or 'New', version of the romance was completed ('perfected') by the addition of the ending of the 'Old' *Arcadia* written fourteen years earlier. But as Florio's judgement so economically reveals, this expedient editorial act created a hybrid text of internal contradictions and strange conjunctions. Apart from being imperfectly perfected, the hybrid *Arcadia* is a work of intimate, familial entertainment bound up with grand instruction, both light-heartedly comic and sombrely tragic. Similar comments could be made on Sidney's life, which serves, indeed, as a microcosm of typically Tudor contradiction and assimilation. In Sidney's biography we find intellectual aspiration combined with political wiliness, deference to the classical past interacting with an intensely modern sense of the new religio-political order, and a pride in insular identity that also demands self-fashioning in the European mould.[1] Sidney's intellectual and literary interests were also famously compendious. According to Fulke Greville, Sidney's friend and biographer, the *Arcadia* manifests the extent of Sidney's 'great harvest of knowledge' (1986: 8), a harvest drawn not just from his humanist classical education, but also from fashionable European literature, cartography, painting, architecture, landscape

---

[1] For two biographies that in different ways make much of the contradictions inherent in Sidney's life, see Duncan-Jones (1991) and Stewart (2000).

gardening, hunting, and horsemanship, to name only a few of the elements that make their appearance in the *Arcadia*.

The *Old Arcadia* (*OA*) was probably begun in 1577 and was completed by 1580. Sidney continued to make minor changes to his 'toyfull booke', as he described it to his brother Robert (Sidney 1912–26: iii. 132), until 1582, when he embarked on the full-scale rewriting that became the *New Arcadia* (*NA*).[2] The *Old Arcadia* begins with the retirement of Duke Basilius from the active life of the ruler, an ill-conceived act based upon an oracle that ultimately imperils his household and realm. Two princes, Musidorus and Pyrocles, arrive in Arcadia and adopt the disguises of a shepherd named Dorus and an Amazon named Cleophila (changed to Zelmane in the *New Arcadia*), in order to gain access to the duke's daughters, Pamela and Philoclea, with whom they have fallen in love. But the stratagem has unexpected results: both the duke and his wife, Gynecia, fall in love with Pyrocles–Cleophila, which ultimately leads to Basilius' mistakenly drinking a love potion that makes him appear dead. In the meantime, Musidorus has sought to elope with Pamela, and Pyrocles has succeeded in making love to Philoclea. But both sets of lovers are apprehended, and when the apparent death of the duke is discovered, Arcadia falls into political disarray. Into this commotion comes Euarchus, King of Macedon and Pyrocles' father, who passes judgement on the princes for their crimes, being initially unaware of their identities. At the very last moment, however, the impending disaster is averted as Basilius awakes.

The *New Arcadia* retains the essence of this plot, while amplifying the original romance's embedded themes of princely behaviour, familial disorder, and political strife through digressions and inset narratives. In accord with its greater dignity and heroic temper, Sidney's revision also moderates the severity of the domestic and political crimes committed by the princes in Arcadia. Most significantly of all, the *New Arcadia* adds the tyrant Cecropia, Basilius' sister, who imprisons the princesses in an attempt to secure the succession of her son Amphialus to the government of Arcadia. Sidney's revision breaks off during the period of the princesses' captivity, and the shape of his intentions for the new work is not known in any detail. Whereas the *Old Arcadia* circulated only in manuscript, the incomplete revision of the *New Arcadia* was published in 1590 under the auspices of Fulke Greville and entitled *The Countess of Pembroke's Arcadia*. The composite version of 1593 was published under the direction of the Countess and the editorship of Hugh Sanford, secretary to her husband, the Earl of Pembroke. This 'broken-backed hybrid' (Woudhuysen 1996: 299) is the *Arcadia* that was known to readers until the rediscovery of the *Old Arcadia* in 1906 and its publication in 1926.[3]

---

[2] For dating and the processes of composition, see Ringler (1962: 365); J. Robertson (1973, pp. xv–xvii); Skretkowicz (1986: 303–17); Woudhuysen (1996: 303–17).

[3] For descriptions of the surviving manuscripts and prints, see J. Robertson (1973, pp. xlii–lxvi); Ringler (1962: 525–38); Skretkowicz (1987, pp. liii–lxiii); Woudhuysen (1996, app.). For the changes made to the *Old Arcadia* material in 1593 in order to ally it with the revised text, see J. Robertson (1973, pp. lx–lxii).

This early embodiment in two manuscript versions and two printed texts—of which only the *Old Arcadia* can be said to be a fully coherent and finished 'work'— means that the *Arcadia* in its material form exemplifies the overlapping publication cultures of manuscript and print. It therefore stands, like much later Tudor literature, on the cusp of two very different literary worlds: one intimate, familiar, and essentially elite, the other public and socially diverse. So it is that on the one hand the *Arcadia* is Sidney's 'toyfull booke', purportedly written for the amusement of his sister, and on the other it is the work of dignified eminence described in Greville's *Dedication*. The historical dominance of the incomplete and composite printed versions means that the textual history of the *Arcadia* is characterized by a rhetoric of hybridity, deficiency, and attempted 'perfection'; this essay will argue that in form and content, as much as in material survival, the *Arcadia* is a hybridized text, at once private and public, comic and serious, English and Continental, modern and retrospective.

There are ten surviving manuscripts of the *Old Arcadia*, and it is clear that transcripts of the work circulated within the Sidney family and its near acquaintances, although it was closely guarded. Indeed, the close keeping of the work was the subject of discussion and some controversy long before it was printed. In the earliest printed reference to *Arcadia* (in 1581), the Countess of Pembroke's servant Thomas Howell lamented that 'so perfite work' (1581: E4^v) should remain hidden from wider knowledge, and in 1587 Sir Henry Sidney's secretary, Edmund Molyneux, commented on how the work was 'choislie kept' and hard to obtain: 'a speciall deere freend he should be that could have a sight, but much more deere that could once obteine a copie of it' (1587: 1554). Yet despite this close keeping and restricted circulation among friends, knowledge of the *Arcadia*'s existence had clearly spread some distance beyond the confines of the family: two writers of early elegies for Sidney, Angel Day and George Whetstone, also make reference to its existence, and there is evidence that Thomas Lodge, Robert Greene, and Barnaby Rich may have seen manuscript copies of the *Old Arcadia*, perhaps through access to Sidney (in the case of Lodge), friends such as Lodowick Bryskett (in the case of Rich) or aristocratic patrons who may have owned a copy (such as George Clifford, Earl of Cumberland, in the case of Greene). A contradictory rhetoric of close keeping and common knowledge thus surrounds the manuscript circulation of the *Old Arcadia*. When Sidney's revision was published in 1590, it perpetuated this world of intimate familiarity through the inclusion of the *Old Arcadia*'s dedication to Sidney's sister Mary, while at the same time casting Sidney's revision as a work of public worth and Protestant virtue through the editorial interventions. Sidney's original dedication frames both the undertaking and its dedicatee in terms appropriate to the original conditions of the tudor romance's 'close' keeping: 'To my deare ladie and sister [...] a principall ornament to the familie of the Sidneis' (A3^r, A4^r). Throughout the dedication, sexual and familial roles are amalgamated, transferred, and broken down, as though in playful anticipation of the sexual hybridity and domestic mayhem that is to ensue in the text itself. Sidney presents himself as at once father (to the text) and loving brother (to its dedicatee): the role he cannot play—that of husband—hovers but is left unspoken in the homage and instruction he offers to Mary as muse and mistress: 'you desired me to doo it, and your desire, to my hart is an absolute commandement' (A3ᵛ). Like an infant, the work is to be kept close to its second mother once the mother–father in whose brain such fancies have been 'begotten' has been 'delivered'. Mother, father, brother, lover: in this dedication, the familial dramas, ambiguous gender roles, and sexual taboos of the *Arcadia* itself press insistently upon the description of its writing, reading, keeping, and showing.

The 1590 *Arcadia* was brought to the press by Sidney's close friend Fulke Greville with the help of Matthew Gwinne and perhaps John Florio. It was based upon what Greville claimed was the unique copy; in fact, there was at least one other, now the only surviving manuscript copy of the *New Arcadia*. Greville's claim to guardianship of the revised *Arcadia* was asserted rapidly after his friend's death in 1586, when he wrote to Sidney's father-in-law, Sir Francis Walsingham, warning him of a planned unauthorized publication of 'sr philip sydneys old arcadia' (Woudhuysen 1996: 416–17). In such a context of intimate, familial keeping, Greville's appearance on the scene, brandishing a version of the work that he claimed was 'a correction of that old one donn 4 or 5 years since which he left in trust with me wherof ther is no more copies, & fitter to be printed then that first which is so common', would seem to be very much that of an interloper seeking to wrest Sidney's offspring from the breast of its second mother by presenting a claim of male friendship and privilege that challenges the authority of the familial bond. In his letter to Walsingham, Greville also refers to a 'direction' in Sidney's hand that should be used to amend this new version; this may have contained indications for adapting the text of the *Old Arcadia* in the ways that were later carried out by editors of the composite 1593 edition.

Greville's intentions in securing the publication of the *New Arcadia* were both personal and ideological. On the one hand, the 1590 *Arcadia* asserted his own privileged position as the guardian of Sidney's revised manuscript and of the author's future intentions for the work, and on the other it allowed him to intervene in and influence the ways in which the *Arcadia* was to be read. Both ends were served by the editorial shaping of the work, most evidently through what is described in the prefatory note included in some copies as 'the division and summing of the chapters [...] for the more ease of the readers' (Sidney 1590: A4ᵛ). This took the form of reducing the text into sections, each of which was introduced by a summary of its action. Assessments of this enterprise differ. From one point of view the summaries are flawed by errors and interrupt the progress of Sidney's narrative; they are swaggering and intrusive, and the system of marginal annotation they employ to link passages with numbered topics is riddled with errors. From a different perspective, the summaries act as a topical index to facilitate wise reading, and thereby provide detailed information concerning Greville's aspirations for the *Arcadia* as a work of moral philosophy; the summaries inserted into the captivity episode in particular indicate the importance laid by Greville on reading the princesses as exemplars of stoic constancy (see Skretkowicz 1986: 111–13, 116; J. Davis 2004: 416).

On both familial and literary grounds, Sidney's sister Mary probably had good reason for intervening in the publication of the *Arcadia*, as she did in 1593 with the help of Hugh Sanford. In this edition the intimate, playful *Old Arcadia* Preface was retained and supplemented by Sanford's Preface reasserting Mary's significance to the enterprise. This time she features as editor, 'correcting the faults' and 'supplying the defectes' that were evident in the 'disfigured face' of the 1590 text. Her task is the 'conclusion, not the perfection of Arcadia' as directed by 'the Authours own writings, or knowen determination' (Sidney 1593: ¶4ʳ). As Sanford makes clear in his Preface, Mary's editorial involvement mirrors and extends the role accorded to her by Sidney, the *Arcadia* being 'done, as it was, for her: as it is, by her' (¶4ᵛ). In accordance with its reasserted place within the Sidney literary fold, the 1593 edition appeared in folio format, with a new title page, while the summaries and marginal numbers were removed. The supplying of the *Arcadia*'s defects did not meet with universal approval: Florio for one lamented that in the composite version 'see we more marring that was well, then mending what was amisse' (R3ʳ). Nevertheless, the Countess's 'completing' of the unperfect *Arcadia* was of critical importance in establishing the canon of Sidney's works; her version of the *Arcadia* was carried through into the 1598 edition that also printed the *Certain Sonnets, Defence of Poetry, The Lady of May*, and *Astrophil and Stella*, and that secured Sidney's lasting reputation as 'a secular writer of erotic works' (Woudhuysen 1996: 235–6), rather than, say, a Protestant translator or political writer.

The hybrid identity of the *Arcadia* as both pastoral and heroic, familiar and public, continued to resonate well into the seventeenth century, thanks to the publication of Greville's *Life* of Sidney in 1652 (now more accurately known by the manuscript title *A Dedication to Sir Philip Sidney*). The works for which the *Dedication* was intended comprise Greville's Senecan tragedies *Mustapha* and *Alaham* along with treatises on subjects such as monarchy, religion, and war. The perils facing monarchy, specifically tyranny and weakness, figure large in Greville's own works, and may explain the *Dedication*'s characterization of the *Arcadia* as illuminating the follies of 'sovereign princes' (1986: 8) in hearkening to 'their own visions', placing the command of their families into the hands of the base, and by private humours rendering the country vulnerable to insurrection and invasion. Greville's is a truly encyclopedic vision of the potential of the *Arcadia*, that in casting Sidney's intention as being to 'turn the barren philosophy precepts into pregnant images of life' (10) brings public affairs and private fortunes equally under the remit of fiction.

Any assessment of the writing and rewriting of the *Arcadia* necessarily addresses the question of Sidney's own political engagement in the period 1579–84. There is a long-standing tradition that the *Arcadia* was written in pastoral retreat during 1579 at the Pembroke seat of Wilton, following Sidney's criticisms of the 'French match' between the Queen and the duc d'Anjou, as voiced in his *Letter to Queen Elizabeth*, and the fallout from a tennis court quarrel with the Earl of Oxford (see Wood 1691–2: i. 183; Duncan-Jones 1991: 163–7). Pastoral literature, however, relocates rather than repudiates the matter of politics: in this genre, retirement serves as a disguised means of political engagement, as the 'greater matters' of state are addressed 'under the vaile of homely persons' (Puttenham 1936: 38). Despite Sidney's physical distance from the court, greater matters, whether of the 'philosophy precepts' type or the specifically Elizabethan, abound in the *Arcadia*, from the princes' debate on solitariness and honourable action, to the 'crises of counsel' and urging of foresight that reflect forward Protestant anxiety about Spanish intentions in the Netherlands (see Worden 1996: 140). Potentially the most serious of the *Arcadia*'s matters is also its most comic: the simultaneously risible yet dreadful affection of Basilius and his wife, Gynecia, for Cleophila, which reduces them to folly and slavery as emblematized by their fawning kisses simultaneously lavished upon Cleophila (*OA* 49). Sidney's interest in the passions of the great is clearly indebted to the controversy over the French match, which threatened to visit one of the *Arcadia*'s recurrent horrors, undue foreign influence, upon England. Philanax's advice to Basilius concerning the oracle echoes that of Sidney to the Queen in the *Letter*, and the inset story of Erona—the only significant digression in the *Old Arcadia*, and still the most important in the *New*—is Sidney's exemplary narrative proving the dangers of 'obstinate' and 'wilful' love in a princess (*OA* 67). The principle articulated by the Erona story—that the amorous bodies of the great are inseparable from their public personae—provides the explanation for the manifold sexual, domestic, and political 'garboils' (*OA* 327) that overtake the plot of the *Old Arcadia*. A 'garboil' is a disturbance or tumult, and it was used in the second half of the sixteenth century to describe religious and social turmoil. Arcadia is engulfed by a rising tide of such commotion, beginning with the social and sexual transformations of the princes that render them unknowable agents—'thou woman or boy, or both', as Dametas says to Cleophila (*OA* 32). Initially, this ambiguity of gender, role, and person is a light-hearted metamorphic theme, elaborated by reference to Ovidian figures such as Apollo, Arethusa, and Caeneus.[4] But as Philoclea's laments reveal, Cleophila is a 'strange' guest in a dangerous, double sense, both a foreigner and an unknowable, unaccountable sexual being (*OA* 111), and this strangeness has personal, familial, and political consequences. Pyrocles' 'metamorphosis' into Cleophila (*OA* 120) leads not only to Philoclea's mental and sexual disquiet, but also to an overturning of domestic government, as Philoclea becomes the amorous rival of both her father and her mother in a Sidneian version of Ovid's disastrous family narratives in the *Metamorphoses*. The hybridity of Cleophila–Pyrocles' sexual identity thus extends to include his–her lovers, in whom generational and gender distinctions are themselves blurred: the father loves the daughter's lover, the mother becomes the daughter's rival for the affections of a woman, and so on. Pyrocles' metamorphosis is also incidentally a cause of disquiet among the Arcadians, who fear the consequences of the duke's retirement, and rise up in unsuccessful revolt, thereby ensuring that private tumults become civic 'garboils'. The political freight carried by the word 'metamorphosis' in the *Arcadia* is underlined by its later deployment in Greville's *Dedication* to describe Sidney's anxiety that the French match would 'metamorphose' England's moderate monarchy into Continental absolutism (1986: 32).

---

[4] Musidorus' surprise is compared to that of Apollo when Daphne is turned into a laurel (*OA* 18); Philoclea is compared to the nymph Arethusa in flight from Alpheus (*OA* 47), and she wishes Cleophila could turn from a woman to a man, as did Caenis when she became Caeneus (*OA* 111).

This theme of disruptive hybridity and metamorphosis is linked to the parallel theme of error, the other main cause of personal and collective turmoil in the *Arcadia*. Basilius' tribulations are firmly ascribed to his foolish interpretation of the oracle, which leads him into the error of retirement and so to the follies of his misplaced love for the hybrid Cleophila. This chain of events renders Basilius himself a politically hybrid and contradictory figure: the duke who is still the duke (as his people insist) yet who has abnegated the dignity and responsibilities of that office in order to indulge in wilful folly. Error is the bane of order in *Arcadia*, as it is in comedy more generally according to Sidney's *Defence*: 'comedy is the imitation of the common errors of our life', manifested in 'our private and domestical matters' (1973: 95–6). Most of the errors such as craftiness, flattery, and vainglory that Sidney cites in the *Defence* through allusion to characters from Terentian comedy are typical of those seen in the parallel households of Basilius and his rustic servant Dametas. These are also, of course, the errors that bedevil courts, and so they later re-emerge in the *New Arcadia* as characteristics of Cecropia's agent Clinias and the delinquent lovers and rulers of the digressions. Error and faultiness are endemic in the public as much as in the private sphere in the *Arcadia*, as exemplified by the Ister bank fable sung by Sidney's pastoral alter ego, Philisides, in the Third Eclogues. In this fable, the beasts make man to be their king by supplying their own attributes (craftiness and flattery among them), but are then rendered subject to his tyranny; the fable thereby articulates a typical charge against government by the people, whose weakness leads them to favour tyrants (see Worden 1996: 230). The Third Eclogues mark the point at which the political and amorous themes of the work converge, as the dark consequences of tyranny in both realms begin to be laid bare: the Ister bank fable is preceded by Dicus' epithalamion celebrating Cupid's defeat by Hymen and by Nico's fabliau warning of adultery and jealousy.

The errors committed by the body politic in the *Arcadia* are treated in a manner at once comical and serious, being depicted on the one hand with a certain insouciance during the Phagonian rebellion in book 2 and on the other with deep solemnity in book 4 following the death of Basilius. The rebellion of the Phagonians is ascribed to the double cause of drunkenness and resentment at Basilius' retirement: they are 'clowns' and 'beasts' armed with pitchforks who nonetheless threaten outright harm by marshalling sporadically sound arguments in a wrongful cause. In elucidating the reasons for their hostility, Sidney employs a languid *occupatio*—'it were tedious to write their far-fetched constructions' (*OA* 127)—but then proceeds to do exactly that at length, including in his summary the justification of rebellion as the rescue of the duke from himself, from bad advice, and from foreign influence (*OA* 123–32). In talking down the rebels, Cleophila deploys ideas familiar from contemporaneous debates on tyranny and rebellion such as *Vindicae contra tyrannos* (1579), written by Sidney's friends Hubert Languet and Philippe du Plessis-Mornay, by warning of the horrors attendant upon 'the tyrannous yoke of your fellow subject' and by recasting the rebels' hostility as 'vehement affection' (*OA* 130–1).[5] While disaster on

---

[5] On Protestant theories of rebellion, see Worden (1996: 281–7).

this occasion can be averted because Cleophila rhetorically disempowers the rebels' cause, and they do not in the main rise above their comic rusticity, the apparent death of Basilius initiates very serious commotions. In the absence of its monarch, Arcadia slides rapidly towards disaster, fractured by 'confused and dangerous divisions' and fatally undermined by self-interest and the failure of great men to know how to act in the public good (*OA* 320–1).

38.1 CROOKED SHIFTS

As Arcadia's near-disaster demonstrates, self-interest is a private error with serious public consequences. In both versions of the *Arcadia*, self-interest is manifested at every level of society, from Basilius' wilful folly to the self-important delusions of his servant Dametas. Particular dangers inhere, however, in the attempts of the *Arcadia*'s young men to advance their self-interests, because those interests are necessarily a hybrid of amorous and political imperatives: this tension between the maintenance of patriarchal order and the fulfilment of young male desire is intrinsic to the operations of Renaissance romance. According to the argument of Greville's *Dedication*, one of the dangers of princely retirement lies in the encouragement it offers to 'the conspiracies of ambitious subalterns to their false ends [...] the ruin of states and princes' (1986: 8). While it is the insurrection of Amphialus in the *New Arcadia* that is intended here, the amorous conspiracies of Pyrocles and Musidorus, who are rendered subaltern figures by being 'transformed [...] in sex and [...] state' by their disguises (*OA* 43), equally pose a threat to the stability of Basilius' life, family, and realm in the *Old Arcadia*; indeed, Greville goes on to state that 'these dark webs of effeminate princes be dangerous fore-runners of innovation [rebellion]' (1986: 9). The rebellion of Amphialus is, arguably, the logical extension of the princes' own actions in the earlier version of the romance, and the darker vision of young male insurrection offered by the *New Arcadia* sheds instructive light upon the conduct of Sidney's princes.

The princes are inextricably linked with the creation and execution of 'crooked shifts' (*NA* 109) during the pursuit of their amorous ambitions. All kinds of 'shifts' (that is, ingenious devices or contrivances) are to be expected in comedy, but the meaning of the word as it is used in the *Arcadia* resides firmly within a more sinister ambit: 'a fraudulent or evasive device, a stratagem; a piece of sophistry, an evasion, subterfuge' (*OED*, 4a). Strategy is an integral part of a young noble's education, and in one of the *New Arcadia* digressions Musidorus brings to bear the knowledge of stratagems he has gained in reading histories, by advising the Arcadian soldiers to disguise themselves as 'the poorest sort' of people in order to deceive their Helot enemies (*NA* 35). But an air of fraudulence still hovers over this, in that it is a theatrical shift rather than a proper military stratagem. Even the most ostensibly comic shifts, such as the gulling of Dametas, Mopsa, and Miso through stories that exploit variously their faults of vainglory, cowardice, greed, and lust, are coloured by the princes' underlying self-interest and their failures of compassion.

Of an even more serious order than their tall tales, sophistry, and disguisings are the strategies that indicate the princes' lack of regard for the laws of Arcadia, and the careless contempt of their methods. Musidorus' disguise is effected by means of the arrest and imprisonment of the shepherd Menalcas, whose clothing he assumes (*OA* 41), and he intends to bring an army upon Basilius in order to force him, 'willing or unwilling', to surrender Philoclea to Pyrocles (*OA* 173). The moral deficiencies of Cleophila's plan simultaneously to rid herself of her inconvenient married lovers and to secure Philoclea are self-evident from the start. All these schemes are unveiled in the trial scene that serves as the climax to both the *Old Arcadia* and the composite 1593 edition. Following the apparent death of Basilius and the princes' attempts on his daughters, Gynecia, Pyrocles, and Musidorus are arrested and brought to trial before Euarchus, Pyrocles' father and Musidorus' uncle, whose arrival halts Arcadia's decline into chaos. The trial scene lays bare the counterfeiting strategies of Pyrocles and Musidorus and subjects them to rigorous judicial investigation. At issue here in book 5 are not just questions of crime and intent, but also the conflict of old and young men, as the princes are dragged—typically, arguing all the way—back within the purlieu of patriarchal power. At the same time as the trial scene stages the reining-in of amorous and subaltern ambition, it also engages closely with the attendant dilemmas experienced by the royal judge Euarchus, who has to subordinate his own person and inclinations to the demands of justice and duty by pursuing his judgment against the princes even once their relationship to him is known. Sidney's bringing Euarchus to the borders of an Arcadia that threatens to implode into civil war, and making him the unwary judge of his own progeny's misdeeds, is an inspired variation on the theme of hybrid identity: it renders the foreign power Arcadia's salvation (parallels with Sidney's hopes for England's role in the Netherlands are evident here), and the father a judge. It also diversifies the emotional landscape of the romance beyond that of amorous love by encompassing love of state and ruler (as exemplified by Philanax) as well as the love of son, and by revealing the contours of, in Greville's telling phrase, a king's 'map of desolation' (1986: 9).

There is no doubt in the world of the *Old Arcadia* that the princes' actions are culpable. Philanax's assessment of their guilt is coloured by his vengeful grief at the perceived death of Basilius, but his assessment of the facts of the case is still an accurate one. His charge of shape- and name-changing as laid against Pyrocles is undoubtedly true (*OA* 387) and the 'vagabonding' princes have indeed 'pilfered' Arcadia's 'jewels' (the princesses), with their 'disguising sleights' (*OA* 399); the princes were clearly blinded by passion (or, worse, the arrogance of the interloping foreign power) if they did not see that their ravishments of Pamela and Philoclea were as much acts of treachery against public persons still in their minority as they were manifestations of private passion. The crucial charge against the cousins is that they have ceased to behave as princes, and, having presented themselves as private men, have rendered themselves subject to the judgment of Arcadia's laws (which, in any case, do not recognize any royal persons except their own).

The princes' crooked shifts thereby almost lead to their actual downfall in a stratagem that no one intended but many now suspect, namely the murder of Basilius and the seizure of Arcadia. Following Gynecia's 'confession', Philanax is determined to find proof of this non-existent stratagem, accusing the princes of being 'of counsel' (*OA* 302) with Gynecia, a charge that in the composite 1593 *Arcadia* creates a chilling parallel between the domestic treacheries of the princes and the familial treachery of Cecropia's attempt to seize power via Amphialus. It is in the treatment of the princes' amorous stratagems in the *Old Arcadia* and in the composite version of 1593 that the disjunctions between 'Old' and 'New' versions are most clearly felt, and the tensions of the hybrid edition most obviously revealed. Whereas in the *Old Arcadia* the princes achieve or come close to the consummation of their loves, in the revised version they are cleansed of sexual impropriety. In the *Old Arcadia* Pyrocles and Philoclea give way to the bliss of 'mutual satisfaction', but in the 1593 version they fall asleep in 'chaste embracements' (*OA* 273; 93 690). Similarly, in the 1593 version the moment when Musidorus is about to break his promise and rape Pamela is removed (*OA* 202; 93 654). Given that Sidney had already moved the poem 'What tongue can her perfections tell' from its location in the *Old Arcadia* consummation scene (*OA* 238–42) to the scene of the sisters bathing in the *New Arcadia* (190–5), it seems highly likely that the editors of the 1593 version were reconstituting authorial intentions (probably gleaned from Greville's 'direction') in making these changes to the princes' most culpable actions.

Sidney's rewriting of the wrongs perpetrated by the princes in Arcadia necessitated further interventions by the editors of the 1593 version. Thus, at the moment of Musidorus and Pamela's discovery, the rebellious 'clowns' who stumble upon them in the *Old Arcadia* are presented as the 'chastisers of Musidorus's broken vow', whereas in the 1593 version the discovery is rendered as the initiation of the rebels' own punishment for insurrection (*OA* 307; 93 754). In his self-defence to Euarchus in the *Old Arcadia*, Pyrocles' desire to protect Philoclea's reputation compounds the problem of his undoubted strategizing, in that he claims on the one hand that she is 'most unjustly accused', yet on the other admits responsibility—'Whatsoever hath been done hath been my violence, which notwithstanding could not prevail against her chastity' (*OA* 380)—and he is therefore open to the charge of equivocation. For the editors of the 1593 version, the logical solution was to rewrite this self-accusation, thereby smoothing out the narrative inconsistency and moderating the evidence of Pyrocles' sexual misdemeanour and his equivocation in law. In this version, therefore, 'violence' is changed to 'only attempt' and 'could not prevail' to 'was never intended' (93: 811). Inevitably, inconsistencies remain in the presentation of Pyrocles' guilt, particularly in the treatment of the violence or force of which he accuses himself (a necessary element in the protection of Philoclea's honour, but inconsistent with the events as they are presented in the 1593 version). So his claim that 'whatsoever hath been informed, was my force' in the *Old Arcadia* is changed to 'fault' in the 1593 version, but the climax of his speech remains the same, invoking a violence that is at odds with the facts as they now stand: 'I cannot, nor ever will deny the love of Philoclea, whose violence wrought violent effects in me' (*OA* 395; 93 826). Similarly, the editors of the 1593 version removed the *Old Arcadia*'s judgment upon Pyrocles that he should be thrown from a high tower for his lust, having Euarchus assert instead that the two princes are 'equally culpable' and should be beheaded for planning the abduction of the princesses, but then in the summary of the judgment, Pyrocles' original punishment resurfaces (*OA* 408; 93 838).

Similar unevennesses occur in relation to the princes' proofs of their heroism. Even if Sidney's intentions for the *New Arcadia* had retained the original denouement of the plot and the trial scene (a fact by no means certain in itself), it is inevitable that the trial would have made extensive reference to the heroism displayed by the princes during the episode of Cecropia's castle. The editors of the 1593 version recognized this problem, and made a handful of references to the new matter, such as Musidorus' allusion to their service to Basilius 'in the late war with Amphialus' (93 831–2), but a full integration of the material was clearly beyond their intention or capacity, and inevitably the logic of the judgments in the 1593 version suffers as a result. Given the slightness of the editors' integration of the matter of the *New Arcadia* into the trial scene, it is remarkable that one of the few other instances where they do seek to do this features Philanax, and concerns the exercising of pity (both emotional and judicial) in relation to the accused. Until the revelation that Basilius lives, Philanax maintains a rigorous adherence to his vengeful anger and resists the urge to pity, thereby bringing down upon his head the hostility of the narrator (and of Pyrocles) but simultaneously providing a powerful seam of psychological drama that Sidney sustains from the moment of the Pyrocles' discovery to the revival of Basilius. The editors of the 1593 version clearly noted the importance of Philanax's struggle between rigour and pity in books 4 and 5, and used the events of the *New Arcadia* to enhance it by making Philanax recall Philoclea's intercession on his behalf when he was captured by Amphialus; this sharpens Philanax's difficulty, as it inclines him to a 'tender pity' that is restrained only by his 'perfect persuasion' of the plot against Basilius (93 751).

A comparable tension between pity and persuasion is also manifested in Euarchus once the princes are revealed to be his son and nephew. Persuaded of the truth of their crimes, Euarchus must prefer justice to the claims of blood, or indeed sacred royalty; his compactly moving lament 'alas, shall justice halt' (*OA* 411) is merely a brief punctuation of a speech that otherwise reasserts the all-encompassing necessity of 'sacred rightfulness' and refuses mercy.[6] But Euarchus' fatherly body betrays him, and his tears of pain render him a 'pitifull spectacle' even as he is charged with tyranny by his nephew (*OA* 412) and, similarly, judged to be 'pitiless' and his dominion insupportable by the beholders (*OA* 414). In this figure of the weeping judge, Sidney deftly encapsulates the conjunction of the judicial and the tragic forms of pity, and has laid the groundwork for the turn to tragedy that is manifested in his revised *Arcadia*.

---

[6] Worden (1996: 178) sees in Euarchus' adherence to justice a specific contrast with Elizabeth's overly clement handling of Mary, Queen of Scots.

38.2 Sonnets in Blood

Whereas the *Old Arcadia* lends itself to assessment against the terms of Terentian comedy, its successor advertises from the outset an affinity with epic and tragedy (see Ringler 1962, pp. xxxvii–viii; Parker 1972; Carey 1987: 249–50). The epic dimension is manifested through the inclusion of well-known persons and tropes from classical epic, notably the fountain in Kalander's garden that features Aeneas at his mother Venus' breast (*NA* 14). The material that is added to the *New Arcadia* concerning the princes' extra-Arcadian adventures also places them on a par with classical epic heroes. As Musidorus travels in search of Pyrocles, he discovers that his cousin's deeds have been celebrated in the ways of ancient epic, via the erection of monuments and the memorializing of these acts in the collective memory. Memory, indeed, is an epic trope that figures large in the *New Arcadia*, from the amorous remembrances of Urania uttered by Strephon and Claius with which the revised version opens; to the tales of their past deeds told by the princes to vivify their heroic personae and to stir the passions of the princesses; to the memories of Parthenia's beauty and Erona's plight that sustain Argalus and Plangus respectively.[7] As these last examples suggest, however, the generic attractions of romance ultimately undermine those of epic, so that amorous memories can exercise a greater force than heroic ones; the imperatives of love efface those of manly action (hence Pyrocles' Amazon disguise); and events that would in epic inspire rhetorical set pieces, such as the Olympian games encountered by Musidorus, are passed over, the 'huge and sportful assembly' becoming in this case 'tedious loneliness' to the prince, since Pyrocles was lost (*NA* 67). Tragedy, on the other hand, is highly congenial to Sidney's revisioning of romance in the *New Arcadia*. Taking up the theatrical metaphors of the *Old Arcadia*, and its flirtation with tragic ironies and reversals, Sidney continues the shift in emphasis away from comedy to tragedy that was seen in the 'tragical end' (*OA* 280) that threatens book 5 of the *Old Arcadia* before the deus ex machina that reveals Basilius is alive after all.

Women are key to the extension of the tragic sensibilities of the *New Arcadia*, particularly in their role as the prime agents of tragic articulation. Pamela's observation in captivity that 'you see how many acts our tragedy hath: fortune is not yet aweary of vexing us' (*NA* 451) is worthy of one of Webster's heroines, and Helen of Corinth collapses entirely the distinctions of female gender and tragic genre in her description of her heart as 'nothing but a stage for tragedies' (*NA* 64). The incident she is recalling at this point—the killing of her spurned lover Philoxenus by his friend Amphialus, and the death from sorrow of Philoxenus' father—is indeed a 'miserable representation', as she terms it, well worthy of the tragic stage. Indeed, images of wasted life, treated with the cold disregard of tragic action, cluster around Helen in actuality as well as memory at this point: her narrative is delivered to Musidorus

---

[7] The importance of memory in the *New Arcadia* is anticipated in the *Old*, for example in the discussion between Pyrocles and Musidorus (*OA* 372–3).

through the window of her coach, which is surrounded by the bodies of her retainers, 'some slain, some lying under their dead horses and striving to get from under them' (*NA* 59). Such a scene is common in the chivalric romances such as *Amadis de Gaule*, upon which Sidney drew in writing the *Arcadia*. However, his observation that Helen, having witnessed this situation, continues in conversation with Musidorus 'without making more of the matter' transforms the easy bloodletting of chivalric romance—in which the suffering of opponents is regarded as an untroubling consequence of their being on the wrong side—into a manifestation of the extreme self-obsession caused by passion, which deprives the sufferer of all pity (a key heroic virtue, as typified by Aeneas), and therefore leads to unfathomable acts of cruelty. The innocent also die as a consequence of Tiridates' 'cruel and tyrannous' love for Erona, which causes him to make war upon her country through an 'extremity of hatred' initiated by the 'extremity of his love'. Such a flagrant breach of the ethical golden mean by a ruler unleashes destruction upon the people; of Erona's population, Tiridates spares 'not man, woman and child', writing 'the sonnets of his love in the blood, and tun[ing] them in the cries of her subjects' (*NA* 206). At a private level, Demagoras' rapelike disfiguring of Parthenia with poison, conducted with 'unmerciful force' against her vain resistance (*NA* 30), manifests this same blunting of the capacity for mercy, and offers a cautionary example of the moral disfigurement that threatens all of the *Arcadia*'s lovers should they fall sway to passion's tyranny. Sidney's description of tragedy in the *Defence* underlines the importance of bodily danger and mutilation to his conception of the genre, which he describes as operating with surgical violation as it 'openeth the greatest wounds, and sheweth forth the ulcers that are covered with tissue' (1912–26: 96). In praising the capacity of tragedy to move even pitiless tyrants, Sidney cites the example of Alexander Pheraeus, a cruel man who was yet moved to tears by the sight of the suffering of Hecuba and Andromache in Euripides' *Troades*. Sidney's own quasi-tragedy also practises such 'sweet violence' (1973: 96) upon women, notably in the incarceration, torture, and staged executions of Pamela and Philoclea by Cecropia—acts which constitute the sharpest proof of Cecropia's 'absolute tyrannies' (*NA* 420). It is during this incarceration that the *New Arcadia* cements its characterization of Pamela as a princely stoic, and Philoclea as feelingly tender: the scourging of Philoclea, for example, is metaphorized as an assault by kites upon a white dove, a deed that moves even senseless objects (such as walls) to the pity that eludes Cecropia (*NA* 420), while Pamela conquers through her virtuous quietude (*NA* 421–2). The spectacular mistreatment of the female body is an Ovidian as well as a tragic trope, and both discourses are united in the scene of Pamela's supposed beheading, which is conceived by Cecropia as a 'new play', a tragedy, staged in the castle hall as a grotesque parody of Tudor entertainments and hospitality rituals. Pursuing his theme of Cecropia's castle as a dehumanized location of displaced pity, Sidney risks a moment of comic insurrection by having the executioner botch his job: at the last moment, the sword experiences an excess of pity and hits flat-long, requiring a second blow. Philoclea's mourning speech in response to this event is uttered in the best traditions of Senecan and Ovidian lament, being prefaced by the 'storm of amazement' and sensory deprivation that are the precursors to tragic locquacity; her association with the 'lamentable Philomela' is fully expected when it comes (*NA* 426–7).

In the opportunities it offers for the displaying of the princesses' tender flesh and the exercising of their soulful rhetoric, the episode of their imprisonment is violently sweet indeed. Yet the generic hybridity of the *New Arcadia*—in particular the insistently comic strain emanating from the underlying 'Old' version—ultimately inhibits the progress of this skein of tragic action and constrains its dignity. The reappearance of Philoclea in Zelmane's room after her apparent death, and the revelation that the executions were deceptions, reimports a green-world mentality into tragic action and muddies the work's generic distinctions. From this point, the imprisoning rooms of Cecropia's castle seem more reminiscent of the pastoral prison of the princesses' lodges in Arcadia, an impression that is furthered by Philoclea's regally dismissive rustic simile for Cecropia, the 'good woman' who revealed her deceptions to the princesses 'with the same pity as folks keep fowl when they are not fat enough for their eating' (*NA* 437). The sudden reassertion of the green world is particularly pronounced in the 1593 *Arcadia*, which breaks off part-way through the fight between Zelmane and Anaxius only to resume with Dorus and Zelmane in an archetypally pastoral scenario—sitting in the shade of a sycamore, discussing their mutual joys and sorrows. The shift from a scene of male proximity in violence to one of proximity in friendship is circumstantial of course, determined by the broken-backed composite text, but would have been no less pronounced and peculiar to the original readers for that.

While the dictates of the original romance plot require that the tragic skein threatening the deaths of Pamela and Philoclea must revert to comedy, the material concerning the new characters (in particular Amphialus, Argalus, and Parthenia) is subject to no such constraints, and therefore competes with the central narrative as a source of readerly pity. The death of Argalus, for example, is particularly powerful in its adaptation of the conventions governing tragic speech. Although the sentiment of his parting words is heroic to the last, they are also futile, being audible to neither wife nor adversary, and in a touching victory of love over war, the hero's farewell is swallowed up in his wife's parting kisses. For a narrative in which woes of greater and lesser seriousness are endlessly talked out, Parthenia's silence ('sorrow lost the wit of utterance'; *NA* 378) marks a greater grief than any yet encountered. And the pity of war is nowhere better expressed than in Parthenia's dissident, wifely, reinterpretation of the 'great praises' uttered concerning her husband, as being 'records of her loss' (*NA* 379). Even Amphialus, who is 'pilloried' by Sidney, according to one point of view, for his failure to resist tyranny and his anti-heroic actions, is granted the title of a 'pitiful spectacle', being a worthy prince whose bloody downfall is rich in the requisite horror (*NA* 442).[8] Sidney is in many ways at his best and most heartfelt when portraying such horror, as seen in the collision of pity and furious grief, anger and beauty in the death of the boy Ismenus at Philanax's hands, or when juxtaposing the artistic and ritualistic beauties of war with its cruel and bloody realities, a contrast that is

---

[8] See Skretkowicz's note in his 1987 edition (*NA* 442).

encapsulated in the idea of terror bravely decked: 'rich furniture, gilt swords, shining armours […] now all universally defiled with dust, blood, broken armours, mangled bodies' (*NA* 345). In the brave decking of terror during the climactic captivity episode, Sidney's *Arcadia* achieves the most striking of its many hybridities, and comes close to artistic, if not textual, perfection.

PRIMARY WORKS

FLORIO, JOHN (trans.) (1603), *The Essayes* by Michel de Montaigne.

GREVILLE, FULKE (1986), *A Dedication to Sir Philip Sidney*, in *The Prose Works of Fulke Greville, Lord Brooke*, ed. J. Gouws (Oxford: Clarendon Press).

HOWELL, THOMAS (1581), *Howell his Devises*.

MOLYNEUX, EDMUND (1587), 'Historical Remembrance of the Sidneys, the Father and the Son', in Raphael Holinshed, *The Third Volume of Chronicles*.

PUTTENHAM, GEORGE (1936), *The Arte of English Poesie*, ed. Gladys Doidge Willcock and Alice Walker (Cambridge: Cambridge University Press).

SIDNEY, PHILIP, 93 (1977), *The Countess of Pembroke's Arcadia* (1593), ed. Maurice Evans (Harmondsworth: Penguin).

—— *NA* (1987), *The Countess of Pembroke's Arcadia (The New Arcadia)*, ed. Victor Skretkowicz (Oxford: Clarendon Press).

—— *OA* (1973), *The Countess of Pembroke's Arcadia (The Old Arcadia)*, ed. Jean Robertson (Oxford: Clarendon Press).

—— (1590), *The Countesse of Pembrokes Arcadia*.

—— (1593), *The Countesse of Pembrokes Arcadia*.

—— (1912–26), *The Complete Works of Sir Philip Sidney*, ed. Albert Feuillerat, 4 vols (Cambridge: Cambridge University Press).

—— (1962), *The Poems of Sir Philip Sidney*, ed. William A. Ringler (Oxford: Clarendon Press).

—— (1973), *Miscellaneous Prose of Sir Philip Sidney*, ed. Katherine Duncan-Jones and Jan van Dorsten (Oxford: Clarendon Press).

WOOD, ANTHONY À (1691–2), *Athenae Oxonienses*, 2 vols.

PART IV

1580–1603

CHAPTER 39

GABRIEL HARVEY'S CHOLERIC WRITING

JENNIFER RICHARDS

To place Gabriel Harvey at the beginning of this part of the book is to assert his centrality to Elizabethan literary culture. This would be a large claim, but the argument that follows will show it to be closer to the truth than we might suspect for a writer whose work is unfamiliar today. To be sure, one part of Harvey's writing has become well known again: his activity as a professional reader, or 'facilitator', thanks to the evidence of his marginalia found throughout his large and diverse library, a good part of which survives. These fragments of writing have attracted much attention in the last two decades; his vernacular literary writings have not.

Why is this? Harvey's antagonists in his own time and beyond would propose a simple solution: his literary talent never equalled his self-importance. We can be a little more generous though and recognize that posterity has not been kind to the modes and genres that most interested him; Harvey is not unique in this. In most respects, the literary 'kinds' in which he composed are remote from conventional understanding of what is truly significant about Elizabethan literature, especially when it is assumed to reach its quintessence at a late stage. Harvey did not write an *Arcadia* or a *Faerie Queene*; nor did he contribute to the extraordinary flowering of the public theatre in the 1590s. On the contrary, he was more likely to be the satirical subject of this last mode, especially if his identification as the original for Shakespeare's tediously pedantic Holofernes in *Love's Labour's Lost* (*c*.1594–5) is correct. Instead, he wrote poems in Latin eulogizing potential aristocratic patrons, letters about vernacular poetry which include examples of his own experiments with classical verse forms, semi-autobiographical prose fiction, lectures on rhetoric, and satirical pamphlets. Most of these forms are only of specialist interest, with the partial exception of the last. Unfortunately, even this promising choice had disastrous consequences for Harvey's reputation.

Gabriel Harvey's satirical writing was provoked by his clash with Thomas Nashe, a writer of astonishing originality. Though this squabble is not especially flattering to either party, it is Harvey who is left looking staid and cumbersome in contrast to his vivacious antagonist. Harvey's first attack on Nashe and on Robert Greene in his *Four Letters and Certain Sonnets* (1592) is dismissed by C. S. Lewis as 'worm's work', and his personality as 'arrogant, unclubbable, unpopular, tactless, vindictive, laboriously jocose' (1954: 354, 351). This is echoed half a century later by Neil Rhodes, who finds Harvey's temperament 'an oleaginous mixture of vanity, obsequiousness and pomposity', and his writing as tediously academic (1992: 58, 120). Nashe, in contrast, is admired by Lewis and Rhodes for his linguistic resourcefulness and originality. In contrast to Harvey, Nashe is seen to display the 'qualities' that are 'celebrated in modernist and postmodernist texts' (123). He is representative of a new generation of writers who had received a rhetorical education, yet who, unlike his opponent, had the 'imaginative freedom to exploit and test' the values of this (59).

These judgements make sense when we know a bit more about Harvey, the Cambridge don who worried about the damage his English writings might do to his academic reputation, and who was mocked as 'Pedantius' in a university comedy of the same name in 1580–1 (Sarah Knight 2006). On paper, he had a distinguished academic career with an appointment as lecturer in Greek at the University of Cambridge in 1573 and then as Praelector of Rhetoric from 1574 to 1576. In 1584, after concluding his study of the civil law at Cambridge, he accepted a medical fellowship at Pembroke College (Stern 1979: 74–5). But for all this, Harvey does not seem to have managed his career very well; he certainly seems to have lacked social skills, despite the fact that his manuscript letter-book represents a series of 'civil conversations' in which he plays the 'starring role' (Katharine Wilson 2006: 43–51). In 1573 he fell out with the fellows of his college, Pembroke Hall, one of whom, Thomas Neville, tried to block his progression to the MA. The charges he levies against Harvey are obviously trumped up. Harvey is accused, among others things, of being 'not familiar like a fellow' as well as 'a great and continual patron of paradoxis and a main defender of straung opinions' (Harvey 1884: 4, 10). However, his prickly self-defence, outlined in a letter to Dr John Young, Master of Pembroke Hall, goes some way to explain why he was regarded by his contemporaries and then much later by Lewis as 'unclubbable': 'I was wunt to be as familiar, and as sociable and as gud a fellow too, as ani,' he insists. 'Marri so, that at usual and convenient times, as after dinner and supper, at commenti fiers, yea and at other times too, if the lest occasion were offrid, I continuid as long as ani, and was as fellowli as the best. [...] I have bene merri in cumpani: I have bene ful hardly drawn out of cumpani' (4).

Outside the university, Harvey did not fare much better. In the late 1570s he was employed as a professional reader in the household of the Earl of Leicester, advising, among others, his nephew Philip Sidney before his embassy to the Holy Roman

Emperor, Rudolph II, in 1577 (Grafton and Jardine 1990: 37), but there is no evidence of this as long-term employment. In *Have With You to Saffron Walden* (1596), Nashe implies that the Earl of Leicester 'sent for another Secretarie to *Oxford*' after realizing that Harvey was 'more meete to make sport with, than anie way deeply to be employd' (Nashe 1596: M4ʳ). While in the 1580s, after his inception as a Doctor of Civil Law at the University of Oxford in 1585, he pursued a brief and undistinguished legal career in the Court of Arches in London. When the quarrel with Nashe broke out in the 1590s, he was in his early forties, and had returned to London probably only to settle the estate of his recently deceased brother John (Stern 1979: 100). In contrast, at the start of the 1590s Nashe was in his early twenties, fresh from Cambridge, and eager to eke out a living as a writer. At the end of the 1580s he had made enough of a reputation to be employed by Bishop Bancroft, alongside Robert Greene and John Lyly, to answer in kind the popular anti-episcopal satires of the anonymous 'Martin Marprelate' (1588–9).

This is not a personality contest, of course. Nashe is valued by literary scholars not because he seems more 'clubbable', far from it, but because he represents a break with the rhetorical tradition that shaped mid-Tudor and early Elizabethan literary culture, defining its moral purpose as service to the commonwealth. As Lorna Hutson argues so compellingly in Chapter 43 in this volume, Nashe's originality rests on his parody of this educational aspiration. His mature writings expose the moral bankruptcy of a print culture directed solely to 'serving the interest of those who held religious and political office'. Early writings like 'To the Gentleman Students of Both Universities' (Oxford and Cambridge), Nashe's dazzling debut in print included as part of the prefatory material to Robert Greene's prose fiction *Menaphon* (1589), may well have been written for just such an end, advertising his wish to use 'his pen in some suitable commonwealth cause'. This publication may even have helped him to secure employment as an anti-Martinist. However, after 1592, when it was much harder for him to gain patronage, Nashe turned his attention instead to subverting these aspirations: the ironic persona of *Pierce Penniless* (1592) 'can't climb aboard the gravy train of profitable moral propaganda', Hutson reminds us, 'without addressing the devil' (see Hutson 1989; and Chapter 43 in this volume).

Even in early work like his Preface to *Menaphon*, though, we can discover the basis of Nashe's later discontent. In this letter, Nashe honours the achievements of the early humanists Desiderius Erasmus and Thomas More and their mid-Tudor successors John Cheke et al., who had recovered the value and place of rhetoric at the centre of the curriculum. But Nashe also laments the decline of this project, its failure to invigorate a national literature. His letter offers a scathing attack on contemporaries who borrow too heavily from classical and Italian literatures and the 'idiote art-masters' who have encouraged them in this. Particular scorn is reserved for the 'mœchanicall mate' who 'abhorres the english he was borne too', borrowing his words from the 'inkhorne' (1589: 2*1ʳ). Such a writer, Nashe complains, fails to digest his reading; he fails to discriminate what is worth imitating, and like a greedy diner he spews forth his 'cholerick incumbrances' in prose and verse (2*1ʳ). This is a moral–political as well as a literary judgement. According to Nashe, this training makes men neither eloquent nor virtuous. On the contrary, it leaves them unbalanced, spluttering forth like irascible men dominated by the fiery humour of choler (see Figure 39.1). Like a good Galenic physician, Nashe prescribes a 'remedie of contraries' to bring 'moderation in a matter of follie': writers who are 'surfetted unawares with the sweete sacietie of eloquence' are advised to study the prose of simpletons, 'our Gothamists barbarisme' (2^*2^r).

This bold letter seems to have sparked the Harvey–Nashe quarrel, although it was Richard Harvey, Gabriel's clergyman brother, who responded at first. Gabriel Harvey is not included in Nashe's attack; on the contrary, his Latin verse is commended in this letter ($A1^r$). Nonetheless, Richard took umbrage at Nashe's presumption in publishing his literary judgements in the Preface to a series of sermons, *A Theological Discourse of the Lamb of God and his Enemies* (1590). Nashe is not the subject of these sermons, which aim to moderate religious debate, tempering satirists like Martin Marprelate who are 'girded and wrapped in with splene and brought up cheefly in the chapters *De contradicentibus*' (Harvey 1590: $Q3^r$). But Richard made the mistake of excoriating Nashe in his Preface for 'peremptorily censoring his betters at pleasure' in his letter 'To the Gentlemen Students' ($A2^v$). In printing this letter, he argues, Nashe has behaved as insolently in the civil realm as Martin in the religious.

Richard made the mistake of excoriating Nashe publicly in a treatise which defends the importance of moderate debate. The irony of this was not lost on Nashe and Greene: to them Richard must have seemed no better than the splenetic 'Martin'. The intemperance of his Preface drew upon all of the Harvey brothers the scorn of Greene, who mocked them as the upwardly mobile sons of a Saffron Walden rope-maker in his estates satire *A Quip for an Upstart Courtier* (1592). It also made Richard the object of Nashe's derision in *Pierce Penniless's Supplication to the Devil* (1592), where he is personified as the Vice Wrath and denounced as an infamous 'ideot' and 'tyred Jade' who has accused this author, Nashe, 'of want of learning', 'upbraiding' him 'for reviving' the 'reverend memorie' of More, Cheke, and others, 'as if they were no meate but for his Masterships mouth' (Nashe 1592: $F2^v$). Yet, unlike Richard, Nashe is careful not to replicate the Vice he reprehends. 'I would not have you thinke that all this that is set downe here, is in good earnest,' his knowing persona Pierce Penilesse teases Richard. '[A]m I subject to the sinne of Wrath I write against or no, in whetting my penne on this block?', he asks after 'Spurgalling' this 'Asse' ($F4^r$).

Nashe's spat with Richard Harvey pales in comparison with the quarrel that erupted between him and Gabriel, however. Greene died in 1592, just after the printing of *A Quip*, and Harvey's harping on about the destitution of his final days seemed egregiously vitriolic *and* foolish, given Nashe's brilliant response to Richard's own intemperate moralizing. 'Howe unlike *Tullies* sweete Offices,' Harvey complains pompously of Greene's and Nashe's writing in *Four Letters* (1592: $D2^v$). They have failed to imbibe the moral philosophy of this Roman orator, whose study of social duties was a core text of the Tudor grammar school; their writing is neither decorous (honest) nor useful to the commonwealth. In response, Nashe would dismiss this as feeble nostalgia, decrying Harvey as a 'stale soker at *Tullies Offices*' and an 'Ape of *Tully*' (1593: $G4^v$, $F2^v$). He exposes Harvey's moralizing as both dated and

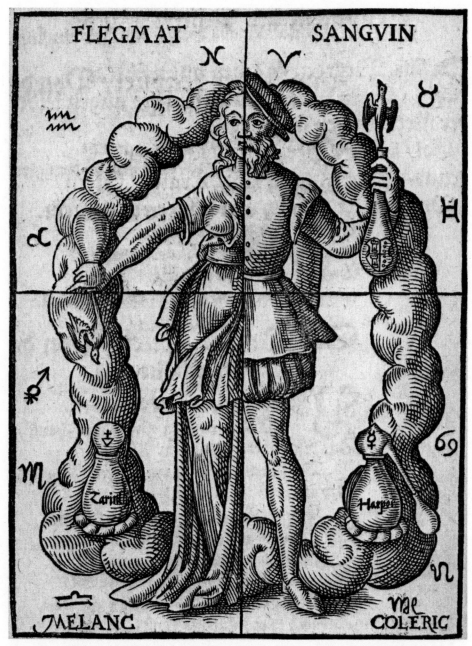

Fig. 39.1 Diagram of the four humours. Choler (bottom right) is gendered masculine. Leonard Thurneisser zum Thurn, *Quinta essentia* (1574), O3ᵛ.

platitudinous and cuts through his rhetoric of 'Humanity' to reveal its more insidious implications. Harvey insists that *his* moral values and *his* practice of debate support an orderly commonwealth. But Nashe exposes this as hypocritical. Like his brother Richard, Harvey fails to represent the moderation he espouses. This 'indigested Chaos of Doctourship' (1592: G4ᵛ), Nashe complains, may repeat moral sayings, but this does not mean that he understands them. He may castigate invective, yet he was still a 'Libeller before I was borne' (I4ʳ). With this criticism Nashe makes a tentative step towards the defence of invective as essential to the health of the commonwealth, a cure for choleric writers like Harvey.

The nimble and quick-witted Nashe is an effective critic and his skilful demystification of Harvey's 'Humanity' seems more modern than his antagonist's ponderous emphasis on moderation and limitation: 'better an hundred Ouides were banished', Harvey argues rather alarmingly in *Four Letters*, 'then the state of Augustus endangered, or a soveraigne Empire infected' (1592: D3ʳ). While in *Pierce's Supererogation* (1593), Harvey will ally himself explicitly with an older culture of 'confutation', the decline of which is blamed on satirists like Nashe. Erasmus and Thomas More 'were supposed fine, and pleasant Confuters in their time' (1593: B3ᵛ), Harvey recalls. So too were Cheke and Ascham. But these scholars have been overtaken by a new generation who argue for the sake of argument, and who relish a *'dominiering Eloquence'* instead of the 'smooth, and clenly, and neate, and fine elegancy' that was valued 'before' (C1ʳ).

Nonetheless, my purpose in returning to this quarrel is not to reinforce our sense of Nashe as 'modern' and Harvey as behind the times, but to point to the difficulty of reading the latter's moral–political idiom of moderation and to reflect on what is lost with its rejection. The spirit of Nashe commends itself to current critical sympathy for a 'newer' intellectual and literary culture, whereby speech or writing that is explicitly irreverent, demystifying, and seemingly 'popular' connotes in itself a step towards a more disputative 'public sphere'. This preference makes it hard for us to see both why moderation mattered in the late Tudor commonwealth, or indeed in any commonwealth, but also the different ways in which this complex virtue was understood. It also makes it hard for us to judge the innovation of Harvey's literary writings and his ongoing attempt to limit a *'dominiering Eloquence'*. But before tackling these issues I want first to recognize why it is so hard to sympathize with someone recommending 'moderation' as insistently as Harvey does.

39.1 HARVEY'S CHOLER

Anger is a tricky emotion to reproduce for rhetorical effect. Too little and you won't persuade your audience of your moral outrage, too much and you lose their goodwill and trust completely. Thomas Wilson is alert to these difficulties. Among the few figures of 'Stomacke greefe' or *Iraecundia* he lists in *The Art of Rhetoric* are *laesio*, when 'we speake to hurt our adversaries, by setting forth their evil behaviour', and *exercratio*, when 'wee curse the extreme wickednesse of some past good Roisters'. Wilson is not concerned to provide an extensive list of the figures of 'Stomacke greefe' on the grounds that these 'come without any great learning'. There is no art in expressing one's anger, he suggests, with the exception of the 'apt bestowing' of its figures. In this, he adds, 'judgement is right needfull' (Wilson 1585: D6^r).

The 'apt bestowing' of these figures is an art that Harvey seems to have lacked. Stung by the attack on his family by Greene and Nashe, he launched a counter-attack, linking both antagonists with the decline of 'all good Learning, & civill Governement' in this 'Martinish and Counter-martinish age'. In this period, he reflects ruefully in *Four Letters*, 'the Spirit of Contradiction reigneth', and 'everie one superaboundeth in his owne humor, even to the annihilating of any other, without rime, or reason' (1592: E3^r). Given his understanding of the dangers of this 'spirit of Contradiction', it behoves him to counter Greene and Nashe with discretion. Harvey signals his awareness of this need in the Preface. The intention he expresses here to temper his own style so that he 'might neither seme blinded with affection, nor enraged with passion: nor partiall to frend, nor prejudiciall to enemy [...] but mildly & calmely shew, how discredite reboundeth upon the autors' (A2^v) indicates that a different humour governs this pamphlet-writer. Harvey clearly *intends* to represent the virtue which he argues his antagonists lack, moderation. Indeed, his own moderation is clearly on display. Thus, in one letter, following his criticism of Greene's excess, he confesses that he has also reprimanded his close friend Spenser for attempting the political satire *Mother Hubberd's Tale* (1591), 'in heat of choller' (B1^r). While in another letter he acknowledges that he, too, has made mistakes. He recalls the trouble that followed the printing of *Three Proper, and Witty, Familiar Letters*, when he was forced to apologize to the university authorities for mocking scholarship in his 'earthquake letter', and also to make account of himself to Edward de Vere, Earl of Oxford, the suspected subject of his satirical poem 'Tuscanism'. The cause of this satirical writing was the frustration of his university ambitions, he explains in *Four Letters*, but also the humoral imbalance of youthfulness and an overzealous and untutored reading of invectives and satires. 'Shall I touch the ulcer?', he asks: 'young bloud is hot; youth hasty: ingenuity open: abuse impatiente: choler stomachous: temptations busie: the Invective vaine, a sturring, and tickelinge vaine: the Satyricall humour, a puffinge, and swellinge humor' (C2^{r-v}).

Nonetheless, this humility is not enough to counter the impression that Harvey is unable to control his anger, or its rhetorical expression. Early in this pamphlet he attacks the recently deceased Greene. He shamelessly relates how, after enquiring about the health of Greene, 'who was reported to lye dangerously sicke in a shoemakers house neere Dow-gate', he received the news that he had died, 'not of the plague, or the pockes', as had been rumoured, 'but of a surfett of pickle herringe and rennish [Rhine] wine' (A4^r). This is an example of *laesio*; he is 'setting forth' Greene's 'evil behaviour' for his readers to condemn. The problem lies not in Harvey's use of this figure per se, but in the grotesque and very personal detail of Greene's supposed licentiousness: Greene's drinking and gambling and whoring. Greene, it is suggested, has quite literally gorged himself to death, or rather burned himself out: 'The hoattest bloud of choller may be cooled: and as the fiercest fury of wild-fire, so the fiercest wild-fire of Fury, consumeth it selfe' (B4^v). More generally, Greene's dissolute and lascivious conduct is mocked and discovered as a cause of his libellous writing; both are regarded as highly dangerous to the commonwealth. To raise money to sustain his lifestyle, or maybe just because he could not help it, Greene would 'counterfeit an hundred dogged Fables, Libles, Calumnies, Slaunders, Lies'. This is dangerous stuff, for 'who can tell', Harvey asks, 'what huge outrages might amount of such quarrellous, and tumultuous causes?' (B1^r).

This detail might not matter, of course, if Harvey were not arguing against such a spirit in this very pamphlet. Quite simply, the fact that he gives expression to his 'Stomacke greefe' with such relish makes his moralizing appear hypocritical. 'There is a certaine thing, called Modestie, if they could light upon it,' Harvey advises, and 'some pretty smacke of discretion would relish well' (E2^r). 'Would Christ, they had more discretion in them, and lesse rancour against other, that never wished them the least evill,' he sighs a few pages later (E4^r). Yet the examples just cited suggest that Harvey lacked discretion too. Thomas Nashe, who is implicated in this criticism, sets about exposing this lack in *Strange News* (1592; 2nd edn. 1593). What is so effective about his attack is that he makes Harvey condemn himself from his own mouth. '*Yong bloud is hot, youth hastie, ingenuitie open, abuse impatient, choller stomachous, temptations busie,*' he quotes Harvey as saying in *Four Letters*, and then glosses thus:

> In a word, the Gentleman was vext, and cutte his bridle for verie anger.
> *The tickling and stirring invective vaine, the puffing and swelling Satiricall spirit* came upon him, as it came on *Coppinger* and *Arthington*, when they mounted into the pease-cart in Cheap-side and preacht: needes hee must cast up certayne crude humours of English Hexameter Verses, they lay uppon his stomacke, a Noble-man stood in his way as he was vomiting, and from top to toe he all to berayd him with *Tuscanisme*.   (1593: G1^r)

Harvey is a fanatic, akin to the 'two confused puritan gentlemen' (Collinson 1990: 424) Edmund Coppinger and Thomas Arthington, who mistook themselves for prophets. He is also the choleric man who vomits forth his rancour on any hapless passer-by, regardless of their social rank.

Harvey's 'Stomacke greefe' is purportedly there to see for anyone who cares to read *Four Letters*, and Nashe has no trouble exposing it. But Nashe is interested in improving not only Harvey's humour but also his rhetoric. In this respect, he does not simply reveal his inability to express his anger with judgement. More damagingly, he aligns Harvey with the choleric writer mocked in the Preface to *Menaphon*: the greedy reader who does not digest his reading properly. Throughout *Four Letters* Harvey piles up neatly balanced moral sayings which establish the authority of his position through repeated appeals to received wisdom and custom. These commonplaces all seem to lead to the same narrow defence of moderation: if writers cannot moderate themselves in speech or action, then they 'must bee ruled by other; and pay for their folly' (1592: B2^r), or even 'banished':

No publike security without private moderation: and the more bondes of government, the more indefeasible assurance. Due Circumspection may do much good: and an aboundant Cautele can do little hurt. Youth is youth: & age corruptible: better an hundred Ovides were banished then the state of Augustus endangered, or a soveraigne Empire infected. Especially in a tumultuous age.   (D3^r)

Nashe debunks brilliantly this emphasis in Harvey's *Four Letters*. This kind of gorging makes him particularly unsuitable to act as a moralist, Nashe argues, because he does not understand the moral sentences he regurgitates. To illustrate this tendency Nashe selectively cites several of Harvey's *sententiae* on moderation, digesting them differently so as to expose his trite reiteration of them: 'A libertie they have thou sayst, but no liberty without bounds, no licence without limitation. Jesu what mister wonders dost thou tell us? every thing hath an end, and a pudding hath two' (1593: E1^r). The moral given expression here ('No liberty without bounds') is unremarkable, Nashe argues. Harvey is simply stating the obvious. Moreover, though he defends the importance of limitation, he does not understand what this is. Nashe, in contrast, insinuates that *he* does. First, he offers a moral defence of poetry worthy of Harvey: 'there is no other unlascivious use or end of poetry, 'but to infamize vice , and magnifie vertue'. Anything else is a '*Dirige* in pricksong without any dittie set to it, that haply may tickle the eare, but never edifies' (E3^{r-v}). Then he complicates and undermines this so as to make the bigger point that Harvey's moralizing, rather than safeguarding the commonwealth as he repeatedly claims, is profoundly threatening to it. In the excerpt cited below Nashe offers two examples which provocatively run counter to the moral argument he seems to be making, and in so doing he shows how necessary it is to digest overly familiar moral sayings:

In the Romaine common-wealths it was lawful for Poets to reprove that enormitie in the highest chairs of authoritie, which none else durst touch, alwais the sacred Majestie of their *Augustus* kept inviolate: for that was a Plannet exalted above their Hexameter horizon, & it was capitall to them in the highest degree to dispute of his setting and rising, or search inquisitively into his predominance and influence.

The secrets of God must not be searcht into. Kings are Gods on earth, their actions must not be sounded by their subjects.

Seneca Neroes Tutor, founde his death in no verse but *Octavia*. *Imperious* Lucan sprinkled but one drop of bloud on his imperiall chayre, and perisht by him also.

Ovid once saw *Augustus* in a place where he would not have beene seene, he was exilde presently to those countries no happy man hears of.   (E3^v)

'Kings are Gods on earth', Nashe argues, and for this reason their 'actions must not be sounded by their subjects'. And yet the examples that follow this statement suggest other reasons why they should not be 'sounded'. Seneca was unwise not because Nero was divine, but because he was a tyrant. Ditto Augustus. Nashe reveals starkly the limits and problems of Harvey's reasoning by making links that his antagonist cannot see, arguing that if you are willing to banish an Ovid in the age of Augustus you are more likely to be protecting a tyranny than a commonwealth.

39.2 HARVEY'S PHYSIC

Harvey is perhaps an easy target. In contrast to his nimble-witted opponent he blunders about in print, never able to insult with quite the same acuity as Nashe. His sympathetic biographer Virginia Stern recognizes that in this quarrel, and in *Four Letters* in particular, he comes across as 'sanctimonious' and 'puritanical' (1979: 97). With less sympathy, Lewis likens this row to a meeting between 'a half drunk street-corner humorist' and 'a respectable person' from 'Peebles' (1954: 413). It is 'useless for the respectable person to show that the charges brought against him are untrue', he argues, 'that he does not beat his wife, is not a cinema star in disguise, is not wearing a false nose'. In the same way, no matter how often Harvey claims to represent civil government we still end up suspecting that he is, as Nashe implies, a rakehell. This is not a contest between equals.

Yet, even Lewis was able to anticipate that Harvey might find a 'future rehabilitator' who would not deem his work 'absolutely hopeless' (1954: 354), and to some extent this has come true. Harvey owned a large and diverse library, which included classical and modern histories, contemporary and ancient literary writings, but also works of cosmology, medicine, jurisprudence, and the natural sciences. Many of these are carefully annotated in his fine italic hand. Evidence of this kind of sustained reading in early modern England is hard to come by, and for this reason Harvey's substantial library has made him a major figure in a new and burgeoning field, the history of reading. The Harvey who emerges from the margins of his books is the same Harvey lampooned by Nashe, only his habits and interests take on a different resonance. Harvey is no longer a 'foolish pedant', but rather a moderately successful professional reader, who was employed to tease out 'counsel from texts read with or for patrons' (Popper 2005: 359). On this view, it is his ability to 'extract and shrink to durable, concise, axiomatic form the pragmatic lessons of the text' that makes him employable (Grafton and Jardine 1990: 68).[1]

Many of these pragmatic lessons are recorded in Harvey's manuscript common-place book, a kind of writing which enabled scholars to bridge the gap 'between study and action' by storing examples and sayings 'poised for use at a moment's notice' (Wolfe 2004: 148). Arguably, such a book reveals its author's values much more readily than his or her more polished literary writings (Lewis 1954: 351). In Harvey's case, practical application is valued repeatedly, and this extends to the examples of exceptional self-restraint he records. Thus, he marvels at the spectacular stoicism of antiquity's most famous military leaders: Hannibal, who, on campaign, slept on the bare ground with scarcely anything to cover him, or Scipio and Alexander the Great, who ate their bread on the move: 'All these used continual exercise: A thin spare Diett: & litle sleepe. (Active and sturring men),' he notes admiringly (Harvey 1913: 92–3). Attention to this distillation of Harvey's reading can change our sense of

---

[1] Even his interest in science can shed a different light on the quarrel with Nashe. See Popper (2005); Wolfe (2004, ch. 4).

his moral–political thinking. This book includes *sententiae*, or 'frutes of discretion', taken 'owt off The Flowers of philosophy' by Seneca (103–9), many of which are reused with some variation in *Four Letters*, and this may suggest that his moralizing is rhetorical rather than deeply held: 'Speak frendly, yea thowgh it be to thy Enemy'; 'Malice drinkith upp the greatist part of [her owne] poyson' (103).

This rehabilitation of Harvey is only partial. After all, the arguments I have just summarized tend to reinforce Nashe's key argument, that Harvey is an unsubtle reader who does not digest moral sayings well enough to embody them.[2] This may explain why recent attention to his reading practice has not prompted a return to his writing in any sustained way. Everything that I have written so far suggests that there are good reasons why this is so. *Four Letters* is problematic insofar as Harvey usurps the role of moral commentator, urging his enemies to temper their ill humour, but failing to do so himself. We can argue, of course, that he never intended to embody moderation; he is regurgitating sayings for rhetorical effect.

Nonetheless, I do not want to make one text representative of Harvey's failings, especially since *Four Letters* too easily obscures the common ground that this university 'rhetor' in fact shared with the young Nashe. Indeed, Harvey sounds uncannily like Nashe in one of his Cambridge lectures on rhetoric, printed in 1577 as *Ciceronianus*. Like his antagonist-to-be, he argues that habits of *imitatio* inhibit eloquence, and even anticipates his own parody as a greedy reader in *Strange News* (1593). He describes how he dined at 'exquisite banquets' with the best of the Roman authors, Virgil, Horace, Ovid, and so on (Harvey 1945: 45–7), but confesses to devouring one author with 'insatiable eagerness', Cicero (49). This makes him a fussy reader; in his youth he refused to taste modern authors like Erasmus or Thomas More because he mistakenly thought they smelled 'of impurity and filth and rottenness' (61). Yet, though this parody of his youthful excess may anticipate Nashe, the remedy he recommends is very different, and it on this that I now propose to focus.

As I have already noted, Nashe prescribes a cure of contraries: he argues that writers 'surfetted unawares with sweete societie of eloquence' should study 'our Gothamists barbarisme' (1589: 2*2ʳ). Harvey's remedy is also one of contraries, although in a very different way. In his Latin rhetorical writings, both *Ciceronianus* and *Rhetor* (also printed in 1577), Harvey argues that rhetoricians do indeed need a more varied diet, and he urges them to read as widely as possible among the best (Roman) authors. But he also argues that this reading should be carefully digested: the rhetorical figures and moral sayings collected from one's reading must be analysed and then tested 'in practice' (*exercitatio*), that is, in one's writing and conversation (see especially Harvey 1577: 75–6). Harvey understands that this kind of testing will enable the student to become a proper Ciceronian, a scholar who imitates not the figures of speech mistakenly deemed the source of Cicero's eloquence, but the discursive process by which he became eloquent. Thus, *Ciceronianus* also details his, so to speak, healthier rereading of Cicero's work. Once he realized the dangers of slavish imitation, Harvey explains,

---

[2] On Harvey as a poor reader, see Wolfe (2004: 129–30); Pincombe (2001: 101).

he 'got into the habit of criticizing' Cicero's style, 'mildly, to be sure, and rather playfully, but still criticizing (Leviter quidem, & quasi ludendo: sed reprehendere nihilominus)' (Harvey 1945: 70–1).

I want to pause over Harvey's description of his criticism of Cicero as 'mild' since this marks his difference from Nashe. What Harvey seems to mean by this is that criticism should be expressed in a 'civil' and decorous way, maintaining a proper sense of the value of an author as a stylist (in this case Cicero) without slavishly adhering to him. This is very much how Harvey conducts himself as a reader in the margins of contemporary works of literature, evaluating, disagreeing with, and commending the advice or examples he finds. In his copy of George Gascoigne's essay 'Certain Notes of Instruction in English Verse' in *The Posies* (1575), Harvey gently criticizes its author's personality ('Sum vanity: & more levity'), but also tests some of his 'instructions' against the practice of friends like Spenser. Following Gascoigne's list of archaisms, for example, Harvey writes, 'All theise in Spenser, & manie like: but with discretion: & tolerably, thowgh sumtime not greatly commendably' (1913: 165, 170). By the same token, Harvey invites criticism of his own work. Asked by an admiring Spenser in *Three Proper, and Witty, Familiar Letters* (1580) if he will expound the rules of his metrical experiments in English, Harvey refuses, explaining that he 'dare[s] geve no Preceptes, nor set downe any Certaine General Arte', but adds that he is 'not greatly squaimishe of my Particular Examples' (1580: D4^v–E1^r). And so he offers examples for Spenser to comment on, some seriously, some inviting mockery (which Nashe would duly supply). Meanwhile, the Preface to *Rhetor* includes a letter from Bartholomew Clerke extolling just this practice of friendly criticism.[3]

This is a different kind of moderation to the one proposed in *Four Letters*, and it represents Harvey's deep engagement with Cicero's moral–political thought as defined, most influentially, in his *De officiis* ('On Social Duties'). For Cicero moderation includes the restraint of the passions, but also a range of other behaviours, among them *verecundia*, or 'shamefastnesse', wherein we 'offende nobodie', and *modestia*, or 'discretion'. This last quality is 'the knowledge of setting those thinges, which ar done, or said, in their proper places' (Cicero 1556: E7^v, G8^r). For Harvey, moderation involves not just the restraint of strong emotion but also the exercise of discrimination, of mixing and matching, of adjusting according to context or person, and of working out what is best in practice.

This aspect of Harvey is little understood, partly, no doubt, because he did not always practise it, but it is important to recall because it qualifies the image of him as a self-aggrandizing pedagogue popularized by Nashe. In general, Harvey is more playful, more self-mocking, and far more anti-Scholastic than his critics, contemporary and modern, have allowed. This Harvey values flexibility and practical application above more traditional scholarship. He understands this as 'healthy' for the commonwealth but also, as my last example from Harvey's writings of the 1570s suggests, for the individual. As he argues in his long, experimental, and frankly bizarre

---

[3] For discussion of this, see Jennifer Richards (2008).

poem 'The Scholar's Love, or Reconcilement of Contraries' in his letter-book, this kind of moderation is crucial to managing one's body and emotions, which, according to contemporary humoral physiology, are always in flux.

From the outset, nothing is certain about this poem, not even the identity of its author: this might be Harvey, as his use of the first-person pronoun initially suggests ('The very first meeter that ever I made'), but it could also be that master of disguise Thomas More, as Harvey claims a few lines later (1884: 101). The main cause of this poem's instability, though, is the state of its author's mind. This poem 'was in a rage devised and deliverid pro and contra according to the quality of [its author's] first and last humor. Anno 1573, mense Septembri' (101). 'Scholar's Love', as its title suggests, relates the tribulations of a philosopher's love affair and the fickleness of his beloved, the enigmatic Ellena. It opens with a conventional blazon applauding the beauty of his mistress, though this soon descends into parody ('Her lovely dugges, in spite of bugges'; 103); such effusiveness is abruptly curtailed once the narrator realizes that she has changed her mind: 'An union? | An Oonnyon' (113). On the one hand, this poem reflects the author's changing humour, not least by dramatically varying its rhyme scheme. On the other hand, it tries to understand positively this experience of contrariety, recognizing that 'All societies consist of contraryes' (117). The narrator comes to terms with his experience partly by reading Aristotle, but more importantly, by listening to everyday stories. One of these is the tale of the apprentice Jack Simkins about how the family of his master get on with one another:

> We all agree togither like kattes and dogges;
> Yet dine we togither and supp we togither,
> And sometyme lawghe togither, and sumtyme crye togither.
>
> (118)

A second is the story of Mistress Infirmity, who is brought before Master Commissary on account of a sexual misdemeanour, yet who speaks as eloquently as a natural philosopher, urging her judge to acknowledge that she is changed ('My heate is well coolid'), and to own up to his own 'fleshe and bludde' (122). 'And wheretoe serve contrary | Humors in mans boddy', the scholar concludes, 'But to make us appliant | To every descant?' (123).

Does this more playful aspect of Harvey's temperament disappear in the harsher atmosphere of the 1590s? The example of the censorious *Four Letters* suggests that it does. We might explain this change psychologically: Greene's *Quip* appeared shortly after the death of his beloved younger brother John (Stern 1979: 97). Yet, as this pamphlet makes clear, Harvey is also lamenting the decline of civil conversation and the emergence of a new culture of confutation in which 'every Martin Junior, and Puny Pierce, [is] a monarch in the kingdome of his owne humour' (Harvey 1592: H1ᵛ). Admittedly, he repeatedly fails to show us an alternative in *Four Letters*, though, as I have argued, his earlier writings do. But we could argue that *Four Letters* is demonstrating the effects of this breakdown. After all, Harvey reflects on his own excess knowingly, albeit briefly, in his final letter. This last letter, he admits, is 'wholly superfluous, but violently extorted after the rest: all wearisome unto me' (84).

This suggestion that Harvey possesses some insight into his own immoderation may feel strained for *Four Letters*, but it is certainly appropriate for his next work, *Pierce's Supererogation* (1593). This is an immediate response to Nashe's *Strange News* (1593), but it also includes, unexpectedly, 'An Advertisement for Pap-hachet, and Martin Mar-prelate', his answer to an earlier satirical pamphlet, John Lyly's splenetic *Pap with an Hatchet* (1589). In this way, Harvey makes explicit the link between the anti-Martinists Lyly and Nashe. In *Pierce's Supererogation*, Harvey has finally moved away from the dialogue form. There is no pretence here of addressing a familiar friend, no dramatization of different voices. Nonetheless, I would argue that it becomes clear in this pamphlet that some of Harvey's more strident attacks in *Four Letters* are directed not at stifling dialogue and debate, as Nashe had implied in *Strange News*, but at keeping the threat of tyranny at bay, and so preserving the possibility for dialogue. '[B]etter an hundred Ovides were banished', Harvey argues in *Four Letters*, 'then the state of Augustus endangered, or a soveraigne Empire infected.' This argument is reworked a year later, in 1593: 'One Ovid was too-much for Roome; and one Greene too-much for London: but one Nashe more intollerable then both: not bicause his witt is anye thinge comparable, but bicause his will is more outragious' (G1^r). The reiteration of this argument suggests that Harvey's position has hardened. However, as he explains, Nashe would be 'utterly insupportable' in an 'absolute' monarchy, presumably like Augustan Rome; but in fact he is also insupportable in just about any kind of commonwealth: 'Germany, Denmarke, Sweden, Polony, Boemia, Hungary, Moscovy, are noe foiles of any such wittes: but neither Fraunce, nor Spaine, nor Turky, nor any puissant kingdom, in one, or other Monarchy of the old, or new world, could ever abide any such pernicious writers, depravers of common discipline' (1593: G1^r). Moreover, he explains more clearly in 1593 why this is so: the satirist also embodies the spirit of tyranny. Like 'Alexander the great', he complains, Nashe will 'have all men his subjectes, and all his subjectes called Alexanders' (C1^v). In other words, there can be no dialogue with a satirist like Nashe who 'will confute me, bicause he will' and 'conquer me, bicause he can' (H3^v).

In this pamphlet Harvey makes clear his concern with how the conduct of subjects is involved in the practice of government and its decline, an argument he had made only implicitly in *Four Letters*. One of the effects of this is to make him appear protective of existing political hierarchies and reluctant to expose corruption, not even of the bishops who encouraged the anti-Martinists in the first place. On the contrary, he often appears deferential to power, praising, for example, the Homeric verse of the King of Scots, James VI (1592: G4^r). Harvey's criticism of Nashe's 'licentious follie', which, he argues, thrives 'not in a popular state, or a petty principalitie, but in a soverain Monarchie, that tendereth politique government' (H2^v), may well be read as inhibiting freely critical speech. And yet, he is not equating 'moderation' with unthinking 'obedience'. His worry is that the kind of domineering eloquence represented by Nashe destroys the possibility for 'politique government' protected in a 'soverain Monarchie'. He supports this point by making James VI stand as a republican example, anticipating the lost opportunity for conversation with him if gentlemen cannot match his learning: 'When young Kings have such a care of their flourishing Prime; and like Cato, are ready to render an accompt of their vacant howers [...] how should gentlemen of yeeres, employ the golden talent of their Industry, and travaile?' (G4^r).

Harvey is not just urging moderation in debate, however. He is also concerned with the kind of 'discretion' outlined by Cicero in *De officiis*, the skill of adjusting according to context or person. This argument is articulated as a political principle in 'An Advertisement for Pap-hachet, and Martin Mar-prelate'. In this Harvey is presenting an alternative to the satirical mimicry of the anti-Martinists. (Harvey cannot distinguish between anti-Martinists and Martinists, between Nashe and Lyly on the one hand and those they attack on the other.) Just as Nashe is criticized for adopting a popular voice in the context of a sovereign monarchy in the main body of *Pierce's Supererogation*, so here the hotter Protestants are criticized for attempting to 'build a reformation in a monarchy, upon a popular foundation' (1593: M1^v). 'Popular Elections, and offices, aswell in Churches, as in Commonwealthes, are for popular states,' he argues; 'Monarchies, and Aristocracies, are to celebrate their elections, and offices, according to their forme of government' (K4^v). Harvey is defending the gradual process by which stable government was founded and by which it can be suddenly changed again by extremists on any side. He is less interested in limiting dissent than in exposing those tendencies in government at any level that will deny the exercise of discretion, the working out of what fits best with current customs, and which he argues characterized the deliberations of the 'auncient Fathers, and Doctors of the Church'.

[W]hat wiser Senates, or hollyer Congregations, or any way more reverend assemblies, then some Generall, and some Provinciall Councels? Where they to a superficiall opinion, seeme to sett-up a Glosse, against, or beside the Text; it would bee considered, what their considerations were; and whether it can appeare, that they directly, or indirectly proceeded without a respective regard of the Commonwealth, or a tender care of the Church, or a reverend Examination of that Text. [...] They are not the simplest, or dissolutest men, that thinke, Discretion must have leave to cutt his coate according to his cloth; and commend their humility, patience, wisdome, and whole conformity, that were ready to accept any requisite order not unlawfull, and to admit any decent, or seemly rites of indifferent nature. (L1^v)

The new reformers are committed to the immediate imposition of ancient Church government, but their lack of discretion, Harvey surmises, will lead to the very trajectory that turned 'The first Bishops of Roome', 'undoubtedly vertuous men, and godly Pastors', into popes and tyrants: the reformers will 'pull-downe Bishops; set up the Minister; make him Bishop of his Parish, and head of the Consistorie (call him, how you list, that must be his place): what will become of him within a fewe generations, but a high Priest in a low Jerusalem, or a great Pope in a small Roome'

(P1ʳ).[4] The same is true of Nashe. It is the defence of this kind of moderation that lies at the heart of Harvey's attack on immoderate satires, whether written by Martinists or their enemies. On his view, satirists share the same domineering impulse that leads to tyranny.

There is another valuable aspect to this distrust of the satirist. Harvey's commitment to negotiation makes him modern in a particular way, for it arises from his sceptical refusal to accept that anyone or any group can have the answer and, alongside this, his understanding of the ubiquity of the tyrannical impulse which can corrupt even the 'best' of freedom fighters, including the Brutus who expelled the Roman tyrant Tarquin and the Brutus who assassinated Julius Caesar: 'Some Stoiques, and melancholie persons have a spice of ambition by themselves: and even *Junius Brutus*, the first, was somway a kinde of *Tarquinius Superbus*: and *Junius Brutus* the second, is not altogither a mortified Creature, but bewrayeth as it were some reliques of fleshe, and bloud' (L4ʳ). The complexity of Harvey's reflection here requires us to qualify our understanding of what is at stake in the quarrel with Nashe, and to rethink what we determine as 'imaginative freedom'.

PRIMARY WORKS

CICERO (1556), *Marcus Tullius Ciceroes Thre Bokes of Duties*, trans. N. Grimald.
HARVEY, GABRIEL (1577), *Rhetor*, <http://comp.uark.edu/~mreynold/rhetor.html>, accessed 16 Feb. 2008.
——(1580), *Three Proper, and Wittie, Familiar Letters: Lately Passed Between Two Universitie Men*.
——(1592), *Foure Letters, and Certaine Sonnets*.
——(1593), *Pierces Supererogation*.
——(1884), *Letter-Book of Gabriel Harvey, A.D. 1573–1580*, ed. E. J. Long Scott (London: Nichols).
——(1913), *Gabriel Harvey's Marginalia*, ed. G. C. Moore Smith (Stratford upon Avon: Shakespeare Head).
——(1945), *Gabriel Harvey's Ciceronianus*, trans. Clarence A. Forbes (Lincoln: University of Nebraska).
HARVEY, RICHARD (1590), *A Theologicall Discourse of the Lamb of God and his Enemies*.
NASHE, THOMAS (1589), 'To the Gentlemen Students of Both Universities', in *Menaphon* by Robert Greene.
——(1592), *Pierce Penilesse his Supplication to the Divell*.
——(1593), *The Apologie of Pierce Pennilesse; or, Strange Newes*.
——(1596), *Have With You to Saffron-Walden; or, Gabriell Harveys Hunt Is Up*.
WILSON, THOMAS (1585), *The Arte of Rhetorique*.

---

[4] Harvey's argument is prescient; this hardening of new structures was already happening in Puritan churches, as elders elected to answer to their congregations became 'permanent clerical officials', as Patrick Collinson notes (1990: 106).

CHAPTER 40

THE INTIMACY OF MANUSCRIPT AND THE PLEASURE OF PRINT

LITERARY CULTURE FROM *THE SCHOOLMASTER* TO *EUPHUES*

FRED SCHURINK

ROGER ASCHAM's *The Schoolmaster* (published 1570) and John Lyly's *Euphues* (1578) were two of the most popular and influential works of Elizabethan England. Surprisingly perhaps, Ascham's educational manual and Lyly's fictional narrative have quite a few elements in common. The most obvious link is the name Euphues, which Lyly took from Ascham's handbook. But the two works also share a number of themes, including education, style, and travel to Italy. In their concern with these subjects, *The Schoolmaster* and *Euphues* are typical of mid-Tudor writing, and of the impact of humanism on literature in the period in particular. However, there is a significant divergence in their treatment of these topics. Because of the differences in their approach to some of the central concerns of the literature of the mid-Tudor period, as well as the immense popularity of *The Schoolmaster* and *Euphues* in the 1570s and the 1580s respectively, these works of Ascham and Lyly have often been taken to mark a decisive shift in the literary culture of sixteenth-century England. In this chapter, I want to revisit the question of the relationship between *The Schoolmaster* and *Euphues*, and its connection to broader developments in the literature of the period. After sketching out briefly the prevailing view of the relation between the two works, I will consider both *The Schoolmaster* and *Euphues* in some detail. In my discussion I will attempt to offer a different, but complementary, interpretation of the connection between the texts and the shift in literary culture they mark. My focus will be the form of the two works, in the sense of both their textual formation or genre and their material format (manuscript or print), in relation to the conditions of the production and consumption of literature in the period.

The most influential account of the relationship between *The Schoolmaster* and *Euphues* remains that of Richard Helgerson, who argued that while Lyly reproduces the forms of humanist education, he 'undermines' both 'the content of the humanist curriculum' and 'the humanist didactic method' (1976: 61). Helgerson claimed that Lyly shows a transgressive attraction to the Italian culture condemned by Ascham; locates the role of wit in speech rather than in memory; secretly delights in his portrayal of Euphues' transgressions; reproduces the imperfection of the world that the work depicts through its antithetic style; and vindicates experience over example. By taking on the ideas of *The Schoolmaster* in *Euphues* and its sequel, Lyly also rebelled against the father figures of mid-Tudor humanism, including Ascham, his kinsman and patron William Cecil, Lord Burghley, and his grandfather William Lily, who gave his name to the authorized grammar of Tudor England.

Helgerson's account is compelling in many ways, and it has been developed further by critics in recent years (e.g. Maslen 1997: 214–20; Pincombe 2001: 107–24). However, *Euphues* and its sequel, *Euphues and his England* (1580), less clearly challenge the ideas of *The Schoolmaster* than Helgerson and others suggest. In particular, their focus on the narrative part of *Euphues* alone is misleading: a large part of the book is devoted to didactic material, which closely resembles *The Schoolmaster* in form and content (see Dolven 2007: 85–6). Moreover, the nature of the work as a collection of commonplace topics invited readers to dissolve any pattern that might have existed in the narrative once more into the elements of which it was constituted—an invitation eagerly taken up by the anonymous author of an early seventeenth-century manuscript that includes *sententiae*, models of virtuous conduct, and comparisons from *Euphues and his England* and marks them with 'γνώμη' ('wise saying') or Latin commonplace headings such as 'Modestia' and 'In senectutem' ('Against Old Age') in the margin (BL, Harley MS 677, fos 80ᵛ–85ʳ; see Schurink 2004: 227–30). In such a context, Lyly's works could end up looking rather like *The Schoolmaster*. In fact, *Euphues* did appear together with Ascham's work in a seventeenth-century list headed 'Schoolbooks and philosophy given to Kingsnorton library' (Hunter 1962: 285). Finally, the accounts of Helgerson and others have a tendency to isolate the ideas conveyed by the works from the form in which they were presented and from the material and some of the social contexts of their publication.

While *The Schoolmaster* is known to modern readers as a printed book, the work had its origins in a manuscript culture. A manuscript copy of what has been called 'the first draft' of the text survives in the Royal Collection in the British Library.[1] Probably written by the end of 1564, it formerly belonged to the collector John Lumley, first Baron Lumley. The text consists of a shorter version of the first book of *The Schoolmaster*. Omitting the Preface (discussed below), it says only that it was intended for the education of Ascham's son.[2] The fact that Ascham allowed a copy to be made of the manuscript, nevertheless, suggests that he intended it for circulation, as do some aspects of its content, such as the panegyric of Queen Elizabeth. In this respect, as in others, the manuscript version of *The Schoolmaster* is closely related to works from the Advice to a Son tradition, which offered advice on manners and morals in the form of a letter or short treatise addressed by a father to his son.[3] Although some of these works were eventually printed, it was essentially a manuscript genre. This was consistent with the ostensibly private nature of the texts, in which a father presented instructions to his son, and with the epistolary form—although authors were, in fact, very much aware that they were addressing themselves to a wider readership and used the role of the father as a convenient rhetorical device. Ascham knew some of the most celebrated examples of this genre, the letters of Sir Thomas Wyatt the elder to his son, and imitated them in a letter of 1559 to his youthful brother-in-law Christopher Howe (Ascham 1570a: B1ᵛ; Powell 2003: 17–19). *The Schoolmaster* is quite different in scope and nature from the letters by Wyatt and by Ascham himself, even in the earlier version; but it has sufficient common characteristics with them to suggest that both Ascham and his first readers would have considered the work in relation to a genre which flourished in the manuscript culture of the time.

The lengthy Preface added in the printed version of *The Schoolmaster* (published posthumously by Ascham's wife, Margaret, in 1570) offers a quite different account of the genesis of the text, focusing on the role of Ascham's patrons Sackville and Burghley in the conception of the work. While it thus effaces the actual history of the work as part of a manuscript culture, it rhetorically invokes the intimacy and familiarity of manuscript and speech at the same time.[4] The Preface vividly evokes the origin of *The Schoolmaster* in a particular occasion by giving the precise date (10 December 1563), place (Windsor Castle), persons present (Burghley, the diners—all named—and the Queen), and cause (the news of the escape of some scholars from Eton for fear of beating). It presents the work as the outcome of a conversation of Ascham with the Privy Counsellor Sir Richard Sackville in the privy chamber, in

[1] Ascham (1564?); see Parks (1937–8). Ryan (1963: 330–1) and Beal (1980: i. AsR3) argue that the manuscript is a scribal copy and not Ascham's holograph, as suggested by Parks.
[2] See Parks (1937–8: 313); this claim was repeated by Ascham in a letter to Queen Elizabeth of 10 October 1567 (Ascham 1864–5: ii. 158).
[3] I am grateful to Jason Powell for this point; see Powell (2003: 4–40); Burghley et al. (1962).
[4] Ascham appears here to be adapting the very similar prefatory strategies of other mid-Tudor humanists, notably Thomas Wilson in *The Art of Rhetoric* (1553) and William Thomas in *Principal Rules of the Italian Grammar* (1550) and other works (see Shrank 2004a: 302–5).

which they discuss exactly the subjects which will later constitute the main topics of the first book (Ascham 1570b: B2ᵛ). When the matter proves too large for their after-dinner conversation, Sackville suggests that Ascham elaborate somewhat on them in writing:

> bicause this place, and this tyme, will not suffer so long taulke, as these good matters require, therefore I pray you, at my request, and at your leysure, put in some order of writing, the cheife pointes of this our taulke, concerning, the right order of teachinge, and honestie of living, for the good bringing up of children & yong men.   (B2ᵛ)

The oral exchange between the two men is thus converted into a manuscript treatise commissioned by Sackville, which Ascham intends to present as a New Year's gift: 'I so mindefull, somewhat to satisfie the honest request of so deare a frend. I thought to praepare some litle treatise for a Newyeares gift that Christmas' (B3ʳ). Even the eventual decision to publish the work is attributed to Sackville, who adds: 'And surelie, beside contentinge me, you shall both please and profit verie many others' (B2ᵛ).

The Preface also suggests why Ascham wanted to invoke the intimacy and famil-iarity of private conversation and manuscript gift exchange. When Sackville first asks Ascham to 'point [...] out a Scholemaster, who by your order, shall teache my sonne and yours'—a commission which Ascham eventually fulfils by writing *The Schoolmaster*—he promises that 'for all the rest, [he] will provide, yea though they three do cost me a couple of hundred poundes by yeare: and beside, you shall finde me as fast a Frend to you and yours, as perchance any you have' (B2ᵛ). *The Schoolmaster* is presented here as part of an exchange involving Ascham's expertise, on the one hand, and Sackville's 'friendship', on the other (Stewart 1997: 112). This transaction is specifically presented as taking the form of a private conversation and then a presentation manuscript. Gifts, including manuscripts, were an essential part of the early modern economy of friendship (Zemon-Davies 2000: 30–2). Printed books were mass-produced and consequently lacked individual features; they were available to an anonymous readership distinguished only by their ability to read and pay for the book. Each manuscript, on the other hand, was a unique artefact, and represented time and effort on the part of the author, especially if it was in his or her own handwriting. A manuscript gift book was thus a sign and expression of the unique service of an author–scribe to a patron. But what was the nature of the 'friendship' between Ascham and Sackville? Ascham's statement that Sackville 'would have bene, not onelie a glad commender of [*The Schoolmaster*], but also a sure and certaine comfort [support], to me and mine, for it' (B3ᵛ) reveals that the rhetoric of friendship conceals a service relationship between the two men. Ascham was in dire financial need throughout the 1560s, and his attempts to gain financial and other support from his patrons through the composition of *The Schoolmaster* were vital to his own fortunes and those of his family (Ryan 1963: 228–40).

According to Ascham's account in the Preface, Sackville's request had its origins in the dinner-time conversation about the severity of schoolmasters started by Burgh-ley, in whose room the debate took place. Burghley both proposed the subject and first put forward the argument which Ascham develops in *The Schoolmaster*, that schoolmasters should use more discretion because beating puts children off learning. There can be no doubt that he is also the unnamed benefactor who Ascham claims encouraged him to take up the work again after the death of Sackville (B3^v–B4^r). Burghley had long been Ascham's patron, and the attribution of the genesis of the work to him and the expectation of his continued assistance expressed in the Preface strongly suggest that Ascham intended Burghley as the dedicatee of *The Schoolmaster* as well: 'he hath many times comforted me and mine, and, I trust to God, shall comfort more and more' (B3^v). Margaret Ascham did, in fact, dedicate the work to Burghley after her husband's death, and he successfully petitioned the Queen on behalf of Ascham's sons on a number of occasions. In particular, it was Burghley who took care of the education of Ascham's eldest son, Giles, whom he recommended for admission to Westminster School, for whom he obtained a scholarship to Trinity College, Cambridge, and whom he got elected to a fellowship at the same college (Ryan 1963: 287–92). Burghley also helped Giles and his brother Dudley obtain the stipend which their father had earned as Latin secretary. *The Schoolmaster* thus achieved Ascham's stated aim to provide for the education of his children and their financial stability: 'For, seing at my death, I am not like to leave them any great store of living, therefore in my life time, I thought good to bequeath unto them, in this litle booke, as in my Will and Testament, the right waie to good learning: which if they followe, with the feare of God, they shall verie well cum to sufficiencie of living' (B4^r). Despite Ascham's rhetoric, however, it was less the method of education presented in *The Schoolmaster* than the patronage relationships created by it which supported the education of his children; and indeed less their education than the backing of Burghley and the Queen which eventually brought Giles and his brothers to a 'sufficiencie of living'.

Ascham not only intended to present himself to his patrons in *The Schoolmaster*; he also meant the book for a wider readership in print. In the Preface he associates both himself and his educational theory with the political elite of Elizabethan England. Having set the debate that engendered the book in Secretary of State Burghley's room in the Queen's palace at Windsor, he makes a special point of listing the titles and positions of all the participants in the exchange:

Syr *William Peter*, Syr *J. Mason*, D. *Wotton*, Syr *Richard Sackville* Treasurer of the Exchecker, Syr *Walter Mildmaye* Chauncellor of the Exchecker, M. *Haddon* Master of Requestes, M. *John Astely* Master of the Jewell house, M. *Bernard Hampton*, M. *Nicasius*, and *I*. Of which number, the most part were of hir Majesties most honourable privie Counsell, and the reast serving hir in verie good place.   (B1^r)

Presenting himself as a close associate of key figures at the court of Elizabeth helped to establish Ascham's authority, and thus to advance the ideas set out in *The Schoolmaster*. As I have argued, Ascham also locates the origin of the specific subject and argument of *The Schoolmaster* in two of the most powerful men in the reign, Burghley and Sackville. More broadly, Ascham validates his own concern with education and confirms its status as a key issue to the commonwealth by showing how the most important political figures of the country dedicated their precious spare time to discussion of the topic. Ascham's strategy evidently worked. His posthumous success in receiving the sanction of the authorities for *The Schoolmaster* and establishing it as the most authoritative English book on education is evidenced not only by its printing history and influence, but also by a very unusual stipulation attached to the licence for printing Richard Mulcaster's educational treatise *Positions* in the Stationers' Register of 1581: 'Provyded alwaies That yf this booke conteine any thinge prejudiciall or hurtfull to the booke of maister Askham that was printed by master Daie Called the Scolemayster That then this Lycence shalbe voyd' (Arber 1875–94: ii. 390, cited in Stewart 1997: 115).

Ascham's extensive Preface at first appears rather tenuously connected to the main text, which presents his ideas on the education and bringing up of children and young men and method of teaching Latin; but in fact it carefully prepares the reader for his treatment of the principal theme of the work, education. Just as Ascham portrays friendship and service relationships as central to the genesis and reception of *The Schoolmaster* by highlighting the origins of the work within an oral and manuscript culture in the Preface, so also does he present friendship and service as both the necessary prerequisites and outcomes of education in the main body of the work. Contrary to the common belief that *The Schoolmaster* is a manual for grammar schools (e.g. B. Nelson 2001: 9), the full title of the work, as well as its content, reveal that Ascham is concerned mainly with the household education of young noblemen by private tutors (a common meaning of the word 'schoolmaster' in the sixteenth-century; see 'Schoolmaster', *OED*, 1e): 'The Scholemaster Or plaine and perfite way of teachyng children, to understand, write, and speake, the Latin tong, but specially purposed for the private bryngyng up of youth in Jentlemen and Noble mens houses'.[5] Children of the gentry and the nobility were often educated in the household of someone else, normally a social superior, who could offer them protection and advance their careers. Ascham himself was placed in the household of the Suffolk lawyer and parliamentarian Sir Humphrey Wingfield, where he was educated alongside the children of Sir Humphrey and others by a private tutor. At the pinnacle of this system were the royal wards, fatherless minors of the nobility, whose property was administered by the Crown and who were educated in the household of the Master of the Wards. This office was held for nearly all of Elizabeth's reign by Ascham's patron Burghley, who provided a humanistic education to a number of leading noblemen of Elizabethan England with the aim of preparing them for positions of responsibility in the government of the country (Simon 1966).

In addition to the patronage relationship involved in placing a child in the household of another, this form of education created a bond between the tutor, his pupils, and their parents, in whose service the tutor was employed. This is reflected in the examples of Ascham's theory of education in *The Schoolmaster*, notably in the

---

[5] Ascham's intention was, however, recognized by his contemporaries, including John Brinsley (1622: D3ᵛ).

long digression on John Whitney. Ostensibly introduced to support a key aspect of Ascham's educational scheme, double translation, this passage in fact focuses not so much on method as on the friendship between the two men. Whitney is described as Ascham's 'bedfeloe'; together, they read Cicero's *De amicitia* ('On Friendship'); and a long poem on the death of Whitney emphasizes how the two men were united in friendship (1570*b*: K4^r–L1^r). In his account of Whitney, then, Ascham presents an ideal of education in which master and pupil are united in friendship, and the experience of education further strengthens their bond (see also Stewart 1997: 126). As before, it is likely that Ascham's 'friendship' with this 'yong jentleman' (K4^v) in the household of Princess Elizabeth also concealed a (prospective) patronage relationship. Such a relation was clearly in evidence between Ascham and his most famous pupil, Queen Elizabeth. Ascham holds Elizabeth up as an exemplar of the achievements of his method of education in *The Schoolmaster* (H1^{r-v} and *passim*). He emphasizes in particular his involvement in her continued study of the classical languages, relating how he went up to the privy chamber after the dinner in Burghley's room to 'red than togither [with Elizabeth] in the Greke tonge, as I well remember, that noble Oration of *Demosthenes* against *Aeschines*, for his false dealing in his Ambassage to king *Philip* of Macedonie' (B2^r). The friendly relationship between the Queen and her former tutor established by their experience of learning and teaching thus continues to be sustained by their joint study.

As with Whitney, the content of their reading matter is equally significant: Demosthenes' *On the False Embassy* is concerned with war and diplomacy. Ascham had commented on Elizabeth's political acumen in reading companion speeches by the Greek orator (Ascham 1864–5: i. 447, trans. in Ascham 1989: 210; see also 1864–5: ii. 63), and the translations of Demosthenes' other orations on Philip of Macedon by Thomas Wilson and Nicholas Carr (published in 1570 and 1571) specifically applied these texts to the political situation of Elizabethan England.[6] Wilson advises that every scholar should read Demosthenes: 'the wysest man lyving may learne of Demosthenes, how to benefite hymselfe and to doe good to hys Countrye, and to mayntayne also the safety of it' (1570: 2*1^r). For Ascham, as for his predecessor Sir Thomas Elyot, author of the educational treatise *The Governor* (1531), and Ascham's patron Burghley, the education and study of the elite are ultimately directed towards a different form of service, to queen and country. The close relationship of education with royal service and the government of the commonwealth is revealed by the inclusion of the various 'governors' and their offices in the Preface discussed above. It is also figured by the concern of the royal servants at Windsor with the incident at nearby Eton and, more generally, by the setting of the work at court—the book was, in fact, entered into the Stationers' Register, and referred to by Ascham himself, as 'the scholemaster of Wynsore' (Arber 1875–94: i. 410; Ascham 1864–5: ii. 176; 1989: 267). Friendship, service, and patronage are thus central to Ascham's design in *The Schoolmaster* at every level: central to education, as well as to literary composition; and central to the outcome

---

[6] On Wilson, see Blanshard and Sowerby (2005) and Shrank (2004*b*: 200–5); on Carr, Binns (1990: 231–5).

of education, as well as to its process. Equally fundamental to the book, however, is Ascham's own role in all this: as an author, as a tutor, and ultimately as a servant to the commonwealth.

John Lyly's *Euphues* also includes a treatise on the education of children, 'Euphues and his Ephaebus', a free, but full, translation of *De liberis educandis*, attributed to the ancient Greek author Plutarch. The pseudo-Plutarchan essay on the education of children was a favourite of the Tudor humanists, and was translated, and then imitated in *The Governor*, by Elyot. Another version of the work, with many additions, was produced by the master of Westminster School Edward Grant, who taught Ascham's son Giles and published Ascham's life and letters in 1576 (see Schurink 2008). And there can be no doubt that Ascham himself was influenced by the essay in *The Schoolmaster*, either directly or via an intermediary source such as Elyot (Ryan 1963: 260–1). Many of the key themes of Ascham's treatise are foreshadowed in *De liberis educandis*: the importance of education, and of good tutors in particular; the value of instruction in good morals, and the application of learning to the benefit of the commonwealth; the encouragement of children to learning by praise, not by beating; and the vices to which young men are prone (particularly idleness, prodigality, and lasciviousness).

Euphues is not, of course, a didactic treatise alone. The longest and to many readers most memorable part of the work—indeed, the only part generally read and printed nowadays—is the fictional narrative with which the work opens. In the bridging passage between the story of Euphues and the didactic treatise 'Euphues and his Ephaebus', the change in character of the work is presented as part of Euphues' repentance and reformation:

> And callyng to minde his former losenes, & how in his youth, he had mispent his time, he thought to give a Caveat to all parents, how they might bring their children up in vertue, and a commaundement to al youth, how they should frame themselves to their fathers instructions: in the which is plainly to be seene, what wit can, & will do, if it be well employed, which discourse following, although it bring lesse pleasure to your youthfull mindes then his first course, yet will it bring more profite, in the one being contened the race of a lover, in the other, the reasons of a Philosopher.   (Lyly 1578: I3^r)

If the first part of *Euphues* constitutes an account of the main character's 'mispent' youth, the second is his attempt to atone for his sins by showing others how to fulfil their potential. In addition to 'Euphues and his Ephaebus', this part of the book includes 'Euphues and Atheos', in which Euphues convinces an unbeliever of the existence of God, and a collection of letters of advice by the reformed Euphues to his former friends. The differences between the fiction of the opening section and the advice of 'Euphues and his Ephaebus', however, are also a reflection of the different modes or genres of the two parts. Two distinctions to which Lyly calls attention stand out: between description and prescription and between pleasure and profit. On the one hand, Lyly expresses anxiety about the potential danger of the descriptive nature of the narrative to its readers; on the other, he emphasizes the pleasure of reading the story of Euphues, and reading about love in particular.

The two parts of *Euphues* express and explore their themes in quite different ways. Narrative by its very nature has to show events as they unfold over time. Moreover, stories have to incorporate some of the imperfections of the world: without some conflict or problem there is nothing to drive the narrative. As Lyly notes (correctly, if tendentiously), 'If then the first sight of Euphues, shal seeme to[o] light to be read of the wise, or to[o] foolish to be regarded of the learned, they ought not to impute it to the iniquitie of the author, but to the necessitie of the history' (A2ᵛ). *Euphues* is consequently largely devoted to the protagonist's 'losenes' and 'mispent [...] time'. In the simplest terms, it illustrates what happens when good wit (Greek: *euphuēs*) spurns the advice of good counsel (*euboulos*), forms a friendship with self-love (*philautos*), and gives himself over to idleness and wantonness (personified by Lucilla). It thus explores the question of what the consequences are of the misuse of a good nature or inclination (*phusis*). As an advice manual, 'Euphues and his Ephaebus' in contrast offers its readers counsel ('how they might') and rules for behaviour ('how they should'), telling them what to do ('a commaundement') and what not ('a Caveat'). It focuses on the question 'what wit can, & will do, if it be well employed'; in other words, the potential of good wit. As a manual of advice, it does not—indeed, should not—concern itself with cases where the potential is abused.[7]

The depiction of Euphues' disobedience and misbehaviour in the fictional part of the work was sufficiently troubling to Lyly to feel the need to offer an explanation in the dedication, where he uses the analogy of a painter: 'Seing then that in every counterfaite [pictorial representation] as well the blemish as the bewtie is coloured: I hope I shal not incur the displeasure of the wise, in that in the discourse of Euphues I have aswel touched the vanities of his love, as the vertues of his lyfe' (A2ʳ). This is a somewhat unusual defence of the portrayal of a character's immoral behaviour; the standard Tudor argument was that bad characters serve as a warning to readers to avoid their actions.[8] This point is made by Eubulus, also in pictorial terms, in his speech to Euphues. Various ancient peoples, he claims, displayed pictures showing the repulsiveness of 'dronken men and other wicked men' (B3ʳ) to warn young men to avoid like behaviour. By presenting an example of an unruly young man, the fictional part of *Euphues* could thus be seen to perform the same moral function as the advice manual of 'Euphues and his Ephaebus'. But except for a single throwaway comment by the narrator—'Heere ye may beholde gentlemen, how lewdly wit standeth in his owne lyght' (B7ᵛ)—and Eubulus' counsel to Euphues, itself questioned by the narrative, the notion is not developed. Euphues himself introduces the concept of exemplarity only after his repentance, and his use of the future tense rather conspicuously glances over the less edifying spectacle of his earlier life: 'I will bee as it were an example my

---

[7] As many critics have noted, by showing the failure of innate talent perfected by a humanist education (Euphues) when confronted with the world outside the classroom, Lyly does question the efficacy of a humanist education; see e.g. Mentz (2006: 133).

[8] There is an excellent discussion of exemplarity in mid-Tudor literature in Pigman (2000: 468–70).

selfe, desiring you all to imitate me' (N4^v).[9] The point Lyly makes in the dedication, too, is rather different. The comparison with a painting suggests that to provide an accurate or realistic representation of his protagonist he has to depict his flaws. The comparison is not very apt, however, as Euphues is not a real person, and *Euphues* no portrait. A few pages later Lyly, in fact, offers a different, and perhaps more convincing, reason, that a flaw may add to the attractiveness of a portrayal: 'in all perfecte shapes, a blemmish bringeth rather a liking every way to the eyes, then a loathing any waye to the minde' (B1^r).

Lyly's argument in the dedication, nevertheless, reveals a deep-seated anxiety. Why does he fear to 'incur the displeasure of the wise'? The answer lies once more in the notion of exemplarity. Bad examples were intended to warn readers off their course of action, particularly if evil characters were punished at the end of the work and repented (as Euphues does, of course). But what if some readers chose to imitate their behaviour, and follow them on the road to perdition, just as they were encouraged to imitate the virtuous conduct of good examples? There was real anxiety about this issue in Tudor England, and by no means was everyone convinced that readers might not take the representation of vice as an incitement to immoral behaviour. Ascham, for example, warned that 'The best examples have never such forse to move to any goodnes, as the bad, vaine, light and fond, have to all ilnes' (H1^v). Euphues himself acknowledges this danger at the very moment he expresses the hope that his counsel will be effective: 'If my lewde lyfe Gentlemen have given you offence, lette my good counsayle make amendes, if by my folly any be allured to lust, let them by my repentaunce be drawne to continencie' (G3^r). Clearly, negative exemplarity put more weight on the judgement of the reader, and the danger remained that the punishment meted out to a character for their depraved behaviour might not wholly obliterate the impression of the attraction of the reprehensible acts (sex, drinking, gambling) portrayed in the fictional narrative.[10]

The other major distinction the narrator draws between the first and the second parts of the work is between pleasure and profit, or, more precisely, between the 'lesse pleasure [...] yet [...] more profite' offered by the 'discourse following' and the more pleasure and less profit offered by 'his first course' (i.e. the path followed by Euphues in his youth). Lyly's wordplay in this passage ('discourse' balanced by 'his [...] course') suggests a link between the opposition between pleasure and profit, on the one hand, and the generic difference between the advice manual of 'Euphues and his Ephaebus' and the story of Euphues' youthful indiscretions, on the other. The title page elaborates further on this connection: 'Very pleasant for all Gentlemen to reade, and most necessary to remember: wherin are contained the delights that Wyt followeth in his youth by the pleasauntnesse of Love, and the happynesse he reapeth in age, by the perfectnesse of Wisedome'. The first half of the first phrase ('Very pleasant [...] to reade') is linked with the first half of the second ('the delights that Wyt followeth in

---

[9] The same applies to Lucilla: 'though I have infected some by example, yet I hope I shall comforte many by repentaunce' (G3^r); see also Katharine Wilson (2006: 61–2); Dolven (2007: 86).

[10] This was the argument, for instance, of John Rainolds, in *The Overthrow of Stage Plays* (1599); see Hunter (1994: 114–15).

his youth by the pleasauntnesse of Love') through the parallelism of the construction, as well as the repetition of derivatives of the root 'pleas-'; similarly, the second half of the first phrase ('most necessary to remember') is coupled with the second half of the second ('the perfectnesse of Wisedome'). The contrast is entirely conventional: the subject of love has an immediate appeal to the reader, but is ephemeral; wisdom, on the other hand, should be subjected to multiple reading and stored in the memory of the student to guide future behaviour. Moreover, the title page specifically connects the pleasure of reading the text ('Very pleasant [...] to reade') with the pleasure of love ('the pleasauntnesse of Love'). On one level, this simply suggests that it is enjoyable to read about love, because it is such a pleasant subject. However, the finely balanced phrases also seem to suggest a more intimate relationship between the pleasure of love and the pleasure of reading. The implication is that reading is almost a substitute for love, not just in the sense that reading about love might be as good as love itself, but also that there is something uniquely pleasurable about reading as a leisure activity.

The connection between the pleasure of literature and the pleasure of love is also reflected in the text of *Euphues*. On a number of occasions, love and love poetry are presented as the parallel products of wit. After his liaison with Lucilla has ended, Euphues ruefully reflects: 'I addicted my selfe wholy to the service of women to spende my lyfe in the lappes of Ladyes, my lands in maintenance of braverie, my witte in the vanities of idle Sonnets' (F3^r). Love poetry, like love itself, is one of the 'delights that Wyt followeth in his youth' (together with the third sign of wasted wit: prodigality). The text, moreover, specifically connects Euphues (wit) with a particular style of speaking and writing. On the very first page of the narrative, readers are informed that the protagonist 'gave himselfe almost to nothing, but practising of those things commonly which are incident to these sharp wits, fine phrases, smoth quipping, merry taunting, using jesting without meane, & abusing mirth without measure' (B1^r). If these attributes are the 'delights' of Euphues (the character), however, they are also the pleasures of *Euphues* (the work): literature about love, and specifically the style of *Euphues*, are a pleasure shared by the protagonist of the work and its readers.

The other way in which the story of *Euphues* represents the link between the pleasure of reading (and hearing) and the pleasure of love is in the highly sexualized exchanges between Euphues and Lucilla. The love between them has its origins in a conversation on the subject proposed as an after-dinner entertainment by Lucilla (a striking contrast to the graver dialogue between the royal servants in Burghley's room in the Preface to *The Schoolmaster*). When Euphues, overcome with passion, suddenly breaks off his speech, Lucilla confesses that his 'witte hath bewitched me, [... his] fyled speach without fraude, hath wrapped me in this misfortune' (C5^v); while on his return to her house she tells him, in conspicuously sexual terms, that 'your discourse being left unperfect, caused us all to long (as women are wont for things that like them) to have an ende thereof' (D3^{r-v}). But Lucilla is far from the passive victim of Euphues' witty talk on love (see also Katharine Wilson 2006: 59). As the last quotation demonstrates, she leads him on, as much as she is herself led on by him. Her speech balances promise and denial so carefully that Euphues is once more overwhelmed by passion:

Euphues was brought into a greate quandarie and as it were a colde shivering, to heare this newe kinde of kindenesse, such sweete meate, such sower sauce, such faire wordes, such faint promises, such hotte love, such colde desire, such certayne hope, such sodaine chaunge, and stoode lyke one that had looked on Medusaes heade, and so had bene tourned into a stone.

(D8^r)

In fact, the teasing nature of speech is woven into the very fabric of *Euphues* in the form of its antithetic style of carefully balanced clauses, once more with the result that the pleasure of the text is shared by the characters and the readers of the work alike.

The emphasis on the pleasure of reading is even more pronounced in *Euphues and his England*, the sequel to *Euphues*. Leaving out the didactic material of the first part completely, it consists of fictional narrative alone. While the story still has a moral framework, the change in form is accompanied by a much more open embrace of pleasure. Thus, Lyly prefaces the book with an address '*To the Ladies* and Gentlewoemen of England', in which he rhetorically invokes the figure of the woman reader, interested in pleasure alone, to portray his book as a 'toy' for recreation rather than a moral guide for edification (as the first part presented itself): 'I would you woulde read bookes that have more shewe of pleasure, then ground of profit, then should Euphues be as often in your hands, being but a toy, as Lawne on your heads, being but trash, the one will be scarse liked after once reading, and the other is worne out after the first washing' (Lyly 1580: ¶1^r, ¶2^r). In the corresponding address to the gentlemen readers, Lyly compares the behaviour of a reader with that of a lover, and employs the metaphor of the garden (normally used to instruct readers to shun immoral 'weeds' and pick only good 'flowers') to suggest readers take from the text whatever pleases them most:

Lovers when they come into a Gardeine, some gather Nettles, some Roses, one Tyme, an other Sage, and everye one, that, for his Ladyes favour, that shee favoureth: insomuch as there is no Weede almoste, but it is worne. If you Gentlemen, doe the lyke in reading, I shall bee sure all my discourses shall be regarded, some for the smell, some for the smart, all for a kinde of a loving smacke: Lette everye one followe his fancie, and say that is best, which he lyketh best.

(¶3^v–¶4^r)

In the text itself, characters seek to delight their audience with their wit ('your eares which I seeke to delight', 2B1^{r-v}; 'witte to delight', 2D3^r; 'witte to move delight', 2E4^r), and both characters and readers are entertained by a wealth of inset narratives. The response of the listeners to these stories within the text is striking, moreover. After Euphues has spent many pages telling Philautus an edifying story about a hermit, the latter informs him that he has been feeling seasick and has completely failed to absorb the lesson. Euphues touchily retorts that 'thou remembrest nothing y^t may doe thee good, nor forgettest any thing, which can do thee harme' (E2^r). And indeed, when Philautus is treated to a story about love by Fidus a few pages later, he is captivated (in contrast to Euphues, who promptly falls asleep): 'Philautus tyckled in everye vaine with delyght, was loath to leave so' (I1ᵛ). Moreover, Fidus' account of his life confirms not only that all young men spurn advice, but that wise counsel on love actually increases lust in young men: 'his putting love into my minde, was like the throwing of Buglosse into wine, which encreaseth in him that drinketh it a desire of lust, though it mittigate the force of drunkennesse' (H2ʳ).

The pleasures, and dangers, of Lyly's texts are connected not only with the form and content of *Euphues* and its sequel, but also with two important historical developments in England around 1580. Lyly's works mark a widening of the range of people and institutions supporting literature; first, the appearance of a different kind of patron on the literary scene. *Euphues and his England* was notoriously dedicated to the Earl of Oxford, whose servant Lyly was at the time. One of the most prominent figures at the court of Elizabeth, Oxford was known for his extravagance of dress and expenses; Lyly himself suggested to the Earl that he was the butt of Gabriel Harvey's satirical description of the Italianate Englishman in his poem 'Speculum Tuscanismi' ('Mirror of Tuscanism', 1580). As a royal ward, Oxford had been educated in the household of Burghley, who personally laid down instructions for his studies. However, in contrast to the small and tight group of serious-minded humanist counsellors portrayed in the Preface to *The Schoolmaster*, who had had a virtual monopoly on the patronage of literature during the mid-Tudor period, Oxford (and other influential noblemen, some of them also educated in Burghley's household) were evidently prepared to support a different kind of literature, focused on pleasure and display as much as on the benefit of the commonwealth.[11]

Secondly, *Euphues*, perhaps more than any other work of the period, marks the breakthrough of prose fiction, and literature more widely, in the marketplace of print. So popular was Lyly's work that it received seven editions by 1581, three years after its initial publication, and was printed another dozen times before 1640 (STC2, 17051–67). *Euphues and his England* similarly went through eight editions in the decade following its first publication, and ten more by 1640 (STC2, 17068–79, 17064–7). The success of *Euphues* and its sequel was made possible by the expansion of literacy and the development of the print trade in sixteenth-century England. The two parts of *Euphues* were particularly successful in appealing to a variety of readers, including some who were newly literate, both in their explicit addresses to different readers and tastes in the prefaces and through the range of forms, materials, and approaches they included. Above all, however, the books promoted the pleasure of reading, especially reading about love, to which the descriptive nature of the narrative gave rise. In the passage from the address to the gentlewomen in *Euphues and his England* quoted above, Lyly develops this notion by presenting his book as a pleasurable fashion commodity: a 'toy' or a headdress ('Lawne'). The comparison with fashion accessories is substantiated by the distinctive, conspicuous, and eminently imitable style and story created by Lyly in the two parts of *Euphues*, which created a vogue that was taken up by both readers and other writers.

---

[11] On Oxford, see A. Nelson (2003); a somewhat different view on his role is presented by Hunter (1962: 68–71).

The status of his works as fashionable items for sale also brought dangers, however. In the address to *Euphues* Lyly acknowledges that 'We commonly see the booke that at Christmas lyeth bound on the Stacioners stall, at Easter to be broken in the Haberdasshers shop [...] a fashion is but a dayes wearing, and a booke but an howres reading' (1578: A4^r). As items of fashion, literary works were also subject to changes in style. But if Lyly later became the 'victim of fashion' (Hunter 1962: 257)—and the style of *Euphues*, as well as its story, was increasingly depicted as outdated and irrelevant by the newly popular writers of the 1590s—his *Euphues* volumes invited and orchestrated their own fate in the marketplace of print by drawing attention to their transience. The dangers of fashionable books of pleasure, romances in particular, imagined for readers (but extending to the reputation of the author too) were much more severe, however. Such complaints concentrated in two distinct, but connected, areas. In the first place, there were concerns that the depiction of the reprehensible actions of fictional characters, in particular love, might incite readers to engage in similar activities. I have already alluded to this problem in the context of negative exemplarity; but the anxieties about this issue were aggravated by the availability of printed books to an anonymous readership, distinguished only by its ability to pay a small fee, and by the spread of literacy to new social groups, including women and members of the lower classes. This raised concerns about the ability of the authorities to control the response of readers to the text. Secondly, it was feared that a surplus of books of pleasure would crowd out more serious and deserving publications. Ascham had already warned: 'Suffer these bookes to be read, and they shall soone displace all bookes of godly learnyng' (1570b: I3^v). Both these anxieties reflected concerns about the commodification of literature in print, which perhaps for the first time offered a varied audience access to pleasure reading— a privilege previously confined to elite men. The response was to introduce new distinctions between different types of texts and readers by associating the commodity status of printed books with particular kinds of literature (notably romances such as Lyly's) and consumers (especially women and lower-class men). But again Lyly pre-empts this movement by linking the status of the book as a fashionable item for sale to the gender and, in a different passage from the one quoted above, class of its readers in the address to the gentlewomen in *Euphues and his England*, thus safely distancing the author and his elite male readers (who get their own preface) from this scene of consumption, to which they are spectators (Newcomb 2002: 45 and *passim*).

The two parts of *Euphues* opened up a range of possibilities (and problems and challenges) for literature in terms of both their form and their strategies of publication. This potential was eagerly exploited by other writers of prose fiction in the 1580s and 1590s. Many imitated the popular story of the prodigal son; more still emulated the extraordinarily popular and eminently marketable prose style; and a good number of authors replicated Lyly's strategy of advertising his second book as a sequel to *Euphues* by using its name in the title—even when the content bore little resemblance to Lyly's work: Anthony Munday's *Zelauto* [...] *Given for a Friendly Entertainment to Euphues at his Late Arrival into England* (1580); Robert Greene's

Menaphon: Camilla's Alarum to Slumbering Euphues in his Melancholy Cell at Silexedra (1589); Thomas Lodge's *Rosalind: Euphues' Golden Legacy* (1590) and *Euphues' Shadow* (1592); John Dickenson's *Arisbas: Euphues amid his Slumbers* (1594).[12] Although there was evidently plenty of scope for the development of the potential of the two parts of *Euphues*, then, Lyly himself gave up writing prose fiction following the publication of *Euphues and his England*. For him, neither the exploration of literary form and style nor the popularity conferred by the success of the works in the marketplace of print were an aim in themselves. G. K. Hunter is surely right that Lyly considered 'the end of rhetoric [to be] political power [...] The Queen could not be approached any closer by these means' (1962: 72). The Earl of Oxford became a patron of a company of players in 1580, and it seems likely that he first suggested writing court plays to Lyly. This literary form enabled Lyly to satisfy his patron and gain more direct access to queen and court, while Oxford enhanced his own reputation at the court through the dazzling creations of his client. Consequently, it was left to other writers to develop the literary modes pioneered by Lyly, and to exploit the potential of popularity in print. None, perhaps, did so with more eagerness than Robert Greene, who ruthlessly, and at least initially very successfully, exploited the commercial potential of the popularity of prose fiction in the style of Lyly, and almost single-handedly invented a new phenomenon in the literary world of Elizabethan England: the 'professional writer' who depended for his income on the printers who stood to profit from the sales of his work, rather than on any Maecenas who might offer him promotion or pecuniary reward. But if Greene's career demonstrates the opportunities and rewards offered by the new print market for literature, it also starkly reveals its dangers: Greene died destitute in 1592, a mere 34 years old.[13]

Many of the individual changes in the literary culture of Tudor England represented by *The Schoolmaster* and *Euphues* took place over what may justifiably be characterized as the *longue durée*. Print had been introduced into England a full century before the publication of Ascham and Lyly's works; and manuscript publication retained its importance well into the seventeenth century and beyond. While its patterns changed over time, patronage was similarly a significant feature of the literary culture throughout the period. Manuals of advice and educational treatises, many of them indebted to Ascham's work, continued to be published long after the Tudor period; and Lyly's *Euphues* stands in a tradition of native prose fiction going back at least to the mid-sixteenth century. However, significant changes in the literary culture of Tudor England did take place around 1580, and *The Schoolmaster* and the two parts of *Euphues* shaped and, in turn, were shaped by these changes in the material and social conditions of their production in vital ways. The particular nexus of the familiarity of manuscript, friendship, patronage, counsel, and service

[12] On the influence of the two parts of *Euphues* on the prose fiction of the 1580s and 1590s, see L. Wright (1958: 383–8); Hunter (1962: 257–97).

[13] See Newcomb (2002); Halasz (1997); Mentz (2006). Much recent scholarship has focused on the role of Greene in creating and exploiting the marketplace of print for prose fiction; in this chapter I have tried to highlight the more ambiguous part played in this process by Lyly, who in many ways anticipates Greene's innovations.

to the commonwealth presented by Ascham's work was changed beyond recognition by developments in printing, the growth of literacy, and changes in patronage. Lyly's two parts of *Euphues* capture these changes in literary culture in motion, and they account for many of the unresolved tensions in the work. His works also illustrate (and to some extent created) the convergence of pleasurable fiction and print typical of the decade following their publication. Among the most popular works from the period, *The Schoolmaster* and *Euphues* were instrumental in shaping and defining many of the developments in literature that characterized the middle years of the reign of Elizabeth.

PRIMARY WORKS

ARBER, EDWARD (ed.) (1875–94), *A Transcript of the Registers of the Company of Stationers of London, 1554–1640, A.D.*, 5 vols (London: privately printed).

ASCHAM, ROGER (1564?), First draft of *The Scholemaster*, BL, Royal MS 18.B.XXIV, fos 47^r–78^r.

—— (1570a), *A Report and Discourse of the Affaires and State of Germany*.

—— (1570b), *The Scholemaster*.

—— (1864–5), *The Whole Works of Roger Ascham*, ed. J. A. Giles, 3 vols (London: Smith).

—— (1989), *Letters of Roger Ascham*, trans. Maurice Hatch and Alvin Vos (New York: Lang).

BRINSLEY, JOHN (1622), *A Consolation for oure Grammar Schooles*.

CECIL, WILLIAM, LORD BURGHLEY, SIR WALTER RALEIGH, and FRANCIS OSBORNE (1962), *Advice to a Son: Precepts of Lord Burghley, Sir Walter Raleigh, and Francis Osborne*, ed. Louis B. Wright (Ithaca, NY: Cornell University Press).

LYLY, JOHN (1578), *Euphues: The Anatomy of Wit*.

—— (1580), *Euphues and his England*.

WILSON, THOMAS (1570), *The Three Orations of Demosthenes*.

CHAPTER 41

REVENGE AND ROMANCE

GEORGE PETTIE'S
PALACE OF PLEASURE
AND ROBERT GREENE'S
PANDOSTO

KATHARINE WILSON

GEORGE PETTIE'S 'Tereus and Progne' and Robert Greene's *Pandosto* belong at opposite ends of the generic spectrum. *Pandosto* (published in 1588) is a pastoral with a plot line reminiscent of a fairy tale: a princess cast out to sea as a baby is brought up by shepherds but is finally restored to her kingdom and marries her prince. 'Tereus and Progne', contained in the anthology *A Petite Palace of Pettie his Pleasure* (1576), is a less consoling narrative, nominally based on one of Ovid's *Metamorphoses*. The plot is bleak: when King Tereus rapes and mutilates his sister-in-law Philomela, she and her sister Progne revenge themselves by tricking the King into eating his own son (Ovid 2002: 190–9). Both stories might now seem equally marginal to the literary canon, their relevance largely defined by their usefulness to Shakespeare. *Pandosto* lives on in the back of student texts as the primary source of the late romance *The Winter's Tale* (c.1610–11). In his earlier tragedy *Titus Andronicus* (1594) Shakespeare explicitly offered up the story of Tereus and Progne as a standard of comparison. Shakespeare's raped and mutilated heroine throws a copy of Ovid's text on stage to show that she has suffered a worse fate than Philomela. If we think of these stories at all, then, it is probably as raw material transformed by the alchemy of Shakespeare.

Yet these texts are less remote than they might appear. Pettie and Greene's books, and their many reprints, testify to the extraordinary explosion of popular printed fictions which characterized the last decades of the sixteenth century. Both *Pandosto* and 'Tereus and Progne' can be described as best-selling novellas, and were as aggressively marketed as their modern counterparts. Pettie and Greene's title pages are stuffed with a range of catchy alternative descriptions. The shout lines insist that these books are both fun to read and morally improving—or, to quote the Horatian tag used by both Pettie and Greene, 'Omne tulit punctum qui miscuit utile dulci' ('He who has mixed the sweet and the useful has carried every point'). How seriously we take these claims is another matter. Greene in particular earned a reputation for the extraordinary speed with which he 'yarkt up' pamphlets (Nashe 1958: i. 287), and both he and Pettie were eager to recommend themselves to an increasingly diverse readership as fast as possible.

In particular Pettie and Greene identified themselves with a rapidly expanding section of the reading public—women. Equally, both authors knew they could not afford to alienate their core male readership. Consequently, their texts are teeming with contradictions, and we can only speculate on how they affected their readers. Greene earned his nickname 'the Homer of women' (Nashe 1958: i. 12) by creating dauntless heroines full of eloquent virtue—but he made sure they appeared to focus their attention on pleasing their often less than impressive husbands. Pettie's book contains an enthusiastic dedication addressed exclusively to gentlewomen, and the author frequently adopted the persona of a prurient agony uncle. But he leavened his praise of women's virtue with plenty of misogynistic outbursts from his male protagonists, which he openly endorsed in the last story of his collection. Both Greene and Pettie were engaged in ever more elaborate attempts to jump on every literary bandwagon, while protesting the unbiased integrity of their narratives.

Their devotion to literary fashions leaves its marks on their texts. Pettie and Greene's books are hybrids, their plots and motifs patchworks of the latest trends. Pettie claims to have derived his tale from Ovid, but it owes at least as much to the contemporary spate of imitations of the gory love triangle formed by Tereus, Progne, and Philomela (see Tempera 1998; Pincombe 1999). Greene plundered his own manuscripts and those of his contemporaries as freely as he borrowed from ancient Greek and modern Italian tales. While the resultant narratives look in many ways like modern novels, they also come under the umbrella definition of 'romance', a genre which is notoriously hard to classify. Some generalizations can be useful. Romance is characteristically 'a story already told', which usually recycles familiar plots (C. Saunders 2004: 2). The authors of romances depend on a close interaction with their readers' awareness of the tales and motifs which are being recycled. Modern readers may share some of this familiarity with their Elizabethan counterparts. The fairy tale motifs in *Pandosto* would have awakened expectations in the minds of Elizabethan readers which we might share: a baby princess who was cast out in a boat would undoubtedly be restored to her kingdom—the only question would be how Greene would achieve this end (H. Cooper 2004: 105–13). Similarly, most readers would have known one of the many versions of the story of Tereus and Progne, but could not have anticipated what interpretative slant Pettie would give to it. In other words, these are imitative romances, and the experience of reading would have centred partly on how old formulas were made new.

Yet these texts are far from passionless literary games or exercises. For both authors it is their protagonists' voices and internal dilemmas which dominate the text. Like most modern novels these stories are mixtures of action and reflection, but the relative proportions may surprise. Both texts feature startlingly rapid plot twists and generic shifts. These contrast with lengthy, florid, and often alliterative speeches in which protagonists or narrator debate different causes of action. Such passages are virtuoso performances, designed to dazzle readers with their authors' rhetorical expertise. They also serve to reinforce the ultimate isolation of the speakers. One reason these stories remain so compelling is the protagonists' relentless but usually doomed quest to read their own and others' minds, set against the mercurial operations of fortune, time, or providence. Pettie and Greene show how rhetorical argument can both paralyse speakers and lead them to reinforce their own prejudices. The energy in both their stories is derived from driving infatuation, which leads in one case to cannibalism and in the other (almost) to incest. Neither Pettie nor Greene were averse to stunning their readers with sensational denouements. Yet they tend to lay less stress on the shocking events of their tales than on the motivations which have brought them about, and the impossibility of escape from their consequences. Perhaps the more alarming idea found in both tales is that a single obsession not only ruins marriages, but corrupts families and destroys generations.

41.1 'HARD DIGESTION': PETTIE'S 'TEREUS AND PROGNE'

Few Elizabethan readers can have picked up Pettie's *Petite Palace* with no expectations. William Painter's weighty anthology *The Palace of Pleasure* (1566–7) had provided a treasury of murder, adultery, and intrigue drawn from French and Italian tales, and the spicier moments in Roman history. Most readers would probably have also been familiar with Geoffrey Fenton's gruesome translation of Matteo Bandello's narratives *Certain Tragical Discourses* (1567) (see Maslen 1997: 82–113). Both Painter and Fenton claimed to have their readers' moral education at heart by providing a range of positive and negative examples for readers to copy or avoid. But both authors found unequivocal moral judgement hard to deliver, especially where women were concerned. Take Painter's tale of Didaco and Violenta. This is a romance set in Valencia, a region which Painter drily notes was known as 'the true seate of humanity' (1890:

i. 218–39). Much of the first half of the story is taken up with Didaco's detailed and determined courtship of Violenta. When Didaco is unfaithful, Painter gives equally careful attention to Violenta's meticulous preparations to murder him, which culminate in her ripping out his eyes, heart, and tongue. However, Painter also records her defence: 'sith he [Didaco] had made her to lose her honestie, shee had sought meanes to make him to loose his life' (238). Although the general population are convinced by this reasoning, Violenta is still beheaded, and Painter leaves readers to assess the relative considerations of Violenta's loss of honesty and her cruel revenge.

One of Fenton's stories provided a yet more graphic illustration of the circumscribed nature of women's lives. The courtesan Pandora, her name ironically suitable to her 'giving' nature, gets pregnant by an unfaithful lover and embarks on elaborate attempts at self-inflicted abortion. When she eventually succeeds by jumping off a coffer, grabbing the fetus, 'she beats with all her force against the walls, painting the posts and pavements in the chamber with the blood and brains of the innocent creature newborn' (184). And while Fenton condemns her, he also considers the reasons for her actions. The story ends with disturbing ambiguity; Pandora rejoins the society of gentlewomen, her secret apparently safe. Perhaps the most important point for both writers is the degree of violence exerted by the women. Violenta displays 'excessive crueltie' (239), Pandora is 'without measure' (182); their actions reveal an unnatural ferocity which ultimately condemns them. But both Painter and Fenton leave their readers with the perhaps insoluble question as to what a woman's just response to abusive men might be.

Moving from Painter and Fenton to Pettie seems like moving from high moral seriousness to high camp. *A Petite Palace of Pettie his Pleasure* was published six years after Pettie graduated from Oxford, and the title alone hints at the 'sauciness', as Pettie puts it, which often intrudes into the collection. Painter had offered his readers a royal residence; Pettie's collection sounds more like a cosy bungalow, a Reader's Digest version of the great classic, stamped on every page with Pettie's own name and irrepressible authorial personality. Before readers even reach the stories, the playful tone which predominates in many of the narratives is suggested by an epistolary sequence in which the modest author 'G.P.' is only persuaded to publish his 'tragical trifles' at the request of his admiring friend 'R.B.' and an importunate printer.

This sequence probably does not show a glimpse of the publishing world in action. Many of Pettie's readers must have been aware that a similar series of letters had prefaced George Gascoigne's scandalous (and phenomenally popular) fiction about upper-class adultery 'A Discourse of the Adventures Passed by Master F.J.', first published in his anthology *A Hundred Sundry Flowers* in 1573 and revised in 1575. In all probability, both Gascoigne and Pettie were creating their notoriety by means of a miniature 'publication fiction'. Gascoigne had claimed his novella was a *roman-à-clef*, which appears to have been why it was heavily criticized and eventually banned by the authorities (see Clegg 1997: 103–22). Pettie too dropped heavy hints that he was writing about familiar figures 'darkly figured forth' (1938: 5)—or wished to be seen to be doing so. Whether Pettie's protagonists were too well disguised or not shocking enough, his work appears to have remained uncontroversially popular.

But Pettie does not seem to have wanted to capitalize on his early literary success, and (like Gascoigne) pursued a military career.

If Painter and Fenton contemplated the condition of women obliquely, Pettie was determined to insinuate himself into every corner of their lives. Before the stories begin, readers encounter the exuberant address to gentlewomen, in which the printer (disingenuously) establishes a hierarchy of consumers: 'I care not to displease twentie men, to please one woman' (3). Despite the tragical matter of his tales, Pettie in his own authorial persona often claims a flirtatious intimacy with his target readership. This encompasses cheerful speculation about the quality of their sex lives, requests for kisses, and boasts of his own prowess: 'the girles of our parish think that welch *Sir Richard* him selfe can not make a better preache then I can' (102). While Painter and Fenton touted the diversity of their subject matter, Pettie chose a topic designed to resonate with women readers—marriage. According to Pettie at the start of the collection, marriage represents a perfect balance between male and female, reflected in the balanced alliterative prose he used to describe it: 'in this stately state of Matrimonie, there is nothing fearefull, nothing fayned [...] so the love of the wife planted in the breast of her husband [...] one sence and one soule serveth them both' (11–12).

Yet in the twelve tales which follow, his protagonists' attempts to enact this lofty ideal are revealed as hideously compromised. Even the best intentions can have disastrous consequences. Pettie depicts not only unfaithful women (and some men), but also potentially happy marriages destroyed by combinations of excessive love: a faithful husband kills his chaste but jealous wife by accident, a loving father kills his daughter to prevent her from being raped. At the mid-point of the anthology Pettie does fulfil his self-appointed brief: 'Admetus and Alcest' is the story of how Alcest sacrificed her life for her husband. That the best wife is a dead wife is pointedly suggested by the ensuing tales. The courtships become increasingly perverse, with the women apparently to blame. In 'Minos and Pasiphae' Pasiphae discards her human lover in favour of a bull. The titles of the last two stories, 'Pygmalion's Friend and his Image' and 'Alexius', contrast sharply with the paired lovers who featured in earlier titles. Pygmalion, spurned by the woman he loves, prefers to masturbate over a statue. While Pettie dutifully condemns Pygmalion's actions, his patronage of women finally and unequivocally dissolves in the last story of the collection. The student Alexius excels at grammar—until he discovers women. But then he gets disillusioned, and his enthusiastic praise changes to misogynistic ranting, openly commended by Pettie. Because Alexius has realized what Pettie has been hinting at throughout the anthology: women refuse to decline tidily like Latin nouns, and balanced prose cannot make balanced marriages. The tale ends with Alexius on a solitary pilgrimage—and Pettie cheering from the sidelines. As so often in early modern literature, the male author writing for male readers emerges to dominate the 'woman's book'.

Yet Pettie cannot be easily dismissed as a satirical misogynist. Like Painter and Fenton, he was determined to analyse the extremes which drive human—and especially female—behaviour, and his ruminations often lead to bizarre fluctuations of tone. Look at the opening tale, in which Camma's jealous and lustful suitor Sinorix murders Camma's loving husband. Camma revenges herself by giving Sinorix poison, which she also takes herself. But Pettie cannot quite convince himself that she was contemplating a fate worse than death: 'Had not the losse of her chastitie been lesse then of her lyfe?' (37). He can only conclude,

But it is naturally incident to women to enter into extremities [...] they are either to lovinge or lothinge, to curteous or to coy [...] for as I must condemne her crueltie, so can I not but commende her constancie, & chastitie, and thinke her worthy to bee compared to *Lucrece*, *Penelope*, or what woman soever that ever had any preheminence of praise for her virtue.

(37–8)

And this is the problem—for all his apparent championship of women, Pettie finds it hard to regard the heroines of his stories as other than unnecessarily disruptive, however provoked. He can suggest a balanced viewpoint by marshalling their unruly activities into comfortingly alliterative clauses. But his almost bathetic loss of interest in compiling a canon of exemplary women for Camma to join suggests where his true sympathies lie.

Yet Camma's actions look both restrained and exemplary compared to those of her alter ego Progne, whose story follows next. The tales which make up the anthology are grouped into broadly thematic pairs, and Camma's and Progne's tales together present aspects of 'good' and 'bad' revenging wives. Or perhaps it would be as fair to say that 'Sinorix and Camma' is the warm-up act to the gore liberally splattered throughout 'Tereus and Progne'. Following Ovid, Pettie recounts how the Thracian king Tereus marries King Pandion's daughter Progne. When Tereus fetches her sister Philomela for a visit, he is overcome by lust for her. After imprisoning her, he rapes her and cuts out her tongue in order to stifle her reproaches. Philomela, however, weaves the story of her abuse into a tapestry and sends it to her sister, who rescues her under cover of celebrating the festival of Bacchus. The sisters then revenge themselves on Tereus by baking Progne and Tereus' son Itys in a pie and serving it to his unsuspecting father. When they flee from him after revealing the secret, all three are transformed into birds.

'Tereus and Progne' stands out in the anthology for many reasons. No trace of Pettie's characteristic banter remains. Instead the author often seems to be wringing his hands at the depths of human depravity he is obliged to recount, or shying away from the grisly details of his plot. He seems determined to sideline many of the most dramatic elements of the tale. The story is the only Ovidian metamorphosis in his collection, yet Pettie consigns the element of magical transformation to a casual aside. When Shakespeare used the narrative in *Titus Andronicus*, he stressed Philomela's extraordinary creativity and articulacy in the face of exceptional cruelty and enforced silence. But for Pettie, Philomela herself is almost an afterthought, and her role in the tale subordinate to the destruction of her sister's marriage and morals. Like Painter and Fenton, Pettie uses his narrative to unpack the stages of revenge through which his protagonist passes. But far more than his predecessors, he unravels her speech and thought. While Painter and Fenton attempted objectivity, Pettie gets inside Progne's head.

The harshness of Pettie's narrative contrasts vividly with the more humane myth-making of his predecessors. Chaucer's mutilation of the story was perhaps the most extreme. Relying on his readers' knowledge of the original, he included Philomela in his *Legend of Good Women* (*c*.1372–86) by the simple expedient of excising the revenge and allowing the tale to fade away with the sisters locked in a touching embrace. While Gower followed Ovid more closely in his *Confessio amantis* (*c*.1390), he justified Progne's actions by showing her appealing to divine justice to sanction her revenge. The most forthright treatment was provided by Gascoigne in *The Complaint of Phylomene* (1576). Unlike his fastidious predecessors, Gascoigne created a version which was both gory, gothic, and unequivocally biased towards the women. As far as Gascoigne was concerned, Progne's revenge was rubber-stamped by Nemesis and her offence 'not so deepe' as that of Tereus (1907: ii. 201).

Pettie initially appears less certain, especially of the greater significance of his narrative. More than Painter and Fenton, Pettie is determined to stress the universal applicability of his tales. Yet, as he begins his story, he still seems unsure how represen-tative it is: 'though it manifest not our manyfolde misery, yet shall it at least set foorth the frailty of our felicity' (42). Pettie's apparent confusion may be a smokescreen. As he elaborates on the general difficulties of mankind, he slyly inserts telling details: 'in our infancy our tender bodies are subjecte to many infirmities [...] wee are plyed sore to silence, which is of hard digestion to us' (41). Pettie invites his readers to unpack the clues to a tale in which silence, digestion, and a child's 'tender body' play such major roles. But he can never quite guarantee the link between his story and the human condition.

However, Pettie soon abandons ontological questions to focus on the creation and destruction of a marriage, a love story gone horribly wrong. Ovid's Tereus married Progne in order to secure a dynastic peace, and their wedding was accompanied by portents of doom. Pettie turns the tale into boy meets girl. When Progne initially appears to Tereus in a dream, her extraordinary beauty impels him to seek her out, and the pair subsequently enjoy five years of marriage. Only the behaviour of Progne and Philomela's father, Pandion, hints at the theme which Pettie unfolds throughout the tale: the perversion of love corrupts not only the couple involved but all their family. The seeds of destruction lurk in even the most innocent types of affection. Pandion grieves at his loss of Progne by marriage, and when he later entrusts Philomela to Tereus' safe keeping, he assures him that 'my life can not last one minute longer, then I shall heare shee doth well' (47). For Tereus, Philomela, and Progne, all the fundamental reference points are familial. Tereus promises to look after Philomela 'as if shee were his owne sister or childe' (48). As if in answer, Philomela's first accusation after Tereus has raped her is 'hast thou thus betrayed my father and sister' (48). After imprisoning Philomela, Tereus returns to Progne, claiming to be the bearer of bad news. Progne thinks immediately of her father, then of her sister. When Tereus persuades her Philomela is dead, Progne allows herself to be consoled by her husband's monstrous promise: 'I wilbe to you in steede of a father & a sister' (50). What Tereus does not know is that his determination to subsume family relationships will end in his consumption of his own son.

No question is ever raised about Tereus' guilt in the actual rape, itself represented as a bestial metamorphosis. Pettie throws up his hands in horror at the assault of the 'ravening Woulfe' Tereus on the 'seely Lambe' Philomela (48). But as he hurries over Tereus' crimes, one metamorphosis generates a worse example: the conversion of Progne into a 'tirannous Tiger' (54) whose crimes surpass those of her husband. The shift of focus is marked by a minor incident (not in any of Pettie's sources) which confirms Pettie's devotion to both romance and male sensibilities. Imprisoned in her grange, Philomela looks out of the window hoping to find some way of sending her tapestry to Progne. Luckily she spots 'a gentleman whom she thought would not sticke to put him selfe in some perill to redresse a Ladies wronge' (50). He duly carries out the task, and his chivalrous act would appear to represent Pettie's hope for the male population.

By contrast Progne is as completely consumed by vengeance as Tereus was by lust. Pettie never lets his readers imagine that she is moved by righteous anger on her sister's behalf. Barely stopping to reflect on Philomela's extraordinary suffering, Progne places herself firmly in a tradition of abandoned women. Tereus' actions have turned her into another Dido, Medea, or Ariadne, deserted by unfaithful menfolk. What upsets Progne most is not just Tereus' infidelity, but his choice of her sister, and this is what motivates her to regard herself as an instrument of divine vengeance. Yet Progne's brief appeal to the deities sounds almost random, a last-minute justification of her plan: 'Or why may not the gods use mee as an instrument to execute their vengeance on him?' (52). By now Pettie has no qualms about scripting his readers' reactions: 'I think your selves wil say that her fury exceeded his folly' (53). Alliteration smoothes the metamorphosis of Tereus' crime into apparently excusable 'folly', in comparison to his wife's mad rage.

So upset is Pettie that he finds himself as piously (if temporarily) silenced as Philomela, proclaiming, 'My tounge is not able to tell' (53) the crime Progne is about to commit. Fortunately he manages to conquer his reticence sufficiently to create a denouement as mawkishly heart-wrenching as it is horrific. The infant Itys toddles onto the scene, baffled by his mother, Progne's, rage: 'why do you beate me mam, I have learned my Criscrosse today so I have, and my father sayth hee will buie mee a golden coate, and then you shannot kisse mee so you shannot' (54). When Progne has beheaded, quartered, and served her son to Tereus, Philomela emerges from behind an arras and flings Itys' head in his father's face. As Tereus pursues the fleeing women, Pettie acknowledges his source for the first time: 'as *Ovid* reporteth' (55), all three are turned into birds. For Ovid the transformation was an act of mercy in the course of which the women escaped and Philomela was given the voice of a nightingale. But Pettie is remorseless; for him the change shows that all three protagonists 'were not worthy humaine shape or the use of reason' (55).

Pettie tries to tidy up the situation with alliteration, and makes a half-hearted attempt at even-handedness: 'It were hard here gentlewomen for you to give sentence, who more offended of the husband or the wife [...] in him sutch falsenesse, in her sutch furiousnesse [...] that I thinke them both worthy to bee condemned to the most botomles pit in Hell' (55). But the glancing acknowledgement of Tereus' 'beastly cruelty' pales in comparison with that of his murderous wife. For Pettie, Progne is primarily a desperate housewife who turns herself into a revenger in the classical tradition. As her fury exceeds its cause, she destroys both her marriage and the humanity of her husband, her sister and herself. Many commentators on the legend would have concurred in seeing Progne's crime as that of overreaction. After all, she herself suffered no direct injury, and could have kept her marriage and status intact (Tempera 1998: 72). Yet Pettie also allows Progne's version of events to speak for itself. In Progne's eyes Tereus has effectively committed incest with her sister and therefore destroyed her, her family, and her marriage. Her action in serving him his own flesh forms as vivid a tableau of his crime as Philomela's tapestry, and the final transformation into birds is only a commentary on the changes effected by lust. Progne usurps Tereus' role as an instrument of violence and Philomela's role as visual communicator. Her dominance of the tale makes Pettie's appalled moralizing appear prudish by comparison.

'Tereus and Progne' is both domestic tragedy and miniature apocalypse, a touchstone for the other stories in the collection. As her devotion to vengeance becomes all-consuming, Progne comes to symbolize the type of female 'extremity' which Pettie was determined to condemn. And by placing a mythic prototype second in his anthology, Pettie allowed its aftershock to resonate through the less bloody transgressions of the women of the later narratives. The effect is cumulative; as the female sex is revealed as faithless, lustful, or (like Pasiphae) bestial, Pygmalion's onanistic idolatry looks excusable and Alexius' misogyny ideal. For all Pettie's proclaimed devotion to women, his attempts to enter their heads assures him (and his male readers) that solitude and theology are altogether safer options.

41.2 'KINGES LUSTES ARE LAWES': GREENE'S *PANDOSTO*

After 'Tereus and Progne', Greene's writing seems to present a more humane world. When Greene published a novella about a woman called Philomela, it had no direct relationship to the Ovidian story, although he must have known his readers would be mentally comparing the two. The emphasis in Greene's *Philomela* (published in 1592) seems designed to present an alternative to female vengeance. Although Philomela is wrongly accused of adultery, her patience and virtue ensure that she eventually achieves contentment—after the death of her abusive husband. The text has much in common with *Pandosto*, which appears similarly restorative in import: shepherdesses are revealed as princesses, fathers and daughters reunited, and the ruling dynasty handed over to the younger generation. Yet, like Pettie's tale, *Pandosto* is charged with the violent consequences of excess, or to use one of Greene's favourite words, 'overloving', in courtships, marriages, and families, and the happy ending of his story contains its own cataclysm.

Greene was Pettie's heir in so many ways, not least because he was one of the primary authors whose works Greene ruthlessly plagiarized (Vincent 1939). Pettie had ensured that his identity was indissolubly woven into the title of his work. His successor imprinted his own name on many of his titles (such as *Greene's Groatsworth of Wit* or *Greene's Farewell to Folly*) and marketed 'Robert Greene' as a recognizable brand name which invoked its own set of readerly expectations. The missing link between Pettie and Greene is provided by John Lyly. In his best-selling *Euphues* books (1578 and 1580) Lyly developed Pettie's alliterative style into 'euphuism' while (in the first book) imitating the plot of 'Alexius'. Greene in turn responded by imitating Lyly's style but reversing his plot in favour of women in his first novel, *Mamillia* (1583). His popular success led him to dominate the literary marketplace throughout the rest of the decade, first with prose and dramatic romances and finally with supposedly autobiographical tales of dissipation and repentance, some of which were probably composed by Greene's imitators. The death of the historical author barely dented the productivity of 'Robert Greene', and dispatches from the underworld kept his name alive well into the next century (see Figure 41.1).

Both his contemporaries and his successors seem to have regarded *Pandosto* as their favourite work by Greene. For his earliest readers, its popularity may have lain in part in its topicality. While many romances featured women falsely accused of adultery, the story of a queen condemned and her daughter saved from exile might have stirred memories of Anne Boleyn's fall from grace and Elizabeth's rise to power (H. Cooper 2004: 274–80, 396–7). More remarkable is the astonishing afterlife the text enjoyed in subsequent centuries; this was a tale which could be rewritten for every genre and royal dynasty (Newcomb 2002). Its genesis remains a mystery. Published at the height of Greene's career in 1588, it may have been drafted years earlier; the Stationers' Register records a 'Triumphe of Time' (the subtitle of *Pandosto*) in 1585 (Newcomb 2002: 55–9).

Pandosto belongs to a group of pastorals circulating in the mid-1580s, and the links between their authors are still mysterious. It shares features with Thomas Lodge's (printed) novels, and more provocatively, with Sir Philip Sidney's manuscript romance known as *The Old Arcadia*, probably composed in the late 1570s. What we can say for certain is that Greene, Lodge, and Sidney were all familiar with recently translated ancient Greek romances like Longus' *Daphnis and Chloe*, which Greene draws on in *Pandosto* (Wolff 1912). Such narratives inspired Greene to inject the moralizing alliterative fictional world which he had inherited from Pettie and Lyly with tragicomic plots in which separated young lovers escape repressive elders, and endure trials and capricious fortune before being joyously reunited. Whether Greene can have seen Sidney's Arcadian interpretation of Greek romance can only be a subject for speculation (see Newcomb 2002: 62–6; Woudhuysen 1996: 264, 300–3, 328–31; Katharine Wilson 2006: 112–17). But the internal evidence is suggestive. Both Greene and Sidney created plots in which at least one prince disguised as a shepherd courts and eventually marries an exiled princess cared for by rustics in the countryside. And

60 GREENE IN CONCEIPT.

New raised from his graue to write
the Tragique Historie of faire
Valeria of London.

WHEREIN IS TRVLY DISCOVERED
the rare and lamentable issue of a Husbands do-
tage, a wiues leudnesse, & childrens disobedience.

Received and reported by I. D.

Veritas non quærit angulos, umbra gaudet.

Printed at London by RICHARD BRADOCKE for
William Iones, dwelling at the signe of the Gunne
neare Holborne conduit. 1598.

Fig. 41.1 The ghost of Robert Greene depicted writing, wrapped in his burial shroud.
John Dickenson, *Greene in Conceipt* (1598), title page, A1ʳ.

both plots are triggered by the credulity of a lecherous ruler—although Sidney is more merciful to foolish Duke Basilius than Greene is to incestuous King Pandosto.

If Greene had even a vague knowledge of the *Arcadia*, there are hints of a more provocative social dimension to *Pandosto*. Greene was himself an anomalous social figure, an Oxford graduate from a humble background making his living by the new and often derided medium of print. His romance is equally hard to place: a 'popular' fiction which would have found the majority of its readers among Greene's moneyed social superiors (Newcomb 2002: 21–6). While Greene's desire to become an established author made him a fundamentally conservative figure, *Pandosto* is distinctive among Greene's works for the attention he gives to the lower ranks of society. Pettie invited his readers into the claustrophobic world of a dysfunctional royal family. Sidney showed aristocrats effortlessly outsmarting foolish servants. Greene by contrast was always alerting his readers to the impact of lusty and unpredictable aristocrats on their powerless underlings. In Greene's world princes make lousy shepherds, and country people praise rural poverty while eagerly aspiring to riches. Rustic virtue is also materially rewarded. In *Pandosto*, a cupbearer is offered a dukedom and a shepherd a knighthood. Greene's examples of upward mobility are sufficiently incongruous as to be unthreatening to the social order, yet they also suggest some sympathy with the servants and shepherds struggling for a better lot.

Greene's own aspirations towards status are signalled from the start of the book. As the title page proclaims, it is the creation of a university graduate: 'Robert Greene, Master of Arts in Cambridge'. Although the dedication and address to the gentlemen readers are larded with modesty topoi, Greene chose as his intended patron a prominent aristocrat—George Clifford, Earl of Cumberland. Greene's erudition is reinforced by the fact that his name is stamped between two Latin mottoes. Greene uses his usual tag 'Omne tulit punctum' but also 'Temporis filia veritas' ('Truth is the daughter of time'). The latter text is echoed in the subtitle 'The Triumph of Time', and the gloss, 'that although by the meanes of sinister fortune, Truth may be concealed yet by Time in spight of fortune it is most manifestly revealed'. This is a book equipped with not just multiple but competing controlling powers: Fortune, the deity most common to Greek romance, is quashed by the more elemental power of Time. The battle for dominance of the text is in turn taken up by the human protagonists. The running title of the text is 'The History of Dorastus and Fawnia', the latter being the two young lovers who defeat the eponymous king Pandosto.

Like Pettie, Greene shows how one man's obsession ruins all around him. Like Tereus, Pandosto suffers a vengeance unwittingly delivered by the next generation, and loses his young son in the course of the text. But Pandosto also has a daughter, Fawnia, who (like Progne and Philomela) refuses to be a casualty of male lust and violence. Fawnia admittedly is saved from danger by a variety of lucky chances as much as by her own virtuous resistance. As in Greek romance, the action in the book is supposedly organized by the unpredictable turns of Fortune's wheel, and Greene frequently nudges his readers towards recognizing the 'tragic' and 'comic' elements of which it is composed. But if the text ends in comedy, it is shot through with loss and tragedy to the last page. The reason is one emotion which is alien to Pettie's tale—guilt. Pettie's bloodied protagonists were changed into birds because of their lack of humanity; in Greene's world it is the knowledge of transgression which is finally overpowering.

The internal landscapes of the protagonists' minds dominate the first half of the plot. Like Pettie, Greene tells a story of the disintegration of married love and its appalling ramifications. King Pandosto becomes wrongly convinced that his faithful wife, Bellaria, has fallen in love with his best friend, Egistus. He is increasingly tormented by the clichés which are his (and Greene's) stock-in-trade: 'thinking that Love was above all Lawes and therefore to be staied with no Law, that it was hard to put fire and flaxe together without burning' (1881–6: iv. 238). The alliterative balance of the prose is a mark of Greene's inheritance from Pettie and Lyly, but the lack of outlandish comparisons characteristic of euphuism are indicative of his later simpler prose.

Greene's literary maturity is further suggested by his breadth of outlook and awareness of an ever more socially diverse readership. Confiding in his cupbearer Franion, Pandosto tries to persuade him to poison Egistus. Franion is well aware of the constraints of his position: 'Kings are knowne to command, servants are blameless to consent' (242). But, unlike his master, he remains capable of exercising moral choice: 'prefer thy content before riches, and a cleare minde before dignity; so being poore thou shalt have rich peace, or else rich, thou shalt enjoy disquiet' (242). Warned by Franion, Egistus flees with him, incentivizing him with promises of a dukedom. Meanwhile, it is Bellaria (who never enters into Egistus' calculations) who is imprisoned by Pandosto, and infuriates him further by giving birth to what her husband believes is Egistus' daughter. Greene shows men locked in their own thoughts but capable of action; the casualty is the woman at the heart of the negotiations. However, like the other aristocrats in the tale, the jailed Bellaria has little idea that her social inferiors can suffer too. Unwittingly echoing Franion, she imagines a life of poverty and simplicity: 'Ah happy life, where poore thoughts and meane desire live in secure content, not fearing Fortune because too low for Fortune' (249).

Yet like many of the women of Greene's romances, Bellaria counters her necessary passivity with active strategy. Unable to stop her daughter from being exposed in a boat, she vindicates herself by applying to the Delphic oracle, and receives an unequivocal endorsement of her and Egistus' innocence. Unlike his Shakespearean counterpart Leontes, Pandosto believes the oracle, and husband and wife are on the point of reconciliation. But in a conflict of emotion typical of Greene, news is brought of the death of Pandosto and Bellaria's young son Garinter. Bellaria falls down dead, while the repentant Pandosto is left to entomb his wife and son.

The burial of Bellaria and Garinter marks the end of the first half of the narrative, as Greene exchanges the claustrophobic court of Bohemia for the pastures of Sicilia. Yet the tumultuous events at court are constantly reasserting themselves. Greene had already left clear signs of unfinished business: the response from the Delphic oracle had ended with 'and the King shall live without an heire: if that which is lost be not found' (258). Accordingly, the princess exposed in a boat is rescued by the shepherd Porrus, who is 'so poore, as a sheepe was halfe his substaunce' (258). Fawnia by contrast is bedecked with royal jewels, an unmistakable indicator of her romance heritage. Porrus (like Franion) is obliged to struggle with conscience and self-interest, and also reaches the sort of moral compromise which eludes the nobles in this text—he decides to keep the riches but take the child home and raise her himself. However, the appearance of unexpected daughters causes problems, and Greene takes the opportunity to insert a wry parody of his earlier plot. For the second time in her life the baby arouses a jealous rage, not from Pandosto this time but from Porrus' wife, Mopsa. When Porrus appears with the child she 'beg[ins] to be somewhat jelousse, yet marveiling that her husband should be so wanton abroad, sith he was so quiet at home' (267). Porrus only escapes a beating when he presents Mopsa with the purse of gold accompanying the child, and Greene delivers a characteristically economically focused version of the foundling myth. As the girl the shepherds call Fawnia grows up, Porrus buys a farm and sheep and starts acquiring land. By the time she reaches 16, the fame of her beauty and modesty have spread to court, and Greene (or perhaps Porrus) notes that she is courted by rich farmers' sons.

Greene's comic cameo of the home life of Porrus and Mopsa invites comparison with the turbulent marriage of Pandosto and Bellaria. It also highlights the central stratagem of the second half of the text—the repetition of scenes with substituted participants. Most of the latter part of the tale is concerned with the courtship of Fawnia, first by Egistus' son Dorastus and then by her father, Pandosto. The relative values of the suitors are called into question by Greene's juxtaposition of the two. Dorastus is fleeing from an arranged marriage when a chance meeting with Fawnia leaves him astonished by his attraction for such a 'country slut' (276). Unwittingly echoing Pandosto's earlier belief, he concludes that love is above the law. Furthermore, he reassures himself by citing an Ovidian metamorphosis: after all, he reasons, Jupiter loved the maid Io (Ovid 2002: 51–8). What he does not say is that Jupiter raped Io, although the idea is not far from his mind. His parting shot to Fawnia is 'Why Fawnia, perhappes I love thee, and then thou must needes yielde, for thou knowest I can commaund and constraine.' Fawnia, however, is having none of it, and responds that 'constrained love is force, not love: and know this sir, mine honesty is such, as I had rather die than be a concubine, even to a king' (284). Both reflect on their love in parallel monologues, but it is only when Dorastus dresses up as a shepherd that Fawnia agrees to allow him to court her. However, as she pithily remarks, 'shepheards are not called shepheardes because they weare hookes and bagges, but that they are borne poore, and live to keep sheepe' (289). In fact, Dorastus' disguise turns out to be so transparent that the neighbours see through it and warn Porrus that a prince has designs on his daughter's honour. By this stage Fawnia has committed herself to loving Dorastus, although she too takes a pragmatic view of the situation. Despite having earlier amazed Dorastus with a witty encomium on the simplicities of country life, she is also 'hoping in time to be advanced from the daughter of a poore farmer to be the wife of a riche King' (291–2).

Dorastus' apparently playful suggestion of rape is never repeated—by him. But Porrus' opinion that 'Kinges lustes are lawes' (293) overshadows the remainder of the plot, as the young lovers find themselves having to thwart the machinations of two very different fathers. Fearing exposure by her foster-father, Dorastus and Fawnia enlist the help of a sea captain and flee to Bohemia, with the captured Porrus in tow. Once there, Fawnia's reputation as a beauty spreads again, and Pandosto, now a lusty fifty-something, has the pair arrested as spies in order to bring them to court. Like Dorastus, he is smitten but anxious, as he reflects when alone, 'Dooth *Pandosto* then love: Yea: whome: A maid unknowne, yea, and perhapps immodest' (306). Fawnia's response to his advances also recalls her earlier encounters with Dorastus. While Pandosto reminds her that 'my power is such as I may compell by force', she insists, 'the body is subject to victories, but the minde not to be subdued by conquest [...] know this, that I will alwaies rather choose death then dishonour' (310–11).

Greene's presentation of the unknowingly incestuous father's designs on his daughter is in many ways understated. At the same time Greene the dramatist calls his readers' attention in particular to the second encounter between Pandosto and Fawnia. This is set out in dialogue, as if in a play, with Pandosto 'using these familiar speeches' (284). In fact, Pandosto, Dorastus, and Fawnia all use speeches which would have been familiar to readers or audiences of Lyly's first play, *Campaspe*, in which Alexander the Great contemplates raping his captive Campaspe, but eventually resigns his claim on her (Moore Smith 1907). But in Lyly's play there is no direct confrontation between Alexander and Campaspe. Greene cobbles together lines from *Campaspe* to invent a new scene, which serves as a template for both Fawnia's would-be lovers. Pandosto and Dorastus speak the same language; love and violence share the same vocabulary.

What Greene does not do is to turn the text into a tragedy of incest. It is entirely characteristic of his technique that he pulls back from the horrific conclusion at the last moment, only to replace it with a breakneck series of reverses of plot and emotion. Fawnia's honour is saved because Pandosto's spurned love turns to hate. He resolves to execute her, Dorastus, Porrus, and the sea captain, having first tortured and blinded the latter. Only when Porrus reveals the secret of Fawnia's birth does Pandosto understand his own moral blindness. The next metamorphosis of emotion he suffers is equally rapid. As he fervently embraces his bemused daughter, Greene notes wryly, '*Fawnia* was not more joyfull that she had found such a Father, then *Dorastus* was glad he should get such a wife' (316). Pandosto is seemingly reconciled with all, including Egistus; the 'most comical event' of Dorastus and Fawnia's marriage is celebrated; and even Porrus is knighted. But Greene has more tricks up his sleeve, and several new plot lines in his last sentence. The wedding

was no sooner ended, but *Pandosto* (calling to mind how first he betraied his friend *Egistus*, how his jealousie was the cause of *Bellarias* death, that contrarie to the law of nature hee had lusted after his owne Daughter) moved with these desperate thoughts, he fell into a melancholie fit, and, to close up the Comedie with a Tragicall stratageme, hee slewe himselfe; whose death being many daies bewailed of *Fawnia*, *Dorastus*, and his dear friend *Egistus*, *Dorastus*, taking his leave of his father, went with his wife and the dead corpse into *Bohemia*, where, after they were sumptuouslie intoombed, *Dorastus* ended his daies in contented quiet. (317)

A wedding followed by a funeral; comedy followed by tragedy—followed by comedy? Greene's reading of Greek romances led him to heap sensational conclusions on top of each other, but the final state of affairs remains ambiguous. Dorastus achieves 'contented quiet', but only apparently after 'they' (logically his wife and father-in-law) are safely below ground. Greene may be guilty of a grammatical error, but the joint burial is eerily reminiscent of Pandosto's dispatch of Bellaria and Garinter at the end of the first half of the narrative. Greene often ended romances (like *Philomela*) with a lone figure. While appearing to endorse a conventional conclusion in which the young lovers triumph, Greene simultaneously suggests the possibility that, like Pettie's Alexius, or Lyly's Euphues, Dorastus somehow rids himself of women and lives in solitary bliss. Fawnia—who never comments on her father's actions—is thus as effectively silenced as her mother before her.

Romance (and the alliterative prose in which it is written) often depends on doubling and reduplication, and repeated plot devices suggest repeated emotions. Both Pettie and Greene organize their romances—and revenges—around displacement and the breaking of taboo. Greene's imaginative geography in *Pandosto* allows the tides flowing around Bohemia and Sicilia to provide a metaphor for the way in which one protagonist unwittingly enacts the role of another. But this repetition does not bring comfort. Both Pettie and Greene decline to follow a trajectory in which sin is followed by forgiveness or atonement. Thus, one of the commonest features of romance—the appearance of the disguised relative—serves a damning rather than a restorative function, whether the instrument of vengeance turns up as shepherdess or shepherd's pie. Tereus' incestuous violence to his sister-in-law leads him to ingest his son. Pandosto's abuse of his wife is replaced by his incestuous violence towards his daughter. In both Pettie and Greene's narratives the languages of obsession, violence, and love are almost impossible to separate. The powers of fortune and providence are subordinate to the human motivations which drive the narrative.

Both authors are unremitting in their punishment for human evil. Pettie manipulates his narrative so that Progne emerges as more unnatural than her husband, and her violence looks forward to that of a Lady Macbeth. Pettie refuses the comfort Ovid built into his narrative—the creation of Philomela the singing nightingale—in favour of delivering an awful warning to his readers of the horrors incident to marriage. Greene appears to deliver a comic ending in which the romance pattern of exile, reintegration, and return is fulfilled. But while Dorastus and Fawnia return to court, Pandosto's repentance is not enough to allow him to join them. Unlike Pettie, Greene gives his villain a conscience, but shows his inability to master his emotions. Greene is notably severer than Shakespeare in this regard. Pandosto is in some ways closer to Lear than to his counterpart in *The Winter's Tale*, Leontes, who regains his family at the end of the play. If his last works are to be believed, Greene himself spent his final years constantly repenting and reoffending. He allows no such latitude to Pandosto, who put himself beyond the pale by lusting after his daughter; like Progne he exceeded normal moral boundaries. His attempts to seize generic control of the plot are also thwarted. The battle between old Pandosto and young Dorastus and Fawnia begun in the alternative titles of the text reaches its apogee when Pandosto commits suicide. Even this 'Tragicall stratageme' is swiftly displaced by the ongoing comic narrative of Dorastus and Fawnia. Yet the hint Greene gives of Dorastus' similarity to Pandosto leaves open the possibility that the cyclical nature of romance is more sinister than it might first appear. And perhaps it is this multiplicity so characteristic of Renaissance romance that links Pettie and Greene most significantly. In Pettie's tale the Ovidian story is pushed to one side in favour of a series of mini-metamorphoses, the transformations of Tereus and Progne's mental states. *Pandosto* is stuffed with colliding narratives, and the conclusion lies somewhere beyond the compendious last sentence. If romance is a story already told, for Greene it is also a story which never quite ends.

Primary Works

FENTON, GEOFFREY (trans.) (1924), *Bandello: Tragical Tales. The Complete Novels*, ed. Hugh Harris (London: Routledge).

GASCOIGNE, GEORGE (1907), *The Complete Works of George Gascoigne*, ed. J. W. Cunliffe, 2 vols (Cambridge: Cambridge University Press).

GREENE, ROBERT (1881–6), *The Life and Complete Works in Prose and Verse of Robert Greene M.A. in Prose and Verse*, ed. A. B. Grosart, 15 vols (London: Huth Library).

NASHE, THOMAS (1958), *The Works of Thomas Nashe*, ed. R. B. McKerrow, rev. F. P. Wilson, 5 vols (Oxford: Blackwell).

OVID (2002), *Ovid's Metamorphoses*, trans. Arthur Golding, ed. Madeleine Forey (London: Penguin).

PAINTER, WILLIAM (1890), *The Palace of Pleasure*, ed. J. Jacobs, 3 vols (London: David Nutt).

PETTIE, GEORGE (1938), *A Petite Pallace of Pettie his Pleasure*, ed. H. Hartman (London: Oxford University Press).

CHAPTER 42

CHRISTOPHER MARLOWE'S *DOCTOR FAUSTUS* AND NATHANIEL WOODES'S *THE CONFLICT OF CONSCIENCE*

DAVID BEVINGTON

DID Christopher Marlowe know Nathaniel Woodes's *The Conflict of Conscience*, and did he have in mind the double ending of that play when he chose to dramatize the story of Doctor Faustus? Woodes's play was published in 1581 as 'An excellent new Commedie' in two states. The first ends with an announcement by the Nuntius that the protagonist, Philologus, has hanged himself in desperation; in the second state, we learn from the Nuntius that Philologus, 'that would have hanged himself with cord', 'Is now converted unto God' with many penitential tears.[1] By demonstrating how the conventional last-minute salvation of the mankind figure of

---

[1] Spelling and punctuation have here been modernized in the many instances where old spelling is not germane to the point being made, especially since Marlowe is also quoted in this present essay in modern spelling.

the morality play could be taken either way, Woodes seems to offer an alternative reading of salvation history with particular relevance to Calvinist theology. His play is also meaningfully poised between the generic portraiture of the morality play and the particularity of the life of the real-life Italian suicide Francesco Spera, who had converted to the reformed religion in Italy but then had recanted under the intense pressure of the Inquisition, in a way that Marlowe might well have found applicable to his dramatization of the life of John Faustus. The Faust figure was of course extensively mythologized in the German *Faustbuch* and its English translation, perhaps not published until 1592, but the name was still a proper name with some sort of claim to historicity (see Deats 1976; Jackson 1971; Kocher 1943; but cf. J. Jones 1994: 52–71).

Nathaniel Woodes, identified on the title page of *The Conflict of Conscience* as 'Minister in Norwich', plainly shows the influence of Calvinist thought, as indeed is true of so many of Woodes's calling in the 1570s and 1580s. Marlowe went up to Cambridge during these same years, where the teaching of Calvinist doctrine was in full sway. The idea of Marlowe's having known Woodes's play is quite plausible, then, even if it cannot be proven. Whether or not the influence is direct, Woodes's play does at least demonstrate the potential of the morality play for divergent endings in a way that Marlowe exploits to brilliant effect in *Doctor Faustus*.

One remarkable thing about the dual ending of *The Conflict of Conscience* is the verbal economy with which the transformation occurs. The revised materials consists solely of a substituted title page, the Prologue, and the last page of the text. The title page of the second state, though reset, is essentially identical in wording to the first state except that 'the desperation of Francis Spera' is changed to 'the doleful desperation of a miserable worldling, termed by the name of Philologus'. In other words, the biographical name is changed into the generic. A similar alteration is found in the second state of the Prologue, much of which retains the original word-ing, until 'An history of late years done' is changed to 'A strange example done of late'. 'Francis Spera's history' is changed to 'a history strange and true'. 'But Spera's name, for causes just, our author doth omit' becomes 'And here our author thought it meet the true name to omit'. Similarly, to defend the principle that a 'comedy' should not concern itself with 'the vices of one private man', the wording of the Prologue in state one explaining that 'For if that Spera had been one, we would straight deem in mind | That all by Spera spoken were; ourselves we would not find' is changed in state two to 'For if this worldling had been named, we would straight deem in mind | That all by him then spoken were; ourselves we would not find.'

Obviously the change from unhappy to happy ending also requires some further alteration of the Prologue. 'He is clean overthrown' becomes 'was almost overthrown'. 'So that he had no power at all in heart firm faith to have, | Being urged to pray until the Lord, His mercies for to crave' is changed to 'So that he had no power at all in heart firm faith to have | Till at the last God changed his mind His mercies for to crave'. One four-line passage captures the essence of this profound shift from damnation to salvation. The first state reads as follows:

> Then, wretch accurst, no power hath repentance to begin;
> Far happier if that unborn and lifeless he had been,
> As in discourse before your eyes shall plainly provèd be,
> If that with patience you abide, the end thereof to see.
>
> (lines 60–3)

State two offers these lines instead:

> Then, wretch accurst, small power hath repentance to begin;
> This history here example shows of one fast wrapped therein,
> As in discourse before your eyes shall plainly provèd be,
> Yet at the last God him restored, even of His mercy free.
>
> (lines 60–3)

Otherwise, the changes are minor, and even in the passages quoted here most of the original wording is retained. We can imagine the author crossing out a few key phrases on the printed sheets and writing in the needed alterations. Perhaps one other change, from 'But while the treatise we do play, I pray you with us bear' to 'And therefore humbly doth you pray to give attentive ear', moves the emphasis away from performance to reading; even the phrase 'As in discourse before your eyes', found in both states, ambiguously posits either dramatic performance or reading. In general, the author seems hopeful that he will have an attentive audience, whether in a performance space or in the library.

The final speech of the Nuntius, labelled as 'Act six, scene last' in both states, and thus appended to what is otherwise marked as a five-act play, proceeds in the same manner of offering minimal if crucial alterations. 'Oh, doleful news' becomes 'Oh, joyful news' (both states, line 2411). What a change was there! The rhyme scheme and stanzaic pattern (rhyme royal) is retained, with most of the actual rhyming words still in place. The account of the protagonist's refusing sustenance for thirty weeks remains essentially the same, even when he is tied by the hands and force-fed. Yet what in state one is portrayed as a desperately successful suicide gives way in state two to a divine miracle: 'And his own hand, now at the last, hath wrought his endless pain' becomes 'And now the Lord, in mercy great, hath eased him of his pain'. A man who 'by deep despair hath hanged himself with cord' is 'now converted unto God, with many bitter tears' (both states, lines 2423–4). Philologus, having learned to 'profess the faith of Christ', is now 'constant to the end'.

Woodes offers his play for acting, in a scheme (identical on the two title pages) for six actors (Bevington 1962: 57–8, 245–51). The doubling of roles is functional even if inept (one actor is left idle for most of the play), and follows a model of earlier offered-for-acting schemes in such plays from the 1560s and 1570s as *Cambises, Enough Is as Good as a Feast, Horestes, Impatient Poverty, The Life and Repentance of Mary Magdalene, Like Will to Like, The Longer Thou Livest the More Fool Thou Art, Lusty Juventus, The Marriage of Wit and Wisdom, Misogonus, New Custom, Trial of Treasure, Virtuous and Godly Susanna,* and *Wealth and Health.* (Bale's *King John* offers a similar plan in effect by stage directions ordering the characters to shift at various points into their alter egos.) The list for *The Conflict of Conscience* follows the norm by assigning one actor to the protagonist, Philologus, and one to the Vice, Hypocrisy, with only a minor doubling as Theologus (who appears only in Act 5, after Hypocrisy has disappeared from the scene). The other four actors distribute the remaining roles among themselves, with four or five apiece for three actors and two roles (the Cardinal and Caconos) for the sixth actor.

A lack of dramaturgical skill or experience on the part of the author manifests itself at several points. The phrasing on both title pages sounds a bit wistful in its hope that the play might be acted: 'The actors' names divided into six parts, most convenient for such as be disposed either to show this comedy in private houses or otherwise.' The venue is left meaningfully vague, in a locution found nowhere else in offered-for-acting lists. *The Conflict of Conscience* is from a later date than most offered-for-acting plays, and may be derivative and amateur in its effort to write a play of this sort.

In the 1560s, 1570s, and 1580s professional companies demonstrated that the morality play genre could be readily adapted to the propagandistic purposes of the Reformation. Leicester's Men and the Queen's Men in particular seem to have been formed with such a purpose in mind. Leicester's Men may have included in their itinerant repertory *The Longer Thou Livest the More Fool Thou Art* and *Enough Is as Good as a Feast*, both by William Wager. If so, these plays were acted by a troupe that enjoyed powerful connections at court. Wager seems to have been a grammar school governor who had lectured at the hospital of St Mary Woolnoth and may have come in contact with that foundation's singing children (P. White 1993; Craik 1958; Eccles 1981). We can perhaps catch a glimpse of how such a reforming clergyman could have written polemical plays for public performance on tour in the interests of furthering the Reformation.

The Conflict of Conscience, on the other hand, presents no evidence of powerful court connections or indeed of having been performed by any professional acting troupe. It is as though Woodes, a parochial minister in Norwich, modelled *The Conflict of Conscience* on plays he was able to read in print, with casting lists showing how the doubling was to be done if an acting troupe should perhaps be encouraged to adopt it for performance. Signs of amateurism are not hard to find. The doubling of Cardinal and Caconos (a foolish Scots papist who speaks in broad Scots brogue) for one actor inefficiently assigns two roles that are in close proximity and turn up nowhere else in the play: Caconos, in Act 3, scene 4, exits near the end of that scene with a scant seven lines of dialogue before the Cardinal must enter, for his only scene, at the beginning of Act 4, scene 1. The Vice figures, Avarice, Hypocrisy, and Tyranny, attempt to sing at one point, but beg off for lack of a treble (lines 760–3)—an omission that would seem to suggest lack of professional competence even while it acknowledges that Vice scenes of this sort regularly end in song in earlier morality plays. The text of *The Conflict of Conscience* contains a number of marginal notations, some of which read as stage directions ('Step aside', line 354; 'Push Avarice backward', line 358; both seemingly intended for Hypocrisy), but others of which read more like glosses supplied by the clerical author: 'HYPOCRISY:

Fig. 42.1 A Tudor conception of the pains of hell. Faustus is dragged to hell at the end of the play. J.D., *The Most Wonderfull and True Storie* (1597), title page, A1ʳ.

a popish policy' (lines 396–7); 'Utilitas facit esse Deos' ('Usefulness makes us gods', lines 412–13); 'Hypocrisy: Antichristian charity' (lines 400–1); 'Hypocrisy. This is sharp arguments [*sic*]' (lines 426–7); 'Hypocrisy: friendship for gain' (lines 684–5), and so on.[2] Practical stage directions are sparse, when compared with those of other moralities. Physical horseplay is scarce. Some speeches are excessively long, as when Satan delivers a lecture of some 114 lines in the play's opening. Interplay between the actors and the presumed audience, so common and so lively in moralities generally, is minimal in *The Conflict of Conscience*. Latin is sometimes untranslated (e.g. lines 1224–8). The play as a whole reads like the work of a zealous Protestant minister who is out of touch with the world of professional theatre.

What interests us at present is the way in which Woodes's play offers a model for Christopher Marlowe's *Doctor Faustus* in its post-Reformation story of a lapsed convert confronting the terrors of damnation (such as those illustrated in Figure 42.1).

---

[2] Hypocrisy is on stage when these marginal comments are offered, so that they could be asides, but some of them are quite long, as at lines 386–97 and 825–61, and would seem to interfere substantially with the speeches of those who are talking.

Marlowe could have known Woodes's source, the autobiographical account of Francesco Spera. The play dramatizes at some length the trial proceedings in which Philologus is brought forward as an accused heretic to face the questions of Tyranny, the Cardinal, and Avarice, all of them egged on by the Vice Hypocrisy. Philologus answers his accusers with humble submission to their authority but with a firm defence of his faith. He refuses to acknowledge the Pope as supreme head of the Church because the Pope 'leaveth Christ, and himself to glory takes' (line 1167). Philologus bolsters his argument with learned citations. His view of the Holy Sacrament is that 'it is a sign of union' binding Christians to peaceful harmony, and is an 'analogy' signifying 'That Christ feeds our souls as the bread doth our body' (lines 1191–1214). The bread remains bread; Christ's 'Hoc est corpus meum' ('This is my body') is to be read in the same metaphoric sense as his 'Vos estis sal terrae, vos estis Lux mundi, | Ego sum ostium, and a hundreth such more' ('You are the salt of the earth, you are the light of the world, I am the host', lines 1224–8; cf. Vulgate Matt. 5: 13–14). Philologus resolves like Susanna to suffer the fate of martyrs. He appeals above all to his conscience (line 1382) as the basis of his principled stand. Yet at last he breaks down under the enticements offered him by Sensual Suggestion of 'worldly wealth' and 'palaces gorgeous', 'fair children', 'wife most amiable', 'pomp so glorious', 'delicate diet', 'life lascivious', and the rest (lines 1593–8). The Vice Hypocrisy exults in his success and bids a comic farewell to the audience.

The long passage in *The Conflict of Conscience* that perhaps most anticipates Marlowe's *Doctor Faustus* is the debate between Spirit and Suggestion that follows Philologus' lapse into recusancy. 'Philologus, Philologus, Philologus!', says Spirit, as he enters. 'I say, | In time take heed, go not too far, look well thy steps unto' (lines 1673–4). Philologus' answer—'Alas, what voice is this I hear, so dolefully to sound | Into mine ears, and warneth me in time yet to beware?' (lines 1681–2)—sounds especially Marlovian; compare Faustus' 'O, something soundeth in mine ears: "| Abjure this magic, turn to God again!" ' (2. 1. 7–8).[3] What Philologus hears is the voice of his good angel, debating with Suggestion, who counters with 'Look in this glass, Philologus; for nought else do thou care.' Suggestion's glass presents 'Naught else but pleasure, pomp, and wealth' (lines 1686–9). The two counsellors offer rival propositions, in alternating speeches, as in Marlowe's play.

Spirit's advice is holy and grounded in the promise of the Gospels, stressing that Philologus has free will to choose the good:

> Thou art yet free, Philologus; all torments thou mayst scape,
> Only the pleasures of the world thou shalt awhile forbear.
> Renounce thy crime, and sue for grace, and do not captivate
> Thy conscience unto mortal sin. The yoke of Christ do bear.
>
> (lines 1699–1702)

Yet Philologus is unable to resist the blandishments of Sensual Suggestion. This stubbornness prompts a swift rebuke from Conscience:

[3] Citations are from the A-text unless otherwise specified.

> Alas, alas, thou woeful wight, what fury doth thee move
> So willingly to cast thyself into consuming fire?
> What Circes hath bewitchèd thee, thy worldly wealth to love
> More than the blessed state of soul?
>
> (lines 1728–31)

When Philologus refuses to listen to godly counsel, Conscience exits with a terrifying denunciation:

> O cursèd creature! O frail flesh! O meat for worms! O dust!
> O bladder puffèd full of wind! O vainer than these all!

The upshot is that 'the Lord him to correct in furious wrath is bent' (lines 1909–16). Philologus is to be sent to hell because of his stubborn refusal to heed the counsel of his good angel.

This long debate is identical in the two printed states of *The Conflict of Conscience*, and yet radically opposite endings are possible to the dramatist. The first version would seem to have been the product of the Calvinist minister from Norwich who saw, in Spera's autobiographical story, an account of unregenerate evil in the protagonist. The surest explanation for Philologus' hardness of heart, when confronted with the spiritual arguments of Spirit and Conscience, is that he is one of those reprobates whom God, in his infinite wisdom, has perceived to be innately evil. At the last, the godly ministers of Woodes's play consign Philologus to his fate. They offer to pray with Philologus, but when he repeatedly insists to them that 'I cannot pray, my spirit is dead, no faith in me remain' (line 2349), and assures them, 'Tush, sirs, you do your labours lose; see where Beelzebub doth come | And doth invite me to a feast; you therefore speak in vain' (lines 1362–3), they sadly conclude that the time has come for them to depart. Yet they are not disillusioned by Philologus' terrible ending. Quite to the contrary, Theologus exults, 'O glorious God, how wonderful those judgement are of thine! | Thou dost behold the secret heart; naught doth thy eyes beguile.' The story of Philologus, as of Spera, is an object lesson. 'Here may the worldlings have a glass, their states for to behold, | And learn in time for to escape the judgements of the Lord' (lines 2384–93). Philologus has failed, but others may learn from his example to turn to God. His tragic story is thoroughly Calvinist in its theology and in its explanation of the paradox of determinism and free will.

Down to this point, the narrative is the same in both states of *The Conflict of Conscience*. Only in an unexpected 'Act six' does the alternative ending appear. It is as though Woodes saw reason to reconsider the implications of his first reprobate ending. It tells of the historical Spera, even if under the name of Philologus, and as such it can accept the tragic necessity of spiritual failure of an individual man. But the morality play genre pulls Woodes towards an opposite consideration: as an Everyman figure, Philologus' generic ending needs finally to be more hopeful. The morality play as a genre promotes the doctrine that as sinners we can be saved by God's grace in spite of our manifest failings. Grace is all in all.

Marlowe's *Doctor Faustus* is poised on this same productive uncertainty as to whether salvation is possible for one who would seem to be an unregenerate sinner. The Good Angel and the Evil Angel make their appearances repeatedly in the play, like Woodes's Conscience and Suggestion, and always as a pair. Marlowe generally gives them equal lines of speech, beginning with the Good Angel. They first come to Faustus after he has indicated his determination to practise necromancy with the help of Valdes and Cornelius, but before he has actually sold his soul to the devil.

GOOD ANGEL   O Faustus, lay that damnèd book aside
   And gaze not on it, lest it tempt thy soul
   And heap God's heavy wrath upon thy head!
   Read, read the Scriptures. That is blasphemy.
EVIL ANGEL   Go forward, Faustus, in that famous art
   Wherein all nature's treasury is contained.
   Be thou on earth as Jove is in the sky,
   Lord and commander of these elements.   (1. 1. 72–9)

By 'That' in line 75 the Good Angel means that damned book of magic that Faustus holds in his hands, having cast aside the Holy Scriptures as a waste of time. The Good Angel gets to speak first, but then the Evil Angel is in a position to have the last word of refutation. Such is the situation again at their next encounter, after Faustus has sold his soul:

GOOD ANGEL   Sweet Faustus, leave that execrable art.
FAUSTUS   Contrition, prayer, repentance—what of them?
GOOD ANGEL   O, they are means to bring thee unto heaven.
EVIL ANGEL   Rather illusions, fruits of lunacy,
   That makes men foolish that do trust them most.
GOOD ANGEL   Sweet Faustus, think of heaven and heavenly things.
EVIL ANGEL   No, Faustus, think of honour and wealth.   (2. 1. 15–21)

An important resemblance between these passages in *Doctor Faustus* and the similar debate in *The Conflict of Conscience* is that the positions of both the Good and Evil Angel are tenable, and are even, in a dramatic sense, true. That is, we as audience are aware of two irreconcilable but equally valid readings of the Holy Scriptures and of theology (especially Calvinist theology): first, that salvation is offered by God to all who truly turn to him, even the most desperate of sinners, and secondly, that some hardened souls are beyond redemption. In theatrical terms, the contradiction is absolute: Faustus can be saved, and Faustus cannot be saved. This paradox may strike us as profoundly and theatrically true throughout the play. As such, the paradox offers unparalleled excitement and uncertainty. Can both be true? At every moment in this extraordinary play, and especially when the two angels appear, it would seem that two contradictory truths both maintain their force (Snyder 1965; Honderich 1973; Sachs 1964; Campbell 1952).

The paradox is vividly theatrical in the angels' next appearance, seemingly in response to Faustus' determination to repent. If heaven 'was made for man', he insists to Mephistopheles, ''twas made for me. | I will renounce this magic and repent'.

> *Enter Good Angel and Evil Angel*
> GOOD ANGEL Faustus, repent yet, God will pity thee.
> EVIL ANGEL Thou art a spirit. God cannot pity thee.
> FAUSTUS Who buzzeth in mine ears I am a spirit?
>   Be I a devil, yet God may pity me;
>   Ay, God will pity me if I repent.
> EVIL ANGEL Ay, but Faustus never shall repent.
>   *Exeunt angels*
> FAUSTUS My heart's so hardened I cannot repent.   (2. 3. 9–18)

The Good Angel continues to insist that God will pity Faustus, but the Evil Angel is given the concluding argument. He maintains that Faustus is a 'spirit', implying thereby that Faustus is no longer a 'man' in the fullest sense and therefore cannot hope to come under the promise that heaven 'was made for man'. What does it mean to be a spirit? Does the Evil Angel mean that, having sold his soul to the devil, Faustus is already irrevocably damned, having in that sense passed already out of the mortal human sphere? What are we to make of Faustus' counter-argument that God may pity Faustus even if Faustus is a devil? Is that possible? Hovering over this argument is the question of God's agency. When the Evil Angel says, 'God cannot pity thee,' does he mean simply that Faustus is incorrigible, or does he mean that God could not pardon Faustus even if God were so inclined? Does the Evil Angel imply the heresy of denying freedom of choice to God? In any event, the matter of free will is fearfully pertinent to Faustus' case. 'Ay, but Faustus never shall repent,' the Evil Angel avers, placing a menacing emphasis on the word 'shall', by way of reply to Faustus' 'Ay, God will pity me if I repent.' Much virtue in 'If!' to quote Touchstone in *As You Like It* out of context here. Perhaps, argues the Evil Angel, repentance might be efficacious *if* Faustus could repent, but Faustus *never shall* repent. Determinism operates at the level of Faustus' presumed will. To the Evil Angel, the question is academic as to whether Faustus could be saved *if* he were to repent, because Faustus *never shall* repent.

Even the punctuation in this key passage operates ambiguously. The Good Angel's 'Faustus, repent yet, God will pity thee' in the A-text reading seems to mean, 'Faustus, repent while there is time; God is there and can pity you,' whereas the B-text reading, 'Faustus, repent, yet God will pity thee,' suggests 'Faustus, repent! Even now, God will pity thee.' The B-text reading perhaps captures better a sense of dramatic excitement, but both feed our anxiety as audience members as to whether salvation is possible still (the Good Angel's position) or inherently and absolutely impossible, given Faustus' status as a 'spirit' (the Evil Angel's position).

The repeated dual responses of the two angels thus operate in *Doctor Faustus* like the dual ending of *The Conflict of Conscience*. Throughout both plays, salvation or damnation remains dramatically and theologically possible at any given moment.

FAUSTUS. Is't not too late?
> *Enter Good and Evil [Angel]*
EVIL ANGEL Too late.
GOOD ANGEL Never too late, if Faustus can repent.
EVIL ANGEL If thou repent, devils shall tear thee in pieces.
GOOD ANGEL Repent, and they shall never raze thy skin.   (2. 3. 77–81)

The word 'can' again captures the insistent paradox of determinism and free will: it is not too late *if* Faustus 'can' repent. But can he? The Evil Angel appears to know his man.

For us as audience, anticipation of the tragic outcome depends to a significant extent on the opening chorus speaking as prologue. Faustus' grim fate is not left in doubt:

CHORUS Till, swoll'n with cunning of a self-conceit,
>   His waxen wings did mount above his reach,
>   And melting heavens conspired his overthrow.
>   For, falling to a devilish exercise,
>   And glutted more with learning's golden gifts,
>   He surfeits upon cursèd necromancy.   (Prologue, lines 20–5)

Faustus' overthrow is assured by this chorus. The overthrow is inevitable because the 'melting heavens' have 'conspired his overthrow'. That is, the heavens are operative in melting Faustus' Icarus-like wings and thus have determined to punish him for his presumption in mounting 'above his reach'. The heavens have evidently conspired thus before the process began. The A-text reading, 'melting heavens', thus attributes direct agency to Providence. The B-text reading, 'And melting, heavens conspired his overthrow', is perhaps more intelligible as implicitly attributing the melting to the warmth of the sun, but the result is the same. The idea is arguably heretical: it pushes Calvinist insistence on the absolute omnipotence and omniscience of God in a dangerous direction by hinting that the heavens have made Faustus what he is, a dangerous aspirer, and are in that sense the author of evil. In any event, Faustus is declared to be a reprobate and beyond hope of redemption from the start of the play. Woodes's first-state Prologue in *The Conflict of Conscience* has the same effect, but Woodes then changes the prediction in state two to one of hope. Marlowe chooses not to follow that redemptive path.

As a result, dramatic tension in *Doctor Faustus* is essentially unlike that of a play like *Othello* in which, if we imagine ourselves as seeing the play for the first time, we do not know the outcome. *Doctor Faustus* is more like *Romeo and Juliet*, where the opening chorus assures us that nothing can resolve the 'fearful passage' of the young couple's 'death-marked love' except their deaths. We experience dramatic tension in the form of wishing that Friar Laurence's letter will somehow reach Romeo in time in Padua or that Juliet will awaken in time to prevent Romeo's suicide, even if we know that these things cannot happen. Dramatic tension of this sort is every bit as effective in the theatre as the tension of not knowing, and it is the kind of tension Marlowe exploits so effectively in *Doctor Faustus*.

Marlowe's play is filled with such galvanizing moments of dramatic uncertainty, and not just when the Good and Evil Angels are on hand to provide alternative counsels.

FAUSTUS Now, Faustus, must thou needs be damned,
    And canst thou not be saved.
    What boots it then to think of God or heaven?
    Away with such vain fancies and despair!
    Despair in God and trust in Beelzebub.
    Now go not backward. No, Faustus, be resolute.
    Why waverest thou? O, something soundeth in mine ears:
    'Abjure this magic, turn to God again!'
    Ay, and Faustus will turn to God again.
    To God? He loves thee not.   (2. 1. 1–10)

Even as Faustus concedes the inevitability of his damnation, we see him struggling with a longing to turn to God again. The theatrical presentation of this soul-struggle is so vivid because it posits the possibility of choice, even if the internal debate ends in self-defeat.

Again, when Faustus is about to sign his contract with the devil, the sudden appearance on his arm of '*Homo, fuge*' drives him into a frantic consideration of his alternatives. The moment is indeed so fraught with the seeming possibility of repentance that Mephistopheles brings on a show of rich apparel and dancing to distract his victim. Still once again, at his next appearance in 2. 3, Faustus seems ready once more to repent:

> When I behold the heavens, then I repent
> And curse thee, wicked Mephistopheles,
> Because thou hast deprived me of those joys.

> (2. 3. 1–3)

Such moments of soul-struggle invite the Good and Evil Angels to give substance to the divided sensibility of Faustus' choice.

Perhaps not coincidentally, when Faustus experiences disappointment in his desire to know the movement of the heavens, and most of all to know why we have not 'conjunctions, oppositions, aspects, eclipses all at one time, but in some years we have more, in some less' (2. 3. 62–4), and has been fobbed off with the vacuous explanation that these mysteries are the result of unequal motion with respect to the whole, Faustus makes his most intense effort to extricate himself from impending damnation: 'Ah, Christ, my Saviour, | Seek to save distressèd Faustus' soul!' (lines 82–3). The plea takes the form of a prayer, and is posited on the bedrock Protestant position that only through sincere penitence and a direct appeal to God can the miserable sinner hope for the gift of heavenly grace. Is this not what Faustus' Christian learning has taught him? He has been, after all, a leading theologian, renowned throughout Europe. Yet his plea is not answered. Instead, Lucifer and Beelzebub join forces with Mephistopheles in confronting Faustus with their power over him. The very fact that such mighty reinforcements are called for would seem to establish beyond doubt that Faustus' spiritual destiny hangs in the balance. Why would they come if his damnation is assured? At the same time, we know, as audience, from the opening chorus, that salvation is for him impossible. We are confronted with an absolute paradox, one that gathers intensity in dramatic excitement.

A theological explanation offers itself in Calvin's teaching, to be sure, namely, that Faustus does indeed have free choice and is responsible for his own spiritual welfare or failure, and yet his fate is predestinately sealed from the beginning of time in the infinite but unknowable wisdom of the Almighty (Sellin 1974). At the same time, the dramatic presentation in the theatre flirts with a more heretical alternative, that the heavens have conspired, and that God, having consigned Faustus to his damnable fate, leaves him to the cruelties of Lucifer and Beelzebub. Certainly God makes no appearance in the play, though he is appealed to once again in Faustus' last desperate moments:

> O, I'll leap up to my God! Who pulls me down?
> See, see where Christ's blood streams in the firmament!
> One drop would save my soul, half a drop. Ah, my Christ!
>
> (5. 2. 77–9)

The Good and Evil Angels disappear from the play after 2. 3, leaving Faustus to his soul-destroying pleasures and occasional lapses into terror in Acts 3 and 4. In its final moments, *Doctor Faustus* returns once more to soul-struggle and to the question of possible choice, albeit at a terrifyingly late hour when the chance of spiritual success seems virtually to have vanished. Yet even at this point the option is presented theatrically as viable. The Old Man is Faustus' opposite number and nemesis, but he also offers his counsel of repentance and renunciation of suicide as the best hope of salvation:

OLD MAN Ah, stay, good Faustus, stay thy desperate steps!
   I see an angel hovers o'er thy head,
   And with a vial full of precious grace
   Offers to pour the same into thy soul.
   Then call for mercy and avoid despair.
FAUSTUS Ah, my sweet friend, I feel thy words
   To comfort my distressèd soul.
   Leave me a while to ponder on my sins.   (5. 1. 53–60)

The Old Man is quite explicit about Christ's offer of mercy as potentially applicable even to Faustus at this late hour. Faustus responds in the same spirit, even if we know that his resolution to meditate on his sinful state cannot prevail. When he bids the Old Man to leave him to his meditations, and is alone, he appears to be in a panic of uncertainty.

FAUSTUS Accursèd Faustus, where is mercy now?
    I do repent, and yet I do despair.
    Hell strives with grace for conquest in my breast.
    What shall I do to shun the snares of death?   (5. 1. 63–6)

Even this late in the play, salvation for Faustus is both possible and impossible.

Faustus' scholarly friends offer him the same hope, the same theological assurance that one must never account it too late to turn to God. To his insistence that 'Faustus' offence can ne'er be pardoned' (5. 2. 15), their reply is 'Yet, Faustus, call on God' (line 28). One scholar asks, even now, 'O, what shall we do to save Faustus?' (line 51). The Third Scholar declares, 'God will strengthen me. I will stay with Faustus' (lines 53–4). The Second Scholar urges, 'Pray thou, and we will pray that God may have mercy upon thee' (lines 60–1). Prayer still can be efficacious. In his final reply to the scholars' implorings, Faustus indicates that he has not entirely given up hope, even if that hope is desperately uncertain: 'Gentlemen, farewell. If I live till morning, I'll visit you; if not, Faustus is gone to hell' (lines 62–3). Even in his last hour alive, Faustus' impulses are hopelessly divided: 'O, I'll leap up to my God! Who pulls me down?' (line 77).

My argument, then, is that the dramatic excitement of *Doctor Faustus* as a play is intensely real even while we understand intellectually that only one outcome is possible. The dramatic excitement is indeed like that of *The Conflict of Conscience*, even if Woodes's play is poorly written by comparison. What both plays represent is the way in which English drama offered to Marlowe and to other late Elizabethan dramatists, including Shakespeare (especially in *Macbeth*), a potential for tragic greatness founded in the wrenching paradoxes of Calvinist theology. Calvin of course did not mean these paradoxes to be discomforting; for those who entertained hope of being part of the Elect, the promise of salvation was intensely beautiful. Yet one can well imagine that Marlowe, for all his exposure to Calvinist thought at Cambridge, saw instead a formula for a tragedy of spiritual failure. Woodes may well have helped him formulate this response to the spiritual battles of the age. But Marlowe was able to go much further as a dramatist, not only because he was a gifted poet but also because he seems to have understood in a deeply personal way how one's faith in spiritual truths could be shaken by doubt. *Doctor Faustus* confirms, for purposes of the play, that hell is real, but it also dramatizes the spiritual dilemma of one who has encountered sceptical uncertainty. A mere willingness to believe, even a fear of the consequences of loss of faith, is not enough in itself to restore faith. One cannot will oneself to believe in divine mysteries. Hence the dramatic power of contradictory forces in this remarkable play.

PRIMARY WORKS

MARLOWE, CHRISTOPHER (1993), *Doctor Faustus, A- and B-Texts (1604, 1616)*, ed. David Bevington and Eric Rasmussen (Manchester: Manchester University Press).

WOODES, NATHANIEL (1952), *The Conflict of Conscience*, ed. H. Davis and F. P. Wilson (Oxford: Oxford University Press).

himself none of the meetest men, to censure Sir *Thomas Moore*, Sir *John Cheeke*, Doctor *Watson*, Doctor *Haddon*, Maister *Ascham*, Doctor *Car*, my brother Doctor *Harvey*, and such like; yet the jolly man will needs be playing the douty *Martin* in his kinde, and limit every man's commendation according to his fancy.   (A2ᵛ–A3ʳ)

Richard Harvey's comparison of Nashe to Marprelate reveals the extent to which permission to pass judgement in the literary sphere was felt, by some at least, to be governed by hierarchies of authority no less strict than the episcopal hierarchies threatened by Martin's Presbyterianism (Black 1997: 720–2). To say that Nashe is 'play[ing] the douty *Martin* in his kinde' by judging the prose style of Cheke, Ascham, and the rest is to imply that the sphere of 'humanitie' is ancillary to that of religion and politics, and that those who engage in critiques of significant literary figures in print are, by definition, threatening the peace and prosperity of the commonwealth.

Richard Harvey's taking exception to Nashe's censuring his betters in the *studia humanitatis* is partly, as Jennifer Richards has shown, an objection to the latter's failure to observe the civil, self-deferential rules of courteous speech which, since the 1540s, had been adopted by those whose objectives were to widen public debate and achieve consensus on matters of political, economic, and linguistic–literary reform (Richards 2003: 115–21; cf. Shrank 2004b: 148–61). Indeed, Richards's discovery of the centrality of Ciceronian and Castiglionian models of civil conversation to mid-Tudor policy-making and, subsequently, to the fashioning of print dialogues on any controversial subject is enormously illuminating for our understanding of exactly what was at stake in the quarrel subsequently pursued between Nashe and Richard Harvey's brother Gabriel.

So critics would now probably conclude that the obscurity surrounding what Nashe has to say about prose style in the Preface to *Menaphon* has little to do with his views on style, and a lot to do with his authorial self-fashioning. For all Nashe's apparent interest in evaluating English writers according to purely stylistic criteria (commenting, for example, that Turbervile is 'not the worst of his time, although in translating he attributed too much to the necessitie of rhyme' (Nashe 1966: iii. 319), he is actually far more implicated in Richard Harvey's position of identifying the welfare of the *studia humanitatis* with the protection of the hierarchies of Church and State than at first appears. Hints throughout the Preface to *Menaphon* suggest that Nashe was aiming the show he made of his literary discernment at a likely literary patron—quite probably a bishop—who might see fit to employ his pen in some suitable commonwealth cause. He concluded the Preface with an appeal to potential employers to 'Reade favourably, to incourage me in the firstlings of my folly, and persuade your selves, I will persecute those Idiots and their heirs unto the third generation, that have made Art bankeroute of her ornaments, and sent Poetry a begging up and down the Countrey' (324). Among 'those Idiots' he had, a few pages earlier, included 'durtie mouthed Martin', whose pamphlets appeared to be more in demand than 'the best poeme that ever *Tasso* eternisht' (315–16). Nor did his bid for employment miss its mark: *An Almond for a Parrot* appeared in late 1589, to all appearances a product of Nashe's pen, and he went on to enjoy the protection and patronage of John Whitgift, Archbishop of Canterbury, at least until 1592 (McGinn 1944).

For all his commendatory contribution to the publishing success of a free-floating piece of commercial fiction, then, Nashe seems never to have been planning a career in Greene's mode himself. Indeed, any praise Nashe subsequently lavished on Greene's talents was always distinctly double-edged. As well as hinting at how effective a tormentor of 'our reformatorie Churchmen' he might be, Nashe was expedient enough to think of using the Preface to advertise another piece of literary apprentice work, his *Anatomy of Absurdity*, to show to the bishops his 'skill in surgery', or in discovering 'the diseases of Arte' (1966: iii. 324). The *Anatomy* is, as R. B. McKerrow, D. C. Allen, and most recently Matthew Steggle have all pointed out, a pretentious compilation of invective against vice, drawn from, among others, Erasmus' *Parabolae*, Textor's *Epithets*, and Thomas de Hibernia's *Manipulus florum* ('Handful of Flowers'), a compendium of examples for preachers. It seems that Nashe, then, no less than Richard and Gabriel Harvey, envisaged liberal studies as properly protected by and serving the interests of those who held religious and political office (1966: iv. 2; Allen 1935; Steggle 2006).

The reading I have just sketched gives us a Nashe who is politic and pragmatic—whose concern that 'Arte' should not be 'bankeroute of her ornaments', nor 'Poetry' sent 'a-begging up and down the Country', is simultaneously a concern with his own authorial ethos and his employability in some service by those close to the Privy Council. It is a reading, however, that I find plausible only for the Nashe who wrote *The Anatomy of Absurdity*, the Preface to Greene's *Menaphon*, and *An Almond for a Parrot*. As far as I can see, the drying up of ecclesiastical patronage after 1592 encouraged Nashe to become the kind of writer that Philip Schwyzer has characterized as radically and even self-destructively experimental. The question of whether Nashe himself would have been 'disturbed by the moral implications of some of his experiments' as Schwyzer suggests (1994: 619), remains an open one, but even if we bracket off that question, it can still make sense to speak of the morally disturbing, radically experimental qualities characteristic of Nashe's writing after *The Anatomy*, *An Almond*, and the Preface to *Menaphon* only if we concede that there were more orthodox, acceptable modes of addressing a print readership which Nashe was willing (at some personal cost) to subvert. This is more or less what I argued nearly twenty years ago, when I suggested that it makes sense to see Nashe's writings after *Pierce Penniless* less as giving us the 'repertoire of a single, personal voice' and more as riskily stylizing and parodying the rhetorical and material media of different voices of authority (Hutson 1989: 4). Much, however, has changed since then, and the premises of my argument may well seem to have been called into question by the ways in which recent cross-disciplinary developments in the historical and literary study of books and readers, rhetoric and politics have revealed the close affinity between the moral, patriotic, and pragmatic concerns of policy-making and literary production in the mid- to late sixteenth century.

Nashe's writing might now more plausibly be seen as continuous with, rather than subversive of, the moral and patriotic concerns that explicitly motivated much of the literary production of the 1550s, 1560s, and 1570s. Jason Scott-Warren, for example, has recently suggested that Nashe's last work, *Lenten Stuff*, 'reads at times like a contribution to the wealth of writings from this period devoted to "projects", worthy schemes to set the poor on work producing commodities, such as silk, coal, or indeed herrings' (2005: 97). This is a reading that would make *Lenten Stuff* a entertaining commercial spin-off of the kinds of patriotic 'plat', or project, inspired by Sir Thomas Smith's *A Discourse on the Commonweal of this Realm of England*. Of course, Scott Warren is not saying that Nashe's work *is* a politic project or plat for the common weal ('his tone is, as ever, unguessable'), and, conversely, my own work very likely overstated the case for reading Nashe as a writer for whom the moral and political agenda of mid-Tudor literary production was a site of repression. Nevertheless, to congratulate the author of *Lenten Stuff* for having 'invented the media publicity stunt' in 'marketing his own celebrity' is to overlook the pamphlet's emotive and creative engagement with the real history of the Privy Council's attempts to silence its author as a result of his troublesome and now lost play *The Isle of Dogs*. It is not just that Nashe 'thinks of his own project' in *Lenten Stuff* as 'getting something for nothing' (Scott-Warren 2005: 97), but that he creates a kind of self-evacuating semiotic plenitude in defiance of those readers determined to construe his verbal 'nothing' as the matter of criminal and political culpability. If, Nashe complained in a digression in *Lenten Stuff*, he were to write 'and leave some tearmes in suspense', then

out steps me an infant squib of the Innes of Court, that hath not halfe greased his dining cappe [...] and he, to approve himselfe an extravagant statesman, catcheth hold of a rush, and absolutely concludeth, it is meant of the Emperor of Ruscia, and that it will utterly marre all the traffike into that country if all the Pamphlets be not called in and suppressed, wherein that libelling word is mentioned. (Nashe 1996: iii. 213)

Nashe's beautiful literary re-creation of the practice of interpreting to incriminate— the lawyer mutating a 'rush' into 'Russia' in order to advance his career—may allude to *The Isle of Dogs* affair, which resulted in Jonson's imprisonment and Nashe's having to flee London, but it may equally recall any number of earlier troubles arising from Nashe's inventive immoderation in print. In 1592 Robert Beale, Clerk of the Queen's Counsel, wrote to Lord Treasurer William Burghley to warn him that one of the Queen's subjects—one Thomas Nashe, indeed—had 'so reviled the whole nation of Denmark' in his *Pierce Penniless* as to have endangered the English polity: 'The realm had otherwise enemies enough, without making any more by such contumelious pamphlets. Wherefore such invectives could not but serve the enemy's turn, whatsoever was pretended otherwise' (Nashe 1996: v. 142). In 1594 Nashe claimed that his fiction *The Unfortunate Traveller* had fallen foul of 'busie wits abrode' who sought 'to anagrammatize the name of Wittenberge to one of the Universities of England'; these were men, wrote Nashe, who stretch the 'words on tenter hooks so miserably, that a man were as good [...] write on cheverell as on paper' (ii. 182). 'Cheverel' is pliable kidskin, or kid-leather, and Nashe characteristically exploits the material sense of 'tenterhooks' as a metaphor for distorting an author's sense (tenterhooks were the hooks on which animal hides were stretched), provoking both a smile and a wince.

Nashe could not, then (any more than any other writer), have turned seamlessly and inconsequentially from fashioning himself as a government servant (employed by the bishops against Marprelate) to fashioning himself as a print 'celebrity', as it were, in the quarrel with Harvey and the writing of *Lenten Stuff*. In the employ of the bishops, his writing was intimately concerned with the renewed urgency of the political question of what it was permissible to say in print. *An Almond for a Parrot* shows acute awareness of the effects of censorship implicit in the statutes which had recently defined as treason any 'devising, writing, printing or setting forth' any matter defamatory of the Queen's Majesty, in which was included 'defamation of her majesty's government' (Clegg 1997: 32–5; Hargreave 1793: i. 193). Martin's mockery of episcopal rule and exclusion of 'her Highnesse from all Ecclesasticall governement' thus 'come[s] in compasse of treason', as Nashe pointed out with cruel legal precision (iii. 353). But by the time of *Lenten Stuff*, Nashe's own writings were being repeatedly construed as dangerously subversive for similar reasons: again and again we find Nashe denying any intention to defame the country's governors. 'O, for a Legion of mice-eyed decipherers and calculators upon characters, now to augurate what I meane by this,' he wrote defiantly of his fantastical false trail of red herring fictions (218). These 'decipherers' sit 'up night and day sifting out treasons': such spies and intelligencers had seized his own papers 'to see whether they contained anything treasonable' on the Privy Council's order after the scandal of *The Isle of Dogs* (iii. 218; v. 30–1).

Nashe's literary experiments rarely failed to create friction with the authorities, whether Privy Council, aldermen, or, finally, bishops. The significance of recalling this in a study about Nashe's relation to mid-Tudor literature has to do with recollecting that the sense of what fiction, literary 'device', and 'invention' might do had long been closely tied, especially in the realm of print, to the imperatives of what Cathy Shrank has called 'writing the nation', or achieving the 'commonwealth' in moral, economic, and linguistic terms (2004*b*). These were imperatives to which Nashe, as we saw from the Preface to *Menaphon*, actually subscribed, though he increasingly made fun of their expedient invocation as part of a spurious rhetoric of moral authority. For Nashe, as critics have repeatedly noted, pushes language not in the direction of tendentious meaning, but in the direction of the material and perceptual pleasures of meaning's disruption. Neil Rhodes wrote of Nashe's style that it thrives on the perception of surprising physical resemblances between what we think of as discrete and heterogeneous areas of experience so that 'a continual kaleidoscoping of images and ideas brings the unexpected into juxtaposition with the familiar' (1980: 19). John Carey, likewise, commented on the 'testing collision' of literary stereotype and 'exuberantly documented reality' that we find in Nashe's prose, likening its effects to Eliot's famous remarks on the metaphysical wit of Donne's poetry, which involves a 'recognition, implicit in the expression of every experience, of other kinds of experience which are possible' (1970: 364). The puzzle, then, is why a prose poet of Nashe's quality, whose writing generally subordinated meaning to metaphorical effect, and whose own allegiances were fairly conservative, should have elicited such censorious, as well as admiring, responses from contemporaries: 'What talke I so longe of *Jacke Wilton*?', wrote Nashe of the scandal caused by his *Unfortunate Traveller*; 'he hath had but a sleight wringing of the eares in comparison of the heavie penance my poore Teares [i.e. *Christ's Tears over Jerusalem*] here have endured' (ii. 183). The 'heavie penance' imposed on *Christ's Tears* was no less perilous to Nashe than the punishment he narrowly escaped as a result of *The Isle of Dogs*. Someone drew the Lord Mayor of London's attention to the defamatory implications of some of Nashe's preacherly denunciations of sin, and Nashe was imprisoned in Newgate, very possibly awaiting trial for treason (Duncan-Jones 1998; Hutson 1987).

If Nashe has always fared well among critics who, like Lewis, Carey, and Rhodes, are more concerned with the effects of literary language than with analysing the political and material conditions of authorship, it is certainly possible that the scandalous reactions repeatedly provoked by his writing were not just responses to a violation of the Ciceronian rhetoric of civility, as Jennifer Richards has described, but were also the effects a widespread habit of assuming that literary 'feigning' is always politically and autobiographically referential. This tendency, I will go on to suggest, is by no means simply the result of a naive response to the authority conferred by print (although we may take as a measure of how seriously print as a medium was taken the fact that every single bishop named in Marprelate's first *Epistle* felt compelled to respond to its charges; Black 1997: 710). It is, rather, part of the legacy of the uses of literary and rhetorical skills in the 1550s and 1560s to achieve so much in the religious, economic, and political spheres. While the achievements of mid-sixteenth-century vernacular literature were momentous—Sir Thomas Smith's *Discourse on the Commonweal*, for example, initiated the government policy that encouraged men of liberal education to compose the 'plats', or projects, which ultimately transformed the economy (see Thirsk 1978: 24–50)—we need to be aware of the negative as well as the positive consequences of a widespread tendency to read fictions as immediately and primarily motivated by, and referring to, contemporary political reality.

C. S. Lewis is, understandably, blamed for devaluing the literary achievement of the mid-sixteenth century in order to glorify the century's closing decade. But Lewis may be seen, rather, as reacting against an influential distaste, expressed by twentieth-century poet–critics, for the artifice and ornament of Elizabethan writing. Poet–critics like Yvor Winters praised the 'native plain style' of the mid-sixteenth century above the 'rhetoric for its own sake' of Elizabethan lyric verse (1967: 3). Lewis acknowledged his contemporaries' revulsion for 'Decoration, externally laid on and inorganic' but countered their implicitly expressive theory of poetry with an insistence on the importance of rhetorical 'invention' (1954: 271). He also characterized the emergence of what he polemically called the 'Golden' literature (the literature disliked by his contemporaries as too full of artifice) by a 'general outlook' expressed in 'a more or less common defence and theory of poetry', which defence, he argued, was not of 'man's right to sing but his right to feign' (318). At stake in the emergent defence of the literary, then, was the question of what it meant to 'feign', to invent fiction.

There is no danger now, of course, of modern literary critics or historians failing to appreciate the significance of rhetoric in the sixteenth-century literary achievement. But we may be in danger of underestimating what it would mean, in the later part of the century, to establish the conditions in which it was possible to 'feign', or invent fiction, in print without assuming some prophylactic posture of apology or repentance that simultaneously asserts the referentiality of the fiction. Shrank has rightly proposed that what we need in order to understand mid-Tudor literary activity is an expanded sense of what constitutes the fictive: 'the selection of a particular text for translation, with its necessary adaptation, accompanying apparatus of dedicatory letters and prefatory matter, can constitute a conscious, crafted and "fictive" act', she writes (2004b: 12). Appreciating the 'fictive acts' of mid-Tudor literature requires analysing the uses of devices—such as reliance on genre and generic expectation, creating a persona, establishing a form of address that constitutes the relationship between writer and reader, or between imagined interlocutors, deploying the rhetorical forms of proof, and so forth—that are being more or less successfully presented not as independently imagined worlds, but as contributions to contemporary actuality. Thus, for example, Shrank herself draws our attention to Thomas Wilson's translation of Demosthenes' orations to the Athenians urging war against Philip of Macedon. This text, published in 1570, 'promote[d] English intervention on behalf of the Protestant Dutch in their wars of independence against Spain', and, as Blair Worden argues, may have influenced Sidney's conception of the *Arcadia*, a political romance about danger in the federation of Greek states (Shrank 2004b: 202; Worden 1996).

Work like Shrank's and Worden's stresses the continuities between texts like Sidney's *Arcadia* and Wilson's *Orations of Demosthenes*, where an older literary criticism would rather have stressed the profound transformation in conceptions of the relationship of fiction to political actuality which they also evince. For an older literary criticism, Sidney's *Arcadia* represents a break in terms of its implicit 'defence of poesy', its sense of the significance of having space in which to feign, as he says in his *Apology for Poetry* (c.1580), 'forms such as never were in Nature' (2002: 85), which, while they may exercise the judgement and deliberation of readers, nevertheless are not subordinate or ancillary to the text's claims about its own analogical reference to historical truth. It is partly just a matter of emphasis, but before the interdisciplinary turn of both literary and historical studies of which Worden's and Shrank's work are exemplary instances, a change in attitudes to vernacular fiction-making was thought to have taken place in the 1570s and 1580s, a thesis most famously and persuasively articulated in Richard Helgerson's study of Gascoigne, Sidney, Greene, and Lyly, *The Elizabethan Prodigals* (1976). Now, however, we have so thoroughly broken down the disciplinary boundaries that prevented us from seeing the political dimensions of texts conventionally regarded as 'literary', and the literary and fictive dimensions of texts (dialogues, orations, treatises) once regarded as furthering some cause of political or pedagogical reform, that Helgerson's thesis might seem irrelevant. The continuity of political interests between Wilson's *Orations of Demosthenes* and Sidney's first *Arcadia* are more important than their obvious differences in degrees of fictional autonomy. One effect of this change of critical emphasis is to undermine the sense that poesy or fiction-making needed defending at the beginning of the 1580s. Another, perhaps more serious, effect is to make it impossible for us to see that the kinds of mid-Tudor 'fictive acts' Shrank analyses so well were themselves successful in terms that could produce tangible difficulties for anyone who aspired to feign things in print without seeming to make truth-claims through political referents. As Helgerson himself pointed out, the 'prodigal' fictions of Gascoigne, Lyly, and Greene were never wholly separable from their real-world referents. 'Neither a fully autonomous artwork nor a veiled account of true events' is how Helgerson described Lyly's *Euphues* (1976: 11).

Philip Sidney, of course, famously asserted that poets do not tell lies, because they do not make assertions about the real world. But Sidney made this assertion polemically, defending it against the prevailing belief that literary or poetic skill should properly serve the moral and political ends of the commonwealth, which might well require that service to take the form of what Shrank calls a 'fictive act'—that is, enhancing, through literary devices, the credibility and rhetorical effectiveness of the patriotic text. Conversely, in the 1560s a supreme example of the patriotic 'fictive act' might be a successful patriotic *forgery*, a text which used literary and rhetorical devices brilliantly to persuade readers of its authoritative discrediting of someone who posed a serious threat to the realm. Such a text is Thomas Wilson's effective forgery of George Buchanan's 'Scottish' vernacular in *A Detection of the Doings of Mary Queen of Scots* (1571). In this text, the reader's skill in reading poetry and recognizing genres and conventions are elicited as part of the text's forensic proving of its case against the poetry's alleged author, who is completely identified with the persona speaking in the poems. As this is a study aimed at understanding the legacy of the mid-Tudor literary achievement for Thomas Nashe, a writer who continually had difficulty dissociating himself from the satiric fictional personae he created, I want to turn now, briefly, to considering how a successful 'fictive act' such as Wilson's 1571 *Detection* might be seen to be encouraging highly literate readers to use their literary skill to erase any sense of the ironic or fictional distance between an author and a persona.

Wilson's *Detection* was a masterful piece of feigning in a number of senses. It was, as James Emerson Philips notes, 'the fountainhead of all later attacks on the Scottish Queen's character and conduct' (1964: 61). Wilson used fictive devices to disguise the text's provenance: he presented it as coming from the pen of Scotland's most distinguished humanist scholar and poet, George Buchanan, who had indeed written a Latin narrative of the facts, the *Detectio*, but the vernacular composite text of 1571 was 'completely a product, in its published form, of English activities to discredit Mary without violating Elizabeth's official attitude of benevolent neutrality towards her reluctant guest' (Philips 1964: 61). Buchanan's Latin *Detectio* had been printed in 1571 by John Day with the addition of an *Actio contra Mariam* by Wilson. In the vernacular *Detection*, however, Wilson translated not only Buchanan's and his own Latin, but the French letters and poems ascribed to the Queen of

Scots, into a pseudo-Scots which encouraged the reader to identify all the text's elements as proofs in a prosecution of the Scots queen by her realm's most eminent scholar.

The most skilful aspect of Wilson's composition of *A Detection* is his integration of the mimetic strategies of forensic rhetoric (which appeals to auditors' and readers' powers of evaluating likelihood based on their reading and experience) with a reliance on readers' readiness to conflate author and poetic persona. Wilson's argument of the conjectural issue—the probability or otherwise of the alleged fact that Mary knowingly conspired with Bothwell to murder her husband—turns again and again on the preparation for a reading of the 'poesy' presented later which will both draw on a sophisticated awareness of genre and tradition, and, at the same time, banish the usual sense of the fictive, ironic *distance* (produced by generic conformity and innovation) between the voice of the poetic persona and that of the ostensible poet. Thus, for example, Wilson-as-Buchanan begins by insisting on the redundancy of every circumstantial proof he might now allege, given our familiarity with a narrative that speaks for itself. He concedes that we do not know Mary's motive, or the 'cause' that incited her to become a husband-killer, but there is, he states, little point in investigating motive when the circumstances fit together so coherently as to make guilt manifest (1571: F4^v). However, he then goes on to discover proofs of the cause, or motive, not (as he hastens to assure us) by drawing on an ancient and extensive literature full of examples which prove the irrationality of women in love, but, much more authentically, by *her own words*:

Will ye aske of me the causes of the chainge of her affectioun? quhat if I ken tham nat? [...] Sic are the natures of some wemen [...] they have vehement affections baith ways [...] I could out of the monumentes of antiquitie rehearse innumerable examples, *but of hir selfe I had raithest beleve hir selfe.*

Call to mind that part of hir letters to Bothwell quhairin sche maketh hir selfe Medea, that is, a woman that nouther in love nor in hatrit can kepe any meane.

(G1^v–G2^r; my emphasis)

The ostensible rejection of the 'foreine probations' of literature for the more authentic evidence of 'hir selfe' as witnessed in her letters cleverly occludes the way in which the intelligibility of this testimony of a woman's motive relies on a familiarity with the very 'monumentes of antiquitie' that have been apparently rejected. Here the author is directing the reader in how to understand a reference several pages later, when, in what is given as the translation of 'An other letter to Bothwell of her love to him' (U2^{r-v}), the writer states that she (as we assume) is breaking a promise in writing this letter, having been commanded not to write, but she writes because she is fearful of his love, and jealous of 'hir that has not the thirde pairt of the willing obedience unto you that I beir'. She fears, she goes on, that this other woman has 'wonne aganis my will that advauntage over me, quhilk the second love of Jason wan' (U2^v).

At issue here is not, of course, the question of whether or not Mary wrote the French version of the letter presented to the reader as 'avowit to be written with the

Scottishe Quenis awne hand' (Q4^r). What is of concern is the way in which Wilson relies on generic expectation—on a familiarity with the uses of literary *fiction*—to establish the very authenticity of self-incrimination ('of hir self I had raithest believe hir self'). In directing the reader's attention to the letter-writer's likening of herself to Medea, Wilson provides a generic context in which to read the sonnets, also translated by him into pseudo-Scots. These sonnets, as Rosalind Smith has written, combine the genre of complaint with that of Petrarchan erotic poetry, and are crucially circulated under feminine signature. The femininity of this particular combination, she observes, would seem unsurprising to the reader of vernacular English literature in print in 1571, in view of the fact that the year 1567 saw both the publication of George Turbervile's translation of Ovid's *Heroides*—a collection of fictitious verse epistles by abandoned heroines of antiquity to their princely but wayward lovers—and Isabella Whitney's *A Copy of a Letter*, which adapted the Ovidian epistolary fiction to a witty proof of the abandoned woman poet's virtue and worth. Among Ovid's abandoned women, of course, were queens and murderesses—Dido gave up her kingdom for Aeneas, and Medea committed crimes for Jason. The sequence, like Whitney's *Copy of a Letter*, works 'to establish "certain profe" of the speaker's love as a means of winning her lover's favour, through a catalogue of the speaker's sacrifices and constancy in love, as against her rival's avarice, self-interest, and inconstancy' (R. Smith 2005: 51). But where Whitney's poetic persona emerges out of her witty transformation of the Ovidian conventions that make it legible in the first place, the voice of the casket sonnets is not permitted to emerge as that of a poetic fiction, a persona. The act of feigning, of producing an innovative poetic version of the conventional Ovidian heroine's voice, incriminates the alleged author, who is wholly identified with the poem's speaker.

Wilson introduces the poems as 'Certaine French Sonnettes written by the quene of Scottes to Bothwell, befoir hir mariage with him, and (as it is sayd) quhile hir husband lyvit, But *certainly befoir his divorce from his wife as the wordes tham selves shew*' (Q4^r). Instead of inviting the reader to appreciate grammatical elements like tense as aspects of the poet's invention and persona-creation, Wilson insists that the present participle in Sonnet 3—'N'estant, à mon regret, comme elle vostre femme' ('Nat being (to my displeasure) your wife as she'; Q4^v, R3^r)—be read as empirical evidence that, *at the time when the sequence was composed*, Bothwell was still married to Jean Gordon. This in turn casts a sinister light on the poem's dramatic creation of an urgent present in which the poet's rival in love is only *now* beginning to see that she has undervalued her beloved:

> Et *maintenant* elle commence à voir
> Qu'elle estoit bien de mauvais jugement
> De n'estimer l'amour d'un tel amant.
>
> (And *now* sche beginneth to see,
> That sche was of veray evill jugement
> [Not] to esteeme the love of sic ane lover.)
>
> (R1^r, R3^v)

The poem's speaker then swears that, by contrast to that of her rival, her own love will show so clearly that he will no longer doubt it ('je juray [...] que en fin mon amour paroistra | Sy tres à clair qu jamais n'en doutra' (R1ᵛ). The surrounding murder narrative itself fills the space opened by imagining what form such a proof of love might, in retrospect, have taken.

Wilson's fictive act was enormously successful. Gabriel Harvey's marginal notes show that he believed Wilson's forgery of Buchanan's prosecutorial voice, as many modern readers have done (Stern 1979: 205). The voice of a queen confessing adulterous devotion to a suspected murderer likewise emerged so powerfully from the juxtaposition of judicial narrative and Heroidean poetic persona that it had a discernible impact on imitation of Ovid's *Heroides* in the English lyric poetry of complaint. For almost fifty years, in the gap between Isabella Whitney's 1573 complaint poems and Mary Wroth's 'unfashionably late sonnet sequences and complaints of 1621', not a single English woman poet, as Ros Smith points out, publicly assumes the fictive persona of a Heroidean abandoned woman (2005: 54).

Wilson's *Detection* shows how the crafted, fictive act of the patriotically motivated writer might appeal to readers' very familiarity with literary convention and classical poetic personae as a strategy of persuasion and mimetic illusion. Writers of the 1570s and 1580s, as Richard Helgerson showed, were ambitious to use their literary skills in service of the kind Wilson performed; their fictions, accordingly, were designed to advertise both their skill in feigning and their skill in presenting that 'feigning' as a political secret to be detected or decoded. George Gascoigne later laughed at readers who, missing 'the sense of the figurative speeches', were apt to confuse the poet with his fictional persona, imagining, for example, that a pastoral poem by 'the noble Erle of Surrey (beginning thus: *In winters just returne)*' had been 'made indeed by a Shepeherd' (Gascoigne 2000: 355, 366). But Gascoigne was being disingenuous. As Robert Maslen has shown, the reason that George Gascoigne's readers initially interpreted *The Adventures of Master F.J.*, including its poems, less as autonomous fiction than as having been written 'to the scandalizing of some worthie personages' (Gascoigne 2000: 362–3) was because Gascoigne himself had originally encouraged such an *à clef* reading. '*The Adventures of Master F.J.*', Maslen writes:

demonstrates its author's aptitude for the detection as well as the perpetration of the secret abuses it describes [...] By setting him to work as he asked them to, the English authorities [...] acknowledged the legitimacy of Gascoigne's brilliant display, in a domestic setting, of the duplicitous skills required by a public servant in England.   (1997: 156–7)

The Thomas Nashe who wrote a preface to Greene's *Menaphon* was a product of the same mid- to late Tudor habit of regarding fiction and poesy as contributing to the duplicitous skills required by a patriotic public servant in Elizabethan England. It can seem to make sense, as a consequence, to write about Nashe, and especially about the Harvey–Nashe quarrel, in terms exclusively concerned with the politics and ethics of self-fashioning or self-representation in print. Richards has given an excellent account of Gabriel Harvey's attempt to use the rhetoric of honesty and civility in his avenging of his brother against attacks in print by Robert Greene (in *A Quip for an Upstart Courtier*) and by Nashe (in *Pierce Penniless*). Nashe, she shows, makes use of the same terms of civility in *Strange News of the Intercepting Certain Letters* to expose 'the hypocrisy of Harvey's self-fashioning as a civil gentleman', demystifying Harvey's carefully cultivated *sprezzatura*. Nashe's victory, she observes, does not invalidate Harvey's practice of friendship and civility in print per se, but shows up its failures in the circumstance of this particular exchange (Richards 2003: 121).

But the implications of the Harvey–Nashe quarrel are broader than an internal critique of the ethics and politics of civil conversation and self-presentation in print would suggest. They can be seen, in fact, as embodying exactly the same issues as those Lewis identified as articulated in defences of poetry in the previous decade: 'not man's right to sing, but his right to feign, to "make things up" ' (1954: 318). This is not to say that Nashe was consciously promoting his own freedom to invent, but that his restless experimentalism and inventiveness inevitably raise questions of reference and political and religious answerability. Nashe's *Unfortunate Traveller*, for example, is clearly a fiction, but it is not the kind of fiction that could be incorporated into what Katharine Wilson calls the 'continuous career development' of the repentant prodigal autobiography (2006: 13). It is rather, as Margaret Ferguson showed, a reflexive, funny, and unsettling exposure of the power games at play in its own narrative's claim to moral and metaphysical authority (1981).

Harvey's response to Nashe reveals a quite reasonable fear that the disruptive energies of his restless experimentation with and mockery of rhetorical forms might have subversive effects on a political establishment already struggling to contain the fallout from Marprelate's devastating assault on the episcopacy. After all, as Philip Schwyzer has pointed out, both *Christ's Tears* and *The Unfortunate Traveller* offer 'highly subversive images of God' (1994: 617). *Christ's Tears over Jerusalem* presents Christ speaking in admonition of Jerusalem's sins, and, by implication, those of London. *The Unfortunate Traveller* mocks the moralizing narrative conventions of chronicle history, presenting itself as the autobiography of the thoroughly unreliable Jack Wilton, page (with a play on the printed page) to the English court. The different stylistic registers Jack uses to describe a series of plagues, battles, and executions in sixteenth-century Europe makes it hard for the pious Christian reader to interpret any of these events as proofs of the existence of a God, vengeful or otherwise. Indeed, where *Christ's Tears* unsettles the reader by daring to speak for God, *The Unfortunate Traveller* exposes the temerity of that enterprise, undermining any possibility of distinguishing those who legitimately claim to speak in God's name from those who are merely impostors. Nevertheless, what Nashe really cannot be accused of in either of these works is the pragmatic self-fictionalizing or self-promotion that Harvey ascribes to him.

Pierce's Supererogation, Harvey's massive confutation of all that Nashe's writing stands for, clearly subscribes to the view that Nashe was primarily engaged in the creation of 'self-referential personalities' (Wilson 2006: 44) or 'self-forgeries' (Neilson 1993: 44) of the kind that Harvey himself produced in his unpublished fictional writings. Harvey's title refers back to the Epistle to the Reader in Nashe's *Strange News*, in which Nashe joked that he was leaving off important business to reply to Harvey's attack on him in *Four Letters* because of 'the strong fayth you have conceiv'd, that I would do works of supererogation in answering the Doctor' (i. 259). 'Supererogation' here is a theological term referring to the performance of good works beyond that which God commands or requires; the bold transposition of the theological term into this secular, laddish context is typical of Nashe, as is the witty play on 'fayth' that precipitates it. But the joke could also seem, like much of the rest of *Strange News*, arrogant and defensive. What Harvey does, in writing *Pierce's Supererogation*, is to put into circulation a definitive interpretation of Nashe's writings as self-referential fictions: the angry Nashe of *Strange News* is conflated with Pierce Penniless, the satirical persona he created in his best-selling pamphlet of 1592, and the conflation Harvey creates is a monster of arrogance and '*domineering eloquence*'. This figure is also referred to by Harvey as 'young Apuleius', who is compared to Alexander the Great for having 'a huge intention, to have all men his subjectes, and all his subjects called Alexanders' (1593: 16).

Nashe, however, in spite of his bluster in *Strange News*, had never intended to create an authorial persona of this kind in writing *Pierce Penniless*. When faced in 1592 with want of means and patronage, his response was not to try and sell his humanist credentials, but to invent, in *Pierce Penniless his Supplication to the Devil*, a discourse which hilariously turned the economics of the patronage system on its head by having an indigent author of the title, Pierce Penniless, expose the diabolic forces upholding the official system. Nashe's title itself indicates the radical quality of his assault on the conventions of print patronage: 'Pierce Pennilesse' plays on the name 'Piers Plowman', traditionally associated, since William Langland's fourteenth-century poem, with the literature of complaint against social injustice. In Elizabethan England, however, complaint literature itself had transmuted into officially commissioned moral propaganda on the values of thrift and solvency—and nothing but this, or attacks on Puritans, could guarantee patronage. Thus, Nashe's Pierce is not the plain-speaking ploughman, but a bankrupt or penniless *purse*, who cannot climb aboard the gravy train of profitable moral propaganda without addressing the Devil, who (since its real motive is profit) is clearly such literature's arch-patron. Finally replying to *Pierce's Supererogation* in *Have with You to Saffron Walden*, Nashe gives up trying to deny Harvey's identification of him with Pierce Penniless—he dramatizes himself as '*Pierce Pennilesse Respondent*', comically drawing attention to the appellation as incrimination—he is now 'answerable' for it, as well as to it—while still distinguishing himself from it (the opening words of the book's dialogue address him as 'Tom'—'What, *Tom*, thou art very welcome. Where hast thou bin this long time[?]'; 1966: iii. 25). Harvey, he says, in titling his own book *Pierce his Supererogation; or, Nashe's Saint Fame*, 'borrows my name, and the name of *Piers Pennilesse* (one of my Bookes), which he knew to be most saleable [...] to helpe his bedred Stuff to limpe out of *Powles Churchyard*, that else would have laine unreprivably spittled at the Chandlers' (35). As to Harvey's Apuleius, Nashe's response is once again to expose, in a parody of legal process, the incriminating effects of Harvey's fictionalization of him: 'Sa ho: hath *Apuleius* ever an Attorney here? One *Apuleius* [...] he endites to be an engrosser of arts and inventions [...] *Non est inventus*: there's no such man to be found' (118).

In writing *Pierce Penniless* Nashe exploited the pleasurable openness not just of language and the vernacular poetic tradition, but of the medium of print, its conventions of layout and typography: part of the funny, disorienting challenge of the supplication to the Devil derives from its exact reproduction of the typographic layout of a credit-hunting dedicatory epistle. Nashe's poetic fictions were not just designed to enhance their author's credit in the world; they produced, from their play with language and print media, completely new ways of experiencing the social, moral, political, and material world of the 1590s. His was a kind of fiction that would, quite simply, have been inconceivable in the middle years of the sixteenth century, but its conceivability even in its own time was, as the response of Harvey and of various voices in authority bear witness, by no means uncontroversial.

Primary Works

BUCHANAN, GEORGE (attrib.) (1571), *Ane Detectioun of the Duinges of Marie Quene of Scottes* by Thomas Wilson.

GASCOIGNE, GEORGE (2000), *An Hundreth Sundrie Flowres*, ed. G. W. Pigman III (Oxford: Clarendon Press).

HARVEY, GABRIEL (1593), *Pierces Supererogation*.

HARVEY, RICHARD (1590), *A Theologicall Discourse of the Lamb of God and his Enemies*.

NASHE, THOMAS (1966), *The Works of Thomas Nashe*, ed. R. B. McKerrow, rev. F. P. Wilson, 5 vols (Oxford: Blackwell).

SIDNEY, PHILIP (2002), *An Apology for Poetry*, ed. Geoffrey Shepherd, rev. R. W. Maslen (Manchester: Manchester University Press).

WILSON, THOMAS (1571), *Ane Detectioun of the Duinges of Marie Quene of Scottes*, attrib. to George Buchanan.

—— (1994), *The Art of Rhetoric* (1560), ed. Peter E. Medine (Pennsylvania: Pennsylvania State University Press).

CHAPTER 44

'HEAR MY TALE OR KISS MY TAIL!' *THE OLD WIFE'S TALE, GAMMER GURTON'S NEEDLE,* AND THE POPULAR CULTURES OF TUDOR COMEDY

ANDREW HISCOCK

THERE was a Laundres of the Towne, whose daughter used often to the Court, to bring home shirts and bandes, which Jemy had long time loved and solicited, but to no ende, shee would not yeelde him an inch of her maydenhead: now Jemy vowed he would have it all. Well, she consented at last, and to be short, soone at night, at nine a clocke being in the winter, when she knew her mother to bee gon to watch with a sicke body, hee should come and all that night lye with her: Jemy though witlesse, wanted no knavish meaning in this, thought long till it was a night. But in the afternoone, the mayde goes up to the Castle, and gathers a great basket of Nettles, and comming home strawes them under the bed. Night comes, nine a clocke strickes, Jemy on his horse comes riding forward, sets him up and knockes at the doore, she lets him in, and bids him welcome bonny man: to bed hee goes, and Jemy was used to lye naked, for it is the use of a number, amongst which number she knew Jemy was one, who no sooner was in bed, but she her selfe knockt at the doore, and her selfe asked who was there, which Jemy hearing was afraide of her mother: also Sir sayes she, creepe under the bed, my mother comes. Jemy bustled not a little, under he creepes stark naked, where hee was stung with nettles: judge you that have feeling of such matters, there he lay turning this way and that way, heer be stung his leg, heere his shoulder, there his buttockes: but the Mayde having lockt the doore to him, went to bed, and there lay hee in durance (as they say) till morning: when the day broke, up gets the Mayde, to Court she goes, and tels the Kinges Chamberlaine of the matter, and he tolde the King, who laughed thereat right hartily.   (Armin 1600: C3^r)

I

In many ways, the comedies, farces, and romances composed during the Tudor period continue to invite audiences to reflect upon the politics of popular representation in the same way that jest books, ballads, cony-catching pamphlets, and prose narratives did for an evolving publishing market in the sixteenth century. It is striking that some authors, such as George Peele, Robert Greene, and Thomas Deloney, appear to have moved back and forth across two or more of these sub-genres in the final decades of the century, and there are clear narrative continuities in the ways in which non-elite members in these fictive worlds are served up for wider consumption. Interestingly, the account above of the maid, the fool, and a harvesting of nettles comes from a much larger compendium, *Fool upon Fool* (1600), which was itself penned by an Elizabethan stage fool, Robert Armin. In this fairly representative example of comic expectations from the period, foolishness is extravagantly expressed in the *doings* of those most distantly located away from the milieu of the political elite. And it becomes increasingly apparent that all too often such figures are delineated in terms of urgent physical need, coarse intellectual reflection, and irrational motivation, and thus clearly serve as an ongoing source of entertainment for privileged audiences within and without these narratives.

If much has been made down the centuries of the thrust in comedy towards the possibility of social harmoniousness (which, more often than not, means the restoration of habitual power relations), this act of closure is reserved conventionally for those who have successfully navigated a series of carefully orchestrated tests, trials, and humiliations. Nonetheless, despite the potentially redemptive spectacle of the arduous labours of provisionally deluded heroes and heroines, there remained a nagging concern (expressed regularly by those who were willing to afford any attention at all to questions of literary genre in the sixteenth century) that comedy sought out *low* company: base jests, asinine intrigues, rural clowns, and, potentially at least, undemanding audiences. In *The Book Named the Governor* (1531), Thomas Elyot acknowledged that there were those who supposed comedies to be 'a doctrinall of rybaudrie', whereas such productions should constitute a warning to the spectators that they 'may prepare them selfe to resist or prevente occasion' (Elyot 1531: 50ʳ–v). In subsequent decades George Gascoigne looked for 'the rewards and punishments of virtues and vices' in his stage entertainment (*The Glass of Government*, 1575: A3ʳ), and Philip Sidney, for 'delightful teaching' (*An Apology for Poetry*, 1595: K3ʳ). However, if, as Sidney complained, 'Our Tragedies and Comedies [are] not without cause cried out against,' it seems that *lowly* comedy offered only the slimmest pickings: 'But our Comedians, thinke there is no delight without laughter, which is very wrong [...] For what is it to make folkes gape at a wretched begger and a beggerly Clowne?' (I4ᵛ, K2ᵛ, K3ʳ).

Ultimately, the cumulative effect of surveying the currents of received thinking among these self-crowned arbiters of literary and cultural taste in sixteenth-century England may be that, in returning to these play texts, jests, and ballads from the period, we are also drawn to ponder the ways in which Tudor comic narratives can uncover the seemingly irrepressible appetite in society for a kind of cognitive shorthand when dealing with members of a social status group and, indeed, the ways in which the undertaking of comedy itself may rely upon such operations of reduction, elision, and erasure. Moreover, when we take into consideration the enormously buoyant markets for broadsides, jest books, and crime narratives as the Tudor period unfolded, it becomes all too possible that sections within the wider populace might be found to be actively investing in foreshortened and/or grossly distorted narratives of popular representation which often circulated within official culture or elite milieux—milieux from which members of this 'wider populace' might be partially or wholly excluded.

II

Given this context of cultural and generic expectations, it may be timely to be reminded of Gramsci's caveat that 'The people is not a culturally homogeneous unit, but it is culturally stratified in a complex way' (Burke 1994: 29). And this challenge to nuance our engagement with the politics of popular representation provides an excellent frame of reference with which to consider plays such as Mr S.'s *Gammer Gurton's Needle* (published 1575) and George Peele's *The Old Wife's Tale* (published 1595).[1] Both Elizabethan play texts in many ways afford strategic, if sometimes contrasting, points of entry into the diverse spectrum of Tudor comedy. This genre, as we have seen, could be greeted by the *literati* of the sixteenth century with down-turned faces, but its creative range nevertheless spanned the possibilities of farce and clownery,

[1] Norland (1995: 280) speculates that the title page of Mr S.'s comedy may have been set by the printer, Thomas Colwell, much earlier in the early 1560s.

witty exchange and improbable reversal, romantic adventure and fantastical caper—and all apparently gravitating (once frauds and deceptions had been exposed to the light) towards the possibility of a 'happy ending' and the reconceptualization of social harmony. The status of popular representation has a radically different status in each play, but in both cases we are surely being asked to enter a dramatic world in which, at least provisionally, those belonging to inferior status groups are not solely, or even principally, functions in the greater destinies of aristocratic players. In *Gammer Gurton's Needle* and *The Old Wife's Tale* such socially subordinate characters are allowed to participate fully in the plays' problematization of what popular and elite conditions of existence might be.

In the midst of the broad, often Grand Guignol, farce of *Gammer Gurton's Needle* (a feature which has mostly monopolized critical engagement with the play hitherto), pressing questions of social policing and economic disempowerment clearly emerge as we penetrate the fractious atmosphere of village life. Furthermore, in *The Old Wife's Tale*, the old wife in question, Madge Clunch, rather than being significant discursively as a subject of cultural domination, is strategically deployed as the bearer of narrative and the keeper (albeit a rather insecure one) of mysterious knowledge. Interestingly, Peele's dramatic structure is comically beset by the textual lacunae of Madge—a figure whose seemingly uncontrollable narrative energies are clearly counterpointed in the play with the extravagant ambitions of the sorcerer Sacrapant, who seeks to stage-manage the lives of others.[2] However, as soon becomes apparent, neither is able to assert complete mastery over their chosen subject:

OLD WOMAN O Lord I quite forgot, there was a Conjurer, and this Conjurer could doo anything, and hee turned himselfe into a great Dragon, and carried the Kinges Daughter away in his mouth to a Castle that hee made of stone, and there he kept hir I know not how long, till at last all the Kinges men went out so long, that hir two Brothers went to seeke hir. O I forget: she (he I would say) turned a proper yong man to a Beare in the night, and a man in the day, and keeps by a crosse that parts three severall waies, and he made his Lady run mad: gods me bones who comes here?   (B1^v)

The question of the politics of popular representation in Tudor comedy not only feeds a larger discussion about the ways in which the creative industries of the period engaged with prevailing habits of thinking about 'the lower orders'. It can also throw light upon the ongoing theorization of popular culture itself, which has often been beleaguered by the intellectual premises of critics who have deeply invested in the depiction of remorselessly divided societies governed by arbitrary and/or impoverishing cultural relationships. Thus, in the 1960s R. W. Ingram wished to foreclose any irksome anxiety about the vulgarity of Mr S.'s comedy by archly reassuring his

---

[2] For an interesting account of the sorcerer as one who 'dares imagine himself a heroic figure', see Goldstone (1960: 204).

readers that 'Groundlings may well be capable of more noise before such events than a sophisticated audience, but both groups react spontaneously to them when they are well presented and handled. It is a mark of *Gammer Gurton's Needle* that there is nothing prurient, sniggering, or cheaply repetitive about the treatment of such material' (Ingram 1967: 259). Earlier in the twentieth century, drawing upon the authority of Matthew Arnold among others, F. R. Leavis had insisted more generally that down the centuries the survival of 'true' cultural achievement had been directly linked to the taste cultures of social elites: 'In any period it is upon a very small minority that the discerning appreciation of art and literature depends: it is (apart from cases of the simple and familiar) only a few who are capable of unprompted, first-hand judgment' (Leavis 1930: 1).

However, as Stuart Hall has contended, it has been convenient, rather than insightful, to rely upon such oppositional theses, and to fantasize a 'whole, authentic, autonomous "popular culture" which lies outside the field of force of the relations of cultural power and domination' (2005: 67). And, equally forcefully from a more historicized perspective, Peter Burke argued in his landmark study *Popular Culture in Early Modern Europe*, 'In 1500 [...] popular culture was everyone's culture; a second culture for the educated [...] the point which needs to be made here is that educated people did not yet associate ballads and chapbooks and festivals with the common people, precisely because they participated in these forms of culture' (1994: 270, 27). Thus, rather than inviting us to celebrate a free-standing and homogeneous popular culture, to lament the loss of an organic *Volkskultur*, or anxiously to dissect scenes of cultural subordination, Tudor texts such as *Gammer Gurton's Needle* and *The Old Wife's Tale* may encourage us to interrogate widely available, but freighted, terms such as 'taste culture' and 'festive comedy'.

Conventionally, as theorists have long stressed, comic narratives should take us away from the august presence of tragic heroes and heroines to engage with the largely resolvable crises unfolding in frenzied urban or pastoral landscapes. In such a vision uncontaminated by generic hybridity, tragedy should compel us to reflect upon the human condition as communicated through the traumas of a cultural elite. However, placing to one side for the moment the study of earlier dramatic forms such as the cycle pageants and moral plays like *Mankind*, Tudor tragedies such as John Pickering's *Horestes* (1567) and Thomas Preston's *Cambises* (1570) refuse resolutely to cooperate with these generic expectations. Similarly, both *Gammer Gurton's Needle* and *The Old Wife's Tale* problematize in some detail contemporary expectations surrounding cultural privilege and effectively unpick our appetites for descending theories of power in comic narrative. Like the cycle plays of the Middle Ages, these Tudor comedies constitute an elite reading of popular culture prepared specifically for public consumption. Indeed, at the end of the eighteenth century Thomas Warton referred to *The Old Wife's Tale* as a 'very scarce and curious piece' (1791: 135), whose narrative, it had nonetheless to be admitted, bore remarkable similarities with that of a later production for a much more select audience, Milton's *Comus*.

III

The comedy of *Gammer Gurton's Needle* obliges audiences throughout to restrict their mockery (as Sidney feared) to the unruly society of the poor and those who have to do business with them. It is worth observing that affairs of the heart appear to have little substance in this farce. Instead of Peele's burlesquing of chivalric romance, in Mr S.'s comedy we have the crazed Gammer taking centre-stage, frantically trying to secure her 'fayre longe strayght ne'le that was myne onely treasure | [...] last end of my pleasure' (1575: A4ʳ). In contrast, Peele shows himself determined in *The Old Wife's Tale* to quicken the representation of popular experience by yoking it to the 'fantastical' theatrical conventions governing the intrigues of questing knights and distressed maidens as produced on the stage at the time. Interestingly, these conventions seem to have been met with a gnashing of teeth among contemporary critics, whatever their enduring appeal with Tudor audiences. Sidney reserved particular scorn for these congested and improbable tales for the stage: 'By and by, we heare newes of shipwracke in the same place, and then wee are to blame, if we accept it not for a Rock. Upon the backe of that, comes out a hidious Monster with fire and smoke, and then the miserable beholders, are bounde to take it for a Cave' (1595: K1ʳ). Similarly, in the prefatory address to his own drama *Promos and Cassandra* (1578), George Whetstone complained that the undiscerning dramatist of such extravagant romances 'is most vaine, indiscreete, and out of order: he fyrst groundes his worke, on impossibilities: then in three howers ronnes he throwe the worlde' (A2ᵛ). Furthermore, Stephen Gosson (who had himself, he confesses, penned a number of dramas for London audiences) not only points up in *Plays Confuted in Five Actions* (1582) what he considered to be, and what Samuel Johnson would later call with reference to *Cymbeline*, the 'unresisting imbecility' of such dramas (Johnson 1989: 235), he also highlights the imaginative leaps which audiences in the theatre were forced to make in the digestion of such fare:

> Sometime you shall see nothing but the adventures of an amorous knight, passing from countrie to countrie for the love of his lady, encountring many a terible monster made of broune paper, and at his retourne, is so wonderfully changed, that he can not be knowne but by some posie in his tablet, or by a broken ring, or a handkircher, or a piece of a cockle shell, what learne you by that?   (Gosson 1582: C6ʳ)

It is indeed possible that the published text of *The Old Wife's Tale* was edited for the purposes of touring, as some critics have speculated. However, even in this (possibly incomplete) version, Peele is clearly both responding to contemporary tastes among theatre audiences, and parodying their appetites for wonderful twists and turns of fortune, improbable courtships, supernatural interventions, and eagerly anticipated denouements of release and redemption. In this play, we are asked initially to attend to the dramatic frame of the Clunch household deep in the forest and the hospitality it offers to the young travelling pages. Antic, Frolic, and Fantastic (of uncertain social station) have lost their way in the woods and show themselves principally hungry for narrative: 'of the Gyant and the Kings Daughter, and I know not what, I have seene the day when I was a litle one, you might have drawne mee a mile after you with such a discourse' (1595: B1ʳ).[3] Peele's tale of magic and sorcery quickly transports us away from this secluded homely environment to an equally disorienting enchanted forest inhabited by strange beasts and perverse magicians. Nor, it seems, should we be concerned to attribute the unfolding of 'an old wives winters tale' solely to the delights of the lower orders. Shakespeare is certainly eager not to do so in his late romance; and, indeed, Peter Burke emphasizes that 'Nobles and peasants seem to have shared the taste for romances of chivalry. In the sixteenth century, the Norman squire, the Sieur de Gouberville, read *Amadis de Gaule* aloud to his peasants when it rained. Broadsides and chap-books seem to have been read by rich and poor, educated and uneducated' (1994: 26). And in the context of these enquiries, we might also turn to a notable mid-Elizabethan specimen, one enterprising Captain Cox, who is reported to have numbered among his book collection: 'King Arthurz book [...] Bevys of Hampton [...] Virgils life [...] Collyn cloout. The Fryar and the boy, Elynor Rumming [...] the Sheperdz kalender. The Ship of Foolz [...] Beside hiz auncient playz, Yooth and charitee, Hikskorner, Nugize, Impacient poverty, and heerwith doctor Boords breviary of health' (L. Wright 1958: 84). By the time plays such as *Gammer Gurton's Needle* and *The Old Wife's Tale* were being presented, there was clearly a long-standing and widespread interest in the magical and improbably romantic tales which invariably seem to have involved almost free-standing narrative functions such as beast combats and the rescue of abducted princesses. And these, in the case of Cox at least, formed a textual continuum with the ownership of interludes such as *Hickscorner*, *Newguise*, and *Impatient Poverty*.

If, more recently, Slavoj Žižek has invited us to believe that 'through fantasy, we learn how to desire' (1991: 6), it is clear that in the early modern period this appetite was being experienced not only through relevant book purchases, but through a host of other forms of cultural entertainment. Much has been made in recent criticism of the longevity of medieval dramaturgical practices—that the Kendal Corpus Christi pageants, for example, appear to have escaped the vigilance of the Reformists and lasted on into the early seventeenth century. However, more generally, there is evidence that guilds and companies maintained their stored wagons even when there was a moratorium on performance; and, indeed, that the elaborate costumes associated with earlier dramatic traditions might be recycled for other kinds of public theatre, whatever the nature of the 'late innovation'. Thus, if there were no possibility in the final decades of the sixteenth century of seeing Herod's knights slaying innocents or of Christ and his forces completing the Harrowing of Hell, elsewhere in the widely

[3] For a revealing discussion of these 'transitional' figures, see Lamb (2002: 33). These enquiries focusing upon the pages and the status of the storytelling 'old wife' are further developed in Lamb (2006: 45–62).

performed St George entertainments we surely find close kin to the fantastical knight errant Huanebango (Juan y Bango) in Peele's *The Old Wife's Tale*.

IV

As was apparent from the jesting tale at the very beginning of this discussion, textual representations of popular culture often pay particular attention to the question of labour—and this may or may not have a domestic context. The first information that we discover about Gammer Gurton is that she is 'sat pesynge and patching of Hodg her mans briche', while as an employer in the village she has set her maid Tyb to cleaning and her landworker Hodge 'to ditchinge' (1575: A2^{r-v}). This decision to draw dramatic attention early on to the workaday lives of non-elite characters operates within conventions already well established in medieval drama, and the referencing of relationships of economic subordination clearly offers opportunities for highlighting oppositional dynamics in society and stimulating cultural critique. Such considerations are placed provisionally centre-stage, for example, in William Wager's moral interlude *Enough Is as Good as a Feast* (1570). Here, a Tenant is produced *in medias res*, complaining in 'Cotswold speech' that

> My Londlord is so covetouse as the devil of hel:
> Except chil give him such a shameful rent.
> As cham not able, away ich must incontinent.
> Oh masters, is not this even a lamentable thing?
> To zee how Londlords their poor tenants do wring.
>
> (C1^{r-v})

However, in a number of Tudor comedies such as *Gammer Gurton's Needle* and *The Old Wife's Tale*, the dramatic stress may not principally fall upon the victim's experience of economic domination in quite the same manner. Instead, we may be drawn into stage worlds in which comic misrule tips over into acts of violation and criminal proceedings among the lower orders. In *The Old Wife's Tale* the focus turns explicitly to social unrest when Wiggen and his company of belligerent parishioners make an unexpected entrance into the world of sorcerers, captive maidens, and questing suitors to do battle with the truculent authorities who refuse to bury a penniless member of the community.[4] Although the episode may be seen to engage

---

[4] David Bevington has drawn attention to the ways in which social moralities might connect with 'a growing sense of restiveness in their lower-class London audiences' (1968: 137). However, more solemnly, Curtis Perry contends with reference to *Gammer Gurton's Needle* that 'the basic elements of the play's story—poverty, unruly vagabondage, clerical incompetence, and the greedy hankering over trifling commodities—are also ubiquitous social concerns provoked by the economic crises of the 1540s and

with larger commitments within the drama concentrating upon loss and exclusion, this strategic insight into civil disorder certainly serves to unsettle Peele's seemingly charmed dramatic world. This representation of warring factions varies significantly from the account of existence among the lower orders which has been established hitherto by the often beguiling evocation of the Clunch household.

Interestingly, when we consider *Gammer Gurton's Needle* in terms of a 'charmed' dramatic world and comic misrule, it quickly becomes apparent that under the careful supervision of the Bedlam the villagers respond to the changeful world about them in terms of superstition and recrimination. Diccon participates fully in such performances, declaring of the traumatized Gammer and her maid Tyb, 'By gogs soule there they syt as still as stones in the streite | As though they had ben taken with fairies or els with some il sprite' (A3^r). And if Hodge exclaims to Gurton's maid Tib on the loss of the needle, 'Perchaunce some felon sprit may haunt our house,' he is also later convinced that the Bedlam is able to 'cal up a great blacke devill' (A3^r, C2^v). Mr S.'s comedy strategically punctures any faith which might be placed in such assertions by constantly reminding the audience of Diccon's role as catalyst but, in keeping with the expectations surrounding the artful capers of the Vice as he emerged in the final decades of the century, the Bedlam exults in blurring the distinctions between observable fact and imaginative possibility. From his privileged position as stage manager and allowed fool, he effectively constitutes the narrative lens through which we witness the developing consciousness of a community capable of both thoroughly arbitrary modes of reasoning and arrestingly imaginative courses of action. Interestingly, his decision to bind the whole village together in an absurd narrative of grand larceny is reminiscent of the aspirations of another, earlier comic hero of the farce *Jack Juggler* (1565) who determines to 'make Jenkine bylive yf I can | That he is not him-selfe but an other man!' (A4^r–v). Both Juggler and Diccon humiliate their credulous neighbours with fantastical speculations, but we are asked to attend to the expert rhetorical manoeuvres with which both jesters creatively edit the experience of those around them.

More generally, comic reversal lies at the heart of any consideration of Tudor comedy, and in *Gammer Gurton's Needle* this narrative technique is explicitly linked to questions of social marginality, agency, and competition. The comic expectations surrounding the anarchic Vice and the witty Fool converge upon the figure of Diccon, who, like many of his antecedents, is allowed to move between social strata and yet also to establish the boundaries of interaction for others. The trickster takes it upon himself to highlight transgressions supposedly committed by his fellow villagers and to propose suitably extravagant courses of revenge for the aggrieved. However, what becomes most particularly striking about Diccon's role are not only his vir-tuosic skills of equivocation (which, by this stage, had become commonplace for the Vice), but his seeming immunity from prosecution, his irrepressible ability to

1550s […] Gammer Gurton's affection for her needle is designed to allude to contemporary reformist invective against an emergent commodity culture' (2002: 217).

exploit the stunted minds of his fellow villagers, and his sustained refusal to bow in any convincing manner to the authority of any representative from the culture of officialdom.

V

If many recent critical studies have all too often sought to shape a popular culture in monolithic terms, as contemporary theoretical debates have often stressed, the shifting representation of the popular must be fractionalized with considerations of age, region, economic status, and gender. Given the limits of time and space, this discussion can only signal the rich potential of these lines of enquiry. However, like the questions of gender expectation and the representation of economic subordination in early modern drama that continue to enjoy lively scholarly interest, the fact that Tudor dramatists were often at pains to identify popular culture in specifically regional terms should also give us pause. Given that the Tudor stage did not privilege an ornate *mise-en-scène* in performance as would be the case, for example, in the next century with the performance of court masques, the concern with regional presentation mostly relies upon a principle of linguistic difference. This dramatic convention, witnessed above in Wager's *Enough Is as Good as a Feast* and already well established by the sixteenth century, was put to a variety of uses in early English drama. We may be reminded of Mak in the Wakefield *Second Shepherds' Pageant*, for example, when he initially tries to create an anonymous and socially elevated identity for himself with the extravagant adoption of a southern dialect:

> What! Ich be a yoman, I tell you, of the kyng I must have reverence;
> Why, who be ich?

> (*Wakefield* 2000: 201, 206–7)

By the Tudor period, it appears to have become almost an expectation that the non-elite character would be identified through a West Country dialect (often identifiable in terms of 'chave' ('I have'), 'cham' ('I am')).

And if critically it has been speculated that Mr S.'s comedy may be located in the Cambridgeshire village of Girton, it should be noted that Hodge expresses himself in a broad stage Zummerset which passes unremarked in Gammer's society: 'See so cham arayed with dablynge in the durt | She that set me to ditchinge, ich wold she had the squ[i]rt' (1575: A2ᵛ). While much has been made theoretically of the positioning of subordinate groups through language, cultural appetites for differentiation and the fetishization of a popular class are frequently problematized in Tudor comedy. Quite apart from the long-standing mockery of the low-bred, ill-educated, non-urban, and thus clowning, characters that would live on English drama for centuries to come, there is also an emphasis upon linguistic 'performance' (in terms of creativity, expertise, as well as solecism) which repeatedly underpins the depiction of popular culture on the sixteenth-century stage. And, of course, such *coloratura* performances are widely in evidence as village life descends progressively into comic riot in *Gammer Gurton's Needle*:

GAMMER Nay fy on thee [thou] rampe, thou ryg, with al that take thy parte.
DAME CHAT A vengeaunce on those lips [that] laieth such things to my charge.
GAMMER A vengence on those callats hips, whose conscience is so large.
CHAT Come out Hogge.
GAMMER Come out hogge, and let me have right.
CHAT Thou arrant Witche.
GAMMER Thou bawdie bitche, chil make thee cursse this night.   (C3ʳ)

In a more general account focusing upon the ways in which popular cultures may be adjudged by the larger society which scrutinizes them, Dick Hebdige acknowledges that

Subcultures [may be seen to] represent 'noise' (as opposed to sound): interference in the orderly sequence [...] We should therefore not underestimate the signifying power of the spectacular subculture not only as a metaphor for potential anarchy 'out there' but as an actual mechanism of semantic disorder: a kind of temporary blockage in the system of representation.   (2005: 355)

Clearly, in a carefully orchestrated narrative such as that of *Gammer Gurton's Needle*, the frantic verbal cut-and-thrust between the characters can communicate both the alienness and the unruliness of a community which appears to defy incorporation into the habitual power relations of the larger society. Nonetheless, these encounters can also point to the arresting vitality of these villagers, whose histrionics can make the representatives of official culture appear bland, if not unappealing.

Moreover, in such comedies the linguistic tours de force, such as those excerpted above, may often be accompanied by equally energetic physical scrummidges. The Ancilla in Henry Medwall's *Fulgens and Lucres* (c.1497) censures the advances of the garrulous servants A and B with violence: 'Et utroque flagellato recedit Ancilla' ('And, when both are beaten, the Maid withdraws'; 1234). And in *Common Conditions* (1576–7)—which like *The Old Wife's Tale* couples together narratives of popular culture with those of romantic questing—the company of tinkers, Shifte, Drifte, and Unthrifte, mostly assert themselves on stage through knockabout spats:

   They fight.
UNTHRIFT Stay, stay, no more brawling now one with another.
SHIFT By gog bould Drift, I'le breake your noddell if you were my brother,
      And thou be a honest fellow Thrift let us but try.
DRIFT Come and thou dare, for I pas not a turd for thee I.   (B1ᵛ)

However, rather than concentrating upon such clowning communities, in *Gammer Gurton's Needle* we are asked to attend to the sleights of hand of the Bedlam. It becomes immediately apparent that Diccon's tales progressively release an unruly power of cultural accusation and violation, a power to antagonize and to divide. Furthermore, not only are we confronted with the disorders of the villagers' experiences, those who are placed in positions of authority are also found wanting in self-government.

Parting company with more heavily moralized comic narratives of the period such as Wager's *Enough Is as Good as a Feast* (1560), *Gammer Gurton's Needle* dispenses with solemn acts of closure ushered in by irreproachable Virtues such as Mercy or Justice. Instead, in a grand finale, Diccon is left to parley with a distinctly suspect official culture, whether in the shape of Dr Rat or the less-than-vigorous peacemaking of Master Bayly. The comic and indolent *clericus* complains that he is always on the run ('Here to a drab, there to a theefe') to sort out the shabby lives of his flock, and if he demurs, he is 'sure to lacke therfore, a tythe pyg or a goose' (D1^r). It is thus material appetite, rather than spiritual vocation, which leads Dr Rat on to become embroiled in the tangle of his parishioners' lives. Official culture is more substantially represented by the later arrival of Master Bayly, but his unfailing geniality ultimately unveils someone determined to soothe sources of social unrest quickly, rather than to attend judiciously to the excesses of the imaginative lives of the villagers:

> I wil injoyne him here, some open kind of penaunce:
> Of this condition, where ye know my fee is twenty pence
> For the bloodshed, I am agreed with you here to dispence.
>
> (C3^v)

VI

So what is to be made of these on-stage communities of popular culture and of the conventions which Tudor drama employed to denote them? Contemporary scholarship, like its early modern forebears, has sometimes despaired of securing a convenient taxonomy, a convenient *morally instructive* taxonomy, for the brawling, cussing, and fantastical folk who inhabit these comedies. Introducing *Gammer Gurton's Needle* to a new readership at the beginning of the twentieth century, Henry Bradley confessed that 'The very rudimentary kind of humour which turns on physically disgusting suggestions is no longer amusing to educated people, and there is so much of this poor stuff in the play that the real wit of some scenes, and the clever portraiture of character throughout, have not received their fair share of acknowledgement' (1912: 202). Much more recently, discomfort lives on as irrepressible critical desires to yoke Tudor comedies together into overarching accounts in terms of theme and artistic aim remain thwarted. Tellingly, Joel B. Altman has argued that 'we cannot find a place in the moral life of the period for the plays we really cherish. We can only—if implicitly—regard them as inspired aberrations' (Altman 1978: 6).

In his *Art of Rhetoric* (1553), Thomas Wilson contended that 'The occasion of laughter [...] is the fondnes, the filthines, the deformitee and all suche evill behavior, as we se to bee in other' (74^v), and it is revealing that this familiar theoretical emphasis upon comedy as a comforting 'evacuation' recurs as a theme in many of the plays under consideration. Indeed, in *Gammer Gurton's Needle*, Hodge pleads, 'Canst not tarrye a lytle thought | Tyll ich make a curtesie of water,' and the besoiled peasant is dismissed by Diccon as a 'shytten knave' (B3^v). Thomas Wilson's concern that comedy should isolate the world of our everyday selves from a crazed dramatic reality on stage can certainly be seen to characterize frequent critical dealings with the likes of Dame Chat, Gammer Gurton, and Dr Rat. In a lively engagement with the play, Kent Cartwright affirms that Mr S. takes us into a world of 'clay, filth, mud, and tatters' (1999: 95).[5] Elsewhere, in critical narratives of estranged and estranging comic worlds, the popular cultures in question can often emerge discursively as autonomous, and thus containable, subcultures. As has been witnessed in the course of this discussion, the convoluted plot of *Gammer Gurton's Needle* describes the dissolution of a community under pressure from an antic disposition. In order for comedy to realize its full potential, Sidney (like many theorists down the centuries) believed that audiences must remain sufficiently disengaged from the intrigue to exploit the moral faculties of recognition and judgement: 'Comedy is an imitation of the common errors of our life, which [the playwright] representeth, in the most ridiculous and scornefull sort that may be' (F3^r). However, more recently, in their analyses of contemporary debates surrounding popular culture, Chandra Mukerji and Michael Schudson have argued that 'There is no Archimedean point outside culture from which to observe it objectively and no protection within the university for those wishing to be ignorant of the popular cultural environment' (1991: 53). What becomes apparent from the more general survey of Tudor comedy is the recurring strategy of successive generations of dramatists to try to secure this 'Archimedean point' with the resources of meta-dramatic techniques.

In this context, *The Old Wife's Tale* joins the ranks of a large number of Tudor romances, comedies, and pageant-like entertainments which sustain interests in contrasting, but interconnected, planes of theatrical existence. Peele's meta-dramatic narrative (which turns upon the figure of Madge Clunch) is but one example of a whole host of plays from the second half of the sixteenth century which seek to respond to allegorical and typological emphases inherited from the drama of earlier generations. Broadly contemporary with Peele's drama of sorcery and abductions, the anonymous romance pageant *The Rare Triumphs of Love and Fortune* (1589) begins with the entry of the Olympian gods, and the subsequent narrative is triggered by a challenge for Venus and Fortune to see who can exert most power over a royal mortal. Elsewhere, in the earlier *Albyon Knyghte* (1566), the initial debate between Justice and Injury

---

[5] John W. Velz calls it 'this most excremental of all Tudor plays' (1984: 8), and William B. Toole, 'comedy of the lowest order' (1973: 256).

provides a moral and spiritual vantage point from which to judge the undertakings of the protagonist. And in R.B.'s *Apius and Virginia* (1575) audiences are introduced once again to a tension between discrete, but intimately related, conditions of existence: 'Here let him make as though he went out and let Consience and Justice come out of him, and let Consience hold in his hande a Lamp burning and let Justice have a sworde and hold it before Apius brest' (C1ʳ).

The imbrication of two dramatic realities in this way not only yielded opportunities for thematic emphasis, moral instruction, symbolic commentary, and affective disengagement on the part of the audience, but it also seems to have constituted an irresistible temptation on occasions for dramatists to engineer awe-inspiring *coups de théâtre*. At the beginning of the Tudor period, the capers of A and B in Henry Medwall's lightly classicized *Fulgens and Lucres* demonstrate an explicit interest in this tension between the dramatic frame of popular enquiry—'Ye, but I pray the, what-calt, tell me this: | Who is he that now comyth yn?' (2000: 195–6)—and the ethical crises which may oppress members of the social elite. In *The Old Wife's Tale* this kind of complex narrative strategy is developed in an equally arresting manner as the characters can be seen to straddle two planes of existence leading to what Joel Altman has famously proposed as a more pervasive schema for Tudor literature in general—the union of 'edifying precepts vividly set forth [...] [with] a play of mind that overran the boundaries traditionally set by the orthodoxy of the outside world' (1978: 30).

> *Enter the two Brothers.*
> FROLIC Soft Gammer, here some come to tell your tale for you.
> FANTASTIC Let them alone, let us heare what they will say.
> 1. BROTHER Upon these chalkie Cliffs of *Albion*
>   We are arived now with tedious toile,
>   And compassing the wide world round about
>   To seeke our sister, to seeke faire *Delya* forth,
>   Yet cannot we so much as heare of hir.   (B1ᵛ–B2ʳ)

In conclusion, whatever the meta-dramatic conundrums that plays such as *The Old Wife's Tale* may pose or the nature of the cultural appetites (or prejudices) to which *Gammer Gurton's Needle* may respond, we return to the thorny question concerning the very function and status of the representation of popular culture in Tudor comedy.[6] It is interesting to note that both literary and historical scholarship pursuing broader enquiries into popular culture has frequently concerned itself with the desire to engage in myths of belonging and to occlude a culturally riven reality. In the early part of the twentieth century F. R. Leavis and Denys Thompson famously lamented that 'what we have lost is the organic community with the living culture it

---

[6] Indeed, David Hall reminds us that 'The historian of popular culture is in pursuit of an elusive quarry. No one knows exactly what this quarry looks likes or even who "the people" are whose culture is at issue. Anyone who intervenes to serve as guide is suspect; the intermediary is by definition different from the subject' (1984: 5).

embodied' (1934: 1); and more recently (but equally solemnly), the theorist Dominic Strinati has argued that 'The comforts and cathartic effects of popular culture enable people to resign themselves to the harsh and unfulfilling reality of living in a capitalist society' (2005: 62). Certainly, there is every reason to believe that in Tudor times comedy was viewed as a therapeutic force at work for the collective mind. In order to support this argument, we need not only turn to the familiar topos of the 'Induction' to *The Taming of the Shrew*, where it is affirmed that

MESSENGER [...] they thought it good you hear a play
  And frame your mind to mirth and merriment,
  Which bars a thousand harms and lengthens life.   (Ind. 2. 131–3)

The Prologue to the earlier *Jack Juggler* also seeks to

> intermix honest mirthe, in such wise
> That your stre[n]gth may be refreshed
> soo the mynd and wittes to keep
> Pregnant, freshe industrius, quike and lustie,
> Honest mirthe, and pastime, is requisite and necessarie.

> (1565: A1ᵛ)

And the figure of Comedy enters at the beginning of *Mucedorus* (1598) clearly with the same aims in mind:

> Musicke revives, and mirth is tollerable.
> *Comedie* play thy part, and please,
> Mak merry them that coms to joy with thee.

> (A2ʳ)[7]

With such questions of mirth and self-government, we return to speculations of Tudor critics which opened this discussion—speculations which would extend well beyond the Tudor period. The bookseller William London in *A Catalogue of the Most Vendible Books in England* (1657) bemoaned the fact that 'too many idly sit down in the Chaire of Ignorance, travelling by the fire side, with the *Wandering Knight Sir John Mandevil*, or it may be *Bevis of Southampton*; whilest the Laws of Nations, admirable foundations of Common-wealths, pass undiscovered or dived into' (A4ᵛ). And a little later, in *Sighs from Hell* (1666), his contemporary John Bunyan recollected his youth when he yearned for 'a Ballad, a News-book, *George* on Horsback or *Bevis of Southampton* [...] [I would seek out] some book that teaches Curious Arts, that tells of old Fables; but for the Holy Scriptures, I cared not. And as it was with me then, so it is with my brethren now' (147–8). Tudor comedies such as *Gammer Gurton's Needle* and *The Old Wife's Tale* not only respond to enduring audience appetites for improbability and imaginative transcendence, but we must also remain open to the

---

[7] More generally, R. W. Maslen (2008: 119–21) has pointed out that the therapy of mirth was an ongoing area of published medical enquiry during the sixteenth century for a number of figures such as Sir Thomas Elyot, William Cunningham, Andrew Boorde, and William Bullein.

possibility that such productions can also lead to the unsettling of widely received habits of thinking on popular culture and to the interrogation of pervasive theories of social control.

OLD WOMAN Once uppon a time there was a King or a Lord, or a Duke that had a faire daughter, the fairest that ever was; as white as snowe, and as redd as bloud: and once uppon a time his daughter was stollen away, and hee sent all his men to seeke out his daughter, and hee sent so long, that he sent all his men out of his Land.

FROLIC Who drest his dinner then?

OLD WOMAN Nay either heare my tale, or kisse my taile.

FANTASTIC Well sed, on with your tale Gammer.   (B1ᵛ)

PRIMARY WORKS

ARMIN, ROBERT (1600), *Foole upon Foole.*

BUNYAN, JOHN (1666), *Sighs from Hell.*

Common Conditions (1576/7), *A pleasant comedie called common conditions.*

ELYOT, THOMAS (1531), *The Boke Named the Governour.*

GASCOIGNE, GEORGE (1575), *The Glasse of Governement.*

GOSSON, STEPHEN (1582), *Playes Confuted in Five Actions.*

Jack Juggler (1565), *A New Enterlude for Chyldren to Playe, Named Jacke Jugeler Both Wytte, and Very Playsent.*

LONDON, WILLIAM (1657), *A Catalogue of the Most Vendible Books in England.*

MEDWALL, HENRY (2000), *Fulgens and Lucres*, in Greg Walker (ed.), *Medieval Drama* (Oxford: Blackwell).

MR S. (1575), *Gammer Gurtons Nedle.*

MUCEDORUS (1598), *A Most Pleasant Comedie of Mucedorus.*

PEELE, GEORGE (1595), *The Old Wives Tale.*

R.B. (1575), *Apius and Virginia.*

SHAKESPEARE, WILLIAM (1987), *The Taming of the Shrew*, ed. Brian Morris (London: Methuen).

SIDNEY, PHILIP (1595), *An Apologie for Poetrie.*

WAGER, WILLIAM (1570), *Inough Is as Good as a Feast.*

Wakefield (2000), 'The Second Shepherds' Play', in Greg Walker (ed.), *Medieval Drama* (Oxford: Blackwell), 42–57.

WHETSTONE, GEORGE (1578), *Promos and Cassandra.*

WILSON, THOMAS (1553), *The Arte of Rhetorique.*

EPILOGUE

EDMUND SPENSER AND THE PASSING OF TUDOR LITERATURE

HELEN COOPER

Of Faerie lond yet if he more inquire,
By certaine signes here set in sundry place
He may it find; ne let him then admire,
But yield his sence to be too blunt and bace
That no'te without an hound fine footing trace.
And thou, O fairest Princesse under sky,
In this faire mirrhour maist behold thy face,
And thine owne realmes in lond of Faery,
And in this antique Image thy great auncestry.

(*FQ* 2, proem 4)[1]

THIS famous stanza from the proem to book 2 of *The Faerie Queene* announces Spenser's conception for his whole work. It is to be a 'mirrhour', not only for Elizabeth but for her 'realmes', England (including Wales in this period) and Ireland; and furthermore, through the 'antique Image' presented in the poem, it will reflect all that has made the contemporary nation what it is. He creates it, in other words, not just as England's national epic, but as an anatomy of the nation for his own times and in the light of how that present has come into being. He will present its own

---

[1] References to *The Faerie Queene* (Spenser 1981) will be given as *FQ* throughout this essay.

'auncestry' alongside the Queen's, in terms of its history, its traditions, and its literary inheritance, for the body politic has a genealogy just as Elizabeth's own person does. It is a poem at once contemporary, in its concerns with the young Anglican Church, the condition of Ireland, and foreign relations; historical and legendary–historical, in its recurrent reversion to chronicle from the founding of Britain forwards; and mythological, in its animation of the topographical structure of the nation, in the mapping of its rivers. It is a key text—it is *the* key text—in the great Elizabethan movement towards what Richard Helgerson calls 'the writing of England' (Helgerson 1992, title page).[2]

The writing of England also had large implications for the nature of the poem's language and style. 'Why a Gods name', Spenser demanded of Gabriel Harvey in 1580, 'may not we, as else the Greekes, have the kingdome of oure owne Language?' (Spenser 1912b: 611). An expression of exasperation at the attempt to impose classical rules of prosody on English verse, the remark also more broadly expresses exasperation at the relegation of English to the status of a subaltern language, at the reluctance to allow it its own authority and independence. Elizabeth's realms extend to include the kingdom of the language; and that too has its own past, its own genealogy. Spenser's use of English refashions the nation's greatest model of poetic excellence, Geoffrey Chaucer, into a living tradition that links the past with his own present, that presents the language complete with its own 'auncestry'.

Like Sir Philip Sidney, Spenser was intent to show that English could produce as good a literature as the ancient world or contemporary Europe. That meant an incorporation of Virgil and Ovid, an emulation or overgoing of the French Clément Marot and the Italian Ludovico Ariosto; but importantly, it also meant incorporating native English traditions in the English language. That was how the *Shepheardes Calender* could become home-grown pastoral, and *The Faerie Queene* an indigenous epic. Any early reader of Spenser who lacked education in Latin and the Continental languages but who had a good background in Tudor writing would have found little in his major works alien or unfamiliar—far less, indeed, than do scholars who try to make them fit classical models. The richness of the Tudor context for *The Faerie Queene* has for long been overshadowed by scholarship on its classical and Italian connections, and more recently by the New Historicist emphasis on its immediate political context. Situated in its own historical and linguistic moment as the culmination of earlier Tudor literature, however, the work reveals a different set of qualities, variously overlapping with and complementary to what is conventionally thought of as humanist, that underline Spenser's commitment to the poetics of nationhood. *The Faerie Queene* was not only the celebration of national pride in the years after the Armada; it was also a *summa* of all that had made England and its literature what they were.

---

[2] See also Claire McEachern, who starts from the insight that 'the Tudor–Stuart nation is profoundly preoccupied with its own historicity' (1996: 33); and, for the earlier decades, Shrank (2004b), which is especially valuable on attitudes to the language.

45.1 Heroical Poetry

Spenser's choice of form for his masterwork is therefore well chosen. 'Heroical poetry', the standard Elizabethan term that comprehended both epic and romance, allowed the poem a size and scope such as enabled it to encompass much of what had gone before, as well as what was going on in his own time. In generic terms, epic had not yet been displaced by tragedy as the most admired literary form: the heroic was 'the best and most accomplished kind of Poetry', in Sidney's terms (2002: 99). Virgil remained the master poet of the European poetic tradition, and the Renaissance rediscovery of Homer gave archaic epic an up-to-the-minute interest. Chivalric romances were the most fashionable and widely read of all narrative forms, even if the texts that were most widely read were not always the most fashionable. Prints of Middle English metrical romances formed the bulk of popular fiction for Tudor readers at large (see H. Cooper 2004: 409–29); Malory's great Arthuriad, the first and only full account of the romance Arthur in English, had been written in the last years of the Plantagenet dynasty and disseminated almost solely through print, its first edition appearing within weeks of Henry Tudor's seizure of the throne. Humanists who claimed to despise such works could nonetheless indulge their delight in stories of adventure in the often more wildly improbable late classical and Continental European romances: the Greek prose *Aethiopica* of Heliodorus and *Daphnis and Chloe* of Longus (recently translated into English by way of Latin and French respectively); the Italian verse Ariosto and Tasso; and that Renaissance equivalent of the soap opera, the Spanish prose *Amadis de Gaule* and its perpetually proliferating imitations and sequels. For Spenser, heroical poetry encompassed equally the admired classical epics, the scorned but universally known native tradition, and the respectable new arrivals. His main borrowing from Virgil lies in the core conception of a national epic; from Ariosto (and, before him, from the thirteenth-century Arthurian prose romances), the meandering and interlinking multiple stories that could pursue the simultaneous adventures of different heroes and heroines in an infinitely capacious structure. The exemplary heroes of the Elizabethan age included Achilles, Aeneas, and Tasso's Rinaldo, all mentioned by Sidney; but Spenser's own set comes from nearer home. He gives a high profile to Arthur, who still carried notable cultural capital as England's one great empire-builder and the forebear of the Tudors, even though he was now tending to slide downmarket (the humanist Sidney rather patronizingly refers to him as 'honest King Arthur'). He invokes Bevis of Southampton, who had fought a dragon in terms Spenser diligently quarries for Redcrosse in book 1 (see A. King 2000: 129–45). For Guyon and his accompanying palmer he appropriates the figure of Guy, or Guyon, of Warwick, legendary ancestor of the earls of Warwick (and therefore of Ambrose and Robert Dudley), who had divided his career between being a knight errant and a palmer; and Guyon furthermore is knighted by Huon of Bordeaux, familiar from Lord Berners's Henrician translation, who had ended his own romance career in fairyland (see *FQ* 2. 1. 6). For many of Spenser's readers, his heroical poem would have invoked home-grown

English romance at least as strongly as it recalled the *Aeneid* or the *Orlando Furioso*.

The opening of the first canto makes the work's affiliations with chivalric romance unmistakable:

> A Gentle Knight was pricking on the plaine,
> Y cladd in mightie armes and silver shielde,
> Wherein old dints of deepe wounds did remaine,
> The cruell markes of many'a bloudy fielde;
> Yet armes till that time did he never wield.

$$(1. 1. 1)$$

Like many of the metrical romances avidly read by the Tudor populace, it declares itself immediately as the story of a knight errant. The title of book 1, however, has already suggested something more, or other than, chivalric romance. This is to be 'the legende of the Knight of the Red Crosse, or of Holinesse'—an idea confirmed in the following stanza:

> But on his brest a bloudie Crosse he bore,
> The deare remembrance of his dying Lord,
> For whose sweete sake that glorious badge he wore...
> Upon his shield the like was also scor'd.

$$(1. 1. 2)$$

The coat of arms identifies this knight, long before he is named in the poem, as St George. The iconography Spenser assembles over book 1, complete with the maiden and her distinctively English feature of a lamb, was still widely available in Reformation England, not least in woodcuts in surviving earlier printed books such as Alexander Barclay's *Life of St George* (Figure E.1), or illustrated missals. The presence in some of these woodcuts of her parents watching the dragon-fight from the walls of their castle further makes them look as if, as in Spenser, they are trapped inside by the monster (Williams 1990).[3] In Spenser's poetic reinterpretation, however, the knight's well-used armour is the 'whole armour of God' of Ephesians 6, and its bearer is therefore also a Christian Everyman, thus potentially a saint by the new Calvinist definition of election. Non-biblical saints had been a major problem ever since the Reformation—or rather, they were eliminated as a problem by largely being eliminated altogether. St George, as the patron saint of England, and in particular of the Order of the Garter (the reincarnation of the Round Table, and, with that, the model for Spenser's Order of Maidenhead), was difficult to dispose of quite so easily, however implausible his history. The Garter Chapel at Windsor Castle supposedly housed the saint's heart; Henry VII had acquired a leg (Gunn 1990: 110). The 'George', a medallion worn on a chain around the neck and showing the saint spearing the dragon, was the distinguishing feature of the Elizabethan Garter knights, and was proudly displayed on their portraits. George's red cross figured

---

[3] See also the reproduction which serves as frontispiece to Hawes (1974). On Una's parents, see the Letter to Ralegh and *FQ* 1. 11. 3.

Here begynnyth the lyfe of the gloryous martyr saynt George/patrone of the Royalme of En-
glonde/traslate by alexander barclay/at cōmaun
dement of the ryght hyghe/ and myghty Prynce
Thomas/duke of Norfolke/tresorer ⁊ Erle mar-
chall of Englonde.

Fig. E.1 St George of England slays the dragon. Alexander Barclay, *Lyfe of St George* (1515), title page, A1ʳ.

prominently in proclamations of English Protestant triumphalism, in Ireland and in Elizabeth's Continental adventures (see McCabe 2002: 101–20).[4] A chivalric epic of Elizabethan knighthood could scarcely exist without him; but allegory allows Spenser to cut the Gordian knot, to keep St George even while substituting a raft of new meanings for his Roman sainthood. Allegory is commonly thought of as an analytical tool, useful for dissecting human behaviour or emotion, but it is often at its most powerful when it is synthetic, combining meanings. One of the most comprehensive of such syntheses, available to Spenser through Robert Crowley's print of Langland in 1550, was the figure of Piers Plowman, who represents at various stages man in God's image, Adam or the earthly labourer; the personification of charity; and God in man's image, Christ incarnate as Jesus.[5] Spenser's Redcrosse Knight is at once a struggling human holiness, and England itself in its theological orientation, an England that has newly established a unique relationship with divine Truth through the Anglican Church.

If Redcrosse represents Englishness in the Protestantized version of its martial patron saint, however, the origins Spenser gives him represent a very different tradition of Englishness, and one that goes back directly to Langland. Where *The Faerie Queene* is the Elizabethan anatomy of England, with the knight as its representative character, Langland's earlier anatomy had made the ploughman its central figure. Spenser's decision to allegorize nobility of inward nature as nobility of blood largely eliminates any possibility of direct imitation,[6] but the tradition of the good ploughman as the true heart of the nation remained powerful in the Tudor age not only through the printing of *Piers Plowman* itself, but also through a series of further works that offered the same representation: hence Spenser's claim, in the Envoy to the *Shepheardes Calender*, that he is following 'the Pilgrim that the Plowman playde a whyle'. The reference may be to Langland or to the pseudo-Chaucerian *Plowman's Tale*, but ploughman literature took many other forms too, including Latimer's sermons on the plough: examples that all (Crowley's print included) emphasized the nature of the true ploughman as inherently Protestant. Spenser's St George (from Greek: *georgos*, a husbandman) brings together the two types, the knight and the tiller of the English soil, in the account of his origins told to him by Contemplation (1. 10. 65–6). Sprung from 'ancient race | Of *Saxon* kings' but stolen by a fairy who leaves a 'base' changeling in his place, the infant George was found in a furrow by a ploughman, and so preserved to emerge in the present of the poem as the young and inexperienced champion of Truth. His biography thus parallels the history Foxe and others claimed for the Church of England, that it was directly descended from the

---

[4] Cf. the Portuguese expedition of 1589 under Norris and Drake going 'Under the sanguine Crosse, brave Englands badge, | To propagate religious pietie', as described by George Peele (1592) in 'A Farewell to the Most Famous Generalles' (lines 25–6).

[5] On Spenser and Langland, see J. Anderson (1976); W. Davis (2002, esp. 153).

[6] See *FQ* 6. 3. 1: Spenser ascribes the equation of lineage with virtue to Chaucer, though Chaucer, following Boethius and Dante, recurrently insists on their independence; *Canterbury Tales*, 3. 1109–76; 'Gentilesse'; and *Boece*, bk 3, pr. 6, m. 6.

original purity of the Saxon Church, but had been displaced by a corrupt Catholicism and was only now returning to take up its true function in the world.[7] *Piers Plowman* seemed to give a glimpse of that process of preservation, offering a trace of the true Church that Foxe and others perceived as re-emerging in the age of John Wyclif after the 'long darkness' of Roman domination. The foundling St George has been brought up by the ploughman, as if to train him in Piers's own brand of English holiness, and would be destined for the same vocation, 'in ploughmans state to byde', if it were not for his own sense of a higher destiny:

> Till prickt with courage, and thy forces pryde,
> To Faery court thou cam'st to seeke for fame,
> And prove thy puissaunt armes, as seemes thee best became.

> (1. 10. 66)

The Letter to Ralegh adds a few more details to how Redcrosse's career turns towards chivalric knighthood. The inspiration for the scene, appropriately enough in this first book of Spenser's Arthuriad, lies in Malory's *Morte D'Arthur*, the work that supplied the model for the series of tales of individual knights (see Rovang 1996). The episode most often cited as the source is the story of Sir Gareth, youngest brother of Sir Gawain, who comes to court pretending to be clownish, and who, like Redcrosse, asks the first adventure as a boon—an adventure that consists, like Redcrosse's, in accompanying a damsel to rescue the occupants of a castle under siege. Spenser, however, conflates the story of the young Gareth with that of the young Torre: a man raised by a cowherd, who is genuinely ignorant of his own royal lineage, but who, like Redcrosse, cannot be content without knighthood and a life in arms (Malory 1969: 7. 3; 3. 3–4; A. King 2000: 145–53).[8]

If Redcrosse recuperates the nation's patron saint and combines the chivalric history of England with the ploughman tradition, the opening stanza may carry a further allusion that is political to an almost dangerous degree, for the knight pricking over a plain who turns out to be St George already had an existence in Tudor prophecy:

> I se come over a bent rydaunde
> A goodly man as armyde knyght.
> he shoke his spere ferselye in hand,
> Right cruelly and kene;
> Styfly & stowre as he wolde stonde,
> he bare a shylde of sylver shene.
> A crosse of gowles therin did be.

> (Erceldoune 1875: 52)

Henry VIII's prohibition of political prophecies had been repeated under Elizabeth, but they were nonetheless widely disseminated orally and in manuscript (see van Es 2002: 164–96). St George enters the scene in the prophecies of Thomas of Erceldoune,

---

[7] See Foxe (1841, esp. i. 516–17; and, on the ploughman tradition, ii. 728–47).

[8] Citations to Malory are as printed by Caxton and his successors and known to Spenser (Malory 1969).

a set concerned with Anglo-Scottish relations, and current in various forms from the late thirteenth to the mid-seventeenth century. The lines quoted come from a version recorded in 1529, where his function is to be at odds with St Andrew, representing Scotland: a harmless statement of fact, one would think, except that a recasting of the prophecy in the mid-century predicted the imminent union of the Crowns of England and Scotland under the son of a 'French wife' who would rule 'all Bretaine' (Erceldoune 1875: 51; see H. Cooper 2004: 192–7). The lines were probably a false prophecy about a child of Mary of Guise, but they were readily interpreted as referring to James Stuart and his mother, Mary, Queen of Scots, widow of the Dauphin. It is at least possible, therefore, that the prophetic element in *The Faerie Queene* consists not only of a panegyrical prediction of the house of Tudor—the present given a providential endorsement by its imaginary prophecy in the past, such as Virgil had incorporated into the *Aeneid* and Ariosto into the *Orlando Furioso*—but of a highly dangerous speculation about the future once the Tudor line has ceased. The very first stanza of Spenser's work could be read as encoding an acknowledgement of what threatens to be the major problem facing the narrative, of what happens to the body politic after the death of the childless mortal body of the Queen. It is impossible to know for certain whether, or in what form, Spenser might have known of the prophecy, though it burst out of hiding as soon as Elizabeth died, to be cited by various commentators as a rare example of a true prediction. The initially hostile encounter between St George and St Andrew and their ensuing reconciliation, as found in the 1529 text, was familiar enough for Dekker to use it to represent the union of the kingdoms in a pageant designed for James's reception into London (a reception that was in the event cancelled on account of the plague).[9] Spenser's mirror of the realm might yet, in a counterfactual extrapolation of the text, have extended to cover the whole of Britain.

45.2 MORALIZED SONG

If Spenser, in a line he borrowed from Ariosto, will write of gender-inclusive 'Knights and Ladies gentle deeds' (proem 1) more typical of romance than of classical epic, he also announces in that same stanza that this will not be for the sake of the narrative: 'Fierce warres and faithfull loves shall moralize my song.' That the poem will be 'moralized' builds into his scheme from the beginning what for Ariosto and Tasso, and indeed Virgil, had been largely imposed *ex post facto*, that his narrative will encode serious meanings directly applicable to his readers. He did not need, however, to look abroad for such a concept, which in those instances lay more in supplemental glosses than in the narratives themselves. Earlier English writings provided him with

[9] The agent of reconciliation in both cases is a beautiful woman on horseback, the Virgin Mary in the 1529 text, a female Genius of the city of London in Dekker (1955).

a number of models for story designed from the ground up as allegory. Langland's *Piers Plowman* was one such, and one moreover that offered, as Spenser set out to do, an entire anatomy of England, theological, economic, and political. Closer to chivalric romance in narrative content was a series of works running throughout the century that testify to a fashion for allegorical romance beyond Spenser's own poem, some of which may have influenced him directly. The earliest was Stephen Hawes's *Example of Vertue*, which was popular enough to go through at least three editions by 1530, and which bears strong narrative similarities to the story of Redcrosse. Stephen Batman's *The Travailed Pilgrim*, a translation of Olivier de La Marche's 1483 *Le Chevalier délibéré*, followed in 1569; and in 1581 William Goodyear translated Jean de Cartigny's 1557 *Voyage du Chevalier errant* as *The Voyage of the Wandering Knight*, with a dedication to Sir Francis Drake.[10] Goodyear's work was reprinted in 1584, and three times more after Spenser's death; Batman's translation was not reprinted, but Lewes Lewkenor produced another translation of de La Marche's work under the title of *The Resolved Gentleman* in 1594—too late to affect *The Faerie Queene*, but demonstrating a continuing taste for chivalric allegory. The subject matter of the de La Marche–Batman–Lewkenor *Chevalier délibéré* is a somewhat dreary account of the journey of the protagonist–narrator across the field of Time towards Debility and Death (topics that take up half the narrative), complete with examples drawn from recent history—which for Batman includes Henry VIII and Mary, with Elizabeth as a counter-example showing the resurgence of life. Batman's most immediate interest for Spenser may have lain in the numerous allegorical woodcuts that present in pictorial form the iconographic elements of the narrative, and which provide a visual equivalent to the set-piece descriptions in *The Faerie Queene*: an element that it shares with Hawes's *Example of Virtue*. Its woodcut of its protagonist armed for the quest, for instance, shows 'the author' as an 'armed knight' with the armour of Strength, the shield of Hope, and the spear of Adventure, and a horse designated as Will. Hawes's rather simpler woodcuts include a conventional series of the seven deadly sins riding on various beasts, as they do in the House of Lucifera.[11] Both works demonstrate the same integration of emblematic set pieces with narrative movement as Spenser provides verbally in his own poem.

In concentrating most on the youth and adulthood of the protagonist rather than his old age, Hawes's poem and Goodyear's prose offer a better fit with the young Redcrosse of book 1 than does de La Marche's text. Hawes's *Example* is a quest romance in which the protagonist, Youth, sets out to win the daughter of the God of Love, killing a dragon on the way; but if that summary sounds secular, the detail of the narrative turns it towards spiritual quest. For his fight with the dragon, Youth is given 'the armure for the soule | That in his epystole wrote saynt Poule' (Hawes

---

[10] On Hawes, Batman, and Goodyear as possible sources for Spenser, see Kaske (1990); Prescott (1989); Evans (1951).

[11] The Hawes woodcuts are reproduced in Hawes (1974). For a similar series closer to Spenser, see the set from Batman's *Crystal Glass*, reproduced in the *Spenser Encyclopedia* s. v. 'Seven Deadly Sins.' In contrast to standard literary and iconographic tradition, but in common with Langland at the end of his poem (B-text: 20. 114–17), Spenser makes his Lechery male.

1974: lines 1394–5). The dragon's three heads are defined as the World, the Flesh, and the Devil, and so in cutting off the first two, Youth is overcoming his own 'flesshly desyre' (line 1458). The lady is named Cleanness, purity, and their marriage is conducted by St Jerome, staunch advocate of virginity over marriage. By the end, the protagonist has reached the age of 60 and has been renamed Virtue, and he is rewarded with a sight of the kingdom of heaven. Over the course of the poem, Youth has to undergo primarily a process of testing; Cartigny–Goodyear's protagonist by contrast offers a model primarily of repentance. He is a wandering knight in both senses of 'errant': he sets out to find 'true felicitie' in this world with the aid of Folly, but after being led thoroughly astray he is brought back to the right path by God's Grace and Repentance and is carried to the palace of Virtue, from where Faith (like Spenser's Contemplation, at the behest of Fidelia) vouchsafes him a vision of the city of Heaven.

Any reader who turned from texts such as these to *The Faerie Queene* would have found much that was familiar. The moralized worlds of Hawes and the others are, however, largely landscapes of the mind, of spiritual psychology, and all are written in the (male) first person: the reader is invited to make the quest portrayed his own. Spenser's heroes and heroines have to be more than that, as Redcrosse encodes the progress of the Anglican Church as well as a struggling holiness, as Britomart quests for her place in the genealogy of England, and as Artegall battles for good government as well as self-rule. All of these writers, Spenser included, make their worlds profoundly imperfect, but in doing so Spenser is making a much larger statement. Hawes and Batman and Goodyear are concerned with the human soul within a fallen world, as Bunyan was later; Spenser, like Langland, is also portraying a polity that is far from ideal. His antecedents in allegory include not only the chivalric romances and the morality plays of psychomachia, the soul torn between conflicting impulses of good and evil, but political moralities such as John Bale's *King Johan* and Nicholas Udall's *Respublica*, which show the government itself as open to deception by the wicked who disguise themselves as good—the counterfeit figures who make a third between the evidently good and evil, such as occur abundantly in *The Faerie Queene*. The first of the Tudor fantasy worlds, More's *Utopia*, presented a rational design for a perfect state, described as if it were a part of real geography. Langland's Field of Folk is England itself reflected in dream, in which money has more influence than Holy Church, no one will work for love of their neighbour, the sins are rife, and Antichrist is close at hand. Spenser's Faeryland is manifestly unreal as a place, but as a 'mirrhour' of Elizabeth's realm it presents the world as it is, with all its recalcitrant human, ecclesiastical, and political problems: where Catholicism is the insidious enemy at home and the great power abroad; where Ireland is in a perpetual state of rebellion; where lust is more commonplace than love; and where justice may be no better than brute force. Its ostensible attitude towards the Queen may be panegyrical, but it contains a pointed element of criticism as well, and the tenor of the whole work aligns it closely with literature of advice to the monarch. Spenser fully shared the awareness of Henrician authors such as More and Elyot that advice may at best be ignored and at worst may invite misprision and punishment; intermingled with flattery, however, criticism may have more chance to make itself heard. It is only when political, social, and psychological problems are stripped out, when the land is reduced to its topography, that it can be presented in lyric harmony, in the procession of the English and Irish rivers in 4. 11 24–7; and even they bear witness to the violent history that has unfolded along their banks.

45.3 POETIC GENEALOGIES

The very first lines of poetry that readers of *The Faerie Queene* encountered make a different kind of statement, not about the scope or the method of the work but about its author and the poetic authority he claimed:

> Lo I the man, whose Muse whilome did maske,
> As time her taught, in lowly Shepheardes weeds,
> Am now enforst a far unfitter taske,
> For trumpets sterne to chaunge mine Oaten reeds.

All Spenser's readers with a Latin education would have recognized the spurious extra lines that regularly appeared prefacing the *Aeneid* in Renaissance editions, and the less formally educated could read them in any of its Tudor translations. In both poems, the passage serves to inform the reader that the author is moving on from pastoral to epic; but Spenser, by virtue of the imitation, is also laying a claim to be casting his own career in the Virgilian model, to be offering the work in hand as an *Aeneid* for England. The move to the heroic had already been adumbrated in the *Shepheardes Calender*, in E.K.'s prefatory matter and in 'October', and Spenser is now fulfilling that hope. For him, however, the lines also mean something more, and other, than that Virgilian fulfilment, for his persona in the *Calender* drew his inspiration not only from the 'Romish Tityrus', the pastoral pseudonym Virgil gave himself, but from an English Tityrus too, the 'God of shepheards' and father of English poetry, Chaucer (Spenser 1912*a*, 'June', 81).[12] In the *Calender*, the Chaucerian inheritance is expressed more as a wish than a fact, as Colin longs that 'on me some little drops would flowe, | Of that the spring was in his learned hedde' ('June', 93–4). By the time of *The Faerie Queene*, the Chaucerian link has become much more assured, and Chaucer is given his own name: Ariosto may be more evidently influential, but Chaucer is the only poetic forebear claimed by name in the entire poem. Furthermore, not merely is Spenser Chaucer's imitator, or even his heir, but the spirit of Chaucer has come alive again in

---

[12] See E.K.'s comment: 'Whom he calleth the God of Poetes for his excellencie'. The identification of Chaucer as Tityrus is first made in 'February', 92 ('I suppose he meane Chaucer, whose prayse for pleasaunt tales cannot dye, so long as the memorie of his name shal live, and the name of Poetrie shal endure'); see also 'December', 4, and Envoy, 9. For Virgil as the 'Romish Tityrus', see 'October', 55. John Burrow (1990) gives an excellent account of Spenser's use of Chaucer. For Chaucer as influencing Spenser's 'artistic self-definition', see J. Anderson (1998).

him. The earlier poet is the 'well of English undefyled', 'the pure well head of Poesie' (4. 2. 32, 7. 7. 9), and

> through infusion sweete
> Of thine owne spirit, which doth in me survive,
> I follow here the footing of thy feete.
>
> (4. 2. 34)

Chaucer, at the end of *Troilus*, had represented himself more humbly, as doing no more than kissing the steps of the great classical poets—though the humility does not disguise the fact that he is associating himself with them. Spenser is making an altogether stronger statement, and casting it in terms not only of tracing his master's footsteps, but also of his own trademark imagery of flowing water: the 'little drops' of the *Calender* have now become the well from which Spenser can be infused with his spirit. Chaucer is the source of his inspiration, the head of the river of English poetry, just as the great rivers of England stand as a synecdoche for the realm.[13]

Even those opening lines of Virgilian imitation therefore inscribe Chaucer within them as a forebear alongside Virgil. Their one word that was not standard Elizabethan English, 'whilome', itself carried strong Chaucerian associations: it is the first word of the first line of his own most heroic poem, 'The Knight's Tale' ('Whilom, as olde stories tellen us'; imitated by Spenser for his continuation of 'The Squire's Tale' in 4. 2. 32, in a continuing process of moving forward from father to son, Knight to Squire, Chaucer to Spenser; see J. Anderson 1990: 30). Archaism in the *Shepheardes Calender* had been used to impart a pseudo-Theocritean rusticity, sometimes, as Sidney noted in the *Apology for Poetry*, to a degree that could appear almost wilful;[14] in *The Faerie Queene*, archaism has become a mark of the nationalist and the heroic. 'Heroical poetry' is itself always nostalgic, always backward-looking: its heroes belong to an age of chivalry that was lost from its very inception, or to an originary era that is past by definition. Spenser's diction enables him to draw not only Chaucer into his purview, but also the less adorned style of the romances of English heroes: a Tudor readership would have responded to the resonances of Redcrosse's dragon-fight with Bevis of Hamtoun's through its language as much as its narrative. Furthermore, although Spenser carries through his assertion of a native linguistic kingdom with unusual conviction, the idea is not unique to him. Veré Rubel, in the classic study of Spenser's poetic diction, concludes by noting the unbroken development of the language of poetry from Chaucer through Spenser, and moreover that Tudor writers 'themselves believed that they had a *native* precedent for the language and forms which they used, and outside influences—whether from the classics or the Italian or the French—were merely ancillary' (Rubel 1966: 273). English first took a new direction not in Chaucer's and Spenser's medium of verse, but in prose and drama,

---

[13] Spenser's rivers, like his model of poetic tradition, are hierarchical, in contrast to the chorography of Leland and Drayton and the practice of the mapmakers: see *FQ* 4. 11. 8–53 and Helgerson (1992: 141–3).

[14] 'That same framing of his style to an old rustic language I dare not allow, since [none of the canonical pastoral authors] did affect it' (Sidney 2002: 110).

forms that were free of any anxiety of influence from the great poetic tradition. Although English poetry goes back beyond Chaucer, he was the recognized point of origin, the well-head: the father of the English language, who left his model of eloquence as his richest inheritance.

In an age obsessed by genealogy, moreover, Chaucer was father to the nation in a more literal sense too. The association was hinted at in Stowe's 1561 edition of Chaucer's *Works*, the edition Spenser used (Hieatt 1975: 19–23), where the title page to the *Canterbury Tales* section is largely taken up with a wide border showing the genealogical lines of the Lancastrians, Beauforts–Tudors, and Yorkists, culminating in the union of all three in Henry VIII. In 1598, shortly before Spenser's death, a new folio edition of the *Works* appeared, with a portrait page designed by John Speed (better known as England's mapmaker) that gives Chaucer himself pride of place at the centre of an analogous family tree. It shows him surrounded by the genealogy and heraldry of the lineage of the Lancastrian and Tudor monarchs down to Henry VII, on one side, and the de la Pole dukes of Suffolk on the other (though with the man designated by Richard III as his heir judiciously excised). At the bottom of the page is the tomb of his son Thomas, itself adorned with twenty heraldic shields, eight of which bear some variant of the royal arms of England modified for cadet lines or for marriage. The de la Poles were direct descendants of Chaucer through his granddaughter Alice; the royal lines get into the picture through the liaison and eventual marriage of Chaucer's sister-in-law Katherine Swinford, née Roet, with John of Gaunt. The name at the top centre of the family tree is therefore not in fact Chaucer but his father-in-law, though that is not the impression that the page aims to give. As its alternative designation as the 'progeny page' indicates, it is designed to portray Chaucer not only as the father of English poetry, but as the father of the English nation. As the work of Chaucer's poetic son and heir, Spenser's national epic helped to prepare the way for such a representation.

Spenser's tribute to Chaucer as his predecessor in *The Faerie Queene* 4. 2 is the fourth in a series of backward sweeps that draw history into the poem. Book 2 contains the great summary of Geoffrey of Monmouth's version of the early history of Britain (the version still standard in English chronicles, including Holinshed), from its original habitation by giants forwards. The history is one of alternating triumph and tragedy, imperial expansion and internecine strife; its protagonists include Lear (2. 10. 27–32), Gorboduc (Gorbogud, 10. 34), and Cymbeline (Kimbeline, 10. 50). The birth of Christ is noted under his reign, as is the later legendary bringing of Christianity to Britain by Joseph of Arimathea—who 'preacht the truth, but since it greately did decay' (10. 53). The account breaks off in mid-sentence as it arrives at the diegetic present of the narrative with Arthur's father, Uther Pendragon (2. 10. 68). Spenser declares at the start that the Queen's 'realme and race | From this renowmed Prince derived are' (10. 4), though he never specifies exactly which prince is at issue, presumably either Brut or Arthur. The Tudors claimed a connection with Arthur, but Spenser is perhaps playing coy since one of the few consistent facts about Arthur in all versions of his story was that he died childless. The more immediate Tudor lineage was equally problematic, since Henry VII's seizure of the throne represented the sharpest break in the lineal descent of the crown since the Norman Conquest. Spenser accordingly switches into a faery genealogy from Elfe, created by Prometheus, which only coincides with history once it reaches Elficleos, alias Henry Tudor, and his heirs down to Gloriana herself, and so to the extradiegetic present of the poem (10. 75–6). Later, a teleological account of Saxon and Welsh history culminating in the Tudors, but with the end broken off, is outlined by Merlin in the form of his prophecy in 3. 227–50. A third historical excursus on the founding of Britain occurs in 3. 9, when Britomart tells of her own descent from Aeneas and Brutus in the diaspora following the sack of Troy, of the founding of Troynovaunt–London, and of the city's continuing strength as 'a wonder of the world' (3. 9. 45). Book 4's eulogy of Chaucer continues the sequence in different terms, to bring poetic history up to the literary present of the poem in Spenser himself.

The rhetorical Chaucer was most admired, by followers such as Lydgate and later commentators such as Puttenham and Sidney, for *Troilus and Criseyde*. It was that poem that established rhyme royal as the dominant prosodic form for serious narrative poetry—for Hawes, for the narrative sections of Wyatt's Penitential Psalms, for many of the tragedies of the *Mirror for Magistrates*, for Shakespeare's *Lucrece*. Spenser uses it only in the otherwise un-Chaucerian *Ruins of Time* and *Four Hymns*, but his preference for long stanzas is itself in the Chaucerian as well as the Italian tradition: the nine-line stanza of the *Faerie Queene* overgoes both. He uses riding rhyme, the couplet form that predominates in *The Canterbury Tales*, only rarely, and then as an explicitly lower-style medium, as in *Mother Hubberd's Tale*; 'February' and 'May' use a shorter, four-stress couplet that intermingles iambs and anapaests, and that may itself be an attempt to imitate the rough metrics of the printed Chaucers. In terms of content, both poets have a fondness for complaint (cf. 'June', 85), *The Book of the Duchess* contributes to *Daphnaida*, and *The Parliament of Fowls* gets an honourable mention in the *Mutability Cantos* (7. 7. 9); but for Spenser, Chaucer was above all the poet of *The Canterbury Tales*. His Chaucer is the teller of 'wise' tales, tales 'of truth [...] And some of love, and some of chevalrie' ('February', 91–9), 'mery tales' ('June', 87), 'antique stories' such as the Squire's (4. 2. 32). It was in the 1590s that Chaucer was beginning to be associated primarily with the more rumbustious of the *Tales*, so Spenser's insistence on the variety, wisdom, and venerability of his storytelling seems designed to ward off the shift in critical perception. He cites him as his model for the fable of the oak and the briar, despite E.K.'s objections (and if E.K. was indeed Spenser himself, Edmundus Kalendarius, rather than Edward Kirke, the redefinition of Chaucer becomes all the more pointed). *Mother Hubberd's Tale* implicitly claims descent, by virtue of its title, from *The Canterbury Tales*, though this one is told not in gratitude for recovery from sickness but to cheer a sick man, not in the month of the regeneration of the earth but in 'the month wherein the righteous maid [i.e. Astraea, the maiden Justice] | Fled back to heaven' (1–2), leaving a world diseased and corrupt. Spenser further offers to make good the damage wrought (as he sees it) on *The Tales* by time, by providing supplements or endings to Chaucer's unfinished tales (the Squire's in book 4, 'Sir Thopas' in the 1590 version of 3. 7. 48, in which Thopas destroys his giant); and he famously reclaims 'Sir Thopas' for serious otherworldly vision in Arthur's dream of Gloriana. Above all, *The Tales* offered him a model of the gathering up within a single work a whole array of examples of good love and bad, virginity and married faithfulness, and false accusations and adultery.[15] In his most extended quotation from Chaucer, Britomart is given the lines on the nature of mutual human love from 'The Franklin's Tale' as her first, and therefore defining, words:

> Ne may love be compeld by maisterie;
> For soone as maisterie comes, sweet love anone
> Taketh his nimble wings, and soone away is gone.[16]

Modern criticism tends to read the lines cynically; Spenser, in a world that still believed that human values had a real existence, did not.

Spenser's first tribute to Chaucer had, however, been given a less ambitious setting, within the humbler pastoral mode of *The Shepheardes Calender*. Chaucer himself wrote no eclogues, but Spenser borrows his description of the

> pipes made of grene corn
> As han thise lytel herde-gromes
> That kepen bestis in the bromes
>
> (*The House of Fame*, lines 1224–6)

for his 'February', the eclogue that contains his first eulogy to the earlier poet. Although the idea of an eclogue cycle is Virgilian, Spenser follows at least as much in more recent pastoral footsteps: the neo-Latin Mantuan, whose *Adolescentia* had become a standard school text and which was translated by George Turberville in 1567; the eclogues written or ascribed to Clement Marot, some of them tending markedly to ecclesiastical criticism; and, whether by imitation or through the wider influence of a shared medieval pastoral tradition, the English eclogues of Alexander Barclay (*c*.1513–14, reprinted 1570) and Barnabe Googe (1563) (see H. Cooper 1977: 115–26). Barclay's eclogues, the first to be written in English, slanted the whole genre markedly towards the satiric, an angle that had indeed become commonplace over the course of the Middle Ages. He also made his poems insistently English in detail and reference even when his sources stemmed from Italy. He devoted his first three eclogues to criticism of court life, a topic that might seem paradoxical for pastoral but which is made plausible, as it is in *Colin Clout's Come Home Again* and Melibee's account in *FQ* 6. 9. 24–5, through the device of the shepherd–speaker's having visited the court and been horrified by what he has seen there. Googe's eclogues mix love laments, moral criticism of love, and also, in his account in his third eclogue of the Marian burning of the good shepherds Daphnes and Alexis, ecclesiastical vituperation and panegyric (see Googe 1989: 51–5). Spenser's assumption that the pastoral tradition incorporates moral teaching and commentary on the state of the Church

---

[15] '*The Faerie Queene* is really all about love' (Logan et al. 1990, p. xi).
[16] *FQ* 3. 1. 25; cf. *Canterbury Tales* 5. 764–6.

follows from these traditions much more than from Virgil; and if Virgil is primarily responsible for Spenser's laments over unrequited love, his eulogy of the ruler, and the set-piece poems and singing matches, the rest of what the *Calender* does is inspired by post-Virgilian traditions. The habit of substituting debate for singing match had been standard practice ever since the Carolingian era, and Spenser, with typical eclecticism, places the two traditions side by side. The eclogue is often thought of as the most classical of all the Renaissance genres; but the Middle Ages had redefined pastoral in ways that turned the mode in significantly different directions from the classical, and those differences were transmitted to English humanist poets by way of an abundance of neo-Latin poets including Petrarch and Mantuan, and by way of a lively vernacular tradition that used the shepherd as the voice of the teacher, the pastor, or the suffering common man. The name Spenser gives himself, Colin, recalls Clement Marot's pseudonym as shepherd–poet; but, as Colin Clout, he takes on John Skelton's voice of complaint against corruption in Church and government. The good shepherd Piers of 'February' invokes the ploughman tradition, and the Diggon Davie of 'September' alludes at once to Bishop Richard Davies and Churchyard's plain-speaking Davy Diker. The *Calender* woodcuts themselves are notably reminiscent of the portrayal of shepherds in the work from which it took its name, the *Calendar of Shepherds*—a compendium of lore supposedly told by a wise master shepherd to his fellow herdsmen, which first appeared in print in Scotland in 1503 and in England three years later, and was reprinted every few years into the seventeenth century.

The *Calendar of Shepherds* kept a remarkably stable Catholic element throughout its reprints, including a full calendar of festive days, the Conception of the Virgin and Thomas Becket among them: perhaps it was too familiar a work for anyone in authority to notice. Spenser's poetic teacher for his own *Calender*, Chaucer, had, however, by the later sixteenth century been firmly adopted for the Protestant cause, a process encouraged not only by his criticism of corrupt ecclesiastics but by the ascription to him of various proto-Protestant works. These included the Lollard *Plowman's Tale*, incorporated into editions of Chaucer's works from 1542, and *Jack Upland*, which together inspired John Foxe to claim him as 'a right Wicklevian', able to bring readers to 'the true knowledge of religion' (Foxe 1841: ii. 357–63, iv. 249–50). That Chaucer was not only England's greatest poet, but also a *Protestant* poet, made him doubly attractive as a model for Spenser. The sixteenth-century editions of his works included a prefatory poem, originally written by Hoccleve for Henry V, but now addressed to Henry VIII as 'veray sustaynour' of Holy Church and to the Garter knights as those that 'ben of saynt Georges lyvere [livery]', urging them to suppress heresy and popular theological disputation. It was first incorporated when Henry could still just about be regarded as *fidei defensor*; Spenser presumably read it in Elizabeth's reign as referring to a rather different Church. Of the mid-century attempts to reclaim Chaucer for Catholicism, William Forrest's casting of Katherine of Aragon as a new Griselda had remained unpublished and was forgotten, and the tomb erected for Chaucer in Westminster Abbey in 1556 could change ecclesiastical allegiance with the abbey itself.

Tomb monuments, as Spenser knew as well as did the Shakespeare of the Sonnets, were temporary: 'All such vaine moniments of earthlie masse, | Devour'd of Time, in time to nought doo passe' (*The Ruins of Time*, 419–20). In *The Ruins of Time*, Spenser imagines poetry as resisting Time's ravages; in *The Faerie Queene*, as he contemplates Chaucer, he is not so sure:

> But wicked Time that all good thoughts doth waste,
> And workes of noblest wits to nought out weare,
> That famous moniment hath quite defaste,
> And robd the world of threasure endlesse deare.

(FQ 4. 2. 33)

The overt topic is the missing ending of 'The Squire's Tale', but the defaced monument suggests not just something missing, but the bad condition of what has survived. 'Moniment' is a key word in Spenser's poetry. It means a memorial of the past existing in the present: the ruins of Rome, the tomb of Mausolus, the works of Chaucer. It can therefore signify what has been lost, Rome in her glory, as much as what survives; or, as in the lines just quoted, it can record the process of loss, of time wearing away what remains. The 1598 edition of Chaucer commented on the damage done to Chaucer's prosody over the years of transmission, and for the first time provided a glossary, a physical memorial to a language that had passed out of current use. Spenser's own works were represented as his monument in many of the poetic tributes paid after his death—in compensation, perhaps, for the fact that no memorial was erected for his grave until 1620.[17] By that time, Chaucer's tomb itself, alongside which Spenser had been buried, the son alongside the father, was also showing signs of wear. Spenser's poetry constituted a living memorial to Chaucer, just as it drew in all the English traditions available to him; but poetry designed as a monument rapidly becomes a tribute to the pastness of its own life. Spenser's works constitute a vast monument to the Tudor era, but he built it as a younger world was coming of age.

Primary Works

Barclay, Alexander (1955), *The Life of St George*, ed. William Nelson, EETS, o.s., 230.

Chaucer, Geoffrey (1987), *The Riverside Chaucer*, ed. L. D. Benson (New York: Houghton Mifflin).

Dekker, Thomas (1955), *The Magnificent Entertainment given to King James*, in *The Dramatic Works of Thomas Dekker*, ed. Fredson Bowers, 3 vols (Cambridge: Cambridge University Press, 1953–8), ii.

Erceldoune, Thomas of (1875), *The Romance and Prophecies of Thomas of Erceldoune*, ed. J. A. H. Murray, EETS, o.s., 68.

Foxe, John (1841), *Acts and Monuments*, ed. S. R. Cattley, 8 vols (London: Seeley and Burnside).

---

[17] See the 'Obituary Verse' section in R. Cummings (1971: 100–13).

GOOGE, BARNABY (1989), *Eclogues, Epitaphs and Sonnets*, ed. J. M. Kennedy (Toronto: University of Toronto Press).

HAWES, STEPHEN (1974), *The Example of Vertue*, in *The Minor Poems of Stephen Hawes*, ed. F. W. Gluck and A. B. Morgan, EETS, o.s., 271.

MALORY, THOMAS (1969), *The Morte d'Arthur*, ed. J. Cowen (Harmondsworth: Penguin).

PEELE, GEORGE (1952), 'A Farewell to the Most Famous Generalles', in *The Life and Minor Works of George Peele*, ed. D. H. Horne (New Haven: Yale University Press), 220–3.

SIDNEY, PHILIP (2002), *An Apology for Poetry*, ed. G. Shepherd, 3rd edn, rev. R. W. Maslen (Manchester: Manchester University Press).

SPENSER, EDMUND, *FQ* (1981), *The Faerie Queene*, ed. A. C. Hamilton, H. Yamashita, and T. Suzuki, 2nd edn (London: Longman).

—— (1912*a*), *The Ruins of Time*, in *The Poetical Works of Edmund Spenser*, ed. J. C. Smith and E. de Selincourt (London: Oxford University Press).

—— (1912*b*), *The Shepheardes Calendar*, in *The Poetical Works of Edmund Spenser*, ed. J. C. Smith and E. de Selincourt (London: Oxford University Press).

—— (1912*c*), *Three Proper Wittie Familiar Letters*, in *The Poetical Works of Edmund Spenser*, ed. J. C. Smith and E. de Selincourt (London: Oxford University Press).

BIBLIOGRAPHY

OXFORD DICTIONARY OF NATIONAL BIOGRAPHY (*ODNB*)

Several contributors have referred to articles in the *ODNB* (checked according to the updated 2008 electronic version). Conventionally, authorship is not given for such articles, but we think authors should be given credit for the work they have done for the *ODNB*, and so we have listed them below.

'Astley, John' (Charlotte Merton).
'Baldwin, William' (John N. King).
'Barker, William' (Kenneth R. Bartlett).
'Bryan, Sir Francis' (Susan Brigden).
'Cavendish, George' (A. S. G. Edwards).
'Cheke, Sir John' (Alan Bryson).
'Churchyard, Thomas' (Raphael Lyne).
'Copland, Robert' (Mary C. Erler).
'Cromwell, Thomas' (Howard Leithead).
'Day, John'(Andrew Pettegree).
'Dudley, Robert, Earl of Leicester' (Simon Adams).
'Dyer, Sir Edward' (Steven W. May).
'Elyot, Thomas' (Stanford E. Lehmberg).
'Foxe, John' (Thomas S. Freeman).
'Fulwell, Ulpian' (David Kathman).
'Howard, Henry, Earl of Surrey' (Susan Brigden).
'Howell, Thomas' (Cathy Shrank).
'Kinwelmersh, Francis' (Gillian Austen).
'Latimer, Hugh' (Susan Wabuda).
'Lupton, Thomas' (G. K. Hunter).
'Mason, Sir John' (P. R. N. Carter).
'More, Thomas' (Seymour Baker House).
'Proctor, John' (David Loades).
'Shute, John' (Gerald Beasley).
'Smith, Sir Thomas' (Ian W. Archer).
'Stanihurst, Richard' (Colm Lennon).

'Thomas, William' (Dakota L. Hamilton).
'Tottel, Richard' (Anna Greening).
'Turbervile, George' (Raphael Lyne).
'Udall, Nicholas' (Matthew Steggle).
'Vaux, Thomas' (Henry Woudhuysen).
'Wager, William' (Peter Happé).
'Whithorne, Thomas' (John Bennell).
'Wilson, Thomas' (Susan Doran and Jonathan Woolfson).
'Wyatt, Sir Thomas (*c*.1503–1542)' (Colin Burrow).
'Wyatt, Sir Thomas (b. in or before 1521, d. 1554)' (Ian W. Archer).

OTHER SECONDARY WORKS

ADAIR, E. R. (1924), 'William Thomas: A Forgotten Clerk to the Privy Council', in *Tudor Studies*, ed. R. Seton-Watson (London: Longmans, Green), 133–60.

ADAMS, ROBERT P. (1959), ' "Bold Bawdry and Open Manslaughter": The English New Humanist Attack on Medieval Romance', *HLQ*, 23: 33–48.

ADAMS, SIMON (2002), *Leicester and the Court: Essays on Elizabethan Politics* (Manchester: Manchester University Press).

ADAMSON, SYLVIA, GAVIN ALEXANDER, and KATRIN ETTENHUBER (eds) (2008), *Renaissance Figures of Speech* (Cambridge: Cambridge University Press).

ADORNO, THEODOR W. (1991), 'On Lyric Poetry and Society', in Adorno, *Notes to Literature*, ed. Rolf Tiedemann, trans. Shierry Weber Nicholsen, 2 vols (New York: Columbia University Press), ii. 37–54.

AERS, DAVID (1990), 'Reading *Piers Plowman*: Literature, History and Criticism', *L&H*, 2nd ser., 1: 4–23.

—— (1992), 'A Whisper in the Ear of Early Modernists; or, Reflections on Literary Critics Writing the "History of the Subject" ', in Aers (ed.), *Culture and History 1350–1600: Essays on English Communities, Identities and Writing* (London: Harvester Wheatsheaf), 177–202.

AHL, FREDERICK (1984), 'The Art of Safe Criticism in Greece and Rome', *American Journal of Philology*, 105: 174–208.

ALFORD, STEPHEN (1998), *The Early Elizabethan Polity: William Cecil and the British Succession Crisis, 1558–1569* (Cambridge: Cambridge University Press).

ALLEN, DAVID G., and ROBERT A. WHITE (eds) (1995), *Subjects on the World's Stage: Essays on British Literature of the Middle Ages and the Renaissance* (Cranbury, NJ: Associated University Presses).

ALLEN, DON CAMERON (1935), 'The *Anatomie of Absurditie*: A Study in Literary Apprenticeship', *SP* 22: 170–6.

ALPERS, PAUL (1997), *What Is Pastoral?* (Chicago: University of Chicago Press).

ALSOP, J. D. (1994), 'The Act for the Queen's Regal Power, 1554', *Parliamentary History*, 13: 261–78.

ALTER, ROBERT (1985), *The Art of Biblical Poetry* (New York: Basic Books).

ALTMAN, JOEL B. (1978), *The Tudor Play of Mind: Rhetorical Inquiry and the Development of Elizabethan Drama* (Berkeley and Los Angeles: University of California Press).

ALWES, DEREK B. (2000), 'Robert Greene's Dueling Dedications', *ELR*, 30: 373–95.

AMELANG, JAMES S. (1998), *The Flight of Icarus: Artisan Autobiography in Early Modern Europe* (Stanford, CA: Stanford University Press).

AMOS, MARK ADDISON (2006), 'Violent Hierarchies: Disciplining Women and Merchant Capitalists in *The Book of the Knyght of the Towre*', in William Kuskin (ed.), *Caxton's Trace: Studies in the History of English Printing* (Notre Dame, IN: University of Notre Dame Press), 69–100.

ANDERSON, A. H. (1963), 'Henry, Lord Stafford (1501–1563) in Local and Central Government', *EHR*, 78: 225–42.

ANDERSON, BENEDICT (2006), *Imagined Communities: Reflections on the Origin and Spread of Nationalism*, rev. edn (London: Verso).

ANDERSON, JUDITH H. (1976), *The Growth of a Personal Voice* (New Haven: Yale University Press).

—— (1990), ' "Myn auctour": Spenser's Enabling Fiction and Eumnestes' "immortal scrine" ', in George M. Logan and Gordon Teskey (eds), *Unfolded Tales: Essays on Renaissance Romance* (Ithaca, NY: Cornell University Press), 16–31.

—— (1998), 'Narrative Reflections: Re-envisaging the Poet in *The Canterbury Tales* and *The Faerie Queene*', in Teresa M. Krier (ed.), *Refiguring Chaucer in the Renaissance* (Gainesville: University Press of Florida), 87–105.

ANGLO, SYDNEY (ed.) (1990), *Chivalry in the Renaissance* (Woodbridge: Boydell Press).

—— (2005), *Machiavelli—The First Century: Studies in Enthusiasm, Hostility and Irrelevance* (Oxford: Oxford University Press).

ARMSTRONG, W. A. (1948), 'The Influence of Seneca and Machiavelli on the Elizabethan Tyrant', *RES*, 24: 19–35.

—— (1950), 'The Background and Sources of Preston's *Cambises*', *ES*, 31: 129–35.

—— (1955), 'The Authorship and Political Meaning of *Cambises*', *ES*, 36: 289–99.

ASHENDEN, SAMANTHA, and DAVID OWEN (eds) (1999), *Foucault contra Habermas: Recasting the Dialogue between Genealogy and Critical Theory* (London: Sage).

ASTON, T. H., and C. H. E. PHILPIN (1985), *The Brenner Debate: Agrarian Class Structure and Economic Development in Pre-industrial Europe* (Cambridge: Cambridge University Press).

ATTRIDGE, DEREK (1974), *Well-Weighed Syllables: Elizabethan Verse in Classical Metres* (Cambridge: Cambridge University Press).

—— (2004), *The Singularity of Literature* (London: Routledge).

AUERBACH, ERICH (1968), *Mimesis: The Representation of Reality in Western Literature*, trans. Willard R. Trask (Princeton: Princeton University Press).

AUSTIN, R. G. (1965), 'Surrey's *Aeneid*', *Classical Review*, n.s., 15: 292–4.

AVILA, CARMELA NOCERA (1992), *Tradurre il 'Cortegiano': The Courtyer di Sir Thomas Hoby* (Bari: Adriatica).

AXTON, MARIE, and JAMES P. CARLEY (eds) (2000), *'Triumphs of English': Henry Parker, Lord Morley, Translator to the Tudor Court* (London: British Library).

AXTON, RICHARD, and PETER HAPPÉ (1991), 'Introduction' to *The Plays of John Heywood* (Cambridge: Brewer).

BAGCHI, DAVID V. N. (1989), *Luther's Earliest Opponents: Catholic Controversialists, 1518–1525* (Minneapolis: Fortress Press).

BAILEY, RICHARD (1992), *Images of English: A Cultural History of the Language* (Cambridge: Cambridge University Press).

BAKER, DAVID WEIL (1999), *Divulging Utopia: Radical Humanism in Sixteenth-Century England* (Amherst: University of Massachusetts Press).

BAKER, HOWARD (1939), *Induction to Tragedy: A Study in a Development of Form in 'Gorboduc', 'The Spanish Tragedy', and 'Titus Andronicus'* (New York: Russell and Russell).

BAKER, J. H. (1990), *The Third University of England: The Inns of Court and the Common-Law Tradition* (London: Selden Society).

BAKER-SMITH, DOMINIC (1990), 'Preface' to M. J. B. Allen et al. (eds), *Sir Philip Sidney's Achievements* (New York: AMS).

BAKHTIN, MIKHAIL (1984), *Rabelais and his World*, trans. Helene Iswolsky (Bloomington: Indiana University Press).

BALDWIN, T. W. (1944), *William Shakspere's Small Latine & Lesse Greeke*, 2 vols (Urbana: University of Illinois Press).

BARNETT, RICHARD C. (1969), *Place, Profit, and Power: A Study of the Servants of William Cecil, Elizabethan Statesman* (Chapel Hill: University of North Carolina Press).

BARNETT, STEPHEN JOHN (1999), 'Where Was your Church before Luther? English Claims for the Antiquity of Protestantism Examined', *Church History*, 68: 14–41.

BARR, HELEN (ed.) (1993), *The Piers Plowman Tradition* (London: Dent).

BARRY, JONATHAN (2000), 'Civility and Civic Culture in Early Modern England: The Meanings of Urban Freedom', in Peter Burke, Brian Harrison, and Paul Slack (eds), *Civil Histories: Essays Presented to Sir Keith Thomas* (Oxford: Oxford University Press), 181–96.

BARTLETT, KENNETH R. (1991), *The English in Italy, 1525–1558* (Geneva: Slatkine).

——(2006), 'Thomas Hoby, Translator, Traveler', in Carmine G. Di Biase (ed.), *Travel and Translation in the Early Modern Period* (Amsterdam: Rodopi), 123–41.

BASKERVILL, CHARLES READ (1927), 'Conventional Features of Medwall's *Fulgens and Lucres*', *MP*, 24: 419–42.

——(1932), 'Taverner's *Garden of Wisdom* and the *Apophthegmata* of Erasmus', *SP*, 29: 149–59.

BASKERVILLE, E. J. (1967), 'The English Traveller to Italy, 1547–1560', PhD diss. (Columbia University).

BATES, CATHERINE (1993), ' "A mild admonisher": Sir Thomas Wyatt and Sixteenth-Century Satire', *HLQ*, 56: 243–58.

BAUMANN, UWE (1998), 'Sir Thomas Elyot's *The Image of Governance*: A Humanist's *Speculum Principis* and a Literary Puzzle', in Dieter Stein and Rosanna Sornicola (eds), *The Virtues of Language* (Amsterdam: John Benjamins), 177–99.

BEADLE, RICHARD, and A. J. PIPER (eds) (1996), *New Science Out of Old Books* (Aldershot: Scolar Press).

BEAL, P. (1980), *Index of English Literary Manuscripts*, 4 vols (London: Mansell), i: *1450–1625*.

BEDFORD, R., and P. KELLY (2007), *Early Modern English Lives: Autobiography and Self-Representation 1500–1660* (Aldershot: Ashgate).

BEIER, A. L., DAVID CANNADINE, and JAMES M. ROSENHEIM (eds) (1989), *The First Modern Society: Essays in English History in Honour of Lawrence Stone* (Cambridge: Cambridge University Press).

BEILIN, ELAINE (1987), *Redeeming Eve: Women Writers of the English Renaissance* (Princeton: Princeton University Press).

BENJAMIN, WALTER (1998), *The Origin of German Tragic Drama*, trans. John Osborne (London: Verso).

BENNETT, H. S. (1950), 'Notes on English Retail Book-Prices, 1480–1560', *The Library*, 5th ser., 5: 172–8.

——(1965), *English Books and Readers: 1558–1603* (Cambridge: Cambridge University Press).

——(1969), *English Books and Readers 1475 to 1557*, 2nd edn (Cambridge: Cambridge University Press).

BENNETT, J. A. W. (1946), 'The Early Fame of Gavin Douglas's *Eneados*', *MLN*, 61: 83–8.

BENTLEY, GERALD EADES (1929), 'New Actors of the Elizabethan Period', *MLN*, 44: 368–72.

BENVENISTE, ÉMILE (1971), *Problems in General Linguistics*, trans. M. E. Meek (Coral Gables: University of Miami Press).

BERDAN, JOHN M. (1920), *Early Tudor Poetry 1485–1547* (New York: Macmillan).

BERNARD, JOHN D. (1989), *Ceremonies of Innocence: Pastoralism in the Poetry of Edmund Spenser* (Cambridge: Cambridge University Press).

BETTERIDGE, THOMAS (1999), *Tudor Histories of the English Reformations, 1530–83* (Aldershot: Ashgate).

——(2004), *Literature and Politics in the English Reformation* (Manchester: Manchester University Press).

BEVINGTON, DAVID (1962), *From 'Mankind' to Marlowe: Growth of Structure in the Popular Drama of Tudor England* (Cambridge, MA: Harvard University Press).

——(1968), *Tudor Drama and Politics: A Critical Approach to Topical Meaning* (Cambridge, MA: Harvard University Press).

——(2007), 'Staging the Reformation: Power and Theatricality in the Plays of William Wager', in Peter Happé and Wim Hüsken (eds), *Interludes and Early Modern Society: Studies in Power, Gender and Theatricality* (Amsterdam: Rodopi), 353–78.

BIDDLE, MARTIN (2000), *King Arthur's Round Table: An Archaeological Investigation* (Woodbridge: Boydell Press).

BINDOFF, S. T. (ed.) (1982), *The History of Parliament: The House of Commons, 1509–1558*, 3 vols (London: Secker and Warburg).

BINNS, J. W. (1990), *Intellectual Culture in Elizabethan and Jacobean England: The Latin Writings of the Age*, ARCA: Classical and Medieval Texts, Papers and Monographs, 24 (Leeds: Cairns).

BLACK, JOSEPH (1997), 'The Rhetoric of Reaction: The Marprelate Tracts 1588–1589, Anti-Martinism, and the Uses of Print in Early Modern England', *SCJ*, 28: 707–25.

BLAKE, N. F. (1965), 'The *Vocabulary in French and English* Printed by William Caxton', *ELN*, 2: 7–15.

——(1969), *Caxton and his World* (London: André Deutsch).

——(1973), *Caxton's Own Prose* (London: André Deutsch).

——(1989), 'Manuscript to Print', in Jeremy Griffiths and Derek Pearsall (eds), *Book Production and Publishing in Britain 1375–1475* (Cambridge: Cambridge University Press), 403–32.

——(1991), *William Caxton and English Literary Culture* (London: Hambledon Press).

BLANCHOT, MAURICE (2007), *A Voice from Elsewhere* (Albany: State University of New York Press).

BLANK, PAULA (1996), *Broken English: Dialects and the Politics of Language in Renaissance Writings* (London: Routledge).

BLANSHARD, A. J. L., and T. A. SOWERBY (2005), 'Thomas Wilson's Demosthenes and the Politics of Tudor Translation', *IJCT*, 12: 46–80.

BLAYNEY, PETER W. M. (2003), *The Stationers' Company before the Charter, 1403–1557* (London: Worshipful Company of Stationers and Newspapermakers).

BOFFEY, JULIA (1991), 'Early Printers and English Lyrics: Sources, Selection, and Presentation of Texts', *PBSA*, 85: 11–26.

BOITANI, PIERO (2007), 'Petrarch and the "Barbari Britanni"', in Martin McLaughlin and Peter Hainsworth (eds), *Petrarch in Britain: Interpreters, Imitators and Translators over 700 Years*, Proceedings of the British Academy, 146: 9–25.

BOLWELL, ROBERT W. (1921), *The Life and Works of John Heywood* (New York: Columbia University Press).

BONAHUE, EDWARD T. (1994), ' "I know the place and the persons": The Play of Textual Frames in Baldwin's *Beware the Cat*', *SP*, 91: 283–300.

BORNKAMM, HEINRICH (1965), *The Heart of Reformation Faith*, trans. John W. Doberstein (New York: Harper and Row).

BORO, JOYCE (2004), 'Lord Berners and his Books: A New Survey', *HLQ*, 67: 236–50.

—— (2007), 'Introduction' to *The Castle of Love: A Critical Edition of Lord Berners's Romance*, Medieval and Renaissance Texts and Studies, 336 (Tempe: Arizona Center for Medieval and Renaissance Studies), 46–71.

BOURDIEU, PIERRE (1993), *The Field of Cultural Production: Essays on Art and Literature*, ed. Randal Johnson (Cambridge: Polity Press).

BOYLE, MARJORIE O'ROURKE (1977), *Erasmus on Language and Method in Theology* (Toronto: University of Toronto Press).

BRADDOCK, R. C. (1987), 'The Duke of Northumberland's Army Reconsidered', *Albion*, 19: 13–17.

BRADEN, GORDON (1985), *Renaissance Tragedy and the Senecan Tradition: Anger's Privilege* (New Haven: Yale University Press).

BRADLEY, HENRY (1912), 'William Stevenson, *Gammer Gurtons Nedle*: Critical Essay and Notes', in C. M. Gayley (ed.), *Representative English Comedies*, 4 vols (New York: Macmillan), i. 197–202.

BRADSHAW, BRENDAN (1982), 'The Christian Humanism of Erasmus', *Journal of Theological Studies*, n.s., 33 (1982), 411–47.

BRADSHAW, C. J. (1997), 'John Bale and the Use of Biblical Imagery', *Reformation*, 2: 173–89.

BRANT, CLARE, and DIANE PURKISS (eds) (1992), *Women, Texts and Histories 1575–1760* (London: Routledge).

BRAUNMULLER, A. R., and MICHAEL HATTAWAY (eds) (2003), *The Cambridge Companion to English Renaissance Drama* (Cambridge: Cambridge University Press).

BRENNAN, MICHAEL G. (1982), 'The Date of the Countess of Pembroke's Translation of the Psalms', *RES*, 33: 434–6.

—— (2002), 'The Queen's Proposed Visit to Wilton House in 1599 and the "Sidney Psalms" ', *SiJ*, 20: 27–53.

BRENNER, ROBERT (1989), 'Bourgeois Revolution and Transition to Capitalism', in A. L. Beier, David Cannadine, and James M. Rosenheim (eds), *The First Modern Society: Essays in English History in Honour of Lawrence Stone* (Cambridge: Cambridge University Press), 271–304.

BRIGDEN, SUSAN (1989), *London and the Reformation* (Oxford: Clarendon Press).

—— (1994), 'Henry Howard, Earl of Surrey, and the "Conjured League" ', *HJ*, 37: 507–37.

—— (1996), ' "The shadow that you know": Sir Thomas Wyatt and Sir Francis Bryan at Court and in Embassy', *HJ*, 39: 1–31.

BRITNELL, R. H. (1997), 'Penitence and Prophecy: George Cavendish on the Last State of Cardinal Wolsey', *JEH*, 48: 263–81.

BROWNLOW, F. W. (1968), '*Speke Parrot*: Skelton's Allegorical Denunciation of Cardinal Wolsey', *SP* 65: 124–39.

—— (1971), 'The Book Compiled by Maister Skelton, Poet Laureate, Called *Speake, Parrot*', *ELR*, 1: 3–26.

—— (ed.) (1990), *The Book of the Laurel* by John Skelton (Newark, NJ: Associated University Presses).

BRYSON, ALAN (2001), ' "The speciall men in every shere": The Edwardian Regime, 1547–1553', PhD diss., University of St Andrews.

——— (forthcoming), 'Edward VI's "speciall men": Crown and Locality in Mid-Tudor England', *Historical Research*, 82.

BUDRA, PAUL (2000), *'A Mirror for Magistrates' and the de casibus Tradition* (Toronto: University of Toronto Press).

BURCKHARDT, JAKOB (1944), *The Civilization of the Renaissance in Italy* (Oxford: Phaidon Press).

BURKE, PETER (1977), 'Representations of the Self from Petrarch to Descartes', in Roy Porter (ed.), *Rewriting the Self: Histories from the Renaissance to the Present* (London: Routledge), 17–28.

——— (1994), *Popular Culture in Early Modern Europe* (1978; repr. Aldershot: Scolar Press).

——— (1995), *The Fortunes of the Courtier: The European Reception of Castiglione's 'Cortegiano'* (Cambridge: Polity Press).

BURROW, COLIN (1993*a*), *Epic Romance: Homer to Milton* (Oxford: Clarendon Press).

——— (1993*b*), 'Horace at Home and Abroad: Wyatt and Sixteenth-Century Horatianism', in Charles Martindale and David Hopkins (eds), *Horace Made New: Horatian Influences on British Writing from the Renaissance to the Twentieth Century* (Cambridge: Cambridge University Press).

——— (1997), 'Virgil in English Translation', in C. Martindale (ed.), *The Cambridge Companion to Virgil* (Cambridge: Cambridge University Press), 21–37.

BURROW, JOHN (1990), 'Chaucer', in A. C. Hamilton (ed.), *The Spenser Encyclopedia* (Toronto: Toronto University Press; London: Routledge), 144–8.

BUSH, DOUGLAS (1924), 'The Classical Tales in Painter's *Palace of Pleasure*', *JEGP*, 23: 331–41.

BUSHNELL, REBECCA W. (1990), *Tragedies of Tyrants: Political Thought and Theater in the English Renaissance* (Ithaca, NY: Cornell University Press).

BUTTERWORTH, CHARLES C. (1953), *The English Primers (1529–1545)* (Philadelphia: University of Pennsylvania Press).

BYROM, H. I. (1932), 'The Case for Nicholas Grimald as Editor of "Tottell's" Miscellany', *MLR*, 27: 125–43.

CAHOON, LESLIE (1988), 'The Bed as Battlefield: Erotic Conquest and Military Metaphor in Ovid's *Amores*', *Transactions of the American Philological Association*, 118: 293–307.

CAMPBELL, LILY B. (1952), '*Doctor Faustus*: A Case of Conscience', *PMLA*, 67: 219–39.

CANITZ, A. E. CHRISTA (1996), ' "In our awyn langage": The Nationalist Agenda of Gavin Douglas's *Eneados*', *Vergilius*, 42: 25–37.

CANNY, NICHOLAS (1998), 'The Origins of Empire: An Introduction', in Canny (ed.), *The Origins of Empire* (Oxford: Oxford University Press), 7–8.

CAREY, JOHN (1970), 'Sixteenth- and Seventeenth-Century Prose', in C. Ricks (ed.), *English Poetry and Prose 1540–1674* (London: Sphere).

——— (1987), 'Structure and Rhetoric in Sidney's *Arcadia*', in Denis Kay (ed.), *Sir Philip Sidney: An Anthology of Modern Criticism* (Oxford: Clarendon Press), 245–64.

CARLEY, JAMES P. (ed.) (2000*a*), *The Libraries of Henry VIII* (London: British Library).

——— (2000*b*), 'The Writings of Henry Parker, Lord Morley', in Marie Axton and James P. Carley (eds), *'Triumphs of English': Henry Parker, Lord Morley, Translator to the Tudor Court* (London: British Library), 27–68.

CARLSON, A. J. (1993), '*Mundus muliebris*: The World of Women Reviled and Defended *ca*.195 BC and 1551 AD. And Other Things . . .', *SCJ*, 24: 541–60.

CARLSON, DAVID R. (1991), 'Royal Tutors in the Reign of Henry VII', *SCJ*, 22: 253–79.

CARLSON, DAVID R. (1992), 'The "Grammarians' War" 1519–21: Humanist Careerism in Early Tudor England, and Printing', *Modern History*, 18: 157–81.

—— (1998), 'The Writings of Bernard André (*c*.1450–*c*.1522)', *RenSt*, 12: 229–50.

—— (2006), 'A Theory of the Early English Printing Firm: Jobbing, Book Publishing, and the Problem of Productive Capacity in Caxton's Work', in William Kuskin (ed.), *Caxton's Trace: Studies in the History of English Printing* (Notre Dame, IN: University of Notre Dame Press), 35–68.

CARPENTER, SARAH (1997), 'The Sixteenth-Century Court Audience: Performers and Spectators', *METh*, 19: 3–14.

CARSON, ANNE (1986), *Eros the Bittersweet: An Essay* (Princeton: Princeton University Press).

CARTWRIGHT, KENT (1999), *Theatre and Humanism: English Drama in the Sixteenth Century* (Cambridge: Cambridge University Press).

CAVE, TERENCE (1979), *The Cornucopian Text: Problems of Writing in the French Renaissance* (Oxford: Clarendon Press).

CHAMBERS, E. K. (1923), *The Elizabethan Stage*, 4 vols (Oxford: Clarendon Press).

—— (1969), *English Pastorals* (1895; repr. Freeport, NY: Books for Libraries).

CHAMBERS, R. W. (1935), *Thomas More* (New York: Harcourt Brace).

CHANDLER, JOHN (1993), *John Leland's Itinerary: Travels in Tudor England* (Stroud: Sutton).

CHANEY, EDWARD (2000), *The Evolution of the Grand Tour* (London: Frank Cass).

CHARLTON, H. B. (1946), *The Senecan Tradition in Renaissance Tragedy* (1921; repr. Manchester: Manchester University Press).

CHARLTON, KENNETH (1987), ' "False Fonde Bookes, Ballades and Rimes": An Aspect of Informal Education in Early Modern England', *History of Education Quarterly*, 27: 449–71.

CHARTIER, ROGER (1987), *The Cultural Uses of Print in Early Modern France*, trans. Lydia S. Cochrane (Princeton: Princeton University Press).

—— (1989), 'The Practical Impact of Writing', in Chartier (ed.), *A History of Private Life*, iii: *Passions of the Renaissance*, trans. Arthur Goldhammer (Cambridge, MA: Harvard University Press), 111–59.

CHRISTIANSON, PAUL (1978), *Reformers and Babylon: English Apocalyptic Visions from the Reformation to the Civil War* (Toronto: University of Toronto Press).

—— (1999), 'The Rise of London's Book-Trade', in Lotte Hellinga and J. B. Trapp (eds), *The Cambridge History of the Book in Britain*, iii: *1400–1557* (Cambridge: Cambridge University Press), 128–47.

CLANCHY, MICHAEL (1993), *Memory to Written Record: England, 1066–1307*, 2nd edn (Oxford: Blackwell).

CLARK, PETER (1977), *English Provincial Society from the Reformation to the Revolution: Religion, Politics and Society in Kent 1500–1640* (Hassocks: Harvester Press).

——ALAN G. R. SMITH, and NICHOLAS TYACKE (eds) (1979), *The English Commonwealth 1547–1640: Essays in Politics and Society Presented to Joel Hurstfield* (Leicester: Leicester University Press).

CLEGG, CYNDIA SUSAN (1997), *Press Censorship in Elizabethan England* (Cambridge: Cambridge University Press).

COCKLE, MAURICE J. D. (1978), *A Bibliography of Military Books up to 1642*, 2nd edn (London: Holland Press).

COINER, NANCY (1995), 'Galathea and the Interplay of Voices in Skelton's *Speke, Parrot*', in David G. Allen and Robert A. White (eds), *Subjects on the World's Stage: Essays on British Literature of the Middle Ages and the Renaissance* (Cranbury, NJ: Associated University Presses), 88–99.

COLDIRON, ANNE (2006), 'Taking Advice from a Frenchwoman: Caxton, Pynson, and Christine de Pizan's Moral Proverbs', in William Kuskin (ed.), *Caxton's Trace: Studies in the History of English Printing* (Notre Dame, IN: University of Notre Dame Press), 127–66.

COLE, M. H. (1999), *The Portable Queen: Elizabeth I and the Politics of Ceremony* (Amherst: University of Massachusetts Press).

COLEMAN, D. C. (1977), *The Economy of England, 1450–1750* (Oxford: Oxford University Press).

COLETTI, THERESA (2004), ' "Curtesy doth it you lere": The Sociology of Transgression in the Digby *Mary Magdalene*', *ELH*, 71: 1–28.

COLISH, MARCIA L. (1978), 'Cicero's *De officiis* and Machiavelli's *Prince*', *SCJ*, 9: 80–93.

COLLEY, JOHN SCOTT (1975), '*Fulgens and Lucres*: Politics and Aesthetics', *Zeitschrift für Anglistik und Amerikanistik*, 23: 322–30.

COLLINSON, PATRICK (1983), *Elizabethan Puritanism* (London: Historical Association).

—— (1990), *The Elizabethan Puritan Movement* (1967; Oxford: Oxford University Press).

—— (1997), 'Truth, Lies, and Fiction in Sixteenth-Century Protestant Historiography', in D. R. Kelley and D. H. Sacks (eds), *The Historical Imagination in Early Modern Britain: History, Rhetoric, and Fiction, 1500–1800* (Cambridge: Cambridge University Press), 37–68.

—— (2002), 'Literature and the Church', in D. Loewenstein and J. Mueller (eds), *The Cambridge History of Early Modern English Literature* (Cambridge: Cambridge University Press), 374–98.

—— (2006), 'The Persecution in Kent', in Eamon Duffy and David M. Loades (eds), *The Church of Mary Tudor* (Aldershot: Ashgate), 309–33.

CONLEY, C. H. (1927), *The First English Translators of the Classics* (New Haven: Yale University Press).

CONNOLLY, MARGARET (1998), *John Shirley: Book Production and the Noble Household in Fifteenth-Century England* (Brookfield, VT: Ashgate).

COOPER, HELEN (1977), *Pastoral: Mediaeval into Renaissance* (Ipswich: D. S. Brewer; Toronto: Rowman and Littlefield).

—— (2004), *The English Romance in Time: Transforming Motifs from Geoffrey of Monmouth to the Death of Shakespeare* (Oxford: Oxford University Press).

—— and SALLY MAPSTONE (eds) (1997), *The Long Fifteenth Century: Essays for Douglas Gray* (Oxford: Clarendon Press).

COOPER, LISA (2005), 'Urban Utterances: Merchants, Artisans, and the Alphabet in Caxton's Dialogues in French and English', *New Medieval Literatures*, 7: 127–62.

COPE, JACKSON I. (1993), *The Theater and the Dream: From Metaphor to Form in Renaissance Drama* (Baltimore: Johns Hopkins University Press).

CORMACK, BRADIN (2007), *A Power to Do Justice: Jurisdiction, English Literature, and the Rise of Common Law* (Chicago: University of Chicago Press).

COURTENAY, WILLIAM J. (1982), 'The Early Stages in the Introduction of Oxford Logic into Italy', in A. Maieru (ed.), *English Logic in Italy in the 14th and 15th Centuries* (Naples: Bibliopolis), 13–32.

CRAIK, T. W. (1958), *The Tudor Interlude: Stage, Costume, and Acting* (Leicester: Leicester University Press).

CRANE, D. E. L. (1984), 'Richard Stanyhurst's Translation of Vergil's *Aeneid* 1582', in G. A. M. Janssens and F. G. A. M. Aarts (eds), *Studies in Seventeenth-Century English Literature, History and Bibliography*, *Costerus*, n.s., 46 (Amsterdam: Rodopi), 47–82.

CRANE, MARY THOMAS (1986), '*Intret Cato*: Authority and the Epigram', in Barbara Kiefer Lewalski (ed.), *Renaissance Genres: Essays on Theory, History, and Interpretation* (Cambridge, MA: Harvard University Press), 158–86.

CRANE, MARY THOMAS (1993), *Framing Authority: Sayings, Self, and Society in Sixteenth-Century England* (Princeton: Princeton University Press, 1993).

CRAUN, E. (1971), 'The *de casibus* Complaint in Elizabethan England, 1559–1593', PhD thesis (Princeton University).

CREWE, JONATHAN (1990), *Trials of Authorship: Anterior Forms and Poetic Reconstruction from Wyatt to Shakespeare* (Berkeley: University of California Press).

CROW, BRIAN (1980), 'The Development of the Representation of Human Actions in Medieval and Renaissance Drama', PhD thesis (University of Bristol).

CUMMINGS, BRIAN (2007), 'The Conscience of Thomas More', in Andreas Höfele et al. (eds), *Pluralisierung und Autorität* (Berlin: Lit Verlag), 1–14.

—— and JAMES SIMPSON (eds) (forthcoming), *Culture Reformations: Twenty-First Century Approaches* (Oxford: Oxford University Press).

CUMMINGS, R. M. (ed.) (1971), *Spenser: The Critical Heritage* (New York: Barnes and Noble).

CURRAN, J. E., JR (2002), *Roman Invasions: The British History, Protestant Anti-Romanism, and the Historical Imagination in England, 1530–1660* (Newark: University of Delaware Press).

D'ALTON, C. W. (2003), 'The Suppression of Lutheran Heretics in England, 1526–1529', *JEH*, 54: 728–53.

DANE, JOSEPH A. (2003), *The Myth of Print Culture: Essays on Evidence, Textuality and Bibliographical Method* (Toronto: University of Toronto Press).

—— (2008), *Abstractions of Evidence in the Study of Manuscripts and Early Printed Books* (Brookfield, VT: Ashgate).

DANIELL, DAVID (1994), *William Tyndale: A Biography* (New Haven: Yale University Press).

DAVIDSON, CLIFFORD (ed.) (1986), *The Saint Play in Medieval Europe* (Kalamazoo, MI: Medieval Institute).

DAVIE, DONALD (ed.) (1996), *The Psalms in English* (London: Penguin).

DAVIES, C. S. L. (1977), *Peace, Print and Protestantism 1450–1558* (St Albans: Paladin).

—— (2008), 'A Rose by Another Name', *TLS*, 13 June, 14–15.

DAVIES, W. T. (1940), 'A Bibliography of John Bale', *Oxford Bibliographical Society: Proceedings and Papers*, 5: 203–79.

DAVIS, ALEX (2003), *Chivalry and Romance in the English Renaissance* (Cambridge: Brewer).

DAVIS, JOEL (2004), 'Multiple *Arcadias* and the Literary Quarrel between Fulke Greville and the Countess of Pembroke', *SP*, 101: 401–30.

DAVIS, LLOYD (2006), 'Critical Debates and Early Modern Autobiography', in R. Bedford, L. Davis, and P. Kelly (eds), *Early Modern Autobiography: Theories, Genres, Practices* (Ann Arbor: University of Michigan Press), 19–34.

DAVIS, NICHOLAS (1984), 'The Meaning of the Word "Interlude": A Discussion', *METh*, 6: 5–15.

DAVIS, P. J. (1989), 'The Chorus in Seneca's *Thyestes*', *Classical Quarterly*, 39: 421–35.

—— (2003), *Seneca: Thyestes* (London: Duckworth).

DAVIS, WALTER (2002), 'Spenser and the History of Allegory', *ELR*, 32: 152–67.

DAYBELL, J. (2006), *Women Letter-Writers in Tudor England* (Oxford: Oxford University Press).

DEARING, BRUCE (1952), 'Gavin Douglas' Eneados: A Reinterpretation', *PMLA*, 67: 845–62.

DEATS, SARAH MUNSON (1976), 'Doctor Faustus: From Chapbook to Tragedy', *ELWIU*, 3: 3–16.

DEBAX, JEAN-PAUL (2007), 'Complicity and Hierarchy: A Tentative Definition of the Interlude Genus', in Peter Happé and Wim Hüsken (eds), *Interludes and Early Modern Society: Studies in Power, Gender and Theatricality* (Amsterdam: Rodopi), 23–42.

DE GRAZIA, MARGRETA (2007), *Hamlet without Hamlet* (Cambridge: Cambridge University Press).

DELANEY, P. (1969), *British Autobiography in the Seventeenth Century* (London: Routledge & Kegan Paul).

DELIYANNIS, DEBORAH (2003), 'Charlemagne's Silver Tables: The Ideology of an Imperial Capital', *Early Medieval Europe*, 12: 159–77.

DE NAVE, F. (ed.) (1994), *Antwerp, Dissident Typographical Centre: The Role of Antwerp Printers in the Religious Conflicts in England (16th Century)* (Antwerp: Snoeck-Ducaju and Zoon).

DERRICK, T. J. (1982), 'Introduction' to *The Arte of Rhetorique*, by Thomas Wilson (New York: Garland).

DEVEREUX, E. J. (1968–9), 'The Publication of the English *Paraphrases* of Erasmus', *BJRL*, 51: 348–67.

—— (1990), 'Empty Tuns and Unfruitful Grafts: Richard Grafton's Historical Publications', *SCJ*, 21: 33–56.

DEWAR, MARY (1964), *Sir Thomas Smith: A Tudor Intellectual in Office* (London: Athlone Press).

DILLON, JANETTE (2002), *Performance and Spectacle in Hall's Chronicle* (London: Society for Theatre Research).

DOBIN, HOWARD (1990), *Merlin's Disciples: Prophecy, Poetry, and Power in Renaissance England* (Stanford, CA: Stanford University Press).

DOERKSEN, DANIEL W., and CHRISTOPHER HODGKINS (eds) (2004), *Centered on the Word* (Newark: University of Delaware Press).

DOLVEN, J. (2007), *Scenes of Instruction in Renaissance Romance* (Chicago: University of Chicago Press).

DONAGAN, BARBARA (1995), 'Halcyon Days and the Literature of War: England's Military Education before 1642', *Past and Present*, 147: 65–100.

DONALDSON, PETER S. (1988), *Machiavelli and Mystery of State* (Cambridge: Cambridge University Press).

DORAN, MADELINE (1954), *Endeavors of Art: A Study of Form in Elizabethan Drama* (Madison: University of Milwaukee Press).

DOUGLAS, AUDREY W., and PETER GREENFIELD (eds) (1986), *Records of Early English Drama: Cumberland, Westmorland, Gloucestershire* (Toronto: University of Toronto).

DOVE, M. (1986), *The Perfect Age of Man's Life* (Cambridge: Cambridge University Press).

DOYLE, A. I. (1957), 'The Work of a Late Fifteenth-Century English Scribe, William Ebes', *BJRL*, 39: 298–325.

DUFF, E. G., et al. (1913), *Hand-Lists of English Printers 1501–1556*, 4 vols (London: Bibliographical Society).

DUFFY, EAMON (1992), *The Stripping of the Altars: Traditional Religion in England 1400–1580* (New Haven: Yale University Press).

DUNCAN-JONES, KATHERINE (1991), *Sir Philip Sidney: Courtier Poet* (London: Hamish Hamilton).

—— (1998), '*Christs Teares*, Nashe's "forsaken extremities" ', *RES*, 49: 167–84.

DUPLESSIS, ROBERT (1997), *Transitions to Capitalism in Early Modern Europe* (Cambridge: Cambridge University Press).

DYCK, ANDREW R. (1996), *A Commentary on Cicero, De Officiis* (Ann Arbor: University of Michigan Press).

EBIN, LOIS A. (1988), *Illuminator Makar, Vates: Visions of Poetry in the Fifteenth Century* (Lincoln: University of Nebraska Press).

ECCLES, MARK (1981), 'William Wager and his Plays', *ELN*, 18: 258–62.

ECHARD, SIAN (1998), 'With Carmen's Help: Latin Authorities in the *Confessio Amantis*', *SP*, 95: 1–40.

EDWARDS, A. S. G. (1971), 'Some Borrowings by Cavendish from Lydgate's *Fall of Princes*', *N&Q*, o.s., 216: 207–9.

EDWARDS, A. S. G. (1974), 'The Date of George Cavendish's Metrical Visions', *PQ*, 53: 128–32.

—— (1980*a*), 'Poet and Printer in Sixteenth Century England', *Gutenburg Jahrbuch*, 82–8.

—— (1980*b*), 'Introduction' to *Metrical Visions*, by George Cavendish (Columbia: University of South Carolina Press for the Newberry Library).

—— (1984), *Stephen Hawes* (Boston: Twayne).

—— (1999), 'Skelton's English Poems in Print and Manuscript', *Trivium*, 31: 87–100.

—— (2002), 'William Copland and the Identity of Printed Middle English Romance', in Philippa Hardman (eds), *The Matter of Identity in Medieval Romance* (Cambridge: Brewer), 139–47.

—— (2004), 'Manuscripts of the Verse of Henry Howard, Earl of Surrey', *HLQ*, 67: 283–93.

—— (2006), 'A Pair of Parrots', *TLS*, 29 Sept., 30.

—— and DEREK PEARSALL (1989), 'The Manuscripts of the Major English Poetic Texts', in Jeremy Griffiths and Derek Pearsall (eds), *Book Production and Publishing in Britain 1395–1475* (Cambridge: Cambridge University Press), 257–78.

EDWARDS, H. L. R., and WILLIAM NELSON (1938), 'The Dating of Skelton's Later Poems', *PMLA*, 53: 601–22.

EISENSTEIN, E. L. (1979), *The Printing Press as an Agent of Change: Communications and Cultural Transformations in Early-Modern Europe*, 2 vols (Cambridge: Cambridge University Press).

—— (2002), '*AHR Forum*: An Unacknowledged Revolution Revisited', *AHR*, 107: 87–105.

ELLIS, JIM (2001), 'Orpheus at the Inns of Court', in G. Klawitter (ed.), *The Affectionate Shepherd: Celebrating Richard Barnsfield* (London: Associated University Presses).

ELTIS, D. A. (1991), 'English Military Theory and the Military Revolution of the Sixteenth Century', D.Phil. thesis (University of Oxford).

ELTON, G. R. (1979), 'Reform and the "Commonwealth-Men" of Edward VI's Reign', in Peter Clark, Alan G. R. Smith, and Nicholas Tyacke (eds), *The English Commonwealth 1547–1640: Essays in Politics and Society Presented to Joel Hurstfield* (Leicester: Leicester University Press), 23–38.

EMDEN, A. B. (1974), *A Biographical Register of the University of Oxford, AD 1500 to 1540* (Oxford: Clarendon Press).

EMPSON, WILLIAM (1951), *The Structure of Complex Words* (London: Chatto & Windus).

EVANS, DOROTHY ATKINSON (1951), 'Introduction' to *The Wandering Knight: by Jean Cartigny*, trans. William Goodyear (Seattle: University of Washington Press).

EVENDEN, ELIZABETH (2008), *Patents, Pictures and Patronage: John Day and the Tudor Book Trade* (Aldershot: Ashgate).

—— and T. S. FREEMAN (2002), 'John Foxe, John Day and the Printing of the *Book of Martyrs*', in R. Myers, M. Harris, and G. Mandelbrote (eds), *Lives in Print: Biography and the Book Trade from the Middle Ages to the 21st Century* (London: Oak Knoll), 23–54.

FAIRFIELD, LESLIE P. (1971), 'The Vocacyon of Johan Bale and Early English Autobiography', *RenQ* 24: 327–40.

—— (1972), 'The Mysterious Press of "Michael Wood" ', *The Library*, 5th ser., 27: 220–32.

—— (1976), *John Bale: Mythmaker for the English Reformation* (West Lafayette, IN: Purdue University Press).

FANTHAM, ELAINE (1986), 'Seneca's *Thyestes*', *UTQ*, 55: 435–6.

FARNHAM, WILLARD (1926), 'John Higgins' *Mirror* and *Locrine*', *MP*, 23: 307–13.

—— (1936), *The Medieval Heritage of Elizabethan Tragedy* (Berkeley: University of California Press).

FEBVRE, LUCIEN PAUL VICTOR, and HENRI-JEAN MARTIN (1976), *The Coming of the Book: The Impact of Printing 1450–1800*, ed. Geoffrey Nowell-Smith and David Wootton, trans. David Gerard (London: Verso).

FERGUSON, ARTHUR B. (1960), *The Indian Summer of English Chivalry* (Durham, NC: Duke University Press).

FERGUSON, MARJORIE (1981), 'Nashe's *Unfortunate Traveller*: The "Newes of the Maker" Game', *ELR*, 11: 165–82.

FINKELPEARL, PHILIP (1969), *John Marston of the Middle Temple* (Cambridge, MA: Harvard University Press).

FISH, STANLEY (1980), *Is There a Text in this Class?* (Cambridge, MA: Harvard University Press).

FITCH, JOHN G. (2002–4), 'Introduction' to Seneca, *Tragedies*, ed. and trans. J. G. Fitch, 2 vols (Cambridge, MA: Harvard University Press), i. 1–33.

FITZPATRICK, JOAN (2004), 'Marrying Waterways: Politicizing and Gendering the Landscape in Spenser's *Faerie Queene* River-Marriage Canto', in Philip Schwyzer and Simon Mealor (eds), *Archipelagic Identities: Literature and Identity in the Atlantic Archipelago, 1550–1800* (Aldershot: Ashgate), 81–91.

FOISTER, SUSAN (2006), *Holbein in England* (London: Tate).

FORD, M. (1999), 'Importation of Printed Books into England and Scotland', in Lotte Hellinga and J. B. Trapp (eds), *The Cambridge History of the Book in Britain*, iii: *1400–1557* (Cambridge: Cambridge University Press), 179–201.

FOREST-HILL, LYNN (2008), 'Maidens and Matrons: The Theatricality of Gender in Tudor Interludes', in Peter Happé and Wim Hüsken (eds), *Interludes* (Amsterdam: Rodopi), 43–69.

FOUCAULT, MICHEL (1979), *Discipline and Punish* (New York: Vintage Books).

—— (1984), 'Truth and Power', in Paul Rabinow (ed.), *The Foucault Reader* (New York: Pantheon), 51–75.

FOWLER, T. (1893), *The History of Corpus Christi College* (Oxford: Clarendon Press).

FOX, ALISTAIR (1982), *Thomas More: History and Providence* (Oxford: Blackwell).

—— (1986), 'Prophecies and Politics in the Reign of Henry VIII', in Alistair Fox and John Guy (eds), *Reassessing the Henrician Age: Humanism, Politics and Reform 1500–1550* (Oxford: Blackwell), 77–94.

—— (1989), *Politics and Literature in the Reigns of Henry VII and Henry VIII* (Oxford: Blackwell).

—— (1997), *The English Renaissance: Identity and Representation in Elizabethan England* (Oxford: Blackwell).

FRADENBURG, LOUISE (1996), *Caxton, Foucault, and the Pleasures of History* (New York: Routledge).

—— and CARLA FRECCERO (1996), 'Introduction: Caxton, Foucault, and the Pleasures of History', in Fradenburg and Freccero (eds), *Premodern Sexualities* (New York: Routledge).

FRANCIS, F. C. (1961), *Robert Copland: Sixteenth Century and Printer and Translator* (Glasgow: Jackson).

FRASER, RUSSELL (1970), *The War against Poetry* (Princeton: Princeton University Press).

FREEMAN, THOMAS S. (1999), 'Texts, Lies and Microfilm: Reading and Misreading Foxe's *Book of Martyrs*', *SCJ*, 30: 23–46.

—— (2002), ' "As true a subiect being prysoner": John Foxe's Notes on the Imprisonment of Princess Elizabeth, 1554–5', *EHR*, 117: 104–16.

FREEMAN, THOMAS S. and SUSAN DORAN (forthcoming), *Mary Tudor: New Perspectives* (London: Palgrave Macmillan).

—— and S. E. WALL (2001), 'Racking the Body, Shaping the Text: The Account of Anne Askew in Foxe's *Book of Martyrs*', *RenQ*, 53: 1165–96.

FRENCH, ROGER K. (2000), 'The Medical Ethics of Gabriele de Zerbi', in French (ed.), *Ancients and Moderns in the Medical Sciences* (Aldershot: Ashgate), 72–97.

FRYE, SUSAN (1993), *Elizabeth I: The Competition for Representation* (New York: Oxford University Press).

FUCHS, BARBARA (2002), 'An English Picaro in New Spain: Miles Philips and the Framing of National Identity', *CR: The New Centennial Review*, 2: 55–68.

FURNIVALL, F. J. (ed.) (1907), *Robert Laneham's Letter* (London: Chatto, Windus, and Duffield).

GADD, IAN (forthcoming), ' "A suitable remedy"? Regulating the Printing Press, 1553–1558', in Elizabeth Evenden (ed.), *1556–57: The Crucible of Confessional Conflict* (Aldershot: Ashgate).

—— and ALEXANDRA GILLESPIE (eds) (2004), *John Stow: Author, Editor and Reader* (London: British Library).

GALLOWAY, DAVID (ed.) (1984), *Norwich: Records of Early English Drama* (Toronto: University of Toronto Press).

—— and JOHN WASSON (ed.) (1980), *Records of Plays and Players in Norfolk and Suffolk, 1330–1642*, Malone Society Collections, 11 (Oxford: Oxford University Press).

GAMBERINI, SPARTACO (1970), *Lo studio dell'italiano in Inghilterra nel '500 e nel '600* (Messina: Casa Editrice G. D'Anna).

GARIN, E. (1960), 'La cultura fiorentina nella seconda meta del 300 e i "barbari britanni" ', *La Rassenga della letteratura italiana*, 62: 181–95.

GASKELL, PHILIP (1972), *A New Introduction to Bibliography* (Oxford: Clarendon Press).

GERITZ, ALBERT J. (1998), *Thomas More: An Annotated Bibliography of Criticism, 1935–1997* (Westport, CT: Greenwood Press).

GERRISH, BRIAN A. (1962), *Grace and Reason: A Study in the Theology of Luther* (Oxford: Oxford University Press).

GIBBONS, BRIAN (2003), 'Romance and the Heroic Play', in A. R. Braunmuller and Michael Hattaway (eds), *The Cambridge Companion to English Renaissance Drama* (Cambridge: Cambridge University Press), 207–36.

GILLESPIE, ALEXANDRA (2004), 'Caxton and After', in A. S. G. Edwards (ed.), *A Companion to Middle English Prose* (Woodbridge: Boydell and Brewer), 307–25.

—— (2006), *Print Culture and the Medieval Author* (Oxford: Oxford University Press).

—— (2008), 'Analytical Survey: The History of the Book', *New Medieval Literatures*, 9: 247–86.

GILLESPIE, VINCENT (1981), 'Justification by Good Works: Skelton's *The Garland of Laurel*', *RMSt* 7: 19–31.

—— (1997), 'Justification by Faith: Skelton's *Replycacion*', in Helen Cooper and Sally Mapstone (eds), *The Long Fifteenth Century: Essays for Douglas Gray* (Oxford: Clarendon Press), 273–312.

—— (ed.) (2001), *Syon Abbey with the Libraries of the Carthusians*, Corpus of British Medieval Library Catalogues, 9 (London: British Library).

GILMONT, JEAN-FRANÇOIS, and KARIN MAAG (eds) (1998), *The Reformation and the Book* (Aldershot: Ashgate).

GLEASON, JOHN B. (1989), *John Colet* (Berkeley: University of California Press).

GLUCK, FLORENCE W., and ALICE B. MORGAN (eds) (1974), *The Minor Poems of Stephen Hawes*, EETS, o.s., 271.

GODFREY, BOB (2002), 'Sin, Vice and the Laughter of the Gods: An Erasmian Perspective on an Early Tudor Interlude', in Roberta Mullini (ed.), *Tudor Theatre: For Laughs(?)/Pour rire(?): Puzzling Laughter in Plays of the Tudor Age/Rires et problèmes dans le théâtre des Tudor*, Collection Theta, 6 (Bern: Lang), 96–110.

GOLDRING, ELIZABETH (2007), 'Portraiture, Patronage, and the Progresses: Robert Dudley, Earl of Leicester, and the Kenilworth Festivities of 1575', in Jayne E. Archer, Elizabeth Goldring, and Sarah Knight (eds), *The Progresses, Pageants and Entertainments of Queen Elizabeth I* (Oxford: Oxford University Press), 163–88.

—— (2008), ' "A mercer ye wot az we be": The Authorship of the Kenilworth *Letter* Reconsidered', *ELR*, 38: 1–25.

GOLDSTONE, H. (1960), 'Interplay in Peele's *The Old Wives' Tale*', *Boston University Studies in English*, 4: 202–13.

GÖRLACH, MANFRED (1993), *Introduction to Early Modern English* (1991; Cambridge: Cambridge University Press).

GOUWS, JOHN (1986), 'Fact and Anecdote in Fulke Greville's Account of Sidney's Last Days', in Jan van Dorsten et al. (eds), *Sir Philip Sidney: 1586 and the Creation of a Legend*, Sir Thomas Browne Institute Publications, n.s., 9 (Leiden: Brill and Leiden University Press, 1986), 62–82.

GOY-BLANQUET, DOMINIQUE (2003), *Shakespeare's Early History Plays: From Chronicle to Stage* (Oxford: Oxford University Press).

GRABES, HERBERT (2005), 'British Cultural History and Church History for the Continent: John Bale's *Summarium* (1548) and *Catalogus* (1557–9)', in Andreas Höfele and Werner von Koppenfels (eds), *Renaissance Go-Betweens: Cultural Exchange in Early Modern Europe* (Berlin: de Gruyter), 139–51.

GRAFTON, ANTHONY, and LISA JARDINE (1990), ' "Studied for action": How Gabriel Harvey Read his Livy', *Past and Present*, 129: 30–78.

GRAHAM, KENNETH J. E. (1994), *The Performance of Conviction: Plainness and Rhetoric in the Early English Renaissance* (Ithaca, NY: Cornell University Press).

—— (2005), 'Distributive Measures: Theology and Economics in the Writings of Robert Crowley', *Criticism*, 47: 137–58.

GRANTLEY, DARRYL (2004), *English Dramatic Interludes 1300–1580* (Cambridge: Cambridge University Press).

GREAVES, MARGARET (1964), *The Blazon of Honour: A Study in Renaissance Magnanimity* (London: Methuen).

GREEN, ROBERT W. (ed.) (1959), *Protestantism and Capitalism: The Weber Thesis and its Critics* (Boston: Heath).

GREENBLATT, STEPHEN (1980), *Renaissance Self-Fashioning: From More to Shakespeare* (Chicago: University Press).

GREENE, ROLAND (1990), 'Sir Philip Sidney's Psalms, the Sixteenth Century Psalter, and the Nature of Lyric', *SEL*, 30: 19–40.

GREENE, THOMAS (1982), *The Light in Troy: Imitation and Discovery in Renaissance Poetry* (New Haven: Yale University Press).

GREG, W. W., and E. BOSWELL (eds) (1930), *Records of the Court of the Stationers' Company 1576 to 1602, from Register B* (London: Bibliographical Society).

GRIFFITHS, JANE (2004), 'Text and Authority: John Stow's 1568 Edition of Skelton's Works', in Ian Gadd and Alexandra Gillespie (eds), *John Stow: Author, Editor and Reader* (London: British Library), 127–34.

—— (2006), *John Skelton and Poetic Authority: Defining the Liberty to Speak* (Oxford: Clarendon Press).

GRIFFITHS, JEREMY, and DEREK PEARSALL (eds) (1989), *Book Production and Publishing in Britain 1375–1475* (Cambridge: Cambridge University Press).

GUDDAT-FIGGE, GISELA (1976), *Catalogue of Manuscripts Containing Middle English Romances* (Munich: Fink).

GUNN, STEVEN (1987), 'The French Wars of Henry VIII', in J. Black (ed.), *The Origins of War in Early Modern Europe* (Edinburgh: Donald), 28–51.

—— (1990), 'Chivalry and the Politics of the Early Tudor Court', in Sydney Anglo (ed.), *Chivalry and the Renaissance* (Woodbridge: Boydell Press), 107–28.

—— (2006), 'The Court of Henry VII', in Steven Gunn and Antheun Janse (eds), *The Court as a Stage: England and the Low Countries in the Later Middle Ages* (Woodbridge: Boydell Press), 132–44.

—— and ANTHEUN JANSE (eds) (2006), *The Court as a Stage: England and the Low Countries in the Later Middle Ages* (Woodbridge: Boydell Press).

GUSDORF, G. (1980), 'Conditions and Limits of Autobiography', in J. Olney (ed.), *Autobiography: Essays Theoretical and Critical* (Princeton: Princeton University Press), 28–48.

GUTIERREZ, NANCY A. (1989), '*Beware the Cat*: Mimesis in a Skin of Oratory', *Style*, 23: 49–69.

—— (1993), 'William Baldwin', in David A. Richardson (ed.), *Sixteenth-Century British Non-dramatic Writers: First Series, Dictionary of Literary Biography*, 132 (Detroit: Bruccoli Cark Layman), 19–26.

GUY, JOHN (1988), *Tudor England* (Oxford: Oxford University Press).

—— (1995), 'The Rhetoric of Counsel in Early Modern England', in D. Hoak (ed.), *Tudor Political Culture* (Cambridge: Cambridge University Press), 292–310.

—— (1997), 'Tudor Monarchy and its Critiques', in Guy (ed.), *The Tudor Monarchy* (London: Arnold), 78–109.

—— (2000), *Thomas More* (London: Arnold).

HABER, JAKOB (1900), *John Heywood's 'The Spider and the Flie': Ein Kulturbild aus dem 16. Jahrhundert* (Berlin: Emil Felber).

HACKETT, HELEN (1992), ' "Yet tell me some such fiction": Lady Mary Wroth's *Urania* and the "Femininity" of Romance', in Clare Brant and Diane Purkiss (eds), *Women, Texts and Histories 1575–1760* (London: Routledge), 39–67.

—— (2000), *Women and Romance Fiction in the English Renaissance* (Cambridge: Cambridge University Press).

HADFIELD, ANDREW (1994), *Literature, Politics and National Identity: Reformation to Renaissance* (Cambridge: Cambridge University Press).

—— (1998), *Literature, Travel and Colonial Writing in the English Renaissance 1545–1625* (Oxford: Clarendon Press).

—— (2001), *The English Renaissance 1500–1620* (Oxford: Blackwell).

—— (2003), 'The Power and Rights of the Crown in *Hamlet* and *Lear*: "The King—The King's to Blame" ', *RES*, n.s., 54: 566–86.

HAIGH, CHRISTOPHER (1993), *English Reformations: Religion, Politics, and Society under the Tudors* (Oxford: Clarendon Press).

HALASZ, ALEXANDRA (1997), *The Marketplace of Print: Pamphlets and the Public Sphere in Early Modern England*, Cambridge Studies in Renaissance Literature and Culture, 17 (Cambridge: Cambridge University Press).

—— (1988), 'Wyatt's David', *TSLL*, 30: 320–44.

HALE, J. R. (1983), *Renaissance War Studies* (London: Hambledon Press).

HALL, DAVID (1984), 'Introduction' to S. L. Kaplan (ed.), *Understanding Popular Culture: Europe from the Middle Ages to the Nineteenth Century* (Berlin: Mouton).

HALL, STUART (2005), 'Notes on Deconstructing "the Popular" ', in Raiford Guins and Omayra Zaragoza Cruz (eds), *Popular Culture: A Reader* (London: Sage), 64–71.

HALPORN, BARBARA (2001), 'The *Margarita Philosophica*: A Case Study in Early Modern Book Design', *JEBS*, 3: 152–66.

HAMILTON, DONNA B. (2000), 'Re-engineering Virgil: *The Tempest* and the Printed English *Aeneid*', in Peter Hulme and William H. Sherman (eds), *The Tempest and its Travels* (Philadelphia: University of Philadelphia Press), 114–20.

HAMLIN, HANNIBAL (2004), *Psalm Culture and Early Modern English Literature* (Cambridge: Cambridge University Press).

——(2005), ' "The highest matter in the noblest form": The Influence of the Sidney Psalms', *SiJ* 23: 133–57.

HANHAM, ALISON (2005), 'Who Made William Caxton's Phrase-Book?', *RES*, 56: 712–29.

HANNAY, MARGARET P. (ed.) (1985), *Silent but for the Word: Tudor Women as Patrons, Translators, and Writers of Religious Works* (Kent, OH: Kent State University Press).

——(2001), ' "So may I with the Psalmist truly say": Women's Psalms Discourse', in Barbara Smith and Ursula Appelt (eds), *Write or Be Written: Early Modern Women Poets and Cultural Constraint* (Aldershot: Ashgate), 105–34.

HANNEN, THOMAS A. (1974), 'The Humanism of Sir Thomas Wyatt', in Thomas O. Sloan and Raymond B. Waddington (eds), *The Rhetoric of Renaissance Poetry from Wyatt to Milton* (Berkeley: University of California Press), 37–57.

HAPPÉ, PETER (1986), 'The Protestant Adaptation of the Saint Play', in Clifford Davidson (ed.), *The Saint Play in Medieval Europe* (Kalamazoo, MI: Medieval Institute), 205–40.

——(1996), *John Bale* (New York: Twayne).

——(2000), 'The Vocacyon of Johan Bale: Protestant Rhetoric and the Self', in Henk Dragstra, S. Ottway, and Helen Wilcox (eds), *Betraying Our Selves: Forms of Self-Representation in Early Modern English Texts* (Houndmills: Palgrave Macmillan), 45–58.

——(2001*a*), 'John Bale's Lost Mystery Cycle', *CahiersE*, 60: 1–12.

——(2001*b*), 'A Catalogue of Illustrations in the Books of John Bale', in Sarah Carpenter, Pamela King, and Peter Meredith (eds), *Porci ante Margaritam: Essays in Honour of Meg Twycross*, Leeds Studies in English, n.s., 32 (Leeds: School of English, University of Leeds), 81–118.

——(2007), ' "Rejoice ye in us with joy most joyfully": John Heywood's Plays and the Court', *CahiersE*, 72: 1–8.

——(2008), 'John Heywood and Humanism: *The Foure PP* and *The Spider and the Flye*', in Zsolt Almási and Mike Pincombe (eds), *Writing the Other: Humanism versus Barbarism in Tudor England* (Newcastle: Cambridge Scholars Press), 118–35.

HARARI, Y. N. (2004), *Renaissance Military Memoirs: War, History, and Identity, 1450–1600* (Woodbridge: Boydell Press).

HARDISON, O. B. (1989), *Prosody and Purpose in the English Renaissance* (Baltimore: Johns Hopkins University Press).

HARDMAN, PHILIPPA (ed.) (2002), *The Matter of Identity in Medieval Romance* (Cambridge: Brewer).

HARGRAVE, FRANCIS (ed.) (1793), *A Complete Collection of State Trials, and Proceedings for High Treason*, 6 vols.

HARRIER, RICHARD (1975), *The Canon of Sir Thomas Wyatt's Poetry* (Cambridge, MA: Harvard University Press).

HARRIS, JESSE W. (1940), *John Bale*, Illinois Studies in Language and Literature, 25 (Urbana: University of Illinois Press).

HART, E. F. (1956), 'The Answer-Poem of the Early Seventeenth Century', *RES*, 7: 19–29.

HAWKES, TERENCE (1962), 'The Matter of Metre', *Essays in Criticism*, 12: 413–21.

HAY, DENYS (1971), 'Italy and Barbarian Europe', in A. Molho and J. A. Tedeschi (eds), *Renaissance Studies in Honour of Hans Baron* (Florence: G. C. Sansoni editore), 48–68.

HAYES, DOUGLAS W. (2004), *Rhetorical Subversion in Early English Drama* (New York: Lang).

HAYS, MICHAEL L. (1985), 'A Bibliography of Dramatic Adaptations of Medieval Romances and Renaissance Chivalric Romances First Available in English through 1616', *RORD*, 28: 87–109.

HEADLEY, JOHN M. (1969), 'Form and Style in the *Responsio*', in Thomas More, *Responsio ad Lutherum*, ed. Headley, 2 vols, pt 2, in *The Complete Works of St Thomas More*, v (New Haven: Yale University Press), 804–23.

HEALE, ELIZABETH (1996), 'Lute and Harp in Wyatt's Poetry', in Helen Wilcox, Richard Todd, and Alasdair MacDonald (eds), *Sacred and Profane: Secular and Devotional Interplay in Early Modern British Literature* (Amsterdam: Vrije Universiteit University Press), 3–16.

——(1997), ' "An owl in a sack troubles no man": Proverbs, Plainness, and Wyatt', *RenSt*, 11: 420–33.

——(1998), *Wyatt, Surrey and Early Tudor Poetry* (London: Longman).

——(2003), *Autobiography and Authorship in Renaissance Verse: Chronicles of the Self* (Basingstoke: Palgrave Macmillan).

——(2008), 'The Fruits of War: The Voice of the Soldier in Gascoigne, Riche, and Churchyard', in Stephen Hamrick (ed.), *George Gascoigne*, Early Modern Literary Studies, 14, item 5, <http://extra.shu.ac.uk/emls/14-1/article4.htm>, accessed 4 Jan. 2009.

HEATON, GABRIEL (2007), 'Elizabethan Entertainments in Manuscript: The Harefield Festivities (1602) and the Dynamics of Exchange', in Jayne E. Archer, Elizabeth Goldring, and Sarah Knight (eds), *The Progresses, Pageants and Entertainments of Queen Elizabeth I* (Oxford: Oxford University Press), 227–44.

HEBDIGE, DICK (2005), 'Subculture', in Raiford Guins and Omayra Zaragoza Cruz (ed.), *Popular Culture: A Reader* (London: Sage), 355–71.

HELGERSON, RICHARD (1976), *The Elizabethan Prodigals* (Berkeley: University of California Press).

——(1983), *Self-Crowned Laureates: Spenser, Jonson, Milton and the Literary System* (Berkeley: University of California Press).

——(1992), *Forms of Nationhood: The Elizabethan Writing of England* (Chicago: Chicago University Press).

——(2003), ' "I Miles Philips": An Elizabethan Seaman Conscripted by History', *PMLA*, 118: 573–80.

HELLINGA, LOTTE (1982), *Caxton in Focus* (London: British Library).

HENDERSON, JUDITH RICE (1999), 'John Heywood's *The Spider and the Flie*: Educating Queen and Country', *SP*, 96: 241–74.

HENINGER, S. K., JR (1990), '*The Shepheardes Calender*', in A. C. Hamilton (ed.), *The Spenser Encyclopedia* (London: Routledge).

HENRY, D., and B. WALKER (1963), 'Seneca and the *Agamemnon*: Some Thoughts on Tragic Doom', *CP*, 58: 1–10.

HERINGTON, C. J. (1966), 'Senecan Tragedy', *Arion*, 5: 422–71.

HERMAN, PETER C. (2001), ' "He said *what*!?" Misdeeming *Gorboduc*, or Problematizing Form, Service and Certainty', *Exemplaria*, 13: 287–321.

HEXTER, J. H. (1952), *More's 'Utopia': The Biography of an Idea* (Princeton: Princeton University Press).

HIEATT, A. KENT (1975), *Chaucer, Spenser, Milton: Mythopoeic Continuities and Transformations* (Montreal: McGill-Queen's University Press).

HIGHLEY, CHRISTOPHER, and JOHN N. KING (eds) (2002), *John Foxe and his World* (Aldershot: Ashgate).

HILL, CHRISTOPHER (1997), *Intellectual Origins of the English Revolution Revisited* (Oxford: Clarendon Press).

HILL, EUGENE D. (1992), 'The First Elizabethan Tragedy: A Contextual Reading of *Cambises*', *SP*, 89: 404–33.

HILTON, RODNEY (1977), *Bondmen Made Free: Medieval Peasant Movements and the English Rising of 1381* (1973; repr. London: Methuen).

HOBBS, R. GERALD (1994), 'Martin Bucer and the Englishing of the Psalms', in D. F. Wright (ed.), *Martin Bucer* (Cambridge: Cambridge University Press), 161–75.

HOBSON, CHRISTOPHER Z. (1997), 'Country Mouse and Towny Mouse: Truth in Wyatt', *TSLL*, 39: 230–58.

HÖFELE, ANDREAS, and WERNER VON KOPPENFELS (eds) (2005), *Renaissance Go-Betweens: Cultural Exchange in Early Modern Europe* (Berlin: de Gruyter).

—— STEPHEN LAQUÉ, ENNO RUGE, and GABRIELA SCHMIDT (eds) (2007), *Pluralisierung und Autorität*, 12 (Berlin: Lit Verlag).

HOFFMAN, FENNO, JR (1959), 'Catherine Parr as a Woman of Letters', *HLQ*, 23: 349–67.

HOFFMAN, NANCY JO (1977), *Spenser's Pastorals: 'The Shepheardes Calender' and 'Colin Clout'* (Baltimore: Johns Hopkins University Press).

HOLSTUN, JAMES (2004), 'The Spider, the Fly, and the Commonwealth: Merrie John Heywood and Agrarian Class Struggle', *ELH*, 71: 53–88.

HONDERICH, PAULINE (1973), 'John Calvin and Doctor Faustus', *MLR*, 67: 1–13.

HORNER, OLGA (1993), '*Fulgens and Lucres*: An Historical Perspective', *METh*, 15: 49–86.

HOSINGTON, BRENDA M. (2006), ' "A poore preasant off Ytalyan costume": The Interplay of Travel and Translation in William Barker's *Dyssputacion off the Nobylytye off Wymen*', in Carmine G. Di Biase (ed.), *Travel and Translation in the Early Modern Period* (Amsterdam: Rodopi), 143–56.

HOULBROOKE, RALPH (ed.) (1988), *English Family Life, 1576–1716: An Anthology from Diaries* (Oxford: Oxford University Press).

HOWARD, JEAN E. (2006), 'Textualizing an Urban Life: The Case of Isabella Whitney', in R. Bedford, L. Davis, and P. Kelly (eds), *Early Modern Autobiography: Theories, Genres, Practices* (Ann Arbor: University of Michigan Press), 217–33.

HOYLE, R. (2001), *The Pilgrimage of Grace and the Politics of the 1530s* (Oxford: Oxford University Press).

HUDSON, ANNE (1997), '*Visio Balei*: An Early Literary Historian', in Helen Cooper and Sally Mapstone (eds), *The Long Fifteenth Century: Essays for Douglas Gray* (Oxford: Clarendon Press), 313–29.

HUGHES, FELICITY (1997), 'Gascoigne's Poses', *SEL*, 37: 1–19.

HUGHES, P. L., and J. F. LARKIN (eds) (1964–9), *Tudor Royal Proclamations*, 3 vols (New Haven: Yale University Press).

HUGHEY, RUTH WILLARD (1971), *John Harington of Stepney, Tudor Gentleman: His Life and Works* (Columbus: Ohio State University Press).

HUME, ANTHEA (1969), 'Spenser, Puritanism, and the Maye Eclogue', *RES*, 20: 155–67.

HUNT, ALICE (2007), 'Legitimacy, Ceremony and Drama: Mary Tudor's Coronation and *Respublica*', in Peter Happé and Wim Hüsken (eds), *Interludes and Early Modern Society: Studies in Gender, Power and Theatricality* (Amsterdam: Rodopi), 331–52.

HUNTER, G. K. (1962), *John Lyly: The Humanist as Courtier* (London: Routledge & Kegan Paul).

—— (1967), 'Seneca and the Elizabethans: A Case-Study in "Influence" ', *ShS*, 20: 17–26.

HUNTER, G. K. (1974), 'Seneca and English Tragedy', in C. D. N. Costa (ed.), *Seneca* (London: Routledge & Kegan Paul), 166–204.

——(1994), 'Rhetoric and Renaissance Drama', in P. Mack (ed.), *Renaissance Rhetoric* (Basingstoke: Macmillan), 103–18.

HUTSON, LORNA (1987), 'Thomas Nashe's "Persecution" by the Aldermen in 1593', *N&Q* 34: 199–200.

——(1989), *Thomas Nashe in Context* (Oxford: Oxford University Press).

——(1993), 'Fortunate Travelers: Reading for the Plot in Sixteenth Century England', *Representations*, 41: 83–103.

——(1994), *The Usurer's Daughter: Male Friendship and Fictions of Women Sixteenth-Century England* (London: Routledge).

HUTTAR, CHARLES A. (1966), 'Wyatt and the Several Editions of *The Court of Venus*', *SB* 19: 181–95.

INGRAM, R. W. (1967), '*Gammer Gurton's Needle*: Comedy Not Quite of the Lowest Order?', *SEL* 7: 257–68.

JACKSON, MACDONALD P. (1971), 'Three Old Ballads and the Date of *Doctor Faustus*', *AUMLA* 36: 187–200.

JAMES, HEATHER (2005), 'The Poet's Toys: Christopher Marlowe and the Liberties of Erotic Elegy', *MLQ* 67: 103–27.

JAMES, HENRY, and GREG WALKER (1995), 'The Politics of *Gorboduc*', *EHR* 110: 109–21.

JAMES, SUSAN E. (1999), *Kateryn Parr: The Making of a Queen* (Aldershot: Ashgate).

JAMESON, FREDRIC (1981), *The Political Unconscious: Narrative as a Socially Symbolic Act* (Ithaca, NY: Cornell University Press).

JAVITCH, DANIEL (1978), *Poetry and Courtliness in Renaissance England* (Princeton: Princeton University Press).

JAYNE, SEARS REYNOLDS (1963), *John Colet and Marsilio Ficino* (Oxford: Oxford University Press).

JOHNS, ADRIAN (1998), *The Nature of the Book: Print and Knowledge in the Making* (Chicago: University of Chicago Press).

——(2002), '*AHR Forum*: How to Acknowledge a Revolution', *AHR* 107: 106–25.

JOHNSON, MICHAEL (2006), 'From Edward III to Edward VI: *The Vision of Piers Plowman* and Early Modern England', *Reformation*, 11: 47–78.

JOHNSON, ROBERT CARL (1970), *John Heywood* (New York: Twayne).

JOHNSON, RONALD (1972), *George Gascoigne* (New York: Twayne).

JOHNSON, SAMUEL (1989), *Samuel Johnson on Shakespeare*, ed. H. R. Woudhuysen (London: Penguin).

JOHNSTON, ANDREW, and JEAN-FRANÇOIS GILMONT (1998), 'Printing and the Reformation in Antwerp', in Jean-François Gilmont and Karin Maag (eds), *The Reformation and the Book* (Aldershot: Ashgate), 188–213.

JONES, JOHN HENRY (ed.) (1994), *The English Faust Book: A Critical Edition, Based on the Text of 1592* (Cambridge: Cambridge University Press).

JONES, NORMAN (1993), *The Birth of the Elizabethan Age: England in the 1560s* (Cambridge, MA: Blackwell).

JONES, RICHARD FOSTER (1953), *The Triumph of the English Language: A Survey of Opinions Concerning the Vernacular from the Introduction of Printing to the Restoration* (London: Oxford University Press).

JONES, WHITNEY R. D. (1970), *The Tudor Commonwealth 1529–1559* (London: Athlone Press).

JORDAN, W. K. (1961), 'Social Institutions in Kent, 1480–1660: A Study of the Changing Patterns of Social Aspirations', *Archaeologia Cantiana*, 75: 1–172.

—— (1971), *Edward VI: The Young King* (Cambridge, MA: Harvard University Press).

JORGENS, ELISE BICKFORD (1982), *The Well-Tun'd Word: Musical Interpretations of English Poetry 1597–1651* (Minneapolis: University of Minnesota Press).

JUSTICE, GEORGE L., and NATHAN TINKER (eds) (2002), *Women's Writing and the Circulation of Ideas: Manuscript Publication in England, 1550–1800* (Cambridge: Cambridge University Press).

KASKE, CAROL V. (1990), 'How Spenser Really Used Stephen Hawes in the Legend of Holiness', in G. M. Logan and G. Teskey (eds), *Unfolded Tales: Essays on Renaissance Romance* (Ithaca, NY: Cornell University Press), 119–36.

—— (2004), 'Spenser's *Amoretti* and *Epithalamion*: A Psalter of Love', in Daniel W. Doerksen and Christopher Hodgkins (eds), *Centered on the Word* (Newark: University of Delaware Press), 28–49.

KASSELL, L. (2005), *Medicine and Magic in Elizabethan London: Simon Forman, Astrologer, Alchemist, and Physician* (Oxford: Clarendon Press).

KATHMAN, DAVID (2004), 'Grocers, Goldsmiths, and Drapers: Freemen and Apprentices in the Elizabethan Theater', *SQ*, 55: 1–49.

KAUFMAN, ROBERT (2000), 'Red Kant, or the Persistence of the Third Critique in Adorno and Jameson', *CritI*, 26: 682–724.

KAUTSKY, KARL (1959), *Thomas More and his 'Utopia'* (New York: Russell and Russell).

KELLAR, CLARE (2003), *Scotland, England and the Reformation 1534–61* (Oxford: Clarendon Press).

KELLY, HENRY (1970), *Divine Providence in the England of Shakespeare's Histories* (Cambridge, MA: Harvard University Press).

KENDRICK, T. D. (1950), *British Antiquity* (London: Methuen).

KENNEDY, J. A. (1989), 'Introduction' to *Eclogues, Epitaphs, and Sonnets* by Barnabe Googe (Toronto: University of Toronto Press).

KHOURY, J. (2006), 'Writing and Lying: William Thomas and the Politics of Translation', in Carmine G. Di Biase (ed.), *Travel and Translation in the Early Modern Period* (Amsterdam: Rodopi), 91–102.

KIDD, COLIN (1999), *British Identities before Nationalism: Ethnicity and Nationhood in the Atlantic World, 1600–1800* (Cambridge: Cambridge University Press).

KING, ANDREW (2000), *'The Faerie Queene' and Middle English Romance: The Matter of Just Memory* (Oxford: Clarendon Press).

KING, JOHN N. (1982), *English Reformation Literature: The Tudor Origins of the Protestant Tradition* (Princeton: Princeton University Press).

—— (1989), *Tudor Royal Iconography: Literature and Art in an Age of Religious Crisis* (Princeton: Princeton University Press).

—— (1990), *Spenser's Poetry and the Reformation Tradition* (Princeton: Princeton University Press).

—— (1997), 'Fact and Fiction in Foxe's *Book of Martyrs*', in D. Loades (ed.), *John Foxe and the English Reformation* (Aldershot: Scolar Press), 12–35.

—— (1999), 'The Book Trade under Edward VI and Mary I', in Lotte Hellinga and J. B. Trapp (eds), *The Cambridge History of the Book in Britain*, iii: *1400–1557* (Cambridge: Cambridge University Press), 164–78.

—— (2001), ' "The light of printing": William Tyndale, John Foxe, John Day, and Early Modern Print Culture', *RenQ*, 54: 52–85.

—— (2002), 'John Day: Master Printer of the English Reformation', in Peter Marshall and Alec Ryrie (eds), *The Beginnings of English Protestantism* (Cambridge: Cambridge University Press), 180–208.

KING, JOHN N. (ed.) (2004), *Voices of the English Reformation: A Sourcebook* (Philadelphia: University of Pennsylvania Press).

—— (2005), 'Guides to Reading Foxe's *Book of Martyrs*', *HLQ*, 68: 133–50.

—— (2006), *Foxe's 'Book of Martyrs' and Early Modern Print Culture* (Cambridge: Cambridge University Press).

—— (ed.) (forthcoming), *Tudor Books and Readers: Materiality and the Construction of Meaning* (Cambridge: Cambridge University Press).

—— and MARK RANKIN (2008), 'Print, Patronage, and the Reception of Continental Reform: 1521–1603', *YES*, 38: 49–67.

KINGSFORD, CHARLES LETHBRIDGE (1913), *English Historical Literature in the Fifteenth Century* (Oxford: Clarendon Press).

KINNEY, ARTHUR F. (2000), 'Introduction' to Arthur F. Kinney (ed.), *The Cambridge Companion to English Literature 1500–1600* (Cambridge: Cambridge University Press).

KIRKPATRICK, ROBIN (1995), *English and Italian Literature from Dante to Shakespeare: A Study of Source, Analogue and Divergence* (Harlow: Longman).

KNIGHT, SARAH (2006), ' "It was not mine intent to prostitute my muse in English": Academic Publication in Early Modern England', in David Adams and Adrian Armstrong (eds), *Print and Power in France and England, 1500–1800* (Aldershot: Ashgate, 2006), 39–51.

KNIGHT, STEPHEN (1994), *Robin Hood: A Complete Study of the English Outlaw* (Oxford: Blackwell).

KNOTT, JOHN RAY (1993), *Discourses of Martyrdom in English Literature, 1563–1694* (Cambridge: Cambridge University Press).

—— (1996), 'John Foxe and the Joy of Suffering', *SCJ*, 27: 721–34.

KNOWLTON, E. C. (1921), 'Nature in Middle English', *JEGP*, 20: 186–207.

KOCHER, PAUL H. (1943), 'The Early Date for Marlowe's *Faustus*', *MLN*, 58: 539–42.

KRONTIRIS, TINA (1998), 'Breaking Barriers of Genre and Gender: Margaret Tyler's Translation of *The Mirrour of Knighthood*', *ELR*, 18: 19–39.

KUGEL, JAMES L. (1981), *The Idea of Biblical Poetry* (New Haven: Yale University Press).

KUIN, R. J. P. (ed.) (1983), *Robert Langham: A Letter*, Medieval and Renaissance Texts, 2 (Leiden: Brill).

KUSKIN, WILLIAM (2006*a*), 'Introduction' to Kuskin (ed.), *Caxton's Trace: Studies in the History of English Printing* (Notre Dame, IN: University of Notre Dame Press).

—— (2006*b*), ' "Onely imagined": Vernacular Community and the English Press', in Kuskin (ed.), *Caxton's Trace: Studies in the History of English Printing* (Notre Dame, IN: University of Notre Dame Press), 199–240.

—— (ed.) (2006*c*), *Caxton's Trace: Studies in the History of English Printing* (Notre Dame, IN: University of Notre Dame Press).

—— (2008), *Symbolic Caxton: Literary Culture and Print Capitalism* (Notre Dame, IN: University of Notre Dame Press).

KWAKKEL, ERIK (2003), 'A New Type of Book for a New Type of Reader: The Emergence of Paper in Vernacular Book Production', *Library*, 7th ser., 4: 219–48.

LALLY, STEVEN (ed.) (1987), *The 'Aeneid' of Thomas Phaer and Thomas Twyne* (New York: Garland).

LAMB, MARY ELLEN (2002), 'Old Wives' Tales, George Peele and Narrative Abjection', *CrSurv*, 14: 28–43.

—— (2006), *The Popular Culture of Shakespeare, Spenser and Jonson* (London: Routledge).

LÄMMERHIRT, K. R. (1909), 'Thomas Blenerhassets "Second Part of the *Mirror for Magistrates*": Eine Quellenstudie', PhD thesis (Kaiser-Wilhems-Universität).

LANCASHIRE, ANNE (2002), *London Civic Theatre: City Drama and Pageantry from Roman Times to 1558* (Cambridge: Cambridge University Press).

LANGSAM, G. GEOFFREY (1951), *Martial Verse and Tudor Books* (New York: King's Crown Press).

LATRÉ, GUIDO (2000), 'The 1535 Coverdale Bible and its Antwerp Origins', in Orlaith O'Sullivan and Ellen Herron (eds), *The Bible as Book: The Reformation* (London: British Library and Oak Knoll), 89–102.

LAVEN, P. J. (1954), 'The Life and Writings of William Thomas', MA diss. (University of London).

LAWTON, DAVID (2001), 'The Surveying Subject and the "Whole World" of Belief: Three Case Studies', *New Medieval Literatures*, 4: 9–37.

LEAVER, ROBIN A. (1991), *'Goostly Psalmes and Spirituall Songes': English and Dutch Metrical Psalms from Coverdale to Utenhove 1535–1566* (Oxford: Clarendon Press).

LEAVIS, F. R. (1930), *Mass Civilization and Minority Culture*, Minority Pamphlets, 1 (Cambridge: Gordon Fraser and Minority Press).

—— and DENYS THOMPSON (1934), *Culture and Environment: The Training of Critical Awareness* (London: Chatto & Windus).

LEHMBERG, STANFORD E. (1960), *Sir Thomas Elyot, Tudor Humanist* (Austin: University of Texas Press).

LEININGER, JEFFREY (2002), 'The Dating of Bale's *John*: A Re-examination', *METh*, 24: 116–37.

LERER, SETH (1993), *Chaucer and his Readers: Imagining the Author in Late-Medieval England* (Princeton: Princeton University Press).

—— (1997), *Courtly Letters in the Age of Henry VIII: Literary Culture and the Arts of Deceit*, Cambridge Studies in Renaissance Literature and Culture, 18 (Cambridge: Cambridge University Press).

—— (1999), 'William Caxton', in David Wallace (ed.), *The Cambridge History of Medieval English Literature* (Cambridge: Cambridge University Press), 720–38.

LEVENSON, JILL L. (1984), 'Romeo and Juliet before Shakespeare', *SP*, 81: 325–40.

LEVINE, MORTIMER (1966), *The Early Elizabethan Succession Question, 1558–1568* (Stanford, CA: Stanford University Press).

LEVINSON, MARJORIE (2007), 'What Is New Formalism?', *PMLA*, 122: 558–69.

LEVY, F. J. (1967), *Tudor Historical Thought* (San Marino, CA: Huntington Library).

LEWALSKI, BARBARA (ed.) (1986), *Renaissance Genres: Essays on Theory, History, and Interpretation* (Cambridge, MA: Harvard University Press).

LEWIS, C. S. (1954), *English Literature in the Sixteenth Century Excluding Drama* (Oxford: Clarendon Press).

LIEBLER, NAOMI CONN (ed.) (2007), *Early Modern Prose Fiction: The Cultural Politics of Reading* (London: Routledge).

LINES, CANDACE (2000), '"To take on them judgemente": Absolutism and Debate in John Heywood's Plays', *SP* 97: 401–32.

LOACH, JENNIFER (1986a), 'The Marian Establishment and the Printing Press', *EHR*, 101: 135–48.

—— (1986b), *Parliament and the Crown in the Reign of Mary Tudor* (Oxford: Clarendon Press).

—— (1999), *Edward VI*, ed. George Bernard and Penry Williams (New Haven: Yale University Press).

LOADES, DAVID M. (1965), *Two Tudor Conspiracies* (Cambridge: Cambridge University Press).

—— (1979), *The Reign of Mary Tudor: Politics, Government and Religion in England 1553–58* (London: Longman; 2nd edn, 1991).

—— (1991), 'Illicit Presses and Clandestine Printing in England, 1520–90', in Loades (ed.), *Politics, Censorship, and the English Reformation* (London: Pinter), 109–26.

LOEWENSTEIN, DAVID, and JANEL M. MUELLER (eds) (2002), *The Cambridge History of Early Modern English Literature* (Cambridge: Cambridge University Press).

LOGAN, GEORGE M., and GORDON TESKEY (eds) (1990), *Unfolded Tales: Essays on Renaissance Romance* (Ithaca, NY: Cornell University Press).

LOVE, HAROLD (1998), *The Culture and Commerce of Texts: Scribal Publication in Seventeenth-Century England* (Amherst: University of Massachusetts Press).

LOWRY, MARTIN (1979), *The World of Aldus Manutius* (Oxford: Blackwell).

LOWTH, ROBERT (1753), *A Translation of the Inauguration Speech or First Lecture on the Hebrew Poetry* (London: n.p.).

LUBORSKY, RUTH, and E. INGRAM (1998), *A Guide to English Illustrated Books, 1536–1603*, 2 vols (Tempe, AZ: Medieval and Renaissance Texts and Studies).

LUCAS, CAROLYN (1989), *Writing for Women: The Example of Woman as Reader in Elizabethan Romance* (Milton Keynes: Open University Press).

LUCAS, SCOTT (2002), 'Diggon Davie and Davy Dicar: Edmund Spenser, Thomas Churchyard, and the Poetics of Public Protest', *SSt*, 16: 151–66.

—— (2003), 'The Consolation of Tragedy: *A Mirror for Magistrates* and the Fall of the "Good Duke" of Somerset', *SP*, 100: 44–70.

—— (2007*a*), ' "Let none such office take, save he that can for right his prince forsake": *A Mirror for Magistrates*, Resistance Theory and the Elizabethan Monarchical Republic', in John McDiarmid (ed.), *The Monarchical Republic of Early Modern England: Essays in Response to Patrick Collinson* (Aldershot: Ashgate), 143–69.

—— (2007*b*), 'Comment: The Visionary Genre and the Rise of the Literary: *Books under Suspicion* and Early Modern England', *JBS* 46: 762–5.

—— (2009), '*A Mirror for Magistrates* and the Politics of the English Reformation' (Amherst: University of Massachusetts Press).

LYALL, R. J. (1989), 'Materials: The Paper Revolution', in Jeremy Griffiths and Derek Pearsall (eds), *Book Production and Publishing in Britain 1395–1475* (Cambridge: Cambridge University Press), 11–29.

LYNE, RAPHAEL (2001), *Ovid's Changing Worlds: English 'Metamorphoses', 1567–1632* (Cambridge: Cambridge University Press).

McCABE, RICHARD A. (2002), *Spenser's Monstrous Regiment: Elizabethan Ireland and the Poetics of Difference* (Oxford: Oxford University Press).

—— (2006), 'Shorter Verse Published 1590–95', in Bart van Es (ed.), *A Critical Companion to Spenser Studies* (Houndmills: Palgrave Macmillan), 166–87.

McCANLES, MICHAEL (1982), '*The Shepheardes Calender* as Document and Monument', *SEL*, 22: 5–19.

McCONICA, J. K. (ed.) (1986), *The History of the University of Oxford*, iii: *The Collegiate University* (Oxford: Clarendon Press).

McCOY, RICHARD C. (1985), 'Gascoigne's *Poëmata Castrata*: The Wages of Courtly Success', *Criticism*, 27: 29–55.

—— (1989), *The Rites of Knighthood: The Literature and Politics of Elizabethan Chivalry* (Berkeley: University of California Press).

MacCULLOCH, DIARMAID (1986), *Suffolk and the Tudors: Politics and Religion in an English County 1500–1600* (Oxford: Clarendon Press).

—— (1996), *Thomas Cranmer* (New Haven: Yale University Press).

—— (1999), *Tudor Church Militant: Edward VI and the Protestant Reformation* (London: Allen Lane).

McCusker, Honor (1942), *John Bale: Dramatist and Antiquary* (Bryn Mawr, PA: Bryn Mawr).

McEachern, Claire (1995), '"A whore at the first blush seemeth only a woman": John Bale's *Image of Both Churches* and the Terms of Religious Difference in the Early English Reformation', *JMRS*, 25: 245–69.

—— (1996), *The Poetics of English Nationhood 1590–1612* (Cambridge: Cambridge University Press).

McGinn, D. C. (1944), 'Nashe's Share in the Marprelate Controversy', *PMLA*, 59: 952–84.

McGrath, Lynette (2002), *Subjectivity and Women's Poetry in Early Modern England: 'Why on the ridge should she desire to go?'* (Aldershot: Ashgate).

Machan, Timothy (2006), 'Early Modern Middle English', in William Kuskin (ed.), *Caxton's Trace: Studies in the History of English Printing* (Notre Dame, IN: University of Notre Dame Press), 299–322.

McKenzie, D. F. (1999), *Bibliography and the Sociology of Texts* (Cambridge: Cambridge University Press).

McKeon, Michael (1987), *The Origins of the English Novel 1600–1740* (Baltimore: Johns Hopkins University Press).

McKerrow, R. B. (1958), 'Introduction' to *The Works of Thomas Nashe*, i (Oxford: Blackwell).

McKitterick, David (2003), *Print, Manuscript and the Search for Order, 1450–1830* (Cambridge: Cambridge University Press).

McLaren, Anne (1999), *Political Culture in the Reign of Elizabeth I: Queen and Commonwealth 1558–1585* (Cambridge: Cambridge University Press).

Maclean, Ian (2002), *Logic, Signs and Nature in the Renaissance: The Case of Learned Medicine* (Cambridge: Cambridge University Press).

Maclean, Sally-Beth, and Scott McMillin (1998), *The Queen's Men and their Plays* (Cambridge: Cambridge University Press).

McRae, Andrew (forthcoming), *Literature and Domestic Travel in Early Modern England* (Cambridge: Cambridge University Press).

Mader, Gottfried (1988), '*Quod nolunt velint*: Deference and Doublespeak at Seneca, *Thyestes* 334–335', *CJ*, 94: 31–47.

Major, John M. (1964), *Sir Thomas Elyot and Renaissance Humanism* (Lincoln: University of Nebraska Press).

Manley, Lawrence (1995), *Literature and Culture in Early Modern London* (Cambridge: Cambridge University Press).

Marcus, Leah S. (2000), 'Dramatic Experiments: Tudor Drama, 1490–1567', in Arthur F. Kinney (ed.), *The Cambridge Companion to English Literature 1500–1600* (Cambridge: Cambridge University Press), 132–52.

Marotti, Arthur (1991), 'Patronage, Poetry, and Print', in Andrew Gurr and Philippa Hardman (eds), *Politics, Patronage and Literature in England 1558–1658*, *YES*, 21: 1–26.

—— (1995), *Manuscript, Print, and the English Renaissance Lyric* (Ithaca, NY: Cornell University Press).

Marshall, C. (2002), *The Shattering of the Self* (Baltimore: Johns Hopkins University Press).

Martin, I. (1997), 'The Manuscript and Editorial Traditions of William Thomas's *The Pilgrim*', *BHR*, 59: 621–41.

Martin, J. W. (1981), 'Miles Hogarde: Artisan and Aspiring Author in Sixteenth-Century England', *RQ*, 34: 359–83.

MARTIN, J. W. (1983), 'The Publishing Career of Robert Crowley: A Sidelight on the Tudor Book Trade', *PubHist*, 14: 85–98.

MASELLO, STEVEN J. (1979), ' "A booke of the travaile and lief of me Thomas Hoby, with diverse thinges woorth the notinge, 1547–1564": A Modern Edition with Introduction and Notes', PhD diss. (Loyola University of Chicago).

MASLEN, R. W. (1997), *Elizabethan Fictions: Espionage, Counter-Espionage, and the Duplicity of Fiction in Early Elizabethan Prose Narratives* (Oxford: Clarendon Press).

——(1999), ' "The cat got your tongue": Pseudo-Translation, Conversion, and Control in William Baldwin's *Beware the Cat*', *Tr& Lit*, 8: 3–27.

——(2000*a*), 'Myths Exploited: The *Metamorphoses* of Ovid in Early Elizabethan England', in A. B. Taylor (ed.), *Shakespeare's Ovid* (Cambridge: Cambridge University Press), 15–30.

——(2000*b*), 'William Baldwin and the Politics of Pseudo-Philosophy in Tudor Prose Fiction', *SP*, 97: 29–60.

——(2008), 'The Healing Dialogues of Doctor Bullein', in Andrew Hiscock (ed.), *Tudor Literature*, *YES*, 38: 119–35.

MASON, H. A. (1959), *Humanism and Poetry in the Early Tudor Period* (London: Routledge & Kegan Paul).

MASUCH, M. (1997), *The Origins of the Individualist Self: Autobiography and Self-Identity in England 1591–1791* (Cambridge: Polity Press).

MATTHEWS, W. (1950), *British Diaries: An Annotated Bibliography of British Diaries between 1442 and 1942* (Berkeley: University of California Press).

——(1955), *British Autobiographies: An Annotated Bibliography of British Autobiographies Published or Written before 1951* (Berkeley: University of California Press).

MAY, STEVEN W. (1975), 'Cavendish's Use of Hall's Chronicle', *Neophil*, 59: 293–300.

——(1991), *The Elizabethan Courtier Poets* (Columbia: University of Missouri Press).

——(2004), 'The Seventeenth Earl of Oxford as Poet and Playwright', *Tennessee Law Review*, 72: 221–54.

MAYER, T. F. (1990), *Thomas Starkey and the Common Weal* (Cambridge: Cambridge University Press).

MEAD, WILLIAM EDWARD (1928), 'To the Reader', in *The Pastime of Pleasure* by Stephen Hawes, EETS, O.S., 173.

MEALE, CAROL (1983), 'The Compiler at Work: John Colyns and BL MS Harley 2252', in Derek Pearsall (ed.), *Manuscripts and Readers in Fifteenth Century England* (Cambridge: D. S. Brewer), 82–103.

MEARS, NATALIE (2005), *Queenship and Political Discourse in the Elizabethan Realms* (Cambridge: Cambridge University Press).

MEDINE, PETER E. (1994), 'Introduction' to *The Art of Rhetoric* by T. Wilson (University Park: Pennsylvania State University Press).

MENTZ, S. (2006), *Romance for Sale in Early Modern England: The Rise of Prose Fiction* (Aldershot: Ashgate).

MEREDITH, PETER (1984), ' "Fart pryke in cule" and Cock-Fighting', *METh*, 6: 30–9.

MERRIX, ROBERT P. (1977), 'The Function of the Comic Plot in *Fulgens and Lucres*', *MLS*, 7: 16–26.

METZGER, M. L. (1996), 'Controversy and "Correctness": English Chronicles and the Chroniclers, 1553–1568', *SCJ*, 27: 437–51.

MEYER-LEE, ROBERT J. (2007), *Poets and Power from Chaucer to Wyatt* (Cambridge: Cambridge University Press).

MICHAEL, M. A. (2008), 'Urban Production of Manuscript Books and the Role of the University Towns', in Nigel J. Morgan and Rodney M. Thomson (eds), *Cambridge*

History of the Book in Britain, ii: *1100–1400* (Cambridge: Cambridge University Press), 168–96.

MILLER, EDWIN (1959), *The Professional Writer in Elizabethan England* (Cambridge, MA: Harvard University Press).

MILLER, HELEN (1986), *Henry VIII and the English Nobility* (Oxford: Blackwell).

MIOLA, ROBERT (1988), 'Aeneas and Hamlet', *CML*, 8: 275–90.

—— (1992), *Shakespeare and Classical Tragedy: The Influence of Seneca* (Oxford: Oxford University Press).

MISKIMIN, ALICE S. (1975), *The Renaissance Chaucer* (New Haven: Yale University Press).

MITCHELL, R. J. (1938), *John Tiptoft (1427–1470)* (London: Longmans, Green).

MITCHELL, W. S. (1959), 'William Bullein, Elizabethan Physician and Author', *Medical History*, 3: 188–200.

MONTA, SUSANNA BRIETZ (2005), *Martyrdom and Literature in Early Modern England* (Cambridge: Cambridge University Press).

MOONEY, LINNE R. (2000), 'Professional Scribes? Identifying English Scribes Who Have a Hand in More Than One Manuscript', in Derek Pearsall (ed.), *New Directions in Medieval Manuscript Studies* (Cambridge: D. S. Brewer), 131–41.

—— (forthcoming), 'London Scribes', in Margaret Connolly and Linne R. Mooney (eds), *The Design and Distribution of Late Medieval Manuscripts and Texts in England* (Woodbridge: Boydell Press).

MOORE SMITH, G. C. (1907), 'Lyly, Greene and Shakespeare', *N&Q*, 10th ser., 8: 461–2.

MORETTI, FRANCO (1988), *Signs Taken for Wonders: Essays in the Sociology of Literary Forms*, trans. S. Fischer, D. Forgacs, and D. Miller, rev. edn (London: Verso).

MORGAN, HIRAM (1985), 'The Colonial Venture of Sir Thomas Smith in Ulster, 1571–5', *HJ*, 27: 261–78.

MORRIS, COLIN, and PETER ROBERTS (eds) (2002), *Pilgrimage: The English Experience from Becket to Bunyan* (Cambridge: Cambridge University Press).

MORTIMER, ANTHONY (2002), *Petrarch's 'Canzoniere' in the English Renaissance*, rev. edn (Amsterdam: Rodopi).

MORTIMER, I. (2002), 'Tudor Chronicler or Sixteenth-Century Diarist? Henry Machyn and the Nature of his Manuscript', *SCJ*, 33: 983–1001.

MORTON, A. L. (1952), *The English Utopia* (London: Lawrence and Wishart).

MOSSER, D. (1999), 'The Use of Caxton Texts and Paper Stocks in Manuscripts of the *Canterbury Tales*', in G. Lester (ed.), *Chaucer in Perspective: Middle English Essays in Honour of Norman Blake* (Sheffield: Sheffield Academic Press), 161–77.

MOTTRAM, STEWART (2008), *Empire and Nation in Early English Renaissance Literature* (Woodbridge: Brewer).

MOUSLEY, ANDREW (1990), 'Renaissance Selves and Life Writing: The Autobiography of Thomas Whythorne', *Forum*, 26: 222–30.

MOZLEY, J. F. (1937), *William Tyndale* (London: SPCK).

MUELLER, JANEL M. (1990), 'Devotion as Difference: Intertextuality in Queen Katherine Parr's *Prayers or Meditations* (1545)', *HLQ*, 53: 171–97.

—— (1997a), 'Pain, Persecution, and the Construction of Selfhood in Foxe's *Acts and Monuments*', in Claire McEachern and Debra Shuger (eds), *Religion and Culture in the Renaissance England* (Cambridge: Cambridge University Press), 161–87.

—— (1997b), 'Complications of Intertextuality: Katherine Parr, John Fisher, and the Book of the Crucifix', in Claude J. Summers and Ted-Larry Pebworth (eds), *Representing Women in Renaissance England* (Columbia: University of Missouri Press), 24–41.

MUKERJI, CHANDRA, and MICHAEL SCHUDSON (1991), 'Introduction: Rethinking Popular Culture', in Mukerji and Schudson (eds), *Rethinking Popular Culture: Contemporary Perspectives in Cultural Studies* (Berkeley: University of California Press), 1–61.

MÜLLER, WOLFGANG G. (1981), *Topik des Stilbegriffs: Zur Geschichte des Stilverständnisses von der Antike bis zur Gegenwart* (Darmstadt: Wissenschaftliche Buchgesellschaft).

—— (1983), '*Ars Rhetorica* und *Ars Poetica*: Zum Verhältnis von Rhetorik und Literatur in der englischen Renaissance', in Heinrich F. Plett (ed.), *Renaissance-Rhetorik/Renaissance Rhetoric* (Berlin: de Gruyter), 225–43.

—— (1994), 'Das Problem des Stils in der Poetik der Renaissance', in Heinrich F. Plett (ed.), *Renaissance-Poetik/Renaissance Poetics* (Berlin: de Gruyter), 133–46.

MUNRO, J. J. (ed.) (1908), *Brooke's 'Romeus and Juliet': Being the Original of Shakespeare's 'Romeo and Juliet'*, ed. J. J. Munro (New York: Duffield).

NEARING, H. (1945), 'English Historical Poetry: 1599–1641', PhD thesis (University of Pennsylvania).

NEEDHAM, PAUL (1986), *The Printer and the Pardoner* (Washington: Library of Congress).

—— (1999), 'The Customs Rolls and the Printed-Book Trade', in Lotte Hellinga and J. B. Trapp (eds), *The Cambridge History of the Book in Britain*, iii:*1400–1557* (Cambridge: Cambridge University Press), 148–63.

NELSON, ALAN H. (1980), 'Introduction' to *The Plays* by John Medwall (Cambridge: Brewer).

—— (2003), *Monstrous Adversary: The Life of Edward de Vere, 17th Earl of Oxford*, Liverpool English Texts and Studies, 40 (Liverpool: Liverpool University Press).

NELSON, B. L. (2001), 'Roger Ascham', in E. A. Malone (ed.), *British Rhetoricians and Logicians 1500–1660: First Series*, Dictionary of Literary Biography, 236 (Detroit: Gale Group), 3–11.

NELSON, WILLIAM (1936), 'Skelton's *Speak, Parrot*', *PMLA*, 51: 59–82.

—— (ed.) (1955), *The Life of St George by Alexander Barclay*, EETS, o.s., 230.

—— (1973), *Fact or Fiction: The Dilemma of the Renaissance Storyteller* (Cambridge, MA: Harvard University Press).

NEWCOMB, LORI H. (2002), *Reading Popular Romance in Early Modern England* (New York: Columbia University Press).

NIELSON, JAMES (1993), 'Reading between the Lines: Manuscript Personality and Gabriel Harvey's Drafts', *SEL*, 33: 43–82.

NORBROOK, DAVID (1984), *Poetry and Politics in the English Renaissance* (London: Routledge & Kegan Paul).

NORHNBERG, JAMES (1976), *The Analogy of 'The Faerie Queene'* (Princeton: Princeton University Press).

NORLAND, HOWARD B. (1995), *Drama in Early Tudor Britain 1485–1558* (Lincoln: University of Nebraska Press).

NUSSBAUM, FELICITY A. (1995), *The Autobiographical Subject: Gender and Ideology in Eighteenth-Century England* (Baltimore: Johns Hopkins University Press).

NUTTON, VIVIAN (1979), 'John Caius and the Linacre Tradition', *Medical History*, 23: 373–91.

—— (1987), *John Caius and the Manuscripts of Galen* (Cambridge: Cambridge University Press).

O'CALLAGHAN, MICHELLE (2000), *The 'Shepheardes Nation': Jacobean Spenserians and Early Stuart Political Culture, 1612–1625* (Oxford: Clarendon Press).

O'DONNELL, ANNE M., and JARED WICKS (2000), 'Introduction' to *An Answere unto Sir Thomas Mores Dialoge* by William Tyndale (Washington: Catholic University of America Press).

O'KILL, BRIAN (1977), 'The Printed Works of William Patten (*c*.1510–*c*.1600)', *TCBS*, 7: 28–45.

ONG, WALTER (2002), *Orality and Literacy: The Technologizing of the Word*, 2nd edn (London: Routledge).

ORCHARD, BARRY (1991), *A Look at the Head and the Fifty: History of Tonbridge School* (London: James & James).

ORUCH, J. (1967), 'Spenser, Camden, and the Poetic Marriages of Rivers', *SP*, 64: 606–24.

OSBORN, JAMES M. (1959), *The Beginnings of Autobiography in England* (Los Angeles: University of California and William Andrew Clark Memorial Library).

O'SULLIVAN, ORLAITH, and ELLEN HERRON (eds) (2000), *The Bible as Book: The Reformation* (London: British Library and Oak Knoll).

O'SULLIVAN, W. (1996), 'The Irish "Remnaunt" of John Bale's Manuscripts', in Richard Beadle and A. J. Piper (eds), *New Science Out of Old Books* (Aldershot: Scolar Press), 374–87.

OVERELL, M. A. (2000), 'Vergerio's Anti-Nicodemite Propaganda and England, 1547–1558', *JEH*, 51: 296–318.

—— (2002), 'Edwardian Court Humanism and *Il Beneficio di Cristo*, 1547–1553', in Jonathan Woolfson (ed.), *Reassessing Tudor Humanism* (Basingstoke: Palgrave Macmillan), 151–73.

PADOVAN, MARIA GRAZIA (1982), 'Il primo viaggio in Italia di Sir Thomas Hoby', tesi di laurea (University of Pisa).

PAGDEN, ANTHONY (ed.) (1987), *The Languages of Political Theory in Early-Modern Europe* (Cambridge: Cambridge University Press).

PAINTER, GEORGE (1976), *William Caxton: A Quincentenary Biography of England's First Printer* (London: Chatto & Windus).

PANOFSKY, RICHARD (1975), 'A Descriptive Study of English Mid-Tudor Short Poetry', doctoral thesis (University of California: Santa Barbara).

—— (1977), 'Introduction' to *Epitaphes, Epigrams, Songs and Sonets* by George Turbervile (New York: Scholar's Facsimiles).

PARKER, R. W. (1972), 'Terentian Structure and Sidney's Original *Arcadia*', *ELR*, 2: 61–78.

PARKS, GEORGE B. (1937–8), 'The First Draft of Ascham's *Scholemaster*', *HLQ*, 1: 313–27.

—— (1957), 'William Barker, Tudor Translator', *PMLA*, 51: 126–40.

PARTRIDGE, MARY (2007), 'Thomas Hoby's English Translation of Castiglione's *Book of the Courtier*', *HJ*, 50: 769–86.

PATTERSON, ANNABEL (1987), *Pastoral and Ideology: Virgil to Valéry* (Berkeley: University of California Press).

—— (1994), *Reading Holinshed's Chronicles* (Chicago: University of Chicago Press).

PATTERSON, LEE (1990), 'On the Margin: Postmodernism, Ironic History and Medieval Studies', *Speculum*, 65: 87–108.

PELLING, MARGARET (2000), 'Defensive Tactics: Networking by Female Medical Practitioners in Early Modern London', in Alexandra Shepard and Phil Withington (eds), *Communities in Early Modern England* (Manchester: Manchester University Press), 39–42.

PERRY, CURTIS (2002), 'Commodity and Commonwealth in *Gammer Gurton's Needle*', *SEL*, 42: 217–34.

PETERSON, DOUGLAS L. (1967), *The English Lyric from Wyatt to Donne: A History of the Plain and Eloquent Styles* (Princeton: Princeton University Press).

PETTITT, THOMAS (1984), 'Tudor Interludes and the Winter Revels', *METh*, 6: 16–27.

PHILIPS, JAMES EMERSON (1955), 'A Revaluation of *Horestes* (1567)', *HLQ*, 18: 227–44.

—— (1964), *Images of a Queen: Mary Stuart in Sixteenth Century Literature* (Berkeley: University of California Press).

PIDOUX, PIERRE (1962), *Le Psautier Huguenot*, 2 vols (Basel: Édition Barenreiter).

PIGMAN, G. W., III (ed.) (2000), *George Gascoigne: A Hundreth Sundrie Flowres* (Oxford: Clarendon Press).

PINCOMBE, MIKE (1999), 'Gascoigne's *Phylomene*: A Late Medieval Paraphrase of Ovid's *Metamorphoses*', in Sabine Coelsch-Foisner (ed.), *Elizabethan Literature and Transformation* (Tübingen: Stauffenburg), 71–81.

—— (2000), 'Sackville *Tragicus*: A Case of Poetic Identity', in A. J. Piesse (ed.), *Sixteenth-Century Identities* (Manchester: University of Manchester Press), 112–32.

—— (2001), *Elizabethan Humanism: Literature and Learning in the Later Sixteenth Century* (Harlow: Longman).

PISCINI, A. (1991), 'Lodovico Domenichi', in *Dizionario biografico degli italiani*, 40 (Rome: Istituto della Enciclopedia Italiana), 595–600.

—— (1999), 'Giambattista Gelli', in *Dizionario biografico degli italiani*, 53 (Rome: Istituto della Enciclopedia Italiana), 12–18.

PLAISANCE, MICHEL (1995), 'L'Académie Florentine de 1541 à 1583: Permanence et changement', in D. S. Chambers and F. Quiviger (eds), *Italian Academies of the Sixteenth Century* (London: Warburg Institute), 127–35.

—— (2004), *L'Académie et le Prince: Culture et politique à Florence au temps de Côme Ier et de François de Medicis* (Rome: Vecchiarelli Editore).

PLETT, HEINRICH F. (2004), *Rhetoric and Renaissance Culture* (Berlin: de Gruyter).

POLLARD, A. F. (1900), *England under Protector Somerset: An Essay* (London: Kegan Paul, Trench, Trübner).

POLLARD, GRAHAM (1978), 'The English Market for Printed Books: The Sandars Lectures 1959', *PubHist*, 4: 7–48.

POPPER, NICHOLAS (2005), 'The English Polydaedali: How Gabriel Harvey Read Late Tudor London', *JHI*, 66: 351–81.

PORTER, ROY (ed.) (1977), *Rewriting the Self: Histories from the Renaissance to the Present* (London: Routledge).

POUND, JOHN (1988), *Tudor and Stuart Norwich* (Chichester: Phillimore).

POWELL, JASON (2003), 'The Letters and Original Prose of the Poet Sir Thomas Wyatt: A Study and Critical Edition', D.Phil. thesis (University of Oxford).

—— (2004), 'Thomas Wyatt's Poetry in Embassy: Egerton 2711 and the Production of Literary Manuscripts Abroad', *HLQ*, 67: 261–82.

—— (2007), 'Thomas Wyatt's Ivy Seal', *N&Q*, n.s., 54: 242–4.

PRESCOTT, ANNE LAKE (1985), 'The Pearl of the Valois and Elizabeth I', in Margaret P. Hannay (ed.), *Silent but for the Word: Tudor Women as Patrons, Translators, and Writers of Religious Works* (Kent, OH: Kent State University Press), 61–76.

—— (1989), 'Spenser's Chivalric Restoration: From Bateman's *Travayled Pylgrime* to the Redcrosse Knight', *SP*, 86: 166–97.

PREST, WILFRID (1972), *The Inns of Court under Elizabeth I and the Early Stuarts* (London: Longmans).

PROUTY, CHARLES T. (1942), *George Gascoigne: Elizabethan Courtier, Soldier, and Poet* (New York: Columbia University Press).

PRUVOST, RENÉ (1937), *Matteo Bandello and Elizabethan Fiction* (Paris: Champion).

PUGH, SYRITHE (2005), *Spenser and Ovid* (Aldershot: Ashgate).

QUINT, DAVID (1993), *Epic and Empire: Politics and Generic Form from Virgil to Milton* (Princeton: Princeton University Press).

QUITSLUND, BETH (2005), 'Teaching us how to Sing: The Peculiarity of the Sidney Psalter', *SiJ* 23: 83–110.

RABKIN, NORMAN (1985), 'Stumbling toward Tragedy', in Peter Erickson and Coppelia Kahn (eds), *Shakespeare's 'Rough Magic': Renaissance Essays in Honor of C. L. Barber* (London: Associated University Presses), 28–49.

RAFFEL, BURTON (1992), *From Stress to Stress: An Autobiography of English Prosody* (Hamden, CT: Archon Press).

RAFFIELD, PAUL (2004), *Images and Cultures of Law in Early Modern England: Justice and Political Power, 1558–1660* (Cambridge: Cambridge University Press).

RAPPAPORT, STEVE (1989), *Worlds within Worlds: Structures of Life in Sixteenth-Century London* (Cambridge: Cambridge University Press).

REED, A. W. (1926), *Early Tudor Drama: Medwall, the Rastells, Heywood and the More Circle* (London: Methuen).

REID, W. STANFORD (1971), 'The Battle Hymns of the Lord: Calvinist Psalmody of the Sixteenth Century', *SCJ*, 2: 36–54.

REX, RICHARD (1991), *The Theology of John Fisher* (Cambridge: Cambridge University Press).

RHODES, NEIL (1980), *Elizabethan Grotesque* (London: Routledge & Kegan Paul).

—— (1992), *The Power of Eloquence and Renaissance Literature* (New York: Harvester-Wheatsheaf).

RICHARDS, JENNIFER (2003), *Rhetoric and Courtliness in Early Modern Literature* (Cambridge: Cambridge University Press).

—— (2008), 'Gabriel Harvey, James VI and the Politics of Reading Early Modern Poetry', *HLQ*, 71: 303–21.

RICHARDS, JUDITH M. (1997a), 'Mary Tudor as "Sole Quene": Gendering Tudor Monarchy', *HJ*, 40: 895–924.

—— (1997b), ' "To promote a woman to beare rule": Talking of Queens in Mid-Tudor England', *SCJ*, 28: 101–21.

RIDLEY, F. H. (ed.) (1963), *Aeneid*, trans. Henry Howard, Earl of Surrey (Berkeley: University of California Press).

RIENSTRA, DEBRA, and NOEL KINNAMON (2002), 'Circulating the Sidney–Pembroke Psalter', in George Justice and Nathan Tinker (eds), *Women's Writing and the Circulation of Ideas* (Cambridge: Cambridge University Press), 50–72.

RINGLER, WILLIAM A. (1962), 'Introduction' to *The Poems of Sir Philip Sidney* (Oxford: Clarendon Press).

—— (1992), *Bibliography and Index of English Verse in Manuscript 1501–1558*, prepared and completed by Michael Rudick and Susan J. Ringler (London: Mansell).

RIVINGTON, S. (1925), *The History of Tonbridge School*, 4th edn (Rivingtons: London).

ROBERTS, PETER (2002), 'Politics, Drama and the Cult of Thomas Becket in the Sixteenth Century', in Colin Morris and Peter Roberts (eds), *Pilgrimage: The English Experience from Becket to Bunyan* (Cambridge: Cambridge University Press), 199–237.

ROBERTSON, JEAN (1973), 'Introduction' to *The Countess of Pembroke's Arcadia (The Old Arcadia)* (Oxford: Clarendon Press).

ROBERTSON, KAREN (1990), 'The Body Natural of a Queen: Mary, James, *Horestes*', *Ren&R*, 26: 25–36.

ROBINSON, BENEDICT SCOTT (2002), 'John Foxe and the Anglo-Saxons', in Christopher Highley and John N. King (eds), *John Foxe and his World* (Aldershot: Ashgate), 54–72.

ROSENBERG, ELEANOR (1957), *Leicester: Patron of Letters* (New York: Columbia University Press).

ROSENDALE, TIMOTHY, *Liturgy and Literature in the Making of Protestant England* (Cambridge: Cambridge University Press, 2007).

ROSE-TROUP, F. (1911), 'Two Book Bills of Katherine Parr', *The Library*, 3rd ser., 2: 40–8.

ROSS, TREVOR (1991), 'Dissolution and the Making of the English Literary Canon: The Catalogues of Leland and Bale', *Ren&R*, 15: 57–80.

Rossi, Sergio (1966), 'Un "italianista" nel Cinquecento inglese: William Thomas', *Aevum*, 3–4: 281–314.

Rovang, Paul R. (1996), *Refashioning 'Knights and Ladies Gentle Deeds': The Intertextuality of Spenser's 'Faerie Queene' and Malory's 'Morte d'Arthur'* (London: Associated University Presses).

Rubel, Veré L. (1966), *Poetic Diction in the English Renaissance from Skelton through Spenser* (1941; repr., New York: Kraus).

Rudd, Niall (2007), *The Satires of Horace* (1981; Trowbridge: Bristol Classic Press).

Rupp, E., et al. (eds) (1969), *Luther and Erasmus: Free Will and Salvation* (Philadelphia: Westminster Press).

Ryan, Lawrence V. (1963), *Roger Ascham* (Stanford: Stanford University Press).

Ryrie, Alec (forthcoming), 'Paths Not Taken in the British Reformations', *HJ*.

Sachs, A. (1964), 'The Religious Despair of Doctor Faustus', *JEGP*, 63: 625–47.

Sadler, John (2005), *Border Fury: England and Scotland at War, 1296–1568* (Harlow: Pearson-Longman).

Saengen, Paul, and Michael Heinlen (1991), 'Incunable Description and its Implication for the Analysis of Fifteenth-Century Reading Habits', in Sandra L. Hindman (ed.), *Printing the Written Word: The Social History of Books, c.1450–1520* (Ithaca, NY: Cornell University Press).

Saintsbury, George (1887), *A History of Elizabethan Literature* (London: Macmillan).

Sanford, Rhonda Lemke (2002), *Maps and Memory in Early Modern England: A Sense of Place* (Palgrave: New York).

Saunders, Corinne (ed.) (2004), *A Companion to Romance: From Classical to Contemporary* (Oxford: Blackwell).

Saunders, J. W. (1951), 'The Stigma of Print: A Note on the Social Bases of Tudor Poetry', *EiC*, 1: 139–64.

Scarry, Elaine (1985), *The Body in Pain* (New York: Oxford University Press).

Scattergood, John (1994), 'Simon Fish's Supplication for the Beggars and Protestant Polemics', in F. de Nave (ed.), *Antwerp, Dissident Typographical Centre: The Role of Antwerp Printers in the Religious Conflicts in England (16th Century)* (Antwerp: Snoeck-Ducaju and Zoon), 89–102.

—— (1996), 'The Early Annotations to John Skelton's Poems', in Scattergood, *Reading the Past: Essays on Medieval and Renaissance Literature* (Dublin: Four Courts Press).

—— (2000), 'John Leland's *Itinerary* and the Identity of England', in A. J. Piesse (ed.), *Sixteenth-Century Identities* (Manchester: Manchester University Press), 58–74.

—— (2006), 'Thomas Wyatt's Epistolary Satires and the Consolations of Intertextuality', in Rudolf Suntrup and Jan R. Veenstra (eds), *Building the Past/Konstruktion der eigenen Vergangenheit* (Brussels: Peter Lang).

Schmitt, Charles B. (1977), 'Thomas Linacre in Italy', in Francis Romeril Maddison, Margaret Pelling, and Charles Webster (eds), *Linacre Studies: Essays on the Life and Works of Thomas Linacre, c.1460–1524* (Oxford: Oxford University Press), 36–75.

Schmitz, Götz (1990), *The Fall of Women in Early English Narrative Verse* (Cambridge: Cambridge University Press).

Schurink, F. (2004), 'Education and Reading in Elizabethan and Jacobean England', D.Phil. thesis (University of Oxford).

—— (2008), 'Print, Patronage, and Occasion: Translations of Plutarch's *Moralia* in Tudor England', in Andrew Hiscock (ed.), *Tudor Literature, YES*, 38: 86–101.

Schuster, Louis A. (1973), 'Thomas More's Polemical Career, 1523–1533', in Thomas More, *The Confutation of Tyndale's Answer*, ed. Louis A. Schuster, Richard Marius, James P. Lusardi, and

Richard J. Schoeck, 3 vols, pt 3, in *The Complete Works of St Thomas More*, viii (New Haven: Yale University Press), 1135–1268.

SCHWYZER, PHILIP (1994), 'Summer Fruit and Autumn Leaves: Thomas Nashe in 1593', *ELR*, 24: 582–619.

—— (2004*a*), 'The Beauties of the Land: Bale's Books, Ashe's Abbeys and the Aesthetics of Manhood', *RenQ*, 57: 99–125.

—— (2004*b*), *Literature, Nationalism and Memory in Early Modern England and Wales* (Cambridge: Cambridge University Press).

SCOTT, DAVID (1977), 'William Patten and the Authorship of "Robert Laneham's *Letter*" (1575)', *ELR*, 7: 297–306.

SCOTT, MARIA (2005), *Re-presenting 'Jane' Shore* (Aldershot: Ashgate).

SCOTT-WARREN, J. (2005), *Early Modern English Literature* (Cambridge: Polity Press).

SELLIN, P. R. (1974), 'The Hidden God: Reformation Awe in Renaissance English Literature', in R. S. Kinsman (ed.), *The Darker Vision of the Renaissance: Beyond the Fields of Reason* (Berkeley: University of California Press), 147–96.

SESSIONS, WILLIAM A. (1994), 'Surrey's Wyatt: Autumn 1542 and the New Poet', in Peter C. Herman (ed.), *Rethinking the Henrician Era: Essays on Early Tudor Texts and Contexts* (Urbana: University of Illinois Press), 168–92.

—— (1996), 'Surrey's Psalms in the Tower', in Helen Wilcox, Richard Todd, and Alasdair MacDonald (eds), *Sacred and Profane: Secular and Devotional Interplay in Early Modern British Literature* (Amsterdam: Vrije Universiteit University Press), 17–32.

—— (1999), *Henry Howard, the Poet Earl of Surrey: A Life* (Oxford: Oxford University Press).

—— (2002), 'Literature and the Court', in David Loewenstein and Janel M. Mueller (eds), *The Cambridge History of Early Modern English Literature* (Cambridge: Cambridge University Press), 229–56.

—— (2006), 'Literature and the Court', in David Loewenstein and Janel Mueller (eds), *The Cambridge History of Early Modern Literature* (Cambridge: Cambridge University Press), 229–56.

SEYMOUR, M. C. (1995–7), *A Catalogue of Chaucer Manuscripts*, 2 vols (Aldershot: Scolar Press).

SHAFFERN, ROBERT W. (2006), 'The Pardoner's Promises: Preaching and Policing Indulgences in the Fourteenth-Century English Church', *The Historian*, 68: 49–65.

SHAGAN, ETHAN H. (1999), 'Protector Somerset and the 1549 Rebellions: New Sources and New Perspectives', *EHR*, 114: 34–63.

—— (2003), *Popular Politics and the English Reformation* (Cambridge: Cambridge University Press).

SHANNON, LAURIE (2002), *Sovereign Amity: Figures of Friendship in Shakespearean Contexts* (Chicago: University of Chicago Press).

—— (2004), 'Poetic Companies: Musters of Agency in George Gascoigne's "Friendly Verse"', *GLQ*, 10: 453–83.

—— (forthcoming), *The Zootopian Constitution: Animal Sovereignty and Early Modern Membership* (Chicago: University of Chicago Press).

SHELL, MARC (ed.) (1993), *Elizabeth's Glass* (Lincoln: University of Nebraska Press).

SHERBERG, MICHAEL (2003), 'The Accademia Fiorentina and the Question of the Language: The Politics of Theory in Ducal Florence', *RenQ*, 56: 26–55.

SHIELDS, RONALD E., and JAMES H. FORSE (2002), 'Creating the Image of a Martyr: John Porter, Bible Reader', *SCJ*, 33: 725–34.

SHORE, D. R. (1981), 'The Autobiography of Thomas Whythorne: An Early Elizabethan Context for Poetry', *Ren&R*, 17: 72–86.

SHORE, D. R. (1982), 'Whythorne's Autobiography and the Genesis of Gascoigne's Master F.J.', *JMRS*, 12: 159–78.

SHRANK, CATHY (2000), 'Rhetorical Constructions of a National Community: The Role of King's English in Mid-Tudor Writing', in Alexandra Shepard and Phil Withington (eds), *Communities in Early Modern England* (Manchester: Manchester University Press), 180–98.

—— (2004a), ' "These fewe scribbled rules": Representing Scribal Intimacy in Early Modern Print', *HLQ*, 67: 295–314.

—— (2004b), *Writing the Nation in Reformation England, 1530–1580* (Oxford: Oxford University Press).

—— (2007), ' "Matters of Love as of Discourse": The English Sonnet, 1560–1580', *SP*, 105: 30–49.

—— (2008a), ' "But I, that knew what harbred in that hed": Sir Thomas Wyatt and his Posthumous "Interpreters" ', *Proceedings of the British Academy*, 154: 375–401.

—— (2008b), 'Trollers and Dreamers: Defining the Citizen–Subject in Sixteenth-Century Cheap Print', in Andrew Hiscock (ed.), *Tudor Literature, YES*, 38: 102–18.

—— (forthcoming), 'Community: John Lydgate's *Serpent of Division* and Thomas Norton and Thomas Sackville's *Gorboduc*', in Brian Cummings and James Simpson (eds), *Cultural Reformations: From Lollardy to the English Civil War* (Oxford: Oxford University Press).

SIEMENS, R. G. (1996), ' "As strayght as ony pole": Publius Cornelius, Edmund de la Pole, and Contemporary Court Satire in Henry Medwall's *Fulgens and Lucres*', *ReFo*, 1/2, <http://www.hull.ac.uk/renforum/v1no2/siemens.htm>, accessed 3 Nov. 2008.

SILVERMAN, KAJA (1995), *The Subject of Semiotics* (Oxford: Oxford University Press).

SIMON, JOAN (1966), *Education and Society in Tudor England* (Cambridge: Cambridge University Press).

SIMONS, JOHN (1990), '*The Canterbury Tales* and Fourteenth-Century Peasant Unrest', *L&H*, 2nd ser., 1: 4–12.

SIMPSON, JAMES (2002), *Reform and Cultural Revolution*, Oxford English Literary History, 2 (1350–1547) (Oxford: Oxford University Press).

—— (2007), *Burning to Read: Fundamentalism and its Opponents in England, 1520–1547* (Cambridge, MA: Harvard University Press).

SIRAISI, NANCY G. (1990), *Medieval and Early Renaissance Medicine: An Introduction to Knowledge and Practice* (Chicago: University of Chicago Press).

SKINNER, QUENTIN (1978), *The Foundations of Modern Political Thought*, 2 vols (Cambridge: Cambridge University Press).

—— (1987), 'Sir Thomas More's *Utopia* and the Language of Renaissance Humanism', in Anthony Pagden (ed.), *The Languages of Political Theory in Early-Modern Europe* (Cambridge: Cambridge University Press), 123–57.

—— (2008), 'Paradiastole: Redescribing the Vices as Virtues', in Sylvia Adamson, Gavin Alexander, and Katrin Ettenhuber (eds), *Renaissance Figures of Speech* (Cambridge: Cambridge University Press), 149–66.

SKRETKOWICZ, VICTOR (1986), 'Building Sidney's Reputation: Texts and Editors of the *Arcadia*', in Jan van Dorsten, Dominic Baker-Smith, and Arthur F. Kinney (eds), *Sir Philip Sidney: 1586 and the Creation of a Legend* (Leiden: Brill and Leiden University Press), 111–24.

—— (1987), 'Introduction' to *The Countess of Pembroke's Arcadia (The New Arcadia)* (Oxford: Clarendon Press).

SKURA, MEREDITH (2008), *Tudor Autobiography: Listening for Inwardness* (Chicago: Chicago University Press).

SLACK, PAUL (1979), 'Mirrors of Health and Treasures of Poor Men: The Uses of the Vernacular Medical Literature of Tudor England', in C. Webster (ed.), *Health, Medicine and Mortality in the Sixteenth Century* (Cambridge: Cambridge University Press).

—— (1979), (1999), *From Reformation to Improvement: Public Welfare in Early Modern England* (Oxford: Oxford University Press).

SMITH, BARBARA, and URSULA APPELT (eds) (2001), *Write or Be Written: Early Modern Women Poets and Cultural Constraints* (Aldershot: Ashgate).

SMITH, HALLETT (1946), 'English Metrical Psalms in the Sixteenth Century and their Literary Significance', *HLQ*, 9: 33–43.

SMITH, ROSALIND (2005), *Sonnets and the English Woman Writer, 1560–1621: The Politics of Absence* (Houndmills: Palgrave Macmillan).

SMUTS, R. MALCOLM (2000), 'Occasional Events, Literary Texts and Historical Interpretations', in Rowland Wymer (ed.), *Neo-Historicism* (Woodbridge: Brewer), 179–98.

SNYDER, SUSAN (1965), 'The Left Hand of God: Despair in Medieval and Renaissance Tradition', *Studies in the Renaissance*, 12: 18–59.

SOUTHERN, RICHARD (1973), *The Staging of Plays before Shakespeare* (New York: Theatre Arts Books).

SPRINKER, M. (1980), 'The End of Autobiography', in James Olney (ed.), *Autobiography: Essays Theoretical and Critical* (Princeton: Princeton University Press), 321–42.

STANIVUKOVIC, GORAN (2007), 'English Renaissance Romances as Conduct Books for Young Men', in Naomi Conn Liebler (ed.), *Early Modern Prose Fiction: The Cultural Politics of Reading* (London: Routledge), 60–78.

STARKEY, DAVID (1982), 'The Court: Castiglione's Ideal and Tudor Reality, Being a Discussion of Sir Thomas Wyatt's "Satire Addressed to Sir Francis Bryan" ', *JWCI*, 45: 232–8.

STARNES, D. T. (1927), 'Notes on Elyot's *The Governour*', *RES*, 3: 37–46.

—— (1933), 'Sir Thomas Elyot and the "Sayings of the Philosophers" ', *Texas University Studies in English*, 13: 5–35.

—— (1956), 'Richard Taverner's *The Garden of Wisdom*, Carion's *Chronicles*, and the Cambyses Legend', *University of Texas Studies in English*, 35: 22–31.

STEELE, R. (1909–11), 'Notes on English Books Printed Abroad 1525–48', *Transactions of the Bibliographical Society*, 11: 189–236.

STEGGLE, MATTHEW (2006), 'The *Manipulus Florum* in *The Anatomy of Absurdity*', *N&Q*, 53: 1–43.

STEINER, E. (2003), *Documentary Culture and the Making of Medieval English* (Cambridge: Cambridge University Press).

STEPHENS, JOHN (1986), 'George Gascoigne's *Posies*', *Neophil*, 70: 130–41.

STERN, VIRGINIA F. (1979), *Gabriel Harvey: His Life, Marginalia, and Library* (Oxford: Clarendon Press).

STEWART, ALAN (1997), *Close Readers: Humanism and Sodomy in Early Modern England* (Princeton: Princeton University Press).

—— (2000), *Philip Sidney: A Double Life* (London: Chatto & Windus).

STRATFORD, JENNY (1999), 'The Royal Collections to 1461', in Lotte Hellinga and J. B. Trapp (eds), *The Cambridge History of the Book in Britain*, iii: *1400–1557* (Cambridge: Cambridge University Press), 255–66.

STREITBERGER, W. R. (1985), 'The Development of Henry VIII's Revels Establishment', *METh*, 7: 83–100.

—— (1998), 'Devising the Revels', *ETREED* 1: 55–74.

STRINATI, DOMINIC (2005), *An Introduction to Theories of Popular Culture* (1995; London: Routledge).

STROHM, PAUL (2006), 'York's Paper Crown: "Bare Life" and Shakespeare's First Tragedy', *JMEMSt*, 36: 75–102.

—— (forthcoming), 'Conscience', in Brian Cummings and James Simpson (eds), *Culture Reformations: Twenty-First Century Approaches* (Oxford: Oxford University Press).

SULLIVAN, J. P. (1985), *Literature and Politics in the Age of Nero* (Ithaca, NY: Cornell University Press).

SUMMERS, CLAUDE J., and TED-LARRY PEBWORTH (eds) (1997), *Representing Women in Renaissance England* (Columbia: University of Missouri Press).

SUMMIT, JENNIFER (2007), 'Leland's *Itinerary* and the Remains of the Medieval Past', in Gordon McMullan and David Matthews (eds), *Reading the Medieval in Early Modern England* (Cambridge: Cambridge University Press), 159–76.

SUTTON, A. F. (1994), 'Caxton was a Mercer: His Social Milieu and Friends', in N. Rogers (ed.), *England in the Fifteenth Century: Proceedings of the 1992 Harlaxton Symposium* (Stamford: Paul Watkins), 118–48.

SWANSON, R. N. (2004), 'Caxton's Indulgence for Rhodes, 1480–81', *The Library*, 5: 195–201.

—— (2008), *Indulgences in Late Medieval England: Passports to Paradise?* (Cambridge: Cambridge University Press).

SYLVESTER, RICHARD S. (1959), 'Introduction' to *The Life and Death of Cardinal Wolsey* by George Cavendish, EETS, o.s., 243.

—— (1960), 'Cavendish's *Life of Wolsey*: The Artistry of a Tudor Biographer', *SP*, 57: 44–71.

TALBERT, E. W. (1967), 'The Political Import and the First Two Audiences of *Gorboduc*', in T. P. Harrison et al. (eds), *Studies in Honor of DeWitt T. Starnes* (Austin: University of Texas), 89–115.

TARRANT, R. J. (ed) (1985), *Seneca's 'Thyestes'* (Atlanta, GA: Scholars Press).

TAWNEY, R. H. (1938), *Religion and the Rise of Capitalism: A Historical Study* (London: Penguin).

TAYLOR, A. B. (ed.) (2000), *Shakespeare's Ovid* (Cambridge: Cambridge University Press).

TEMPERA, MARIANGELA (1998), ' "Worse than Procne": The Sister as Avenger in the English Renaissance', in Michele Marrapodi (ed.), *The Italian World of English Renaissance Drama* (London: Associated Universities Press), 71–88.

TESKEY, GORDON (1989), 'Introduction' to George M. Logan and Gordon Teskey (ed.), *Unfolded Tales: Essays on Renaissance Romance* (Ithaca, NY: Cornell University Press), 1–10.

THIRSK, JOAN (1978), *Economic Policy and Projects: The Development of a Consumer Society in Early Modern England* (Oxford: Clarendon Press).

THOMSON, PATRICIA (1964), *Sir Thomas Wyatt and his Background* (London: Routledge & Kegan Paul).

—— (1974), *Wyatt: The Critical Heritage* (London: Routledge & Kegan Paul).

THORP, M. R. (1978), 'Religion and the Wyatt Rebellion of 1554', *Church History*, 47: 363–80.

TIGHE, W. J. (1987), 'The Gentlemen Pensioners, the Duke of Northumberland, and the Attempted Coup of July 1553', *Albion*, 19: 1–11.

TITTLER, ROBERT (1991), *Architecture and Power: The Town Hall and the English Urban Community c.1500–1640* (Oxford: Oxford University Press).

—— (1998), *The Reformation and the Towns in England: Politics and Political Culture, c.1540–1640* (Oxford: Oxford University Press).

TODD, RICHARD (1987), ' "So well attyr'd abroad": A Background to the Sidney–Pembroke Psalter and its Implications for the Seventeenth-Century Lyric', *TSLL*, 29: 74–93.

TOOLE, WILLIAM B. (1973), 'The Aesthetics of Scatology in *Gammer Gurton's Needle*', *ELN*, 10: 252–8.

TOURNOY, GILBERT (1994), 'Humanists, Rulers and Reformers: Relationships between England and the Southern Low Countries in the First Half of the Sixteenth Century', in F. de Nave (ed.), *Antwerp, Dissident Typographical Centre: The Role of Antwerp Printers in the Religious Conflicts in England (16th Century)* (Antwerp: Snoeck-Ducaju and Zoon), 21–9.

TRAISTER, BARBARA H. (2001), *The Notorious Astrological Physician of London: The Works and Days of Simon Forman* (Chicago: University of Chicago Press).

TRAPP, J. B. (1991), *Erasmus, Colet and More: The Early Tudor Humanists and their Books* (London: British Library).

—— and HUBERTUS HERBRÜGGEN (eds) (1977), *'The King's Good Servant': Sir Thomas More 1477/8–1535*, exhibition catalogue (London: National Portrait Gallery).

TRIM, D. J. B. (2002), 'Fighting "Jacob's Wars": The Employment of English and Welsh Mercenaries in the European Wars of Religion: France and the Netherlands, 1562–1610', PhD thesis (University of London).

—— (2004), ' "Knights of Christ"? Chivalric Culture in England *c*.1400–*c*.1550', in D. J. B. Trim and P. J. Balderstone (eds), *Cross, Crown and Community: Religion, Government and Culture in Early Modern England, 1400–1800* (Oxford: Lang), 78–112.

TUCK, RICHARD (1993), *Philosophy and Government 1572–1651* (Cambridge: Cambridge University Press).

TUCKER, MELVIN J. (1969), 'The Ladies in *The Garland of Laurel*', RenQ, 22: 333–45.

TUDEAU-CLAYTON, MARGARET (1998), *Jonson, Shakespeare and Early Modern Virgil* (Cambridge: Cambridge University Press).

—— (1999), 'Richard Carew, William Shakespeare, and the Politics of Translating Virgil in Early Modern England and Scotland', IJCT, 5: 507–27.

TUDOR-CRAIG, PAMELA (1989), 'Henry VIII and David', in Daniel Williams (ed.), *Early Tudor England* (Woodbridge: Boydell Press), 185–205.

TURNER, ROBERT Y. (1961–2), 'Pathos and the *Gorboduc* Tradition, 1560–1590', HLQ 25: 97–120.

TWYCROSS, MEG, with MALCOLM JONES and ALAN FLETCHER (2001), ' "Farte pryke in cule": The Pictures', METh, 23: 100–21.

VAN DER HAAR, DIRK (ed.) (1933), *Richard Stanyhurst's 'Aeneis'* (Amsterdam: Paris).

VANDER MEULEN, DAVID L. (2003–4), 'How to Read Book History', SB, 56: 171–93.

VAN ES, BART (2002), *Spenser's Forms of History* (Oxford: Oxford University Press).

VANHOUTTE, JACQUELINE (1996), 'Engendering England: The Restructuring of Allegiance in the Writings of Richard Morison and John Bale', Ren&R, 20: 49–77.

—— (2000), 'Community, Authority, and the Motherland in Sackville and Norton's *Gorboduc*', SEL, 40: 227–39.

VEESER, H. ARAM (ed.) (1989), *The New Historicism* (New York: Routledge).

VELZ, JOHN W. (1984), 'Scatology and Moral Meaning in Two English Renaissance Plays', SCRev, 1: 4–21.

VENUTI, LAURENCE (1995), *The Translator's Invisibility: A History of Translation* (London: Routledge).

VICKERS, BRIAN (1970), *Classical Rhetoric in English Poetry* (London: Macmillan).

—— (1983), 'The Power of Persuasion: Images of the Orator, Elyot to Shakespeare', in James J. Murphy (ed.), *Renaissance Eloquence: Studies in the Theory and Practice of Renaissance Rhetoric* (Berkeley: University of California Press), 411–35.

VINCENT, C. J. (1939), 'Pettie and Greene', MLN 54: 105–11.

VIROLI, M. (1992), *From Politics to Reason of State: The Acquisition and Transformation of the Language of Politics, 1250–1600* (Cambridge: Cambridge University Press).

WAKELIN, DANIEL (2007), *Humanism, Reading, and English Literature 1430–1530* (Oxford: Oxford University Press).

—— (2008), 'Possibilities for Reading: Classical Translations in Parallel Texts *c*.1520–1558', *SP*, 105: 463–86.

WALKER, GREG (1988), *John Skelton and the Politics of the 1520s* (Cambridge: Cambridge University Press).

—— (1989), 'The "Expulsion of the Minions" of 1519 Reconsidered', *HJ*, 32: 1–16.

—— (1998), *The Politics of Performance in Early Renaissance Drama* (Cambridge: Cambridge University Press).

—— (2005), *Writing under Tyranny: English Literature and the Henrician Reformation* (Oxford: Oxford University Press).

—— (2006), '*Fulgens and Lucres* and Early Tudor Drama', in Garret A. Sullivan, JR, Patrick Cheney, and Andrew Hadfield (eds), *Early Modern English Drama: A Critical Companion* (Oxford: Oxford University Press), 23–34.

WALL, WENDY (1993), *The Imprint of Gender: Authorship and Publication in the English Renaissance* (Ithaca, NY: Cornell University Press).

WALSHAM, ALEXANDRA (2004), 'Preaching without Speaking: Script, Print and Religious Dissent', in Alexandra Walsham and J. Crick (eds), *The Uses of Script and Print 1300–1700* (Cambridge: Cambridge University Press), 211–34.

WANG, YU-CHIAO (2004), 'Caxton's Romances and their Early Tudor Readers', *HLQ*, 67: 173–88.

WARD, A. W. (1967), 'Introduction' to *The Spider and the Flie* by John Heywood (1894; New York: Burt Franklin, 1967).

WARNEKE, SARA (1995), *Images of the Educational Traveller in Early Modern England* (Leiden: Brill).

WARNER, J. CHRISTOPHER (1998), *Henry VIII's Divorce: Literature and the Politics of the Printing Press* (Woodbridge: Boydell Press).

—— (2002), 'Elizabeth I, Saviour of Books: John Bale's Preface to the *Scriptorum Illustrium Maioris Britanniae*', in Christopher Highley and John N. King (eds), *John Foxe and his World* (Aldershot: Ashgate), 91–101.

WARTON, THOMAS (1791), 'Preliminary Notes on *Comus*', in *Poems upon Several Occasions* [...] *with Translations by John Milton* (London: Dodsley), 123–36.

WASSON, JOHN M. (1994), 'A Parish Play in the West Riding of Yorkshire', in Alexandra Johnston and Wim Hüsken (eds), *English Parish Drama* (Amsterdam: Rodopi), 149–57.

WATSON, ROBERT N. (2003), 'Tragedy', in A. R. Braunmuller and Michael Hattaway (eds), *The Cambridge Companion to English Renaissance Drama*, 2nd edn (Cambridge: Cambridge University Press), 292–343.

WATT, TESSA (1991), *Cheap Print and Popular Piety, 1550–1640* (Cambridge: Cambridge University Press).

WEAR, ANDREW (2000), *Knowledge and Practice in English Medicine, 1550–1680* (Cambridge: Cambridge University Press).

WEBB, HENRY J. (1965), *Elizabethan Military Science: The Books and the Practice* (Madison: University of Wisconsin Press).

WEBER, MAX (1930), *The Protestant Ethic and the Spirit of Capitalism*, trans. Talcott Parsons (London: George Allen).

WEST, WILLIAM (2006), 'Old News: Caxton, de Worde, and the Invention of the Edition', in William Kuskin (ed.), *Caxton's Trace: Studies in the History of English Printing* (Notre Dame, IN: University of Notre Dame Press), 241–74.

WESTFALL, SUZANNE R. (1990), *Patrons and Performance: Early Tudor Household Revels* (Oxford: Clarendon Press).

WHEAT, CATHLEEN HAYHURST (1951), 'Luke Shepherd's *Antipi Amicus*', *PQ*, 30: 64–8.

WHEELER, HAROLD (1949), *The Wonderful Story of London* (London: Odhams).

WHIGHAM, FRANK (1984), *Ambition and Privilege: The Social Tropes of Elizabethan Courtesy Theory* (Berkeley: University of California Press).

WHITE, MICHELINE (2005), 'Protestant Women's Writing and Congregational Psalm Singing: From the Song of the Exiled "Handmaid" (1555) to the Countess of Pembroke's *Psalmes* (1599)', *SiJ*, 23: 61–82.

WHITE, PAUL WHITFIELD (1993), *Theatre and Reformation: Protestantism, Patronage and Playing in Tudor England* (Cambridge: Cambridge University Press).

—— (2008), *Drama and Religion in English Provincial Society 1485–1660* (Cambridge: Cambridge University Press).

WHITTERIDGE, G. (1977), 'Some Italian Precursors of the Royal College of Physicians', *Journal of the Royal College of Physicians of London*, 12: 67–80.

WIATT, W. H. (1962), 'The Lost History of Wyatt's Rebellion', *Renaissance News*, 15: 129–33.

WICKHAM, GLYNNE (1963), *Early English Stages 1300 to 1660*, ii/1: *1576 to 1660* (London: Routledge & Kegan Paul).

WILCOX, HELEN, RICHARD TODD, and ALASDAIR MACDONALD (eds) (1996), *Sacred and Profane: Secular and Devotional Interplay in Early Modern British Literature* (Amsterdam: Vrije Universiteit University Press).

WILKINS, DAVID (ed.) (1737), *Concilia Magnae Britanniae et Hiberniae*, 4 vols (London: Bowyer, Richardson, Purser).

WILLIAMS, DANIEL (ed.) (1989), *Early Tudor England* (Woodbridge: Boydell Press).

WILLIAMS, FRANKLIN B. (1990), 'Una's Lamb', in A. C. Hamilton (ed.), *The Spenser Encyclopedia* (Toronto: Toronto University Press; London: Routledge).

WILLIAMS, NEVILLE (1964), *Thomas Howard, Fourth Duke of Norfolk* (New York: Dutton).

WILLIAMS, RAYMOND (1985), *The Country and the City* (1973; repr., London: Hogarth Press).

WILSON, EMILY (2004), 'First, Serve the Children', *TLS*, 16 Apr. (issue 5272), 4–6.

WILSON, JANET (1990), 'A Catalogue of the "Unlawful" Books Found in John Stow's Study on 21 February 1568/9', *Recusant History*, 20: 1–30.

WILSON, K. J. (1976), 'Elyot's Prologues', in *The Letters of Sir Thomas Elyot*, ed. Wilson, *SP*, 73/5, 39–78.

—— (1985), *Incomplete Fictions: The Formation of English Renaissance Dialogue* (Washington: Catholic University of America Press).

WILSON, KATHARINE (2006), *Fictions of Authorship in Late Elizabethan Narratives: Euphues in Arcadia* (Oxford: Clarendon Press).

WINSTON, JESSICA (2005), 'Expanding the Political Nation: *Gorboduc* at the Inns of Court and Succession Revisited', *ETREED*, 8: 11–34.

—— (2006*a*), 'National History to Foreign Calamity: *A Mirror for Magistrates* and Early English Tragedy', in Dermot Cavanagh et al. (eds), *Shakespeare's Histories and Counter-Histories* (Manchester: Manchester University Press), 152–65.

—— (2006*b*), 'Seneca in Early Elizabethan England', *RenQ*, 59: 29–58.

WINTERS, YVOR (1939), 'The 16th Century Lyric in England: A Critical and Historical Reinterpretation', I–III, *Poetry*, 53: 258–72, 320–35; 54: 35–51.

—— (1967), *Forms of Discovery: Critical and Historical Essays on the Forms of Short Poem in English* (Chicago: Swallow Press).

WITHINGTON, PHIL (2001), 'Two Renaissances? Urban Political Culture in Post-Reformation England Reconsidered', *HJ*, 44: 239–67.

—— (2005), *The Politics of Commonwealth: Citizens and Freemen in Early Modern England* (Cambridge: Cambridge University Press).

—— (2007), 'Public Discourse, Corporate Citizenship and State Formation in Early Modern England', *AHR*, 112: 1016–38.

WOLFE, JESSICA (2004), *Humanism, Machinery, and Renaissance Literature* (Cambridge: Cambridge University Press).

WOLFF, SAMUEL LEE (1912), *The Greek Romances in Elizabethan Prose Fiction* (New York: Columbia University Press).

WOOD, ANDY (2002), *Riot, Rebellion and Popular Politics in Early Modern England* (Basingstoke: Palgrave).

WOOD, ELLEN MEIKSINS (2002), *The Origin of Capitalism: A Longer View* (London: Verso).

WOODHOUSE, ELISABETH (1999), 'Kenilworth, the Earl of Leicester's Pleasure Grounds Following Robert Laneham's Letter', *Garden History*, 27: 127–44.

WOODS, SUSANNE (1984), *Natural Emphasis: English Versification from Chaucer to Dryden* (San Marino, CA: Huntington Library).

WOOLF, DANIEL R. (1990), *The Idea of History in Early Stuart England: Erudition, Ideology, and the 'Light of Truth' from the Accession of James I to the Civil War* (Toronto: University of Toronto Press).

—— (1995), 'The Rhetoric of Martyrdom: Generic Contradiction and Narrative Strategy in John Foxe's *Acts and Monuments*', in T. F. Mayer and D. R. Woolf (eds), *The Rhetorics of Life-Writing in Early Modern Europe* (Ann Arbor: University of Michigan Press), 243–8.

WOOLFSON, JONATHAN (1997), 'John Claymond, Pliny the Elder, and the Early History of Corpus Christi College, Oxford', *EHR*, 102: 882–903.

—— (1998), *Padua and the Tudors: English Students in Italy, 1485–1603* (Toronto: Toronto University Press).

WORDEN, BLAIR (1996), *The Sound of Virtue: Philip Sidney's 'Arcadia' and Elizabethan Politics* (New Haven: Yale University Press).

WOUDHUYSEN, H. R. (1996), *Sir Philip Sidney and the Circulation of Manuscripts, 1558–1640* (Oxford: Clarendon Press).

WRIGHT, D. F. (ed.) (1994), *Martin Bucer* (Cambridge: Cambridge University Press).

WRIGHT, LOUIS B. (1933), 'Translations for the Elizabethan Middle Class', *The Library*, 13: 312–26.

—— (1958), *Middle-Class Culture in Elizabethan England* (1935; New York: Cornell University Press).

WRIGHTSON, KEITH (2000), *Earthly Necessities: Economic Lives in Early Modern Britain* (New Haven: Yale University Press).

WYATT, MICHAEL (2005), *The Italian Encounter with Tudor England: A Cultural Politics of Translation* (Cambridge: Cambridge University Press).

YEAMES, A. H. S. (ed.) (1914), 'The Grand Tour of an Elizabethan', *Papers of the British School at Rome*, 7: 92–113.

YOUNG, SIR GEORGE (1928), *An English Prosody on Inductive Lines* (Cambridge: Cambridge University Press).

ZANRÉ, DOMENICO (2004), *Cultural Non-conformity in Early Modern Florence* (Aldershot: Ashgate).

ZEEVELD, W. G. (1936), 'The Influence of Hall on Shakespeare's English Historical Plays', *ELH*, 3: 317–53.

ZELL, M. L. (ed.) (2000), *Early Modern Kent 1540–1640* (Woodbridge: Boydell Press).

ZEMON-DAVIS, N. (2000), *The Gift in Sixteenth-Century France* (Oxford: Oxford University Press).

ZIM, RIVKAH (1987), *English Metrical Psalms: Poetry as Praise and Prayer, 1535–1601* (Cambridge: Cambridge University Press).

ZITNER, SHELDON (1985), 'Surrey's "Epitaph on Thomas Clere": Lyric and History', in Chaviva Hosek and Patricia Parker (eds), *Lyric Poetry: Beyond New Criticism* (Ithaca, NY: Cornell University Press), 106–15.

ŽIŽEK, SLAVOJ (1991), *Looking Awry: An Introduction to Jacques Lacan through Popular Culture* (Cambridge, MA: MIT Press).

ZOCCA, LOUIS (1950), *Elizabethan Narrative Poetry* (New Brunswick, NJ: Rutgers University Press).

ACKNOWLEDGEMENTS OF SOURCES

The editors and publisher wish to thank the following, who have kindly given permission to reproduce the illustrations listed:

Bodleian Library: **8.1** (MS Selden supra 41, 194^v).

British Library: **P.1** (shelfmark C111.aa.30, A1^v), **1.1** (shelfmark C.57.b.25), **3.1** (shelfmark C.71.d.33, U1^r), **4.1** (Harley MS 2252, 135^v), **4.2** (shelfmark G.11165, A6^r), **8.2** (Huth MS 56, M7^v), **15.1** (shelfmark C.95.a.9), **16.1** (shelfmark C.58.a.24), **22.1** (shelfmark C.12.i.82, D1^r), **39.1** (shelfmark 717.l.37.(1.), O3^v).

Cambridge University Library: **12.1** (shelfmark Syn.7.59.119, A1^r), **18.1** (shelfmark SSS.2.8), **20.1** (shelfmark Syn.7.55.28, 2Q^v), **20.2** (shelfmark Syn.7.55.28, B2^v), **29.1** (shelfmark Peterborough.H.3.61, P1^v), **35.1** (shelfmark Syn.7.58.77, P4^r).

Huntington Library: **32.1** (shelfmark 69548, A1^r), **37.1** (shelfmark 12925, L2^v), **41.1** (shelfmark 31354, A1^r).

Kunstsmuseum, Basel: **7.1** (Kupferstichkabinett, Amerbach-Kabinett, Inv. 1662.31).

Lambeth Palace Library: **9.1** (shelfmark (ZZ)1539.3.01, A3^v), **42.1** (shelfmark (ZZ)1597.15.01, A1^r).

Magdalene College, Cambridge: **33.1** (shelfmark Pepys 2972/21 [CM]).

Trinity College, Cambridge: **26.1** (shelfmark Capell*.19[2], D4^r), **32.2** (shelfmark Capell.T.9[1], A7^v), **E.1** (shelfmark VI.1.13, A1^r).

University of Newcastle: **27.1** (shelfmark PI 615.89 BUL, I8^r).

University of Sheffield: **30.1** (shelfmark RBR F 274.205 (F), 2Y2^r).

Warburg Institute Library: **34.1** (shelfmark NCH 407, Q6^r).

INDEX